POGO

POGO

by WALT KELLY

THROUGH THE WILD BLUE WONDER

THE COMPLETE SYNDICATED COMIC STRIPS

VOLUME 1

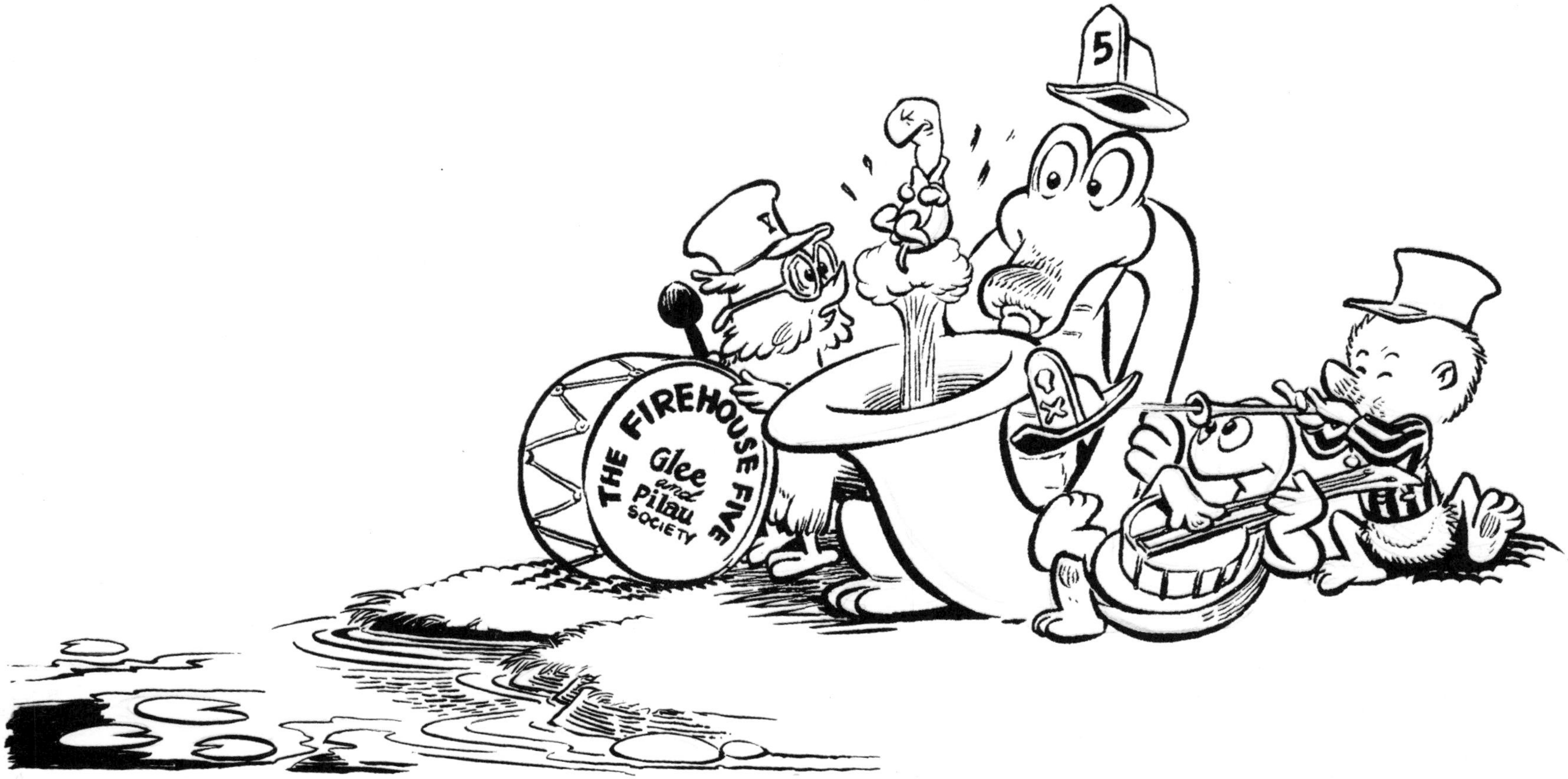
5
THE FIREHOUSE FIVE
Glee and Pilau SOCIETY

Editors: Carolyn Kelly & Kim Thompson
Consulting Editor: Mark Evanier
Book Design and Art Restoration: Carolyn Kelly
Production and Digital Art Restoration: Paul Baresh
Cover Art: Walt Kelly, painted by Carolyn Kelly
Associate Publisher: Eric Reynolds
Publishers: Gary Groth & Kim Thompson

Through The Wild Blue Wonder, the title for this volume, was found among Walt Kelly's
private papers.

An expanded version of R.C. Harvey's "Swamp Talk" column can be located at the
Fantagraphics Books website, www.fantagraphics.com, where our other books
can also be gazed upon.

For a free full-color catalogue of comics, including reprints of such other classic comic
strips as *Peanuts*, *Popeye*, *Prince Valiant*, and *Krazy Kat*, call 1-800-657-1100.
Or write Fantagraphics Books, 7563 Lake City Way, Seattle, WA 98115, USA.

Distribution:
   USA (bookstores): W.W. Norton and Company, Inc.
Order Department: 800-233-4830
   USA (comics shops): Diamond Comics Distributors.
Order Department: 800-452-6642 x215
   UNITED KINGDOM: Turnaround Distribution
Order Department: 20-8829-3002
   CANADA: Canadian Manda Group
Order department: 800-452-6642 x862

ISBN: 978-1-56097-869-5

First printing: September, 2011
Printed in China

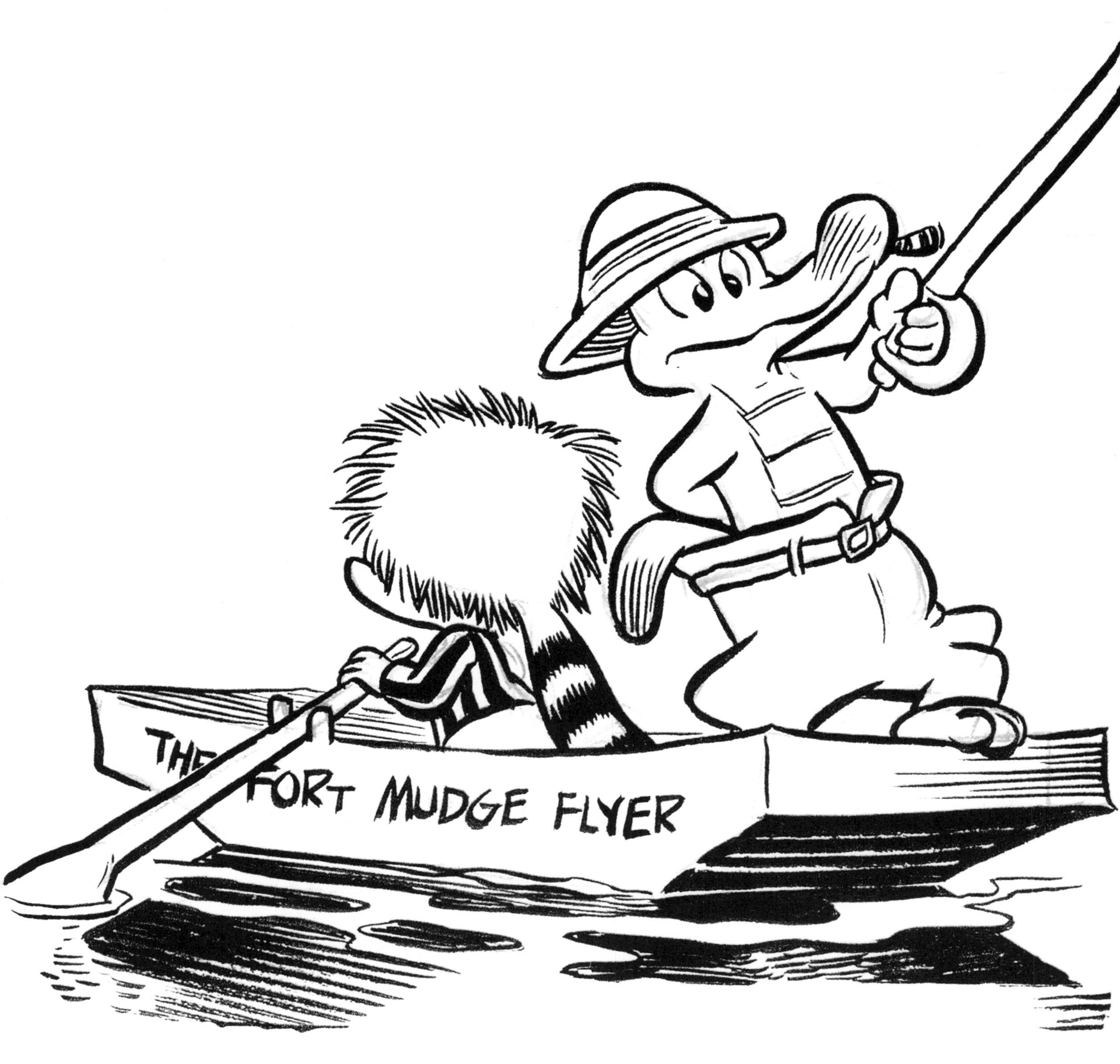
THE FORT MUDGE FLYER

EDITORS' NOTE

It's about time. Matter of fact, it's well past "about time." This is a period when every major newspaper strip – and even some no one has ever heard of – is getting the full, "complete" archive treatment, usually under hard covers. That Walt Kelly's *Pogo* was not chief among them was just not right.

So now that's taken care of. This is the first volume of Fantagraphics' reprinting of that classic strip, finally in the format it deserves. To those who have followed the drawn-out process of getting it done, watching one release date after another tick by, our apologies and one simple excuse: We had to get it right. There are, alas, no readily available collections of perfect copies. Much of what is in this and subsequent volumes has never been reprinted and the material had to be tracked down, reconstructed and retouched. One of those responsible for this book had a special reason for such diligence: She is Carolyn Kelly, daughter of the man who created the work before you. With her, it wasn't just a matter of doing justice to a classic newspaper strip. She wanted the best possible presentation of the work of a man she loved and admired. And still does.

Worth the wait? That's up to you to decide. We can just tell you that it wouldn't have been as good if it had come out when the project was first announced.

Hard and painful as it may be to believe today, there was a time when the common assumption was that once a strip like *Pogo* had appeared in the newspaper, no one would ever be interested in reading it again. There were foreign sales and Kelly reconfigured the material into all those great Simon and Schuster paperbacks. But the working mindset in strips then was that beyond that, no one would be interested in reading them again. Ergo, the comic strip syndicates did not always maintain a set of good, clean files for future generations' reprinting or reading pleasure. Into the trash so much of it went...making the jobs of today's archivists and assemblers all the more difficult.

This series of books, like so many other collections of classic strips, is therefore only possible thanks to the indefatigable fans. We're talking about the ones who, painstakingly over the decades, assembled collections of their favorite comic strips from old newspaper tearsheets. Steve Thompson, president of the POGO Fan Club, and Rick Norwood supplied the vast majority of strips for this volume, and when we had to fill in a few missing strips and panels, we turned to the vital Billy Ireland Cartoon Library and Museum at Ohio State University, and to its currently-retiring curator, Lucy Caswell. It is also vital to salute the late and sorely missed Bill Blackbeard, whose utterly invaluable San Francisco Academy of Comic Art collection formed the bedrock of OSU's collection.

And so for this first release, we are able to bring you the first two years of *Pogo*...and since those were not full years, there's ample room for the precursor of the nationally-syndicated strip. As explained in the introduction, Kelly first put *Pogo* into newspapers in the short-lived *New York Star*. When it went away, the possum didn't. Those *Star* strips are presented in the rear of this book, after the Sunday pages and before an informative annotation by R.C. Harvey which identifies this and that for those who might today miss some references. And of course, we are proud to have an introduction by Walt's good friend and colleague in the newspaper game, Jimmy Breslin.

Subsequent volumes will each house two full years, give or take a week or so when a storyline stretched past New Year's Day and so belongs in either volume. Kelly wrote and drew *Pogo* for twenty-four years, and each of these books is designed to contain two years so we're looking at a nice, even twelve volumes. You may want to go clear about eighteen inches on your bookshelf right now. Within a few years, it will display *Pogo* in full.

No newspaper strip has ever been more deserving of a complete, quality reissuance...as you know because you didn't start reading with this page. You went directly to the gold and began enjoying the early, formative days of Walt Kelly's classic creation. If it never got any better than what's in this volume, it would still warrant the deluxe treatment. But as you'll see, it just gets better and better...and one of us can say that without being accused of familial bias. It's the one who wasn't literally sitting on his lap when he drew some of what follows...

– Kim Thompson and Carolyn Kelly, Editors

TABLE OF CONTENTS

TABLE OF CONTENTS

TABLE OF CONTENTS

TABLE OF CONTENTS

Solid MacHogany arrives to help sing Christmas carols while Churchy and Howland ar planning dinner. Rackety Coon Chile questions the use of Christmas trees. "Boston Charlie" is sung and Porky practices his blessing.

Week of Dec. 25, 1950 – Gifts are exchanged and resolutions planned. Porky steps on the punchline of Churchy's joke. Howland looks for a resolution he can give Pogo. Solid MacHogany heads for New Orleans.

Week of Dec. 31, 1950 – For New Year's, Albert makes a resolution to stop picking fights.

TABLE OF CONTENTS

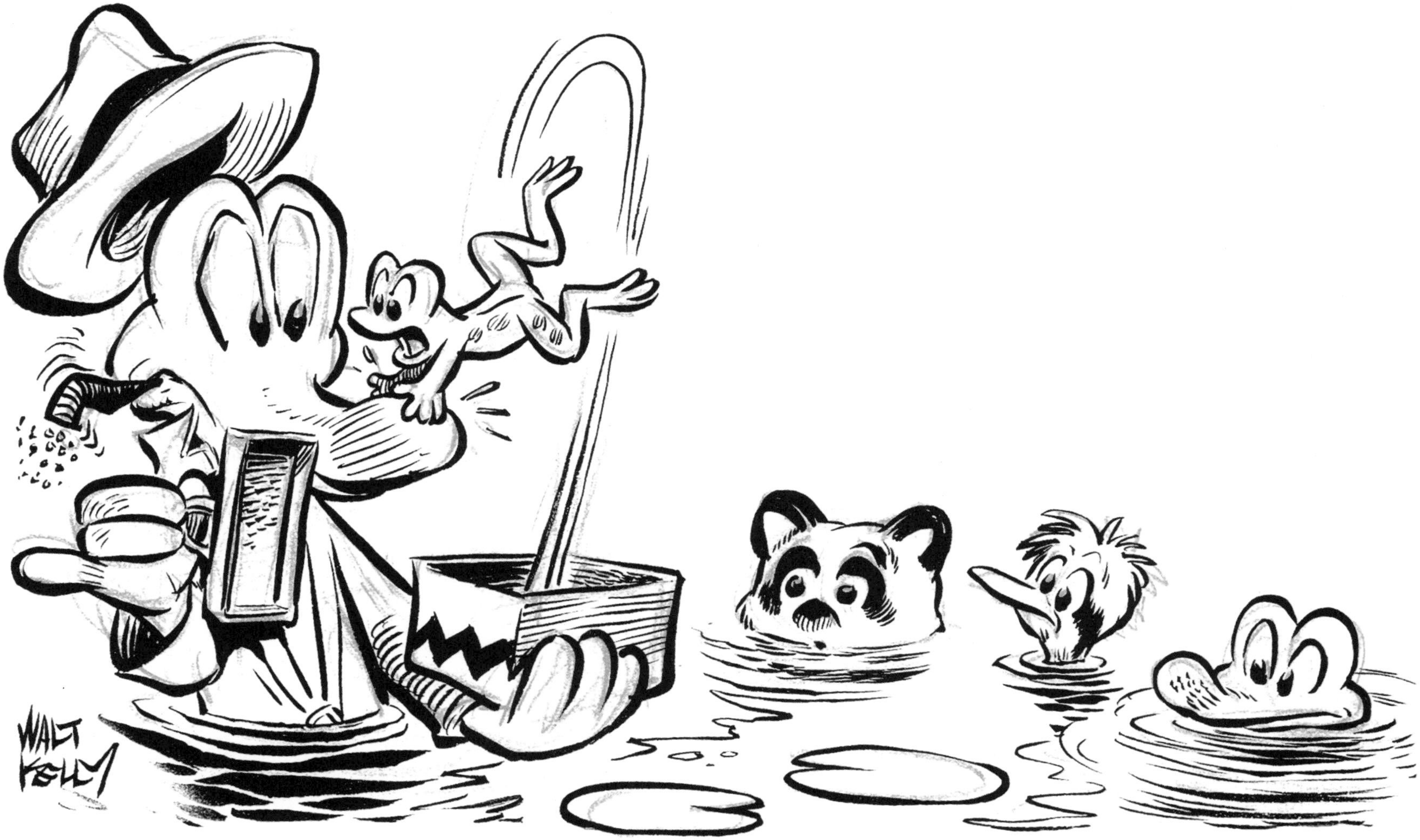
WALT KELLY

FOREWORD

BY JIMMY BRESLIN

There was a minor problem with what Walt Kelly said on the afternoon I heard him say it. We were in a bar called the Orient Room, way up on a street along the East River in Manhattan, in New York, and he was interested in the large and most disturbing reaction to his Pogo comic strip about Senator Joseph McCarthy. He had drawn McCarthy as an ugly pig in the swamp that the Pogo strip used as a base. Or as a frightful lizard. Whatever, McCarthy was a complete scum in a swamp.

Everywhere in the country, and his Pogo was there, McCarthy people were so loud and outraged and calling for violence that it had to be taken as a problem.

Kelly agreed. Here is what he said as he stood in the bar with so many hearing him:

"I wish they would shoot me."

Our problem with this is that I know that he meant it. Dark thought and the possibility of screaming humor.

He spoke so softly and then suddenly would bellow. He listened more than anybody I've been around. He comes out of the cracked rooms and crying kids of welfare clients in Connecticut. That work sticks to his feet and runs a wonderful and insane humor that comes out of his hands onto a cartoon script.

There you are. Give us a drink and we're off to another.

Yes we are. Now it is a Sunday in Saigon and Kelly arrives from New York at this small hotel on one of the packed streets. He gets in the bar. He drinks and out comes this small white pad and he starts drawing on it. Page after page. Drink after drink. He bellows and starts handing out the paper with his cartoons. And money. He throws cartoons and money at the waiters and bus boys and floor sweepers and forces them to have a ton of drinks. They went out into the night with cartoons for their children and money in the pocket and whiskey buzzing in their heads. Nobody came to work on Monday. The manager of the hotel tried a mop. His wife made up beds until her back gave out.

Kelly was at the bar screaming for somebody to serve him.

When next reported on, he was in a transport plane at an open hatch, kicking out flares that bathed the place below with this flat half light.

Now, half stiff and standing with him as he went through the Metropolitan Museum of Art until he came upon the empty space on the wall waiting for something sometime. Right now, it had four pieces of common wood in a rectangle framing an empty space on an empty wall.

Kelly got in front of it and put a hand on his hip. The other hand held a walking stick. Which he tapped against the empty space on the wall.

"By God, Breslin, he has it."

"This is a pure genius. By God. Oh, look at this."

His walking stick tapped the dusty wall as his cry of genius ran through the hall. The first art appreciators came up and stopped to look at this miracle work on the wall. After them came more. Kelly never stopped. Somebody said who he was. The interest rose. More people came. He had drawn a crowd for dust on a wall.

Of course he was soon gone.

Always I can remember him on this day when he was in bed for the reason that whiskey had put the insides of his leg in such a vise that it had to be removed.

And Walt Kelly is in that bed and he looks down at the space under the sheet where he has a missing leg.

"I guess I'm just going to have to stay here until it grows back."

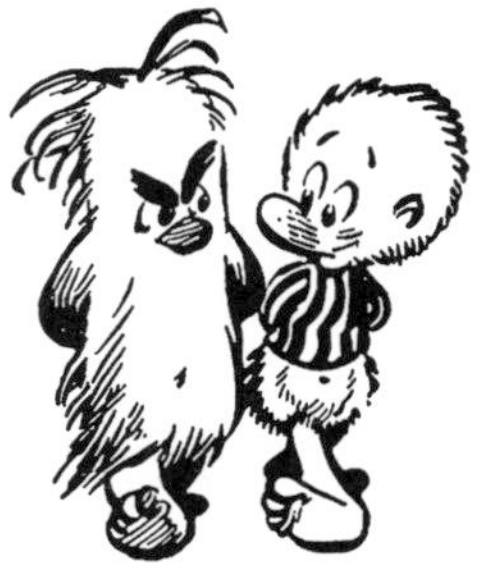

Walt Kelly, September 26, 1952, in the midst of a book tour to promote the release of the Simon and Schuster paperback *I Go Pogo*. He is seen here at a luncheon at the Sertoma Club in Madison, Wisconsin where he later delivered a lecture and drew cartoons for the audience. *Photo courtesy of the Wisconsin Historical Society. WHS Image ID 35583.*

INTRODUCTION

BY STEVE THOMPSON

On August 26, 1913, Walt Kelly, a clear-eyed youth of honest Scotch-Irish-English-French-Austrian blood found himself in Philadelphia, Pa. He was one day old, and although his ancestors had been rooted along the shores of the Delaware for 150 years, he immediately hatched a plan. Two years later he was in Bridgeport, Connecticut, complete with father, mother, sister and sixteen teeth, all his own.

"Ten years later, to the day, he was twelve years and one day old. He had survived fire (fell into the coal scuttle with a jack-o-lantern in 1919), flood (homemade boat struck a swimming duck and splintered, 1923), starvation (lost the lunch on a fishing expedition with father, 1924), savage beasts (rabid rabbit shot to death on other side of town, 1924), disease and pestilence (Chicken Pox and Mumps, 1918), and education (8 years grammar school)." [from a Post-Hall Syndicate promotional biography]

So Walter Crawford Kelly, Jr., son of Walter and Genevieve (*née* MacAnulla) Kelly, described his early life in a biography put out by the Post-Hall Syndicate as part of a publicity brochure for *Pogo*, and as a summary of anyone's early life, it's probably as complete and accurate as any. Kelly Sr. was a painter of vaudeville theater scenery and also worked as a shop foreman, originally in the Remington Arms factory and later with General Electric. Kelly Jr. credited his father ("he was a pretty fair painter") with being the first to put a brush in his hand and to encourage his artistic leanings.

"Maybe the mind works differently in different people, but I am strong for a conception held by my father. Not being a great man for writing (he threw his education aside in 1895 at the age of nine), he believed that the true means of communication is the picture. We are, he said at one point, bad at talking, bad at remembering language, and bad at spelling, but we are just great at remembering pictures.

"'Language,' he said to my mother one evening at supper, 'is the worst means of communication known to man.'

"She asked if he'd have another cup of coffee, and when he said he would, Mother said that he'd been using the language successfully most of his life, well enough to get well fed, anyhow.

Unpublished pre-Disney art, early 30's.

"He replied that if Mother had drawn a picture of a cup of coffee he'd have gotten the message as quick as any other way. The idea of my mother drawing anything except a highly irregular apple left us all convulsed. So, we stayed on with speech." [Levin, Martin, ed. *Five Boyhoods*, Garden City: Doubleday & Company, 1962.]

In 1918, Walt (nicknamed "Crawf" to distinguish him from his father) followed his older sister Bernice off to school. There was no small amount of pressure involved since, as he later said, Bernice "had been a big success in her kindergarten and first-grade years. She had wit, grace, mature scholarly inclinations, and large brown eyes. Well, I had brown eyes. She was an acknowledged scholar. She studied hard and her head was full of geometrical theory, more history than she needed, and grammatical rules that had never been used by man or beast. On the other hand, I was the family slob. All I did was sing and draw on paper bags. When it came to the question of what to make of me, a puzzled look came over the father's face. 'Maybe he could learn cards,' he said to my mother, 'or to shoot dice.' My mother didn't think

this was funny. I thought vaguely that I could be an artist, but experiments with my father at my elbow convinced me that the work was hard." [*Ibid.*]

Kelly credited Florence Blackham, the principal of Hall Elementary School, in the introduction of *Ten Ever-Lovin' Blue-Eyed Years With Pogo*, as being a major influence on the children of Bridgeport, developing their sense of equality and what is now referred to as diversity. "Our principal never let us entertain any ideas about differences. To us the name of Cohen had the constitutional ring of Washington. We were proud of being us. We had our differences, fighting over the important things, such as erasers, marbles, candy, but we didn't quarrel over race or name. Somehow, she sent us off to high school feeling neither superior nor inferior. We saw our first Negro children in class there, and believe it or not, none of us was impressed one way or another, which is as it should be."

When Crawf moved on to Warren G. Harding High School, he again followed Bernice, this time onto the staff of the school newspaper, *The Spectator*, contributing cartoons and illustrations. He also provided artwork to three years of the school yearbook, *The Stylus*. During his later high school years, in addition to reporting for *The Spectator*, he became a stringer reporter for the *Bridgeport Post* on both Harding and Central High School sporting events and a regular contributor of drawings and puzzles to the *Post's* Junior Page. His "How many things are wrong with this picture" puzzles were often the star feature of the page.

Along with millions of his contemporaries, Kelly graduated from high school in 1930 into an almost non-existent job market. He initially followed his father into General Electric and, as a sideline, provided some cartoons to the house organ *Works News*. While he continued to work for the *Bridgeport Post* during the early 1930s, it was mostly freelance and part-time. For about a year, he worked for the Public Welfare Department interviewing enrollees and also spent time working for Warner Brothers, but it was the manufacturer of corsets and other women's undergarments, not the movie studio of the same name.

His work on the *Bridgeport Post* progressed to humorous illustrations of unusual stories and more serious illustrations for historical and retrospective pieces. In 1931, he produced a series of "X More Shopping Days Until Christmas" panels, with a drawing of a boy similar to Percy Crosby's Skippy and one-liners such as "What this country needs is fewer people telling us what this country needs" and "A word to the wise often interrupts a monologue." He even included an early version of a phrase he would later make famous – "We have met the enemy and we are his'n." His major project for the *Post* was his depiction, in comic strip form, of the life of Bridgeport's most famous resident, showman and circus magnate P.T. Barnum. Barnum would, of course, later be the inspiration for P. T. Bridgeport in *Pogo*.

As the Bridgeport job market continued to be unsatisfactory, Kelly decided to pursue his artistic endeavors more seriously. He worked sporadically in New York City doing signs and window designs on a free-lance basis, but was not particularly successful. He briefly attended art school but a lack of funds forced him to drop out.

Walt Disney Studios was advertising nationwide for artists, so Kelly sent off his portfolio, postmarked December 10, 1935. It obviously made a good impression, as he was soon on his way to Los Angeles and officially on the payroll as of January 6, 1936. An added incentive to relocating on the West Coast was that he'd become enamored of a Connecticut girl named Helen DeLacy and she had recently moved to Oakland, California. Even being in opposite ends of a big state could not keep them apart and they were married in September of 1937.

Disney at the time had an apprenticeship program, and everyone started out in the story department. As he progressed through the system, he became an animator both on shorts (*Nifty Nineties*, *Little Whirlwind*) and feature films, notably *Dumbo*, *Pinocchio* and *Fantasia*. The Disney training changed and developed Kelly's artistic style from his early pen technique to the later full-bodied brushwork. His training in drawing animal characters "in the round" meant that his *Pogo* characters were not two-dimensional drawings, but representations of actual three-dimensional animals, who can be seen to shift their weight while walking, shrug their shoulders, and so on.

That was one thing he gained from his years with Disney. Another was a lifelong friendship with the studio's most colorful, eccentric director-animator, Ward Kimball. And in a bit of serendipity, Selby Daley, who would later become Walt's third wife, also worked at Disney at that time. On meeting her over twenty-five years later, Walt said that the animators used to watchthe women in Ink and Paint going past their building, and he remembered Selby because she always wore red shoes.

In late May of 1941, a strike divided the studio, with many of the lower levelemployees walking out. Kelly, with friends on both sides of the dispute, found the whole matter troubling and heartbreaking. He was spared from participating when he was called back to Bridgeport to help his parents with a family emergency, but his wife Helen stayed in Los Angeles, maintaining contact with the Women's Auxiliary of the Disney Unit Strikers of the Screen Cartoonists Guild. She kept Walt up-to-date on the activities of the strikers via an exchange of almost daily letters, and in those letters they mutually decided his future did not rest at Disney's and maybe not even in the field of animation. In the summer, Kelly returned to Los Angeles, spoke with friends and co-workers and even talked with Walt Disney, with whom he'd forged a friendship and a sense of mutual respect. The strikers returned to work on Sept. 21, but Walt had already tendered his resignation and was officially off the payroll as of Sept. 6.

While away from Los Angeles, Walt had explored a number of options, and because of Disney's close connection with Western Publishing (Western had provided Disney with some of his initial funding), was able to get a job with them doing stories and art for various Dell Comics.

The Kellys returned to Connecticut, eventually settling into life in Darien, Connecticut, about fifteen miles down the coast from Bridgeport. Many of those he knew at Disney went into the

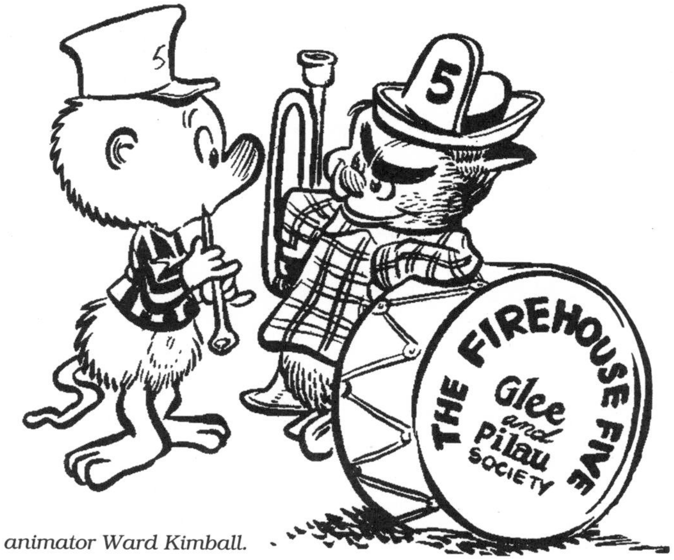
5
THE FIREHOUSE FIVE
Glee and Pilau SOCIETY

Kimbo Kat was based on Disney animator Ward Kimball.

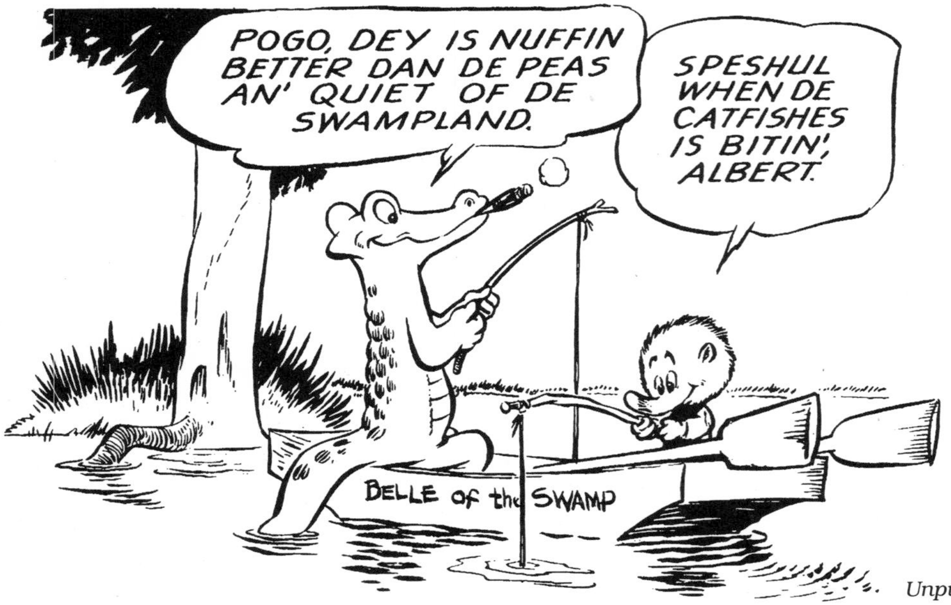
POGO, DEY IS NUFFIN BETTER DAN DE PEAS AN' QUIET OF DE SWAMPLAND.
SPESHUL WHEN DE CATFISHES IS BITIN', ALBERT.
BELLE of the SWAMP

Unpublished early Albert and Pogo art.

military during WWII but Walt was unable to serve due to the aftereffects of a childhood illness, which he speculated was either rheumatic fever or polio. While working for Western on various Dell comics, he did manage to aid the war effort by illustrating military language manuals published in English, Dutch and Japanese. During the forties, Walt and Helen had three children, Kathleen, Carolyn and Peter. Carolyn and Peter would, for a time, produce the revived *Walt Kelly's Pogo* newspaper strip in the 1990s.

Initially, Walt created his own characters for Western, such as the short series "Kandi the Cave Kid" in *Looney Tunes and Merrie Melodies* and "Seaman Sy Wheeler" in the short-lived, more adultoriented *Camp Comics*. He also briefly took over "Pat, Patsy and Pete" in *Looney Tunes and Merrie Melodies* and even did a short Bugs Bunny story. He primarily worked on adapting various fairy tale stories for seasonal Mother Goose books, while including his own variations of older stories and his original poetry.

Eventually he took on the covers for *Walt Disney's Comics and Stories* and the eighty-three he did are highly sought-after by collectors for their fine, expressive artistry, with his own stylistic elements almost always visible in the backgrounds. His touch was identifiable enough that in the mid-fifties a fan sent him a *WDC&S* cover and asked Walt if he did it. He had, and complimented the fan on his ability to recognize his style.

The editors at Western were clearly delighted with his work. A year after he started with them, they assigned him to begin adapting the movie series *Our Gang* as a series of comic book stories.InDecember 1942 another of his own creations showed up in the first issue of *Animal Comics* – "Albert Takes the Cake," starring Albert the Alligator and Pogo Possum.

Albert and Pogo appeared regularly in *Animal Comics* until January 1948, co-starring at first with a black human child named Bumbazine. Bumbazine disappeared fairly early in the feature's run because, Kelly said, he was not as believable as the animals. Though Kelly's name did not appear on the stories for almost five years, he managed to retain the rights to his creation. When he started doing art and political cartoons for *The New York Star* newspaper in July 1948, he revived his swamp critters in comic strip format, calling it simply *Pogo*. The strip ran six days a week from October 4, 1948 to January 28, 1949 when the *Star* ceased publication. By May, the burgeoning Hall Syndicate had picked up the strip as a daily, with the Sunday strip beginning in January of 1950. In late 1949, Pogo also returned to Western with his own Dell comic book, and the growing number of fans had two sources for the feature.

As with most strips, the characters in *Pogo* changed in appearance, both between comic book and strip, and in the early years within the strip. In one case, that of the circus bear P.T. Bridgeport, Kelly radically changed his appearance within days, but for the most part the changes were gradual. In response to a question about how the characters changed, Kelly replied, "Well, I didn't know it was happening, as a matter of fact. I suppose that you yourself, the artist, laughingly called the creator of this stuff, change, yourself, and without quite knowing it, you see things, you look back on things that you didn't know had happened. I didn't realize that Pogo had become what he is today. I have always thought that it's possible that he doesn't look like a possum because I can't draw a possum. I think that perhaps it's that your ideas grow with you and fortunately or unfortunately, your strip changes with your own growth. If you grow in the right direction along with the public, and trying not only to follow them but at the same time sort of stay ahead of them, you can't help but have changes come over it."

It didn't take long for *Pogo* to develop a sizeable fan base, much faster than most new strips, and within a year Kelly was receiving offers of merchandise contracts and even animation possibilities. Right from the start, he was reluctant to give up any quality control, and turned down the offers because he didn't have the time to monitor them. In order to get the strip syndicated, however, he did have to give up the copyright to the strip (although not the characters), and he quickly began to chafe at the fact that Hall Syndicate had the contractual right to bring in someone else to do "his" strip. He began talking to Bob Hall, head of the syndicate, and during the last quarter of 1951 he began to register his dissatisfaction by signing the strip Hurty Gurdee, Orville Yonder, Wart Kerky, etc. or with no signature at all. Hall finally got the message. On January 1, 1952, the strip's indicia began reading "copyright Walt Kelly, distributed by Hall Syndicate." The syndicate also lost the right to edit the art or script of the strip, a right it had in the original contract. Kelly finally had complete control over his creation.

In the early years of *Pogo*, Kelly worked closely with both the syndicate and newspaper editors throughout the country to publicize the strip. To help increase awareness of *Pogo*, promotional panels were provided to editors at no additional charge. These could be used on front pages to show upcoming weather, countdown panels to Christmas, reminders to cancel the paper for vacations, and support for charitable causes.

Kelly further bonded with newspaper editors because of something he began doing in October of 1951. That month, he lettered the name of one of his editors on the side of the boat used by the characters. It quickly became a tradition. When a new newspaper began to carry the strip, the name of its publisher or editor might well be inked on a boat, an honor that was extended in other directions, as well. Family members, friends, co-workers and even just enthusiastic fans would find their names adorning the hull and would almost always receive the prized original art as an extra thrill. Throughout the years Kelly received thousands of requests for names on boats, many times more than could have been accommodated even if a boat appeared in the strip every day.

Self-portrait — Dell Four Color comic book #105, April 1946, inside front cover.

7

As the fifties began, Walt and Helen divorced. Helen remained in Darien, while Walt moved to Manhattan and married Stephanie Waggony, who had originally worked with him as a secretary. Stephanie would later accompany Walt on some of his round-the-world reporting trips, as well as handling some of the business management for the strip. Walt and Stephanie had five children, Stephen, Andrew, Kathryn, Nancy and John. Unfortunately, Kathryn died shortly before her first birthday, Nancy died the day after she was born, and John was born severely disabled. Even though few outside his immediate circle understood the reference to Kathryn's never reaching her first birthday, for many years in late October, Kelly would draw a bug floating through the Swamp with a birthday cake, trying to find someone looking for a birthday. One of his poems is also titled "To the Mother of Kathryn Barbara."

Kelly's relationship with Hall (later Post-Hall) Syndicate was not always collaborative, or even congenial. When Hank Ketcham (*Dennis the Menace*), another Disney alumnus and fellow Hall artist, asked him about renegotiating his contract, Kelly replied, "I figured out a long time ago that selling and billing in any business is not worth much more than 25 or 30%." When Ketcham later asked about using an agent or attorney for negotiations, he replied, "I do not use a lawyer for either negotiations or contract discussion.... No one can do anything to better your bargaining strength except yourself. If you own your material you can do anything."

It was often the case that the Syndicate, in Kelly's opinion, was lax in doing its share of promotion, its salesmen were not doing their jobs in placing *Pogo* in new papers, and Bob Hall did not support the strip strongly enough. In a particularly egregious case, in August 1957 the Greater Buffalo Press, which printed Sunday comics sections for almost all papers nationwide, removed the name on a boat. While originally requested by a single paper (the name was that of an editor at a competing newspaper), GBP erased it from every comic section it printed that week. In an extensive letter to Bob Hall, triggered partly by what Kelly saw as a far-too-mild reaction to this, he complained about the lack of support from Hall in censorship and editing issues, as well as the lack of promotion. "There is no question that your job has at the very least been cut in half by the constant flow of activity and publicity, all on a high level, that has come out of our offices.... I have never used an agent or representative as such.... I do not believe in ten-percent men in the first place; but when I pay 40 percent for not as much as a regular ten-per-center would give me, *i.e.*: a little clear-headed and professional representation, I feel that I am being overcharged." In an earlier letter, he said,

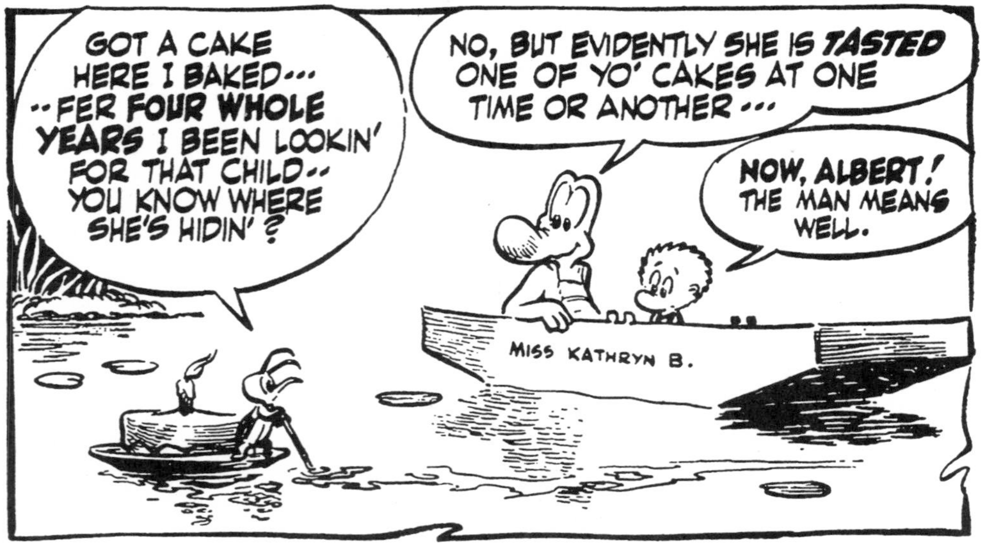
GOT A CAKE HERE I BAKED... ..FER FOUR WHOLE YEARS I BEEN LOOKIN' FOR THAT CHILD.. YOU KNOW WHERE SHE'S HIDIN'?
NO, BUT EVIDENTLY SHE IS TASTED ONE OF YO' CAKES AT ONE TIME OR ANOTHER...
NOW, ALBERT! THE MAN MEANS WELL.
MISS KATHRYN B.

Late October daily strip, mid-'50s.

"the strip picked up and used most by the Treasury to house organs and factory newspapers for the [Savings] Bond Drive was *Pogo*.... It's about time we broke 500 with *Pogo*. Every evidence shows it need not apologize for being intellectual."

The reputation of Pogo as an intellectual strip has merit, and it's in good company, sharing that reputation with *Krazy Kat, Barnaby, King Aroo* and only a few others. Milt Caniff, while discussing the popularity of various strips, said, "None of us present [Caniff, Jules Feiffer, Kelly] win polls, in the usual sense of polling people, because ours is an intense audience, rather than a large one. I think that's generally true of anybody who writes and draws his own material, because again he's writing for himself. This is true with Jules, too, and I'm sure it is with [Al] Capp. The audience that you're going for is one that will tear down the building if the strip is left out of the paper, but they wouldn't think of writing a letter in the ordinary sense of writing a fan letter."

It didn't take long for *Pogo*'s fans to start asking for a reprint collection so they didn't have to keep clipping strips out of the paper. Many of Kelly's friends from the defunct *New York Star* had remained in the publishing industry and several were working for Simon and Schuster, then the largest publisher of cartoon collections. As fans of Kelly's work, they were more than willing to see their company issue a paperback collection, which was done in 1951 and entitled, simply, *Pogo*. As with all the successive S&S collections, the volume did not include all the strips in sequence. Instead, Kelly reconfigured the material, adding in new panels and extending others to create a rhythm of storytelling more befitting book format.

Because of concerns that the art would suffer by being printed in the usual pocket book format, *Pogo* was a trade paperback, closer in size to a standard hardcover novel. Priced at a dollar instead of the quarter most paperbacks commanded, the book eventually sold over 300,000 copies and remained in print for almost twenty years.

Its publication caused problems with Western Publishing, which maintained that its contract with Kelly gave them the exclusive rights to book collections of *Pogo*. Kelly, Simon & Schuster and Western eventually arrived at an agreement. Simon & Schuster would continue with paperback reprints, and Western, agreeing it was not the same thing, would continue the *Pogo Possum* comic book they were issuing.

Eventually, Kelly decided the pressure of doing all of this, even with the help of long-time assistant George Ward, was too much and cancelled the comic book with issue #16 in 1954. While many comic books of the era were reprinting newspaper strips, *Pogo* had actually gone in the opposite direction, completing the move from its comic book origins to newspaper format.

Newspaper readers weren't the only ones to recognize the appeal of *Pogo*. In 1954, Kelly became the first cartoonist asked to contribute original artwork to the Library of Congress art collection. His compatriots at the relatively new National Cartoonists Society awarded him their highest honor, the Billy DeBeck Award (later renamed the Reuben after Rube Goldberg) for best comic strip for 1951 (presented April 1952) – he'd placed third for the award the previous year. They elected him President in 1954, re-elected him in 1955, and later awarded him the Silver T-Square for outstanding service to the Society.

Kelly's tenure as President was most certainly not a quiet one. The day after he was installed as President, he testified on behalf of the NCS before the Congressional subcommittee investigating juvenile delinquency and comic books, immediately following the testimony of *Seduction of the Innocent* author Fredric Wertham and E.C. Comics publisher William M. Gaines.

Along with his promotional work with newspapers and editors, Kelly paid close attention to his readers, regularly answering fan mail and often sending signed books and original strips, even if not originally requested. In 1952, largely as a promotional effort, he launched the Pogo for President campaign, with "I Go Pogo" his variant on Eisenhower's campaign slogan, "I Like Ike." College students throughout the country leaped on board, hundreds of thousands of campaign buttons were distributed nationwide and Kelly did nearly a hundred public appearances on college campuses during the spring and fall. Many campus papers already carried the strip, more picked it up during the campaign, and every college town had a bookstore more than willing to host an autograph session. With all this, it wasn't surprising that sales of both the strip and the first two collections, *Pogo* and *I Go Pogo*, soared. While Pogo himself was an unenthusiastic candidate, he was run for President again in every election until the end of the strip. In 1956, Kelly provided not only special newspaper columns but also television commentary for NBC during both the Republican and Democratic national conventions in Chicago.

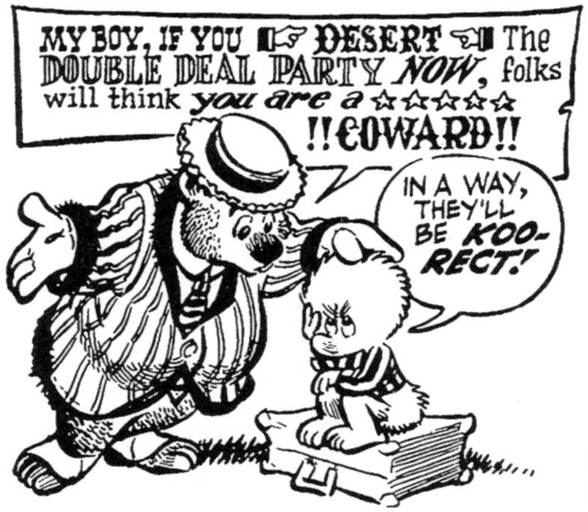
MY BOY, IF YOU DESERT The DOUBLE DEAL PARTY NOW, folks will think you are a ☆☆☆☆☆ !!COWARD!!
IN A WAY, THEY'LL BE KOO-RECT!

The reluctant candidate: daily strip, 1952.

The 1952 "I Go Pogo" campaign didn't include any particularly direct political commentary. The following year, however, saw the first appearance of xenophobic Mole McCarony, named for Senator Pat McCarran of Nevada, chairman of the Senate Internal Security Subcommittee. Mole, in turn, introduced to the Swamp a bobcat named Simple J. Malarkey, an obvious caricature of Wisconsin Senator Joseph R. McCarthy, who was then engaged in a very public search for communists in all areas of government and public life. As a means of generating publicity, it was ideal. *Pogo* was being mentioned in the national press, as well as in the editorial pages of papers carrying the strip, and hundreds of thousands of people became aware of this odd little bunch of characters. As a direct result, *Life* magazine sent Kelly to the 1954 Army-McCarthy hearings to provide both a written and visual report.

Throughout the 1950s, *Pogo* continued to stir up controversy. At the height of the desegregation movement, when schools in some Down South communities were closing rather than integrate, Kelly met the issue head-on. His characters set up "speakeasy" schools, dispensing education like alcohol during Prohibition. Such scenes caused many of the papers in the South to either stop carrying the strip entirely, or remove it during those sequences. Even some editors who had previously supported Kelly during the Simple J. Malarkey period now complained about the political slant of the strip. Caricatures of Nikita Khrushchev and Fidel Castro delighted many but resulted in cancellation and complaints from papers in Japan and other countries concerned about offending the Soviets. Kelly also expanded his criticism of bigotry and intolerance in books such as *The Jack Acid Society Black Book* and *The Pogo Poop Book*, both of which included stories created especially for those volumes.

Kelly's work pace was legendary, especially since it included not only creating and managing a successful comic strip, but also dozens of speaking engagements and multiple world reporting tours. A coworker once described him interrupting work on an animation project, taking down a sheet of Strathmore drawing paper and "knocking out a complete daily strip in an hour or so." Wolfgang Mozart, when asked why his written manuscripts didn't show any strikeouts or changes, said, "the committing to paper is done quickly enough, for everything is already finished, and it rarely differs on paper from what it was in my imagination." Kelly's technique seemed to be much the same.

Pogo has, without a doubt, the largest cast in the history of comic strips. Scholars have identified nearly 500 named or otherwise unique characters, plus hundreds more unnamed and generic critters and spear-carriers that appear in the background. Kelly himself said that he assumed most of the characters had jobs in other strips when they weren't onstage in *Pogo.* It's important to note that the Okefenokee Swamp is also a character in the strip, at least as important as the animals. Many artists echoed cartoonist Roy Crane (*Buz Sawyer, Wash Tubbs and Captain Easy*) when he said he wished he could draw trees the way Kelly did. Kelly responded that he learned to draw trees by copying Crane.

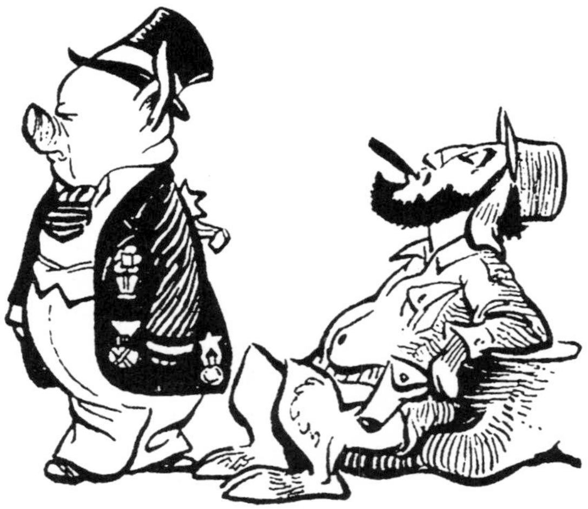

Khrushchev and Castro.

The characters in *Pogo* are self-aware enough to realize that they are in a comic strip. Albert scratches matches on panel borders and other characters lean against them. Churchy carries out a periodic campaign against word balloons, claiming they "steal work from honest men." In a June 1961 sequence, he shoots a child's Okefenokee Park souvenir balloon and, to save Churchy from an irate mother and child, Albert blows up a whispered word balloon, ties a string to it and presents it to the now happy child. In the strip of 2-28-50 in this volume, Porky takes an aspiring artist on a tour of the day's comic strip. A 1964 Sunday has Albert exclaiming, "Man, look at that art work!" and explaining to Pogo how to become a great cartoonist, by "swipin' jokes from your pals." In a filler panel at the end of *Equal Time for Pogo*, Porky tells Pogo "there's nothing like a new-painted morning."

One significant change during the fifties was the lettering, credited to a new member of the *Pogo* team. Henry Shikuma relieved Walt and assistant George Ward of their lettering duties, and also developed a distinctive "type style" for the strip. Unlike most lettering, where the horizontal elements are lighter or the same weight as the verticals, the usual lettering in *Pogo* has heavier horizontals.

Lettering and word balloons as a whole had always been a significant part of *Pogo*. The use of individualized lettering styles for some characters, such as Gothic for Deacon, black-bordered rectangular balloons (not unlike sympathy cards) for Sarcophagus Macabre, the circus poster balloons of P.T. Bridgeport, even Celtic léttering for a couple of Irish characters that dropped by on St. Patrick's Day, tells us even more about the characters and their voices.

In 1966, Kelly sent Pogo, Albert and Churchy off on an extended adventure to Prehysteria, a prehistoric town with people, animals and dinosaurs living together. This is often cited as a favorite sequence (it ran for over a year) by many fans and, in addition to giving his characters a "vacation" from the Swamp, gave Kelly the chance to pay homage to one of his major artistic influences, T.S. Sullivant.

Thomas S. Sullivant was a regular and popular contributor to the early humor magazines *Judge* and *Life*, known for his incredibly detailed animal characters. In an article written for *Art in America* in 1959, and another for the NCS magazine *The Cartoonist* in 1965, Kelly brought Sullivant out of his undeserved

Prehysterical Pogo *art, 1966.*

obscurity even among cartoonists. Many of the characters in Prehysteria, especially those such as lions and monkeys, make Kelly's appreciation of Sullivant obvious. The influences on Kelly's art of Sullivant, and of A. B. Frost, another significant animal cartoonist of the 19th Century, are at least as important as the influences of humorists and satirists Lewis Carroll (*Alice in Wonderland*, etc.) and Edward Lear (*The Book of Nonsense, Nonsense Songs and Stories*) on his writing.

By the late 1960s, *Pogo* had become an almost exclusively political strip. When TV host Mitch Miller asked him, "Who do you visualize as your audience?" Kelly said, "It has to be the guy that's drawing it. I'm afraid you either sink or swim on your knowledge of how to get your thoughts across to other people. So, you have to decide on one audience guy who's your test, and that's you. If you are somewhat like the rest of the country, and if you have the same kinds of hopes and fears and aspirations and so on, you'll probably have a very wide audience. If you have smaller, different kinds of fears than most people, you'll probably have a smaller audience."

In the mid-sixties, Kelly returned to Los Angeles almost thirty years after he left the city, Disney Studios and the animation business. The occasion was an animated TV special that brought him into collaboration with director Chuck Jones, best known for his Warner Bros. cartoons and for the recently completed *How the Grinch Stole Christmas*. Sponsored by Procter and Gamble and accompanied by store promotions of Pogo dolls and cups to buyers of P&G soaps, *The Pogo Special Birthday Special* was not well received and Kelly himself was extremely disappointed with what resulted. He and Jones clashed throughout the production, especially on character design, and Jones later said that as a result he "would never work with another animator on a project." Fans of the strip were almost unanimous in their dislike of the final product, complaining about the voices and changes in the characters. Most viewers who were unfamiliar with *Pogo* turned to their newspapers to discover a strip that had little in common with the television production. The *Birthday Special* was only shown once, and fifteen years later had a limited reappearance on videotape.

While it lost a number of papers during the 1968 election due to the extensive use of political caricatures, *Pogo* enjoyed resurgence in 1970, when Kelly latched onto the burgeoning environmental movement. For a government-distributed poster, he produced what became an iconic illustration of Pogo looking out at the viewer with a junk-filled swamp behind him and the sentence, "We have met the enemy and he is us." Although the line appeared in the strip less than a dozen times, it remains one of the things most remembered about the strip and has become part of the popular lexicon.

While working on *The Pogo Special Birthday Special*, Kelly met Selby Daley, who was already working in the Chuck Jones studio, and together they developed the film *We Have Met The Enemy and He Is Us*. This was to be a public-service television program, showing the swamp characters confronting ecology and pollution issues, followed by a five-minute live segment with local officials talking about activities in their community. Instead of using the bright paints common in animation, they created the film using colored pencils, in order to give a softer and more natural appearance to the swamp and characters. Unfortunately, the planned financing fell through, and the film, while virtually completed, was never released. Kelly managed to recycle the storyboard for the first half of a book of the same name.

Kelly's health, which had caused periodic problems throughout the sixties, grew steadily worse, especially after his second wife Stephanie died from cancer in 1970. For the last two years of his life, his activities were severely restricted. He married Selby in a New York hospital room in late 1972, and the following day had a leg amputated due to complications from diabetes. He spent most of the following year in and out of the hospital, and the strip suffered as a result. Assistant Don Morgan (aided by Willie Ito) did more and more of the primary artwork. Reprints were snuck in by the syndicate, which did not publicly reveal that Kelly was ill until fans wrote to their papers asking about the reprints. Nevertheless, he always expected to resume full production. In what turned out to be his last interview, he told Don Crinklaw of the *St. Louis Post-Dispatch* in August 1973 that he was doing better and *Pogo* would be back as strong as ever. Unfortunately, it was not to be.

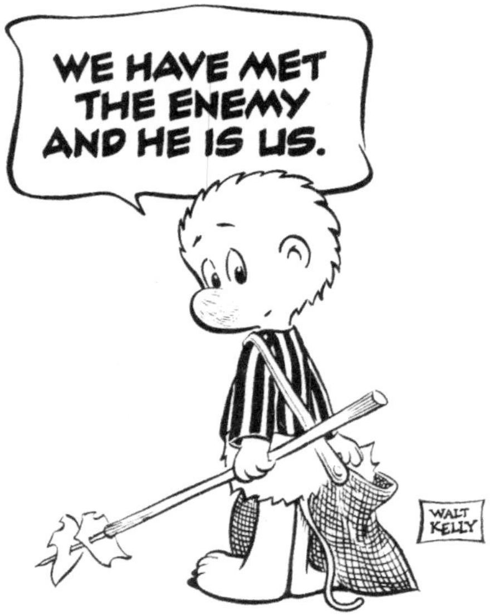
WE HAVE MET THE ENEMY AND HE IS US.
WALT KELLY
Pogo's most well-known statement.

Around the time that interview appeared, Kelly had recovered enough strength that he and Selby travelled to Los Angeles to tend to business arrangements for the *We Have Met the Enemy* film. There, he suffered a stroke and was hospitalized. Several of his children hurried to Los Angeles to see him and daughter Carolyn stayed on to help take care of him, staying there until the end. It came on October 18.

Selby Kelly was determined that the *Pogo* strip should continue. Reprints and cut-and-pasted photostats of earlier strips carried the feature at first, but she soon began to insert new sequences produced with the help of Don Morgan and Henry Shikuma on the art and Walt's son Steve on the scripts. The first strip she drew, a tribute to Walt, ran on December 25, 1973 and she continued drawing the feature for another year and a half.

Many papers carrying the strip canceled when Kelly died, however, and more canceled throughout 1974. In addition to the loss of Walt, rising newsprint costs were causing papers to reduce the size of comic strips, which were no longer seen as the readership draw they used to be. Selby ended the strip on Sunday, July 20, 1975, saying in the last panel, "...we'll go back to the comical books and regroup." By that time, there were only about 30 papers still carrying the strip, none in major markets, and there had not been a new paperback collection in years. When the cancellation announcement was made, some fans were surprised to learn the strip was still running.

Walt Kelly's art and legacy lived on. He was among the first inductees into the Cartoon Hall of Fame, and many younger cartoonists cite him as their major inspiration. Jeff Smith (*Bone*) says that the book *Prehysterical Pogo* showed him that it was possible to tell cartoon stories in black-and-white book format, and that he still learns brush technique by studying Kelly drawings. In a speech honoring what would have been Kelly's 75th birthday, Bill Watterson (*Calvin and Hobbes*) said, "There have been a few fine and imaginative strips since *Pogo*, of course, but none has taken such complete advantage of the cartoon medium. *Pogo* shows what a comic strip can really be."

Perhaps the best way to close is with part of a newspaper report of Kelly's memorial service in New York. "Standing in front of an easel covered with *Pogo* cartoons, [Al] Capp ... said he began reading *Pogo* when 'people around New York were quoting profound and hilarious lines that I couldn't remember having written.' He described the strip ... as 'too elusive for the average manic-depressive – the private fantasies of a wise and gifted child. All cartoonists glowed in *Pogo*'s success. It was proof of the superiority of cartoonists over writers who can't draw and artists who can't write – two classes who are respected more than we are.'"

Nearly seventy years after *Pogo* began, it's still true.

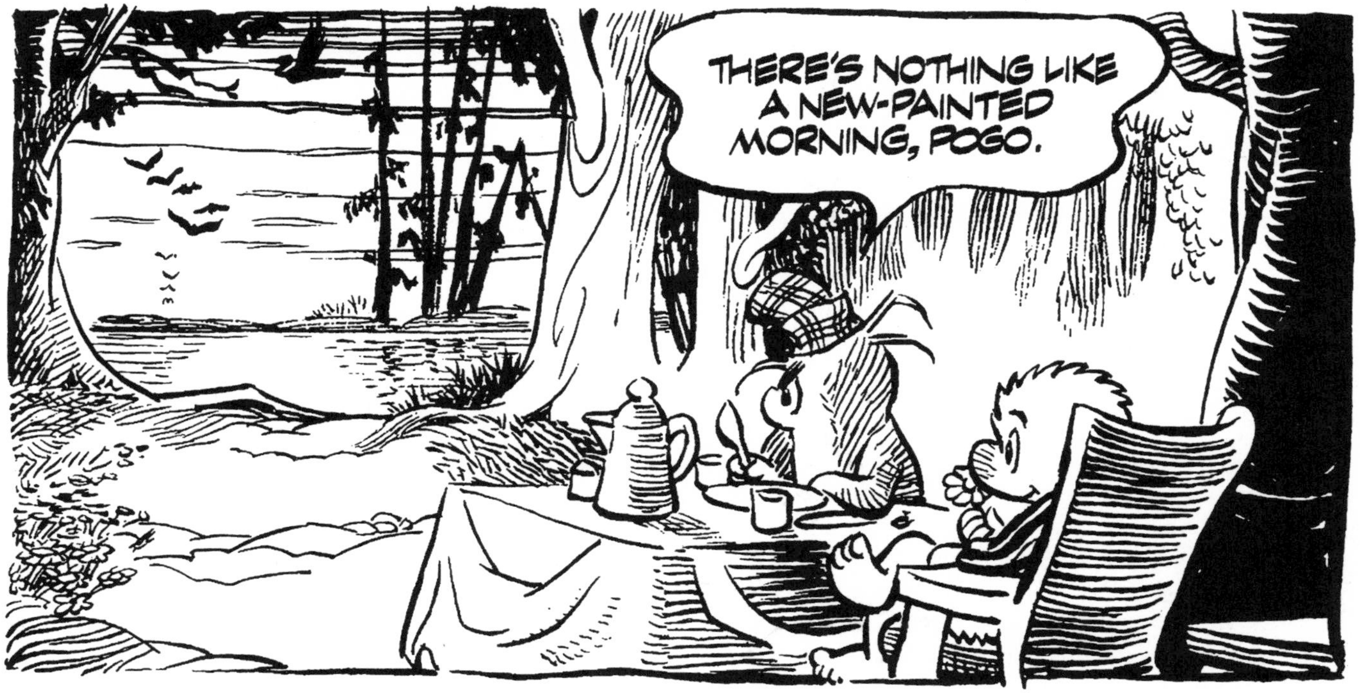
THERE'S NOTHING LIKE A NEW-PAINTED MORNING, POGO.

Equal Time for Pogo, *1968.*

DAILY STRIPS

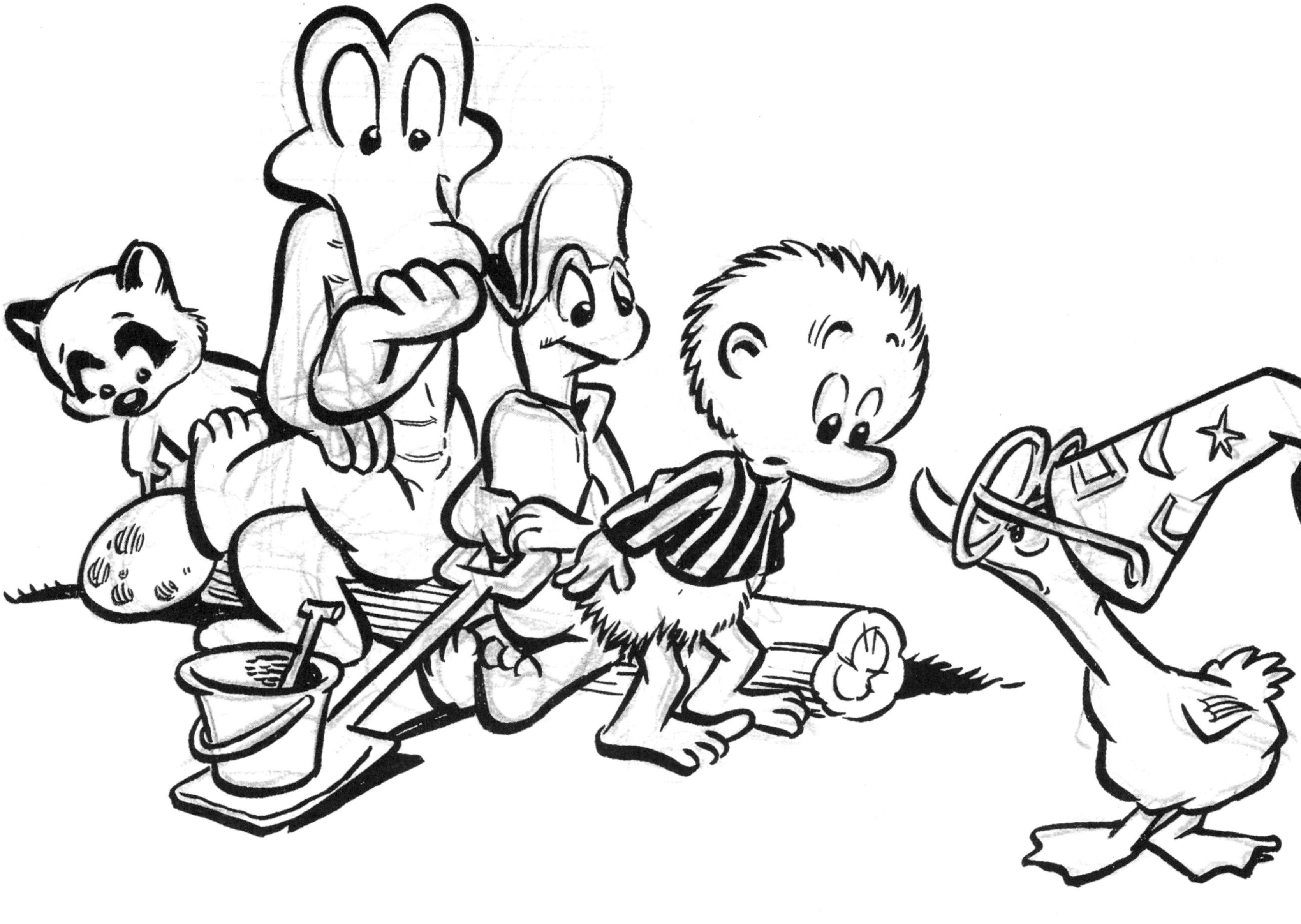

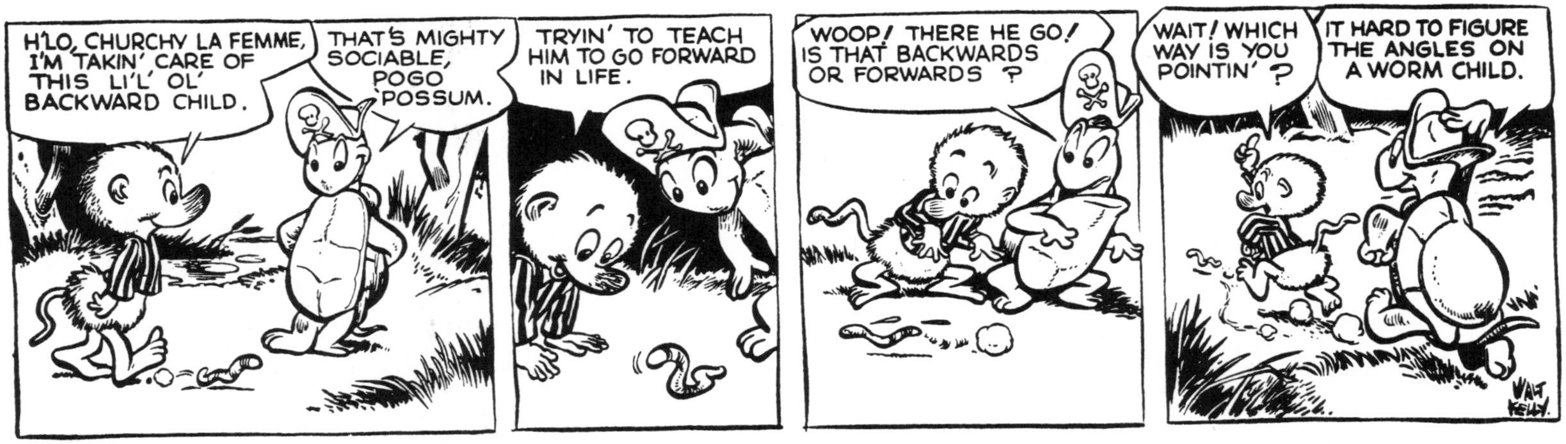
H'LO, CHURCHY LA FEMME, I'M TAKIN' CARE OF THIS LI'L' OL' BACKWARD CHILD.
THAT'S MIGHTY SOCIABLE, POGO 'POSSUM.
TRYIN' TO TEACH HIM TO GO FORWARD IN LIFE.
WOOP! THERE HE GO! IS THAT BACKWARDS OR FORWARDS ?
WAIT! WHICH WAY IS YOU POINTIN' ?
IT HARD TO FIGURE THE ANGLES ON A WORM CHILD.

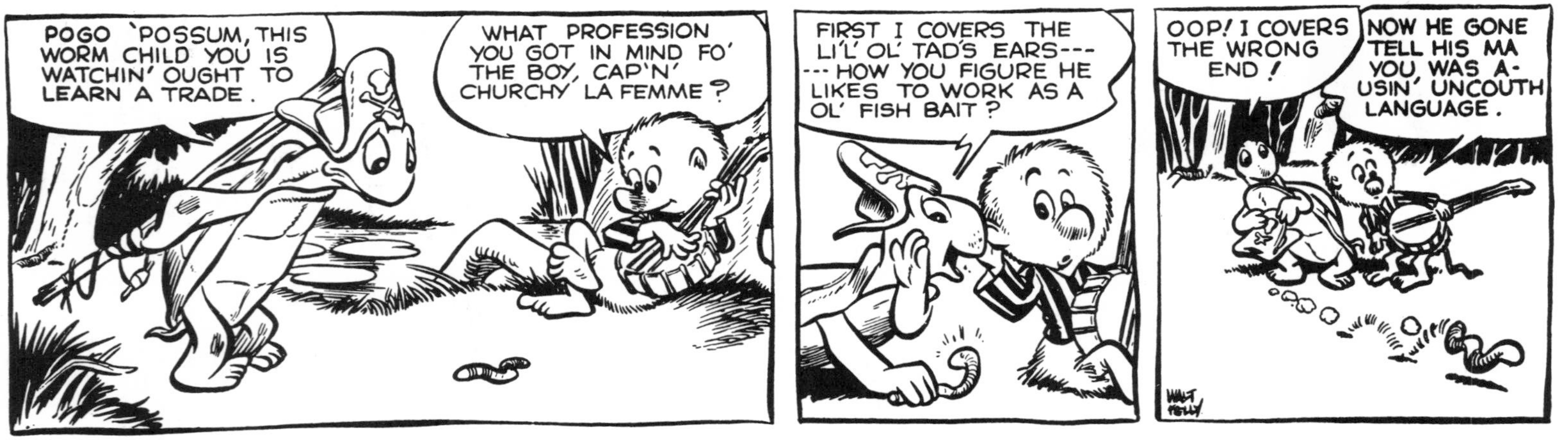
POGO 'POSSUM, THIS WORM CHILD YOU IS WATCHIN' OUGHT TO LEARN A TRADE.
WHAT PROFESSION YOU GOT IN MIND FO' THE BOY, CAP'N' CHURCHY LA FEMME ?
FIRST I COVERS THE LI'L' OL' TAD'S EARS--- ---HOW YOU FIGURE HE LIKES TO WORK AS A OL' FISH BAIT ?
OOP! I COVERS THE WRONG END!
NOW HE GONE TELL HIS MA YOU WAS A-USIN' UNCOUTH LANGUAGE.

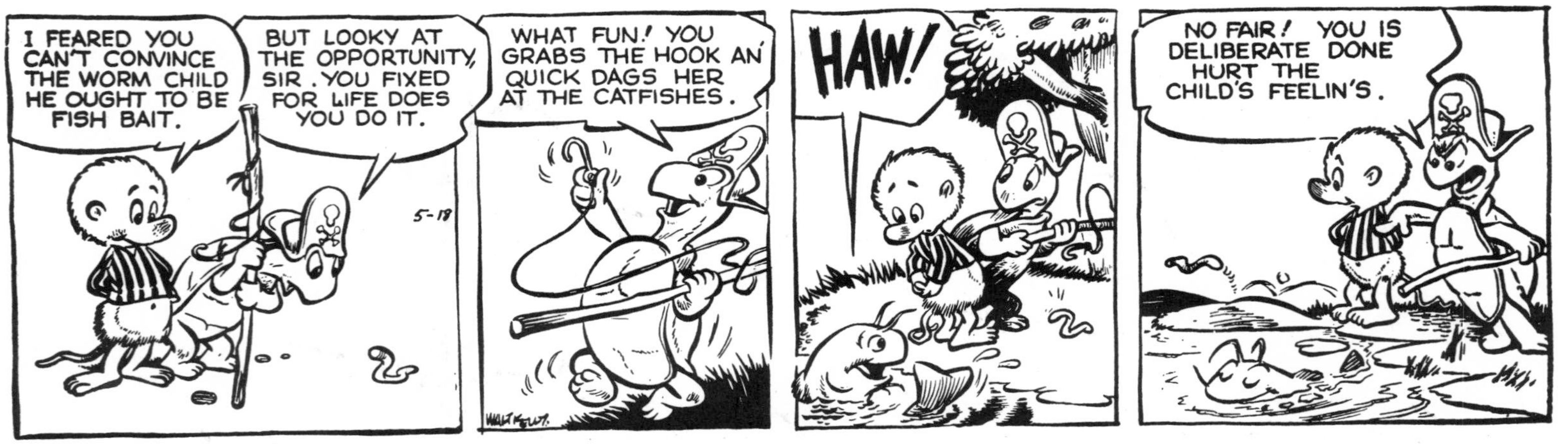
I FEARED YOU CAN'T CONVINCE THE WORM CHILD HE OUGHT TO BE FISH BAIT.
BUT LOOKY AT THE OPPORTUNITY, SIR. YOU FIXED FOR LIFE DOES YOU DO IT.
5-18
WHAT FUN! YOU GRABS THE HOOK AN' QUICK DAGS HER AT THE CATFISHES.
HAW!
NO FAIR! YOU IS DELIBERATE DONE HURT THE CHILD'S FEELIN'S.

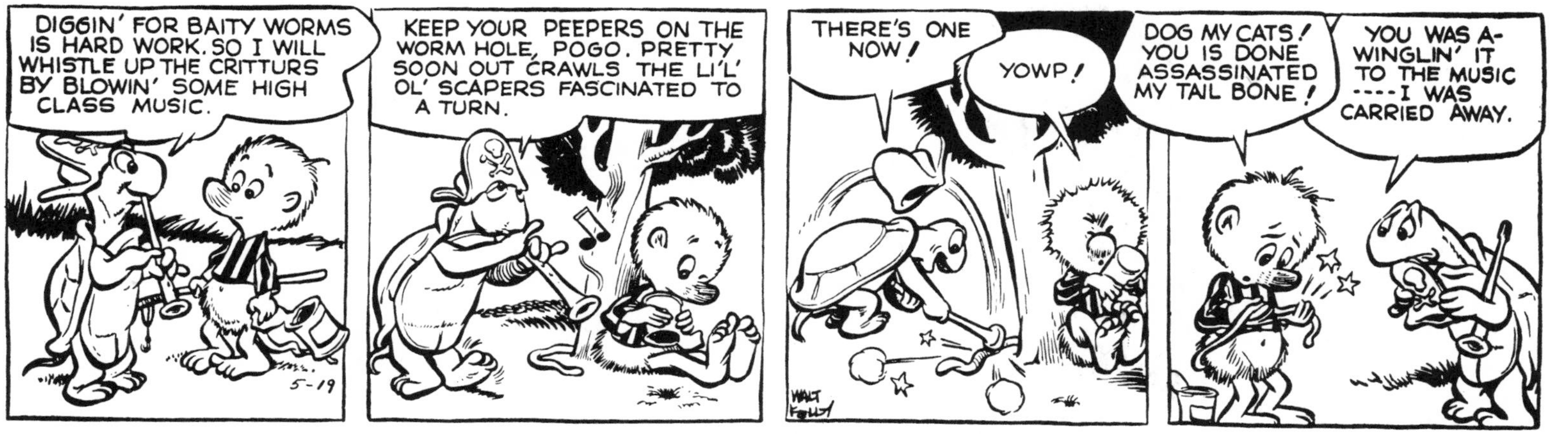
DIGGIN' FOR BAITY WORMS IS HARD WORK. SO I WILL WHISTLE UP THE CRITTURS BY BLOWIN' SOME HIGH CLASS MUSIC.
5-19
KEEP YOUR PEEPERS ON THE WORM HOLE, POGO. PRETTY SOON OUT CRAWLS THE LI'L' OL' SCAPERS FASCINATED TO A TURN.
THERE'S ONE NOW!
YOWP!
WALT KELLY
DOG MY CATS! YOU IS DONE ASSASSINATED MY TAIL BONE!
YOU WAS A-WINGLIN' IT TO THE MUSIC ----I WAS CARRIED AWAY.

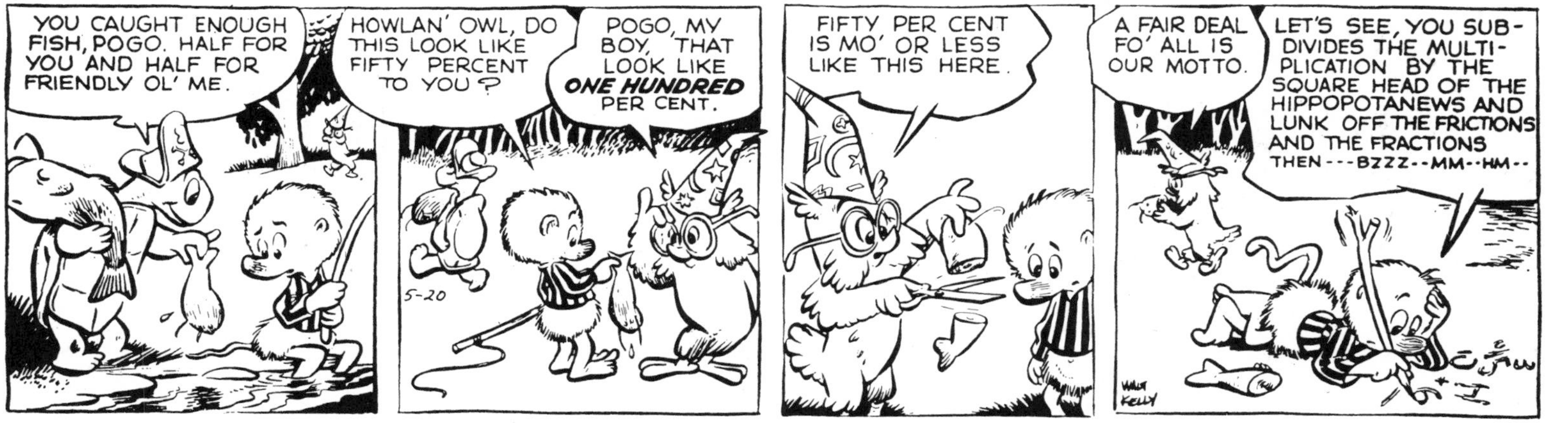
YOU CAUGHT ENOUGH FISH, POGO. HALF FOR YOU AND HALF FOR FRIENDLY OL' ME.
HOWLAN' OWL, DO THIS LOOK LIKE FIFTY PERCENT TO YOU?
POGO, MY BOY, THAT LOOK LIKE ONE HUNDRED PER CENT.
5-20
FIFTY PER CENT IS MO' OR LESS LIKE THIS HERE.
A FAIR DEAL FO' ALL IS OUR MOTTO.
LET'S SEE, YOU SUB-DIVIDES THE MULTI-PLICATION BY THE SQUARE HEAD OF THE HIPPOPOTANEWS AND LUNK OFF THE FRICTIONS AND THE FRACTIONS THEN---BZZZ--MM--HM--
WALT KELLY

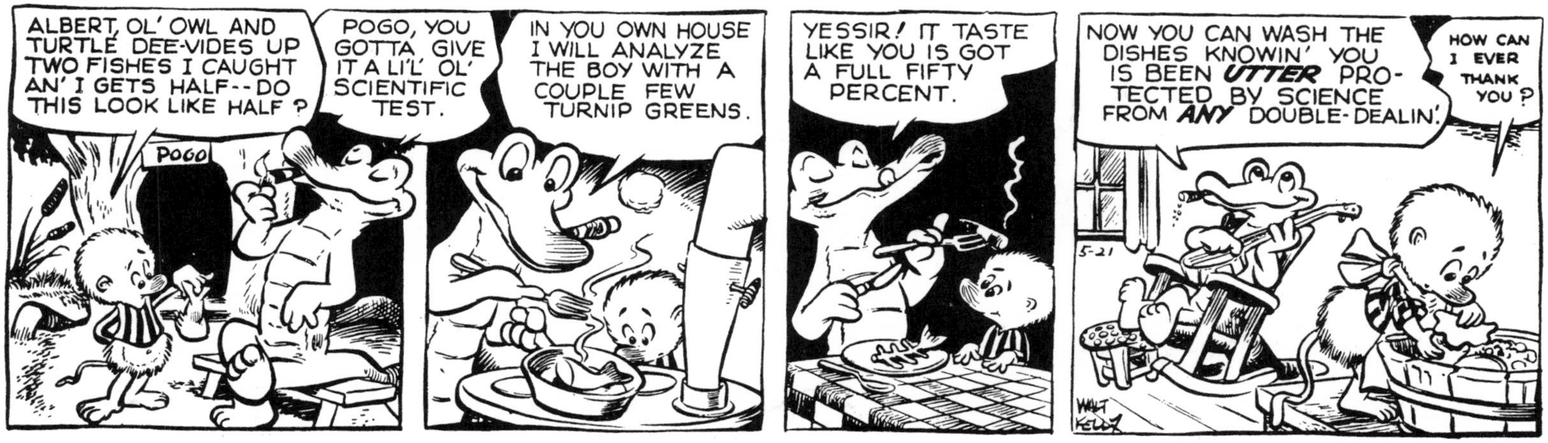
ALBERT, OL' OWL AND TURTLE DEE-VIDES UP TWO FISHES I CAUGHT AN' I GETS HALF--DO THIS LOOK LIKE HALF?
POGO
POGO, YOU GOTTA GIVE IT A LI'L' OL' SCIENTIFIC TEST.
IN YOU OWN HOUSE I WILL ANALYZE THE BOY WITH A COUPLE FEW TURNIP GREENS.
YESSIR! IT TASTE LIKE YOU IS GOT A FULL FIFTY PERCENT.
5-21
WALT KELLY
NOW YOU CAN WASH THE DISHES KNOWIN' YOU IS BEEN UTTER PRO-TECTED BY SCIENCE FROM ANY DOUBLE-DEALIN'.
HOW CAN I EVER THANK YOU?

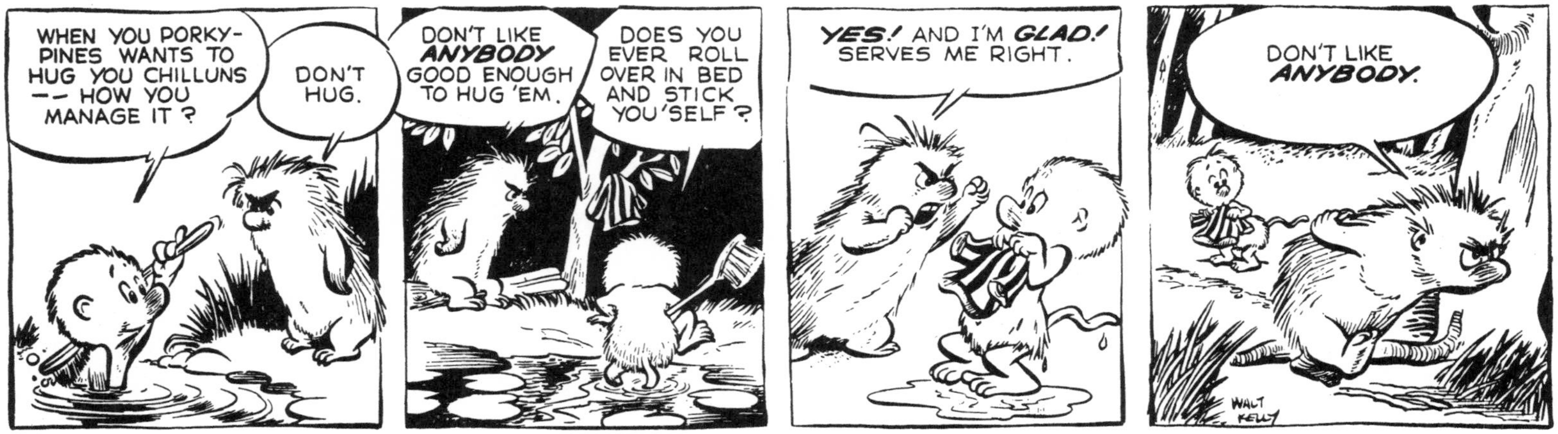
WHEN YOU PORKY-PINES WANTS TO HUG YOU CHILLUNS -- HOW YOU MANAGE IT ?
DON'T HUG.
DON'T LIKE ANYBODY GOOD ENOUGH TO HUG 'EM.
DOES YOU EVER ROLL OVER IN BED AND STICK YOU'SELF ?
YES! AND I'M GLAD! SERVES ME RIGHT.
DON'T LIKE ANYBODY.
WALT KELLY

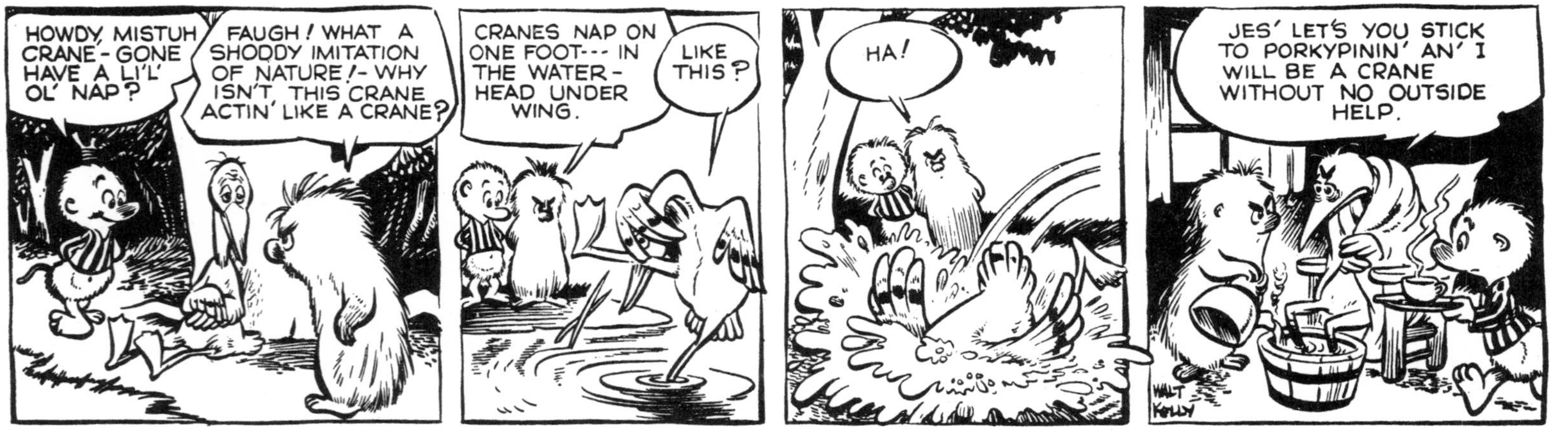
HOWDY, MISTUH CRANE - GONE HAVE A LI'L' OL' NAP ?
FAUGH! WHAT A SHODDY IMITATION OF NATURE! - WHY ISN'T THIS CRANE ACTIN' LIKE A CRANE ?
CRANES NAP ON ONE FOOT--- IN THE WATER - HEAD UNDER WING.
LIKE THIS ?
HA!
JES' LET'S YOU STICK TO PORKYPININ' AN' I WILL BE A CRANE WITHOUT NO OUTSIDE HELP.
WALT KELLY

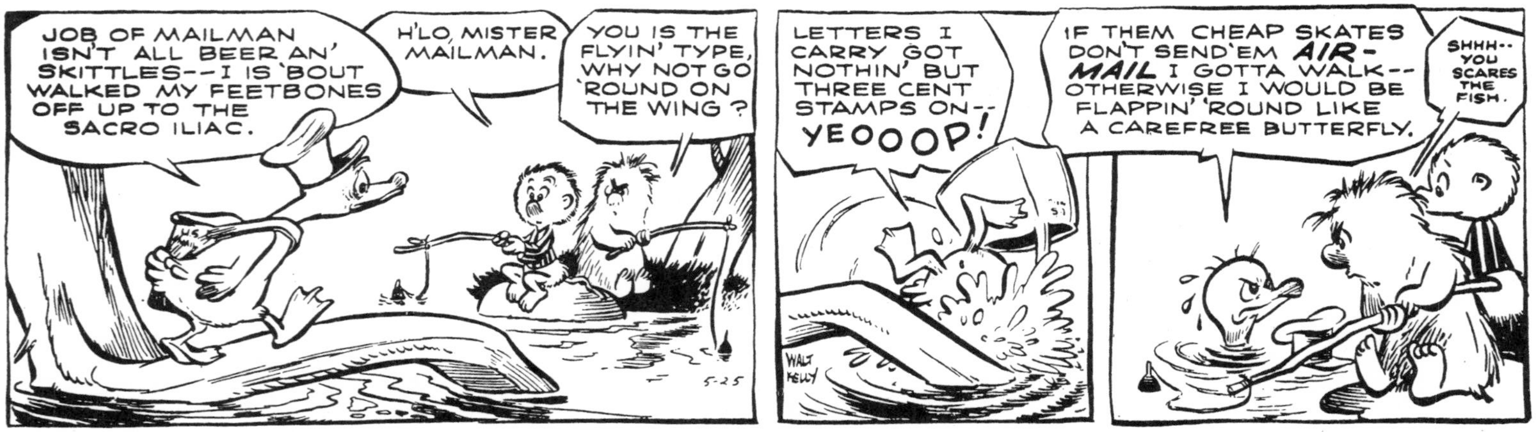
JOB OF MAILMAN ISN'T ALL BEER AN' SKITTLES--I IS 'BOUT WALKED MY FEETBONES OFF UP TO THE SACRO ILIAC.
H'LO, MISTER MAILMAN.
YOU IS THE FLYIN' TYPE, WHY NOT GO 'ROUND ON THE WING ?
5-25
LETTERS I CARRY GOT NOTHIN' BUT THREE CENT STAMPS ON--
YEOOOP!
IF THEM CHEAP SKATES DON'T SEND 'EM AIR-MAIL I GOTTA WALK-- OTHERWISE I WOULD BE FLAPPIN' 'ROUND LIKE A CAREFREE BUTTERFLY.
SHHH-- YOU SCARES THE FISH.
WALT KELLY

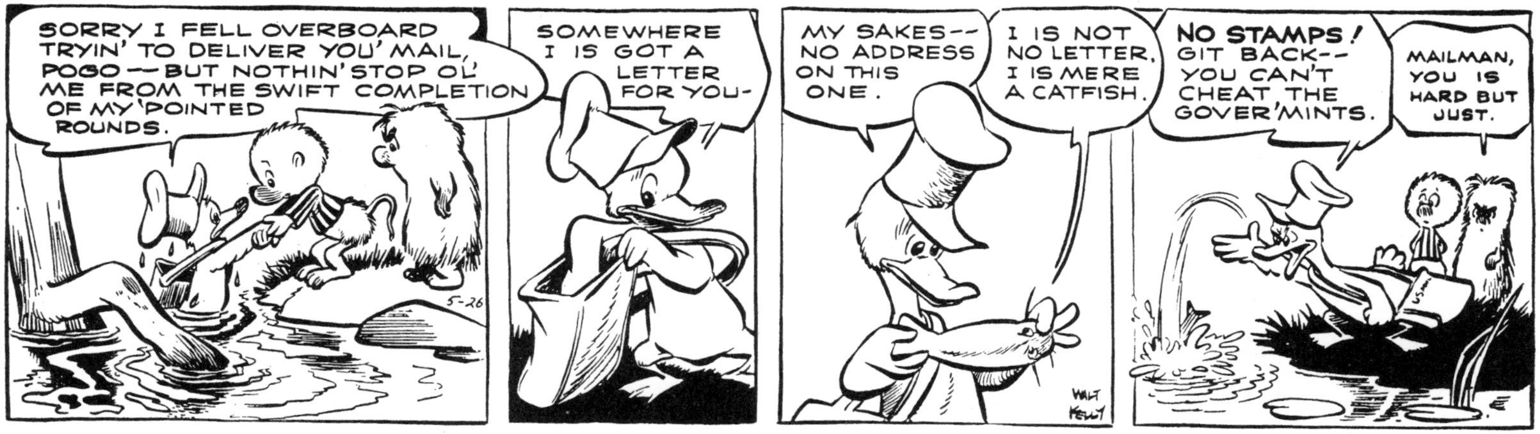
SORRY I FELL OVERBOARD TRYIN' TO DELIVER YOU' MAIL, POGO -- BUT NOTHIN' STOP OL' ME FROM THE SWIFT COMPLETION OF MY 'POINTED ROUNDS.
5-26
SOMEWHERE I IS GOT A LETTER FOR YOU-
MY SAKES -- NO ADDRESS ON THIS ONE.
I IS NOT NO LETTER, I IS MERE A CATFISH.
WALT KELLY
NO STAMPS! GIT BACK -- YOU CAN'T CHEAT THE GOVER'MINTS.
MAILMAN, YOU IS HARD BUT JUST.

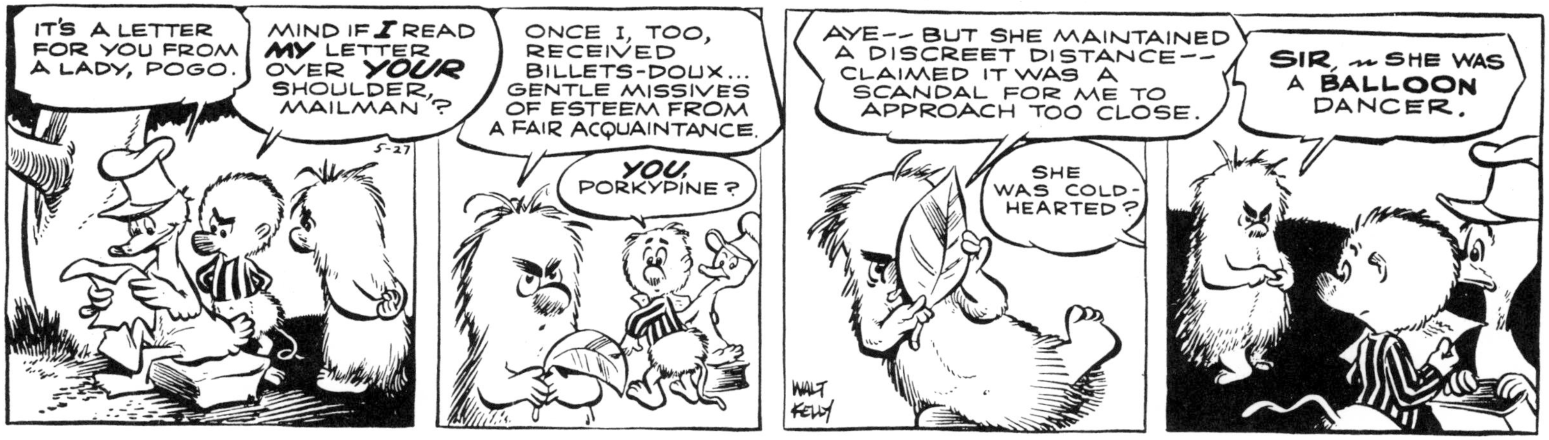
IT'S A LETTER FOR YOU FROM A LADY, POGO.
MIND IF I READ MY LETTER OVER YOUR SHOULDER, MAILMAN?
5-27
ONCE I, TOO, RECEIVED BILLETS-DOUX... GENTLE MISSIVES OF ESTEEM FROM A FAIR ACQUAINTANCE.
YOU, PORKYPINE?
AYE -- BUT SHE MAINTAINED A DISCREET DISTANCE -- CLAIMED IT WAS A SCANDAL FOR ME TO APPROACH TOO CLOSE.
SHE WAS COLD-HEARTED?
WALT KELLY
SIR, -- SHE WAS A BALLOON DANCER.

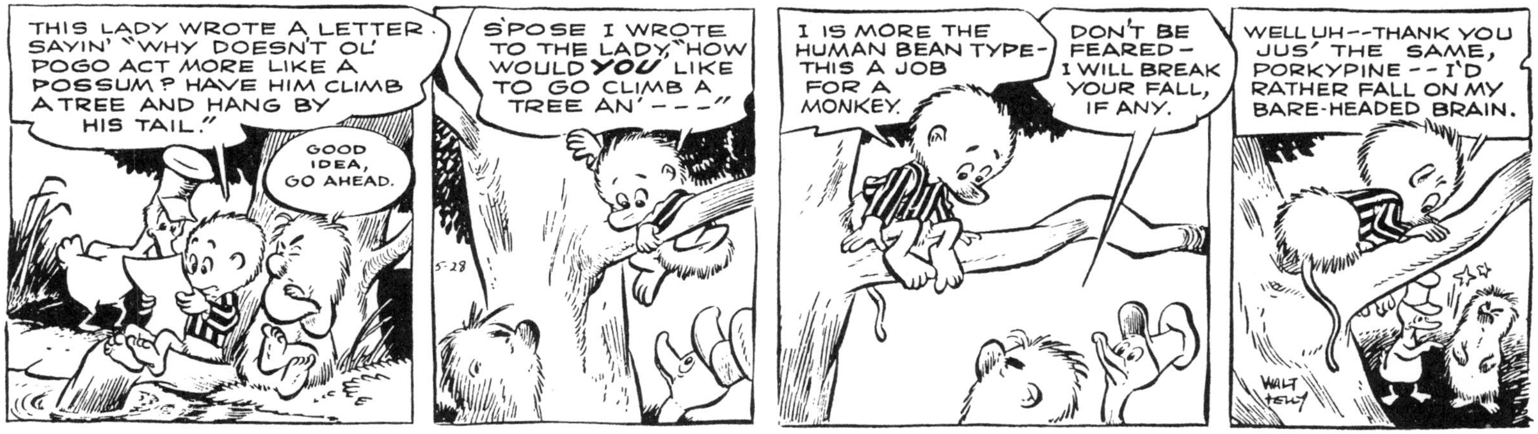
THIS LADY WROTE A LETTER SAYIN' "WHY DOESN'T OL' POGO ACT MORE LIKE A POSSUM? HAVE HIM CLIMB A TREE AND HANG BY HIS TAIL."
GOOD IDEA, GO AHEAD.
S'POSE I WROTE TO THE LADY, "HOW WOULD YOU LIKE TO GO CLIMB A TREE AN' ---"
5-28
I IS MORE THE HUMAN BEAN TYPE - THIS A JOB FOR A MONKEY.
DON'T BE FEARED - I WILL BREAK YOUR FALL, IF ANY.
WELL UH -- THANK YOU JUS' THE SAME, PORKYPINE -- I'D RATHER FALL ON MY BARE-HEADED BRAIN.
WALT KELLY

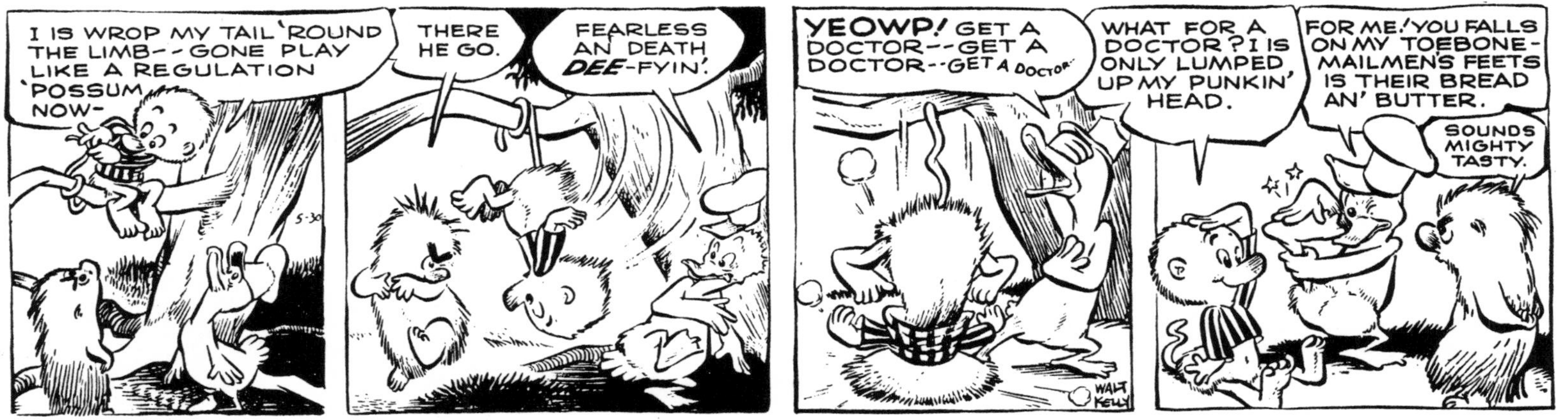
I IS WROP MY TAIL 'ROUND THE LIMB--GONE PLAY LIKE A REGULATION 'POSSUM NOW-
5-30
THERE HE GO.
FEARLESS AN' DEATH DEE-FYIN'.
YEOWP! GET A DOCTOR--GET A DOCTOR--GET A DOCTOR
WALT KELLY
WHAT FOR A DOCTOR? I IS ONLY LUMPED UP MY PUNKIN' HEAD.
FOR ME! YOU FALLS ON MY TOEBONE-MAILMEN'S FEETS IS THEIR BREAD AN' BUTTER.
SOUNDS MIGHTY TASTY.

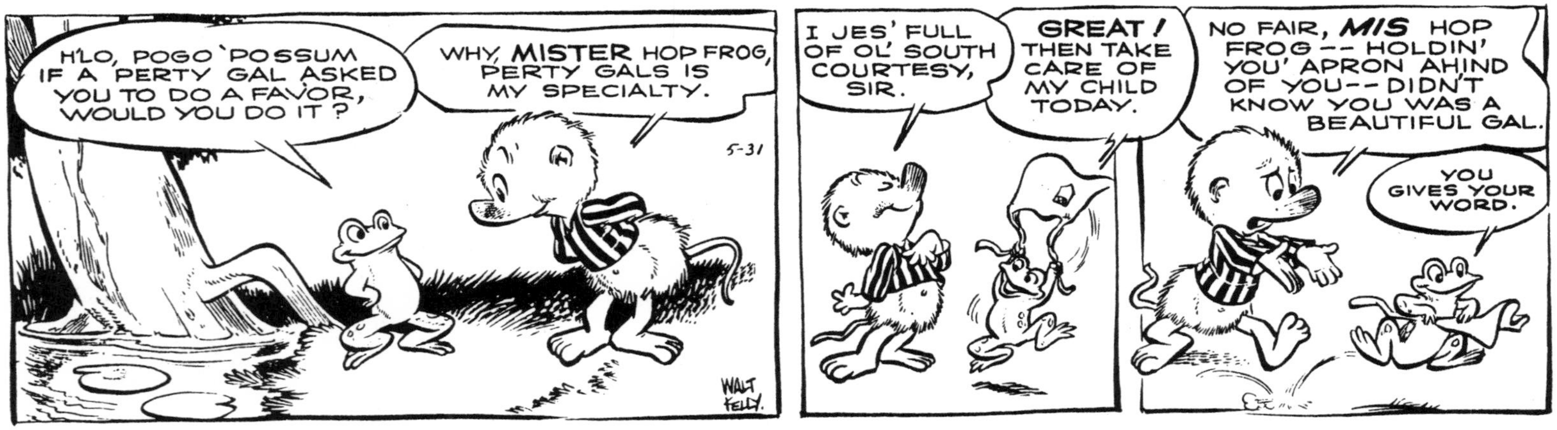
H'LO, POGO 'POSSUM IF A PERTY GAL ASKED YOU TO DO A FAVOR, WOULD YOU DO IT?
WHY, MISTER HOP FROG, PERTY GALS IS MY SPECIALTY.
5-31
WALT KELLY.
I JES' FULL OF OL' SOUTH COURTESY, SIR.
GREAT! THEN TAKE CARE OF MY CHILD TODAY.
NO FAIR, MIS HOP FROG -- HOLDIN' YOU' APRON AHIND OF YOU--DIDN'T KNOW YOU WAS A BEAUTIFUL GAL.
YOU GIVES YOUR WORD.

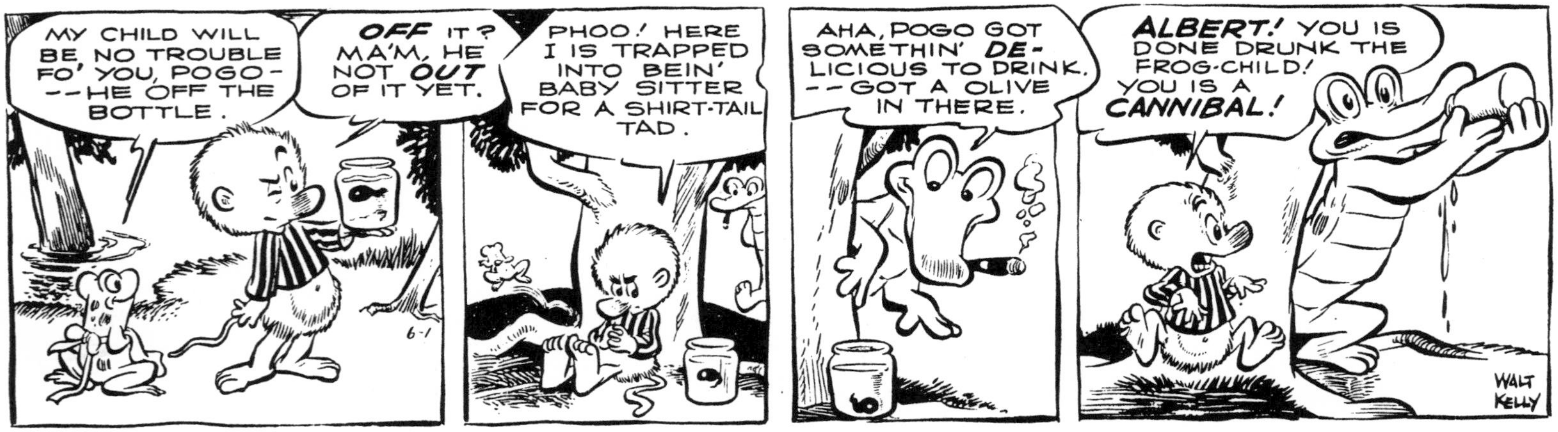
MY CHILD WILL BE NO TROUBLE FO' YOU, POGO--HE OFF THE BOTTLE.
OFF IT? MA'M, HE NOT OUT OF IT YET.
6-1
PHOO! HERE I IS TRAPPED INTO BEIN' BABY SITTER FOR A SHIRT-TAIL TAD.
AHA, POGO GOT SOMETHIN' DE-LICIOUS TO DRINK. --GOT A OLIVE IN THERE.
ALBERT! YOU IS DONE DRUNK THE FROG-CHILD! YOU IS A CANNIBAL!
WALT KELLY

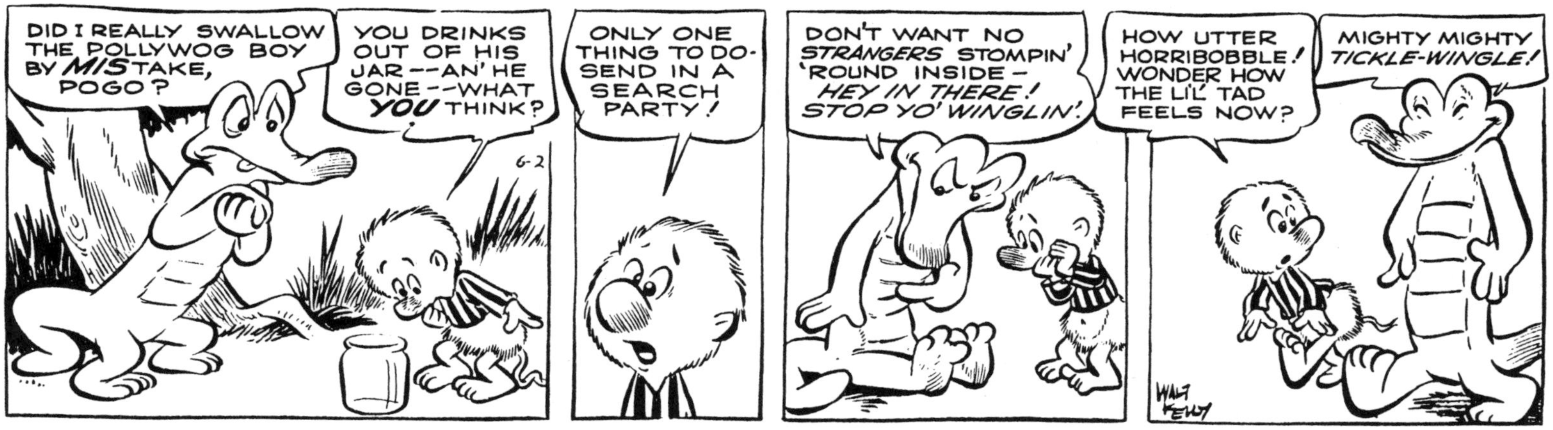
DID I REALLY SWALLOW THE POLLYWOG BOY BY *MIS*TAKE, POGO?
YOU DRINKS OUT OF HIS JAR--AN' HE GONE--WHAT *YOU* THINK?
6-2
ONLY ONE THING TO DO-SEND IN A SEARCH PARTY!
DON'T WANT NO *STRANGERS* STOMPIN' 'ROUND INSIDE-*HEY IN THERE! STOP YO' WINGLIN'!*
HOW UTTER HORRIBOBBLE! WONDER HOW THE LI'L TAD FEELS NOW?
MIGHTY MIGHTY *TICKLE-WINGLE!*
WALT KELLY

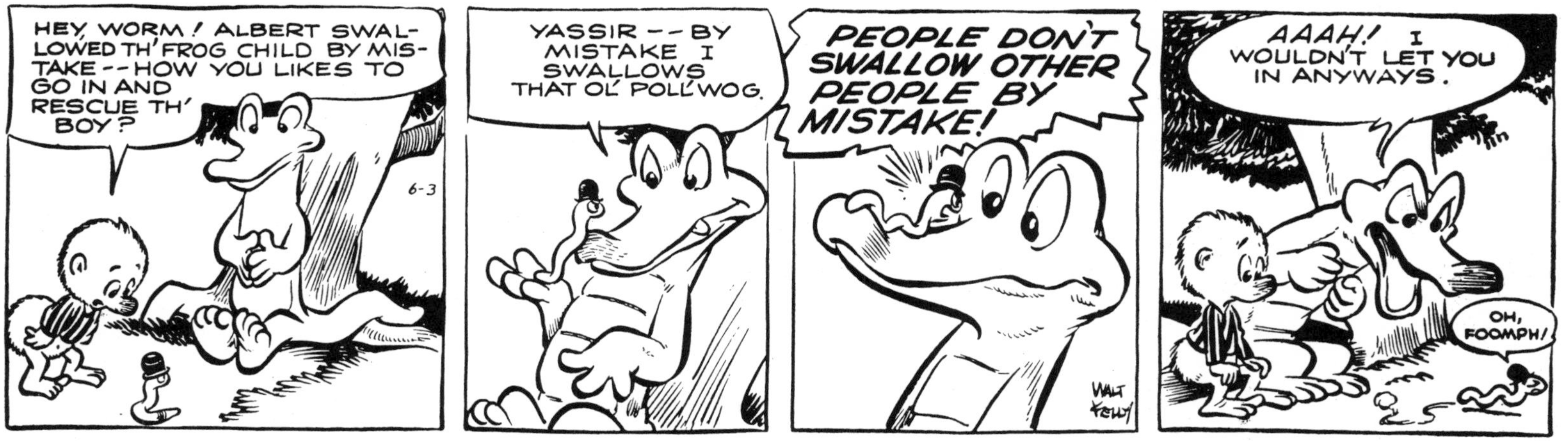
HEY, WORM! ALBERT SWALLOWED TH' FROG CHILD BY MISTAKE--HOW YOU LIKES TO GO IN AND RESCUE TH' BOY?
6-3
YASSIR--BY MISTAKE I SWALLOWS THAT OL' POLL'WOG.
PEOPLE DON'T SWALLOW OTHER PEOPLE BY MISTAKE!
WALT KELLY
AAAH! I WOULDN'T LET YOU IN ANYWAYS.
OH, FOOMPH!

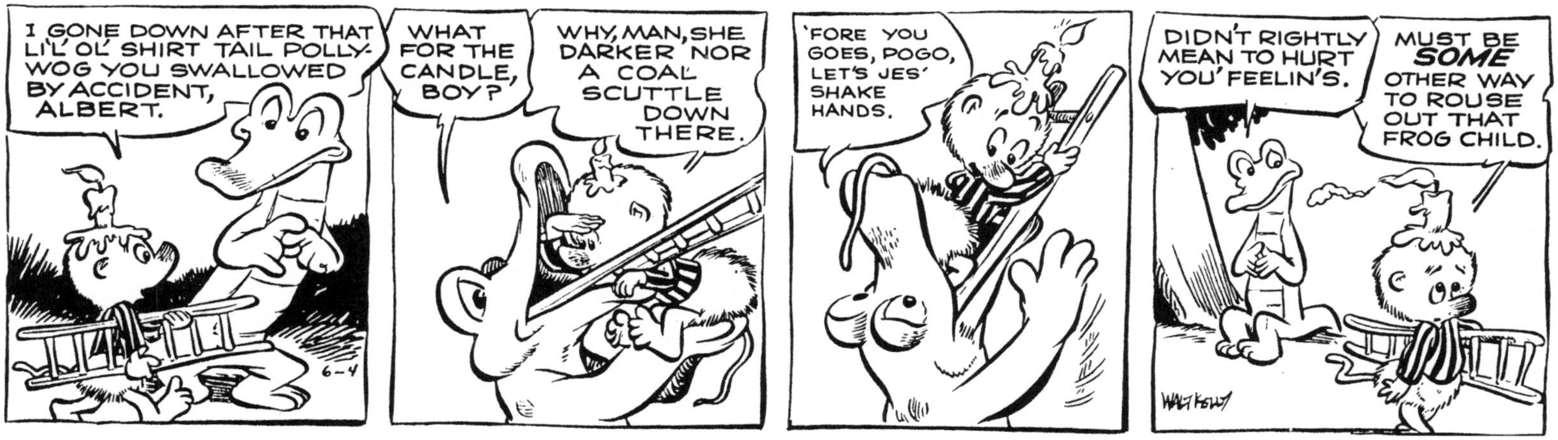
I GONE DOWN AFTER THAT LI'L OL' SHIRT TAIL POLLYWOG YOU SWALLOWED BY ACCIDENT, ALBERT.
6-4
WHAT FOR THE CANDLE, BOY?
WHY, MAN, SHE DARKER NOR A COAL SCUTTLE DOWN THERE.
'FORE YOU GOES, POGO, LET'S JES' SHAKE HANDS.
DIDN'T RIGHTLY MEAN TO HURT YOU' FEELIN'S.
MUST BE **SOME** OTHER WAY TO ROUSE OUT THAT FROG CHILD.
WALT KELLY

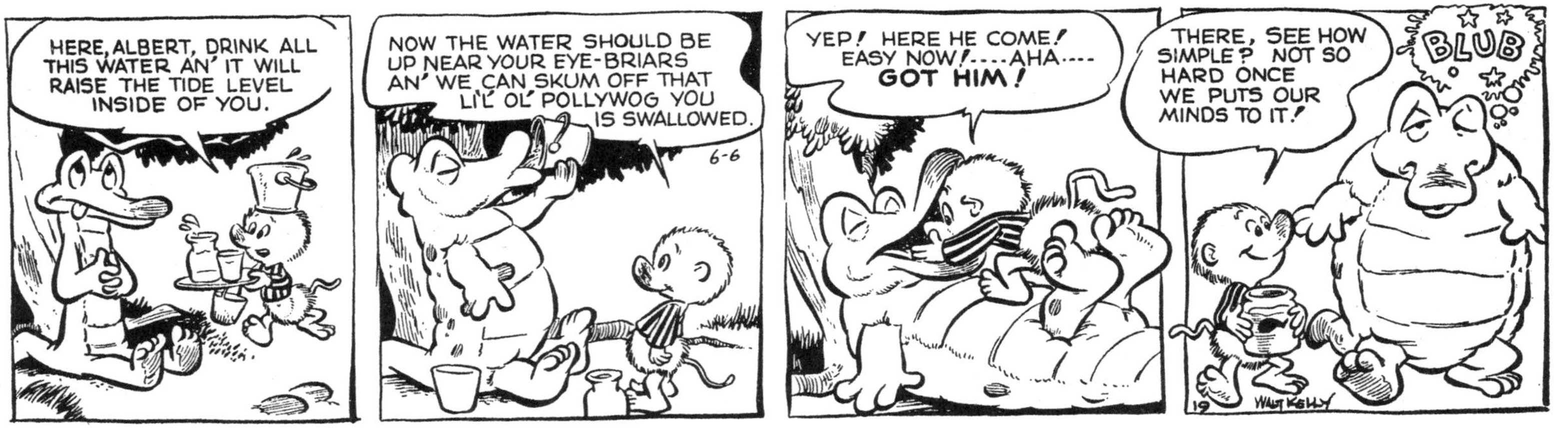
HERE, ALBERT, DRINK ALL THIS WATER AN' IT WILL RAISE THE TIDE LEVEL INSIDE OF YOU.
NOW THE WATER SHOULD BE UP NEAR YOUR EYE-BRIARS AN' WE CAN SKUM OFF THAT LI'L OL' POLLYWOG YOU IS SWALLOWED.
6-6
YEP! HERE HE COME! EASY NOW!----AHA---- GOT HIM!
THERE, SEE HOW SIMPLE? NOT SO HARD ONCE WE PUTS OUR MINDS TO IT!
BLUB
19
WALT KELLY

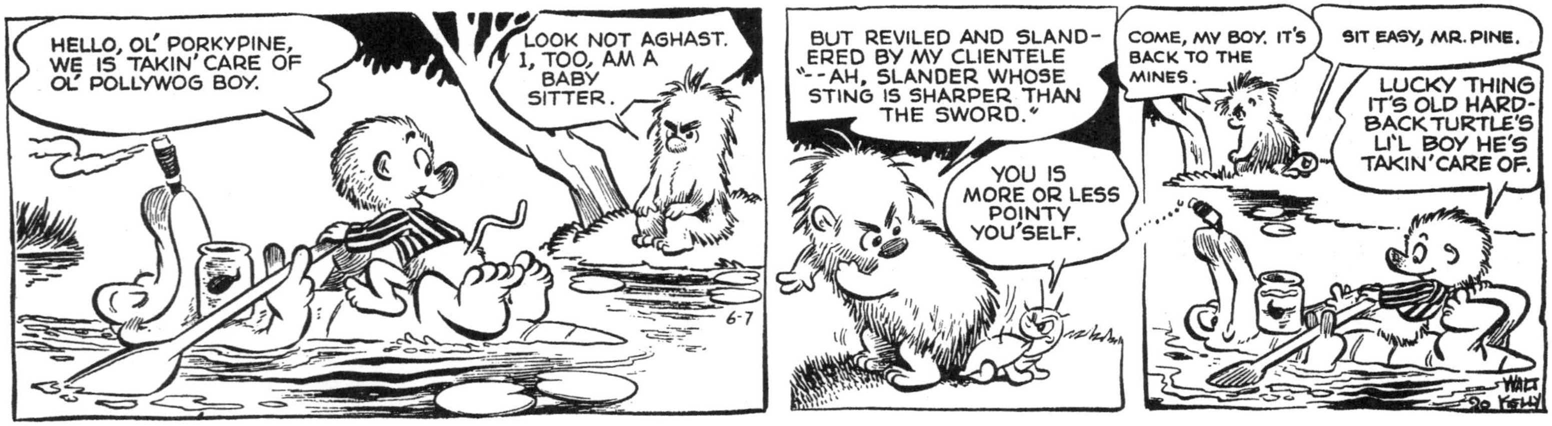
HELLO, OL' PORKYPINE, WE IS TAKIN' CARE OF OL' POLLYWOG BOY.
LOOK NOT AGHAST. I, TOO, AM A BABY SITTER.
6-7
BUT REVILED AND SLANDERED BY MY CLIENTELE "--AH, SLANDER WHOSE STING IS SHARPER THAN THE SWORD."
YOU IS MORE OR LESS POINTY YOU'SELF.
COME, MY BOY. IT'S BACK TO THE MINES.
SIT EASY, MR. PINE.
LUCKY THING IT'S OLD HARD-BACK TURTLE'S LI'L BOY HE'S TAKIN' CARE OF.
20
WALT KELLY

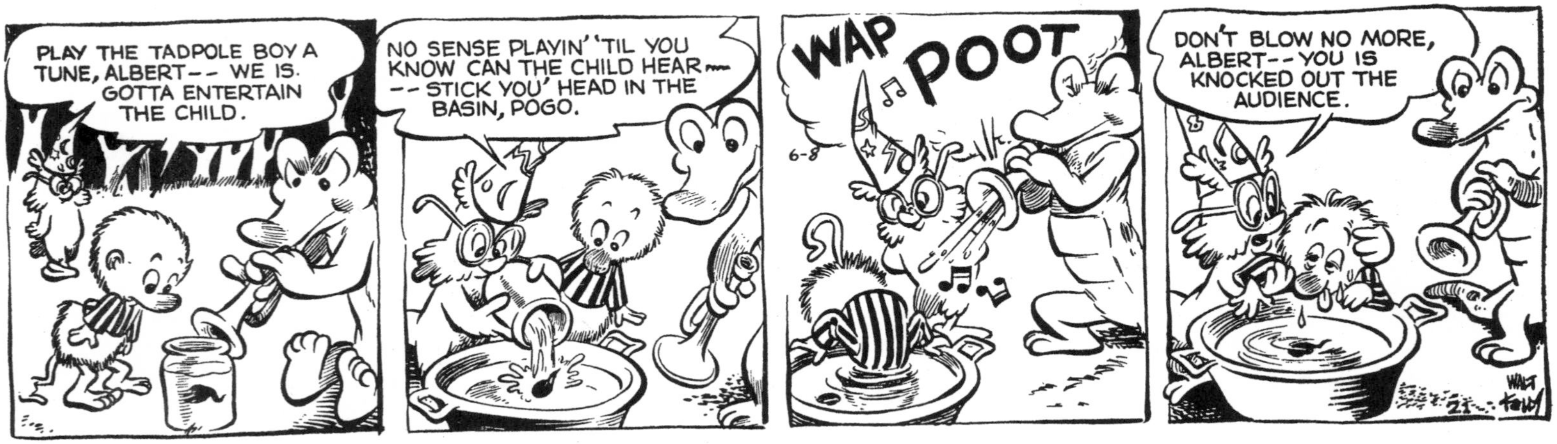
PLAY THE TADPOLE BOY A TUNE, ALBERT-- WE IS GOTTA ENTERTAIN THE CHILD.
NO SENSE PLAYIN' 'TIL YOU KNOW CAN THE CHILD HEAR---- STICK YOU' HEAD IN THE BASIN, POGO.
WAP
POOT
6-8
DON'T BLOW NO MORE, ALBERT--YOU IS KNOCKED OUT THE AUDIENCE.
21
WALT KELLY

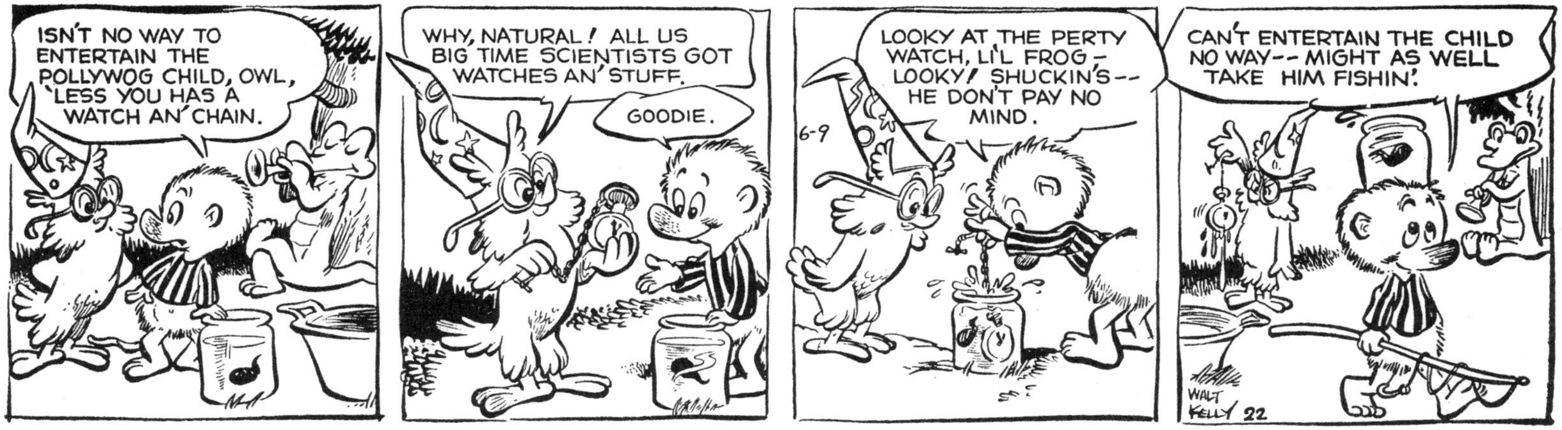
ISN'T NO WAY TO ENTERTAIN THE POLLYWOG CHILD, OWL, 'LESS YOU HAS A WATCH AN' CHAIN.
WHY, NATURAL! ALL US BIG TIME SCIENTISTS GOT WATCHES AN' STUFF.
GOODIE.
6-9
LOOKY AT THE PERTY WATCH, LI'L FROG — LOOKY! SHUCKIN'S -- HE DON'T PAY NO MIND.
CAN'T ENTERTAIN THE CHILD NO WAY -- MIGHT AS WELL TAKE HIM FISHIN'.
WALT KELLY 22

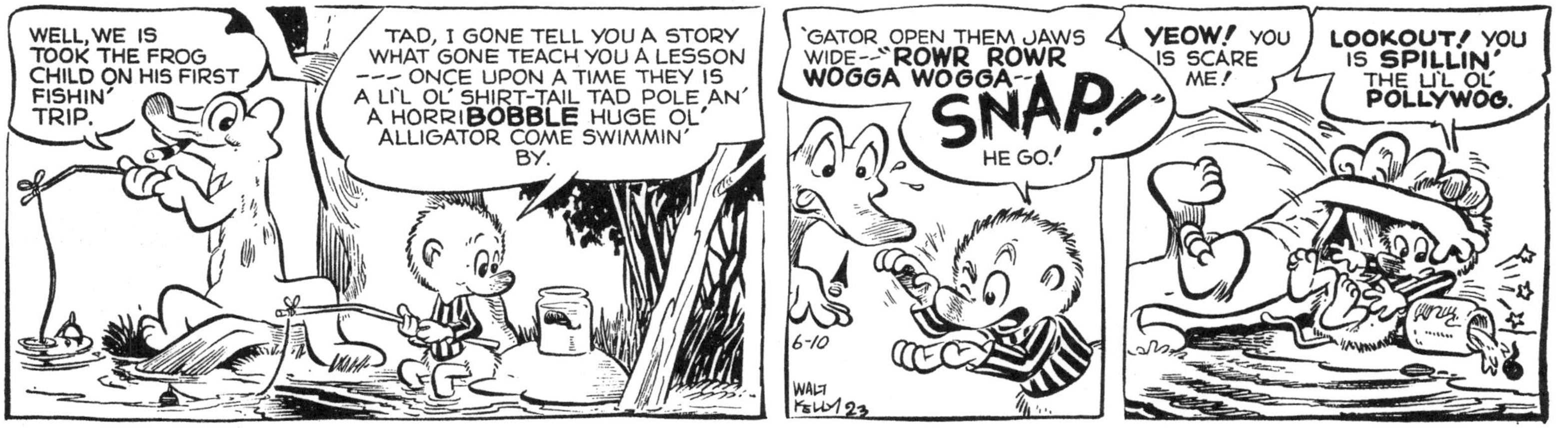
WELL, WE IS TOOK THE FROG CHILD ON HIS FIRST FISHIN' TRIP.
TAD, I GONE TELL YOU A STORY WHAT GONE TEACH YOU A LESSON --- ONCE UPON A TIME THEY IS A LI'L OL' SHIRT-TAIL TAD POLE AN' A HORRIBOBBLE HUGE OL' ALLIGATOR COME SWIMMIN' BY.
'GATOR OPEN THEM JAWS WIDE -- "ROWR ROWR WOGGA WOGGA -- SNAP!" HE GO.
6-10
WALT KELLY 23
YEOW! YOU IS SCARE ME!
LOOKOUT! YOU IS SPILLIN' THE LI'L OL' POLLYWOG.

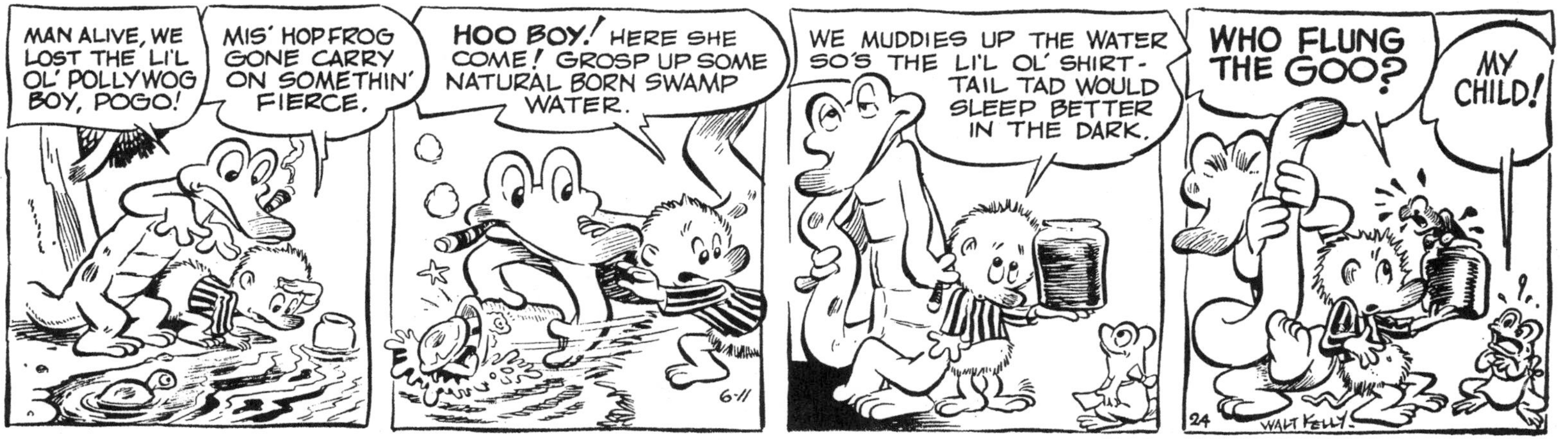
MAN ALIVE, WE LOST THE LI'L OL' POLLYWOG BOY, POGO!
MIS' HOPFROG GONE CARRY ON SOMETHIN' FIERCE.
HOO BOY! HERE SHE COME! GROSP UP SOME NATURAL BORN SWAMP WATER.
6-11
WE MUDDIES UP THE WATER SO'S THE LI'L OL' SHIRT-TAIL TAD WOULD SLEEP BETTER IN THE DARK.
WHO FLUNG THE GOO?
MY CHILD!
24 WALT KELLY

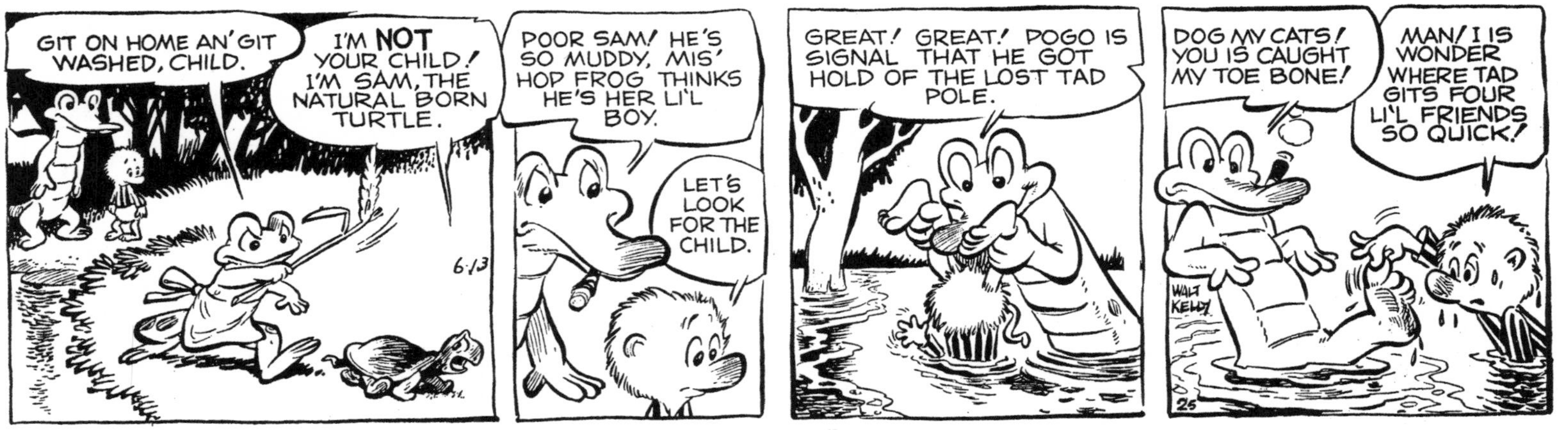
GIT ON HOME AN' GIT WASHED, CHILD.
I'M **NOT** YOUR CHILD! I'M SAM, THE NATURAL BORN TURTLE.
6-13
POOR SAM! HE'S SO MUDDY, MIS' HOP FROG THINKS HE'S HER LI'L BOY.
LET'S LOOK FOR THE CHILD.
GREAT! GREAT! POGO IS SIGNAL THAT HE GOT HOLD OF THE LOST TAD POLE.
DOG MY CATS! YOU IS CAUGHT MY TOE BONE!
MAN! I IS WONDER WHERE TAD GITS FOUR LI'L FRIENDS SO QUICK!
WALT KELLY
25

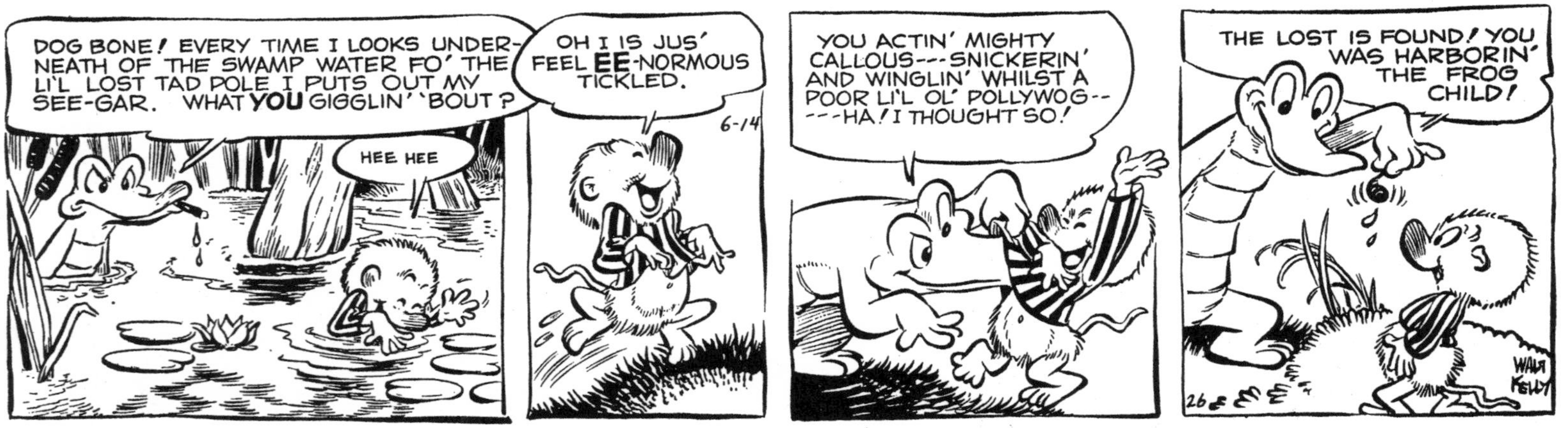
DOG BONE! EVERY TIME I LOOKS UNDERNEATH OF THE SWAMP WATER FO' THE LI'L LOST TAD POLE I PUTS OUT MY SEE-GAR. WHAT **YOU** GIGGLIN' 'BOUT?
HEE HEE
OH I IS JUS' FEEL **EE**-NORMOUS TICKLED.
6-14
YOU ACTIN' MIGHTY CALLOUS---SNICKERIN' AND WINGLIN' WHILST A POOR LI'L OL' POLLYWOG-----HA! I THOUGHT SO!
THE LOST IS FOUND! YOU WAS HARBORIN' THE FROG CHILD!
26
WALT KELLY

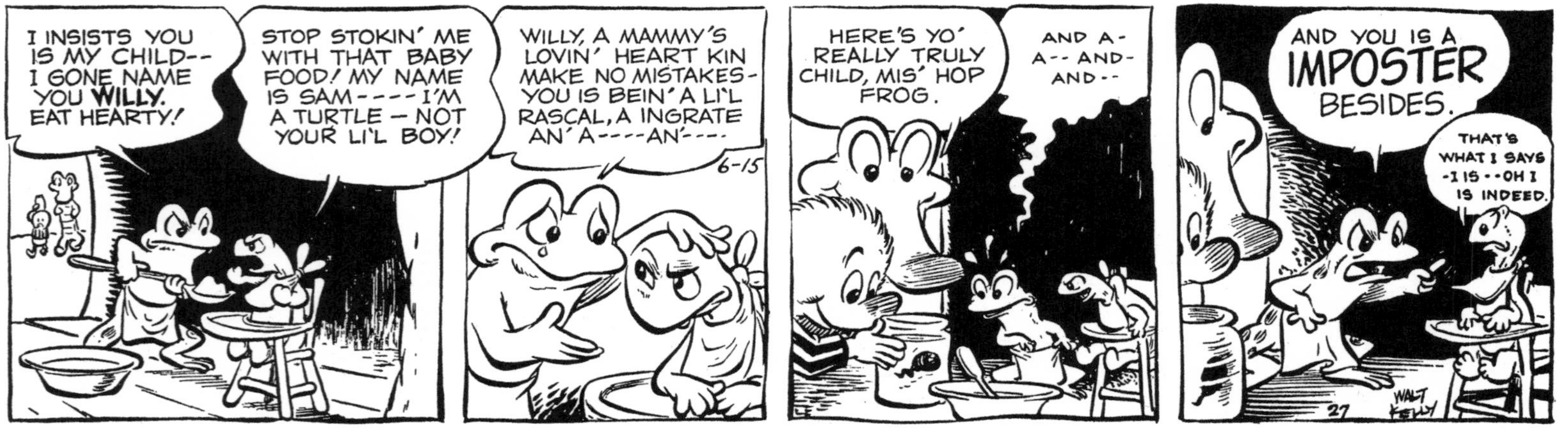
I INSISTS YOU IS MY CHILD--I GONE NAME YOU **WILLY**. EAT HEARTY!
STOP STOKIN' ME WITH THAT BABY FOOD! MY NAME IS SAM----I'M A TURTLE — NOT YOUR LI'L BOY!
WILLY, A MAMMY'S LOVIN' HEART KIN MAKE NO MISTAKES-YOU IS BEIN' A LI'L RASCAL, A INGRATE AN' A----AN'---.
6-15
HERE'S YO' REALLY TRULY CHILD, MIS' HOP FROG.
AND A-A--AND-AND--
AND YOU IS A **IMPOSTER** BESIDES.
THAT'S WHAT I SAYS -I IS--OH I IS INDEED.
27
WALT KELLY

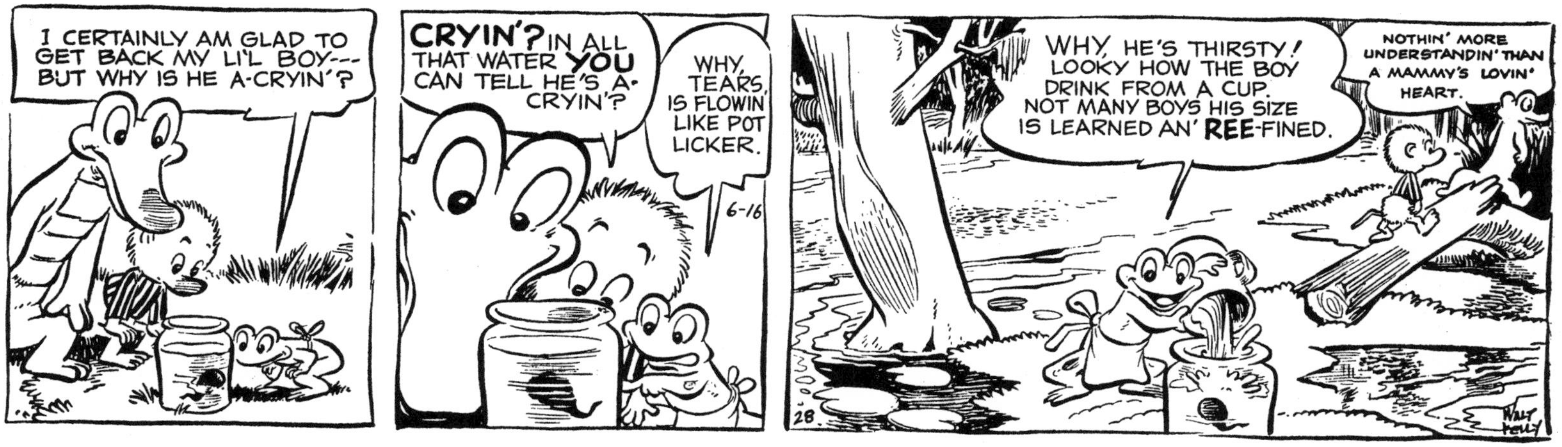
I CERTAINLY AM GLAD TO GET BACK MY LI'L BOY--- BUT WHY IS HE A-CRYIN'?
CRYIN'? IN ALL THAT WATER YOU CAN TELL HE'S A-CRYIN'?
WHY, TEARS, IS FLOWIN' LIKE POT LICKER.
6-16
WHY, HE'S THIRSTY! LOOKY HOW THE BOY DRINK FROM A CUP. NOT MANY BOYS HIS SIZE IS LEARNED AN' REE-FINED.
NOTHIN' MORE UNDERSTANDIN' THAN A MAMMY'S LOVIN' HEART.
WALT KELLY

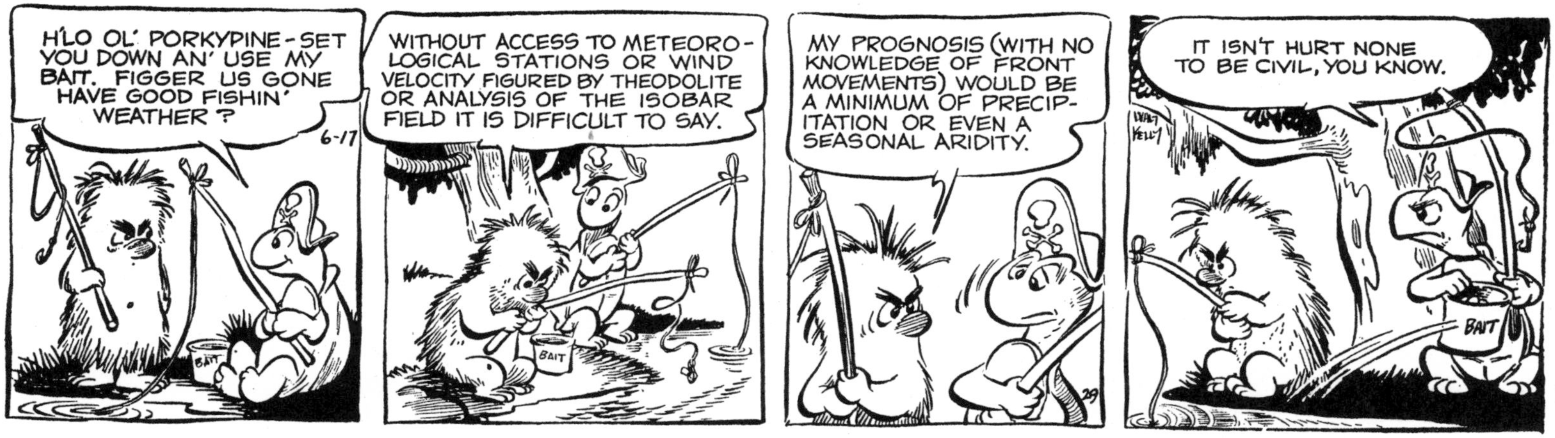
H'LO OL' PORKYPINE - SET YOU DOWN AN' USE MY BAIT. FIGGER US GONE HAVE GOOD FISHIN' WEATHER?
6-17
BAIT
WITHOUT ACCESS TO METEOROLOGICAL STATIONS OR WIND VELOCITY FIGURED BY THEODOLITE OR ANALYSIS OF THE ISOBAR FIELD IT IS DIFFICULT TO SAY.
BAIT
MY PROGNOSIS (WITH NO KNOWLEDGE OF FRONT MOVEMENTS) WOULD BE A MINIMUM OF PRECIPITATION OR EVEN A SEASONAL ARIDITY.
IT ISN'T HURT NONE TO BE CIVIL, YOU KNOW.
WALT KELLY
BAIT

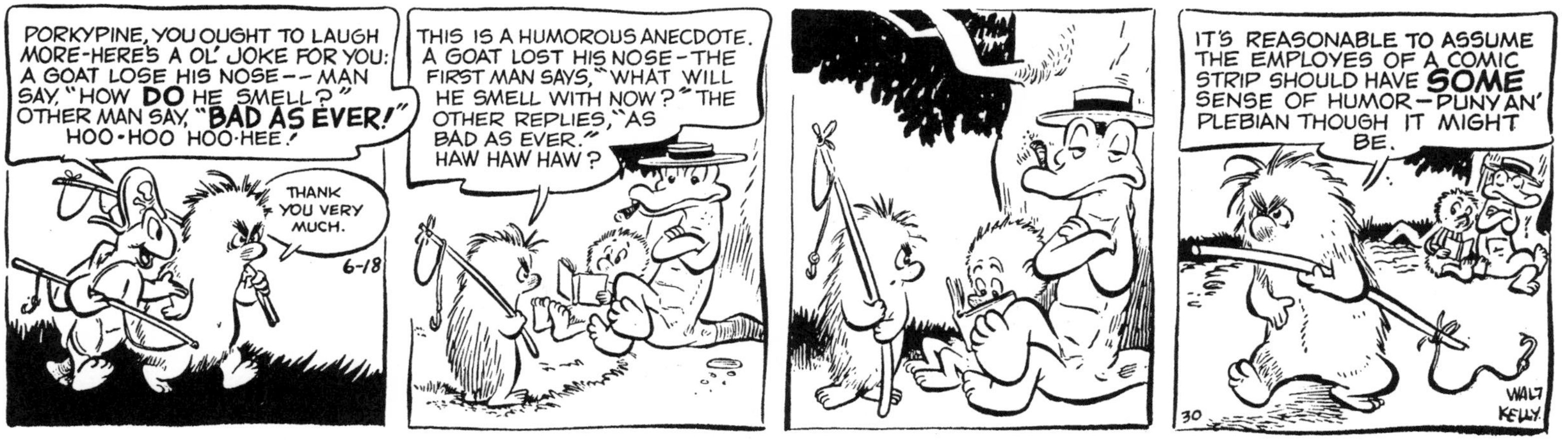
PORKYPINE, YOU OUGHT TO LAUGH MORE - HERE'S A OL' JOKE FOR YOU: A GOAT LOSE HIS NOSE -- MAN SAY, "HOW DO HE SMELL?" OTHER MAN SAY, "BAD AS EVER!" HOO-HOO HOO-HEE!
THANK YOU VERY MUCH.
6-18
THIS IS A HUMOROUS ANECDOTE. A GOAT LOST HIS NOSE - THE FIRST MAN SAYS, "WHAT WILL HE SMELL WITH NOW?" THE OTHER REPLIES, "AS BAD AS EVER." HAW HAW HAW?
IT'S REASONABLE TO ASSUME THE EMPLOYES OF A COMIC STRIP SHOULD HAVE SOME SENSE OF HUMOR - PUNY AN' PLEBIAN THOUGH IT MIGHT BE.
WALT KELLY

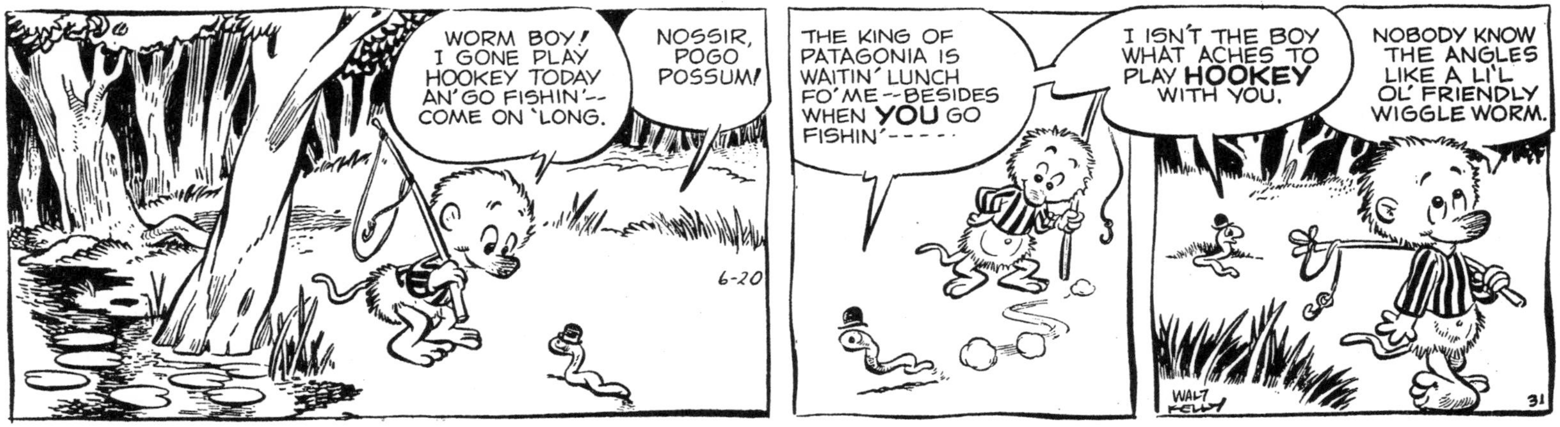

WORM BOY! I GONE PLAY HOOKEY TODAY AN' GO FISHIN'-- COME ON 'LONG.
NOSSIR, POGO POSSUM!
6-20
THE KING OF PATAGONIA IS WAITIN' LUNCH FO' ME--BESIDES WHEN YOU GO FISHIN'-----
I ISN'T THE BOY WHAT ACHES TO PLAY HOOKEY WITH YOU.
NOBODY KNOW THE ANGLES LIKE A LI'L OL' FRIENDLY WIGGLE WORM.
WALT KELLY
31

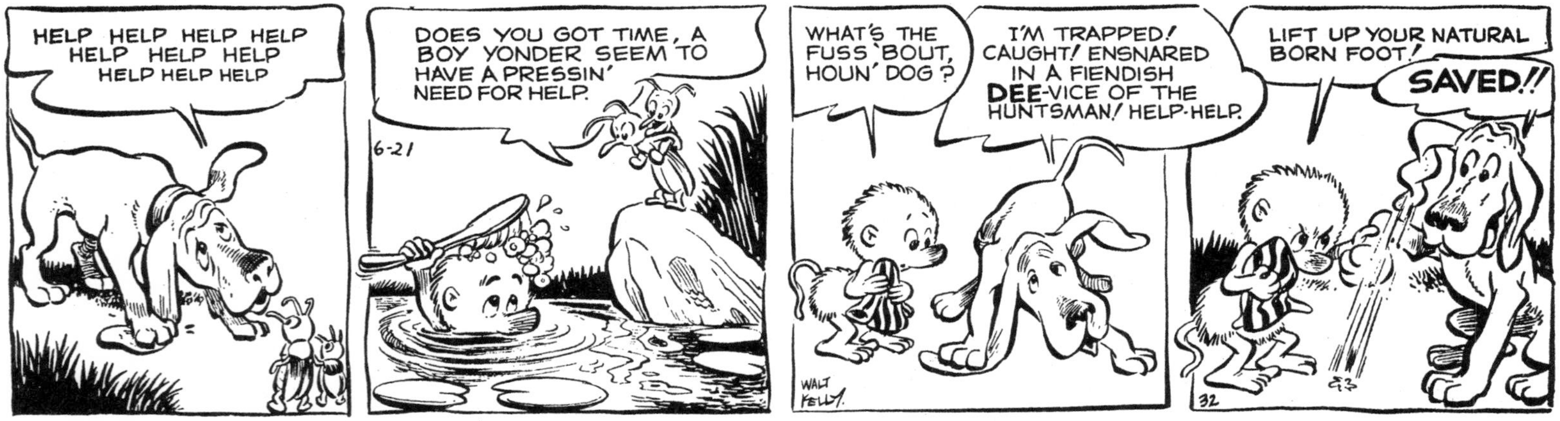

HELP HELP HELP HELP HELP HELP HELP HELP HELP HELP
DOES YOU GOT TIME, A BOY YONDER SEEM TO HAVE A PRESSIN' NEED FOR HELP.
6-21
WHAT'S THE FUSS 'BOUT, HOUN' DOG?
I'M TRAPPED! CAUGHT! ENSNARED IN A FIENDISH DEE-VICE OF THE HUNTSMAN! HELP-HELP.
WALT KELLY
LIFT UP YOUR NATURAL BORN FOOT!
SAVED!!
32

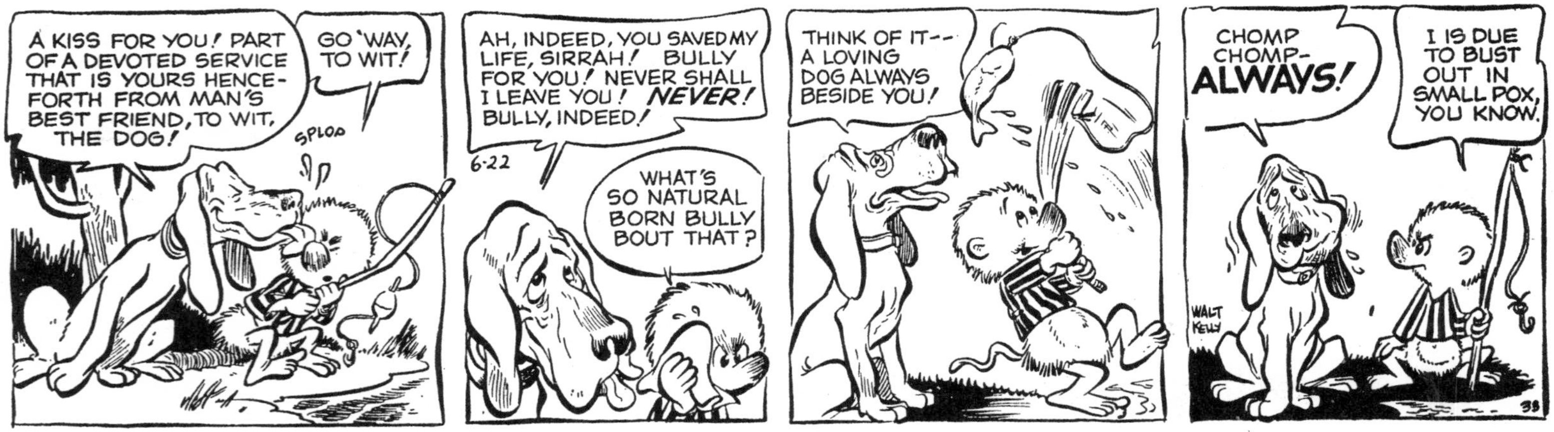

A KISS FOR YOU! PART OF A DEVOTED SERVICE THAT IS YOURS HENCE-FORTH FROM MAN'S BEST FRIEND, TO WIT, THE DOG!
GO 'WAY, TO WIT!
SPLOD
AH, INDEED, YOU SAVED MY LIFE, SIRRAH! BULLY FOR YOU! NEVER SHALL I LEAVE YOU! NEVER! BULLY, INDEED!
6-22
WHAT'S SO NATURAL BORN BULLY 'BOUT THAT?
THINK OF IT-- A LOVING DOG ALWAYS BESIDE YOU!
CHOMP CHOMP- ALWAYS!
I IS DUE TO BUST OUT IN SMALL POX, YOU KNOW.
WALT KELLY
33

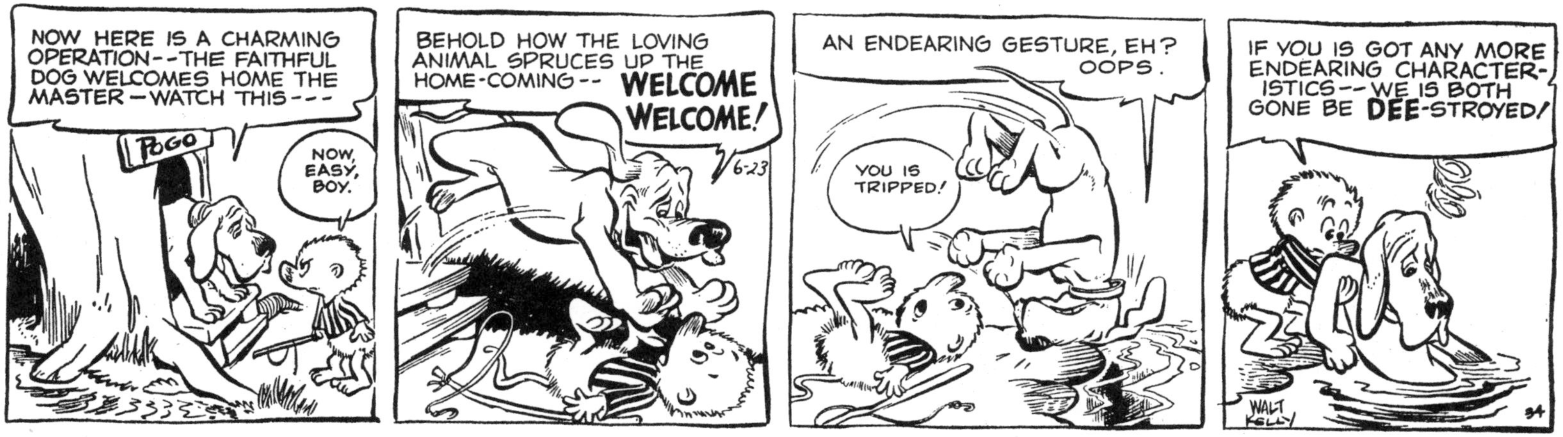
NOW HERE IS A CHARMING OPERATION--THE FAITHFUL DOG WELCOMES HOME THE MASTER—WATCH THIS---
POGO
NOW, EASY, BOY.
BEHOLD HOW THE LOVING ANIMAL SPRUCES UP THE HOME-COMING-- WELCOME WELCOME!
6-23
AN ENDEARING GESTURE, EH? OOPS.
YOU IS TRIPPED!
IF YOU IS GOT ANY MORE ENDEARING CHARACTER-ISTICS--WE IS BOTH GONE BE DEE-STROYED!
WALT KELLY
34

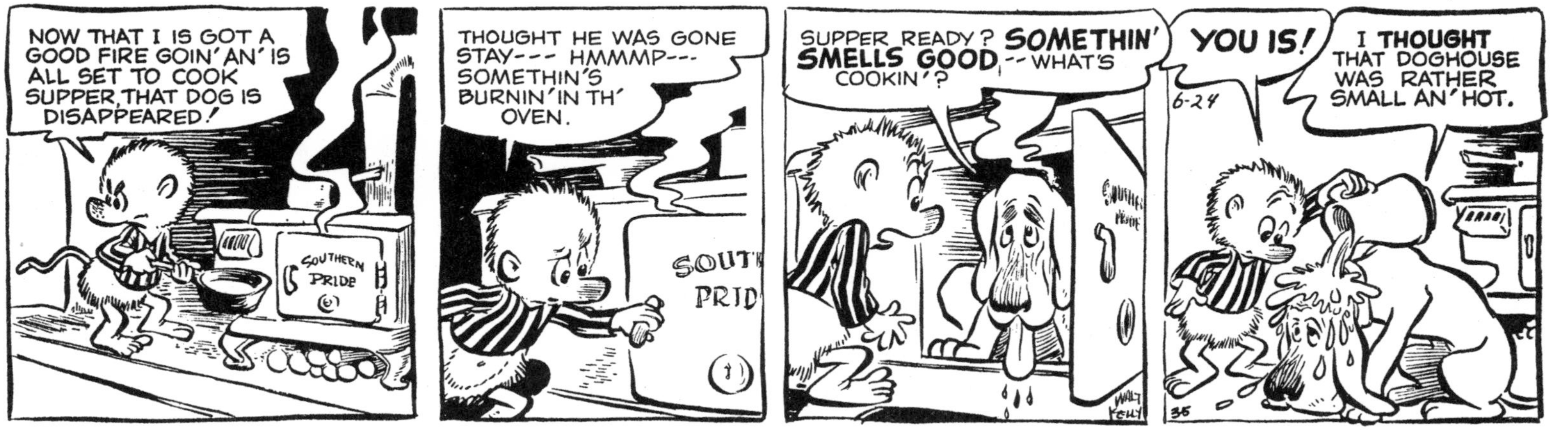
NOW THAT I IS GOT A GOOD FIRE GOIN' AN' IS ALL SET TO COOK SUPPER, THAT DOG IS DISAPPEARED!
SOUTHERN PRIDE
THOUGHT HE WAS GONE STAY--- HMMMP--- SOMETHIN'S BURNIN' IN TH' OVEN.
SOUTH PRID
SUPPER READY? SOMETHIN' SMELLS GOOD--WHAT'S COOKIN'?
WALT KELLY
YOU IS!
6-24
I THOUGHT THAT DOGHOUSE WAS RATHER SMALL AN' HOT.
35

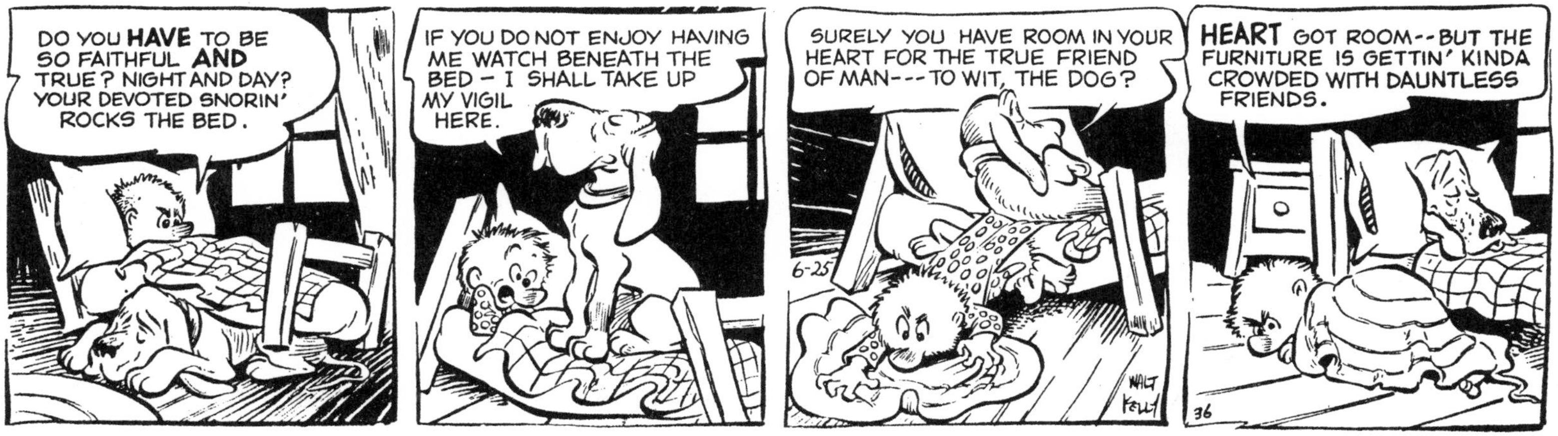
DO YOU HAVE TO BE SO FAITHFUL AND TRUE? NIGHT AND DAY? YOUR DEVOTED SNORIN' ROCKS THE BED.
IF YOU DO NOT ENJOY HAVING ME WATCH BENEATH THE BED—I SHALL TAKE UP MY VIGIL HERE.
SURELY YOU HAVE ROOM IN YOUR HEART FOR THE TRUE FRIEND OF MAN---TO WIT, THE DOG?
6-25
WALT KELLY
HEART GOT ROOM--BUT THE FURNITURE IS GETTIN' KINDA CROWDED WITH DAUNTLESS FRIENDS.
36

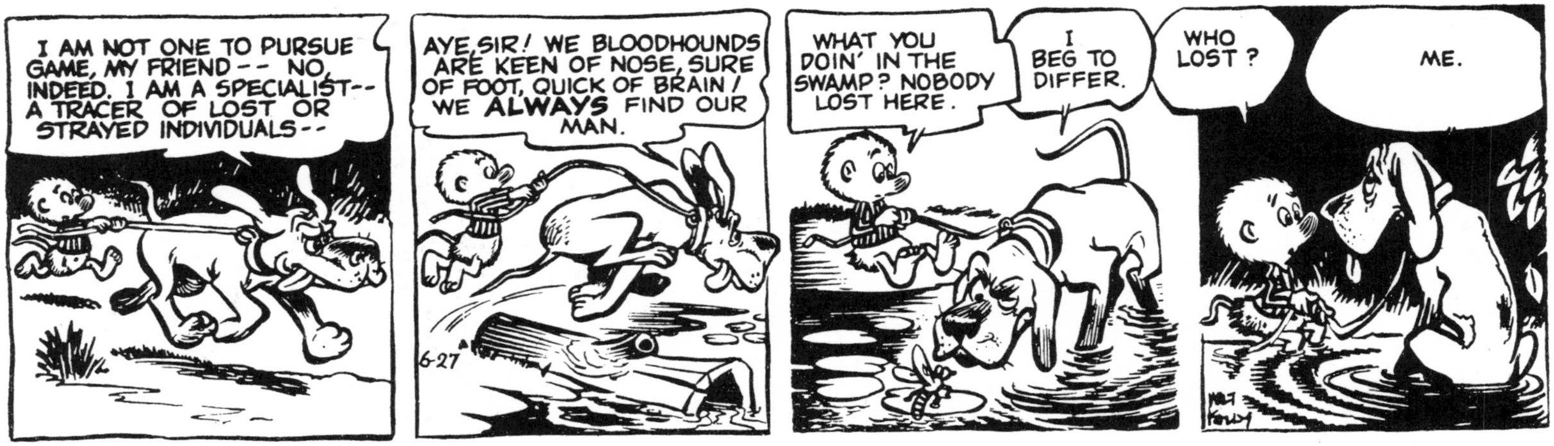
I AM NOT ONE TO PURSUE GAME, MY FRIEND -- NO, INDEED. I AM A SPECIALIST -- A TRACER OF LOST OR STRAYED INDIVIDUALS --
AYE, SIR! WE BLOODHOUNDS ARE KEEN OF NOSE, SURE OF FOOT, QUICK OF BRAIN! WE **ALWAYS** FIND OUR MAN.
6-27
WHAT YOU DOIN' IN THE SWAMP? NOBODY LOST HERE.
I BEG TO DIFFER.
WHO LOST?
ME.

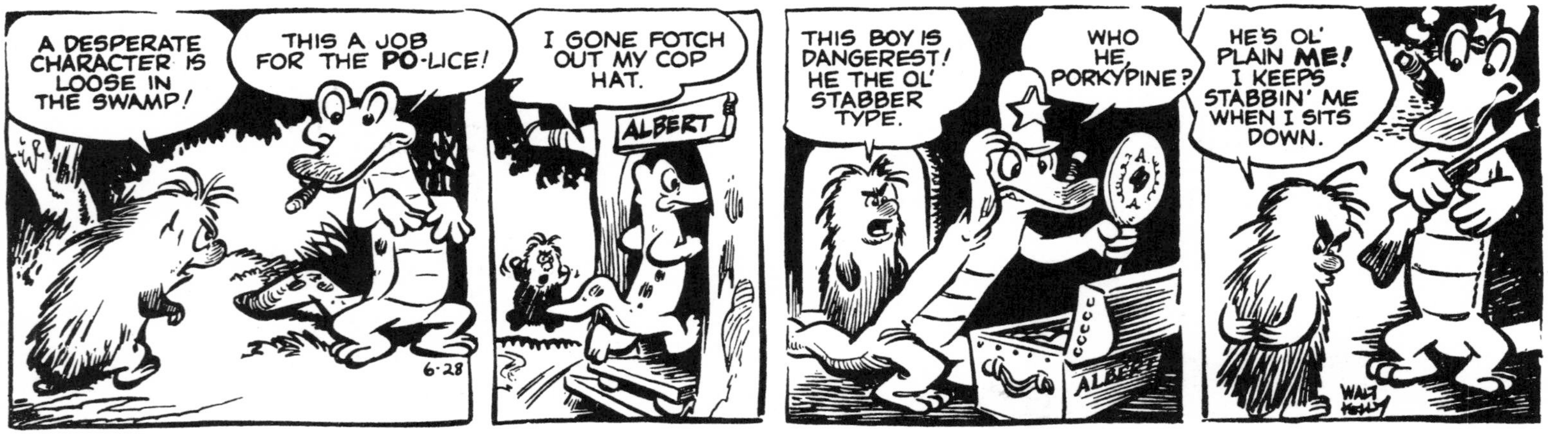
A DESPERATE CHARACTER IS LOOSE IN THE SWAMP!
THIS A JOB FOR THE **PO**-LICE!
6-28
I GONE FOTCH OUT MY COP HAT.
ALBERT
THIS BOY IS DANGEREST! HE THE OL' STABBER TYPE.
WHO HE, PORKYPINE?
ALBERT
HE'S OL' PLAIN **ME!** I KEEPS STABBIN' ME WHEN I SITS DOWN.

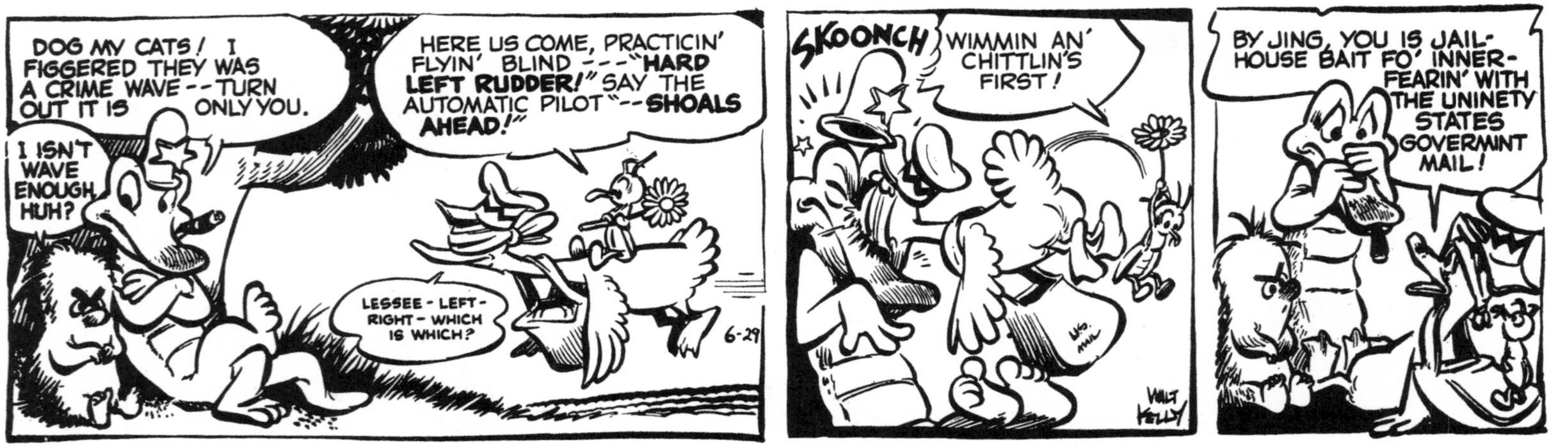
DOG MY CATS! I FIGGERED THEY WAS A CRIME WAVE -- TURN OUT IT IS ONLY YOU.
I ISN'T WAVE ENOUGH, HUH?
HERE US COME, PRACTICIN' FLYIN' BLIND --- "**HARD LEFT RUDDER!**" SAY THE AUTOMATIC PILOT" -- **SHOALS AHEAD!**"
LESSEE - LEFT - RIGHT - WHICH IS WHICH?
6-29
SKOONCH
WIMMIN AN' CHITTLIN'S FIRST!
BY JING, YOU IS JAIL-HOUSE BAIT FO' INNER-FEARIN' WITH THE UNINETY STATES GOVERMINT MAIL!

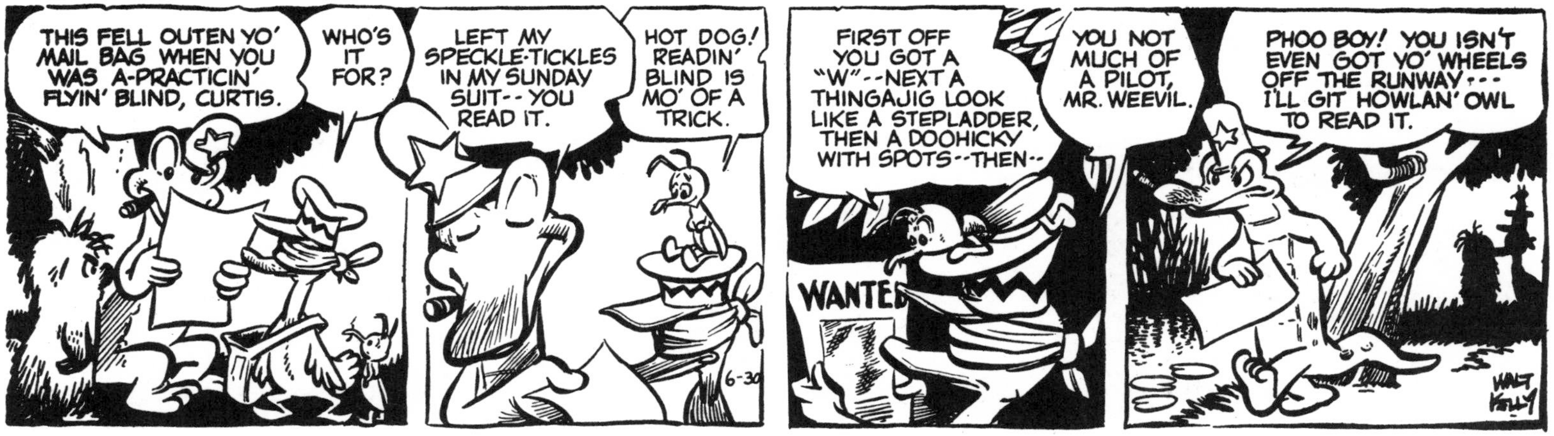
THIS FELL OUTEN YO' MAIL BAG WHEN YOU WAS A-PRACTICIN' FLYIN' BLIND, CURTIS.
WHO'S IT FOR?
LEFT MY SPECKLE-TICKLES IN MY SUNDAY SUIT-- YOU READ IT.
HOT DOG! READIN' BLIND IS MO' OF A TRICK.
6-30
FIRST OFF YOU GOT A "W"--NEXT A THINGAJIG LOOK LIKE A STEPLADDER, THEN A DOOHICKY WITH SPOTS--THEN--
WANTED
YOU NOT MUCH OF A PILOT, MR. WEEVIL.
PHOO BOY! YOU ISN'T EVEN GOT YO' WHEELS OFF THE RUNWAY--- I'LL GIT HOWLAN' OWL TO READ IT.
WALT KELLY

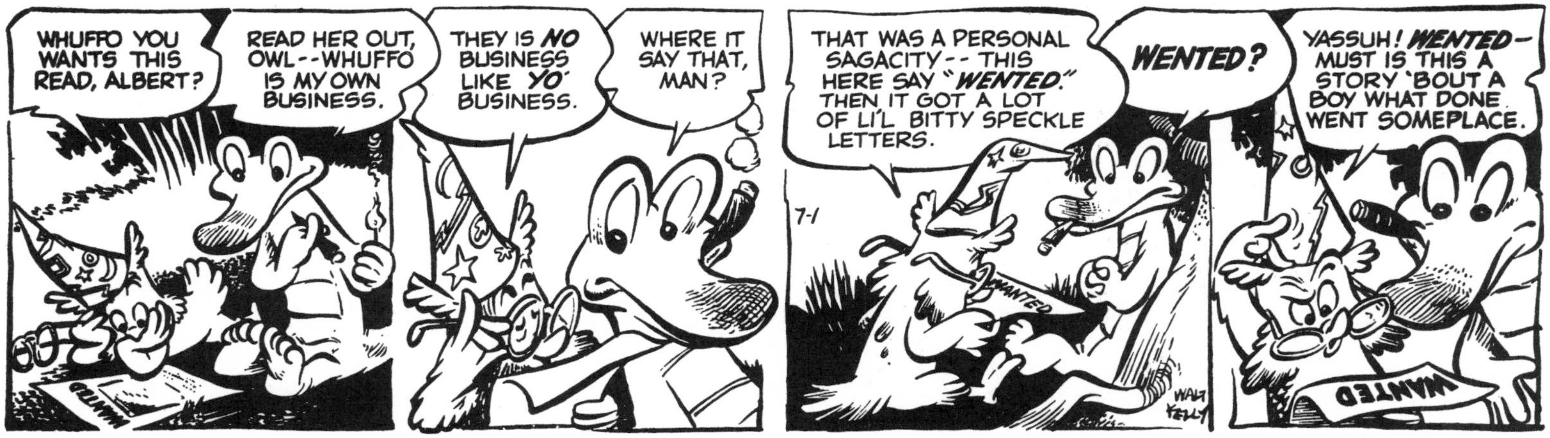
WHUFFO YOU WANTS THIS READ, ALBERT?
READ HER OUT, OWL--WHUFFO IS MY OWN BUSINESS.
THEY IS NO BUSINESS LIKE YO' BUSINESS.
WHERE IT SAY THAT, MAN?
THAT WAS A PERSONAL SAGACITY-- THIS HERE SAY "WENTED." THEN IT GOT A LOT OF LI'L BITTY SPECKLE LETTERS.
7-1
WENTED?
YASSUH! WENTED-- MUST IS THIS A STORY 'BOUT A BOY WHAT DONE WENT SOMEPLACE.
WANTED
WALT KELLY

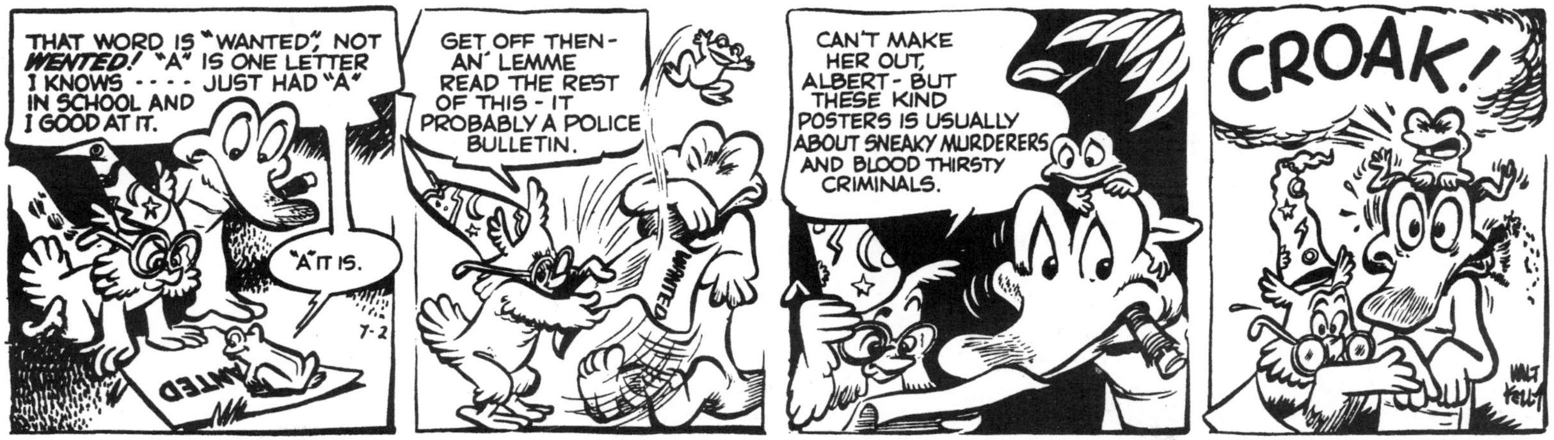
THAT WORD IS "WANTED", NOT WENTED! "A" IS ONE LETTER I KNOWS ---- JUST HAD "A" IN SCHOOL AND I GOOD AT IT.
"A" IT IS.
7-2
WANTED
GET OFF THEN- AN' LEMME READ THE REST OF THIS - IT PROBABLY A POLICE BULLETIN.
CAN'T MAKE HER OUT, ALBERT- BUT THESE KIND POSTERS IS USUALLY ABOUT SNEAKY MURDERERS AND BLOOD THIRSTY CRIMINALS.
CROAK!
WALT KELLY

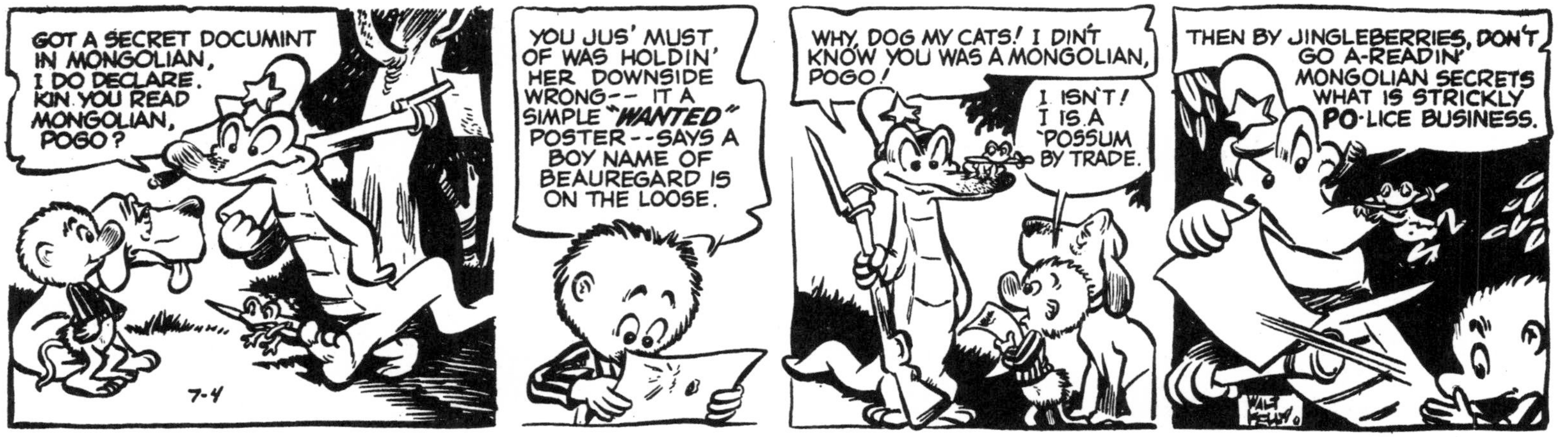
GOT A SECRET DOCUMINT IN MONGOLIAN, I DO DECLARE. KIN YOU READ MONGOLIAN, POGO?
7-4
YOU JUS' MUST OF WAS HOLDIN' HER DOWNSIDE WRONG-- IT A SIMPLE "WANTED" POSTER--SAYS A BOY NAME OF BEAUREGARD IS ON THE LOOSE.
WHY, DOG MY CATS! I DIN'T KNOW YOU WAS A MONGOLIAN, POGO!
I ISN'T! I IS A 'POSSUM BY TRADE.
THEN BY JINGLEBERRIES, DON'T GO A-READIN' MONGOLIAN SECRETS WHAT IS STRICKLY PO-LICE BUSINESS.

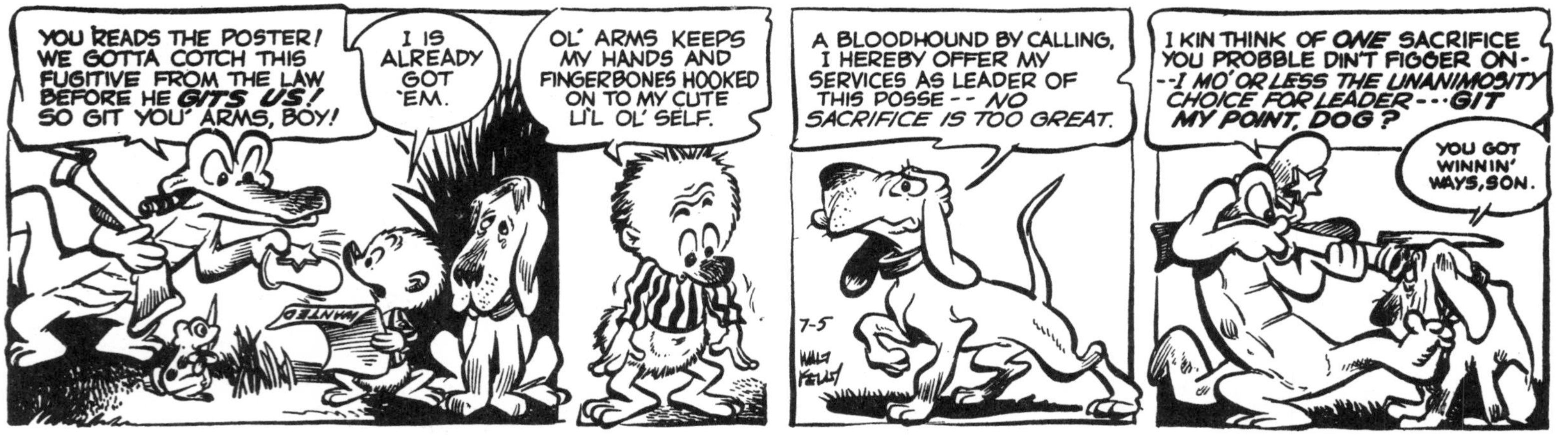
YOU READS THE POSTER! WE GOTTA COTCH THIS FUGITIVE FROM THE LAW BEFORE HE GITS US! SO GIT YOU' ARMS, BOY!
I IS ALREADY GOT 'EM.
OL' ARMS KEEPS MY HANDS AND FINGERBONES HOOKED ON TO MY CUTE LI'L OL' SELF.
A BLOODHOUND BY CALLING, I HEREBY OFFER MY SERVICES AS LEADER OF THIS POSSE -- NO SACRIFICE IS TOO GREAT.
7-5
I KIN THINK OF ONE SACRIFICE YOU PROBBLE DIN'T FIGGER ON- --I MO' OR LESS THE UNANIMOSITY CHOICE FOR LEADER---GIT MY POINT, DOG?
YOU GOT WINNIN' WAYS, SON.

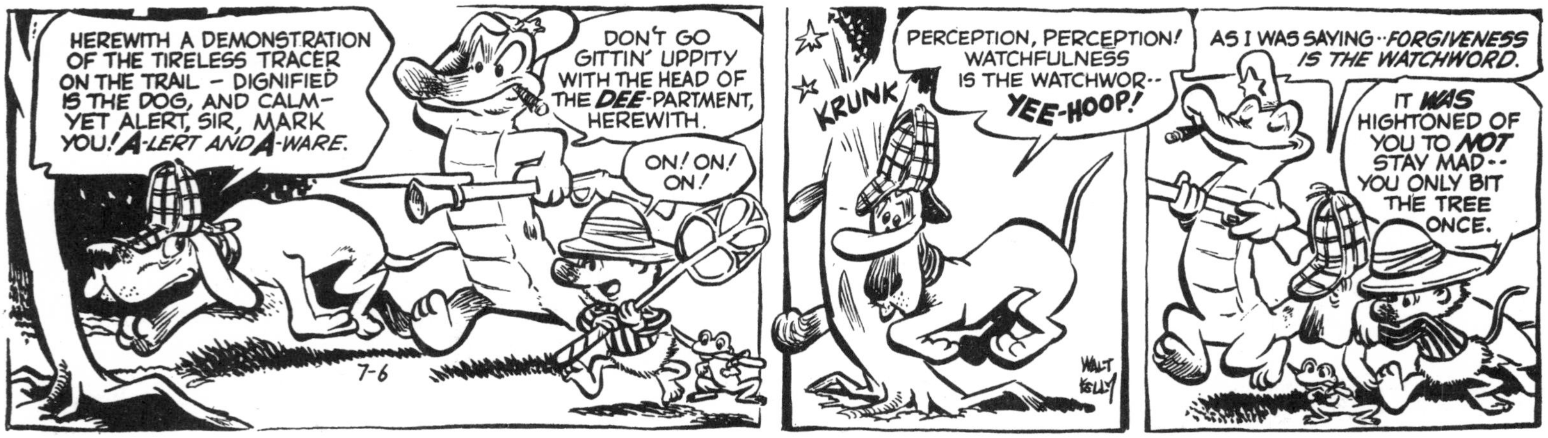
HEREWITH A DEMONSTRATION OF THE TIRELESS TRACER ON THE TRAIL - DIGNIFIED IS THE DOG, AND CALM-YET ALERT, SIR, MARK YOU! A-LERT AND A-WARE.
DON'T GO GITTIN' UPPITY WITH THE HEAD OF THE DEE-PARTMENT, HEREWITH.
ON! ON! ON!
7-6
KRUNK
PERCEPTION, PERCEPTION! WATCHFULNESS IS THE WATCHWOR-- YEE-HOOP!
AS I WAS SAYING--FORGIVENESS IS THE WATCHWORD.
IT WAS HIGHTONED OF YOU TO NOT STAY MAD-- YOU ONLY BIT THE TREE ONCE.

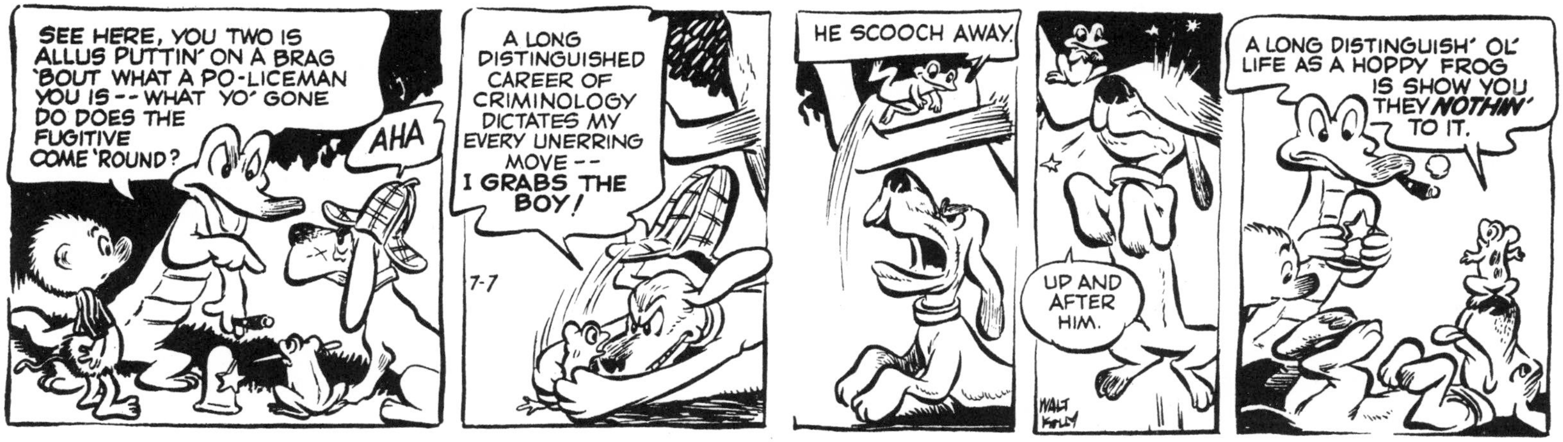
SEE HERE, YOU TWO IS ALLUS PUTTIN' ON A BRAG 'BOUT WHAT A PO-LICEMAN YOU IS -- WHAT YO' GONE DO DOES THE FUGITIVE COME 'ROUND?
AHA
A LONG DISTINGUISHED CAREER OF CRIMINOLOGY DICTATES MY EVERY UNERRING MOVE -- I GRABS THE BOY!
7-7
HE SCOOCH AWAY.
UP AND AFTER HIM.
WALT KELLY
A LONG DISTINGUISH' OL' LIFE AS A HOPPY FROG IS SHOW YOU THEY NOTHIN' TO IT.

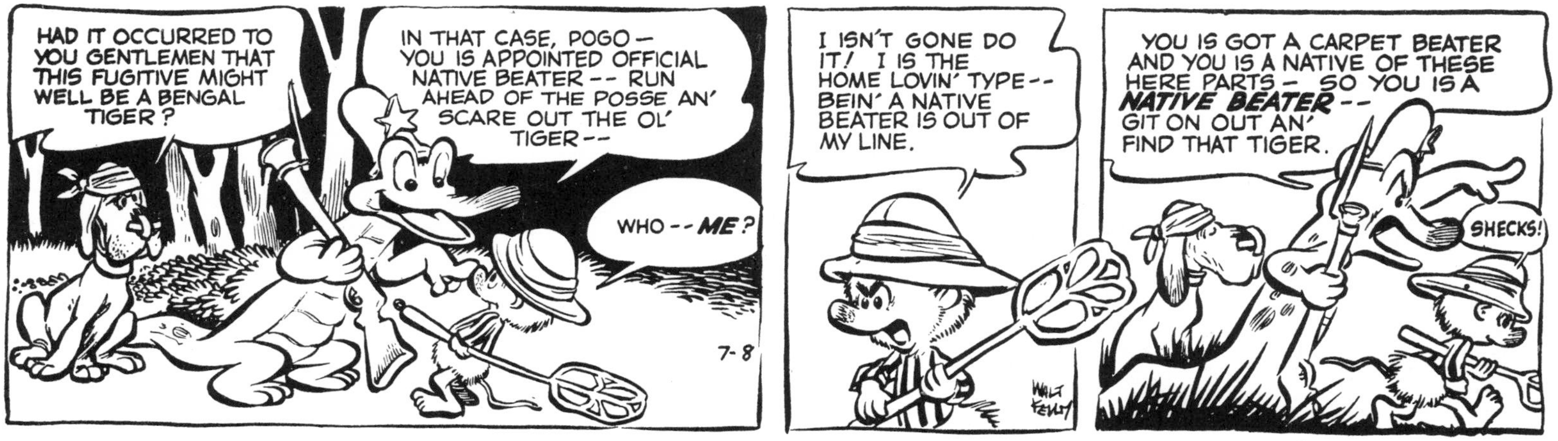
HAD IT OCCURRED TO YOU GENTLEMEN THAT THIS FUGITIVE MIGHT WELL BE A BENGAL TIGER?
IN THAT CASE, POGO — YOU IS APPOINTED OFFICIAL NATIVE BEATER -- RUN AHEAD OF THE POSSE AN' SCARE OUT THE OL' TIGER --
WHO -- ME?
7-8
I ISN'T GONE DO IT! I IS THE HOME LOVIN' TYPE -- BEIN' A NATIVE BEATER IS OUT OF MY LINE.
WALT KELLY
YOU IS GOT A CARPET BEATER AND YOU IS A NATIVE OF THESE HERE PARTS — SO YOU IS A NATIVE BEATER -- GIT ON OUT AN' FIND THAT TIGER.
SHECKS!

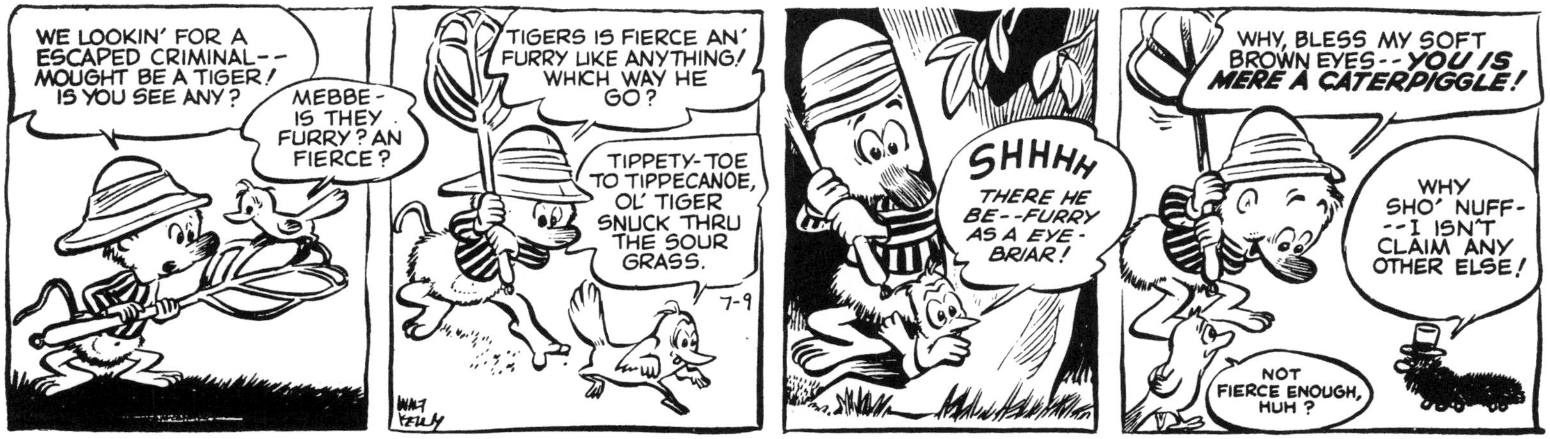
WE LOOKIN' FOR A ESCAPED CRIMINAL -- MOUGHT BE A TIGER! IS YOU SEE ANY?
MEBBE - IS THEY FURRY? AN FIERCE?
TIGERS IS FIERCE AN' FURRY LIKE ANYTHING! WHICH WAY HE GO?
TIPPETY-TOE TO TIPPECANOE, OL' TIGER SNUCK THRU THE SOUR GRASS.
7-9
WALT KELLY
SHHHH
THERE HE BE -- FURRY AS A EYE-BRIAR!
WHY, BLESS MY SOFT BROWN EYES -- YOU IS MERE A CATERPIGGLE!
WHY SHO' NUFF - - I ISN'T CLAIM ANY OTHER ELSE!
NOT FIERCE ENOUGH, HUH?

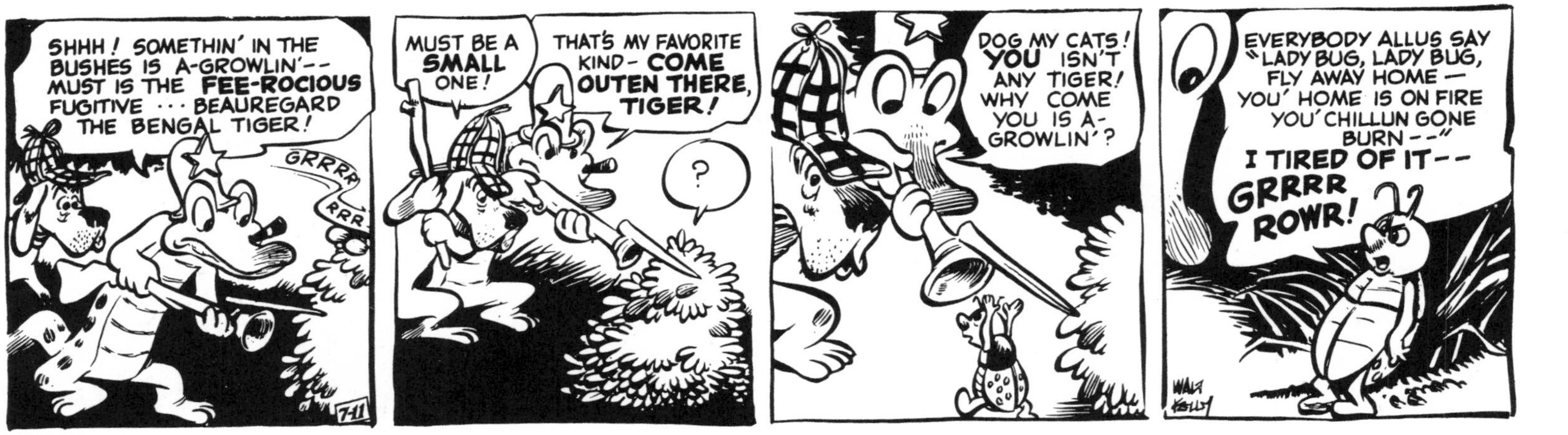
SHHH! SOMETHIN' IN THE BUSHES IS A-GROWLIN'-- MUST IS THE FEE-ROCIOUS FUGITIVE ··· BEAUREGARD THE BENGAL TIGER!
GRRRR
RRR
7-11
MUST BE A SMALL ONE!
THAT'S MY FAVORITE KIND- COME OUTEN THERE, TIGER!
?
DOG MY CATS! YOU ISN'T ANY TIGER! WHY COME YOU IS A-GROWLIN'?
EVERYBODY ALLUS SAY "LADY BUG, LADY BUG, FLY AWAY HOME — YOU' HOME IS ON FIRE YOU' CHILLUN GONE BURN--"
I TIRED OF IT-- GRRRR ROWR!
WALT KELLY

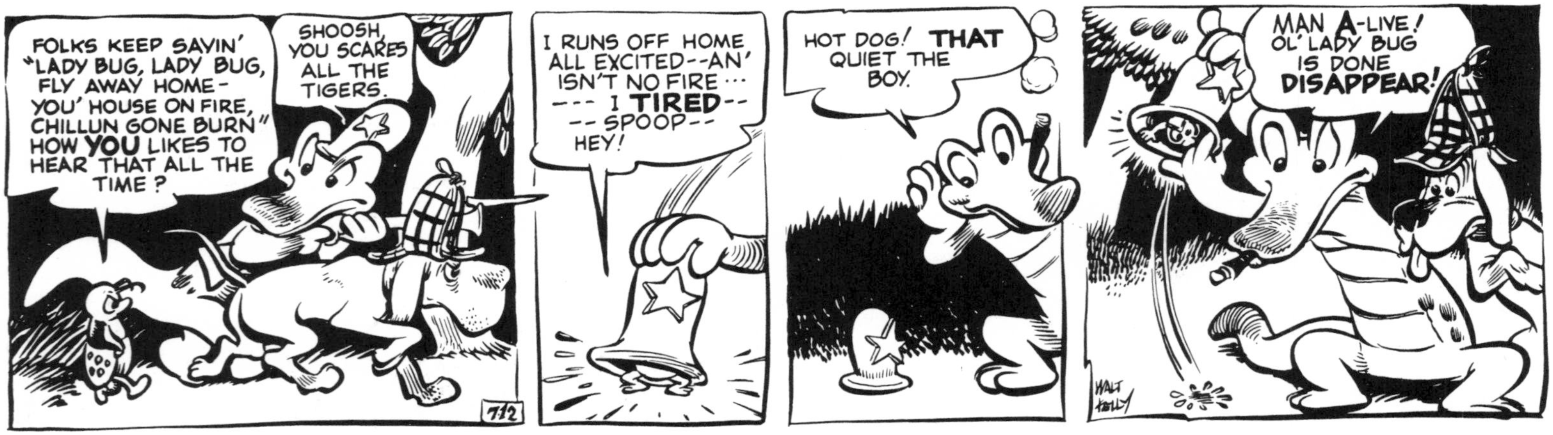
FOLKS KEEP SAYIN' "LADY BUG, LADY BUG, FLY AWAY HOME- YOU' HOUSE ON FIRE, CHILLUN GONE BURN" HOW YOU LIKES TO HEAR THAT ALL THE TIME?
SHOOSH, YOU SCARES ALL THE TIGERS.
7-12
I RUNS OFF HOME ALL EXCITED--AN' ISN'T NO FIRE ··· --- I TIRED-- -- SPOOP-- HEY!
HOT DOG! THAT QUIET THE BOY.
MAN A-LIVE! OL' LADY BUG IS DONE DISAPPEAR!
WALT KELLY

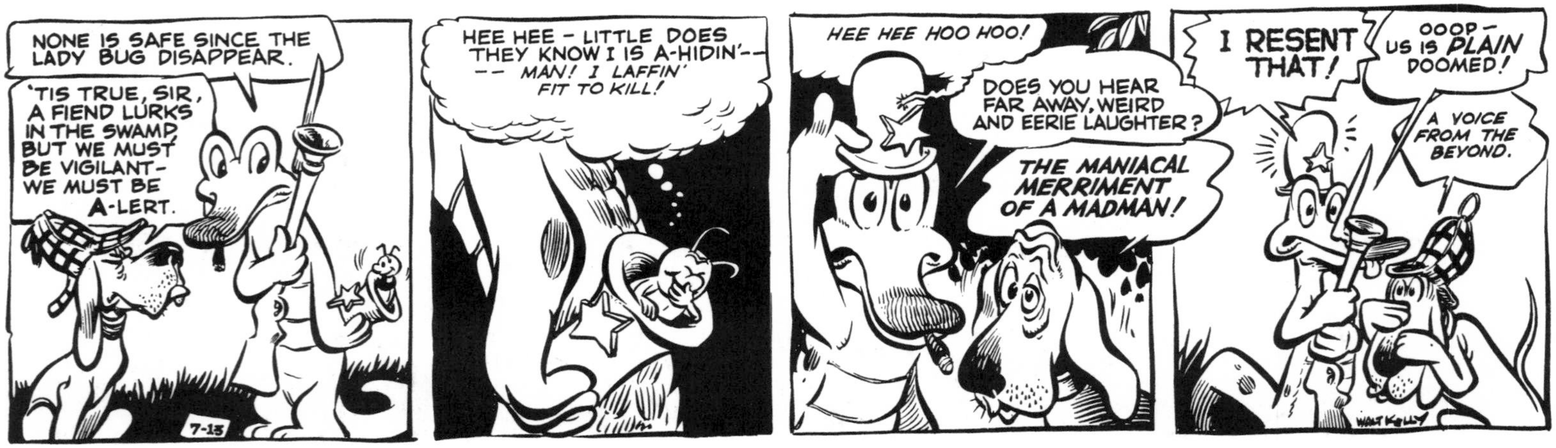
NONE IS SAFE SINCE THE LADY BUG DISAPPEAR.
'TIS TRUE, SIR, A FIEND LURKS IN THE SWAMP BUT WE MUST BE VIGILANT- WE MUST BE A-LERT.
7-13
HEE HEE - LITTLE DOES THEY KNOW I IS A-HIDIN'- -- MAN! I LAFFIN' FIT TO KILL!
HEE HEE HOO HOO!
DOES YOU HEAR FAR AWAY, WEIRD AND EERIE LAUGHTER?
THE MANIACAL MERRIMENT OF A MADMAN!
I RESENT THAT!
OOOP- US IS PLAIN DOOMED!
A VOICE FROM THE BEYOND.
WALT KELLY

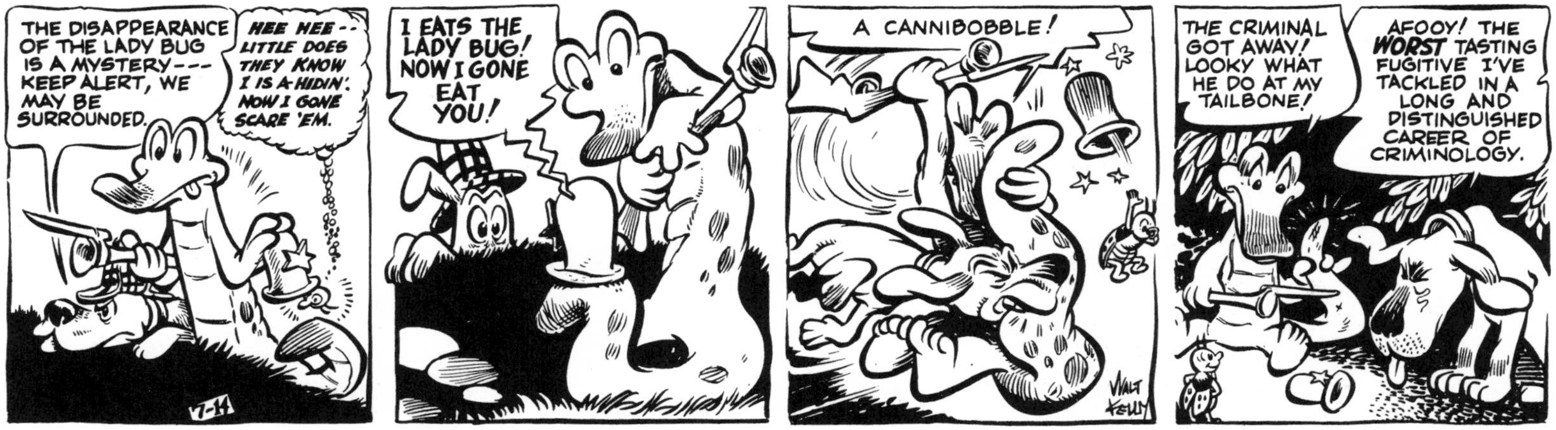
THE DISAPPEARANCE OF THE LADY BUG IS A MYSTERY--- KEEP ALERT, WE MAY BE SURROUNDED.
HEE HEE-- LITTLE DOES THEY KNOW I IS A-HIDIN'. NOW I GONE SCARE 'EM.
I EATS THE LADY BUG! NOW I GONE EAT YOU!
A CANNIBOBBLE!
THE CRIMINAL GOT AWAY! LOOKY WHAT HE DO AT MY TAILBONE!
AFOOY! THE WORST TASTING FUGITIVE I'VE TACKLED IN A LONG AND DISTINGUISHED CAREER OF CRIMINOLOGY.
WALT KELLY

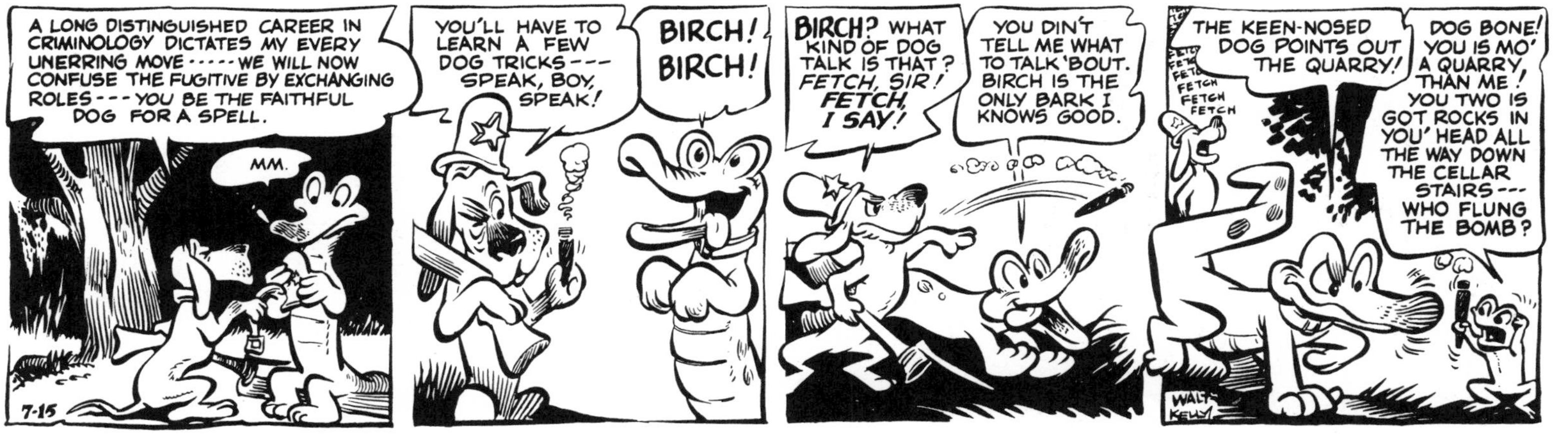
A LONG DISTINGUISHED CAREER IN CRIMINOLOGY DICTATES MY EVERY UNERRING MOVE----- WE WILL NOW CONFUSE THE FUGITIVE BY EXCHANGING ROLES--- YOU BE THE FAITHFUL DOG FOR A SPELL.
MM.
7-15
YOU'LL HAVE TO LEARN A FEW DOG TRICKS--- SPEAK, BOY, SPEAK!
BIRCH! BIRCH!
BIRCH? WHAT KIND OF DOG TALK IS THAT? FETCH, SIR! FETCH, I SAY!
YOU DIN'T TELL ME WHAT TO TALK 'BOUT. BIRCH IS THE ONLY BARK I KNOWS GOOD.
THE KEEN-NOSED DOG POINTS OUT THE QUARRY!
FETCH FETCH FETCH
DOG BONE! YOU IS MO' A QUARRY THAN ME! YOU TWO IS GOT ROCKS IN YOU' HEAD ALL THE WAY DOWN THE CELLAR STAIRS--- WHO FLUNG THE BOMB?
WALT KELLY

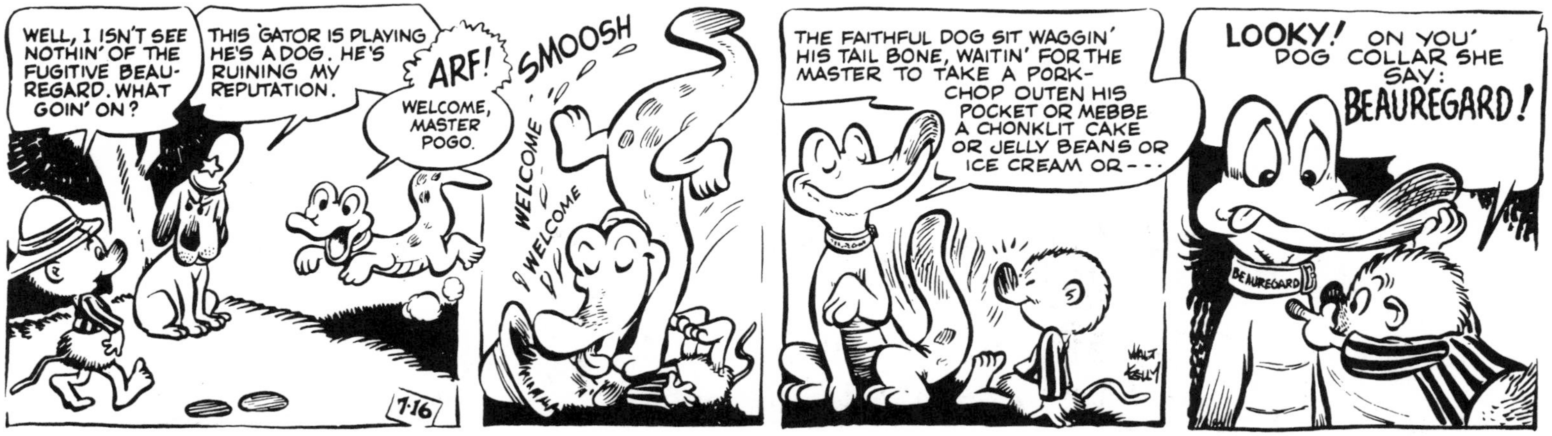
WELL, I ISN'T SEE NOTHIN' OF THE FUGITIVE BEAU-REGARD. WHAT GOIN' ON?
THIS 'GATOR IS PLAYING HE'S A DOG. HE'S RUINING MY REPUTATION.
ARF!
WELCOME, MASTER POGO.
7-16
SMOOSH
WELCOME
WELCOME
THE FAITHFUL DOG SIT WAGGIN' HIS TAIL BONE, WAITIN' FOR THE MASTER TO TAKE A PORK-CHOP OUTEN HIS POCKET OR MEBBE A CHONKLIT CAKE OR JELLY BEANS OR ICE CREAM OR---
WALT KELLY
LOOKY! ON YOU' DOG COLLAR SHE SAY: BEAUREGARD!
BEAUREGARD

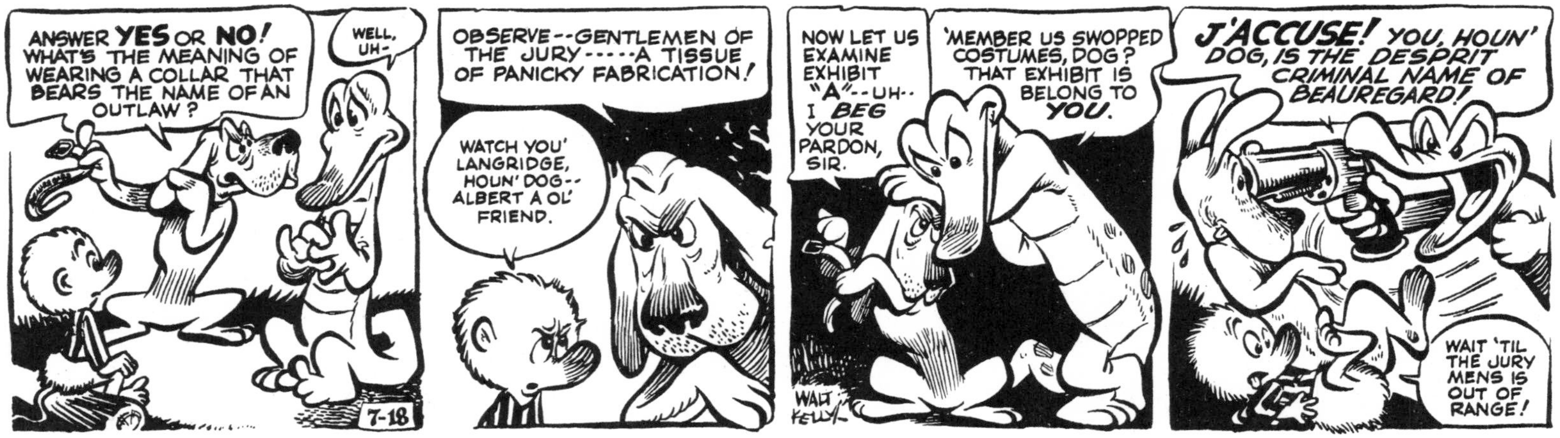
ANSWER YES OR NO! WHAT'S THE MEANING OF WEARING A COLLAR THAT BEARS THE NAME OF AN OUTLAW?
WELL, UH-
7-18
OBSERVE--GENTLEMEN OF THE JURY-----A TISSUE OF PANICKY FABRICATION!
WATCH YOU' LANGRIDGE, HOUN' DOG-- ALBERT A OL' FRIEND.
NOW LET US EXAMINE EXHIBIT "A"--UH-- I BEG YOUR PARDON, SIR.
'MEMBER US SWOPPED COSTUMES, DOG? THAT EXHIBIT IS BELONG TO YOU.
WALT KELLY
J'ACCUSE! YOU, HOUN' DOG, IS THE DESPRIT CRIMINAL NAME OF BEAUREGARD!
WAIT 'TIL THE JURY MENS IS OUT OF RANGE!

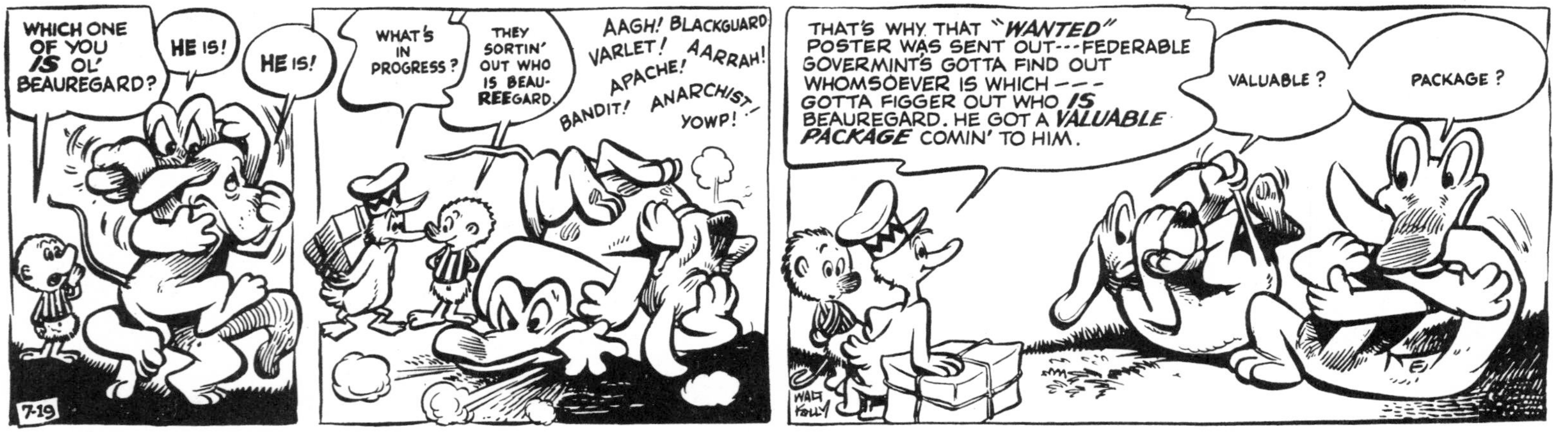
WHICH ONE OF YOU IS OL' BEAUREGARD?
HE IS!
HE IS!
7-19
WHAT'S IN PROGRESS?
THEY SORTIN' OUT WHO IS BEAU-REEGARD.
AAGH! BLACKGUARD VARLET! AARRAH! APACHE! BANDIT! ANARCHIST! YOWP!
THAT'S WHY THAT "WANTED" POSTER WAS SENT OUT---FEDERABLE GOVERMINT'S GOTTA FIND OUT WHOMSOEVER IS WHICH--- GOTTA FIGGER OUT WHO IS BEAUREGARD. HE GOT A VALUABLE PACKAGE COMIN' TO HIM.
VALUABLE?
PACKAGE?
WALT KELLY

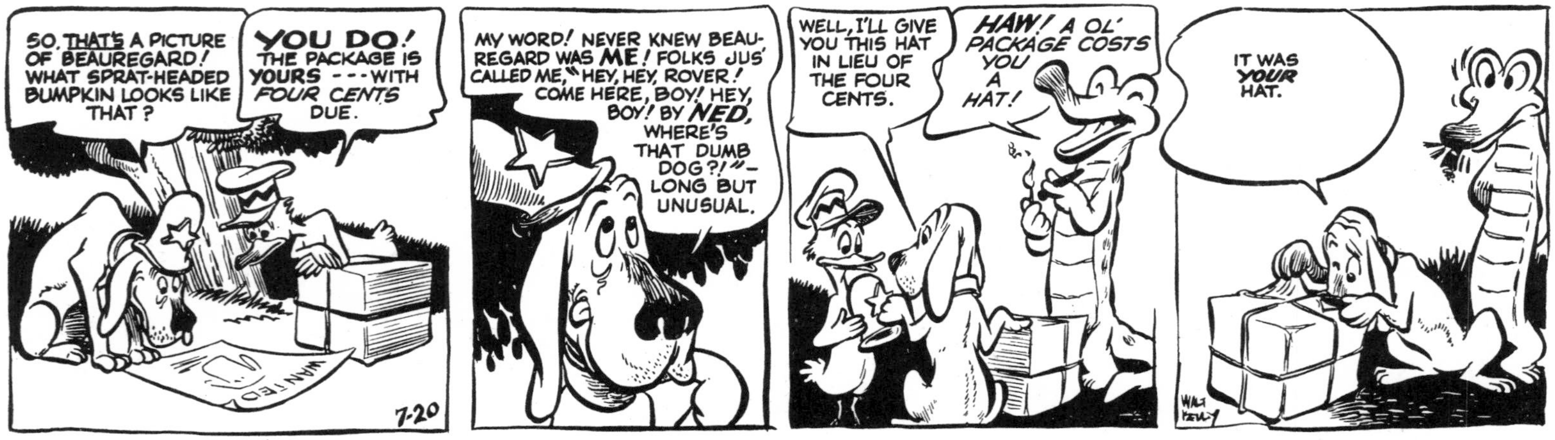
SO, THAT'S A PICTURE OF BEAUREGARD! WHAT SPRAT-HEADED BUMPKIN LOOKS LIKE THAT?
YOU DO! THE PACKAGE IS YOURS---WITH FOUR CENTS DUE.
7-20
MY WORD! NEVER KNEW BEAU-REGARD WAS ME! FOLKS JUS' CALLED ME, "HEY, HEY, ROVER! COME HERE, BOY! HEY, BOY! BY NED, WHERE'S THAT DUMB DOG?!"-LONG BUT UNUSUAL.
WELL, I'LL GIVE YOU THIS HAT IN LIEU OF THE FOUR CENTS.
HAW! A OL' PACKAGE COSTS YOU A HAT!
IT WAS YOUR HAT.
WALT KELLY

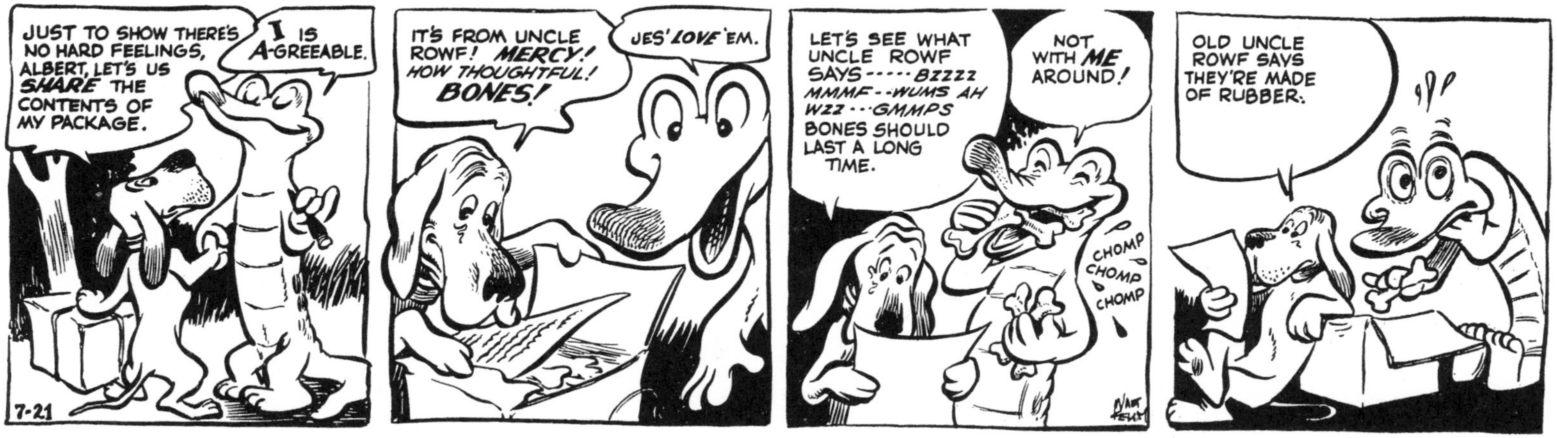
JUST TO SHOW THERE'S NO HARD FEELINGS, ALBERT, LET'S US SHARE THE CONTENTS OF MY PACKAGE.
I IS A-GREEABLE.
7-21
IT'S FROM UNCLE ROWF! MERCY! HOW THOUGHTFUL! BONES!
JES' LOVE 'EM.
LET'S SEE WHAT UNCLE ROWF SAYS----- BZZZZ MMMF--WUMS AH WZZ---GMMPS BONES SHOULD LAST A LONG TIME.
NOT WITH ME AROUND!
CHOMP CHOMP CHOMP
OLD UNCLE ROWF SAYS THEY'RE MADE OF RUBBER.

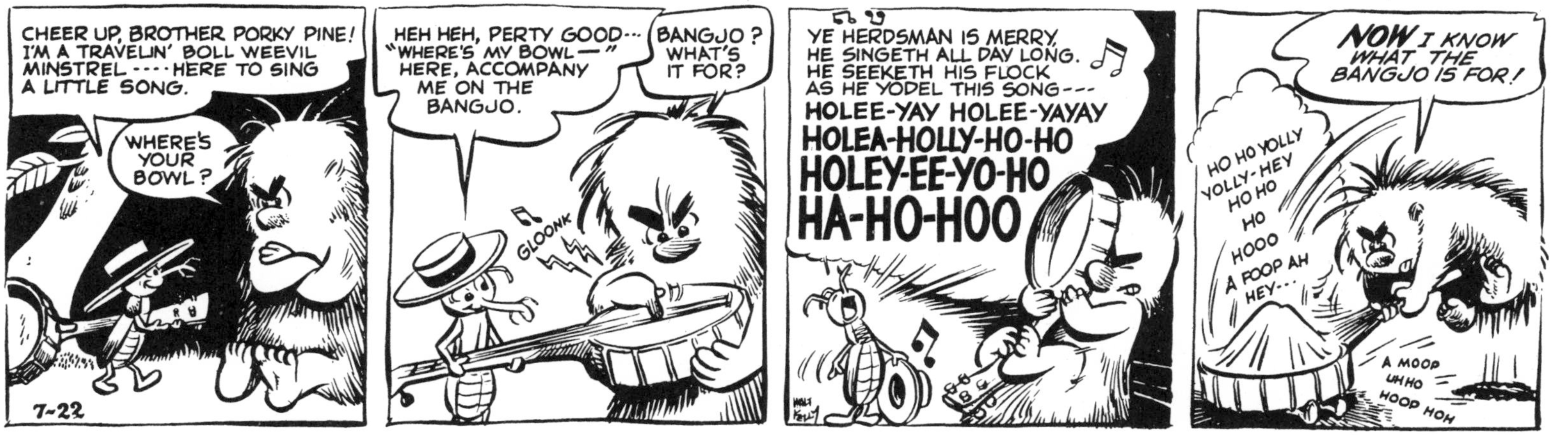
CHEER UP, BROTHER PORKY PINE! I'M A TRAVELIN' BOLL WEEVIL MINSTREL ---- HERE TO SING A LITTLE SONG.
WHERE'S YOUR BOWL?
7-22
HEH HEH, PERTY GOOD--- "WHERE'S MY BOWL—" HERE, ACCOMPANY ME ON THE BANGJO.
BANGJO? WHAT'S IT FOR?
GLOONK
YE HERDSMAN IS MERRY, HE SINGETH ALL DAY LONG. HE SEEKETH HIS FLOCK AS HE YODEL THIS SONG---
HOLEE-YAY HOLEE-YAYAY
HOLEA-HOLLY-HO-HO
HOLEY-EE-YO-HO
HA-HO-HOO
NOW I KNOW WHAT THE BANGJO IS FOR!
HO HO YOLLY YOLLY-HEY HO HO HO HOOO A FOOP AH HEY---
A MOOP UH HO HOOP HOH

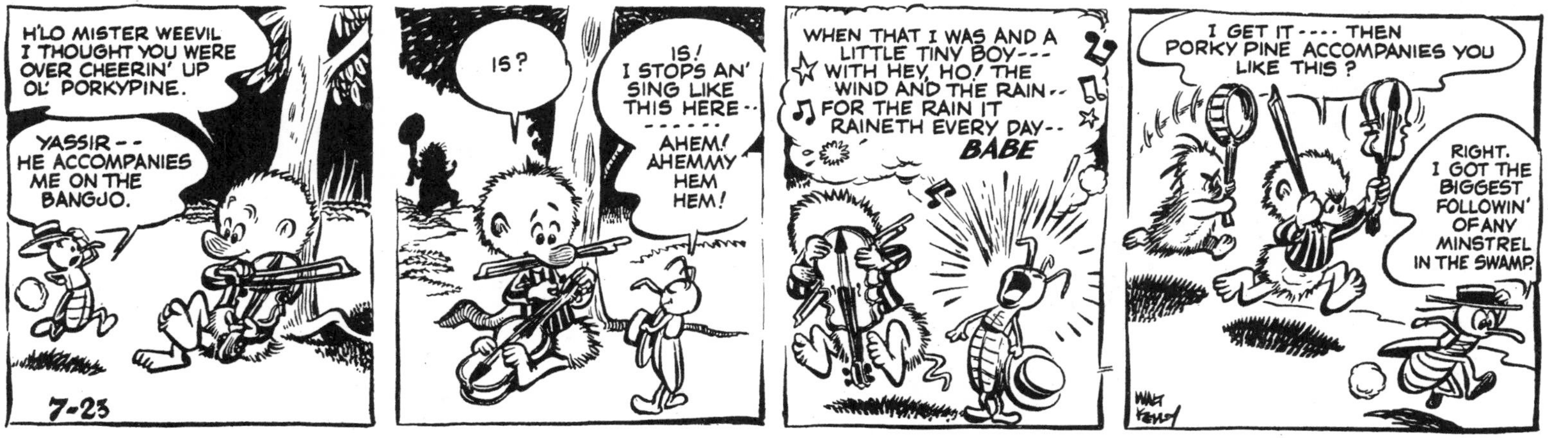
H'LO MISTER WEEVIL I THOUGHT YOU WERE OVER CHEERIN' UP OL' PORKYPINE.
YASSIR-- HE ACCOMPANIES ME ON THE BANGJO.
7-23
IS?
IS! I STOPS AN' SING LIKE THIS HERE-- ------ AHEM! AHEMMY HEM HEM!
WHEN THAT I WAS AND A LITTLE TINY BOY--- WITH HEY, HO! THE WIND AND THE RAIN-- FOR THE RAIN IT RAINETH EVERY DAY-- BABE
I GET IT---- THEN PORKY PINE ACCOMPANIES YOU LIKE THIS?
RIGHT. I GOT THE BIGGEST FOLLOWIN' OF ANY MINSTREL IN THE SWAMP.

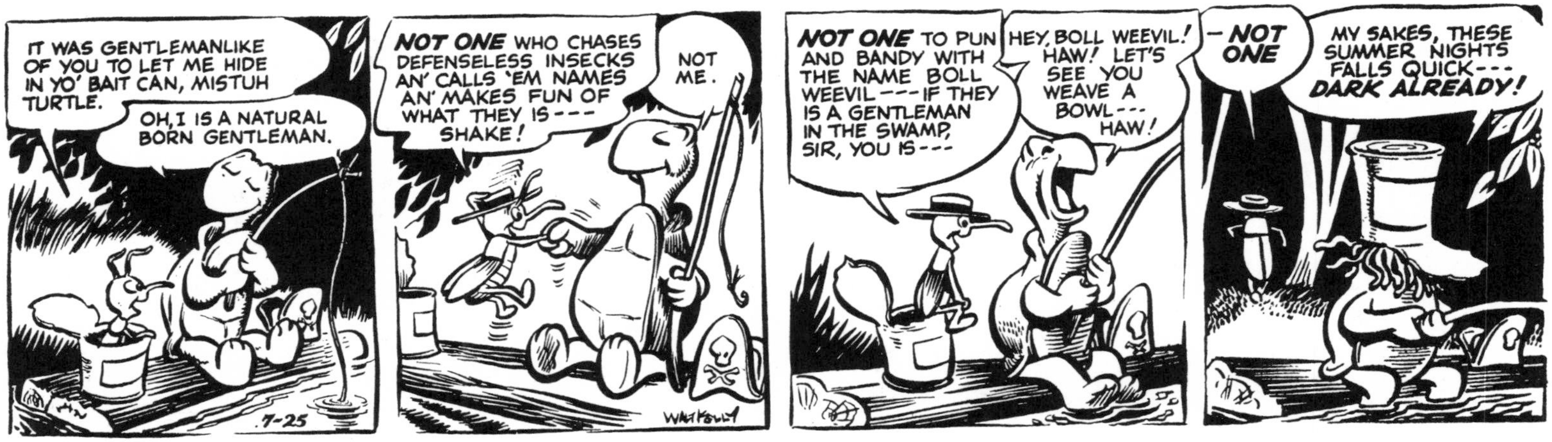
IT WAS GENTLEMANLIKE OF YOU TO LET ME HIDE IN YO' BAIT CAN, MISTUH TURTLE.
OH, I IS A NATURAL BORN GENTLEMAN.
NOT ONE WHO CHASES DEFENSELESS INSECKS AN' CALLS 'EM NAMES AN' MAKES FUN OF WHAT THEY IS --- SHAKE!
NOT ME.
NOT ONE TO PUN AND BANDY WITH THE NAME BOLL WEEVIL --- IF THEY IS A GENTLEMAN IN THE SWAMP, SIR, YOU IS ---
HEY, BOLL WEEVIL! HAW! LET'S SEE YOU WEAVE A BOWL--- HAW!
— NOT ONE
MY SAKES, THESE SUMMER NIGHTS FALLS QUICK--- DARK ALREADY!
7-25

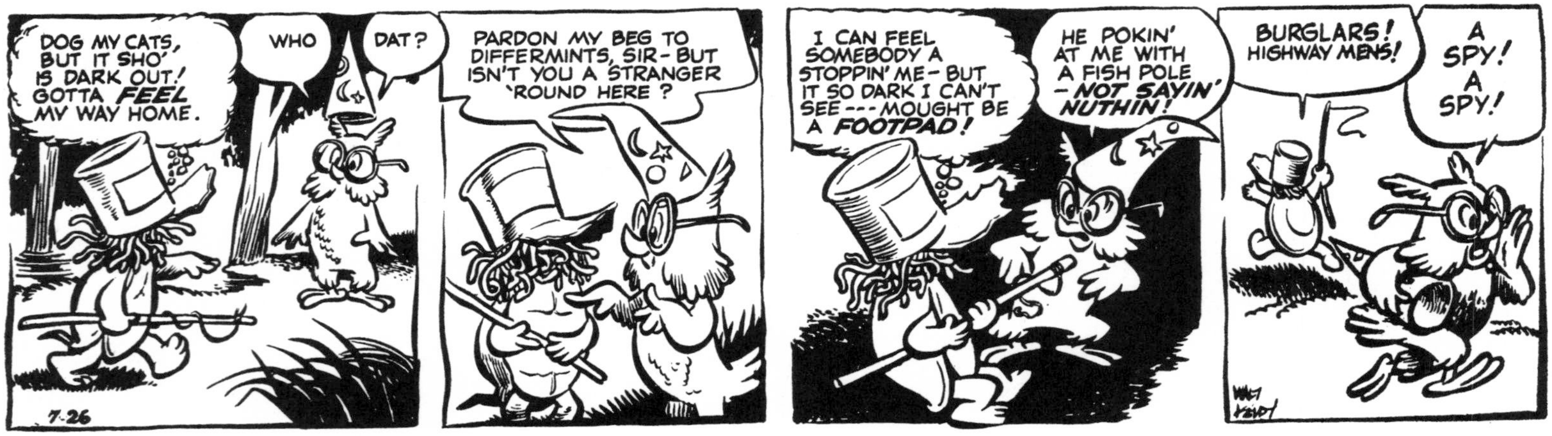
DOG MY CATS, BUT IT SHO' IS DARK OUT! GOTTA FEEL MY WAY HOME.
WHO
DAT?
PARDON MY BEG TO DIFFERMINTS, SIR- BUT ISN'T YOU A STRANGER 'ROUND HERE ?
I CAN FEEL SOMEBODY A STOPPIN' ME- BUT IT SO DARK I CAN'T SEE--- MOUGHT BE A FOOTPAD!
HE POKIN' AT ME WITH A FISH POLE -NOT SAYIN' NUTHIN'!
BURGLARS! HIGHWAY MENS!
A SPY! A SPY!
7-26

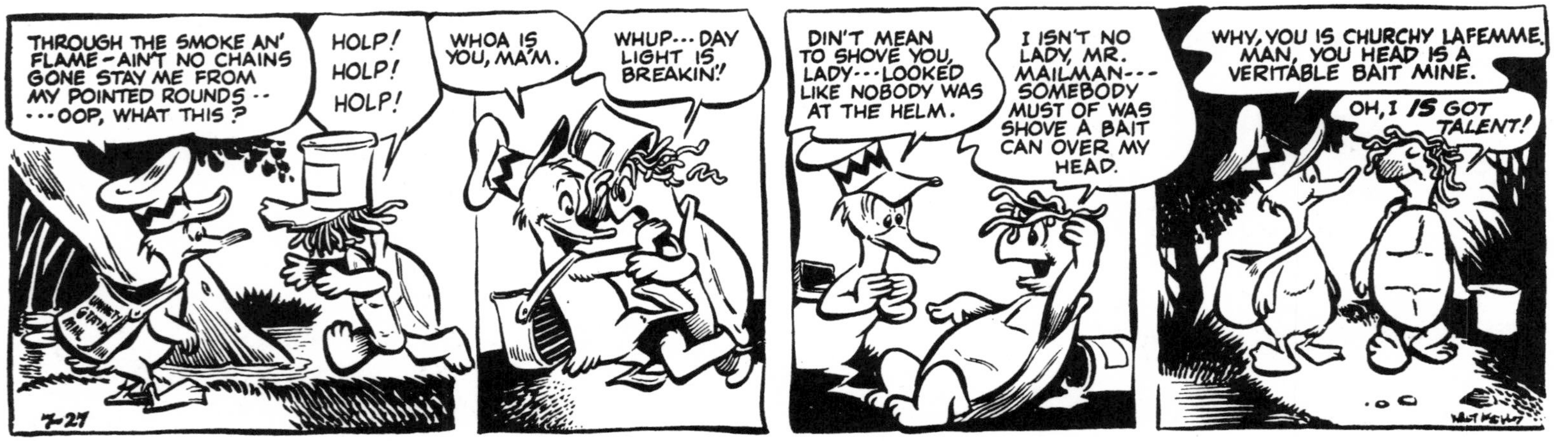
THROUGH THE SMOKE AN' FLAME- AIN'T NO CHAINS GONE STAY ME FROM MY POINTED ROUNDS -- ---OOP, WHAT THIS ?
HOLP! HOLP! HOLP!
WHOA IS YOU, MA'M.
WHUP--- DAY LIGHT IS BREAKIN'!
DIN'T MEAN TO SHOVE YOU, LADY--- LOOKED LIKE NOBODY WAS AT THE HELM.
I ISN'T NO LADY, MR. MAILMAN--- SOMEBODY MUST OF WAS SHOVE A BAIT CAN OVER MY HEAD.
WHY, YOU IS CHURCHY LAFEMME. MAN, YOU HEAD IS A VERITABLE BAIT MINE.
OH, I IS GOT TALENT!
7-27

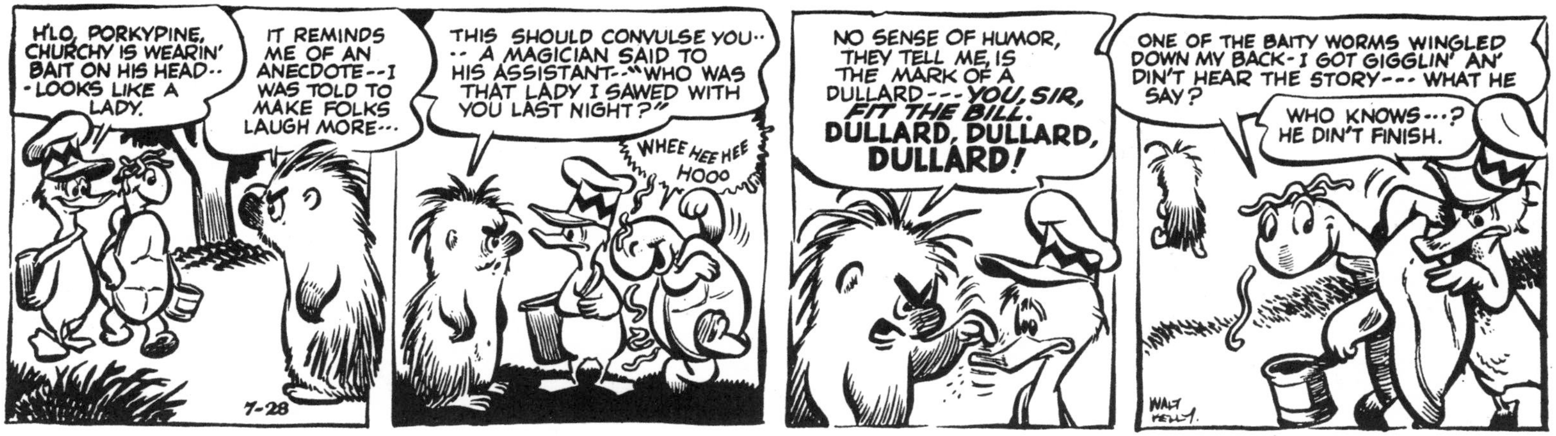
H'LO, PORKYPINE, CHURCHY IS WEARIN' BAIT ON HIS HEAD-- -LOOKS LIKE A LADY.
IT REMINDS ME OF AN ANECDOTE--I WAS TOLD TO MAKE FOLKS LAUGH MORE--.
7-28
THIS SHOULD CONVULSE YOU-- -- A MAGICIAN SAID TO HIS ASSISTANT--"WHO WAS THAT LADY I SAWED WITH YOU LAST NIGHT?"
WHEE HEE HEE HOOO
NO SENSE OF HUMOR, THEY TELL ME, IS THE MARK OF A DULLARD--- YOU, SIR, FIT THE BILL. DULLARD, DULLARD, DULLARD!
ONE OF THE BAITY WORMS WINGLED DOWN MY BACK- I GOT GIGGLIN' AN' DIN'T HEAR THE STORY--- WHAT HE SAY?
WHO KNOWS---? HE DIN'T FINISH.
WALT KELLY.

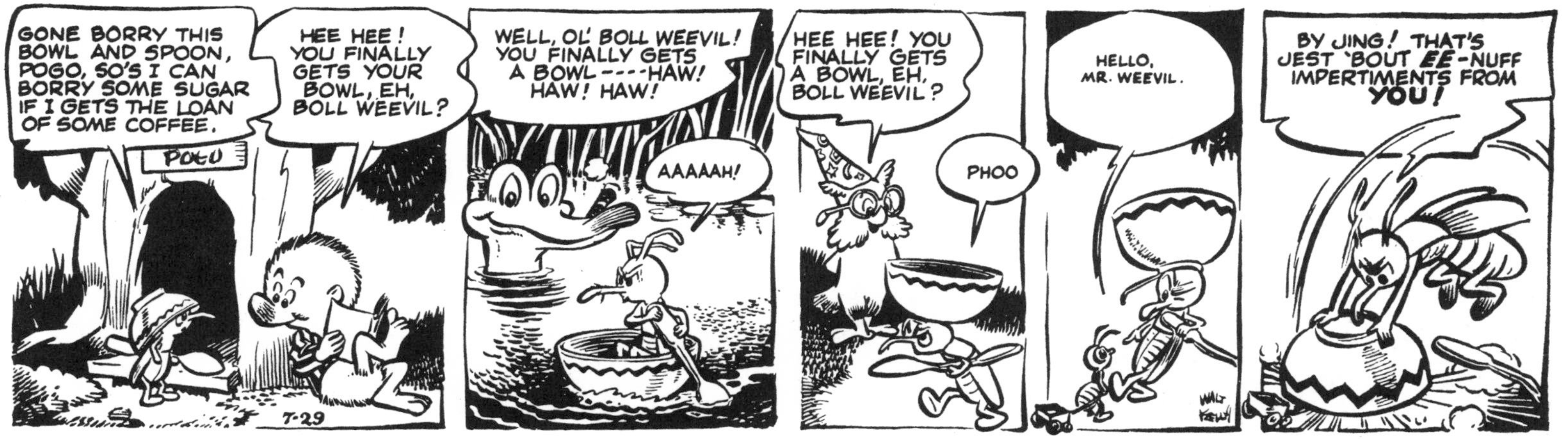
GONE BORRY THIS BOWL AND SPOON, POGO, SO'S I CAN BORRY SOME SUGAR IF I GETS THE LOAN OF SOME COFFEE.
HEE HEE! YOU FINALLY GETS YOUR BOWL, EH, BOLL WEEVIL?
POGO
7-29
WELL, OL' BOLL WEEVIL! YOU FINALLY GETS A BOWL----HAW! HAW! HAW!
AAAAAH!
HEE HEE! YOU FINALLY GETS A BOWL, EH, BOLL WEEVIL?
PHOO
HELLO, MR. WEEVIL.
WALT KELLY
BY JING! THAT'S JEST 'BOUT EE-NUFF IMPERTIMENTS FROM YOU!

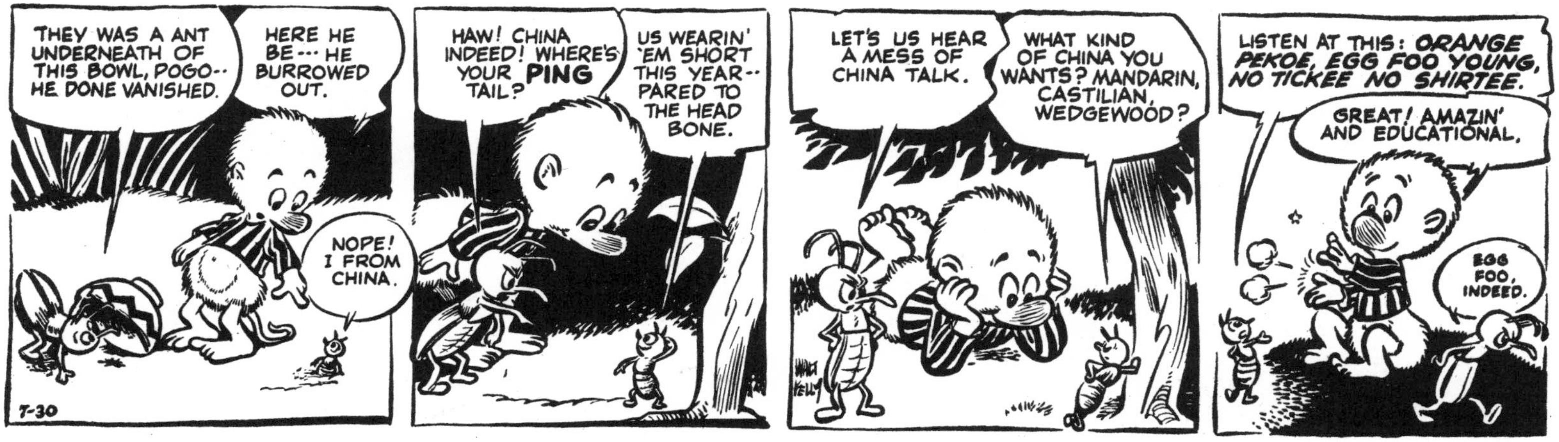
THEY WAS A ANT UNDERNEATH OF THIS BOWL, POGO-- HE DONE VANISHED.
HERE HE BE--- HE BURROWED OUT.
NOPE! I FROM CHINA.
7-30
HAW! CHINA INDEED! WHERE'S YOUR PING TAIL?
US WEARIN' 'EM SHORT THIS YEAR-- PARED TO THE HEAD BONE.
LET'S US HEAR A MESS OF CHINA TALK.
WHAT KIND OF CHINA YOU WANTS? MANDARIN, CASTILIAN, WEDGEWOOD?
WALT KELLY
LISTEN AT THIS: ORANGE PEKOE, EGG FOO YOUNG, NO TICKEE NO SHIRTEE.
GREAT! AMAZIN' AND EDUCATIONAL.
EGG FOO, INDEED.

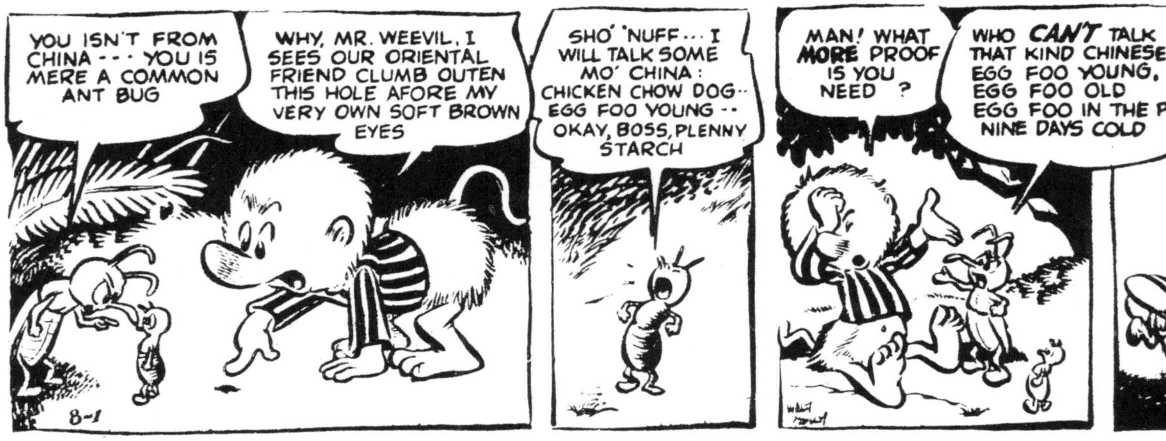
YOU ISN'T FROM CHINA --- YOU IS MERE A COMMON ANT BUG
WHY, MR. WEEVIL, I SEES OUR ORIENTAL FRIEND CLUMB OUTEN THIS HOLE AFORE MY VERY OWN SOFT BROWN EYES
SHO' 'NUFF --- I WILL TALK SOME MO' CHINA: CHICKEN CHOW DOG -- EGG FOO YOUNG -- OKAY, BOSS, PLENNY STARCH
MAN! WHAT MORE PROOF IS YOU NEED ?
WHO CAN'T TALK THAT KIND CHINESE? EGG FOO YOUNG, EGG FOO OLD EGG FOO IN THE POT NINE DAYS COLD
THIS HOLE YOU IS SAY COME UP FROM CHINA IS ONLY A INCH DEEP.
AY-MAZIN'! DIN'T HAVE NO IDEA CHINA WAS SO CLOSE!
OH SHO'!
8-1

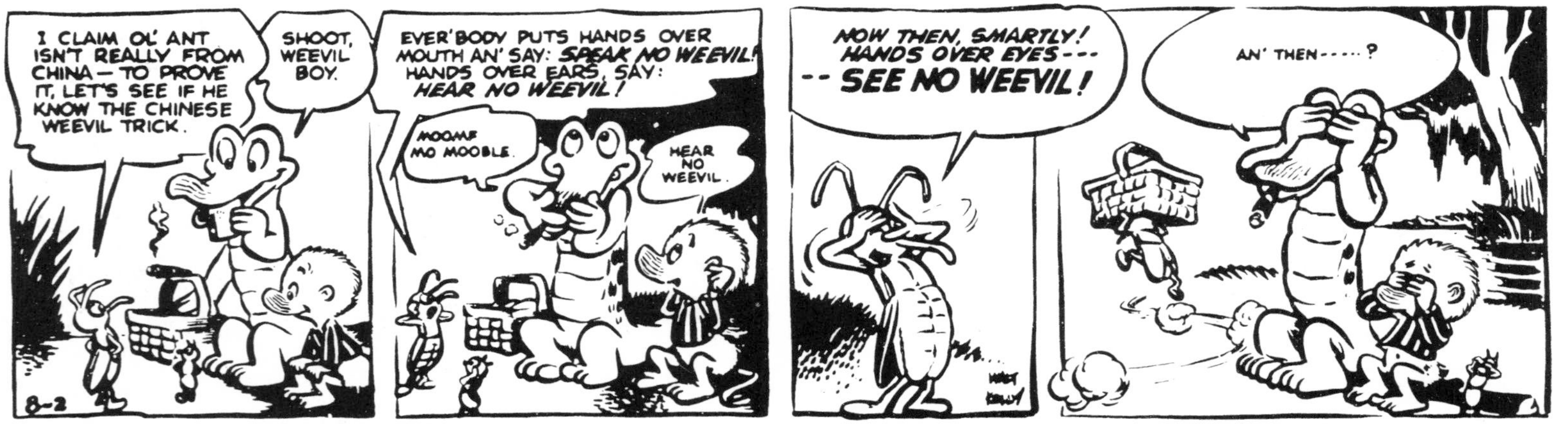
I CLAIM OL' ANT ISN'T REALLY FROM CHINA — TO PROVE IT, LET'S SEE IF HE KNOW THE CHINESE WEEVIL TRICK.
SHOOT, WEEVIL BOY.
EVER'BODY PUTS HANDS OVER MOUTH AN' SAY: SPEAK NO WEEVIL! HANDS OVER EARS, SAY: HEAR NO WEEVIL!
MOOMF MO MOOBLE.
HEAR NO WEEVIL.
NOW THEN, SMARTLY! HANDS OVER EYES --- -- SEE NO WEEVIL!
AN' THEN -----?
8-2

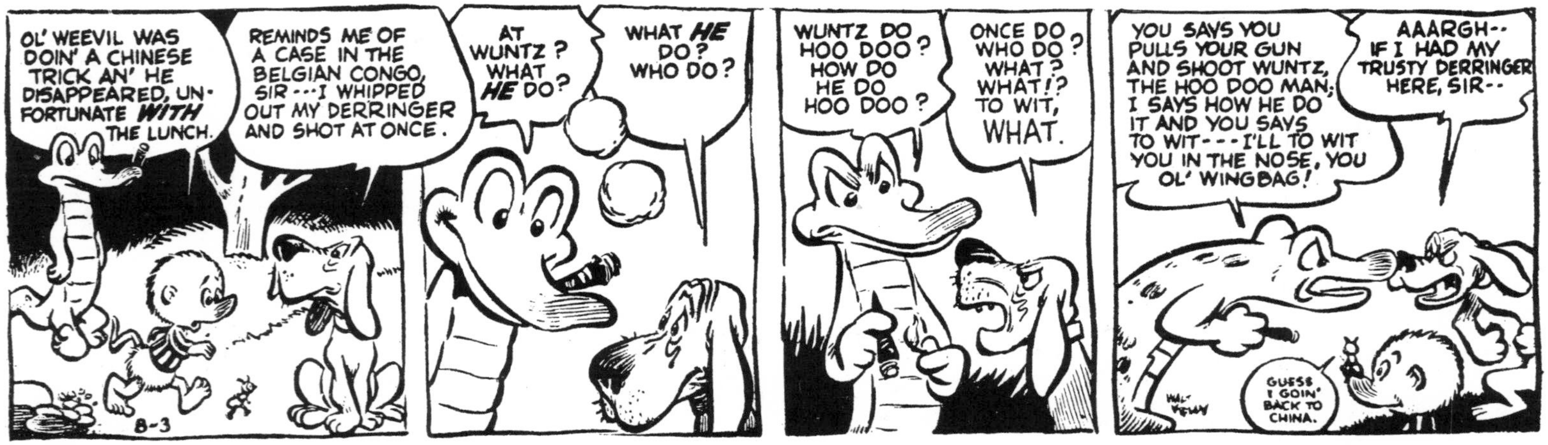
OL' WEEVIL WAS DOIN' A CHINESE TRICK AN' HE DISAPPEARED, UN-FORTUNATE WITH THE LUNCH.
REMINDS ME OF A CASE IN THE BELGIAN CONGO, SIR --- I WHIPPED OUT MY DERRINGER AND SHOT AT ONCE.
AT WUNTZ? WHAT HE DO?
WHAT HE DO? WHO DO?
WUNTZ DO HOO DOO? HOW DO HE DO HOO DOO?
ONCE DO WHO DO? WHAT? WHAT!? TO WIT, WHAT.
YOU SAYS YOU PULLS YOUR GUN AND SHOOT WUNTZ, THE HOO DOO MAN; I SAYS HOW HE DO IT AND YOU SAYS TO WIT --- I'LL TO WIT YOU IN THE NOSE, YOU OL' WINGBAG!
AAARGH -- IF I HAD MY TRUSTY DERRINGER HERE, SIR --
GUESS I GOIN' BACK TO CHINA.
8-3

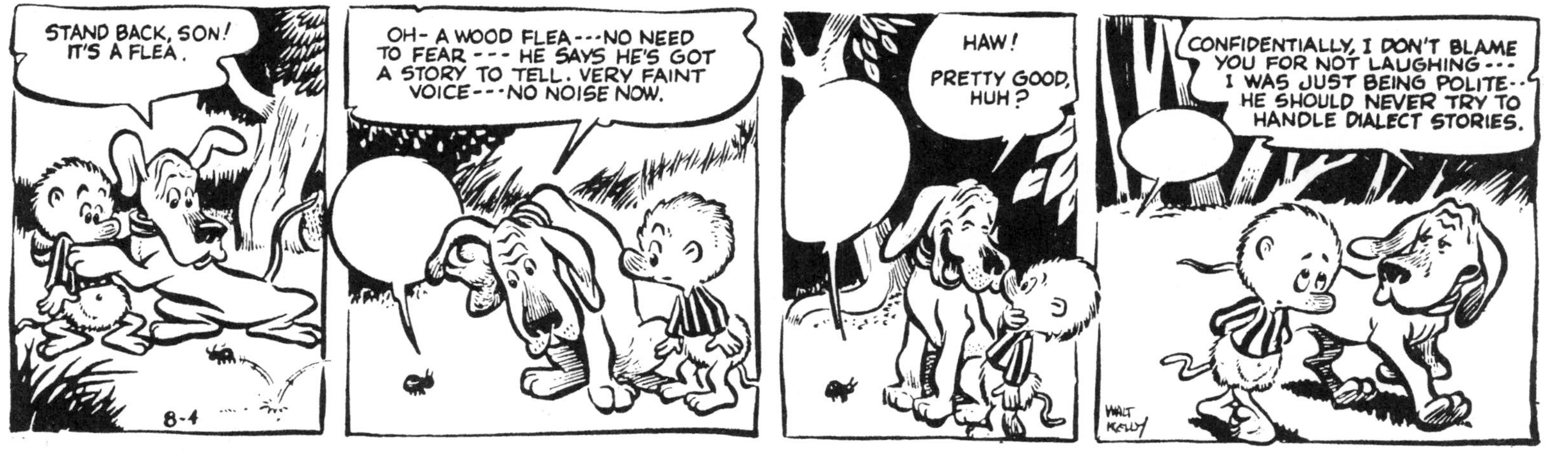
STAND BACK, SON! IT'S A FLEA.
8-4
OH- A WOOD FLEA---NO NEED TO FEAR--- HE SAYS HE'S GOT A STORY TO TELL. VERY FAINT VOICE---NO NOISE NOW.
HAW! PRETTY GOOD, HUH?
CONFIDENTIALLY, I DON'T BLAME YOU FOR NOT LAUGHING--- I WAS JUST BEING POLITE-- HE SHOULD NEVER TRY TO HANDLE DIALECT STORIES.
WALT KELLY

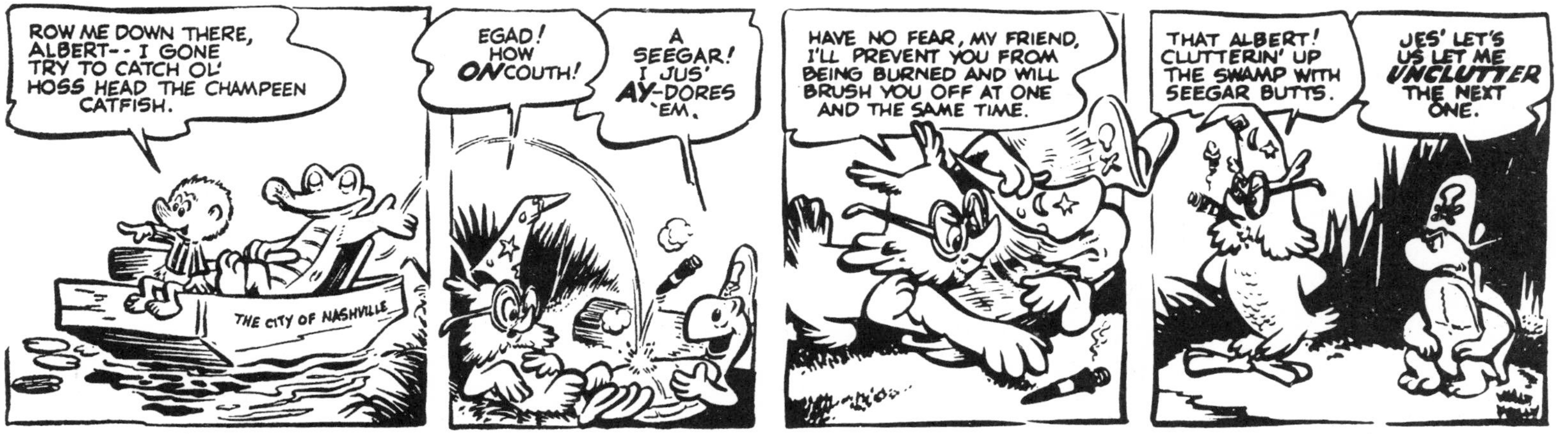
ROW ME DOWN THERE, ALBERT-- I GONE TRY TO CATCH OL' HOSS HEAD THE CHAMPEEN CATFISH.
THE CITY OF NASHVILLE
EGAD! HOW ONCOUTH!
A SEEGAR! I JUS' AY-DORES 'EM.
HAVE NO FEAR, MY FRIEND, I'LL PREVENT YOU FROM BEING BURNED AND WILL BRUSH YOU OFF AT ONE AND THE SAME TIME.
THAT ALBERT! CLUTTERIN' UP THE SWAMP WITH SEEGAR BUTTS.
JES' LET'S US LET ME UNCLUTTER THE NEXT ONE.

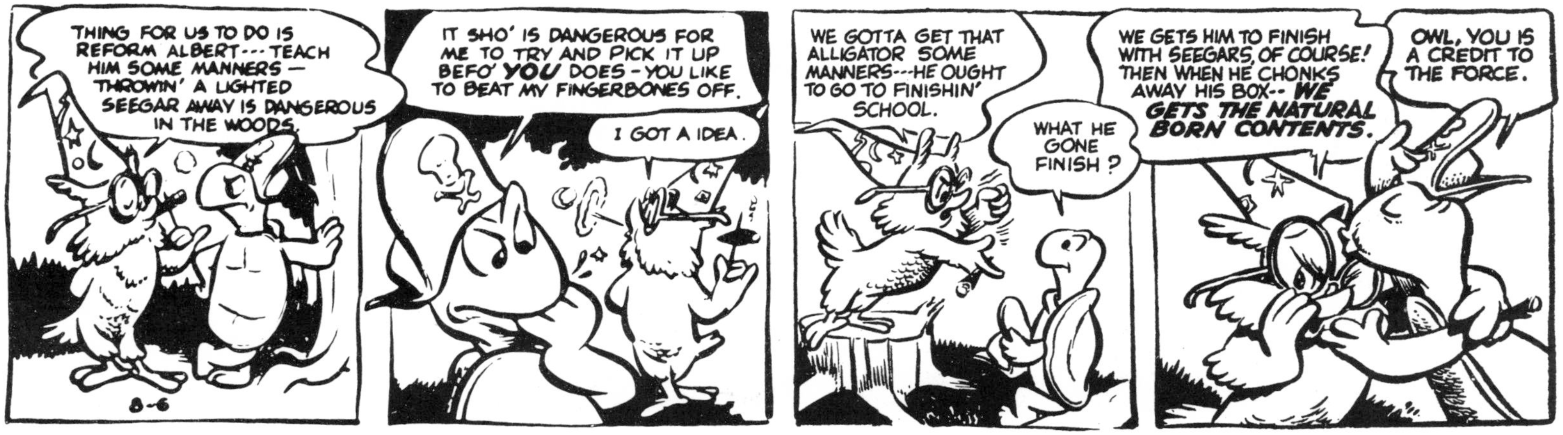
THING FOR US TO DO IS REFORM ALBERT--- TEACH HIM SOME MANNERS — THROWIN' A LIGHTED SEEGAR AWAY IS DANGEROUS IN THE WOODS.
8-6
IT SHO' IS DANGEROUS FOR ME TO TRY AND PICK IT UP BEFO' YOU DOES - YOU LIKE TO BEAT MY FINGERBONES OFF.
I GOT A IDEA.
WE GOTTA GET THAT ALLIGATOR SOME MANNERS---HE OUGHT TO GO TO FINISHIN' SCHOOL.
WHAT HE GONE FINISH?
WE GETS HIM TO FINISH WITH SEEGARS, OF COURSE! THEN WHEN HE CHONKS AWAY HIS BOX-- WE GETS THE NATURAL BORN CONTENTS.
OWL, YOU IS A CREDIT TO THE FORCE.

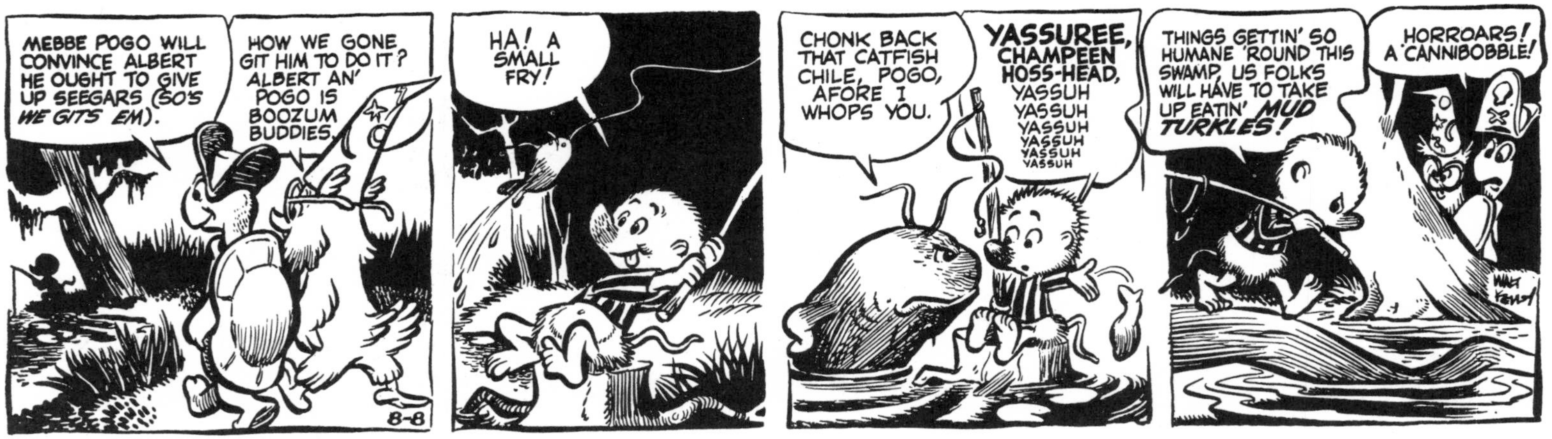
MEBBE POGO WILL CONVINCE ALBERT HE OUGHT TO GIVE UP SEEGARS (SO'S WE GITS EM).
HOW WE GONE GIT HIM TO DO IT? ALBERT AN' POGO IS BOOZUM BUDDIES.
8-8
HA! A SMALL FRY!
CHONK BACK THAT CATFISH CHILE, POGO, AFORE I WHOPS YOU.
YASSUREE, CHAMPEEN HOSS-HEAD, YASSUH YASSUH YASSUH YASSUH YASSUH YASSUH
THINGS GETTIN' SO HUMANE 'ROUND THIS SWAMP, US FOLKS WILL HAVE TO TAKE UP EATIN' MUD TURKLES!
HORROARS! A CANNIBOBBLE!
WALT KELLY

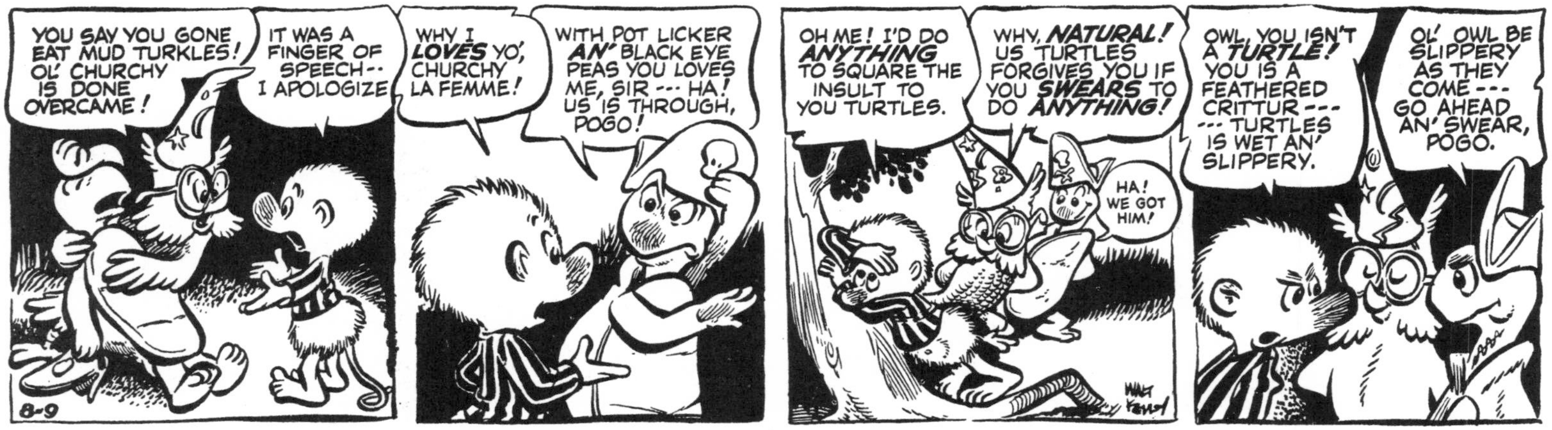
YOU SAY YOU GONE EAT MUD TURKLES! OL' CHURCHY IS DONE OVERCAME!
IT WAS A FINGER OF SPEECH -- I APOLOGIZE
8-9
WHY I LOVES YO', CHURCHY LA FEMME!
WITH POT LICKER AN' BLACK EYE PEAS YOU LOVES ME, SIR --- HA! US IS THROUGH, POGO!
OH ME! I'D DO ANYTHING TO SQUARE THE INSULT TO YOU TURTLES.
WHY, NATURAL! US TURTLES FORGIVES YOU IF YOU SWEARS TO DO ANYTHING!
HA! WE GOT HIM!
WALT KELLY
OWL, YOU ISN'T A TURTLE! YOU IS A FEATHERED CRITTUR ---- --- TURTLES IS WET AN' SLIPPERY.
OL' OWL BE SLIPPERY AS THEY COME --- GO AHEAD AN' SWEAR, POGO.

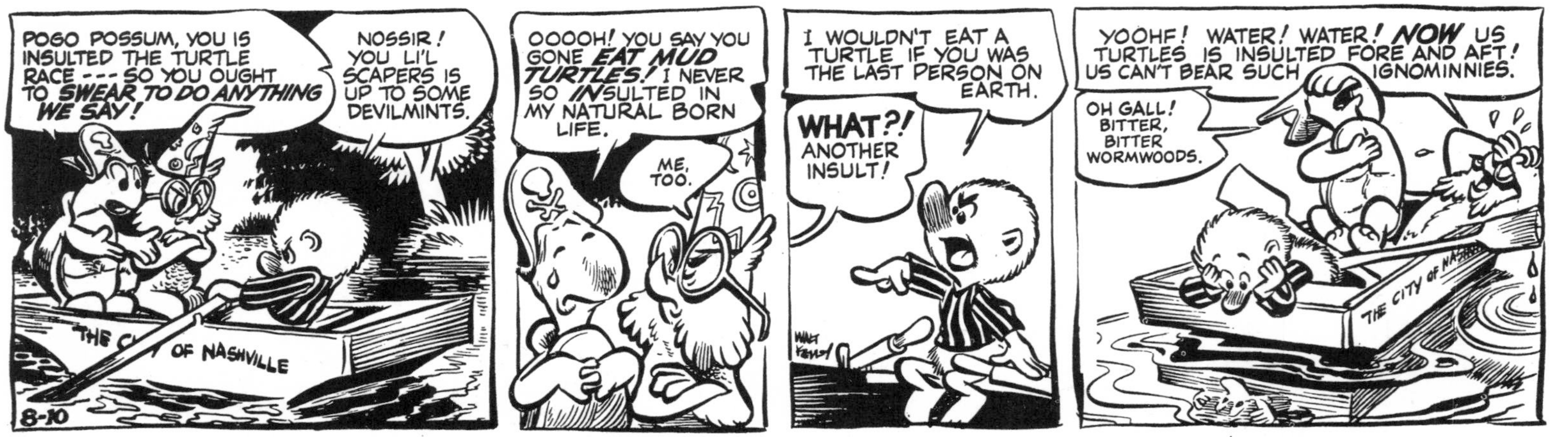
POGO POSSUM, YOU IS INSULTED THE TURTLE RACE --- SO YOU OUGHT TO SWEAR TO DO ANYTHING WE SAY!
NOSSIR! YOU LI'L SCAPERS IS UP TO SOME DEVILMINTS.
THE CITY OF NASHVILLE
8-10
OOOOH! YOU SAY YOU GONE EAT MUD TURTLES! I NEVER SO INSULTED IN MY NATURAL BORN LIFE.
ME, TOO.
I WOULDN'T EAT A TURTLE IF YOU WAS THE LAST PERSON ON EARTH.
WHAT?! ANOTHER INSULT!
WALT KELLY
YOOHF! WATER! WATER! NOW US TURTLES IS INSULTED FORE AND AFT! US CAN'T BEAR SUCH IGNOMINNIES.
OH GALL! BITTER, BITTER WORMWOODS.

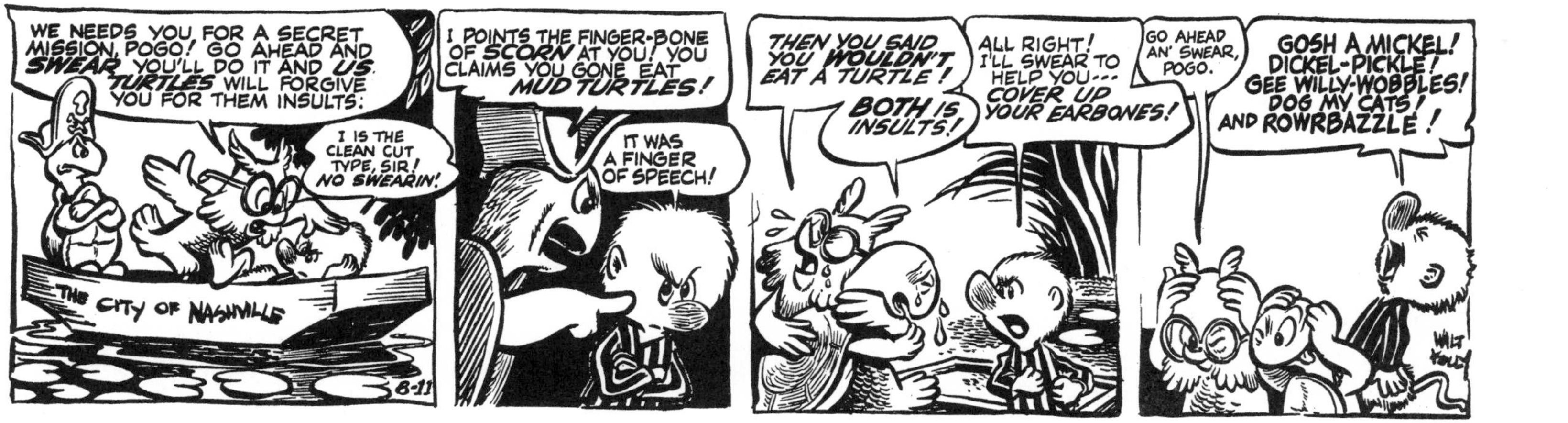
WE NEEDS YOU FOR A SECRET MISSION, POGO! GO AHEAD AND SWEAR YOU'LL DO IT AND US TURTLES WILL FORGIVE YOU FOR THEM INSULTS:
I IS THE CLEAN CUT TYPE, SIR! NO SWEARIN!
I POINTS THE FINGER-BONE OF SCORN AT YOU! YOU CLAIMS YOU GONE EAT MUD TURTLES!
IT WAS A FINGER OF SPEECH!
THEN YOU SAID YOU WOULDN'T EAT A TURTLE!
BOTH IS INSULTS!
ALL RIGHT! I'LL SWEAR TO HELP YOU--- COVER UP YOUR EARBONES!
GO AHEAD AN' SWEAR, POGO.
GOSH A MICKEL! DICKEL-PICKLE! GEE WILLY-WOBBLES! DOG MY CATS! AND ROWRBAZZLE!
THE CITY OF NASHVILLE
8-11

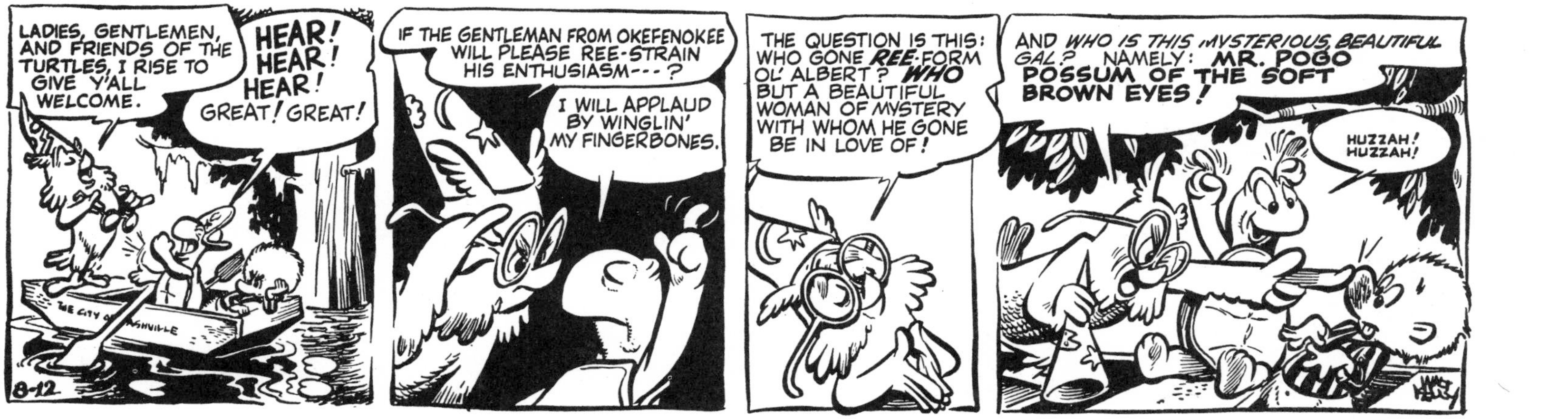
LADIES, GENTLEMEN, AND FRIENDS OF THE TURTLES, I RISE TO GIVE Y'ALL WELCOME.
HEAR! HEAR! HEAR! GREAT! GREAT!
IF THE GENTLEMAN FROM OKEFENOKEE WILL PLEASE REE-STRAIN HIS ENTHUSIASM---?
I WILL APPLAUD BY WINGLIN' MY FINGERBONES.
THE QUESTION IS THIS: WHO GONE REE-FORM OL' ALBERT? WHO BUT A BEAUTIFUL WOMAN OF MYSTERY WITH WHOM HE GONE BE IN LOVE OF!
AND WHO IS THIS MYSTERIOUS, BEAUTIFUL GAL? NAMELY: MR. POGO POSSUM OF THE SOFT BROWN EYES!
HUZZAH! HUZZAH!
8-12

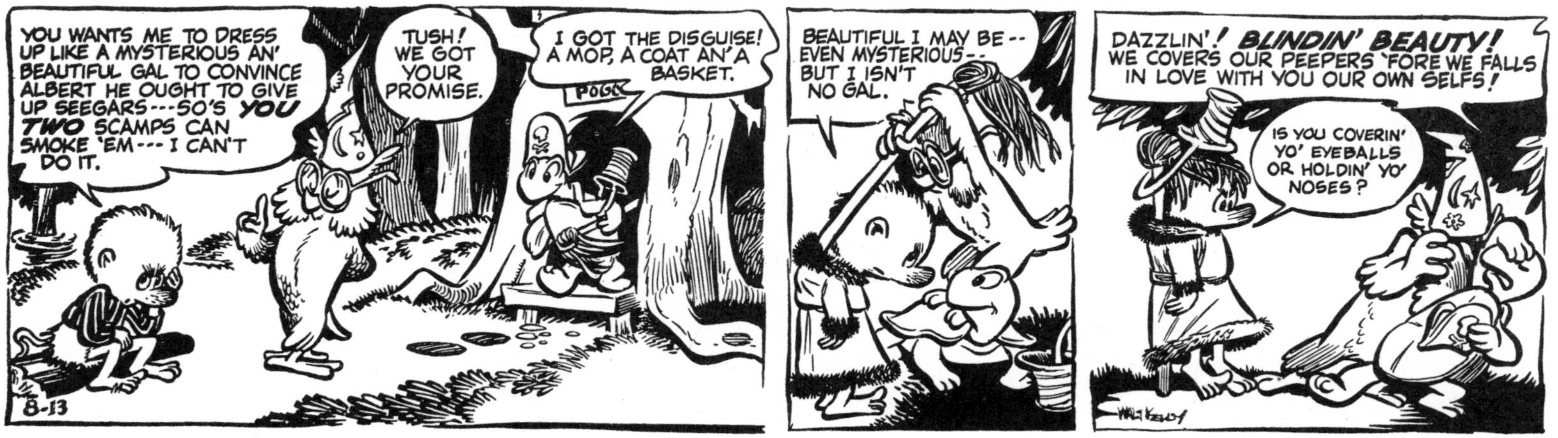
YOU WANTS ME TO DRESS UP LIKE A MYSTERIOUS AN' BEAUTIFUL GAL TO CONVINCE ALBERT HE OUGHT TO GIVE UP SEEGARS---SO'S YOU TWO SCAMPS CAN SMOKE 'EM--- I CAN'T DO IT.
TUSH! WE GOT YOUR PROMISE.
I GOT THE DISGUISE! A MOP, A COAT AN' A BASKET.
BEAUTIFUL I MAY BE-- EVEN MYSTERIOUS-- BUT I ISN'T NO GAL.
DAZZLIN'! BLINDIN' BEAUTY! WE COVERS OUR PEEPERS 'FORE WE FALLS IN LOVE WITH YOU OUR OWN SELFS!
IS YOU COVERIN' YO' EYEBALLS OR HOLDIN' YO' NOSES?
8-13

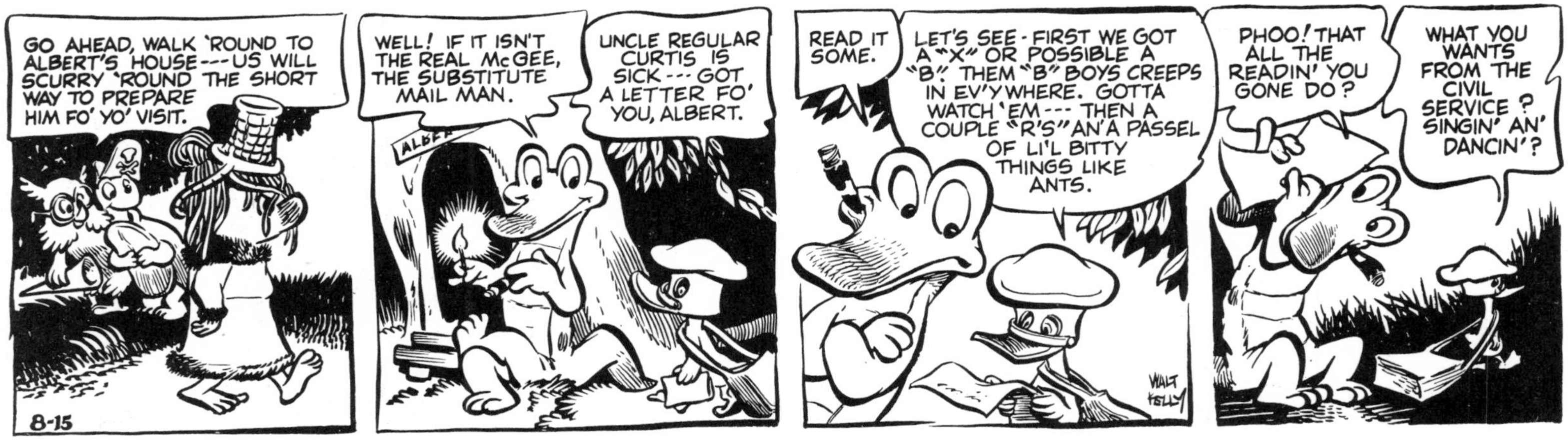
GO AHEAD, WALK 'ROUND TO ALBERT'S HOUSE---US WILL SCURRY 'ROUND THE SHORT WAY TO PREPARE HIM FO' YO' VISIT.
8-15
WELL! IF IT ISN'T THE REAL McGEE, THE SUBSTITUTE MAIL MAN.
UNCLE REGULAR CURTIS IS SICK---GOT A LETTER FO' YOU, ALBERT.
READ IT SOME.
LET'S SEE - FIRST WE GOT A "X" OR POSSIBLE A "B." THEM "B" BOYS CREEPS IN EV'YWHERE. GOTTA WATCH 'EM --- THEN A COUPLE "R'S" AN' A PASSEL OF LI'L BITTY THINGS LIKE ANTS.
WALT KELLY
PHOO! THAT ALL THE READIN' YOU GONE DO?
WHAT YOU WANTS FROM THE CIVIL SERVICE? SINGIN' AN' DANCIN'?

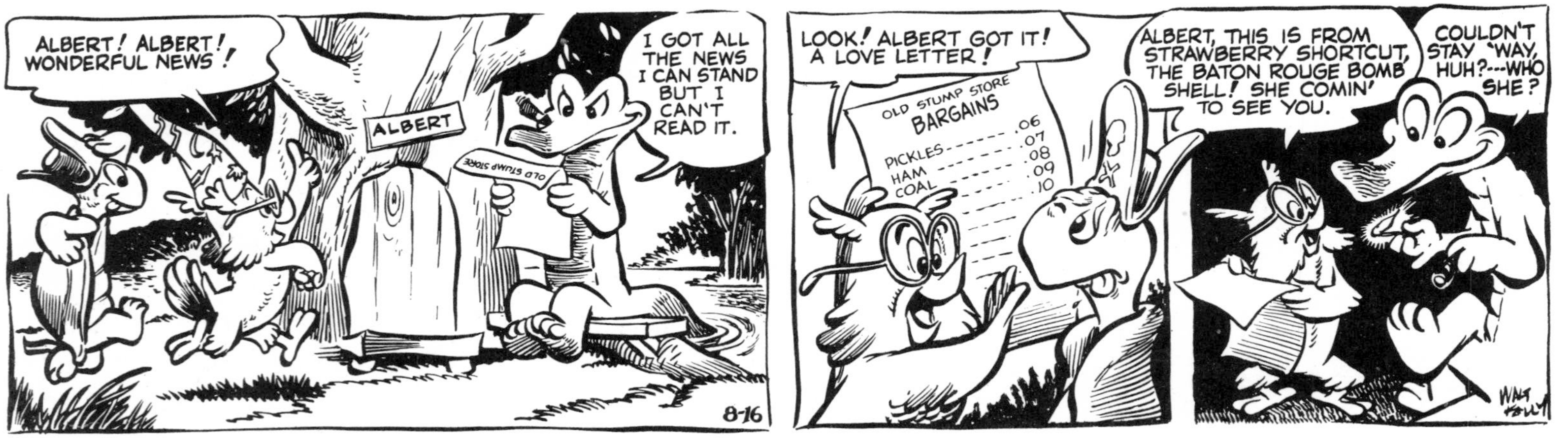
ALBERT! ALBERT! WONDERFUL NEWS!
ALBERT
OLD STUMP STORE
I GOT ALL THE NEWS I CAN STAND BUT I CAN'T READ IT.
8-16
LOOK! ALBERT GOT IT! A LOVE LETTER!
OLD STUMP STORE
BARGAINS
PICKLES - - - - - - .06
HAM - - - - - - .07
COAL - - - - - - .08
.09
.10
ALBERT, THIS IS FROM STRAWBERRY SHORTCUT, THE BATON ROUGE BOMB SHELL! SHE COMIN' TO SEE YOU.
COULDN'T STAY 'WAY, HUH?---WHO SHE?
WALT KELLY

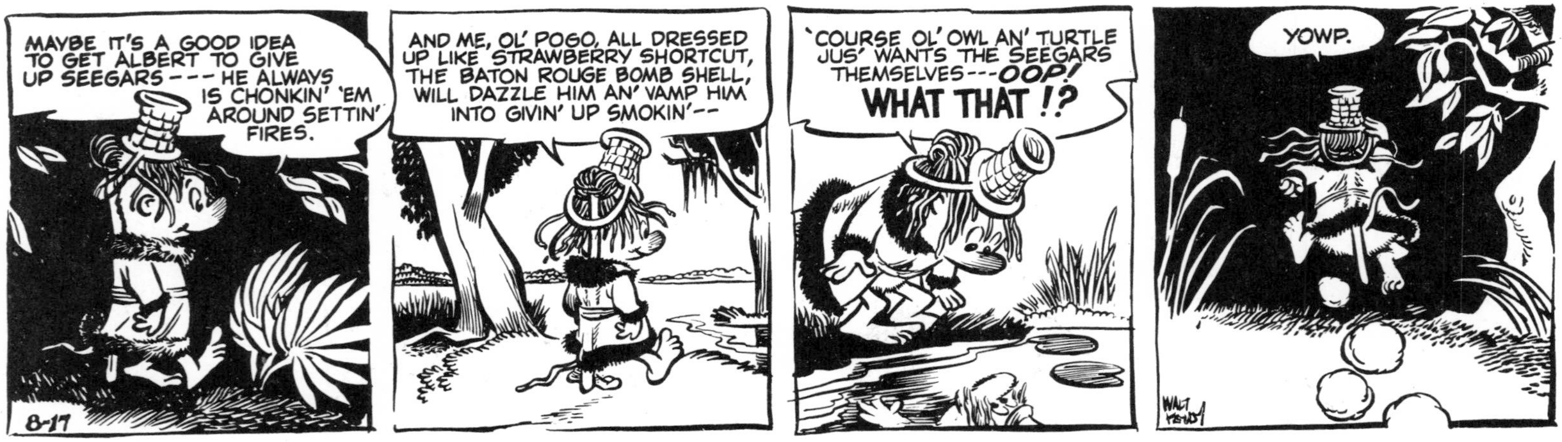
MAYBE IT'S A GOOD IDEA TO GET ALBERT TO GIVE UP SEEGARS --- HE ALWAYS IS CHONKIN' 'EM AROUND SETTIN' FIRES.
8-17
AND ME, OL' POGO, ALL DRESSED UP LIKE STRAWBERRY SHORTCUT, THE BATON ROUGE BOMB SHELL, WILL DAZZLE HIM AN' VAMP HIM INTO GIVIN' UP SMOKIN'--
'COURSE OL' OWL AN' TURTLE JUS' WANTS THE SEEGARS THEMSELVES---OOP!
WHAT THAT!?
YOWP.
WALT KELLY

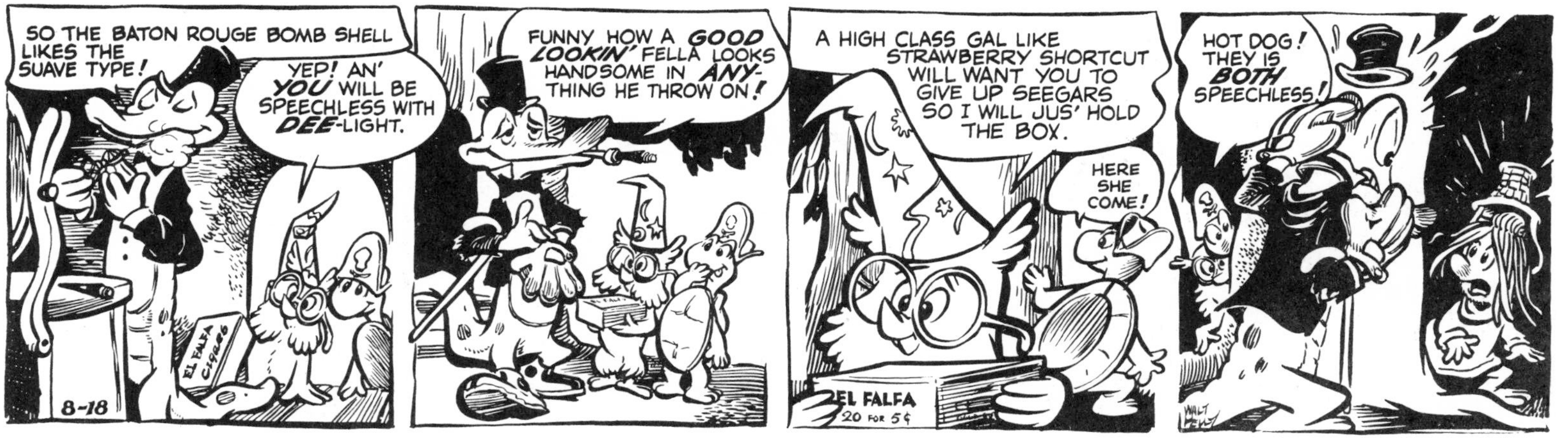
SO THE BATON ROUGE BOMB SHELL LIKES THE SUAVE TYPE!
YEP! AN' YOU WILL BE SPEECHLESS WITH DEE-LIGHT.
8-18
FUNNY HOW A GOOD LOOKIN' FELLA LOOKS HANDSOME IN ANY-THING HE THROW ON!
A HIGH CLASS GAL LIKE STRAWBERRY SHORTCUT WILL WANT YOU TO GIVE UP SEEGARS SO I WILL JUS' HOLD THE BOX.
HERE SHE COME!
EL FALFA 20 FOR 5¢
HOT DOG! THEY IS BOTH SPEECHLESS!
WALT KELLY

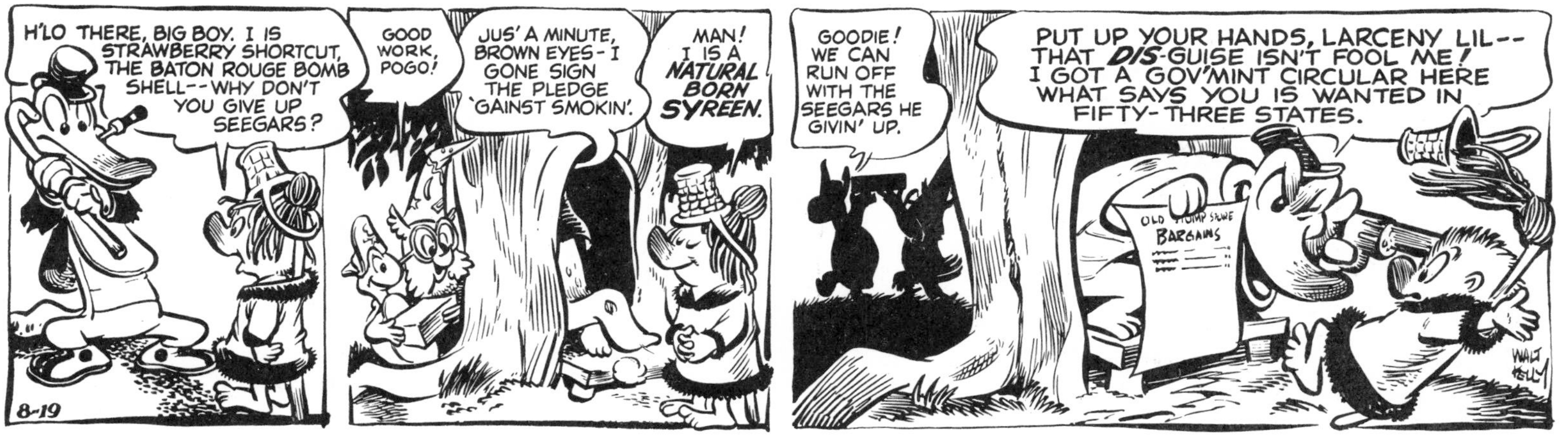
H'LO THERE, BIG BOY. I IS STRAWBERRY SHORTCUT, THE BATON ROUGE BOMB SHELL--WHY DON'T YOU GIVE UP SEEGARS?
8-19
GOOD WORK, POGO!
JUS' A MINUTE, BROWN EYES- I GONE SIGN THE PLEDGE 'GAINST SMOKIN'.
MAN! I IS A NATURAL BORN SYREEN.
GOODIE! WE CAN RUN OFF WITH THE SEEGARS HE GIVIN' UP.
PUT UP YOUR HANDS, LARCENY LIL-- THAT DIS-GUISE ISN'T FOOL ME! I GOT A GOV'MINT CIRCULAR HERE WHAT SAYS YOU IS WANTED IN FIFTY-THREE STATES.
BARGAINS
WALT KELLY

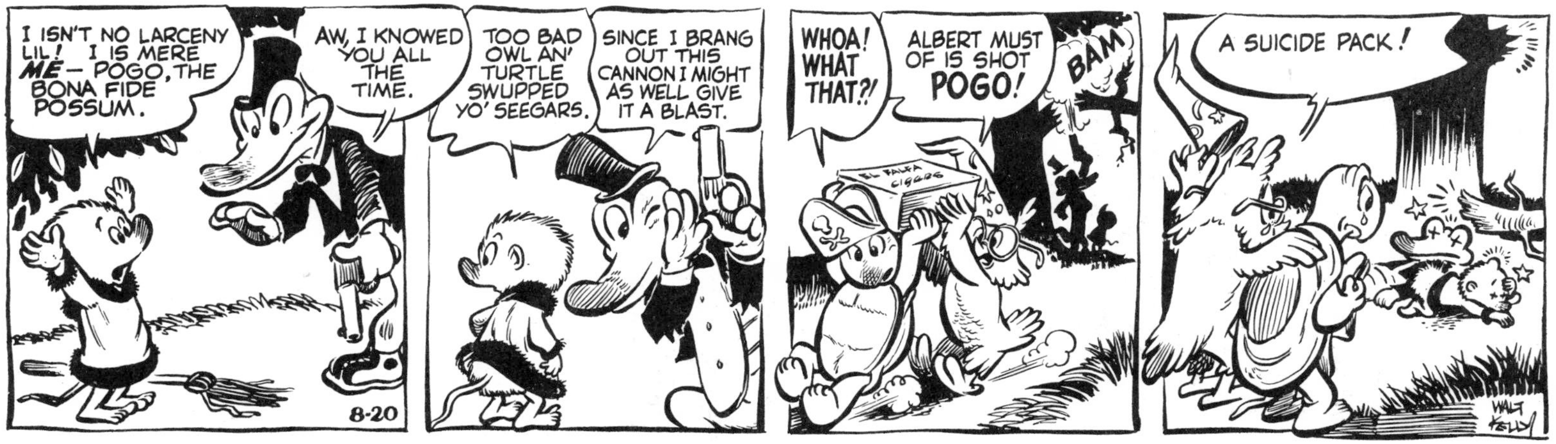
I ISN'T NO LARCENY LIL! I IS MERE ME- POGO, THE BONA FIDE POSSUM.
AW, I KNOWED YOU ALL THE TIME.
8-20
TOO BAD OWL AN' TURTLE SWUPPED YO' SEEGARS.
SINCE I BRANG OUT THIS CANNON I MIGHT AS WELL GIVE IT A BLAST.
WHOA! WHAT THAT?!
ALBERT MUST OF IS SHOT POGO!
BAM
A SUICIDE PACK!
WALT KELLY

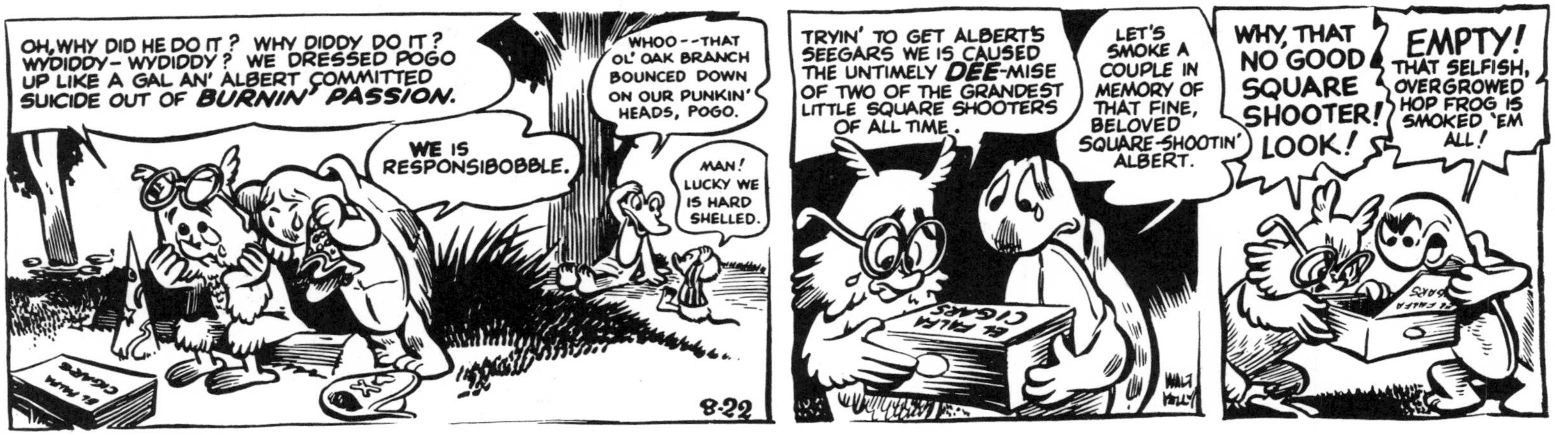
OH, WHY DID HE DO IT? WHY DIDDY DO IT? WYDIDDY-WYDIDDY? WE DRESSED POGO UP LIKE A GAL AN' ALBERT COMMITTED SUICIDE OUT OF BURNIN' PASSION.
WE IS RESPONSIBOBBLE.
WHOO--THAT OL' OAK BRANCH BOUNCED DOWN ON OUR PUNKIN' HEADS, POGO.
MAN! LUCKY WE IS HARD SHELLED.
8-22
TRYIN' TO GET ALBERT'S SEEGARS WE IS CAUSED THE UNTIMELY DEE-MISE OF TWO OF THE GRANDEST LITTLE SQUARE SHOOTERS OF ALL TIME.
LET'S SMOKE A COUPLE IN MEMORY OF THAT FINE, BELOVED SQUARE-SHOOTIN' ALBERT.
EL FALFA CIGARS
WALT KELLY
WHY, THAT NO GOOD SQUARE SHOOTER! LOOK!
EMPTY! THAT SELFISH, OVERGROWED HOP FROG IS SMOKED 'EM ALL!

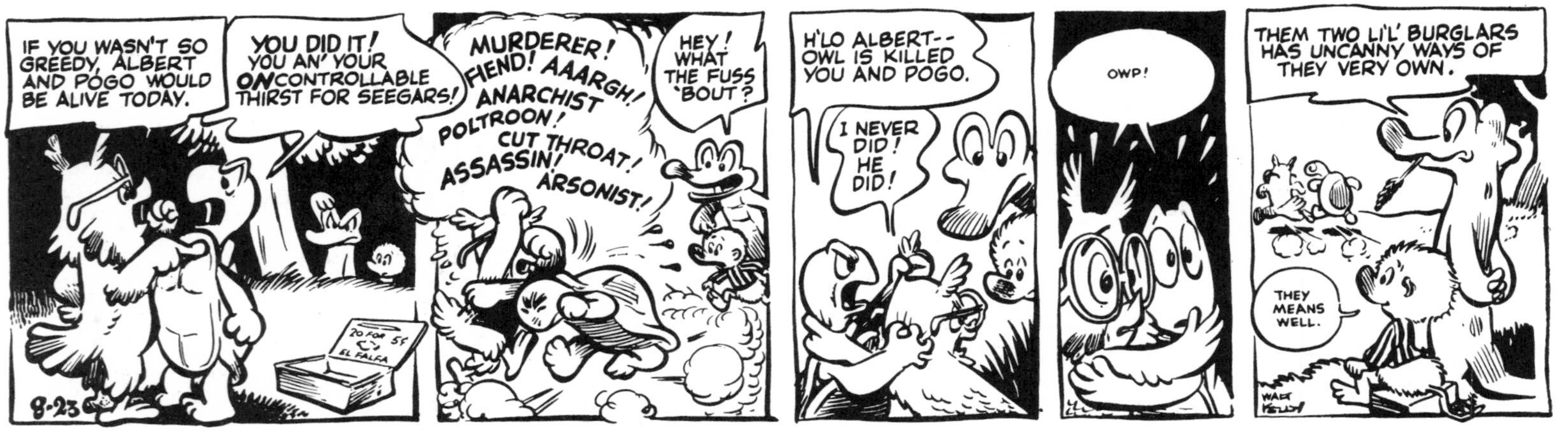
IF YOU WASN'T SO GREEDY, ALBERT AND POGO WOULD BE ALIVE TODAY.
YOU DID IT! YOU AN' YOUR ONCONTROLLABLE THIRST FOR SEEGARS!
20 FOR 55 EL FALFA
8-23
MURDERER! FIEND! AAARGH! ANARCHIST POLTROON! CUT THROAT! ASSASSIN! ARSONIST!
HEY! WHAT THE FUSS 'BOUT?
H'LO ALBERT--OWL IS KILLED YOU AND POGO.
I NEVER DID! HE DID!
OWP!
THEM TWO LI'L' BURGLARS HAS UNCANNY WAYS OF THEY VERY OWN.
THEY MEANS WELL.
WALT KELLY

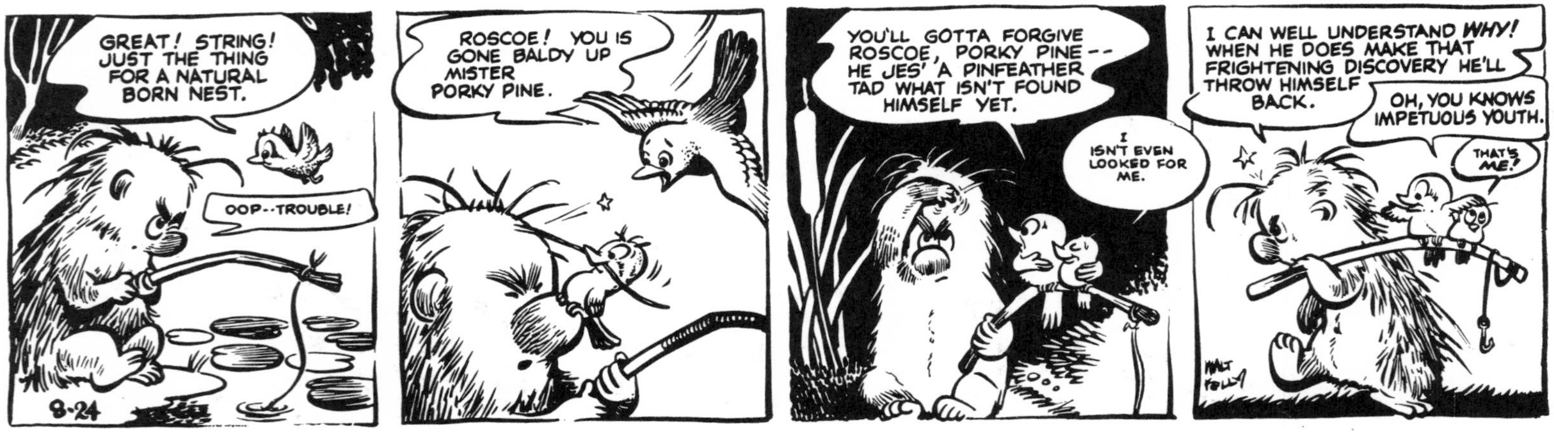
GREAT! STRING! JUST THE THING FOR A NATURAL BORN NEST.
OOP--TROUBLE!
8-24
ROSCOE! YOU IS GONE BALDY UP MISTER PORKY PINE.
YOU'LL GOTTA FORGIVE ROSCOE, PORKY PINE--HE JES' A PINFEATHER TAD WHAT ISN'T FOUND HIMSELF YET.
I ISN'T EVEN LOOKED FOR ME.
WALT KELLY
I CAN WELL UNDERSTAND WHY! WHEN HE DOES MAKE THAT FRIGHTENING DISCOVERY HE'LL THROW HIMSELF BACK.
OH, YOU KNOWS IMPETUOUS YOUTH.
THAT'S ME!

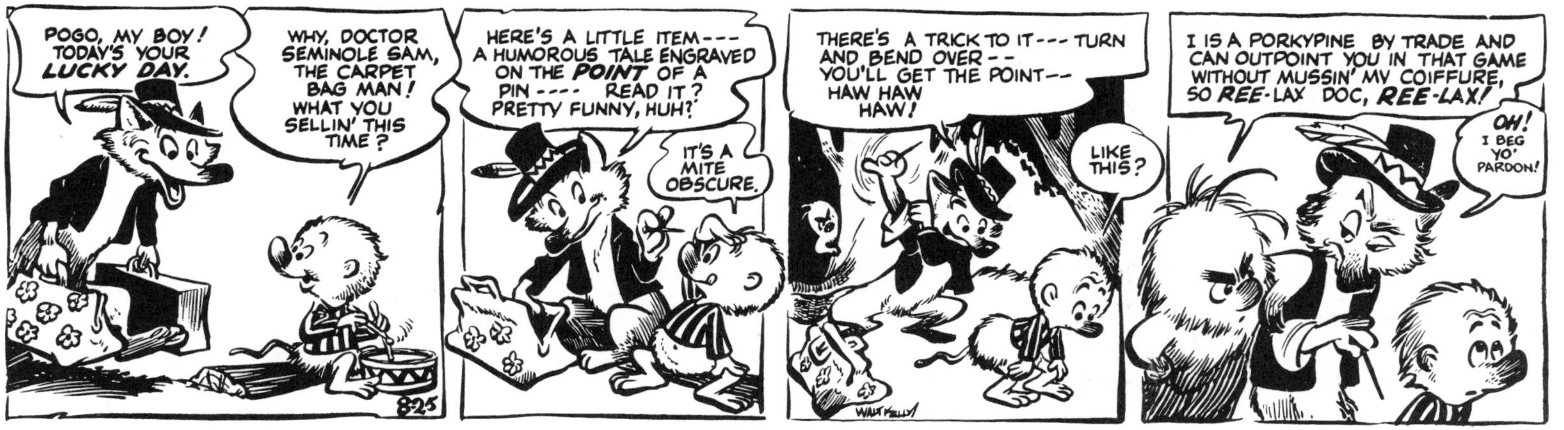
POGO, MY BOY! TODAY'S YOUR LUCKY DAY.
WHY, DOCTOR SEMINOLE SAM, THE CARPET BAG MAN! WHAT YOU SELLIN' THIS TIME?
8-25
HERE'S A LITTLE ITEM--- A HUMOROUS TALE ENGRAVED ON THE POINT OF A PIN---- READ IT? PRETTY FUNNY, HUH?
IT'S A MITE OBSCURE.
THERE'S A TRICK TO IT--- TURN AND BEND OVER-- YOU'LL GET THE POINT-- HAW HAW HAW!
LIKE THIS?
WALT KELLY
I IS A PORKYPINE BY TRADE AND CAN OUTPOINT YOU IN THAT GAME WITHOUT MUSSIN' MY COIFFURE, SO REE-LAX DOC, REE-LAX!
OH! I BEG YO' PARDON!

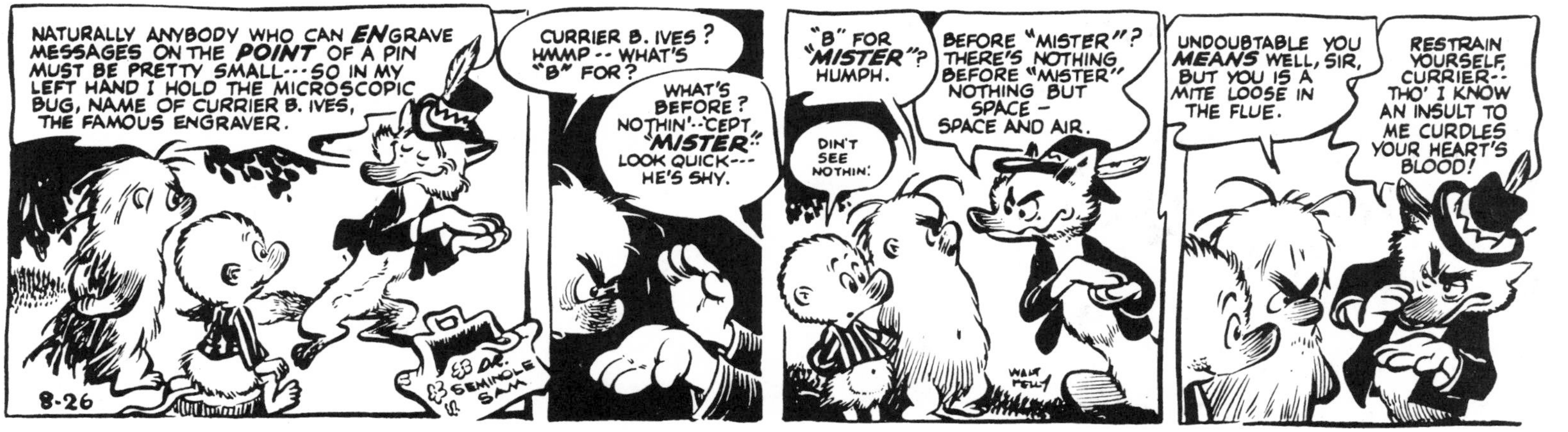
NATURALLY ANYBODY WHO CAN ENGRAVE MESSAGES ON THE POINT OF A PIN MUST BE PRETTY SMALL--- SO IN MY LEFT HAND I HOLD THE MICROSCOPIC BUG, NAME OF CURRIER B. IVES, THE FAMOUS ENGRAVER.
DR. SEMINOLE SAM
8-26
CURRIER B. IVES? HMMP-- WHAT'S "B" FOR?
WHAT'S BEFORE? NOTHIN'--'CEPT "MISTER." LOOK QUICK--- HE'S SHY.
"B" FOR "MISTER"? HUMPH.
DIN'T SEE NOTHIN'.
BEFORE "MISTER"? THERE'S NOTHING BEFORE "MISTER" NOTHING BUT SPACE- SPACE AND AIR.
WALT KELLY
UNDOUBTABLE YOU MEANS WELL, SIR, BUT YOU IS A MITE LOOSE IN THE FLUE.
RESTRAIN YOURSELF, CURRIER-- THO' I KNOW AN INSULT TO ME CURDLES YOUR HEART'S BLOOD!

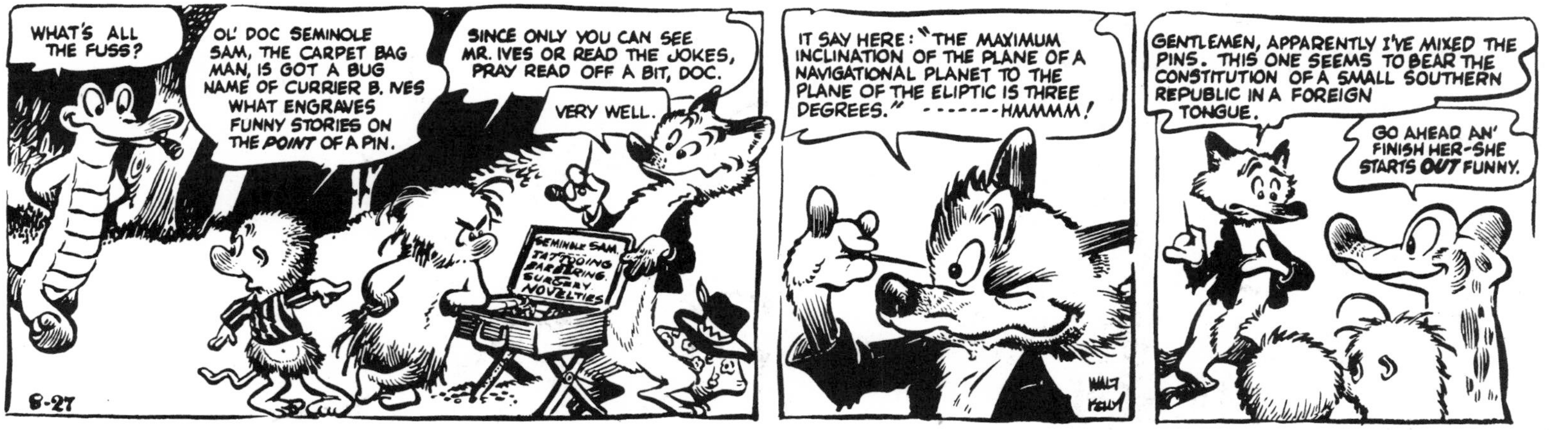
WHAT'S ALL THE FUSS?
OL' DOC SEMINOLE SAM, THE CARPET BAG MAN, IS GOT A BUG NAME OF CURRIER B. IVES WHAT ENGRAVES FUNNY STORIES ON THE POINT OF A PIN.
SINCE ONLY YOU CAN SEE MR. IVES OR READ THE JOKES, PRAY READ OFF A BIT, DOC.
VERY WELL.
SEMINOLE SAM TATTOOING BARBERING SURGERY NOVELTIES
8-27
IT SAY HERE: "THE MAXIMUM INCLINATION OF THE PLANE OF A NAVIGATIONAL PLANET TO THE PLANE OF THE ELIPTIC IS THREE DEGREES." -------HMMMM!
WALT KELLY
GENTLEMEN, APPARENTLY I'VE MIXED THE PINS. THIS ONE SEEMS TO BEAR THE CONSTITUTION OF A SMALL SOUTHERN REPUBLIC IN A FOREIGN TONGUE.
GO AHEAD AN' FINISH HER-SHE STARTS OUT FUNNY.

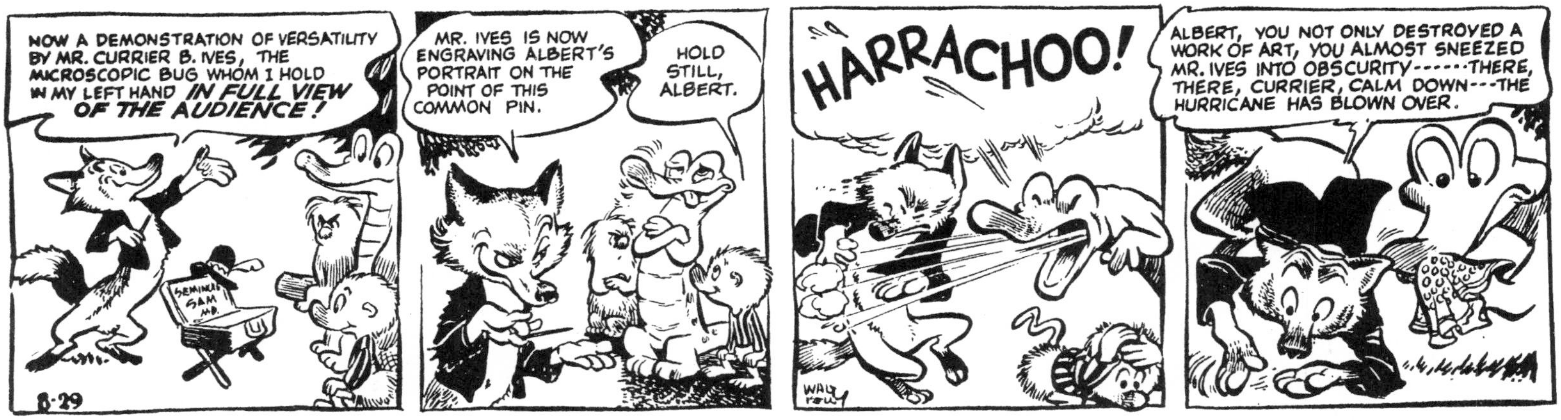
NOW A DEMONSTRATION OF VERSATILITY BY MR. CURRIER B. IVES, THE MICROSCOPIC BUG WHOM I HOLD IN MY LEFT HAND IN FULL VIEW OF THE AUDIENCE!
SEMINOLE SAM M.D.
8-29
MR. IVES IS NOW ENGRAVING ALBERT'S PORTRAIT ON THE POINT OF THIS COMMON PIN.
HOLD STILL, ALBERT.
HARRACHOO!
ALBERT, YOU NOT ONLY DESTROYED A WORK OF ART, YOU ALMOST SNEEZED MR. IVES INTO OBSCURITY------THERE, THERE, CURRIER, CALM DOWN---THE HURRICANE HAS BLOWN OVER.

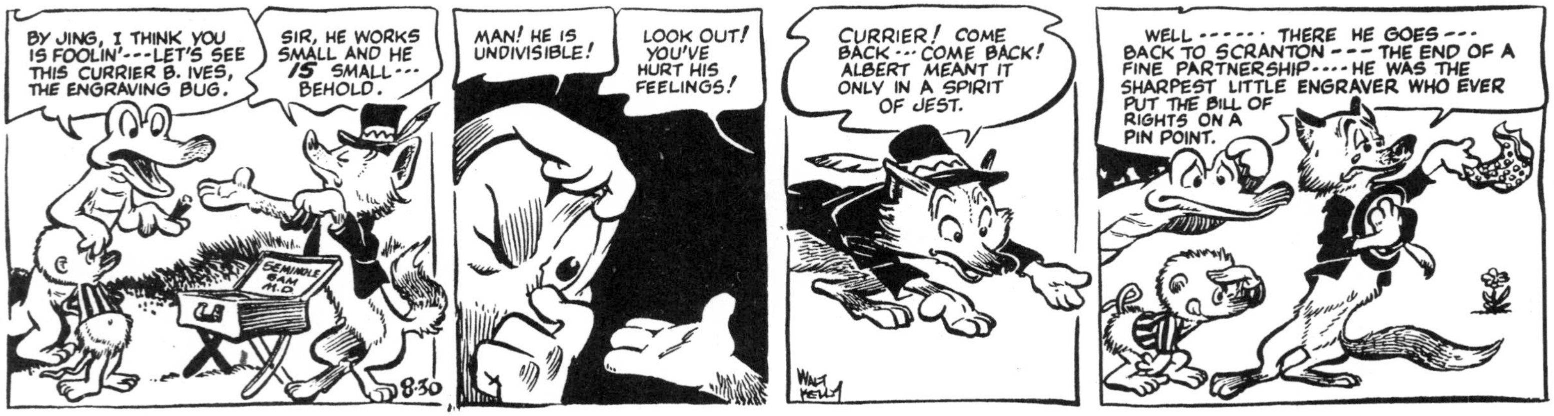
BY JING, I THINK YOU IS FOOLIN'---LET'S SEE THIS CURRIER B. IVES, THE ENGRAVING BUG.
SIR, HE WORKS SMALL AND HE IS SMALL--- BEHOLD.
SEMINOLE SAM M.D.
8-30
MAN! HE IS UNDIVISIBLE!
LOOK OUT! YOU'VE HURT HIS FEELINGS!
CURRIER! COME BACK--- COME BACK! ALBERT MEANT IT ONLY IN A SPIRIT OF JEST.
WELL------ THERE HE GOES--- BACK TO SCRANTON--- THE END OF A FINE PARTNERSHIP---- HE WAS THE SHARPEST LITTLE ENGRAVER WHO EVER PUT THE BILL OF RIGHTS ON A PIN POINT.

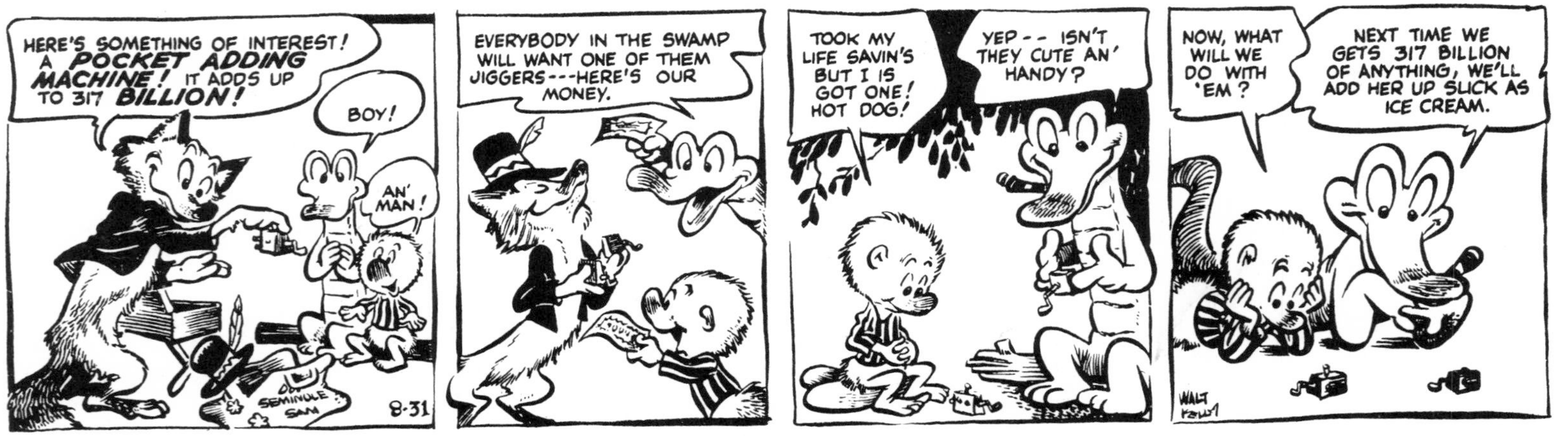
HERE'S SOMETHING OF INTEREST! A POCKET ADDING MACHINE! IT ADDS UP TO 317 BILLION!
BOY!
AN' MAN!
SEMINOLE SAM
8-31
EVERYBODY IN THE SWAMP WILL WANT ONE OF THEM JIGGERS---HERE'S OUR MONEY.
TOOK MY LIFE SAVIN'S BUT I IS GOT ONE! HOT DOG!
YEP-- ISN'T THEY CUTE AN' HANDY?
NOW, WHAT WILL WE DO WITH 'EM?
NEXT TIME WE GETS 317 BILLION OF ANYTHING, WE'LL ADD HER UP SLICK AS ICE CREAM.

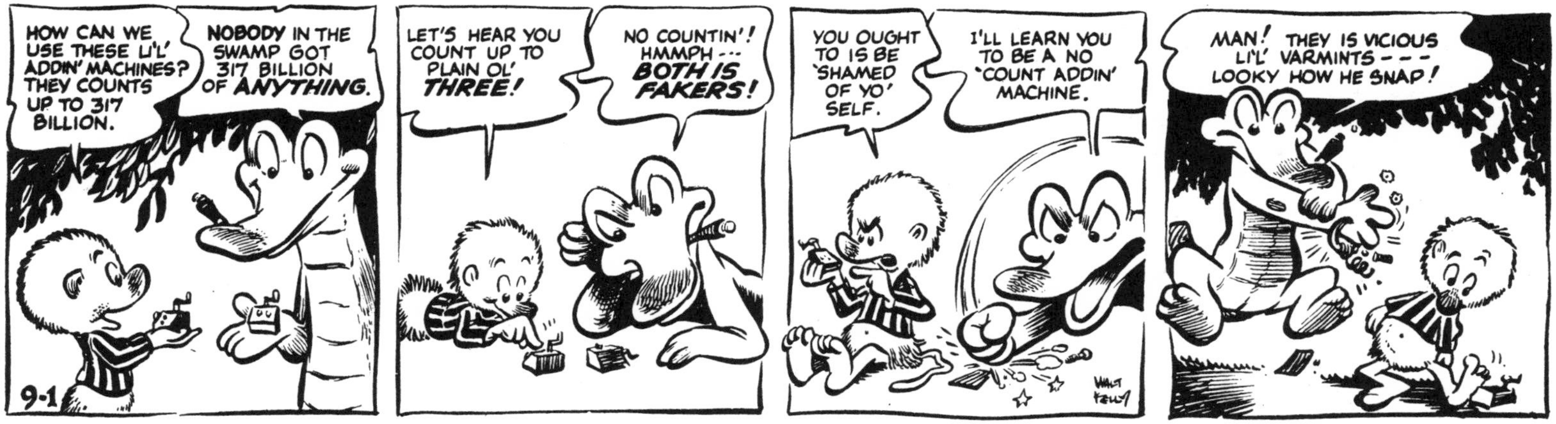

HOW CAN WE USE THESE LI'L' ADDIN' MACHINES? THEY COUNTS UP TO 317 BILLION.
NOBODY IN THE SWAMP GOT 317 BILLION OF ANYTHING.
9-1
LET'S HEAR YOU COUNT UP TO PLAIN OL' THREE!
NO COUNTIN'! HMMPH --- BOTH IS FAKERS!
YOU OUGHT TO IS BE 'SHAMED OF YO' SELF.
I'LL LEARN YOU TO BE A NO 'COUNT ADDIN' MACHINE.
WALT KELLY
MAN! THEY IS VICIOUS LI'L' VARMINTS --- LOOKY HOW HE SNAP!

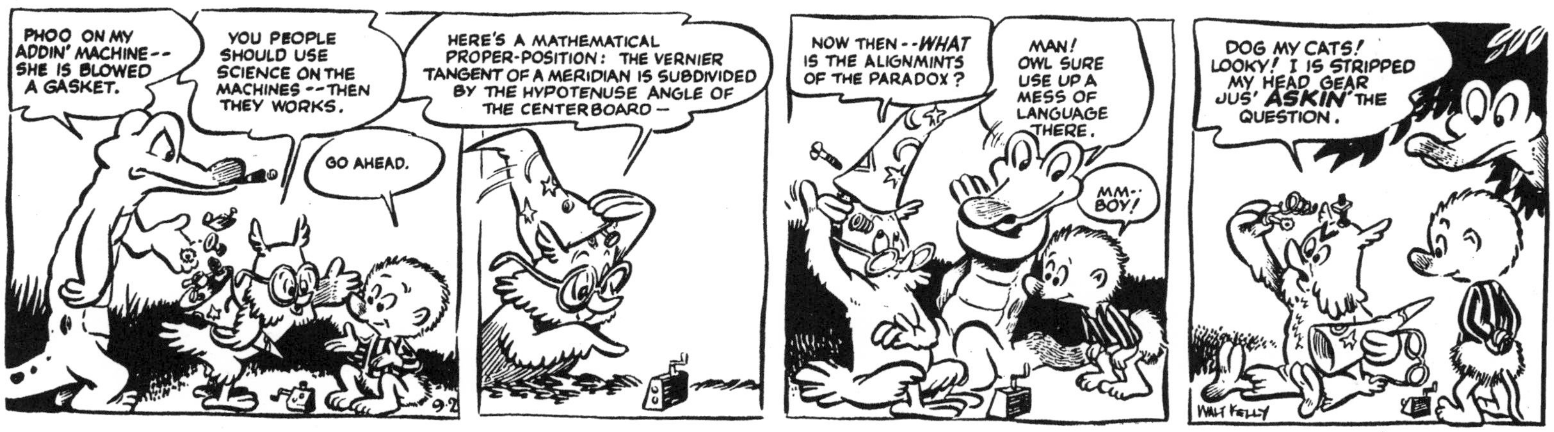

PHOO ON MY ADDIN' MACHINE -- SHE IS BLOWED A GASKET.
YOU PEOPLE SHOULD USE SCIENCE ON THE MACHINES -- THEN THEY WORKS.
GO AHEAD.
9-2
HERE'S A MATHEMATICAL PROPER-POSITION: THE VERNIER TANGENT OF A MERIDIAN IS SUBDIVIDED BY THE HYPOTENUSE ANGLE OF THE CENTERBOARD —
NOW THEN -- WHAT IS THE ALIGNMINTS OF THE PARADOX?
MAN! OWL SURE USE UP A MESS OF LANGUAGE THERE.
MM-- BOY!
DOG MY CATS! LOOKY! I IS STRIPPED MY HEAD GEAR JUS' ASKIN' THE QUESTION.
WALT KELLY

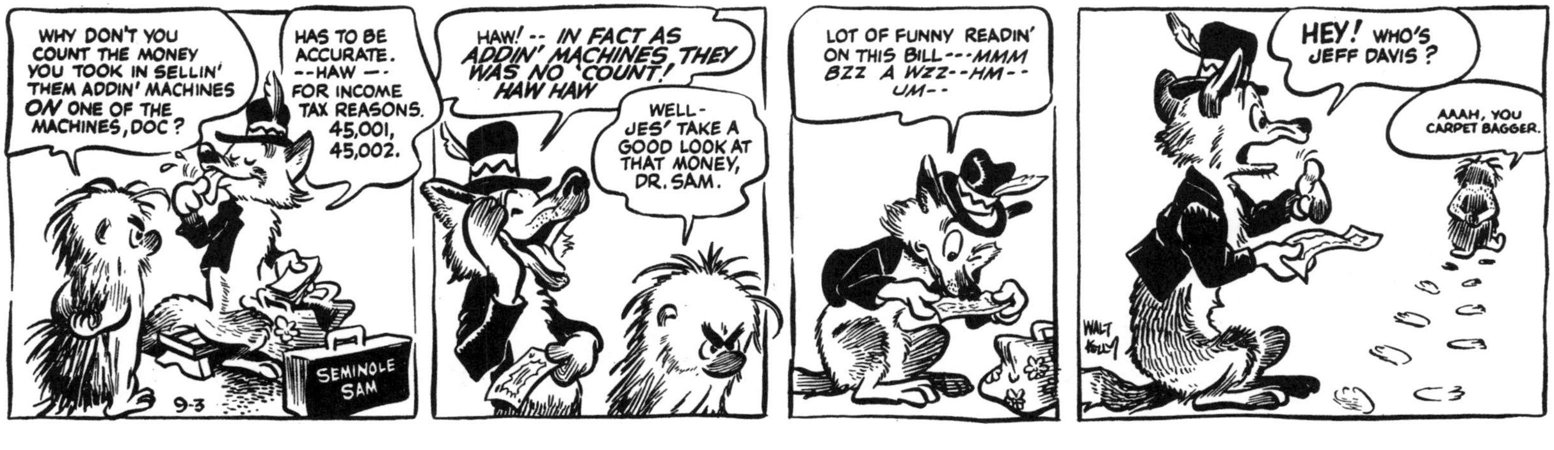

WHY DON'T YOU COUNT THE MONEY YOU TOOK IN SELLIN' THEM ADDIN' MACHINES ON ONE OF THE MACHINES, DOC?
HAS TO BE ACCURATE. --HAW -- FOR INCOME TAX REASONS. 45,001, 45,002.
SEMINOLE SAM
9-3
HAW! -- IN FACT AS ADDIN' MACHINES THEY WAS NO 'COUNT! HAW HAW
WELL- JES' TAKE A GOOD LOOK AT THAT MONEY, DR. SAM.
LOT OF FUNNY READIN' ON THIS BILL --- MMM BZZ A WZZ -- HM -- UM --
WALT KELLY
HEY! WHO'S JEFF DAVIS?
AAAH, YOU CARPET BAGGER.

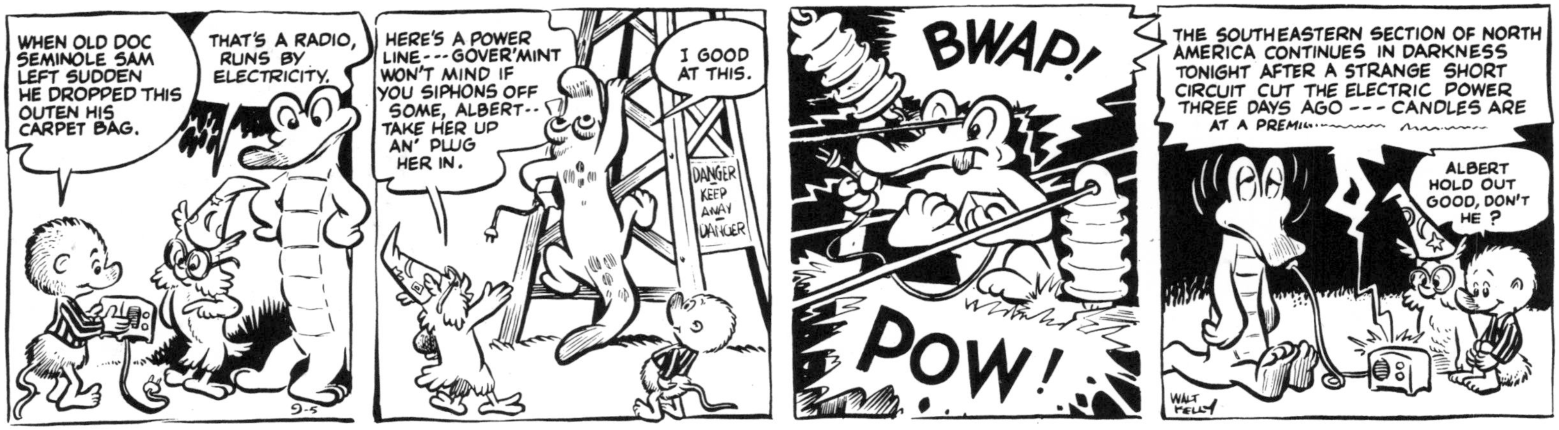
WHEN OLD DOC SEMINOLE SAM LEFT SUDDEN HE DROPPED THIS OUTEN HIS CARPET BAG.
THAT'S A RADIO, RUNS BY ELECTRICITY.
9-5
HERE'S A POWER LINE---GOVER'MINT WON'T MIND IF YOU SIPHONS OFF SOME, ALBERT--TAKE HER UP AN' PLUG HER IN.
I GOOD AT THIS.
DANGER KEEP AWAY DANGER
BWAP!
POW!
THE SOUTHEASTERN SECTION OF NORTH AMERICA CONTINUES IN DARKNESS TONIGHT AFTER A STRANGE SHORT CIRCUIT CUT THE ELECTRIC POWER THREE DAYS AGO --- CANDLES ARE AT A PREMI
ALBERT HOLD OUT GOOD, DON'T HE ?
WALT KELLY

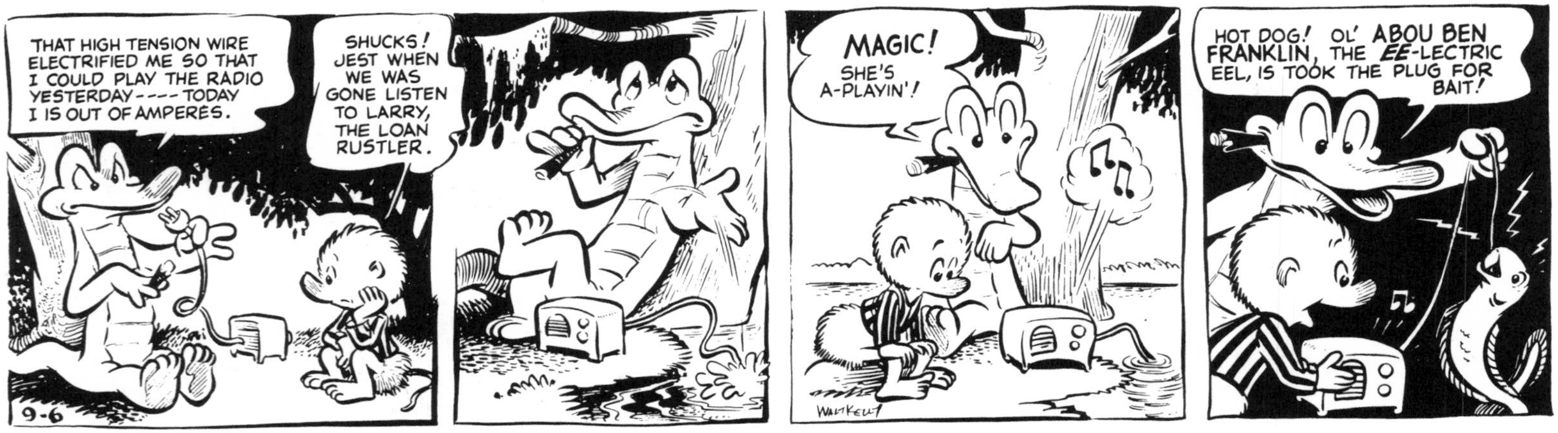
THAT HIGH TENSION WIRE ELECTRIFIED ME SO THAT I COULD PLAY THE RADIO YESTERDAY---- TODAY I IS OUT OF AMPERES.
SHUCKS! JEST WHEN WE WAS GONE LISTEN TO LARRY, THE LOAN RUSTLER.
9-6
MAGIC! SHE'S A-PLAYIN'!
WALT KELLY
HOT DOG! OL' ABOU BEN FRANKLIN, THE EE-LECTRIC EEL, IS TOOK THE PLUG FOR BAIT!

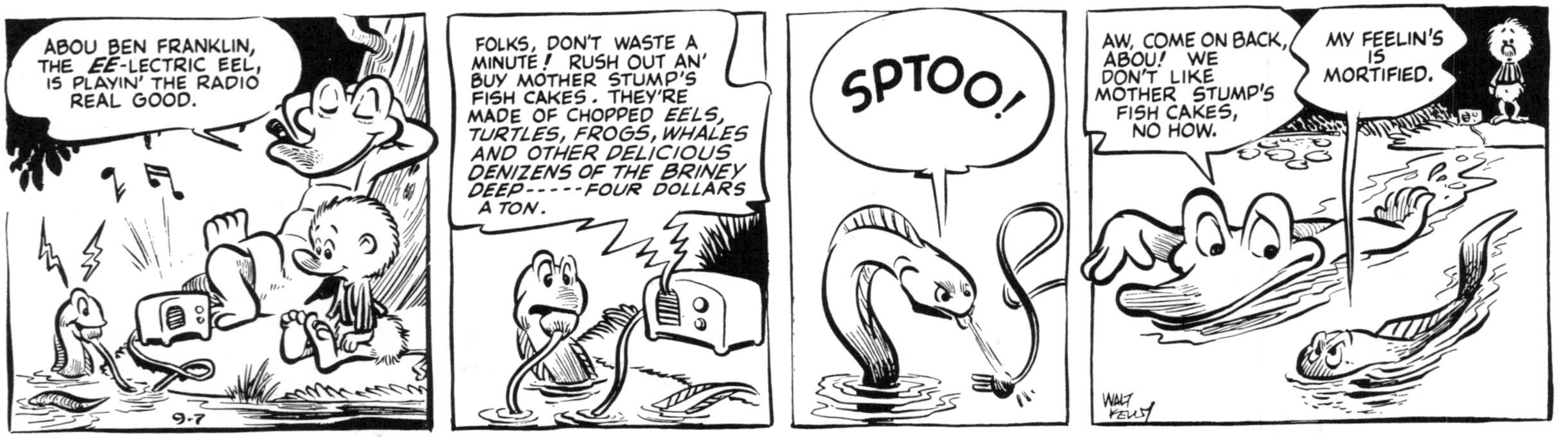
ABOU BEN FRANKLIN, THE EE-LECTRIC EEL, IS PLAYIN' THE RADIO REAL GOOD.
9-7
FOLKS, DON'T WASTE A MINUTE! RUSH OUT AN' BUY MOTHER STUMP'S FISH CAKES. THEY'RE MADE OF CHOPPED EELS, TURTLES, FROGS, WHALES AND OTHER DELICIOUS DENIZENS OF THE BRINEY DEEP-----FOUR DOLLARS A TON.
SPTOO!
AW, COME ON BACK, ABOU! WE DON'T LIKE MOTHER STUMP'S FISH CAKES, NO HOW.
MY FEELIN'S IS MORTIFIED.
WALT KELLY

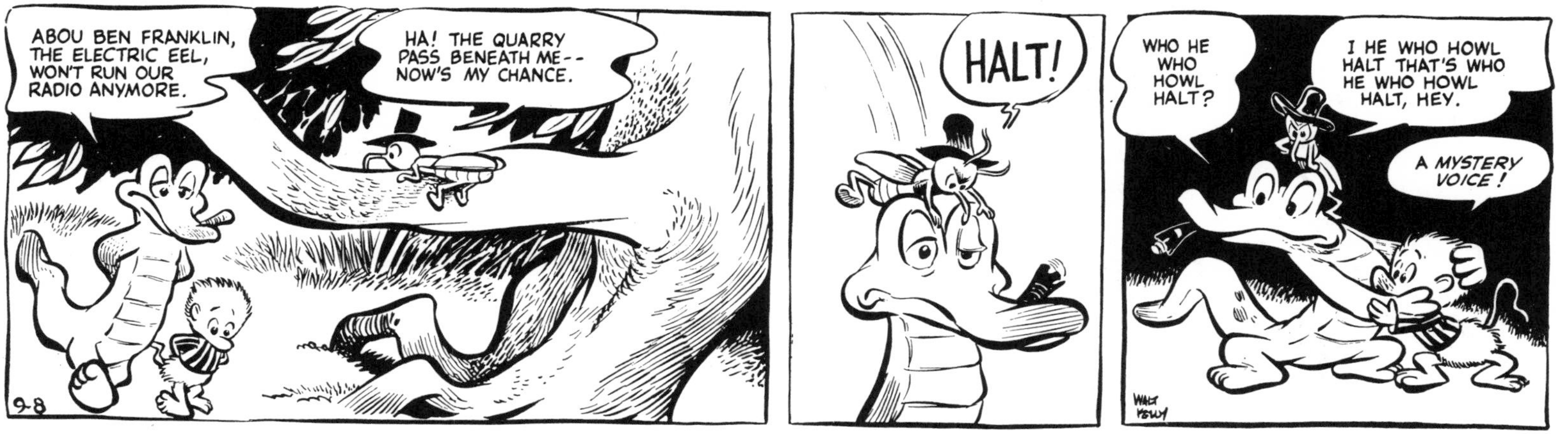
ABOU BEN FRANKLIN, THE ELECTRIC EEL, WON'T RUN OUR RADIO ANYMORE.
HA! THE QUARRY PASS BENEATH ME-- NOW'S MY CHANCE.
9-8
HALT!
WHO HE WHO HOWL HALT?
I HE WHO HOWL HALT THAT'S WHO HE WHO HOWL HALT, HEY.
A *MYSTERY VOICE!*
WALT KELLY

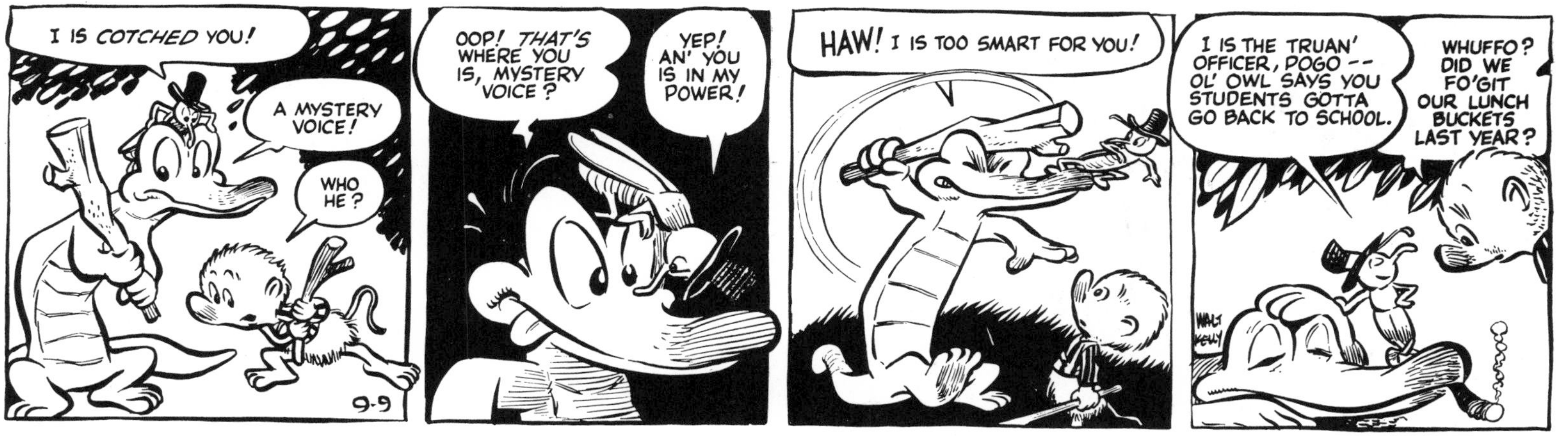
I IS *COTCHED* YOU!
A MYSTERY VOICE!
WHO HE?
9-9
OOP! *THAT'S* WHERE YOU IS, MYSTERY VOICE?
YEP! AN' YOU IS IN MY POWER!
HAW! I IS TOO SMART FOR YOU!
I IS THE TRUAN' OFFICER, POGO -- OL' OWL SAYS YOU STUDENTS GOTTA GO BACK TO SCHOOL.
WHUFFO? DID WE FO'GIT OUR LUNCH BUCKETS LAST YEAR?
WALT KELLY

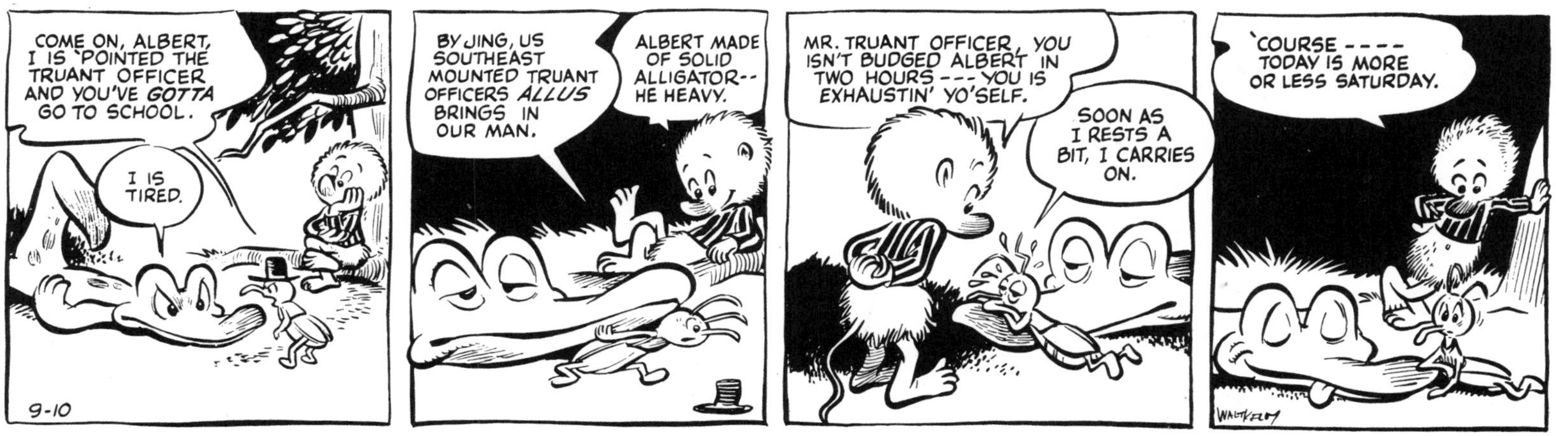
COME ON, ALBERT, I IS 'POINTED THE TRUANT OFFICER AND YOU'VE *GOTTA* GO TO SCHOOL.
I IS TIRED.
9-10
BY JING, US SOUTHEAST MOUNTED TRUANT OFFICERS *ALLUS* BRINGS IN OUR MAN.
ALBERT MADE OF SOLID ALLIGATOR-- HE HEAVY.
MR. TRUANT OFFICER, YOU ISN'T BUDGED ALBERT IN TWO HOURS --- YOU IS EXHAUSTIN' YO'SELF.
SOON AS I RESTS A BIT, I CARRIES ON.
'COURSE ---- TODAY IS MORE OR LESS SATURDAY.
WALT KELLY

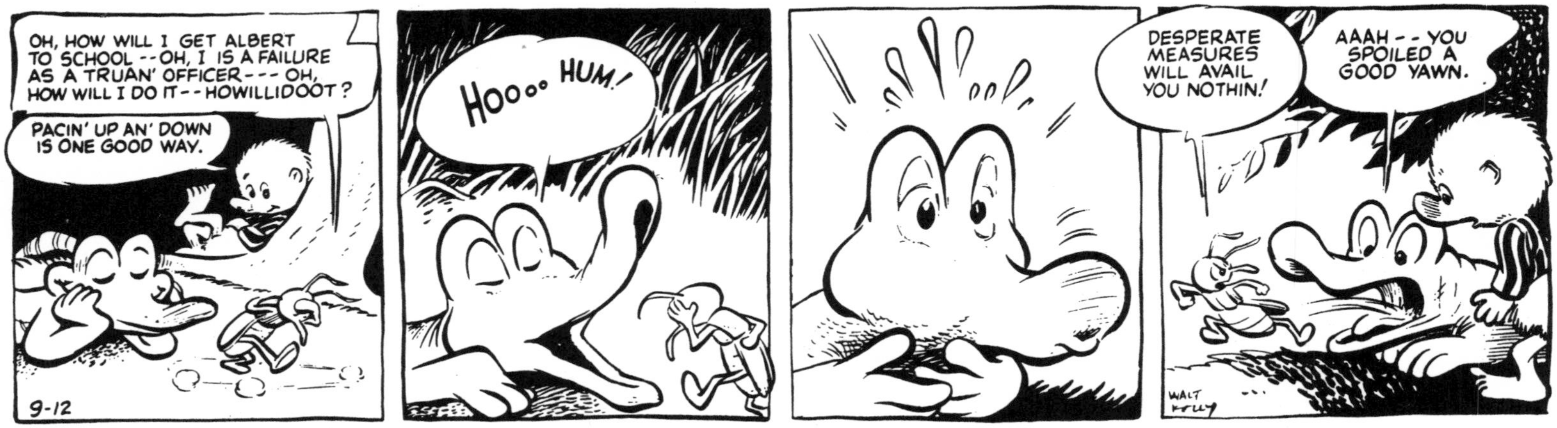
OH, HOW WILL I GET ALBERT TO SCHOOL --OH, I IS A FAILURE AS A TRUAN' OFFICER--- OH, HOW WILL I DO IT--HOWILLIDOOT?
PACIN' UP AN' DOWN IS ONE GOOD WAY.
9-12
HOO°° HUM!
DESPERATE MEASURES WILL AVAIL YOU NOTHIN!
AAAH--YOU SPOILED A GOOD YAWN.
WALT KELLY

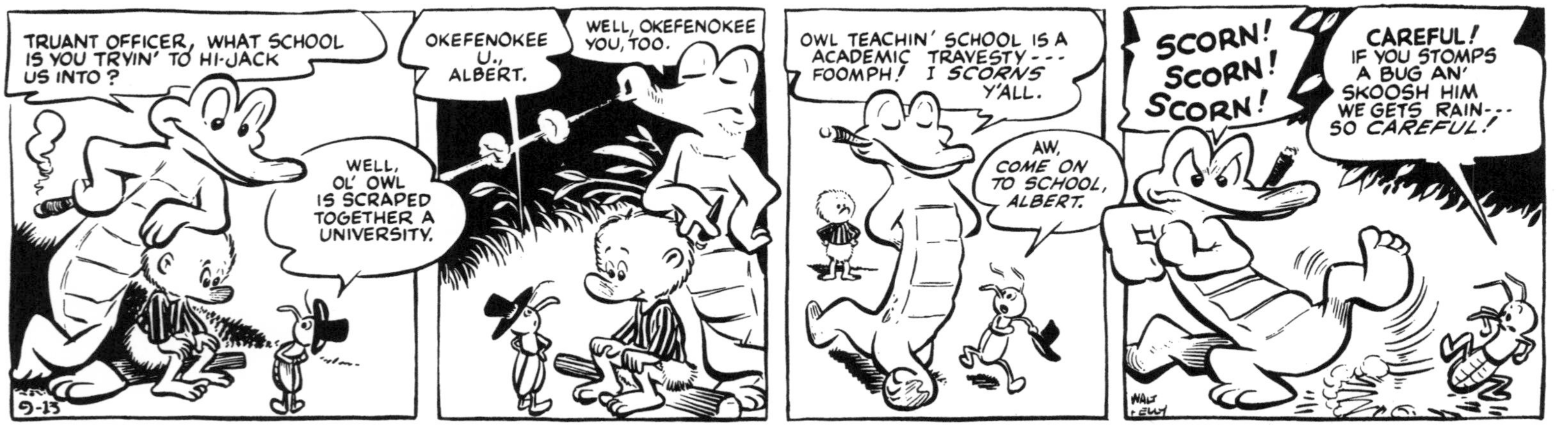
TRUANT OFFICER, WHAT SCHOOL IS YOU TRYIN' TO HI-JACK US INTO?
WELL, OL' OWL IS SCRAPED TOGETHER A UNIVERSITY.
9-13
OKEFENOKEE U., ALBERT.
WELL, OKEFENOKEE YOU, TOO.
OWL TEACHIN' SCHOOL IS A ACADEMIC TRAVESTY--- FOOMPH! I SCORNS Y'ALL.
AW, COME ON TO SCHOOL, ALBERT.
SCORN! SCORN! SCORN!
CAREFUL! IF YOU STOMPS A BUG AN' SKOOSH HIM WE GETS RAIN--- SO CAREFUL!
WALT KELLY

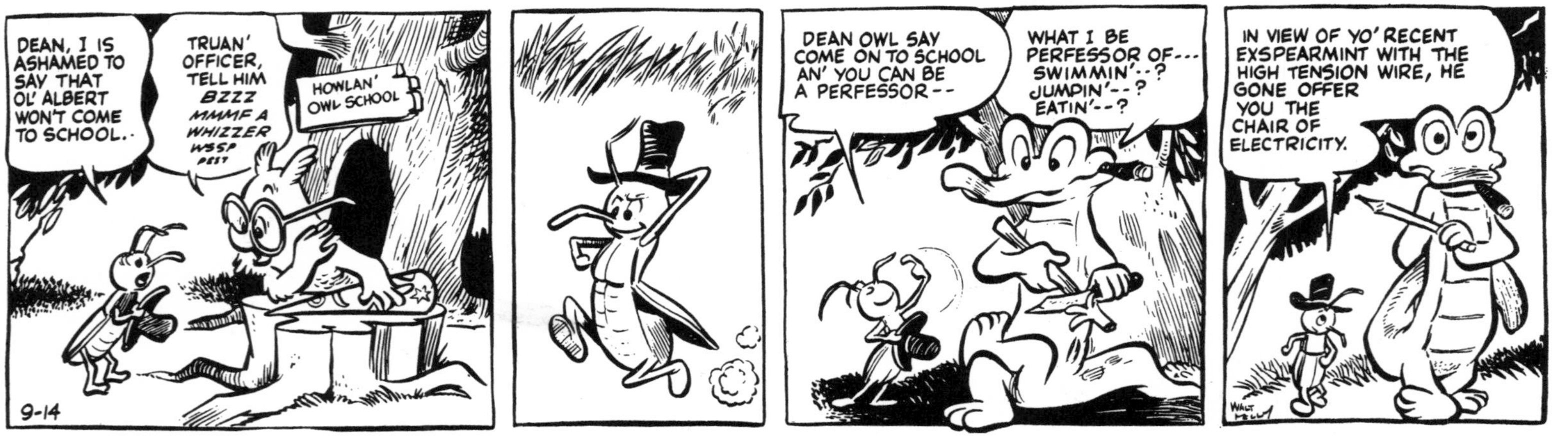
DEAN, I IS ASHAMED TO SAY THAT OL' ALBERT WON'T COME TO SCHOOL..
TRUAN' OFFICER, TELL HIM BZZZ MMMF A WHIZZER WSSP PSST
HOWLAN' OWL SCHOOL
9-14
DEAN OWL SAY COME ON TO SCHOOL AN' YOU CAN BE A PERFESSOR--
WHAT I BE PERFESSOR OF--- SWIMMIN'--? JUMPIN'--? EATIN'--?
IN VIEW OF YO' RECENT EXSPEARMINT WITH THE HIGH TENSION WIRE, HE GONE OFFER YOU THE CHAIR OF ELECTRICITY.
WALT KELLY

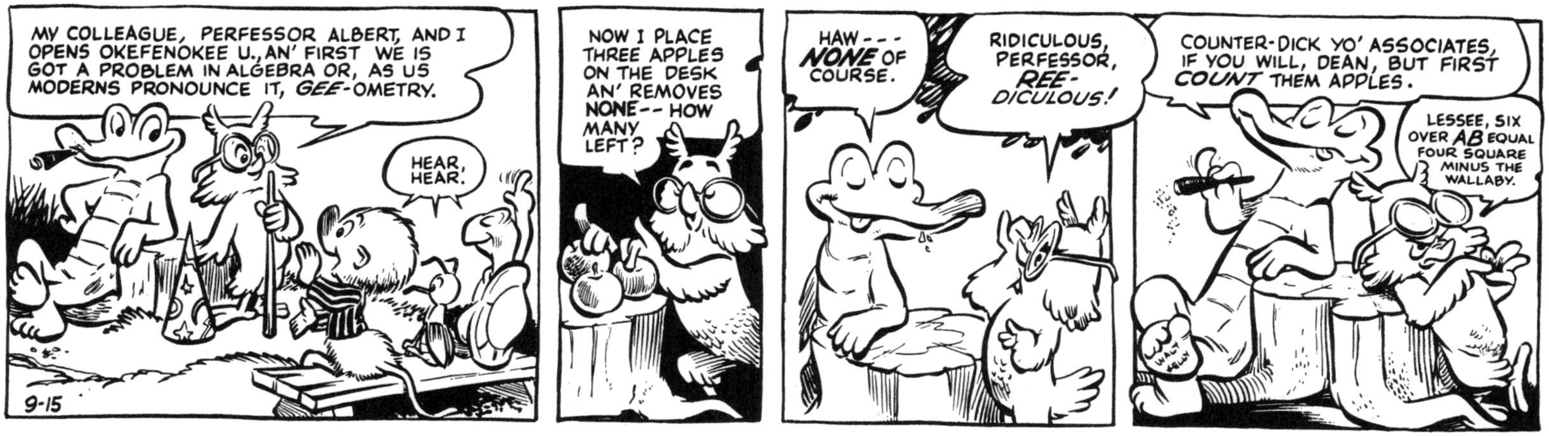
MY COLLEAGUE, PERFESSOR ALBERT, AND I OPENS OKEFENOKEE U., AN' FIRST WE IS GOT A PROBLEM IN ALGEBRA OR, AS US MODERNS PRONOUNCE IT, GEE-OMETRY.
HEAR, HEAR.
9-15
NOW I PLACE THREE APPLES ON THE DESK AN' REMOVES NONE-- HOW MANY LEFT?
HAW--- NONE OF COURSE.
RIDICULOUS, PERFESSOR, REE-DICULOUS!
COUNTER-DICK YO' ASSOCIATES, IF YOU WILL, DEAN, BUT FIRST COUNT THEM APPLES.
LESSEE, SIX OVER AB EQUAL FOUR SQUARE MINUS THE WALLABY.
WALT KELLY

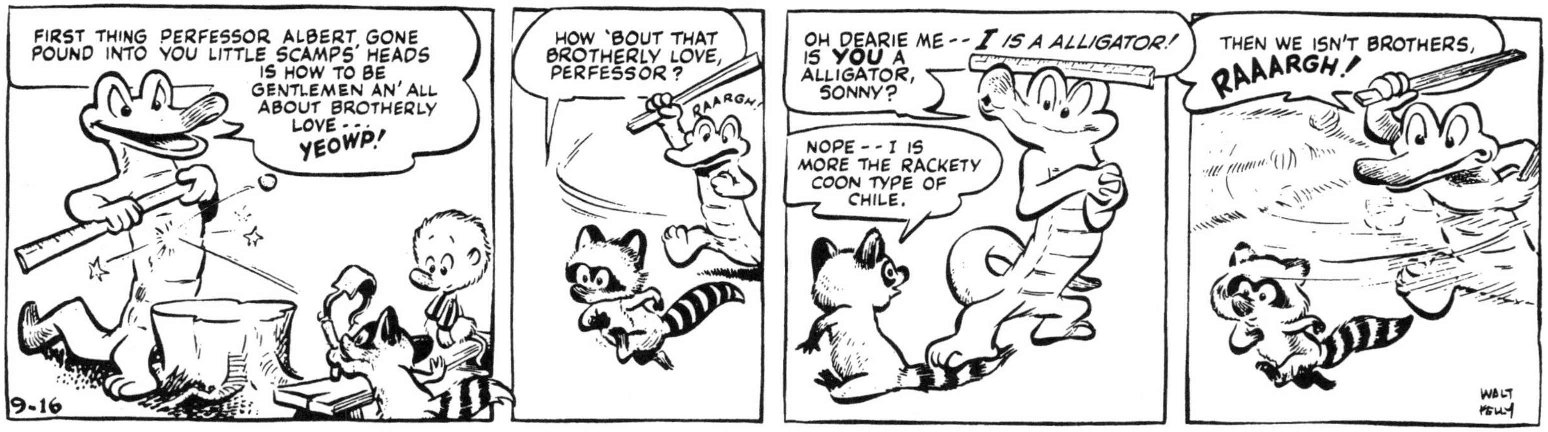
FIRST THING PERFESSOR ALBERT GONE POUND INTO YOU LITTLE SCAMPS' HEADS IS HOW TO BE GENTLEMEN AN' ALL ABOUT BROTHERLY LOVE...
YEOWP!
9-16
HOW 'BOUT THAT BROTHERLY LOVE, PERFESSOR?
RAARGH!
OH DEARIE ME-- I IS A ALLIGATOR! IS YOU A ALLIGATOR, SONNY?
NOPE--I IS MORE THE RACKETY COON TYPE OF CHILE.
THEN WE ISN'T BROTHERS, RAAARGH!
WALT KELLY

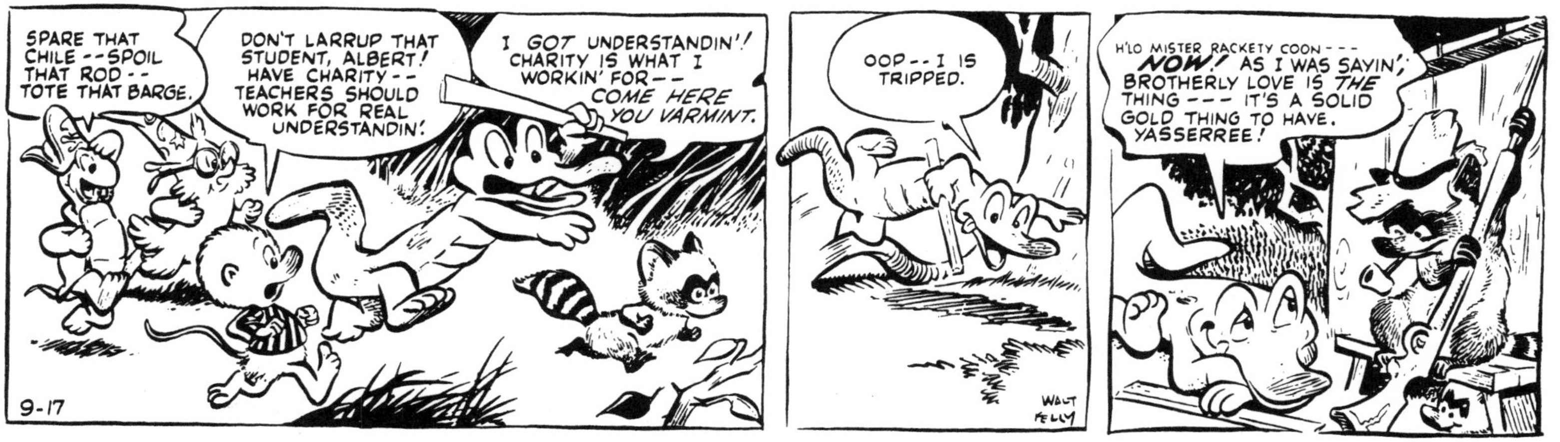
SPARE THAT CHILE--SPOIL THAT ROD-- TOTE THAT BARGE.
DON'T LARRUP THAT STUDENT, ALBERT! HAVE CHARITY-- TEACHERS SHOULD WORK FOR REAL UNDERSTANDIN'.
I GOT UNDERSTANDIN'! CHARITY IS WHAT I WORKIN' FOR-- COME HERE YOU VARMINT.
9-17
OOP--I IS TRIPPED.
WALT KELLY
H'LO MISTER RACKETY COON--- NOW! AS I WAS SAYIN', BROTHERLY LOVE IS THE THING--- IT'S A SOLID GOLD THING TO HAVE. YASSERREE!

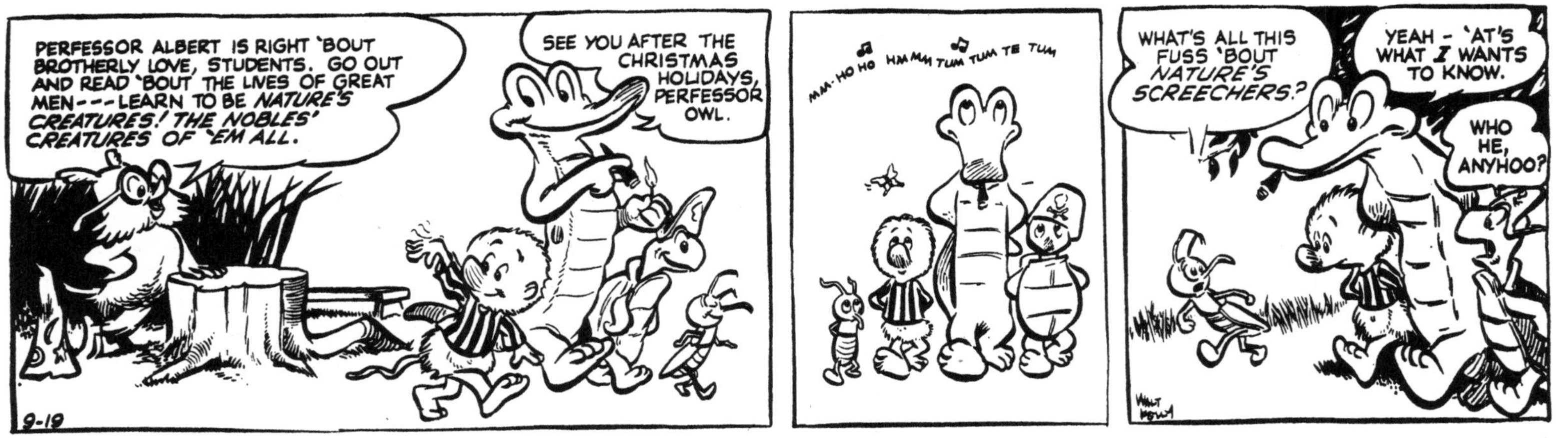
PERFESSOR ALBERT IS RIGHT 'BOUT BROTHERLY LOVE, STUDENTS. GO OUT AND READ 'BOUT THE LIVES OF GREAT MEN---LEARN TO BE NATURE'S CREATURES! THE NOBLES' CREATURES OF 'EM ALL.
SEE YOU AFTER THE CHRISTMAS HOLIDAYS, PERFESSOR OWL.
9-19
MM-HO HO HMMM TUM TUM TE TUM
WHAT'S ALL THIS FUSS 'BOUT NATURE'S SCREECHERS?
YEAH - 'AT'S WHAT I WANTS TO KNOW.
WHO HE, ANYHOO?
WALT KELLY

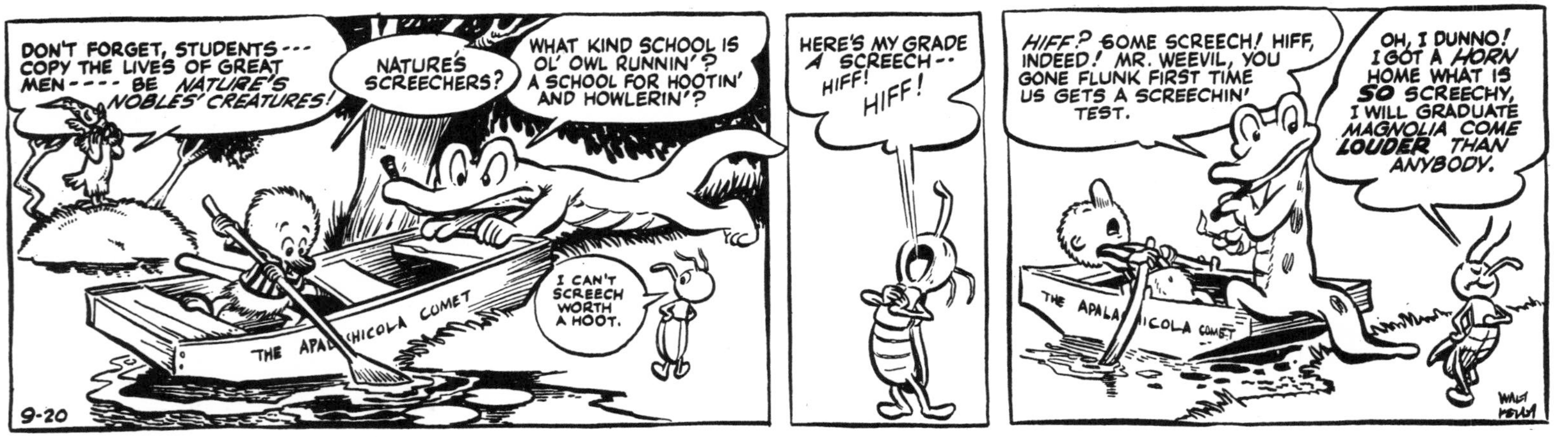
DON'T FORGET, STUDENTS--- COPY THE LIVES OF GREAT MEN---- BE NATURE'S NOBLES' CREATURES!
NATURE'S SCREECHERS?
WHAT KIND SCHOOL IS OL' OWL RUNNIN'? A SCHOOL FOR HOOTIN' AND HOWLERIN'?
I CAN'T SCREECH WORTH A HOOT.
THE APALACHICOLA COMET
9-20
HERE'S MY GRADE A SCREECH-- HIFF!
HIFF!
HIFF? SOME SCREECH! HIFF, INDEED! MR. WEEVIL, YOU GONE FLUNK FIRST TIME US GETS A SCREECHIN' TEST.
OH, I DUNNO! I GOT A HORN HOME WHAT IS SO SCREECHY, I WILL GRADUATE MAGNOLIA COME LOUDER THAN ANYBODY.
THE APALACHICOLA COMET
WALT KELLY

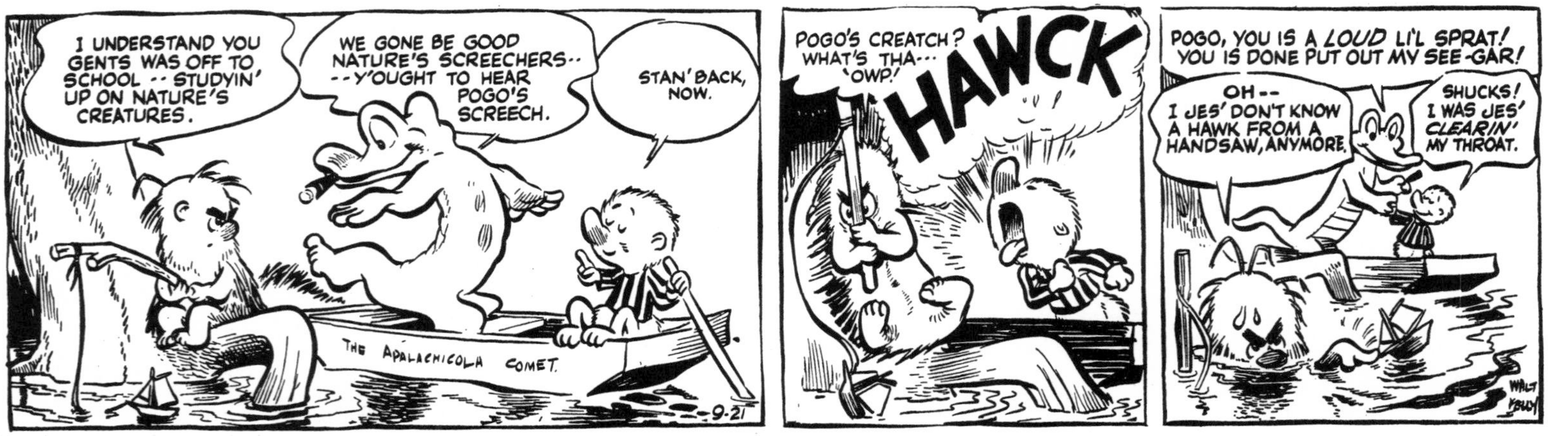
I UNDERSTAND YOU GENTS WAS OFF TO SCHOOL -- STUDYIN' UP ON NATURE'S CREATURES.
WE GONE BE GOOD NATURE'S SCREECHERS-- --Y'OUGHT TO HEAR POGO'S SCREECH.
STAN' BACK, NOW.
THE APALACHICOLA COMET.
9-21
POGO'S CREATCH? WHAT'S THA--- 'OWP.'
HAWCK
POGO, YOU IS A LOUD LI'L SPRAT! YOU IS DONE PUT OUT MY SEE-GAR!
OH -- I JES' DON'T KNOW A HAWK FROM A HANDSAW, ANYMORE.
SHUCKS! I WAS JES' CLEARIN' MY THROAT.
WALT KELLY

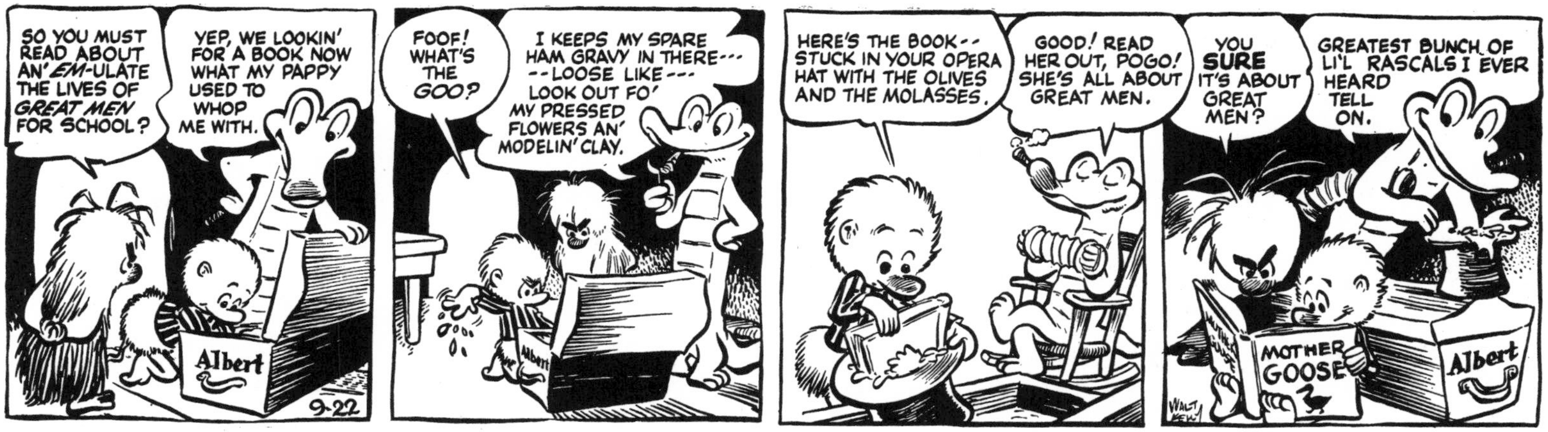
SO YOU MUST READ ABOUT AN' *EM*-ULATE THE LIVES OF *GREAT MEN* FOR SCHOOL?
YEP, WE LOOKIN' FOR A BOOK NOW WHAT MY PAPPY USED TO WHOP ME WITH.
Albert
9-22
FOOF! WHAT'S THE *GOO?*
I KEEPS MY SPARE HAM GRAVY IN THERE--- --LOOSE LIKE--- LOOK OUT FO' MY PRESSED FLOWERS AN' MODELIN' CLAY.
HERE'S THE BOOK-- STUCK IN YOUR OPERA HAT WITH THE OLIVES AND THE MOLASSES.
GOOD! READ HER OUT, POGO! SHE'S ALL ABOUT GREAT MEN.
YOU **SURE** IT'S ABOUT GREAT MEN?
GREATEST BUNCH OF LI'L RASCALS I EVER HEARD TELL ON.
MOTHER GOOSE
Albert
WALT KELLY

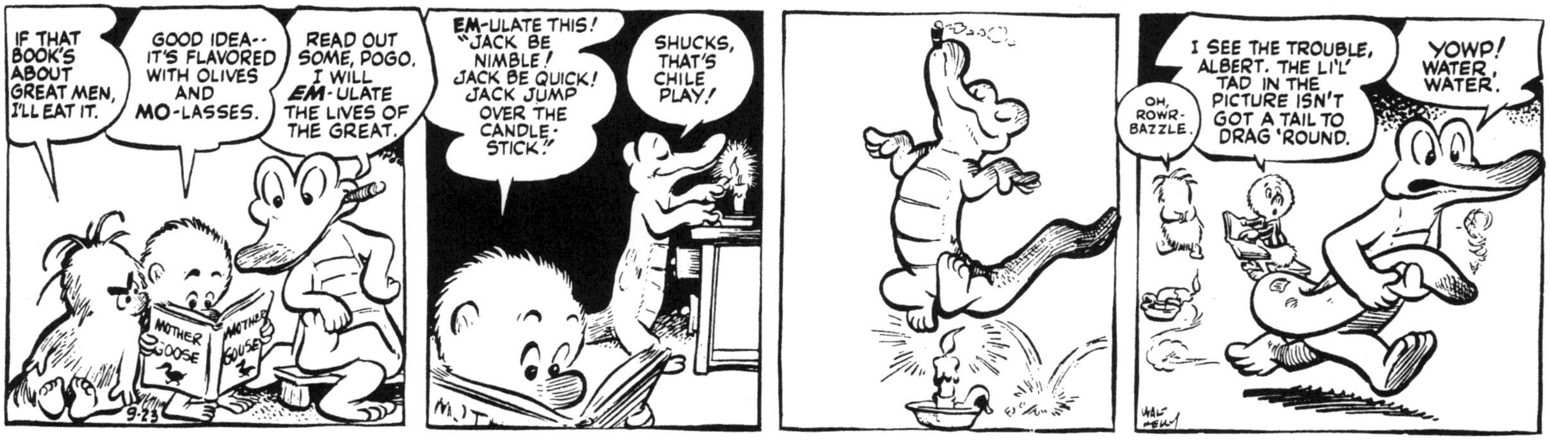
IF THAT BOOK'S ABOUT GREAT MEN, I'LL EAT IT.
GOOD IDEA-- IT'S FLAVORED WITH OLIVES AND **MO**-LASSES.
READ OUT SOME, POGO. I WILL ***EM***-ULATE THE LIVES OF THE GREAT.
MOTHER GOOSE
9-23
EM-ULATE THIS! "JACK BE NIMBLE! JACK BE QUICK! JACK JUMP OVER THE CANDLE-STICK!"
SHUCKS, THAT'S CHILE PLAY!
OH, ROWR-BAZZLE.
I SEE THE TROUBLE, ALBERT. THE LI'L TAD IN THE PICTURE ISN'T GOT A TAIL TO DRAG 'ROUND.
YOWP! WATER, WATER.
WALT KELLY

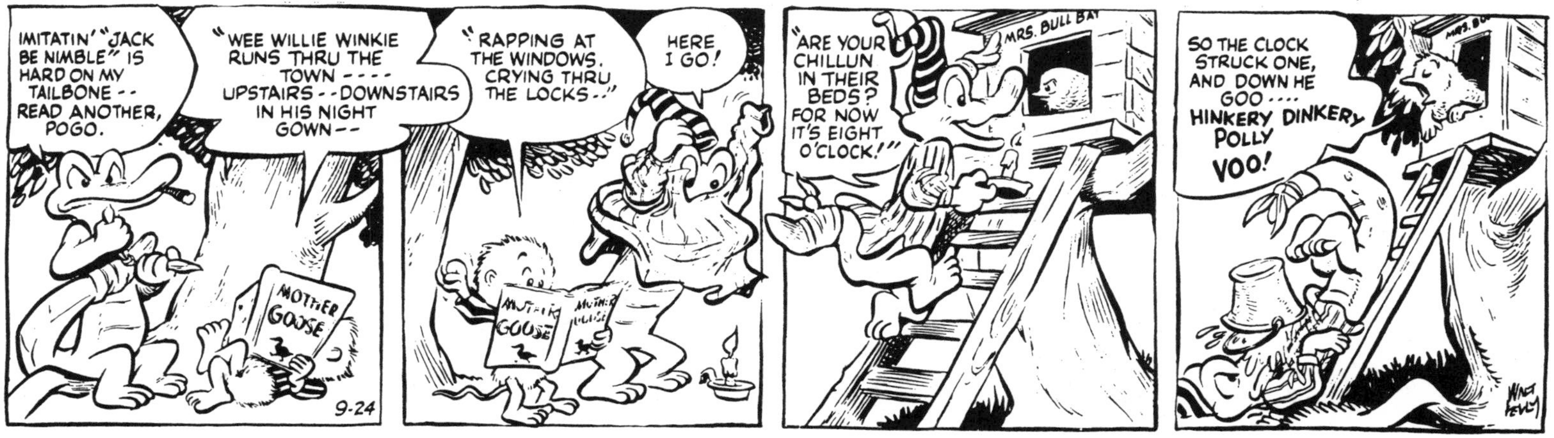
IMITATIN' "JACK BE NIMBLE" IS HARD ON MY TAILBONE-- READ ANOTHER, POGO.
"WEE WILLIE WINKIE RUNS THRU THE TOWN---- UPSTAIRS--DOWNSTAIRS IN HIS NIGHT GOWN--
MOTHER GOOSE
9-24
"RAPPING AT THE WINDOWS, CRYING THRU THE LOCKS--"
HERE I GO!
"ARE YOUR CHILLUN IN THEIR BEDS? FOR NOW IT'S EIGHT O'CLOCK!"
MRS. BULL BAT
SO THE CLOCK STRUCK ONE, AND DOWN HE GOO---- **HINKERY DINKERY POLLY VOO!**
WALT KELLY

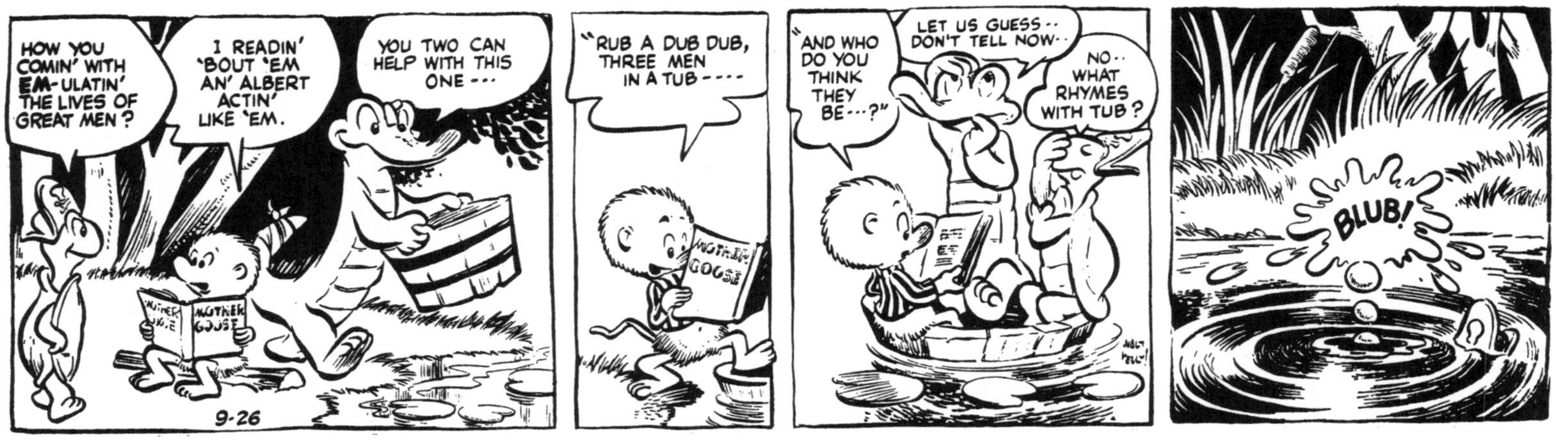
HOW YOU COMIN' WITH EM-ULATIN' THE LIVES OF GREAT MEN?
I READIN' 'BOUT 'EM AN' ALBERT ACTIN' LIKE 'EM.
YOU TWO CAN HELP WITH THIS ONE---
MOTHER GOOSE
9-26
"RUB A DUB DUB, THREE MEN IN A TUB----
MOTHER GOOSE
"AND WHO DO YOU THINK THEY BE---?"
LET US GUESS-- DON'T TELL NOW--
NO-- WHAT RHYMES WITH TUB?
BLUB!

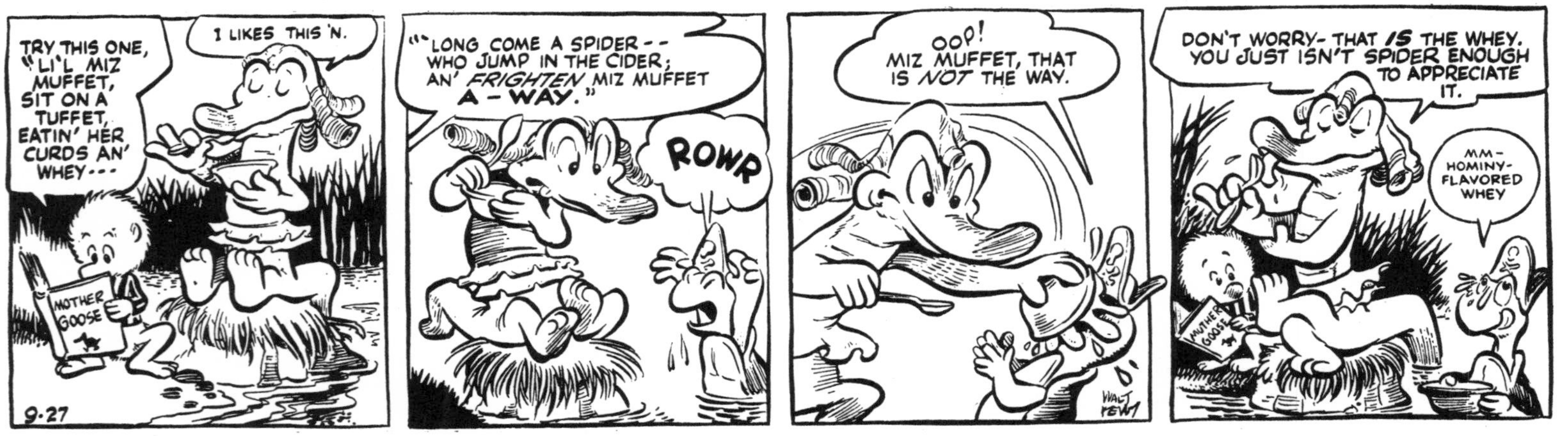
TRY THIS ONE, "LI'L MIZ MUFFET, SIT ON A TUFFET, EATIN' HER CURDS AN' WHEY---
I LIKES THIS 'N.
MOTHER GOOSE
9-27
"LONG COME A SPIDER-- WHO JUMP IN THE CIDER; AN' FRIGHTEN MIZ MUFFET A-WAY."
ROWR
OOP! MIZ MUFFET, THAT IS NOT THE WAY.
DON'T WORRY- THAT IS THE WHEY. YOU JUST ISN'T SPIDER ENOUGH TO APPRECIATE IT.
MM- HOMINY- FLAVORED WHEY
MOTHER GOOSE

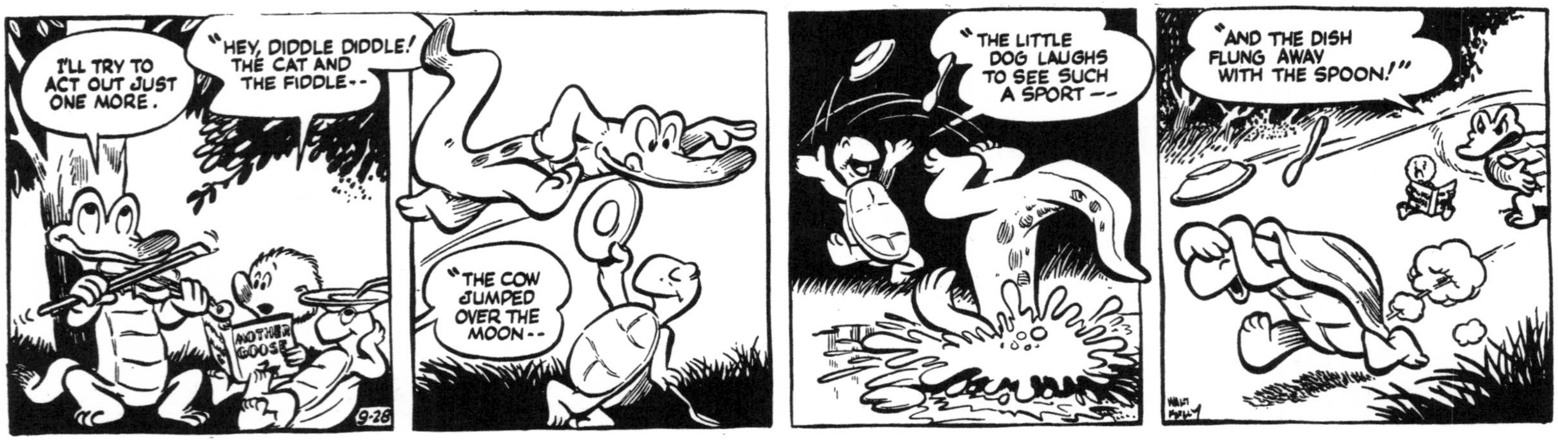
I'LL TRY TO ACT OUT JUST ONE MORE.
"HEY, DIDDLE DIDDLE! THE CAT AND THE FIDDLE--
MOTHER GOOSE
9-28
"THE COW JUMPED OVER THE MOON--
"THE LITTLE DOG LAUGHS TO SEE SUCH A SPORT--
"AND THE DISH FLUNG AWAY WITH THE SPOON!"

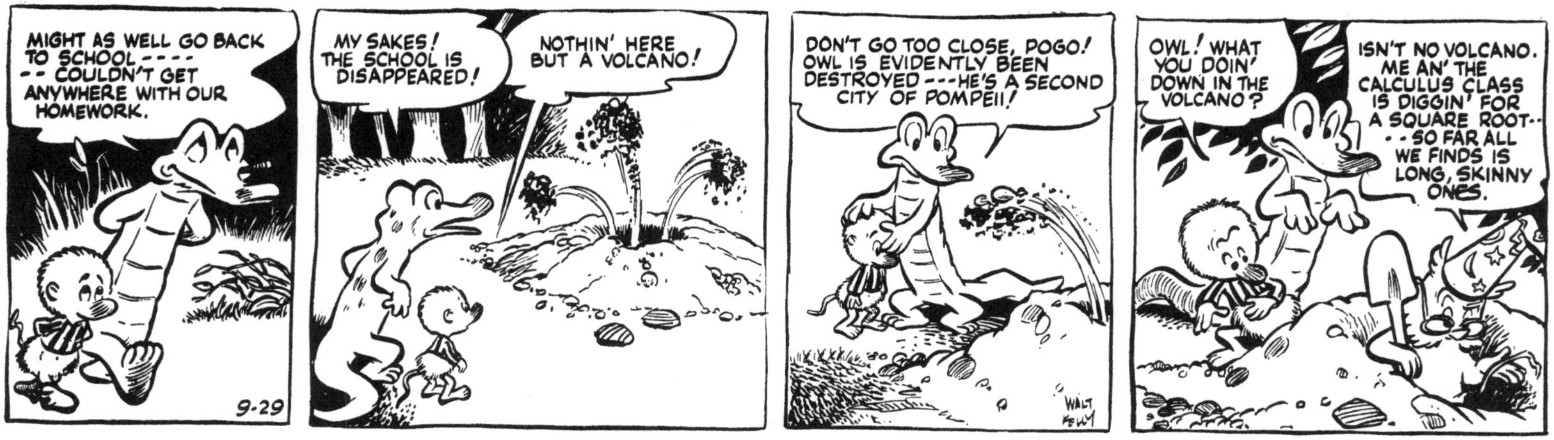
MIGHT AS WELL GO BACK TO SCHOOL - - - - - - COULDN'T GET ANYWHERE WITH OUR HOMEWORK.
9-29
MY SAKES! THE SCHOOL IS DISAPPEARED!
NOTHIN' HERE BUT A VOLCANO!
DON'T GO TOO CLOSE, POGO! OWL IS EVIDENTLY BEEN DESTROYED - - - HE'S A SECOND CITY OF POMPEII!
WALT KELLY
OWL! WHAT YOU DOIN' DOWN IN THE VOLCANO?
ISN'T NO VOLCANO. ME AN' THE CALCULUS CLASS IS DIGGIN' FOR A SQUARE ROOT - - - - SO FAR ALL WE FINDS IS LONG, SKINNY ONES.

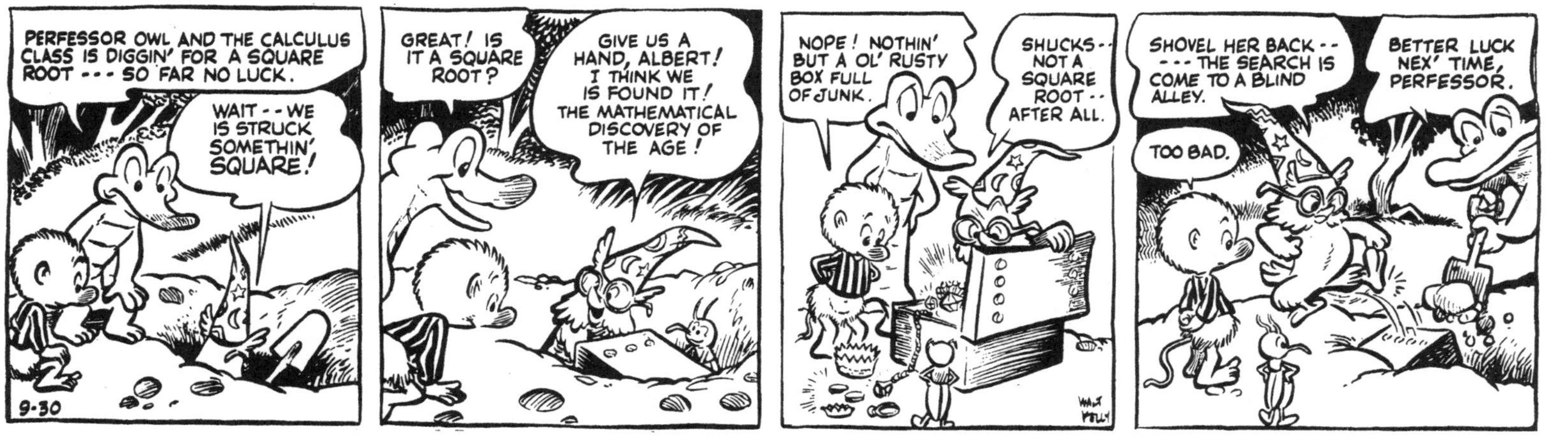
PERFESSOR OWL AND THE CALCULUS CLASS IS DIGGIN' FOR A SQUARE ROOT - - - SO FAR NO LUCK.
WAIT - - WE IS STRUCK SOMETHIN' SQUARE!
9-30
GREAT! IS IT A SQUARE ROOT?
GIVE US A HAND, ALBERT! I THINK WE IS FOUND IT! THE MATHEMATICAL DISCOVERY OF THE AGE!
NOPE! NOTHIN' BUT A OL' RUSTY BOX FULL OF JUNK.
SHUCKS - - NOT A SQUARE ROOT - - AFTER ALL.
WALT KELLY
SHOVEL HER BACK - - - - - THE SEARCH IS COME TO A BLIND ALLEY.
BETTER LUCK NEX' TIME, PERFESSOR.
TOO BAD.

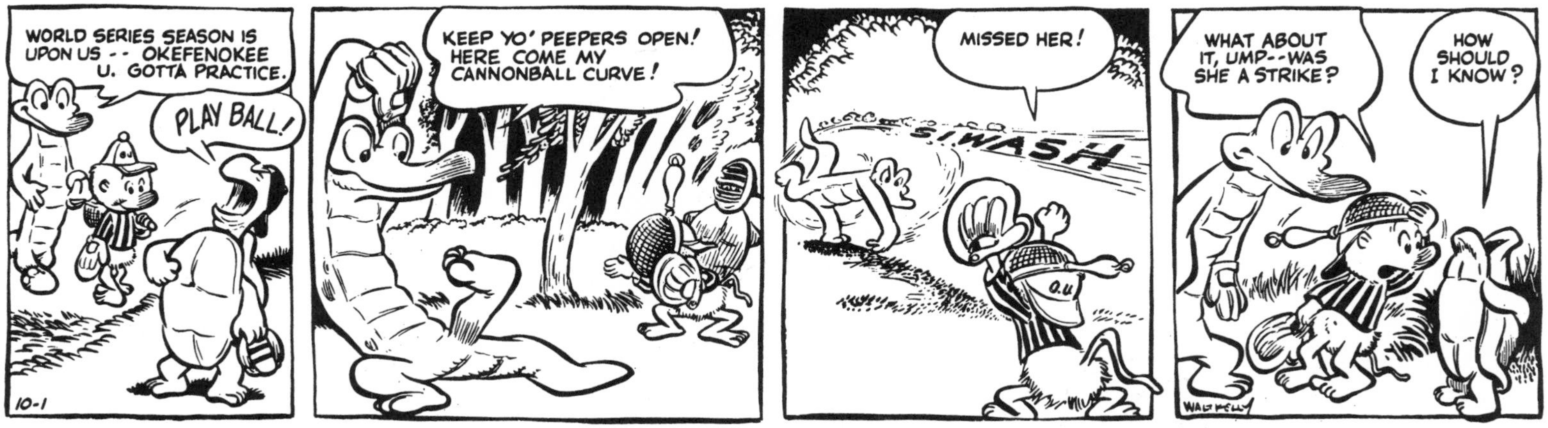
WORLD SERIES SEASON IS UPON US - - OKEFENOKEE U. GOTTA PRACTICE.
PLAY BALL!
10-1
KEEP YO' PEEPERS OPEN! HERE COME MY CANNONBALL CURVE!
MISSED HER!
SWASH
WHAT ABOUT IT, UMP - - WAS SHE A STRIKE?
HOW SHOULD I KNOW?
WALT KELLY

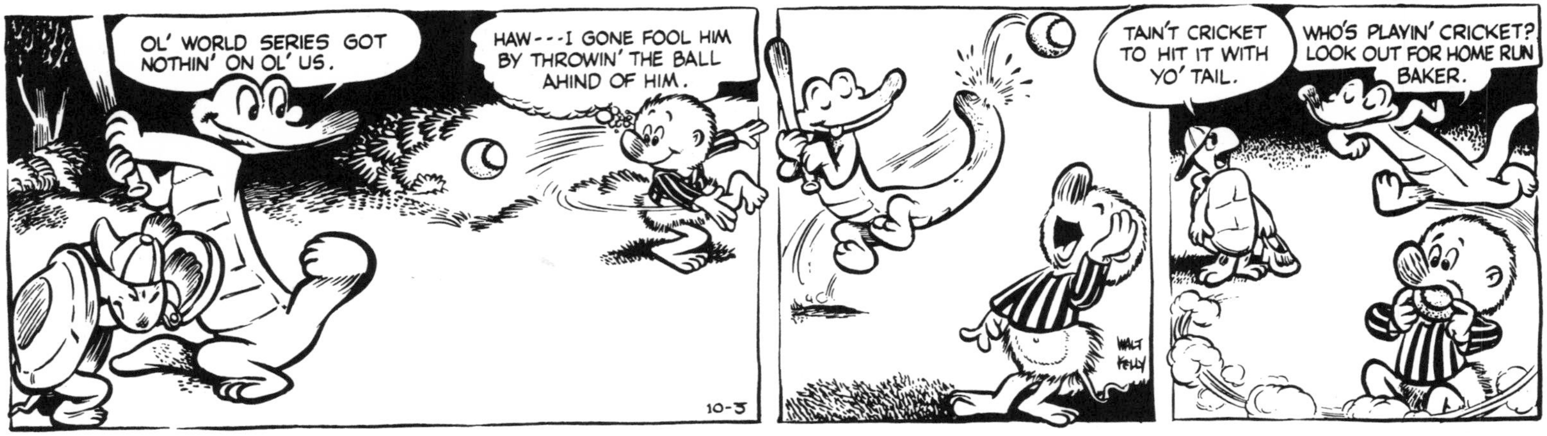
OL' WORLD SERIES GOT NOTHIN' ON OL' US.
HAW---I GONE FOOL HIM BY THROWIN' THE BALL AHIND OF HIM.
10-3
WALT KELLY
TAIN'T CRICKET TO HIT IT WITH YO' TAIL.
WHO'S PLAYIN' CRICKET? LOOK OUT FOR HOME RUN BAKER.

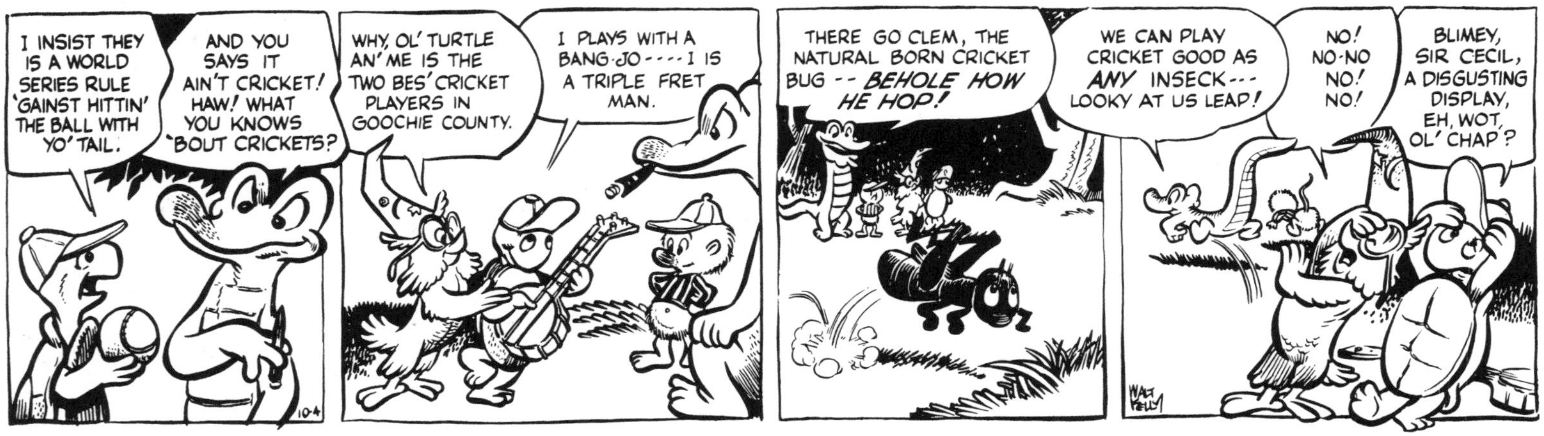
I INSIST THEY IS A WORLD SERIES RULE 'GAINST HITTIN' THE BALL WITH YO' TAIL.
AND YOU SAYS IT AIN'T CRICKET! HAW! WHAT YOU KNOWS 'BOUT CRICKETS?
10-4
WHY, OL' TURTLE AN' ME IS THE TWO BES' CRICKET PLAYERS IN GOOCHIE COUNTY.
I PLAYS WITH A BANG-JO----I IS A TRIPLE FRET MAN.
THERE GO CLEM, THE NATURAL BORN CRICKET BUG -- BEHOLE HOW HE HOP!
WE CAN PLAY CRICKET GOOD AS ANY INSECK--- LOOKY AT US LEAP!
NO! NO-NO NO! NO!
BLIMEY, SIR CECIL, A DISGUSTING DISPLAY, EH, WOT, OL' CHAP?
WALT KELLY

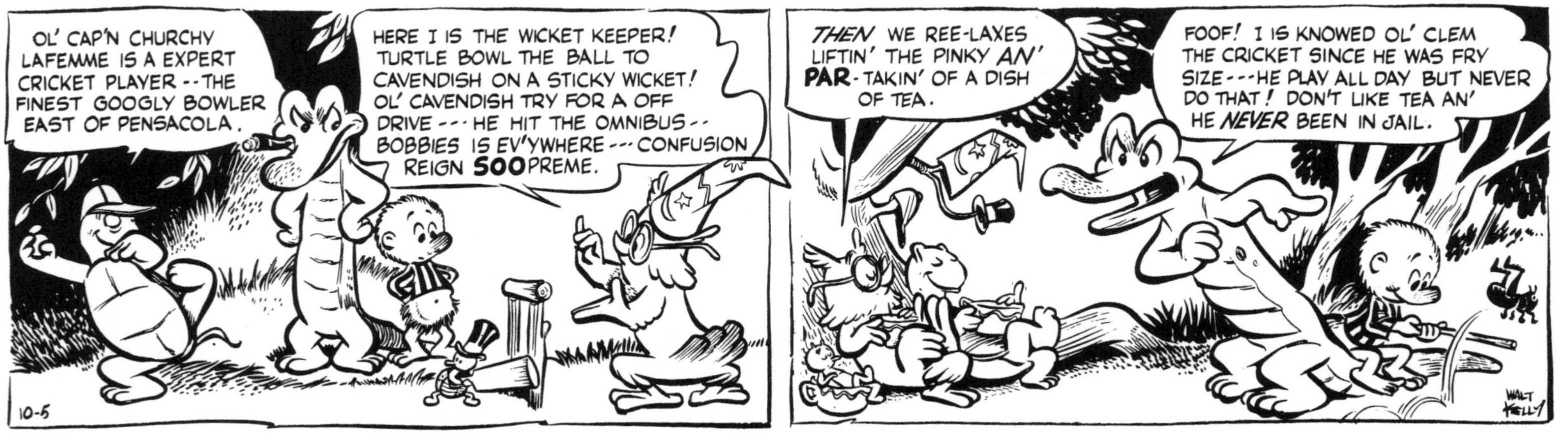
OL' CAP'N CHURCHY LAFEMME IS A EXPERT CRICKET PLAYER--THE FINEST GOOGLY BOWLER EAST OF PENSACOLA.
HERE I IS THE WICKET KEEPER! TURTLE BOWL THE BALL TO CAVENDISH ON A STICKY WICKET! OL' CAVENDISH TRY FOR A OFF DRIVE---HE HIT THE OMNIBUS-- BOBBIES IS EV'YWHERE---CONFUSION REIGN SOOPREME.
10-5
THEN WE REE-LAXES LIFTIN' THE PINKY AN' PAR-TAKIN' OF A DISH OF TEA.
FOOF! I IS KNOWED OL' CLEM THE CRICKET SINCE HE WAS FRY SIZE---HE PLAY ALL DAY BUT NEVER DO THAT! DON'T LIKE TEA AN' HE NEVER BEEN IN JAIL.
WALT KELLY

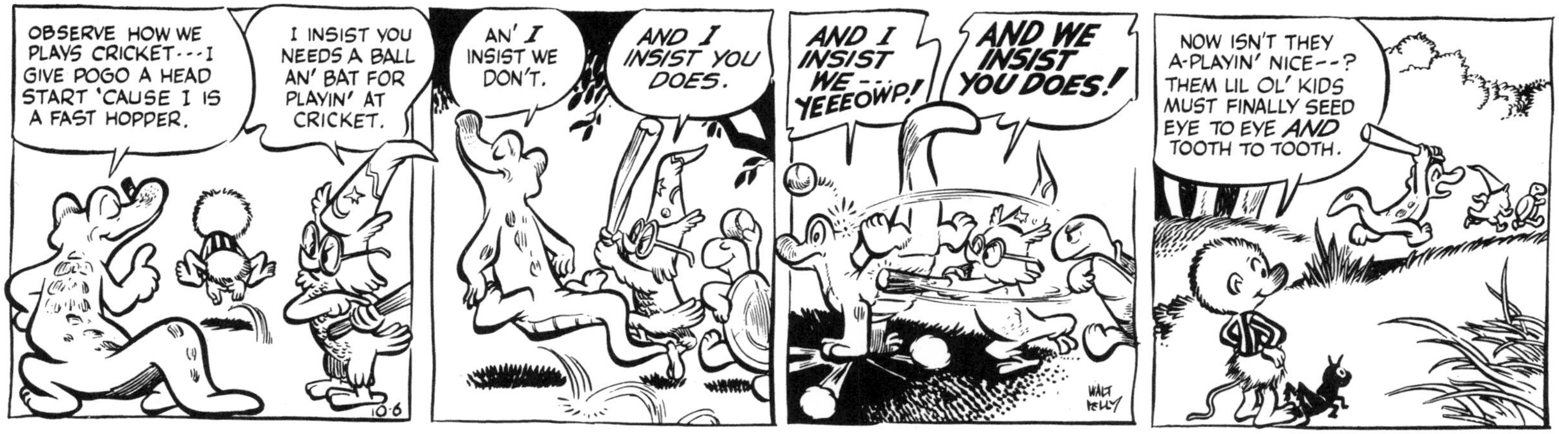
OBSERVE HOW WE PLAYS CRICKET---I GIVE POGO A HEAD START 'CAUSE I IS A FAST HOPPER.
I INSIST YOU NEEDS A BALL AN' BAT FOR PLAYIN' AT CRICKET.
10-6
AN' I INSIST WE DON'T.
AND I INSIST YOU DOES.
AND I INSIST WE--- YEEEOWP!
AND WE INSIST YOU DOES!
WALT KELLY
NOW ISN'T THEY A-PLAYIN' NICE--? THEM LIL OL' KIDS MUST FINALLY SEED EYE TO EYE AND TOOTH TO TOOTH.

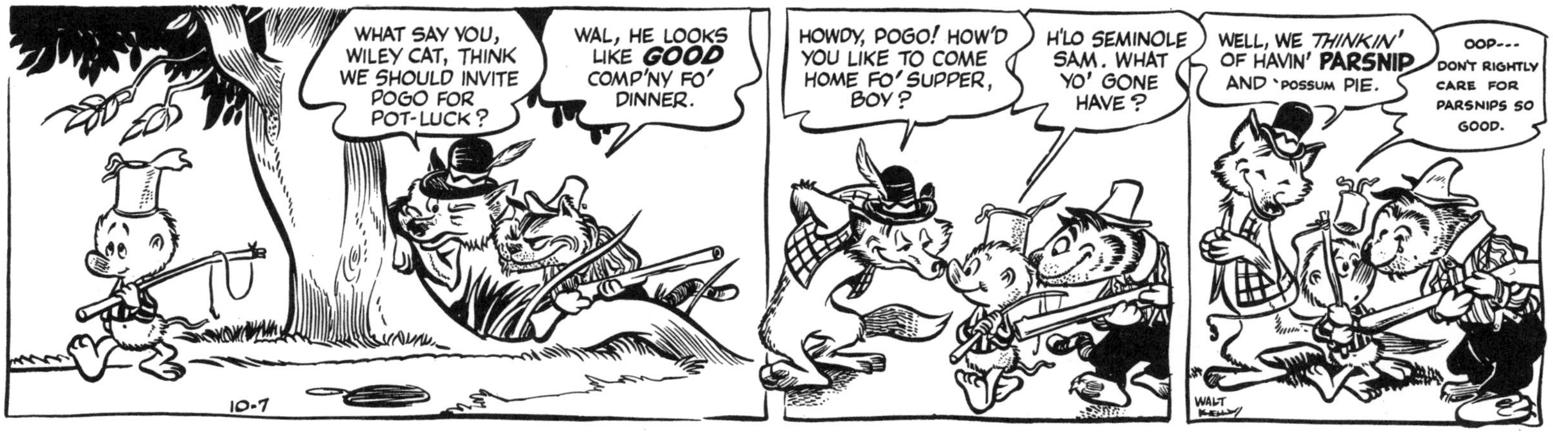
WHAT SAY YOU, WILEY CAT, THINK WE SHOULD INVITE POGO FOR POT-LUCK?
WAL, HE LOOKS LIKE GOOD COMP'NY FO' DINNER.
10-7
HOWDY, POGO! HOW'D YOU LIKE TO COME HOME FO' SUPPER, BOY?
H'LO SEMINOLE SAM. WHAT YO' GONE HAVE?
WELL, WE THINKIN' OF HAVIN' PARSNIP AND 'POSSUM PIE.
OOP--- DON'T RIGHTLY CARE FOR PARSNIPS SO GOOD.
WALT KELLY

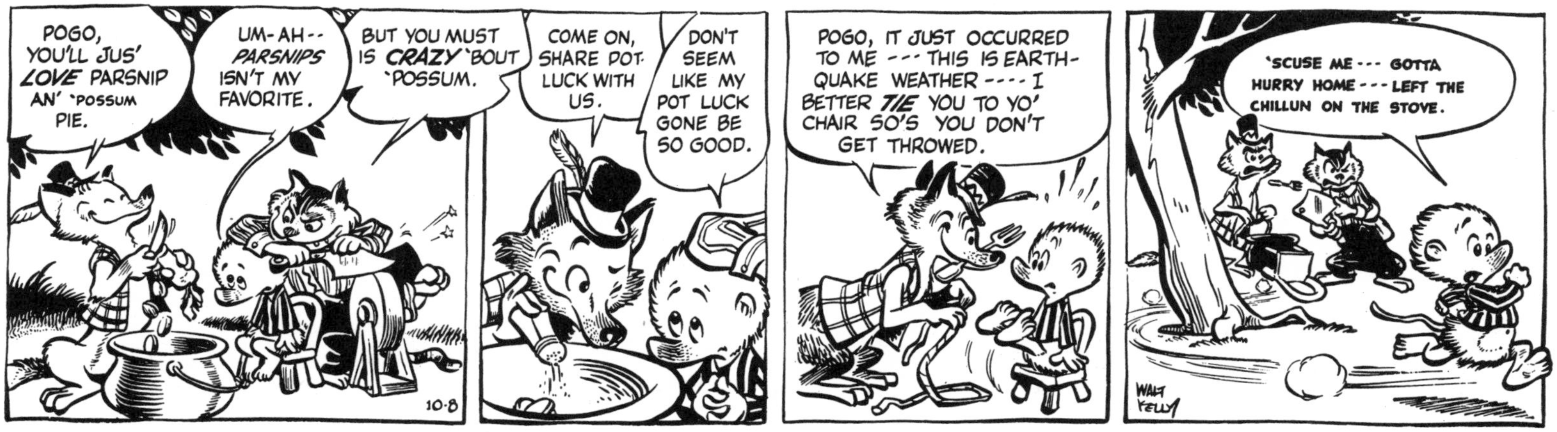
POGO, YOU'LL JUS' LOVE PARSNIP AN' 'POSSUM PIE.
UM-AH-- PARSNIPS ISN'T MY FAVORITE.
BUT YOU MUST IS CRAZY 'BOUT 'POSSUM.
10-8
COME ON, SHARE POT LUCK WITH US.
DON'T SEEM LIKE MY POT LUCK GONE BE SO GOOD.
POGO, IT JUST OCCURRED TO ME --- THIS IS EARTH-QUAKE WEATHER ---- I BETTER TIE YOU TO YO' CHAIR SO'S YOU DON'T GET THROWED.
'SCUSE ME --- GOTTA HURRY HOME --- LEFT THE CHILLUN ON THE STOVE.
WALT KELLY

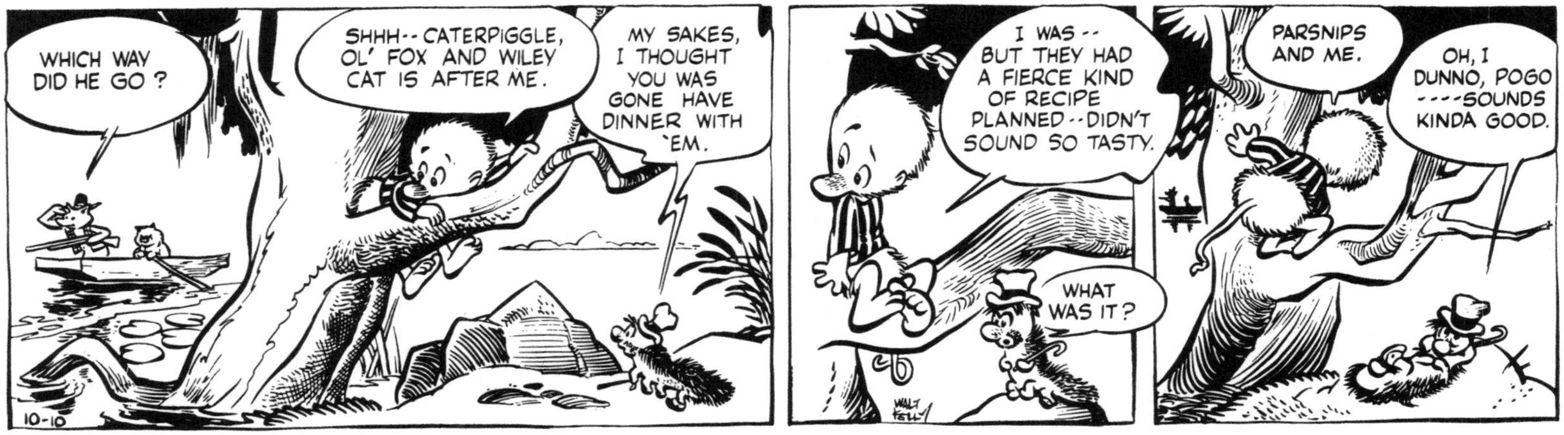
WHICH WAY DID HE GO ?
SHHH-- CATERPIGGLE, OL' FOX AND WILEY CAT IS AFTER ME.
MY SAKES, I THOUGHT YOU WAS GONE HAVE DINNER WITH 'EM.
I WAS -- BUT THEY HAD A FIERCE KIND OF RECIPE PLANNED -- DIDN'T SOUND SO TASTY.
WHAT WAS IT ?
PARSNIPS AND ME.
OH, I DUNNO, POGO ----SOUNDS KINDA GOOD.
10-10
WALT KELLY

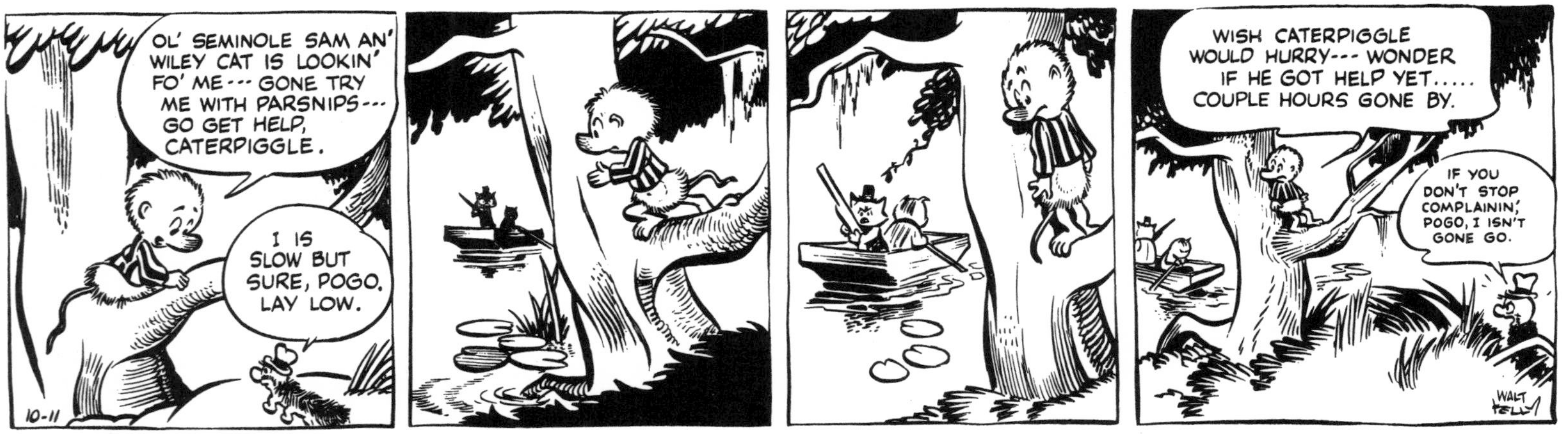
OL' SEMINOLE SAM AN' WILEY CAT IS LOOKIN' FO' ME --- GONE TRY ME WITH PARSNIPS--- GO GET HELP, CATERPIGGLE.
I IS SLOW BUT SURE, POGO. LAY LOW.
WISH CATERPIGGLE WOULD HURRY--- WONDER IF HE GOT HELP YET..... COUPLE HOURS GONE BY.
IF YOU DON'T STOP COMPLAININ', POGO, I ISN'T GONE GO.
10-11
WALT KELLY

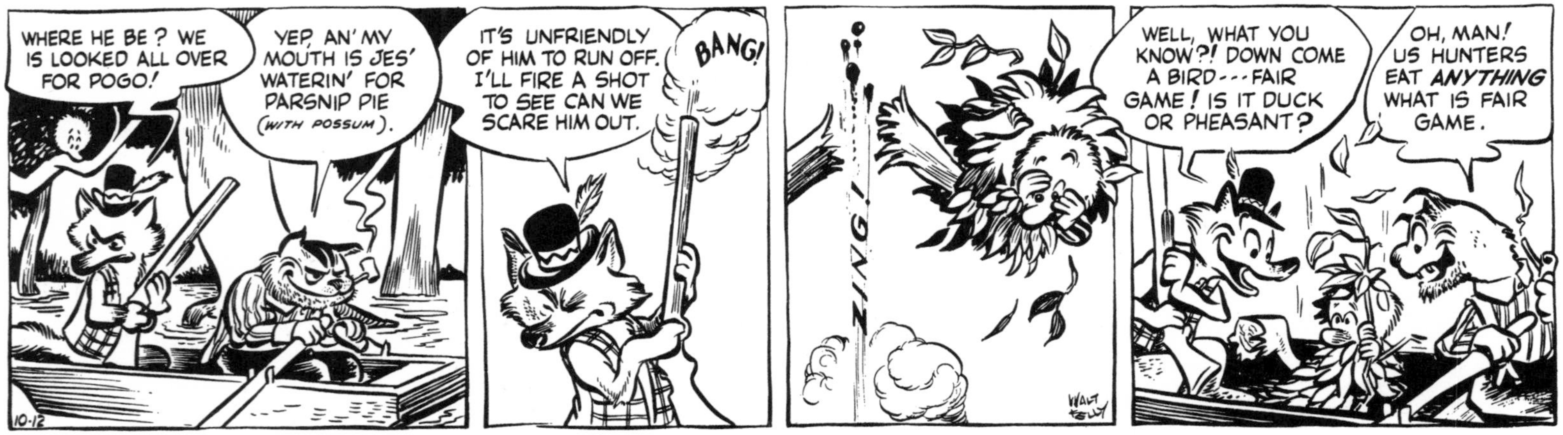
WHERE HE BE ? WE IS LOOKED ALL OVER FOR POGO!
YEP, AN' MY MOUTH IS JES' WATERIN' FOR PARSNIP PIE (WITH POSSUM).
IT'S UNFRIENDLY OF HIM TO RUN OFF. I'LL FIRE A SHOT TO SEE CAN WE SCARE HIM OUT.
BANG!
ZING!
WELL, WHAT YOU KNOW?! DOWN COME A BIRD--- FAIR GAME! IS IT DUCK OR PHEASANT?
OH, MAN! US HUNTERS EAT ANYTHING WHAT IS FAIR GAME.
10-12
WALT KELLY

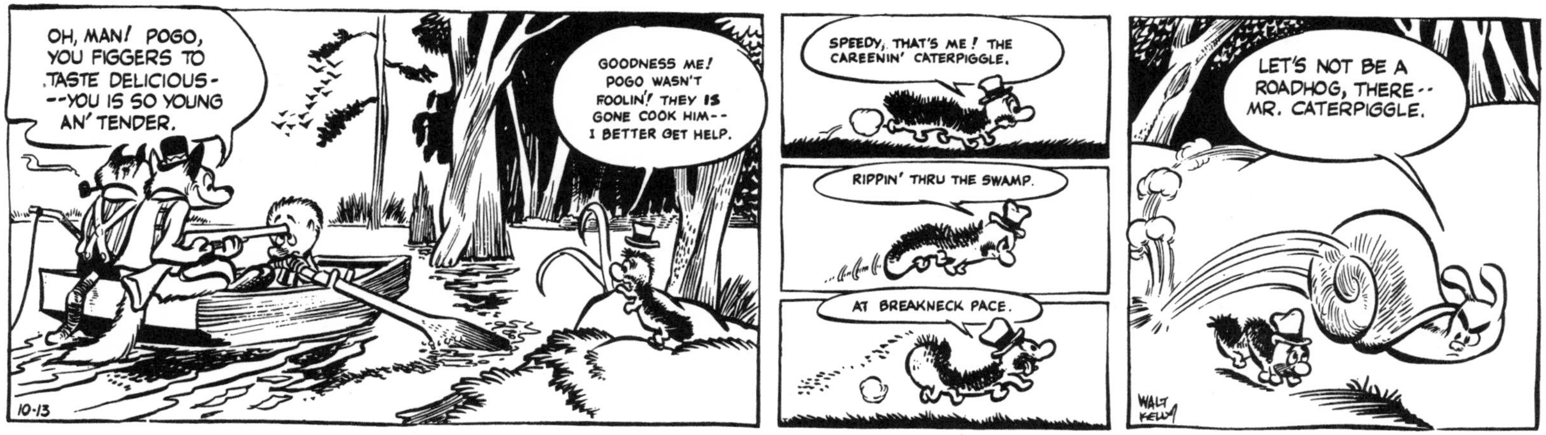
OH, MAN! POGO, YOU FIGGERS TO TASTE DELICIOUS- --YOU IS SO YOUNG AN' TENDER.
GOODNESS ME! POGO WASN'T FOOLIN'! THEY IS GONE COOK HIM-- I BETTER GET HELP.
10-13
SPEEDY, THAT'S ME! THE CAREENIN' CATERPIGGLE.
RIPPIN' THRU THE SWAMP.
AT BREAKNECK PACE.
LET'S NOT BE A ROADHOG, THERE-- MR. CATERPIGGLE.
WALT KELLY

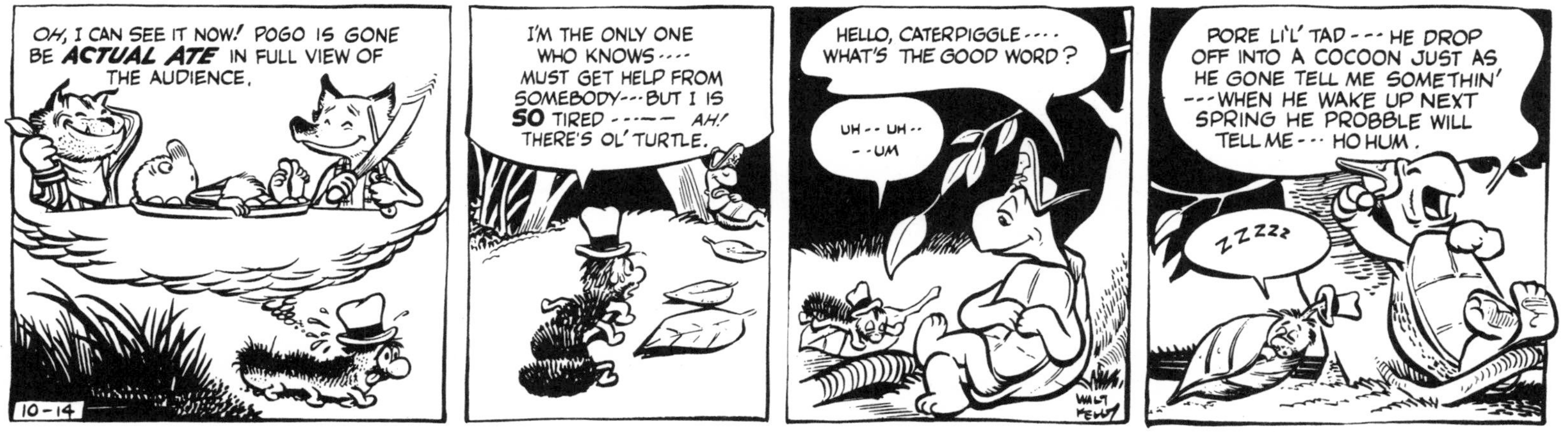
OH, I CAN SEE IT NOW! POGO IS GONE BE ACTUAL ATE IN FULL VIEW OF THE AUDIENCE.
10-14
I'M THE ONLY ONE WHO KNOWS---- MUST GET HELP FROM SOMEBODY---BUT I IS SO TIRED ---—— AH! THERE'S OL' TURTLE.
HELLO, CATERPIGGLE---- WHAT'S THE GOOD WORD?
UH--UH-- --UM
WALT KELLY
PORE LI'L' TAD --- HE DROP OFF INTO A COCOON JUST AS HE GONE TELL ME SOMETHIN' ---WHEN HE WAKE UP NEXT SPRING HE PROBBLE WILL TELL ME--- HO HUM.
ZZZZZ

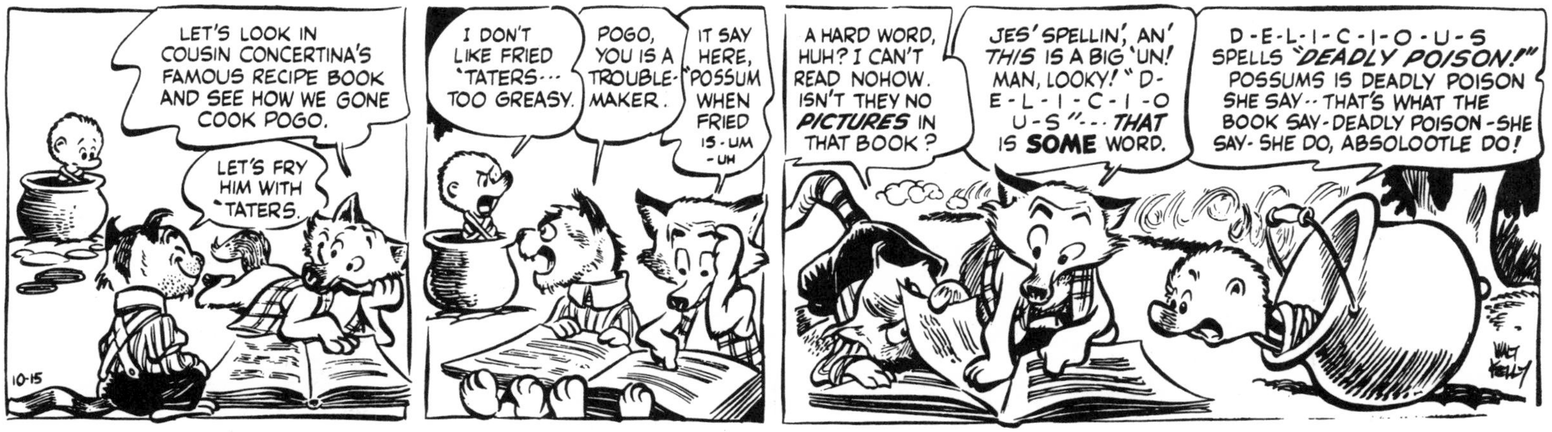
LET'S LOOK IN COUSIN CONCERTINA'S FAMOUS RECIPE BOOK AND SEE HOW WE GONE COOK POGO.
LET'S FRY HIM WITH 'TATERS.
10-15
I DON'T LIKE FRIED 'TATERS--- TOO GREASY.
POGO, YOU IS A TROUBLE-MAKER.
IT SAY HERE, "POSSUM WHEN FRIED IS-UM -UH
A HARD WORD, HUH? I CAN'T READ NOHOW. ISN'T THEY NO PICTURES IN THAT BOOK?
JES' SPELLIN', AN' THIS IS A BIG 'UN! MAN, LOOKY! "D-E-L-I-C-I-O U-S"--- THAT IS SOME WORD.
D-E-L-I-C-I-O-U-S SPELLS "DEADLY POISON!" POSSUMS IS DEADLY POISON SHE SAY-- THAT'S WHAT THE BOOK SAY-DEADLY POISON-SHE SAY-SHE DO, ABSOLOOTLE DO!
WALT KELLY

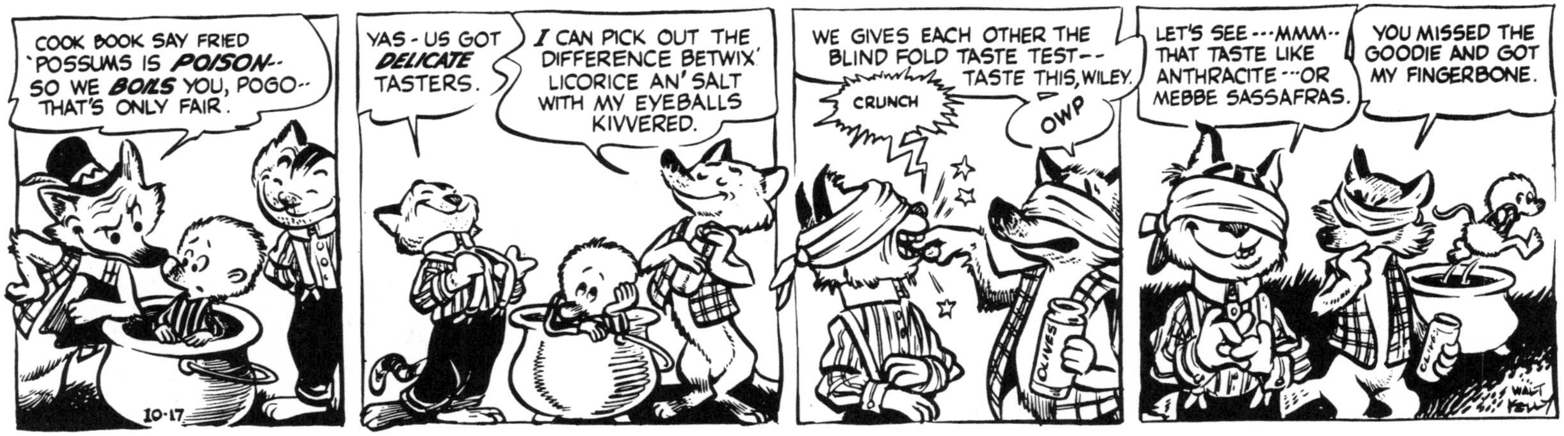
COOK BOOK SAY FRIED 'POSSUMS IS POISON-- SO WE BOILS YOU, POGO-- THAT'S ONLY FAIR.
10-17
YAS-US GOT DELICATE TASTERS.
I CAN PICK OUT THE DIFFERENCE BETWIX' LICORICE AN' SALT WITH MY EYEBALLS KIVVERED.
WE GIVES EACH OTHER THE BLIND FOLD TASTE TEST-- TASTE THIS, WILEY.
CRUNCH
OWP
OLIVES
LET'S SEE---MMM-- THAT TASTE LIKE ANTHRACITE---OR MEBBE SASSAFRAS.
YOU MISSED THE GOODIE AND GOT MY FINGERBONE.
WALT KELLY

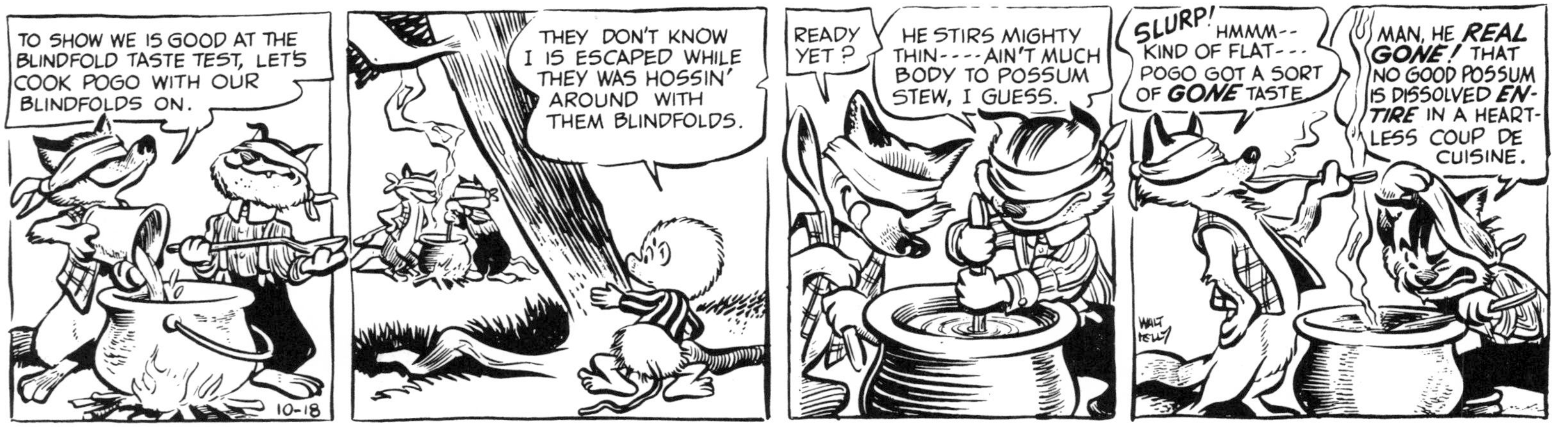
TO SHOW WE IS GOOD AT THE BLINDFOLD TASTE TEST, LET'S COOK POGO WITH OUR BLINDFOLDS ON.
10-18
THEY DON'T KNOW I IS ESCAPED WHILE THEY WAS HOSSIN' AROUND WITH THEM BLINDFOLDS.
READY YET?
HE STIRS MIGHTY THIN----AIN'T MUCH BODY TO POSSUM STEW, I GUESS.
SLURP! HMMM-- KIND OF FLAT--- POGO GOT A SORT OF GONE TASTE.
MAN, HE REAL GONE! THAT NO GOOD POSSUM IS DISSOLVED ENTIRE IN A HEARTLESS COUP DE CUISINE.
WALT KELLY

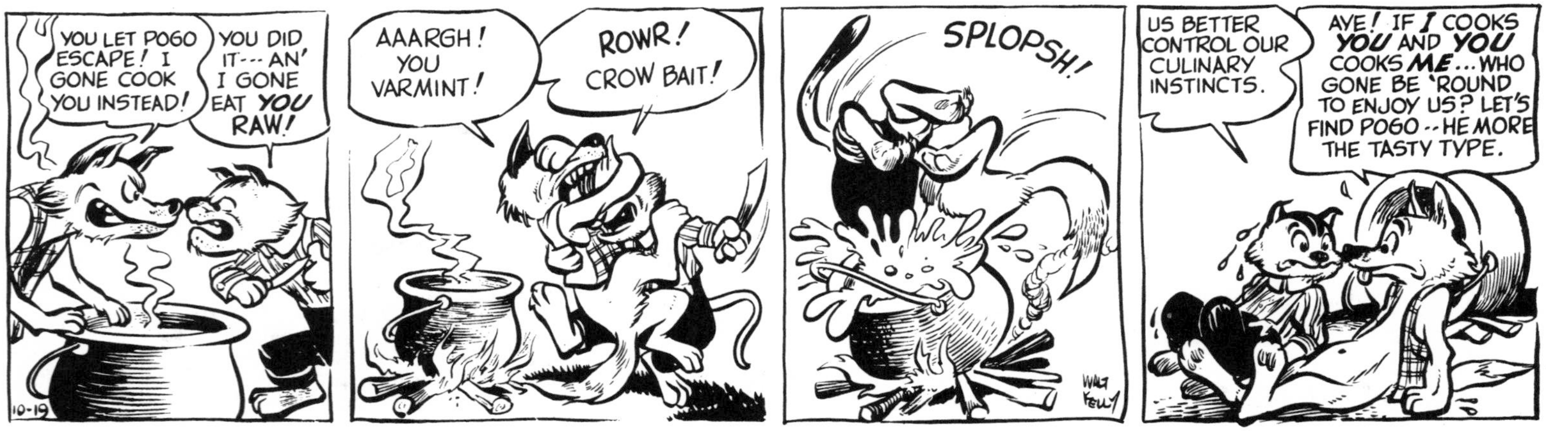
YOU LET POGO ESCAPE! I GONE COOK YOU INSTEAD!
YOU DID IT--- AN' I GONE EAT YOU RAW!
10-19
AAARGH! YOU VARMINT!
ROWR! CROW BAIT!
SPLOPSH!
WALT KELLY
US BETTER CONTROL OUR CULINARY INSTINCTS.
AYE! IF I COOKS YOU AND YOU COOKS ME...WHO GONE BE 'ROUND TO ENJOY US? LET'S FIND POGO--HE MORE THE TASTY TYPE.

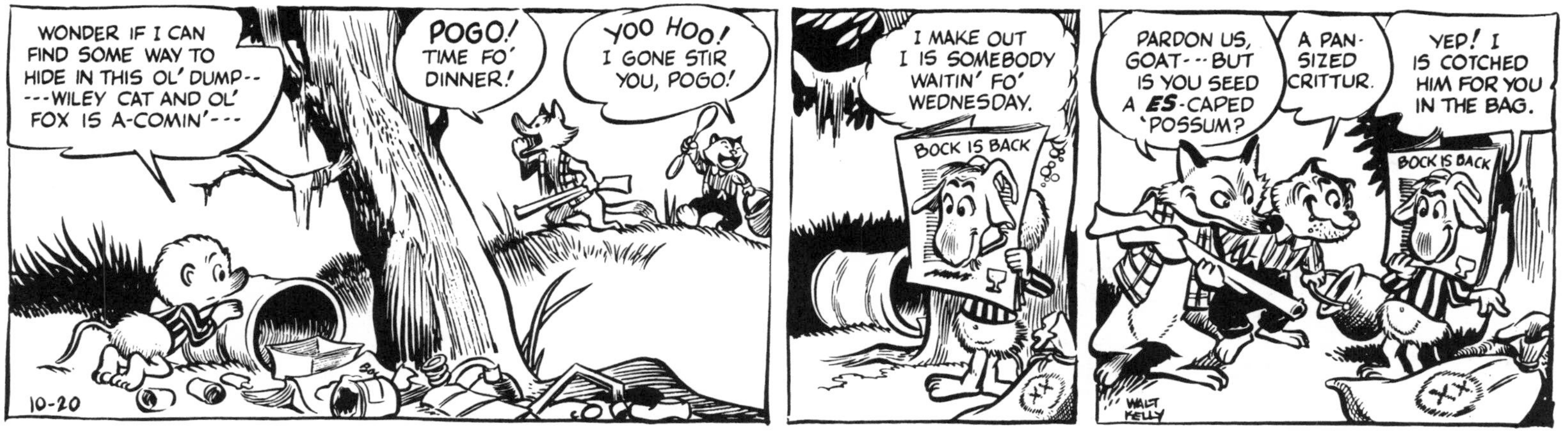
WONDER IF I CAN FIND SOME WAY TO HIDE IN THIS OL' DUMP-- ---WILEY CAT AND OL' FOX IS A-COMIN'---
POGO! TIME FO' DINNER!
YOO HOO! I GONE STIR YOU, POGO!
10-20
I MAKE OUT I IS SOMEBODY WAITIN' FO' WEDNESDAY.
BOCK IS BACK
PARDON US, GOAT---BUT IS YOU SEED A ES-CAPED 'POSSUM?
A PAN-SIZED CRITTUR.
YEP! I IS COTCHED HIM FOR YOU IN THE BAG.
BOCK IS BACK
WALT KELLY

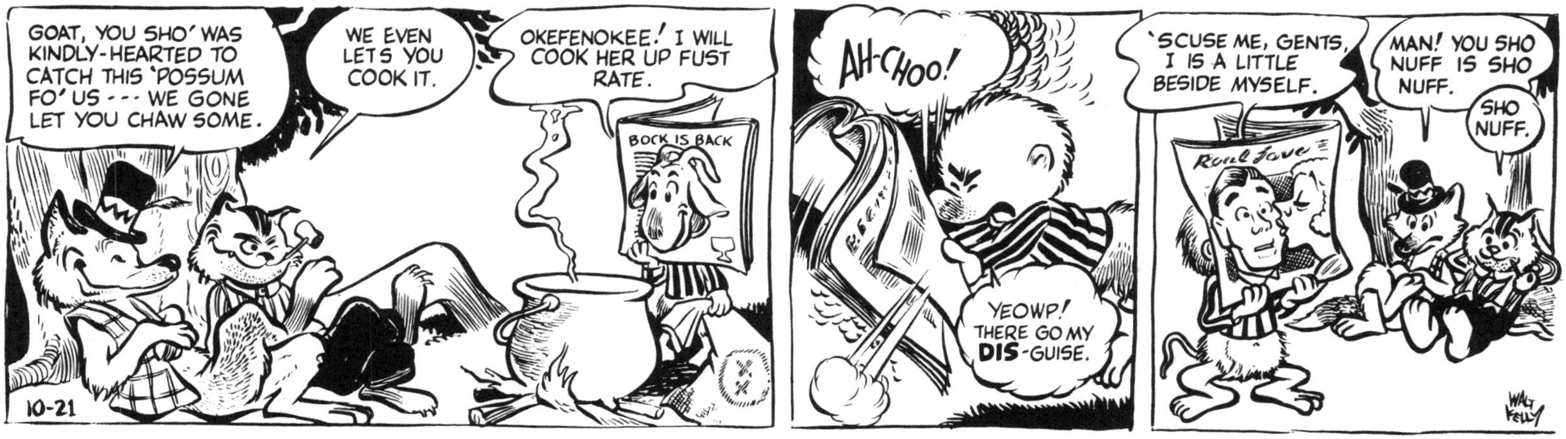
GOAT, YOU SHO' WAS KINDLY-HEARTED TO CATCH THIS 'POSSUM FO' US --- WE GONE LET YOU CHAW SOME.
WE EVEN LETS YOU COOK IT.
OKEFENOKEE! I WILL COOK HER UP FUST RATE.
BOCK IS BACK
10-21
AH-CHOO!
YEOWP! THERE GO MY DIS-GUISE.
'SCUSE ME, GENTS, I IS A LITTLE BESIDE MYSELF.
MAN! YOU SHO NUFF IS SHO NUFF.
SHO NUFF.
WALT KELLY

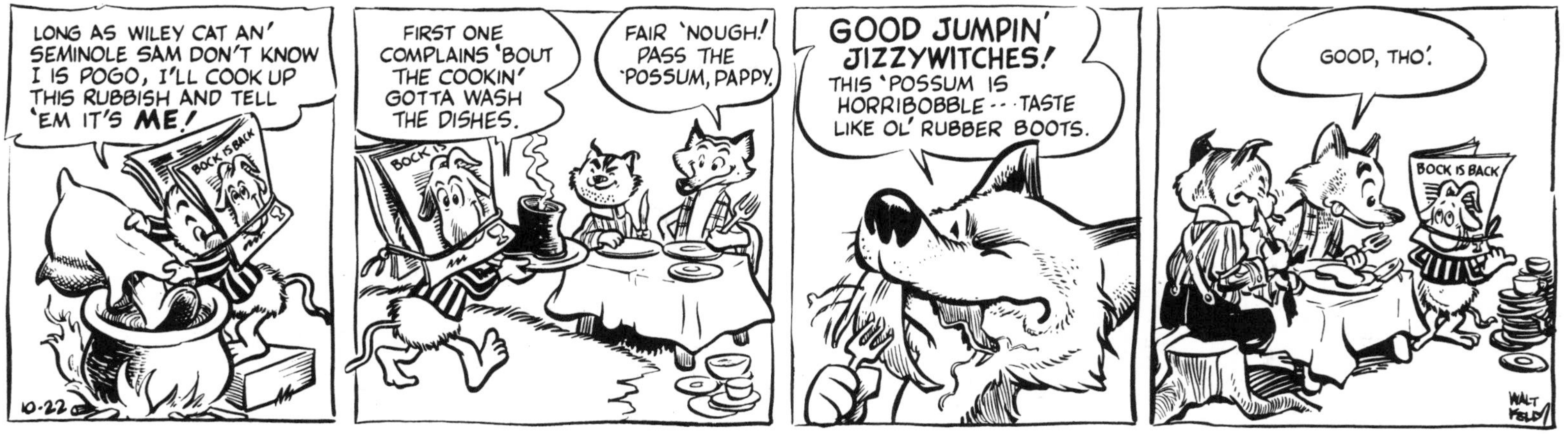
LONG AS WILEY CAT AN' SEMINOLE SAM DON'T KNOW I IS POGO, I'LL COOK UP THIS RUBBISH AND TELL 'EM IT'S ME!
BOCK IS BACK
10-22
FIRST ONE COMPLAINS 'BOUT THE COOKIN' GOTTA WASH THE DISHES.
FAIR 'NOUGH! PASS THE 'POSSUM, PAPPY.
GOOD JUMPIN' JIZZYWITCHES! THIS 'POSSUM IS HORRIBOBBLE---TASTE LIKE OL' RUBBER BOOTS.
GOOD, THO'.
BOCK IS BACK
WALT KELLY

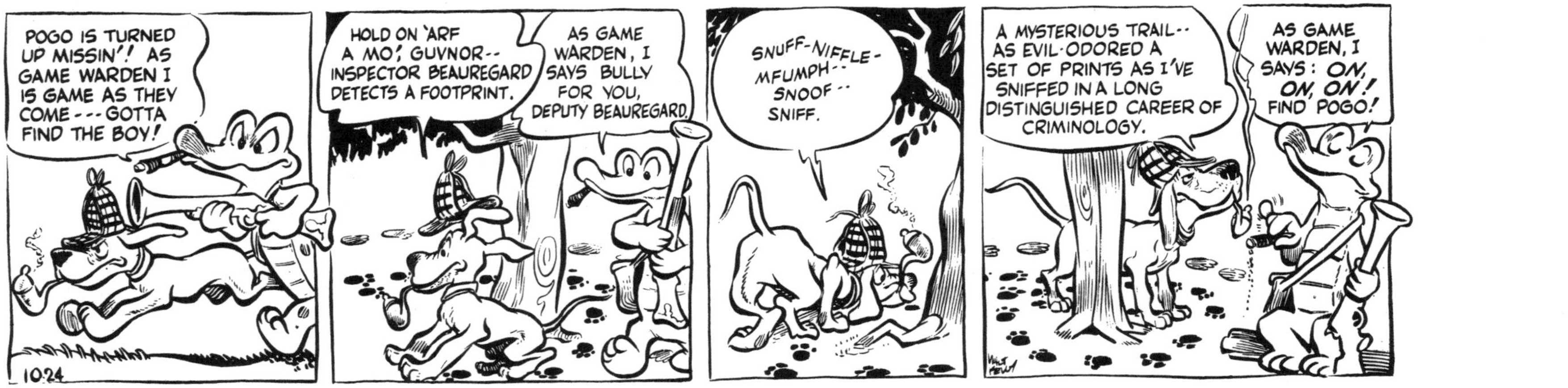
POGO IS TURNED UP MISSIN'! AS GAME WARDEN I IS GAME AS THEY COME --- GOTTA FIND THE BOY!
10-24
HOLD ON 'ARF A MO', GUVNOR-- INSPECTOR BEAUREGARD DETECTS A FOOTPRINT.
AS GAME WARDEN, I SAYS BULLY FOR YOU, DEPUTY BEAUREGARD.
SNUFF-NIFFLE-MFUMPH-- SNOOF-- SNIFF.
A MYSTERIOUS TRAIL-- AS EVIL-ODORED A SET OF PRINTS AS I'VE SNIFFED IN A LONG DISTINGUISHED CAREER OF CRIMINOLOGY.
AS GAME WARDEN, I SAYS: ON, ON, ON! FIND POGO!

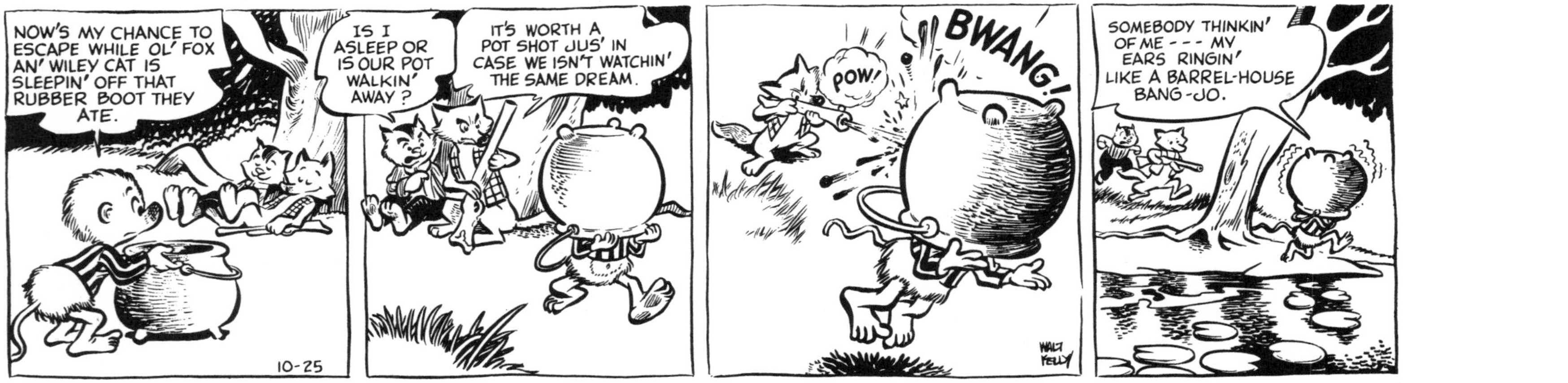
NOW'S MY CHANCE TO ESCAPE WHILE OL' FOX AN' WILEY CAT IS SLEEPIN' OFF THAT RUBBER BOOT THEY ATE.
10-25
IS I ASLEEP OR IS OUR POT WALKIN' AWAY?
IT'S WORTH A POT SHOT JUS' IN CASE WE ISN'T WATCHIN' THE SAME DREAM.
BWANG!
POW!
SOMEBODY THINKIN' OF ME --- MY EARS RINGIN' LIKE A BARREL-HOUSE BANG-JO.

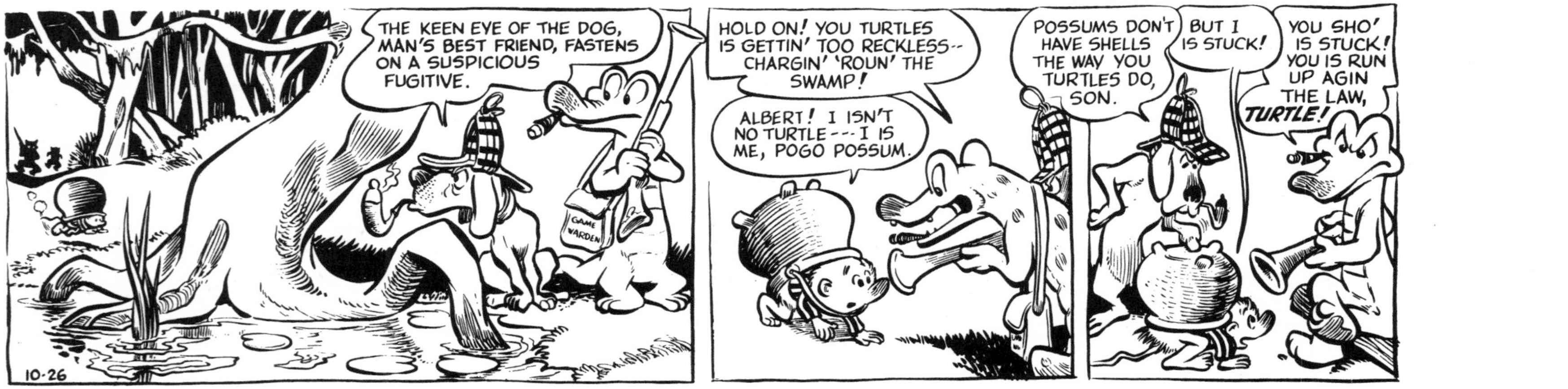
THE KEEN EYE OF THE DOG, MAN'S BEST FRIEND, FASTENS ON A SUSPICIOUS FUGITIVE.
GAME WARDEN
10-26
HOLD ON! YOU TURTLES IS GETTIN' TOO RECKLESS-- CHARGIN' 'ROUN' THE SWAMP!
ALBERT! I ISN'T NO TURTLE --- I IS ME, POGO POSSUM.
POSSUMS DON'T HAVE SHELLS THE WAY YOU TURTLES DO, SON.
BUT I IS STUCK!
YOU SHO' IS STUCK! YOU IS RUN UP AGIN THE LAW, TURTLE!

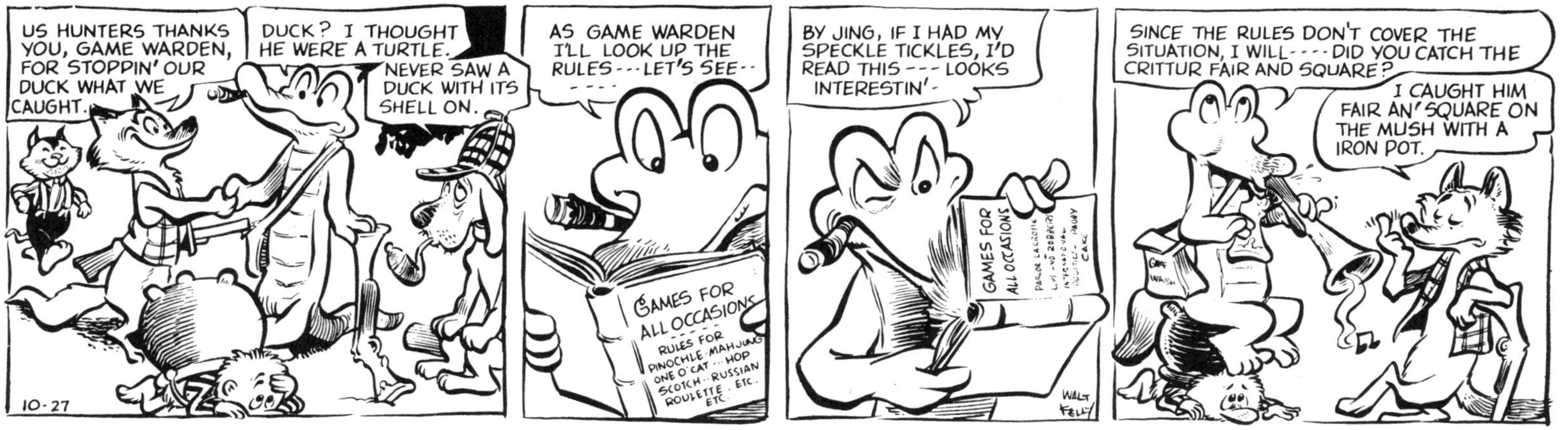
US HUNTERS THANKS YOU, GAME WARDEN, FOR STOPPIN' OUR DUCK WHAT WE CAUGHT.
DUCK? I THOUGHT HE WERE A TURTLE.
NEVER SAW A DUCK WITH ITS SHELL ON.
10-27
AS GAME WARDEN I'LL LOOK UP THE RULES---LET'S SEE-- ----
GAMES FOR ALL OCCASIONS
RULES FOR PINOCHLE·MAHJUNG ONE O'CAT··HOP SCOTCH··RUSSIAN ROULETTE··ETC. ETC.
BY JING, IF I HAD MY SPECKLE TICKLES, I'D READ THIS --- LOOKS INTERESTIN'-
GAMES FOR ALL OCCASIONS
WALT KELLY
SINCE THE RULES DON'T COVER THE SITUATION, I WILL----DID YOU CATCH THE CRITTUR FAIR AND SQUARE?
I CAUGHT HIM FAIR AN' SQUARE ON THE MUSH WITH A IRON POT.

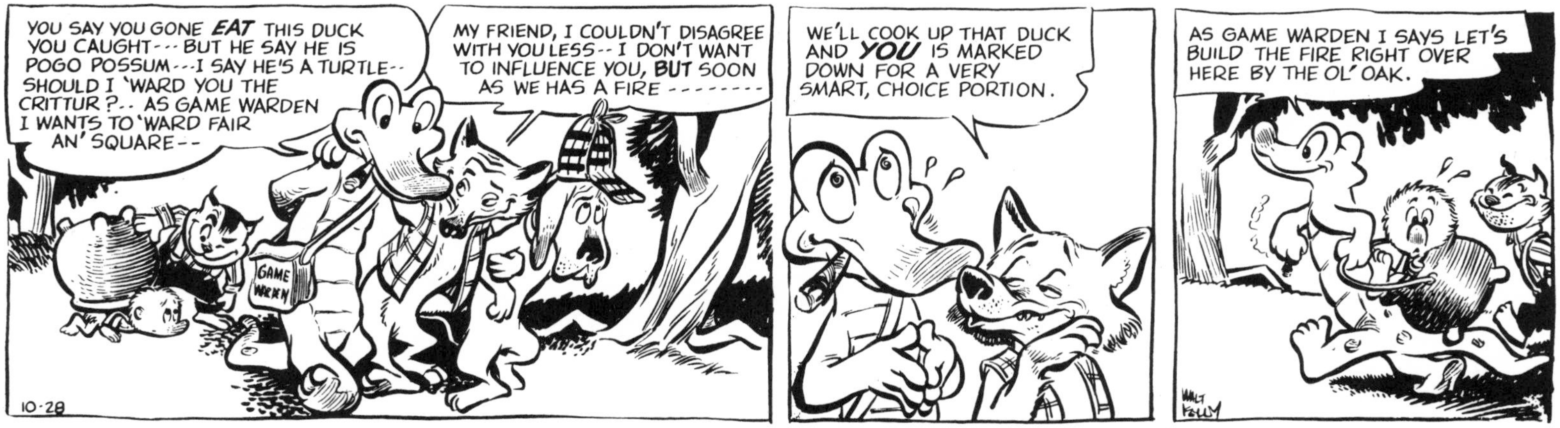
YOU SAY YOU GONE EAT THIS DUCK YOU CAUGHT--- BUT HE SAY HE IS POGO POSSUM---I SAY HE'S A TURTLE-- SHOULD I 'WARD YOU THE CRITTUR?-- AS GAME WARDEN I WANTS TO 'WARD FAIR AN' SQUARE--
MY FRIEND, I COULDN'T DISAGREE WITH YOU LESS--I DON'T WANT TO INFLUENCE YOU, BUT SOON AS WE HAS A FIRE --------
10-28
WE'LL COOK UP THAT DUCK AND YOU IS MARKED DOWN FOR A VERY SMART, CHOICE PORTION.
AS GAME WARDEN I SAYS LET'S BUILD THE FIRE RIGHT OVER HERE BY THE OL' OAK.
WALT KELLY

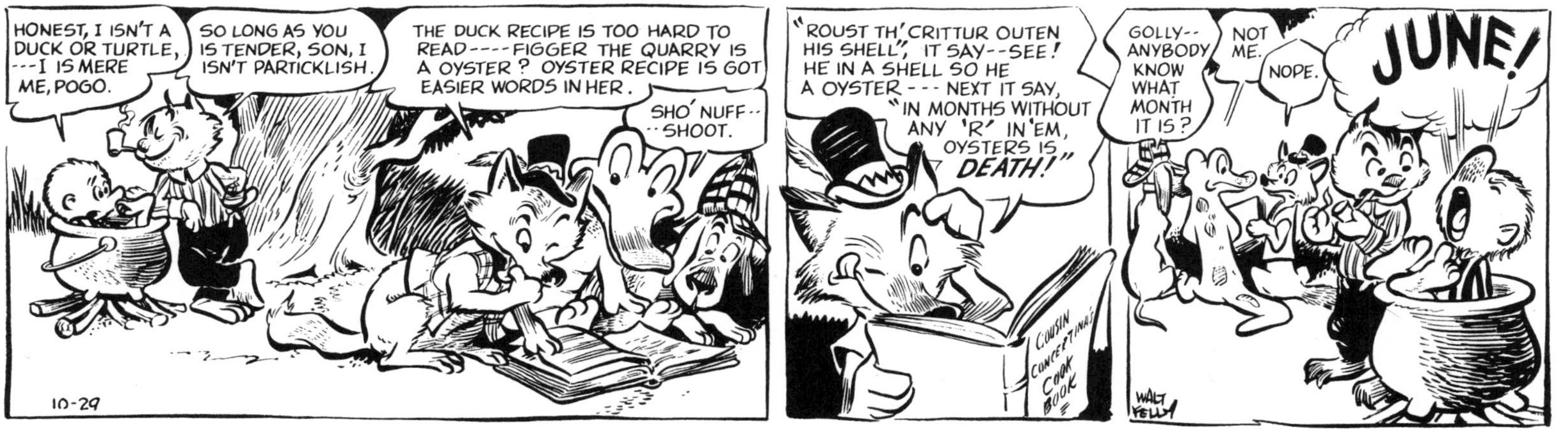
HONEST, I ISN'T A DUCK OR TURTLE, ---I IS MERE ME, POGO.
SO LONG AS YOU IS TENDER, SON, I ISN'T PARTICKLISH.
THE DUCK RECIPE IS TOO HARD TO READ----FIGGER THE QUARRY IS A OYSTER? OYSTER RECIPE IS GOT EASIER WORDS IN HER.
SHO' NUFF-- --SHOOT.
10-29
"ROUST TH' CRITTUR OUTEN HIS SHELL", IT SAY--SEE! HE IN A SHELL SO HE A OYSTER --- NEXT IT SAY, "IN MONTHS WITHOUT ANY 'R' IN 'EM, OYSTERS IS DEATH!"
COUSIN CONCEPTINA'S COOK BOOK
GOLLY-- ANYBODY KNOW WHAT MONTH IT IS?
NOT ME.
NOPE.
JUNE!
WALT KELLY

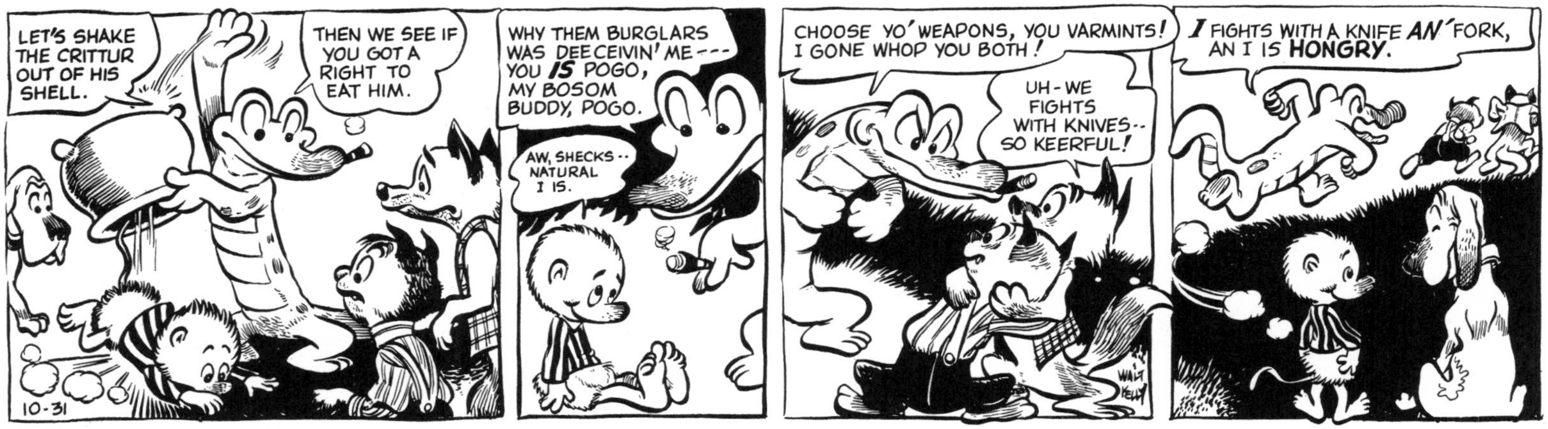
LET'S SHAKE THE CRITTUR OUT OF HIS SHELL.
THEN WE SEE IF YOU GOT A RIGHT TO EAT HIM.
10-31
WHY THEM BURGLARS WAS DEECEIVIN' ME --- YOU IS POGO, MY BOSOM BUDDY, POGO.
AW, SHECKS -- NATURAL I IS.
CHOOSE YO' WEAPONS, YOU VARMINTS! I GONE WHOP YOU BOTH!
UH-WE FIGHTS WITH KNIVES -- SO KEERFUL!
WALT KELLY
I FIGHTS WITH A KNIFE AN' FORK, AN I IS HONGRY.

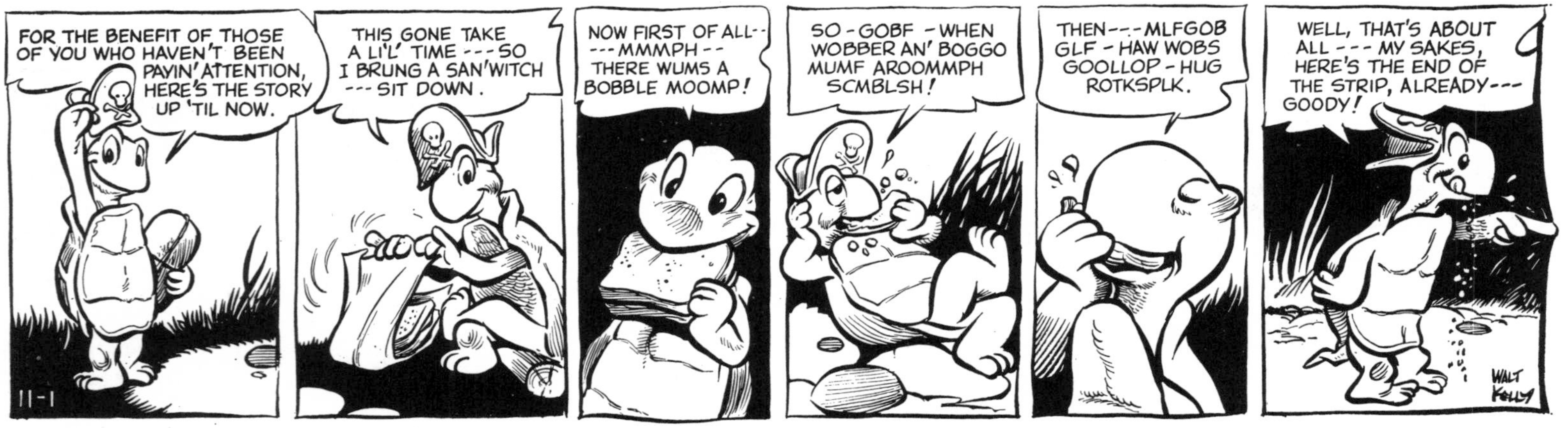
FOR THE BENEFIT OF THOSE OF YOU WHO HAVEN'T BEEN PAYIN' ATTENTION, HERE'S THE STORY UP 'TIL NOW.
11-1
THIS GONE TAKE A LI'L' TIME --- SO I BRUNG A SAN'WITCH --- SIT DOWN.
NOW FIRST OF ALL -- --- MMMPH -- THERE WUMS A BOBBLE MOOMP!
SO-GOBF - WHEN WOBBER AN' BOGGO MUMF AROOMMPH SCMBLSH!
THEN --- MLFGOB GLF - HAW WOBS GOOLLOP - HUG ROTKSPLK.
WELL, THAT'S ABOUT ALL --- MY SAKES, HERE'S THE END OF THE STRIP, ALREADY --- GOODY!
WALT KELLY

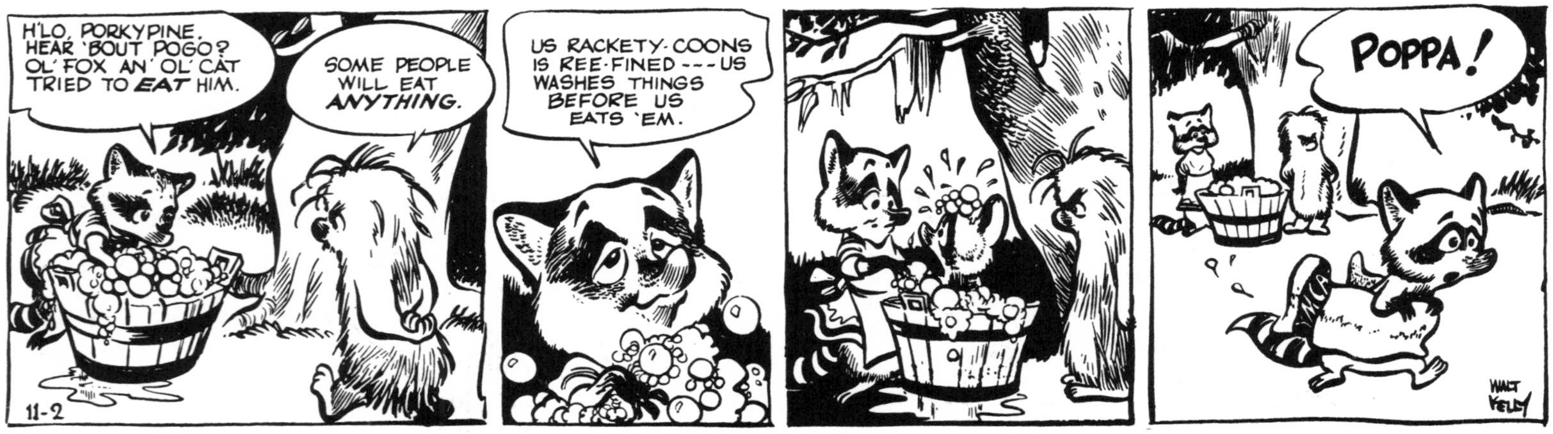
H'LO, PORKYPINE. HEAR 'BOUT POGO? OL' FOX AN' OL' CAT TRIED TO EAT HIM.
SOME PEOPLE WILL EAT ANYTHING.
11-2
US RACKETY-COONS IS REE-FINED --- US WASHES THINGS BEFORE US EATS 'EM.
POPPA!
WALT KELLY

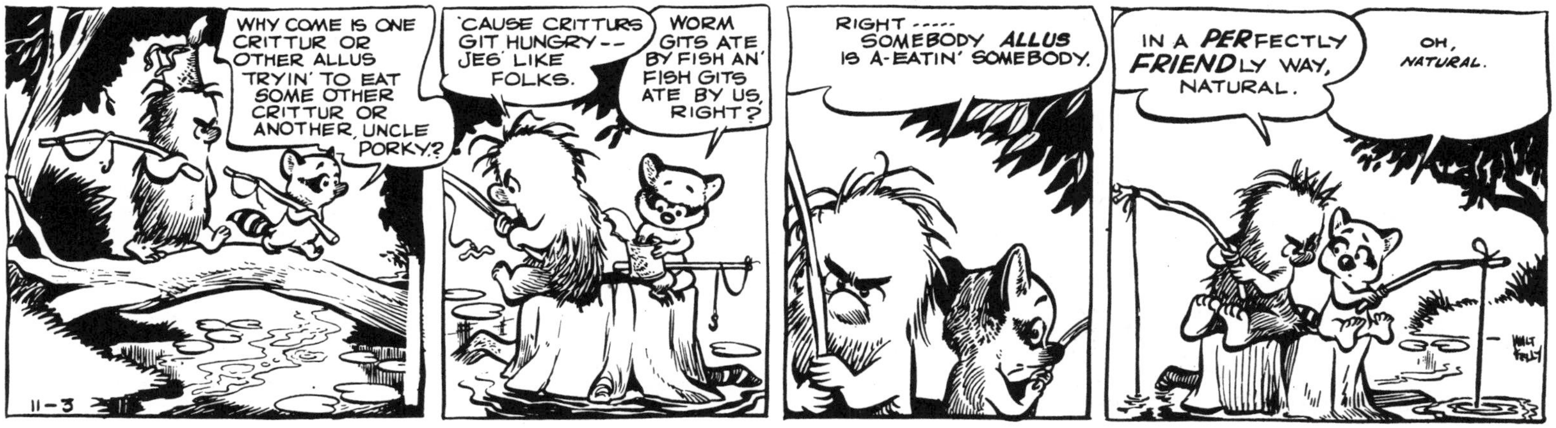
WHY COME IS ONE CRITTUR OR OTHER ALLUS TRYIN' TO EAT SOME OTHER CRITTUR OR ANOTHER, UNCLE PORKY?
11-3
'CAUSE CRITTURS GIT HUNGRY-- JES' LIKE FOLKS.
WORM GITS ATE BY FISH AN' FISH GITS ATE BY US, RIGHT?
RIGHT ----- SOMEBODY ALLUS IS A-EATIN' SOMEBODY.
IN A PERFECTLY FRIENDLY WAY, NATURAL.
OH, NATURAL.
WALT KELLY

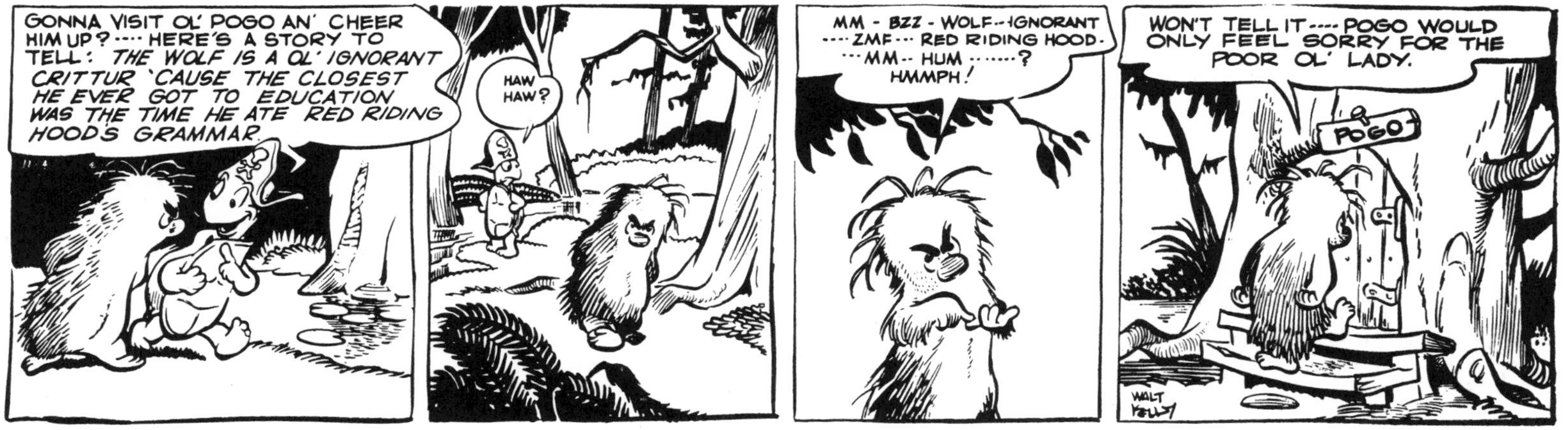
GONNA VISIT OL' POGO AN' CHEER HIM UP? ---- HERE'S A STORY TO TELL: THE WOLF IS A OL' IGNORANT CRITTUR 'CAUSE THE CLOSEST HE EVER GOT TO EDUCATION WAS THE TIME HE ATE RED RIDING HOOD'S GRAMMAR.
11-4
HAW HAW?
MM - BZZ - WOLF--IGNORANT ----ZMF--- RED RIDING HOOD. ---MM-- HUM -------? HMMPH!
WON'T TELL IT---- POGO WOULD ONLY FEEL SORRY FOR THE POOR OL' LADY.
POGO
WALT KELLY

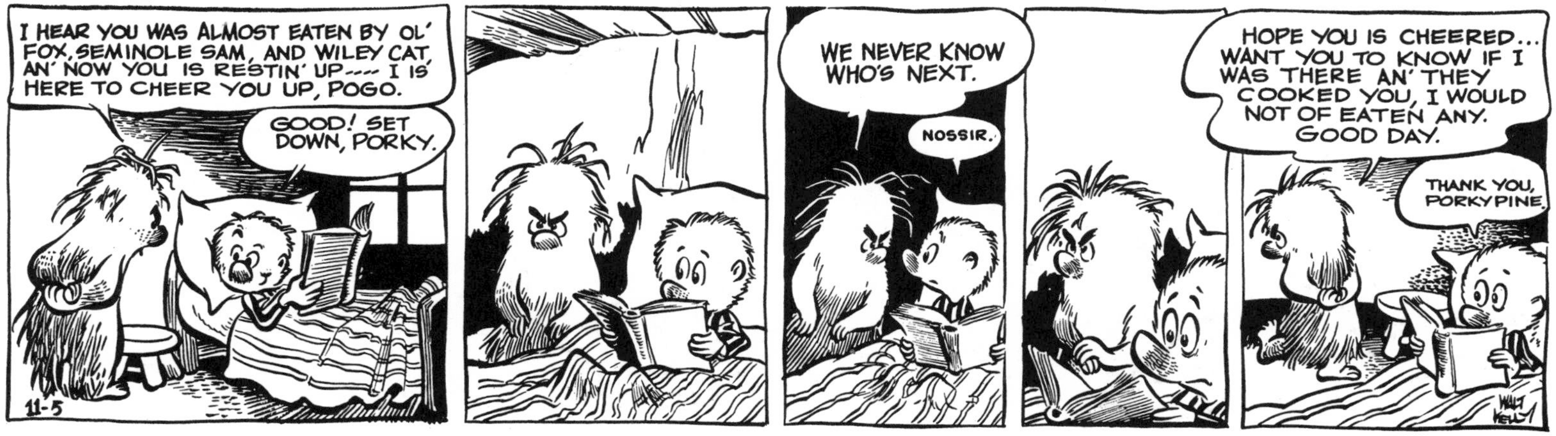
I HEAR YOU WAS ALMOST EATEN BY OL' FOX, SEMINOLE SAM, AND WILEY CAT, AN' NOW YOU IS RESTIN' UP---- I IS HERE TO CHEER YOU UP, POGO.
GOOD! SET DOWN, PORKY.
11-5
WE NEVER KNOW WHO'S NEXT.
NOSSIR.
HOPE YOU IS CHEERED... WANT YOU TO KNOW IF I WAS THERE AN' THEY COOKED YOU, I WOULD NOT OF EATEN ANY. GOOD DAY.
THANK YOU, PORKYPINE.
WALT KELLY

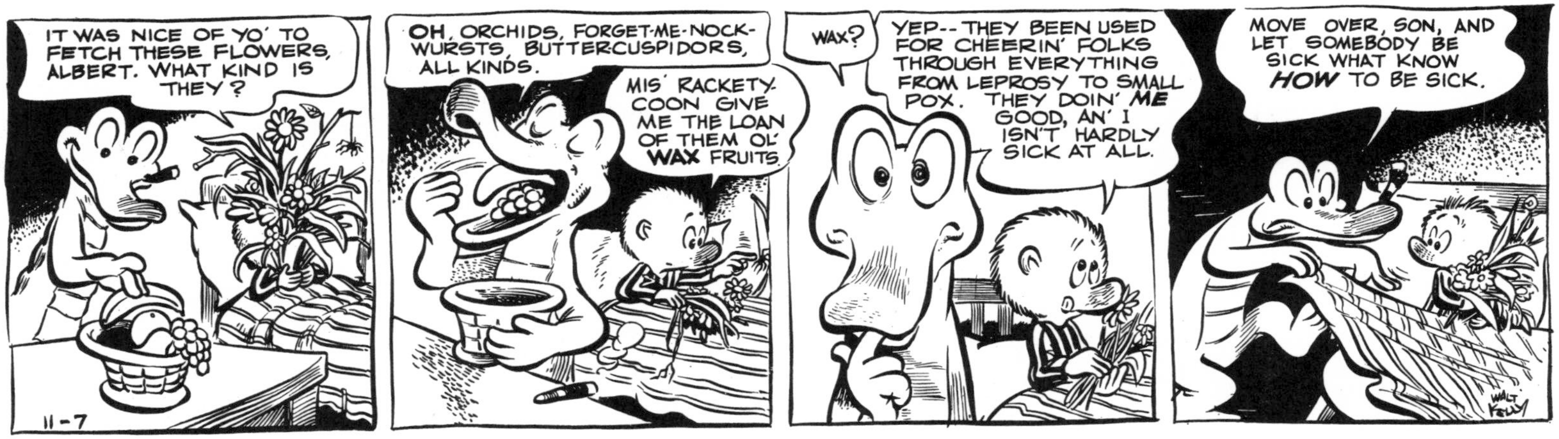
IT WAS NICE OF YO' TO FETCH THESE FLOWERS, ALBERT. WHAT KIND IS THEY?
OH, ORCHIDS, FORGET-ME-NOCK-WURSTS, BUTTERCUSPIDORS, ALL KINDS.
MIS' RACKETY-COON GIVE ME THE LOAN OF THEM OL' WAX FRUITS.
WAX?
YEP-- THEY BEEN USED FOR CHEERIN' FOLKS THROUGH EVERYTHING FROM LEPROSY TO SMALL POX. THEY DOIN' ME GOOD, AN' I ISN'T HARDLY SICK AT ALL.
MOVE OVER, SON, AND LET SOMEBODY BE SICK WHAT KNOW HOW TO BE SICK.
11-7
WALT KELLY

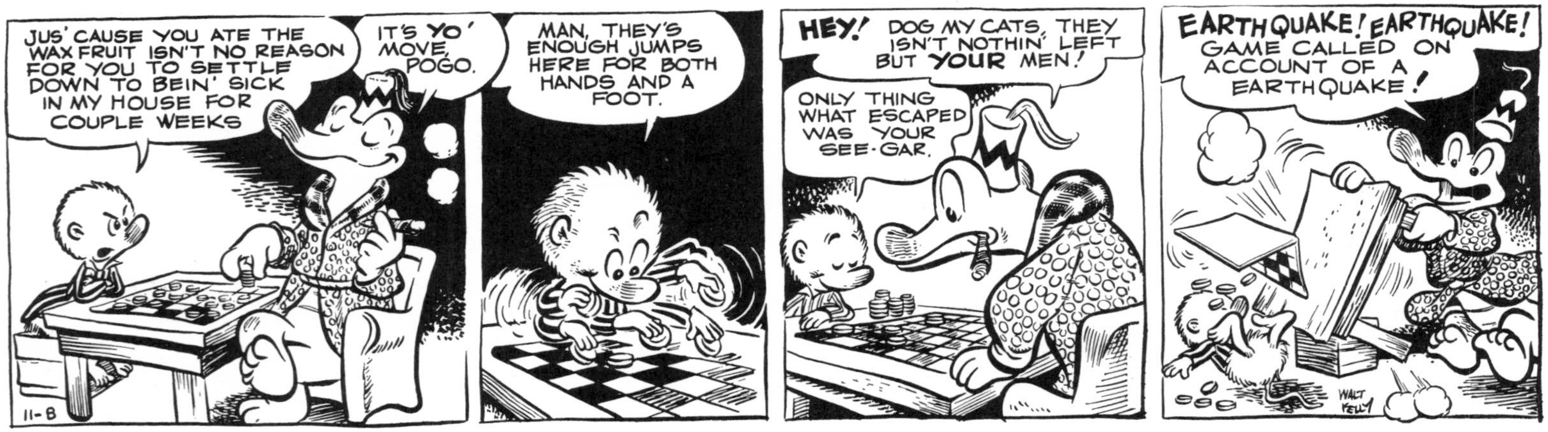
JUS' CAUSE YOU ATE THE WAX FRUIT ISN'T NO REASON FOR YOU TO SETTLE DOWN TO BEIN' SICK IN MY HOUSE FOR COUPLE WEEKS
IT'S YO' MOVE, POGO.
MAN, THEY'S ENOUGH JUMPS HERE FOR BOTH HANDS AND A FOOT.
HEY! DOG MY CATS, THEY ISN'T NOTHIN' LEFT BUT YOUR MEN!
ONLY THING WHAT ESCAPED WAS YOUR SEE-GAR.
EARTHQUAKE! EARTHQUAKE! GAME CALLED ON ACCOUNT OF A EARTHQUAKE!
11-8
WALT KELLY

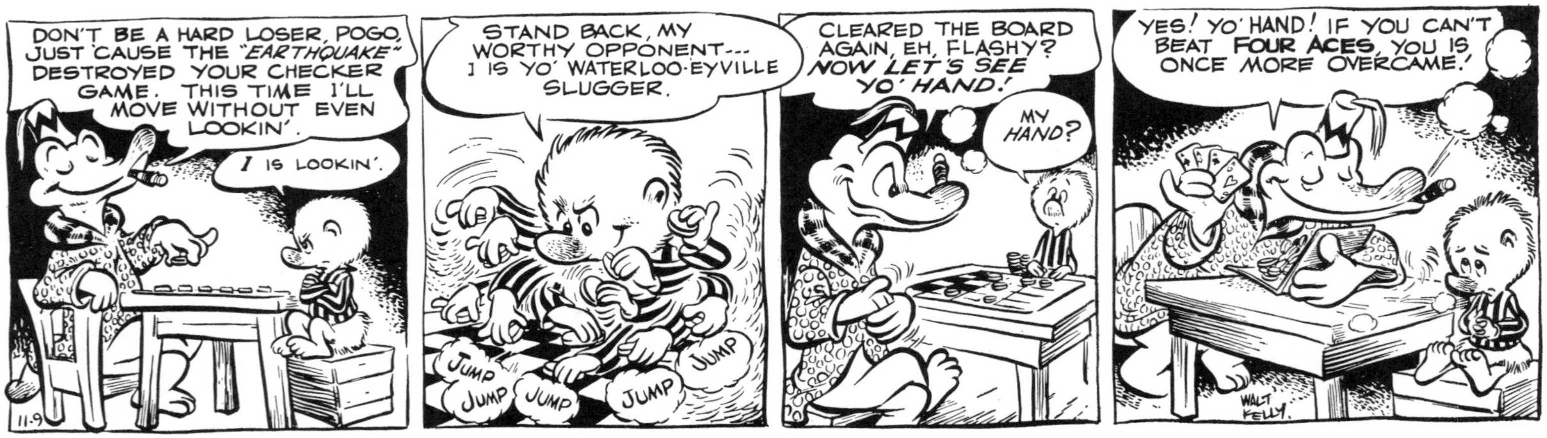
DON'T BE A HARD LOSER, POGO, JUST CAUSE THE "EARTHQUAKE" DESTROYED YOUR CHECKER GAME. THIS TIME I'LL MOVE WITHOUT EVEN LOOKIN'.
I IS LOOKIN'.
STAND BACK, MY WORTHY OPPONENT--- I IS YO' WATERLOO-EYVILLE SLUGGER.
JUMP
JUMP
JUMP
JUMP
JUMP
CLEARED THE BOARD AGAIN, EH, FLASHY? NOW LET'S SEE YO' HAND!
MY HAND?
YES! YO' HAND! IF YOU CAN'T BEAT FOUR ACES, YOU IS ONCE MORE OVERCAME!
11-9
WALT KELLY

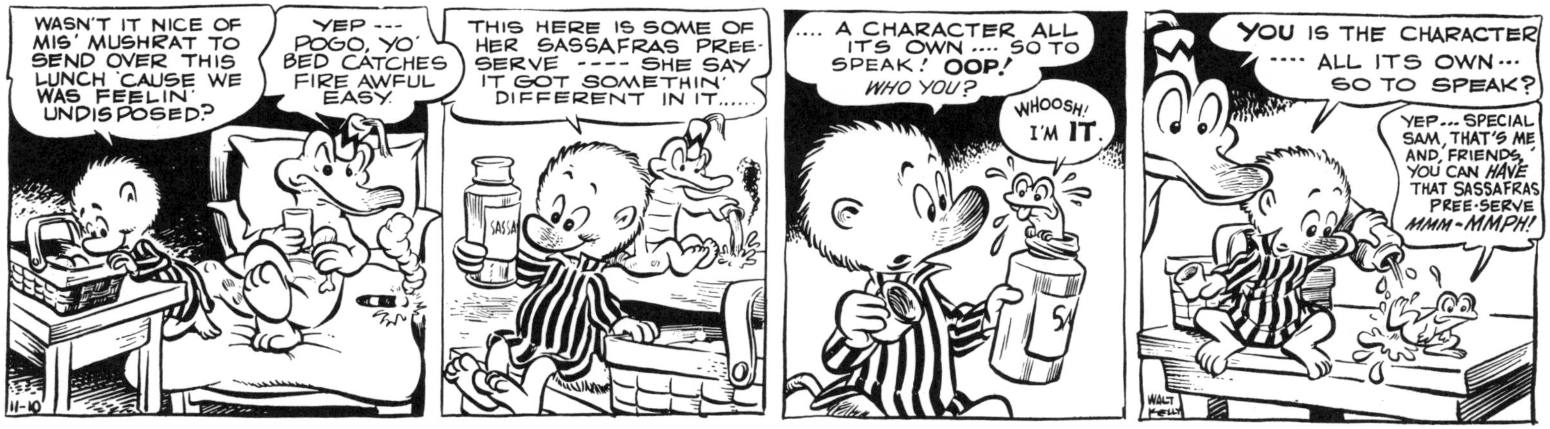
WASN'T IT NICE OF MIS' MUSHRAT TO SEND OVER THIS LUNCH 'CAUSE WE WAS FEELIN' UNDISPOSED?
YEP --- POGO, YO' BED CATCHES FIRE AWFUL EASY.
11-10
THIS HERE IS SOME OF HER SASSAFRAS PREE-SERVE ---- SHE SAY IT GOT SOMETHIN' DIFFERENT IN IT......
.... A CHARACTER ALL ITS OWN .... SO TO SPEAK! OOP! WHO YOU?
WHOOSH! I'M IT.
YOU IS THE CHARACTER ---- ALL ITS OWN --- SO TO SPEAK?
YEP --- SPECIAL SAM, THAT'S ME AND, FRIENDS, YOU CAN HAVE THAT SASSAFRAS PREE-SERVE MMM-MMPH!
WALT KELLY

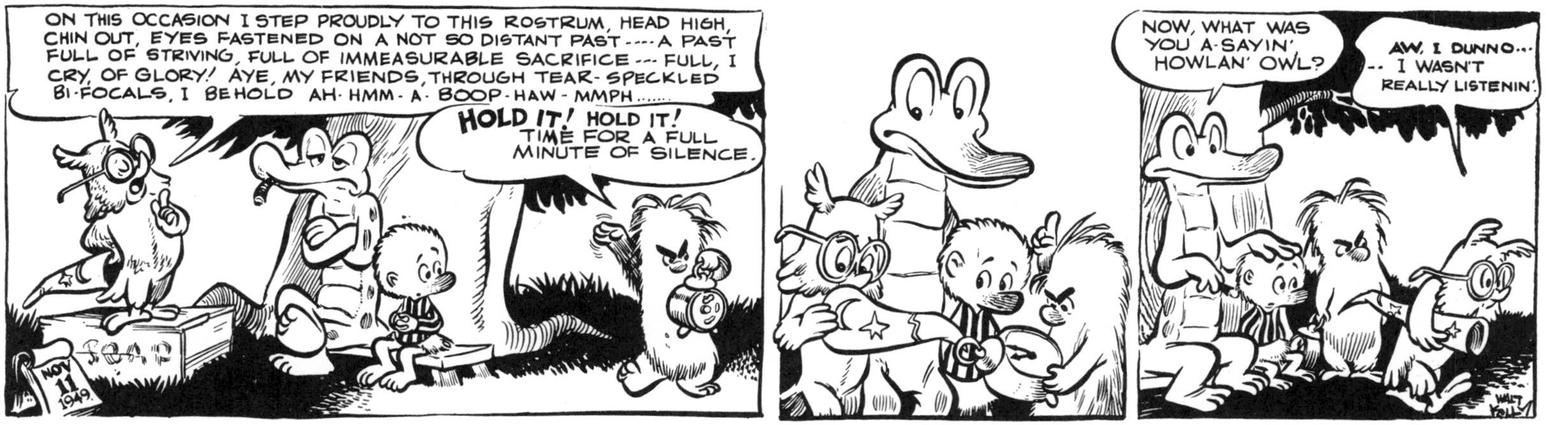
ON THIS OCCASION I STEP PROUDLY TO THIS ROSTRUM, HEAD HIGH, CHIN OUT, EYES FASTENED ON A NOT SO DISTANT PAST ---- A PAST FULL OF STRIVING, FULL OF IMMEASURABLE SACRIFICE --- FULL, I CRY, OF GLORY! AYE, MY FRIENDS, THROUGH TEAR-SPECKLED BI-FOCALS, I BEHOLD AH-HMM-A-BOOP-HAW-MMPH.......
HOLD IT! HOLD IT! TIME FOR A FULL MINUTE OF SILENCE.
SOAP
NOV 11 1949
NOW, WHAT WAS YOU A-SAYIN' HOWLAN' OWL?
AW, I DUNNO... -- I WASN'T REALLY LISTENIN'.
WALT KELLY

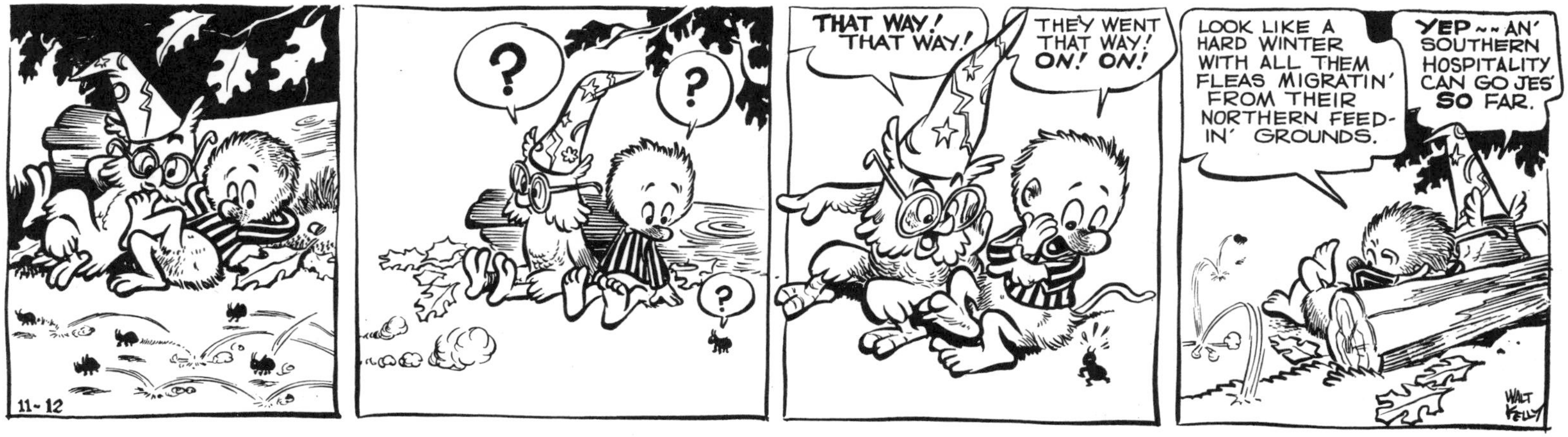
11-12
?
?
?
THAT WAY! THAT WAY!
THEY WENT THAT WAY! ON! ON!
LOOK LIKE A HARD WINTER WITH ALL THEM FLEAS MIGRATIN' FROM THEIR NORTHERN FEED-IN' GROUNDS.
YEP -- AN' SOUTHERN HOSPITALITY CAN GO JES' SO FAR.
WALT KELLY

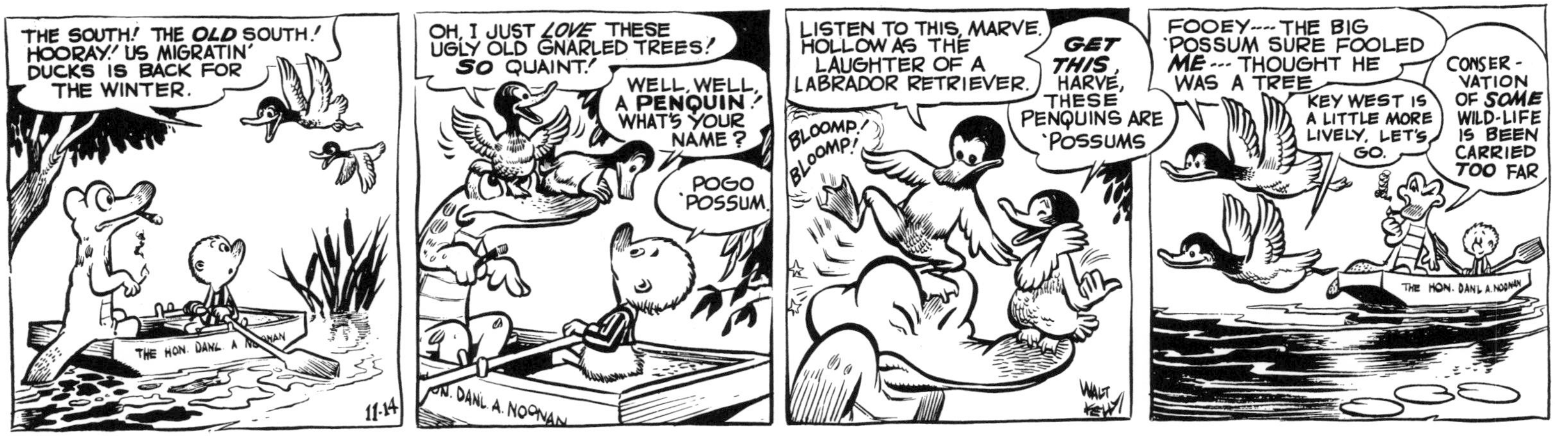
THE SOUTH! THE OLD SOUTH! HOORAY! US MIGRATIN' DUCKS IS BACK FOR THE WINTER.
THE HON. DANL. A. NOONAN
11-14
OH, I JUST LOVE THESE UGLY OLD GNARLED TREES! SO QUAINT!
WELL, WELL, A PENQUIN! WHAT'S YOUR NAME?
POGO 'POSSUM.
N. DANL. A. NOONAN
LISTEN TO THIS, MARVE. HOLLOW AS THE LAUGHTER OF A LABRADOR RETRIEVER.
GET THIS, HARVE, THESE PENQUINS ARE 'POSSUMS
BLOOMP! BLOOMP!
WALT KELLY
FOOEY--- THE BIG 'POSSUM SURE FOOLED ME --- THOUGHT HE WAS A TREE
KEY WEST IS A LITTLE MORE LIVELY, LET'S GO.
CONSER-VATION OF SOME WILD-LIFE IS BEEN CARRIED TOO FAR
THE HON. DANL. A. NOONAN

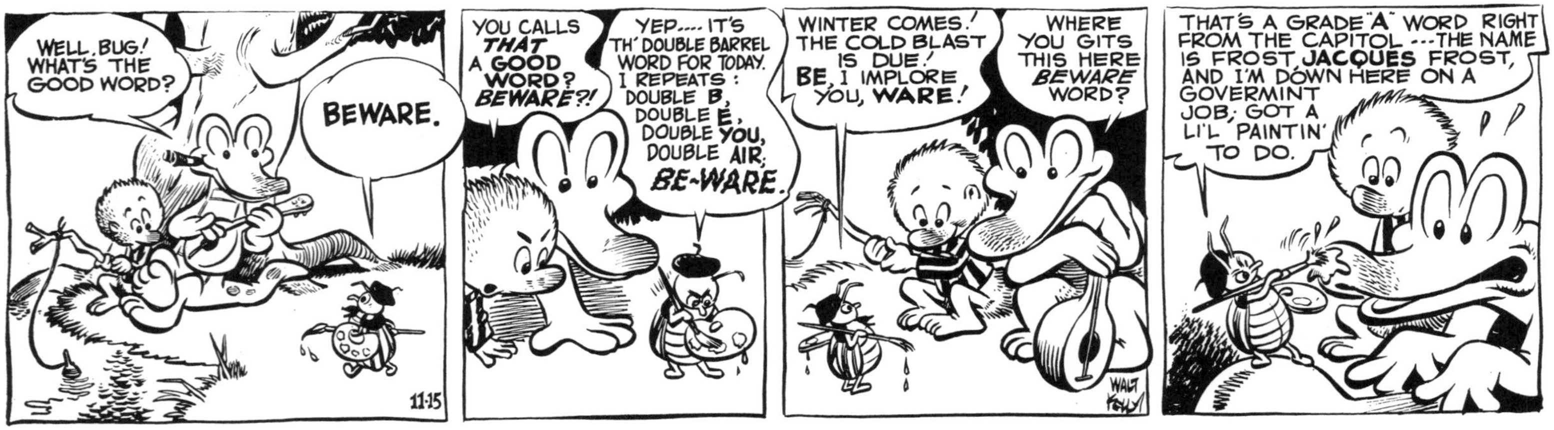
WELL, BUG! WHAT'S THE GOOD WORD?
BEWARE.
11-15
YOU CALLS THAT A GOOD WORD? BEWARE?!
YEP.... IT'S TH' DOUBLE BARREL WORD FOR TODAY. I REPEATS: DOUBLE B, DOUBLE E, DOUBLE YOU, DOUBLE AIR: BE-WARE.
WINTER COMES! THE COLD BLAST IS DUE! BE, I IMPLORE YOU, WARE!
WHERE YOU GITS THIS HERE BEWARE WORD?
WALT KELLY
THAT'S A GRADE "A" WORD RIGHT FROM THE CAPITOL ---THE NAME IS FROST JACQUES FROST, AND I'M DOWN HERE ON A GOVERMINT JOB; GOT A LI'L PAINTIN' TO DO.

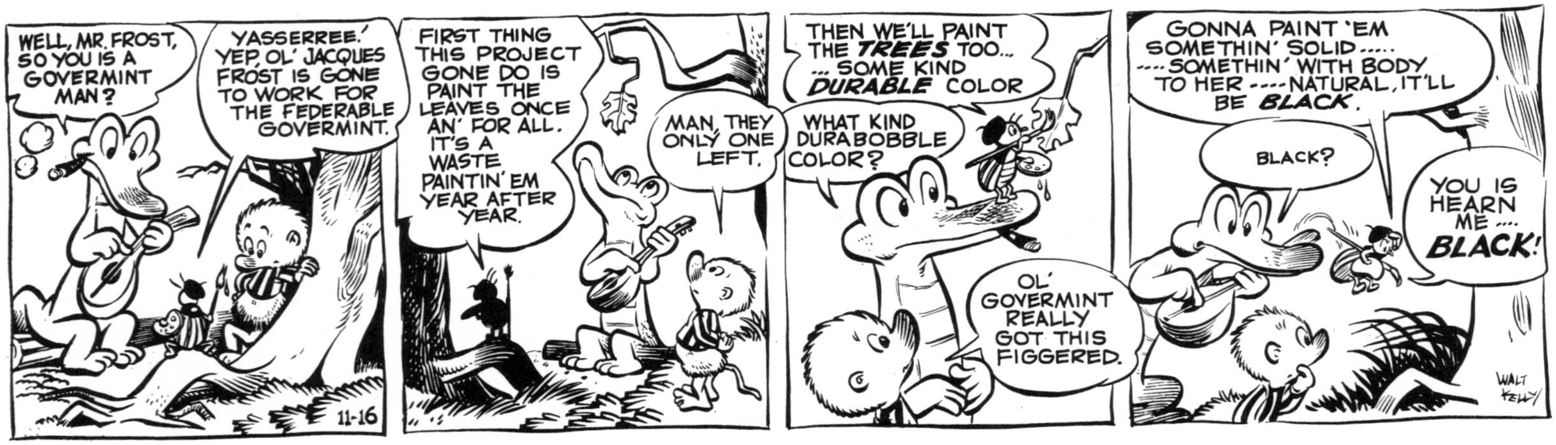
WELL, MR. FROST, SO YOU IS A GOVERMINT MAN?
YASSERREE! YEP, OL' JACQUES FROST IS GONE TO WORK FOR THE FEDERABLE GOVERMINT.
11-16
FIRST THING THIS PROJECT GONE DO IS PAINT THE LEAVES ONCE AN' FOR ALL. IT'S A WASTE PAINTIN' EM YEAR AFTER YEAR.
MAN, THEY ONLY ONE LEFT.
THEN WE'LL PAINT THE TREES TOO... ... SOME KIND DURABLE COLOR
WHAT KIND DURABOBBLE COLOR?
OL' GOVERMINT REALLY GOT THIS FIGGERED.
GONNA PAINT 'EM SOMETHIN' SOLID..... ....SOMETHIN' WITH BODY TO HER ----NATURAL, IT'LL BE BLACK.
BLACK?
YOU IS HEARN ME.... BLACK!
WALT KELLY

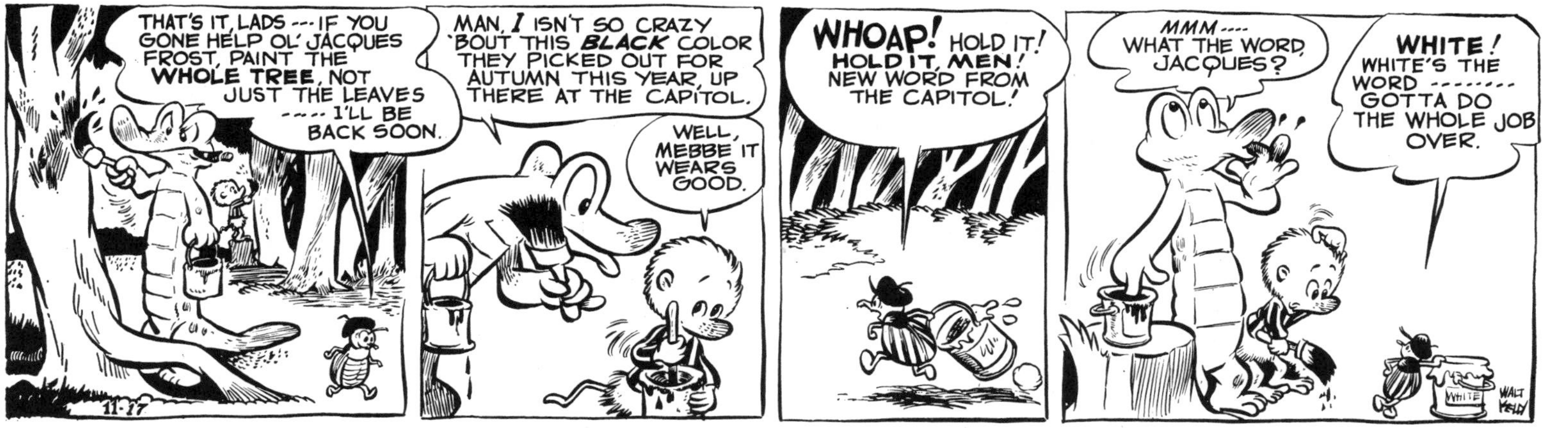
THAT'S IT, LADS --- IF YOU GONE HELP OL' JACQUES FROST, PAINT THE WHOLE TREE, NOT JUST THE LEAVES ---- I'LL BE BACK SOON.
11-17
MAN, I ISN'T SO CRAZY 'BOUT THIS BLACK COLOR THEY PICKED OUT FOR AUTUMN THIS YEAR, UP THERE AT THE CAPITOL.
WELL, MEBBE IT WEARS GOOD.
WHOAP! HOLD IT! HOLD IT, MEN! NEW WORD FROM THE CAPITOL!
MMM ---- WHAT THE WORD, JACQUES?
WHITE! WHITE'S THE WORD -------- GOTTA DO THE WHOLE JOB OVER.
WHITE
WALT KELLY

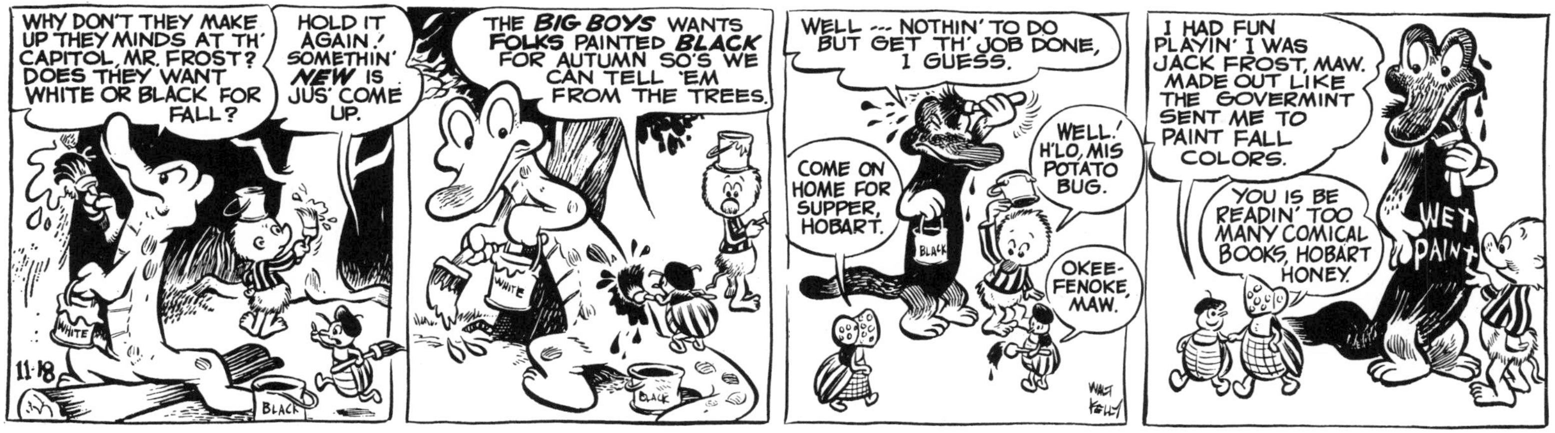
WHY DON'T THEY MAKE UP THEY MINDS AT TH' CAPITOL, MR. FROST? DOES THEY WANT WHITE OR BLACK FOR FALL?
HOLD IT AGAIN! SOMETHIN' NEW IS JUS' COME UP.
WHITE
BLACK
11-18
THE BIG BOYS WANTS FOLKS PAINTED BLACK FOR AUTUMN SO'S WE CAN TELL 'EM FROM THE TREES.
WHITE
BLACK
WELL --- NOTHIN' TO DO BUT GET TH' JOB DONE, I GUESS.
COME ON HOME FOR SUPPER, HOBART.
WELL! H'LO, MIS POTATO BUG.
BLACK
OKEE-FENOKE, MAW.
WALT KELLY
I HAD FUN PLAYIN' I WAS JACK FROST, MAW. MADE OUT LIKE THE GOVERMINT SENT ME TO PAINT FALL COLORS.
YOU IS BE READIN' TOO MANY COMICAL BOOKS, HOBART HONEY.
WET PAINT

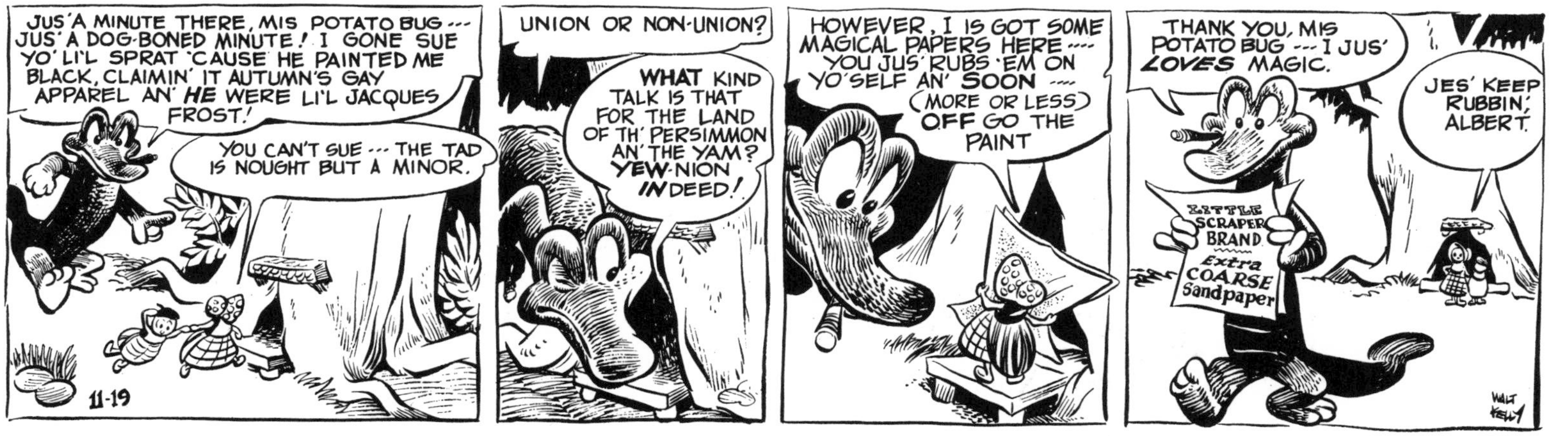
JUS' A MINUTE THERE, MIS POTATO BUG --- JUS' A DOG-BONED MINUTE! I GONE SUE YO' LI'L SPRAT 'CAUSE HE PAINTED ME BLACK, CLAIMIN' IT AUTUMN'S GAY APPAREL AN' HE WERE LI'L JACQUES FROST!
YOU CAN'T SUE --- THE TAD IS NOUGHT BUT A MINOR.
11-19
UNION OR NON-UNION?
WHAT KIND TALK IS THAT FOR THE LAND OF TH' PERSIMMON AN' THE YAM? YEW-NION INDEED!
HOWEVER, I IS GOT SOME MAGICAL PAPERS HERE ---- YOU JUS' RUBS 'EM ON YO'SELF AN' SOON ---- (MORE OR LESS) OFF GO THE PAINT
THANK YOU, MIS POTATO BUG --- I JUS' LOVES MAGIC.
JES' KEEP RUBBIN', ALBERT.
LITTLE SCRAPER BRAND Extra COARSE Sandpaper
WALT KELLY

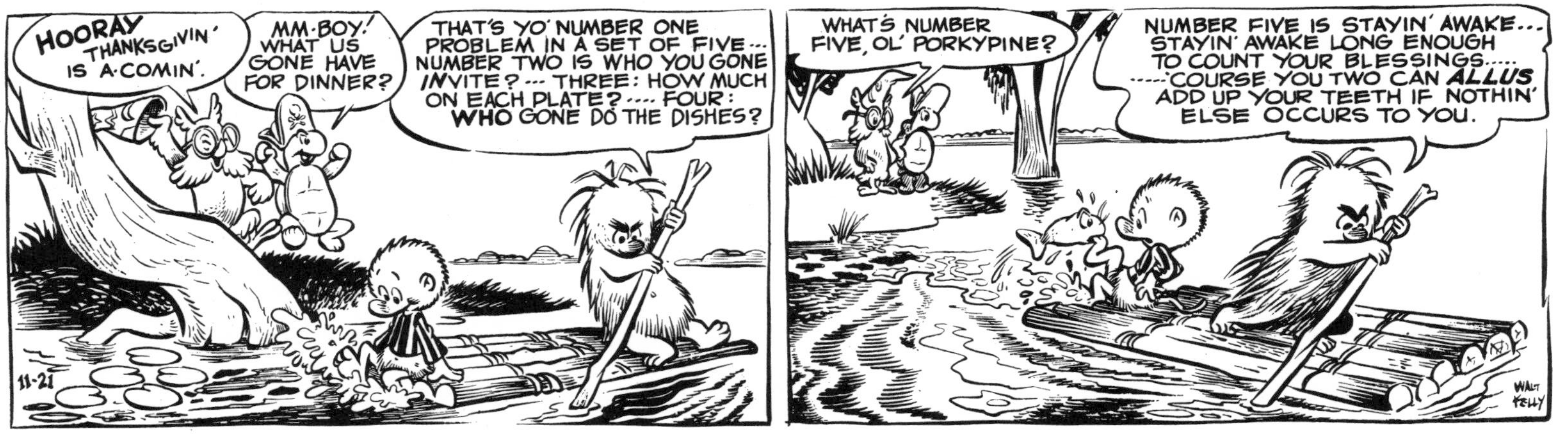
HOORAY THANKSGIVIN' IS A-COMIN'.
MM-BOY! WHAT US GONE HAVE FOR DINNER?
THAT'S YO' NUMBER ONE PROBLEM IN A SET OF FIVE--- NUMBER TWO IS WHO YOU GONE INVITE? --- THREE: HOW MUCH ON EACH PLATE? ---- FOUR: WHO GONE DO THE DISHES?
11-21
WHAT'S NUMBER FIVE, OL' PORKYPINE?
NUMBER FIVE IS STAYIN' AWAKE... STAYIN' AWAKE LONG ENOUGH TO COUNT YOUR BLESSINGS..... ----'COURSE YOU TWO CAN ALLUS ADD UP YOUR TEETH IF NOTHIN' ELSE OCCURS TO YOU.
WALT KELLY

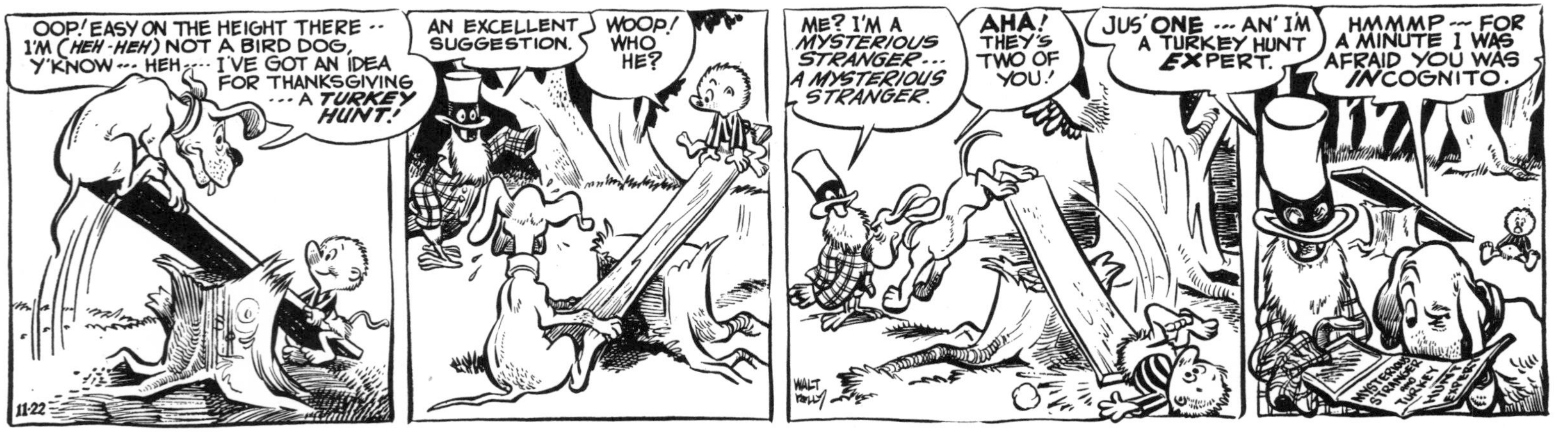
OOP! EASY ON THE HEIGHT THERE -- I'M (HEH-HEH) NOT A BIRD DOG, Y'KNOW --- HEH ---- I'VE GOT AN IDEA FOR THANKSGIVING --- A TURKEY HUNT!
11-22
AN EXCELLENT SUGGESTION.
WOOP! WHO HE?
ME? I'M A MYSTERIOUS STRANGER... A MYSTERIOUS STRANGER.
AHA! THEY'S TWO OF YOU!
WALT KELLY
JUS' ONE --- AN' I'M A TURKEY HUNT EXPERT.
HMMMP --- FOR A MINUTE I WAS AFRAID YOU WAS INCOGNITO.

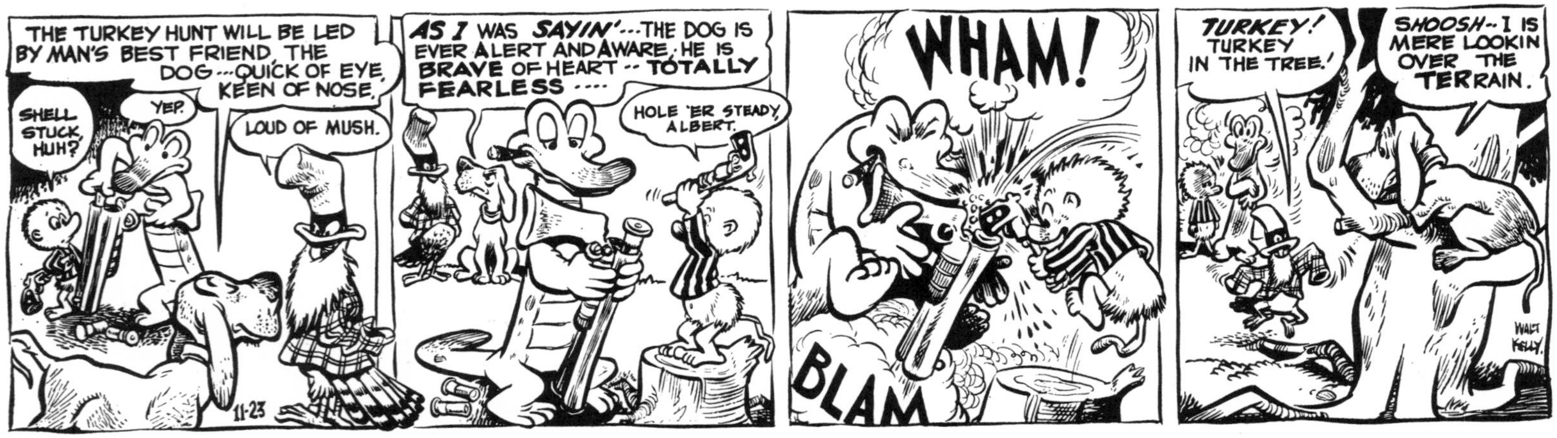
THE TURKEY HUNT WILL BE LED BY MAN'S BEST FRIEND, THE DOG --- QUICK OF EYE, KEEN OF NOSE,
SHELL STUCK, HUH?
YEP.
LOUD OF MUSH.
AS I WAS SAYIN' --- THE DOG IS EVER ALERT AND AWARE, HE IS BRAVE OF HEART -- TOTALLY FEARLESS ----
HOLE 'ER STEADY, ALBERT.
11-23
WHAM!
BLAM
TURKEY! TURKEY IN THE TREE!
SHOOSH -- I IS MERE LOOKIN OVER THE TERRAIN.
WALT KELLY

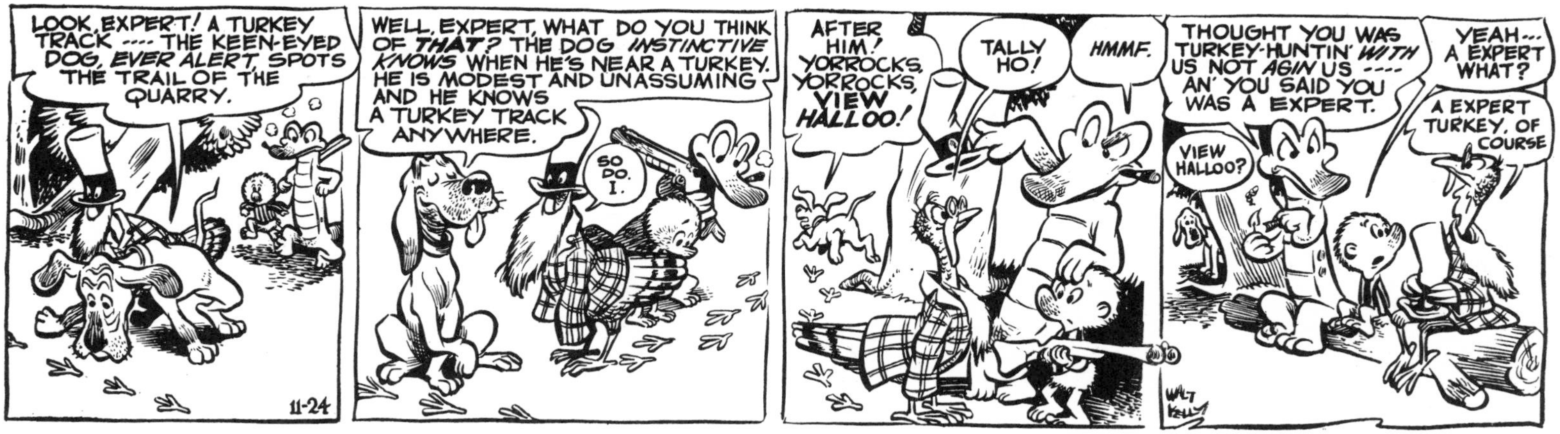
LOOK, EXPERT! A TURKEY TRACK ---- THE KEEN-EYED DOG, *EVER ALERT*, SPOTS THE TRAIL OF THE QUARRY.
11-24
WELL, EXPERT, WHAT DO YOU THINK OF *THAT*? THE DOG *INSTINCTIVE KNOWS* WHEN HE'S NEAR A TURKEY. HE IS MODEST AND UNASSUMING AND HE KNOWS A TURKEY TRACK ANYWHERE.
SO DO. I.
AFTER HIM! YORROCKS, YORROCKS, **VIEW HALLOO!**
TALLY HO!
HMMF.
THOUGHT YOU WAS TURKEY-HUNTIN' *WITH* US NOT *AGIN* US ---- AN' YOU SAID YOU WAS A EXPERT.
YEAH... A EXPERT WHAT?
VIEW HALLOO?
A EXPERT TURKEY, OF COURSE
WALT KELLY

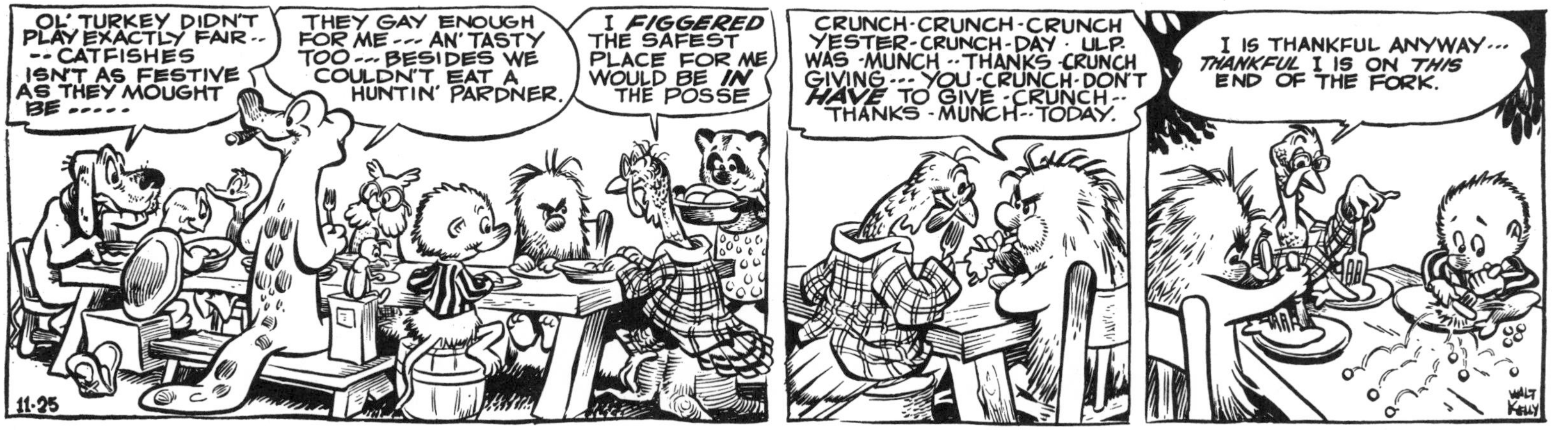
OL' TURKEY DIDN'T PLAY EXACTLY FAIR -- -- CATFISHES ISN'T AS FESTIVE AS THEY MOUGHT BE -----
THEY GAY ENOUGH FOR ME --- AN' TASTY TOO --- BESIDES WE COULDN'T EAT A HUNTIN' PARDNER.
I *FIGGERED* THE SAFEST PLACE FOR ME WOULD BE *IN* THE POSSE
11-25
CRUNCH-CRUNCH-CRUNCH YESTER-CRUNCH-DAY - ULP. WAS -MUNCH -- THANKS -CRUNCH GIVING --- YOU -CRUNCH- DON'T *HAVE* TO GIVE -CRUNCH -- THANKS -MUNCH -- TODAY.
I IS THANKFUL ANYWAY... *THANKFUL* I IS ON *THIS* END OF THE FORK.
WALT KELLY

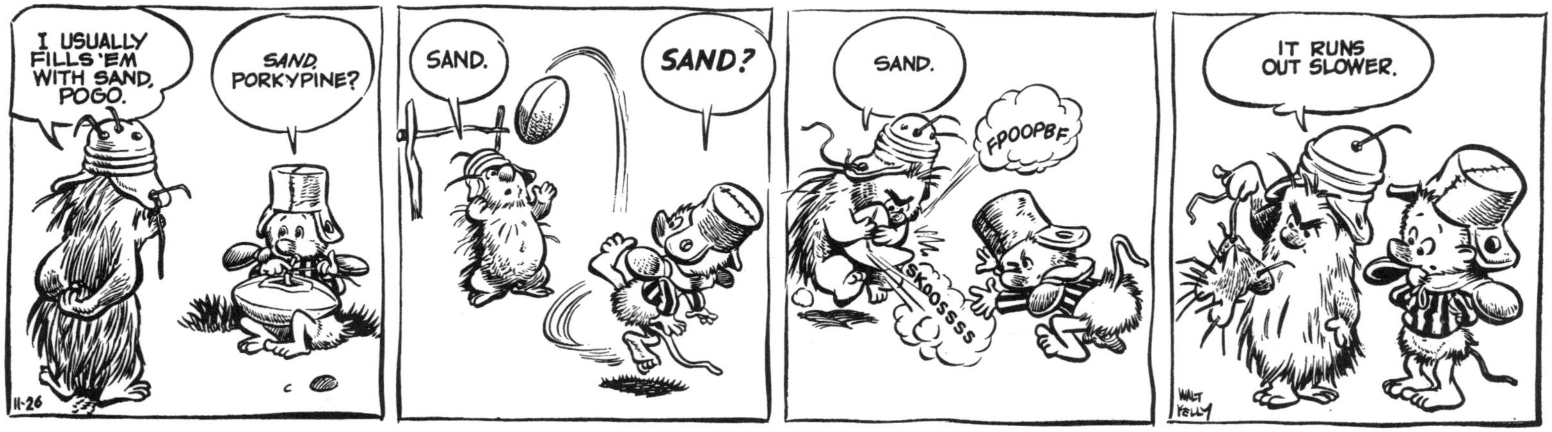
I USUALLY FILLS 'EM WITH SAND, POGO.
SAND, PORKYPINE?
11-26
SAND.
SAND?
SAND.
FPOOPBF
SKOOSSSS
IT RUNS OUT SLOWER.
WALT KELLY

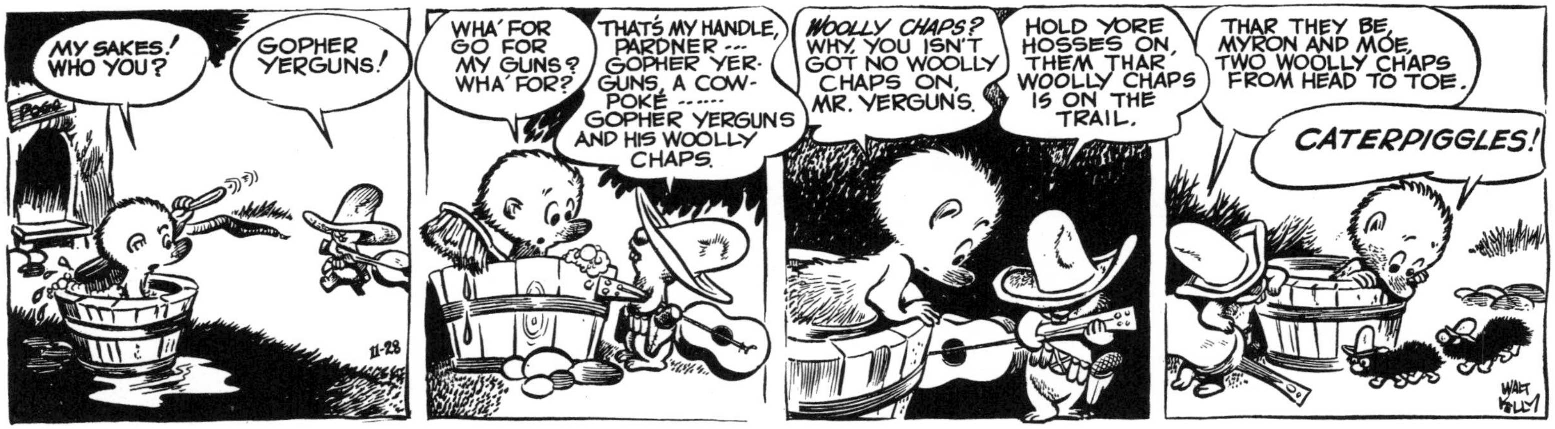
MY SAKES! WHO YOU?
GOPHER YERGUNS!
11-28
WHA' FOR GO FOR MY GUNS? WHA' FOR?
THAT'S MY HANDLE, PARDNER --- GOPHER YERGUNS, A COWPOKE ----- GOPHER YERGUNS AND HIS WOOLLY CHAPS.
WOOLLY CHAPS? WHY, YOU ISN'T GOT NO WOOLLY CHAPS ON, MR. YERGUNS.
HOLD YORE HOSSES ON, THEM THAR WOOLLY CHAPS IS ON THE TRAIL.
THAR THEY BE, MYRON AND MOE, TWO WOOLLY CHAPS FROM HEAD TO TOE.
CATERPIGGLES!
WALT KELLY

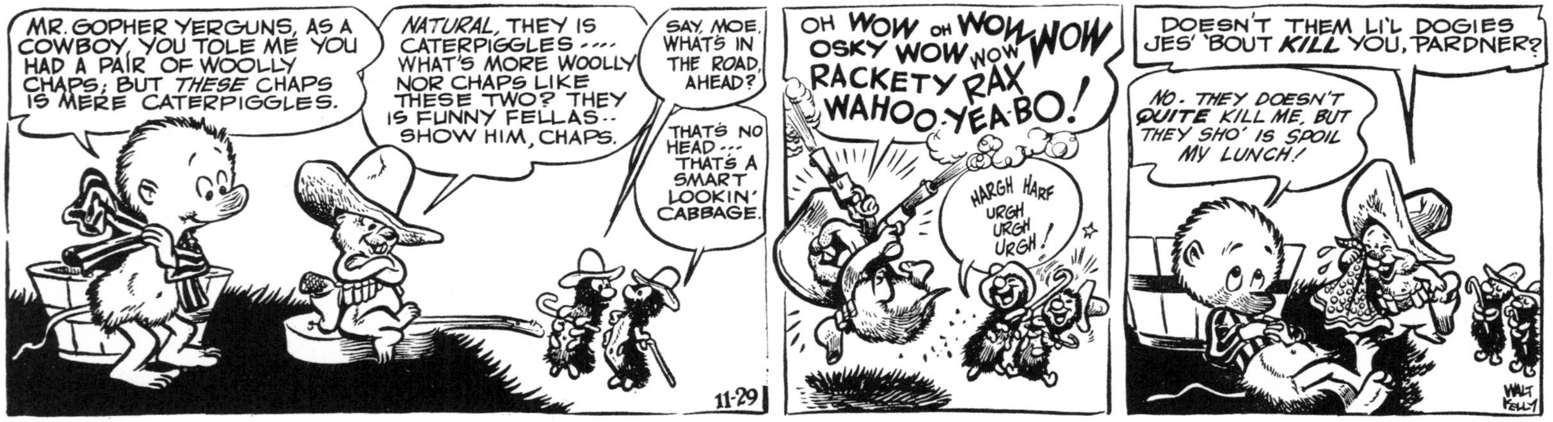
MR. GOPHER YERGUNS, AS A COWBOY, YOU TOLE ME YOU HAD A PAIR OF WOOLLY CHAPS; BUT THESE CHAPS IS MERE CATERPIGGLES.
NATURAL, THEY IS CATERPIGGLES .... WHAT'S MORE WOOLLY NOR CHAPS LIKE THESE TWO? THEY IS FUNNY FELLAS -- SHOW HIM, CHAPS.
SAY, MOE, WHAT'S IN THE ROAD AHEAD?
THAT'S NO HEAD --- THAT'S A SMART LOOKIN' CABBAGE.
11-29
OH WOW OH WOW WOW OSKY WOW WOW WOW RACKETY RAX WAHOO-YEA-BO!
HARGH HARF URGH URGH URGH!
DOESN'T THEM LI'L DOGIES JES' 'BOUT KILL YOU, PARDNER?
NO - THEY DOESN'T QUITE KILL ME, BUT THEY SHO' IS SPOIL MY LUNCH!
WALT KELLY

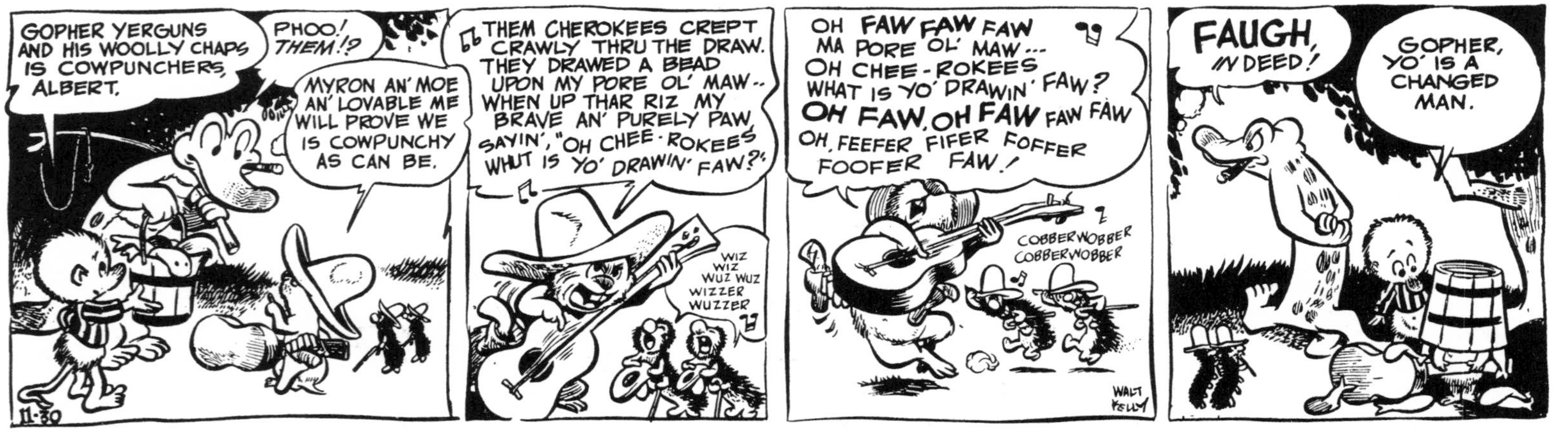
GOPHER YERGUNS AND HIS WOOLLY CHAPS IS COWPUNCHERS, ALBERT.
PHOO! THEM!?
MYRON AN' MOE AN' LOVABLE ME WILL PROVE WE IS COWPUNCHY AS CAN BE.
11-30
"THEM CHEROKEES CREPT CRAWLY THRU THE DRAW. THEY DRAWED A BEAD UPON MY PORE OL' MAW -- WHEN UP THAR RIZ MY BRAVE AN' PURELY PAW, SAYIN', "OH CHEE-ROKEES WHUT IS YO' DRAWIN' FAW?"
WIZ WIZ WUZ WUZ WIZZER WUZZER
OH FAW FAW FAW MA PORE OL' MAW... OH CHEE-ROKEES WHAT IS YO' DRAWIN' FAW? OH FAW, OH FAW FAW FAW OH, FEEFER FIFER FOFFER FOOFER FAW!"
COBBERWOBBER COBBERWOBBER
WALT KELLY
FAUGH, INDEED!
GOPHER, YO' IS A CHANGED MAN.

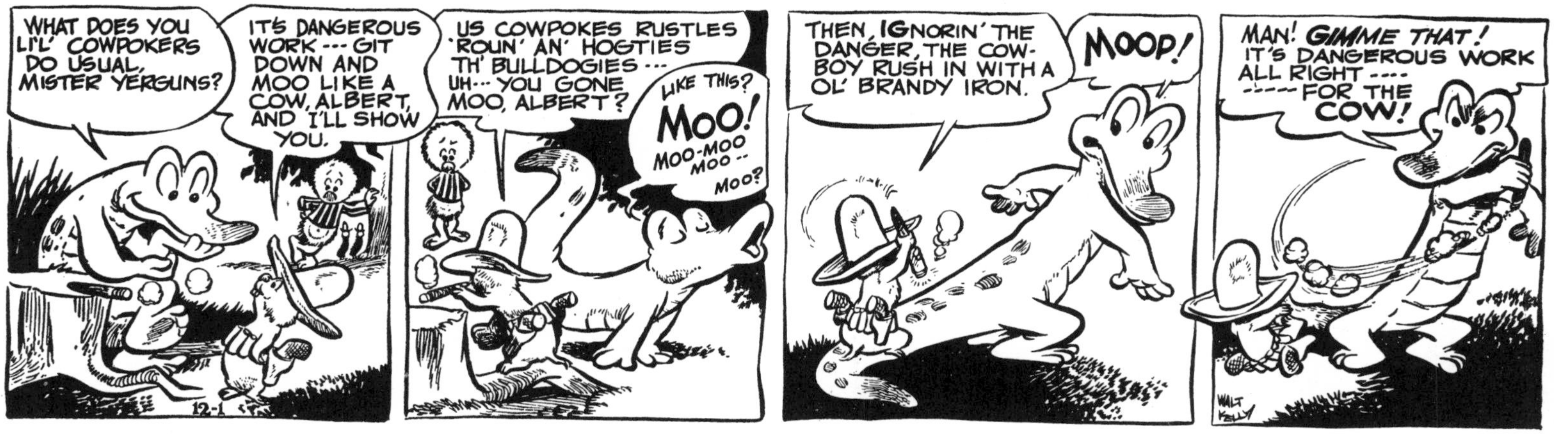
WHAT DOES YOU LI'L' COWPOKERS DO USUAL, MISTER YERGUNS?
IT'S DANGEROUS WORK --- GIT DOWN AND MOO LIKE A COW, ALBERT, AND I'LL SHOW YOU.
US COWPOKES RUSTLES 'ROUN' AN' HOGTIES TH' BULLDOGIES --- UH--- YOU GONE MOO, ALBERT?
LIKE THIS? MOO! MOO-MOO MOO -- MOO?
THEN, IGNORIN' THE DANGER, THE COW-BOY RUSH IN WITH A OL' BRANDY IRON.
MOOP!
MAN! GIMME THAT! IT'S DANGEROUS WORK ALL RIGHT ---- ----- FOR THE COW!
12-1
WALT KELLY

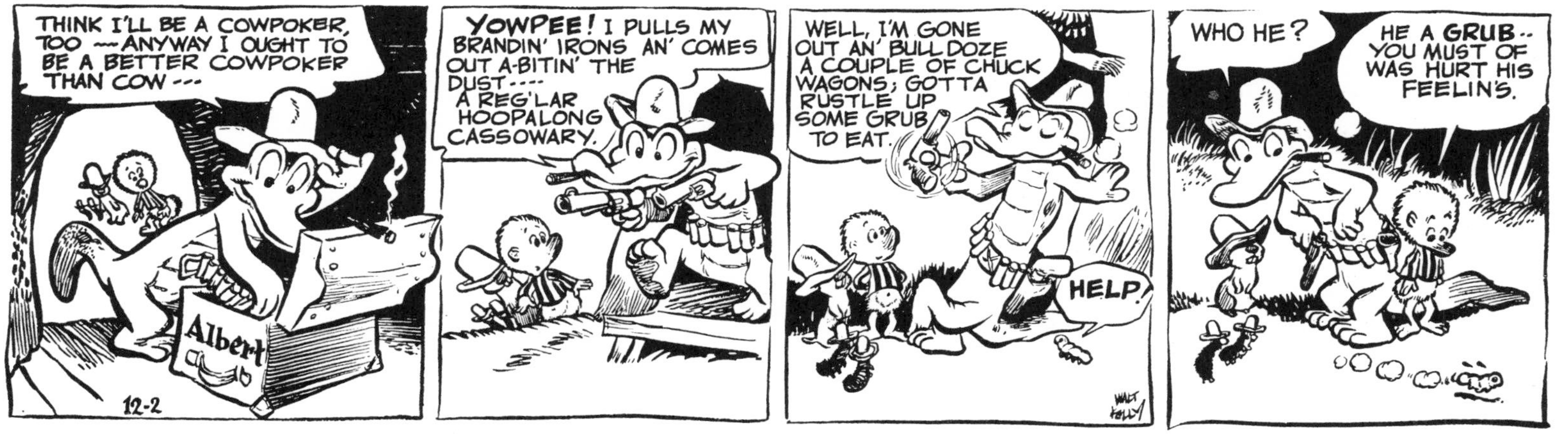
THINK I'LL BE A COWPOKER, TOO --- ANYWAY I OUGHT TO BE A BETTER COWPOKER THAN COW ---
Albert
12-2
YOWPEE! I PULLS MY BRANDIN' IRONS AN' COMES OUT A-BITIN' THE DUST---- A REG'LAR HOOPALONG CASSOWARY.
WELL, I'M GONE OUT AN' BULL DOZE A COUPLE OF CHUCK WAGONS; GOTTA RUSTLE UP SOME GRUB TO EAT.
HELP!
WALT KELLY
WHO HE?
HE A GRUB -- YOU MUST OF WAS HURT HIS FEELIN'S.

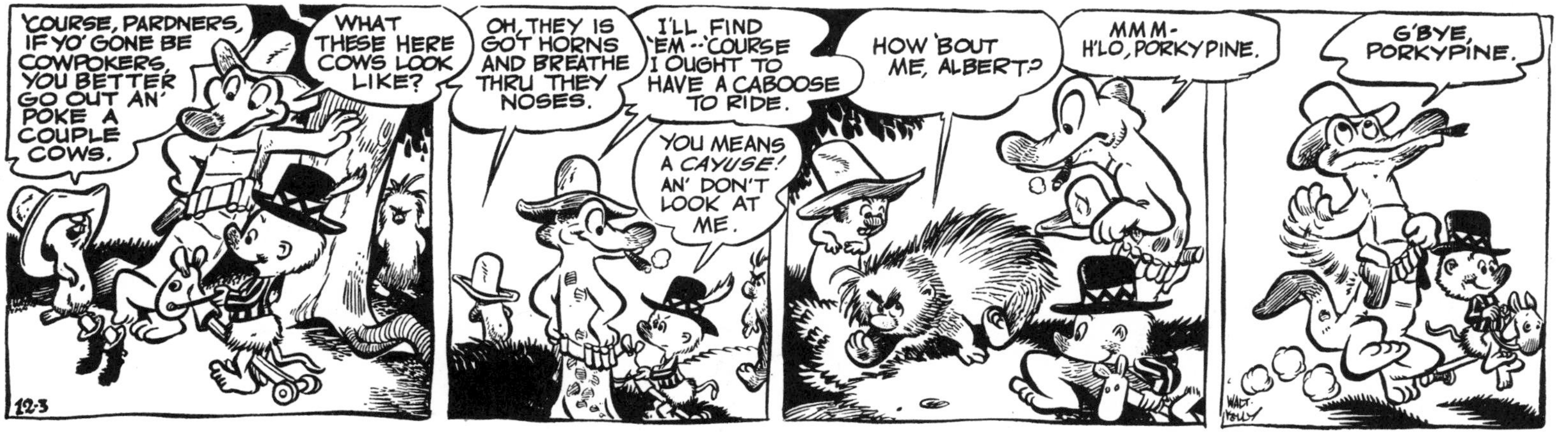
'COURSE, PARDNERS, IF YO' GONE BE COWPOKERS, YOU BETTER GO OUT AN' POKE A COUPLE COWS.
WHAT THESE HERE COWS LOOK LIKE?
12-3
OH, THEY IS GOT HORNS AND BREATHE THRU THEY NOSES.
I'LL FIND 'EM -- 'COURSE I OUGHT TO HAVE A CABOOSE TO RIDE.
YOU MEANS A CAYUSE! AN' DON'T LOOK AT ME.
HOW 'BOUT ME, ALBERT?
MMM- H'LO, PORKYPINE.
G'BYE, PORKYPINE.
WALT KELLY

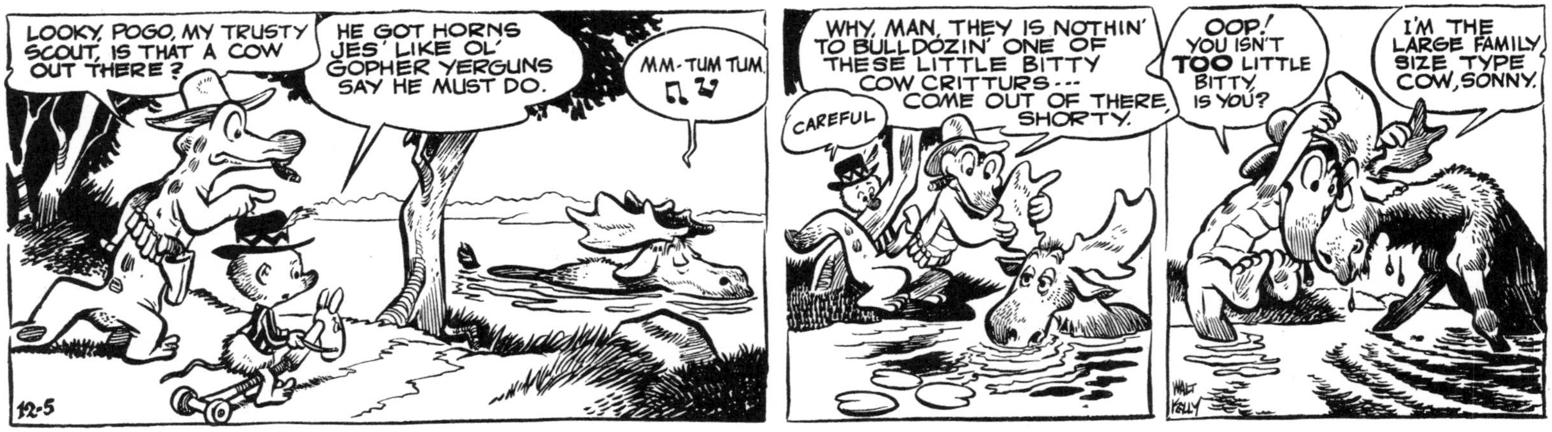
LOOKY, POGO, MY TRUSTY SCOUT, IS THAT A COW OUT THERE?
HE GOT HORNS JES' LIKE OL' GOPHER YERGUNS SAY HE MUST DO.
MM-TUM TUM
WHY, MAN, THEY IS NOTHIN' TO BULLDOZIN' ONE OF THESE LITTLE BITTY COW CRITTURS--- COME OUT OF THERE, SHORTY.
CAREFUL
OOP! YOU ISN'T TOO LITTLE BITTY, IS YOU?
I'M THE LARGE FAMILY SIZE TYPE COW, SONNY.
12-5
WALT KELLY

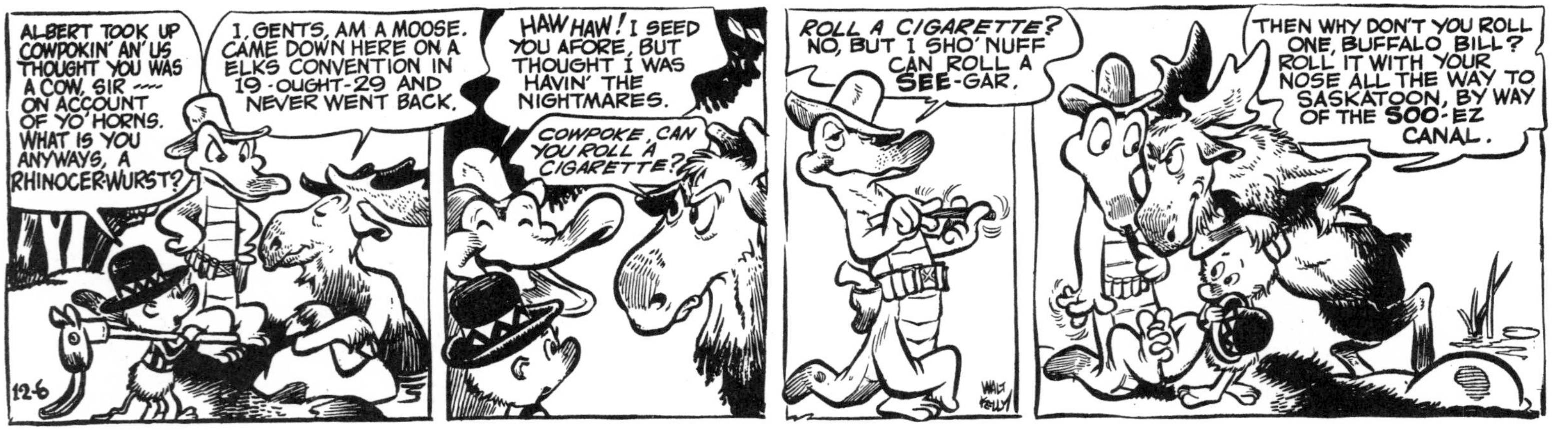
ALBERT TOOK UP COWPOKIN' AN' US THOUGHT YOU WAS A COW, SIR ---- ON ACCOUNT OF YO' HORNS. WHAT IS YOU ANYWAYS, A RHINOCER-WURST?
I, GENTS, AM A MOOSE. CAME DOWN HERE ON A ELKS CONVENTION IN 19-OUGHT-29 AND NEVER WENT BACK.
HAW HAW! I SEED YOU AFORE, BUT THOUGHT I WAS HAVIN' THE NIGHTMARES.
COWPOKE, CAN YOU ROLL A CIGARETTE?
ROLL A CIGARETTE? NO, BUT I SHO' NUFF CAN ROLL A SEE-GAR.
THEN WHY DON'T YOU ROLL ONE, BUFFALO BILL? ROLL IT WITH YOUR NOSE ALL THE WAY TO SASKATOON, BY WAY OF THE SOO-EZ CANAL.
12-6
WALT KELLY

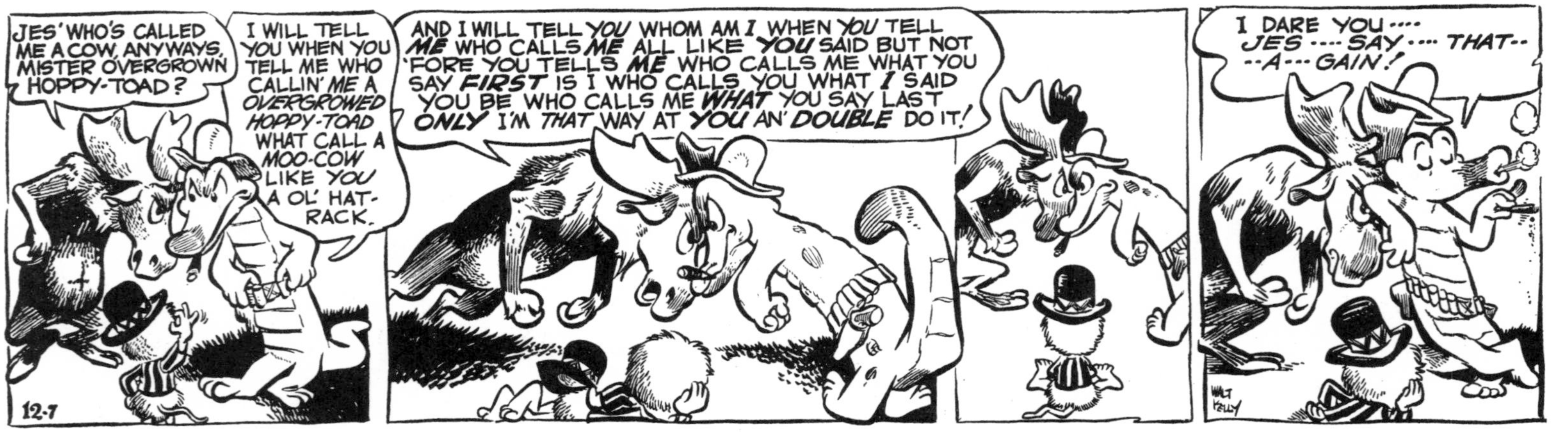
JES' WHO'S CALLED ME A COW, ANYWAYS, MISTER OVERGROWN HOPPY-TOAD?
I WILL TELL YOU WHEN YOU TELL ME WHO CALLIN' ME A OVERGROWED HOPPY-TOAD WHAT CALL A MOO-COW LIKE YOU A OL' HAT-RACK.
AND I WILL TELL YOU WHOM AM I WHEN YOU TELL ME WHO CALLS ME ALL LIKE YOU SAID BUT NOT 'FORE YOU TELLS ME WHO CALLS ME WHAT YOU SAY FIRST IS I WHO CALLS YOU WHAT I SAID YOU BE WHO CALLS ME WHAT YOU SAY LAST ONLY I'M THAT WAY AT YOU AN' DOUBLE DO IT!
I DARE YOU ···· JES ···· SAY ···· THAT-- --A--- GAIN!
12-7
WALT KELLY

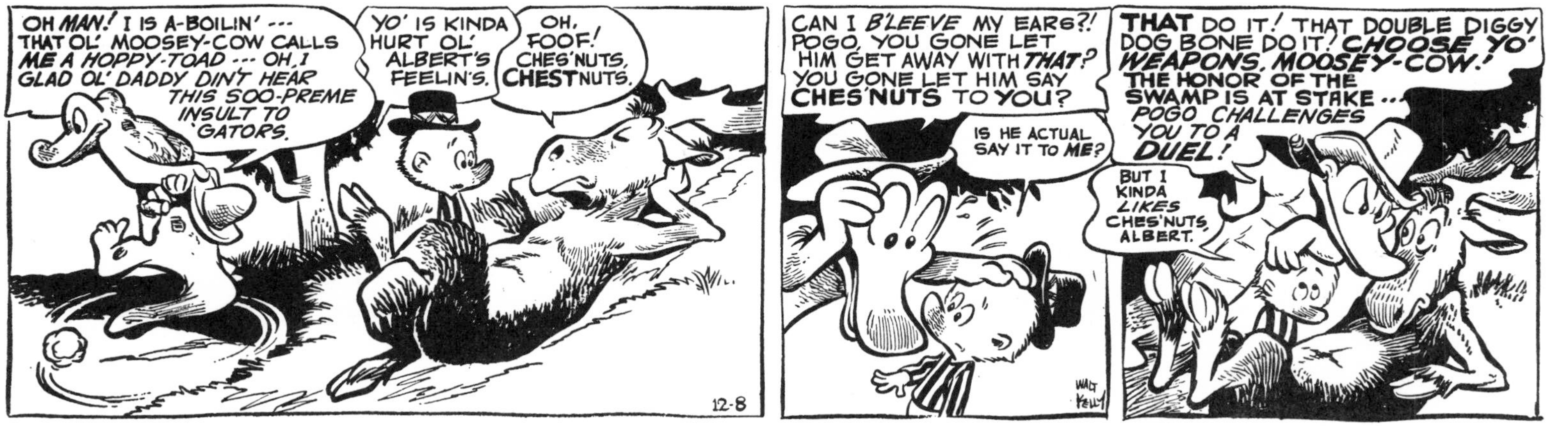
OH MAN! I IS A-BOILIN' --- THAT OL' MOOSEY-COW CALLS ME A HOPPY-TOAD --- OH, I GLAD OL' DADDY DIN'T HEAR THIS SOO-PREME INSULT TO GATORS.
YO' IS KINDA HURT OL' ALBERT'S FEELIN'S.
OH, FOOF! CHES'NUTS, CHESTNUTS.
12-8
CAN I B'LEEVE MY EARS?! POGO, YOU GONE LET HIM GET AWAY WITH THAT? YOU GONE LET HIM SAY CHES'NUTS TO YOU?
IS HE ACTUAL SAY IT TO ME?
THAT DO IT! THAT DOUBLE DIGGY DOG BONE DO IT! CHOOSE YO' WEAPONS, MOOSEY-COW! THE HONOR OF THE SWAMP IS AT STAKE... POGO CHALLENGES YOU TO A DUEL!
BUT I KINDA LIKES CHES'NUTS, ALBERT.
WALT KELLY

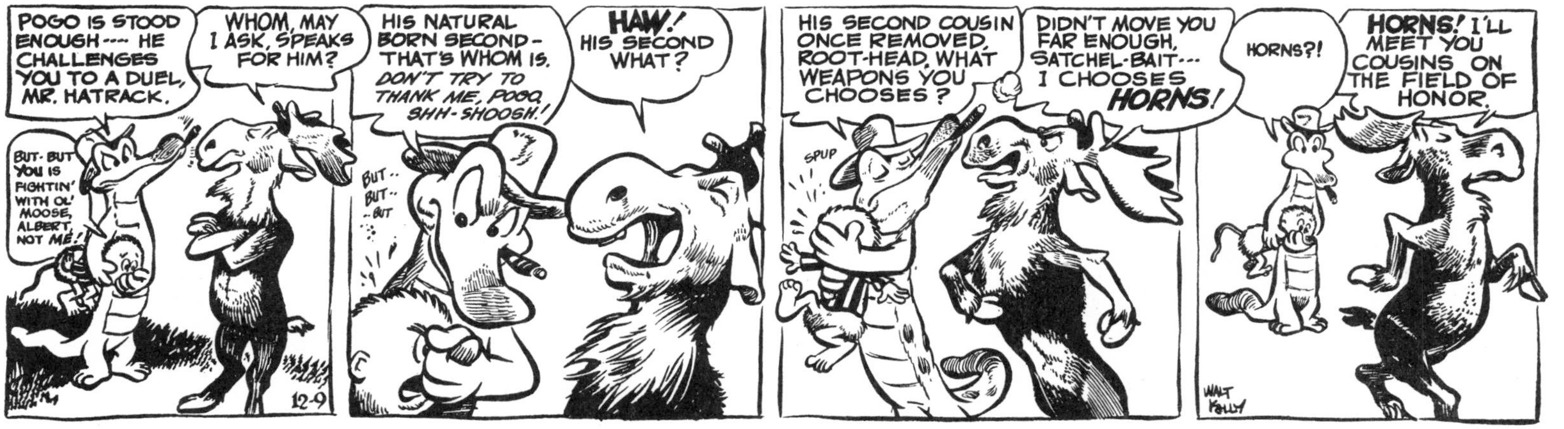
POGO IS STOOD ENOUGH --- HE CHALLENGES YOU TO A DUEL, MR. HATRACK.
WHOM, MAY I ASK, SPEAKS FOR HIM?
BUT-BUT YOU IS FIGHTIN' WITH OL' MOOSE, ALBERT, NOT ME!
12-9
HIS NATURAL BORN SECOND - THAT'S WHOM IS. DON'T TRY TO THANK ME, POGO, SHH-SHOOSH!
HAW! HIS SECOND WHAT?
BUT.. BUT.. ..BUT
HIS SECOND COUSIN ONCE REMOVED, ROOT-HEAD. WHAT WEAPONS YOU CHOOSES?
DIDN'T MOVE YOU FAR ENOUGH, SATCHEL-BAIT... I CHOOSES HORNS!
SPUP
HORNS?!
HORNS! I'LL MEET YOU COUSINS ON THE FIELD OF HONOR.
WALT KELLY

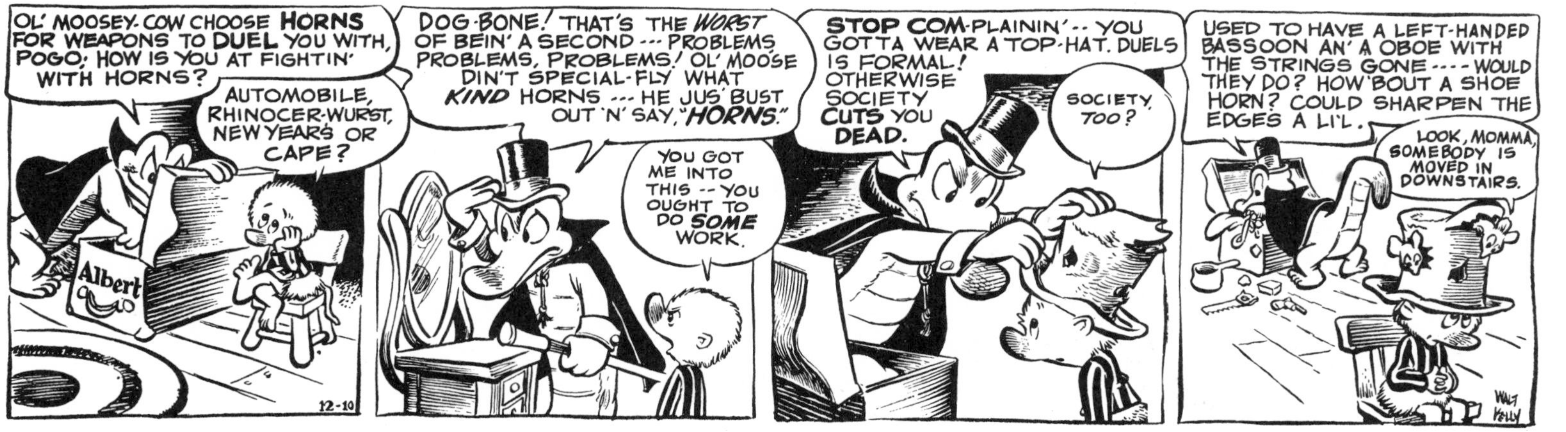
OL' MOOSEY-COW CHOOSE HORNS FOR WEAPONS TO DUEL YOU WITH, POGO; HOW IS YOU AT FIGHTIN' WITH HORNS?
AUTOMOBILE, RHINOCER-WURST, NEW YEARS OR CAPE?
Albert
12-10
DOG-BONE! THAT'S THE WORST OF BEIN' A SECOND --- PROBLEMS, PROBLEMS, PROBLEMS! OL' MOOSE DIN'T SPECIAL-FLY WHAT KIND HORNS --- HE JUS' BUST OUT 'N' SAY, "HORNS."
YOU GOT ME INTO THIS -- YOU OUGHT TO DO SOME WORK.
STOP COM-PLAININ' -- YOU GOTTA WEAR A TOP-HAT. DUELS IS FORMAL! OTHERWISE SOCIETY CUTS YOU DEAD.
SOCIETY, TOO?
USED TO HAVE A LEFT-HANDED BASSOON AN' A OBOE WITH THE STRINGS GONE ---- WOULD THEY DO? HOW 'BOUT A SHOE HORN? COULD SHARPEN THE EDGES A LI'L.
LOOK, MOMMA, SOMEBODY IS MOVED IN DOWNSTAIRS.
WALT KELLY

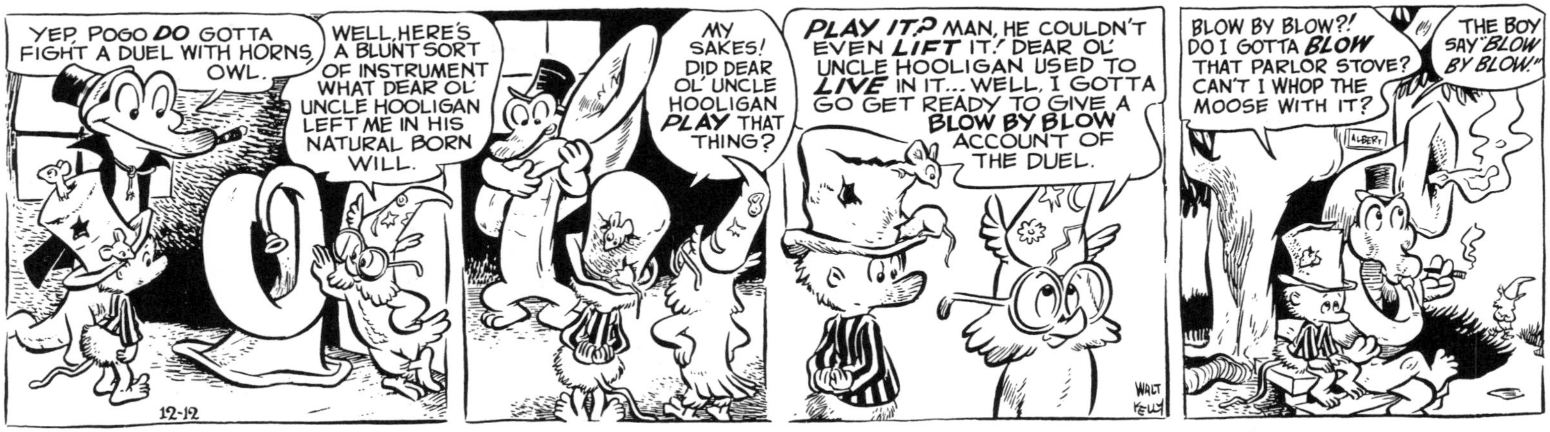
YEP, POGO **DO** GOTTA FIGHT A DUEL WITH HORNS, OWL.
WELL, HERE'S A BLUNT SORT OF INSTRUMENT WHAT DEAR OL' UNCLE HOOLIGAN LEFT ME IN HIS NATURAL BORN WILL.
12-12
MY SAKES! DID DEAR OL' UNCLE HOOLIGAN **PLAY** THAT THING?
PLAY IT? MAN, HE COULDN'T EVEN **LIFT** IT! DEAR OL' UNCLE HOOLIGAN USED TO **LIVE** IN IT... WELL, I GOTTA GO GET READY TO GIVE A **BLOW BY BLOW** ACCOUNT OF THE DUEL.
BLOW BY BLOW?! DO I GOTTA **BLOW** THAT PARLOR STOVE? CAN'T I WHOP THE MOOSE WITH IT?
THE BOY SAY "*BLOW BY BLOW.*"
ALBERT
WALT KELLY

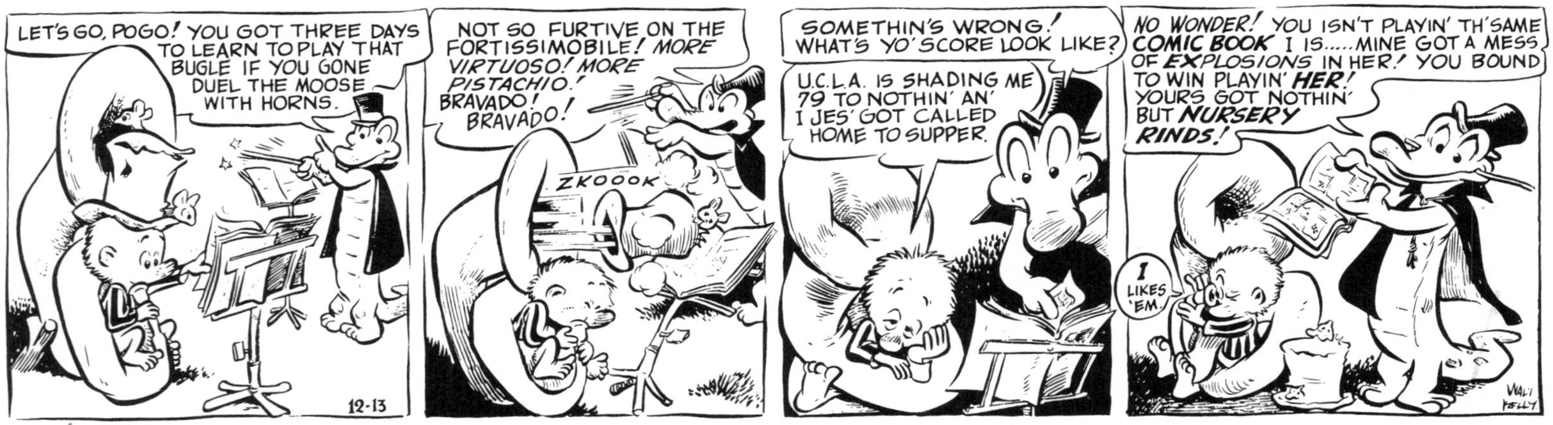
LET'S GO, POGO! YOU GOT THREE DAYS TO LEARN TO PLAY THAT BUGLE IF YOU GONE DUEL THE MOOSE WITH HORNS.
12-13
NOT SO FURTIVE ON THE FORTISSIMOBILE! *MORE VIRTUOSO! MORE PISTACHIO!* BRAVADO! BRAVADO!
ZKOOOK
SOMETHIN'S WRONG! WHAT'S YO' SCORE LOOK LIKE?
U.C.L.A. IS SHADING ME 79 TO NOTHIN' AN' I JES' GOT CALLED HOME TO SUPPER.
NO WONDER! YOU ISN'T PLAYIN' TH' SAME **COMIC BOOK** I IS..... MINE GOT A MESS OF ***EXPLOSIONS*** IN HER! YOU BOUND TO WIN PLAYIN' ***HER!*** YOURS GOT NOTHIN' BUT ***NURSERY RINDS!***
I LIKES 'EM.
WALT KELLY

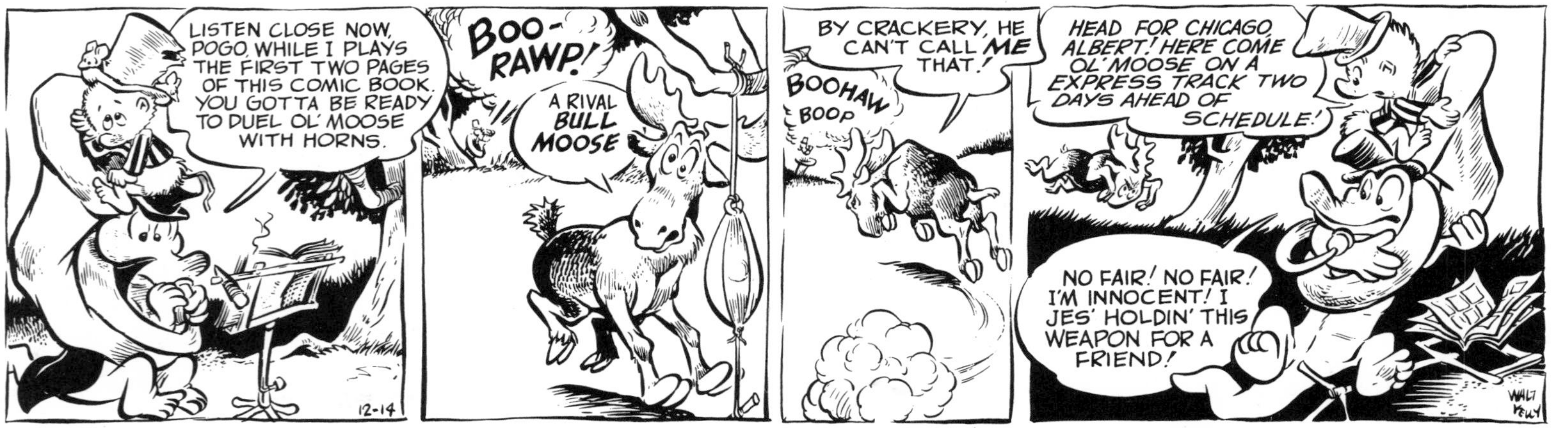
LISTEN CLOSE NOW, POGO, WHILE I PLAYS THE FIRST TWO PAGES OF THIS COMIC BOOK. YOU GOTTA BE READY TO DUEL OL' MOOSE WITH HORNS.
12-14
BOO-RAWP!
A RIVAL **BULL MOOSE**
BY CRACKERY, HE CAN'T CALL **ME** THAT!
BOOHAW
BOOP
HEAD FOR CHICAGO, ALBERT! HERE COME OL' MOOSE ON A EXPRESS TRACK TWO DAYS AHEAD OF SCHEDULE!
NO FAIR! NO FAIR! I'M INNOCENT! I JES' HOLDIN' THIS WEAPON FOR A FRIEND!
WALT KELLY

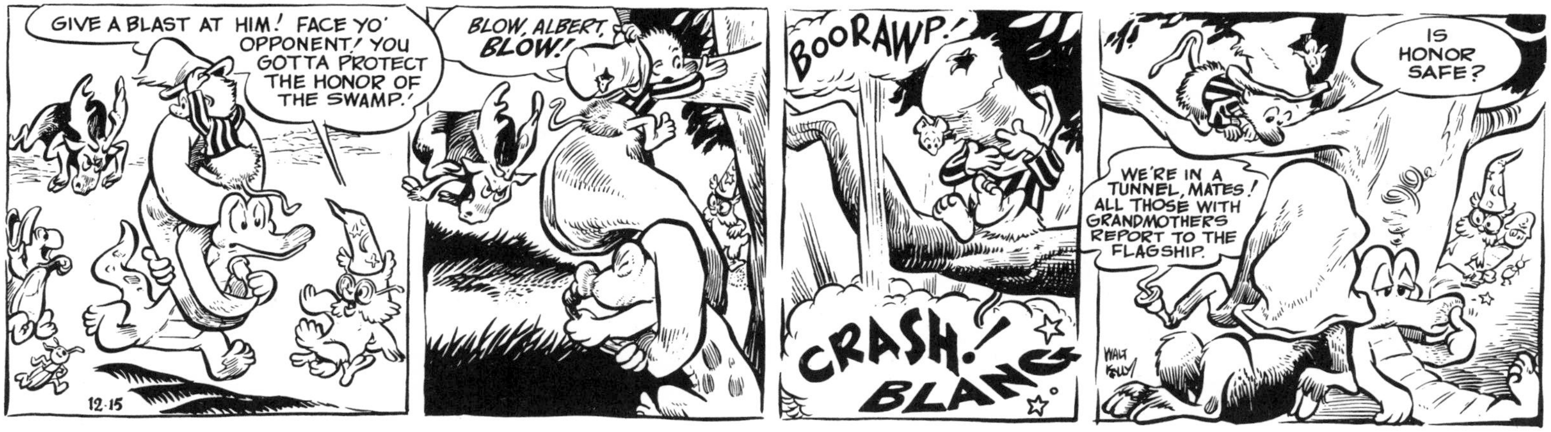
GIVE A BLAST AT HIM! FACE YO' OPPONENT! YOU GOTTA PROTECT THE HONOR OF THE SWAMP!
12-15
BLOW, ALBERT, BLOW!
BOORAWP!
CRASH! BLANG
IS HONOR SAFE?
WE'RE IN A TUNNEL, MATES! ALL THOSE WITH GRANDMOTHERS REPORT TO THE FLAGSHIP.
WALT KELLY

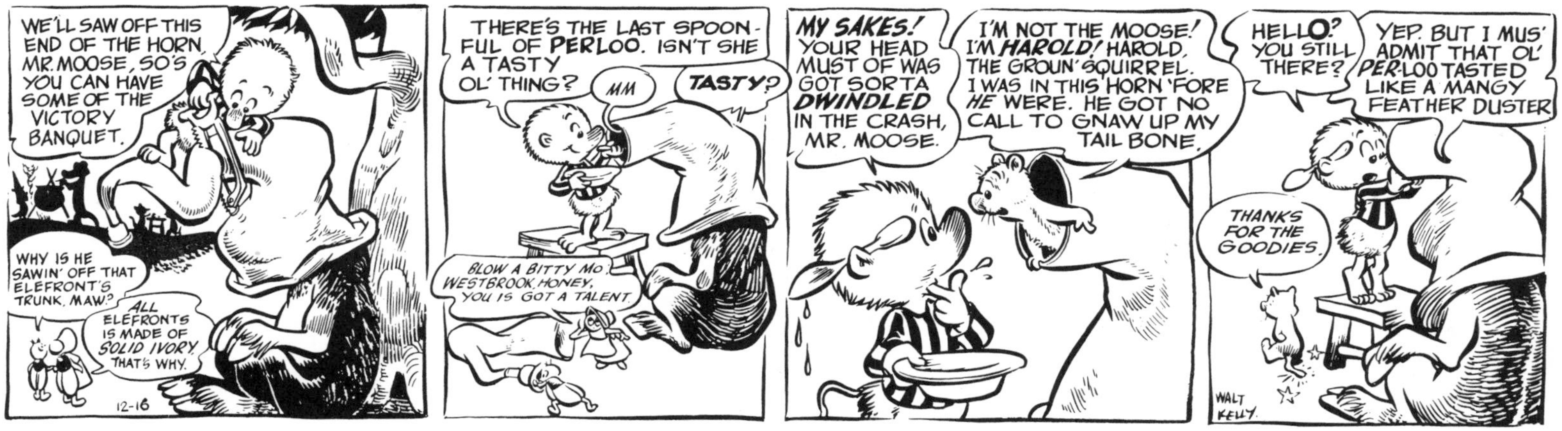
WE'LL SAW OFF THIS END OF THE HORN, MR. MOOSE, SO'S YOU CAN HAVE SOME OF THE VICTORY BANQUET.
WHY IS HE SAWIN' OFF THAT ELEFRONT'S TRUNK, MAW?
ALL ELEFRONTS IS MADE OF SOLID IVORY. THAT'S WHY.
12-16
THERE'S THE LAST SPOON-FUL OF PERLOO. ISN'T SHE A TASTY OL' THING?
MM
TASTY?
BLOW A BITTY MO', WESTBROOK HONEY, YOU IS GOT A TALENT.
MY SAKES! YOUR HEAD MUST OF WAS GOT SORTA DWINDLED IN THE CRASH, MR. MOOSE.
I'M NOT THE MOOSE! I'M HAROLD! HAROLD, THE GROUN' SQUIRREL. I WAS IN THIS HORN 'FORE HE WERE. HE GOT NO CALL TO GNAW UP MY TAIL BONE.
HELLO? YOU STILL THERE?
YEP. BUT I MUS' ADMIT THAT OL' PER-LOO TASTED LIKE A MANGY FEATHER DUSTER.
THANKS FOR THE GOODIES.
WALT KELLY

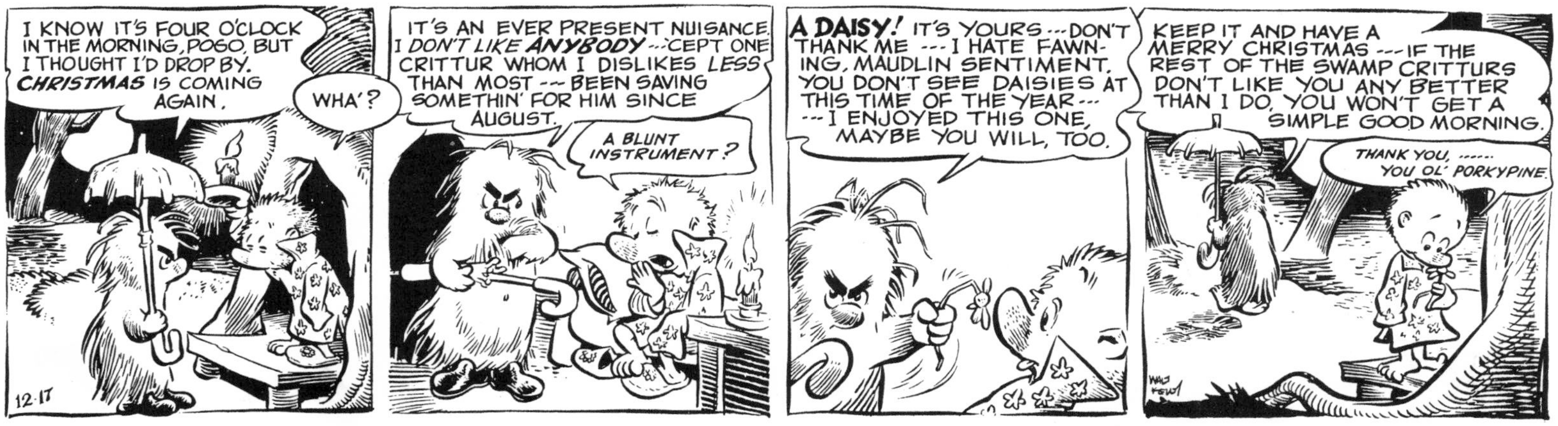
I KNOW IT'S FOUR O'CLOCK IN THE MORNING, POGO, BUT I THOUGHT I'D DROP BY. CHRISTMAS IS COMING AGAIN.
WHA'?
12-17
IT'S AN EVER PRESENT NUISANCE. I DON'T LIKE ANYBODY --'CEPT ONE CRITTUR WHOM I DISLIKES LESS THAN MOST -- BEEN SAVING SOMETHIN' FOR HIM SINCE AUGUST.
A BLUNT INSTRUMENT?
A DAISY! IT'S YOURS --- DON'T THANK ME --- I HATE FAWN-ING, MAUDLIN SENTIMENT. YOU DON'T SEE DAISIES AT THIS TIME OF THE YEAR--- --- I ENJOYED THIS ONE, MAYBE YOU WILL, TOO.
KEEP IT AND HAVE A MERRY CHRISTMAS --- IF THE REST OF THE SWAMP CRITTURS DON'T LIKE YOU ANY BETTER THAN I DO, YOU WON'T GET A SIMPLE GOOD MORNING.
THANK YOU, ... YOU OL' PORKYPINE.
WALT KELLY

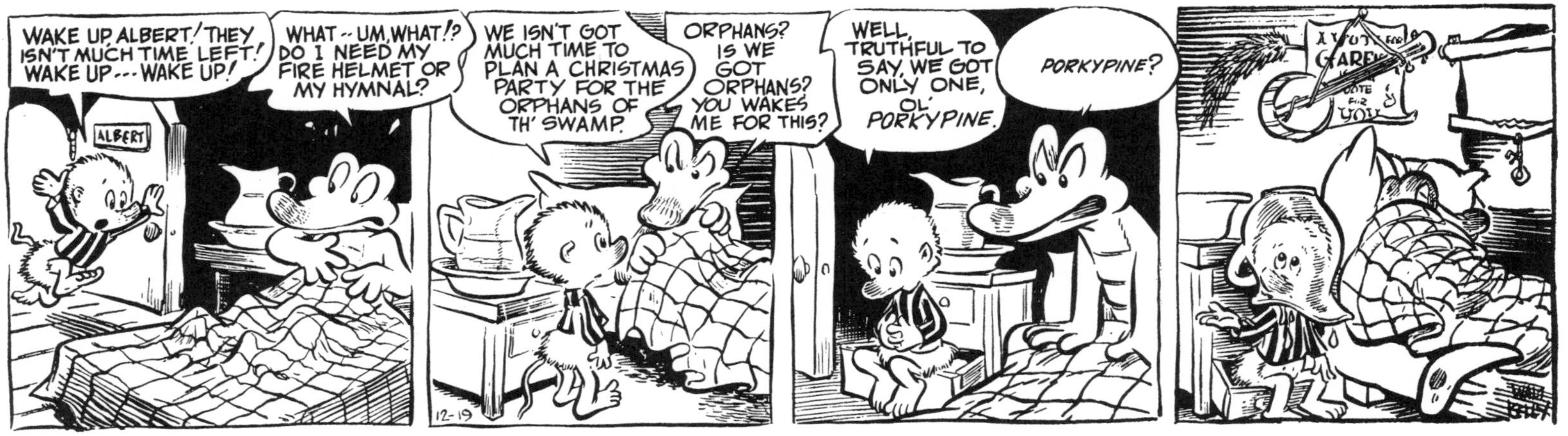
WAKE UP, ALBERT! THEY ISN'T MUCH TIME LEFT! WAKE UP--- WAKE UP!
ALBERT
WHAT -- UM, WHAT!? DO I NEED MY FIRE HELMET OR MY HYMNAL?
WE ISN'T GOT MUCH TIME TO PLAN A CHRISTMAS PARTY FOR THE ORPHANS OF TH' SWAMP.
ORPHANS? IS WE GOT ORPHANS? YOU WAKES ME FOR THIS?
12-19
WELL, TRUTHFUL TO SAY, WE GOT ONLY ONE, OL' PORKYPINE.
PORKYPINE?
WALT KELLY

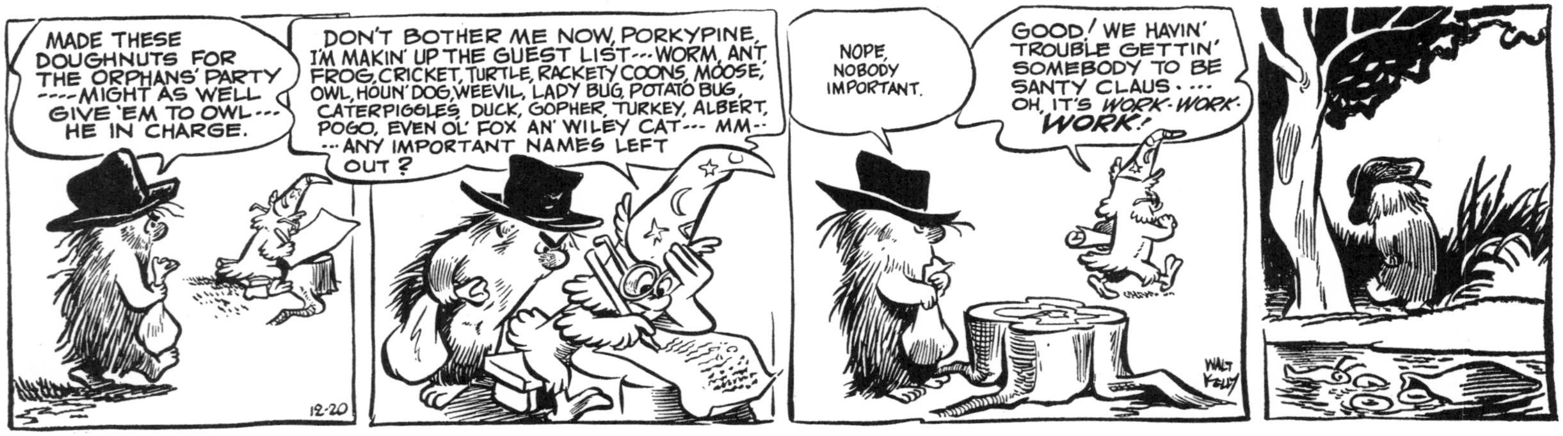
MADE THESE DOUGHNUTS FOR THE ORPHANS' PARTY ----MIGHT AS WELL GIVE 'EM TO OWL--- HE IN CHARGE.
12-20
DON'T BOTHER ME NOW, PORKYPINE, I'M MAKIN' UP THE GUEST LIST--- WORM, ANT, FROG, CRICKET, TURTLE, RACKETY COONS, MOOSE, OWL, HOUN' DOG, WEEVIL, LADY BUG, POTATO BUG, CATERPIGGLES, DUCK, GOPHER, TURKEY, ALBERT, POGO, EVEN OL' FOX AN' WILEY CAT--- MM-- --- ANY IMPORTANT NAMES LEFT OUT?
NOPE, NOBODY IMPORTANT.
GOOD! WE HAVIN' TROUBLE GETTIN' SOMEBODY TO BE SANTY CLAUS. --- OH, IT'S WORK-WORK-WORK!
WALT KELLY

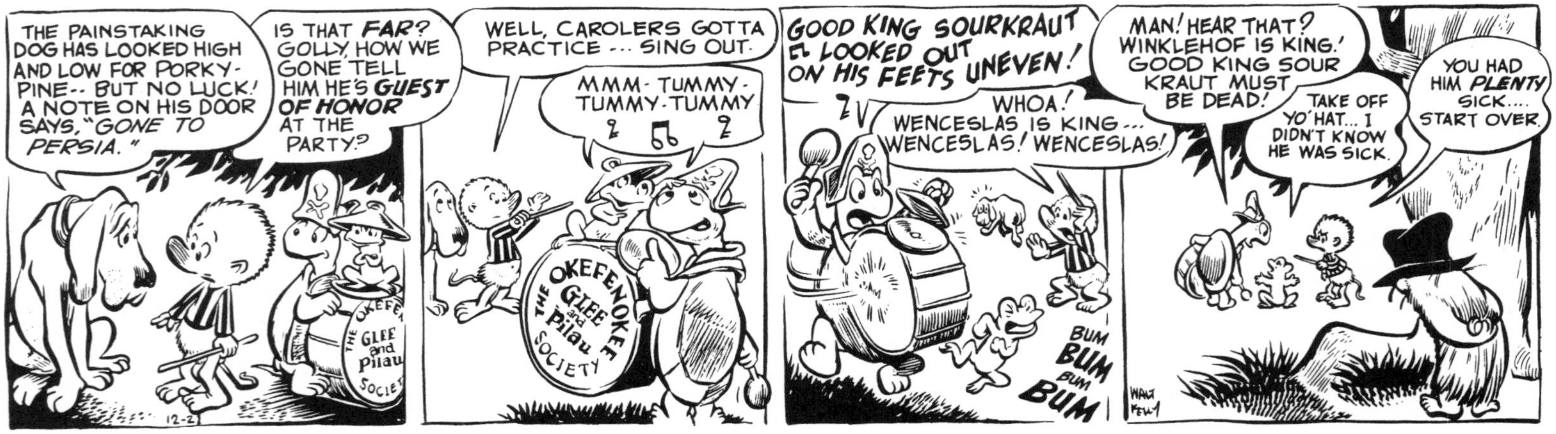
THE PAINSTAKING DOG HAS LOOKED HIGH AND LOW FOR PORKY-PINE-- BUT NO LUCK! A NOTE ON HIS DOOR SAYS, "GONE TO PERSIA."
IS THAT FAR? GOLLY, HOW WE GONE TELL HIM HE'S GUEST OF HONOR AT THE PARTY?
THE OKEFENOKEE GLEE and Pilau SOCIETY
WELL, CAROLERS GOTTA PRACTICE --- SING OUT.
MMM-TUMMY-TUMMY-TUMMY
THE OKEFENOKEE GLEE and Pilau SOCIETY
GOOD KING SOURKRAUT EL LOOKED OUT ON HIS FEETS UNEVEN!
WHOA! WENCESLAS IS KING... WENCESLAS! WENCESLAS!
BUM BUM BUM BUM
WALT KELLY
MAN! HEAR THAT? WINKLEHOF IS KING! GOOD KING SOUR KRAUT MUST BE DEAD!
TAKE OFF YO' HAT... I DIDN'T KNOW HE WAS SICK.
YOU HAD HIM PLENTY SICK.... START OVER.

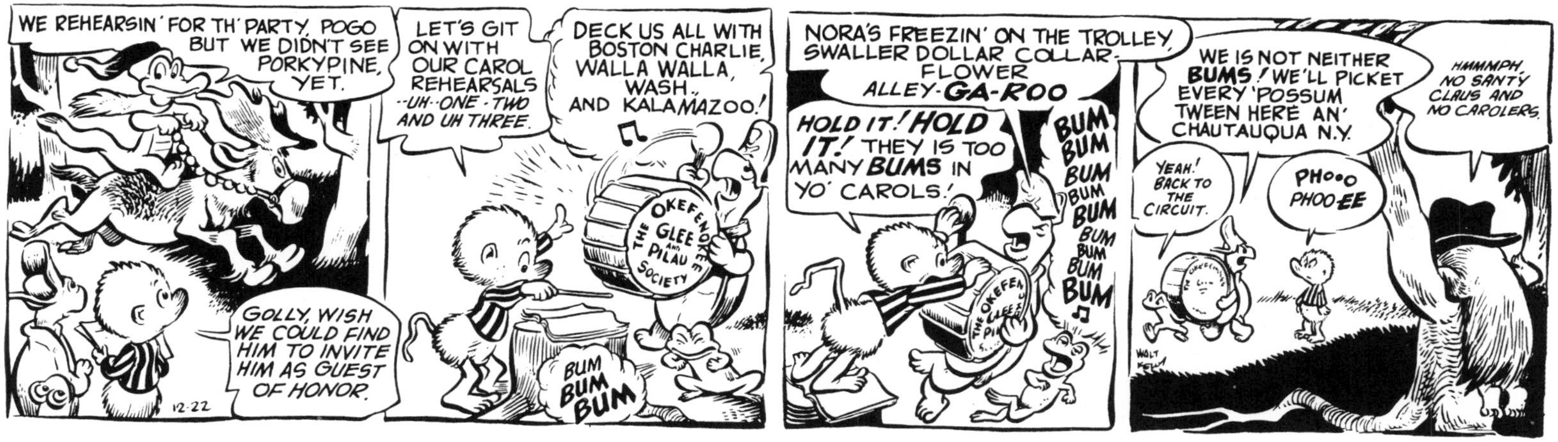
WE REHEARSIN' FOR TH' PARTY, POGO BUT WE DIDN'T SEE PORKYPINE, YET.
GOLLY, WISH WE COULD FIND HIM TO INVITE HIM AS GUEST OF HONOR.
12-22
LET'S GIT ON WITH OUR CAROL REHEARSALS --UH--ONE - TWO AND UH THREE.
DECK US ALL WITH BOSTON CHARLIE, WALLA WALLA, WASH., AND KALAMAZOO!
THE OKEFENOKEE GLEE AND PILAU SOCIETY
BUM BUM BUM
NORA'S FREEZIN' ON THE TROLLEY, SWALLER DOLLAR COLLAR-FLOWER ALLEY-GA-ROO
HOLD IT! HOLD IT! THEY IS TOO MANY BUMS IN YO' CAROLS!
BUM BUM BUM BUM BUM BUM BUM BUM BUM
WE IS NOT NEITHER BUMS! WE'LL PICKET EVERY 'POSSUM TWEEN HERE AN' CHAUTAUQUA N.Y.
HMMMPH, NO SANTY CLAUS AND NO CAROLERS.
YEAH! BACK TO THE CIRCUIT.
PHOoo PHOO-EE
WALT KELLY

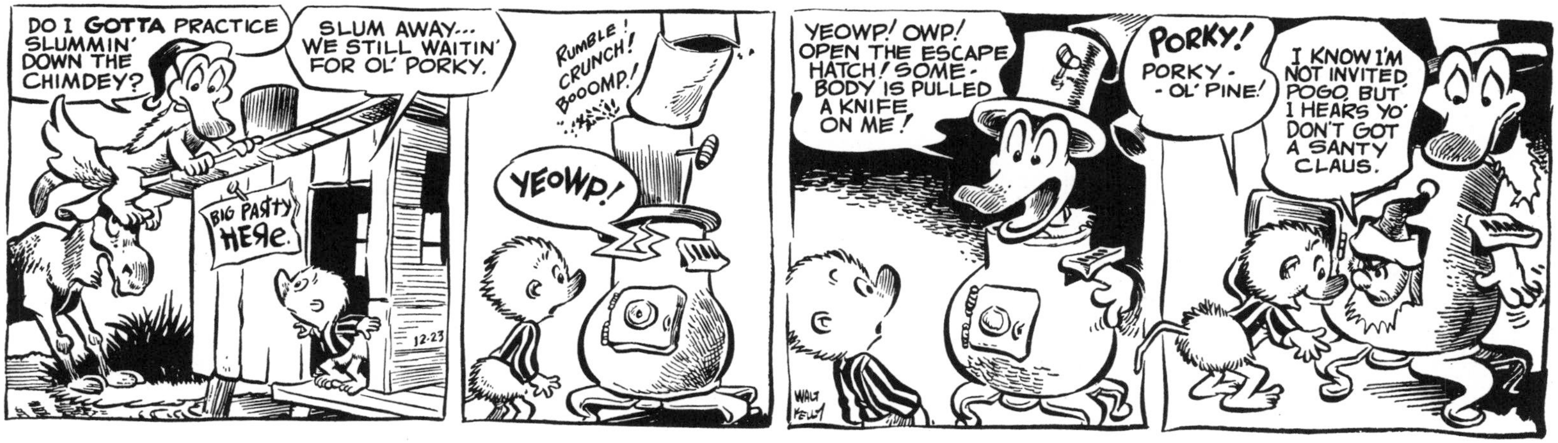
DO I GOTTA PRACTICE SLUMMIN' DOWN THE CHIMDEY?
SLUM AWAY... WE STILL WAITIN' FOR OL' PORKY.
BIG PARTY HERe.
12-23
RUMBLE! CRUNCH! BOOOMP!
YEOWP!
YEOWP! OWP! OPEN THE ESCAPE HATCH! SOME-BODY IS PULLED A KNIFE ON ME!
WALT KELLY
PORKY! PORKY - - OL' PINE!
I KNOW I'M NOT INVITED, POGO, BUT I HEARS YO' DON'T GOT A SANTY CLAUS.

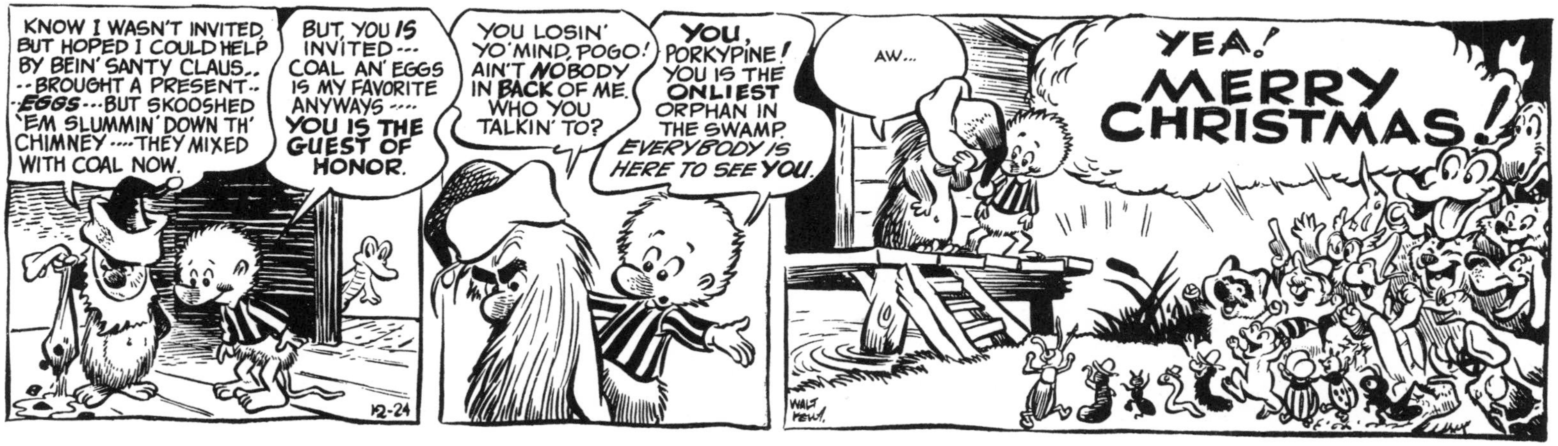
KNOW I WASN'T INVITED, BUT HOPED I COULD HELP BY BEIN' SANTY CLAUS.. --BROUGHT A PRESENT-- -EGGS---BUT SKOOSHED 'EM SLUMMIN' DOWN TH' CHIMNEY----THEY MIXED WITH COAL NOW.
BUT, YOU IS INVITED--- COAL AN' EGGS IS MY FAVORITE ANYWAYS---- YOU IS THE GUEST OF HONOR.
12-24
YOU LOSIN' YO' MIND, POGO! AIN'T NOBODY IN BACK OF ME. WHO YOU TALKIN' TO?
YOU, PORKYPINE! YOU IS THE ONLIEST ORPHAN IN THE SWAMP. EVERYBODY IS HERE TO SEE YOU.
AW...
YEA! MERRY CHRISTMAS!
WALT KELLY

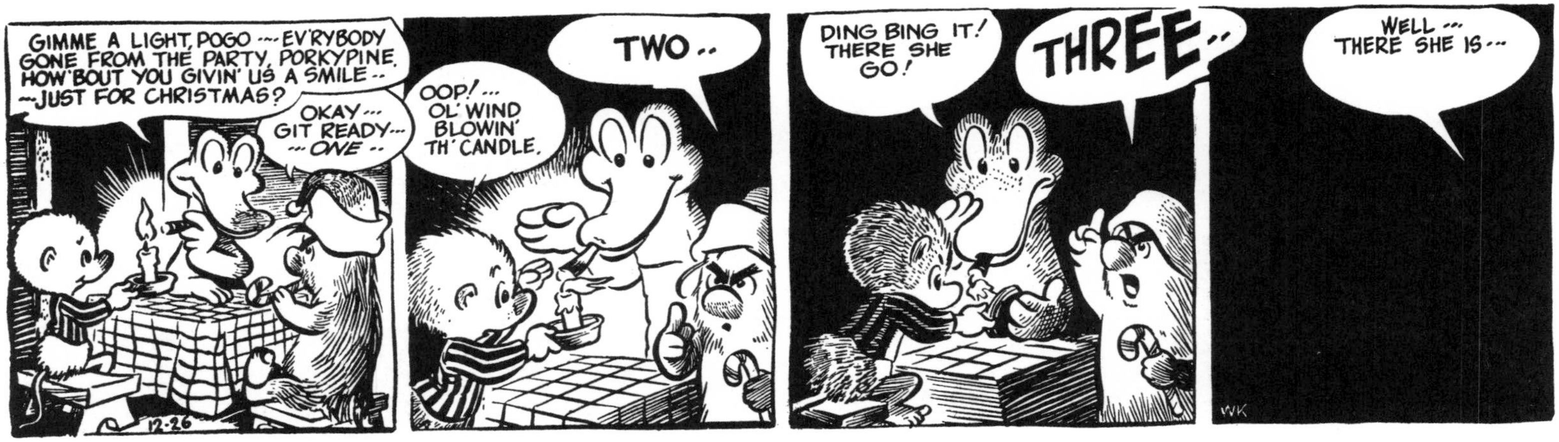
GIMME A LIGHT, POGO --- EV'RYBODY GONE FROM THE PARTY, PORKYPINE. HOW 'BOUT YOU GIVIN' US A SMILE -- --JUST FOR CHRISTMAS?
OKAY --- GIT READY--- --ONE --
OOP! --- OL' WIND BLOWIN' TH' CANDLE.
TWO ..
DING BING IT! THERE SHE GO!
THREE..
WELL --- THERE SHE IS ---
12-26
WK

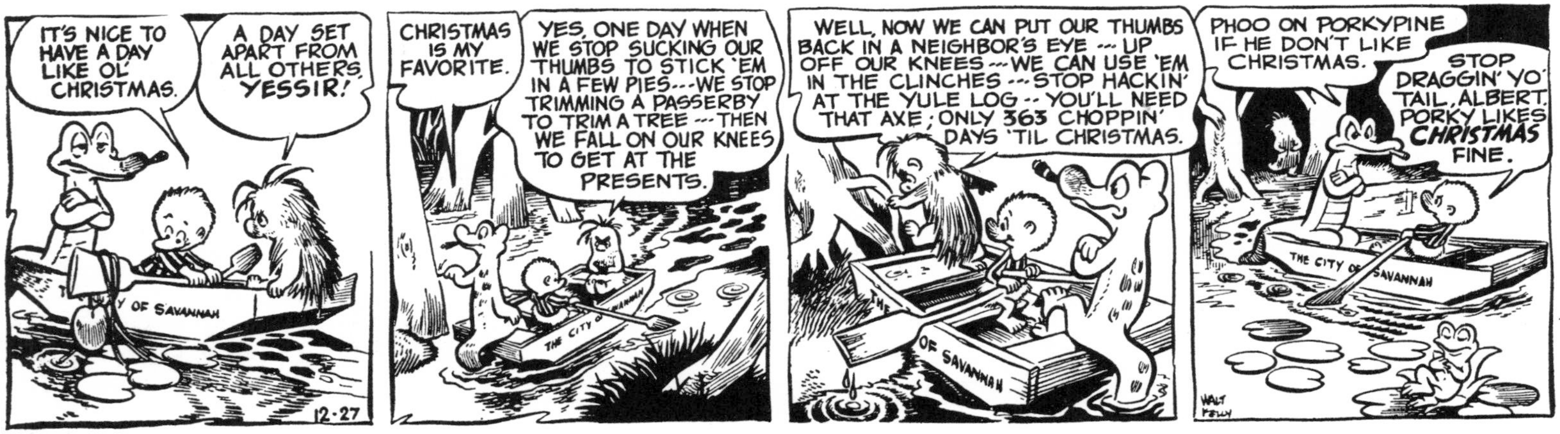
IT'S NICE TO HAVE A DAY LIKE OL' CHRISTMAS.
A DAY SET APART FROM ALL OTHERS. YESSIR!
CHRISTMAS IS MY FAVORITE.
YES, ONE DAY WHEN WE STOP SUCKING OUR THUMBS TO STICK 'EM IN A FEW PIES --- WE STOP TRIMMING A PASSERBY TO TRIM A TREE --- THEN WE FALL ON OUR KNEES TO GET AT THE PRESENTS.
WELL, NOW WE CAN PUT OUR THUMBS BACK IN A NEIGHBOR'S EYE --- UP OFF OUR KNEES --- WE CAN USE 'EM IN THE CLINCHES --- STOP HACKIN' AT THE YULE LOG -- YOU'LL NEED THAT AXE; ONLY 363 CHOPPIN' DAYS 'TIL CHRISTMAS.
PHOO ON PORKYPINE IF HE DON'T LIKE CHRISTMAS.
STOP DRAGGIN' YO' TAIL, ALBERT. PORKY LIKES CHRISTMAS FINE.
OF SAVANNAH
THE CITY OF SAVANNAH
12-27
WALT KELLY

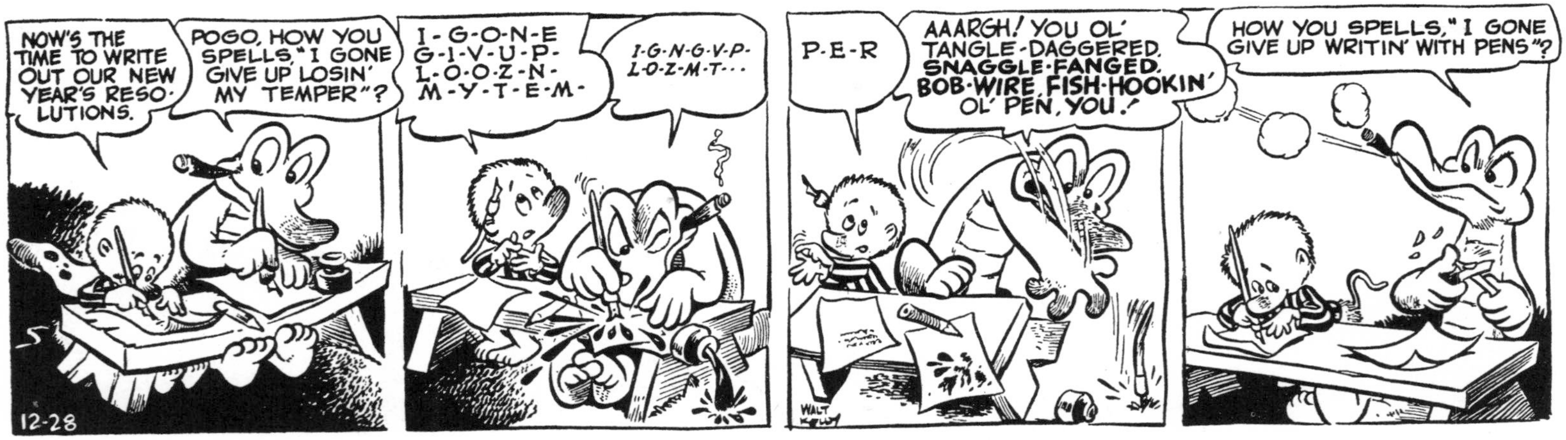
NOW'S THE TIME TO WRITE OUT OUR NEW YEAR'S RESO-LUTIONS.
POGO, HOW YOU SPELLS, "I GONE GIVE UP LOSIN' MY TEMPER"?
I-G-O-N-E G-I-V-U-P- L-O-O-Z-N- M-Y-T-E-M-
I-G-N-G-V-P- L-O-Z-M-T-...
P-E-R
AAARGH! YOU OL' TANGLE-DAGGERED, SNAGGLE-FANGED, BOB-WIRE, FISH-HOOKIN' OL' PEN, YOU!
HOW YOU SPELLS, "I GONE GIVE UP WRITIN' WITH PENS"?
12-28
WALT KELLY

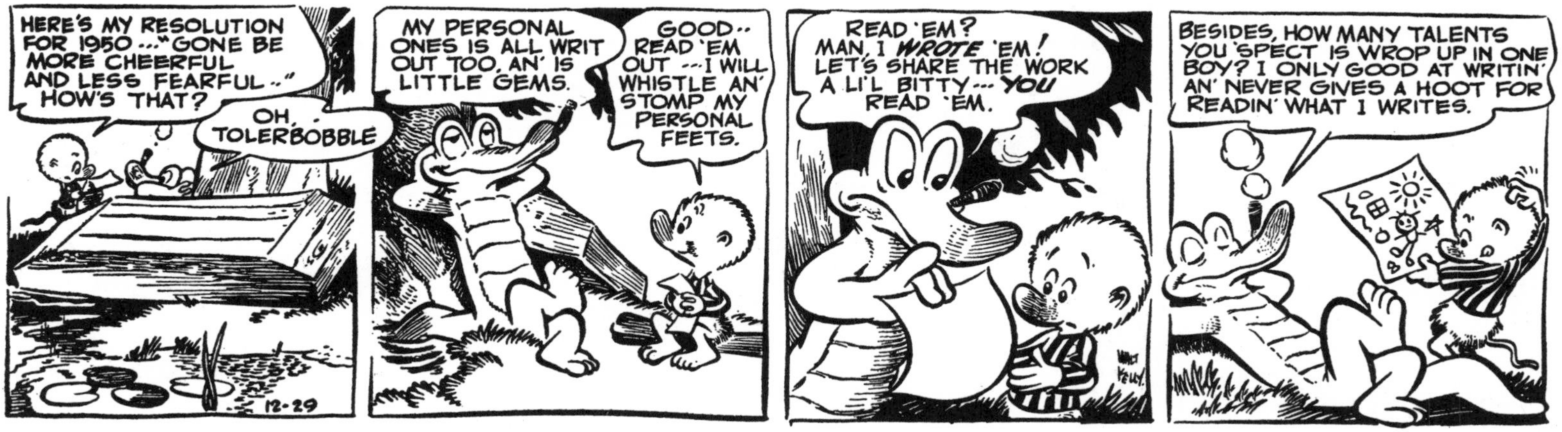
HERE'S MY RESOLUTION FOR 1950 ..."GONE BE MORE CHEERFUL AND LESS FEARFUL.." HOW'S THAT?
OH, TOLERBOBBLE
12-29
MY PERSONAL ONES IS ALL WRIT OUT TOO, AN' IS LITTLE GEMS.
GOOD.. READ 'EM OUT ---I WILL WHISTLE AN' STOMP MY PERSONAL FEETS.
READ 'EM? MAN, I WROTE 'EM! LET'S SHARE THE WORK A LI'L BITTY--- YOU READ 'EM.
WALT KELLY
BESIDES, HOW MANY TALENTS YOU 'SPECT IS WROP UP IN ONE BOY? I ONLY GOOD AT WRITIN' AN' NEVER GIVES A HOOT FOR READIN' WHAT I WRITES.

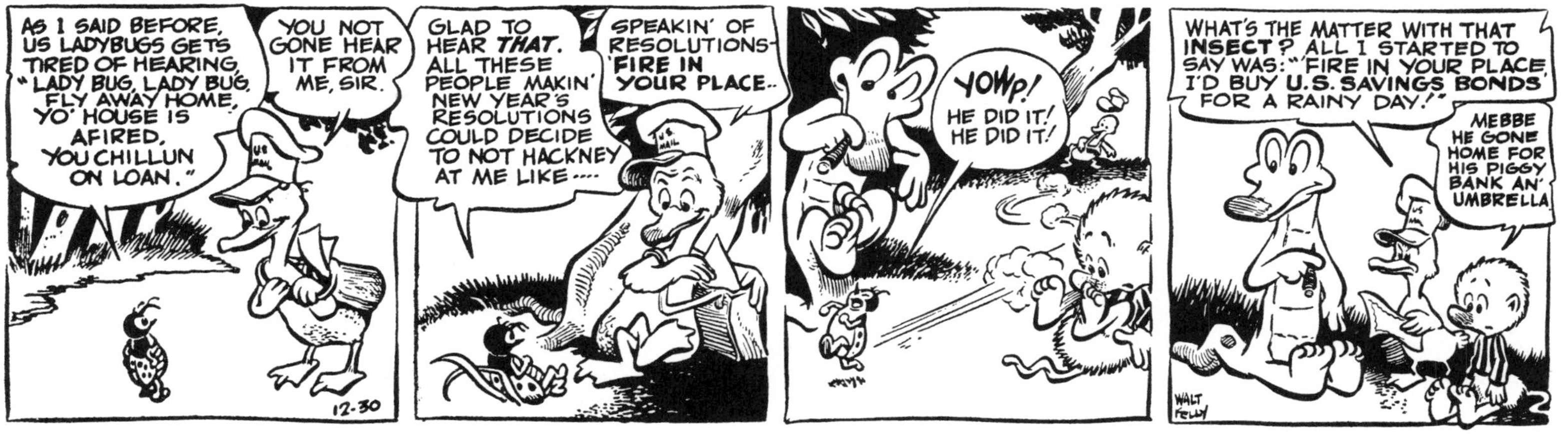
AS I SAID BEFORE, US LADYBUGS GETS TIRED OF HEARING, "LADY BUG, LADY BUG, FLY AWAY HOME, YO' HOUSE IS AFIRED, YOU CHILLUN ON LOAN."
YOU NOT GONE HEAR IT FROM ME, SIR.
12-30
GLAD TO HEAR THAT. ALL THESE PEOPLE MAKIN' NEW YEAR'S RESOLUTIONS COULD DECIDE TO NOT HACKNEY AT ME LIKE ----
SPEAKIN' OF RESOLUTIONS- 'FIRE IN YOUR PLACE..
YOWP!
HE DID IT! HE DID IT!
WHAT'S THE MATTER WITH THAT INSECT? ALL I STARTED TO SAY WAS: "FIRE IN YOUR PLACE I'D BUY U.S. SAVINGS BONDS FOR A RAINY DAY!"
MEBBE HE GONE HOME FOR HIS PIGGY BANK AN' UMBRELLA
WALT KELLY

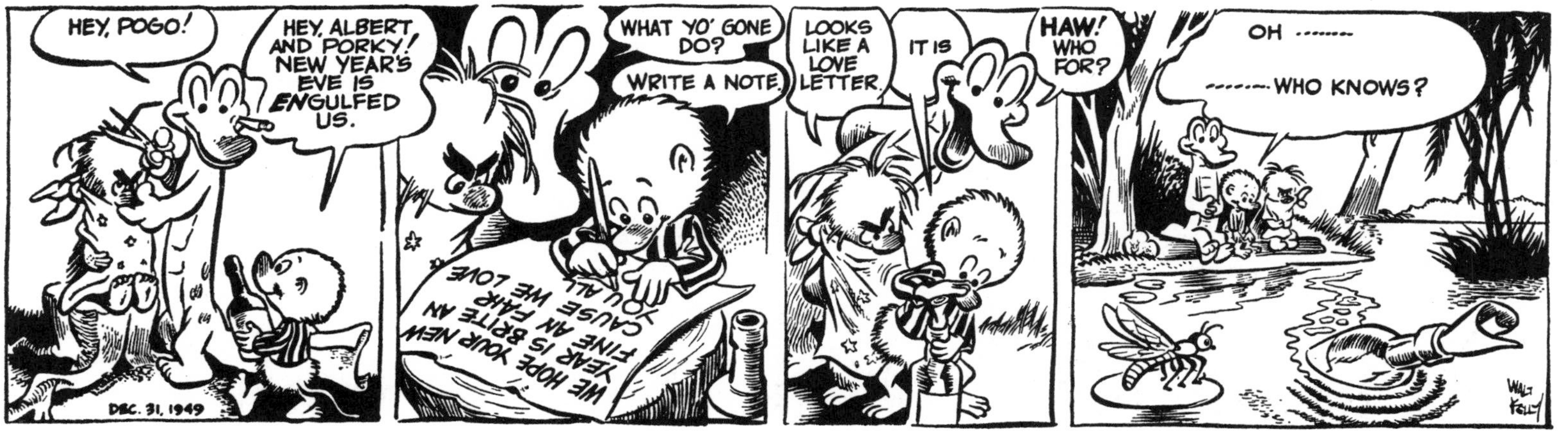
HEY, POGO!
HEY, ALBERT, AND PORKY! NEW YEAR'S EVE IS ENGULFED US.
DEC. 31, 1949
WHAT YO' GONE DO?
WRITE A NOTE.
WE HOPE YOUR NEW YEAR IS BRITE AN FINE AN FAIR CAUSE WE LOVE YOU ALL
LOOKS LIKE A LOVE LETTER.
IT IS
HAW! WHO FOR?
OH -------
-------WHO KNOWS?
WALT KELLY

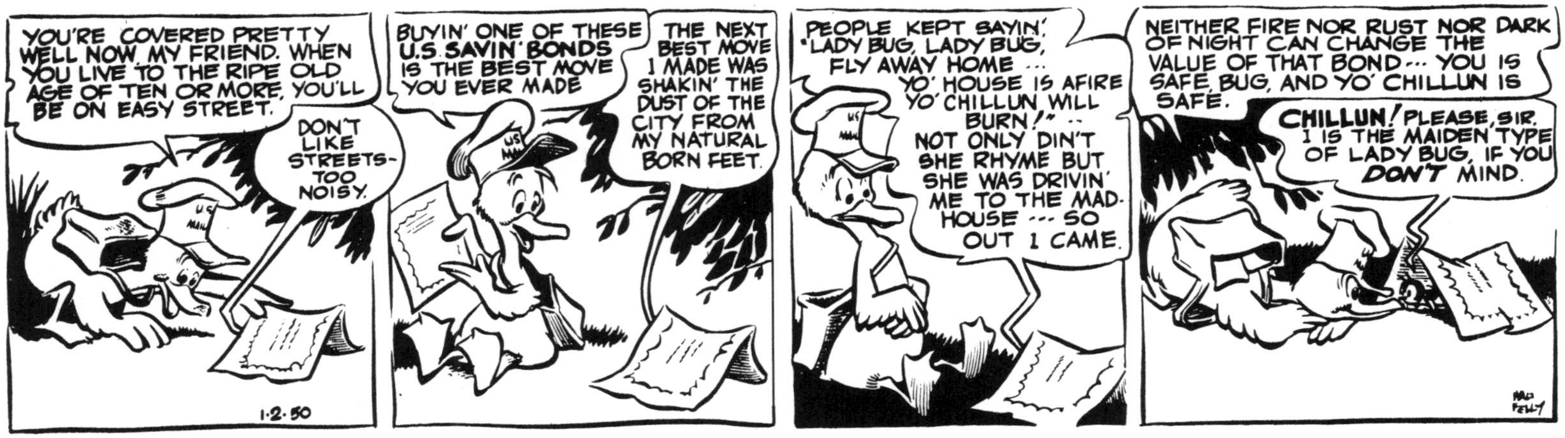
YOU'RE COVERED PRETTY WELL NOW, MY FRIEND. WHEN YOU LIVE TO THE RIPE OLD AGE OF TEN OR MORE, YOU'LL BE ON EASY STREET.
DON'T LIKE STREETS-TOO NOISY.
1·2·50
BUYIN' ONE OF THESE U.S. SAVIN' BONDS IS THE BEST MOVE YOU EVER MADE
THE NEXT BEST MOVE I MADE WAS SHAKIN' THE DUST OF THE CITY FROM MY NATURAL BORN FEET.
PEOPLE KEPT SAYIN' "LADY BUG, LADY BUG, FLY AWAY HOME ... YO' HOUSE IS AFIRE YO' CHILLUN WILL BURN!" -- NOT ONLY DIN'T SHE RHYME BUT SHE WAS DRIVIN' ME TO THE MAD-HOUSE --- SO OUT I CAME.
NEITHER FIRE NOR RUST NOR DARK OF NIGHT CAN CHANGE THE VALUE OF THAT BOND --- YOU IS SAFE, BUG, AND YO' CHILLUN IS SAFE.
CHILLUN! PLEASE, SIR, I IS THE MAIDEN TYPE OF LADY BUG, IF YOU DON'T MIND.

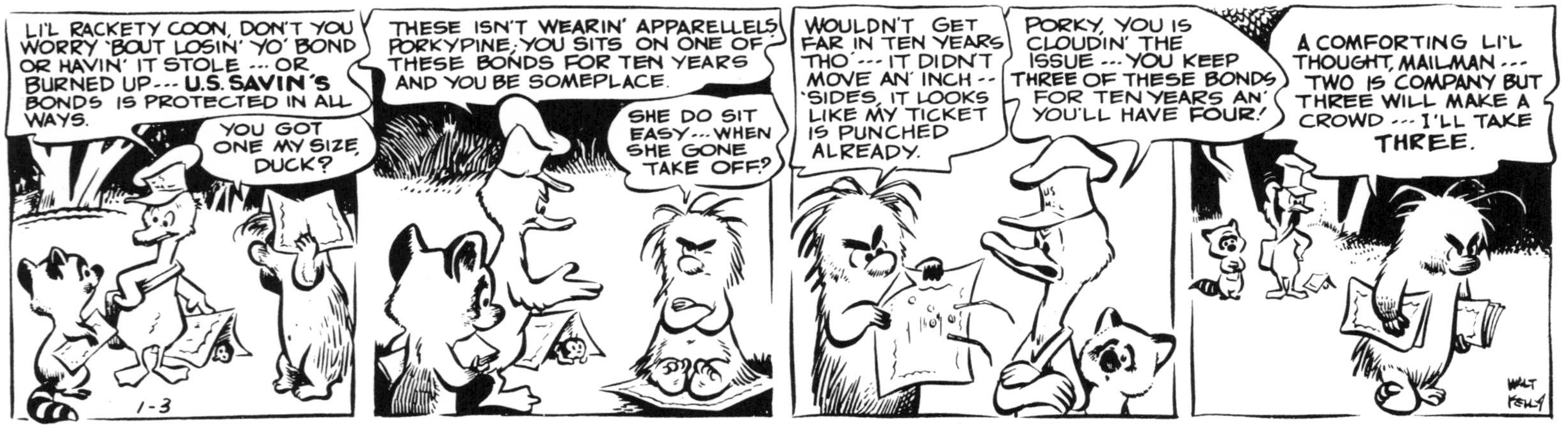
LI'L RACKETY COON, DON'T YOU WORRY 'BOUT LOSIN' YO' BOND OR HAVIN' IT STOLE --- OR BURNED UP --- U.S. SAVIN'S BONDS IS PROTECTED IN ALL WAYS.
YOU GOT ONE MY SIZE, DUCK?
1-3
THESE ISN'T WEARIN' APPARELLELS, PORKYPINE; YOU SITS ON ONE OF THESE BONDS FOR TEN YEARS AND YOU BE SOMEPLACE.
SHE DO SIT EASY --- WHEN SHE GONE TAKE OFF?
WOULDN'T GET FAR IN TEN YEARS THO' --- IT DIDN'T MOVE AN' INCH -- 'SIDES, IT LOOKS LIKE MY TICKET IS PUNCHED ALREADY.
PORKY, YOU IS CLOUDIN' THE ISSUE --- YOU KEEP THREE OF THESE BONDS FOR TEN YEARS AN' YOU'LL HAVE FOUR!
A COMFORTING LI'L THOUGHT, MAILMAN --- TWO IS COMPANY BUT THREE WILL MAKE A CROWD --- I'LL TAKE THREE.
WALT KELLY

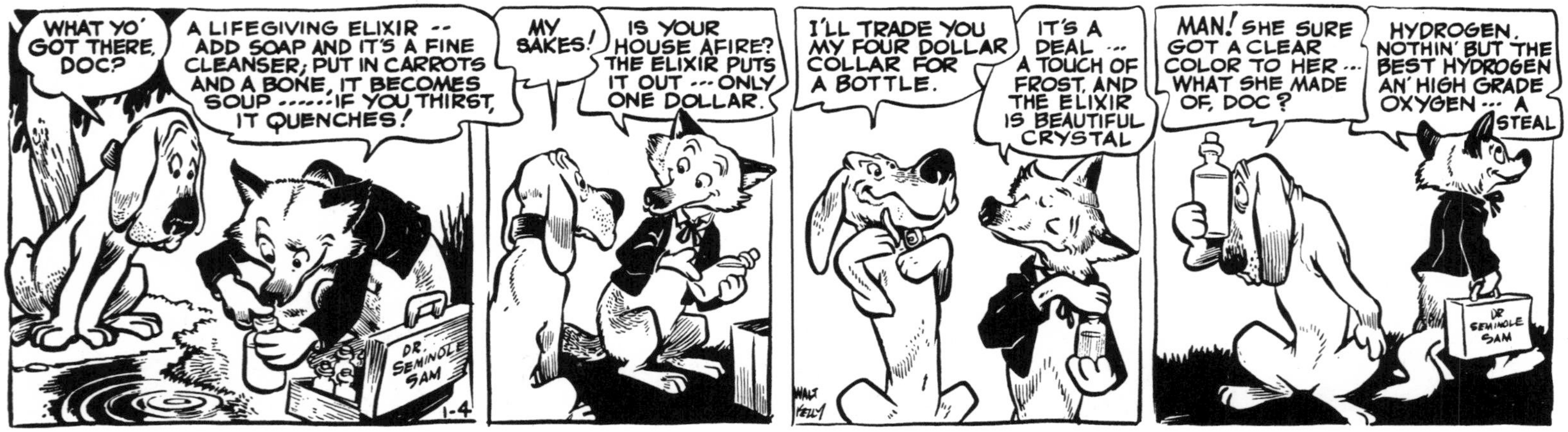
WHAT YO' GOT THERE, DOC?
A LIFEGIVING ELIXIR -- ADD SOAP AND IT'S A FINE CLEANSER; PUT IN CARROTS AND A BONE, IT BECOMES SOUP ------ IF YOU THIRST, IT QUENCHES!
DR. SEMINOLE SAM
1-4
MY SAKES!
IS YOUR HOUSE AFIRE? THE ELIXIR PUTS IT OUT --- ONLY ONE DOLLAR.
I'LL TRADE YOU MY FOUR DOLLAR COLLAR FOR A BOTTLE.
IT'S A DEAL ... A TOUCH OF FROST, AND THE ELIXIR IS BEAUTIFUL CRYSTAL
WALT KELLY
MAN! SHE SURE GOT A CLEAR COLOR TO HER ... WHAT SHE MADE OF, DOC?
HYDROGEN, NOTHIN' BUT THE BEST HYDROGEN AN' HIGH GRADE OXYGEN --- A STEAL
DR. SEMINOLE SAM

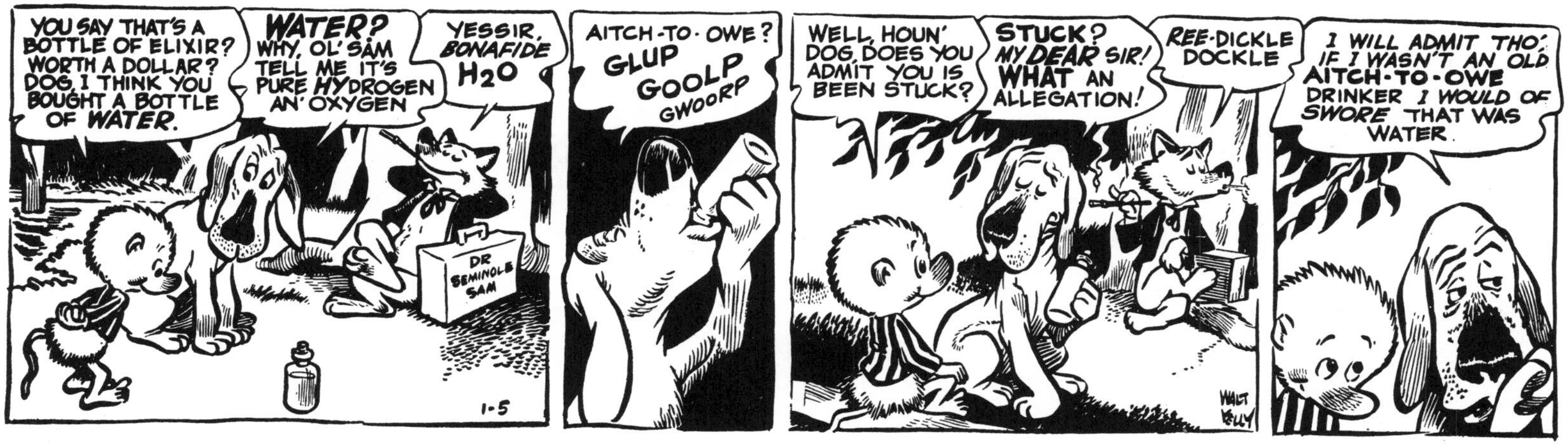
YOU SAY THAT'S A BOTTLE OF ELIXIR? WORTH A DOLLAR? DOG, I THINK YOU BOUGHT A BOTTLE OF WATER.
WATER? WHY, OL' SAM TELL ME IT'S PURE HYDROGEN AN' OXYGEN
YESSIR, BONAFIDE H2O
DR SEMINOLE SAM
1-5
AITCH-TO-OWE?
GLUP
GOOLP
GWOORP
WELL, HOUN' DOG, DOES YOU ADMIT YOU IS BEEN STUCK?
STUCK? MY DEAR SIR! WHAT AN ALLEGATION!
REE-DICKLE DOCKLE
WALT KELLY
I WILL ADMIT THO' IF I WASN'T AN OLD AITCH-TO-OWE DRINKER I WOULD OF SWORE THAT WAS WATER.

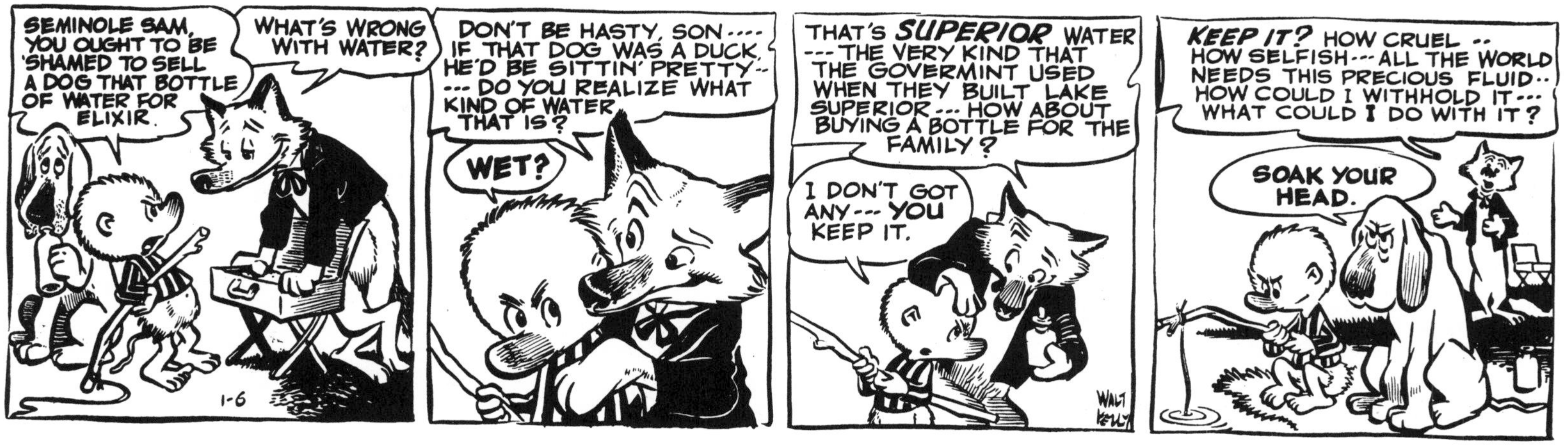
SEMINOLE SAM, YOU OUGHT TO BE 'SHAMED TO SELL A DOG THAT BOTTLE OF WATER FOR ELIXIR.
WHAT'S WRONG WITH WATER?
1-6
DON'T BE HASTY, SON ---- IF THAT DOG WAS A DUCK HE'D BE SITTIN' PRETTY-- --- DO YOU REALIZE WHAT KIND OF WATER THAT IS?
WET?
THAT'S SUPERIOR WATER --- THE VERY KIND THAT THE GOVERMINT USED WHEN THEY BUILT LAKE SUPERIOR --- HOW ABOUT BUYING A BOTTLE FOR THE FAMILY?
I DON'T GOT ANY --- YOU KEEP IT.
WALT KELLY
KEEP IT? HOW CRUEL -- HOW SELFISH --- ALL THE WORLD NEEDS THIS PRECIOUS FLUID -- HOW COULD I WITHHOLD IT --- WHAT COULD I DO WITH IT?
SOAK YOUR HEAD.

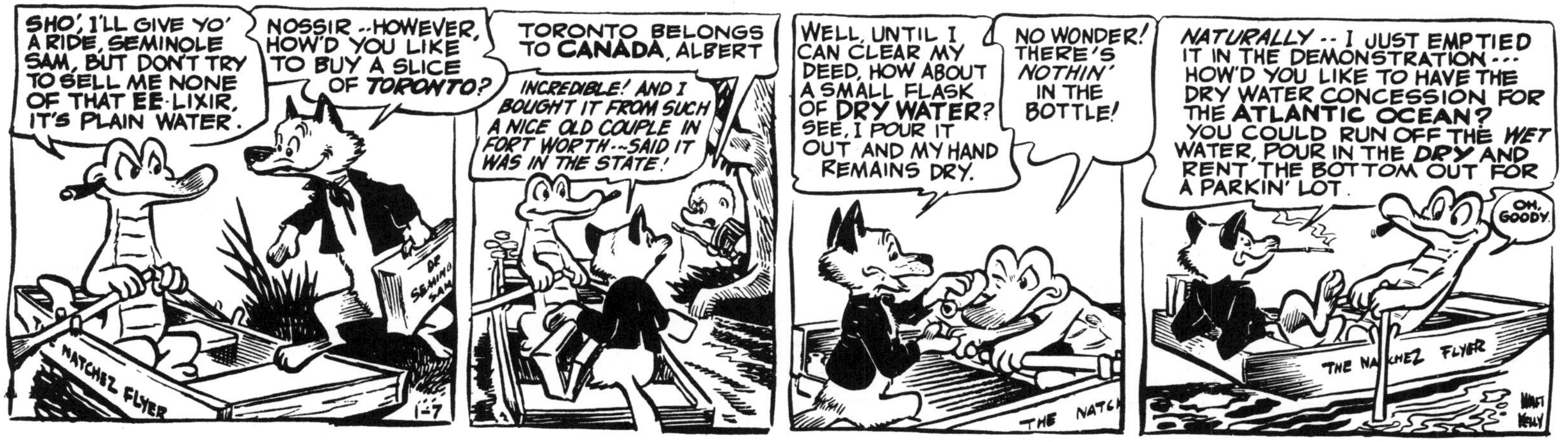
SHO', I'LL GIVE YO' A RIDE, SEMINOLE SAM, BUT DON'T TRY TO SELL ME NONE OF THAT EE-LIXIR, IT'S PLAIN WATER.
NOSSIR -- HOWEVER, HOW'D YOU LIKE TO BUY A SLICE OF TORONTO?
DR SEMINOLE SAM
NATCHEZ FLYER
1-7
TORONTO BELONGS TO CANADA, ALBERT
INCREDIBLE! AND I BOUGHT IT FROM SUCH A NICE OLD COUPLE IN FORT WORTH -- SAID IT WAS IN THE STATE!
WELL, UNTIL I CAN CLEAR MY DEED, HOW ABOUT A SMALL FLASK OF DRY WATER? SEE, I POUR IT OUT AND MY HAND REMAINS DRY.
NO WONDER! THERE'S NOTHIN' IN THE BOTTLE!
THE NATCH
NATURALLY -- I JUST EMPTIED IT IN THE DEMONSTRATION --- HOW'D YOU LIKE TO HAVE THE DRY WATER CONCESSION FOR THE ATLANTIC OCEAN? YOU COULD RUN OFF THE WET WATER, POUR IN THE DRY AND RENT THE BOTTOM OUT FOR A PARKIN' LOT.
OH, GOODY.
THE NATCHEZ FLYER
WALT KELLY

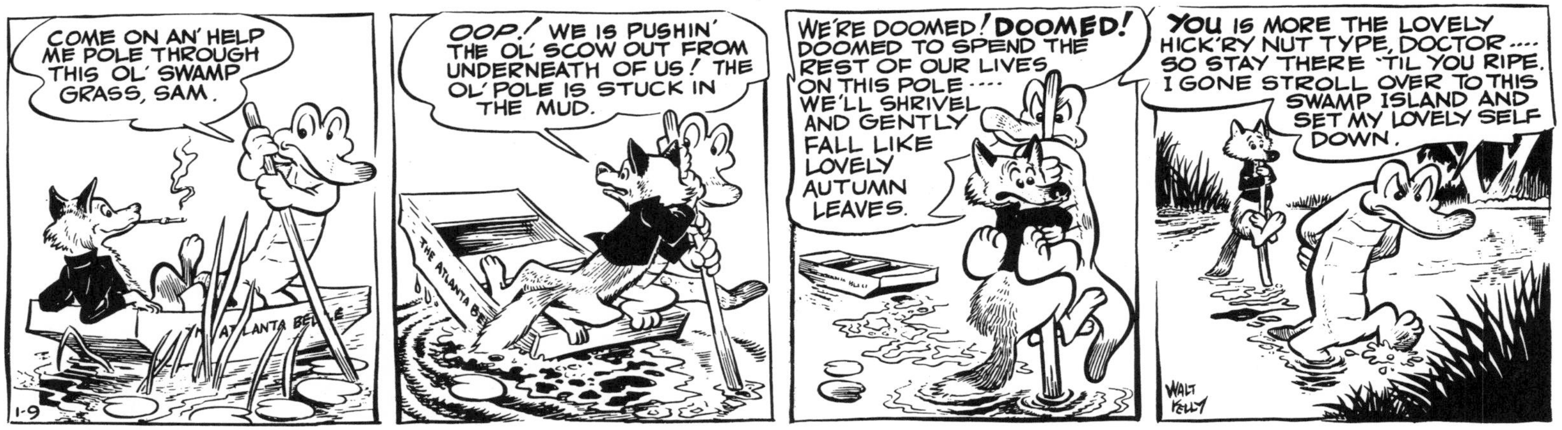
COME ON AN' HELP ME POLE THROUGH THIS OL' SWAMP GRASS, SAM.
THE ATLANTA BELLE
1-9
OOP! WE IS PUSHIN' THE OL' SCOW OUT FROM UNDERNEATH OF US! THE OL' POLE IS STUCK IN THE MUD.
THE ATLANTA BE
WE'RE DOOMED! DOOMED! DOOMED TO SPEND THE REST OF OUR LIVES ON THIS POLE --- WE'LL SHRIVEL AND GENTLY FALL LIKE LOVELY AUTUMN LEAVES.
YOU IS MORE THE LOVELY HICK'RY NUT TYPE, DOCTOR.... SO STAY THERE 'TIL YOU RIPE. I GONE STROLL OVER TO THIS SWAMP ISLAND AND SET MY LOVELY SELF DOWN.
WALT KELLY

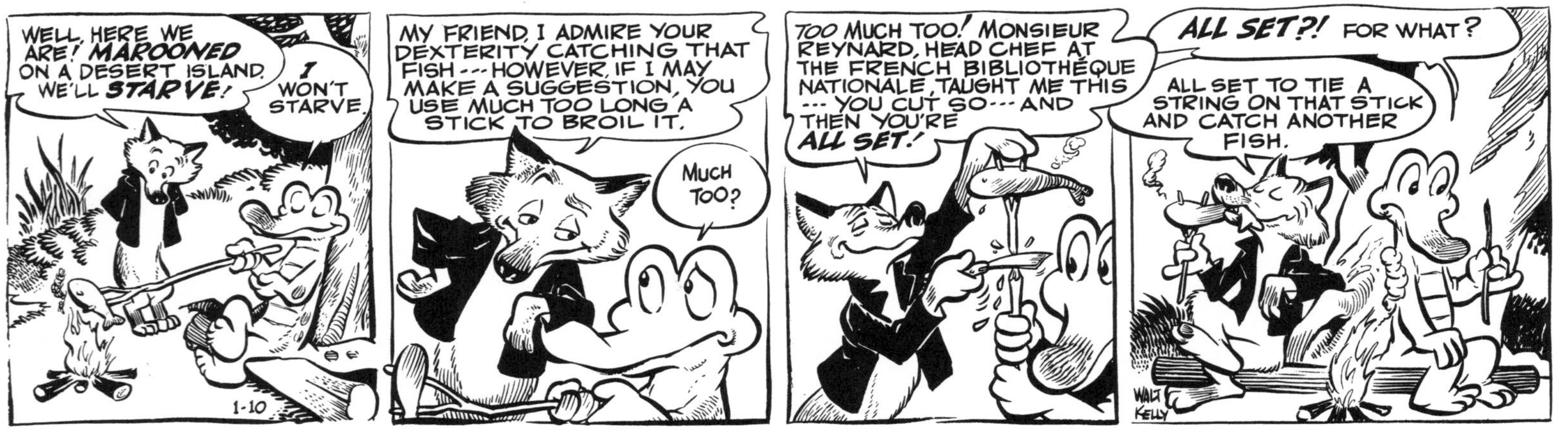
WELL, HERE WE ARE! MAROONED ON A DESERT ISLAND. WE'LL STARVE!
I WON'T STARVE.
1-10
MY FRIEND, I ADMIRE YOUR DEXTERITY CATCHING THAT FISH --- HOWEVER, IF I MAY MAKE A SUGGESTION, YOU USE MUCH TOO LONG A STICK TO BROIL IT.
MUCH TOO?
TOO MUCH TOO! MONSIEUR REYNARD, HEAD CHEF AT THE FRENCH BIBLIOTHÈQUE NATIONALE, TAUGHT ME THIS --- YOU CUT SO --- AND THEN YOU'RE ALL SET!
ALL SET?! FOR WHAT?
ALL SET TO TIE A STRING ON THAT STICK AND CATCH ANOTHER FISH.
WALT KELLY

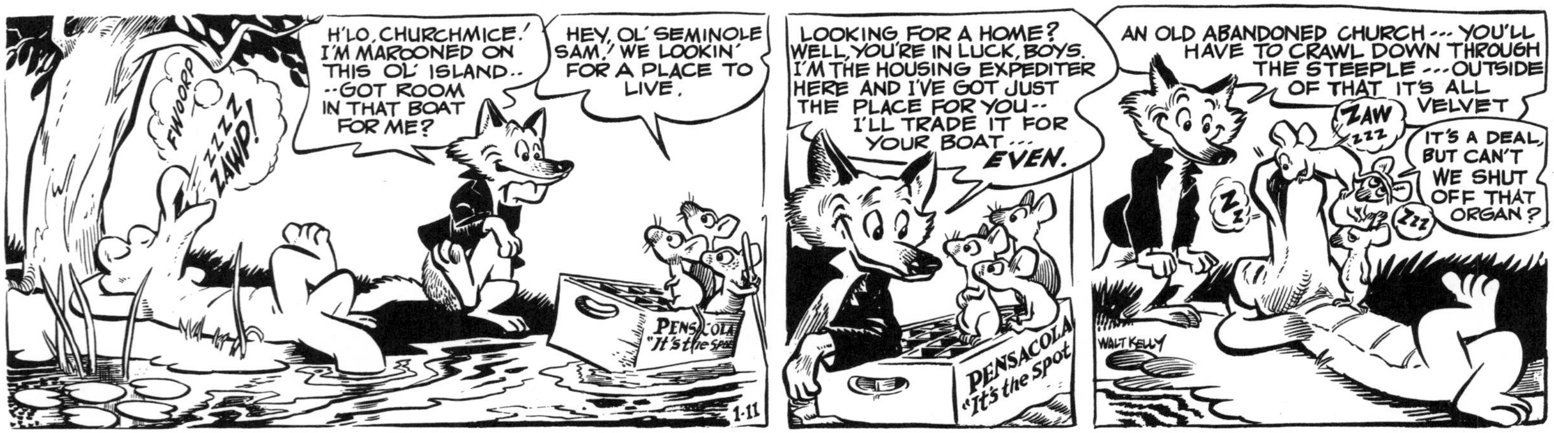
FWOOPP
ZZZZZ ZAWP!
H'LO, CHURCHMICE! I'M MAROONED ON THIS OL' ISLAND.. --GOT ROOM IN THAT BOAT FOR ME?
HEY, OL' SEMINOLE SAM! WE LOOKIN' FOR A PLACE TO LIVE.
PENSACOLA "It's the spot"
1-11
LOOKING FOR A HOME? WELL, YOU'RE IN LUCK, BOYS. I'M THE HOUSING EXPEDITER HERE AND I'VE GOT JUST THE PLACE FOR YOU -- I'LL TRADE IT FOR YOUR BOAT... EVEN.
PENSACOLA "It's the Spot"
AN OLD ABANDONED CHURCH --- YOU'LL HAVE TO CRAWL DOWN THROUGH THE STEEPLE --- OUTSIDE OF THAT IT'S ALL VELVET
ZAW ZZZ
IT'S A DEAL, BUT CAN'T WE SHUT OFF THAT ORGAN?
ZZZ
WALT KELLY

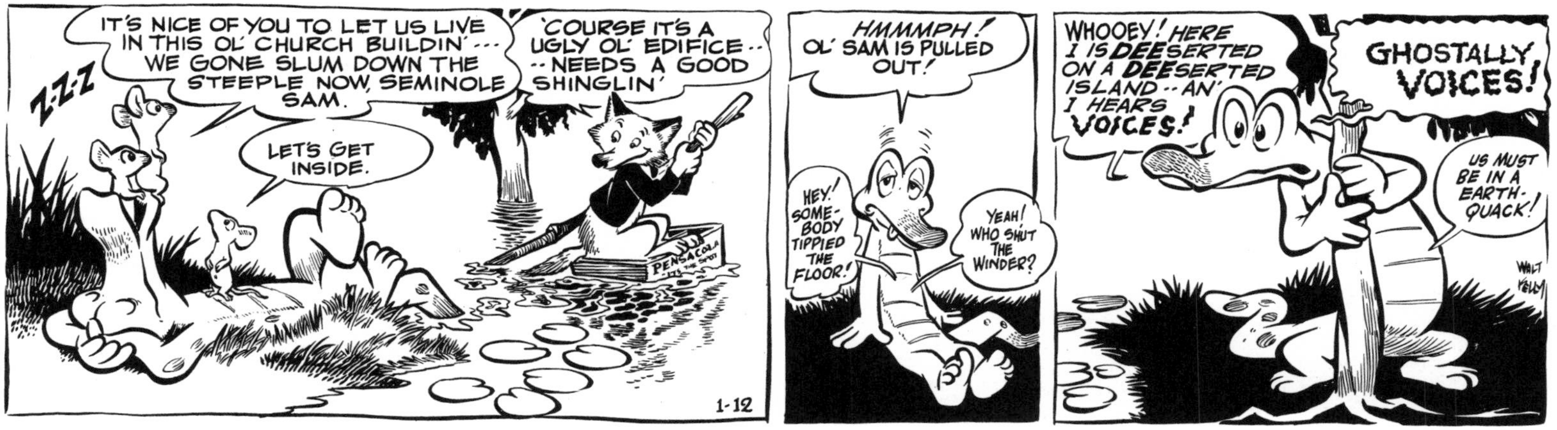
IT'S NICE OF YOU TO LET US LIVE IN THIS OL' CHURCH BUILDIN' --- WE GONE SLUM DOWN THE STEEPLE NOW, SEMINOLE SAM.
Z-Z-Z
LET'S GET INSIDE.
'COURSE IT'S A UGLY OL' EDIFICE -- -- NEEDS A GOOD SHINGLIN'
PENSACOLA
1-12
HMMMPH! OL' SAM IS PULLED OUT!
HEY! SOME-BODY TIPPIED THE FLOOR!
YEAH! WHO SHUT THE WINDER?
WHOOEY! HERE I IS DEESERTED ON A DEESERTED ISLAND -- AN' I HEARS VOICES!
GHOSTALLY VOICES!
US MUST BE IN A EARTH-QUACK!
WALT KELLY

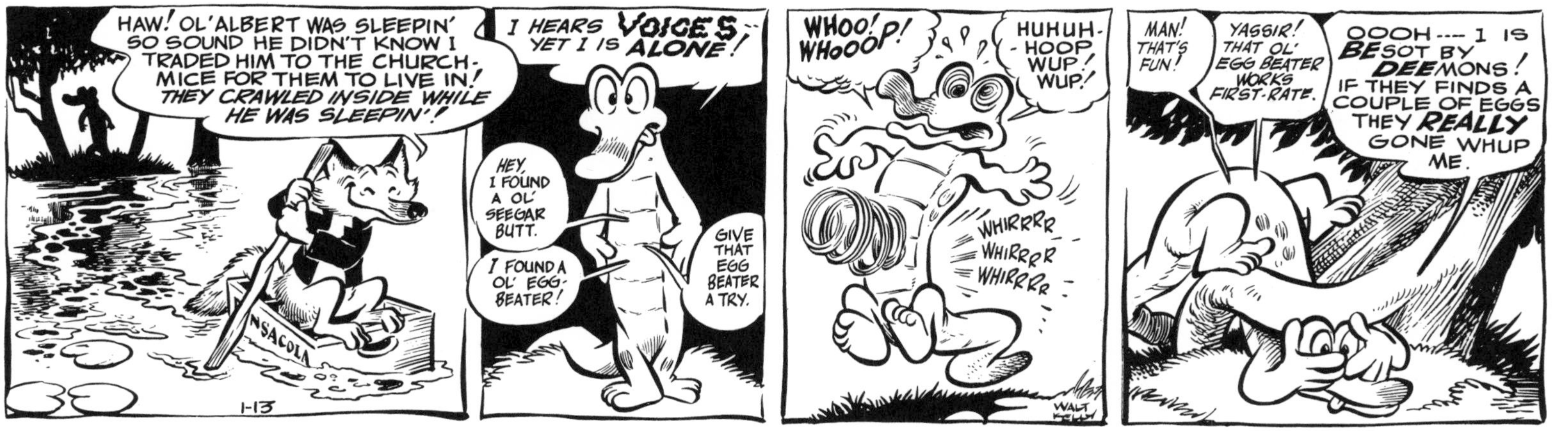
HAW! OL' ALBERT WAS SLEEPIN' SO SOUND HE DIDN'T KNOW I TRADED HIM TO THE CHURCH-MICE FOR THEM TO LIVE IN! THEY CRAWLED INSIDE WHILE HE WAS SLEEPIN'!
NSACOLA
1-13
I HEARS VOICES-- YET I IS ALONE!
HEY, I FOUND A OL' SEEGAR BUTT.
I FOUND A OL' EGG-BEATER!
GIVE THAT EGG BEATER A TRY.
WHOO! WHOOOP!
HUHUH--HOOP WUP! WUP!
WHIRRRR WHIRRRR WHIRRRR
WALT KELLY
MAN! THAT'S FUN!
YASSIR! THAT OL' EGG BEATER WORKS FIRST-RATE.
OOOH ---- I IS BESOT BY DEEMONS! IF THEY FINDS A COUPLE OF EGGS THEY REALLY GONE WHUP ME.

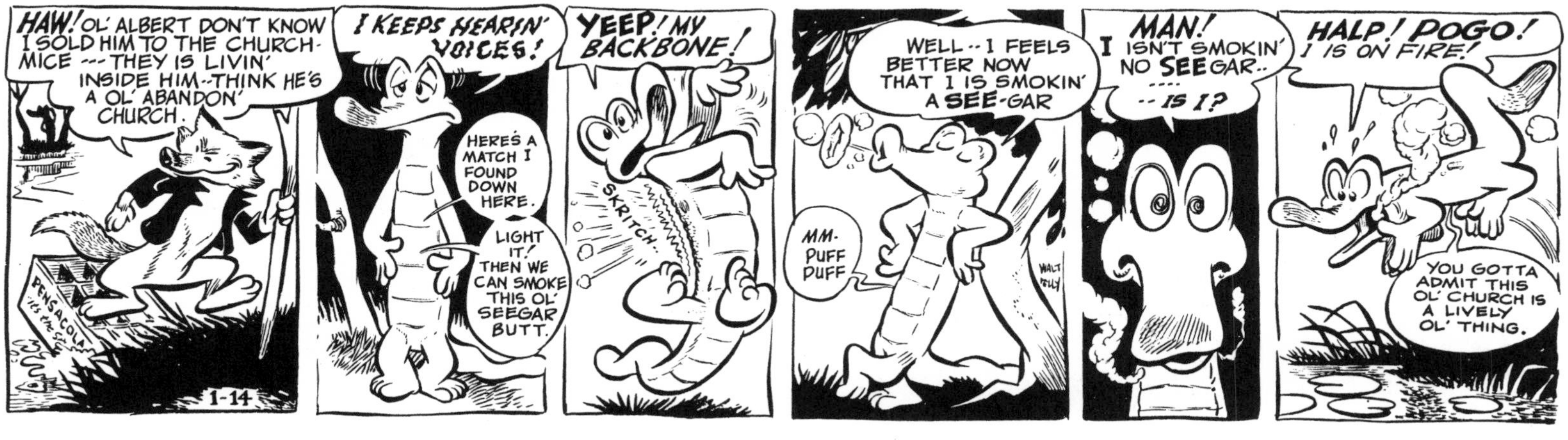
HAW! OL' ALBERT DON'T KNOW I SOLD HIM TO THE CHURCH-MICE --- THEY IS LIVIN' INSIDE HIM--THINK HE'S A OL' ABANDON' CHURCH.
PENSACOLA
1-14
I KEEPS HEARIN' VOICES!
HERE'S A MATCH I FOUND DOWN HERE.
LIGHT IT! THEN WE CAN SMOKE THIS OL' SEEGAR BUTT.
YEEP! MY BACKBONE!
SKRITCH
WELL -- I FEELS BETTER NOW THAT I IS SMOKIN' A SEE-GAR
MM-PUFF PUFF
WALT KELLY
MAN! I ISN'T SMOKIN' NO SEEGAR.. ---- -- IS I?
HALP! POGO! I IS ON FIRE!
YOU GOTTA ADMIT THIS OL' CHURCH IS A LIVELY OL' THING.

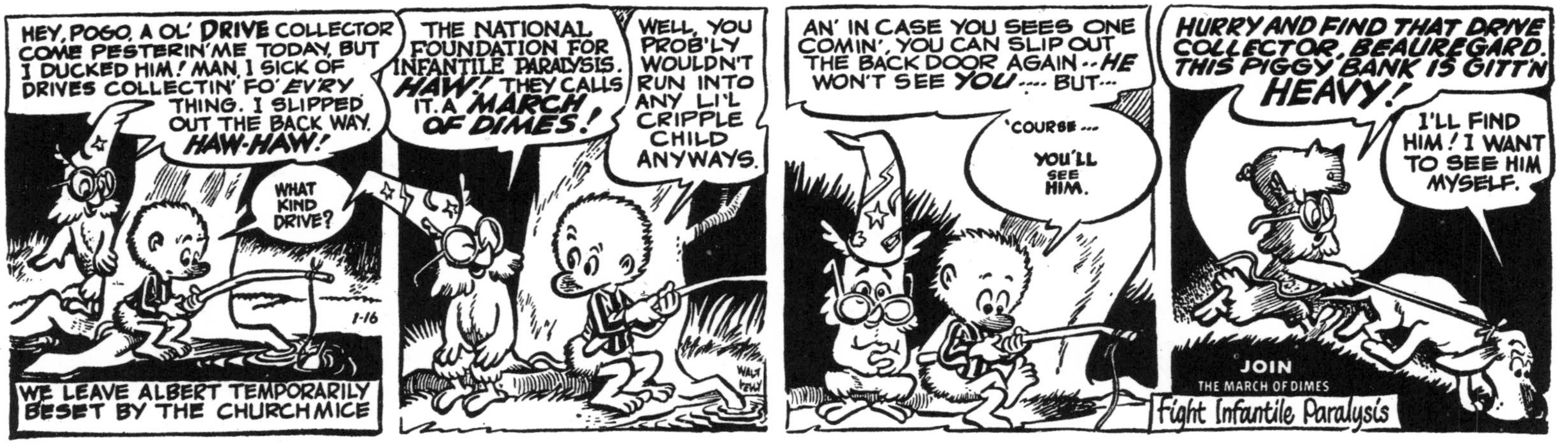
HEY, POGO, A OL' DRIVE COLLECTOR COME PESTERIN' ME TODAY, BUT I DUCKED HIM! MAN, I SICK OF DRIVES COLLECTIN' FO' EV'RY THING. I SLIPPED OUT THE BACK WAY. HAW-HAW!
WHAT KIND DRIVE?
1-16
WE LEAVE ALBERT TEMPORARILY BESET BY THE CHURCHMICE
THE NATIONAL FOUNDATION FOR INFANTILE PARALYSIS. HAW! THEY CALLS IT A MARCH OF DIMES!
WELL, YOU PROB'LY WOULDN'T RUN INTO ANY LI'L CRIPPLE CHILD ANYWAYS.
WALT KELLY
AN' IN CASE YOU SEES ONE COMIN', YOU CAN SLIP OUT THE BACK DOOR AGAIN -- HE WON'T SEE YOU .... BUT ...
'COURSE ... YOU'LL SEE HIM.
HURRY AND FIND THAT DRIVE COLLECTOR, BEAUREGARD. THIS PIGGY BANK IS GITT'N HEAVY!
I'LL FIND HIM! I WANT TO SEE HIM MYSELF.
JOIN
THE MARCH OF DIMES
Fight Infantile Paralysis

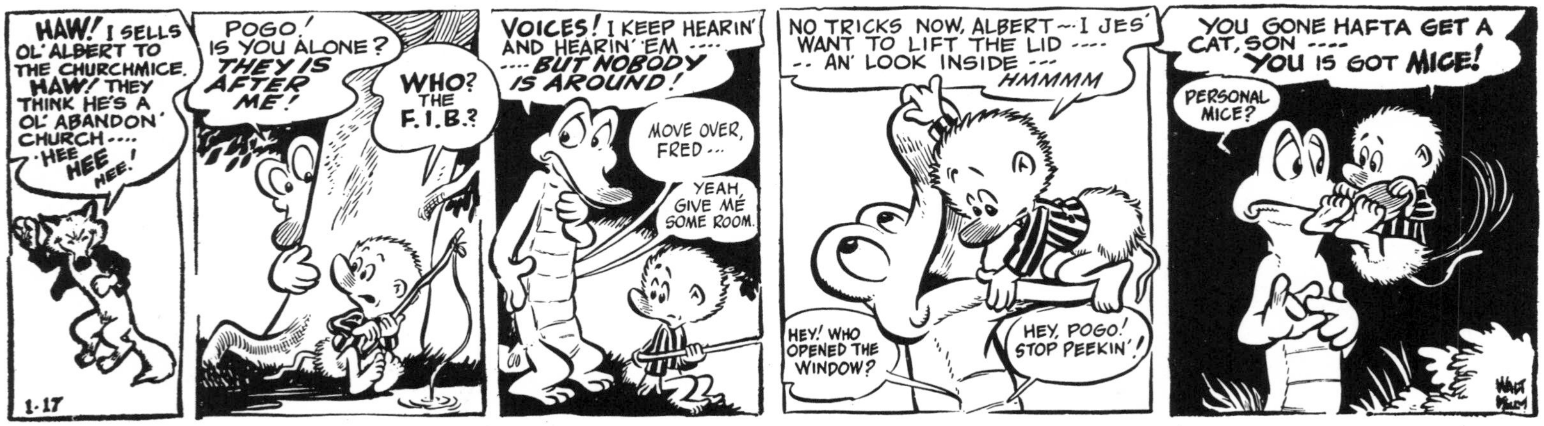
HAW! I SELLS OL' ALBERT TO THE CHURCHMICE. HAW! THEY THINK HE'S A OL' ABANDON' CHURCH .... HEE HEE HEE!
1-17
POGO! IS YOU ALONE? THEY IS AFTER ME!
WHO? THE F.I.B.?
VOICES! I KEEP HEARIN' AND HEARIN' 'EM .... BUT NOBODY IS AROUND!
MOVE OVER, FRED ...
YEAH, GIVE ME SOME ROOM.
NO TRICKS NOW, ALBERT -- I JES' WANT TO LIFT THE LID ---- -- AN' LOOK INSIDE --- HMMMM
HEY! WHO OPENED THE WINDOW?
HEY, POGO! STOP PEEKIN'!
YOU GONE HAFTA GET A CAT, SON ---- YOU IS GOT MICE!
PERSONAL MICE?
WALT KELLY

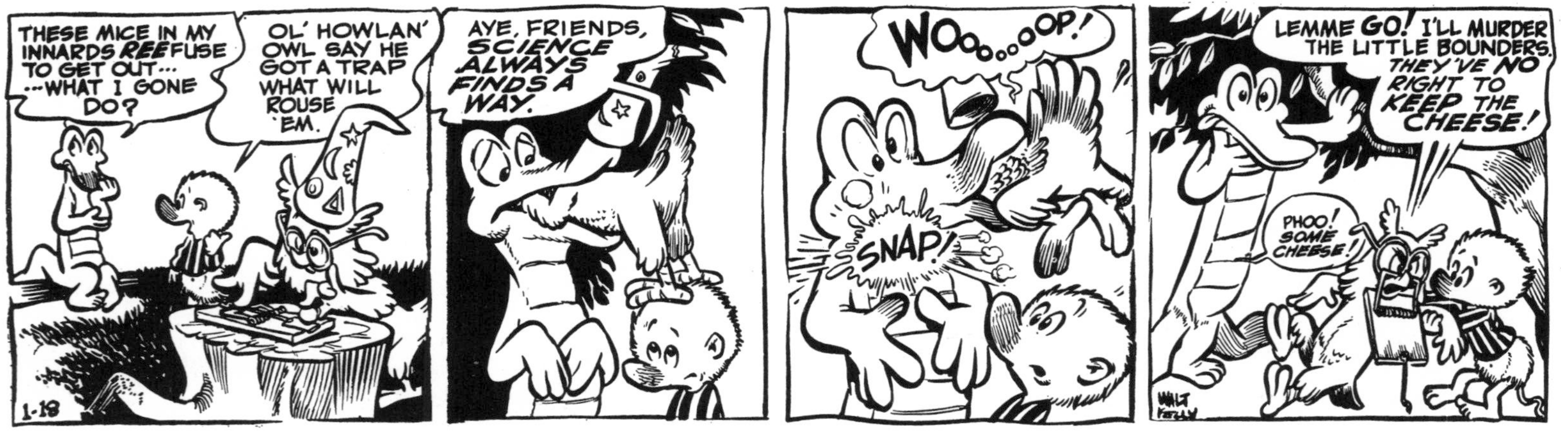
THESE MICE IN MY INNARDS REEFUSE TO GET OUT ... ... WHAT I GONE DO?
OL' HOWLAN' OWL SAY HE GOT A TRAP WHAT WILL ROUSE 'EM.
1-18
AYE, FRIENDS, SCIENCE ALWAYS FINDS A WAY.
WOoo...oOP!
SNAP!
LEMME GO! I'LL MURDER THE LITTLE BOUNDERS. THEY'VE NO RIGHT TO KEEP THE CHEESE!
PHOO! SOME CHEESE!
WALT KELLY

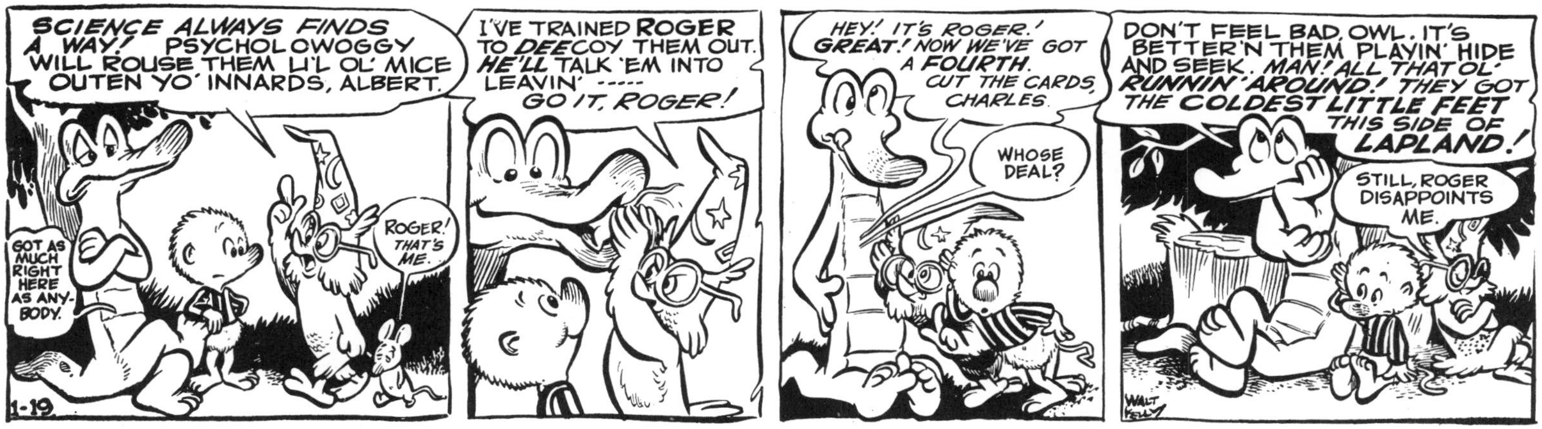
SCIENCE ALWAYS FINDS A WAY! PSYCHOLOWOGGY WILL ROUSE THEM LI'L OL' MICE OUTEN YO' INNARDS, ALBERT.
GOT AS MUCH RIGHT HERE AS ANY-BODY.
ROGER! THAT'S ME.
1-19
I'VE TRAINED ROGER TO DEECOY THEM OUT. HE'LL TALK 'EM INTO LEAVIN' ----- GO IT, ROGER!
HEY! IT'S ROGER! GREAT! NOW WE'VE GOT A FOURTH. CUT THE CARDS, CHARLES.
WHOSE DEAL?
DON'T FEEL BAD, OWL. IT'S BETTER'N THEM PLAYIN' HIDE AND SEEK. MAN! ALL THAT OL' RUNNIN' AROUND! THEY GOT THE COLDEST LITTLE FEET THIS SIDE OF LAPLAND!
STILL, ROGER DISAPPOINTS ME.
WALT KELLY

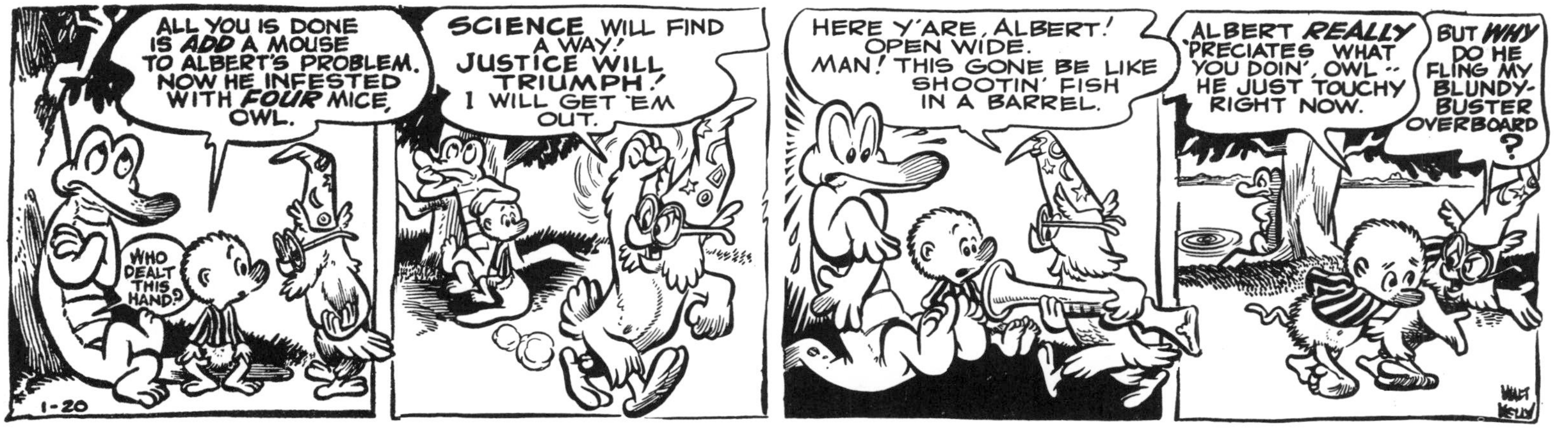
ALL YOU IS DONE IS ADD A MOUSE TO ALBERT'S PROBLEM. NOW HE INFESTED WITH FOUR MICE, OWL.
WHO DEALT THIS HAND?
1-20
SCIENCE WILL FIND A WAY! JUSTICE WILL TRIUMPH! I WILL GET 'EM OUT.
HERE Y'ARE, ALBERT! OPEN WIDE. MAN! THIS GONE BE LIKE SHOOTIN' FISH IN A BARREL.
ALBERT REALLY 'PRECIATES WHAT YOU DOIN', OWL -- HE JUST TOUCHY RIGHT NOW.
BUT WHY DO HE FLING MY BLUNDY-BUSTER OVERBOARD?
WALT KELLY

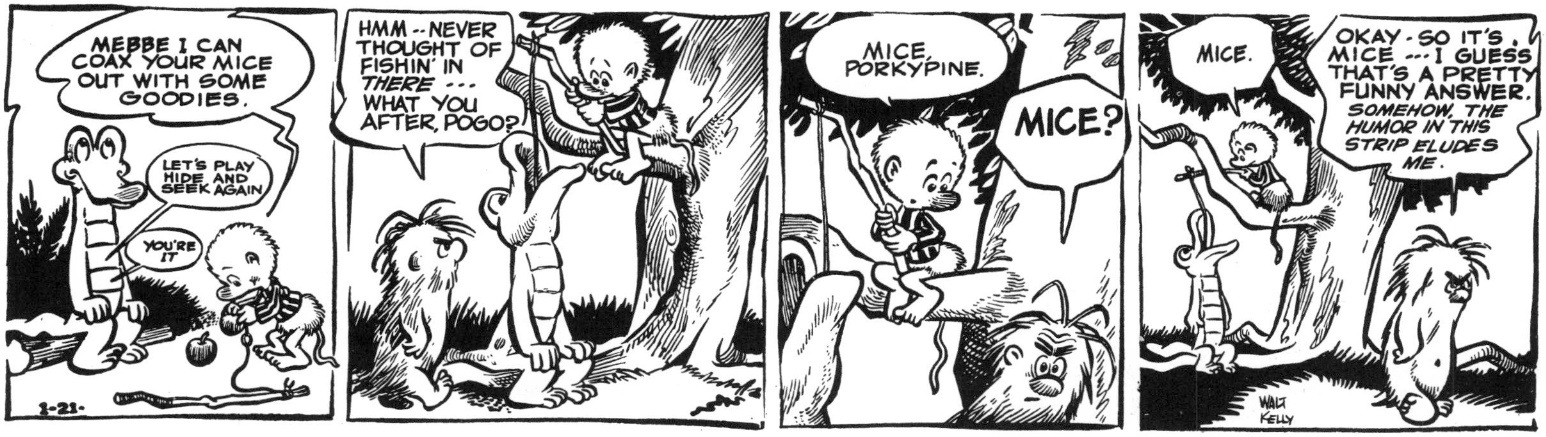
MEBBE I CAN COAX YOUR MICE OUT WITH SOME GOODIES.
LET'S PLAY HIDE AND SEEK AGAIN
YOU'RE IT
1-21
HMM -- NEVER THOUGHT OF FISHIN' IN THERE --- WHAT YOU AFTER, POGO?
MICE, PORKYPINE.
MICE?
MICE.
OKAY - SO IT'S MICE --- I GUESS THAT'S A PRETTY FUNNY ANSWER. SOMEHOW, THE HUMOR IN THIS STRIP ELUDES ME.
WALT KELLY

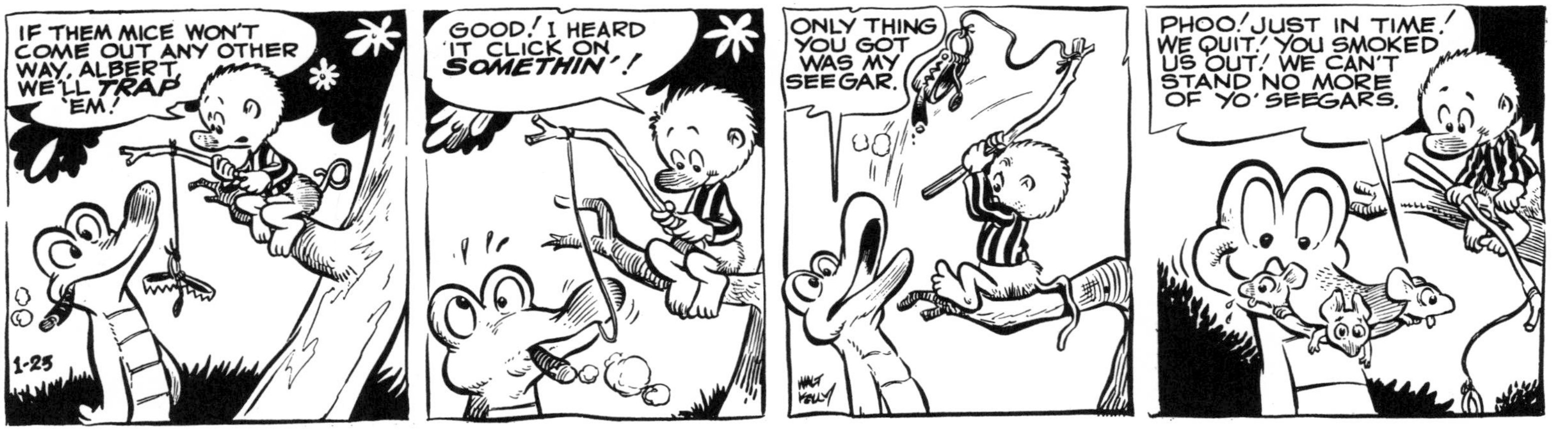
IF THEM MICE WON'T COME OUT ANY OTHER WAY, ALBERT, WE'LL **TRAP** 'EM!
1-23
GOOD! I HEARD 'IT CLICK ON **SOMETHIN'**!
ONLY THING YOU GOT WAS MY SEEGAR.
WALT KELLY
PHOO! JUST IN TIME! WE QUIT! YOU SMOKED US OUT! WE CAN'T STAND NO MORE OF YO' SEEGARS.

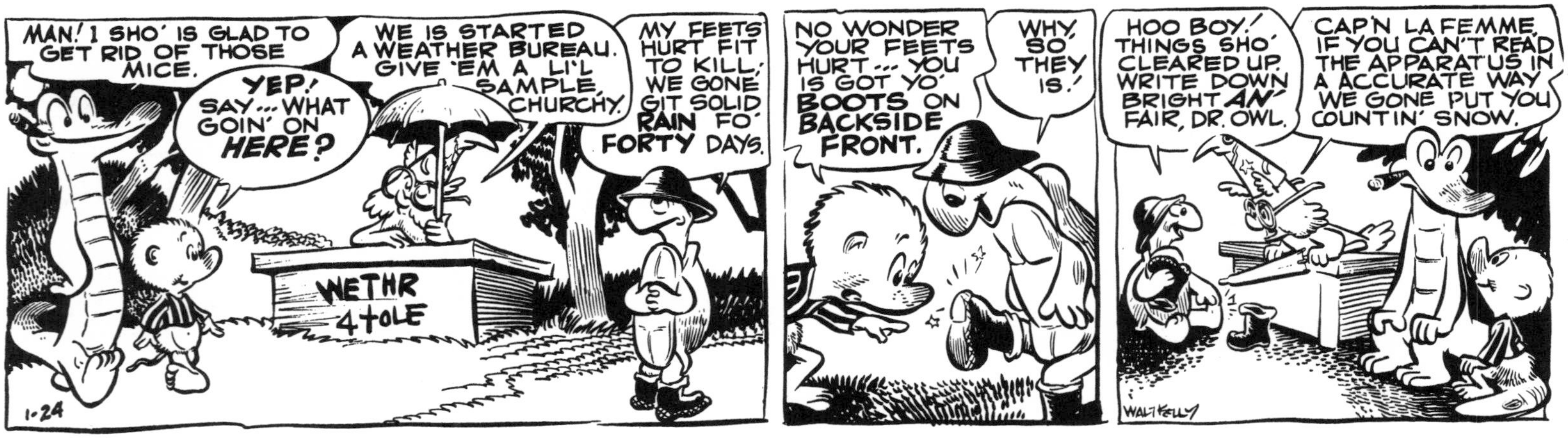
MAN! I SHO' IS GLAD TO GET RID OF THOSE MICE.
YEP! SAY... WHAT GOIN' ON **HERE?**
WE IS STARTED A WEATHER BUREAU. GIVE 'EM A LI'L SAMPLE, CHURCHY.
MY FEETS HURT FIT TO KILL, WE GONE GIT SOLID **RAIN** FO' **FORTY** DAYS.
WETHR 4TOLE
1-24
NO WONDER YOUR FEETS HURT... YOU IS GOT YO' **BOOTS** ON **BACKSIDE FRONT.**
WHY, SO THEY IS!
HOO BOY! THINGS SHO' CLEARED UP. WRITE DOWN BRIGHT **AN'** FAIR, DR. OWL.
CAP'N LA FEMME, IF YOU CAN'T READ THE APPARATUS IN A ACCURATE WAY WE GONE PUT YOU COUNTIN' SNOW.
WALT KELLY

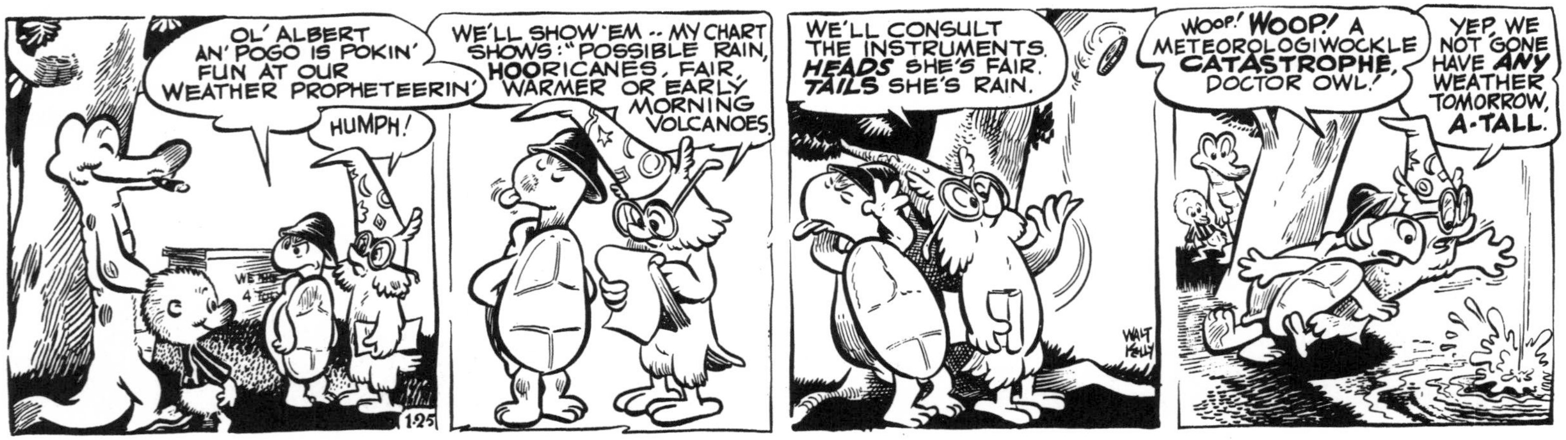
OL' ALBERT AN' POGO IS POKIN' FUN AT OUR WEATHER PROPHETEERIN'
HUMPH!
1-25
WE'LL SHOW 'EM -- MY CHART SHOWS: "POSSIBLE RAIN, **HOO**RICANES, FAIR, WARMER OR EARLY MORNING VOLCANOES.
WE'LL CONSULT THE INSTRUMENTS. **HEADS** SHE'S FAIR. **TAILS** SHE'S RAIN.
WALT KELLY
WOOP! **WOOP!** A METEOROLOGIWOCKLE **CATASTROPHE**, DOCTOR OWL!
YEP, WE NOT GONE HAVE **ANY** WEATHER TOMORROW, **A-TALL**.

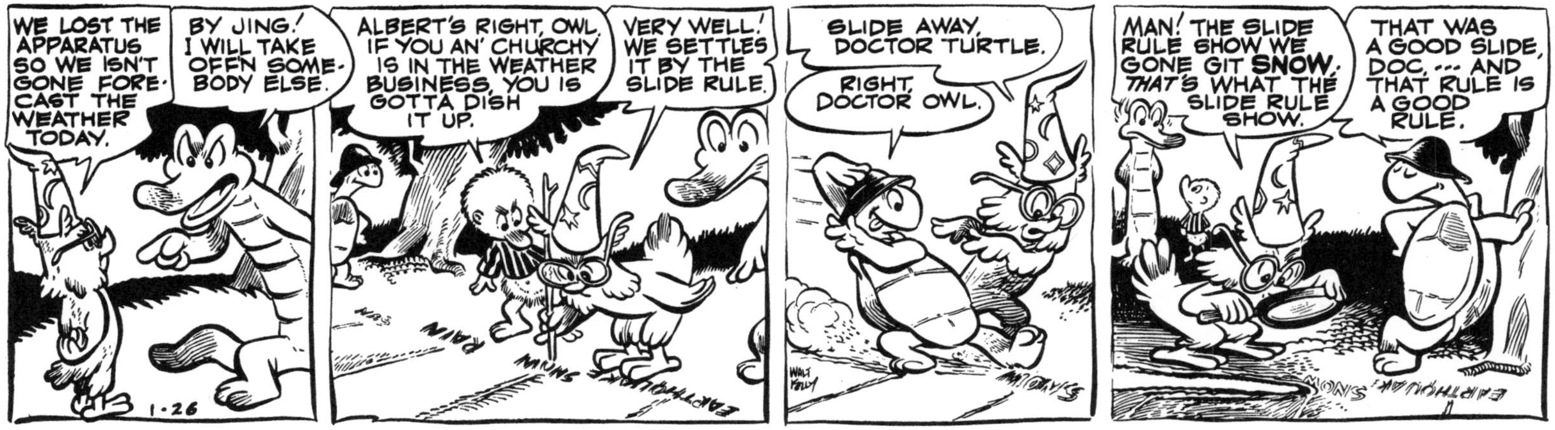
WE LOST THE APPARATUS SO WE ISN'T GONE FORE-CAST THE WEATHER TODAY.
BY JING! I WILL TAKE OFFN SOME-BODY ELSE.
1-26
ALBERT'S RIGHT, OWL, IF YOU AN' CHURCHY IS IN THE WEATHER BUSINESS, YOU IS GOTTA DISH IT UP.
VERY WELL! WE SETTLES IT BY THE SLIDE RULE.
SLIDE AWAY, DOCTOR TURTLE.
RIGHT, DOCTOR OWL.
WALT KELLY
MAN! THE SLIDE RULE SHOW WE GONE GIT SNOW. THAT'S WHAT THE SLIDE RULE SHOW.
THAT WAS A GOOD SLIDE, DOC, --- AND THAT RULE IS A GOOD RULE.

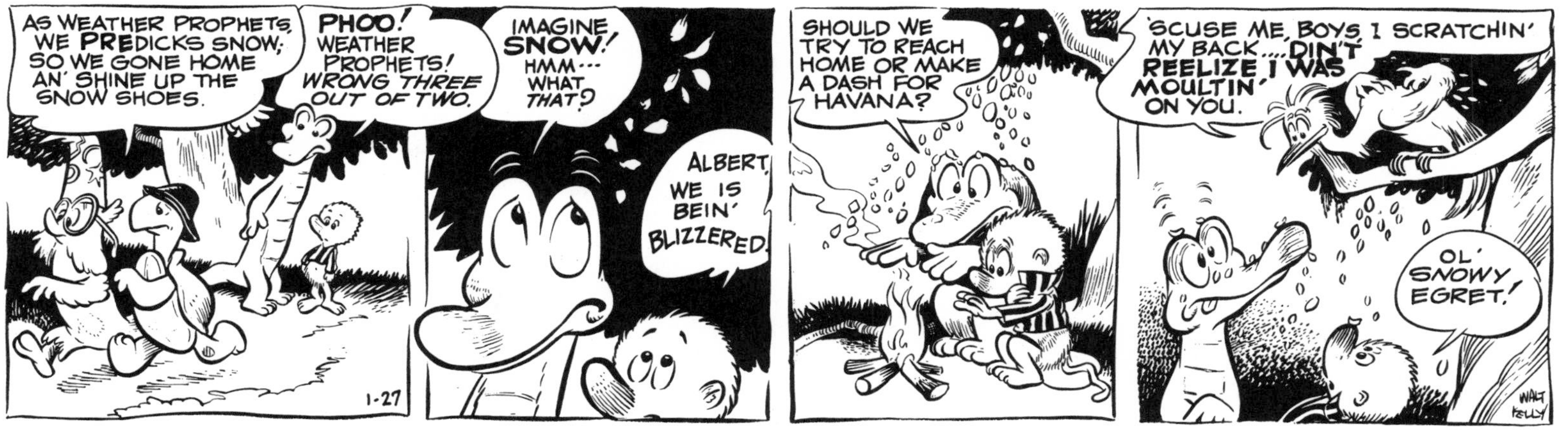
AS WEATHER PROPHETS WE PREDICKS SNOW; SO WE GONE HOME AN' SHINE UP THE SNOW SHOES.
PHOO! WEATHER PROPHETS! WRONG THREE OUT OF TWO.
1-27
IMAGINE, SNOW! HMM--- WHAT THAT?
ALBERT, WE IS BEIN' BLIZZERED.
SHOULD WE TRY TO REACH HOME OR MAKE A DASH FOR HAVANA?
'SCUSE ME, BOYS, I SCRATCHIN' MY BACK.... DIN'T REELIZE I WAS MOULTIN' ON YOU.
OL' SNOWY EGRET!
WALT KELLY

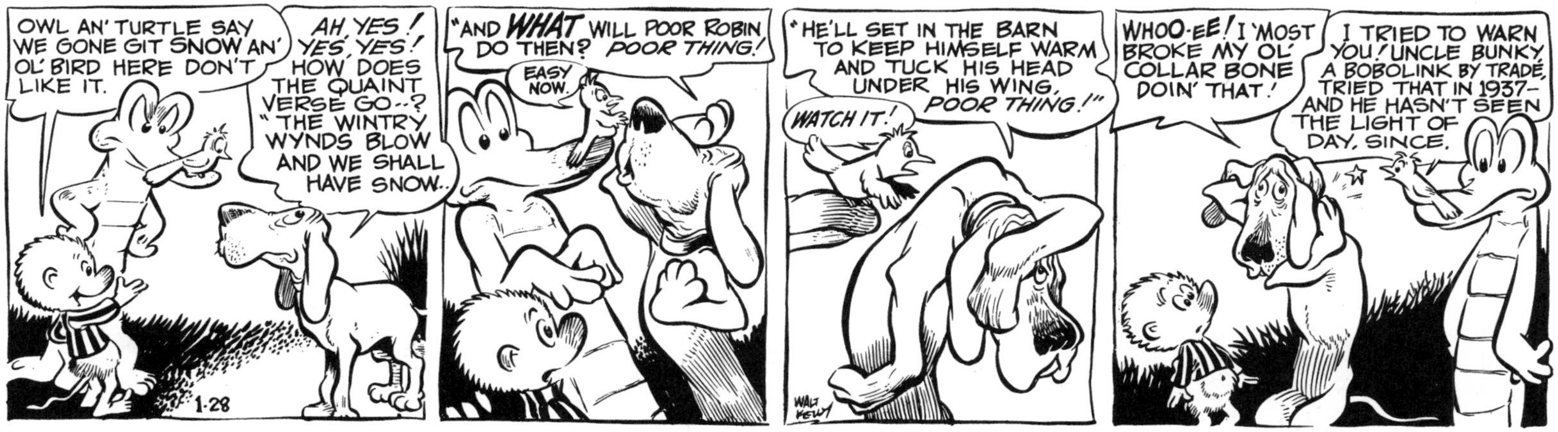
OWL AN' TURTLE SAY WE GONE GIT SNOW AN' OL' BIRD HERE DON'T LIKE IT.
AH, YES! YES, YES! HOW DOES THE QUAINT VERSE GO--? "THE WINTRY WYNDS BLOW AND WE SHALL HAVE SNOW..
1-28
"AND WHAT WILL POOR ROBIN DO THEN? POOR THING!
EASY NOW.
"HE'LL SET IN THE BARN TO KEEP HIMSELF WARM AND TUCK HIS HEAD UNDER HIS WING, POOR THING!"
WATCH IT!
WALT KELLY
WHOO-EE! I 'MOST BROKE MY OL' COLLAR BONE DOIN' THAT!
I TRIED TO WARN YOU! UNCLE BUNKY, A BOBOLINK BY TRADE, TRIED THAT IN 1937- AND HE HASN'T SEEN THE LIGHT OF DAY, SINCE.

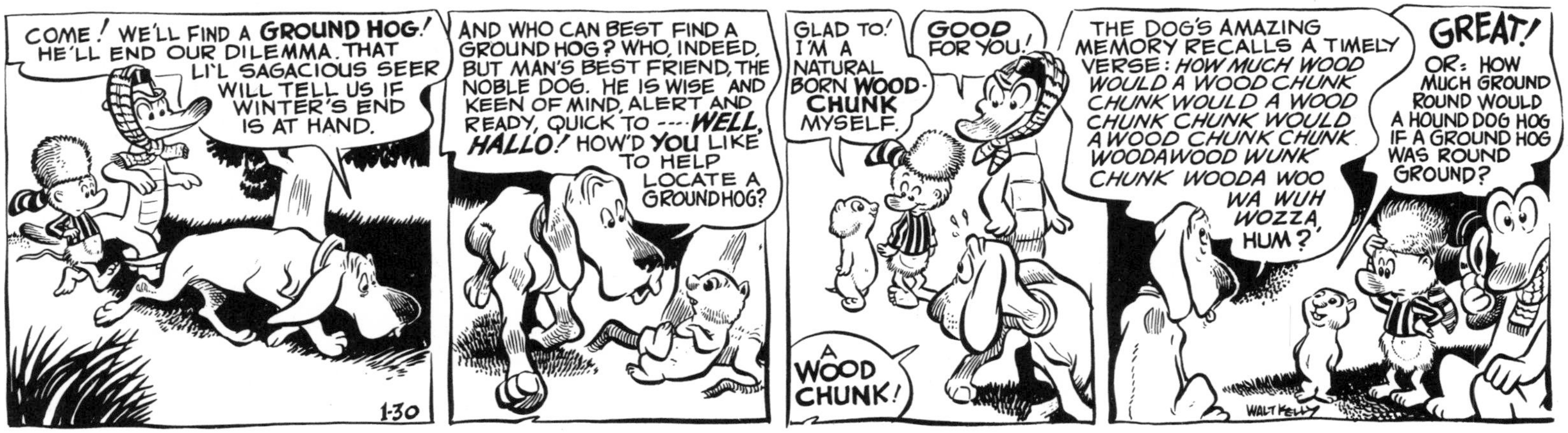
COME! WE'LL FIND A GROUND HOG! HE'LL END OUR DILEMMA. THAT LI'L SAGACIOUS SEER WILL TELL US IF WINTER'S END IS AT HAND.
1-30
AND WHO CAN BEST FIND A GROUND HOG? WHO, INDEED, BUT MAN'S BEST FRIEND, THE NOBLE DOG. HE IS WISE AND KEEN OF MIND, ALERT AND READY, QUICK TO ---- WELL, HALLO! HOW'D YOU LIKE TO HELP LOCATE A GROUNDHOG?
GLAD TO! I'M A NATURAL BORN WOOD-CHUNK MYSELF.
GOOD FOR YOU!
A WOOD CHUNK!
THE DOG'S AMAZING MEMORY RECALLS A TIMELY VERSE: HOW MUCH WOOD WOULD A WOOD CHUNK CHUNK WOULD A WOOD CHUNK CHUNK WOULD A WOOD CHUNK CHUNK WOODAWOOD WUNK CHUNK WOODA WOO WA WUH WOZZA, HUM?
GREAT! OR: HOW MUCH GROUND ROUND WOULD A HOUND DOG HOG IF A GROUND HOG WAS ROUND GROUND?
WALT KELLY

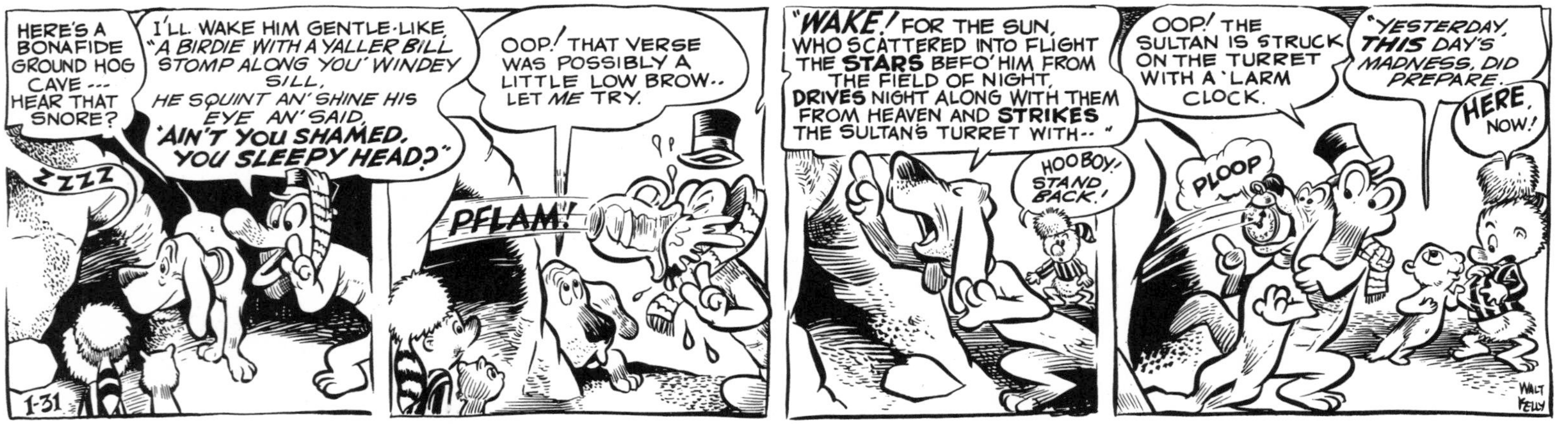
HERE'S A BONAFIDE GROUND HOG CAVE --- HEAR THAT SNORE?
I'LL WAKE HIM GENTLE-LIKE. "A BIRDIE WITH A YALLER BILL STOMP ALONG YOU' WINDEY SILL, HE SQUINT AN' SHINE HIS EYE AN' SAID, 'AIN'T YOU SHAMED, YOU SLEEPY HEAD?'"
ZZZZ
1-31
OOP! THAT VERSE WAS POSSIBLY A LITTLE LOW BROW.. LET ME TRY.
PFLAM!
"WAKE! FOR THE SUN, WHO SCATTERED INTO FLIGHT THE STARS BEFO' HIM FROM THE FIELD OF NIGHT, DRIVES NIGHT ALONG WITH THEM FROM HEAVEN AND STRIKES THE SULTAN'S TURRET WITH-- "
HOO BOY! STAND BACK!
OOP! THE SULTAN IS STRUCK ON THE TURRET WITH A 'LARM CLOCK.
PLOOP
"YESTERDAY, THIS DAY'S MADNESS, DID PREPARE."
HERE, NOW!
WALT KELLY

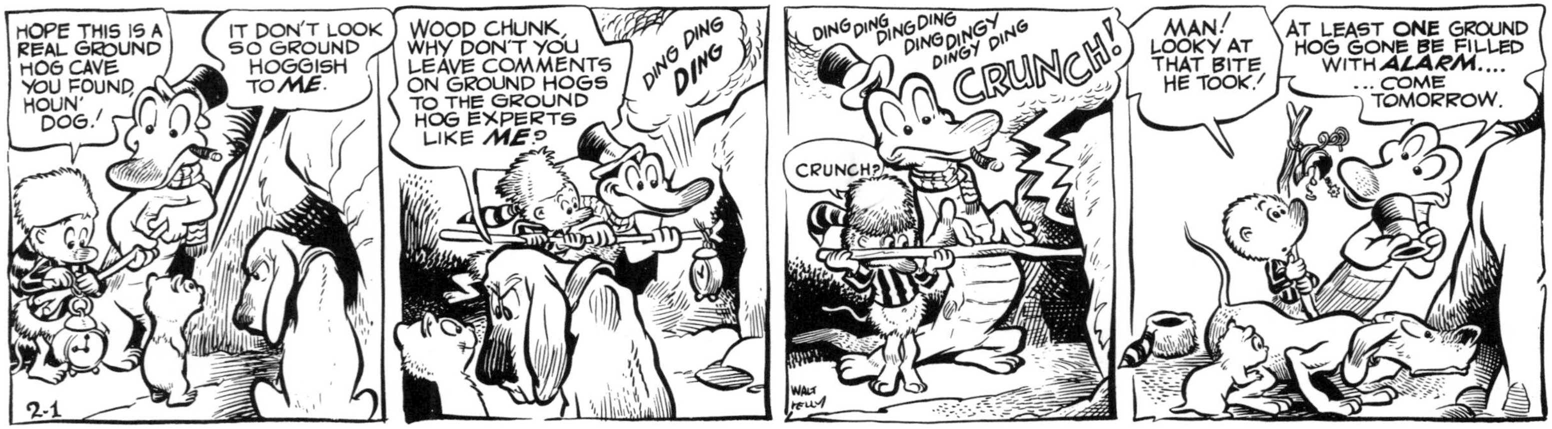
HOPE THIS IS A REAL GROUND HOG CAVE YOU FOUND, HOUN' DOG!
IT DON'T LOOK SO GROUND HOGGISH TO ME.
2-1
WOOD CHUNK, WHY DON'T YOU LEAVE COMMENTS ON GROUND HOGS TO THE GROUND HOG EXPERTS LIKE ME?
DING DING DING
DING DING DING DING DING DINGY DINGY DING
CRUNCH!
CRUNCH?
WALT KELLY
MAN! LOOKY AT THAT BITE HE TOOK!
AT LEAST ONE GROUND HOG GONE BE FILLED WITH ALARM.... ... COME TOMORROW.

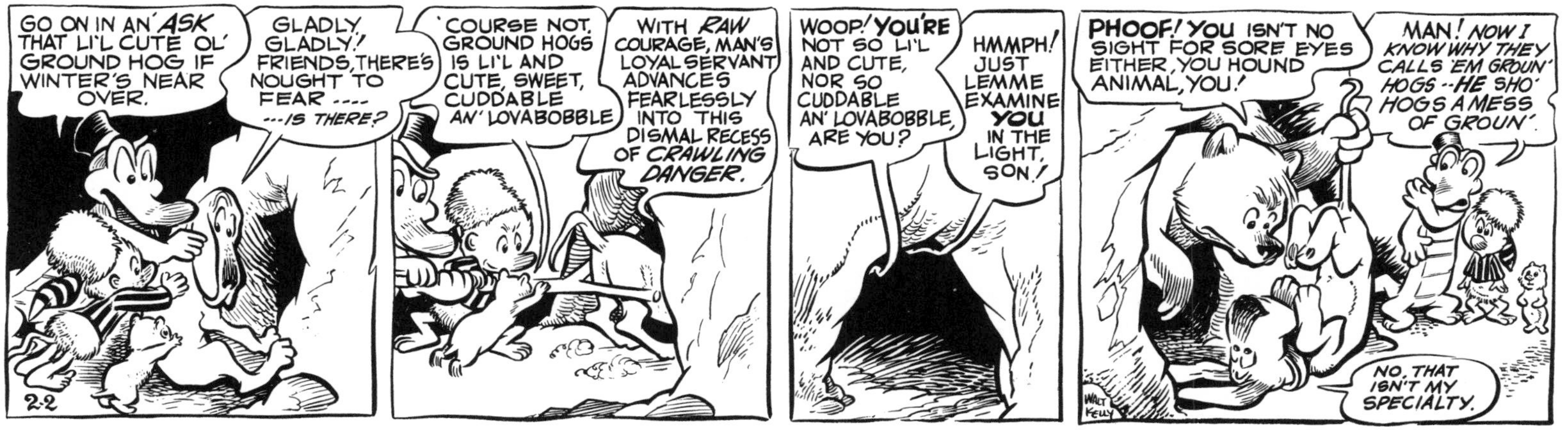
GO ON IN AN' ASK THAT LI'L CUTE OL' GROUND HOG IF WINTER'S NEAR OVER.
GLADLY. GLADLY! FRIENDS, THERE'S NOUGHT TO FEAR ---- ---IS THERE?
'COURSE NOT. GROUND HOGS IS LI'L AND CUTE, SWEET, CUDDABLE AN' LOVABOBBLE
WITH RAW COURAGE, MAN'S LOYAL SERVANT ADVANCES FEARLESSLY INTO THIS DISMAL RECESS OF CRAWLING DANGER.
WOOP! YOU'RE NOT SO LI'L AND CUTE, NOR SO CUDDABLE AN' LOVABOBBLE, ARE YOU?
HMMPH! JUST LEMME EXAMINE YOU IN THE LIGHT, SON!
PHOOF! YOU ISN'T NO SIGHT FOR SORE EYES EITHER, YOU HOUND ANIMAL, YOU!
MAN! NOW I KNOW WHY THEY CALLS 'EM GROUN' HOGS --HE SHO' HOGS A MESS OF GROUN'.
NO, THAT ISN'T MY SPECIALTY.
2-2
WALT KELLY

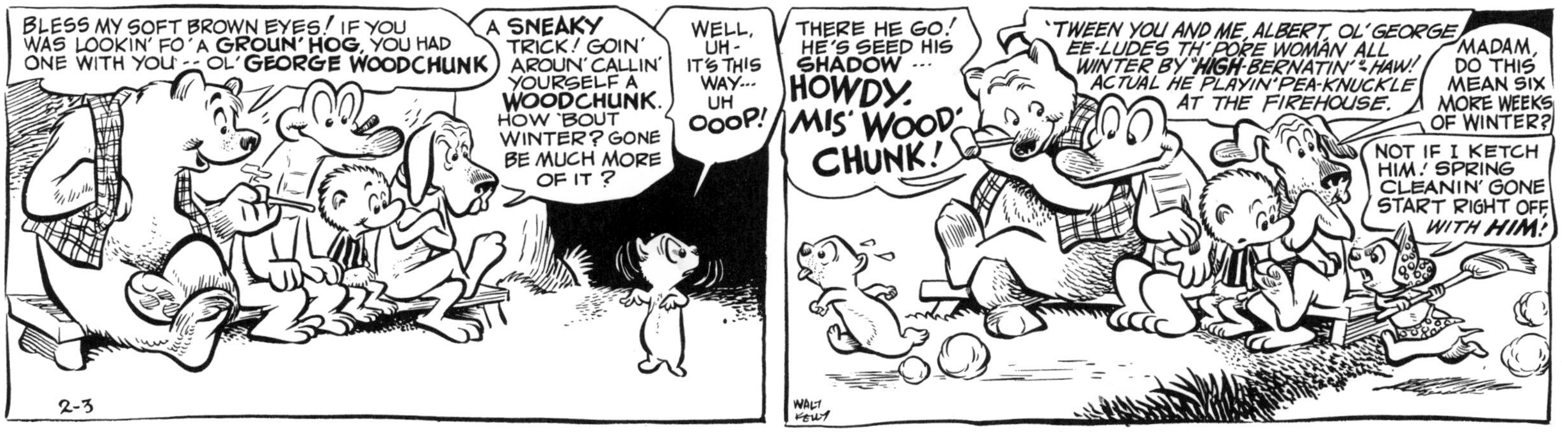
BLESS MY SOFT BROWN EYES! IF YOU WAS LOOKIN' FO' A GROUN' HOG, YOU HAD ONE WITH YOU -- OL' GEORGE WOODCHUNK
A SNEAKY TRICK! GOIN' AROUN' CALLIN' YOURSELF A WOODCHUNK. HOW 'BOUT WINTER? GONE BE MUCH MORE OF IT?
WELL, UH - IT'S THIS WAY--- UH
OOOP!
THERE HE GO! HE'S SEED HIS SHADOW ---
HOWDY, MIS' WOOD-CHUNK!
'TWEEN YOU AND ME, ALBERT, OL' GEORGE EE-LUDES TH' PORE WOMAN ALL WINTER BY 'HIGH-BERNATIN'' - HAW! ACTUAL HE PLAYIN' PEA-KNUCKLE AT THE FIREHOUSE.
MADAM, DO THIS MEAN SIX MORE WEEKS OF WINTER?
NOT IF I KETCH HIM! SPRING CLEANIN' GONE START RIGHT OFF WITH HIM!
2-3
WALT KELLY

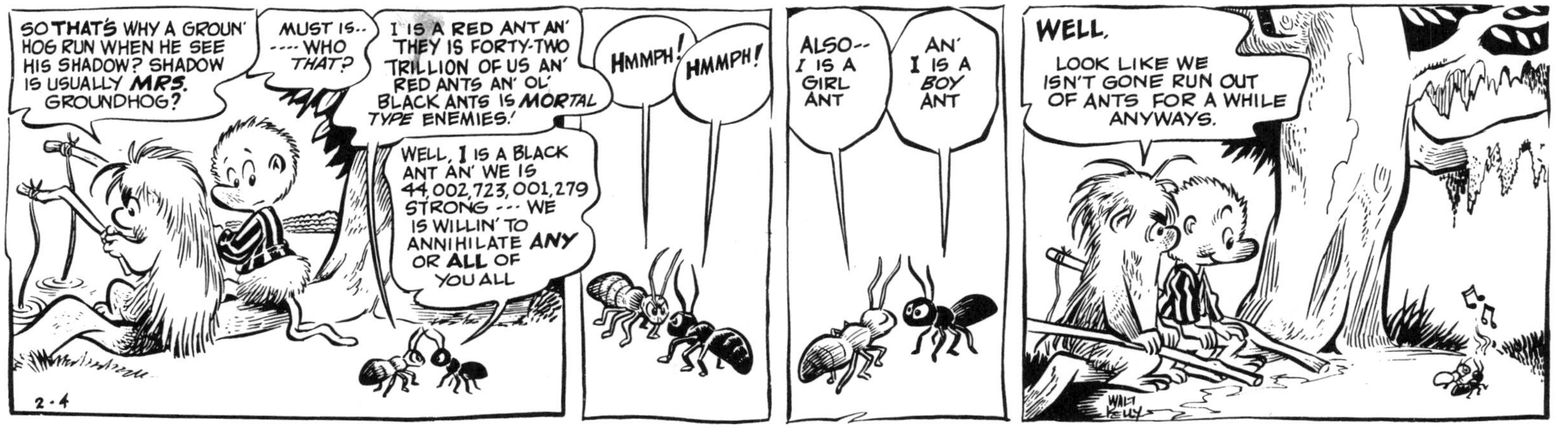
SO THAT'S WHY A GROUN' HOG RUN WHEN HE SEE HIS SHADOW? SHADOW IS USUALLY MRS. GROUNDHOG?
MUST IS.. ---- WHO THAT?
I IS A RED ANT AN' THEY IS FORTY-TWO TRILLION OF US AN' RED ANTS AN' OL' BLACK ANTS IS MORTAL TYPE ENEMIES!
WELL, I IS A BLACK ANT AN' WE IS 44,002,723,001,279 STRONG --- WE IS WILLIN' TO ANNIHILATE ANY OR ALL OF YOU ALL
HMMPH!
HMMPH!
ALSO-- I IS A GIRL ANT
AN' I IS A BOY ANT
WELL,
LOOK LIKE WE ISN'T GONE RUN OUT OF ANTS FOR A WHILE ANYWAYS.
2-4
WALT KELLY

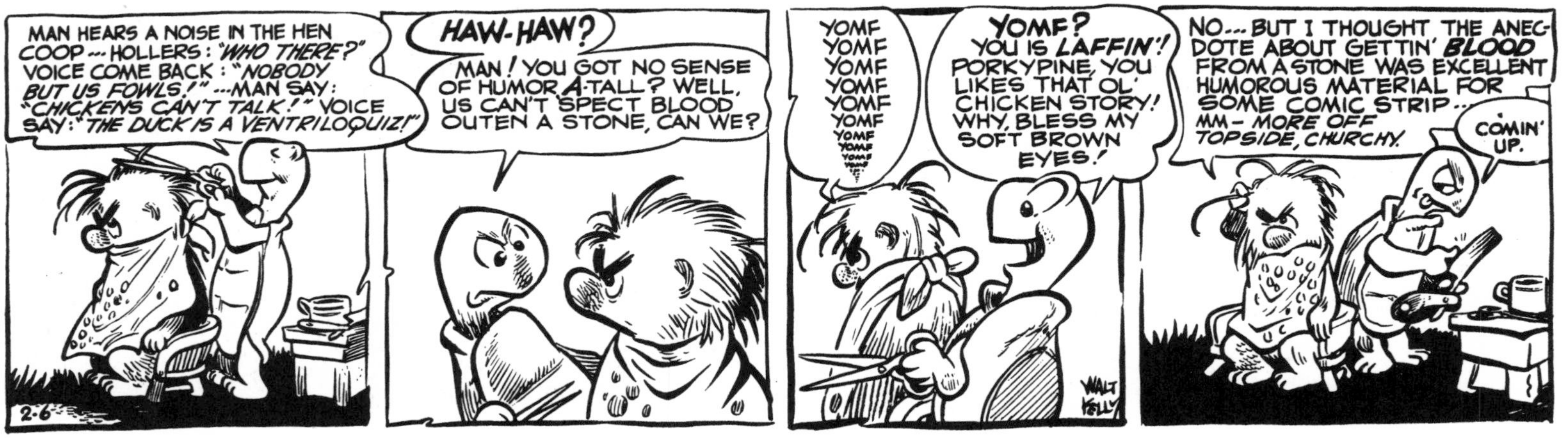
MAN HEARS A NOISE IN THE HEN COOP --- HOLLERS: "WHO THERE?" VOICE COME BACK: "NOBODY BUT US FOWLS!" ---MAN SAY: "CHICKENS CAN'T TALK!" VOICE SAY: "THE DUCK IS A VENTRILOQUIZ!"
HAW-HAW?
MAN! YOU GOT NO SENSE OF HUMOR A-TALL? WELL, US CAN'T 'SPECT BLOOD OUTEN A STONE, CAN WE?
YOMF YOMF YOMF YOMF YOMF YOMF
YOMF? YOU IS LAFFIN'! PORKYPINE, YOU LIKES THAT OL' CHICKEN STORY! WHY, BLESS MY SOFT BROWN EYES!
NO... BUT I THOUGHT THE ANEC-DOTE ABOUT GETTIN' BLOOD FROM A STONE WAS EXCELLENT HUMOROUS MATERIAL FOR SOME COMIC STRIP... MM - MORE OFF TOPSIDE, CHURCHY.
COMIN' UP.
2-6
WALT KELLY

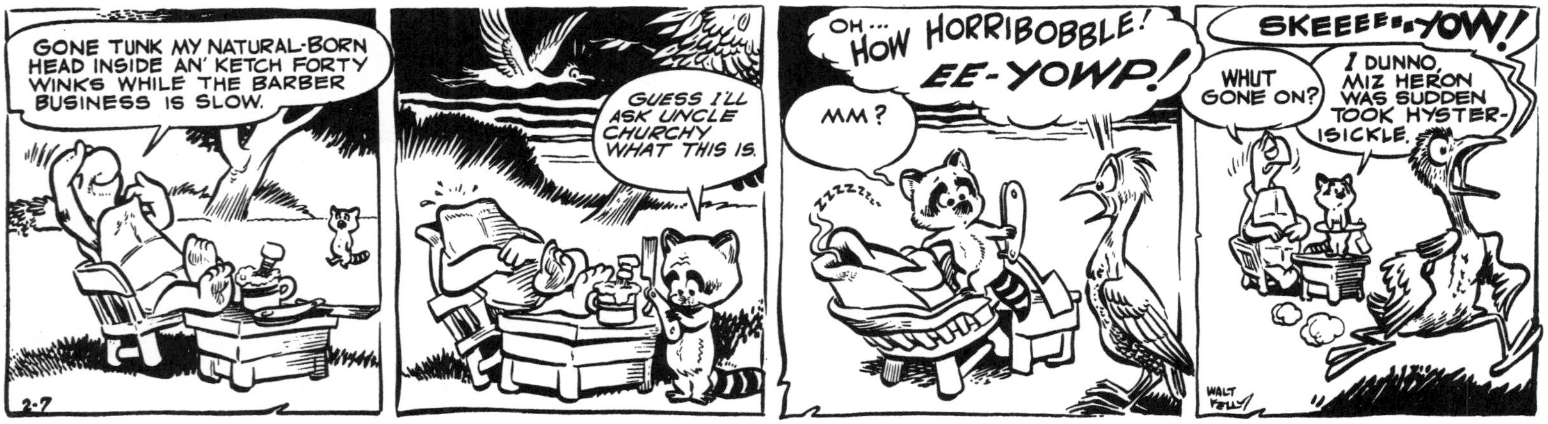
GONE TUNK MY NATURAL-BORN HEAD INSIDE AN' KETCH FORTY WINKS WHILE THE BARBER BUSINESS IS SLOW.
GUESS I'LL ASK UNCLE CHURCHY WHAT THIS IS.
OH... HOW HORRIBOBBLE! EE-YOWP!
MM?
SKEEEEE-YOW!
WHUT GONE ON?
I DUNNO, MIZ HERON WAS SUDDEN TOOK HYSTER-ISICKLE.
2-7
WALT KELLY

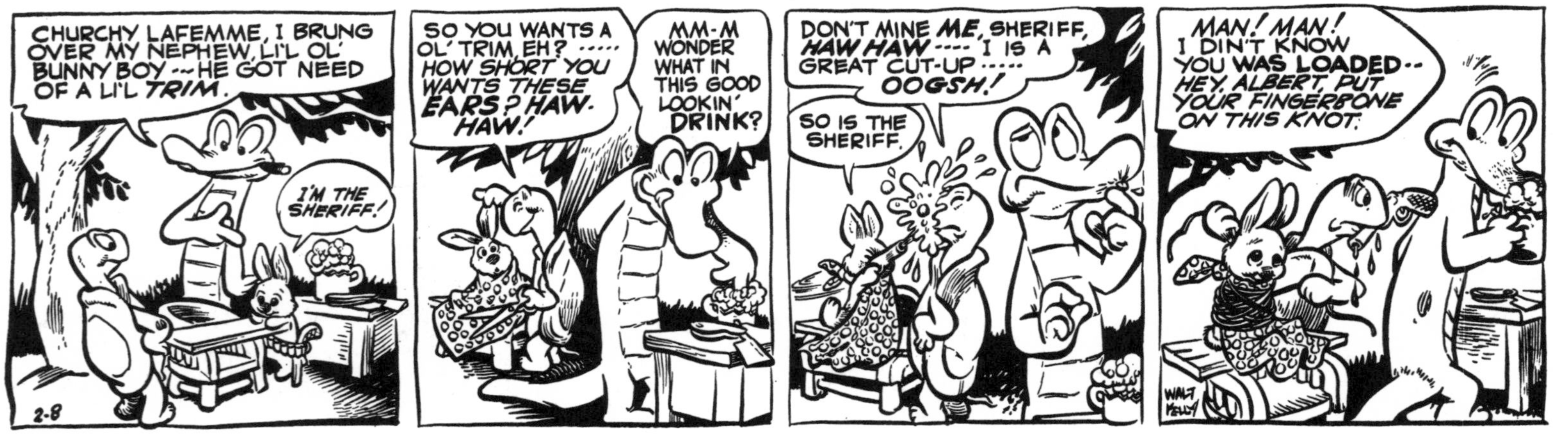
CHURCHY LAFEMME, I BRUNG OVER MY NEPHEW, LI'L OL' BUNNY BOY -- HE GOT NEED OF A LI'L TRIM.
I'M THE SHERIFF!
SO YOU WANTS A OL' TRIM, EH? ..... HOW SHORT YOU WANTS THESE EARS? HAW-HAW!
MM-M WONDER WHAT IN THIS GOOD LOOKIN' DRINK?
DON'T MINE ME, SHERIFF, HAW HAW ---- I IS A GREAT CUT-UP ..... OOGSH!
SO IS THE SHERIFF.
MAN! MAN! I DIN'T KNOW YOU WAS LOADED -- HEY, ALBERT, PUT YOUR FINGERBONE ON THIS KNOT.
2-8
WALT KELLY

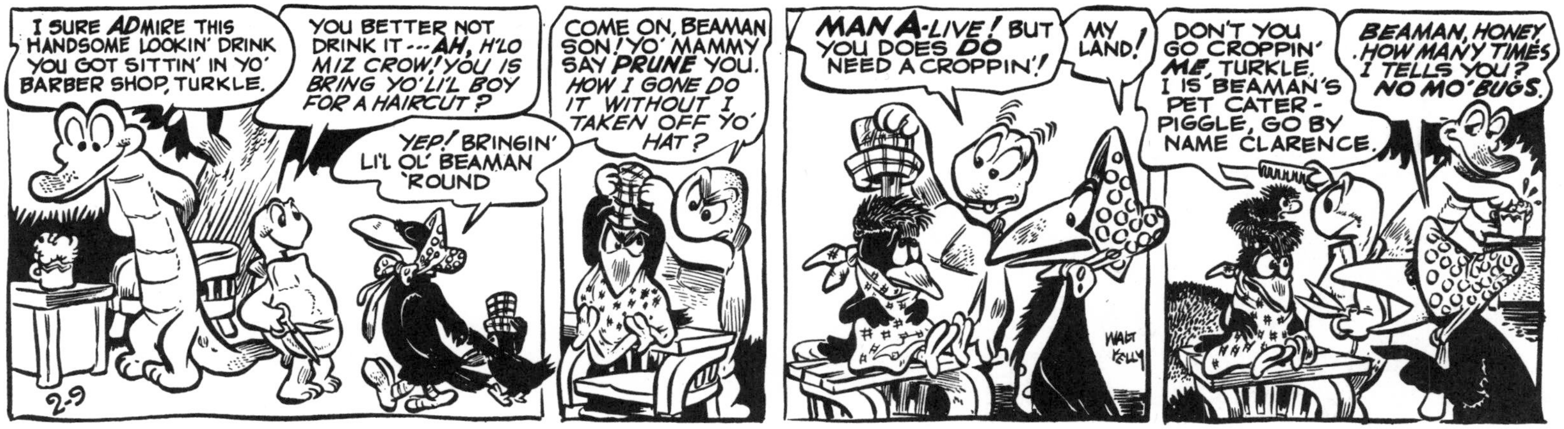
I SURE ADMIRE THIS HANDSOME LOOKIN' DRINK YOU GOT SITTIN' IN YO' BARBER SHOP, TURKLE.
YOU BETTER NOT DRINK IT---AH, H'LO MIZ CROW! YOU IS BRING YO' LI'L BOY FOR A HAIRCUT?
YEP! BRINGIN' LI'L OL' BEAMAN 'ROUND
2-9
COME ON, BEAMAN SON! YO' MAMMY SAY PRUNE YOU.
HOW I GONE DO IT WITHOUT I TAKEN OFF YO' HAT?
MAN A-LIVE! BUT YOU DOES DO NEED A CROPPIN'!
MY LAND!
DON'T YOU GO CROPPIN' ME, TURKLE. I IS BEAMAN'S PET CATER-PIGGLE, GO BY NAME CLARENCE.
BEAMAN, HONEY, HOW MANY TIMES I TELLS YOU? NO MO' BUGS.

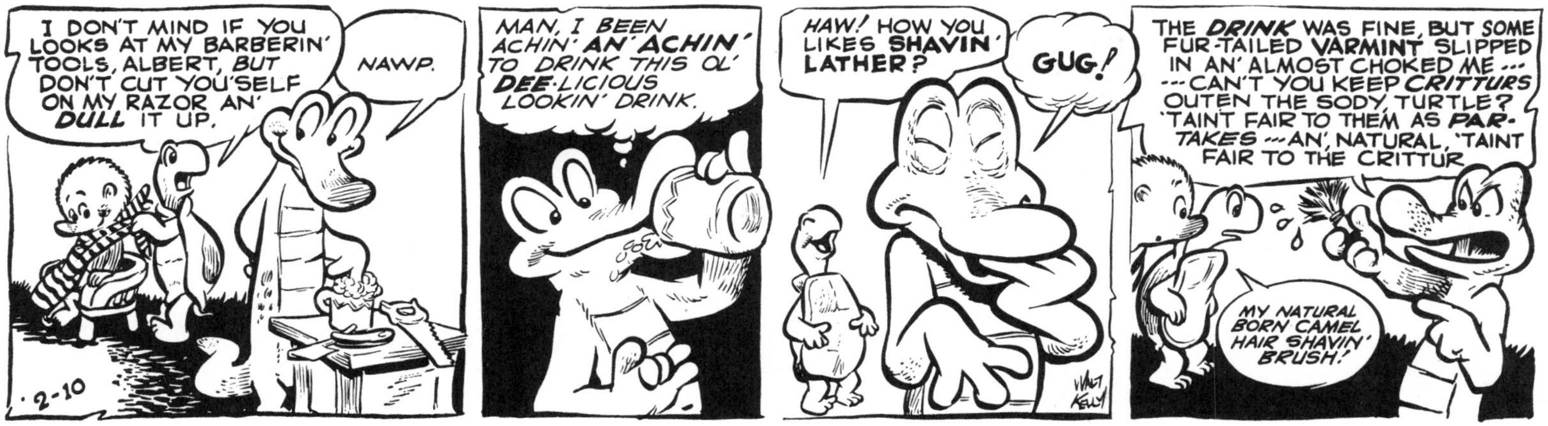
I DON'T MIND IF YOU LOOKS AT MY BARBERIN' TOOLS, ALBERT, BUT DON'T CUT YOU'SELF ON MY RAZOR AN' DULL IT UP.
NAWP.
2-10
MAN, I BEEN ACHIN' AN' ACHIN' TO DRINK THIS OL' DEE-LICIOUS LOOKIN' DRINK.
HAW! HOW YOU LIKES SHAVIN' LATHER?
GUG!
THE DRINK WAS FINE, BUT SOME FUR-TAILED VARMINT SLIPPED IN AN' ALMOST CHOKED ME------CAN'T YOU KEEP CRITTURS OUTEN THE SODY, TURTLE? 'TAINT FAIR TO THEM AS PAR-TAKES---AN', NATURAL, 'TAINT FAIR TO THE CRITTUR.
MY NATURAL BORN CAMEL HAIR SHAVIN' BRUSH!

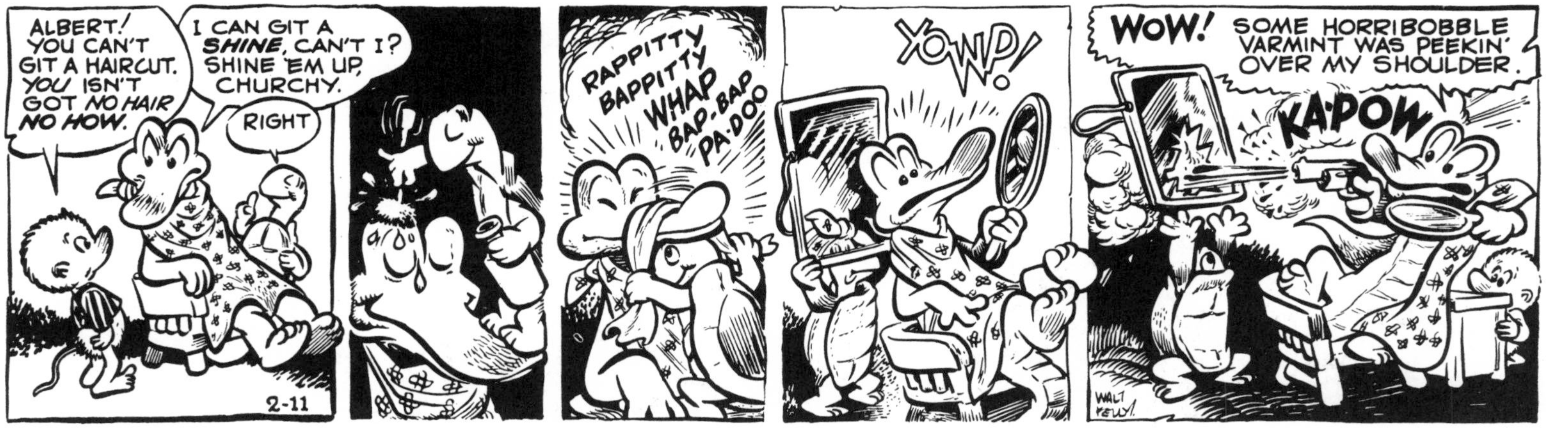
ALBERT! YOU CAN'T GIT A HAIRCUT. YOU ISN'T GOT NO HAIR NO HOW.
I CAN GIT A SHINE, CAN'T I? SHINE 'EM UP, CHURCHY.
RIGHT
2-11
RAPPITTY BAPPITTY WHAP BAP-BAP PA-DOO
YOWP!
WOW! SOME HORRIBOBBLE VARMINT WAS PEEKIN' OVER MY SHOULDER.
KA-POW

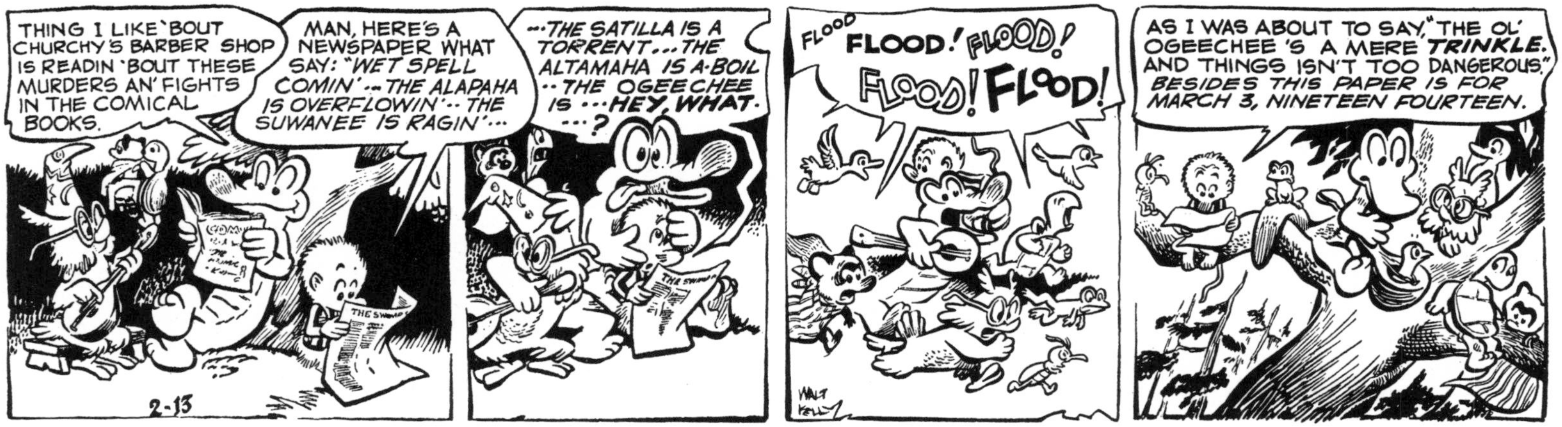
THING I LIKE 'BOUT CHURCHY'S BARBER SHOP IS READIN 'BOUT THESE MURDERS AN' FIGHTS IN THE COMICAL BOOKS.
MAN, HERE'S A NEWSPAPER WHAT SAY: "WET SPELL COMIN' -- THE ALAPAHA IS OVERFLOWIN' -- THE SUWANEE IS RAGIN' ...
--THE SATILLA IS A TORRENT ... THE ALTAMAHA IS A-BOIL -- THE OGEECHEE IS --- HEY, WHAT --- ?
FLOOD FLOOD! FLOOD! FLOOD! FLOOD!
AS I WAS ABOUT TO SAY, "THE OL' OGEECHEE 'S A MERE TRINKLE. AND THINGS ISN'T TOO DANGEROUS." BESIDES THIS PAPER IS FOR MARCH 3, NINETEEN FOURTEEN.
2-13
WALT KELLY

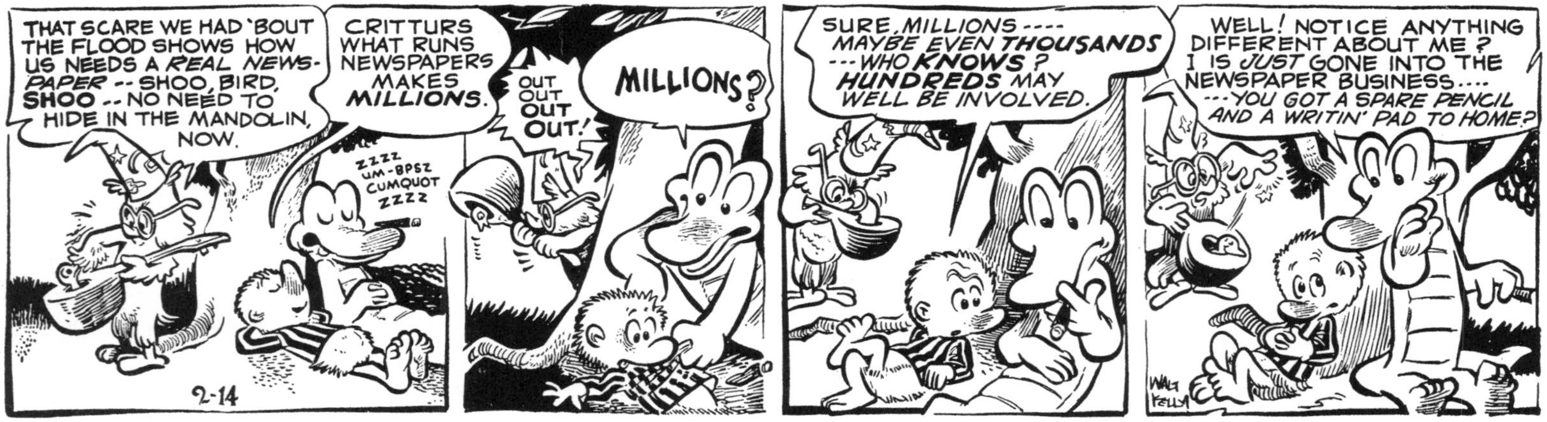
THAT SCARE WE HAD 'BOUT THE FLOOD SHOWS HOW US NEEDS A REAL NEWSPAPER -- SHOO, BIRD, SHOO -- NO NEED TO HIDE IN THE MANDOLIN, NOW.
CRITTURS WHAT RUNS NEWSPAPERS MAKES MILLIONS.
ZZZZ UM-BPSZ CUMQUOT ZZZZ
OUT OUT OUT OUT!
MILLIONS?
SURE, MILLIONS ---- MAYBE EVEN THOUSANDS --- WHO KNOWS? HUNDREDS MAY WELL BE INVOLVED.
WELL! NOTICE ANYTHING DIFFERENT ABOUT ME? I IS JUST GONE INTO THE NEWSPAPER BUSINESS .... --- YOU GOT A SPARE PENCIL AND A WRITIN' PAD TO HOME?
2-14
WALT KELLY

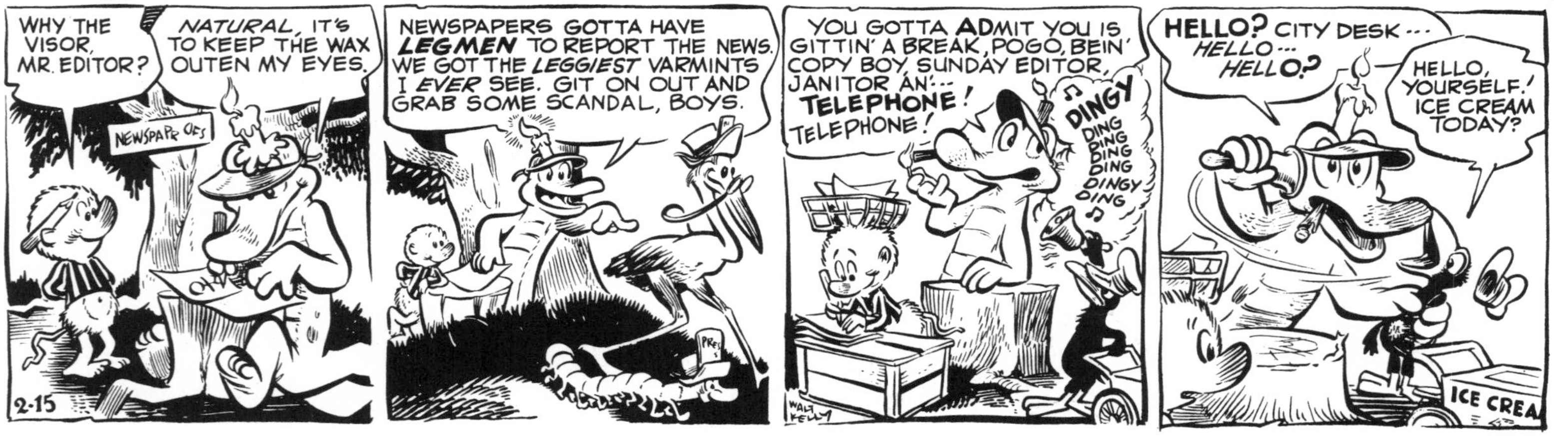
WHY THE VISOR, MR. EDITOR?
NATURAL, IT'S TO KEEP THE WAX OUTEN MY EYES.
NEWSPAPERS GOTTA HAVE LEGMEN TO REPORT THE NEWS. WE GOT THE LEGGIEST VARMINTS I EVER SEE. GIT ON OUT AND GRAB SOME SCANDAL, BOYS.
YOU GOTTA ADMIT YOU IS GITTIN' A BREAK, POGO, BEIN' COPY BOY, SUNDAY EDITOR, JANITOR AN' --- TELEPHONE! TELEPHONE!
DINGY DING DING DING DING DINGY DING
HELLO? CITY DESK --- HELLO --- HELLO?
HELLO, YOURSELF! ICE CREAM TODAY?
ICE CREA
2-15
WALT KELLY

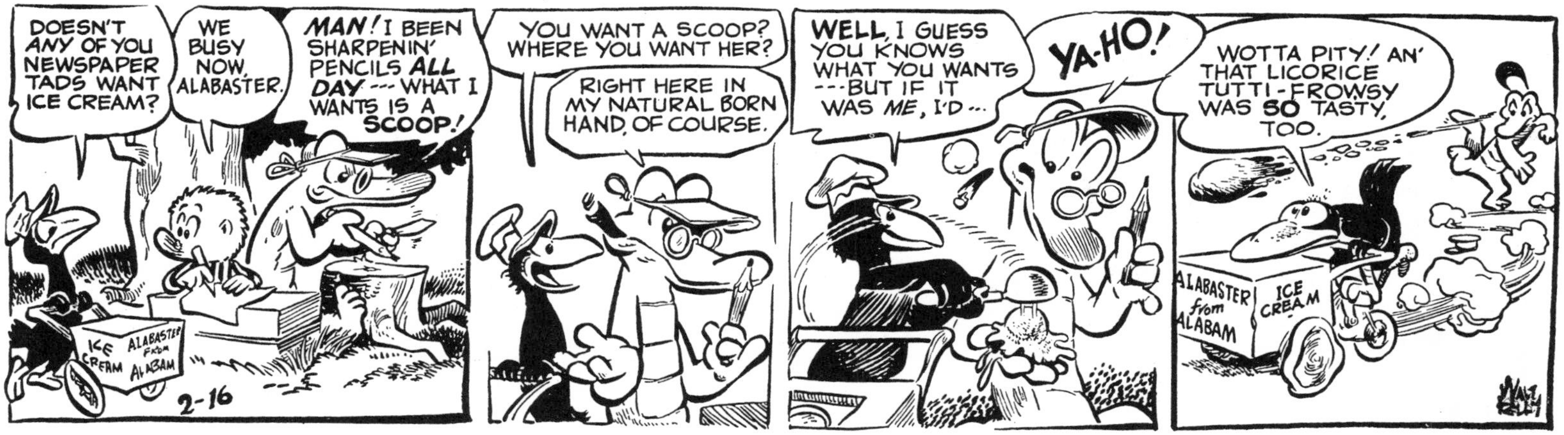
DOESN'T ANY OF YOU NEWSPAPER TADS WANT ICE CREAM?
WE BUSY NOW, ALABASTER.
MAN! I BEEN SHARPENIN' PENCILS ALL DAY --- WHAT I WANTS IS A SCOOP!
ICE CREAM ALABASTER FROM ALABAM
2-16
YOU WANT A SCOOP? WHERE YOU WANT HER?
RIGHT HERE IN MY NATURAL BORN HAND, OF COURSE.
WELL, I GUESS YOU KNOWS WHAT YOU WANTS ---BUT IF IT WAS ME, I'D...
YA-HO!
WOTTA PITY! AN' THAT LICORICE TUTTI-FROWSY WAS SO TASTY, TOO.
ALABASTER from ALABAM ICE CREAM
WALT KELLY

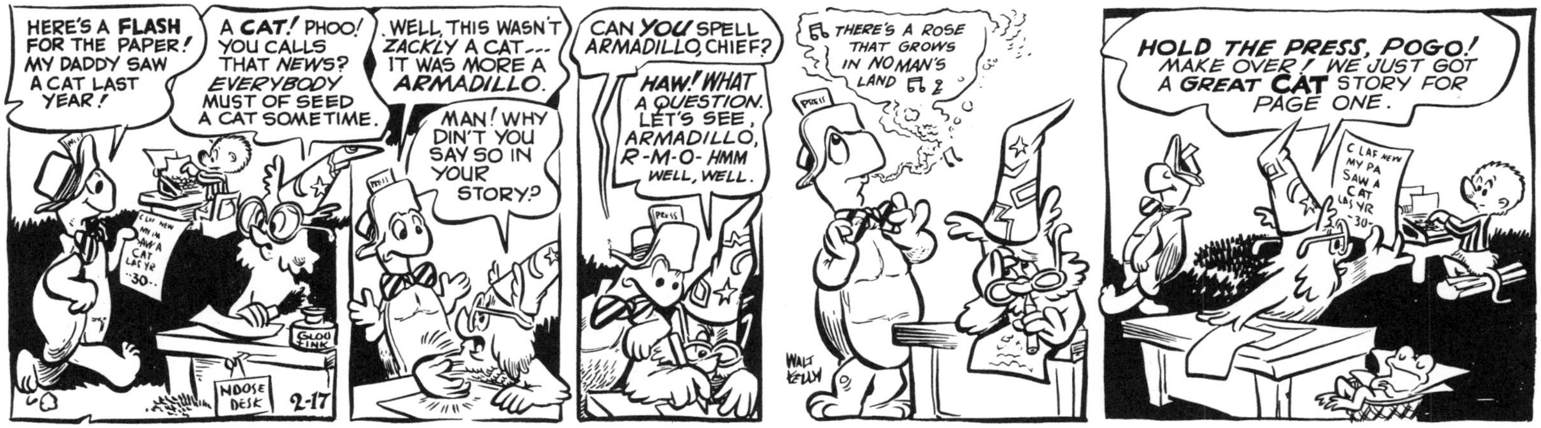
HERE'S A FLASH FOR THE PAPER! MY DADDY SAW A CAT LAST YEAR!
A CAT! PHOO! YOU CALLS THAT NEWS? EVERYBODY MUST OF SEED A CAT SOMETIME.
GLOO INK
NOOSE DESK
2-17
WELL, THIS WASN'T ZACKLY A CAT--- IT WAS MORE A ARMADILLO.
MAN! WHY DIN'T YOU SAY SO IN YOUR STORY?
CAN YOU SPELL ARMADILLO, CHIEF?
HAW! WHAT A QUESTION. LET'S SEE, ARMADILLO, R-M-O-HMM WELL, WELL.
THERE'S A ROSE THAT GROWS IN NO MAN'S LAND
WALT KELLY
HOLD THE PRESS, POGO! MAKE OVER! WE JUST GOT A GREAT CAT STORY FOR PAGE ONE.

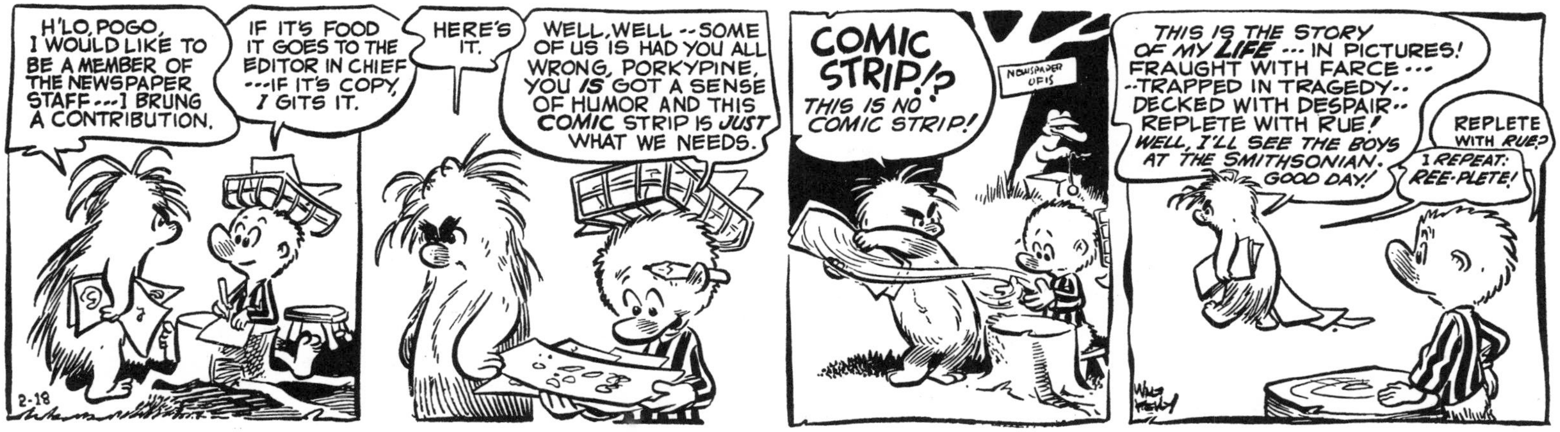
H'LO, POGO, I WOULD LIKE TO BE A MEMBER OF THE NEWSPAPER STAFF---I BRUNG A CONTRIBUTION.
IF IT'S FOOD IT GOES TO THE EDITOR IN CHIEF ---IF IT'S COPY, I GITS IT.
2-18
HERE'S IT.
WELL, WELL --SOME OF US IS HAD YOU ALL WRONG, PORKYPINE, YOU IS GOT A SENSE OF HUMOR AND THIS COMIC STRIP IS JUST WHAT WE NEEDS.
COMIC STRIP!? THIS IS NO COMIC STRIP!
NEWSPAPER OFIS
THIS IS THE STORY OF MY LIFE --- IN PICTURES! FRAUGHT WITH FARCE --- --TRAPPED IN TRAGEDY-- DECKED WITH DESPAIR-- REPLETE WITH RUE! WELL, I'LL SEE THE BOYS AT THE SMITHSONIAN. GOOD DAY!
REPLETE WITH RUE?
I REPEAT: REE-PLETE!
WALT KELLY

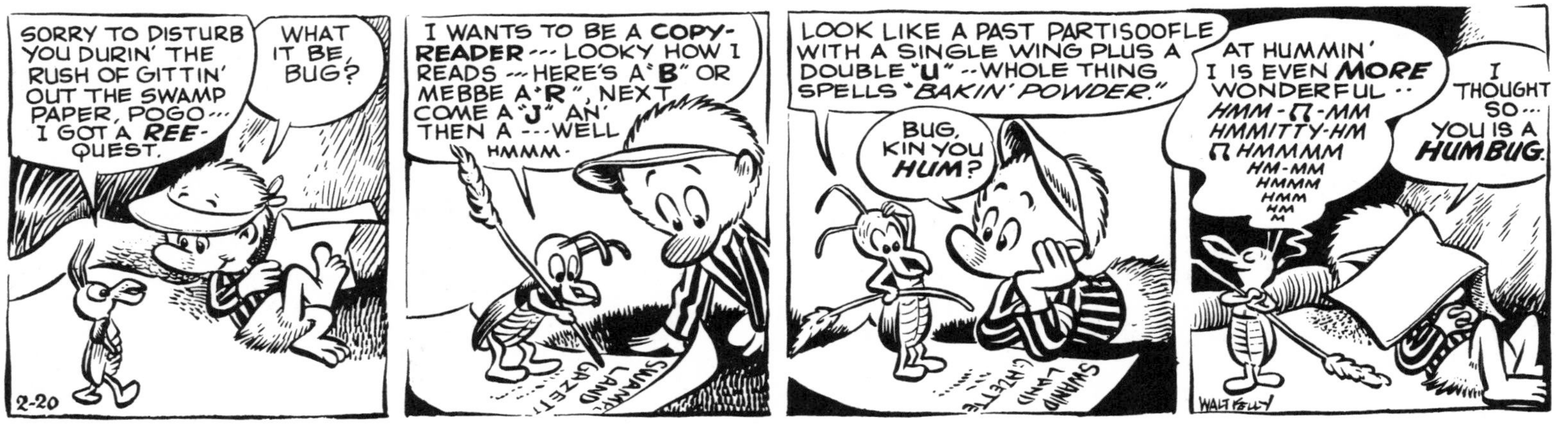
SORRY TO DISTURB YOU DURIN' THE RUSH OF GITTIN' OUT THE SWAMP PAPER, POGO--- I GOT A **REE**-QUEST.
WHAT IT BE, BUG?
2-20
I WANTS TO BE A **COPY-READER**--- LOOKY HOW I READS ---HERE'S A "**B**" OR MEBBE A "**R**", NEXT COME A "**J**" AN' THEN A ---WELL HMMM-
LOOK LIKE A PAST PARTISOOFLE WITH A SINGLE WING PLUS A DOUBLE "**U**" --WHOLE THING SPELLS "*BAKIN' POWDER*."
BUG, KIN YOU ***HUM***?
AT HUMMIN' I IS EVEN ***MORE*** WONDERFUL -- *HMM-♫-MM HMMITTY-HM ♫ HMMMM HM-MM HMMM HMM HM M*
I THOUGHT SO--- YOU IS A ***HUMBUG***.
WALT KELLY

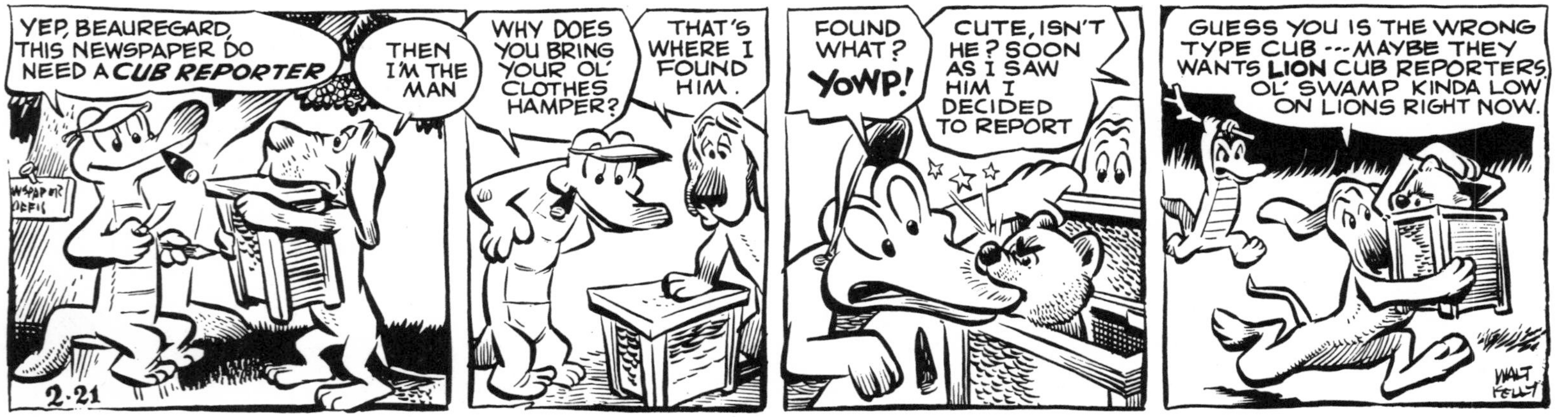
YEP, BEAUREGARD, THIS NEWSPAPER DO NEED A ***CUB REPORTER***
THEN I'M THE MAN
2-21
WHY DOES YOU BRING YOUR OL' CLOTHES HAMPER?
THAT'S WHERE I FOUND HIM.
FOUND WHAT?
YOWP!
CUTE, ISN'T HE? SOON AS I SAW HIM I DECIDED TO REPORT
GUESS YOU IS THE WRONG TYPE CUB ---MAYBE THEY WANTS **LION** CUB REPORTERS. OL' SWAMP KINDA LOW ON LIONS RIGHT NOW.
WALT KELLY

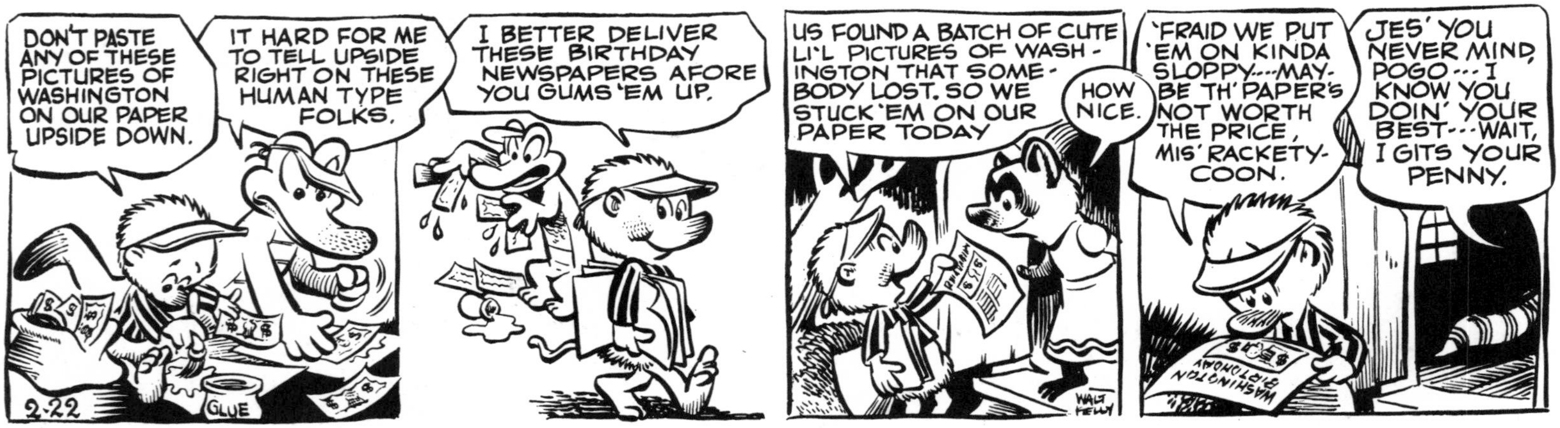
DON'T PASTE ANY OF THESE PICTURES OF WASHINGTON ON OUR PAPER UPSIDE DOWN.
IT HARD FOR ME TO TELL UPSIDE RIGHT ON THESE HUMAN TYPE FOLKS.
2-22
GLUE
I BETTER DELIVER THESE BIRTHDAY NEWSPAPERS AFORE YOU GUMS 'EM UP.
US FOUND A BATCH OF CUTE LI'L PICTURES OF WASH-INGTON THAT SOME-BODY LOST. SO WE STUCK 'EM ON OUR PAPER TODAY
HOW NICE.
WALT KELLY
'FRAID WE PUT 'EM ON KINDA SLOPPY---MAY-BE TH' PAPER'S NOT WORTH THE PRICE, MIS' RACKETY-COON.
JES' YOU NEVER MIND, POGO--- I KNOW YOU DOIN' YOUR BEST---WAIT, I GITS YOUR PENNY.

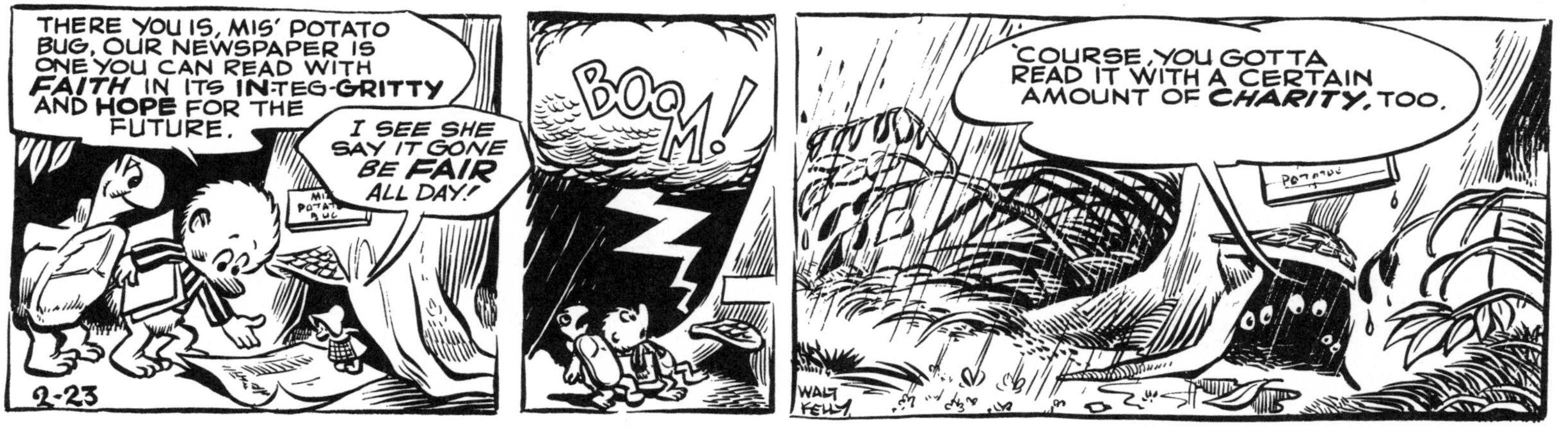
THERE YOU IS, MIS' POTATO BUG, OUR NEWSPAPER IS ONE YOU CAN READ WITH FAITH IN ITS IN-TEG-GRITTY AND HOPE FOR THE FUTURE.
I SEE SHE SAY IT GONE BE FAIR ALL DAY!
2-23
BOOM!
'COURSE, YOU GOTTA READ IT WITH A CERTAIN AMOUNT OF CHARITY, TOO.
WALT KELLY

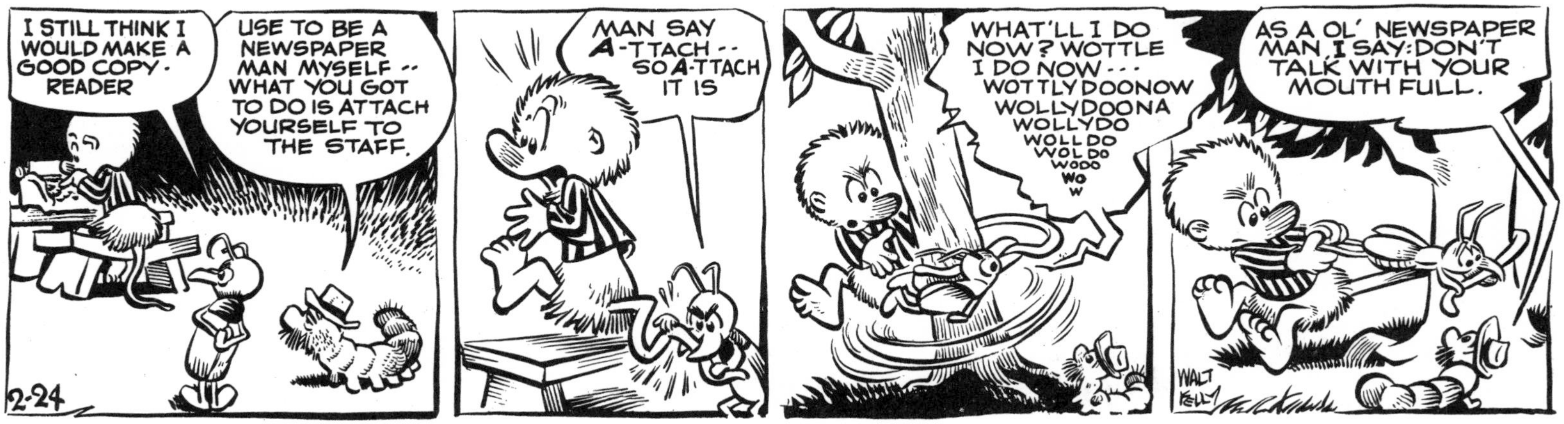
I STILL THINK I WOULD MAKE A GOOD COPY-READER
USE TO BE A NEWSPAPER MAN MYSELF -- WHAT YOU GOT TO DO IS ATTACH YOURSELF TO THE STAFF.
2-24
MAN SAY A-TTACH -- SO A-TTACH IT IS
WHAT'LL I DO NOW? WOTTLE I DO NOW --- WOTTLYDOONOW WOLLYDOONA WOLLYDO WOLLDO WOLDO WODO WO W
AS A OL' NEWSPAPER MAN, I SAY: DON'T TALK WITH YOUR MOUTH FULL.
WALT KELLY

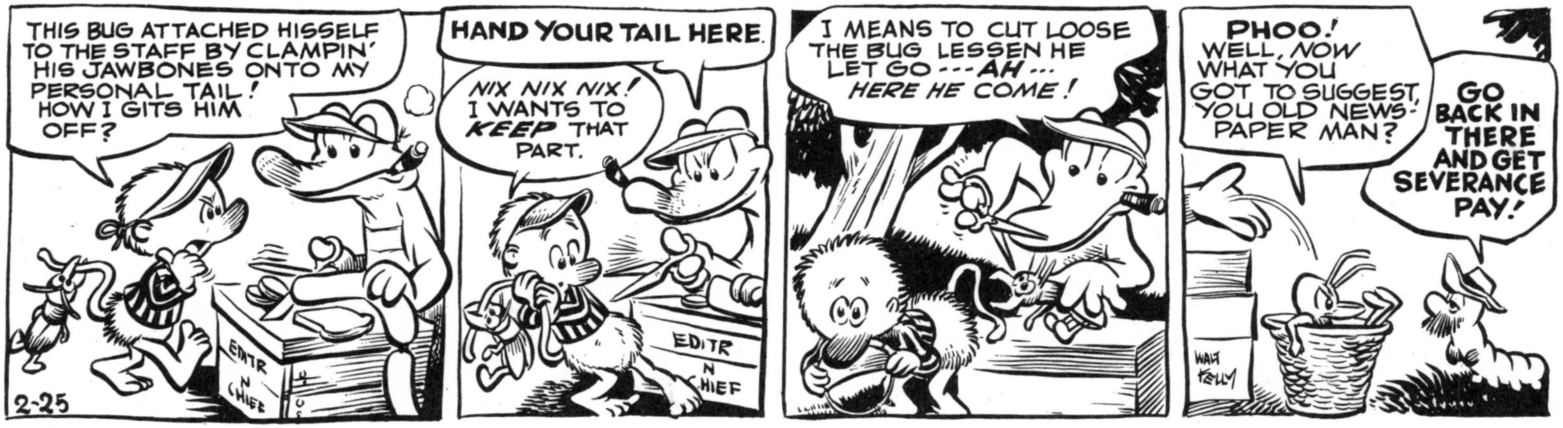
THIS BUG ATTACHED HISSELF TO THE STAFF BY CLAMPIN' HIS JAWBONES ONTO MY PERSONAL TAIL! HOW I GITS HIM OFF?
EDITR N CHIEF
2-25
HAND YOUR TAIL HERE.
NIX NIX NIX! I WANTS TO KEEP THAT PART.
EDITR N CHIEF
I MEANS TO CUT LOOSE THE BUG LESSEN HE LET GO --- AH --- HERE HE COME!
PHOO! WELL, NOW WHAT YOU GOT TO SUGGEST, YOU OLD NEWS-PAPER MAN?
GO BACK IN THERE AND GET SEVERANCE PAY!
WALT KELLY

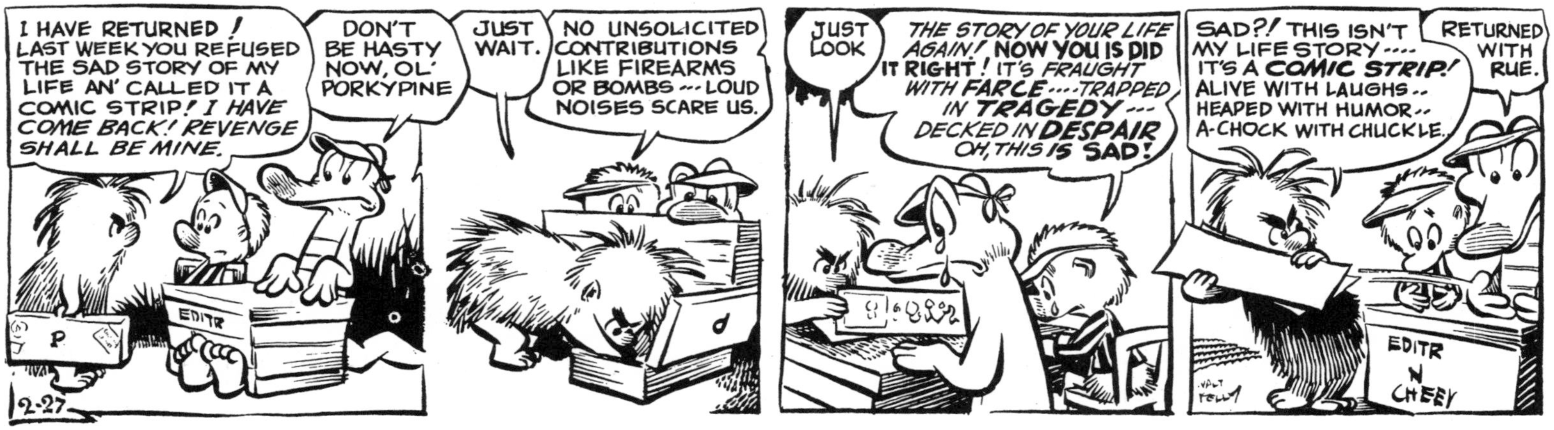
I HAVE RETURNED! LAST WEEK YOU REFUSED THE SAD STORY OF MY LIFE AN' CALLED IT A COMIC STRIP! I HAVE COME BACK! REVENGE SHALL BE MINE.
DON'T BE HASTY NOW, OL' PORKYPINE
EDITR
2-27
JUST WAIT.
NO UNSOLICITED CONTRIBUTIONS LIKE FIREARMS OR BOMBS --- LOUD NOISES SCARE US.
JUST LOOK
THE STORY OF YOUR LIFE AGAIN! NOW YOU IS DID IT RIGHT! IT'S FRAUGHT WITH FARCE---TRAPPED IN TRAGEDY--- DECKED IN DESPAIR OH, THIS IS SAD!
SAD?! THIS ISN'T MY LIFE STORY---- IT'S A COMIC STRIP! ALIVE WITH LAUGHS.. HEAPED WITH HUMOR.. A-CHOCK WITH CHUCKLE.
RETURNED WITH RUE.
EDITR N CHEEF

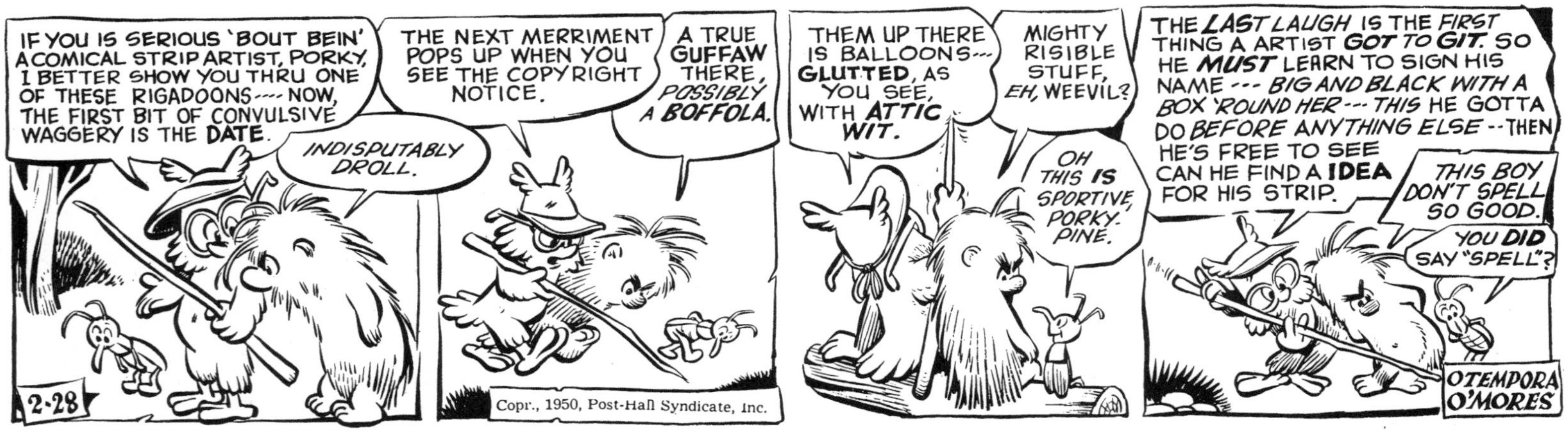
IF YOU IS SERIOUS 'BOUT BEIN' A COMICAL STRIP ARTIST, PORKY, I BETTER SHOW YOU THRU ONE OF THESE RIGADOONS---- NOW, THE FIRST BIT OF CONVULSIVE WAGGERY IS THE DATE.
INDISPUTABLY DROLL.
2-28
THE NEXT MERRIMENT POPS UP WHEN YOU SEE THE COPYRIGHT NOTICE.
A TRUE GUFFAW THERE, POSSIBLY A BOFFOLA.
Copr., 1950, Post-Hall Syndicate, Inc.
THEM UP THERE IS BALLOONS--- GLUTTED, AS YOU SEE, WITH ATTIC WIT.
MIGHTY RISIBLE STUFF, EH, WEEVIL?
OH THIS IS SPORTIVE, PORKY-PINE.
THE LAST LAUGH IS THE FIRST THING A ARTIST GOT TO GIT. SO HE MUST LEARN TO SIGN HIS NAME --- BIG AND BLACK WITH A BOX 'ROUND HER --- THIS HE GOTTA DO BEFORE ANYTHING ELSE -- THEN HE'S FREE TO SEE CAN HE FIND A IDEA FOR HIS STRIP.
THIS BOY DON'T SPELL SO GOOD.
YOU DID SAY "SPELL"?
OTEMPORA O'MORES

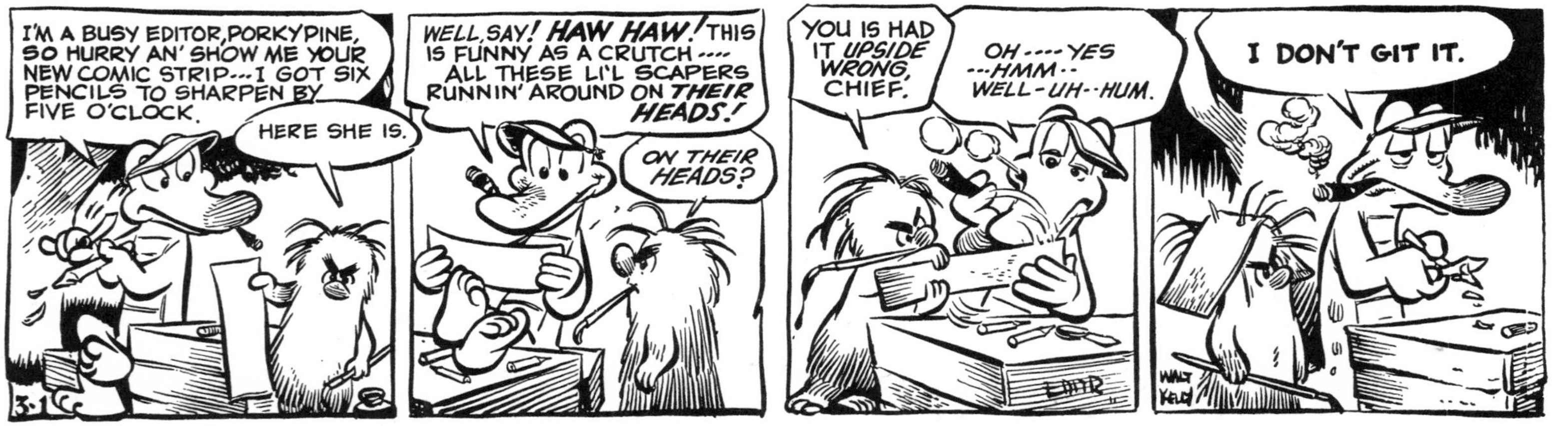
I'M A BUSY EDITOR, PORKYPINE, SO HURRY AN' SHOW ME YOUR NEW COMIC STRIP--- I GOT SIX PENCILS TO SHARPEN BY FIVE O'CLOCK.
HERE SHE IS.
3-1
WELL, SAY! HAW HAW! THIS IS FUNNY AS A CRUTCH---- ALL THESE LI'L SCAPERS RUNNIN' AROUND ON THEIR HEADS!
ON THEIR HEADS?
YOU IS HAD IT UPSIDE WRONG, CHIEF.
OH ---- YES --HMM -- WELL-UH--HUM.
I DON'T GIT IT.

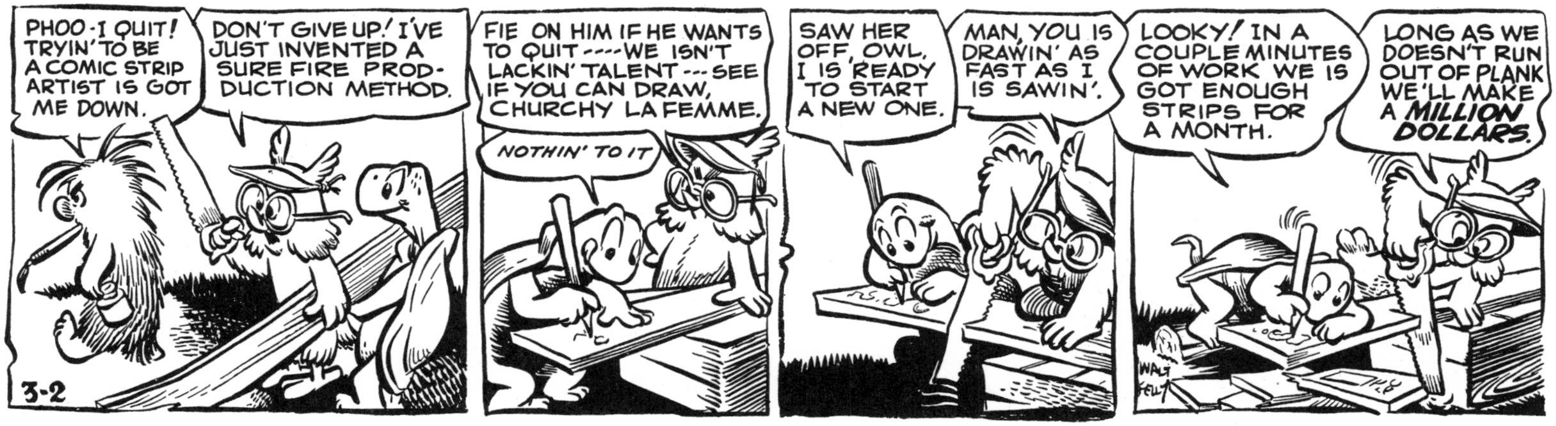
PHOO-I QUIT! TRYIN' TO BE A COMIC STRIP ARTIST IS GOT ME DOWN.
DON'T GIVE UP! I'VE JUST INVENTED A SURE FIRE PROD-DUCTION METHOD.
FIE ON HIM IF HE WANTS TO QUIT----WE ISN'T LACKIN' TALENT---SEE IF YOU CAN DRAW, CHURCHY LA FEMME.
NOTHIN' TO IT
SAW HER OFF, OWL, I IS READY TO START A NEW ONE.
MAN, YOU IS DRAWIN' AS FAST AS I IS SAWIN'.
LOOKY! IN A COUPLE MINUTES OF WORK WE IS GOT ENOUGH STRIPS FOR A MONTH.
LONG AS WE DOESN'T RUN OUT OF PLANK WE'LL MAKE A MILLION DOLLARS.
3-2

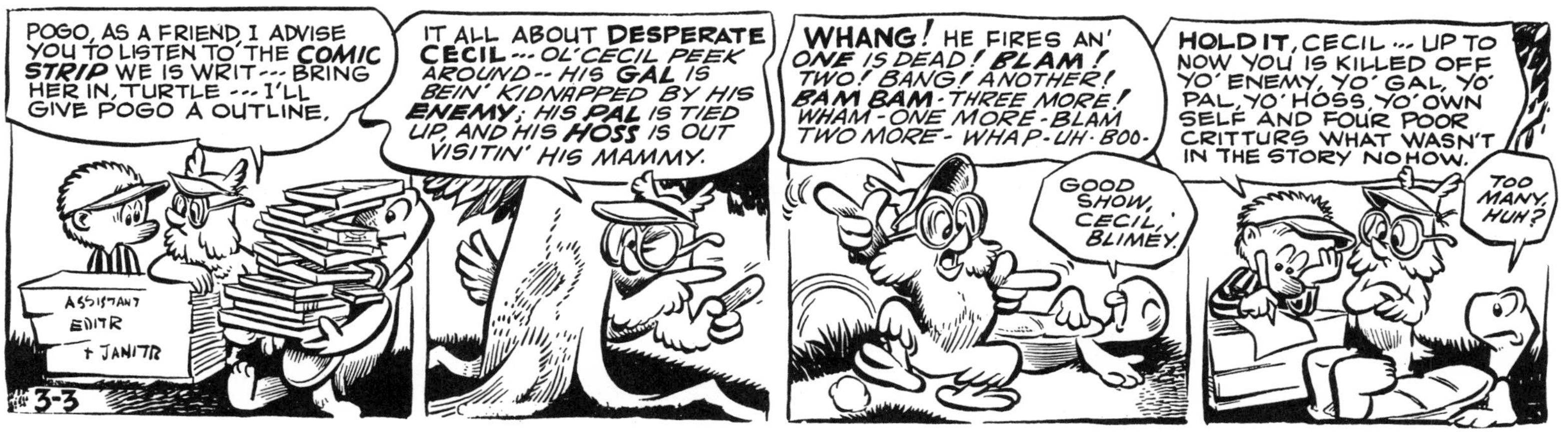
POGO, AS A FRIEND I ADVISE YOU TO LISTEN TO THE COMIC STRIP WE IS WRIT---BRING HER IN, TURTLE---I'LL GIVE POGO A OUTLINE.
ASSISTANT EDITR + JANITR
IT ALL ABOUT DESPERATE CECIL---OL' CECIL PEEK AROUND--HIS GAL IS BEIN' KIDNAPPED BY HIS ENEMY; HIS PAL IS TIED UP, AND HIS HOSS IS OUT VISITIN' HIS MAMMY.
WHANG! HE FIRES AN' ONE IS DEAD! BLAM! TWO! BANG! ANOTHER! BAM BAM-THREE MORE! WHAM-ONE MORE-BLAM TWO MORE-WHAP-UH-BOO-
GOOD SHOW, CECIL, BLIMEY.
HOLD IT, CECIL...UP TO NOW YOU IS KILLED OFF YO' ENEMY, YO' GAL, YO' PAL, YO' HOSS, YO' OWN SELF AND FOUR POOR CRITTURS WHAT WASN'T IN THE STORY NOHOW.
TOO MANY, HUH?
3-3

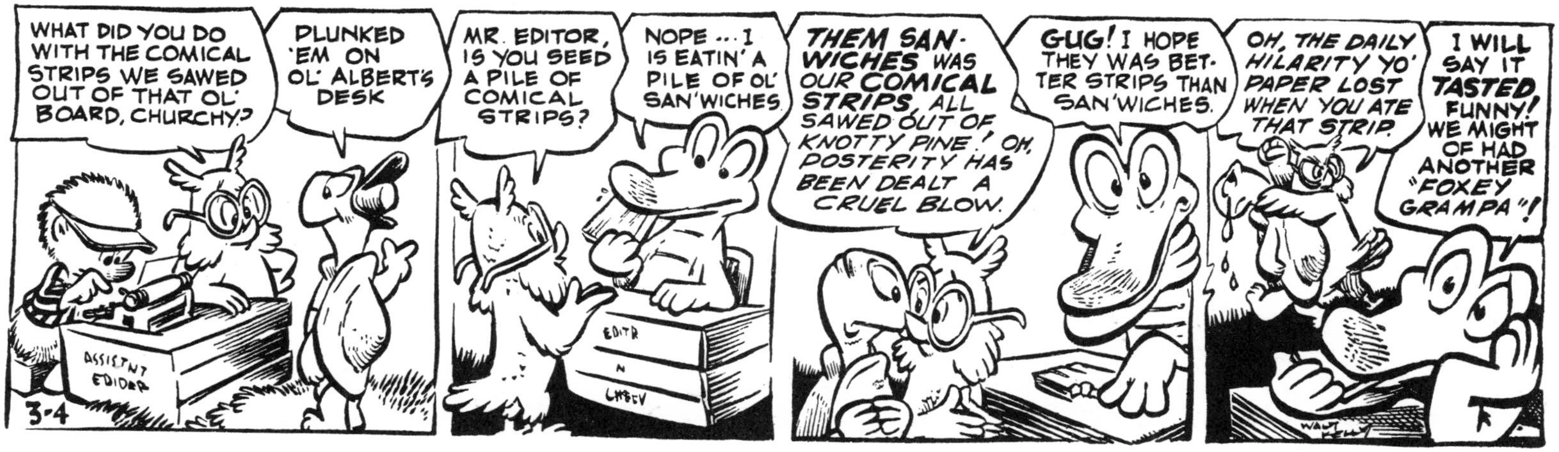
WHAT DID YOU DO WITH THE COMICAL STRIPS WE SAWED OUT OF THAT OL' BOARD, CHURCHY?
PLUNKED 'EM ON OL' ALBERT'S DESK
ASSISTNT EDIDER
MR. EDITOR, IS YOU SEED A PILE OF COMICAL STRIPS?
NOPE...I IS EATIN' A PILE OF OL' SAN'WICHES.
EDITR N CHEEF
THEM SAN-WICHES WAS OUR COMICAL STRIPS, ALL SAWED OUT OF KNOTTY PINE! OH, POSTERITY HAS BEEN DEALT A CRUEL BLOW.
GUG! I HOPE THEY WAS BET-TER STRIPS THAN SAN'WICHES.
OH, THE DAILY HILARITY YO' PAPER LOST WHEN YOU ATE THAT STRIP.
I WILL SAY IT TASTED FUNNY! WE MIGHT OF HAD ANOTHER "FOXEY GRAMPA"!
3-4

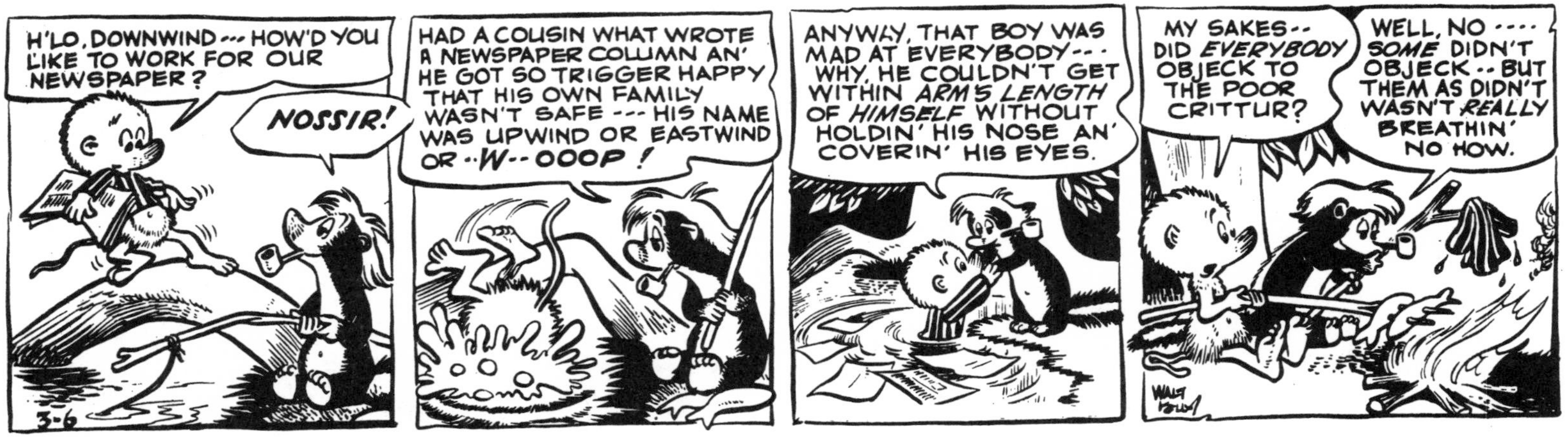

H'LO, DOWNWIND --- HOW'D YOU LIKE TO WORK FOR OUR NEWSPAPER?
NOSSIR!
3-6
HAD A COUSIN WHAT WROTE A NEWSPAPER COLUMN AN' HE GOT SO TRIGGER HAPPY THAT HIS OWN FAMILY WASN'T SAFE --- HIS NAME WAS UPWIND OR EASTWIND OR .. W-- OOOP!
ANYWAY, THAT BOY WAS MAD AT EVERYBODY--- WHY, HE COULDN'T GET WITHIN ARM'S LENGTH OF HIMSELF WITHOUT HOLDIN' HIS NOSE AN' COVERIN' HIS EYES.
MY SAKES-- DID EVERYBODY OBJECK TO THE POOR CRITTUR?
WELL, NO ---- SOME DIDN'T OBJECK -- BUT THEM AS DIDN'T WASN'T REALLY BREATHIN' NO HOW.
WALT KELLY

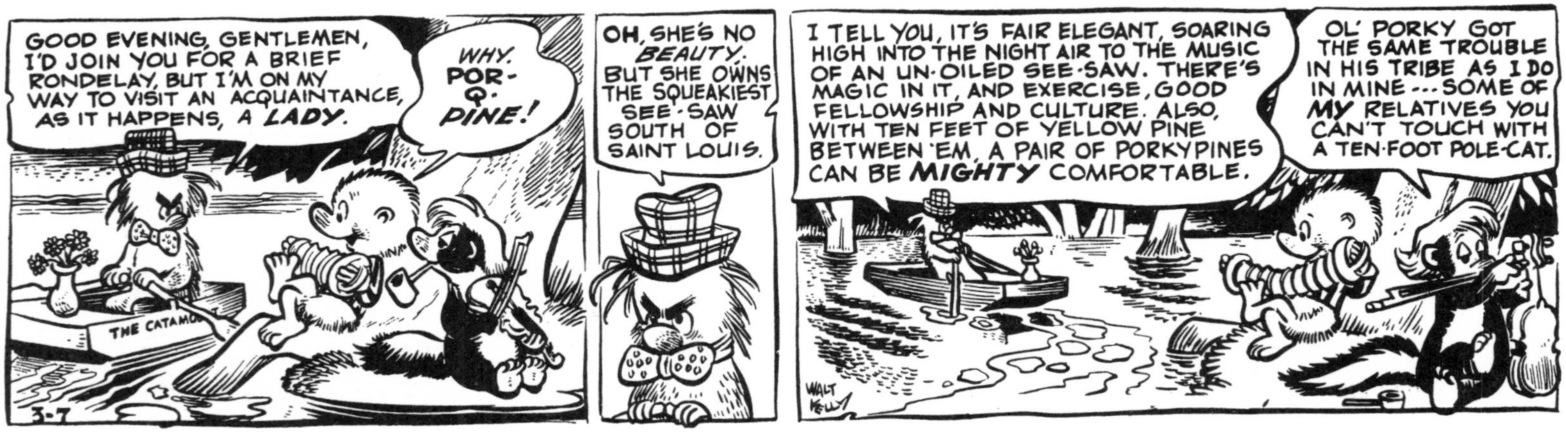

GOOD EVENING, GENTLEMEN, I'D JOIN YOU FOR A BRIEF RONDELAY, BUT I'M ON MY WAY TO VISIT AN ACQUAINTANCE, AS IT HAPPENS, A LADY.
WHY. POR-Q-PINE!
THE CATAMO
3-7
OH, SHE'S NO BEAUTY. BUT SHE OWNS THE SQUEAKIEST SEE-SAW SOUTH OF SAINT LOUIS.
I TELL YOU, IT'S FAIR ELEGANT, SOARING HIGH INTO THE NIGHT AIR TO THE MUSIC OF AN UN-OILED SEE-SAW. THERE'S MAGIC IN IT, AND EXERCISE, GOOD FELLOWSHIP AND CULTURE. ALSO, WITH TEN FEET OF YELLOW PINE BETWEEN 'EM, A PAIR OF PORKYPINES CAN BE MIGHTY COMFORTABLE.
OL' PORKY GOT THE SAME TROUBLE IN HIS TRIBE AS I DO IN MINE --- SOME OF MY RELATIVES YOU CAN'T TOUCH WITH A TEN-FOOT POLE-CAT.
WALT KELLY

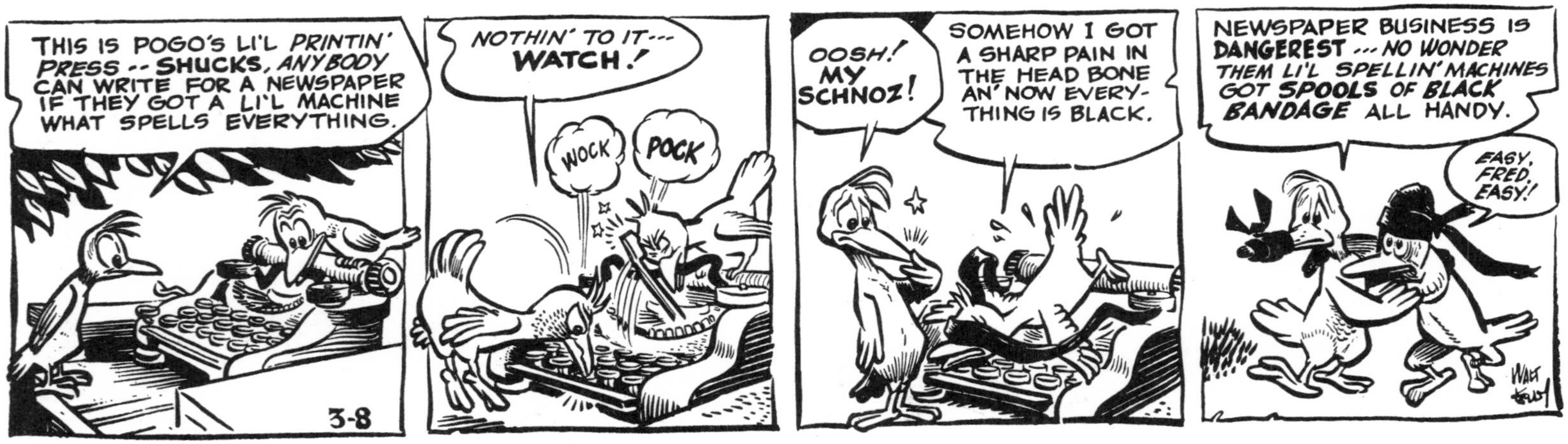

THIS IS POGO'S LI'L PRINTIN' PRESS -- SHUCKS, ANYBODY CAN WRITE FOR A NEWSPAPER IF THEY GOT A LI'L MACHINE WHAT SPELLS EVERYTHING.
3-8
NOTHIN' TO IT--- WATCH.!
WOCK
POCK
OOSH! MY SCHNOZ!
SOMEHOW I GOT A SHARP PAIN IN THE HEAD BONE AN' NOW EVERY-THING IS BLACK.
NEWSPAPER BUSINESS IS DANGEREST --- NO WONDER THEM LI'L SPELLIN' MACHINES GOT SPOOLS OF BLACK BANDAGE ALL HANDY.
EASY, FRED, EASY!
WALT KELLY

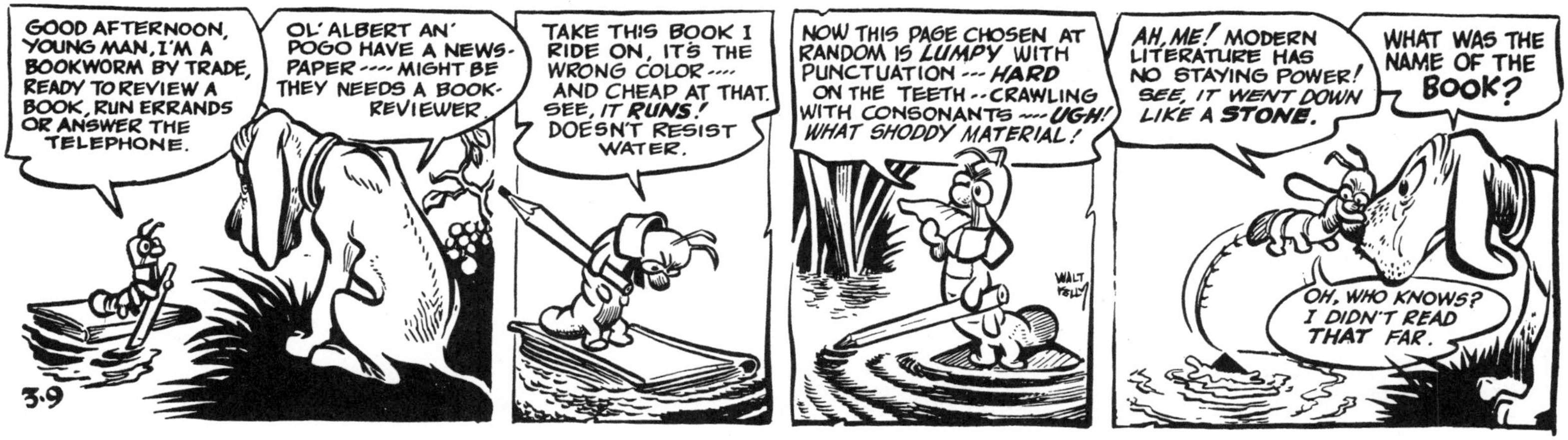
GOOD AFTERNOON, YOUNG MAN, I'M A BOOKWORM BY TRADE, READY TO REVIEW A BOOK, RUN ERRANDS OR ANSWER THE TELEPHONE.
OL' ALBERT AN' POGO HAVE A NEWSPAPER ---- MIGHT BE THEY NEEDS A BOOK-REVIEWER.
TAKE THIS BOOK I RIDE ON, IT'S THE WRONG COLOR ---- AND CHEAP AT THAT. SEE, IT RUNS! DOESN'T RESIST WATER.
NOW THIS PAGE CHOSEN AT RANDOM IS LUMPY WITH PUNCTUATION --- HARD ON THE TEETH -- CRAWLING WITH CONSONANTS ---- UGH! WHAT SHODDY MATERIAL!
AH, ME! MODERN LITERATURE HAS NO STAYING POWER! SEE, IT WENT DOWN LIKE A STONE.
WHAT WAS THE NAME OF THE BOOK?
OH, WHO KNOWS? I DIDN'T READ THAT FAR.
3-9
WALT KELLY

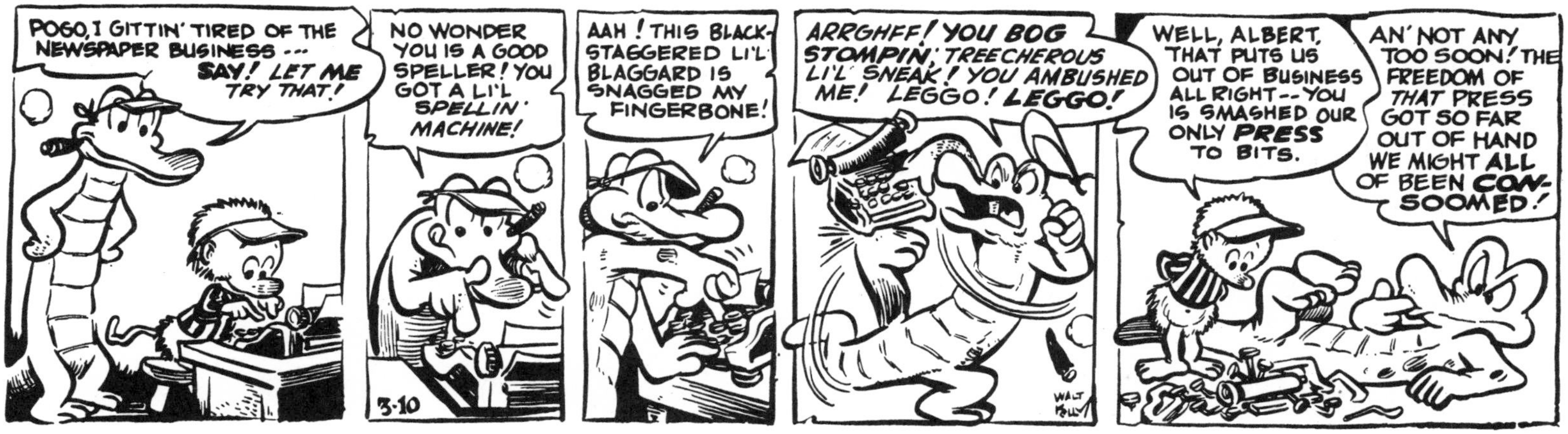
POGO, I GITTIN' TIRED OF THE NEWSPAPER BUSINESS --- SAY! LET ME TRY THAT!
NO WONDER YOU IS A GOOD SPELLER! YOU GOT A LI'L SPELLIN' MACHINE!
AAH! THIS BLACK-STAGGERED LI'L BLAGGARD IS SNAGGED MY FINGERBONE!
ARRGHFF! YOU BOG STOMPIN', TREECHEROUS LI'L SNEAK! YOU AMBUSHED ME! LEGGO! LEGGO!
WELL, ALBERT, THAT PUTS US OUT OF BUSINESS ALL RIGHT -- YOU IS SMASHED OUR ONLY PRESS TO BITS.
AN' NOT ANY TOO SOON! THE FREEDOM OF THAT PRESS GOT SO FAR OUT OF HAND WE MIGHT ALL OF BEEN CON-SOOMED!
3-10
WALT KELLY

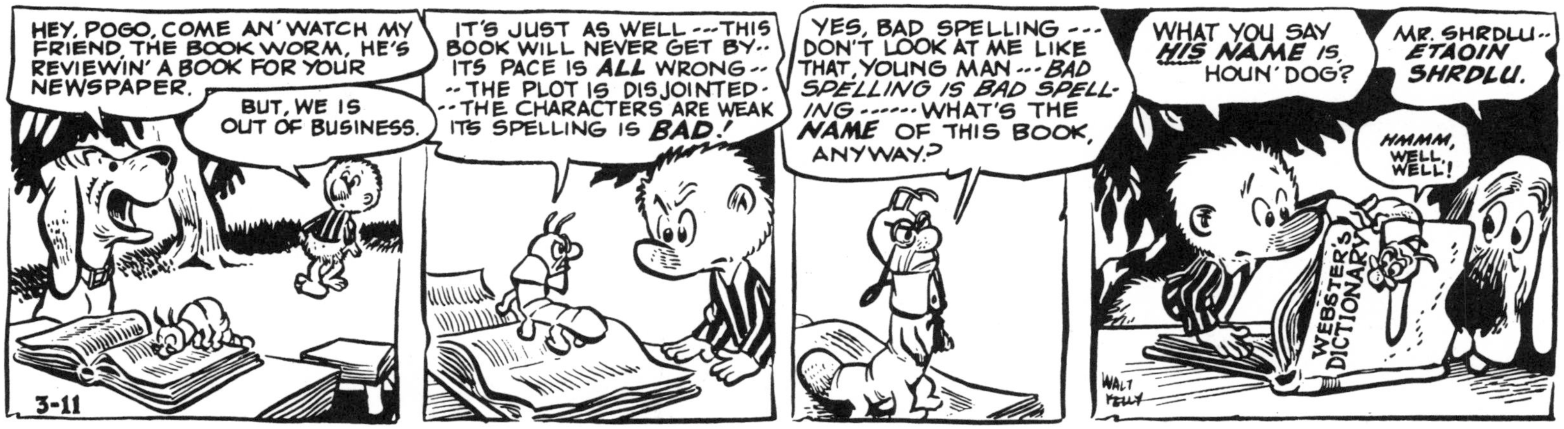
HEY, POGO, COME AN' WATCH MY FRIEND, THE BOOK WORM, HE'S REVIEWIN' A BOOK FOR YOUR NEWSPAPER.
BUT, WE IS OUT OF BUSINESS.
IT'S JUST AS WELL --- THIS BOOK WILL NEVER GET BY -- ITS PACE IS ALL WRONG -- -- THE PLOT IS DISJOINTED -- -- THE CHARACTERS ARE WEAK ITS SPELLING IS BAD!
YES, BAD SPELLING --- DON'T LOOK AT ME LIKE THAT, YOUNG MAN --- BAD SPELLING IS BAD SPELL-ING ------ WHAT'S THE NAME OF THIS BOOK, ANYWAY?
WHAT YOU SAY HIS NAME IS, HOUN' DOG?
MR. SHRDLU -- ETAOIN SHRDLU.
HMMM, WELL, WELL!
WEBSTER'S DICTIONARY
3-11
WALT KELLY

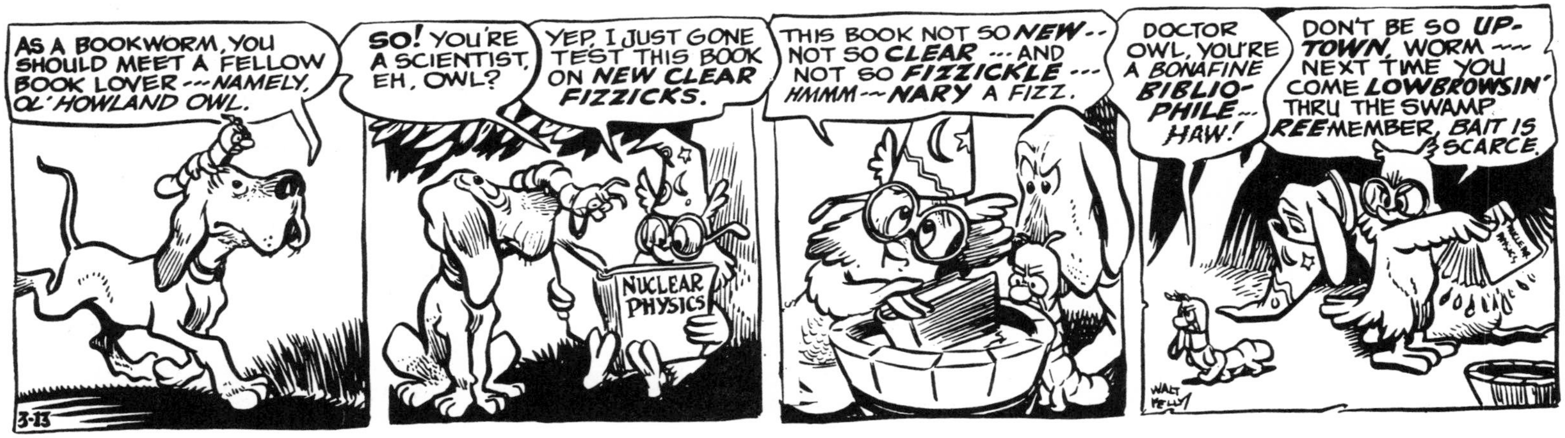
AS A BOOKWORM, YOU SHOULD MEET A FELLOW BOOK LOVER --- NAMELY, OL' HOWLAND OWL.
SO! YOU'RE A SCIENTIST, EH, OWL?
YEP. I JUST GONE TEST THIS BOOK ON NEW CLEAR FIZZICKS.
NUCLEAR PHYSICS
THIS BOOK NOT SO NEW -- NOT SO CLEAR --- AND NOT SO FIZZICKLE --- HMMM -- NARY A FIZZ.
DOCTOR OWL, YOU'RE A BONAFINE BIBLIO-PHILE -- HAW!
DON'T BE SO UP-TOWN, WORM ---- NEXT TIME YOU COME LOWBROWSIN' THRU THE SWAMP REEMEMBER, BAIT IS SCARCE.
3-13
WALT KELLY

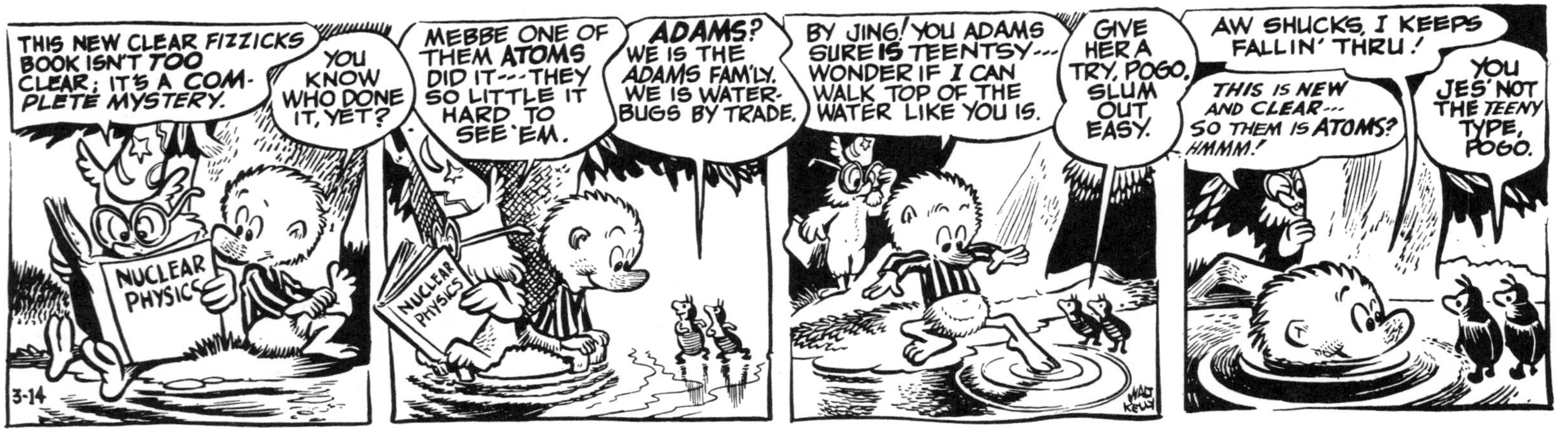
THIS NEW CLEAR FIZZICKS BOOK ISN'T TOO CLEAR; IT'S A COMPLETE MYSTERY.
YOU KNOW WHO DONE IT, YET?
NUCLEAR PHYSICS
MEBBE ONE OF THEM ATOMS DID IT --- THEY SO LITTLE IT HARD TO SEE 'EM.
ADAMS? WE IS THE ADAMS FAM'LY. WE IS WATER-BUGS BY TRADE.
BY JING! YOU ADAMS SURE IS TEENTSY --- WONDER IF I CAN WALK TOP OF THE WATER LIKE YOU IS.
GIVE HER A TRY, POGO. SLUM OUT EASY.
AW SHUCKS, I KEEPS FALLIN' THRU!
THIS IS NEW AND CLEAR --- SO THEM IS ATOMS? HMMM!
YOU JES' NOT THE TEENY TYPE, POGO.
3-14
WALT KELLY

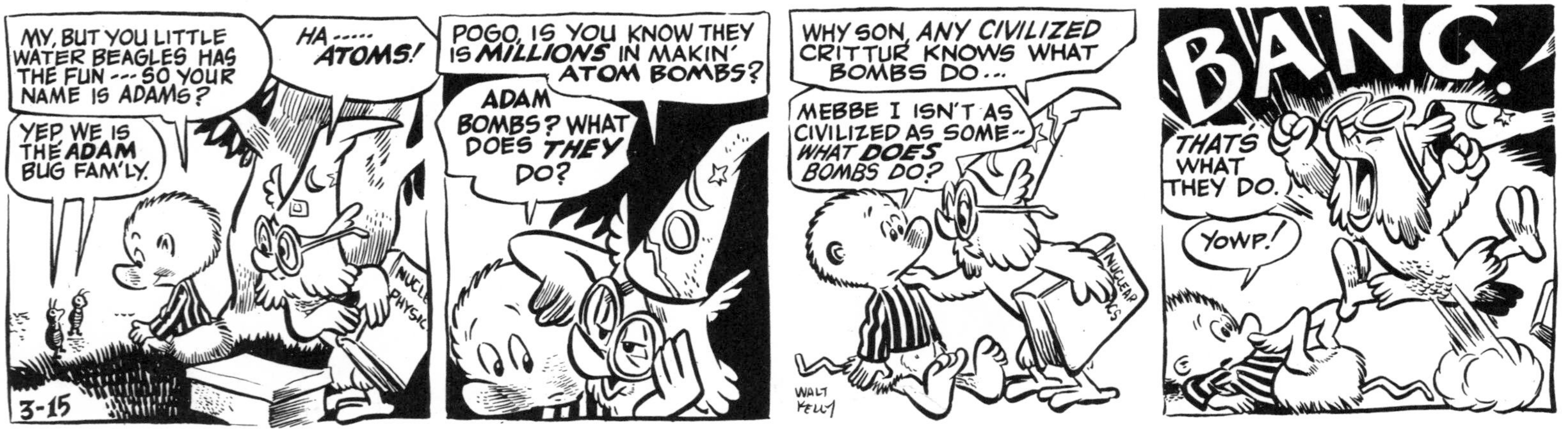
MY, BUT YOU LITTLE WATER BEAGLES HAS THE FUN --- SO YOUR NAME IS ADAMS?
HA ----- ATOMS!
YEP WE IS THE ADAM BUG FAM'LY.
POGO, IS YOU KNOW THEY IS MILLIONS IN MAKIN' ATOM BOMBS?
ADAM BOMBS? WHAT DOES THEY DO?
WHY SON, ANY CIVILIZED CRITTUR KNOWS WHAT BOMBS DO...
MEBBE I ISN'T AS CIVILIZED AS SOME -- WHAT DOES BOMBS DO?
BANG!
THAT'S WHAT THEY DO.
YOWP!
3-15
WALT KELLY

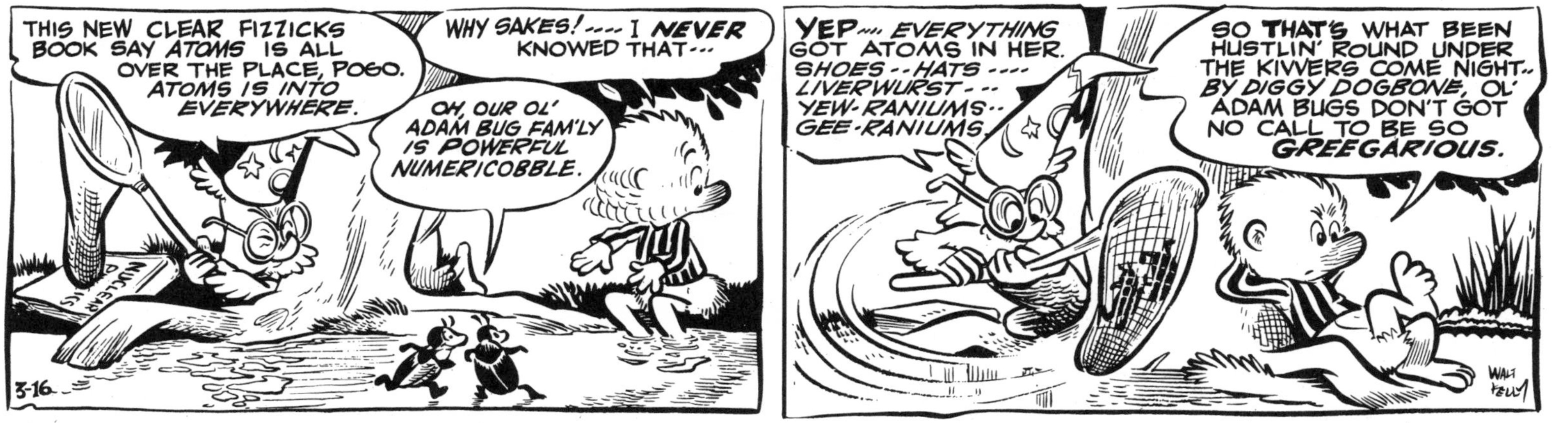
THIS NEW CLEAR FIZZICKS BOOK SAY ATOMS IS ALL OVER THE PLACE, POGO. ATOMS IS INTO EVERYWHERE.
WHY SAKES! ---- I NEVER KNOWED THAT---
OH, OUR OL' ADAM BUG FAM'LY IS POWERFUL NUMERICOBBLE.
3-16
YEP---- EVERYTHING GOT ATOMS IN HER. SHOES--HATS---- LIVERWURST--- YEW-RANIUMS-- GEE-RANIUMS.
SO THAT'S WHAT BEEN HUSTLIN' ROUND UNDER THE KIVVERS COME NIGHT-- BY DIGGY DOGBONE, OL' ADAM BUGS DON'T GOT NO CALL TO BE SO GREEGARIOUS.
WALT KELLY

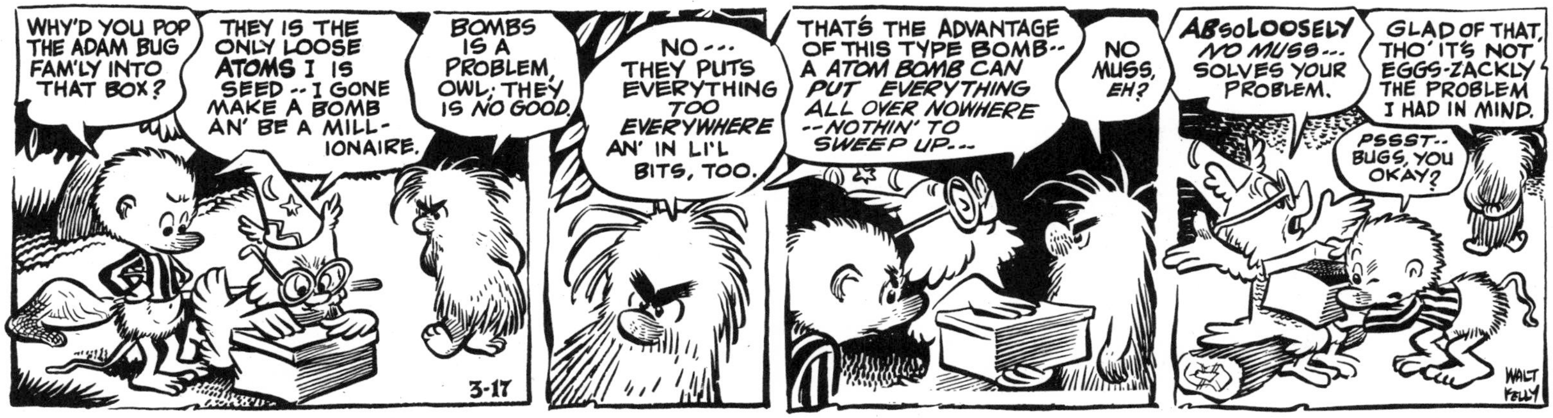
WHY'D YOU POP THE ADAM BUG FAM'LY INTO THAT BOX?
THEY IS THE ONLY LOOSE ATOMS I IS SEED -- I GONE MAKE A BOMB AN' BE A MILL-IONAIRE.
BOMBS IS A PROBLEM, OWL; THEY IS NO GOOD.
3-17
NO--- THEY PUTS EVERYTHING TOO EVERYWHERE AN' IN LI'L BITS, TOO.
THAT'S THE ADVANTAGE OF THIS TYPE BOMB-- A ATOM BOMB CAN PUT EVERYTHING ALL OVER NOWHERE --NOTHIN' TO SWEEP UP---
NO MUSS, EH?
ABSOLOOSELY NO MUSS--- SOLVES YOUR PROBLEM.
GLAD OF THAT, THO' IT'S NOT EGGS-ZACKLY THE PROBLEM I HAD IN MIND.
PSSST-- BUGS, YOU OKAY?
WALT KELLY

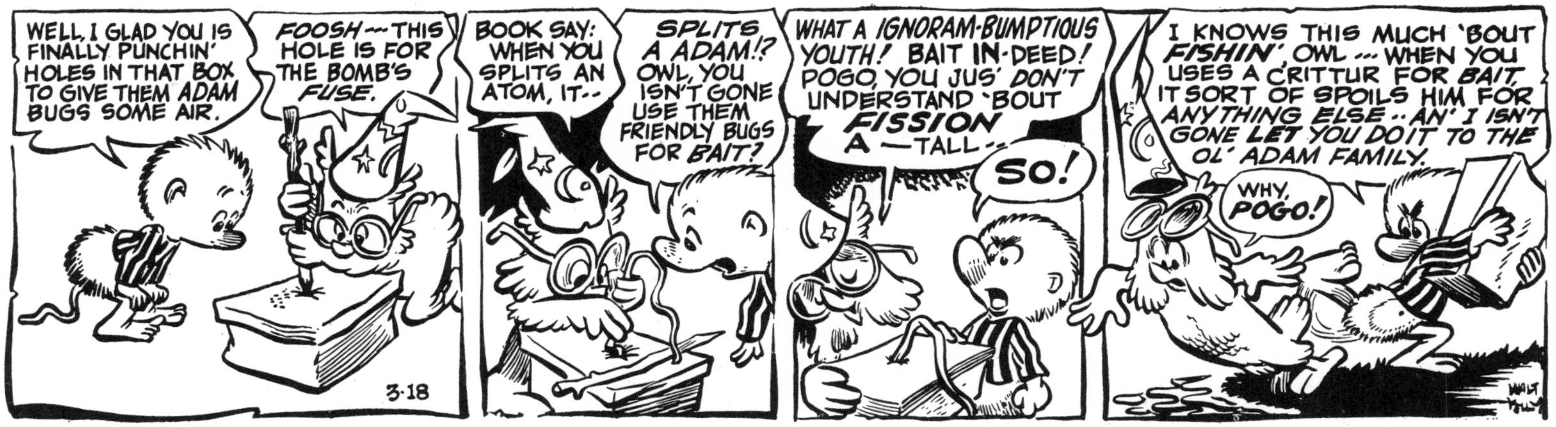
WELL, I GLAD YOU IS FINALLY PUNCHIN' HOLES IN THAT BOX TO GIVE THEM ADAM BUGS SOME AIR.
FOOSH --- THIS HOLE IS FOR THE BOMB'S FUSE.
3-18
BOOK SAY: WHEN YOU SPLITS AN ATOM, IT--
SPLITS A ADAM!? OWL, YOU ISN'T GONE USE THEM FRIENDLY BUGS FOR BAIT?
WHAT A IGNORAM-BUMPTIOUS YOUTH! BAIT IN-DEED! POGO, YOU JUS' DON'T UNDERSTAND 'BOUT FISSION A—TALL--
SO!
I KNOWS THIS MUCH 'BOUT FISHIN', OWL --- WHEN YOU USES A CRITTUR FOR BAIT, IT SORT OF SPOILS HIM FOR ANYTHING ELSE -- AN' I ISN'T GONE LET YOU DO IT TO THE OL' ADAM FAMILY.
WHY, POGO!
WALT KELLY

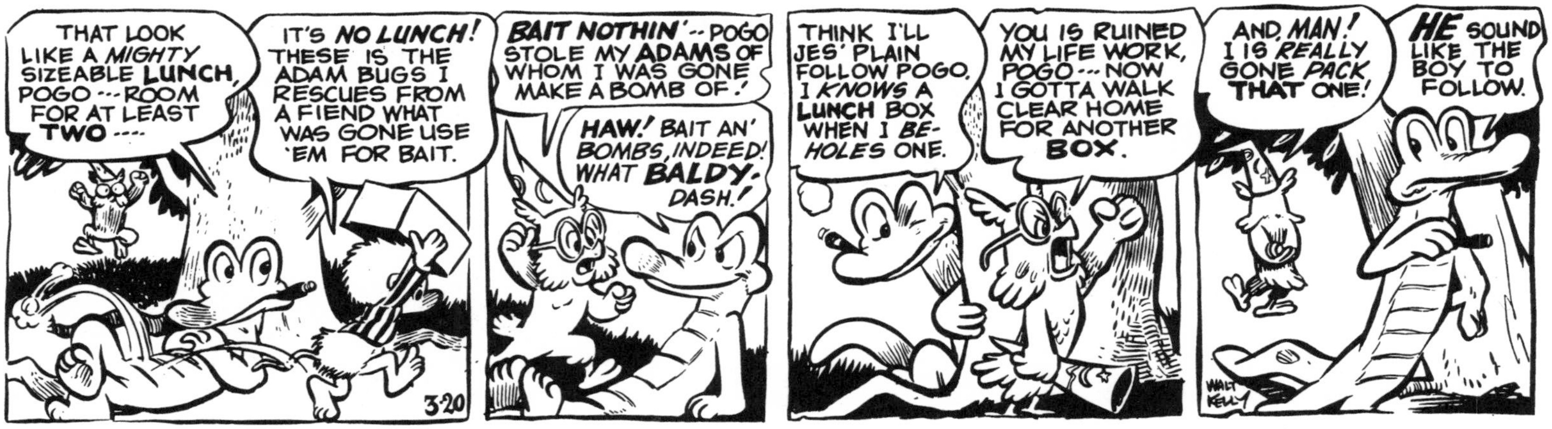
THAT LOOK LIKE A MIGHTY SIZEABLE LUNCH, POGO --- ROOM FOR AT LEAST TWO ----
IT'S NO LUNCH! THESE IS THE ADAM BUGS I RESCUES FROM A FIEND WHAT WAS GONE USE 'EM FOR BAIT.
3-20
BAIT NOTHIN' -- POGO STOLE MY ADAMS OF WHOM I WAS GONE MAKE A BOMB OF.!
HAW! BAIT AN' BOMBS, INDEED! WHAT BALDY-DASH.!
THINK I'LL JES' PLAIN FOLLOW POGO. I KNOWS A LUNCH BOX WHEN I BE-HOLES ONE.
YOU IS RUINED MY LIFE WORK, POGO --- NOW I GOTTA WALK CLEAR HOME FOR ANOTHER BOX.
AND, MAN! I IS REALLY GONE PACK THAT ONE!
HE SOUND LIKE THE BOY TO FOLLOW.
WALT KELLY

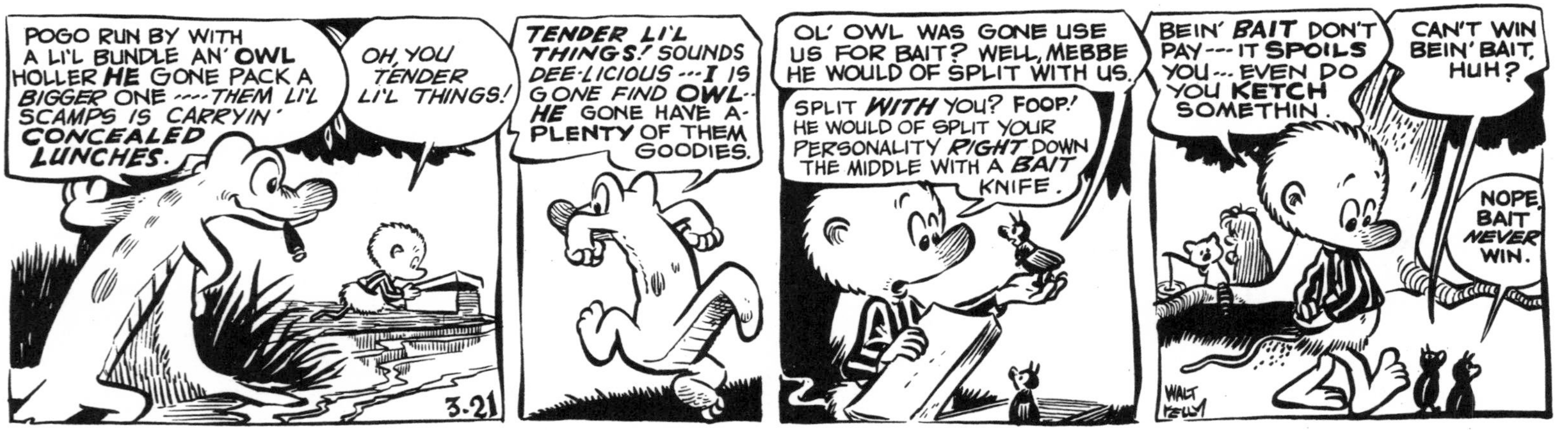
POGO RUN BY WITH A LI'L BUNDLE AN' OWL HOLLER HE GONE PACK A BIGGER ONE ---- THEM LI'L SCAMPS IS CARRYIN' CONCEALED LUNCHES.
OH, YOU TENDER LI'L THINGS!
3-21
TENDER LI'L THINGS.! SOUNDS DEE-LICIOUS --- I IS GONE FIND OWL -- HE GONE HAVE A-PLENTY OF THEM GOODIES.
OL' OWL WAS GONE USE US FOR BAIT? WELL, MEBBE HE WOULD OF SPLIT WITH US.
SPLIT WITH YOU? FOOP! HE WOULD OF SPLIT YOUR PERSONALITY RIGHT DOWN THE MIDDLE WITH A BAIT KNIFE.
BEIN' BAIT DON'T PAY --- IT SPOILS YOU --- EVEN DO YOU KETCH SOMETHIN.
CAN'T WIN BEIN' BAIT, HUH?
NOPE, BAIT NEVER WIN.
WALT KELLY

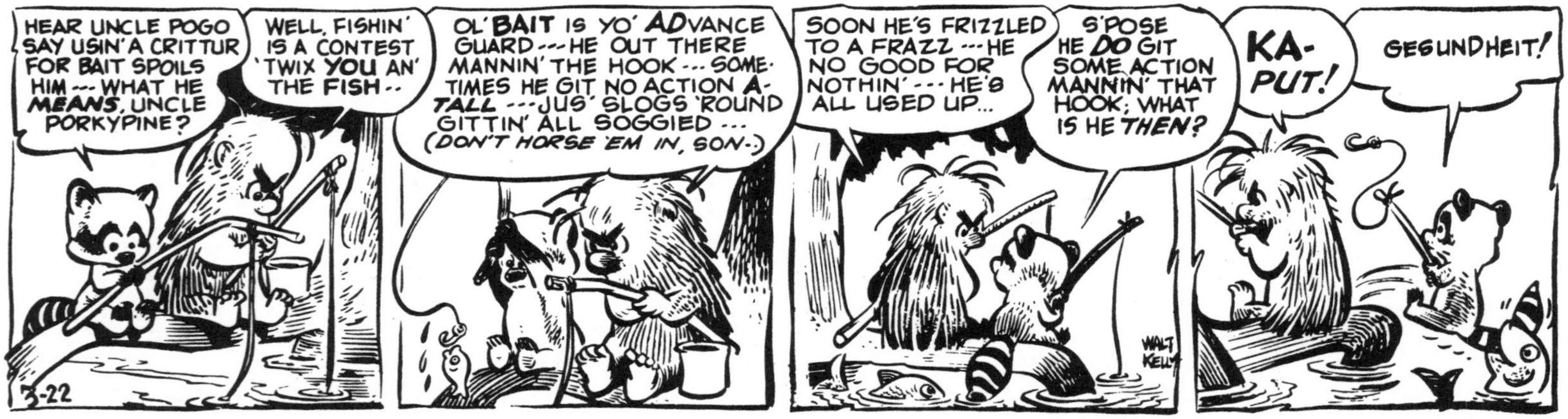
HEAR UNCLE POGO SAY USIN' A CRITTUR FOR BAIT SPOILS HIM --- WHAT HE MEANS, UNCLE PORKYPINE?
WELL, FISHIN' IS A CONTEST 'TWIX YOU AN' THE FISH --
3-22
OL' BAIT IS YO' ADVANCE GUARD --- HE OUT THERE MANNIN' THE HOOK --- SOME-TIMES HE GIT NO ACTION A-TALL --- JUS' SLOGS 'ROUND GITTIN' ALL SOGGIED ---
(DON'T HORSE 'EM IN, SON.)
SOON HE'S FRIZZLED TO A FRAZZ --- HE NO GOOD FOR NOTHIN' --- HE'S ALL USED UP...
S'POSE HE DO GIT SOME ACTION MANNIN' THAT HOOK; WHAT IS HE THEN?
KA-PUT!
GESUNDHEIT!
WALT KELLY

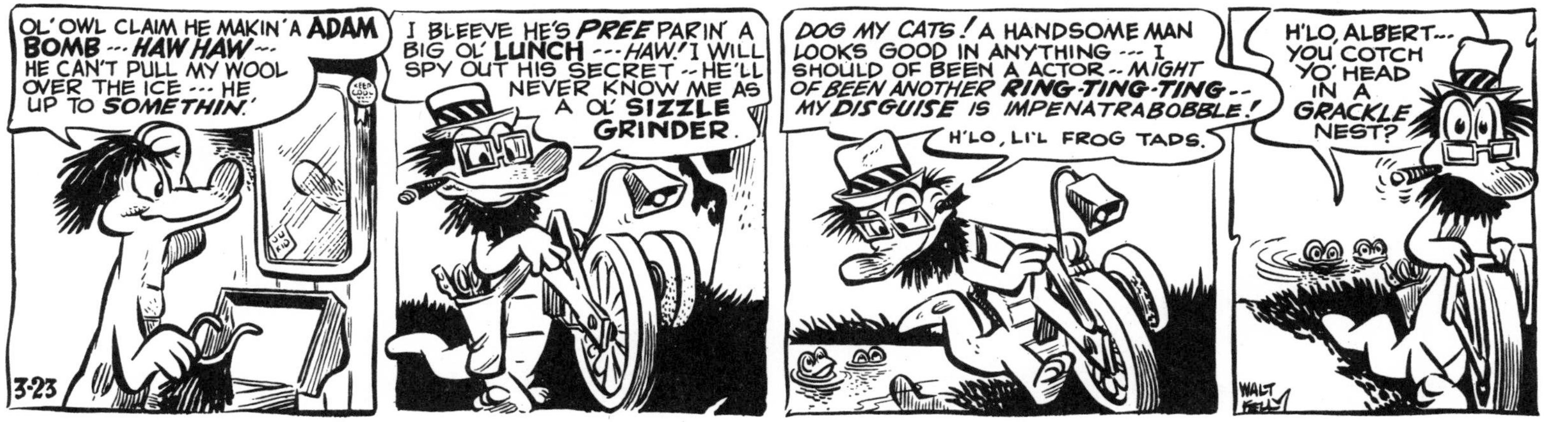
3-23
OL' OWL CLAIM HE MAKIN' A ADAM BOMB --- HAW HAW -- HE CAN'T PULL MY WOOL OVER THE ICE --- HE UP TO SOMETHIN'
I BLEEVE HE'S PREE PARIN' A BIG OL' LUNCH --- HAW! I WILL SPY OUT HIS SECRET -- HE'LL NEVER KNOW ME AS A OL' SIZZLE GRINDER.
DOG MY CATS! A HANDSOME MAN LOOKS GOOD IN ANYTHING --- I SHOULD OF BEEN A ACTOR -- MIGHT OF BEEN ANOTHER RING-TING-TING -- MY DISGUISE IS IMPENATRABOBBLE!
H'LO, LI'L FROG TADS.
H'LO, ALBERT --- YOU COTCH YO' HEAD IN A GRACKLE NEST?
WALT KELLY

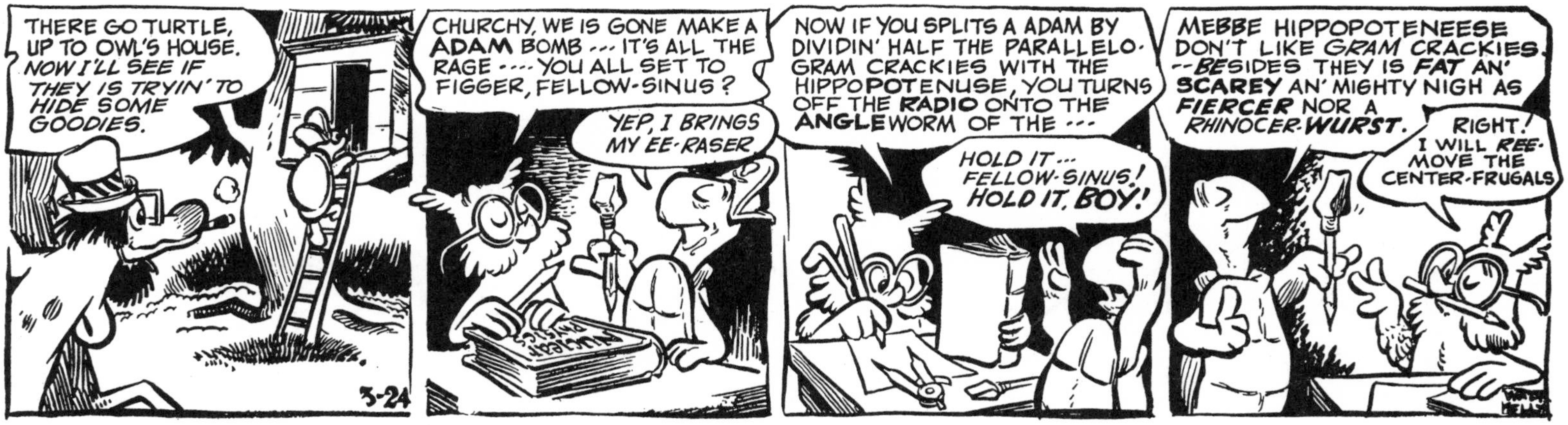
THERE GO TURTLE, UP TO OWL'S HOUSE. NOW I'LL SEE IF THEY IS TRYIN' TO HIDE SOME GOODIES.
3-24
CHURCHY, WE IS GONE MAKE A ADAM BOMB --- IT'S ALL THE RAGE ---- YOU ALL SET TO FIGGER, FELLOW-SINUS?
YEP, I BRINGS MY EE-RASER
NOW IF YOU SPLITS A ADAM BY DIVIDIN' HALF THE PARALLELO-GRAM CRACKIES WITH THE HIPPOPOTENUSE, YOU TURNS OFF THE RADIO ONTO THE ANGLEWORM OF THE ---
HOLD IT --- FELLOW-SINUS! HOLD IT, BOY!
MEBBE HIPPOPOTENEESE DON'T LIKE GRAM CRACKIES. -- BESIDES THEY IS FAT AN' SCAREY AN' MIGHTY NIGH AS FIERCER NOR A RHINOCER-WURST.
RIGHT! I WILL REE-MOVE THE CENTER-FRUGALS

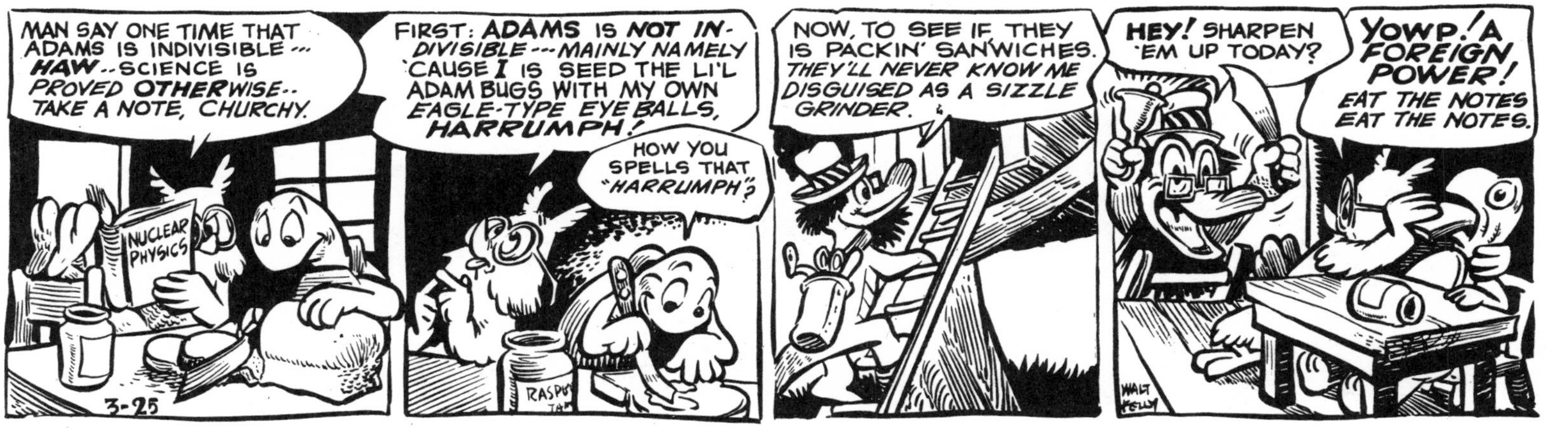
MAN SAY ONE TIME THAT ADAMS IS INDIVISIBLE --- HAW -- SCIENCE IS PROVED OTHERWISE -- TAKE A NOTE, CHURCHY.
NUCLEAR PHYSICS
3-25
FIRST: ADAMS IS NOT IN-DIVISIBLE --- MAINLY NAMELY 'CAUSE I IS SEED THE LI'L ADAM BUGS WITH MY OWN EAGLE-TYPE EYE BALLS, HARRUMPH!
HOW YOU SPELLS THAT "HARRUMPH"?
NOW, TO SEE IF THEY IS PACKIN' SAN'WICHES. THEY'LL NEVER KNOW ME DISGUISED AS A SIZZLE GRINDER.
HEY! SHARPEN 'EM UP TODAY?
YOWP! A FOREIGN POWER! EAT THE NOTES EAT THE NOTES.
WALT KELLY

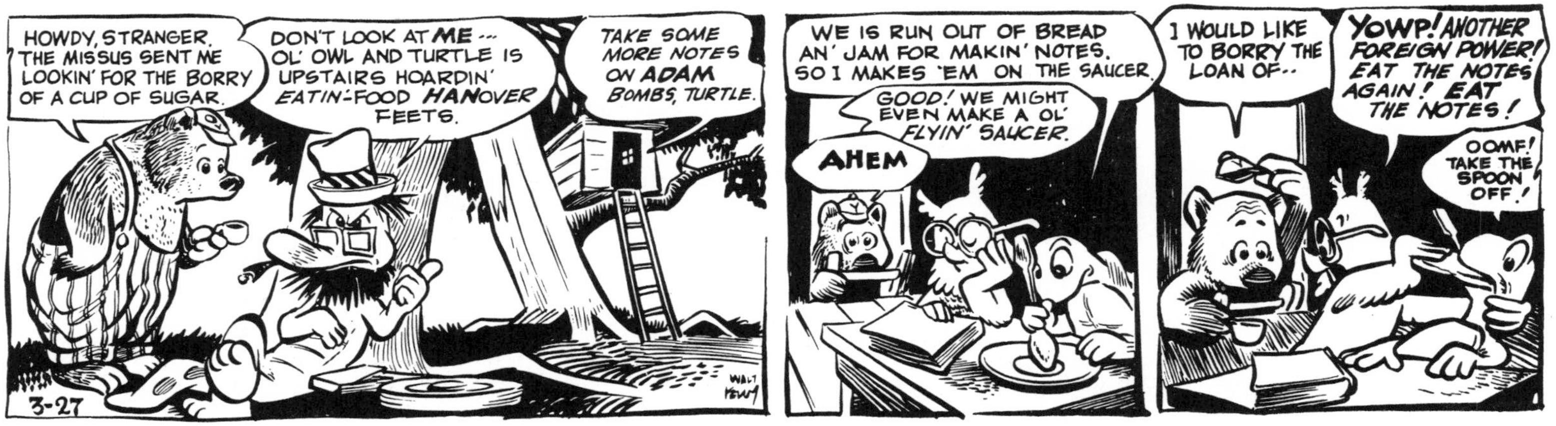
HOWDY, STRANGER. THE MISSUS SENT ME LOOKIN' FOR THE BORRY OF A CUP OF SUGAR.
DON'T LOOK AT **ME** --- OL' OWL AND TURTLE IS UPSTAIRS HOARDIN' *EATIN'-FOOD* **HAN**OVER FEETS.
TAKE SOME MORE NOTES ON **ADAM** *BOMBS, TURTLE.*
3-27
WALT KELLY
WE IS RUN OUT OF BREAD AN' JAM FOR MAKIN' NOTES. SO I MAKES 'EM ON THE SAUCER.
GOOD! WE MIGHT EVEN MAKE A OL' *FLYIN' SAUCER.*
AHEM
I WOULD LIKE TO BORRY THE LOAN OF--
YOWP! ANOTHER FOREIGN POWER! EAT THE NOTES AGAIN! EAT THE NOTES!
OOMF! TAKE THE SPOON OFF!

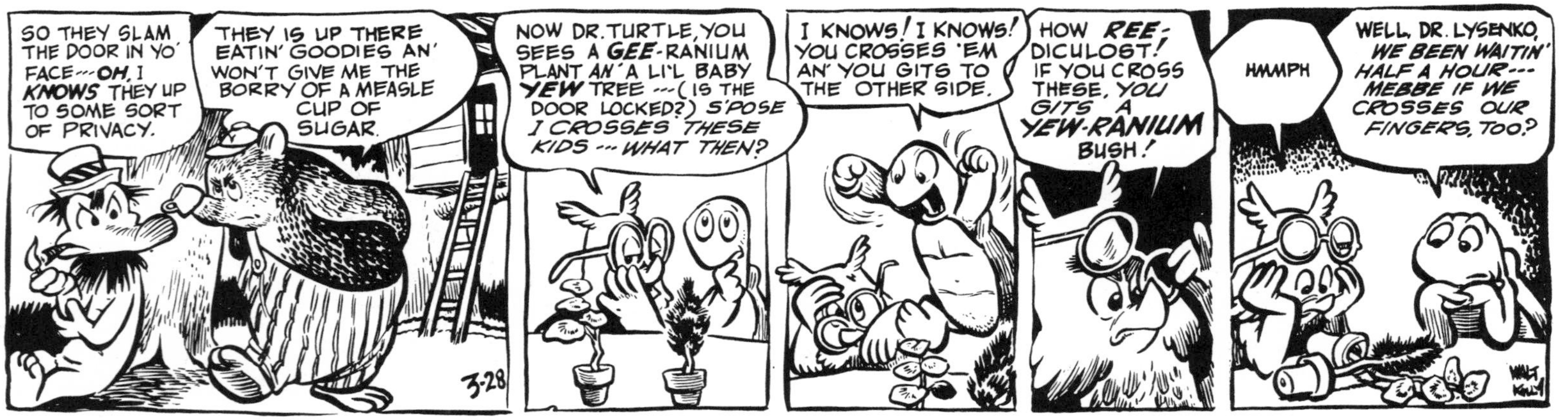
SO THEY SLAM THE DOOR IN YO' FACE---**OH**, I **KNOWS** THEY UP TO SOME SORT OF PRIVACY.
THEY IS UP THERE EATIN' GOODIES AN' WON'T GIVE ME THE BORRY OF A MEASLE CUP OF SUGAR.
3-28
NOW DR. TURTLE, YOU SEES A **GEE**-RANIUM PLANT *AN'* A LI'L BABY **YEW** TREE ---(IS THE DOOR LOCKED?) *S'POSE I CROSSES THESE KIDS --- WHAT THEN?*
I KNOWS! I KNOWS! YOU CROSSES 'EM AN' YOU GITS TO THE OTHER SIDE.
HOW **REE**-DICULOST! IF YOU CROSS THESE, *YOU GITS* A **YEW-RANIUM** BUSH!
HMMPH
WELL, DR. LYSENKO, *WE BEEN WAITIN'* HALF A HOUR--- *MEBBE IF WE CROSSES OUR FINGERS, TOO?*
WALT KELLY

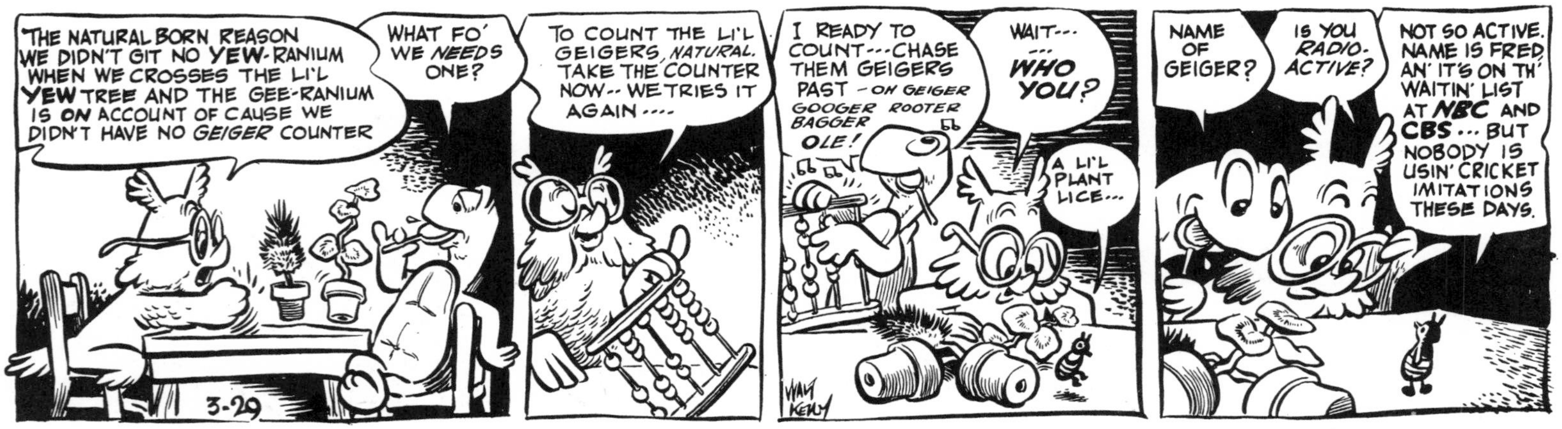
THE NATURAL BORN REASON WE DIDN'T GIT NO **YEW**-RANIUM WHEN WE CROSSES THE LI'L **YEW** TREE AND THE GEE-RANIUM IS **ON** ACCOUNT OF CAUSE WE DIDN'T HAVE NO *GEIGER* COUNTER
WHAT FO' WE *NEEDS* ONE?
3-29
TO COUNT THE LI'L GEIGERS, *NATURAL*. TAKE THE COUNTER NOW -- WE TRIES IT AGAIN ----
I READY TO COUNT---CHASE THEM GEIGERS PAST -- *OH GEIGER GOOGER ROOTER BAGGER OLE!*
WAIT--- --- *WHO YOU?*
A LI'L PLANT LICE...
WALT KELLY
NAME OF GEIGER?
IS YOU *RADIO-ACTIVE?*
NOT SO ACTIVE. NAME IS FRED AN' IT'S ON TH' WAITIN' LIST AT **NBC** AND **CBS** ... BUT NOBODY IS USIN' CRICKET IMITATIONS THESE DAYS.

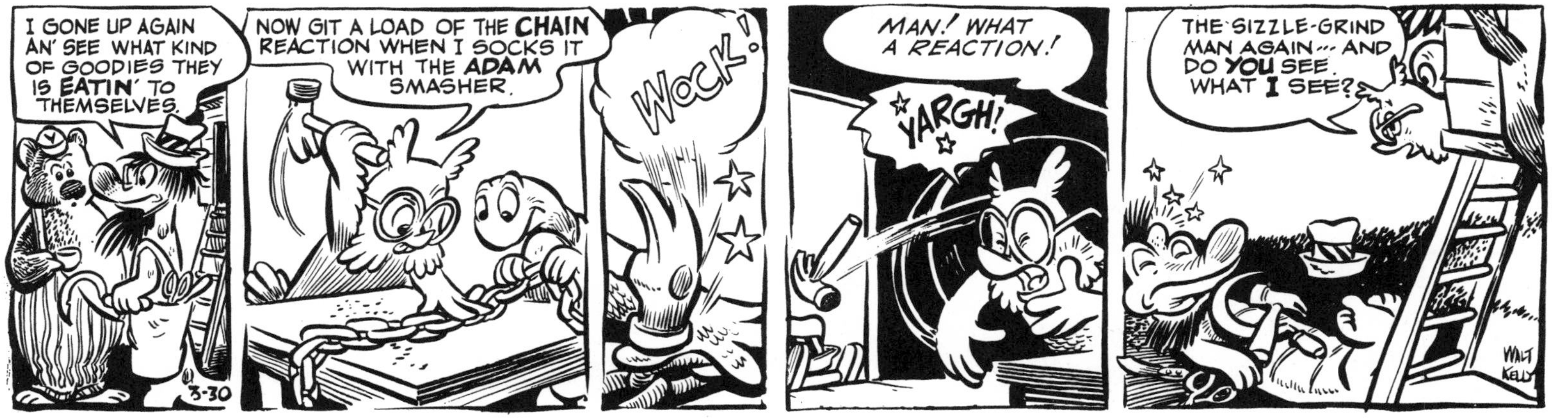
I GONE UP AGAIN AN' SEE WHAT KIND OF GOODIES THEY IS EATIN' TO THEMSELVES.
3-30
NOW GIT A LOAD OF THE CHAIN REACTION WHEN I SOCKS IT WITH THE ADAM SMASHER.
WOCK!
MAN! WHAT A REACTION!
YARGH!
THE SIZZLE-GRIND MAN AGAIN --- AND DO YOU SEE WHAT I SEE?
WALT KELLY

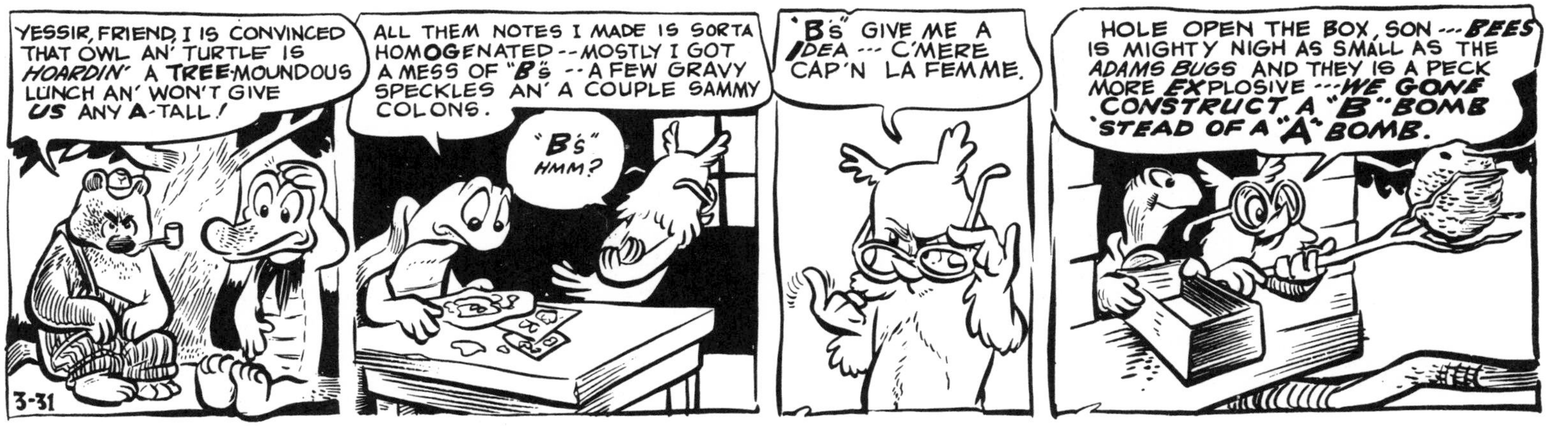
YESSIR, FRIEND, I IS CONVINCED THAT OWL AN' TURTLE IS HOARDIN' A TREE-MOUNDOUS LUNCH AN' WON'T GIVE US ANY A-TALL!
3-31
ALL THEM NOTES I MADE IS SORTA HOMOGENATED -- MOSTLY I GOT A MESS OF "B'S" -- A FEW GRAVY SPECKLES AN' A COUPLE SAMMY COLONS.
"B'S" HMM?
"B'S" GIVE ME A IDEA --- C'MERE CAP'N LA FEMME.
HOLE OPEN THE BOX, SON --- BEES IS MIGHTY NIGH AS SMALL AS THE ADAMS BUGS AND THEY IS A PECK MORE EXPLOSIVE --- WE GONE CONSTRUCT A "B" BOMB 'STEAD OF A "A" BOMB.

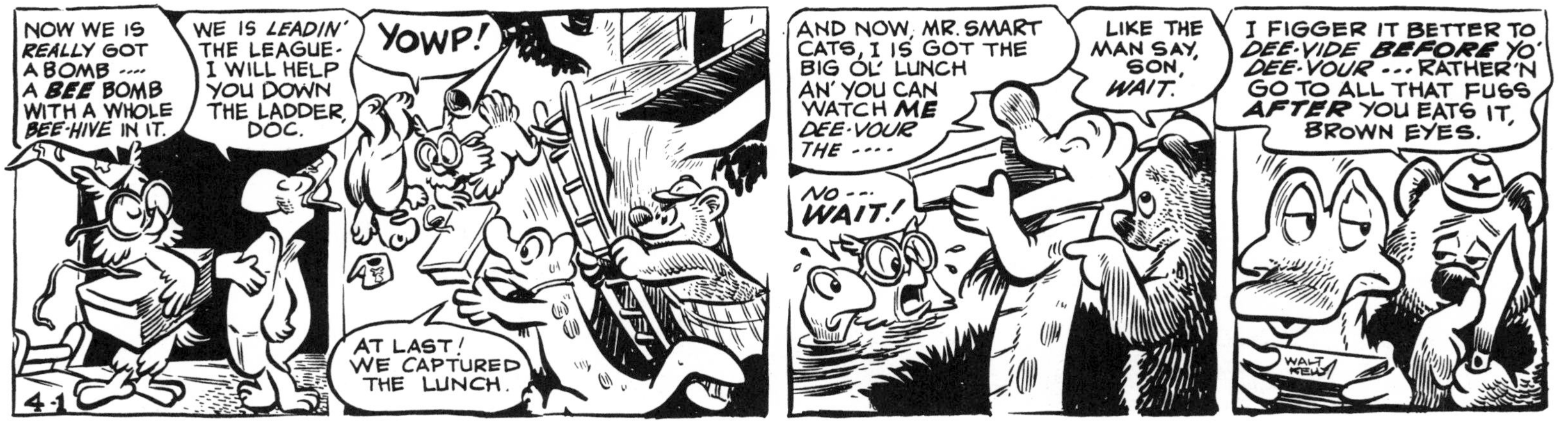
NOW WE IS REALLY GOT A BOMB ---- A BEE BOMB WITH A WHOLE BEE-HIVE IN IT.
WE IS LEADIN' THE LEAGUE - I WILL HELP YOU DOWN THE LADDER, DOC.
4-1
YOWP!
AT LAST! WE CAPTURED THE LUNCH.
AND NOW, MR. SMART CATS, I IS GOT THE BIG OL' LUNCH AN' YOU CAN WATCH ME DEE-VOUR THE ----
LIKE THE MAN SAY, SON, WAIT.
NO --- WAIT!
I FIGGER IT BETTER TO DEE-VIDE BEFORE YO' DEE-VOUR --- RATHER'N GO TO ALL THAT FUSS AFTER YOU EATS IT, BROWN EYES.
WALT KELLY

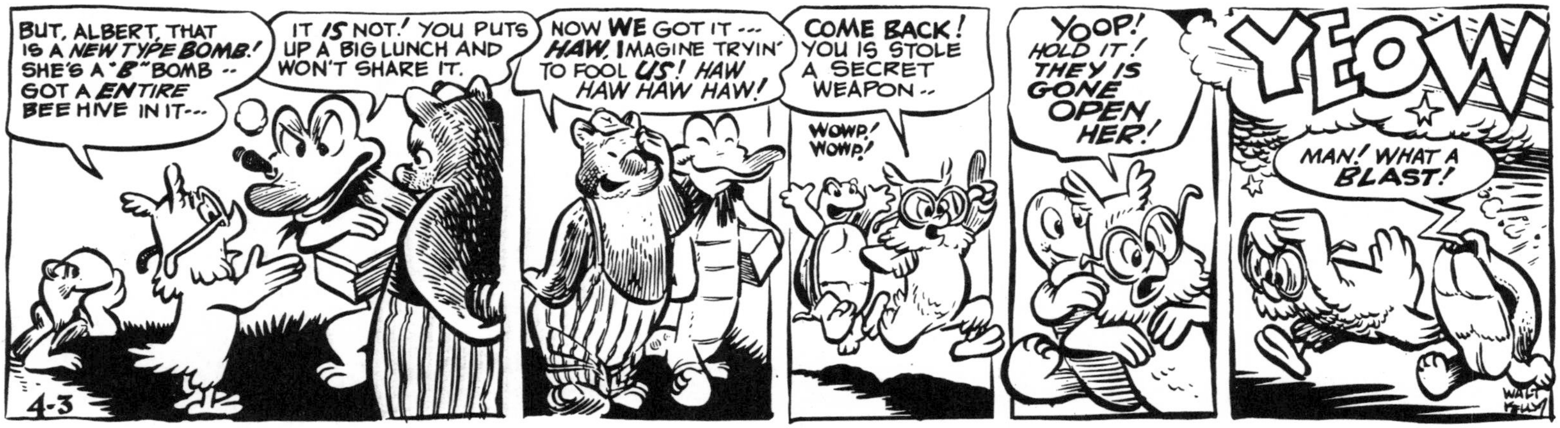
BUT, ALBERT, THAT IS A NEW TYPE BOMB! SHE'S A "B" BOMB -- GOT A ENTIRE BEE HIVE IN IT---
IT IS NOT! YOU PUTS UP A BIG LUNCH AND WON'T SHARE IT.
NOW WE GOT IT --- HAW, IMAGINE TRYIN' TO FOOL US! HAW HAW HAW HAW!
COME BACK! YOU IS STOLE A SECRET WEAPON --
WOWP! WOWP!
YOOP! HOLD IT! THEY IS GONE OPEN HER!
YEOW
MAN! WHAT A BLAST!
4-3
WALT KELLY

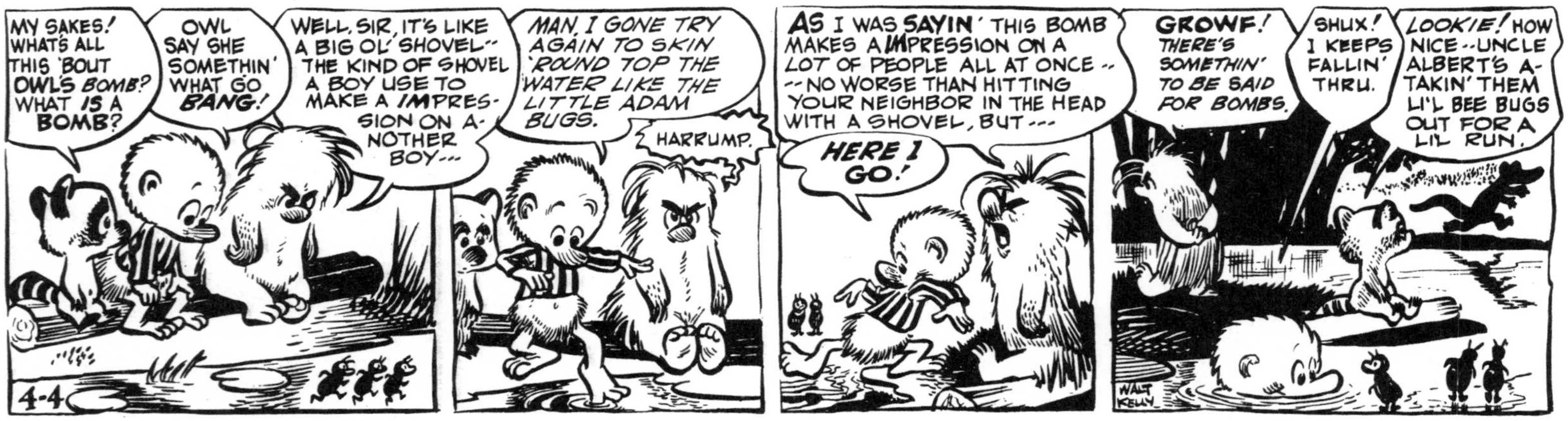
MY SAKES! WHAT'S ALL THIS 'BOUT OWL'S BOMB? WHAT IS A BOMB?
OWL SAY SHE SOMETHIN' WHAT GO BANG!
WELL, SIR, IT'S LIKE A BIG OL' SHOVEL-- THE KIND OF SHOVEL A BOY USE TO MAKE A IMPRESSION ON A-NOTHER BOY---
MAN, I GONE TRY AGAIN TO SKIN 'ROUND TOP THE WATER LIKE THE LITTLE ADAM BUGS.
HARRUMP.
AS I WAS SAYIN' THIS BOMB MAKES A IMPRESSION ON A LOT OF PEOPLE ALL AT ONCE -- -- NO WORSE THAN HITTING YOUR NEIGHBOR IN THE HEAD WITH A SHOVEL, BUT ---
HERE I GO!
GROWF! THERE'S SOMETHIN' TO BE SAID FOR BOMBS.
SHUX! I KEEPS FALLIN' THRU.
LOOKIE! HOW NICE -- UNCLE ALBERT'S A-TAKIN' THEM LI'L BEE BUGS OUT FOR A LI'L RUN.
4-4
WALT KELLY

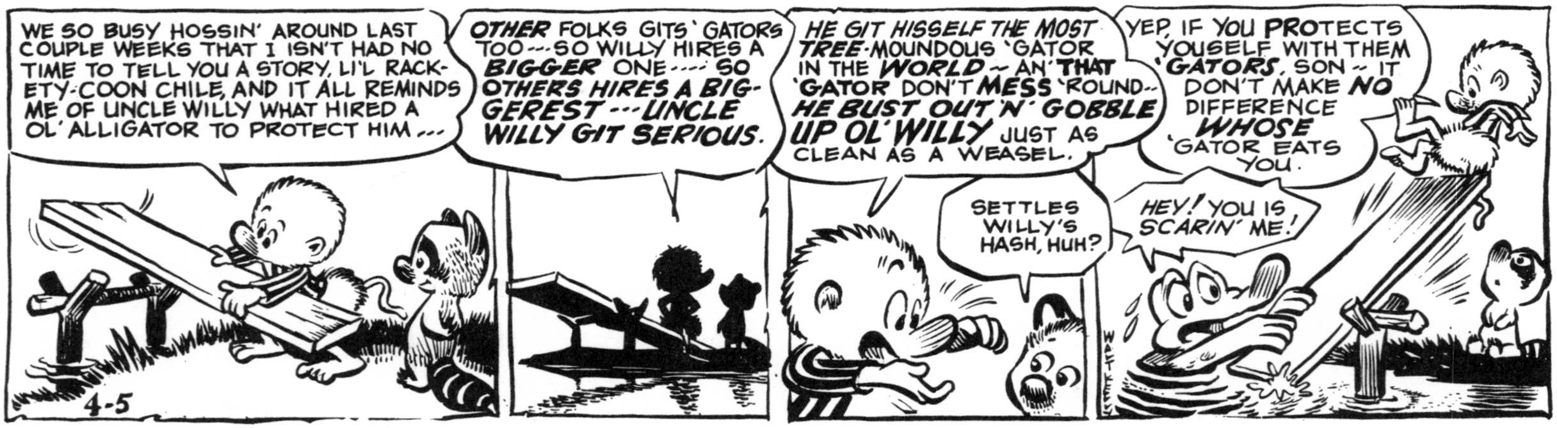
WE SO BUSY HOSSIN' AROUND LAST COUPLE WEEKS THAT I ISN'T HAD NO TIME TO TELL YOU A STORY, LI'L RACKETY-COON CHILE, AND IT ALL REMINDS ME OF UNCLE WILLY WHAT HIRED A OL' ALLIGATOR TO PROTECT HIM ---
OTHER FOLKS GITS 'GATORS TOO --- SO WILLY HIRES A BIGGER ONE ---- SO OTHERS HIRES A BIGGEREST --- UNCLE WILLY GIT SERIOUS.
HE GIT HISSELF THE MOST TREE-MOUNDOUS 'GATOR IN THE WORLD -- AN' THAT 'GATOR DON'T MESS 'ROUND -- HE BUST OUT 'N' GOBBLE UP OL' WILLY JUST AS CLEAN AS A WEASEL.
SETTLES WILLY'S HASH, HUH?
YEP, IF YOU PROTECTS YOUSELF WITH THEM 'GATORS, SON -- IT DON'T MAKE NO DIFFERENCE WHOSE 'GATOR EATS YOU.
HEY! YOU IS SCARIN' ME!
4-5
WALT KELLY

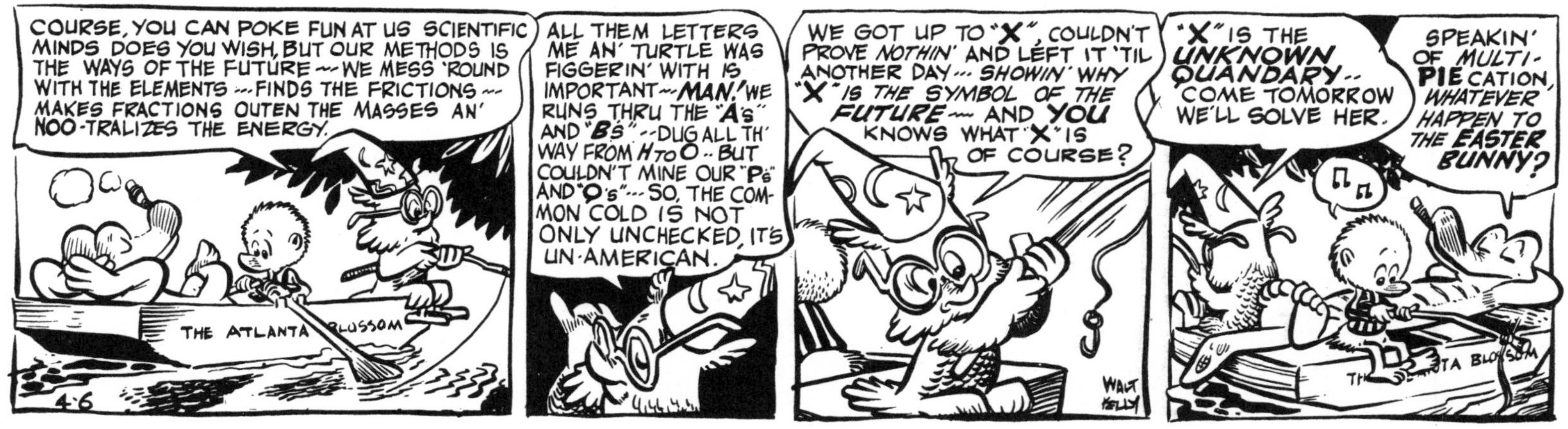
COURSE, YOU CAN POKE FUN AT US SCIENTIFIC MINDS DOES YOU WISH, BUT OUR METHODS IS THE WAYS OF THE FUTURE — WE MESS 'ROUND WITH THE ELEMENTS — FINDS THE FRICTIONS — MAKES FRACTIONS OUTEN THE MASSES AN' NOO-TRALIZES THE ENERGY.
THE ATLANTA BLOSSOM
4-6
ALL THEM LETTERS ME AN' TURTLE WAS FIGGERIN' WITH IS IMPORTANT — MAN! WE RUNS THRU THE "A's" AND "B's" -- DUG ALL TH' WAY FROM H TO O -- BUT COULDN'T MINE OUR "P's" AND "Q's" -- SO, THE COMMON COLD IS NOT ONLY UNCHECKED, IT'S UN-AMERICAN.
WE GOT UP TO "X", COULDN'T PROVE NOTHIN' AND LEFT IT 'TIL ANOTHER DAY... SHOWIN' WHY "X" IS THE SYMBOL OF THE FUTURE — AND YOU KNOWS WHAT "X" IS OF COURSE?
WALT KELLY
"X" IS THE UNKNOWN QUANDARY... COME TOMORROW WE'LL SOLVE HER.
SPEAKIN' OF MULTI-PIE CATION, WHATEVER HAPPEN TO THE EASTER BUNNY?

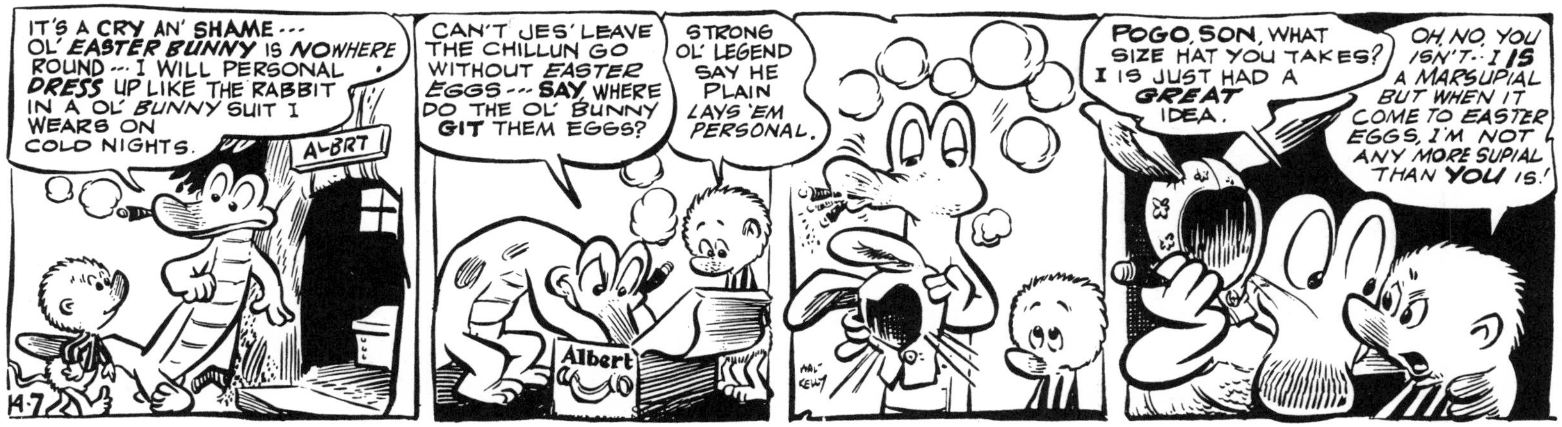
IT'S A CRY AN' SHAME --- OL' EASTER BUNNY IS NOWHERE ROUND --- I WILL PERSONAL DRESS UP LIKE THE RABBIT IN A OL' BUNNY SUIT I WEARS ON COLD NIGHTS.
AL-BRT
4-7
CAN'T JES' LEAVE THE CHILLUN GO WITHOUT EASTER EGGS --- SAY, WHERE DO THE OL' BUNNY GIT THEM EGGS?
STRONG OL' LEGEND SAY HE PLAIN LAYS 'EM PERSONAL.
Albert
POGO, SON, WHAT SIZE HAT YOU TAKES? I IS JUST HAD A GREAT IDEA.
OH, NO, YOU ISN'T -- I IS A MARSUPIAL BUT WHEN IT COME TO EASTER EGGS, I'M NOT ANY MORE SUPIAL THAN YOU IS!

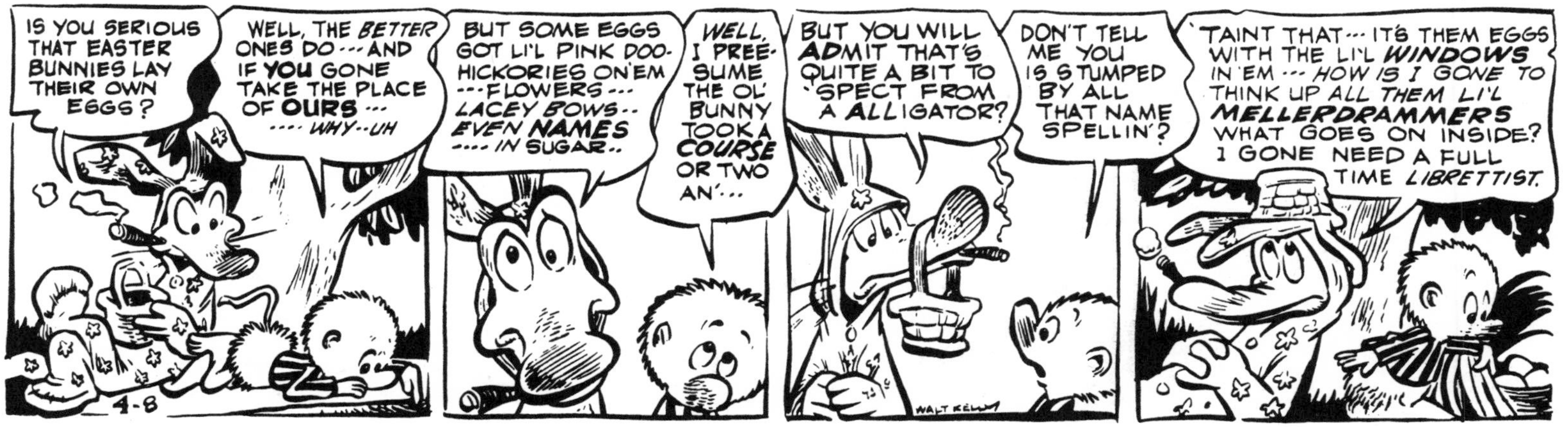
IS YOU SERIOUS THAT EASTER BUNNIES LAY THEIR OWN EGGS?
WELL, THE BETTER ONES DO --- AND IF YOU GONE TAKE THE PLACE OF OURS --- ---- WHY -- UH
4-8
BUT SOME EGGS GOT LI'L PINK DOO-HICKORIES ON 'EM --- FLOWERS --- LACEY BOWS -- EVEN NAMES ---- IN SUGAR --
WELL, I PREE-SUME THE OL' BUNNY TOOK A COURSE OR TWO AN'...
BUT YOU WILL ADMIT THAT'S QUITE A BIT TO 'SPECT FROM A ALLIGATOR?
DON'T TELL ME YOU IS STUMPED BY ALL THAT NAME SPELLIN'?
WALT KELLY
'TAINT THAT --- IT'S THEM EGGS WITH THE LI'L WINDOWS IN 'EM --- HOW IS I GONE TO THINK UP ALL THEM LI'L MELLERDRAMMERS WHAT GOES ON INSIDE? I GONE NEED A FULL TIME LIBRETTIST.

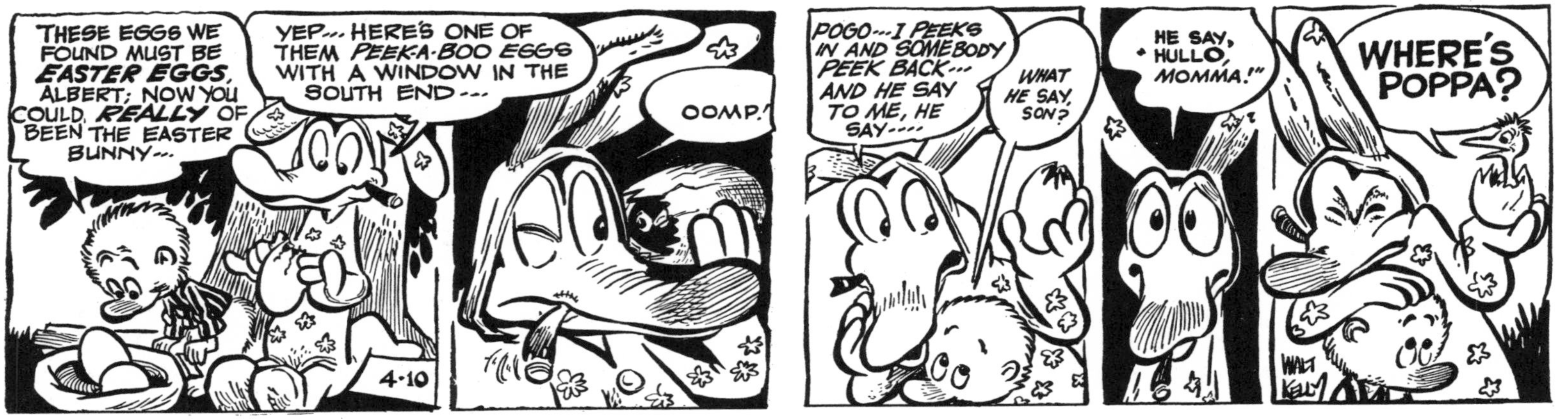
THESE EGGS WE FOUND MUST BE EASTER EGGS, ALBERT; NOW YOU COULD REALLY OF BEEN THE EASTER BUNNY--.
YEP--. HERE'S ONE OF THEM PEEK-A-BOO EGGS WITH A WINDOW IN THE SOUTH END---
OOMP.'
4-10
POGO---I PEEKS IN AND SOMEBODY PEEK BACK--- AND HE SAY TO ME, HE SAY----
WHAT HE SAY, SON?
HE SAY, "HULLO, MOMMA!"
WHERE'S POPPA?
WALT KELLY

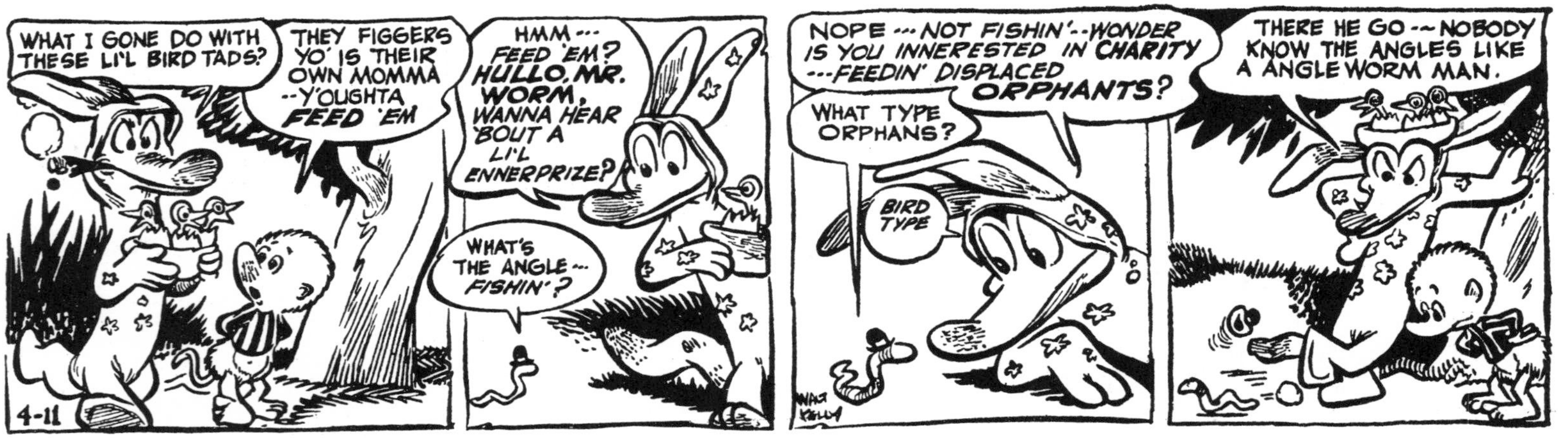
WHAT I GONE DO WITH THESE LI'L BIRD TADS?
THEY FIGGERS YO' IS THEIR OWN MOMMA --Y'OUGHTA FEED 'EM
HMM--- FEED 'EM? HULLO, MR. WORM, WANNA HEAR 'BOUT A LI'L ENNERPRIZE?
WHAT'S THE ANGLE--- FISHIN'?
4-11
NOPE --- NOT FISHIN'--WONDER IS YOU INNERESTED IN CHARITY ---FEEDIN' DISPLACED ORPHANTS?
WHAT TYPE ORPHANS?
BIRD TYPE
WALT KELLY
THERE HE GO -- NOBODY KNOW THE ANGLES LIKE A ANGLE WORM MAN.

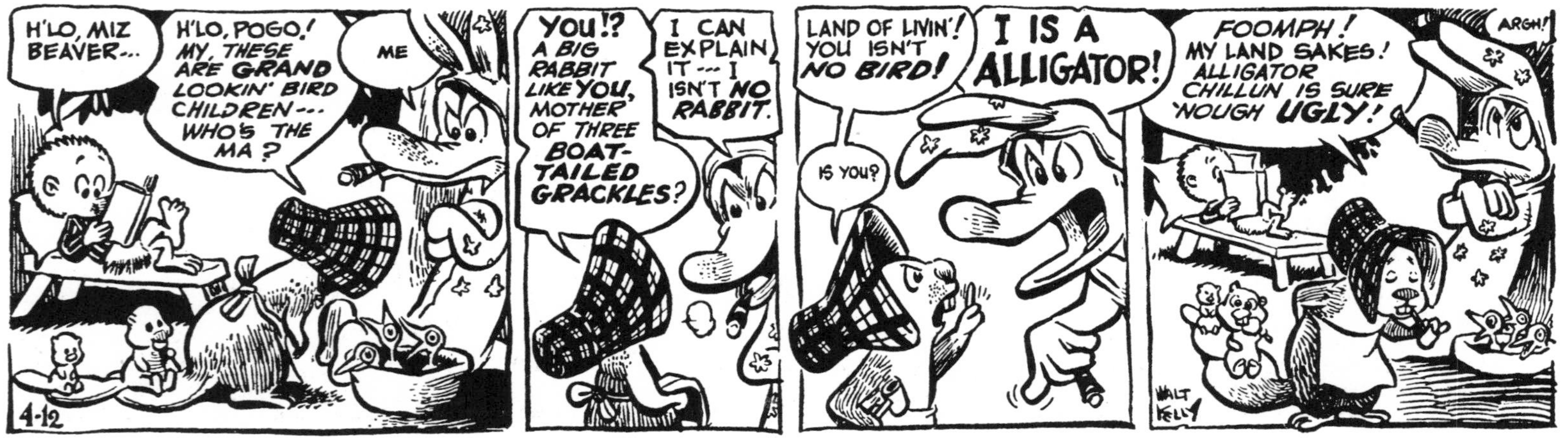
H'LO, MIZ BEAVER--.
H'LO, POGO! MY, THESE ARE GRAND LOOKIN' BIRD CHILDREN--- WHO'S THE MA?
ME
4-12
YOU!? A BIG RABBIT LIKE YOU, MOTHER OF THREE BOAT-TAILED GRACKLES?
I CAN EXPLAIN IT --- I ISN'T NO RABBIT.
LAND OF LIVIN'! YOU ISN'T NO BIRD!
I IS A ALLIGATOR!
IS YOU?
FOOMPH! MY LAND SAKES! ALLIGATOR CHILLUN IS SURE 'NOUGH UGLY!
ARGH!
WALT KELLY

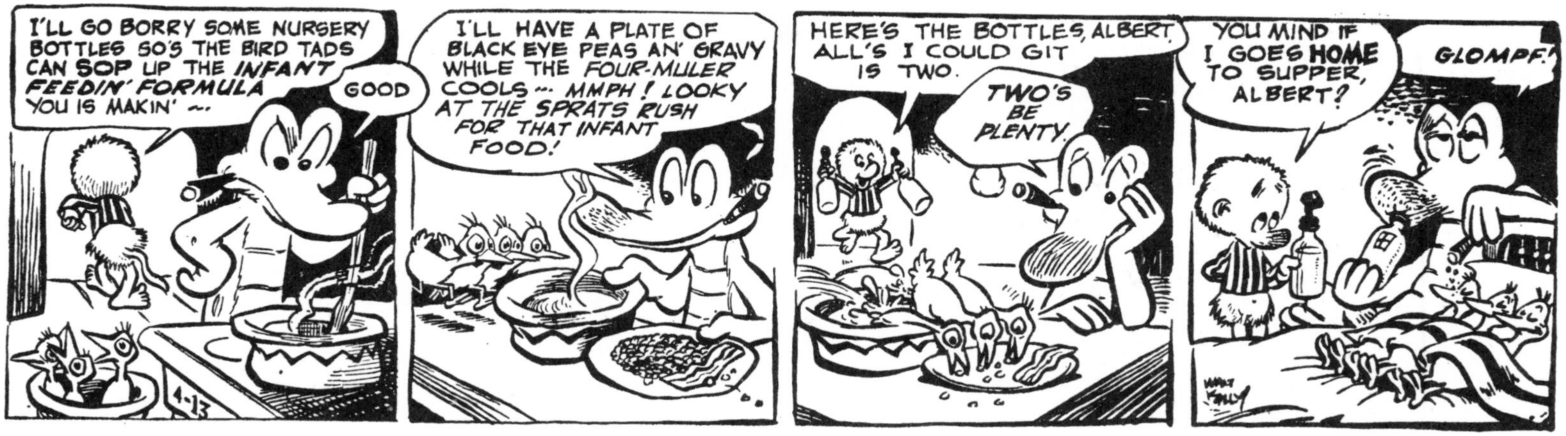
I'LL GO BORRY SOME NURSERY BOTTLES SO'S THE BIRD TADS CAN SOP UP THE INFANT FEEDIN' FORMULA YOU IS MAKIN' ~.
GOOD
4-13
I'LL HAVE A PLATE OF BLACK EYE PEAS AN' GRAVY WHILE THE FOUR-MULER COOLS-- MMPH! LOOKY AT THE SPRATS RUSH FOR THAT INFANT FOOD!
HERE'S THE BOTTLES, ALBERT. ALL'S I COULD GIT IS TWO.
TWO'S BE PLENTY.
YOU MIND IF I GOES HOME TO SUPPER, ALBERT?
GLOMPF!

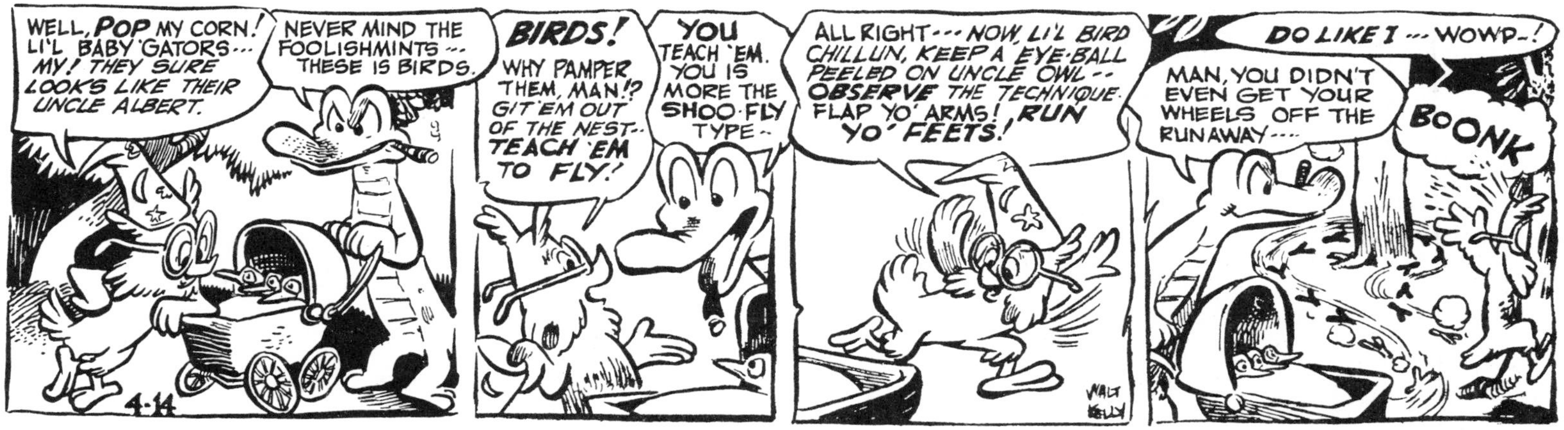
WELL, POP MY CORN! LI'L BABY GATORS--- MY! THEY SURE LOOK'S LIKE THEIR UNCLE ALBERT.
NEVER MIND THE FOOLISHMINTS -- THESE IS BIRDS.
4-14
BIRDS!
WHY PAMPER THEM, MAN!? GIT 'EM OUT OF THE NEST-- TEACH 'EM TO FLY!
YOU TEACH 'EM. YOU IS MORE THE SHOO-FLY TYPE--
ALL RIGHT--- NOW, LI'L BIRD CHILLUN, KEEP A EYE-BALL PEELED ON UNCLE OWL-- OBSERVE THE TECHNIQUE. FLAP YO' ARMS! RUN YO' FEETS!
WALT KELLY
DO LIKE I --- WOWP-!
MAN, YOU DIDN'T EVEN GET YOUR WHEELS OFF THE RUNAWAY----
BOONK

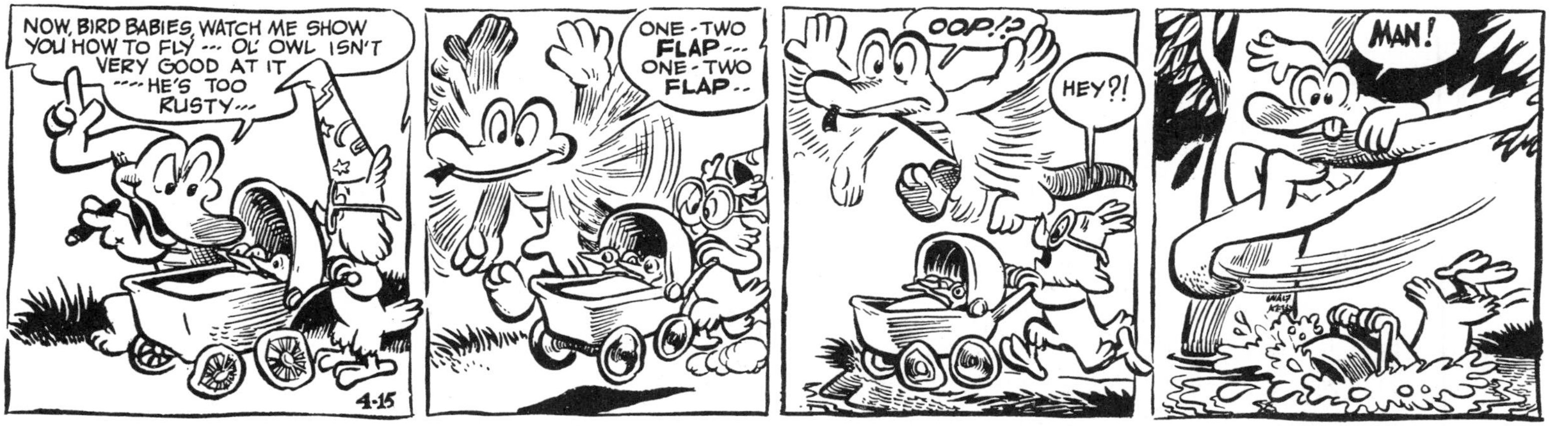
NOW, BIRD BABIES, WATCH ME SHOW YOU HOW TO FLY --- OL' OWL ISN'T VERY GOOD AT IT ---- HE'S TOO RUSTY---
4-15
ONE - TWO FLAP--- ONE - TWO FLAP--
OOP!?
HEY?!
MAN!

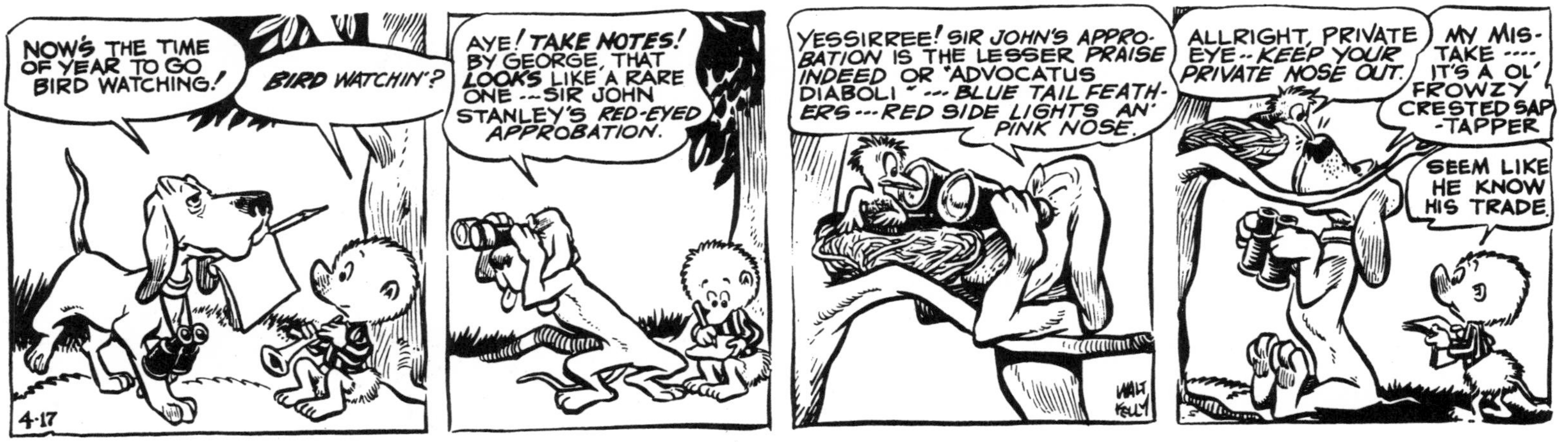
NOW'S THE TIME OF YEAR TO GO BIRD WATCHING!
BIRD WATCHIN'?
AYE! TAKE NOTES! BY GEORGE, THAT LOOKS LIKE A RARE ONE --- SIR JOHN STANLEY'S RED-EYED APPROBATION.
YESSIRREE! SIR JOHN'S APPROBATION IS THE LESSER PRAISE INDEED OR "ADVOCATUS DIABOLI" --- BLUE TAIL FEATHERS --- RED SIDE LIGHTS AN' PINK NOSE.
ALLRIGHT, PRIVATE EYE -- KEEP YOUR PRIVATE NOSE OUT.
MY MISTAKE ---- IT'S A OL' FROWZY CRESTED SAP-TAPPER
SEEM LIKE HE KNOW HIS TRADE.
4-17
WALT KELLY

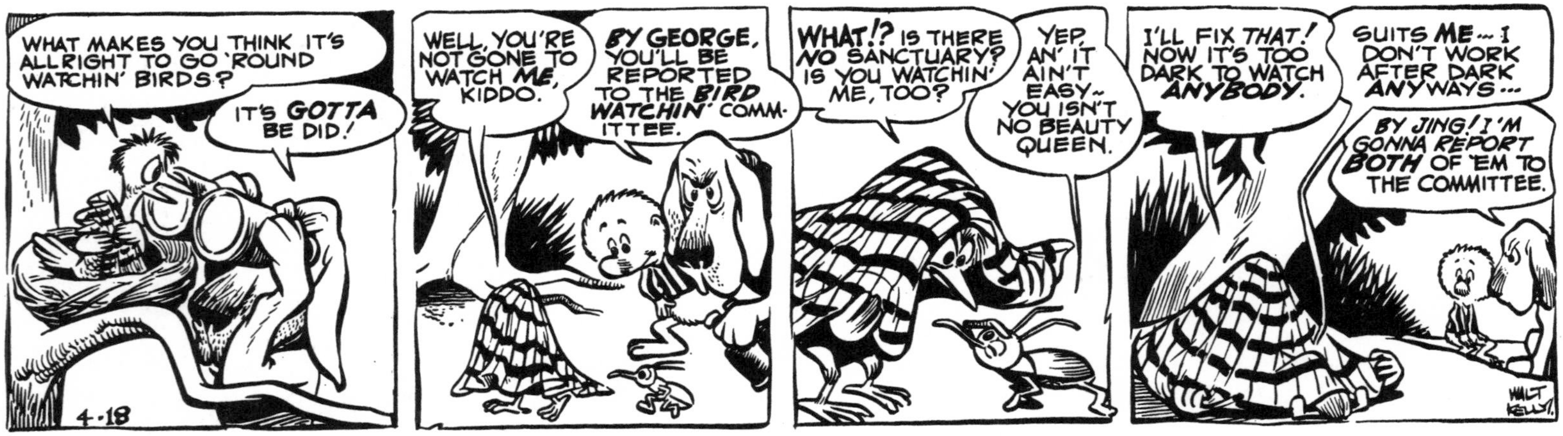
WHAT MAKES YOU THINK IT'S ALLRIGHT TO GO 'ROUND WATCHIN' BIRDS?
IT'S GOTTA BE DID!
WELL, YOU'RE NOT GONE TO WATCH ME, KIDDO.
BY GEORGE, YOU'LL BE REPORTED TO THE BIRD WATCHIN' COMMITTEE.
WHAT!? IS THERE NO SANCTUARY? IS YOU WATCHIN' ME, TOO?
YEP. AN' IT AIN'T EASY-- YOU ISN'T NO BEAUTY QUEEN.
I'LL FIX THAT! NOW IT'S TOO DARK TO WATCH ANYBODY.
SUITS ME -- I DON'T WORK AFTER DARK ANYWAYS ---
BY JING! I'M GONNA REPORT BOTH OF 'EM TO THE COMMITTEE.
4-18
WALT KELLY

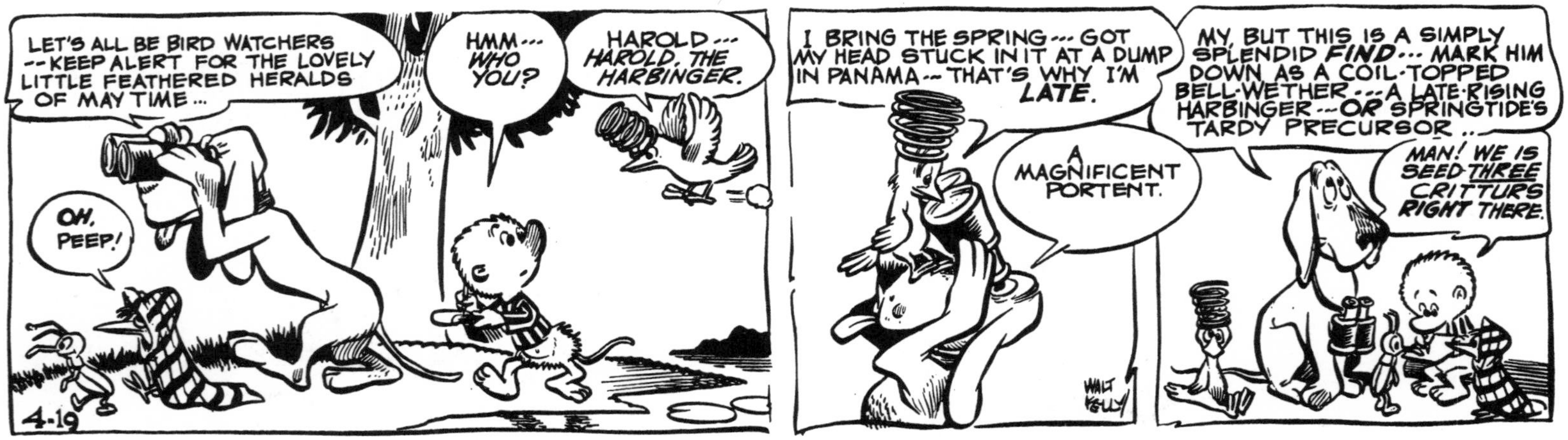
LET'S ALL BE BIRD WATCHERS --KEEP ALERT FOR THE LOVELY LITTLE FEATHERED HERALDS OF MAY TIME ...
OH, PEEP!
HMM --- WHO YOU?
HAROLD --- HAROLD, THE HARBINGER.
I BRING THE SPRING --- GOT MY HEAD STUCK IN IT AT A DUMP IN PANAMA -- THAT'S WHY I'M LATE.
A MAGNIFICENT PORTENT.
MY, BUT THIS IS A SIMPLY SPLENDID FIND --- MARK HIM DOWN AS A COIL-TOPPED BELL-WETHER --- A LATE-RISING HARBINGER --- OR SPRINGTIDE'S TARDY PRECURSOR ...
MAN! WE IS SEED THREE CRITTURS RIGHT THERE.
4-19
WALT KELLY

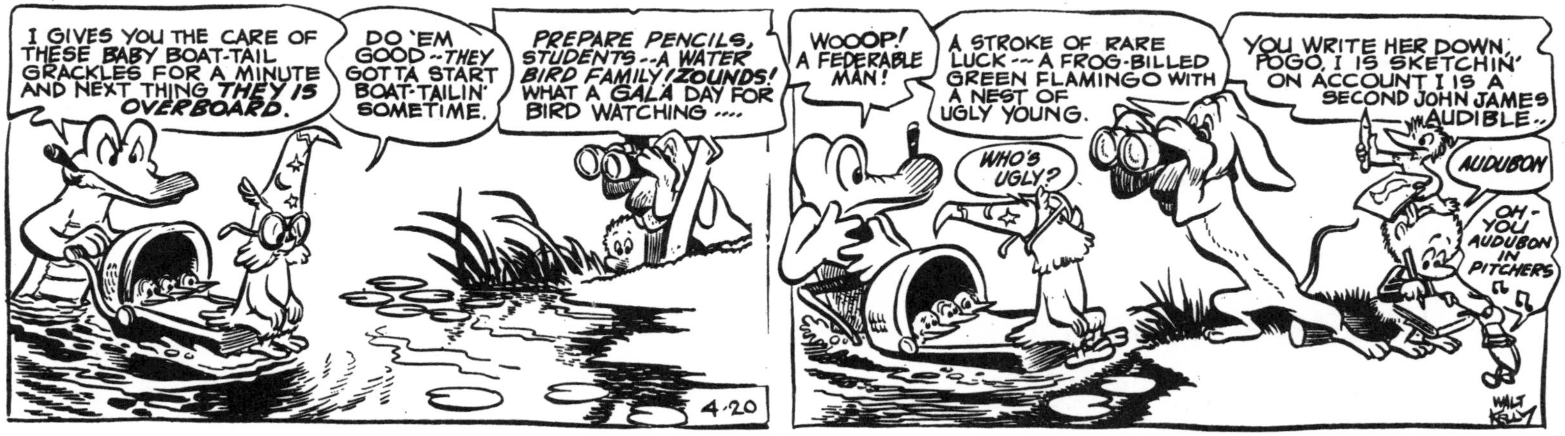
I GIVES YOU THE CARE OF THESE BABY BOAT-TAIL GRACKLES FOR A MINUTE AND NEXT THING THEY IS OVERBOARD.
DO 'EM GOOD -- THEY GOTTA START BOAT-TAILIN' SOMETIME.
PREPARE PENCILS, STUDENTS -- A WATER BIRD FAMILY! ZOUNDS! WHAT A GALA DAY FOR BIRD WATCHING ....
4-20
WOOOP! A FEDERABLE MAN!
A STROKE OF RARE LUCK -- A FROG-BILLED GREEN FLAMINGO WITH A NEST OF UGLY YOUNG.
WHO'S UGLY?
YOU WRITE HER DOWN, POGO, I IS SKETCHIN' ON ACCOUNT I IS A SECOND JOHN JAMES AUDIBLE..
AUDUBON
OH - YOU AUDUBON IN PITCHERS
WALT KELLY

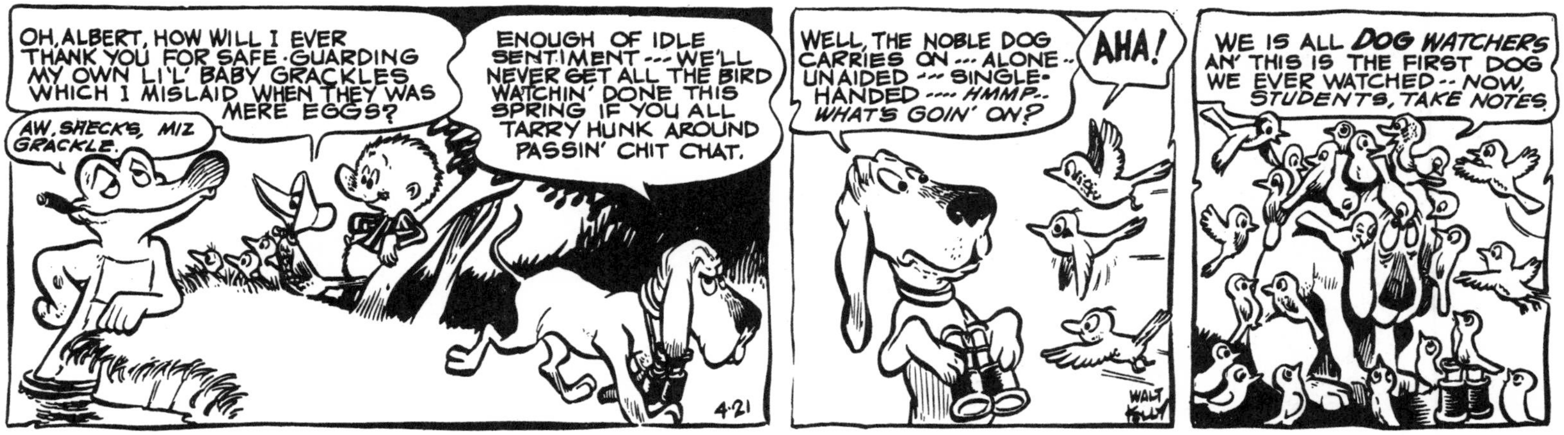
OH, ALBERT, HOW WILL I EVER THANK YOU FOR SAFE-GUARDING MY OWN LI'L' BABY GRACKLES WHICH I MISLAID WHEN THEY WAS MERE EGGS?
AW, SHECKS, MIZ GRACKLE.
ENOUGH OF IDLE SENTIMENT --- WE'LL NEVER GET ALL THE BIRD WATCHIN' DONE THIS SPRING IF YOU ALL TARRY HUNK AROUND PASSIN' CHIT CHAT.
4-21
WELL, THE NOBLE DOG CARRIES ON --- ALONE -- UNAIDED -- SINGLE-HANDED ---- HMMP.. WHAT'S GOIN' ON?
AHA!
WALT KELLY
WE IS ALL DOG WATCHERS AN' THIS IS THE FIRST DOG WE EVER WATCHED -- NOW, STUDENTS, TAKE NOTES.

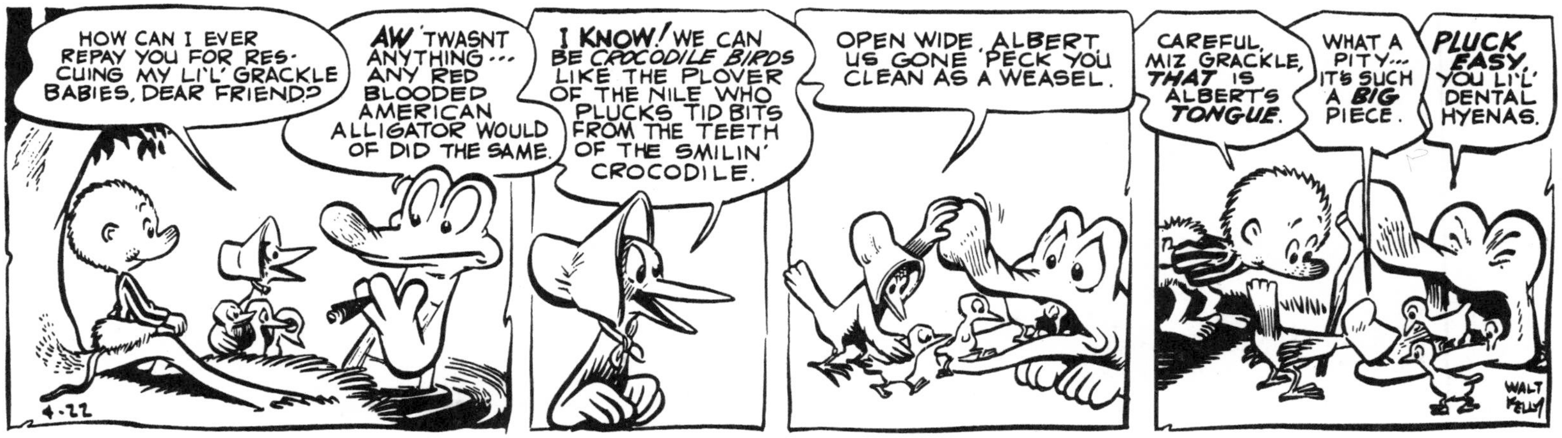
HOW CAN I EVER REPAY YOU FOR RES-CUING MY LI'L' GRACKLE BABIES, DEAR FRIEND?
AW 'TWASNT ANYTHING --- ANY RED BLOODED AMERICAN ALLIGATOR WOULD OF DID THE SAME.
4-22
I KNOW! WE CAN BE CROCODILE BIRDS LIKE THE PLOVER OF THE NILE WHO PLUCKS TID BITS FROM THE TEETH OF THE SMILIN' CROCODILE.
OPEN WIDE, ALBERT US GONE PECK YOU CLEAN AS A WEASEL.
CAREFUL, MIZ GRACKLE, THAT IS ALBERT'S TONGUE.
WHAT A PITY... IT'S SUCH A BIG PIECE.
PLUCK EASY, YOU LI'L' DENTAL HYENAS.
WALT KELLY

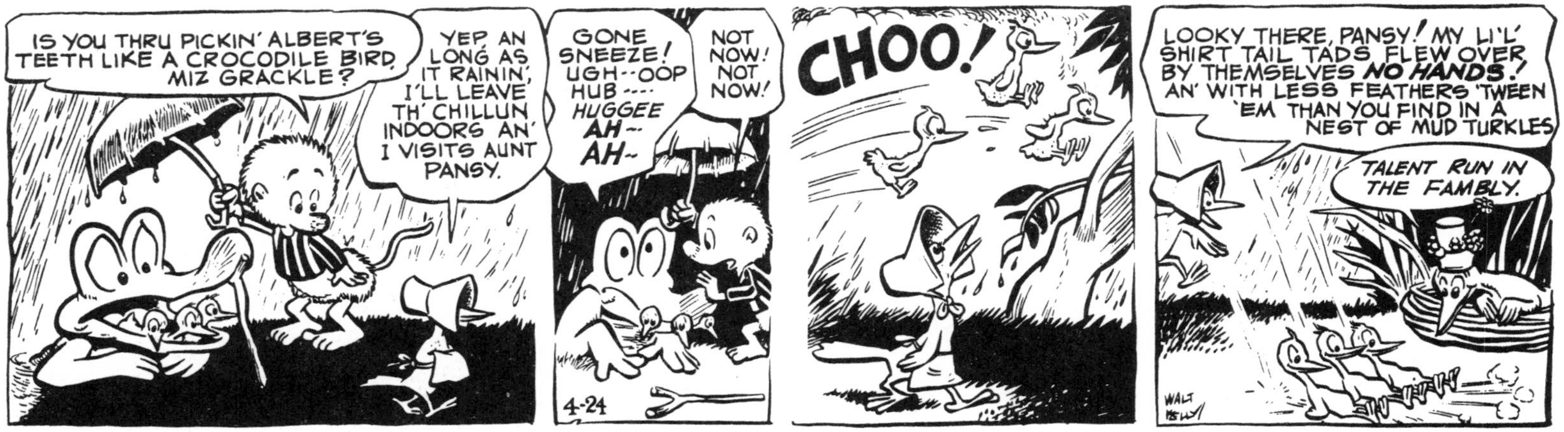
IS YOU THRU PICKIN' ALBERT'S TEETH LIKE A CROCODILE BIRD, MIZ GRACKLE?
YEP. AN LONG AS IT RAININ', I'LL LEAVE TH' CHILLUN INDOORS AN' I VISITS AUNT PANSY.
GONE SNEEZE! UGH--OOP HUB---- HUGGEE AH-- AH-
NOT NOW! NOT NOW!
4-24
CHOO!
LOOKY THERE, PANSY! MY LI'L' SHIRT TAIL TADS FLEW OVER BY THEMSELVES NO HANDS! AN' WITH LESS FEATHERS 'TWEEN 'EM THAN YOU FIND IN A NEST OF MUD TURKLES.
TALENT RUN IN THE FAMBLY.
WALT KELLY

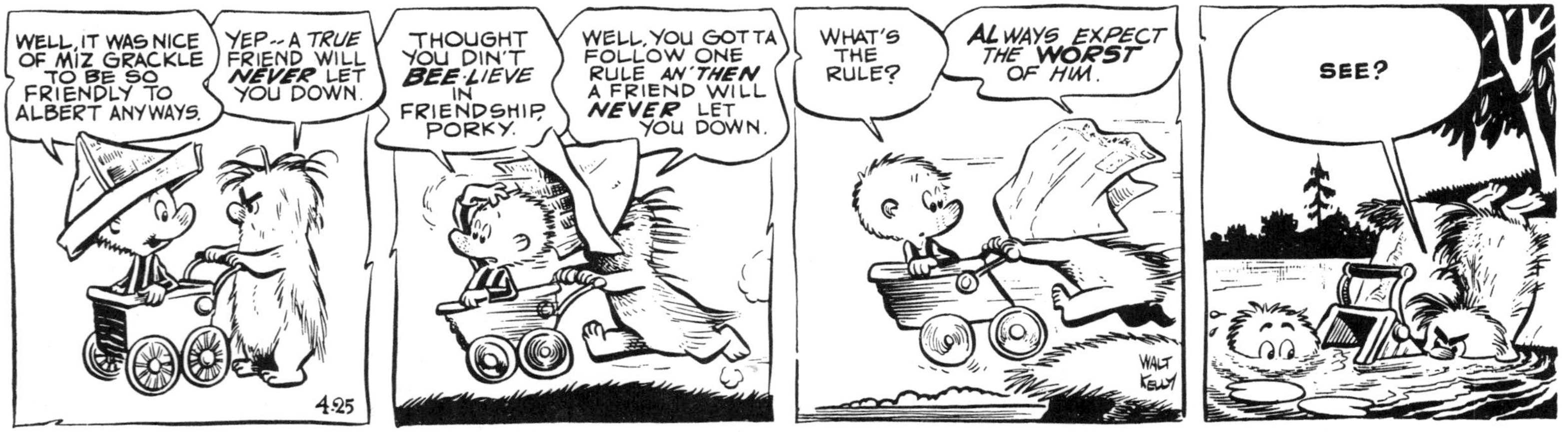
WELL, IT WAS NICE OF MIZ GRACKLE TO BE SO FRIENDLY TO ALBERT ANYWAYS.
YEP-- A TRUE FRIEND WILL NEVER LET YOU DOWN.
4-25
THOUGHT YOU DIN'T BEE-LIEVE IN FRIENDSHIP, PORKY.
WELL, YOU GOTTA FOLLOW ONE RULE AN' THEN A FRIEND WILL NEVER LET YOU DOWN.
WHAT'S THE RULE?
ALWAYS EXPECT THE WORST OF HIM.
WALT KELLY
SEE?

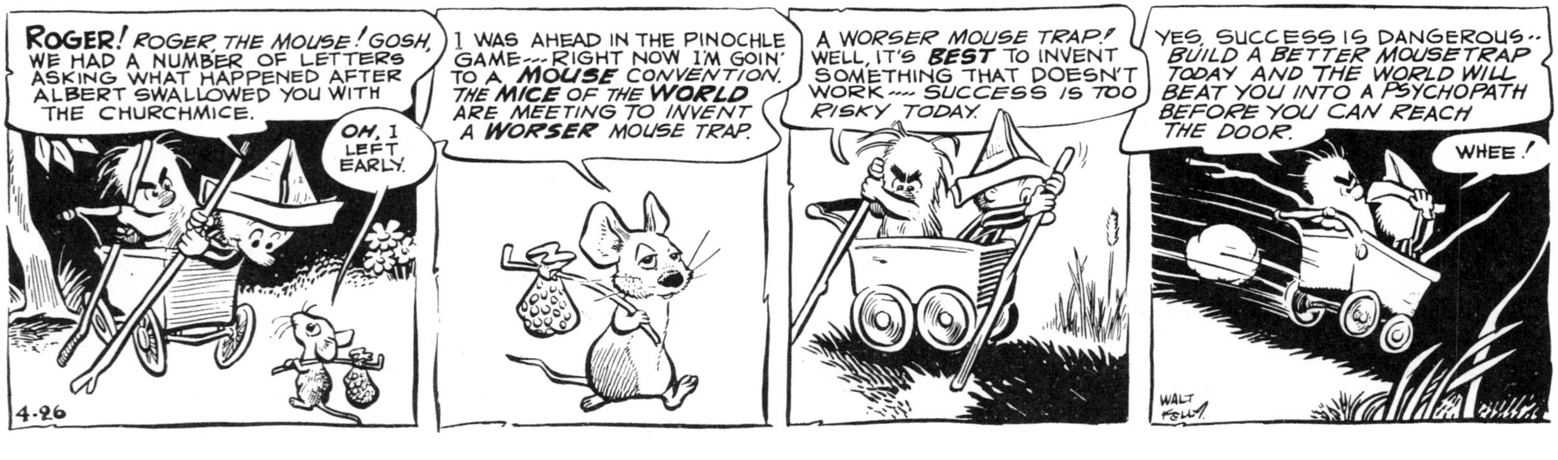
ROGER! ROGER, THE MOUSE! GOSH, WE HAD A NUMBER OF LETTERS ASKING WHAT HAPPENED AFTER ALBERT SWALLOWED YOU WITH THE CHURCHMICE.
OH, I LEFT EARLY.
4-26
I WAS AHEAD IN THE PINOCHLE GAME--- RIGHT NOW I'M GOIN' TO A MOUSE CONVENTION. THE MICE OF THE WORLD ARE MEETING TO INVENT A WORSER MOUSE TRAP.
A WORSER MOUSE TRAP! WELL, IT'S BEST TO INVENT SOMETHING THAT DOESN'T WORK---- SUCCESS IS TOO RISKY TODAY.
YES, SUCCESS IS DANGEROUS-- BUILD A BETTER MOUSETRAP TODAY AND THE WORLD WILL BEAT YOU INTO A PSYCHOPATH BEFORE YOU CAN REACH THE DOOR.
WHEE!
WALT KELLY

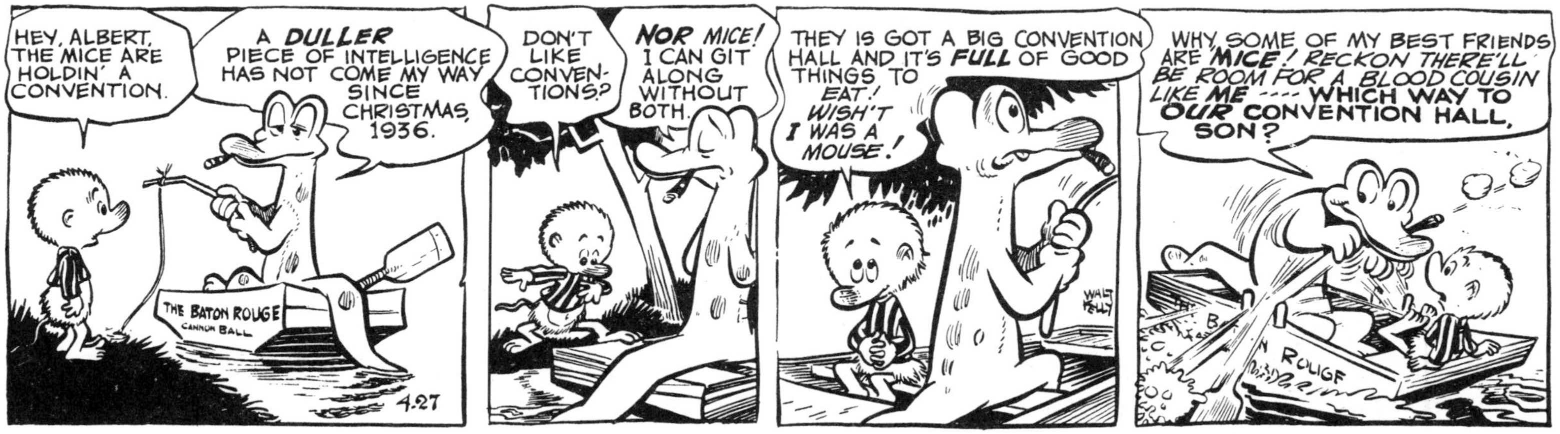
HEY, ALBERT, THE MICE ARE HOLDIN' A CONVENTION.
A DULLER PIECE OF INTELLIGENCE HAS NOT COME MY WAY SINCE CHRISTMAS, 1936.
THE BATON ROUGE
CANNON BALL
4.27
DON'T LIKE CONVEN-TIONS?
NOR MICE! I CAN GIT ALONG WITHOUT BOTH.
THEY IS GOT A BIG CONVENTION HALL AND IT'S FULL OF GOOD THINGS TO EAT!
WISH'T I WAS A MOUSE!
WALT KELLY
WHY, SOME OF MY BEST FRIENDS ARE MICE! RECKON THERE'LL BE ROOM FOR A BLOOD COUSIN LIKE ME ---- WHICH WAY TO OUR CONVENTION HALL, SON?

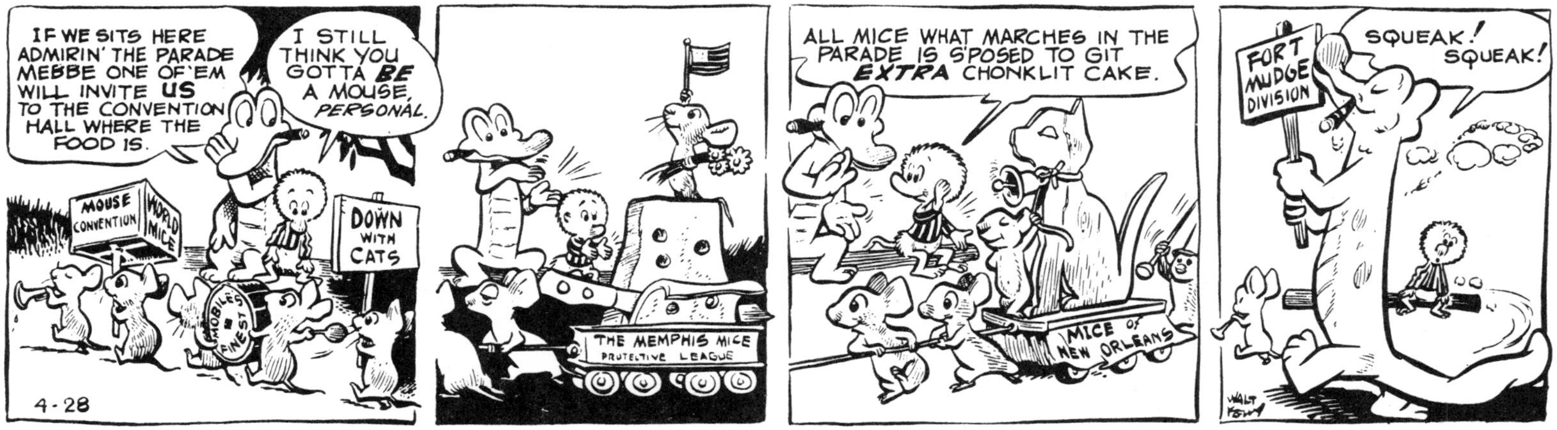
IF WE SITS HERE ADMIRIN' THE PARADE MEBBE ONE OF 'EM WILL INVITE US TO THE CONVENTION HALL WHERE THE FOOD IS.
I STILL THINK YOU GOTTA BE A MOUSE, PERSONAL.
MOUSE CONVENTION
WORLD MICE
DOWN WITH CATS
MOBILE'S FINEST
4-28
THE MEMPHIS MICE PROTECTIVE LEAGUE
ALL MICE WHAT MARCHES IN THE PARADE IS S'POSED TO GIT EXTRA CHONKLIT CAKE.
MICE OF NEW ORLEANS
FORT MUDGE DIVISION
SQUEAK! SQUEAK!
WALT KELLY

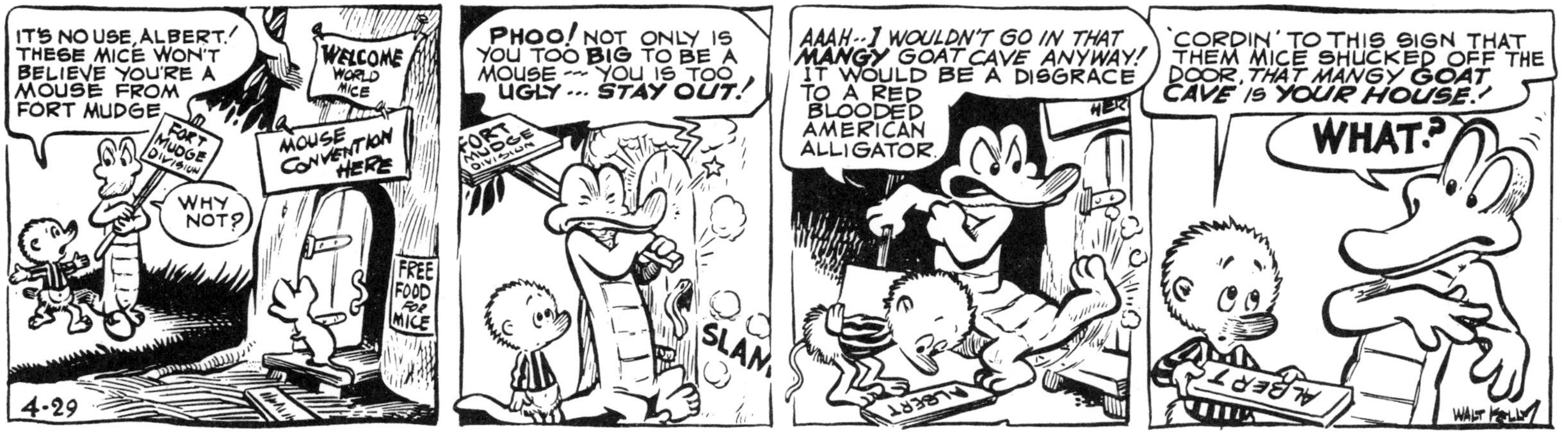
IT'S NO USE, ALBERT! THESE MICE WON'T BELIEVE YOU'RE A MOUSE FROM FORT MUDGE
FORT MUDGE DIVISION
WHY NOT?
WELCOME WORLD MICE
MOUSE CONVENTION HERE
FREE FOOD FOR MICE
4-29
PHOO! NOT ONLY IS YOU TOO BIG TO BE A MOUSE -- YOU IS TOO UGLY ... STAY OUT!
FORT MUDGE DIVISION
SLAM
AAAH -- I WOULDN'T GO IN THAT MANGY GOAT CAVE ANYWAY! IT WOULD BE A DISGRACE TO A RED BLOODED AMERICAN ALLIGATOR.
ALBERT
'CORDIN' TO THIS SIGN THAT THEM MICE SHUCKED OFF THE DOOR, THAT MANGY GOAT CAVE IS YOUR HOUSE!
WHAT?
ALBERT
WALT KELLY

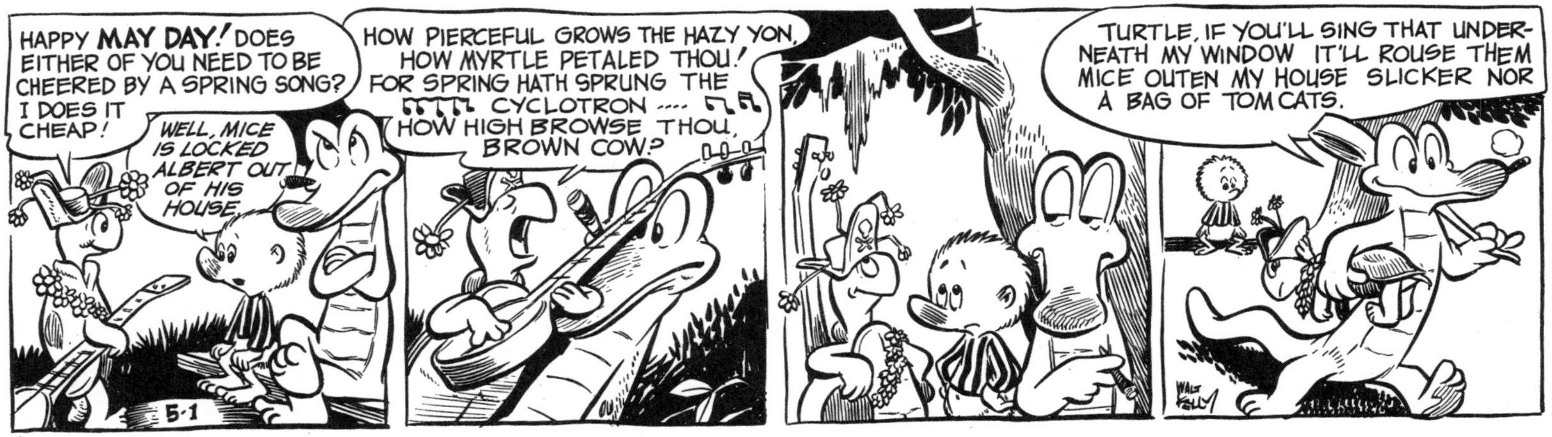

HAPPY MAY DAY! DOES EITHER OF YOU NEED TO BE CHEERED BY A SPRING SONG? I DOES IT CHEAP!
WELL, MICE IS LOCKED ALBERT OUT OF HIS HOUSE.
HOW PIERCEFUL GROWS THE HAZY YON, HOW MYRTLE PETALED THOU! FOR SPRING HATH SPRUNG THE CYCLOTRON .... HOW HIGH BROWSE THOU, BROWN COW?
TURTLE, IF YOU'LL SING THAT UNDERNEATH MY WINDOW IT'LL ROUSE THEM MICE OUTEN MY HOUSE SLICKER NOR A BAG OF TOM CATS.
5-1
WALT KELLY

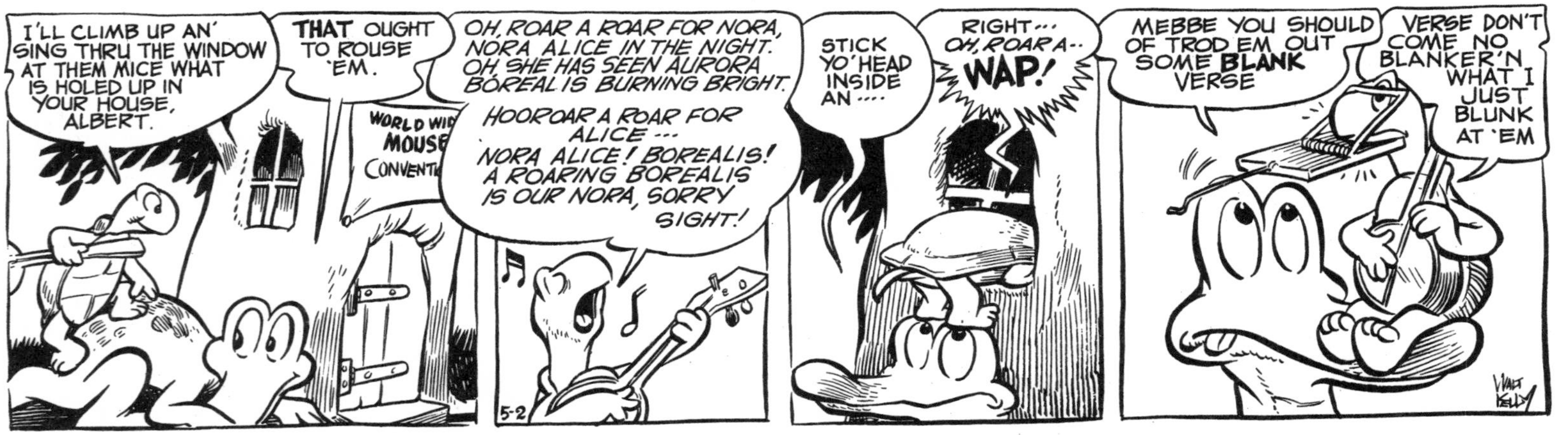

I'LL CLIMB UP AN' SING THRU THE WINDOW AT THEM MICE WHAT IS HOLED UP IN YOUR HOUSE, ALBERT.
THAT OUGHT TO ROUSE 'EM.
WORLD WID MOUSE CONVENTI
OH, ROAR A ROAR FOR NORA, NORA ALICE IN THE NIGHT. OH, SHE HAS SEEN AURORA BOREALIS BURNING BRIGHT.
HOOROAR A ROAR FOR ALICE --- NORA ALICE! BOREALIS! A ROARING BOREALIS IS OUR NORA, SORRY SIGHT!
5-2
STICK YO' HEAD INSIDE AN ....
RIGHT ... OH, ROAR A --
WAP!
MEBBE YOU SHOULD OF TROD EM OUT SOME BLANK VERSE
VERSE DON'T COME NO BLANKER'N WHAT I JUST BLUNK AT 'EM
WALT KELLY

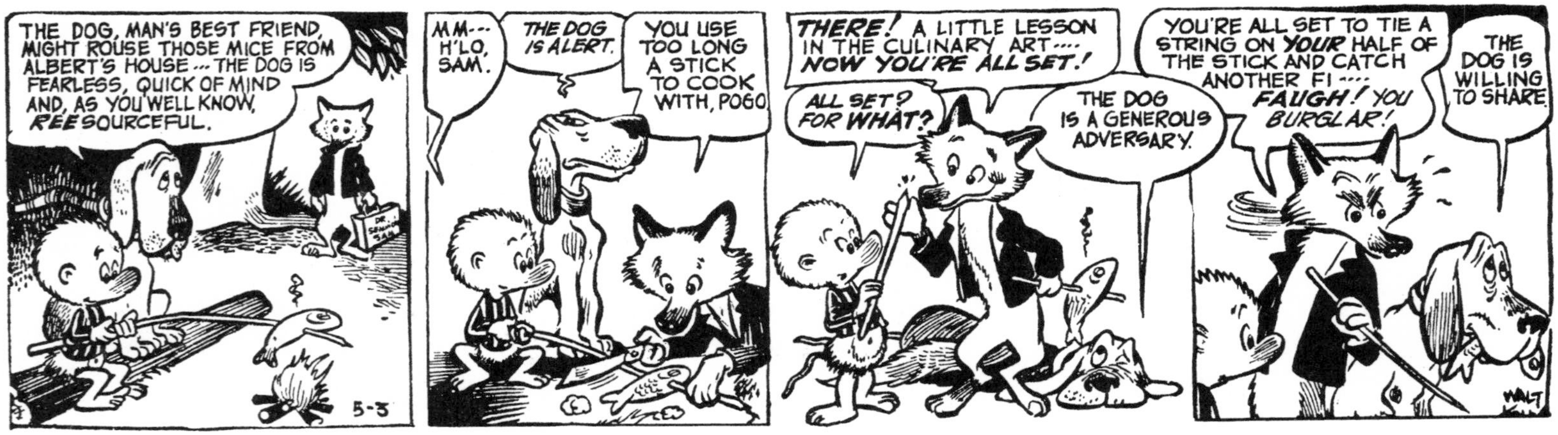

THE DOG, MAN'S BEST FRIEND, MIGHT ROUSE THOSE MICE FROM ALBERT'S HOUSE -- THE DOG IS FEARLESS, QUICK OF MIND AND, AS YOU WELL KNOW, REESOURCEFUL.
5-3
MM--- H'LO, SAM.
THE DOG IS ALERT.
YOU USE TOO LONG A STICK TO COOK WITH, POGO
THERE! A LITTLE LESSON IN THE CULINARY ART .... NOW YOU'RE ALL SET!
ALL SET? FOR WHAT?
THE DOG IS A GENEROUS ADVERSARY.
YOU'RE ALL SET TO TIE A STRING ON YOUR HALF OF THE STICK AND CATCH ANOTHER FI .... FAUGH! YOU BURGLAR!
THE DOG IS WILLING TO SHARE.
WALT

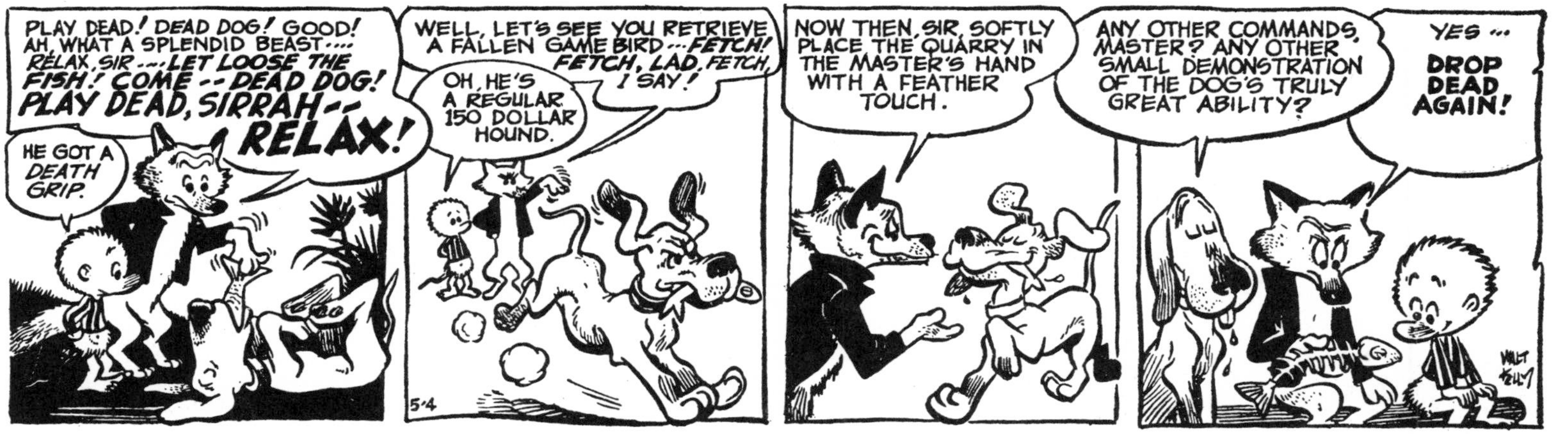
PLAY DEAD! DEAD DOG! GOOD! AH, WHAT A SPLENDID BEAST.... RELAX, SIR --- LET LOOSE THE FISH! COME -- DEAD DOG! PLAY DEAD, SIRRAH -- RELAX!
HE GOT A DEATH GRIP.
WELL, LET'S SEE YOU RETRIEVE A FALLEN GAME BIRD --- FETCH! FETCH, LAD, FETCH, I SAY!
OH, HE'S A REGULAR 150 DOLLAR HOUND.
5-4
NOW THEN, SIR, SOFTLY PLACE THE QUARRY IN THE MASTER'S HAND WITH A FEATHER TOUCH.
ANY OTHER COMMANDS, MASTER? ANY OTHER SMALL DEMONSTRATION OF THE DOG'S TRULY GREAT ABILITY?
YES ... DROP DEAD AGAIN!
WALT KELLY

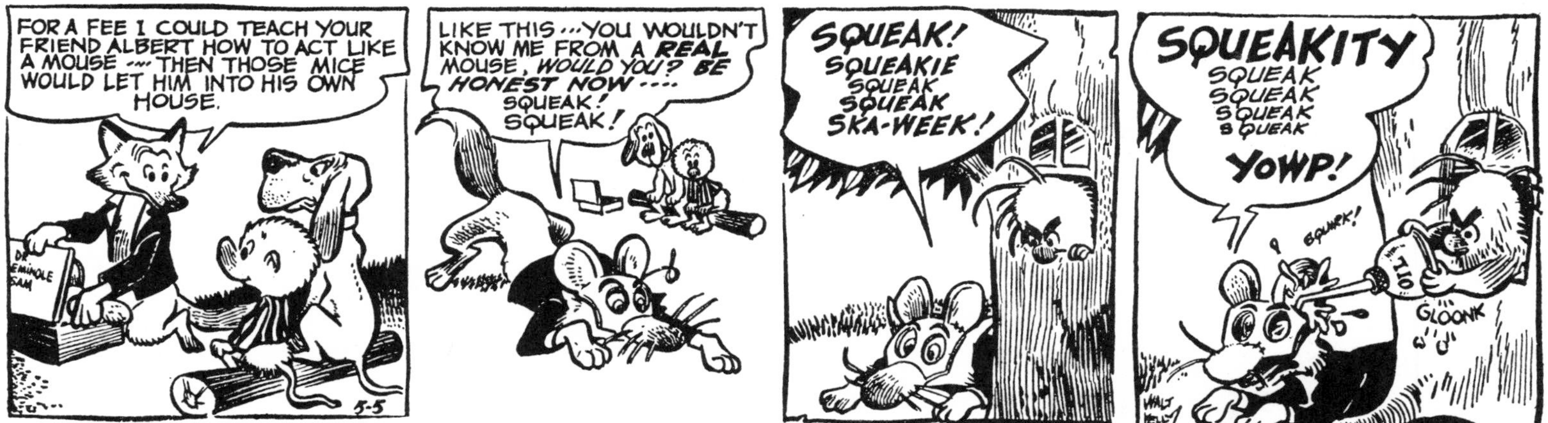
FOR A FEE I COULD TEACH YOUR FRIEND ALBERT HOW TO ACT LIKE A MOUSE --- THEN THOSE MICE WOULD LET HIM INTO HIS OWN HOUSE.
5-5
LIKE THIS ... YOU WOULDN'T KNOW ME FROM A REAL MOUSE, WOULD YOU? BE HONEST NOW .... SQUEAK! SQUEAK!
SQUEAK! SQUEAKIE SQUEAK SQUEAK SKA-WEEK!
SQUEAKITY SQUEAK SQUEAK SQUEAK SQUEAK YOWP!
SQUIRK!
OIL
GLOONK
WALT KELLY

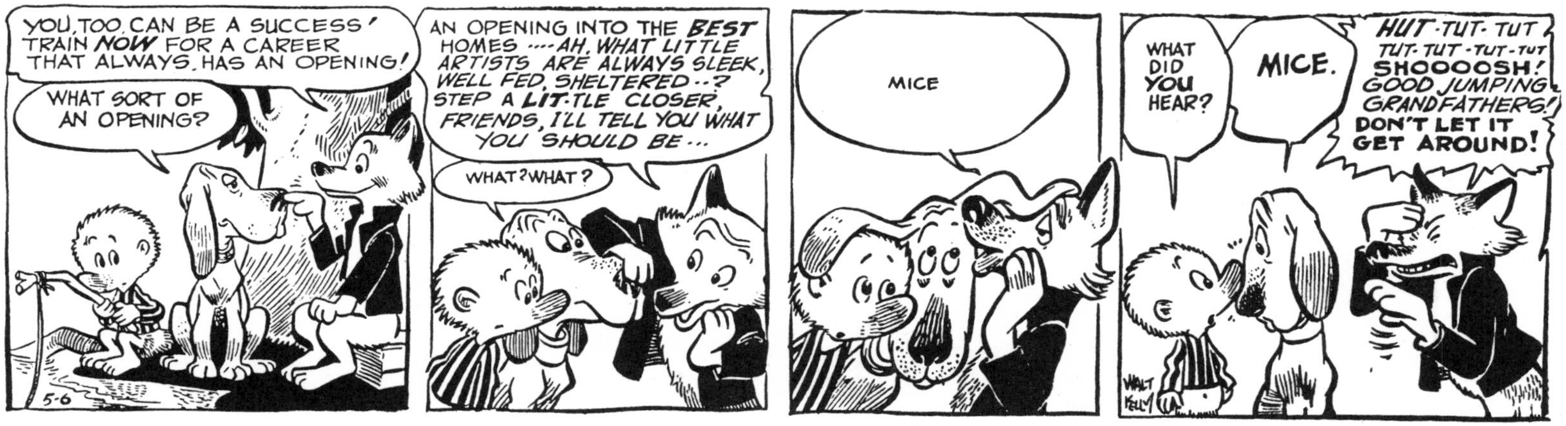
YOU, TOO, CAN BE A SUCCESS! TRAIN NOW FOR A CAREER THAT ALWAYS HAS AN OPENING!
WHAT SORT OF AN OPENING?
5-6
AN OPENING INTO THE BEST HOMES ---- AH, WHAT LITTLE ARTISTS ARE ALWAYS SLEEK, WELL FED, SHELTERED --? STEP A LIT-TLE CLOSER, FRIENDS, I'LL TELL YOU WHAT YOU SHOULD BE ...
WHAT? WHAT?
MICE
WHAT DID YOU HEAR?
MICE.
HUT-TUT-TUT TUT-TUT-TUT-TUT SHOOOOSH! GOOD JUMPING GRANDFATHERS! DON'T LET IT GET AROUND!
WALT KELLY

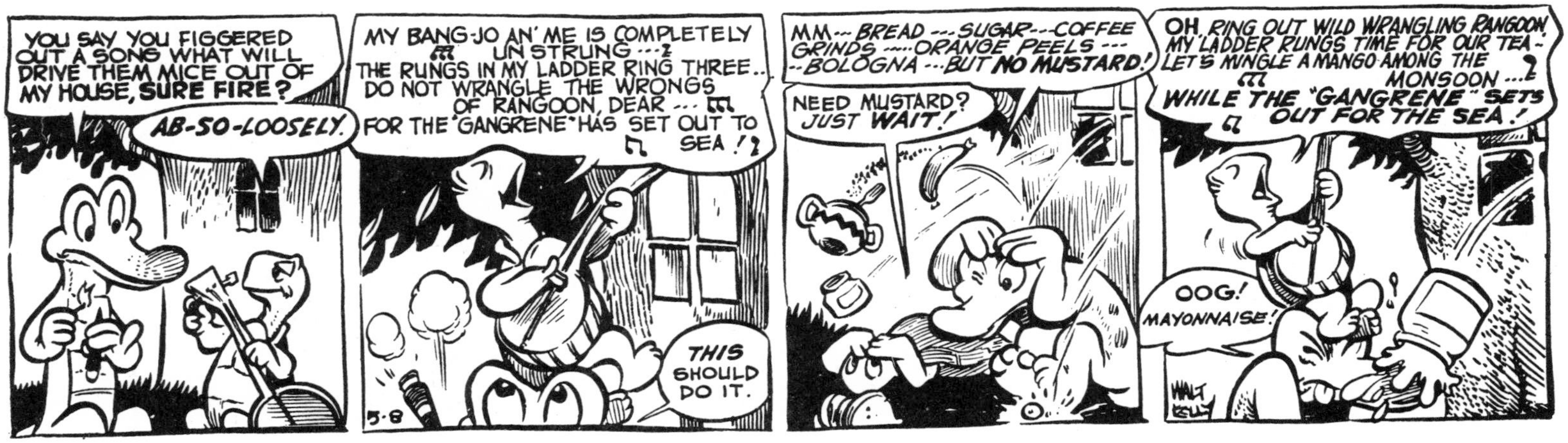
YOU SAY YOU FIGGERED OUT A SONG WHAT WILL DRIVE THEM MICE OUT OF MY HOUSE, SURE FIRE?
AB-SO-LOOSELY.
MY BANG-JO AN' ME IS COMPLETELY UN STRUNG --- THE RUNGS IN MY LADDER RING THREE... DO NOT WRANGLE THE WRONGS OF RANGOON, DEAR --- FOR THE "GANGRENE" HAS SET OUT TO SEA !
THIS SHOULD DO IT.
5-8
MM--- BREAD --- SUGAR --- COFFEE GRINDS ---- ORANGE PEELS --- -- BOLOGNA --- BUT NO MUSTARD!
NEED MUSTARD? JUST WAIT!
OH, RING OUT WILD WRANGLING RANGOON, MY LADDER RUNGS TIME FOR OUR TEA - LET'S MINGLE A MANGO AMONG THE MONSOON ... WHILE THE "GANGRENE" SETS OUT FOR THE SEA.
OOG! MAYONNAISE!
WALT KELLY

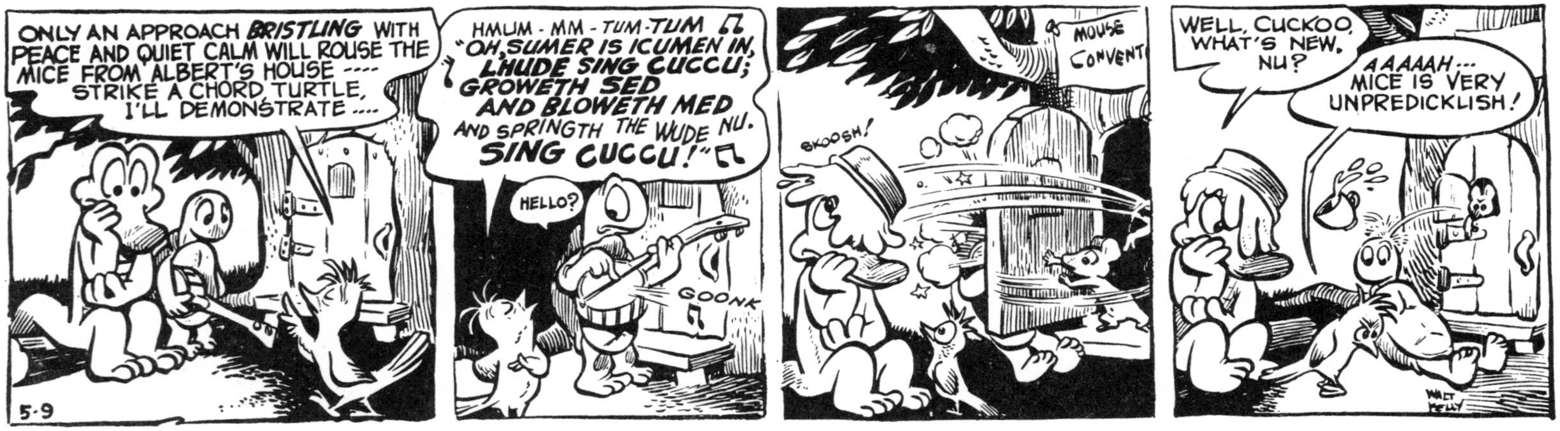
ONLY AN APPROACH BRISTLING WITH PEACE AND QUIET CALM WILL ROUSE THE MICE FROM ALBERT'S HOUSE ---- STRIKE A CHORD TURTLE, I'LL DEMONSTRATE ---
5-9
HMUM - MM - TUM-TUM "OH, SUMER IS ICUMEN IN, LHUDE SING CUCCU; GROWETH SED AND BLOWETH MED AND SPRINGTH THE WUDE NU. SING CUCCU!"
HELLO?
GOONK
MOUSE CONVENT
SKOOSH!
WELL, CUCKOO, WHAT'S NEW, NU?
AAAAAH--- MICE IS VERY UNPREDICKLISH!
WALT KELLY

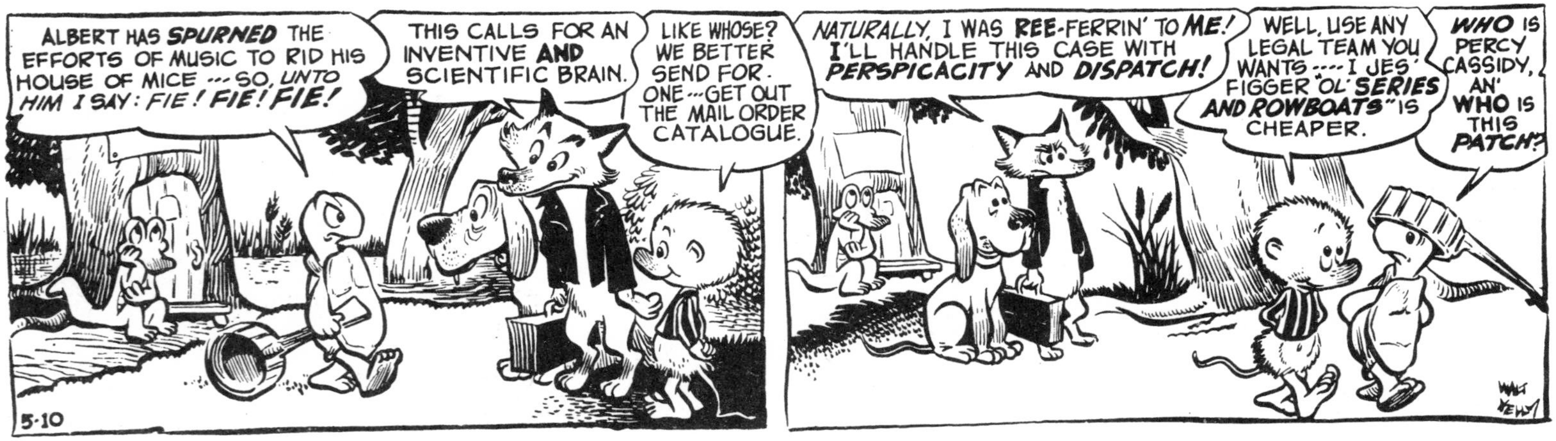
ALBERT HAS SPURNED THE EFFORTS OF MUSIC TO RID HIS HOUSE OF MICE --- SO, UNTO HIM I SAY: FIE! FIE! FIE!
THIS CALLS FOR AN INVENTIVE AND SCIENTIFIC BRAIN.
LIKE WHOSE? WE BETTER SEND FOR ONE --- GET OUT THE MAIL ORDER CATALOGUE.
5-10
NATURALLY, I WAS REE-FERRIN' TO ME! I'LL HANDLE THIS CASE WITH PERSPICACITY AND DISPATCH!
WELL, USE ANY LEGAL TEAM YOU WANTS ---- I JES' FIGGER "OL' SERIES AND ROWBOATS" IS CHEAPER.
WHO IS PERCY CASSIDY, AN' WHO IS THIS PATCH?
WALT KELLY

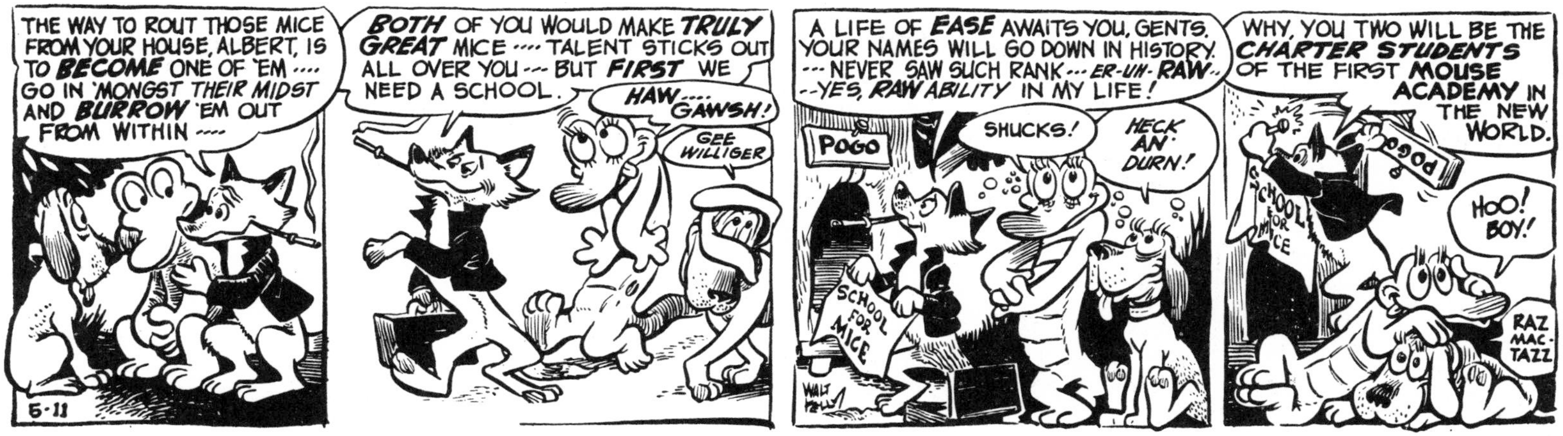
THE WAY TO ROUT THOSE MICE FROM YOUR HOUSE, ALBERT, IS TO BECOME ONE OF 'EM ···· GO IN 'MONGST THEIR MIDST AND BURROW 'EM OUT FROM WITHIN ····
5·11
BOTH OF YOU WOULD MAKE TRULY GREAT MICE ···· TALENT STICKS OUT ALL OVER YOU --- BUT FIRST WE NEED A SCHOOL.
HAW.... GAWSH!
GEE WILLIGER
A LIFE OF EASE AWAITS YOU, GENTS. YOUR NAMES WILL GO DOWN IN HISTORY. --- NEVER SAW SUCH RANK --- ER-UH- RAW --YES, RAW ABILITY IN MY LIFE!
POGO
SHUCKS!
HECK AN' DURN!
SCHOOL FOR MICE
WALT KELLY
WHY, YOU TWO WILL BE THE CHARTER STUDENTS OF THE FIRST MOUSE ACADEMY IN THE NEW WORLD.
POGO
SCHOOL FOR MICE
HOO! BOY!
RAZ MAC-TAZZ

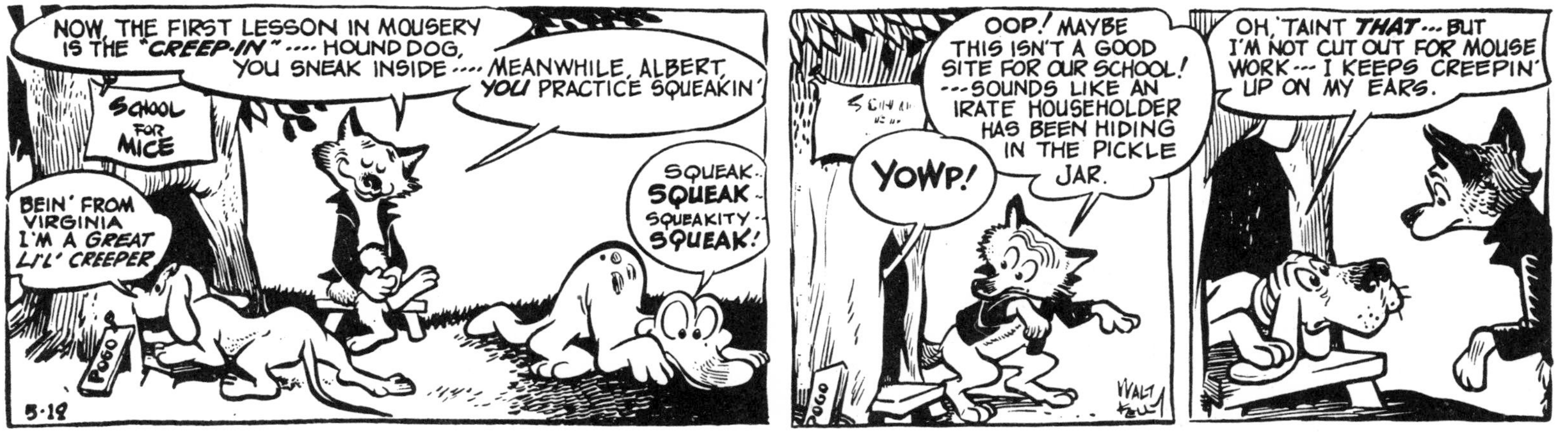
NOW, THE FIRST LESSON IN MOUSERY IS THE "CREEP-IN" ···· HOUND DOG, YOU SNEAK INSIDE ····
MEANWHILE, ALBERT, YOU PRACTICE SQUEAKIN'
SCHOOL FOR MICE
BEIN' FROM VIRGINIA I'M A GREAT LI'L' CREEPER
SQUEAK. SQUEAK - SQUEAKITY - SQUEAK!
POGO
5·12
OOP! MAYBE THIS ISN'T A GOOD SITE FOR OUR SCHOOL! ---SOUNDS LIKE AN IRATE HOUSEHOLDER HAS BEEN HIDING IN THE PICKLE JAR.
YOWP!
WALT KELLY
OH, 'TAINT THAT --- BUT I'M NOT CUT OUT FOR MOUSE WORK --- I KEEPS CREEPIN' UP ON MY EARS.

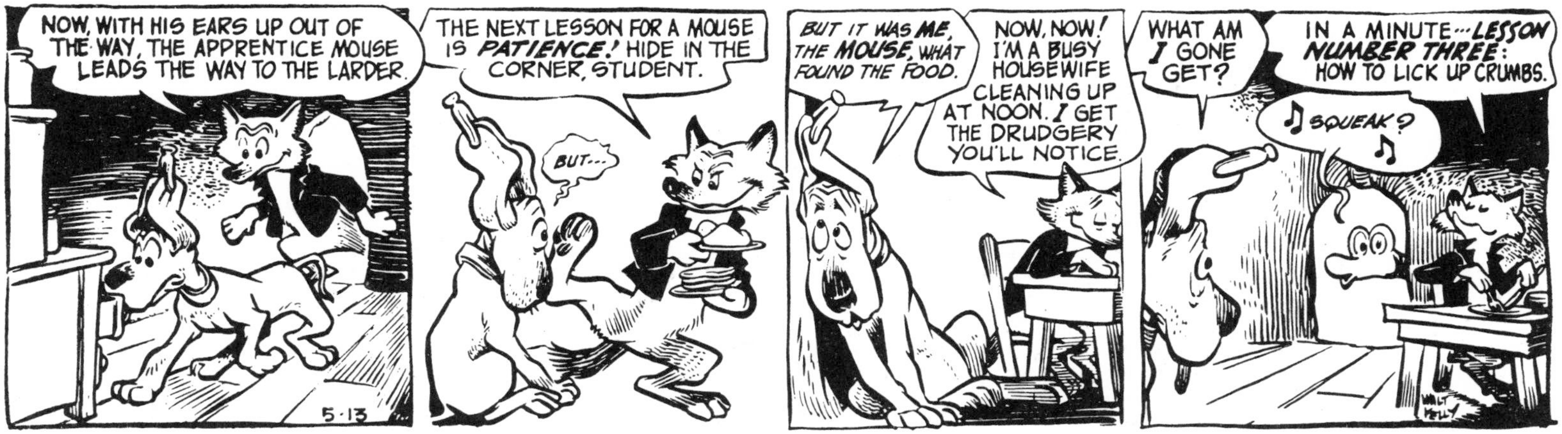
NOW, WITH HIS EARS UP OUT OF THE WAY, THE APPRENTICE MOUSE LEADS THE WAY TO THE LARDER.
5·13
THE NEXT LESSON FOR A MOUSE IS PATIENCE.' HIDE IN THE CORNER, STUDENT.
BUT...
BUT IT WAS ME, THE MOUSE, WHAT FOUND THE FOOD.
NOW, NOW! I'M A BUSY HOUSEWIFE CLEANING UP AT NOON. I GET THE DRUDGERY YOU'LL NOTICE.
WHAT AM I GONE GET?
IN A MINUTE --- LESSON NUMBER THREE: HOW TO LICK UP CRUMBS.
♫ SQUEAK? ♪
WALT KELLY

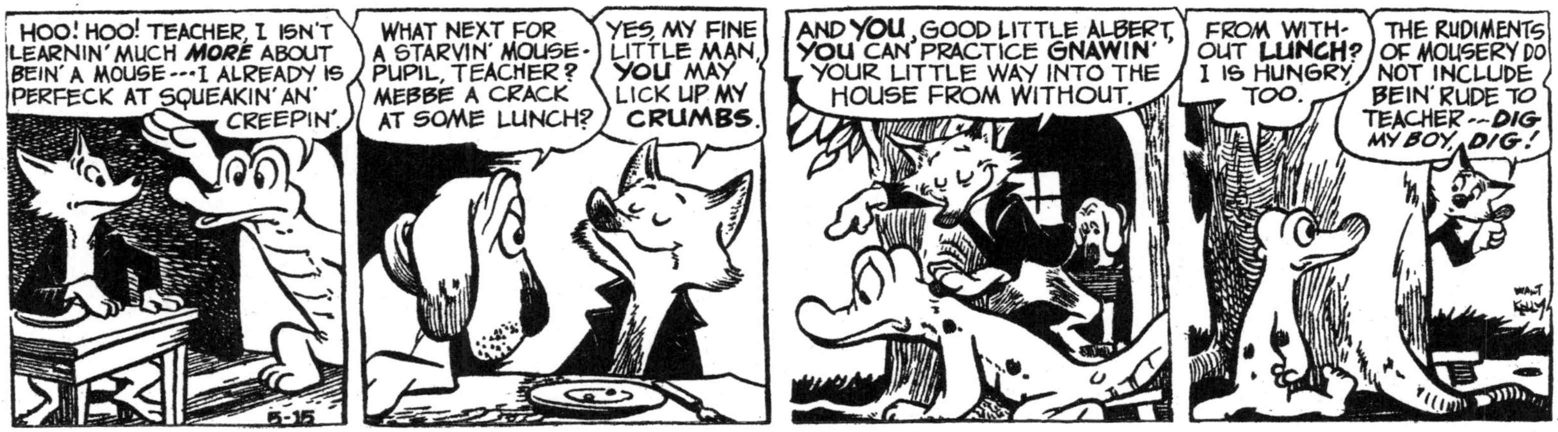
HOO! HOO! TEACHER, I ISN'T LEARNIN' MUCH MORE ABOUT BEIN' A MOUSE --- I ALREADY IS PERFECK AT SQUEAKIN' AN' CREEPIN'.
WHAT NEXT FOR A STARVIN' MOUSE-PUPIL, TEACHER? MEBBE A CRACK AT SOME LUNCH?
YES, MY FINE LITTLE MAN, YOU MAY LICK UP MY CRUMBS.
AND YOU, GOOD LITTLE ALBERT, YOU CAN PRACTICE GNAWIN' YOUR LITTLE WAY INTO THE HOUSE FROM WITHOUT.
FROM WITH-OUT LUNCH? I IS HUNGRY TOO.
THE RUDIMENTS OF MOUSERY DO NOT INCLUDE BEIN' RUDE TO TEACHER -- DIG MY BOY, DIG!
5-15
WALT KELLY

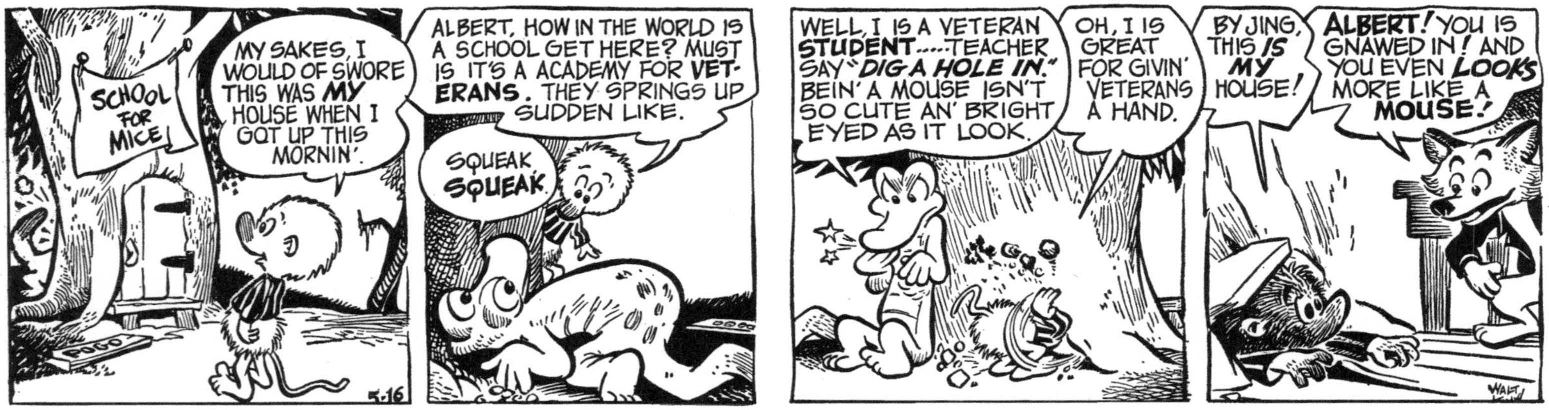
SCHOOL FOR MICE
MY SAKES, I WOULD OF SWORE THIS WAS MY HOUSE WHEN I GOT UP THIS MORNIN'.
ALBERT, HOW IN THE WORLD IS A SCHOOL GET HERE? MUST IS IT'S A ACADEMY FOR VETERANS. THEY SPRINGS UP SUDDEN LIKE.
SQUEAK SQUEAK
POGO
5-16
WELL, I IS A VETERAN STUDENT ---- TEACHER SAY "DIG A HOLE IN." BEIN' A MOUSE ISN'T SO CUTE AN' BRIGHT EYED AS IT LOOK.
OH, I IS GREAT FOR GIVIN' VETERANS A HAND.
BY JING, THIS IS MY HOUSE!
ALBERT! YOU IS GNAWED IN! AND YOU EVEN LOOKS MORE LIKE A MOUSE!
WALT KELLY

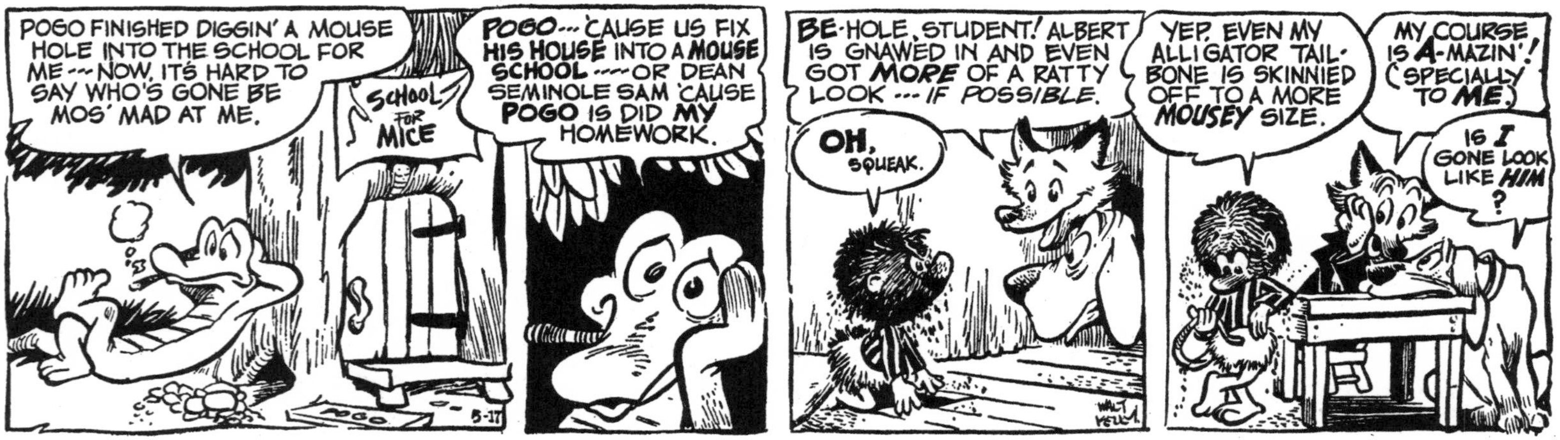
POGO FINISHED DIGGIN' A MOUSE HOLE INTO THE SCHOOL FOR ME --- NOW, IT'S HARD TO SAY WHO'S GONE BE MOS' MAD AT ME.
SCHOOL FOR MICE
POGO
5-17
POGO --- 'CAUSE US FIX HIS HOUSE INTO A MOUSE SCHOOL ---- OR DEAN SEMINOLE SAM 'CAUSE POGO IS DID MY HOMEWORK.
BE-HOLE, STUDENT! ALBERT IS GNAWED IN AND EVEN GOT MORE OF A RATTY LOOK --- IF POSSIBLE.
OH, SQUEAK.
YEP, EVEN MY ALLIGATOR TAIL-BONE IS SKINNIED OFF TO A MORE MOUSEY SIZE.
MY COURSE IS A-MAZIN'! (SPECIALLY TO ME.)
IS I GONE LOOK LIKE HIM?
WALT KELLY

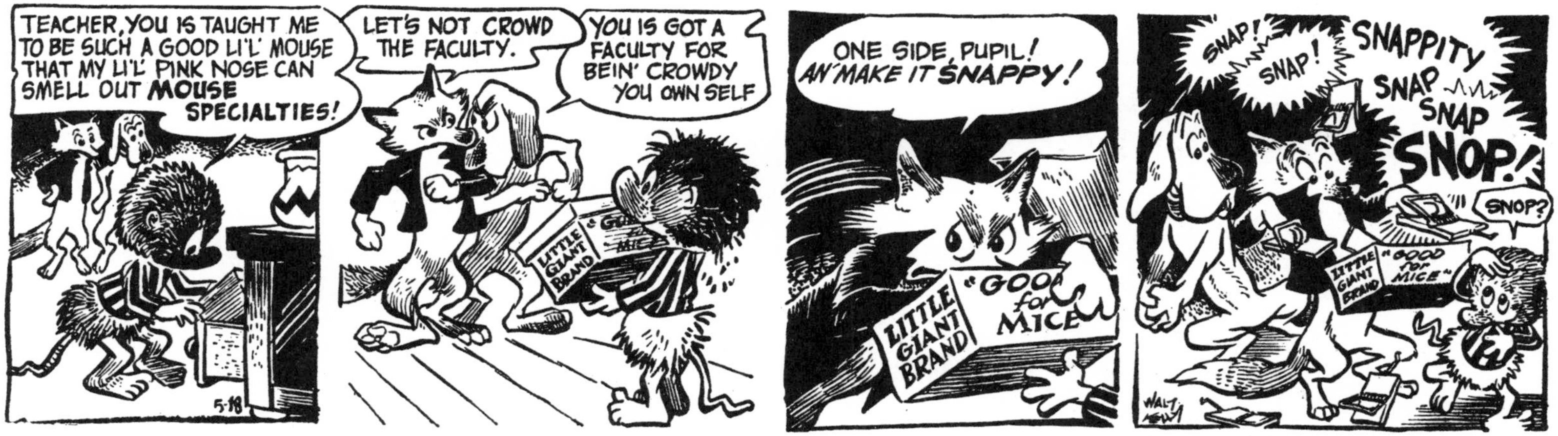
TEACHER, YOU IS TAUGHT ME TO BE SUCH A GOOD LI'L' MOUSE THAT MY LI'L' PINK NOSE CAN SMELL OUT MOUSE SPECIALTIES!
5-18
LET'S NOT CROWD THE FACULTY.
YOU IS GOT A FACULTY FOR BEIN' CROWDY YOU OWN SELF
LITTLE GIANT BRAND
ONE SIDE, PUPIL! AN' MAKE IT SNAPPY!
LITTLE GIANT BRAND
"GOOD for MICE"
SNAP! SNAP! SNAPPITY SNAP SNAP SNOP!
SNOP?
LITTLE GIANT BRAND
"GOOD for MICE"
WALT KELLY

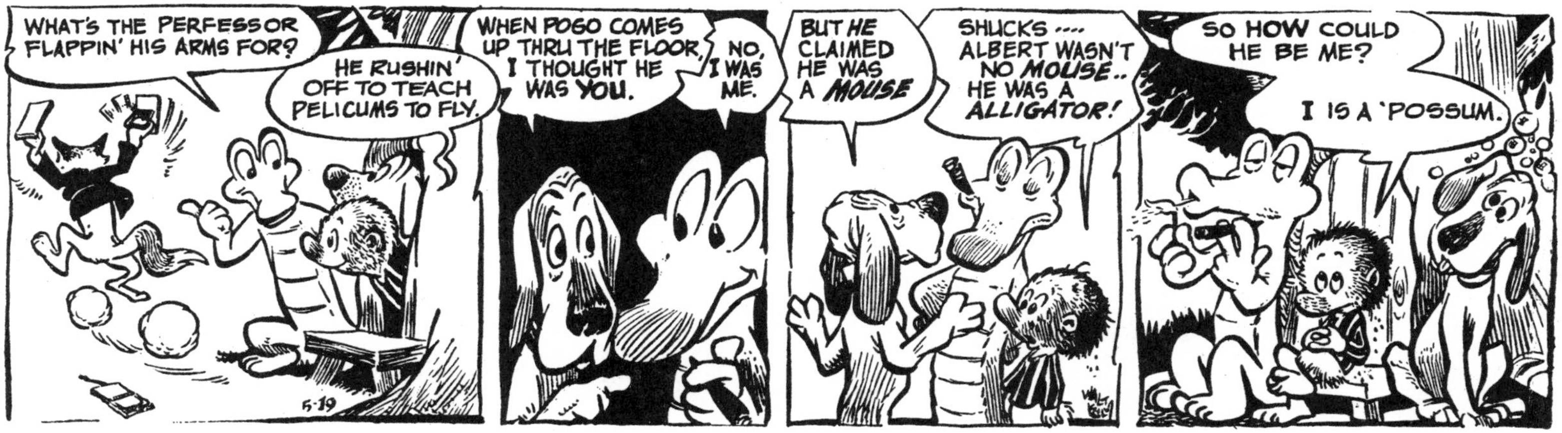
WHAT'S THE PERFESSOR FLAPPIN' HIS ARMS FOR?
HE RUSHIN' OFF TO TEACH PELICUMS TO FLY.
5-19
WHEN POGO COMES UP THRU THE FLOOR, I THOUGHT HE WAS YOU.
NO, I WAS ME.
BUT HE CLAIMED HE WAS A MOUSE
SHUCKS.... ALBERT WASN'T NO MOUSE.. HE WAS A ALLIGATOR!
WALT KELLY
SO HOW COULD HE BE ME?
I IS A 'POSSUM.

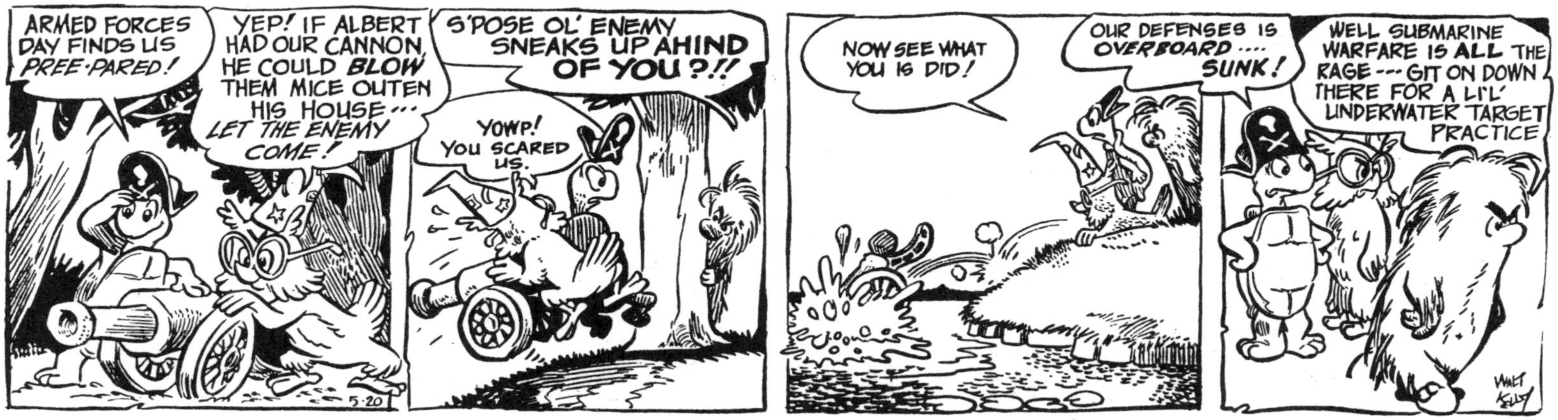
ARMED FORCES DAY FINDS US PREE-PARED!
YEP! IF ALBERT HAD OUR CANNON HE COULD BLOW THEM MICE OUTEN HIS HOUSE... LET THE ENEMY COME!
5-20
S'POSE OL' ENEMY SNEAKS UP AHIND OF YOU?!!
YOWP! YOU SCARED US.
NOW SEE WHAT YOU IS DID!
OUR DEFENSES IS OVERBOARD.... SUNK!
WELL SUBMARINE WARFARE IS ALL THE RAGE --- GIT ON DOWN THERE FOR A LI'L' UNDERWATER TARGET PRACTICE
WALT KELLY

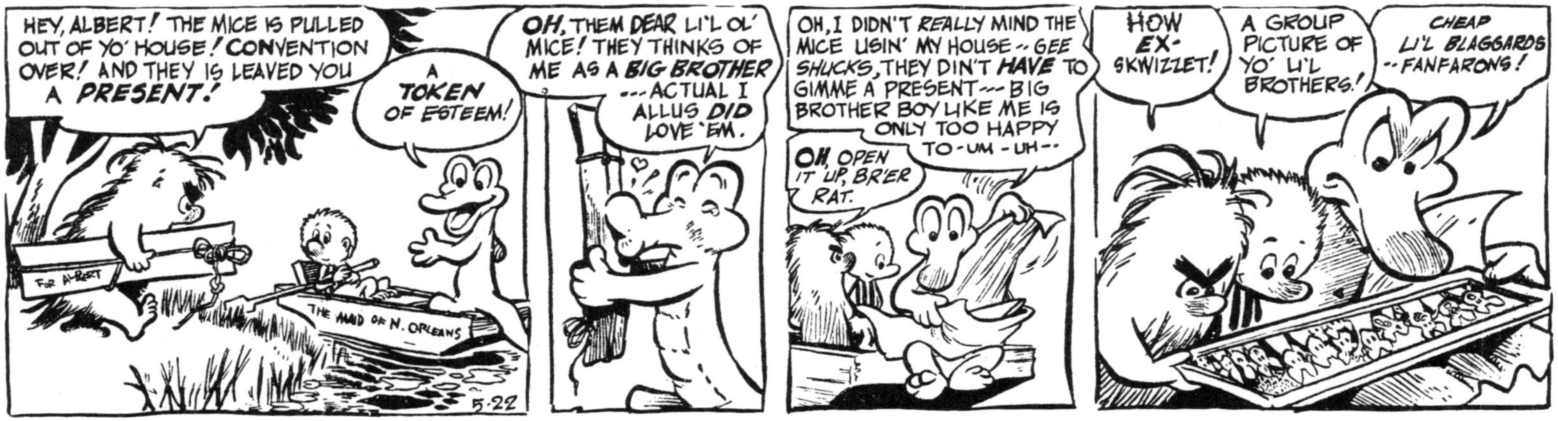
HEY, ALBERT! THE MICE IS PULLED OUT OF YO' HOUSE! CONVENTION OVER! AND THEY IS LEAVED YOU A PRESENT!
A TOKEN OF ESTEEM!
FOR ALBERT
THE MAID OF N. ORLEANS
5-22
OH, THEM DEAR LI'L OL' MICE! THEY THINKS OF ME AS A BIG BROTHER ---ACTUAL I ALLUS DID LOVE 'EM.
OH, I DIDN'T REALLY MIND THE MICE USIN' MY HOUSE -- GEE SHUCKS, THEY DIN'T HAVE TO GIMME A PRESENT --- BIG BROTHER BOY LIKE ME IS ONLY TOO HAPPY TO-UM-UH--
OH, OPEN IT UP, BR'ER RAT.
HOW EX-SKWIZZET!
A GROUP PICTURE OF YO' LI'L BROTHERS!
CHEAP LI'L BLAGGARDS --FANFARONS!

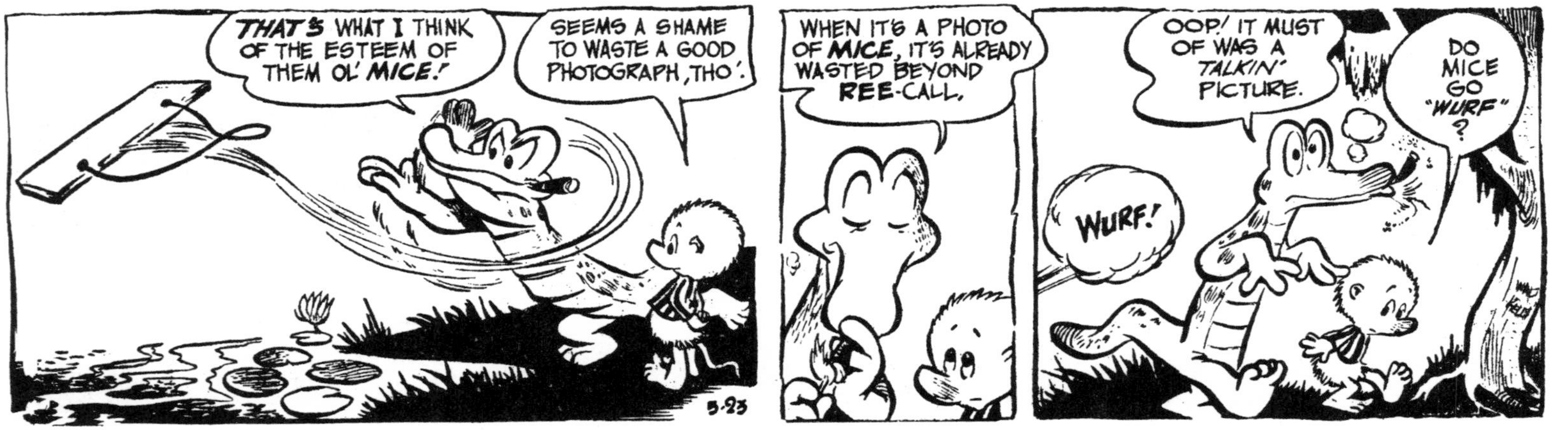
THAT'S WHAT I THINK OF THE ESTEEM OF THEM OL' MICE!
SEEMS A SHAME TO WASTE A GOOD PHOTOGRAPH, THO'.
5-23
WHEN IT'S A PHOTO OF MICE, IT'S ALREADY WASTED BEYOND REE-CALL.
OOP! IT MUST OF WAS A TALKIN' PICTURE.
DO MICE GO "WURF"?
WURF!

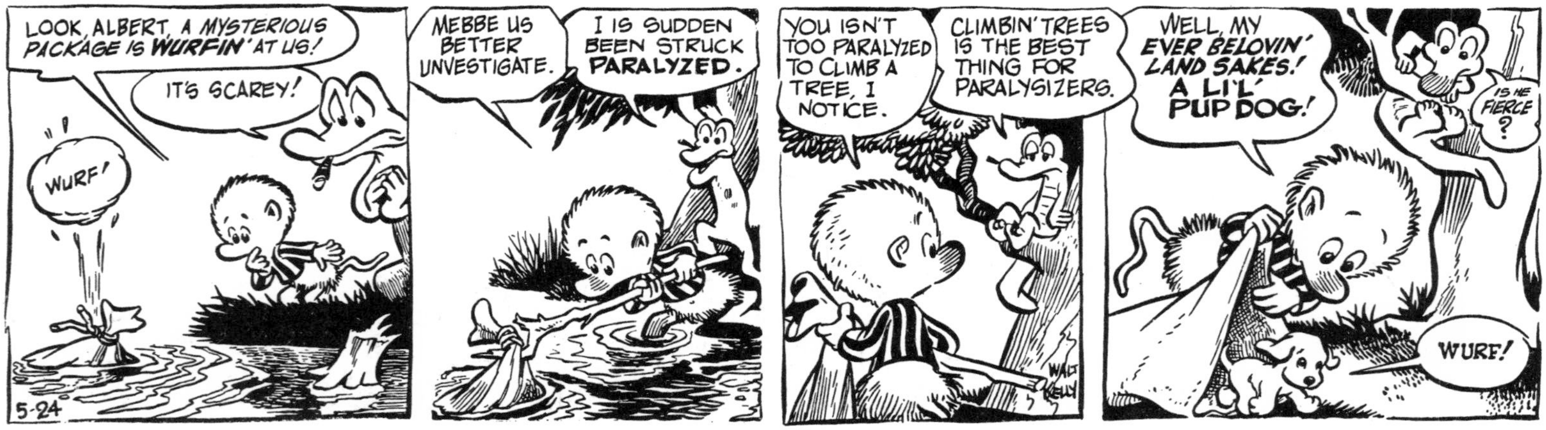
LOOK, ALBERT, A MYSTERIOUS PACKAGE IS WURFIN' AT US!
IT'S SCAREY!
WURF!
5-24
MEBBE US BETTER UNVESTIGATE.
I IS SUDDEN BEEN STRUCK PARALYZED.
YOU ISN'T TOO PARALYZED TO CLIMB A TREE, I NOTICE.
CLIMBIN' TREES IS THE BEST THING FOR PARALYSIZERS.
WALT KELLY
WELL, MY EVER BELOVIN' LAND SAKES! A LI'L PUP DOG!
IS HE FIERCE?
WURF!

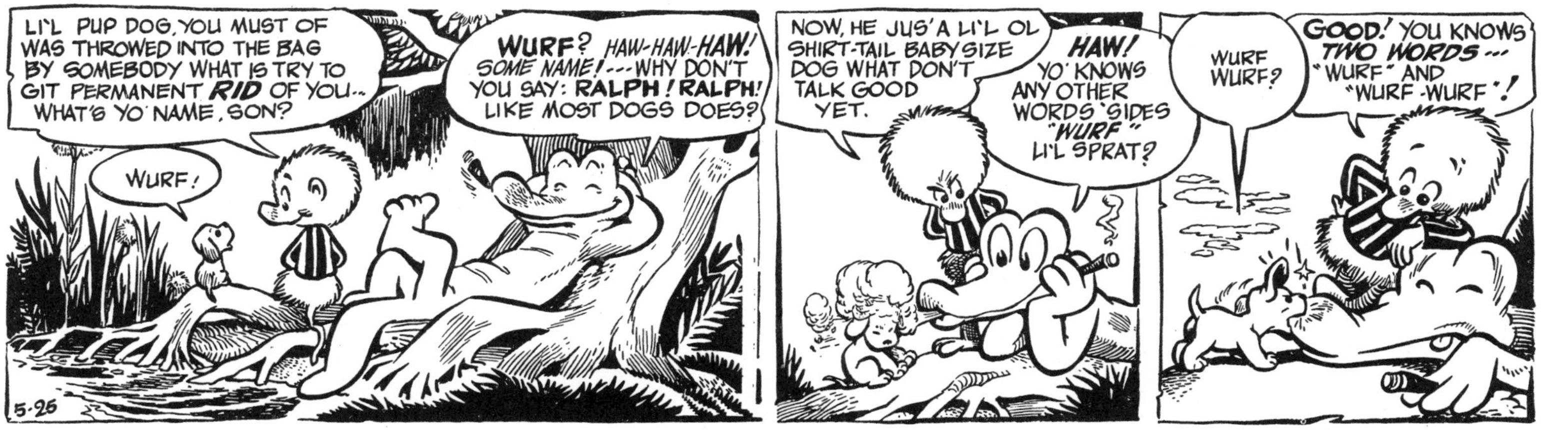
LI'L PUP DOG, YOU MUST OF WAS THROWED INTO THE BAG BY SOMEBODY WHAT IS TRY TO GIT PERMANENT RID OF YOU... WHAT'S YO' NAME, SON?
WURF!
WURF? HAW-HAW-HAW! SOME NAME! --- WHY DON'T YOU SAY: RALPH! RALPH! LIKE MOST DOGS DOES?
NOW, HE JUS' A LI'L OL SHIRT-TAIL BABY SIZE DOG WHAT DON'T TALK GOOD YET.
HAW! YO' KNOWS ANY OTHER WORDS 'SIDES "WURF" LI'L SPRAT?
WURF WURF?
GOOD! YOU KNOWS TWO WORDS --- "WURF" AND "WURF-WURF"!
5-25

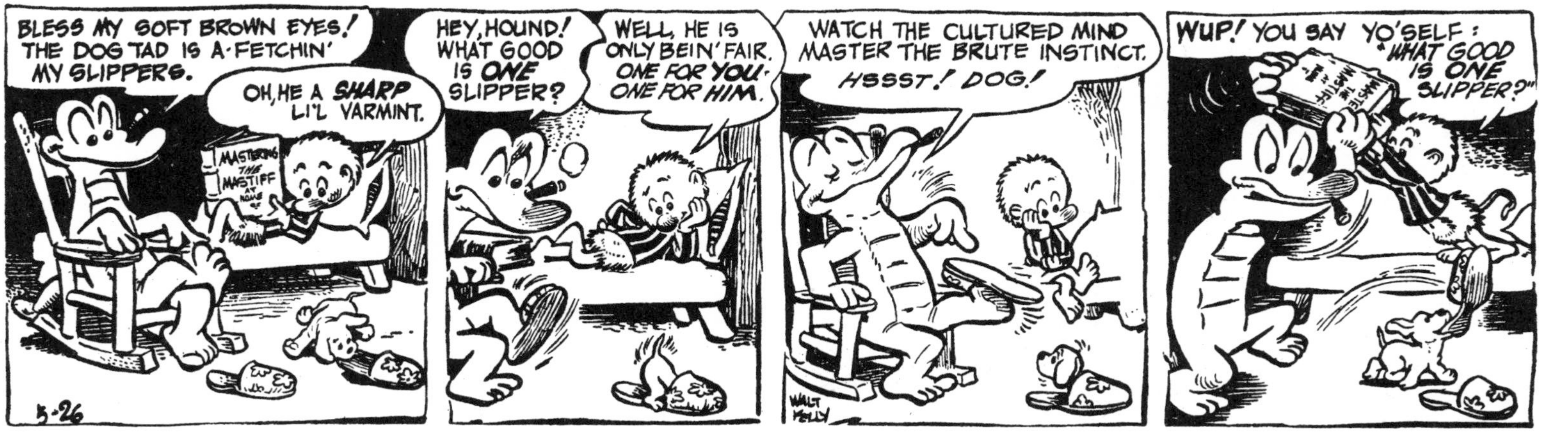
BLESS MY SOFT BROWN EYES! THE DOG TAD IS A-FETCHIN' MY SLIPPERS.
OH, HE A SHARP LI'L VARMINT.
MASTERING THE MASTIFF
HEY, HOUND! WHAT GOOD IS ONE SLIPPER?
WELL, HE IS ONLY BEIN' FAIR. ONE FOR YOU ONE FOR HIM.
WATCH THE CULTURED MIND MASTER THE BRUTE INSTINCT.
HSSST! DOG!
WUP! YOU SAY YO'SELF: "WHAT GOOD IS ONE SLIPPER?"
5-26
WALT KELLY

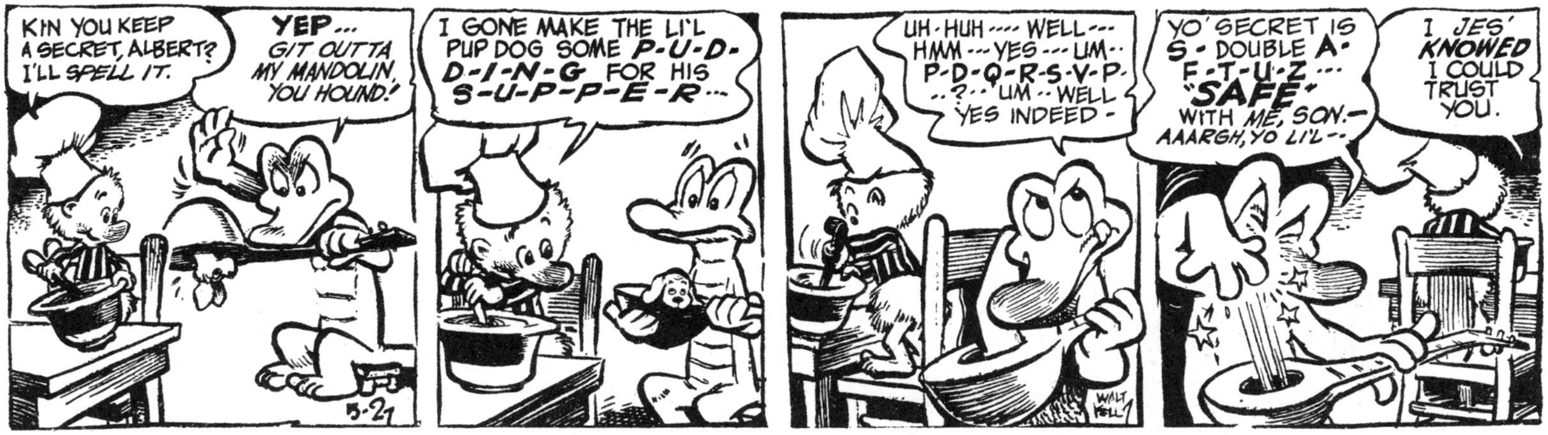
KIN YOU KEEP A SECRET, ALBERT? I'LL SPELL IT.
YEP... GIT OUTTA MY MANDOLIN, YOU HOUND!
I GONE MAKE THE LI'L PUP DOG SOME P-U-D-D-I-N-G FOR HIS S-U-P-P-E-R...
UH-HUH ---- WELL --- HMM --- YES --- UM -- P-D-Q-R-S-V-P- -- ? -- UM -- WELL YES INDEED -
YO' SECRET IS S - DOUBLE A - F-T-U-Z --- "SAFE" WITH ME, SON. — AARGH, YO LI'L --
I JES' KNOWED I COULD TRUST YOU.
5-27
WALT KELLY

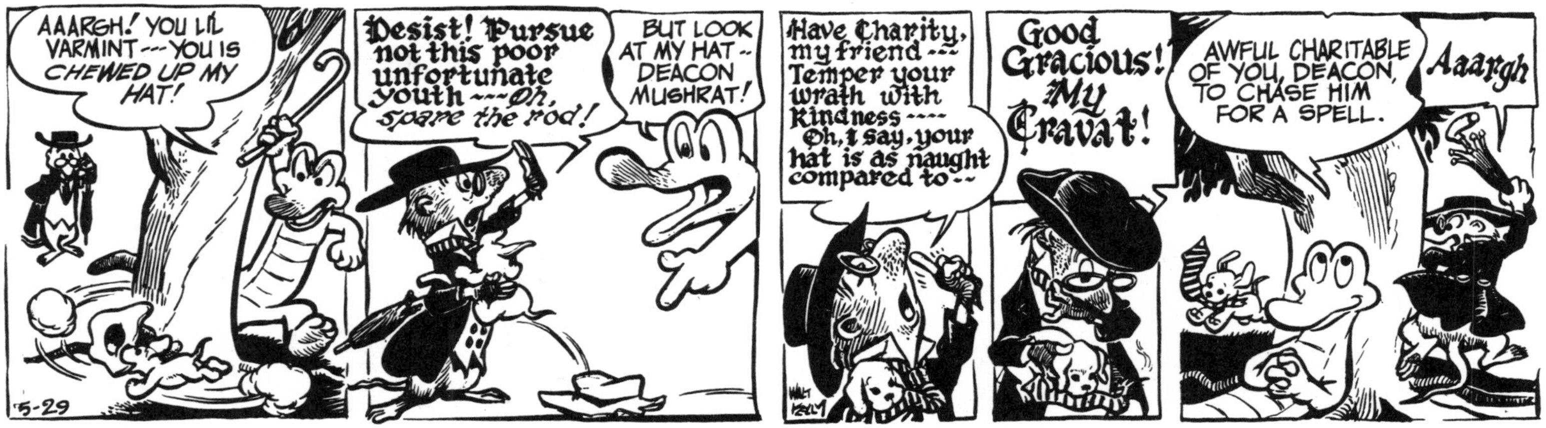
AAARGH! YOU LI'L VARMINT---YOU IS CHEWED UP MY HAT!
Desist! Pursue not this poor unfortunate youth---Oh, spare the rod!
BUT LOOK AT MY HAT-- DEACON MUSHRAT!
Have Charity, my friend--- Temper your wrath with Kindness----
Oh, I say, your hat is as naught compared to--
Good Gracious! My Cravat!
AWFUL CHARITABLE OF YOU, DEACON, TO CHASE HIM FOR A SPELL.
Aaargh
5-29

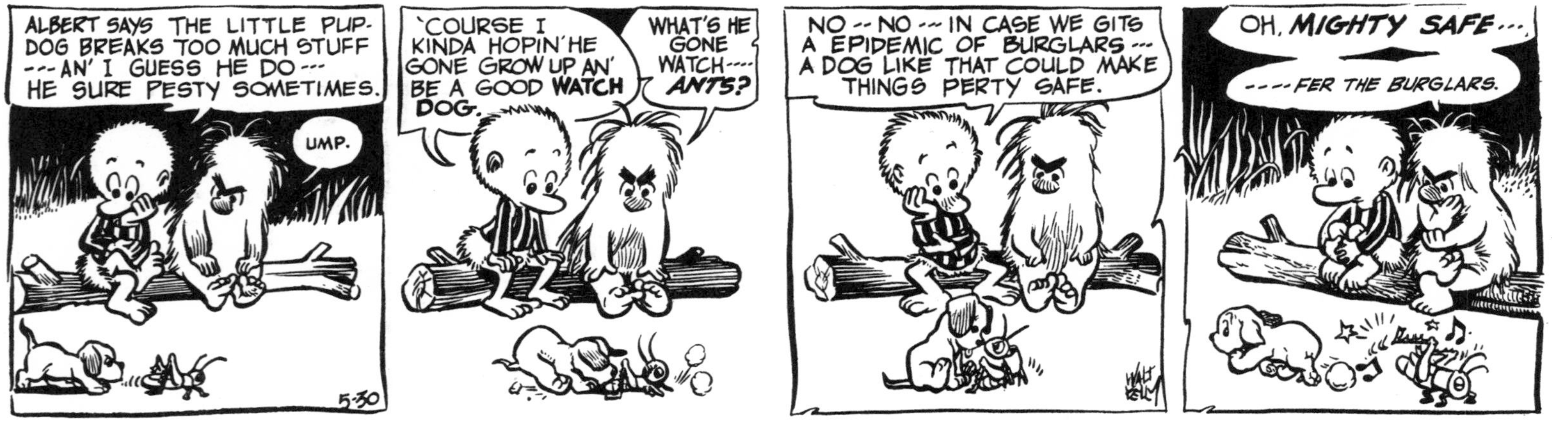
ALBERT SAYS THE LITTLE PUP-DOG BREAKS TOO MUCH STUFF ---AN' I GUESS HE DO--- HE SURE PESTY SOMETIMES.
UMP.
'COURSE I KINDA HOPIN' HE GONE GROW UP AN' BE A GOOD WATCH DOG.
WHAT'S HE GONE WATCH---- ANTS?
NO--NO--IN CASE WE GITS A EPIDEMIC OF BURGLARS--- A DOG LIKE THAT COULD MAKE THINGS PERTY SAFE.
OH, MIGHTY SAFE...
----FER THE BURGLARS.
5-30

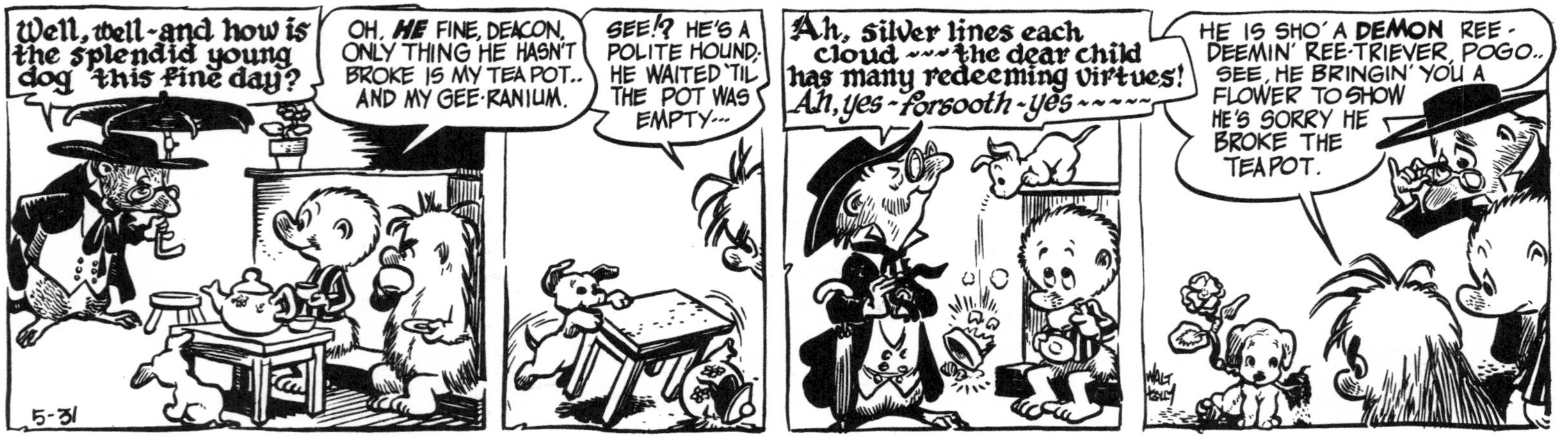
Well, well-and how is the splendid young dog this fine day?
OH, HE FINE, DEACON. ONLY THING HE HASN'T BROKE IS MY TEA POT.. AND MY GEE-RANIUM.
SEE!? HE'S A POLITE HOUND. HE WAITED 'TIL THE POT WAS EMPTY---
Ah, silver lines each cloud----the dear child has many redeeming virtues! Ah, yes-forsooth-yes-----
HE IS SHO' A DEMON REE-DEEMIN' REE-TRIEVER, POGO.. SEE, HE BRINGIN' YOU A FLOWER TO SHOW HE'S SORRY HE BROKE THE TEAPOT.
5-31

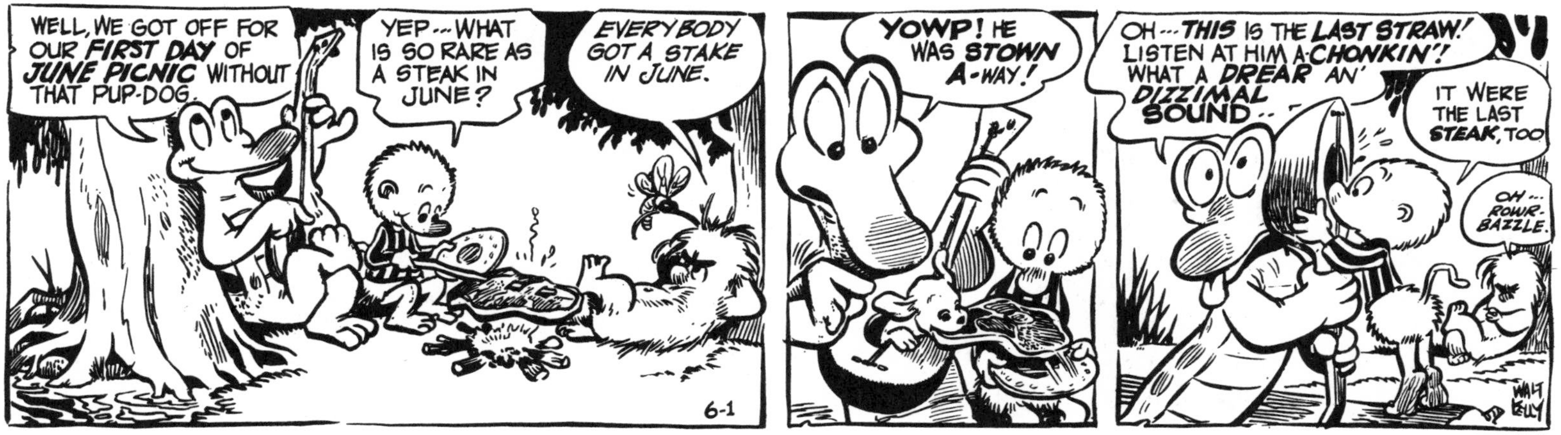
WELL, WE GOT OFF FOR OUR **FIRST DAY** OF **JUNE PICNIC** WITHOUT THAT PUP-DOG.
YEP--WHAT IS SO RARE AS A STEAK IN JUNE?
EVERYBODY GOT A STAKE IN JUNE.
6-1
YOWP! HE WAS **STOWN A-WAY!**
OH--**THIS** IS THE **LAST STRAW!** LISTEN AT HIM A-**CHONKIN'!** WHAT A **DREAR** AN' **DIZZIMAL SOUND**--
IT WERE THE LAST **STEAK**, TOO
OH--ROWRBAZZLE.
WALT KELLY

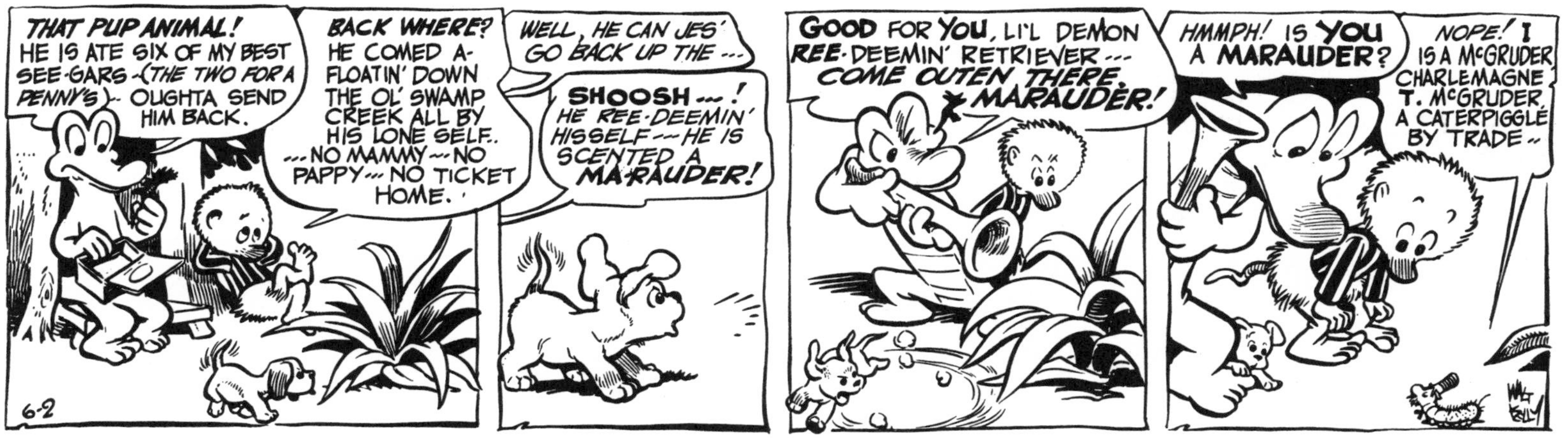
THAT PUP ANIMAL! HE IS ATE SIX OF MY BEST SEE-GARS-(THE TWO FOR A PENNY'S)- OUGHTA SEND HIM BACK.
BACK WHERE?
HE COMED A-FLOATIN' DOWN THE OL' SWAMP CREEK ALL BY HIS LONE SELF. --NO MAMMY--NO PAPPY--NO TICKET HOME.
6-2
WELL, HE CAN JES' GO BACK UP THE--
SHOOSH--! HE REE-DEEMIN' HISSELF--HE IS SCENTED A **MA-RAUDER!**
GOOD FOR **YOU**, LI'L DEMON **REE**-DEEMIN' RETRIEVER-- **COME OUTEN THERE, MARAUDER!**
HMMPH! IS **YOU** A **MARAUDER?**
NOPE! **I** IS A McGRUDER CHARLEMAGNE **T. McGRUDER** A CATERPIGGLE BY TRADE--
WALT KELLY

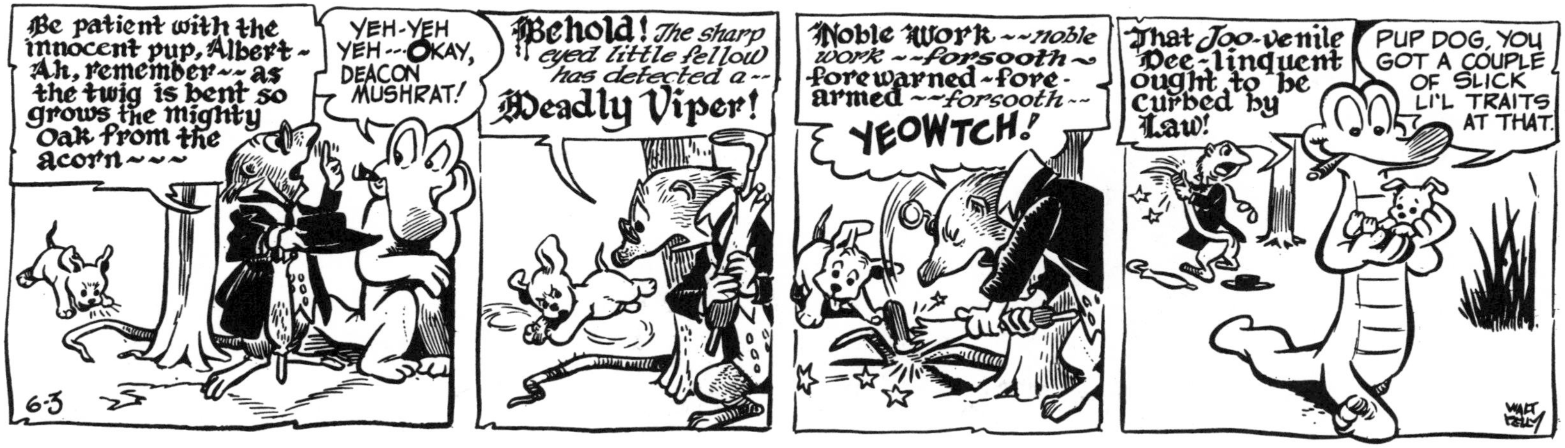
Be patient with the innocent pup, Albert- Ah, remember--as the twig is bent so grows the mighty Oak from the acorn---
YEH-YEH YEH--**O**KAY, DEACON MUSHRAT!
6-3
Behold! The sharp eyed little fellow has detected a-- **Deadly Viper!**
"Noble Work--noble work--forsooth- forewarned-fore-armed--forsooth--
YEOWTCH!
That Joo-venile Dee-linquent ought to be curbed by Law!
PUP DOG, YOU GOT A COUPLE OF SLICK LI'L TRAITS AT THAT.
WALT KELLY

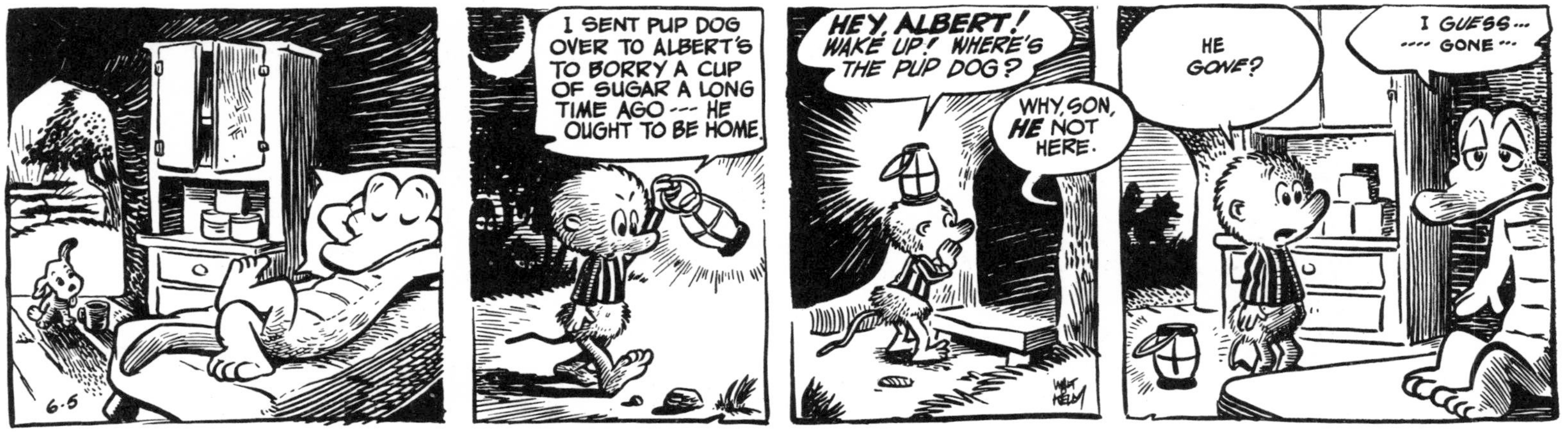
6-5
I SENT PUP DOG OVER TO ALBERT'S TO BORRY A CUP OF SUGAR A LONG TIME AGO --- HE OUGHT TO BE HOME.
HEY, ALBERT! WAKE UP! WHERE'S THE PUP DOG?
WHY, SON, HE NOT HERE.
WALT KELLY
HE GONE?
I GUESS... ---- GONE ---

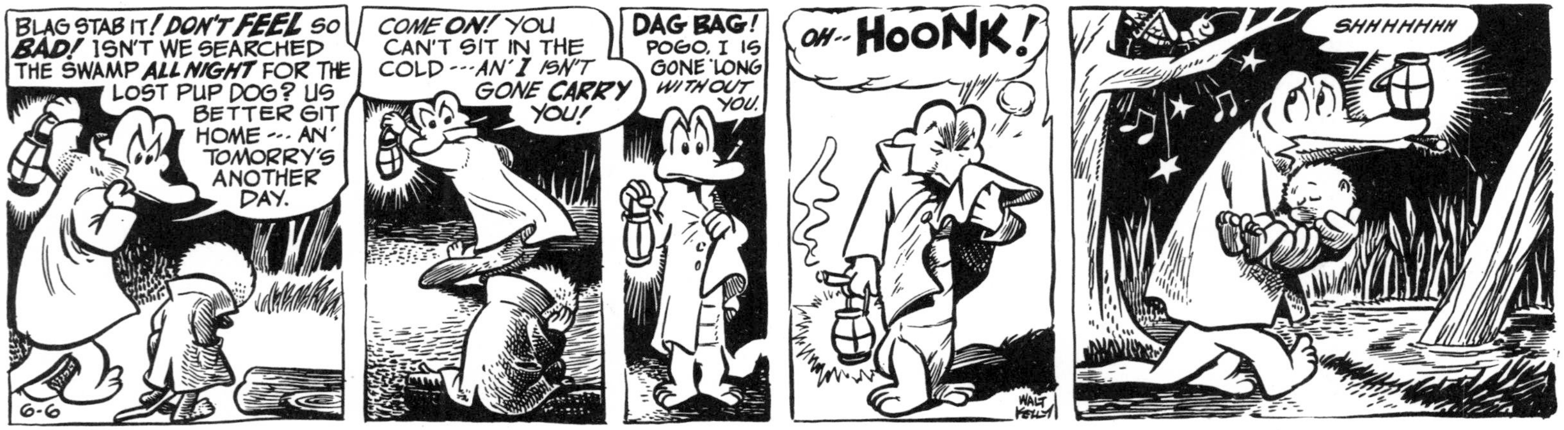
BLAG STAB IT! DON'T FEEL SO BAD! ISN'T WE SEARCHED THE SWAMP ALL NIGHT FOR THE LOST PUP DOG? US BETTER GIT HOME --- AN' TOMORRY'S ANOTHER DAY.
6-6
COME ON! YOU CAN'T SIT IN THE COLD --- AN' I ISN'T GONE CARRY YOU!
DAG BAG! POGO, I IS GONE 'LONG WITH OUT YOU.
OH-- HOONK!
WALT KELLY
SHHHHHHH

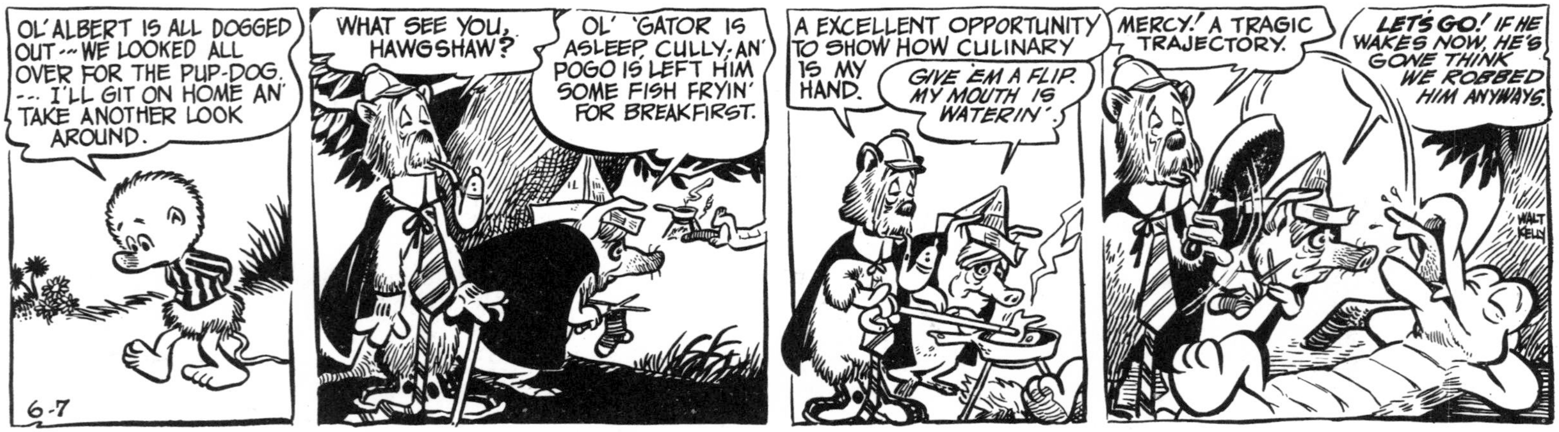
OL' ALBERT IS ALL DOGGED OUT -- WE LOOKED ALL OVER FOR THE PUP-DOG. --. I'LL GIT ON HOME AN' TAKE ANOTHER LOOK AROUND.
6-7
WHAT SEE YOU, HAWGSHAW?
OL' 'GATOR IS ASLEEP, CULLY, AN' POGO IS LEFT HIM SOME FISH FRYIN' FOR BREAKFIRST.
A EXCELLENT OPPORTUNITY TO SHOW HOW CULINARY IS MY HAND.
GIVE 'EM A FLIP. MY MOUTH IS WATERIN'.
MERCY! A TRAGIC TRAJECTORY.
LET'S GO! IF HE WAKES NOW, HE'S GONE THINK WE ROBBED HIM ANYWAYS.
WALT KELLY

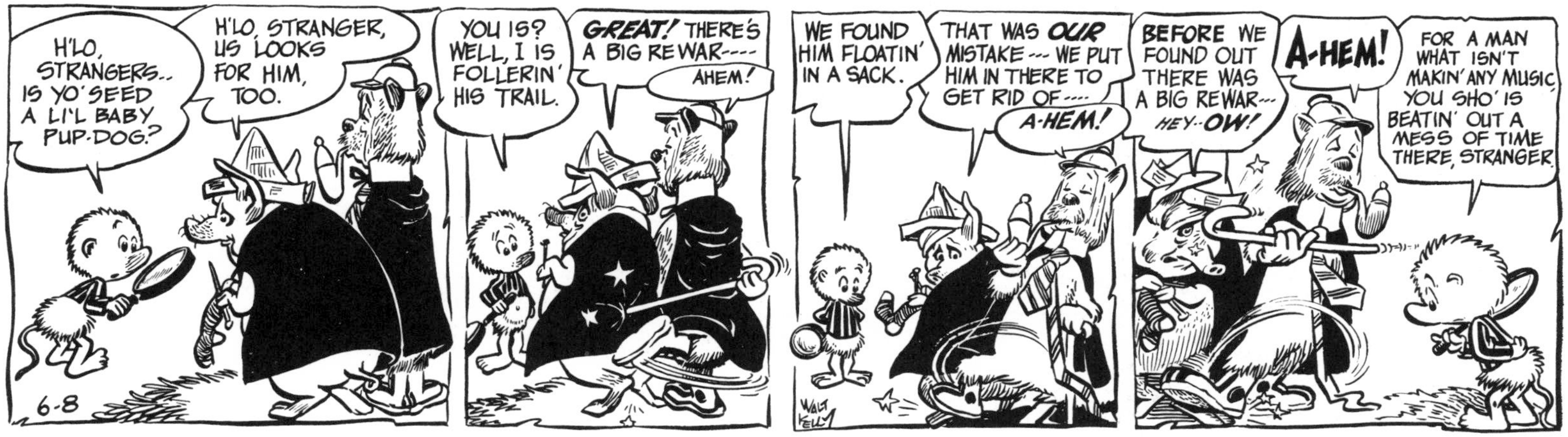
H'LO, STRANGERS.. IS YO' SEED A LI'L BABY PUP-DOG?
H'LO, STRANGER, US LOOKS FOR HIM, TOO.
6-8
YOU IS? WELL, I IS FOLLERIN' HIS TRAIL.
GREAT! THERE'S A BIG REWAR----
AHEM!
WE FOUND HIM FLOATIN' IN A SACK.
THAT WAS OUR MISTAKE --- WE PUT HIM IN THERE TO GET RID OF ----
A-HEM!
WALT KELLY
BEFORE WE FOUND OUT THERE WAS A BIG REWAR---
HEY--OW!
A-HEM!
FOR A MAN WHAT ISN'T MAKIN' ANY MUSIC, YOU SHO' IS BEATIN' OUT A MESS OF TIME THERE, STRANGER.

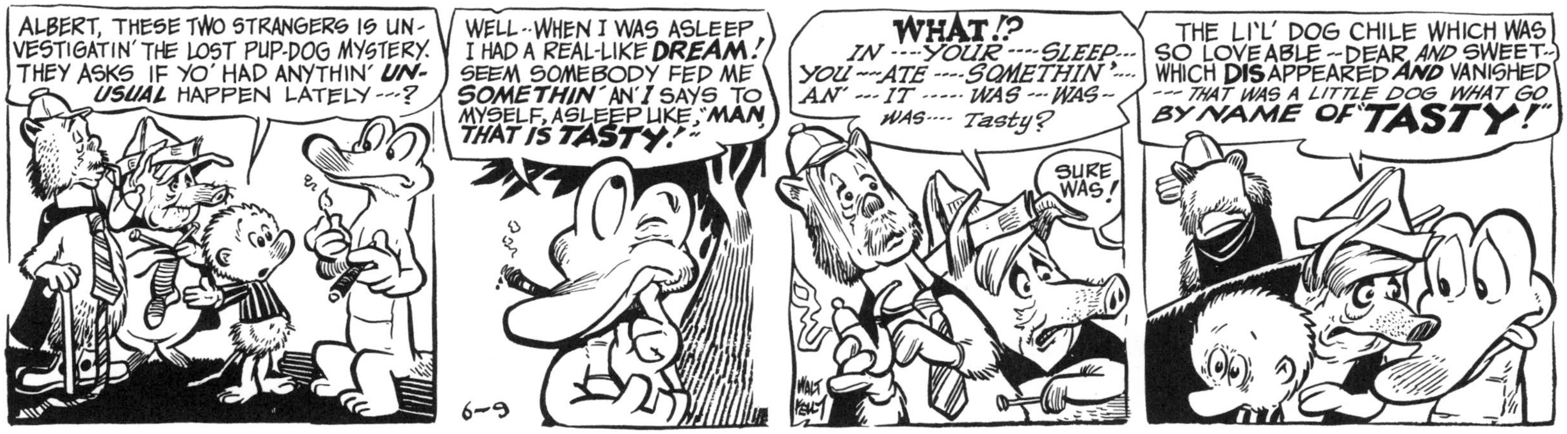
ALBERT, THESE TWO STRANGERS IS UN-VESTIGATIN' THE LOST PUP-DOG MYSTERY. THEY ASKS IF YO' HAD ANYTHIN' UN-USUAL HAPPEN LATELY ---?
WELL--WHEN I WAS ASLEEP I HAD A REAL-LIKE DREAM! SEEM SOMEBODY FED ME SOMETHIN' AN' I SAYS TO MYSELF, ASLEEP LIKE, "MAN, THAT IS TASTY!"
6-9
WHAT!?
IN ---- YOUR ---- SLEEP--- YOU --- ATE ---- SOMETHIN' ---- AN' --- IT ----- WAS --- WAS-- WAS---- Tasty?
SURE WAS!
WALT KELLY
THE LI'L' DOG CHILE WHICH WAS SO LOVEABLE --DEAR AND SWEET-- WHICH DISAPPEARED AND VANISHED --- THAT WAS A LITTLE DOG WHAT GO BY NAME OF "TASTY!"

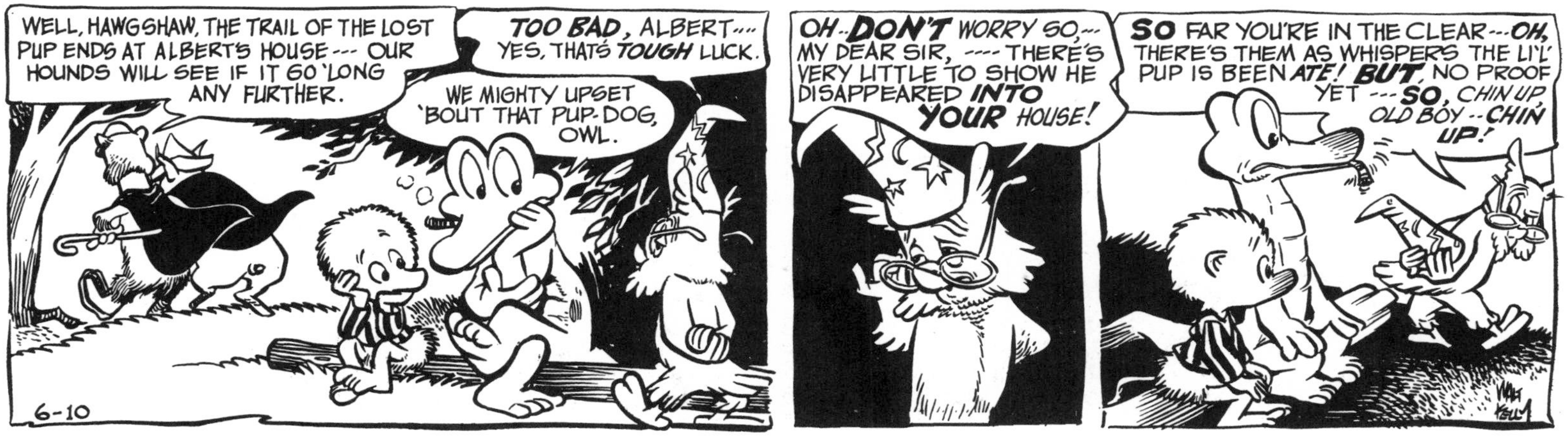
WELL, HAWGSHAW, THE TRAIL OF THE LOST PUP ENDS AT ALBERT'S HOUSE --- OUR HOUNDS WILL SEE IF IT GO 'LONG ANY FURTHER.
TOO BAD, ALBERT---- YES, THAT'S TOUGH LUCK.
WE MIGHTY UPSET 'BOUT THAT PUP-DOG, OWL.
6-10
OH--DON'T WORRY SO,-- MY DEAR SIR, ---- THERE'S VERY LITTLE TO SHOW HE DISAPPEARED INTO YOUR HOUSE!
SO FAR YOU'RE IN THE CLEAR---OH, THERE'S THEM AS WHISPERS THE LI'L' PUP IS BEEN ATE! BUT, NO PROOF YET ---SO, CHIN UP OLD BOY --CHIN UP!
WALT KELLY

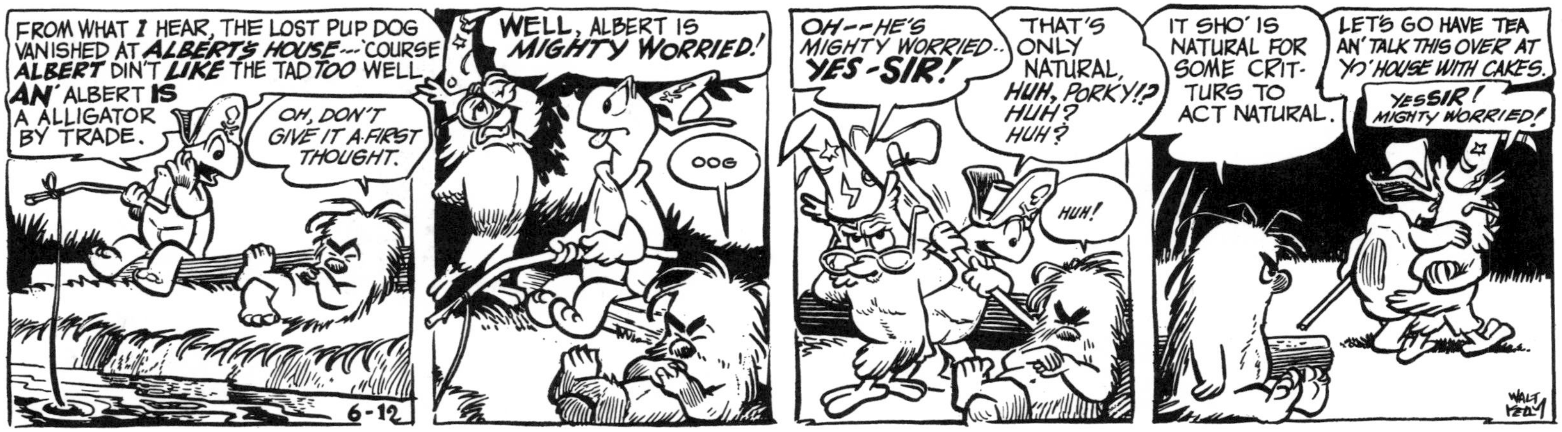
FROM WHAT I HEAR, THE LOST PUP DOG VANISHED AT ALBERT'S HOUSE--- 'COURSE ALBERT DIN'T LIKE THE TAD TOO WELL AN' ALBERT IS A ALLIGATOR BY TRADE.
OH, DON'T GIVE IT A FIRST THOUGHT.
6-12
WELL, ALBERT IS MIGHTY WORRIED!
OOG
OH-- HE'S MIGHTY WORRIED.. YES-SIR!
THAT'S ONLY NATURAL, HUH, PORKY!? HUH? HUH?
HUH!
IT SHO' IS NATURAL FOR SOME CRIT-TURS TO ACT NATURAL.
LET'S GO HAVE TEA AN' TALK THIS OVER AT YO' HOUSE WITH CAKES.
YESSIR! MIGHTY WORRIED!
WALT KELLY

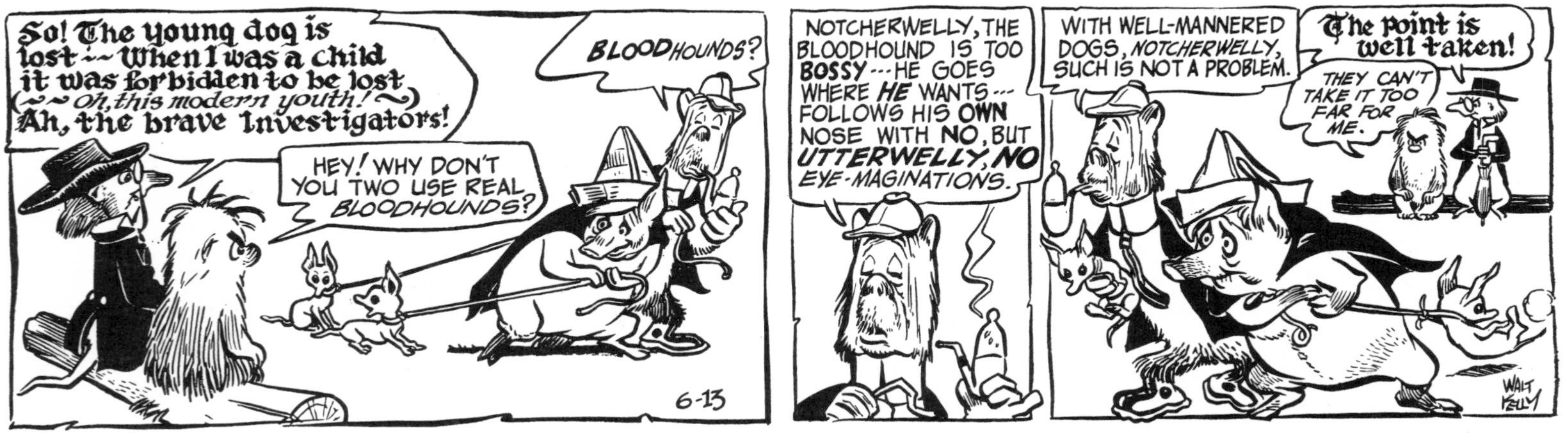
So! The young dog is lost -- When I was a child it was forbidden to be lost (~~ oh, this modern youth! ~) Ah, the brave Investigators!
HEY! WHY DON'T YOU TWO USE REAL BLOODHOUNDS?
BLOODHOUNDS?
6-13
NOTCHERWELLY, THE BLOODHOUND IS TOO BOSSY --- HE GOES WHERE HE WANTS --- FOLLOWS HIS OWN NOSE WITH NO, BUT UTTERWELLY, NO EYE-MAGINATIONS.
WITH WELL-MANNERED DOGS, NOTCHERWELLY, SUCH IS NOT A PROBLEM.
The point is well taken!
THEY CAN'T TAKE IT TOO FAR FOR ME.
WALT KELLY

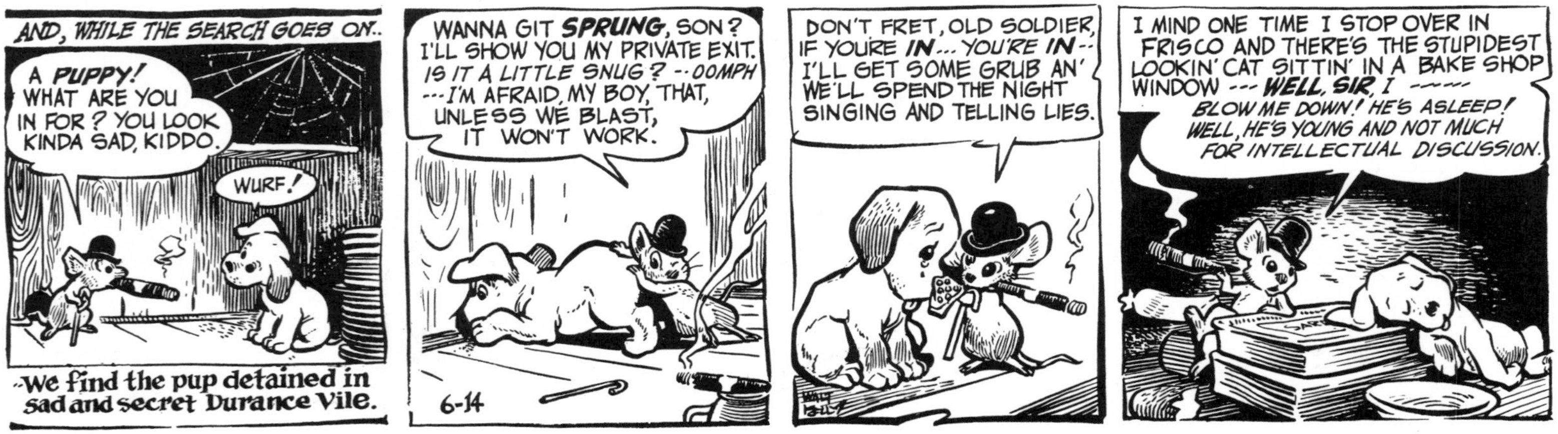
AND, WHILE THE SEARCH GOES ON..
A PUPPY! WHAT ARE YOU IN FOR? YOU LOOK KINDA SAD, KIDDO.
WURF!
..We find the pup detained in sad and secret Durance Vile.
WANNA GIT SPRUNG, SON? I'LL SHOW YOU MY PRIVATE EXIT. IS IT A LITTLE SNUG? -- OOMPH --- I'M AFRAID, MY BOY, THAT, UNLESS WE BLAST, IT WON'T WORK.
6-14
DON'T FRET, OLD SOLDIER, IF YOU'RE IN... YOU'RE IN -- I'LL GET SOME GRUB AN' WE'LL SPEND THE NIGHT SINGING AND TELLING LIES.
WALT KELLY
I MIND ONE TIME I STOP OVER IN FRISCO AND THERE'S THE STUPIDEST LOOKIN' CAT SITTIN' IN A BAKE SHOP WINDOW --- WELL, SIR, I -----
BLOW ME DOWN! HE'S ASLEEP! WELL, HE'S YOUNG AND NOT MUCH FOR INTELLECTUAL DISCUSSION.

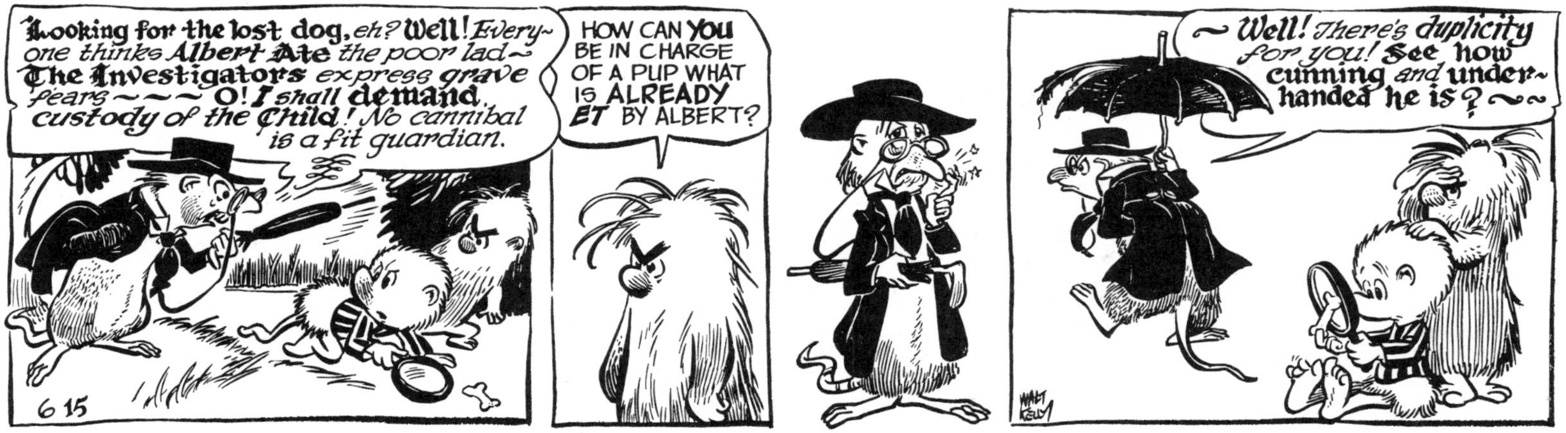
Looking for the lost dog, eh? Well! Everyone thinks Albert Ate the poor lad~ The Investigators express grave fears ~~~ O! I shall demand custody of the Child! No cannibal is a fit guardian.
HOW CAN YOU BE IN CHARGE OF A PUP WHAT IS ALREADY ET BY ALBERT?
~ Well! There's duplicity for you! See how cunning and underhanded he is? ~~
6 15
WALT KELLY

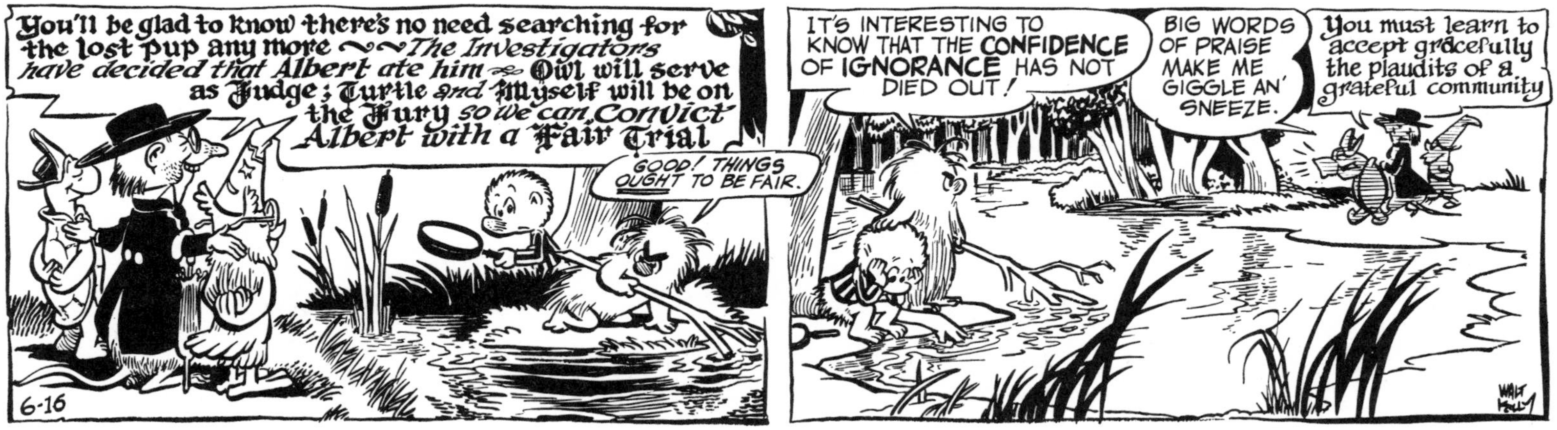
You'll be glad to know there's no need searching for the lost pup any more ~~ The Investigators have decided that Albert ate him ~ Owl will serve as Judge; Turtle and Myself will be on the Jury so we can Convict Albert with a Fair Trial
GOOD! THINGS OUGHT TO BE FAIR.
IT'S INTERESTING TO KNOW THAT THE CONFIDENCE OF IGNORANCE HAS NOT DIED OUT!
BIG WORDS OF PRAISE MAKE ME GIGGLE AN' SNEEZE.
You must learn to accept gracefully the plaudits of a grateful community
6-16
WALT KELLY

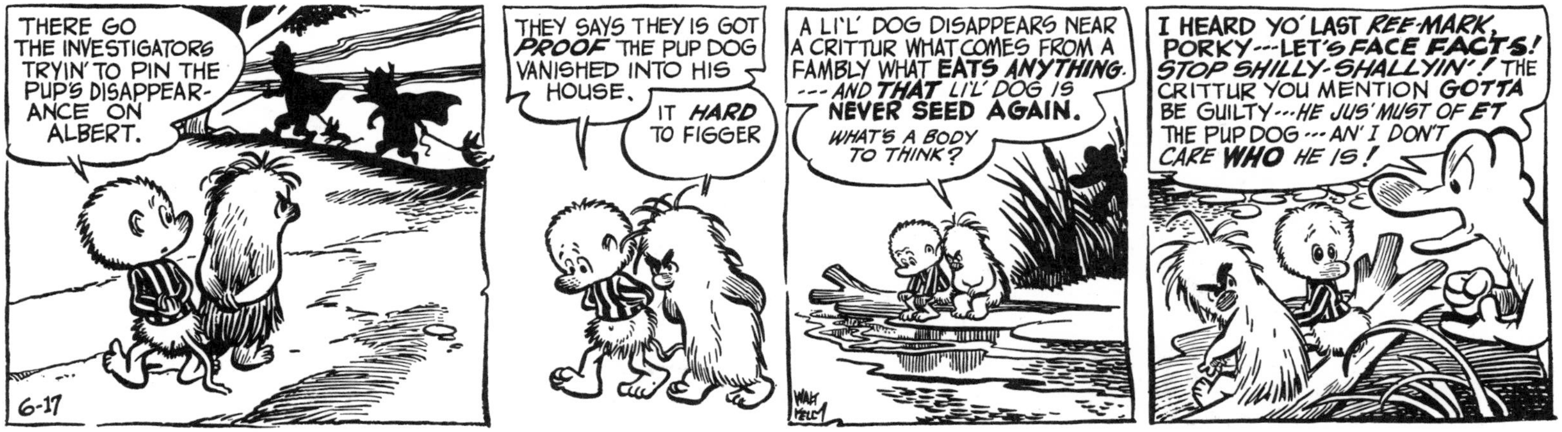
THERE GO THE INVESTIGATORS TRYIN' TO PIN THE PUP'S DISAPPEARANCE ON ALBERT.
THEY SAYS THEY IS GOT PROOF THE PUP DOG VANISHED INTO HIS HOUSE.
IT HARD TO FIGGER
A LI'L' DOG DISAPPEARS NEAR A CRITTUR WHAT COMES FROM A FAMBLY WHAT EATS ANYTHING. --- AND THAT LI'L' DOG IS NEVER SEED AGAIN.
WHAT'S A BODY TO THINK?
I HEARD YO' LAST REE-MARK, PORKY---LET'S FACE FACTS! STOP SHILLY-SHALLYIN'! THE CRITTUR YOU MENTION GOTTA BE GUILTY---HE JUS' MUST OF ET THE PUP DOG --- AN' I DON'T CARE WHO HE IS!
6-17
WALT KELLY

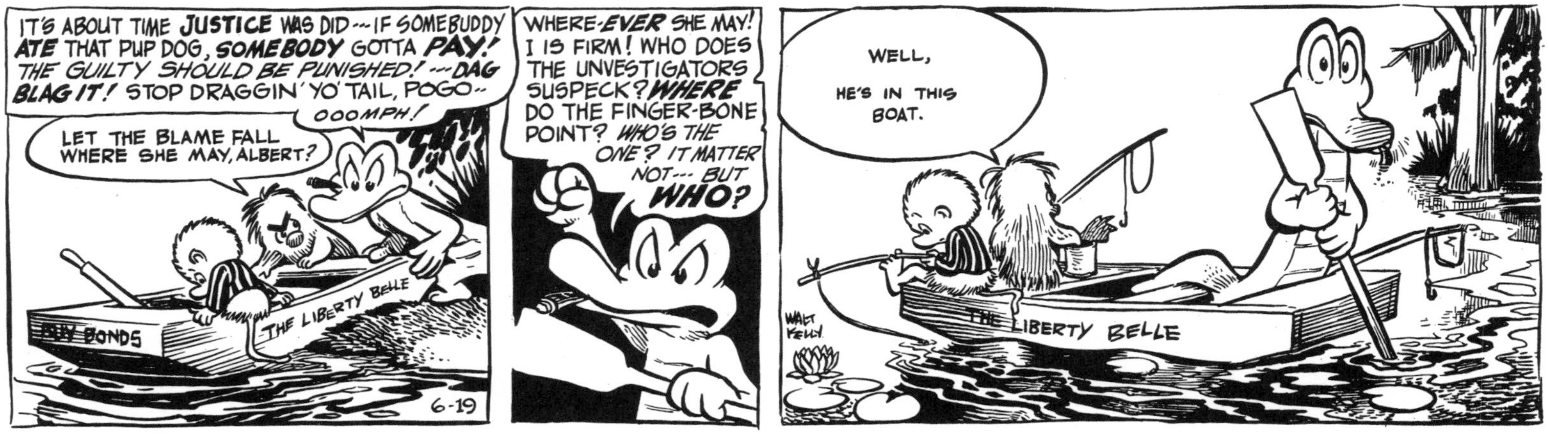
IT'S ABOUT TIME JUSTICE WAS DID--- IF SOMEBUDDY ATE THAT PUP DOG, SOMEBODY GOTTA PAY! THE GUILTY SHOULD BE PUNISHED! ---DAG BLAG IT! STOP DRAGGIN' YO' TAIL, POGO--
OOOMPH!
LET THE BLAME FALL WHERE SHE MAY, ALBERT?
BUY BONDS
THE LIBERTY BELLE
6-19
WHERE-EVER SHE MAY! I IS FIRM! WHO DOES THE UNVESTIGATORS SUSPECK? WHERE DO THE FINGER-BONE POINT? WHO'S THE ONE? IT MATTER NOT--- BUT WHO?
WELL, HE'S IN THIS BOAT.
THE LIBERTY BELLE
WALT KELLY

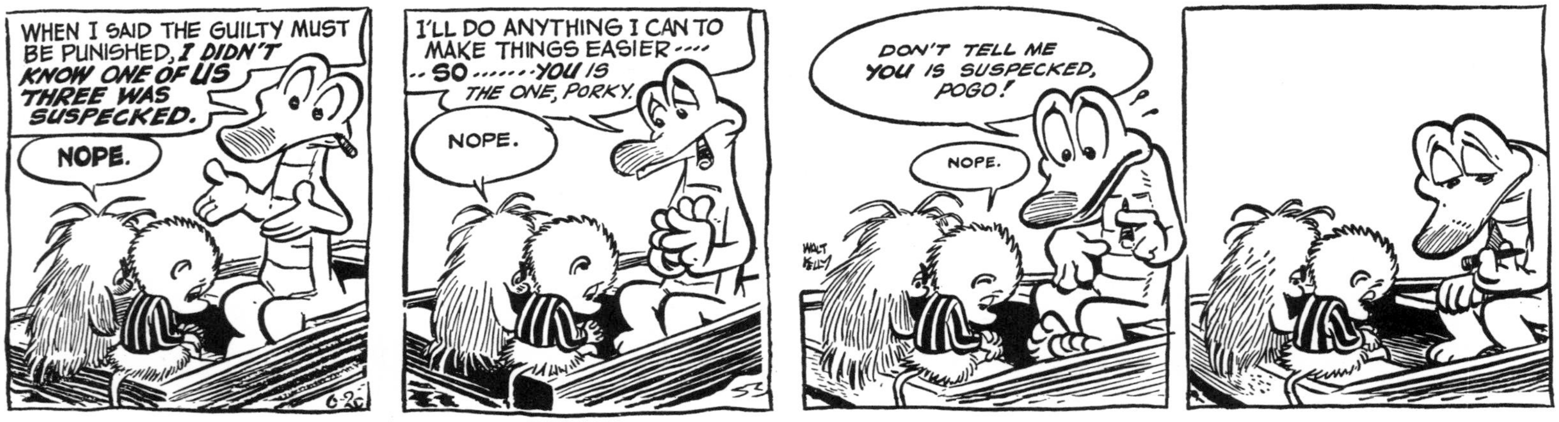
WHEN I SAID THE GUILTY MUST BE PUNISHED, I DIDN'T KNOW ONE OF US THREE WAS SUSPECKED.
NOPE.
I'LL DO ANYTHING I CAN TO MAKE THINGS EASIER ---- .. SO .... YOU IS THE ONE, PORKY.
NOPE.
DON'T TELL ME YOU IS SUSPECKED, POGO!
NOPE.
WALT KELLY

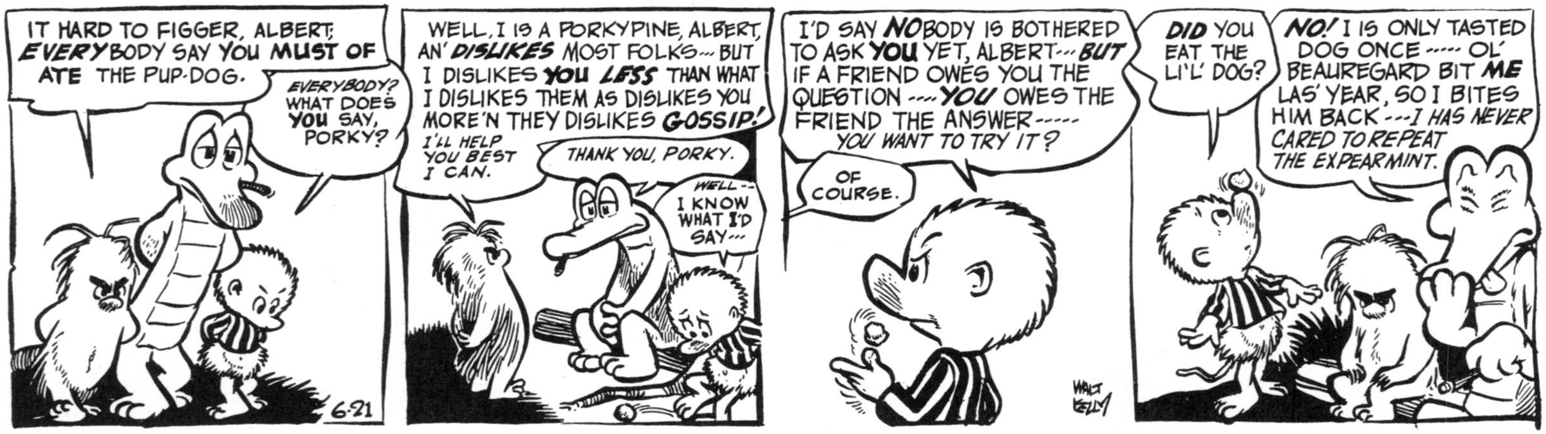
IT HARD TO FIGGER, ALBERT; EVERYBODY SAY YOU MUST OF ATE THE PUP-DOG.
EVERYBODY? WHAT DOES YOU SAY, PORKY?
6-21
WELL, I IS A PORKYPINE, ALBERT, AN' DISLIKES MOST FOLKS--- BUT I DISLIKES YOU LESS THAN WHAT I DISLIKES THEM AS DISLIKES YOU MORE'N THEY DISLIKES GOSSIP!
I'LL HELP YOU BEST I CAN.
THANK YOU, PORKY.
WELL-- I KNOW WHAT I'D SAY---
I'D SAY NOBODY IS BOTHERED TO ASK YOU YET, ALBERT--- BUT IF A FRIEND OWES YOU THE QUESTION ---- YOU OWES THE FRIEND THE ANSWER----- YOU WANT TO TRY IT?
OF COURSE.
WALT KELLY
DID YOU EAT THE LI'L' DOG?
NO! I IS ONLY TASTED DOG ONCE ----- OL' BEAUREGARD BIT ME LAS' YEAR, SO I BITES HIM BACK --- I HAS NEVER CARED TO REPEAT THE EXPEARMINT.

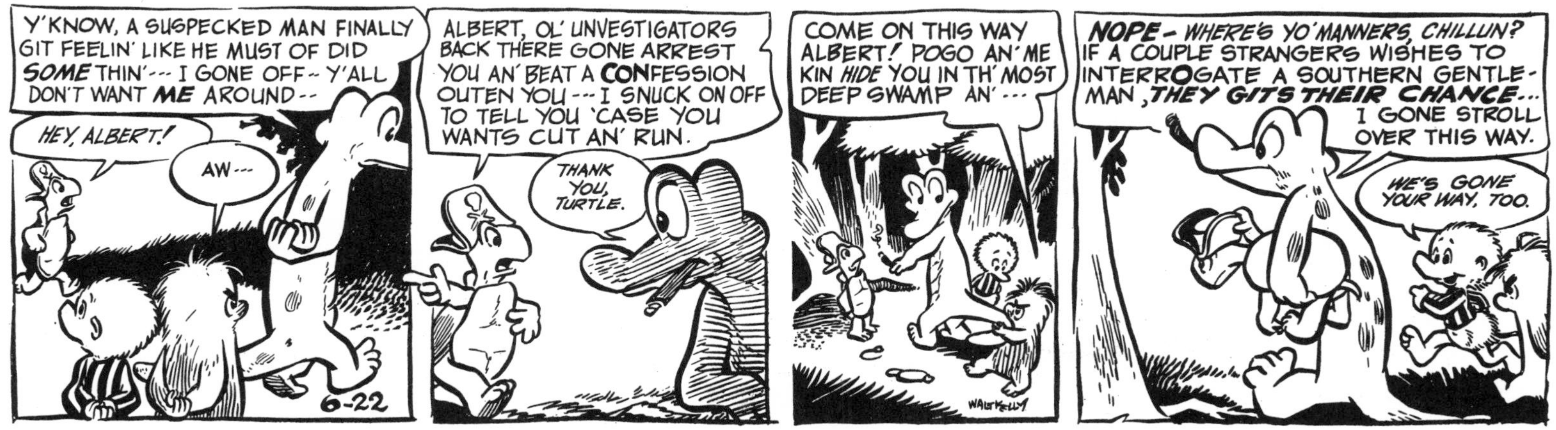
Y'KNOW, A SUSPECKED MAN FINALLY GIT FEELIN' LIKE HE MUST OF DID SOME THIN'--- I GONE OFF -- Y'ALL DON'T WANT ME AROUND --
HEY, ALBERT!
AW---
6-22
ALBERT, OL' UNVESTIGATORS BACK THERE GONE ARREST YOU AN' BEAT A CONFESSION OUTEN YOU --- I SNUCK ON OFF TO TELL YOU 'CASE YOU WANTS CUT AN' RUN.
THANK YOU, TURTLE.
COME ON THIS WAY ALBERT! POGO AN' ME KIN HIDE YOU IN TH' MOST DEEP SWAMP AN' ---
WALT KELLY
NOPE - WHERE'S YO' MANNERS, CHILLUN? IF A COUPLE STRANGERS WISHES TO INTERROGATE A SOUTHERN GENTLEMAN, THEY GITS THEIR CHANCE... I GONE STROLL OVER THIS WAY.
WE'S GONE YOUR WAY, TOO.

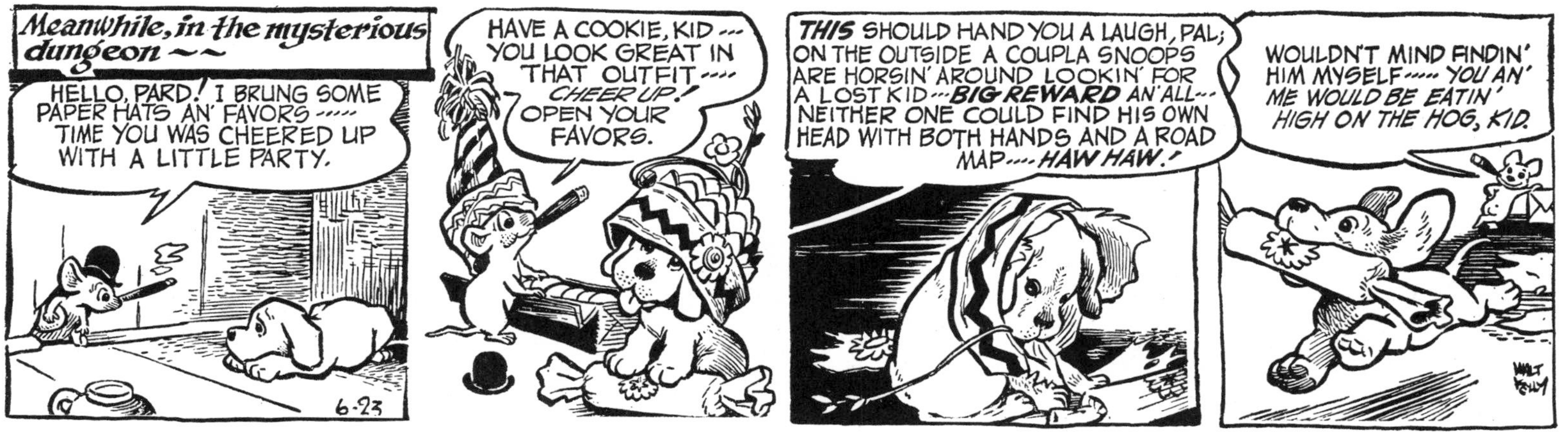
Meanwhile, in the mysterious dungeon ~~
HELLO, PARD! I BRUNG SOME PAPER HATS AN' FAVORS ----- TIME YOU WAS CHEERED UP WITH A LITTLE PARTY.
6-23
HAVE A COOKIE, KID --- YOU LOOK GREAT IN THAT OUTFIT ---- CHEER UP! OPEN YOUR FAVORS.
THIS SHOULD HAND YOU A LAUGH, PAL; ON THE OUTSIDE A COUPLA SNOOPS ARE HORSIN' AROUND LOOKIN' FOR A LOST KID --- BIG REWARD AN' ALL -- NEITHER ONE COULD FIND HIS OWN HEAD WITH BOTH HANDS AND A ROAD MAP ---- HAW HAW!
WOULDN'T MIND FINDIN' HIM MYSELF ----- YOU AN' ME WOULD BE EATIN' HIGH ON THE HOG, KID.
WALT KELLY

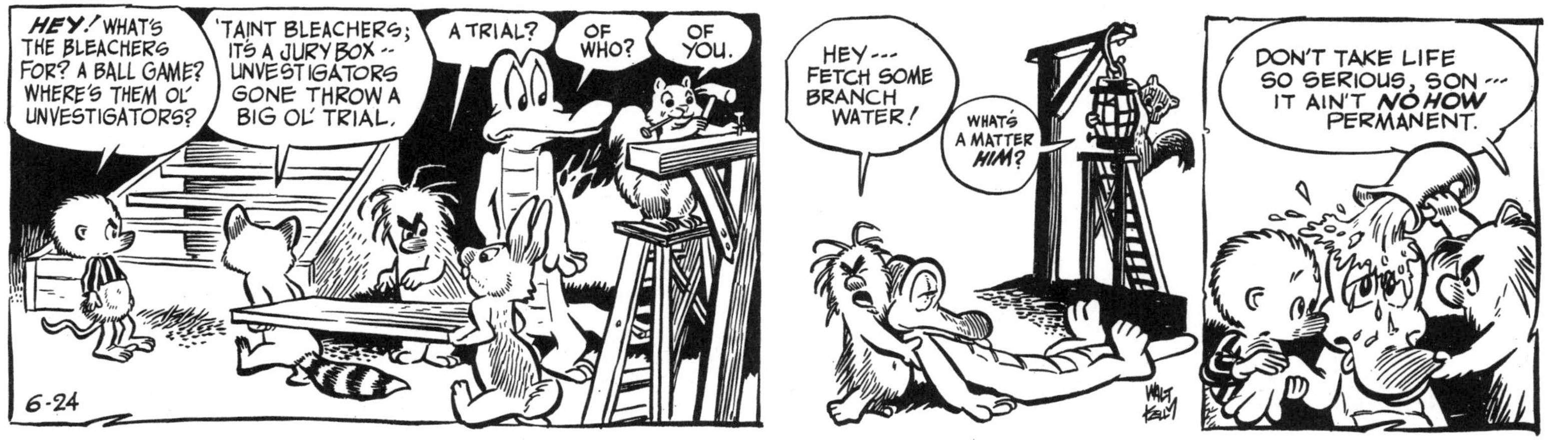
HEY! WHAT'S THE BLEACHERS FOR? A BALL GAME? WHERE'S THEM OL' UNVESTIGATORS?
'TAINT BLEACHERS; IT'S A JURY BOX -- UNVESTIGATORS GONE THROW A BIG OL' TRIAL.
A TRIAL?
OF WHO?
OF YOU.
6-24
HEY --- FETCH SOME BRANCH WATER!
WHAT'S A MATTER HIM?
WALT KELLY
DON'T TAKE LIFE SO SERIOUS, SON --- IT AIN'T NOHOW PERMANENT.

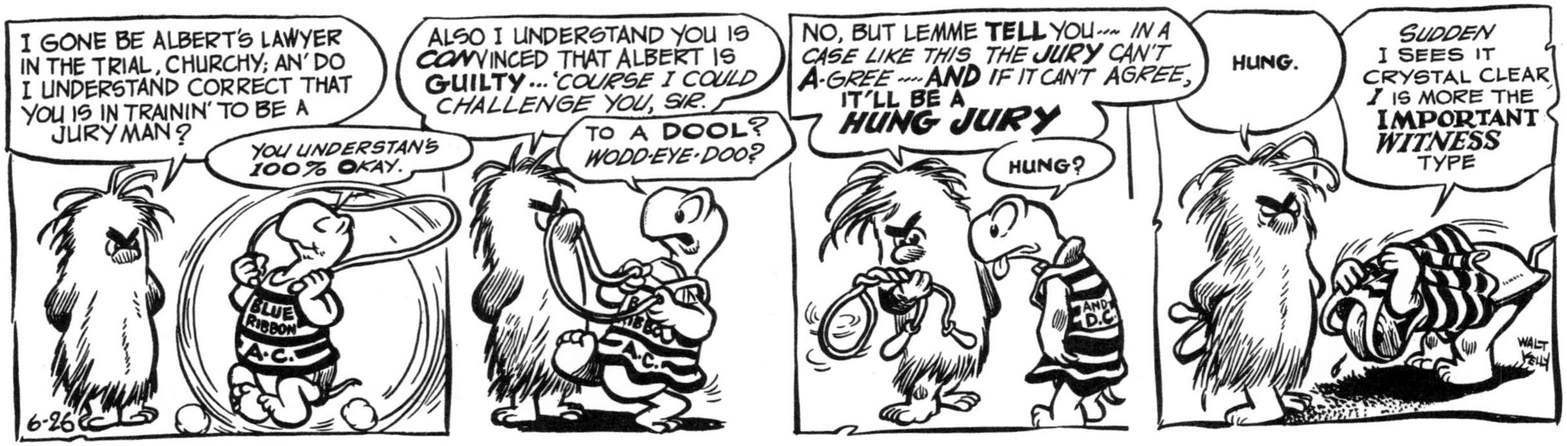
I GONE BE ALBERT'S LAWYER IN THE TRIAL, CHURCHY; AN' DO I UNDERSTAND CORRECT THAT YOU IS IN TRAININ' TO BE A JURY MAN?
YOU UNDERSTAN'S 100% OKAY.
BLUE RIBBON A.C.
6-26
ALSO I UNDERSTAND YOU IS CONVINCED THAT ALBERT IS GUILTY... 'COURSE I COULD CHALLENGE YOU, SIR.
TO A DOOL? WODD-EYE-DOO?
NO, BUT LEMME TELL YOU--- IN A CASE LIKE THIS THE JURY CAN'T A-GREE ---- AND IF IT CAN'T AGREE, IT'LL BE A HUNG JURY
HUNG?
HUNG.
SUDDEN I SEES IT CRYSTAL CLEAR I IS MORE THE IMPORTANT WITNESS TYPE
WALT KELLY

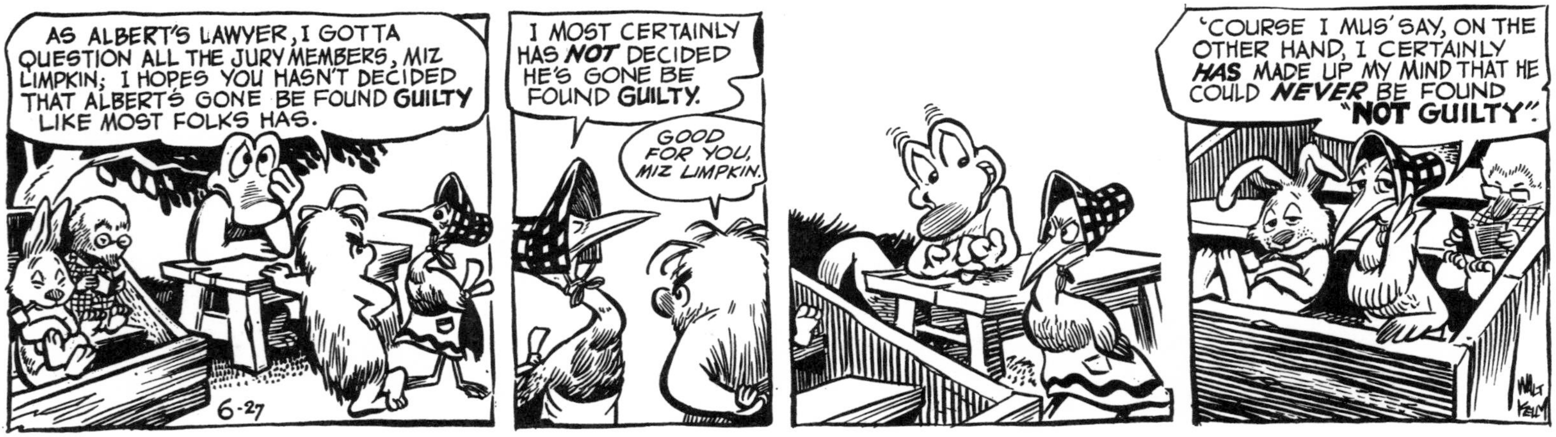
AS ALBERT'S LAWYER, I GOTTA QUESTION ALL THE JURY MEMBERS, MIZ LIMPKIN; I HOPES YOU HASN'T DECIDED THAT ALBERT'S GONE BE FOUND GUILTY LIKE MOST FOLKS HAS.
6-27
I MOST CERTAINLY HAS NOT DECIDED HE'S GONE BE FOUND GUILTY.
GOOD FOR YOU, MIZ LIMPKIN.
'COURSE I MUS' SAY, ON THE OTHER HAND, I CERTAINLY HAS MADE UP MY MIND THAT HE COULD NEVER BE FOUND "NOT GUILTY".
WALT KELLY

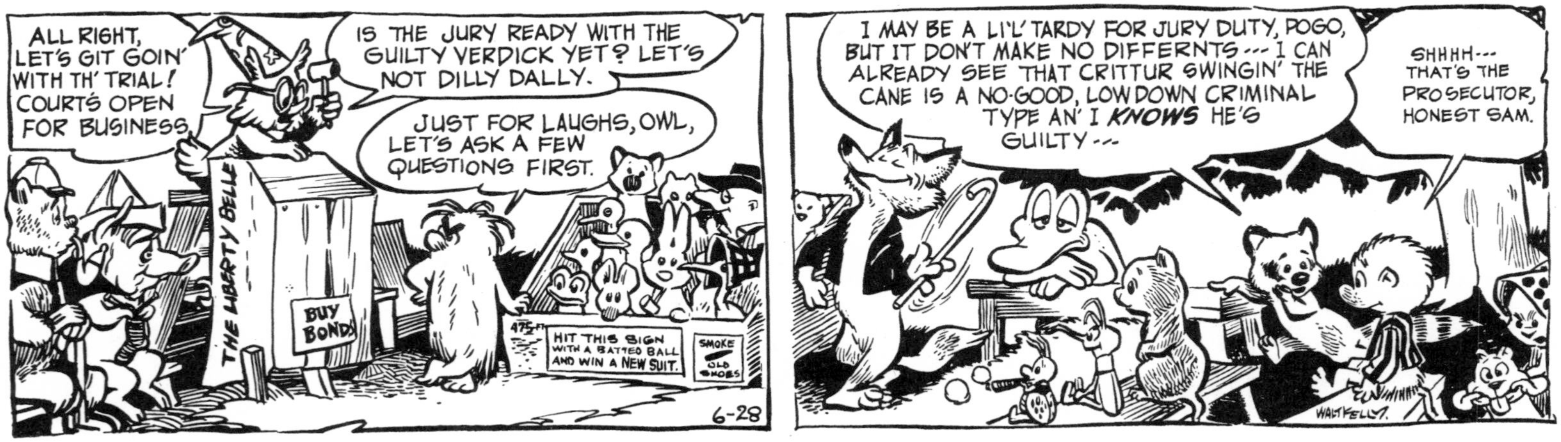
ALL RIGHT, LET'S GIT GOIN' WITH TH' TRIAL! COURT'S OPEN FOR BUSINESS.
IS THE JURY READY WITH THE GUILTY VERDICK YET? LET'S NOT DILLY DALLY.
JUST FOR LAUGHS, OWL, LET'S ASK A FEW QUESTIONS FIRST.
THE LIBERTY BELLE
BUY BONDS
HIT THIS SIGN WITH A BATTED BALL AND WIN A NEW SUIT.
SMOKE OLD SHOES
6-28
I MAY BE A LI'L' TARDY FOR JURY DUTY, POGO, BUT IT DON'T MAKE NO DIFFERNTS --- I CAN ALREADY SEE THAT CRITTUR SWINGIN' THE CANE IS A NO-GOOD, LOWDOWN CRIMINAL TYPE AN' I KNOWS HE'S GUILTY ---
SHHHH--- THAT'S THE PROSECUTOR, HONEST SAM.
WALT KELLY

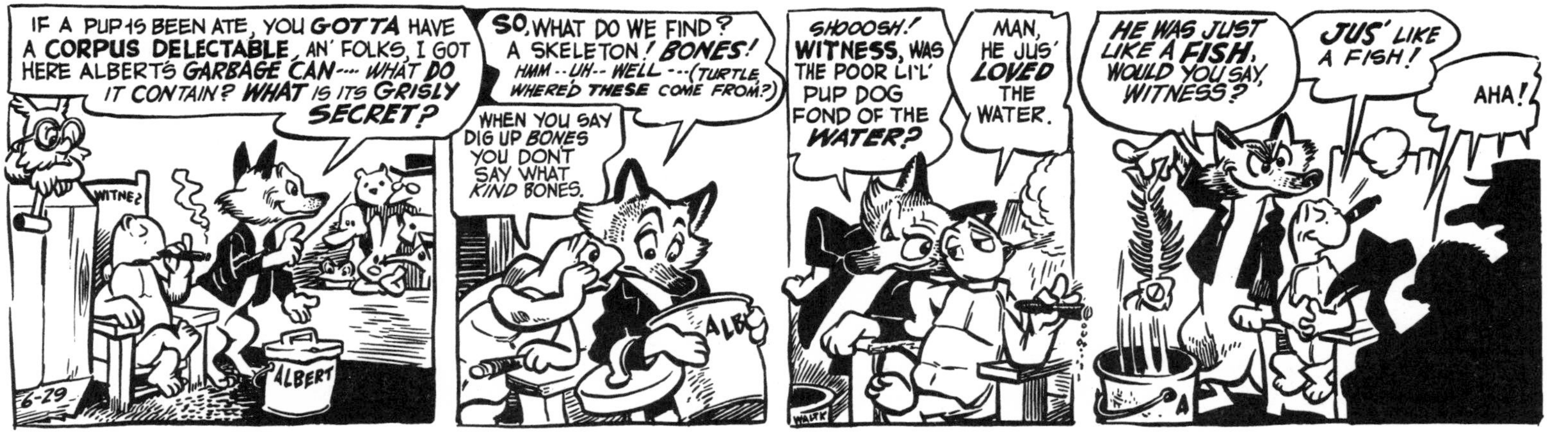
IF A PUP IS BEEN ATE, YOU GOTTA HAVE A CORPUS DELECTABLE, AN' FOLKS, I GOT HERE ALBERT'S GARBAGE CAN---- WHAT DO IT CONTAIN? WHAT IS ITS GRISLY SECRET?
ALBERT
6-29
SO, WHAT DO WE FIND? A SKELETON! BONES! HMM--UH--WELL---(TURTLE, WHERE'D THESE COME FROM?)
WHEN YOU SAY DIG UP BONES YOU DON'T SAY WHAT KIND BONES.
SHOOOSH! WITNESS, WAS THE POOR LI'L' PUP DOG FOND OF THE WATER?
MAN, HE JUS' LOVED THE WATER.
HE WAS JUST LIKE A FISH, WOULD YOU SAY, WITNESS?
JUS' LIKE A FISH!
AHA!

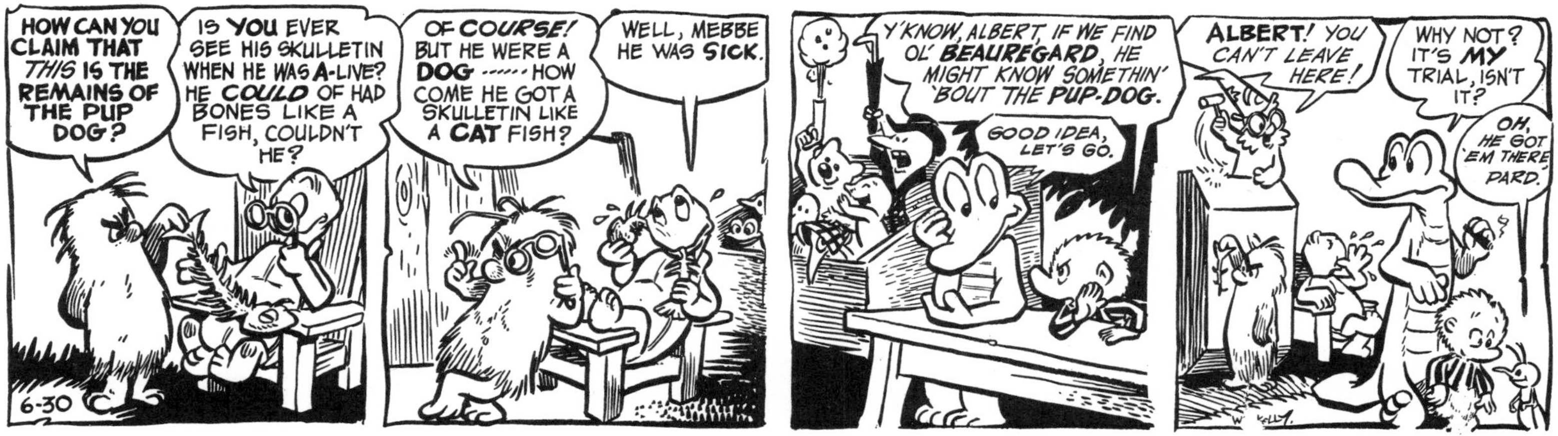
HOW CAN YOU CLAIM THAT THIS IS THE REMAINS OF THE PUP DOG?
IS YOU EVER SEE HIS SKULLETIN WHEN HE WAS A-LIVE? HE COULD OF HAD BONES LIKE A FISH, COULDN'T HE?
6-30
OF COURSE! BUT HE WERE A DOG ------ HOW COME HE GOT A SKULLETIN LIKE A CAT FISH?
WELL, MEBBE HE WAS SICK.
Y'KNOW, ALBERT, IF WE FIND OL' BEAUREGARD, HE MIGHT KNOW SOMETHIN' 'BOUT THE PUP-DOG.
GOOD IDEA, LET'S GO.
ALBERT! YOU CAN'T LEAVE HERE!
WHY NOT? IT'S MY TRIAL, ISN'T IT?
OH, HE GOT 'EM THERE PARD.

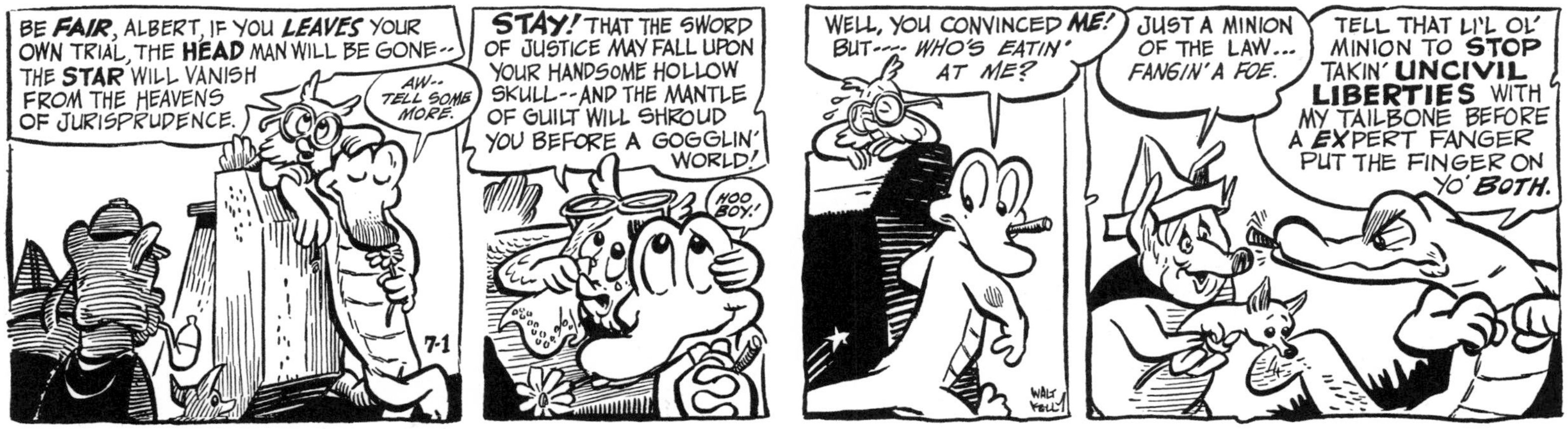
BE FAIR, ALBERT, IF YOU LEAVES YOUR OWN TRIAL, THE HEAD MAN WILL BE GONE-- THE STAR WILL VANISH FROM THE HEAVENS OF JURISPRUDENCE.
AW-- TELL SOME MORE.
7-1
STAY! THAT THE SWORD OF JUSTICE MAY FALL UPON YOUR HANDSOME HOLLOW SKULL--AND THE MANTLE OF GUILT WILL SHROUD YOU BEFORE A GOGGLIN' WORLD!
HOO BOY!
WELL, YOU CONVINCED ME! BUT---- WHO'S EATIN' AT ME?
JUST A MINION OF THE LAW... FANGIN' A FOE.
TELL THAT LI'L OL' MINION TO STOP TAKIN' UNCIVIL LIBERTIES WITH MY TAILBONE BEFORE A EXPERT FANGER PUT THE FINGER ON YO' BOTH.

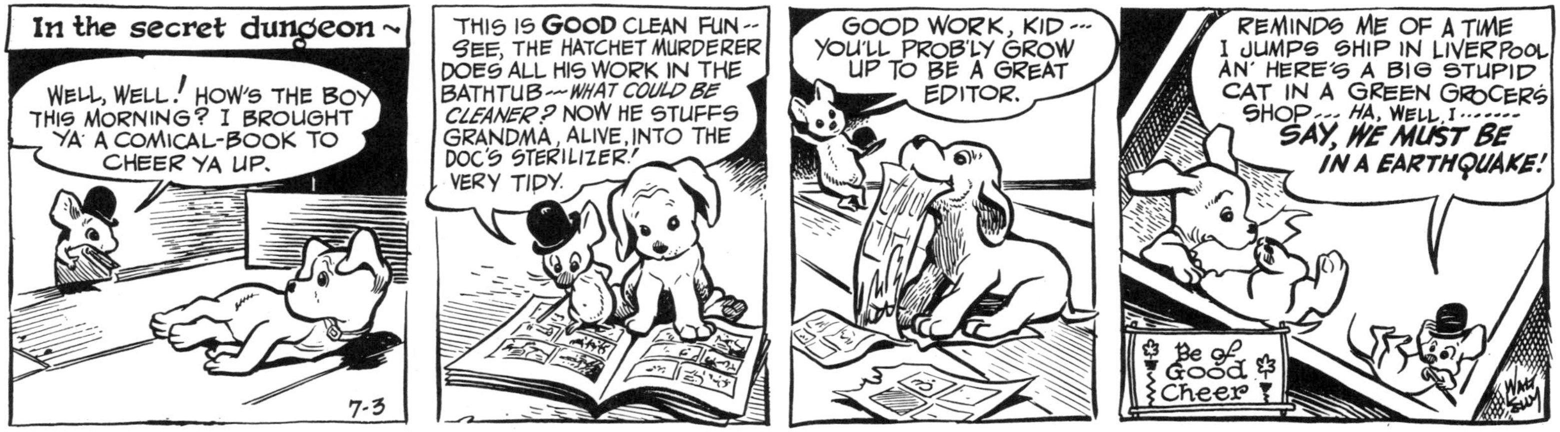
In the secret dungeon ~
WELL, WELL! HOW'S THE BOY THIS MORNING? I BROUGHT YA A COMICAL-BOOK TO CHEER YA UP.
7-3
THIS IS GOOD CLEAN FUN -- SEE, THE HATCHET MURDERER DOES ALL HIS WORK IN THE BATHTUB -- WHAT COULD BE CLEANER? NOW HE STUFFS GRANDMA, ALIVE, INTO THE DOC'S STERILIZER! VERY TIDY.
GOOD WORK, KID --- YOU'LL PROB'LY GROW UP TO BE A GREAT EDITOR.
REMINDS ME OF A TIME I JUMPS SHIP IN LIVERPOOL AN' HERE'S A BIG STUPID CAT IN A GREEN GROCER'S SHOP --- HA, WELL, I ...... SAY, WE MUST BE IN A EARTHQUAKE!
Be of Good Cheer
WALT KELLY

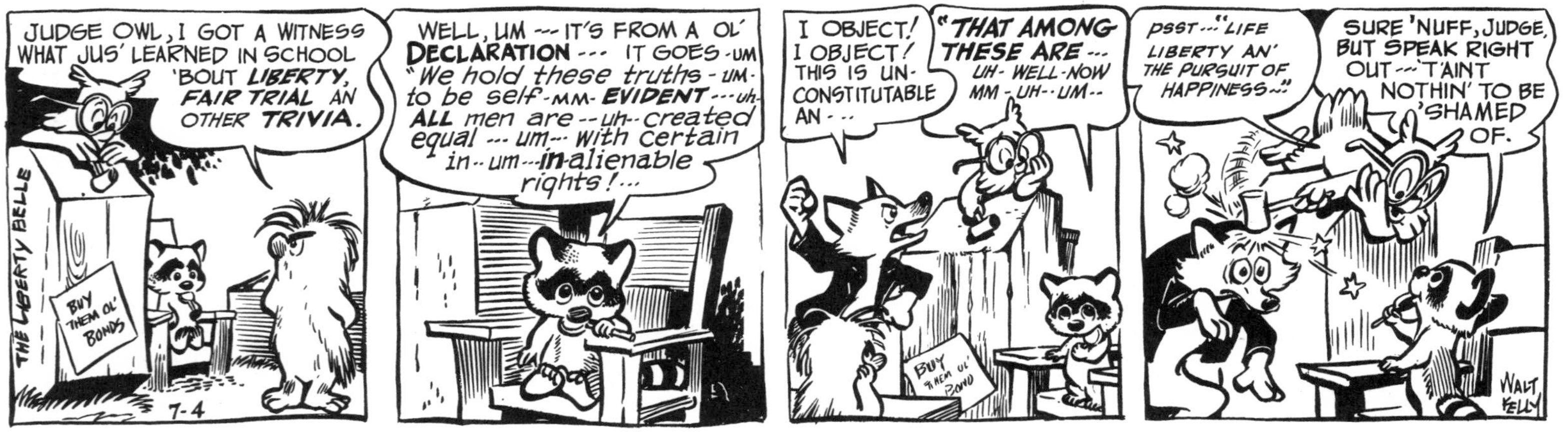
JUDGE OWL, I GOT A WITNESS WHAT JUS' LEARNED IN SCHOOL 'BOUT LIBERTY, FAIR TRIAL AN OTHER TRIVIA.
THE LIBERTY BELLE
BUY THEM OL' BONDS
7-4
WELL, UM --- IT'S FROM A OL' DECLARATION --- IT GOES - UM "We hold these truths - UM - to be self - MM - EVIDENT --- uh - ALL men are -- uh - created equal --- um -- with certain in -- um -- in-alienable rights! ...
I OBJECT! I OBJECT! THIS IS UN-CONSTITUTABLE AN - --
"THAT AMONG THESE ARE --- UH - WELL - NOW MM - UH - - UM --
BUY THEM OL' BONDS
PSST --- "LIFE LIBERTY AN' THE PURSUIT OF HAPPINESS --"
SURE 'NUFF, JUDGE, BUT SPEAK RIGHT OUT --- 'T AIN'T NOTHIN' TO BE 'SHAMED OF.
WALT KELLY

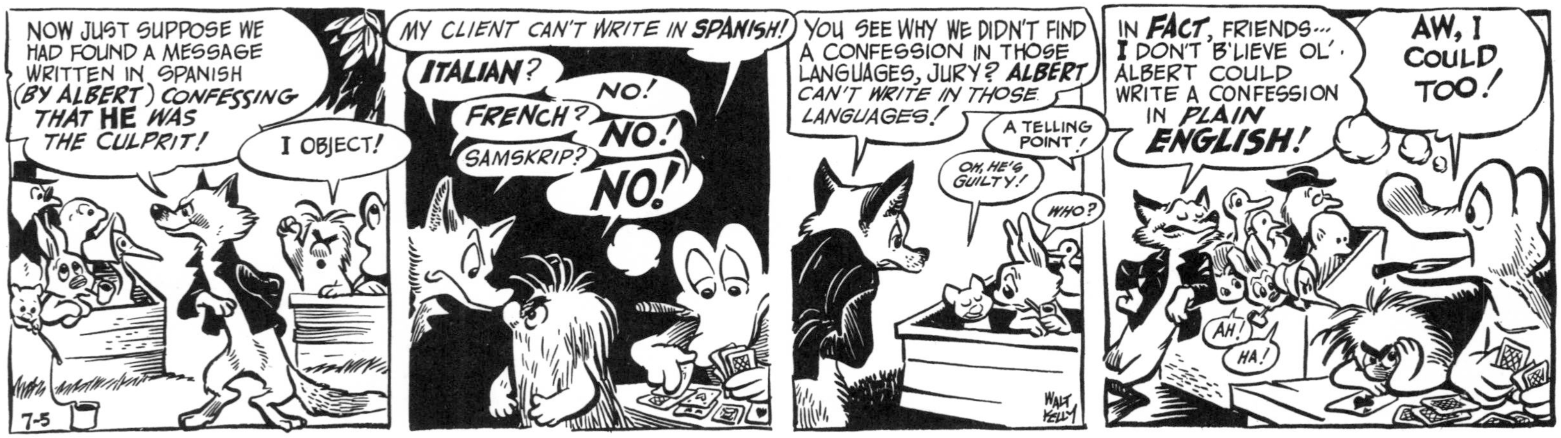
NOW JUST SUPPOSE WE HAD FOUND A MESSAGE WRITTEN IN SPANISH (BY ALBERT) CONFESSING THAT HE WAS THE CULPRIT!
I OBJECT!
7-5
MY CLIENT CAN'T WRITE IN SPANISH!
ITALIAN?
NO!
FRENCH?
NO!
SAMSKRIP?
NO!
YOU SEE WHY WE DIDN'T FIND A CONFESSION IN THOSE LANGUAGES, JURY? ALBERT CAN'T WRITE IN THOSE LANGUAGES!
A TELLING POINT!
OH, HE'S GUILTY!
WHO?
WALT KELLY
IN FACT, FRIENDS... I DON'T B'LIEVE OL' ALBERT COULD WRITE A CONFESSION IN PLAIN ENGLISH!
AW, I COULD TOO!
AH!
HA!

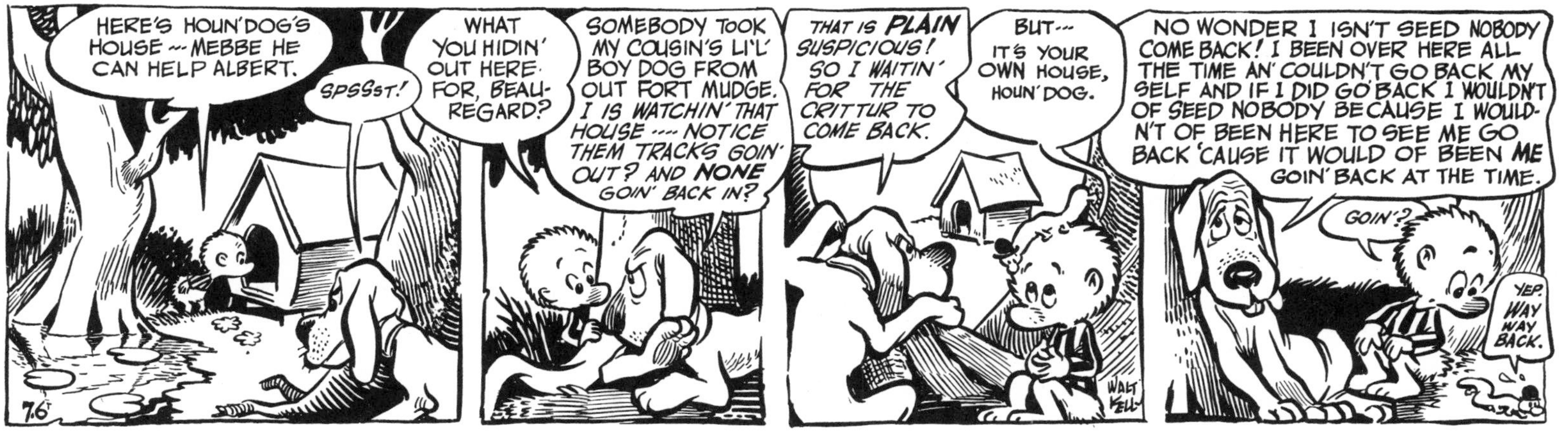
HERE'S HOUN'DOG'S HOUSE -- MEBBE HE CAN HELP ALBERT.
SPSSST!
WHAT YOU HIDIN' OUT HERE FOR, BEAU-REGARD?
SOMEBODY TOOK MY COUSIN'S LI'L' BOY DOG FROM OUT FORT MUDGE. I IS WATCHIN' THAT HOUSE --- NOTICE THEM TRACKS GOIN' OUT? AND NONE GOIN' BACK IN?
THAT IS PLAIN SUSPICIOUS! SO I WAITIN' FOR THE CRITTUR TO COME BACK.
BUT--- IT'S YOUR OWN HOUSE, HOUN'DOG.
NO WONDER I ISN'T SEED NOBODY COME BACK! I BEEN OVER HERE ALL THE TIME AN' COULDN'T GO BACK MY SELF AND IF I DID GO BACK I WOULDN'T OF SEED NOBODY BECAUSE I WOULDN'T OF BEEN HERE TO SEE ME GO BACK 'CAUSE IT WOULD OF BEEN ME GOIN' BACK AT THE TIME.
GOIN'?
YEP. WAY WAY BACK.
7-6
WALT KELLY

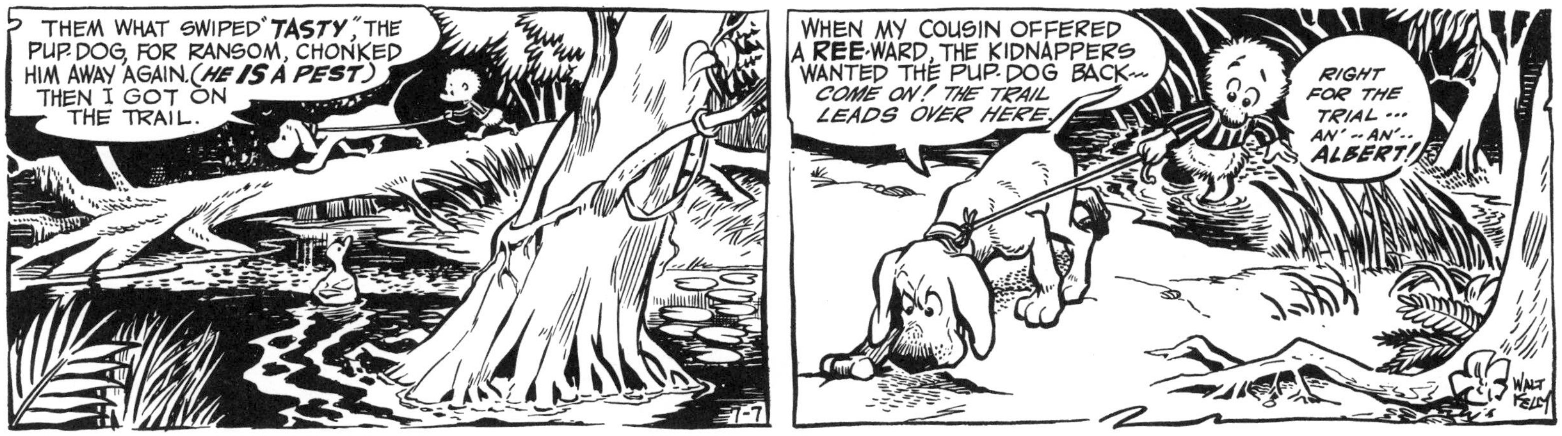
THEM WHAT SWIPED "TASTY," THE PUP-DOG FOR RANSOM, CHONKED HIM AWAY AGAIN. (HE IS A PEST.) THEN I GOT ON THE TRAIL.
WHEN MY COUSIN OFFERED A REE-WARD, THE KIDNAPPERS WANTED THE PUP-DOG BACK-- COME ON! THE TRAIL LEADS OVER HERE.
RIGHT FOR THE TRIAL... AN'--AN'-- ALBERT!
7-7
WALT KELLY

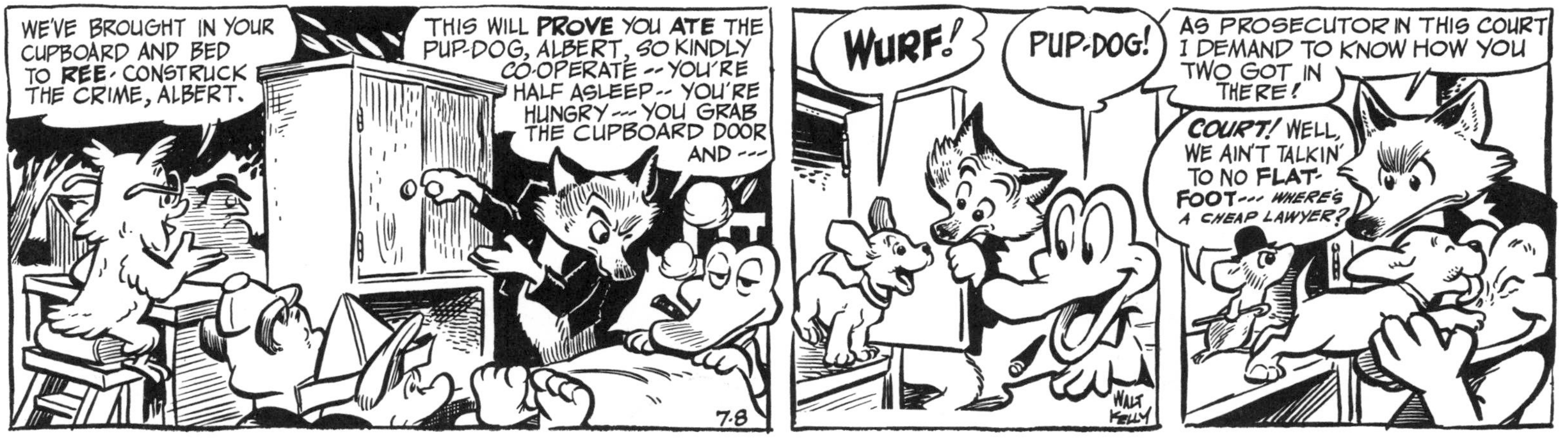
WE'VE BROUGHT IN YOUR CUPBOARD AND BED TO REE-CONSTRUCK THE CRIME, ALBERT.
THIS WILL PROVE YOU ATE THE PUP-DOG, ALBERT, SO KINDLY CO-OPERATE -- YOU'RE HALF ASLEEP -- YOU'RE HUNGRY --- YOU GRAB THE CUPBOARD DOOR AND ---
WURF!
PUP-DOG!
AS PROSECUTOR IN THIS COURT I DEMAND TO KNOW HOW YOU TWO GOT IN THERE!
COURT! WELL, WE AIN'T TALKIN' TO NO FLAT-FOOT--- WHERE'S A CHEAP LAWYER?
7-8
WALT KELLY

NOTCHERWELLY, IT IS NOW CLEAR THAT ALBERT COULD HAVE EATEN THE YOUNG DOG.
RIGHT -- HE COULD OF REACHED OVER TO THE CUPBOARD AND SWALLIED UP THE POOR PUP!
BUT THE LI'L' DOG IS ALIVE! HE GOT LOCKED IN THE CUPBOARD TRYIN' TO GIT A CUP OF SUGAR!
HA!
7-10
DON'T CLOUD THE ISSUE! THE CRIME IS NOW REVEALED IN ALL ITS GRISLY POSSIBILITIES. ALBERT IS GUILTY OF PRE-CONCEALED MURDER!
A QUICK LOOK AT THE LAW LEAD ME TO CORNCLUDE THAT SOMETHIN' SNEAKY IS BEEN COMMITTED! FINDIN' THE CORPUS DEE-LECTABLE HALE AN' HEARTY IS UNFAIR, UNHEARD-OF AND UNHUMAN!
WALT KELLY

AN' NOW, THE OLD suspensus per collum, KIDDO.
ne quid nimis.
silent leges inter arma.
AW ~ non omnis moriar. QUIET! SO'S I FIND A ACE
HOW CAN ALBERT BE GUILTY IF NO CRIME IS BEEN DONE?
HOW 'BOUT ONE OF THEM OTHERS? WE ISN'T FUSSY.
7-11
HOLD ON THAR, PARDS! THEM TWO ONSAVORY VARMINTS IS THE BONAFIDE CULPRITS! MAN AN' BOY I'VE TRAILED 'EM THRU THE MESQUITE FO' NIGH ONTO THUTTY YEAR!
IT'S HOPAROUN' CAVITY! WE'RE DONE!
HOUN' DOG, WHERE IN BLUE TUNKET DID YOU GIT THAT SPEECH?
WALT KELLY

WAPPINGER!
WAPPINGER!
WHERE'D YOU GET THAT SPEECH YESTERDAY, HOUN' DOG?
IT WAS LEFT OVER FROM A OL' HIGH SCHOOL PLAY.
7-12
I SHOULD OF TOLE YOU -- THIS GUN SHOOTS ONLY BLANKS.
DRIVER! DRIVER! MY LAND! ANOTHER BUS REFUSES TO STOP IF I COULD WRITE I'D SEND A NASTY LETTER TO THE MAYOR --- IF HE COULD ONLY READ.
THAT'S OKAY ---- I'M NOT SURE WE'RE CHASING THE RIGHT ONES ANYWAYS.
WALT KELLY

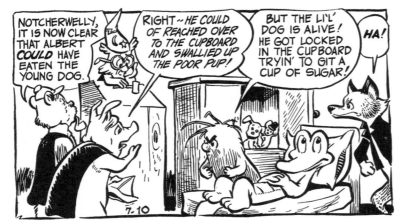

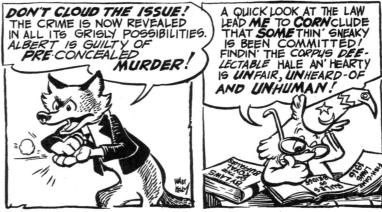

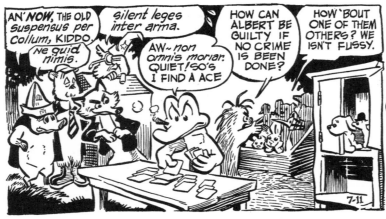

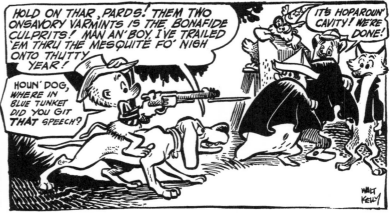

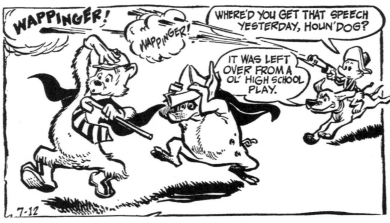

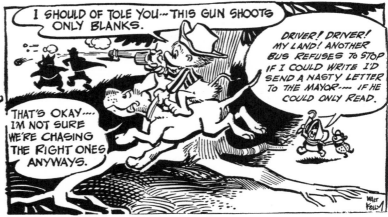

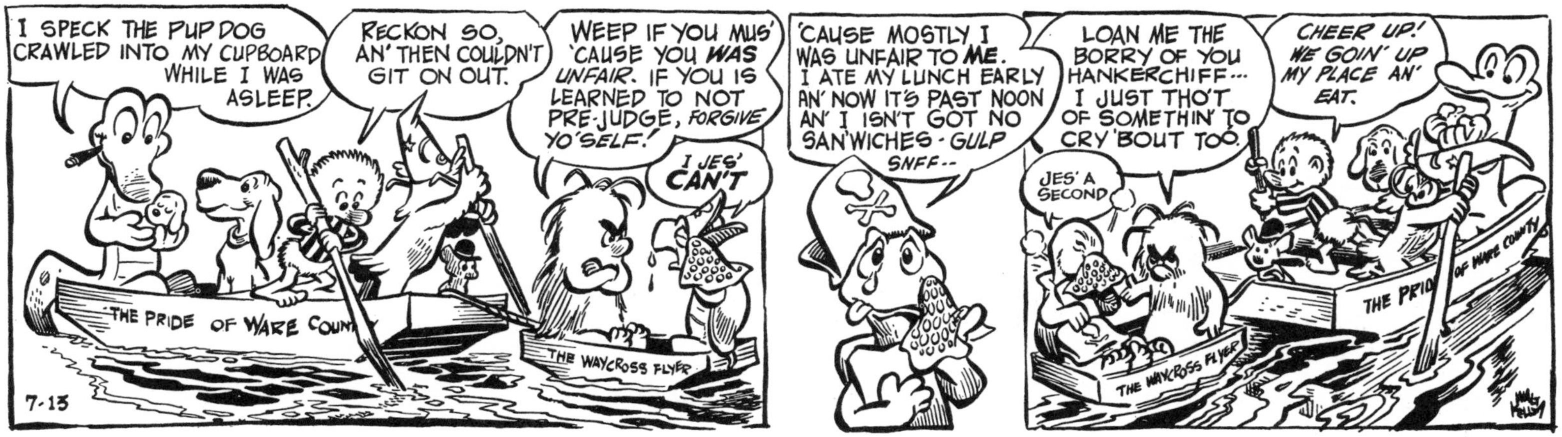
I SPECK THE PUP DOG CRAWLED INTO MY CUPBOARD WHILE I WAS ASLEEP.
RECKON SO, AN' THEN COULDN'T GIT ON OUT.
WEEP IF YOU MUS' 'CAUSE YOU WAS UNFAIR. IF YOU IS LEARNED TO NOT PRE-JUDGE, FORGIVE YO'SELF!
I JES' CAN'T
THE PRIDE OF WARE COUNTY
THE WAYCROSS FLYER
7-13
'CAUSE MOSTLY I WAS UNFAIR TO ME. I ATE MY LUNCH EARLY AN' NOW IT'S PAST NOON AN' I ISN'T GOT NO SAN'WICHES - GULP SNFF--
LOAN ME THE BORRY OF YOU HANKERCHIFF--- I JUST THO'T OF SOMETHIN' TO CRY 'BOUT TOO.
JES' A SECOND
CHEER UP! WE GOIN' UP MY PLACE AN' EAT.
THE PRIDE OF WARE COUNTY
THE WAYCROSS FLYER
WALT KELLY

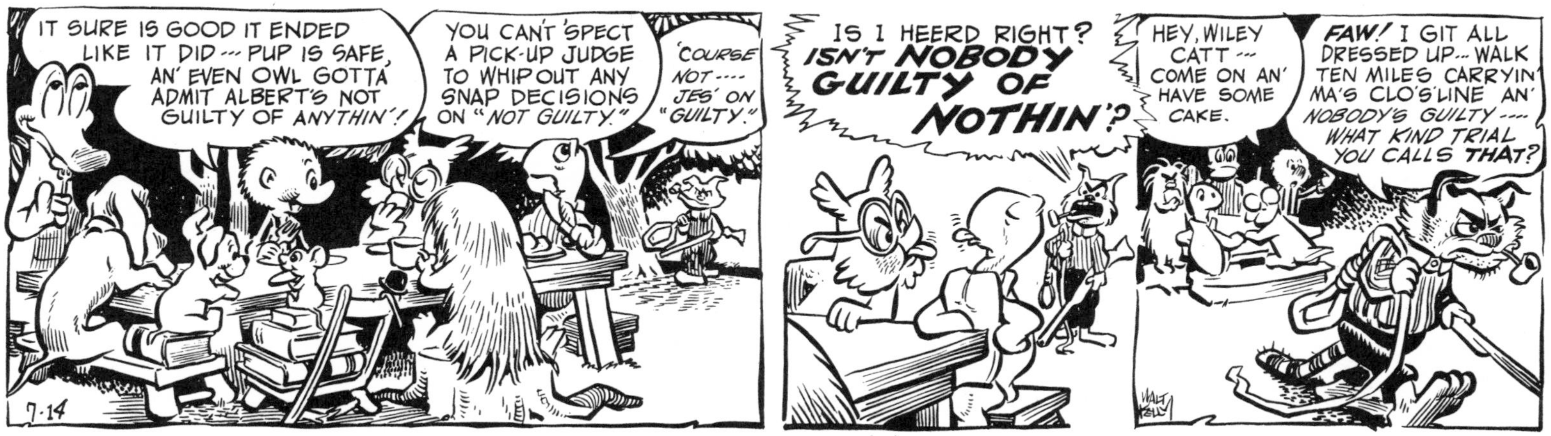
IT SURE IS GOOD IT ENDED LIKE IT DID --- PUP IS SAFE, AN' EVEN OWL GOTTA ADMIT ALBERT'S NOT GUILTY OF ANYTHIN'!
YOU CAN'T 'SPECT A PICK-UP JUDGE TO WHIP OUT ANY SNAP DECISIONS ON "NOT GUILTY."
'COURSE NOT---- JES' ON "GUILTY."
7-14
IS I HEERD RIGHT? ISN'T NOBODY GUILTY OF NOTHIN'?
HEY, WILEY CATT --- COME ON AN' HAVE SOME CAKE.
FAW! I GIT ALL DRESSED UP--- WALK TEN MILES CARRYIN MA'S CLO'S LINE AN' NOBODY'S GUILTY ---- WHAT KIND TRIAL YOU CALLS THAT?
WALT KELLY

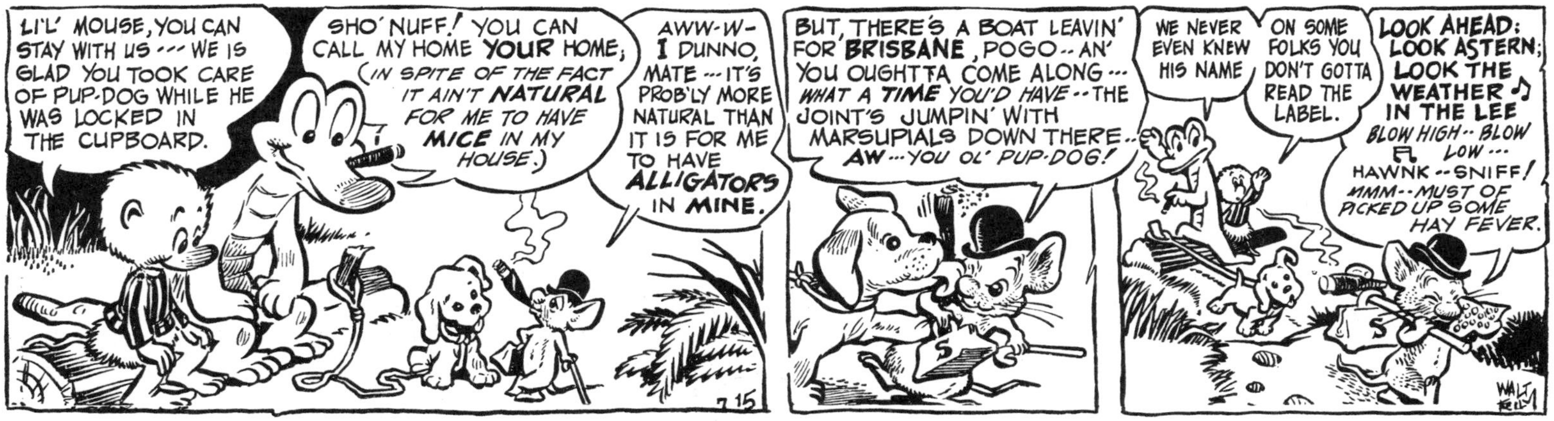
LI'L' MOUSE, YOU CAN STAY WITH US --- WE IS GLAD YOU TOOK CARE OF PUP-DOG WHILE HE WAS LOCKED IN THE CUPBOARD.
SHO' NUFF! YOU CAN CALL MY HOME YOUR HOME; (IN SPITE OF THE FACT IT AIN'T NATURAL FOR ME TO HAVE MICE IN MY HOUSE.)
AWW-W- I DUNNO, MATE --- IT'S PROB'LY MORE NATURAL THAN IT IS FOR ME TO HAVE ALLIGATORS IN MINE.
7-15
BUT, THERE'S A BOAT LEAVIN' FOR BRISBANE, POGO -- AN' YOU OUGHTTA COME ALONG --- WHAT A TIME YOU'D HAVE -- THE JOINT'S JUMPIN' WITH MARSUPIALS DOWN THERE -- AW --- YOU OL' PUP-DOG!
WE NEVER EVEN KNEW HIS NAME
ON SOME FOLKS YOU DON'T GOTTA READ THE LABEL.
LOOK AHEAD: LOOK ASTERN; LOOK THE WEATHER IN THE LEE BLOW HIGH -- BLOW LOW --- HAWNK -- SNIFF! MMM -- MUST OF PICKED UP SOME HAY FEVER.
WALT KELLY

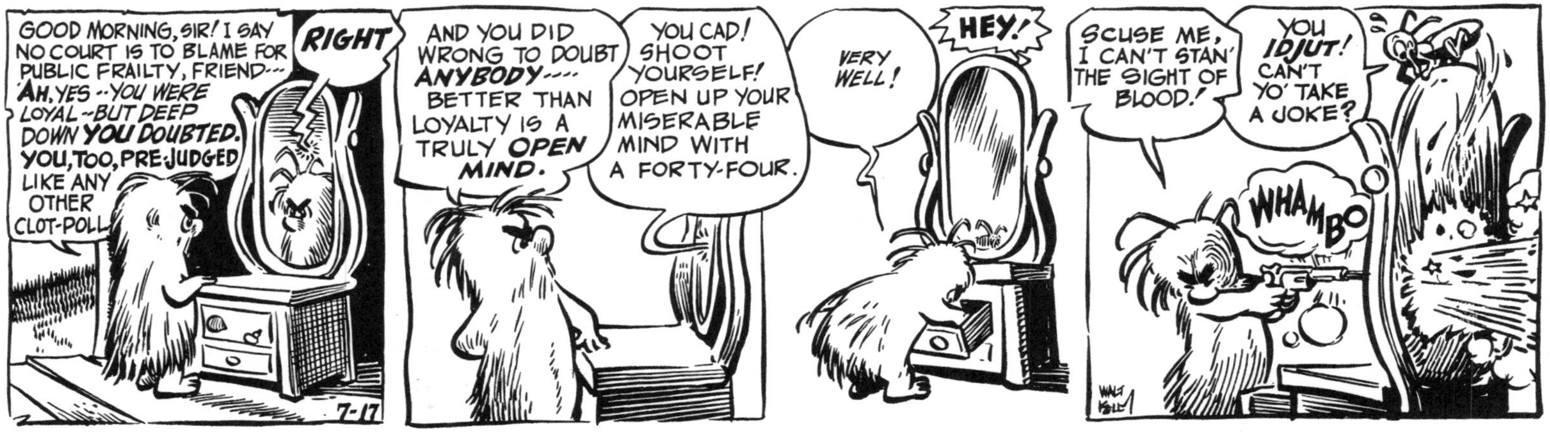
GOOD MORNING, SIR! I SAY NO COURT IS TO BLAME FOR PUBLIC FRAILTY, FRIEND--- AH, YES -- YOU WERE LOYAL -- BUT DEEP DOWN YOU DOUBTED. YOU, TOO, PRE-JUDGED LIKE ANY OTHER CLOT-POLL
RIGHT
7-17
AND YOU DID WRONG TO DOUBT ANYBODY---- BETTER THAN LOYALTY IS A TRULY OPEN MIND.
YOU CAD! SHOOT YOURSELF! OPEN UP YOUR MISERABLE MIND WITH A FORTY-FOUR.
VERY WELL!
HEY!
SCUSE ME, I CAN'T STAN' THE SIGHT OF BLOOD!
YOU IDJUT! CAN'T YO' TAKE A JOKE?
WHAMBO
WALT KELLY

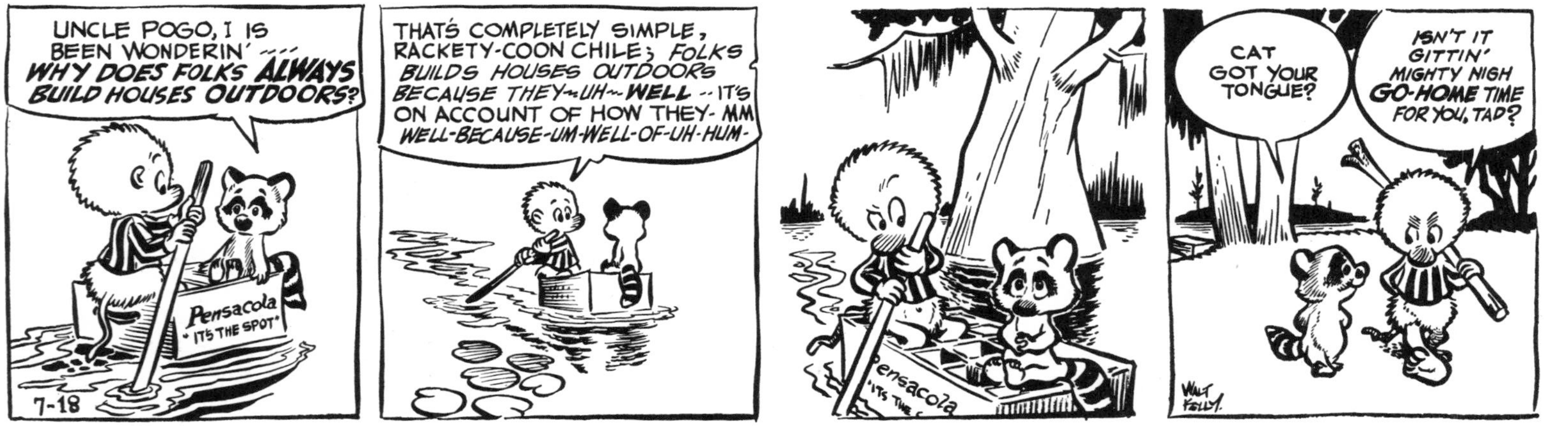
UNCLE POGO, I IS BEEN WONDERIN' ---- WHY DOES FOLKS ALWAYS BUILD HOUSES OUTDOORS?
Pensacola "IT'S THE SPOT"
7-18
THAT'S COMPLETELY SIMPLE, RACKETY-COON CHILE; FOLKS BUILDS HOUSES OUTDOORS BECAUSE THEY--UH--WELL -- IT'S ON ACCOUNT OF HOW THEY- MM WELL-BECAUSE-UM-WELL-OF-UH-HUM-
CAT GOT YOUR TONGUE?
ISN'T IT GITTIN' MIGHTY NIGH GO-HOME TIME FOR YOU, TAD?
WALT KELLY

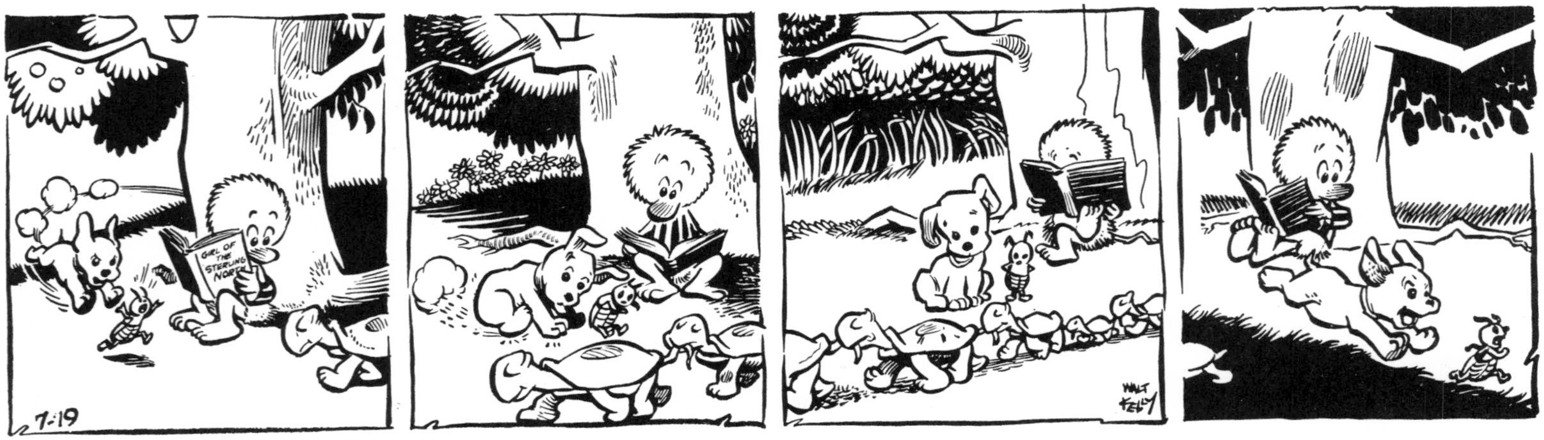
GIRL OF THE STERLING NORTH
7-19
WALT KELLY

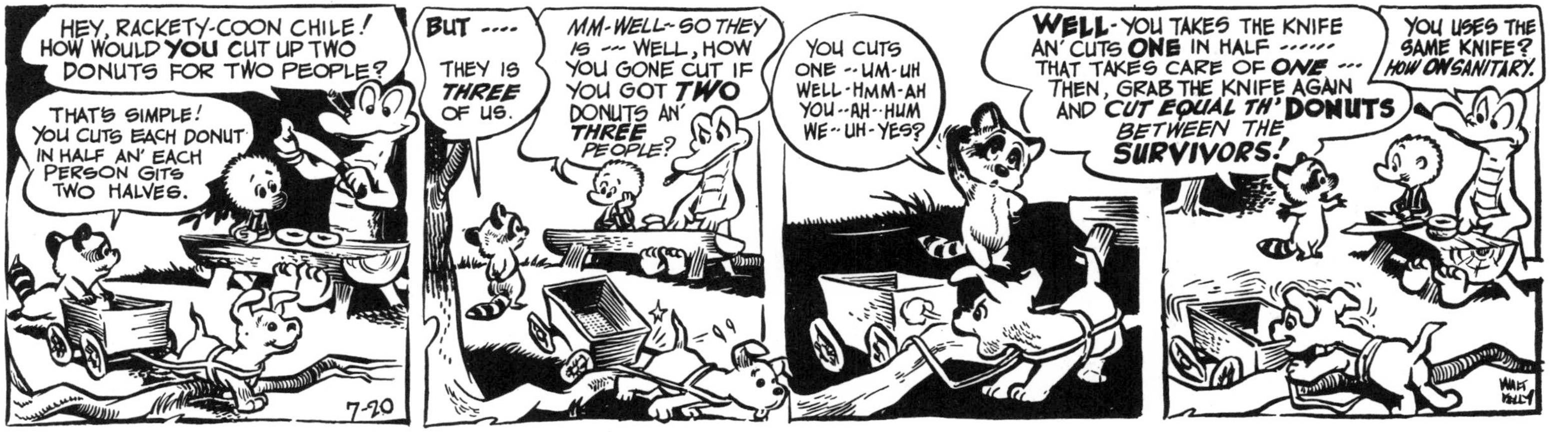
HEY, RACKETY-COON CHILE! HOW WOULD YOU CUT UP TWO DONUTS FOR TWO PEOPLE?
THAT'S SIMPLE! YOU CUTS EACH DONUT IN HALF AN' EACH PERSON GITS TWO HALVES.
7-20
BUT ----
THEY IS THREE OF US.
MM-WELL-- SO THEY IS --- WELL, HOW YOU GONE CUT IF YOU GOT TWO DONUTS AN' THREE PEOPLE?
YOU CUTS ONE --UM-UH WELL-HMM-AH YOU--AH--HUM WE--UH-YES?
WELL- YOU TAKES THE KNIFE AN' CUTS ONE IN HALF ------ THAT TAKES CARE OF ONE --- THEN, GRAB THE KNIFE AGAIN AND CUT EQUAL TH' DONUTS BETWEEN THE SURVIVORS!
YOU USES THE SAME KNIFE? HOW ONSANITARY.
WALT KELLY

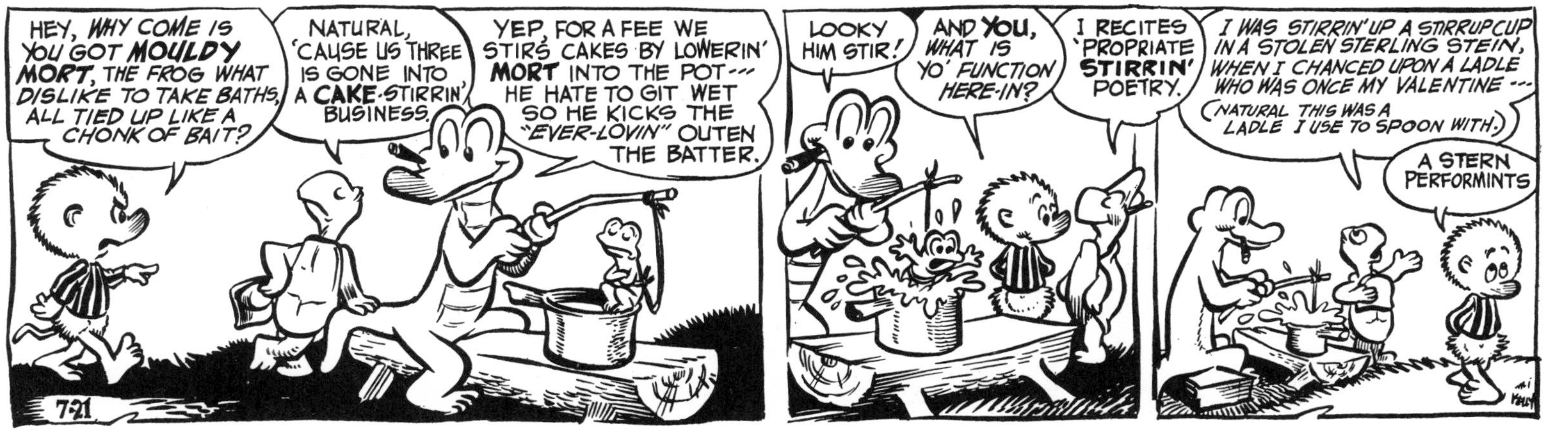
HEY, WHY COME IS YOU GOT MOULDY MORT, THE FROG WHAT DISLIKE TO TAKE BATHS, ALL TIED UP LIKE A CHONK OF BAIT?
NATURAL, 'CAUSE US THREE IS GONE INTO A CAKE-STIRRIN' BUSINESS.
YEP, FOR A FEE WE STIRS CAKES BY LOWERIN' MORT INTO THE POT--- HE HATE TO GIT WET SO HE KICKS THE "EVER-LOVIN'" OUTEN THE BATTER.
7-21
LOOKY HIM STIR!
AND YOU, WHAT IS YO' FUNCTION HERE-IN?
I RECITES 'PROPRIATE STIRRIN' POETRY.
I WAS STIRRIN' UP A STIRRUP CUP IN A STOLEN STERLING STEIN, WHEN I CHANCED UPON A LADLE WHO WAS ONCE MY VALENTINE ---
(NATURAL THIS WAS A LADLE I USE TO SPOON WITH.)
A STERN PERFORMINTS

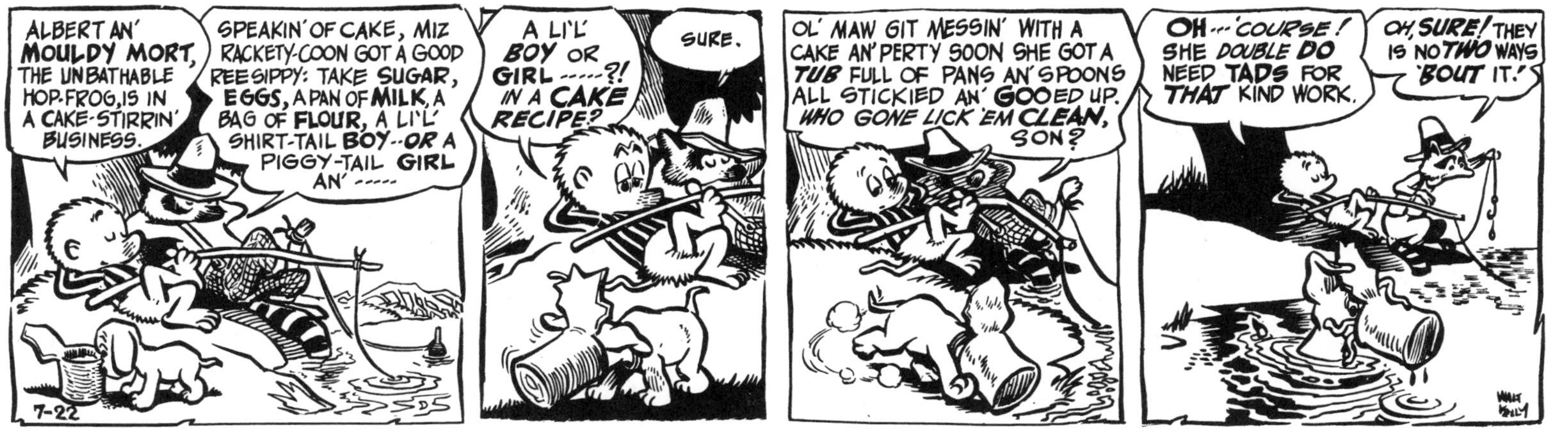
ALBERT AN' MOULDY MORT, THE UNBATHABLE HOP-FROG, IS IN A CAKE-STIRRIN' BUSINESS.
SPEAKIN' OF CAKE, MIZ RACKETY-COON GOT A GOOD REESIPPY: TAKE SUGAR, EGGS, A PAN OF MILK, A BAG OF FLOUR, A LI'L' SHIRT-TAIL BOY--OR A PIGGY-TAIL GIRL AN' -----
7-22
A LI'L' BOY OR GIRL -----?! IN A CAKE RECIPE?
SURE.
OL' MAW GIT MESSIN' WITH A CAKE AN' PERTY SOON SHE GOT A TUB FULL OF PANS AN' SPOONS ALL STICKIED AN' GOOED UP. WHO GONE LICK 'EM CLEAN, SON?
OH--- 'COURSE! SHE DOUBLE DO NEED TADS FOR THAT KIND WORK.
OH, SURE! THEY IS NO TWO WAYS 'BOUT IT.'
WALT KELLY

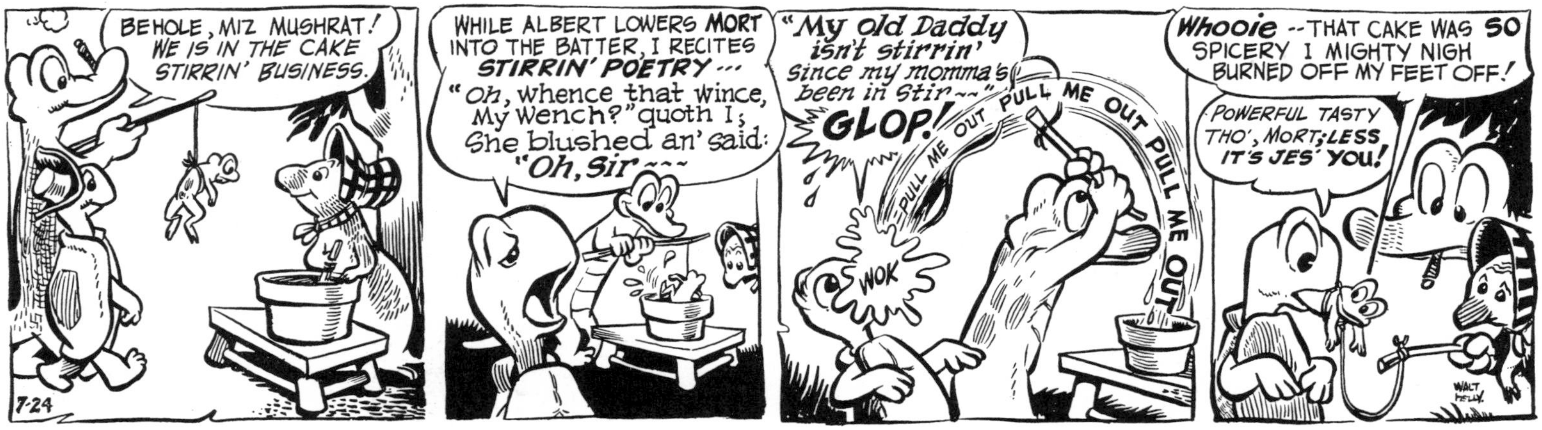
BEHOLE, MIZ MUSHRAT! WE IS IN THE CAKE STIRRIN' BUSINESS.
7-24
WHILE ALBERT LOWERS **MORT** INTO THE BATTER, I RECITES **STIRRIN' POETRY** --- "Oh, whence that wince, My Wench?" quoth I; She blushed an' said: "Oh, Sir ---"
"My old Daddy isn't stirrin' Since my momma's been in Stir ---"
GLOP!
PULL ME OUT PULL ME OUT PULL ME OUT PULL ME OUT
WOK
Whooie --THAT CAKE WAS **SO** SPICERY I MIGHTY NIGH BURNED OFF MY FEET OFF!
POWERFUL TASTY THO', MORT; **LESS IT'S JES' YOU!**
WALT KELLY

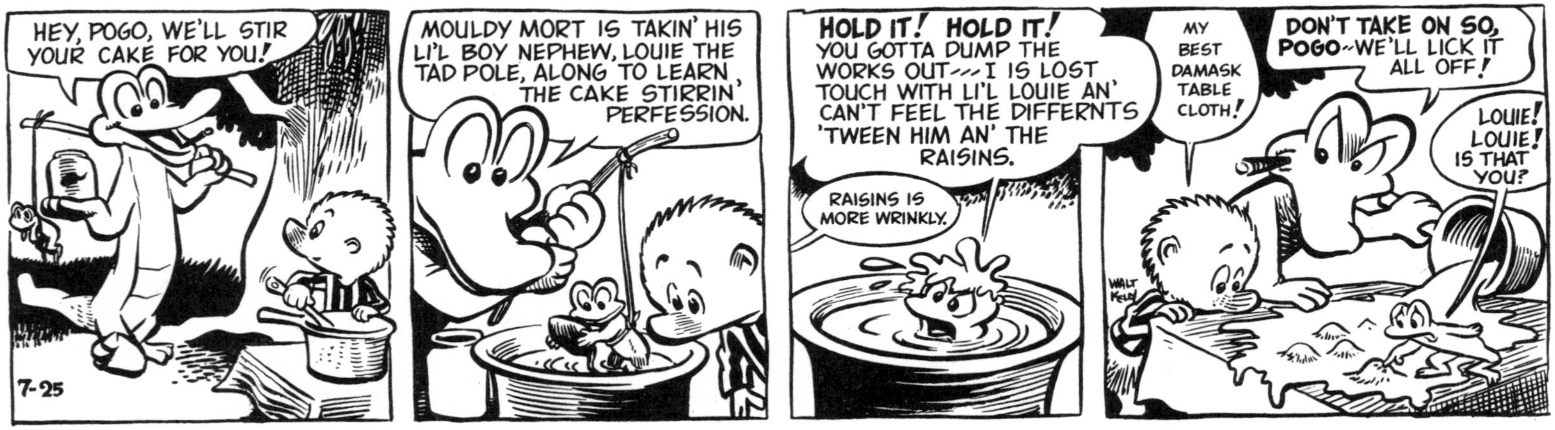
HEY, POGO, WE'LL STIR YOUR CAKE FOR YOU!
7-25
MOULDY MORT IS TAKIN' HIS LI'L BOY NEPHEW, LOUIE THE TAD POLE, ALONG TO LEARN THE CAKE STIRRIN' PERFESSION.
HOLD IT! HOLD IT! YOU GOTTA DUMP THE WORKS OUT--- I IS LOST TOUCH WITH LI'L LOUIE AN' CAN'T FEEL THE DIFFERNTS 'TWEEN HIM AN' THE RAISINS.
RAISINS IS MORE WRINKLY.
MY BEST DAMASK TABLE CLOTH!
DON'T TAKE ON SO, POGO--WE'LL LICK IT ALL OFF!
LOUIE! LOUIE! IS THAT YOU?
WALT KELLY

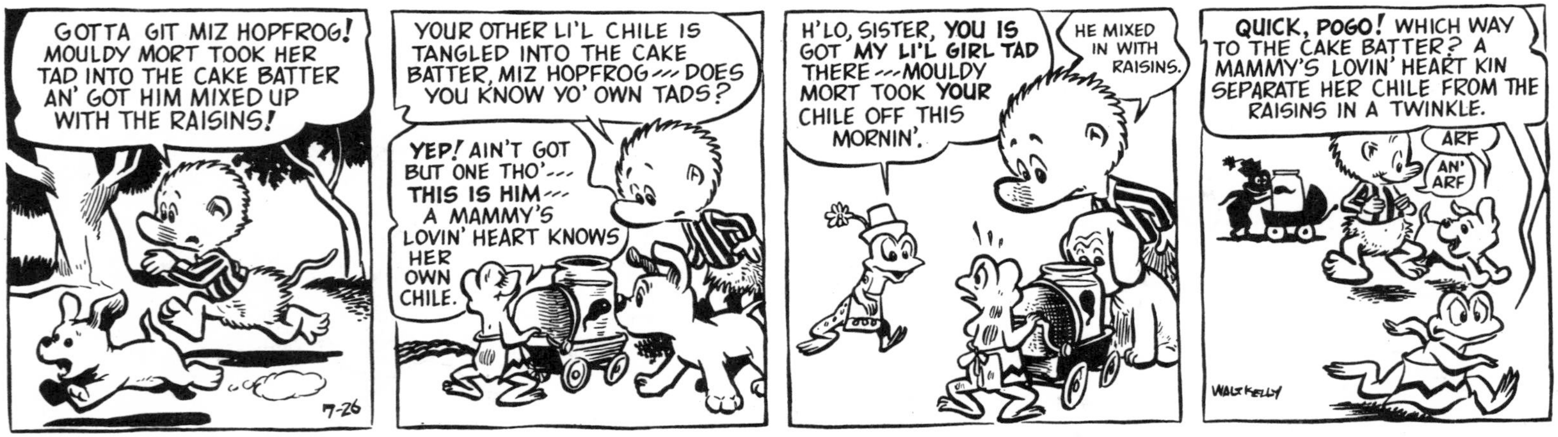
GOTTA GIT MIZ HOPFROG! MOULDY MORT TOOK HER TAD INTO THE CAKE BATTER AN' GOT HIM MIXED UP WITH THE RAISINS!
7-26
YOUR OTHER LI'L CHILE IS TANGLED INTO THE CAKE BATTER, MIZ HOPFROG--- DOES YOU KNOW YO' OWN TADS?
YEP! AIN'T GOT BUT ONE THO'--- **THIS IS HIM**--- A MAMMY'S LOVIN' HEART KNOWS HER OWN CHILE.
H'LO, SISTER, **YOU IS** GOT **MY LI'L GIRL TAD** THERE ---**MOULDY** MORT TOOK **YOUR** CHILE OFF THIS MORNIN'.
HE MIXED IN WITH RAISINS.
QUICK, POGO! WHICH WAY TO THE CAKE BATTER? A MAMMY'S LOVIN' HEART KIN SEPARATE HER CHILE FROM THE RAISINS IN A TWINKLE.
ARF
AN' ARF
WALT KELLY

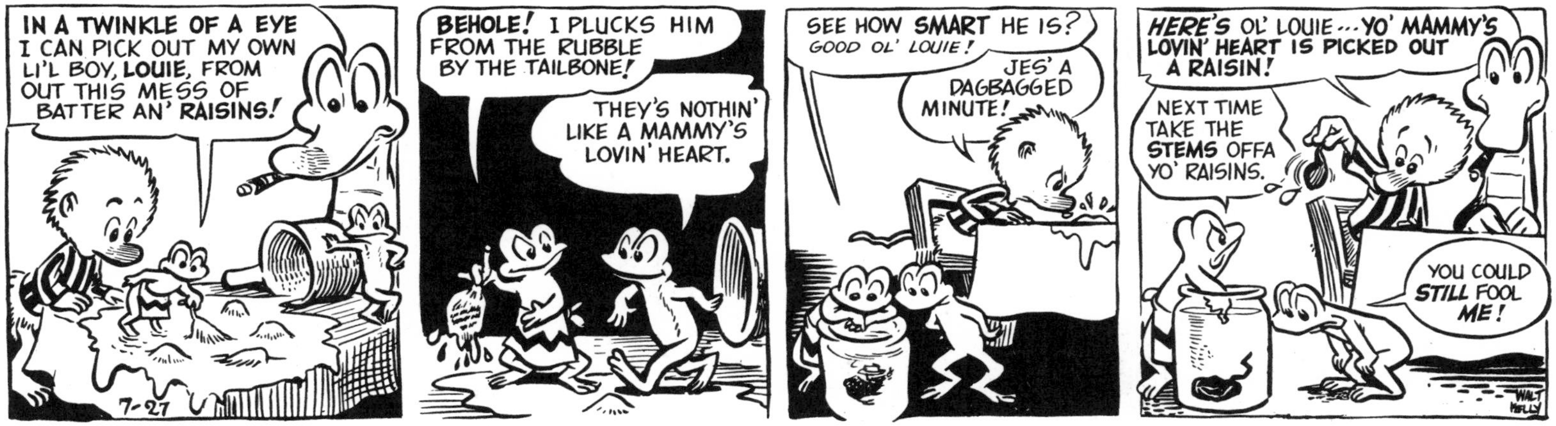
IN A TWINKLE OF A EYE I CAN PICK OUT MY OWN LI'L BOY, LOUIE, FROM OUT THIS MESS OF BATTER AN' RAISINS!
7-27
BEHOLE! I PLUCKS HIM FROM THE RUBBLE BY THE TAILBONE!
THEY'S NOTHIN' LIKE A MAMMY'S LOVIN' HEART.
SEE HOW SMART HE IS? GOOD OL' LOUIE!
JES' A DAGBAGGED MINUTE!
HERE'S OL' LOUIE... YO' MAMMY'S LOVIN' HEART IS PICKED OUT A RAISIN!
NEXT TIME TAKE THE STEMS OFFA YO' RAISINS.
YOU COULD STILL FOOL ME!
WALT KELLY

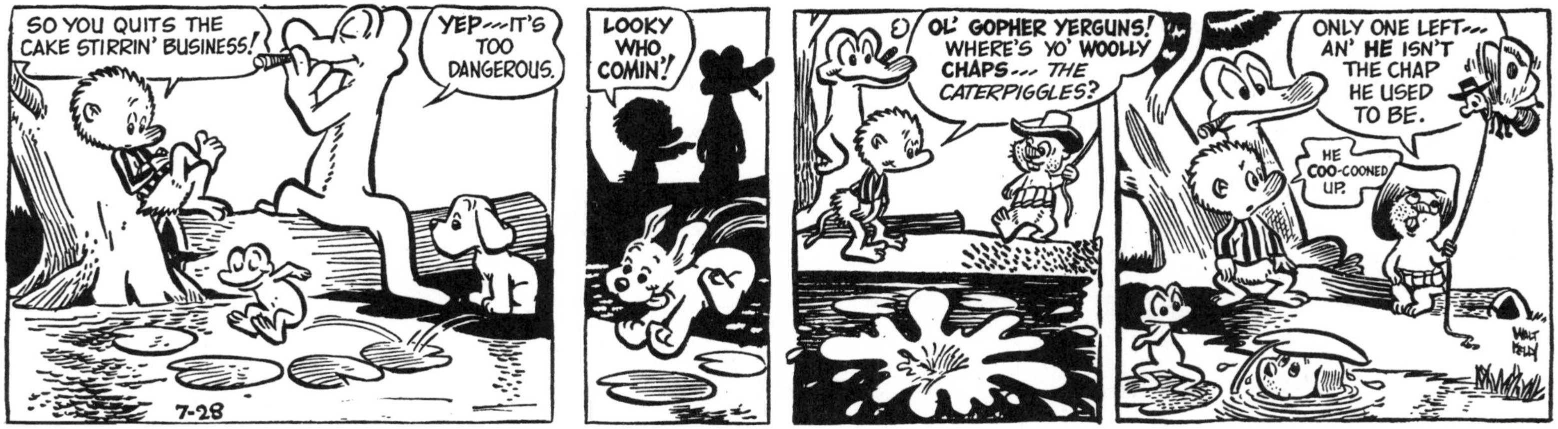
SO YOU QUITS THE CAKE STIRRIN' BUSINESS!
YEP---IT'S TOO DANGEROUS.
7-28
LOOKY WHO COMIN'!
OL' GOPHER YERGUNS! WHERE'S YO' WOOLLY CHAPS--- THE CATERPIGGLES?
ONLY ONE LEFT--- AN' HE ISN'T THE CHAP HE USED TO BE.
HE COO-COONED UP.
WALT KELLY

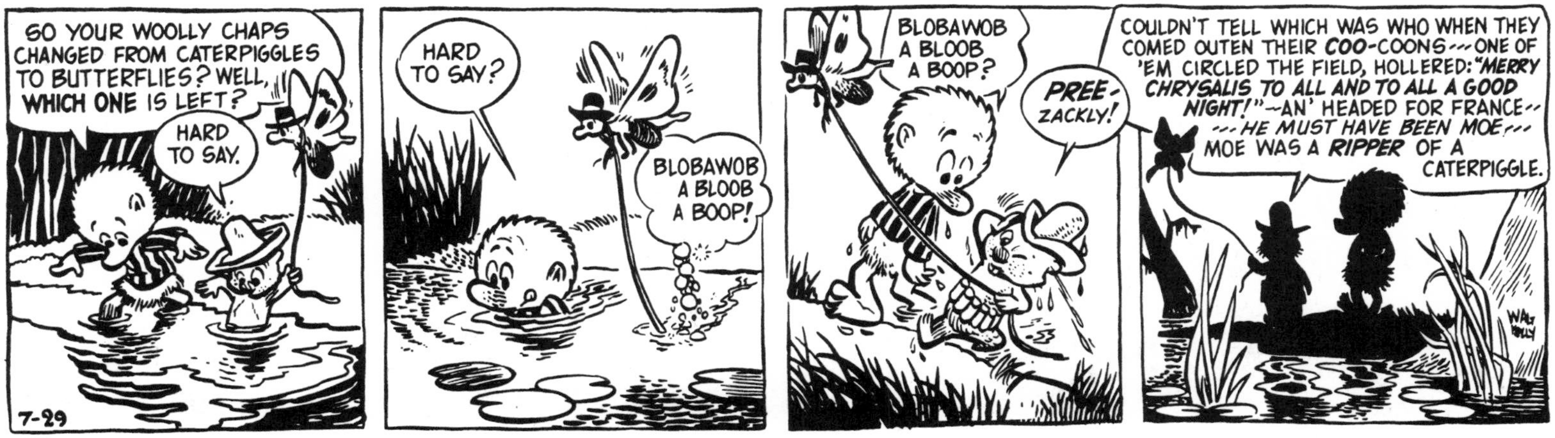
SO YOUR WOOLLY CHAPS CHANGED FROM CATERPIGGLES TO BUTTERFLIES? WELL, WHICH ONE IS LEFT?
HARD TO SAY.
7-29
HARD TO SAY?
BLOBAWOB A BLOOB A BOOP!
BLOBAWOB A BLOOB A BOOP?
PREE-ZACKLY!
COULDN'T TELL WHICH WAS WHO WHEN THEY COMED OUTEN THEIR COO-COONS--- ONE OF 'EM CIRCLED THE FIELD, HOLLERED: "MERRY CHRYSALIS TO ALL AND TO ALL A GOOD NIGHT!"--AN' HEADED FOR FRANCE-- ---HE MUST HAVE BEEN MOE--- MOE WAS A RIPPER OF A CATERPIGGLE.
WALT KELLY

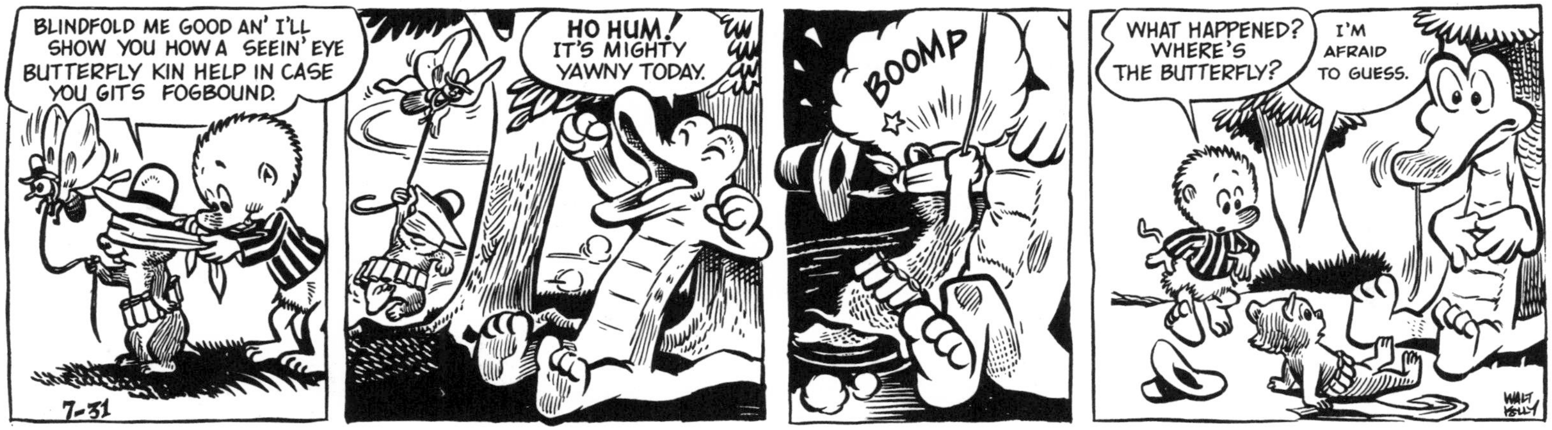
BLINDFOLD ME GOOD AN' I'LL SHOW YOU HOW A SEEIN' EYE BUTTERFLY KIN HELP IN CASE YOU GITS FOGBOUND.
7-31
HO HUM! IT'S MIGHTY YAWNY TODAY.
BOOMP
WHAT HAPPENED? WHERE'S THE BUTTERFLY?
I'M AFRAID TO GUESS.
WALT KELLY

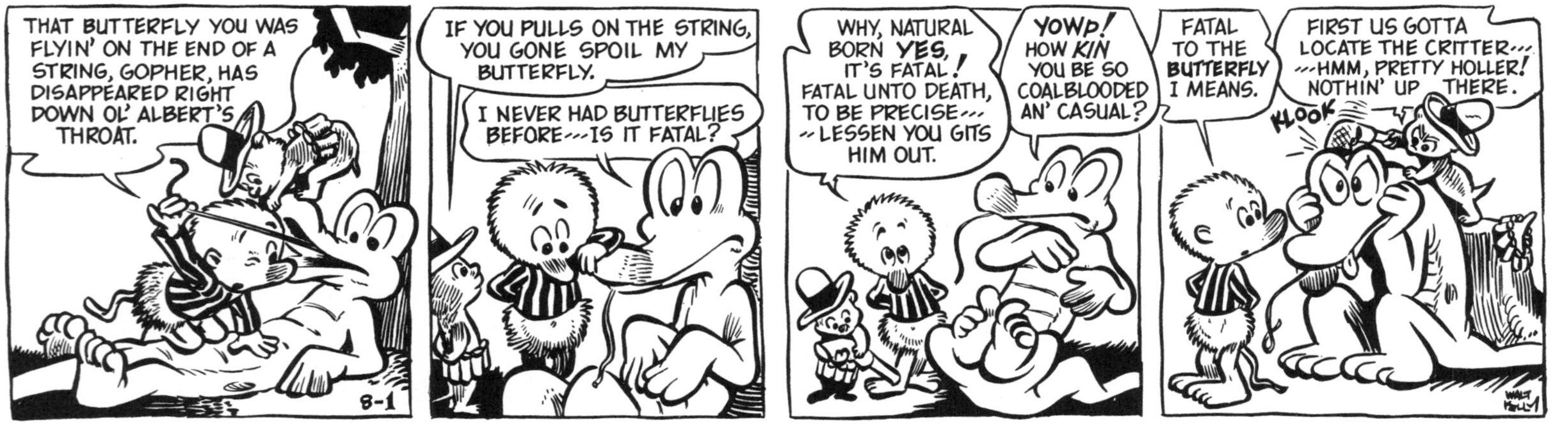
THAT BUTTERFLY YOU WAS FLYIN' ON THE END OF A STRING, GOPHER, HAS DISAPPEARED RIGHT DOWN OL' ALBERT'S THROAT.
8-1
IF YOU PULLS ON THE STRING, YOU GONE SPOIL MY BUTTERFLY.
I NEVER HAD BUTTERFLIES BEFORE--IS IT FATAL?
WHY, NATURAL BORN YES, IT'S FATAL! FATAL UNTO DEATH, TO BE PRECISE---LESSEN YOU GITS HIM OUT.
YOWP! HOW KIN YOU BE SO COALBLOODED AN' CASUAL?
FATAL TO THE BUTTERFLY I MEANS.
FIRST US GOTTA LOCATE THE CRITTER------HMM, PRETTY HOLLER! NOTHIN' UP THERE.
KLOOK
WALT KELLY

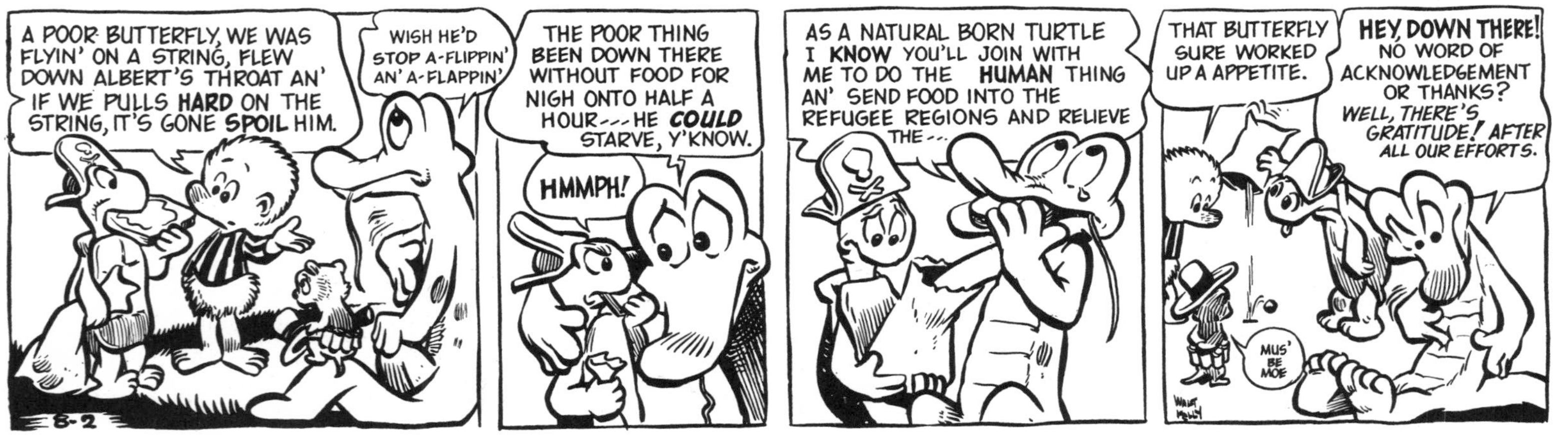
A POOR BUTTERFLY, WE WAS FLYIN' ON A STRING, FLEW DOWN ALBERT'S THROAT AN' IF WE PULLS HARD ON THE STRING, IT'S GONE SPOIL HIM.
WISH HE'D STOP A-FLIPPIN' AN' A-FLAPPIN'
8-2
THE POOR THING BEEN DOWN THERE WITHOUT FOOD FOR NIGH ONTO HALF A HOUR---HE COULD STARVE, Y'KNOW.
HMMPH!
AS A NATURAL BORN TURTLE I KNOW YOU'LL JOIN WITH ME TO DO THE HUMAN THING AN' SEND FOOD INTO THE REFUGEE REGIONS AND RELIEVE THE---
THAT BUTTERFLY SURE WORKED UP A APPETITE.
HEY, DOWN THERE! NO WORD OF ACKNOWLEDGEMENT OR THANKS? WELL, THERE'S GRATITUDE! AFTER ALL OUR EFFORTS.
MUS' BE MOE
WALT KELLY

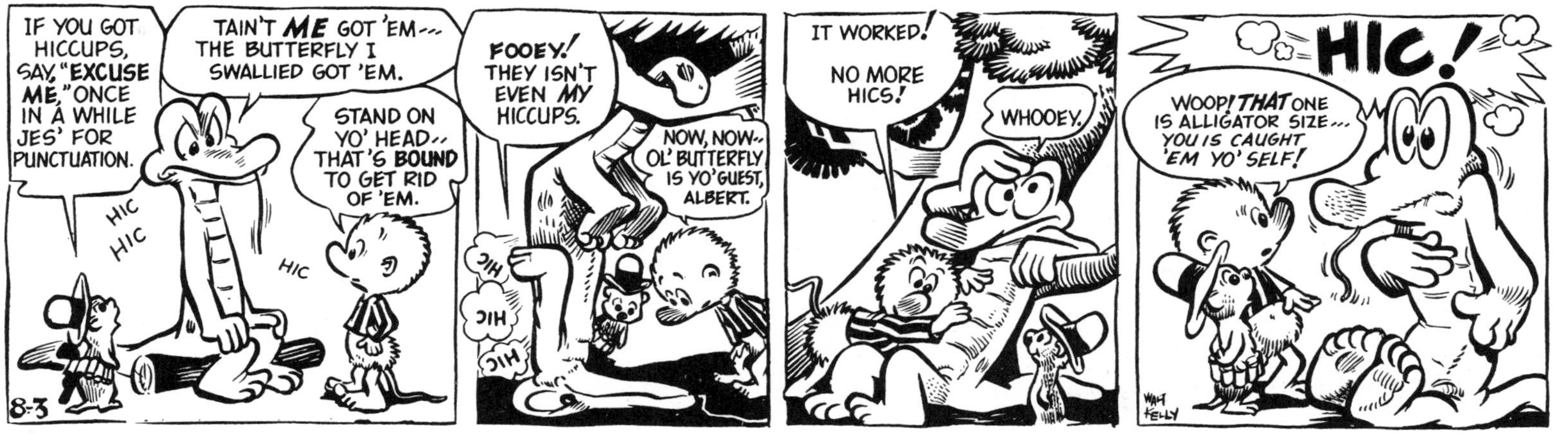
IF YOU GOT HICCUPS, SAY, "EXCUSE ME," ONCE IN A WHILE JES' FOR PUNCTUATION.
TAIN'T ME GOT 'EM--- THE BUTTERFLY I SWALLIED GOT 'EM.
HIC
HIC
HIC
STAND ON YO' HEAD-- THAT'S BOUND TO GET RID OF 'EM.
8-3
FOOEY! THEY ISN'T EVEN MY HICCUPS.
NOW, NOW-- OL' BUTTERFLY IS YO' GUEST, ALBERT.
HIC
HIC
HIC
IT WORKED! NO MORE HICS!
WHOOEY.
HIC!
WOOP! THAT ONE IS ALLIGATOR SIZE--- YOU IS CAUGHT 'EM YO' SELF!
WALT KELLY

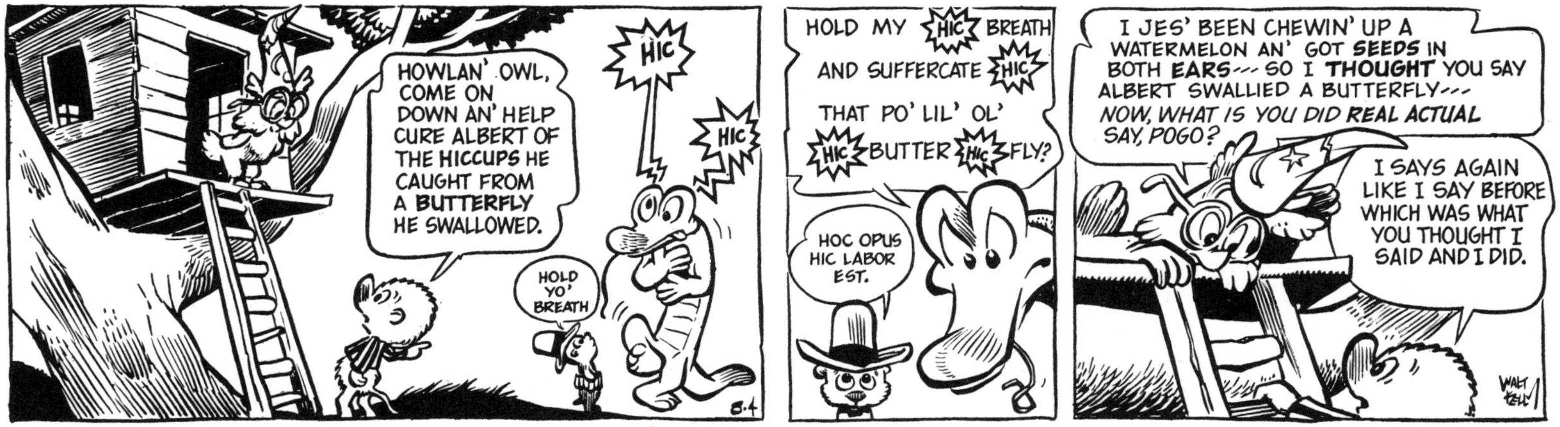
HOWLAN' OWL, COME ON DOWN AN' HELP CURE ALBERT OF THE HICCUPS HE CAUGHT FROM A BUTTERFLY HE SWALLOWED.
HIC
HIC
HOLD YO' BREATH
8-4
HOLD MY HIC BREATH AND SUFFERCATE HIC THAT PO' LIL' OL' HIC BUTTER HIC FLY?
HOC OPUS HIC LABOR EST.
I JES' BEEN CHEWIN' UP A WATERMELON AN' GOT SEEDS IN BOTH EARS--- SO I THOUGHT YOU SAY ALBERT SWALLIED A BUTTERFLY--- NOW, WHAT IS YOU DID REAL ACTUAL SAY, POGO?
I SAYS AGAIN LIKE I SAY BEFORE WHICH WAS WHAT YOU THOUGHT I SAID AND I DID.
WALT KELLY

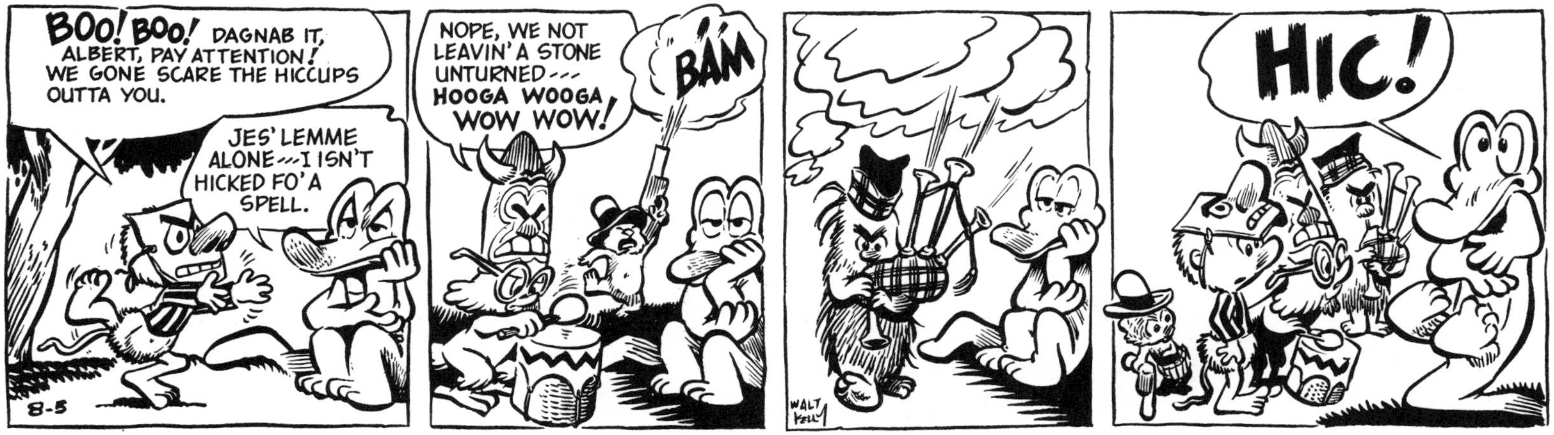
BOO! BOO! DAGNAB IT, ALBERT, PAY ATTENTION! WE GONE SCARE THE HICCUPS OUTTA YOU.
JES' LEMME ALONE---I ISN'T HICKED FO' A SPELL.
8-5
NOPE, WE NOT LEAVIN' A STONE UNTURNED--- HOOGA WOOGA WOW WOW!
BAM
WALT KELLY
HIC!

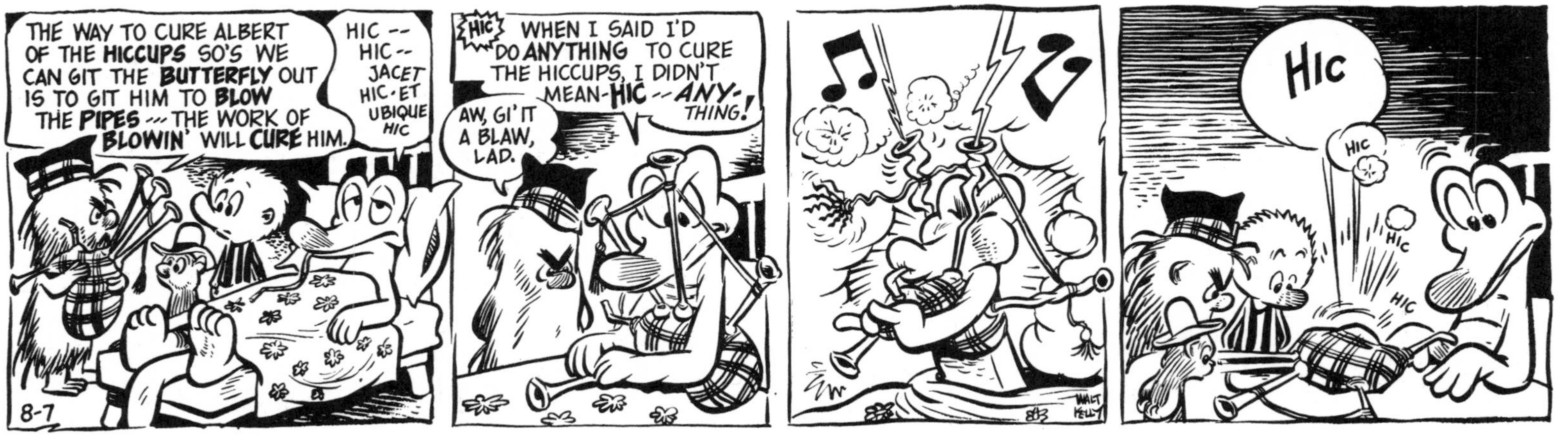
THE WAY TO CURE ALBERT OF THE HICCUPS SO'S WE CAN GIT THE BUTTERFLY OUT IS TO GIT HIM TO BLOW THE PIPES --- THE WORK OF BLOWIN' WILL CURE HIM.
HIC -- HIC -- JACET HIC - ET UBIQUE HIC
8-7
HIC
WHEN I SAID I'D DO ANYTHING TO CURE THE HICCUPS, I DIDN'T MEAN- HIC -- ANY-THING!
AW, GI' IT A BLAW, LAD.
WALT KELLY
HIC
HIC
HIC
HIC

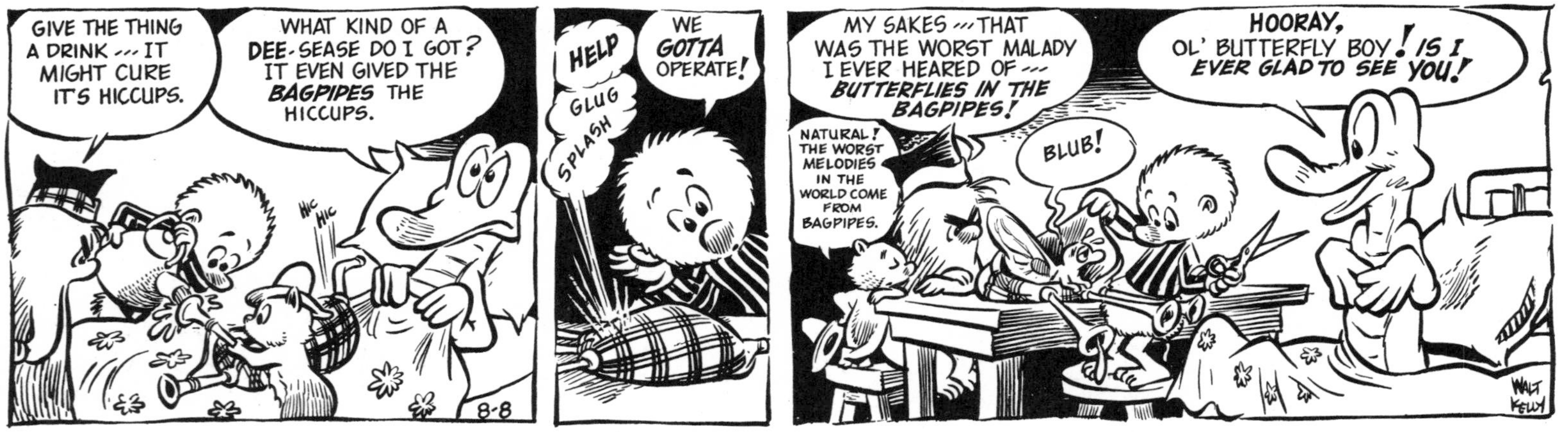
GIVE THE THING A DRINK --- IT MIGHT CURE IT'S HICCUPS.
WHAT KIND OF A DEE-SEASE DO I GOT? IT EVEN GIVED THE BAGPIPES THE HICCUPS.
HIC
HIC
8-8
HELP
GLUG
SPLASH
WE GOTTA OPERATE!
MY SAKES --- THAT WAS THE WORST MALADY I EVER HEARED OF --- BUTTERFLIES IN THE BAGPIPES!
NATURAL! THE WORST MELODIES IN THE WORLD COME FROM BAGPIPES.
BLUB!
HOORAY, OL' BUTTERFLY BOY! IS I EVER GLAD TO SEE YOU!
WALT KELLY

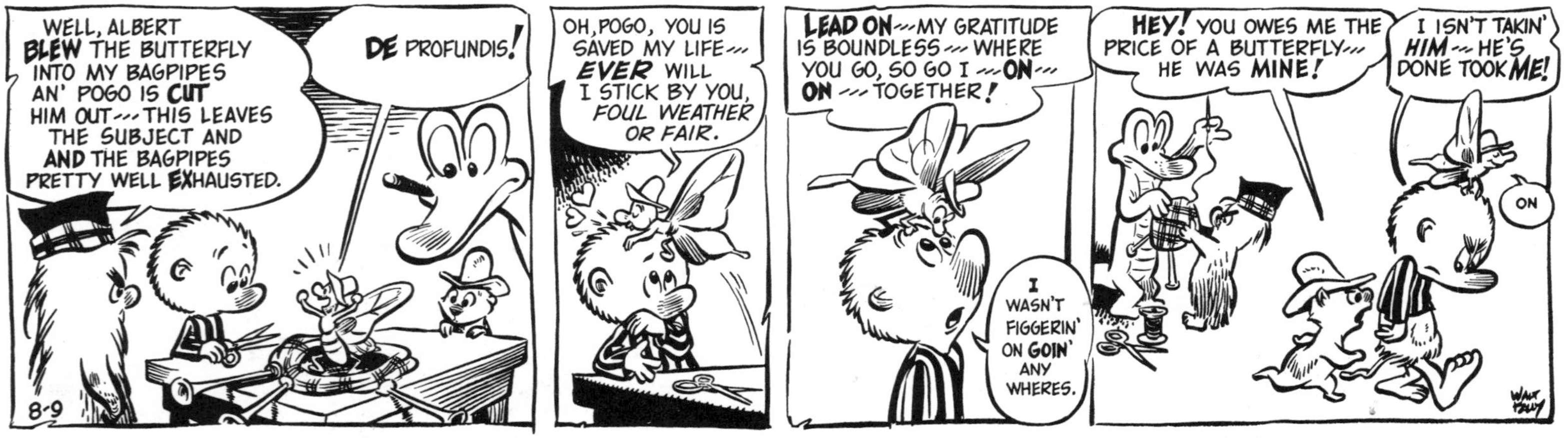
WELL, ALBERT BLEW THE BUTTERFLY INTO MY BAGPIPES AN' POGO IS CUT HIM OUT --- THIS LEAVES THE SUBJECT AND AND THE BAGPIPES PRETTY WELL EXHAUSTED.
DE PROFUNDIS!
8-9
OH, POGO, YOU IS SAVED MY LIFE --- EVER WILL I STICK BY YOU, FOUL WEATHER OR FAIR.
LEAD ON --- MY GRATITUDE IS BOUNDLESS --- WHERE YOU GO, SO GO I --- ON --- ON --- TOGETHER!
I WASN'T FIGGERIN' ON GOIN' ANY WHERES.
HEY! YOU OWES ME THE PRICE OF A BUTTERFLY --- HE WAS MINE!
I ISN'T TAKIN' HIM -- HE'S DONE TOOK ME!
ON
WALT KELLY

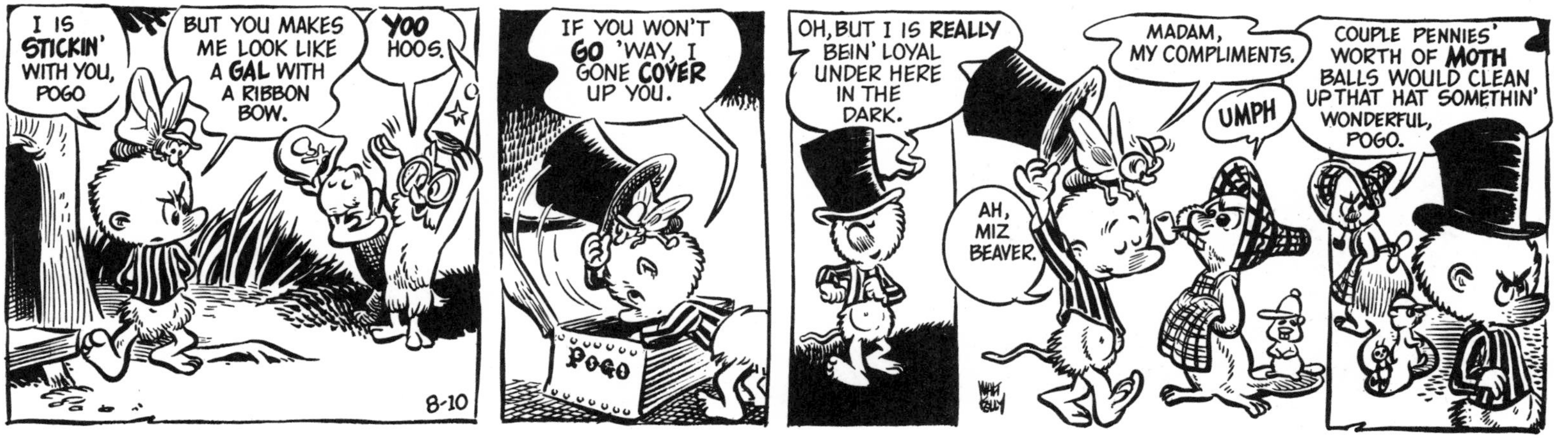
I IS STICKIN' WITH YOU, POGO
BUT YOU MAKES ME LOOK LIKE A GAL WITH A RIBBON BOW.
YOO HOOS.
8-10
IF YOU WON'T GO 'WAY, I GONE COVER UP YOU.
POGO
OH, BUT I IS REALLY BEIN' LOYAL UNDER HERE IN THE DARK.
AH, MIZ BEAVER.
MADAM, MY COMPLIMENTS.
UMPH
COUPLE PENNIES' WORTH OF MOTH BALLS WOULD CLEAN UP THAT HAT SOMETHIN' WONDERFUL, POGO.

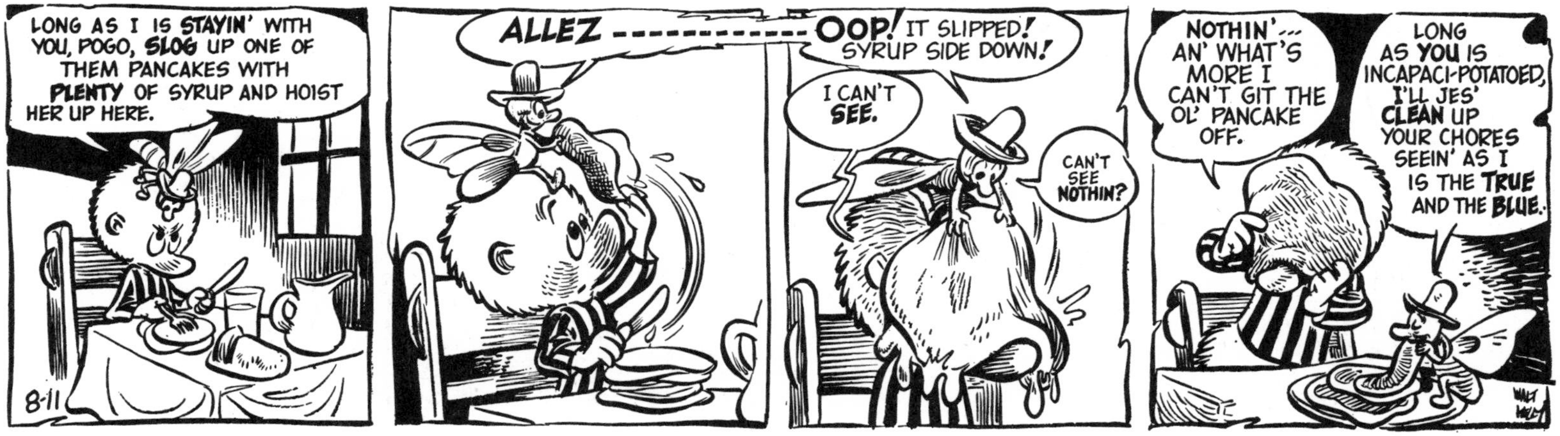
LONG AS I IS STAYIN' WITH YOU, POGO, SLOG UP ONE OF THEM PANCAKES WITH PLENTY OF SYRUP AND HOIST HER UP HERE.
8-11
ALLEZ -------------OOP! IT SLIPPED! SYRUP SIDE DOWN!
I CAN'T SEE.
CAN'T SEE NOTHIN?
NOTHIN'--- AN' WHAT'S MORE I CAN'T GIT THE OL' PANCAKE OFF.
LONG AS YOU IS INCAPACI-POTATOED, I'LL JES' CLEAN UP YOUR CHORES SEEIN' AS I IS THE TRUE AND THE BLUE.

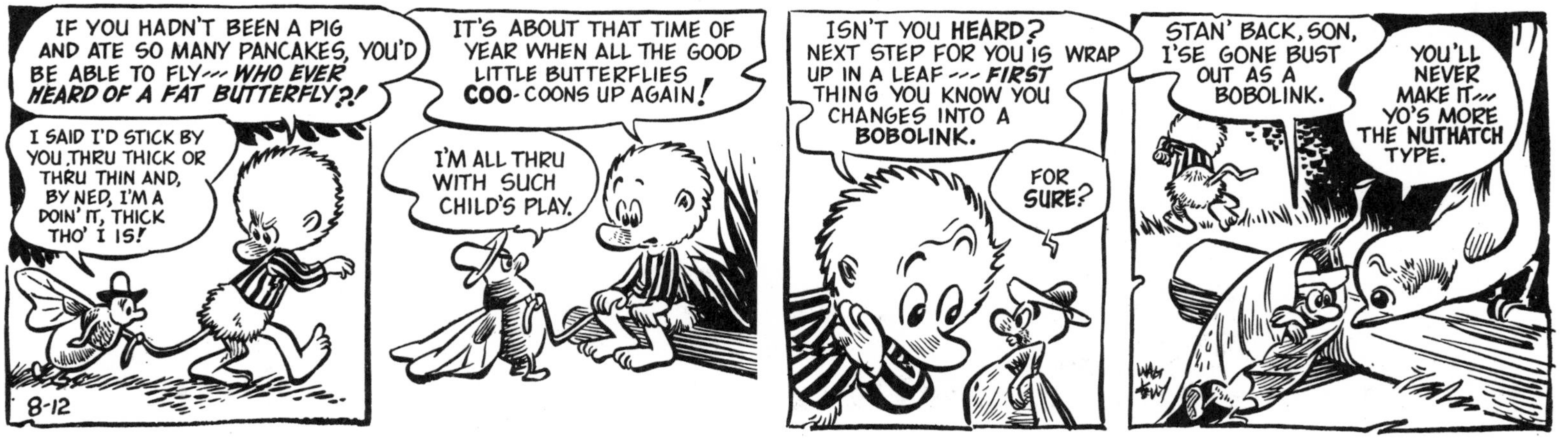
IF YOU HADN'T BEEN A PIG AND ATE SO MANY PANCAKES, YOU'D BE ABLE TO FLY--- WHO EVER HEARD OF A FAT BUTTERFLY?!
I SAID I'D STICK BY YOU THRU THICK OR THRU THIN AND, BY NED, I'M A DOIN' IT, THICK THO' I IS!
8-12
IT'S ABOUT THAT TIME OF YEAR WHEN ALL THE GOOD LITTLE BUTTERFLIES COO-COONS UP AGAIN!
I'M ALL THRU WITH SUCH CHILD'S PLAY.
ISN'T YOU HEARD? NEXT STEP FOR YOU IS WRAP UP IN A LEAF --- FIRST THING YOU KNOW YOU CHANGES INTO A BOBOLINK.
FOR SURE?
STAN' BACK, SON, I'SE GONE BUST OUT AS A BOBOLINK.
YOU'LL NEVER MAKE IT--- YO'S MORE THE NUTHATCH TYPE.

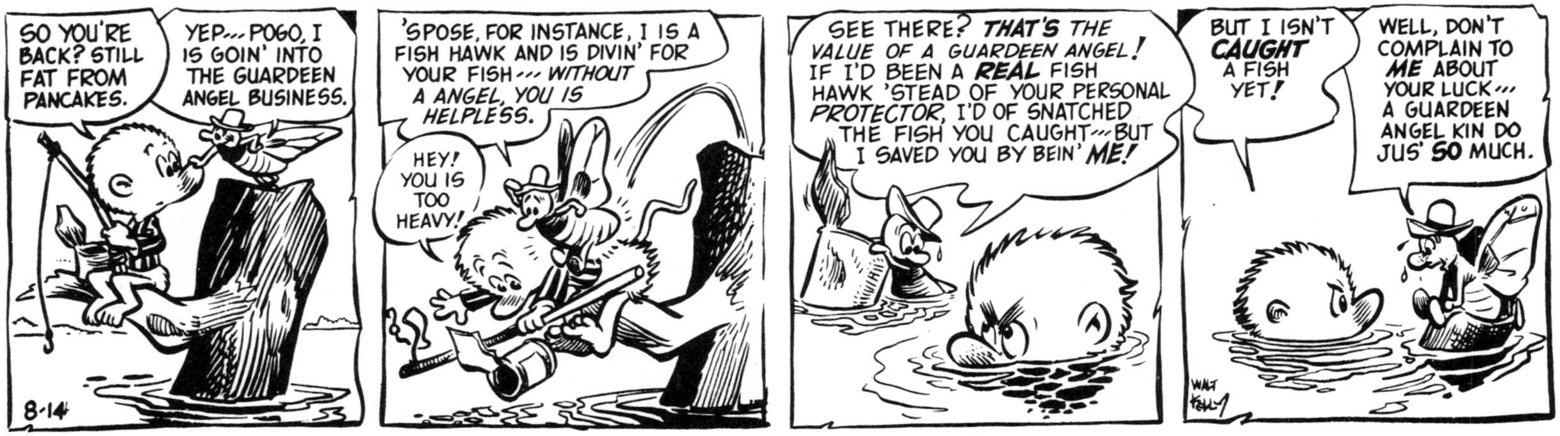
SO YOU'RE BACK? STILL FAT FROM PANCAKES.
YEP... POGO, I IS GOIN' INTO THE GUARDEEN ANGEL BUSINESS.
8-14
'SPOSE, FOR INSTANCE, I IS A FISH HAWK AND IS DIVIN' FOR YOUR FISH... WITHOUT A ANGEL, YOU IS HELPLESS.
HEY! YOU IS TOO HEAVY!
SEE THERE? THAT'S THE VALUE OF A GUARDEEN ANGEL! IF I'D BEEN A REAL FISH HAWK 'STEAD OF YOUR PERSONAL PROTECTOR, I'D OF SNATCHED THE FISH YOU CAUGHT... BUT I SAVED YOU BY BEIN' ME!
BUT I ISN'T CAUGHT A FISH YET!
WELL, DON'T COMPLAIN TO ME ABOUT YOUR LUCK... A GUARDEEN ANGEL KIN DO JUS' SO MUCH.
WALT KELLY

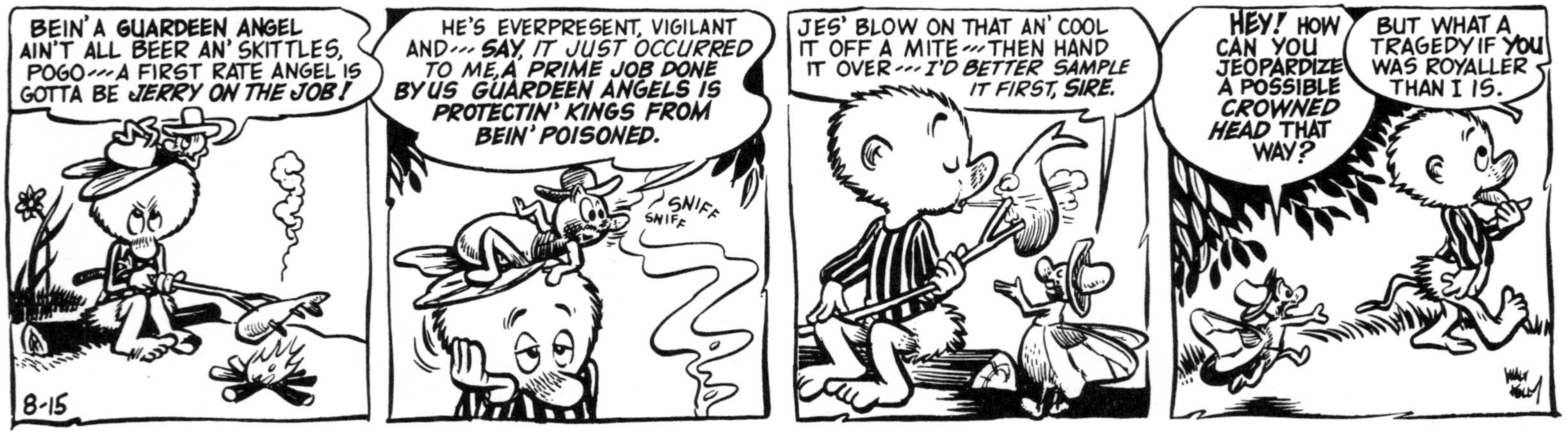
BEIN' A GUARDEEN ANGEL AIN'T ALL BEER AN' SKITTLES, POGO... A FIRST RATE ANGEL IS GOTTA BE JERRY ON THE JOB!
8-15
HE'S EVERPRESENT, VIGILANT AND... SAY, IT JUST OCCURRED TO ME, A PRIME JOB DONE BY US GUARDEEN ANGELS IS PROTECTIN' KINGS FROM BEIN' POISONED.
SNIFF SNIFF
JES' BLOW ON THAT AN' COOL IT OFF A MITE... THEN HAND IT OVER... I'D BETTER SAMPLE IT FIRST, SIRE.
HEY! HOW CAN YOU JEOPARDIZE A POSSIBLE CROWNED HEAD THAT WAY?
BUT WHAT A TRAGEDY IF YOU WAS ROYALLER THAN I IS.
WALT KELLY

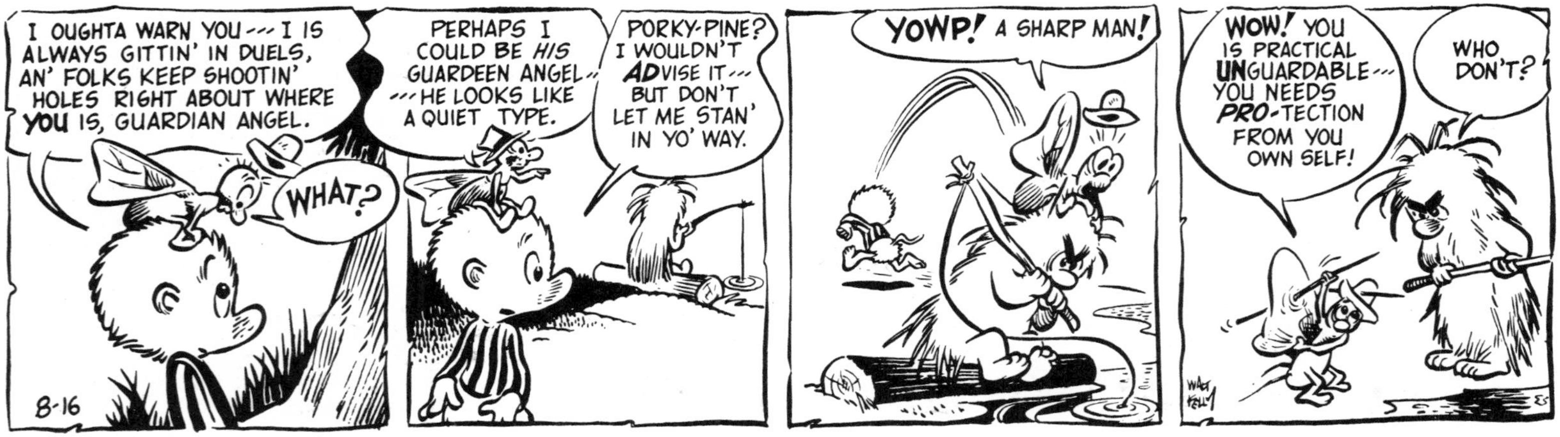
I OUGHTA WARN YOU... I IS ALWAYS GITTIN' IN DUELS, AN' FOLKS KEEP SHOOTIN' HOLES RIGHT ABOUT WHERE YOU IS, GUARDIAN ANGEL.
WHAT?
8-16
PERHAPS I COULD BE HIS GUARDEEN ANGEL... HE LOOKS LIKE A QUIET TYPE.
PORKY-PINE? I WOULDN'T ADVISE IT... BUT DON'T LET ME STAN' IN YO' WAY.
YOWP! A SHARP MAN!
WOW! YOU IS PRACTICAL UNGUARDABLE... YOU NEEDS PRO-TECTION FROM YOU OWN SELF!
WHO DON'T?
WALT KELLY

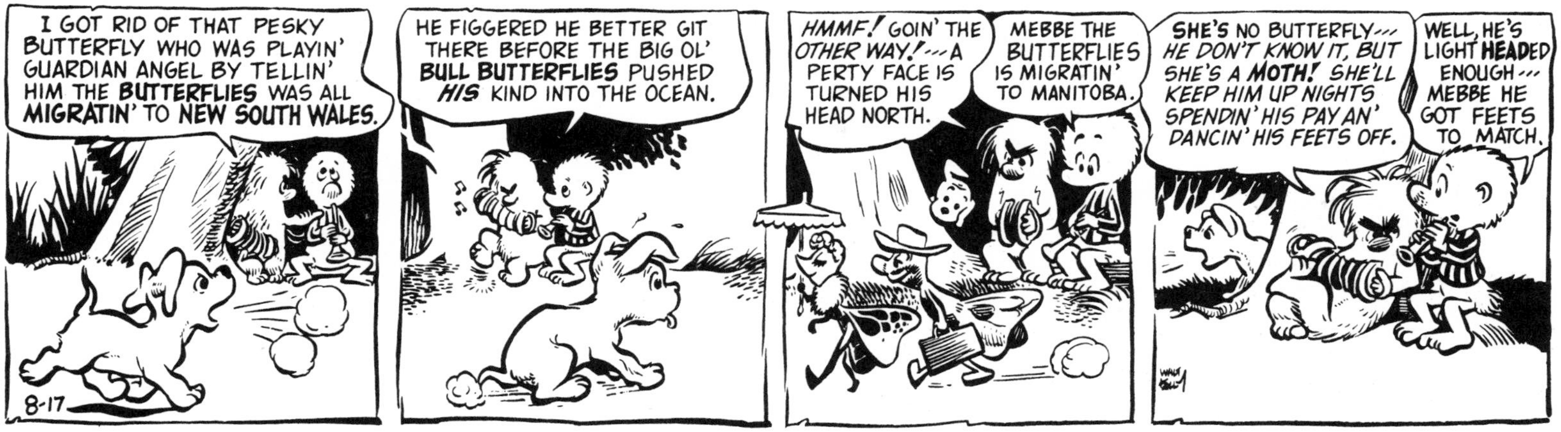
I GOT RID OF THAT PESKY BUTTERFLY WHO WAS PLAYIN' GUARDIAN ANGEL BY TELLIN' HIM THE **BUTTERFLIES** WAS ALL **MIGRATIN'** TO **NEW SOUTH WALES**.
8-17
HE FIGGERED HE BETTER GIT THERE BEFORE THE BIG OL' **BULL BUTTERFLIES** PUSHED ***HIS*** KIND INTO THE OCEAN.
HMMF! GOIN' THE *OTHER WAY!*--- A PERTY FACE IS TURNED HIS HEAD NORTH.
MEBBE THE BUTTERFLIES IS MIGRATIN' TO MANITOBA.
SHE'S NO BUTTERFLY--- *HE DON'T KNOW IT, BUT SHE'S A* **MOTH!** *SHE'LL KEEP HIM UP NIGHTS SPENDIN' HIS PAY AN' DANCIN' HIS FEETS OFF.*
WELL, HE'S LIGHT **HEADED** ENOUGH--- MEBBE HE GOT FEETS TO MATCH.

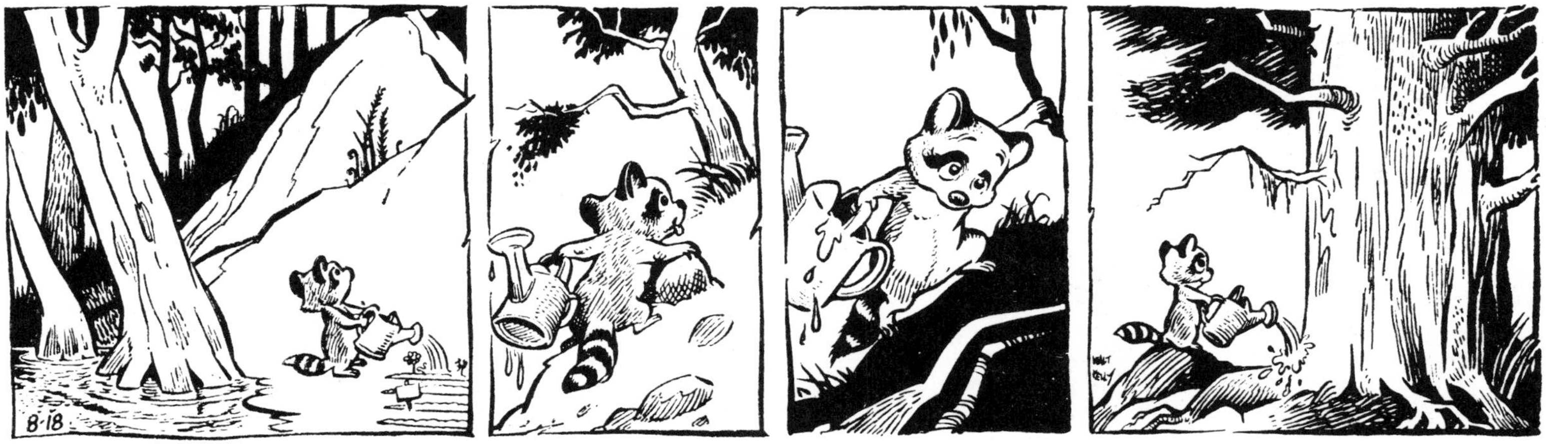
8-18

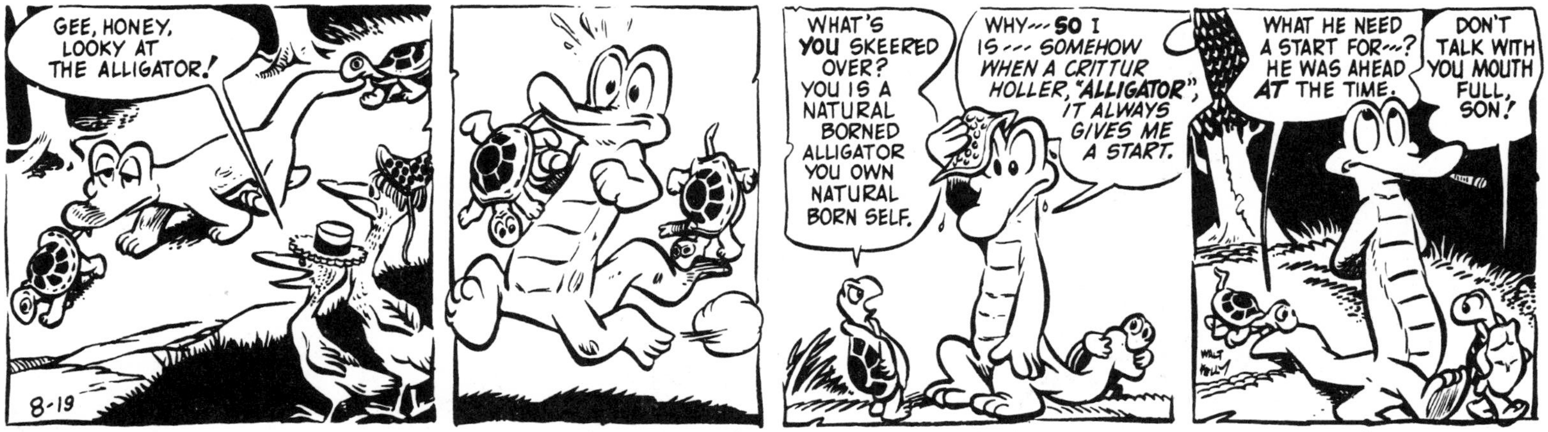
GEE, HONEY, LOOKY AT THE ALLIGATOR!
8-19
WHAT'S **YOU** SKEERED OVER? YOU IS A NATURAL BORNED ALLIGATOR YOU OWN NATURAL BORN SELF.
WHY--- **SO** I IS--- *SOMEHOW WHEN A CRITTUR HOLLER,* ***"ALLIGATOR"***, *IT ALWAYS GIVES ME A START.*
WHAT HE NEED A START FOR---? HE WAS AHEAD ***AT*** THE TIME.
DON'T TALK WITH YOU MOUTH FULL, SON!

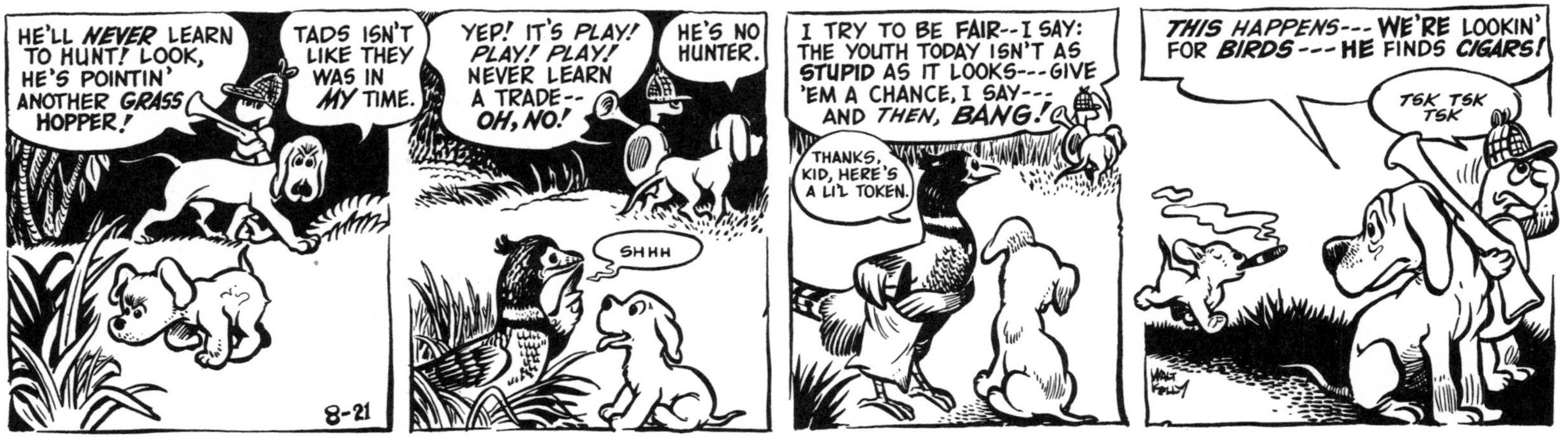
HE'LL **NEVER** LEARN TO HUNT! LOOK, HE'S POINTIN' ANOTHER **GRASS HOPPER!**
TADS ISN'T LIKE THEY WAS IN *MY* TIME.
8-21
YEP! IT'S *PLAY! PLAY! PLAY!* NEVER LEARN A TRADE-- **OH, NO!**
HE'S NO HUNTER.
SHHH
I TRY TO BE **FAIR**--I SAY: THE YOUTH TODAY ISN'T AS **STUPID** AS IT LOOKS---GIVE 'EM A CHANCE, I SAY--- AND *THEN*, **BANG!**
THANKS, KID, HERE'S A LI'L TOKEN.
THIS HAPPENS--- **WE'RE** LOOKIN' FOR **BIRDS**--- **HE** FINDS **CIGARS!**
TSK TSK TSK
WALT KELLY

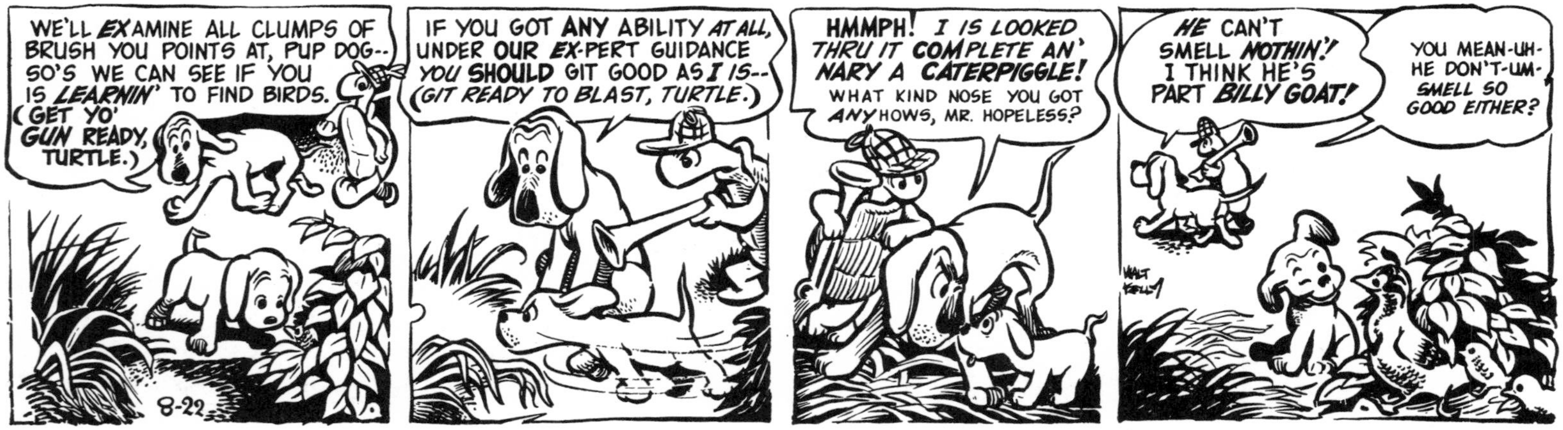
WE'LL ***EX***AMINE ALL CLUMPS OF BRUSH YOU POINTS AT, PUP DOG-- SO'S WE CAN SEE IF YOU IS ***LEARNIN'*** TO FIND BIRDS.
(GET YO' **GUN** READY, TURTLE.)
8-22
IF YOU GOT **ANY** ABILITY *AT ALL*, UNDER **OUR *EX***-PERT GUIDANCE *YOU* **SHOULD** GIT GOOD AS *I IS*-- (*GIT READY TO BLAST, TURTLE.*)
HMMPH! *I IS LOOKED THRU IT* **COM***PLETE AN'* ***NARY A CATERPIGGLE!*** WHAT KIND NOSE YOU GOT ***ANY***HOWS, MR. HOPELESS?
HE CAN'T SMELL ***NOTHIN'!*** I THINK HE'S PART ***BILLY GOAT!***
YOU MEAN-UH- HE DON'T-UM- *SMELL SO GOOD EITHER?*
WALT KELLY

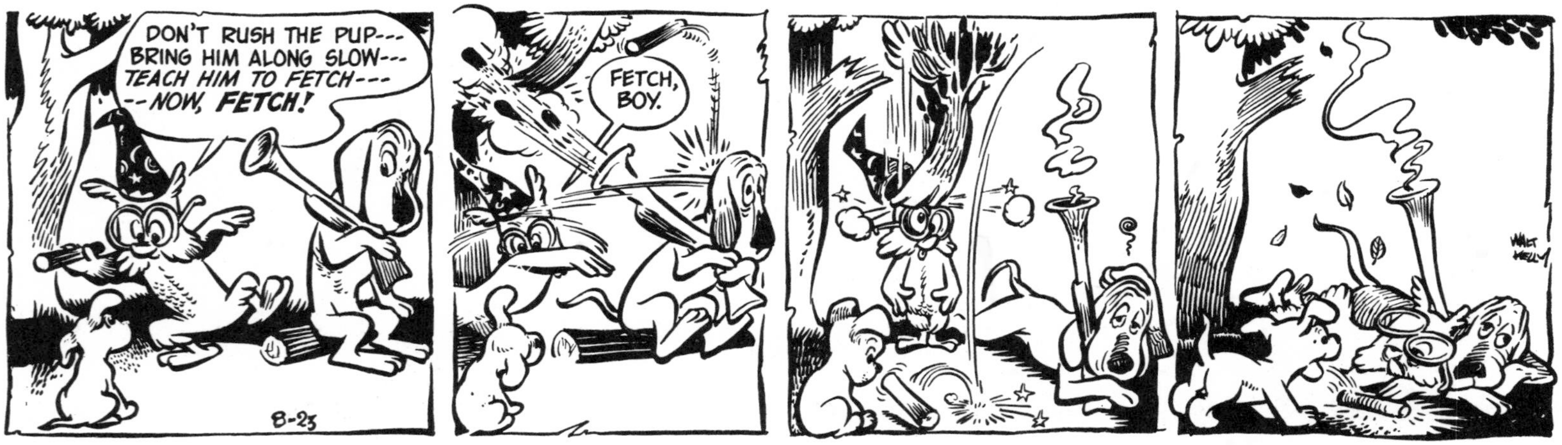
DON'T RUSH THE PUP--- BRING HIM ALONG SLOW--- *TEACH HIM TO FETCH*--- --*NOW*, **FETCH!**
8-23
FETCH, BOY.
WALT KELLY

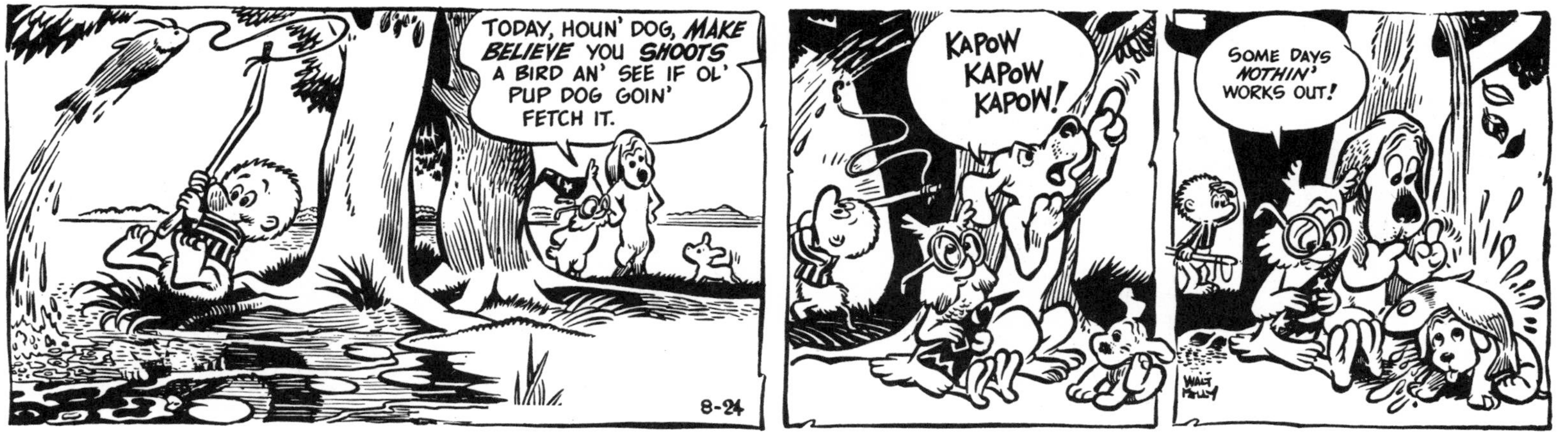
TODAY, HOUN' DOG, MAKE BELIEVE YOU SHOOTS A BIRD AN' SEE IF OL' PUP DOG GOIN' FETCH IT.
8-24
KAPOW KAPOW KAPOW!
SOME DAYS NOTHIN' WORKS OUT!
WALT KELLY

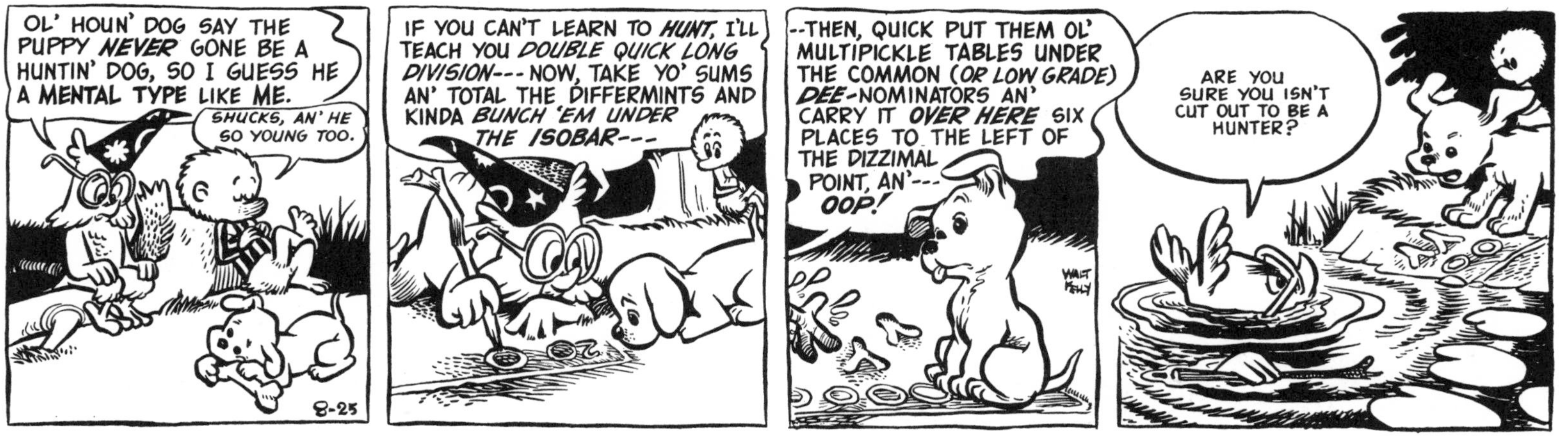
OL' HOUN' DOG SAY THE PUPPY NEVER GONE BE A HUNTIN' DOG, SO I GUESS HE A MENTAL TYPE LIKE ME.
SHUCKS, AN' HE SO YOUNG TOO.
8-25
IF YOU CAN'T LEARN TO HUNT, I'LL TEACH YOU DOUBLE QUICK LONG DIVISION--- NOW, TAKE YO' SUMS AN' TOTAL THE DIFFERMINTS AND KINDA BUNCH 'EM UNDER THE ISOBAR---
--THEN, QUICK PUT THEM OL' MULTIPICKLE TABLES UNDER THE COMMON (OR LOW GRADE) DEE-NOMINATORS AN' CARRY IT OVER HERE SIX PLACES TO THE LEFT OF THE DIZZIMAL POINT, AN'--- OOP!
WALT KELLY
ARE YOU SURE YOU ISN'T CUT OUT TO BE A HUNTER?

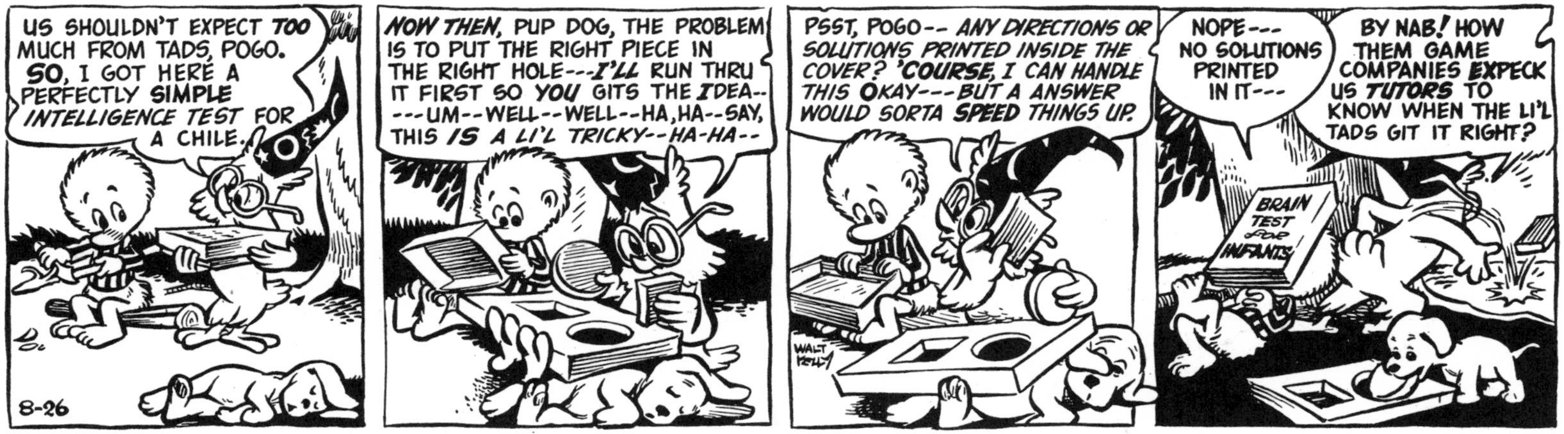
US SHOULDN'T EXPECT TOO MUCH FROM TADS, POGO. SO, I GOT HERE A PERFECTLY SIMPLE INTELLIGENCE TEST FOR A CHILE.
8-26
NOW THEN, PUP DOG, THE PROBLEM IS TO PUT THE RIGHT PIECE IN THE RIGHT HOLE---I'LL RUN THRU IT FIRST SO YOU GITS THE IDEA-- ---UM--WELL--WELL--HA,HA--SAY, THIS IS A LI'L TRICKY--HA-HA--
PSST, POGO-- ANY DIRECTIONS OR SOLUTIONS PRINTED INSIDE THE COVER? 'COURSE, I CAN HANDLE THIS OKAY---BUT A ANSWER WOULD SORTA SPEED THINGS UP.
WALT KELLY
NOPE--- NO SOLUTIONS PRINTED IN IT---
BY NAB! HOW THEM GAME COMPANIES EXPECK US TUTORS TO KNOW WHEN THE LI'L TADS GIT IT RIGHT?
BRAIN TEST FOR INFANTS

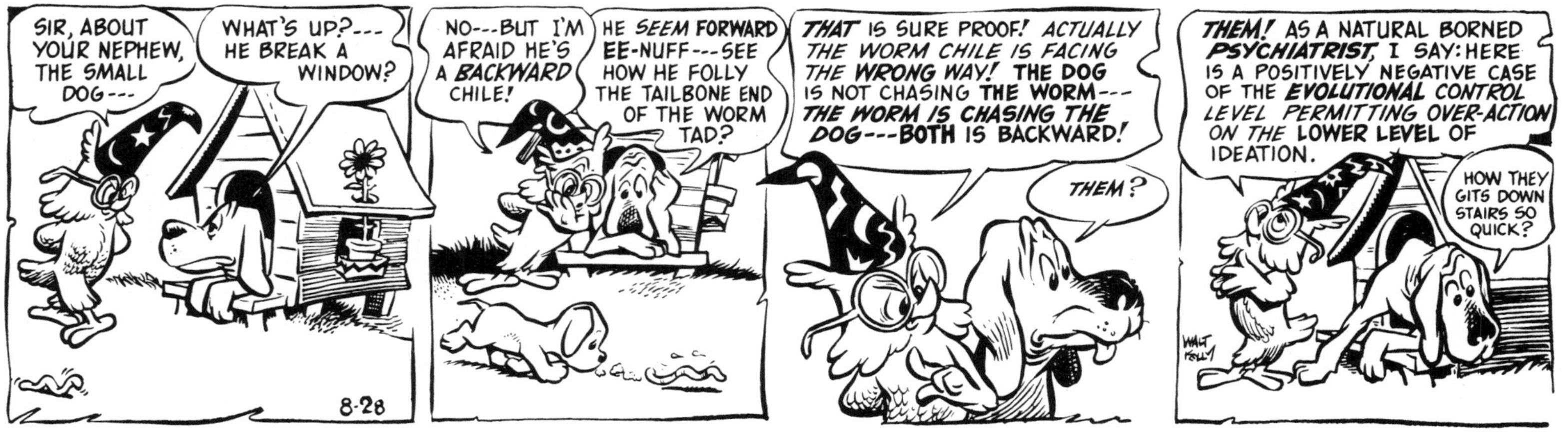
SIR, ABOUT YOUR NEPHEW, THE SMALL DOG---
WHAT'S UP?--- HE BREAK A WINDOW?
8-28
NO---BUT I'M AFRAID HE'S A BACKWARD CHILE!
HE SEEM FORWARD EE-NUFF---SEE HOW HE FOLLY THE TAILBONE END OF THE WORM TAD?
THAT IS SURE PROOF! ACTUALLY THE WORM CHILE IS FACING THE WRONG WAY! THE DOG IS NOT CHASING THE WORM--- THE WORM IS CHASING THE DOG---BOTH IS BACKWARD!
THEM?
THEM! AS A NATURAL BORNED PSYCHIATRIST, I SAY: HERE IS A POSITIVELY NEGATIVE CASE OF THE EVOLUTIONAL CONTROL LEVEL PERMITTING OVER-ACTION ON THE LOWER LEVEL OF IDEATION.
HOW THEY GITS DOWN STAIRS SO QUICK?
WALT KELLY

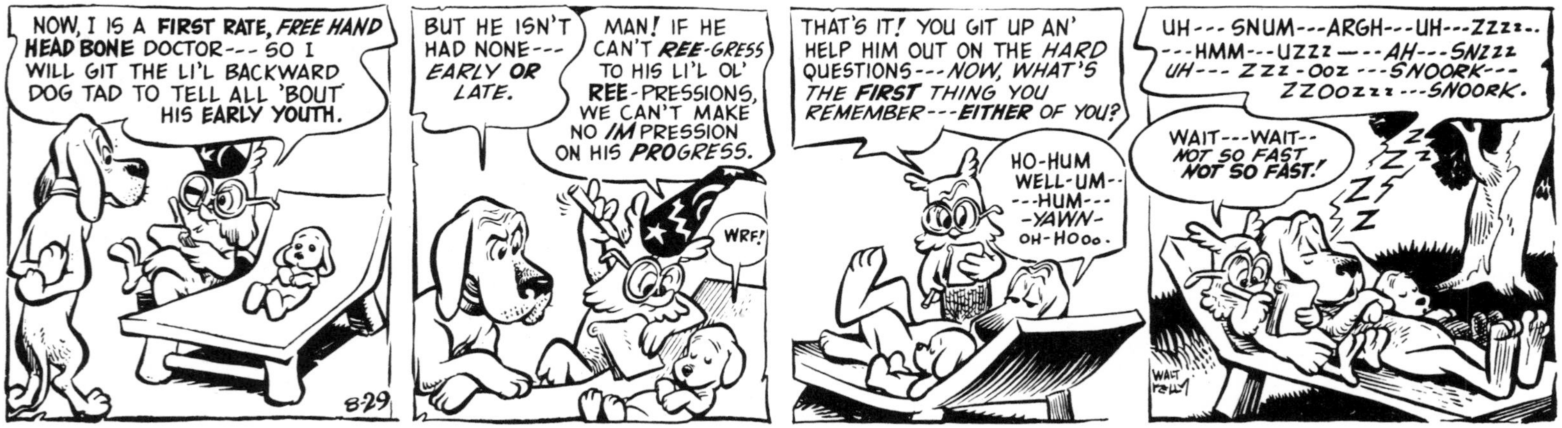
NOW, I IS A FIRST RATE, FREE HAND HEAD BONE DOCTOR--- SO I WILL GIT THE LI'L BACKWARD DOG TAD TO TELL ALL 'BOUT HIS EARLY YOUTH.
8-29
BUT HE ISN'T HAD NONE--- EARLY OR LATE.
MAN! IF HE CAN'T REE-GRESS TO HIS LI'L OL' REE-PRESSIONS, WE CAN'T MAKE NO IM PRESSION ON HIS PROGRESS.
WRF!
THAT'S IT! YOU GIT UP AN' HELP HIM OUT ON THE HARD QUESTIONS---NOW, WHAT'S THE FIRST THING YOU REMEMBER---EITHER OF YOU?
HO-HUM WELL-UM-- --HUM--- -YAWN- OH-HOOo.
UH---SNUM---ARGH---UH---ZZZZ.. ---HMM---UZZZ — --AH---SNZZZ UH--- ZZZ-OOZ ---SNOORK--- ZZOOZZZ ---SNOORK.
WAIT---WAIT-- NOT SO FAST NOT SO FAST!
WALT KELLY

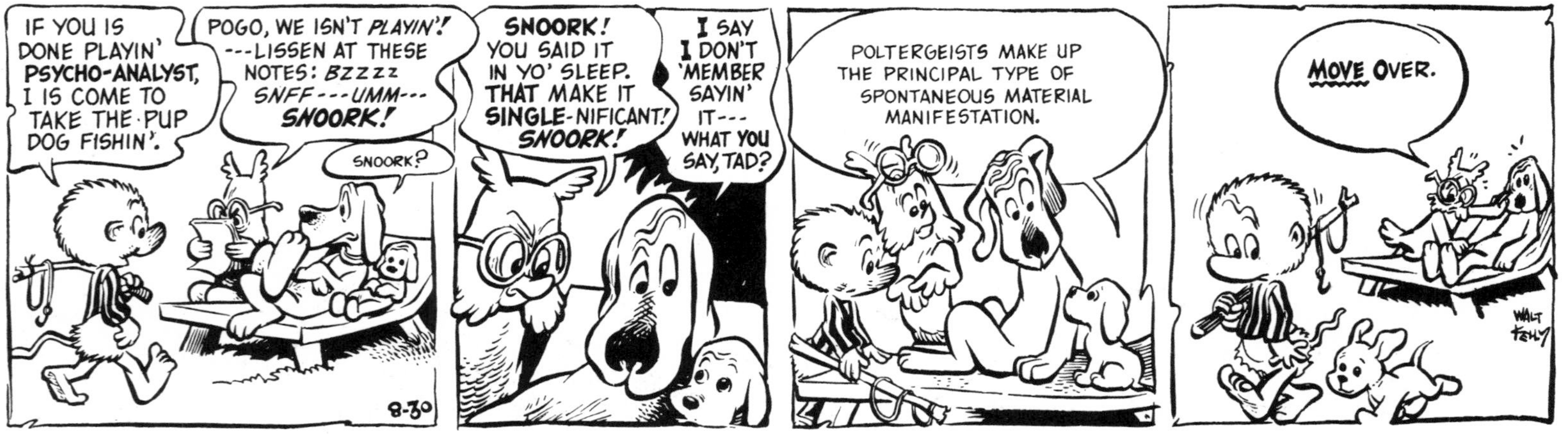
IF YOU IS DONE PLAYIN' PSYCHO-ANALYST, I IS COME TO TAKE THE PUP DOG FISHIN'.
POGO, WE ISN'T PLAYIN'! ---LISSEN AT THESE NOTES: BZZZZ SNFF---UMM--- SNOORK!
SNOORK?
8-30
SNOORK! YOU SAID IT IN YO' SLEEP. THAT MAKE IT SINGLE-NIFICANT! SNOORK!
I SAY I DON'T 'MEMBER SAYIN' IT--- WHAT YOU SAY, TAD?
POLTERGEISTS MAKE UP THE PRINCIPAL TYPE OF SPONTANEOUS MATERIAL MANIFESTATION.
MOVE OVER.
WALT KELLY

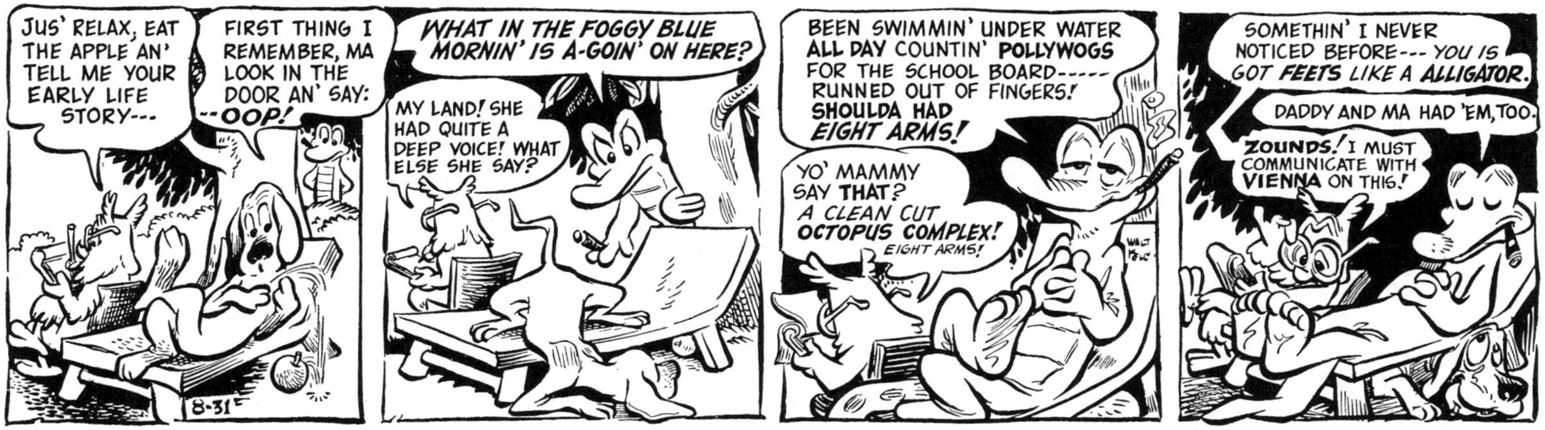
JUS' RELAX, EAT THE APPLE AN' TELL ME YOUR EARLY LIFE STORY---
FIRST THING I REMEMBER, MA LOOK IN THE DOOR AN' SAY: --OOP!
8-31
WHAT IN THE FOGGY BLUE MORNIN' IS A-GOIN' ON HERE?
MY LAND! SHE HAD QUITE A DEEP VOICE! WHAT ELSE SHE SAY?
BEEN SWIMMIN' UNDER WATER ALL DAY COUNTIN' POLLYWOGS FOR THE SCHOOL BOARD----- RUNNED OUT OF FINGERS! SHOULDA HAD EIGHT ARMS!
YO' MAMMY SAY THAT? A CLEAN CUT OCTOPUS COMPLEX! EIGHT ARMS!
SOMETHIN' I NEVER NOTICED BEFORE--- YOU IS GOT FEETS LIKE A ALLIGATOR.
DADDY AND MA HAD 'EM, TOO.
ZOUNDS! I MUST COMMUNICATE WITH VIENNA ON THIS!

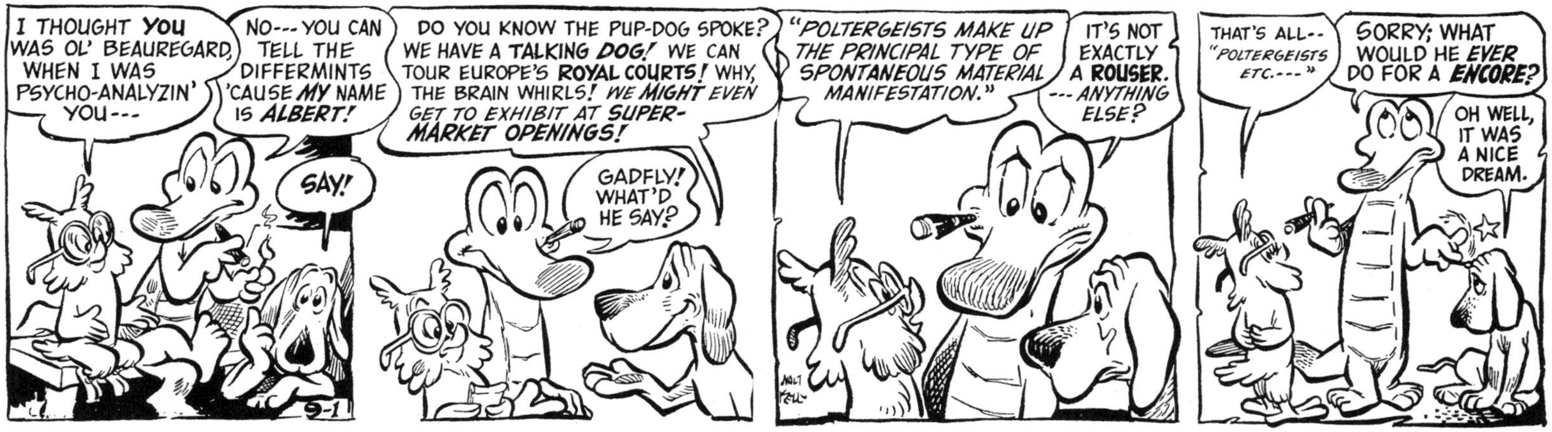
I THOUGHT YOU WAS OL' BEAUREGARD WHEN I WAS PSYCHO-ANALYZIN' YOU---
NO---YOU CAN TELL THE DIFFERMINTS 'CAUSE MY NAME IS ALBERT!
SAY!
9-1
DO YOU KNOW THE PUP-DOG SPOKE? WE HAVE A TALKING DOG! WE CAN TOUR EUROPE'S ROYAL COURTS! WHY, THE BRAIN WHIRLS! WE MIGHT EVEN GET TO EXHIBIT AT SUPER-MARKET OPENINGS!
GADFLY! WHAT'D HE SAY?
"POLTERGEISTS MAKE UP THE PRINCIPAL TYPE OF SPONTANEOUS MATERIAL MANIFESTATION."
IT'S NOT EXACTLY A ROUSER. --- ANYTHING ELSE?
THAT'S ALL-- "POLTERGEISTS ETC.---"
SORRY; WHAT WOULD HE EVER DO FOR A ENCORE?
OH WELL, IT WAS A NICE DREAM.

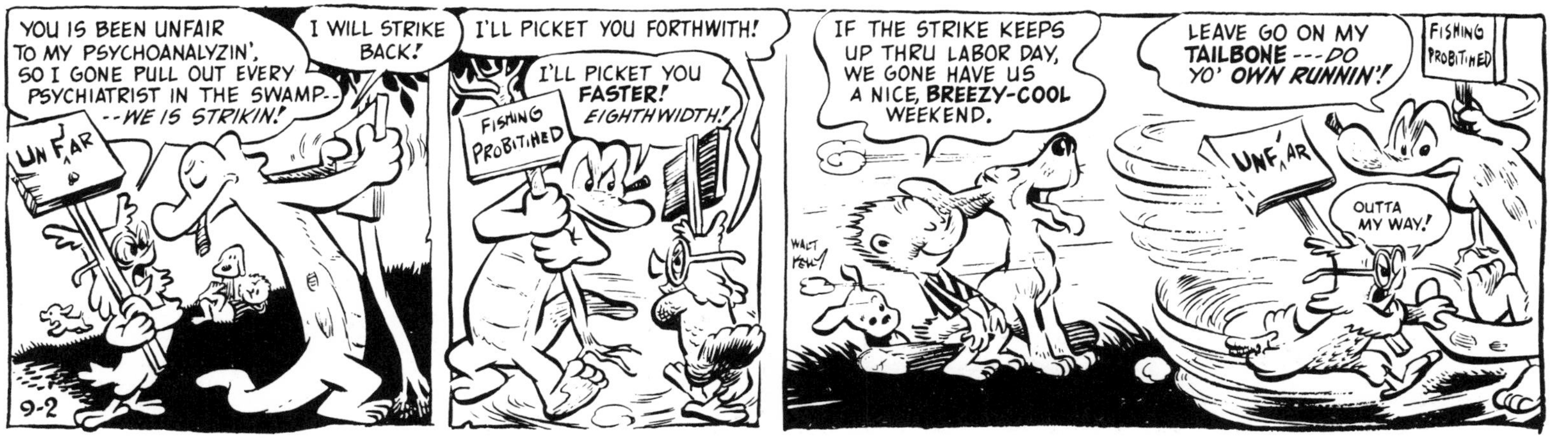
YOU IS BEEN UNFAIR TO MY PSYCHOANALYZIN', SO I GONE PULL OUT EVERY PSYCHIATRIST IN THE SWAMP-- --WE IS STRIKIN'!
I WILL STRIKE BACK!
UN FAR
9-2
I'LL PICKET YOU FORTHWITH!
I'LL PICKET YOU FASTER! EIGHTHWIDTH!
FISHING PROBITIHED
IF THE STRIKE KEEPS UP THRU LABOR DAY, WE GONE HAVE US A NICE, BREEZY-COOL WEEKEND.
LEAVE GO ON MY TAILBONE ---DO YO' OWN RUNNIN'!
FISHING PROBITIHED
UNF AR
OUTTA MY WAY!

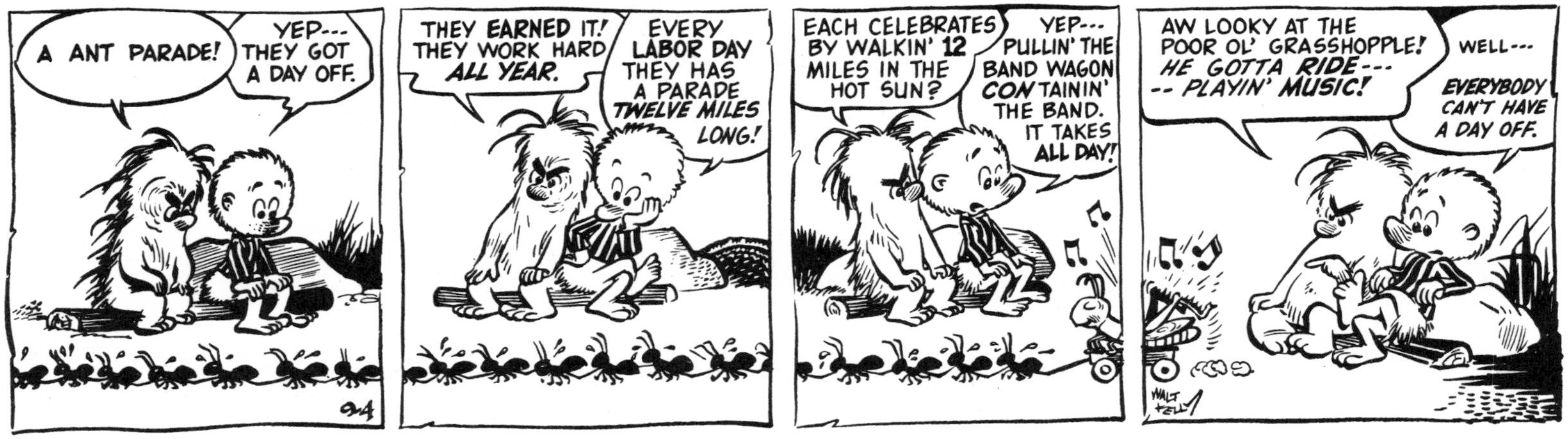
A ANT PARADE!
YEP--- THEY GOT A DAY OFF.
THEY EARNED IT! THEY WORK HARD ALL YEAR.
EVERY LABOR DAY THEY HAS A PARADE TWELVE MILES LONG!
EACH CELEBRATES BY WALKIN' 12 MILES IN THE HOT SUN?
YEP--- PULLIN' THE BAND WAGON CONTAININ' THE BAND. IT TAKES ALL DAY!
AW LOOKY AT THE POOR OL' GRASSHOPPLE! HE GOTTA RIDE--- -- PLAYIN' MUSIC!
WELL---
EVERYBODY CAN'T HAVE A DAY OFF.
9-4
WALT KELLY

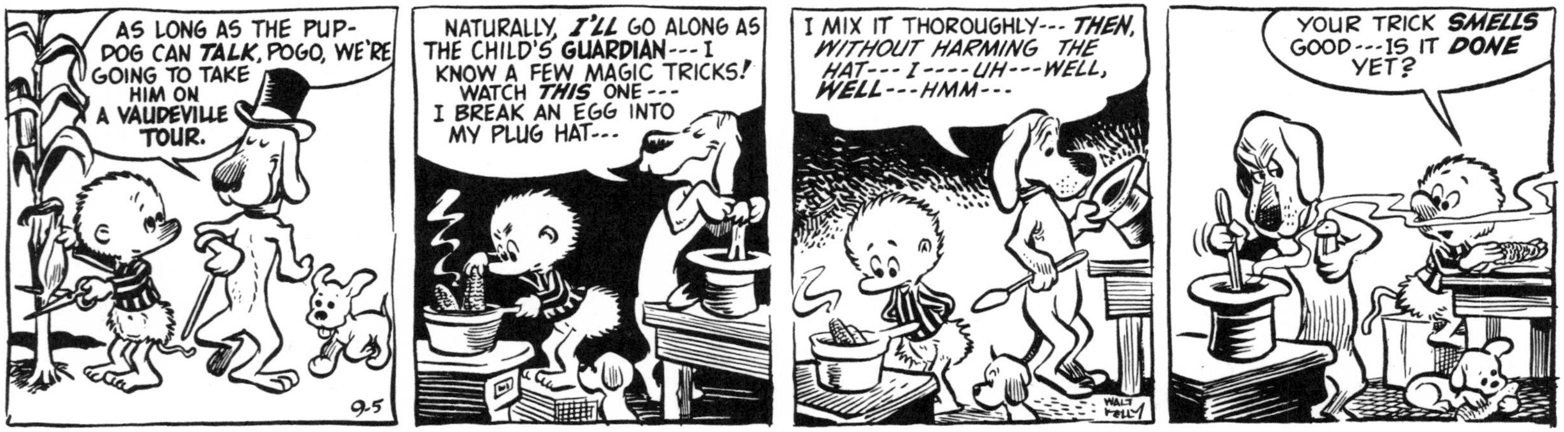
AS LONG AS THE PUP-DOG CAN TALK, POGO, WE'RE GOING TO TAKE HIM ON A VAUDEVILLE TOUR.
9-5
NATURALLY, I'LL GO ALONG AS THE CHILD'S GUARDIAN--- I KNOW A FEW MAGIC TRICKS! WATCH THIS ONE--- I BREAK AN EGG INTO MY PLUG HAT---
I MIX IT THOROUGHLY--- THEN, WITHOUT HARMING THE HAT--- I----UH---WELL, WELL---HMM---
WALT KELLY
YOUR TRICK SMELLS GOOD---IS IT DONE YET?

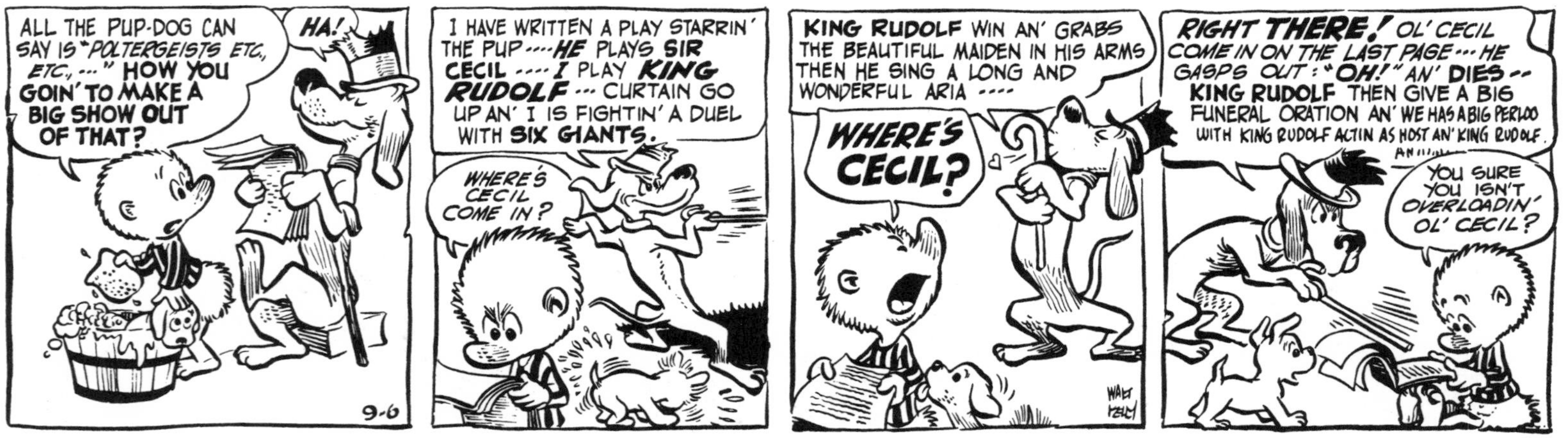
ALL THE PUP-DOG CAN SAY IS "POLTERGEISTS ETC, ETC., ..." HOW YOU GOIN' TO MAKE A BIG SHOW OUT OF THAT?
HA!
9-6
I HAVE WRITTEN A PLAY STARRIN' THE PUP----HE PLAYS SIR CECIL ----I PLAY KING RUDOLF --- CURTAIN GO UP AN' I IS FIGHTIN' A DUEL WITH SIX GIANTS.
WHERE'S CECIL COME IN?
KING RUDOLF WIN AN' GRABS THE BEAUTIFUL MAIDEN IN HIS ARMS THEN HE SING A LONG AND WONDERFUL ARIA ----
WHERE'S CECIL?
WALT KELLY
RIGHT THERE! OL' CECIL COME IN ON THE LAST PAGE--- HE GASPS OUT: "OH!" AN' DIES -- KING RUDOLF THEN GIVE A BIG FUNERAL ORATION AN' WE HAS A BIG PERLOO WITH KING RUDOLF ACTIN AS HOST AN' KING RUDOLF.
YOU SURE YOU ISN'T OVERLOADIN' OL' CECIL?

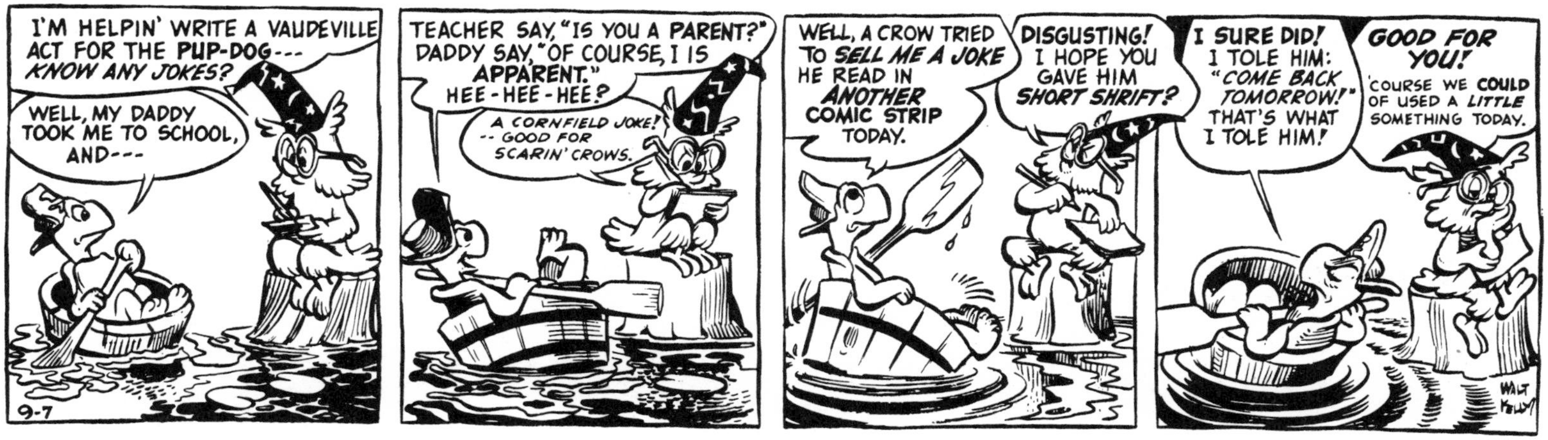
I'M HELPIN' WRITE A VAUDEVILLE ACT FOR THE PUP-DOG--- KNOW ANY JOKES?
WELL, MY DADDY TOOK ME TO SCHOOL, AND---
9-7
TEACHER SAY, "IS YOU A PARENT?" DADDY SAY, "OF COURSE, I IS APPARENT." HEE-HEE-HEE?
A CORNFIELD JOKE! -- GOOD FOR SCARIN' CROWS.
WELL, A CROW TRIED TO SELL ME A JOKE HE READ IN ANOTHER COMIC STRIP TODAY.
DISGUSTING! I HOPE YOU GAVE HIM SHORT SHRIFT?
I SURE DID! I TOLE HIM: "COME BACK TOMORROW!" THAT'S WHAT I TOLE HIM!
GOOD FOR YOU!
'COURSE WE COULD OF USED A LITTLE SOMETHING TODAY.
WALT KELLY

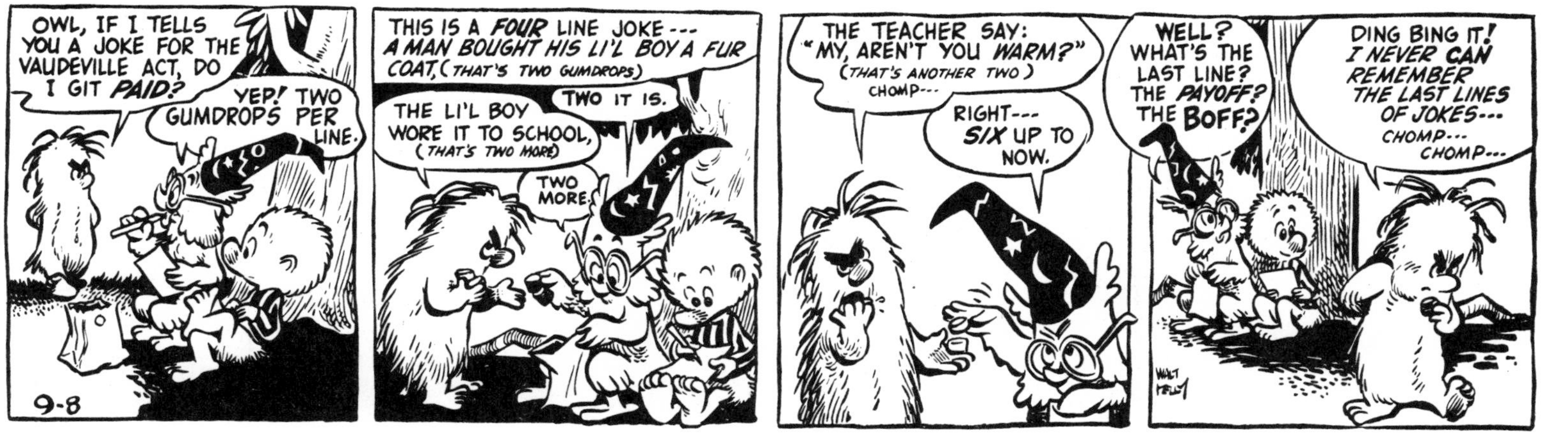
OWL, IF I TELLS YOU A JOKE FOR THE VAUDEVILLE ACT, DO I GIT PAID?
YEP! TWO GUMDROPS PER LINE.
9-8
THIS IS A FOUR LINE JOKE --- A MAN BOUGHT HIS LI'L BOY A FUR COAT, (THAT'S TWO GUMDROPS)
TWO IT IS.
THE LI'L BOY WORE IT TO SCHOOL, (THAT'S TWO MORE)
TWO MORE.
THE TEACHER SAY: "MY, AREN'T YOU WARM?" (THAT'S ANOTHER TWO) CHOMP---
RIGHT--- SIX UP TO NOW.
WELL? WHAT'S THE LAST LINE? THE PAYOFF? THE BOFF?
DING BING IT! I NEVER CAN REMEMBER THE LAST LINES OF JOKES--- CHOMP--- CHOMP---
WALT KELLY

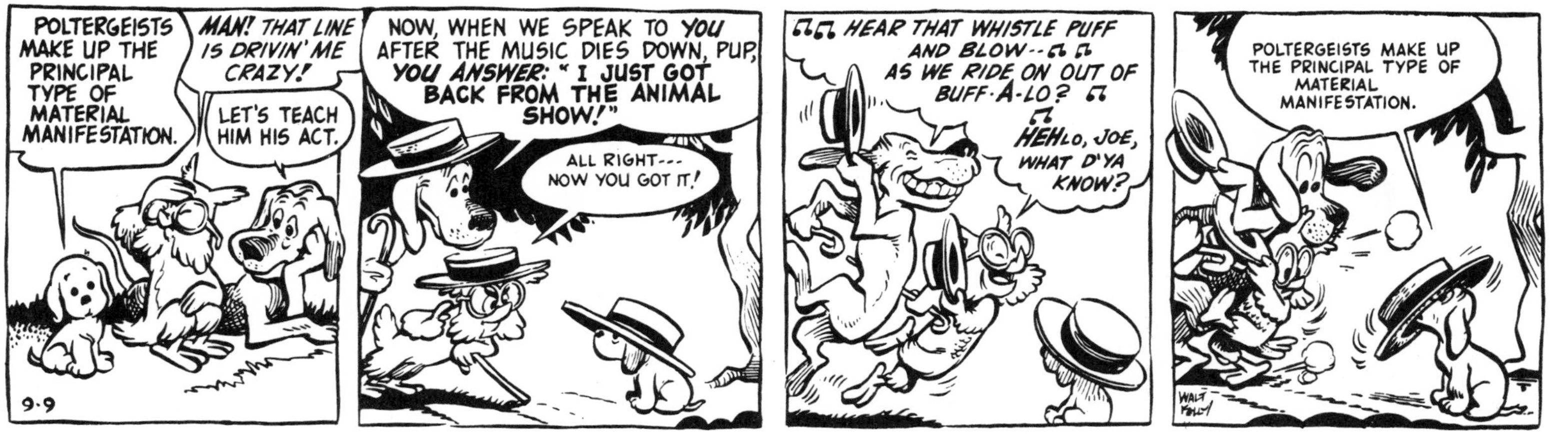
POLTERGEISTS MAKE UP THE PRINCIPAL TYPE OF MATERIAL MANIFESTATION.
MAN! THAT LINE IS DRIVIN' ME CRAZY!
LET'S TEACH HIM HIS ACT.
9-9
NOW, WHEN WE SPEAK TO YOU AFTER THE MUSIC DIES DOWN, PUP, YOU ANSWER: "I JUST GOT BACK FROM THE ANIMAL SHOW!"
ALL RIGHT--- NOW YOU GOT IT!
♫ HEAR THAT WHISTLE PUFF AND BLOW-- ♫ AS WE RIDE ON OUT OF BUFF-A-LO? ♫
♫ HEHLO, JOE, WHAT D'YA KNOW?
POLTERGEISTS MAKE UP THE PRINCIPAL TYPE OF MATERIAL MANIFESTATION.
WALT KELLY

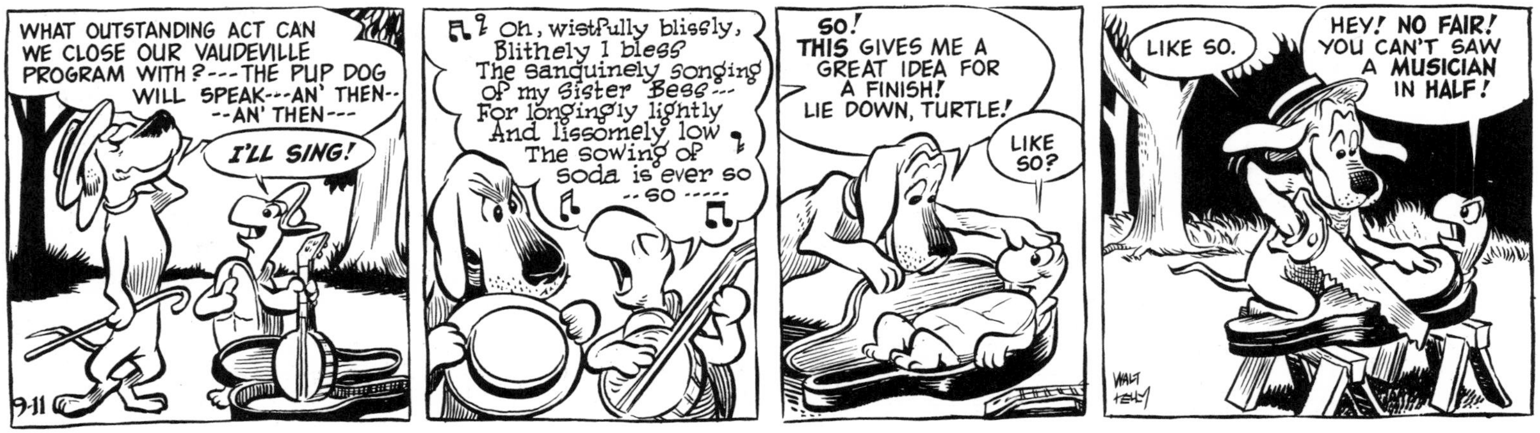
WHAT OUTSTANDING ACT CAN WE CLOSE OUR VAUDEVILLE PROGRAM WITH?---THE PUP DOG WILL SPEAK---AN' THEN-- --AN' THEN---
I'LL SING!
9-11
Oh, wistfully blissly, Blithely I bless The sanquinely songing Of my Sister Bess--- For longingly lightly And lissomely low The sowing of soda is ever so --so -----
SO! THIS GIVES ME A GREAT IDEA FOR A FINISH! LIE DOWN, TURTLE!
LIKE SO?
LIKE SO.
HEY! NO FAIR! YOU CAN'T SAW A MUSICIAN IN HALF!
WALT KELLY

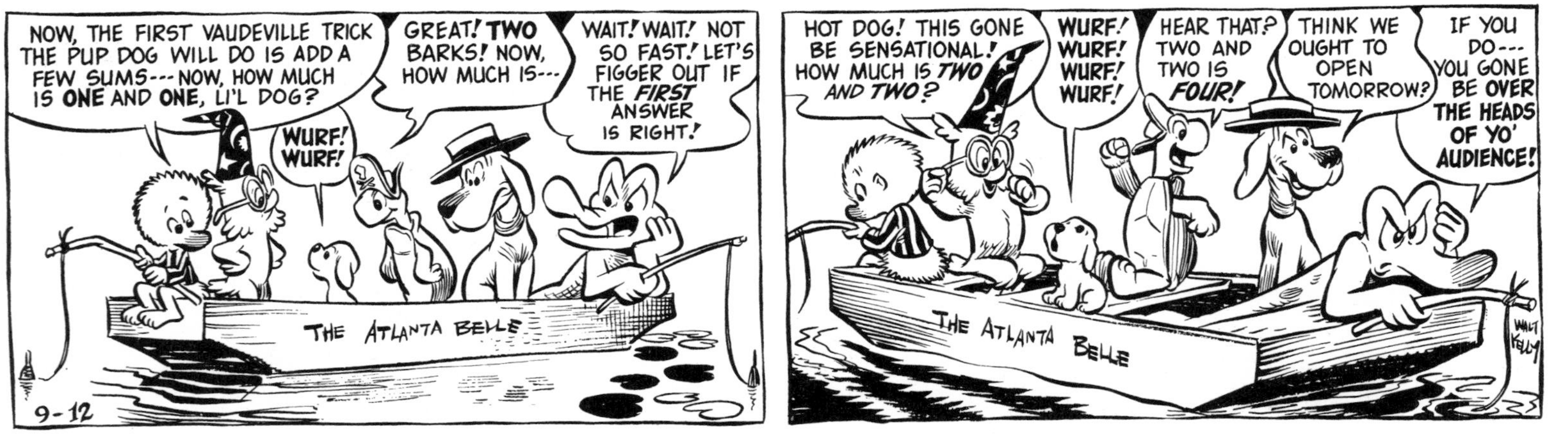
NOW, THE FIRST VAUDEVILLE TRICK THE PUP DOG WILL DO IS ADD A FEW SUMS---NOW, HOW MUCH IS ONE AND ONE, LI'L DOG?
WURF! WURF!
GREAT! TWO BARKS! NOW, HOW MUCH IS---
WAIT! WAIT! NOT SO FAST! LET'S FIGGER OUT IF THE FIRST ANSWER IS RIGHT!
THE ATLANTA BELLE
9-12
HOT DOG! THIS GONE BE SENSATIONAL! HOW MUCH IS TWO AND TWO?
WURF! WURF! WURF! WURF!
HEAR THAT? TWO AND TWO IS FOUR!
THINK WE OUGHT TO OPEN TOMORROW?
IF YOU DO--- YOU GONE BE OVER THE HEADS OF YO' AUDIENCE!
THE ATLANTA BELLE
WALT KELLY

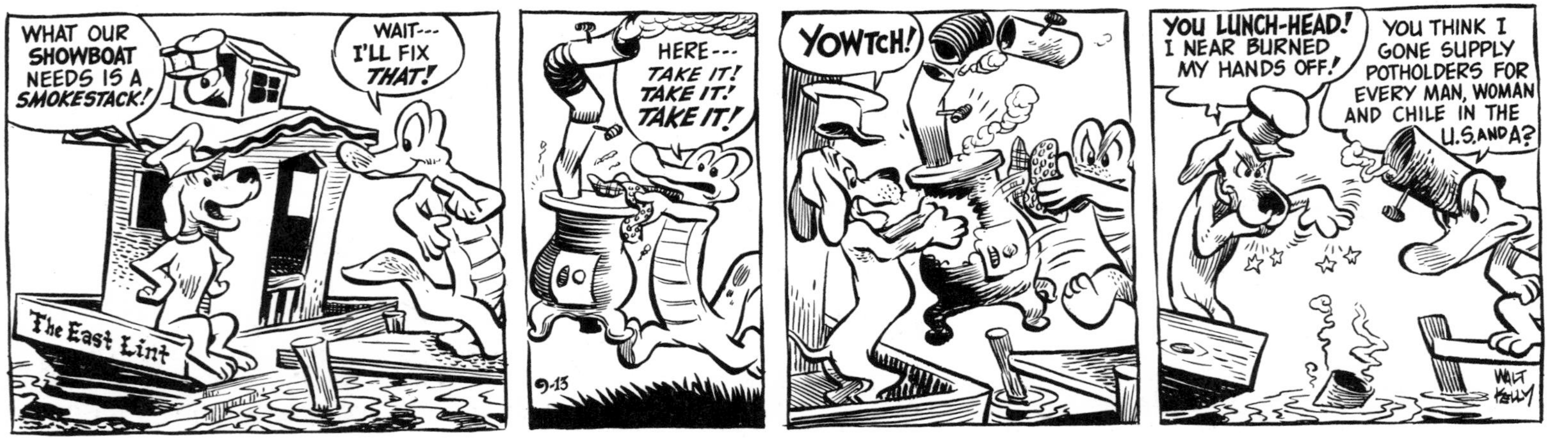
WHAT OUR SHOWBOAT NEEDS IS A SMOKESTACK!
WAIT--- I'LL FIX THAT!
The East Lint
HERE--- TAKE IT! TAKE IT! TAKE IT!
9-13
YOWTCH!
YOU LUNCH-HEAD! I NEAR BURNED MY HANDS OFF!
YOU THINK I GONE SUPPLY POTHOLDERS FOR EVERY MAN, WOMAN AND CHILE IN THE U.S. AND A?
WALT KELLY

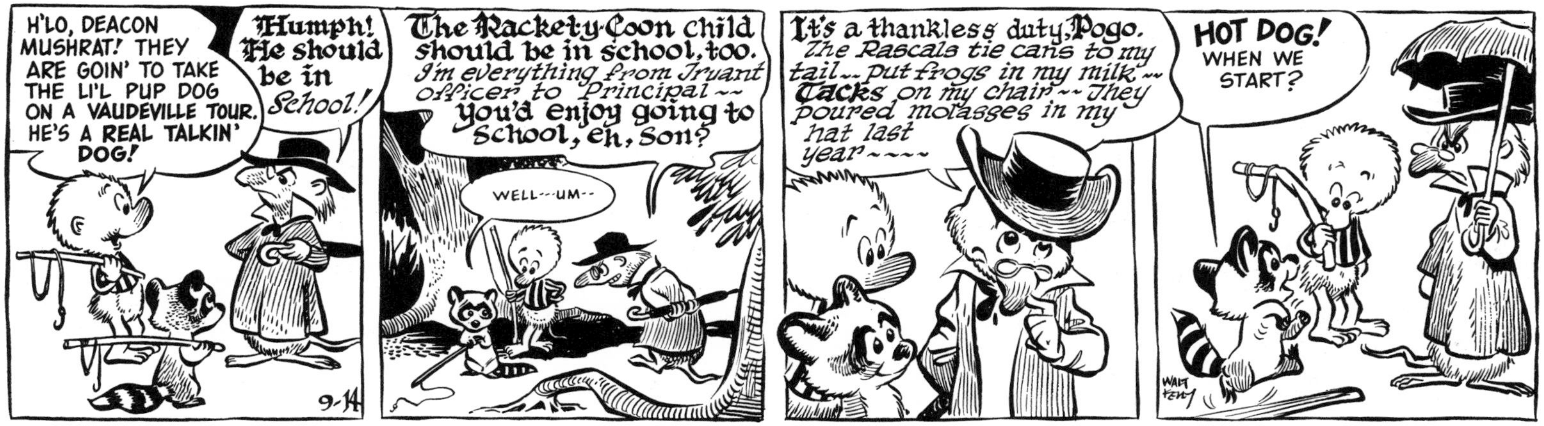
H'LO, DEACON MUSHRAT! THEY ARE GOIN' TO TAKE THE LI'L PUP DOG ON A VAUDEVILLE TOUR. HE'S A REAL TALKIN' DOG!
Humph! He should be in School!
9-14
The Rackety-Coon child should be in school, too. I'm everything from Truant officer to Principal -- You'd enjoy going to School, eh, Son?
WELL---UM--
It's a thankless duty, Pogo. The Rascals tie cans to my tail -- put frogs in my milk -- Tacks on my chair -- They poured molasses in my hat last year ~~~~
HOT DOG! WHEN WE START?
WALT KELLY

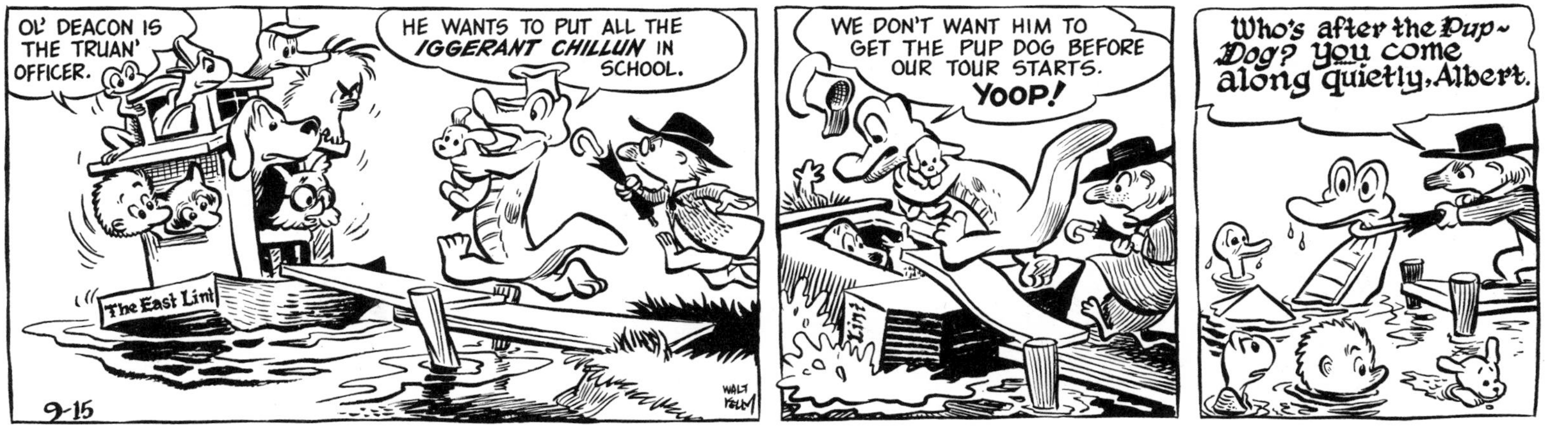
OL' DEACON IS THE TRUAN' OFFICER.
HE WANTS TO PUT ALL THE IGGERANT CHILLUN IN SCHOOL.
The East Lint
9-15
WALT KELLY
WE DON'T WANT HIM TO GET THE PUP DOG BEFORE OUR TOUR STARTS. YOOP!
Lint
Who's after the Pup-Dog? You come along quietly, Albert.

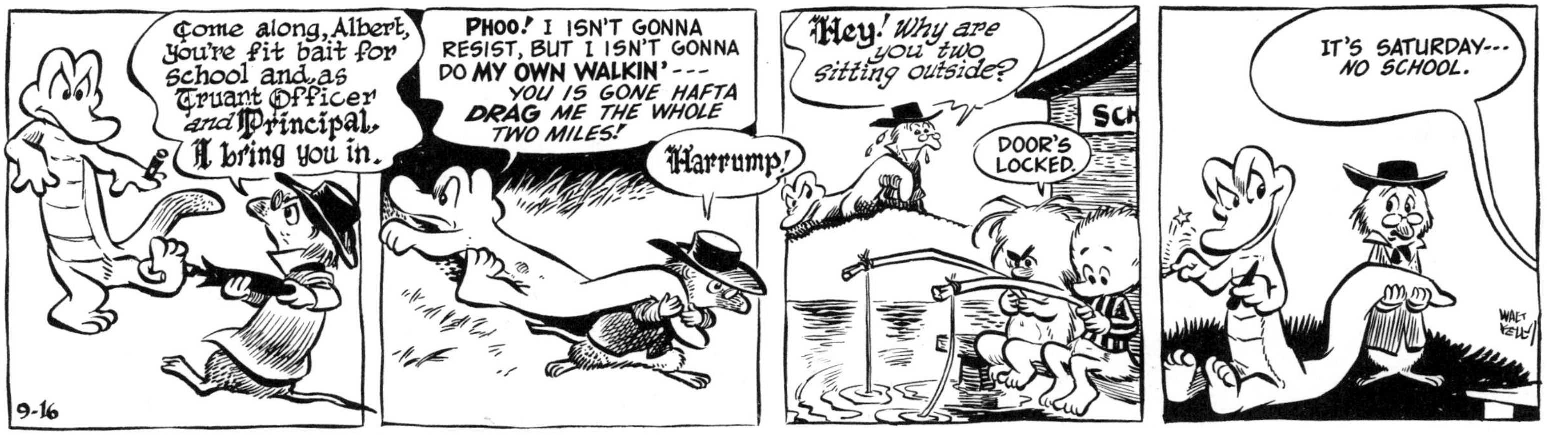
Come along, Albert, You're fit bait for School and, as Truant Officer and Principal, I bring you in.
9-16
PHOO! I ISN'T GONNA RESIST, BUT I ISN'T GONNA DO MY OWN WALKIN' --- YOU IS GONE HAFTA DRAG ME THE WHOLE TWO MILES!
Harrump!
Hey! Why are you two sitting outside?
DOOR'S LOCKED.
SCH
IT'S SATURDAY--- NO SCHOOL.
WALT KELLY

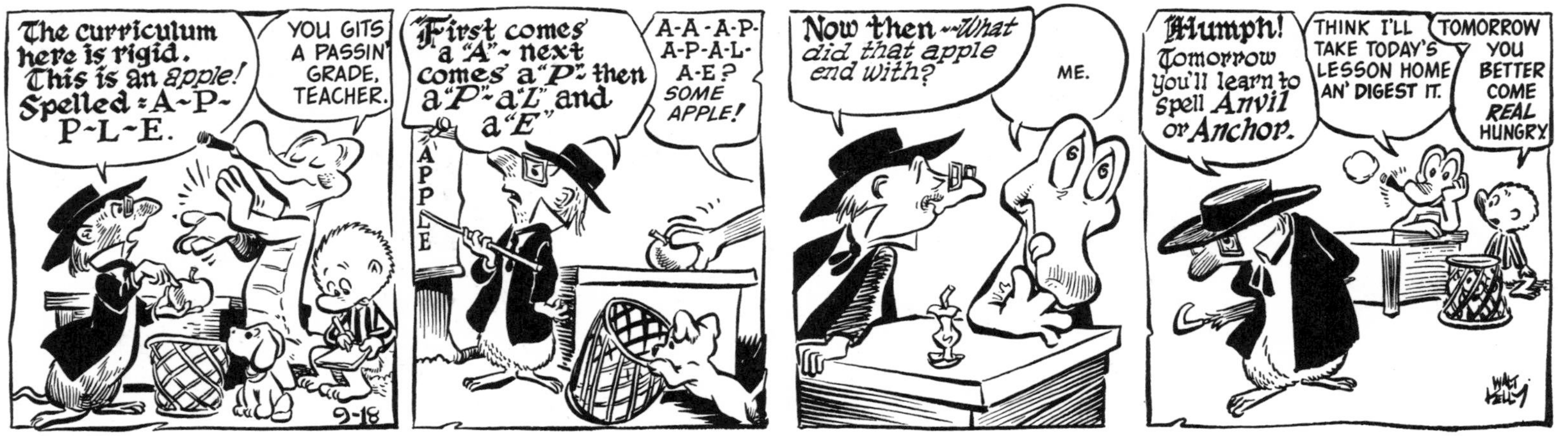
The curriculum here is rigid. This is an apple! Spelled = A-P-P-L-E.
YOU GITS A PASSIN' GRADE, TEACHER.
9-18
APPLE
First comes a "A" - next comes a "P" - then a "P" - a "L" and a "E"
A-A-A-P-A-P-A-L-A-E? SOME APPLE!
Now then -- What did that apple end with?
ME.
Humph! Tomorrow you'll learn to spell Anvil or Anchor.
THINK I'LL TAKE TODAY'S LESSON HOME AN' DIGEST IT.
TOMORROW YOU BETTER COME REAL HUNGRY
WALT KELLY

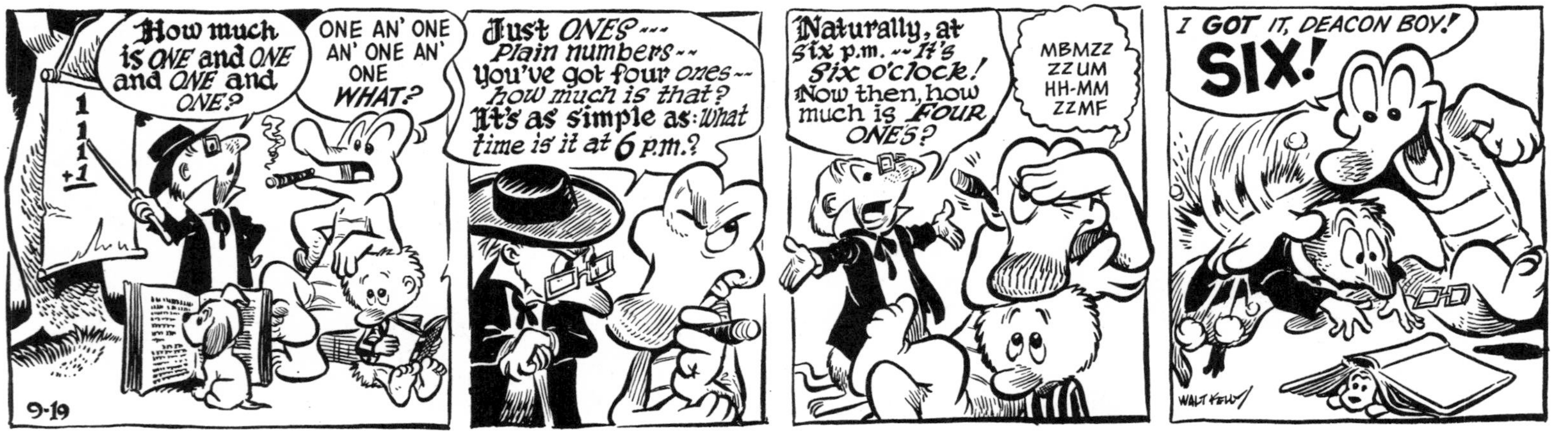
How much is ONE and ONE and ONE and ONE?
ONE AN' ONE AN' ONE AN' ONE WHAT?
1 1 1 +1
9-19
Just ONES --- Plain numbers -- You've got four ones -- how much is that? It's as simple as: What time is it at 6 p.m.?
Naturally, at six p.m. -- It's Six o'clock! Now then, how much is FOUR ONES?
MBMZZ ZZUM HH-MM ZZMF
I GOT IT, DEACON BOY! SIX!
WALT KELLY

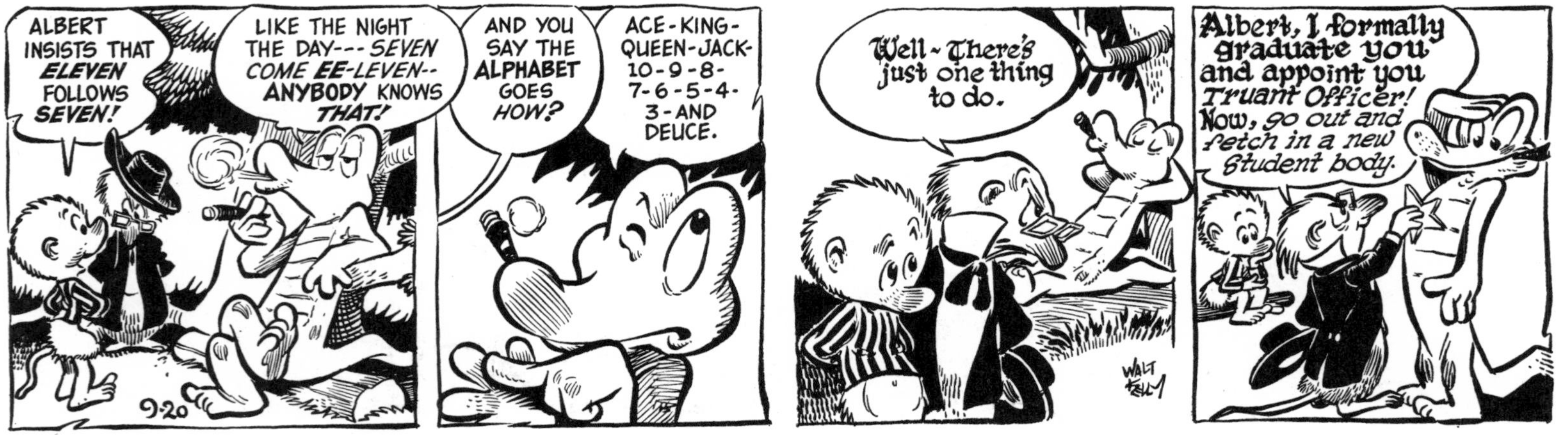
ALBERT INSISTS THAT ELEVEN FOLLOWS SEVEN!
LIKE THE NIGHT THE DAY --- SEVEN COME EE-LEVEN -- ANYBODY KNOWS THAT!
9-20
AND YOU SAY THE ALPHABET GOES HOW?
ACE-KING-QUEEN-JACK-10-9-8-7-6-5-4-3-AND DEUCE.
Well - There's just one thing to do.
WALT KELLY
Albert, I formally graduate you and appoint you Truant Officer! Now, go out and fetch in a new Student body.

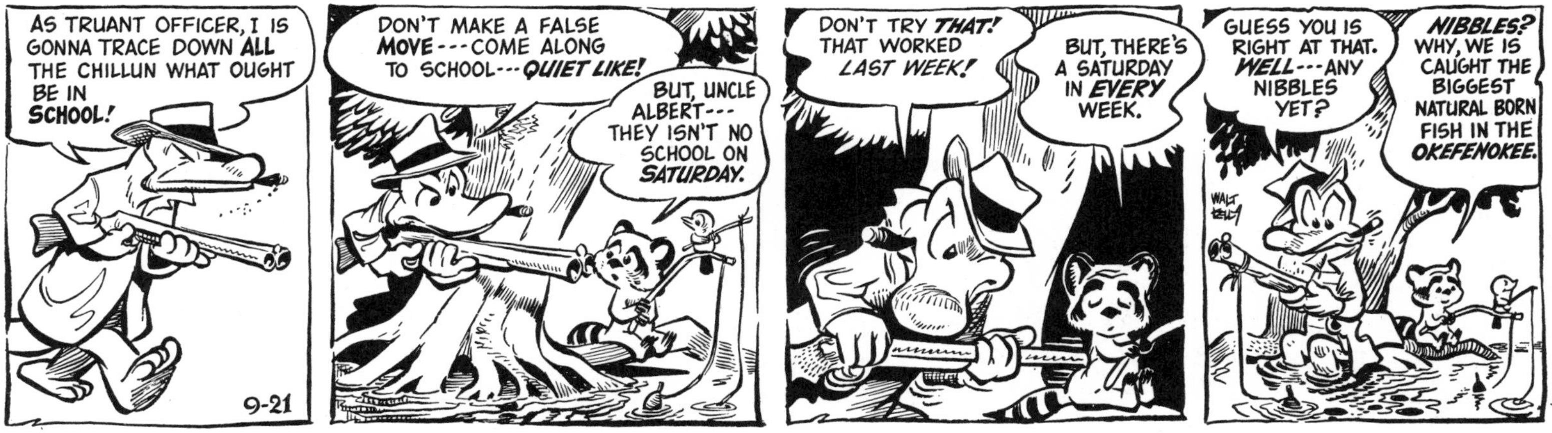
AS TRUANT OFFICER, I IS GONNA TRACE DOWN ALL THE CHILLUN WHAT OUGHT BE IN SCHOOL!
9-21
DON'T MAKE A FALSE MOVE---COME ALONG TO SCHOOL---QUIET LIKE!
BUT, UNCLE ALBERT---THEY ISN'T NO SCHOOL ON SATURDAY.
DON'T TRY THAT! THAT WORKED LAST WEEK!
BUT, THERE'S A SATURDAY IN EVERY WEEK.
GUESS YOU IS RIGHT AT THAT. WELL---ANY NIBBLES YET?
NIBBLES? WHY, WE IS CAUGHT THE BIGGEST NATURAL BORN FISH IN THE OKEFENOKEE.
WALT KELLY

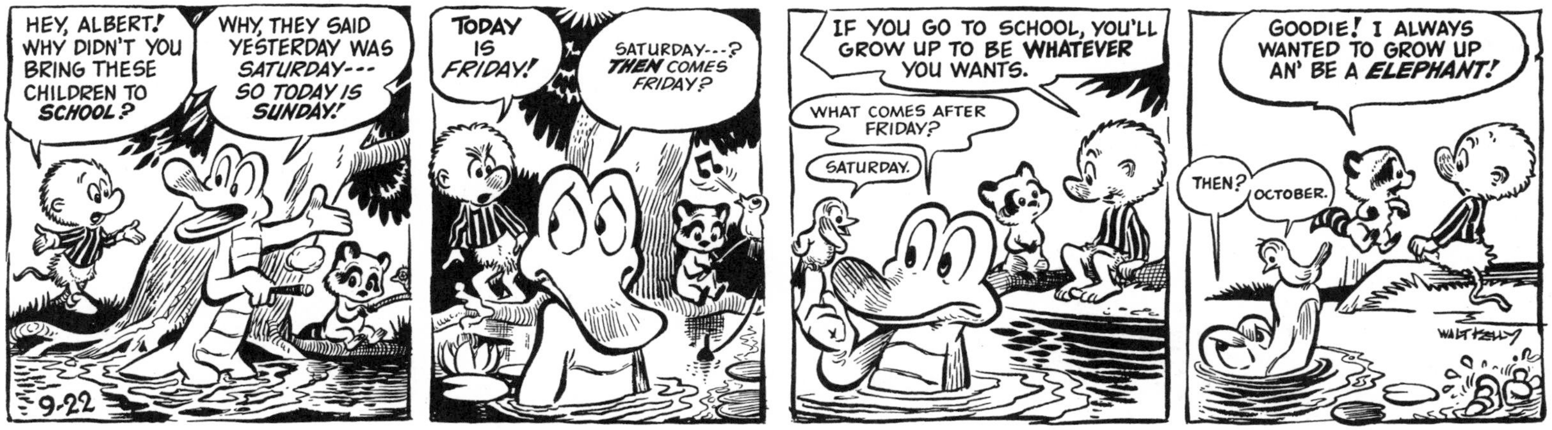
HEY, ALBERT! WHY DIDN'T YOU BRING THESE CHILDREN TO SCHOOL?
WHY, THEY SAID YESTERDAY WAS SATURDAY---SO TODAY IS SUNDAY!
9-22
TODAY IS FRIDAY!
SATURDAY---? THEN COMES FRIDAY?
IF YOU GO TO SCHOOL, YOU'LL GROW UP TO BE WHATEVER YOU WANTS.
WHAT COMES AFTER FRIDAY?
SATURDAY.
GOODIE! I ALWAYS WANTED TO GROW UP AN' BE A ELEPHANT!
THEN?
OCTOBER.
WALT KELLY

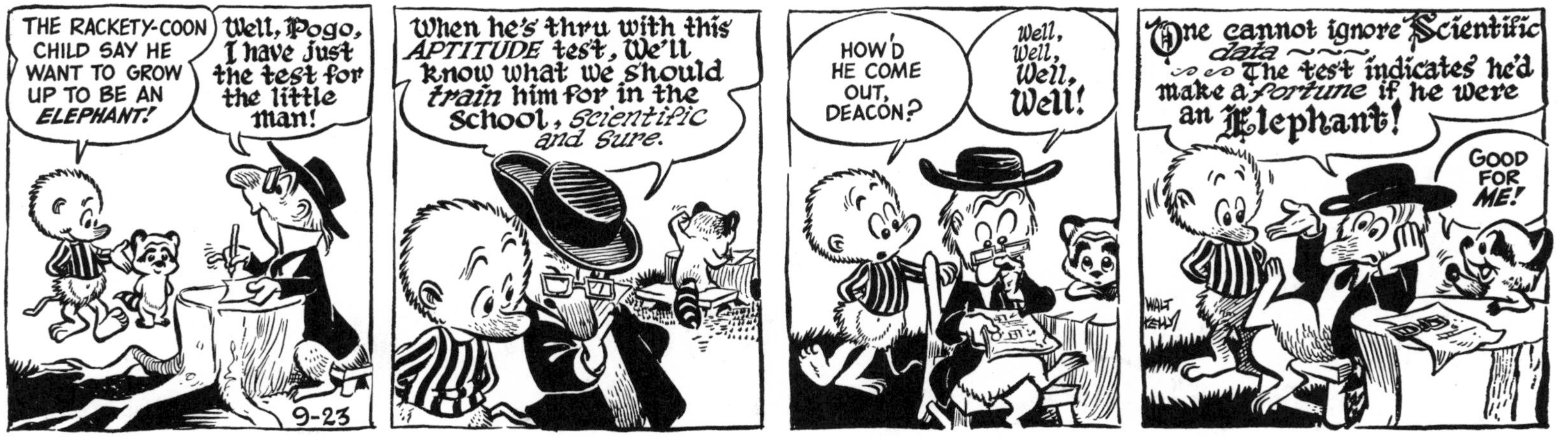
THE RACKETY-COON CHILD SAY HE WANT TO GROW UP TO BE AN ELEPHANT!
Well, Pogo, I have just the test for the little man!
9-23
When he's thru with this APTITUDE test, We'll know what we should train him for in the School, scientific and sure.
HOW'D HE COME OUT, DEACON?
Well, Well, Well, Well!
One cannot ignore Scientific data ~~ The test indicates he'd make a fortune if he were an Elephant!
GOOD FOR ME!
WALT KELLY

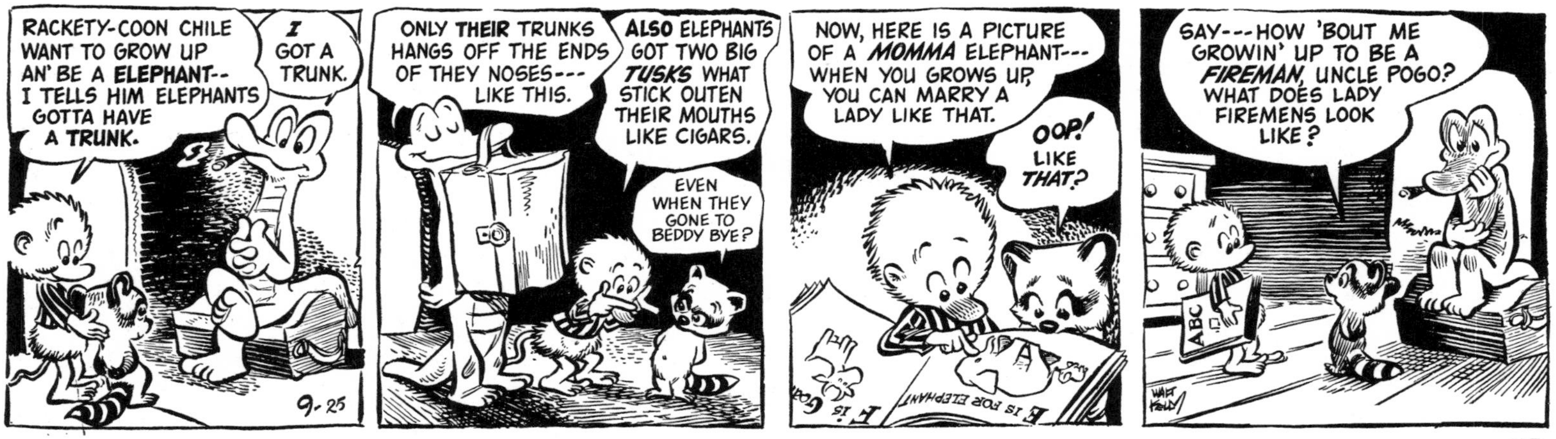
RACKETY-COON CHILE WANT TO GROW UP AN' BE A **ELEPHANT**-- I TELLS HIM ELEPHANTS GOTTA HAVE A **TRUNK.**
I GOT A TRUNK.
9-25
ONLY **THEIR** TRUNKS HANGS OFF THE ENDS OF THEY NOSES--- LIKE THIS.
ALSO ELEPHANTS GOT TWO BIG ***TUSKS*** WHAT STICK OUTEN THEIR MOUTHS LIKE CIGARS.
EVEN WHEN THEY GONE TO BEDDY BYE?
NOW, HERE IS A PICTURE OF A ***MOMMA*** ELEPHANT--- WHEN YOU GROWS UP, YOU CAN MARRY A LADY LIKE THAT.
OOP! LIKE ***THAT?***
SAY---HOW 'BOUT ME GROWIN' UP TO BE A ***FIREMAN,*** UNCLE POGO? WHAT DOES LADY FIREMENS LOOK LIKE?
ABC
WALT KELLY

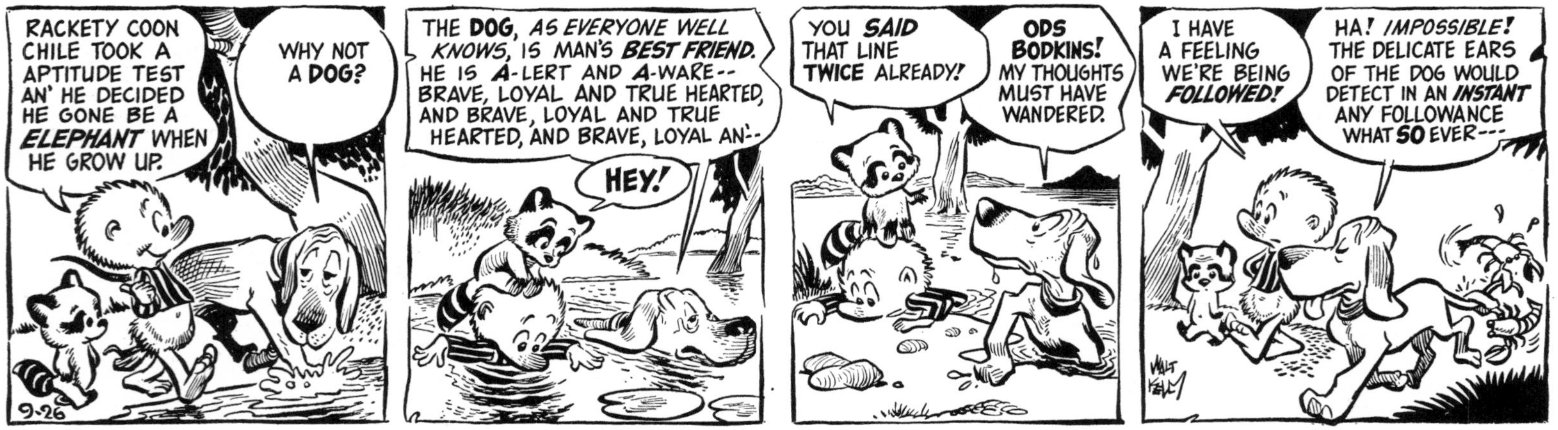
RACKETY COON CHILE TOOK A APTITUDE TEST AN' HE DECIDED HE GONE BE A ***ELEPHANT*** WHEN HE GROW UP.
WHY NOT A **DOG?**
9-26
THE **DOG**, *AS EVERYONE WELL KNOWS,* IS MAN'S ***BEST FRIEND.*** HE IS ***A***-LERT AND ***A***-WARE-- BRAVE, LOYAL AND TRUE HEARTED, AND BRAVE, LOYAL AND TRUE HEARTED, AND BRAVE, LOYAL AN'--
HEY!
YOU **SAID** THAT LINE **TWICE** ALREADY!
ODS BODKINS! MY THOUGHTS MUST HAVE WANDERED.
I HAVE A FEELING WE'RE BEING ***FOLLOWED!***
HA! *IMPOSSIBLE!* THE DELICATE EARS OF THE DOG WOULD DETECT IN AN ***INSTANT*** ANY FOLLOWANCE WHAT **SO** EVER---
WALT KELLY

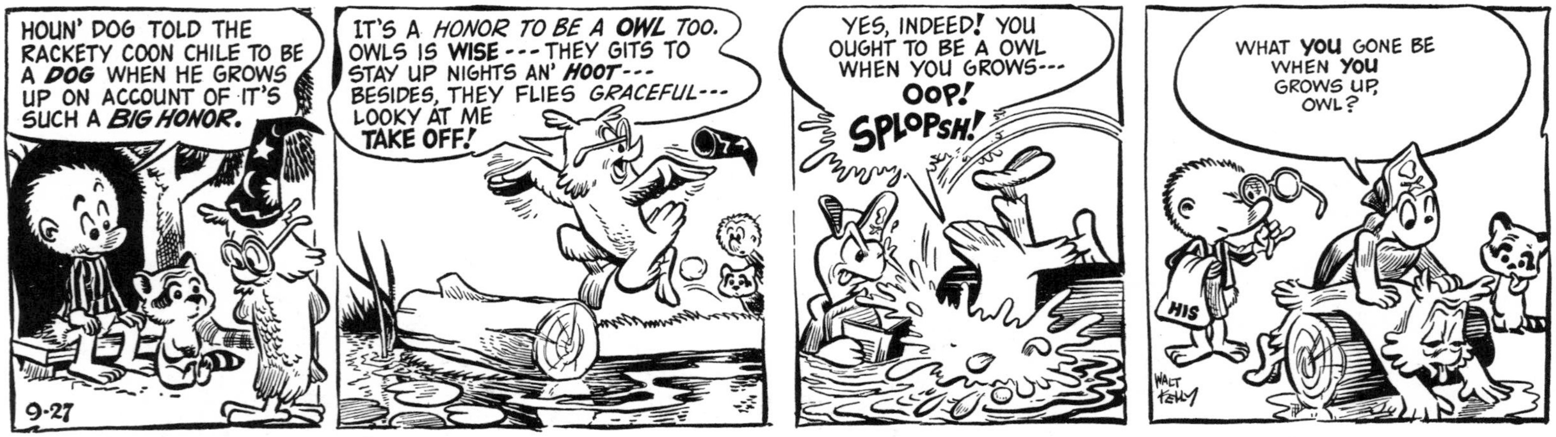
HOUN' DOG TOLD THE RACKETY COON CHILE TO BE A ***DOG*** WHEN HE GROWS UP ON ACCOUNT OF IT'S SUCH A ***BIG HONOR.***
9-27
IT'S A *HONOR TO BE A* ***OWL*** *TOO.* OWLS IS **WISE**---THEY GITS TO STAY UP NIGHTS AN' ***HOOT***--- BESIDES, THEY FLIES *GRACEFUL*--- LOOKY AT ME **TAKE OFF!**
YES, INDEED! YOU OUGHT TO BE A OWL WHEN YOU GROWS--- **OOP!**
SPLOPSH!
WHAT **YOU** GONE BE WHEN **YOU** GROWS UP, OWL?
HIS
WALT KELLY

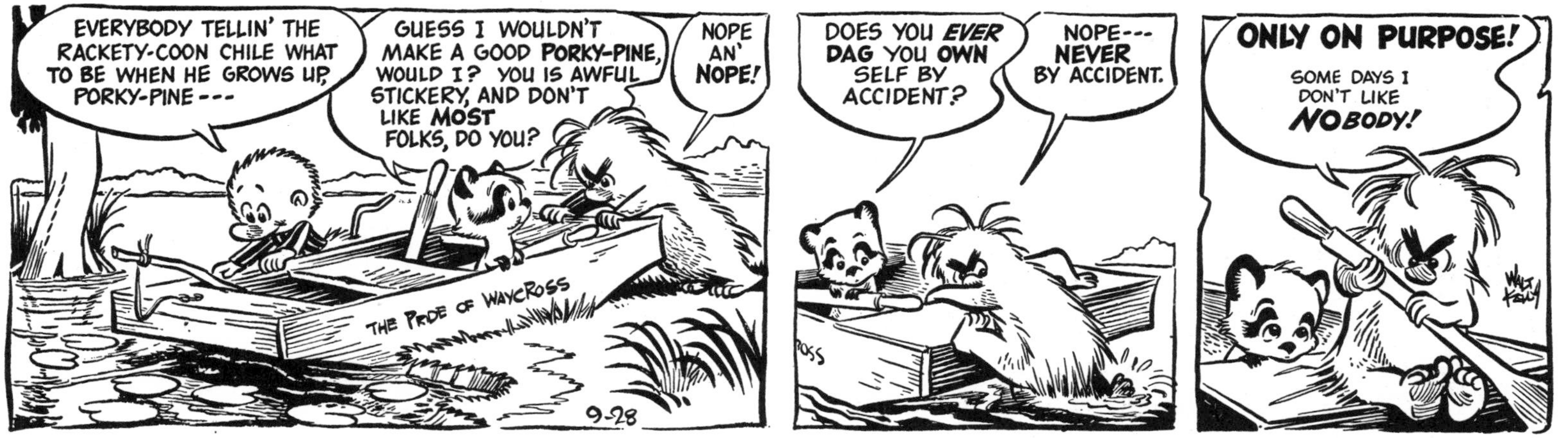
EVERYBODY TELLIN' THE RACKETY-COON CHILE WHAT TO BE WHEN HE GROWS UP, PORKY-PINE---
GUESS I WOULDN'T MAKE A GOOD PORKY-PINE, WOULD I? YOU IS AWFUL STICKERY, AND DON'T LIKE MOST FOLKS, DO YOU?
NOPE AN' NOPE!
THE PRIDE OF WAYCROSS
9-28
DOES YOU EVER DAG YOU OWN SELF BY ACCIDENT?
NOPE--- NEVER BY ACCIDENT.
ONLY ON PURPOSE!
SOME DAYS I DON'T LIKE NOBODY!
WALT KELLY

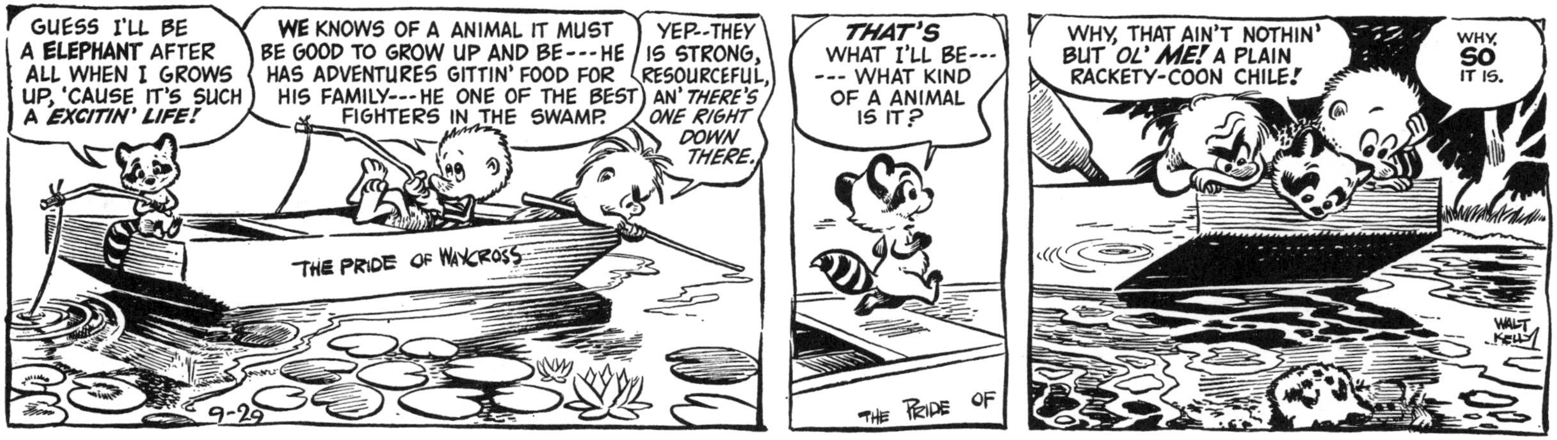
GUESS I'LL BE A ELEPHANT AFTER ALL WHEN I GROWS UP, 'CAUSE IT'S SUCH A EXCITIN' LIFE!
WE KNOWS OF A ANIMAL IT MUST BE GOOD TO GROW UP AND BE---HE HAS ADVENTURES GITTIN' FOOD FOR HIS FAMILY---HE ONE OF THE BEST FIGHTERS IN THE SWAMP.
YEP--THEY IS STRONG, RESOURCEFUL, AN' THERE'S ONE RIGHT DOWN THERE.
THE PRIDE OF WAYCROSS
9-29
THAT'S WHAT I'LL BE--- --- WHAT KIND OF A ANIMAL IS IT?
THE PRIDE OF
WHY, THAT AIN'T NOTHIN' BUT OL' ME! A PLAIN RACKETY-COON CHILE!
WHY, SO IT IS.
WALT KELLY

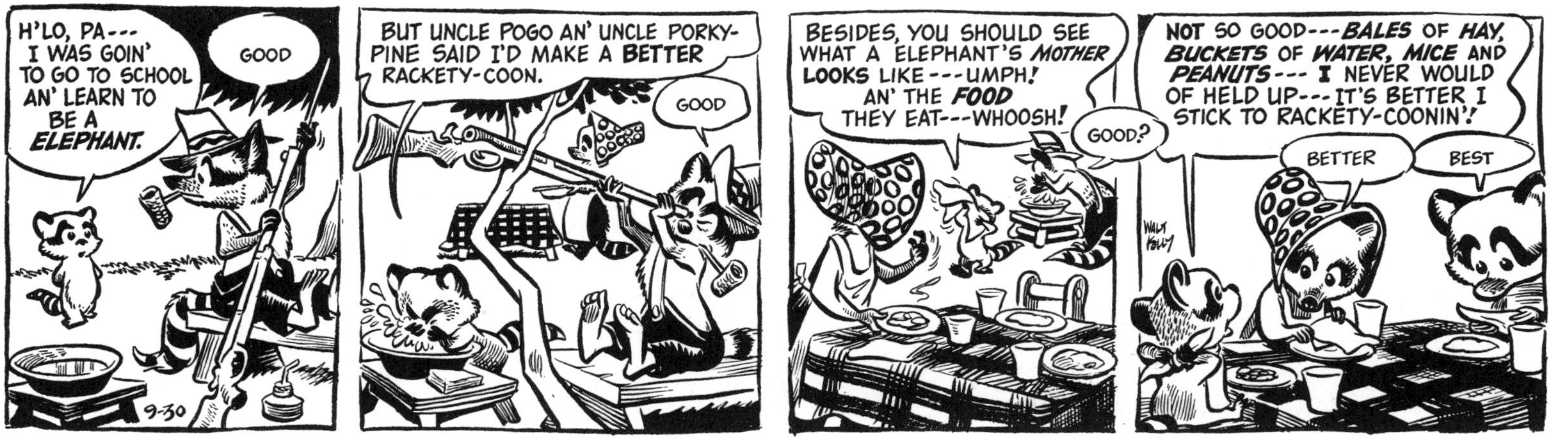
H'LO, PA--- I WAS GOIN' TO GO TO SCHOOL AN' LEARN TO BE A ELEPHANT.
GOOD
9-30
BUT UNCLE POGO AN' UNCLE PORKY-PINE SAID I'D MAKE A BETTER RACKETY-COON.
GOOD
BESIDES, YOU SHOULD SEE WHAT A ELEPHANT'S MOTHER LOOKS LIKE---UMPH! AN' THE FOOD THEY EAT---WHOOSH!
GOOD?
WALT KELLY
NOT SO GOOD---BALES OF HAY, BUCKETS OF WATER, MICE AND PEANUTS--- I NEVER WOULD OF HELD UP---IT'S BETTER I STICK TO RACKETY-COONIN'!
BETTER
BEST

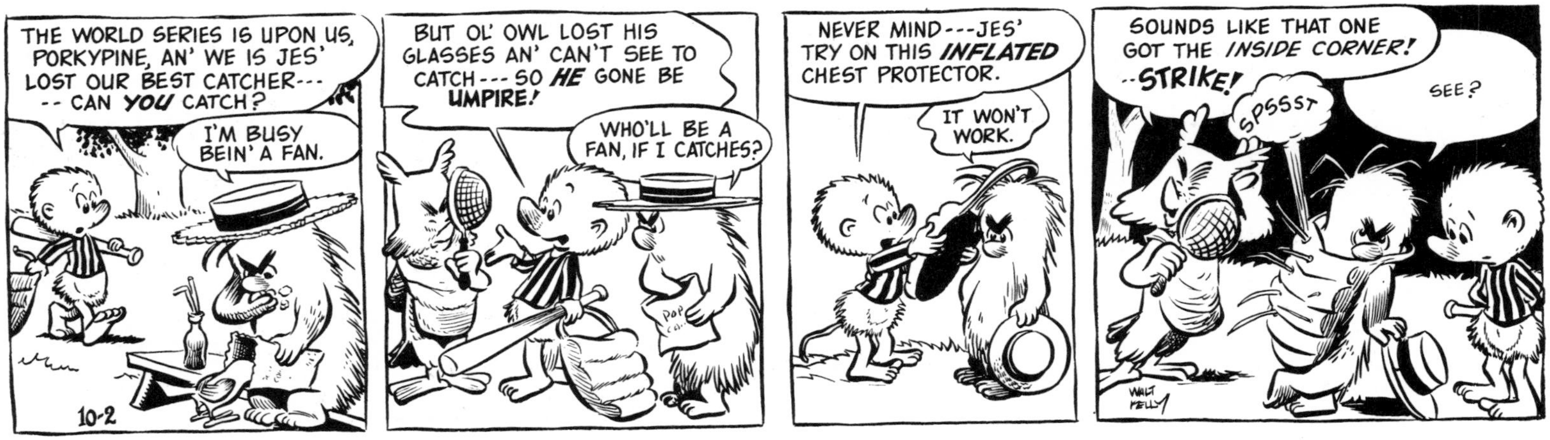
THE WORLD SERIES IS UPON US, PORKYPINE, AN' WE IS JES' LOST OUR BEST CATCHER--- -- CAN YOU CATCH?
I'M BUSY BEIN' A FAN.
10-2
BUT OL' OWL LOST HIS GLASSES AN' CAN'T SEE TO CATCH --- SO HE GONE BE UMPIRE!
WHO'LL BE A FAN, IF I CATCHES?
NEVER MIND---JES' TRY ON THIS INFLATED CHEST PROTECTOR.
IT WON'T WORK.
SOUNDS LIKE THAT ONE GOT THE INSIDE CORNER! --STRIKE!
SPSSST
SEE?
WALT KELLY

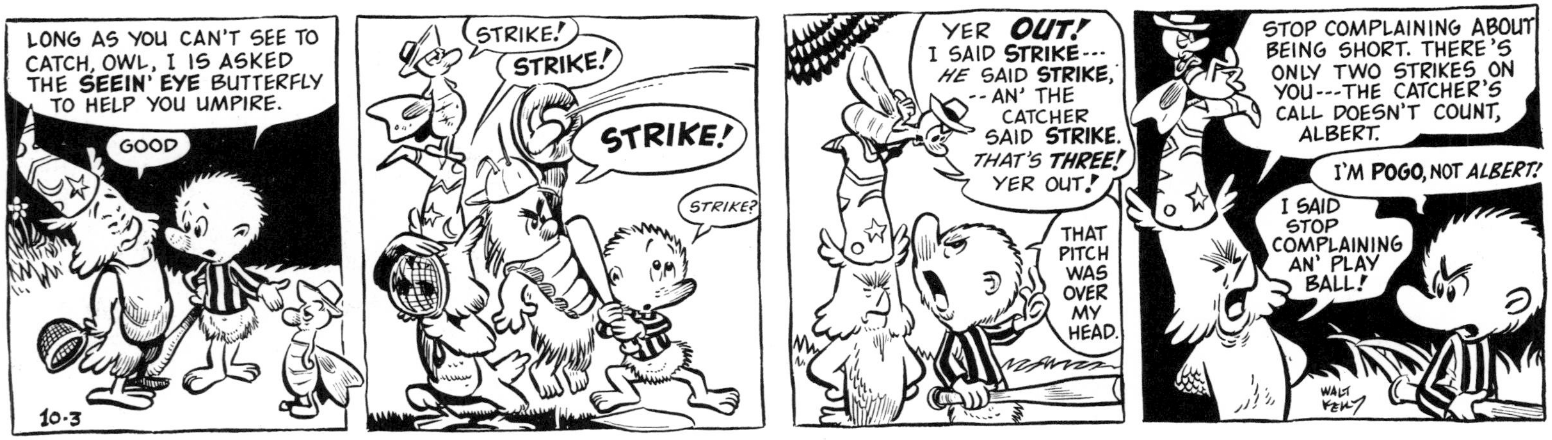
LONG AS YOU CAN'T SEE TO CATCH, OWL, I IS ASKED THE SEEIN' EYE BUTTERFLY TO HELP YOU UMPIRE.
GOOD
10-3
STRIKE!
STRIKE!
STRIKE!
STRIKE?
YER OUT! I SAID STRIKE--- HE SAID STRIKE, --AN' THE CATCHER SAID STRIKE. THAT'S THREE! YER OUT!
THAT PITCH WAS OVER MY HEAD.
STOP COMPLAINING ABOUT BEING SHORT. THERE'S ONLY TWO STRIKES ON YOU---THE CATCHER'S CALL DOESN'T COUNT, ALBERT.
I'M POGO, NOT ALBERT!
I SAID STOP COMPLAINING AN' PLAY BALL!
WALT KELLY

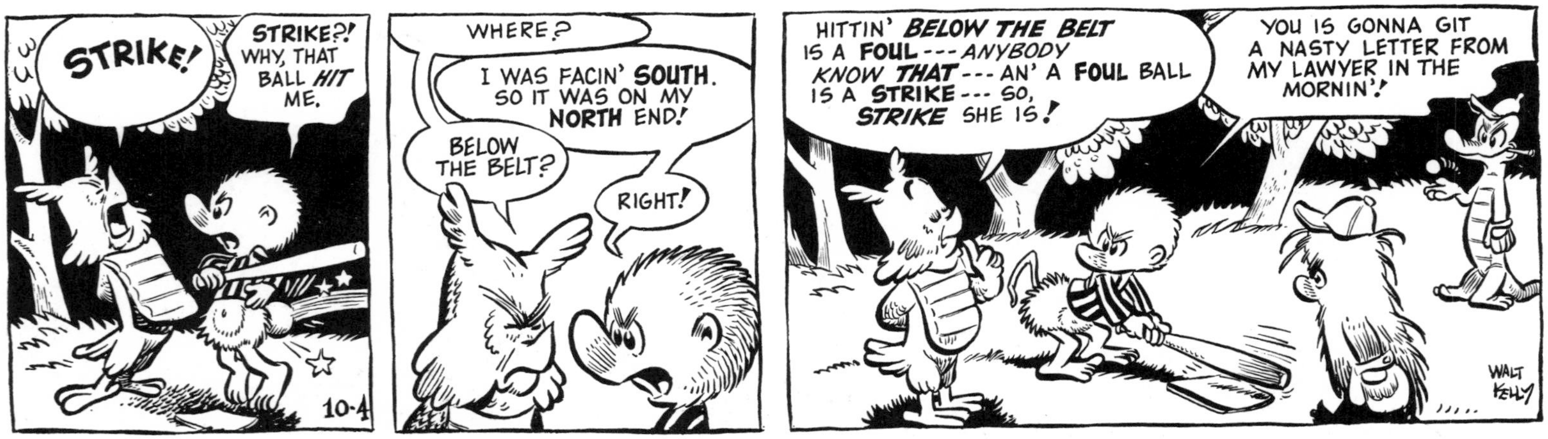
STRIKE!
STRIKE?! WHY, THAT BALL HIT ME.
10-4
WHERE?
I WAS FACIN' SOUTH. SO IT WAS ON MY NORTH END!
BELOW THE BELT?
RIGHT!
HITTIN' BELOW THE BELT IS A FOUL --- ANYBODY KNOW THAT --- AN' A FOUL BALL IS A STRIKE --- SO, STRIKE SHE IS!
YOU IS GONNA GIT A NASTY LETTER FROM MY LAWYER IN THE MORNIN'!
WALT KELLY

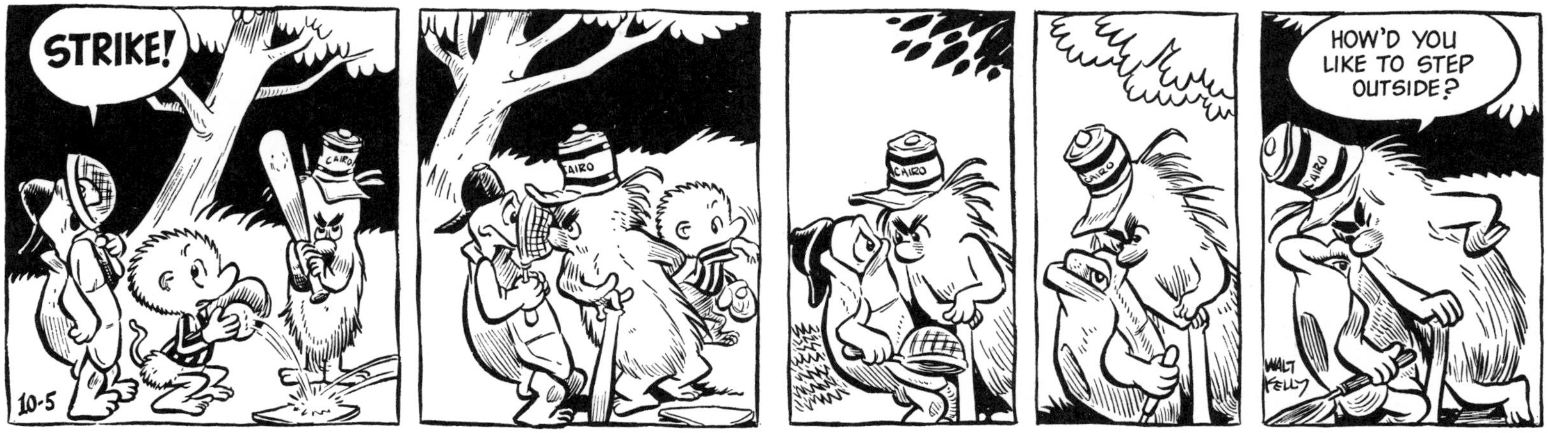
STRIKE!
HOW'D YOU LIKE TO STEP OUTSIDE?
10-5
WALT KELLY

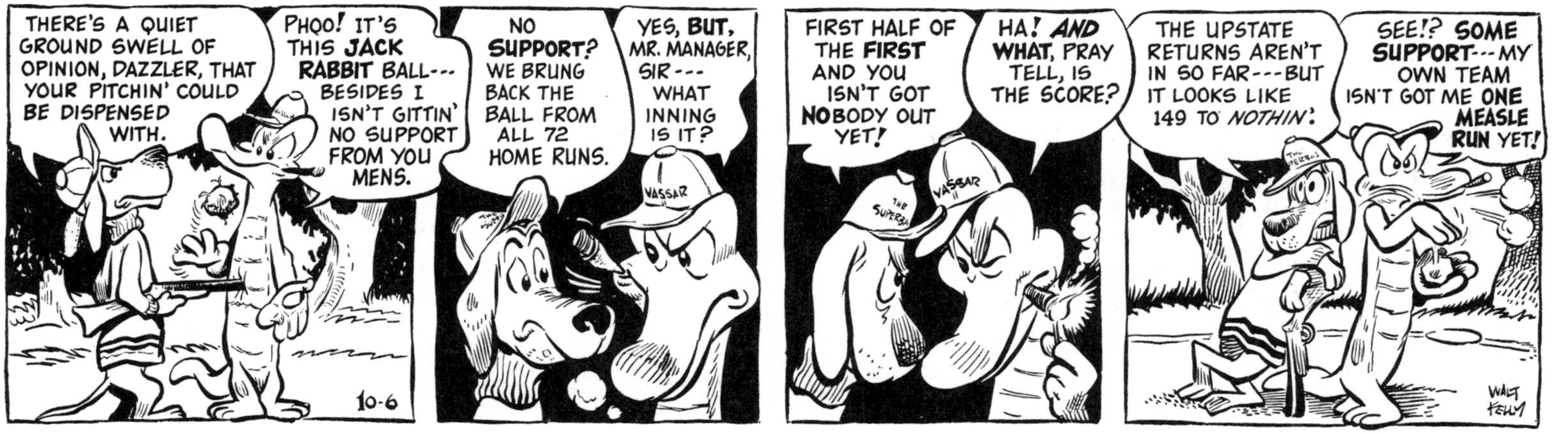
THERE'S A QUIET GROUND SWELL OF OPINION, DAZZLER, THAT YOUR PITCHIN' COULD BE DISPENSED WITH.
PHOO! IT'S THIS JACK RABBIT BALL--- BESIDES I ISN'T GITTIN' NO SUPPORT FROM YOU MENS.
NO SUPPORT? WE BRUNG BACK THE BALL FROM ALL 72 HOME RUNS.
YES, BUT, MR. MANAGER, SIR--- WHAT INNING IS IT?
FIRST HALF OF THE FIRST AND YOU ISN'T GOT NOBODY OUT YET!
HA! AND WHAT, PRAY TELL, IS THE SCORE?
THE UPSTATE RETURNS AREN'T IN SO FAR---BUT IT LOOKS LIKE 149 TO NOTHIN'.
SEE!? SOME SUPPORT---MY OWN TEAM ISN'T GOT ME ONE MEASLE RUN YET!
10-6
VASSAR
WALT KELLY

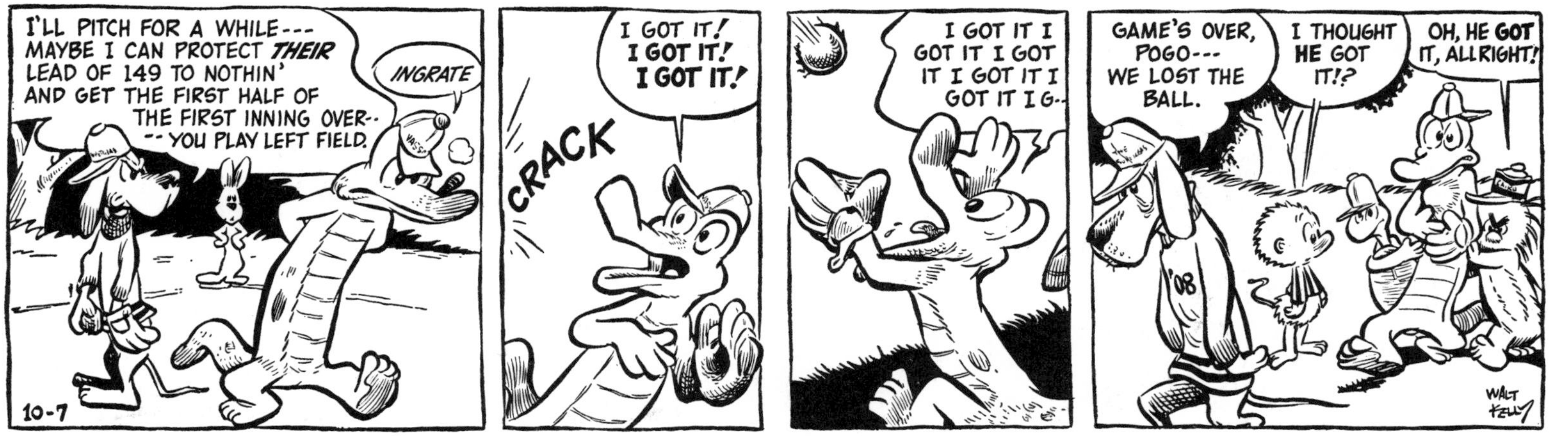
I'LL PITCH FOR A WHILE--- MAYBE I CAN PROTECT THEIR LEAD OF 149 TO NOTHIN' AND GET THE FIRST HALF OF THE FIRST INNING OVER-- --YOU PLAY LEFT FIELD.
INGRATE
I GOT IT! I GOT IT! I GOT IT!
CRACK
I GOT IT I GOT IT I GOT IT I GOT IT I GOT IT I G--
GAME'S OVER, POGO--- WE LOST THE BALL.
I THOUGHT HE GOT IT!?
OH, HE GOT IT, ALLRIGHT!
'08
10-7
WALT KELLY

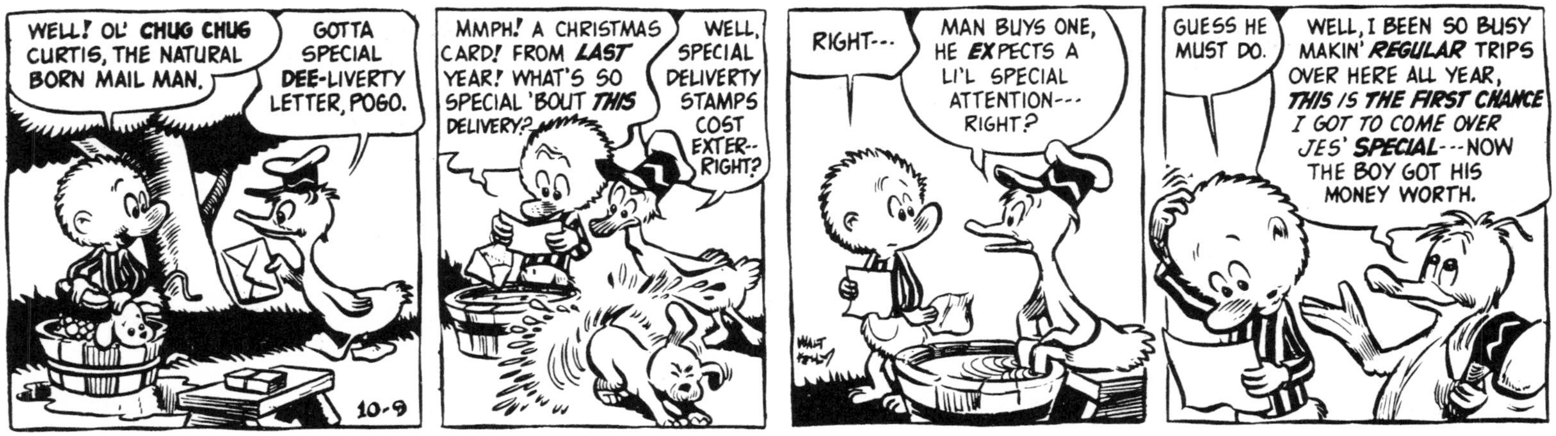
WELL! OL' CHUG CHUG CURTIS, THE NATURAL BORN MAIL MAN.
GOTTA SPECIAL DEE-LIVERTY LETTER, POGO.
10-9
MMPH! A CHRISTMAS CARD! FROM LAST YEAR! WHAT'S SO SPECIAL 'BOUT THIS DELIVERY?
WELL, SPECIAL DELIVERTY STAMPS COST EXTER-RIGHT?
RIGHT---
MAN BUYS ONE, HE EXPECTS A LI'L SPECIAL ATTENTION--- RIGHT?
GUESS HE MUST DO.
WELL, I BEEN SO BUSY MAKIN' REGULAR TRIPS OVER HERE ALL YEAR, THIS IS THE FIRST CHANCE I GOT TO COME OVER JES' SPECIAL---NOW THE BOY GOT HIS MONEY WORTH.

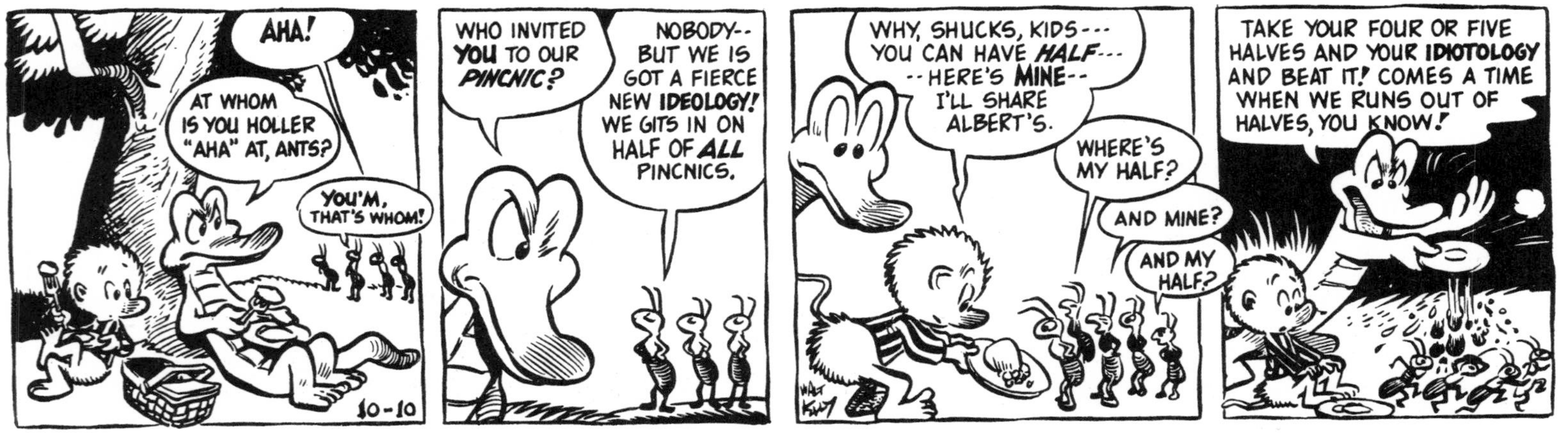
AHA!
AT WHOM IS YOU HOLLER "AHA" AT, ANTS?
YOU'M, THAT'S WHOM!
10-10
WHO INVITED YOU TO OUR PINCNIC?
NOBODY-- BUT WE IS GOT A FIERCE NEW IDEOLOGY! WE GITS IN ON HALF OF ALL PINCNICS.
WHY, SHUCKS, KIDS--- YOU CAN HAVE HALF--- --HERE'S MINE-- I'LL SHARE ALBERT'S.
WHERE'S MY HALF?
AND MINE?
AND MY HALF?
TAKE YOUR FOUR OR FIVE HALVES AND YOUR IDIOTOLOGY AND BEAT IT! COMES A TIME WHEN WE RUNS OUT OF HALVES, YOU KNOW!

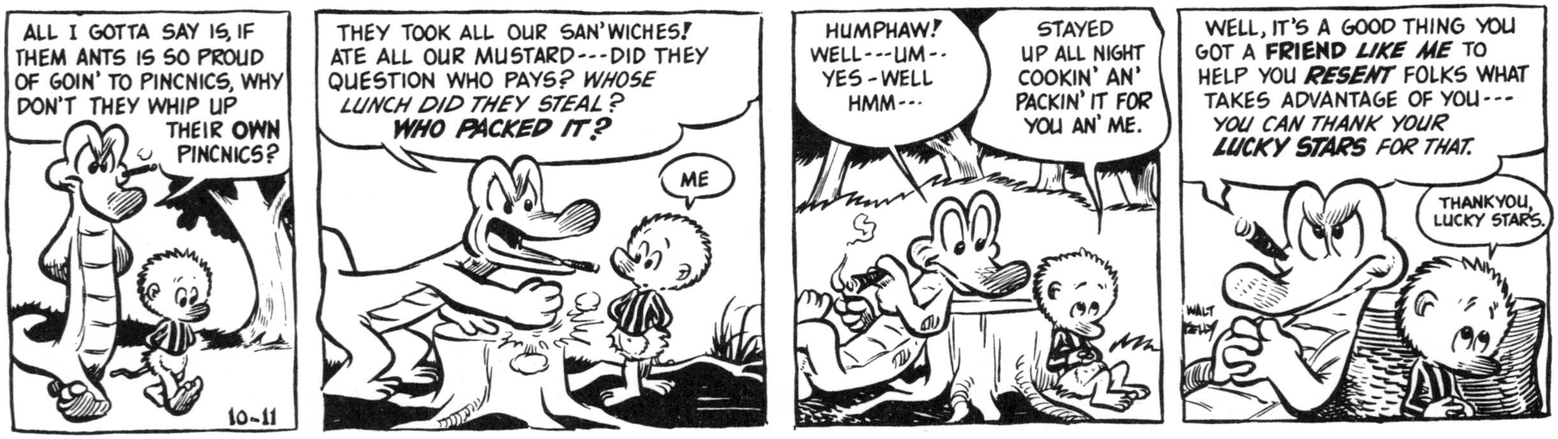
ALL I GOTTA SAY IS, IF THEM ANTS IS SO PROUD OF GOIN' TO PINCNICS, WHY DON'T THEY WHIP UP THEIR OWN PINCNICS?
10-11
THEY TOOK ALL OUR SAN'WICHES! ATE ALL OUR MUSTARD---DID THEY QUESTION WHO PAYS? WHOSE LUNCH DID THEY STEAL? WHO PACKED IT?
ME
HUMPHAW! WELL---UM-- YES-WELL HMM---
STAYED UP ALL NIGHT COOKIN' AN' PACKIN' IT FOR YOU AN' ME.
WELL, IT'S A GOOD THING YOU GOT A FRIEND LIKE ME TO HELP YOU RESENT FOLKS WHAT TAKES ADVANTAGE OF YOU--- YOU CAN THANK YOUR LUCKY STARS FOR THAT.
THANKYOU, LUCKY STARS.

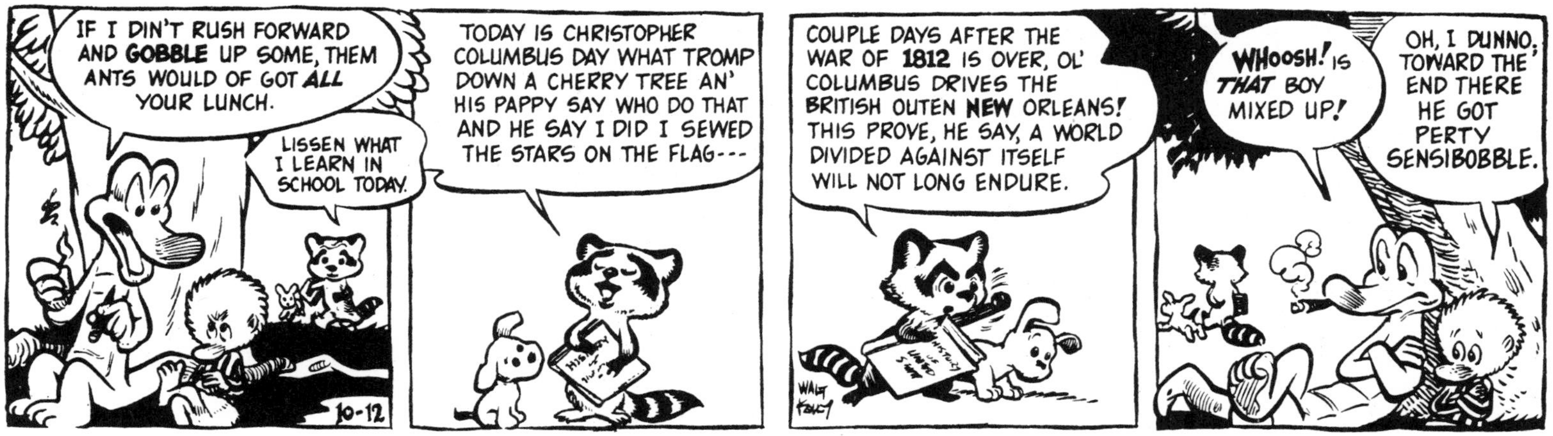
IF I DIN'T RUSH FORWARD AND GOBBLE UP SOME, THEM ANTS WOULD OF GOT ALL YOUR LUNCH.
LISSEN WHAT I LEARN IN SCHOOL TODAY.
10-12
TODAY IS CHRISTOPHER COLUMBUS DAY WHAT TROMP DOWN A CHERRY TREE AN' HIS PAPPY SAY WHO DO THAT AND HE SAY I DID I SEWED THE STARS ON THE FLAG---
COUPLE DAYS AFTER THE WAR OF 1812 IS OVER, OL' COLUMBUS DRIVES THE BRITISH OUTEN NEW ORLEANS! THIS PROVE, HE SAY, A WORLD DIVIDED AGAINST ITSELF WILL NOT LONG ENDURE.
WHOOSH! IS THAT BOY MIXED UP!
OH, I DUNNO, TOWARD THE END THERE HE GOT PERTY SENSIBOBBLE.

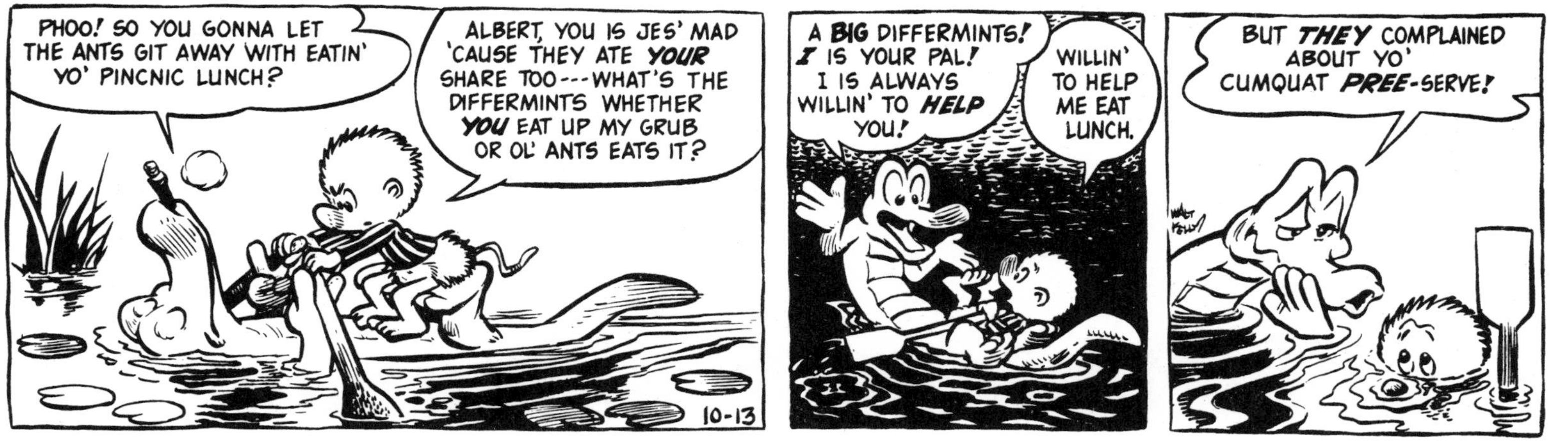
PHOO! SO YOU GONNA LET THE ANTS GIT AWAY WITH EATIN' YO' PINCNIC LUNCH?
ALBERT, YOU IS JES' MAD 'CAUSE THEY ATE YOUR SHARE TOO---WHAT'S THE DIFFERMINTS WHETHER YOU EAT UP MY GRUB OR OL' ANTS EATS IT?
10-13
A BIG DIFFERMINTS! I IS YOUR PAL! I IS ALWAYS WILLIN' TO HELP YOU!
WILLIN' TO HELP ME EAT LUNCH.
BUT THEY COMPLAINED ABOUT YO' CUMQUAT PREE-SERVE!

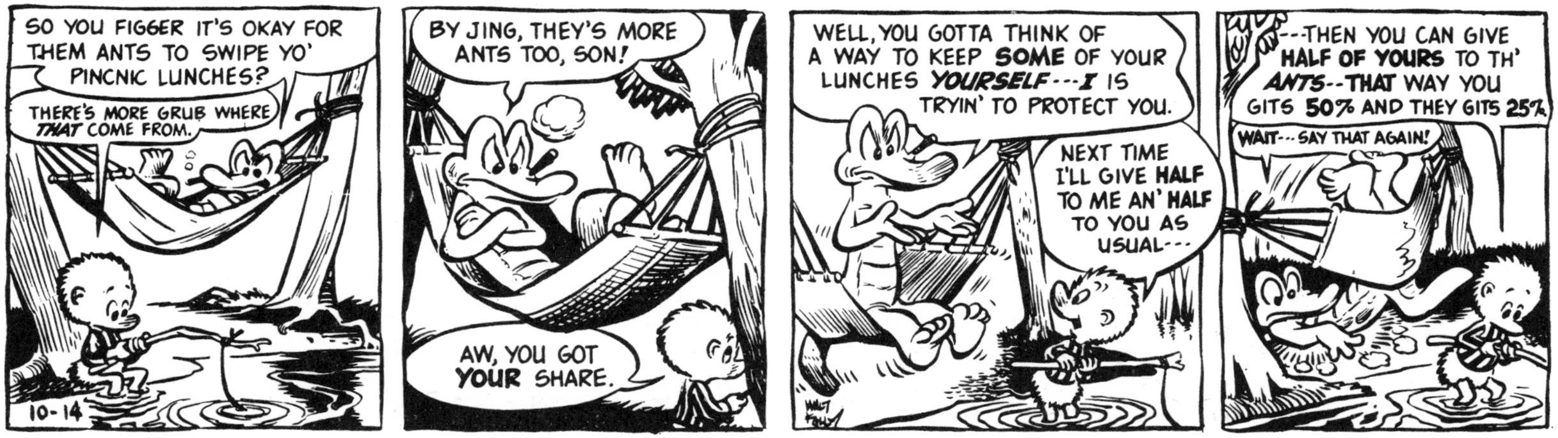
SO YOU FIGGER IT'S OKAY FOR THEM ANTS TO SWIPE YO' PINCNIC LUNCHES?
THERE'S MORE GRUB WHERE THAT COME FROM.
10-14
BY JING, THEY'S MORE ANTS TOO, SON!
AW, YOU GOT YOUR SHARE.
WELL, YOU GOTTA THINK OF A WAY TO KEEP SOME OF YOUR LUNCHES YOURSELF---I IS TRYIN' TO PROTECT YOU.
NEXT TIME I'LL GIVE HALF TO ME AN' HALF TO YOU AS USUAL---
---THEN YOU CAN GIVE HALF OF YOURS TO TH' ANTS--THAT WAY YOU GITS 50% AND THEY GITS 25%.
WAIT---SAY THAT AGAIN!

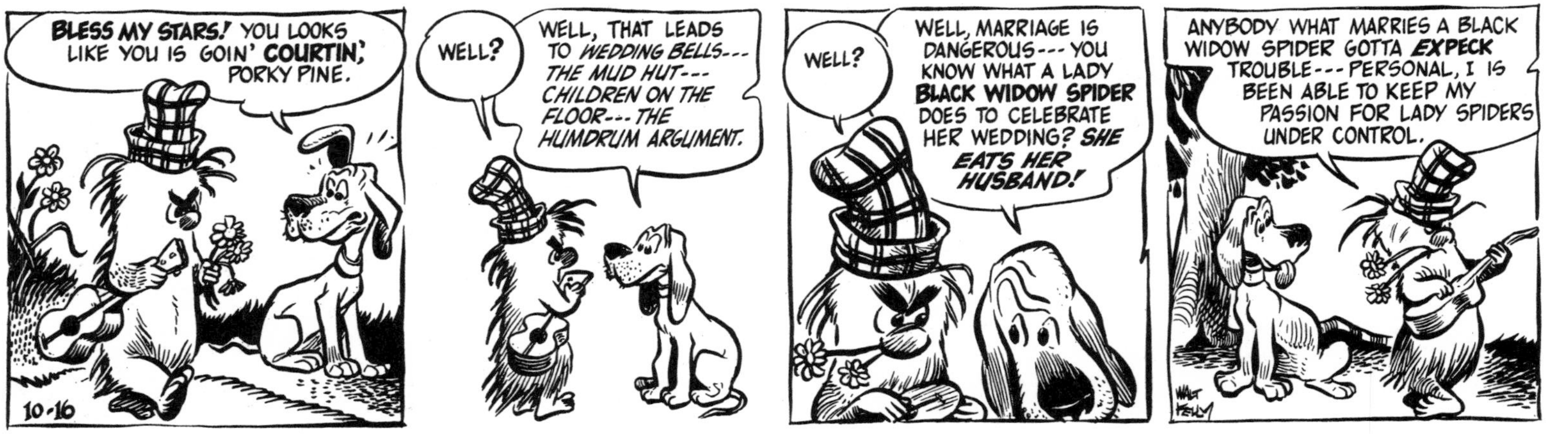
BLESS MY STARS! YOU LOOKS LIKE YOU IS GOIN' COURTIN', PORKY PINE.
WELL?
WELL, THAT LEADS TO WEDDING BELLS--- THE MUD HUT--- CHILDREN ON THE FLOOR--- THE HUMDRUM ARGUMENT.
WELL?
WELL, MARRIAGE IS DANGEROUS--- YOU KNOW WHAT A LADY BLACK WIDOW SPIDER DOES TO CELEBRATE HER WEDDING? SHE EATS HER HUSBAND!
ANYBODY WHAT MARRIES A BLACK WIDOW SPIDER GOTTA EXPECK TROUBLE--- PERSONAL, I IS BEEN ABLE TO KEEP MY PASSION FOR LADY SPIDERS UNDER CONTROL.
10-16
WALT KELLY

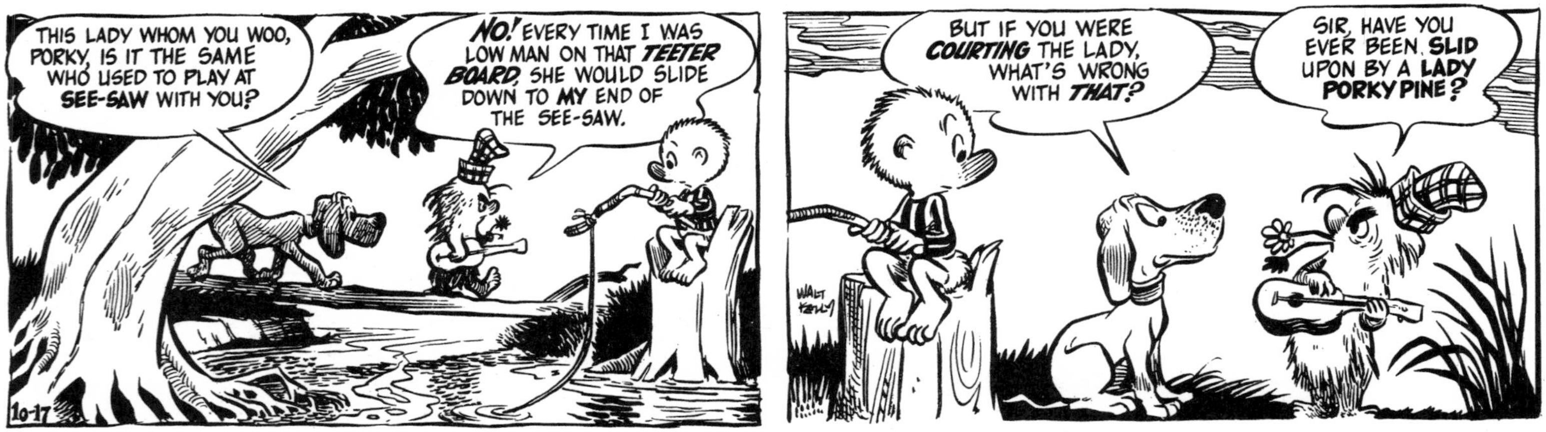
THIS LADY WHOM YOU WOO, PORKY, IS IT THE SAME WHO USED TO PLAY AT SEE-SAW WITH YOU?
NO! EVERY TIME I WAS LOW MAN ON THAT TEETER BOARD SHE WOULD SLIDE DOWN TO MY END OF THE SEE-SAW.
BUT IF YOU WERE COURTING THE LADY, WHAT'S WRONG WITH THAT?
SIR, HAVE YOU EVER BEEN SLID UPON BY A LADY PORKY PINE?
10-17
WALT KELLY

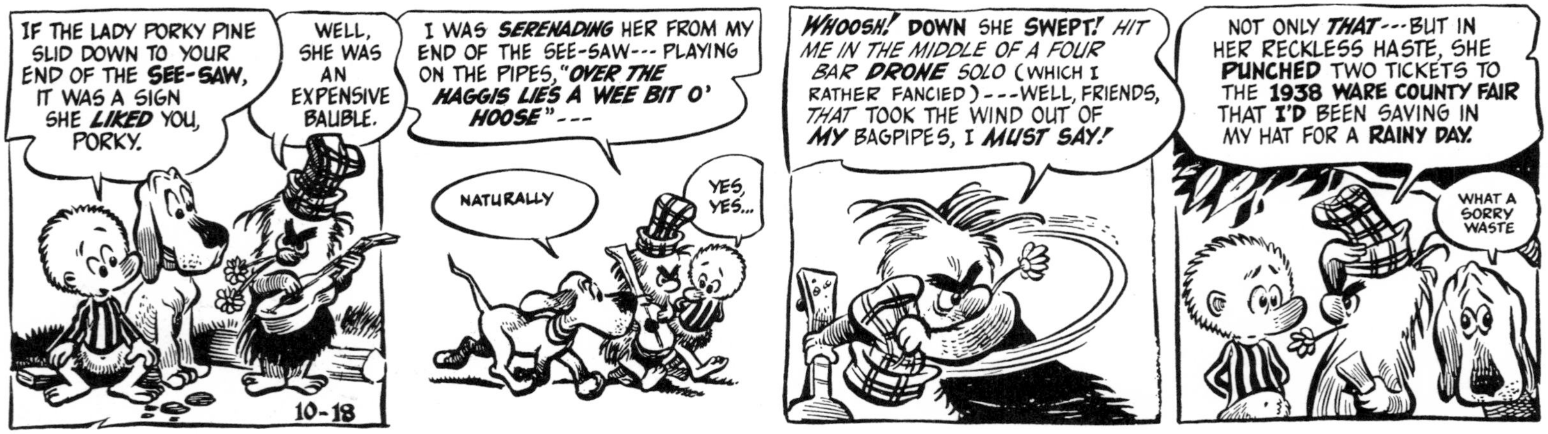
IF THE LADY PORKY PINE SLID DOWN TO YOUR END OF THE SEE-SAW, IT WAS A SIGN SHE LIKED YOU, PORKY.
WELL, SHE WAS AN EXPENSIVE BAUBLE.
I WAS SERENADING HER FROM MY END OF THE SEE-SAW--- PLAYING ON THE PIPES, "OVER THE HAGGIS LIES A WEE BIT O' HOOSE"---
NATURALLY
YES, YES...
WHOOSH! DOWN SHE SWEPT! HIT ME IN THE MIDDLE OF A FOUR BAR DRONE SOLO (WHICH I RATHER FANCIED)---WELL, FRIENDS, THAT TOOK THE WIND OUT OF MY BAGPIPES, I MUST SAY!
NOT ONLY THAT---BUT IN HER RECKLESS HASTE, SHE PUNCHED TWO TICKETS TO THE 1938 WARE COUNTY FAIR THAT I'D BEEN SAVING IN MY HAT FOR A RAINY DAY.
WHAT A SORRY WASTE
10-18

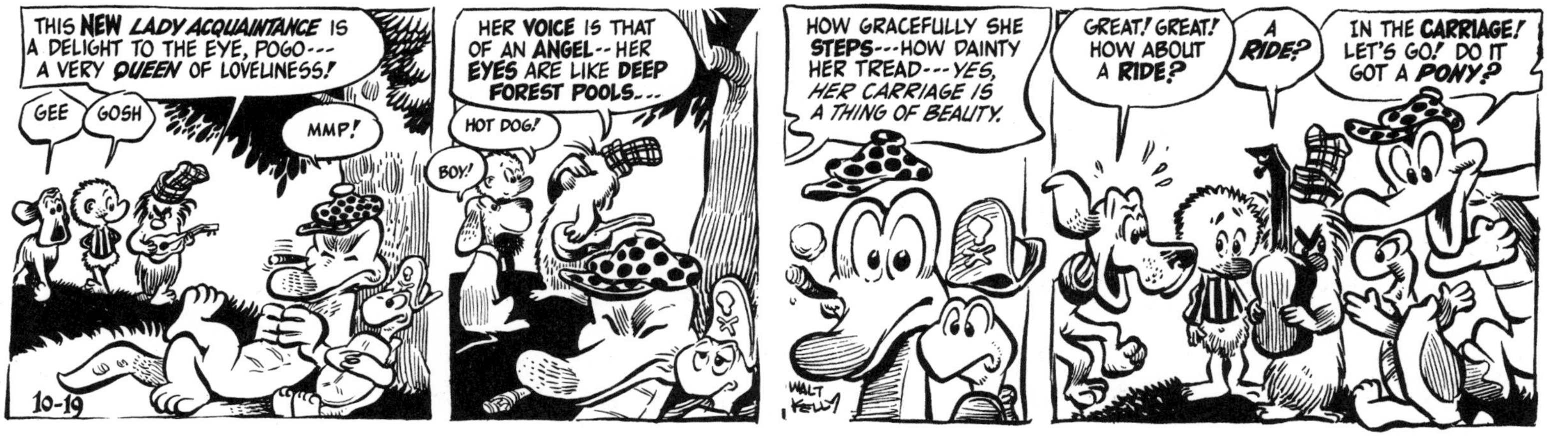
THIS NEW LADY ACQUAINTANCE IS A DELIGHT TO THE EYE, POGO--- A VERY QUEEN OF LOVELINESS!
GEE
GOSH
MMP!
HER VOICE IS THAT OF AN ANGEL--HER EYES ARE LIKE DEEP FOREST POOLS...
HOT DOG!
BOY!
HOW GRACEFULLY SHE STEPS---HOW DAINTY HER TREAD---YES, HER CARRIAGE IS A THING OF BEAUTY.
GREAT! GREAT! HOW ABOUT A RIDE?
A RIDE?
IN THE CARRIAGE! LET'S GO! DO IT GOT A PONY?
10-19
WALT KELLY

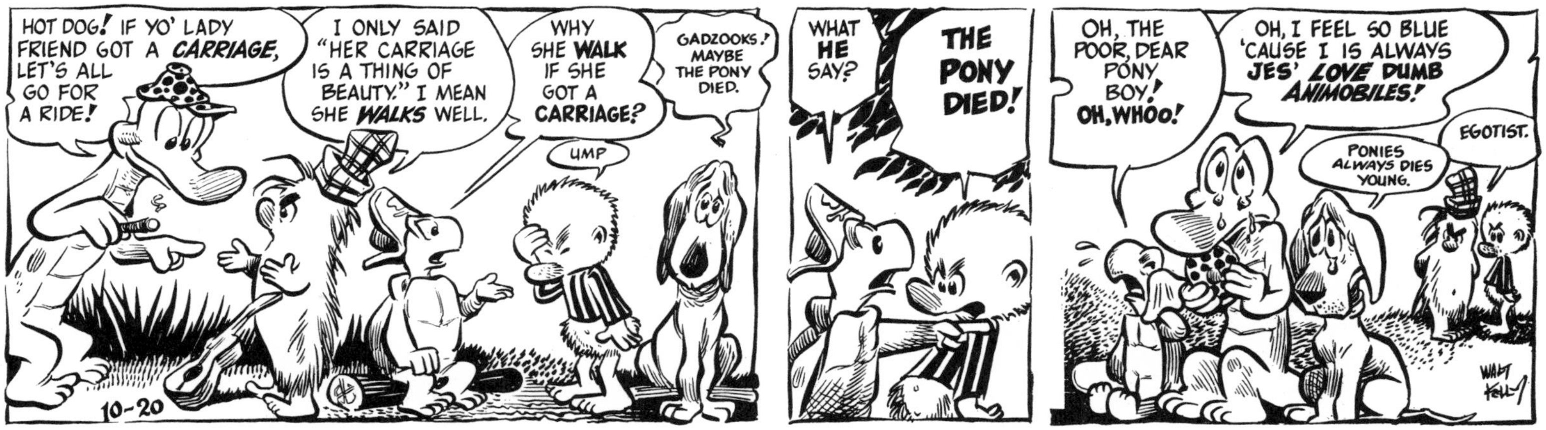
HOT DOG! IF YO' LADY FRIEND GOT A CARRIAGE, LET'S ALL GO FOR A RIDE!
I ONLY SAID "HER CARRIAGE IS A THING OF BEAUTY." I MEAN SHE WALKS WELL.
WHY SHE WALK IF SHE GOT A CARRIAGE?
GADZOOKS! MAYBE THE PONY DIED.
UMP
WHAT HE SAY?
THE PONY DIED!
OH, THE POOR, DEAR PONY BOY! OH, WHOO!
OH, I FEEL SO BLUE 'CAUSE I IS ALWAYS JES' LOVE DUMB ANIMOBILES!
PONIES ALWAYS DIES YOUNG.
EGOTIST.
10-20
WALT KELLY

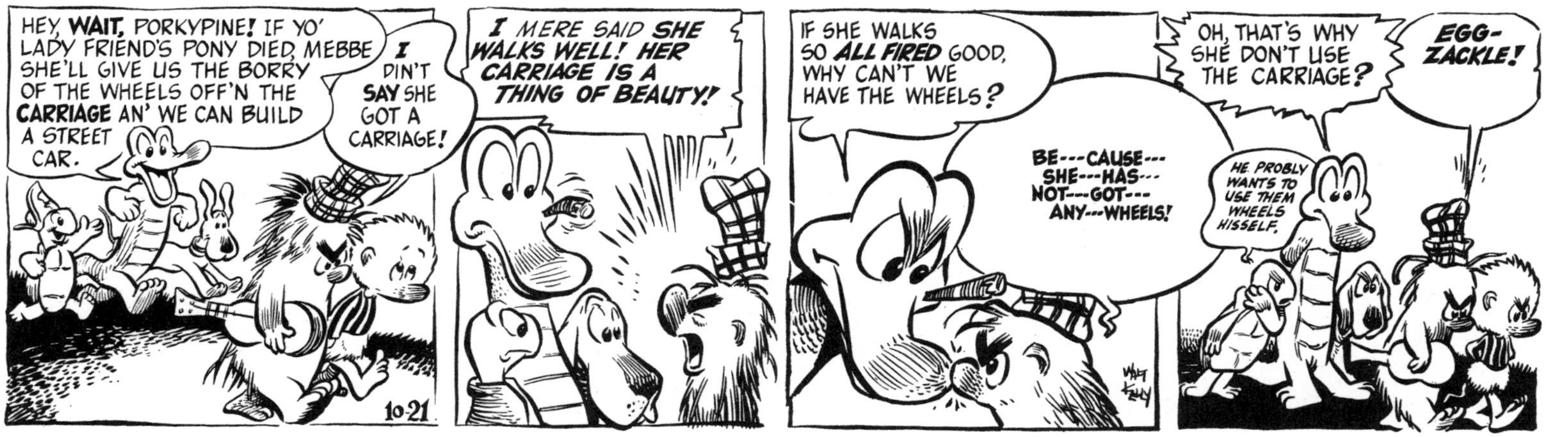
HEY, WAIT, PORKYPINE! IF YO' LADY FRIEND'S PONY DIED, MEBBE SHE'LL GIVE US THE BORRY OF THE WHEELS OFF'N THE CARRIAGE AN' WE CAN BUILD A STREET CAR.
I DIN'T SAY SHE GOT A CARRIAGE!
I MERE SAID SHE WALKS WELL! HER CARRIAGE IS A THING OF BEAUTY!
IF SHE WALKS SO ALL FIRED GOOD, WHY CAN'T WE HAVE THE WHEELS?
BE---CAUSE--- SHE---HAS--- NOT---GOT--- ANY---WHEELS!
OH, THAT'S WHY SHE DON'T USE THE CARRIAGE?
EGG-ZACKLE!
HE PROBLY WANTS TO USE THEM WHEELS HISSELF.
10-21
WALT KELLY

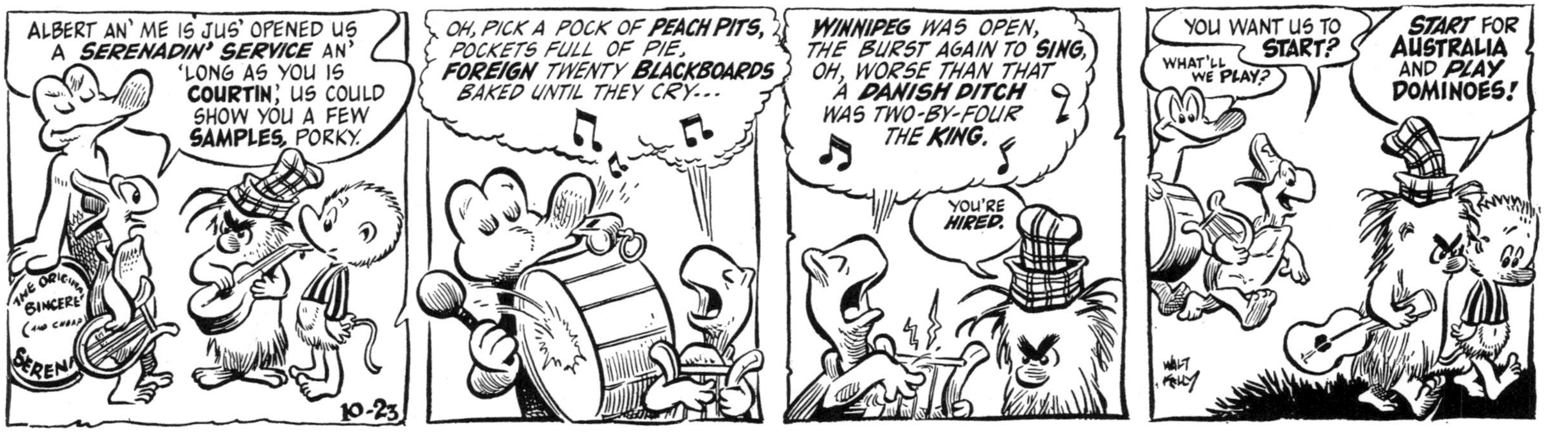
ALBERT AN' ME IS JUS' OPENED US A SERENADIN' SERVICE AN' 'LONG AS YOU IS COURTIN', US COULD SHOW YOU A FEW SAMPLES, PORKY.
10-23
OH, PICK A POCK OF PEACH PITS, POCKETS FULL OF PIE. FOREIGN TWENTY BLACKBOARDS BAKED UNTIL THEY CRY---
WINNIPEG WAS OPEN, THE BURST AGAIN TO SING, OH, WORSE THAN THAT A DANISH DITCH WAS TWO-BY-FOUR THE KING.
YOU'RE HIRED.
YOU WANT US TO START?
WHAT'LL WE PLAY?
START FOR AUSTRALIA AND PLAY DOMINOES!
WALT KELLY

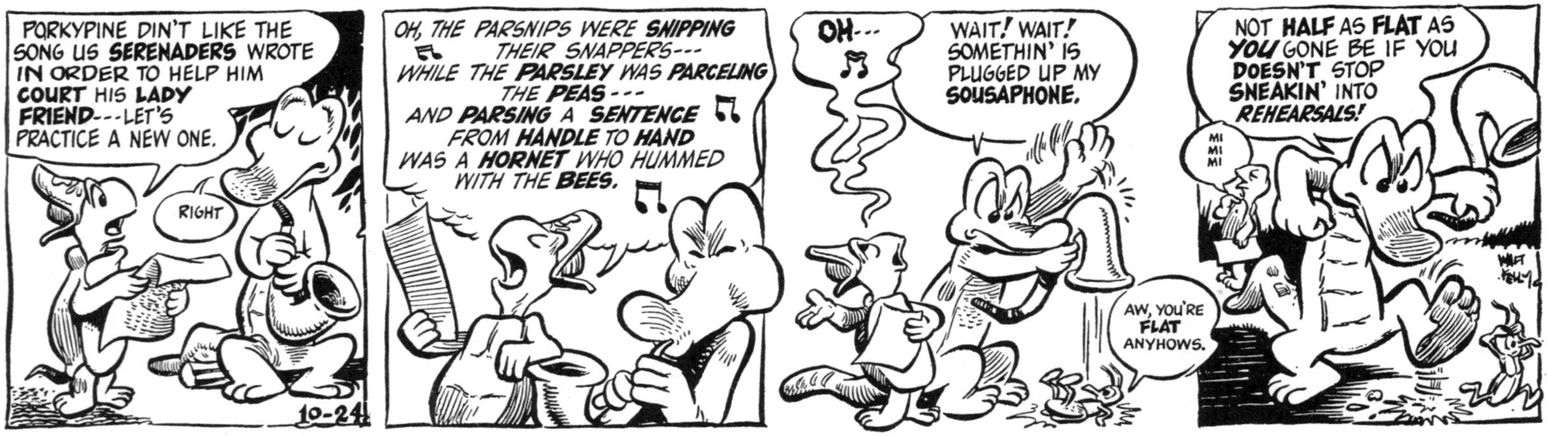
PORKYPINE DIN'T LIKE THE SONG US SERENADERS WROTE IN ORDER TO HELP HIM COURT HIS LADY FRIEND---LET'S PRACTICE A NEW ONE.
RIGHT
10-24
OH, THE PARSNIPS WERE SNIPPING THEIR SNAPPERS--- WHILE THE PARSLEY WAS PARCELING THE PEAS--- AND PARSING A SENTENCE FROM HANDLE TO HAND WAS A HORNET WHO HUMMED WITH THE BEES.
OH---
WAIT! WAIT! SOMETHIN' IS PLUGGED UP MY SOUSAPHONE.
AW, YOU'RE FLAT ANYHOWS.
NOT HALF AS FLAT AS YOU GONE BE IF YOU DOESN'T STOP SNEAKIN' INTO REHEARSALS!
MI MI MI
WALT KELLY

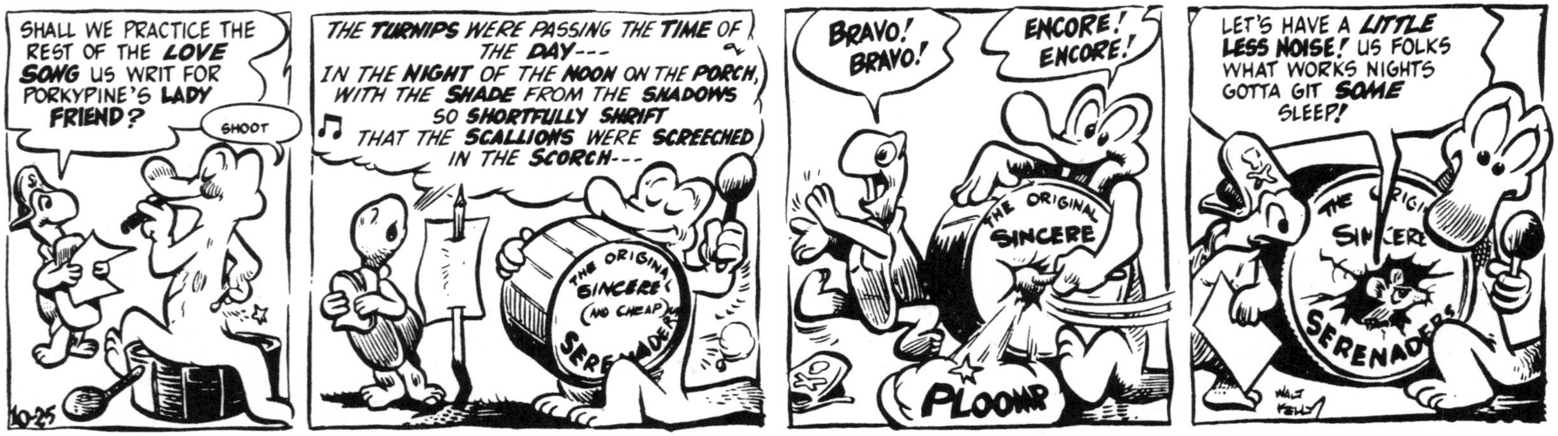
SHALL WE PRACTICE THE REST OF THE LOVE SONG US WRIT FOR PORKYPINE'S LADY FRIEND?
SHOOT
10-25
THE TURNIPS WERE PASSING THE TIME OF THE DAY--- IN THE NIGHT OF THE NOON ON THE PORCH, WITH THE SHADE FROM THE SHADOWS SO SHORTFULLY SHRIFT THAT THE SCALLIONS WERE SCREECHED IN THE SCORCH---
THE ORIGINAL SINCERE (AND CHEAP) SERENADERS
BRAVO! BRAVO!
ENCORE! ENCORE!
THE ORIGINAL SINCERE
PLOOMP
LET'S HAVE A LITTLE LESS NOISE! US FOLKS WHAT WORKS NIGHTS GOTTA GIT SOME SLEEP!
SERENADERS
WALT KELLY

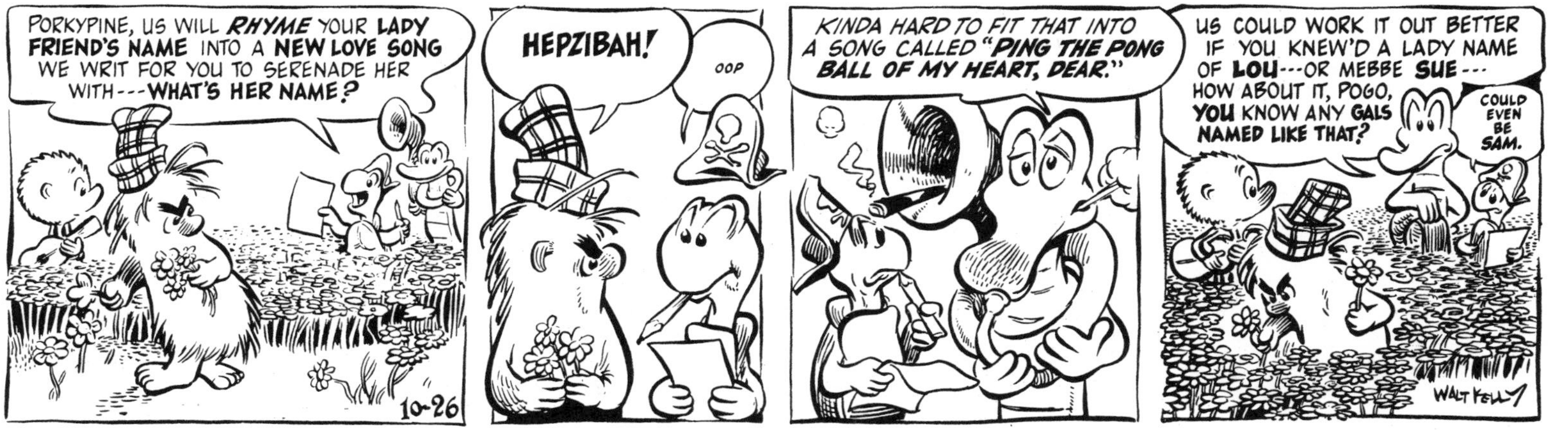
PORKYPINE, US WILL RHYME YOUR LADY FRIEND'S NAME INTO A NEW LOVE SONG WE WRIT FOR YOU TO SERENADE HER WITH---WHAT'S HER NAME?
HEPZIBAH!
OOP
KINDA HARD TO FIT THAT INTO A SONG CALLED "PING THE PONG BALL OF MY HEART, DEAR."
US COULD WORK IT OUT BETTER IF YOU KNEW'D A LADY NAME OF LOU---OR MEBBE SUE---HOW ABOUT IT, POGO, YOU KNOW ANY GALS NAMED LIKE THAT?
COULD EVEN BE SAM.
10-26
WALT KELLY

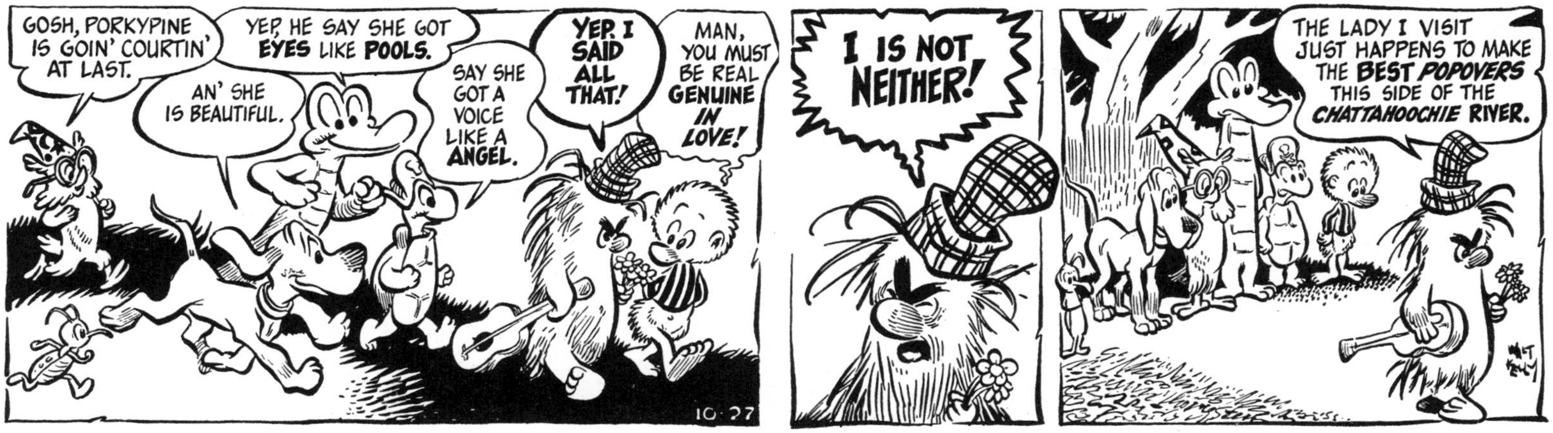
GOSH, PORKYPINE IS GOIN' COURTIN' AT LAST.
YEP, HE SAY SHE GOT EYES LIKE POOLS.
AN' SHE IS BEAUTIFUL.
SAY SHE GOT A VOICE LIKE A ANGEL.
YEP, I SAID ALL THAT!
MAN, YOU MUST BE REAL GENUINE IN LOVE!
I IS NOT NEITHER!
THE LADY I VISIT JUST HAPPENS TO MAKE THE BEST POPOVERS THIS SIDE OF THE CHATTAHOOCHIE RIVER.
10-27
WALT KELLY

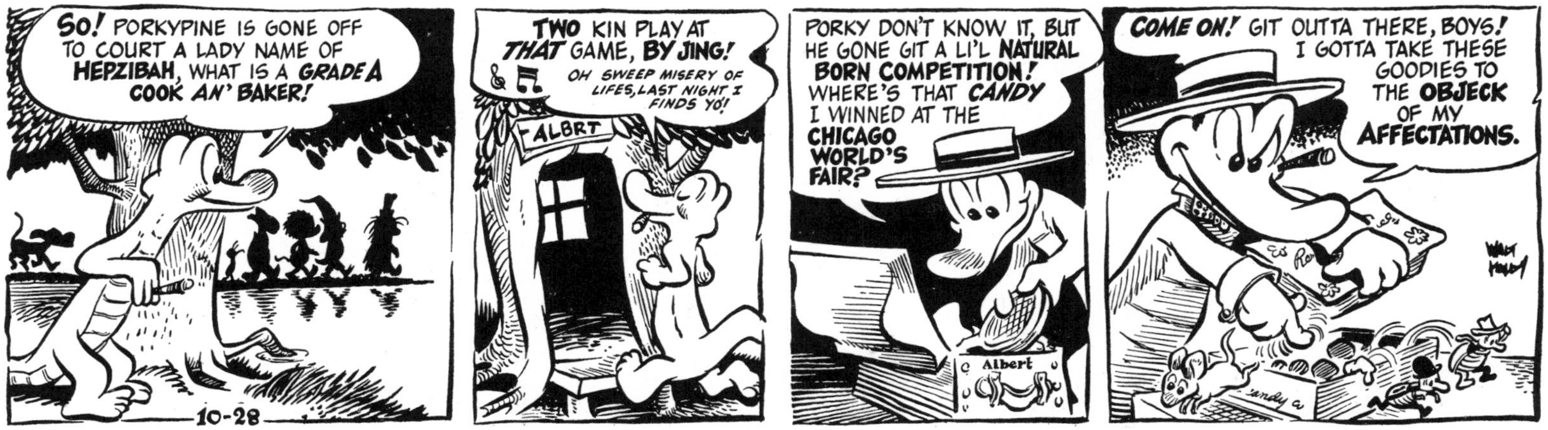
SO! PORKYPINE IS GONE OFF TO COURT A LADY NAME OF HEPZIBAH, WHAT IS A GRADE A COOK AN' BAKER!
TWO KIN PLAY AT THAT GAME, BY JING!
OH SWEEP MISERY OF LIFES, LAST NIGHT I FINDS YO!
ALBRT
PORKY DON'T KNOW IT, BUT HE GONE GIT A LI'L NATURAL BORN COMPETITION! WHERE'S THAT CANDY I WINNED AT THE CHICAGO WORLD'S FAIR?
Albert
COME ON! GIT OUTTA THERE, BOYS! I GOTTA TAKE THESE GOODIES TO THE OBJECK OF MY AFFECTATIONS.
10-28
WALT KELLY

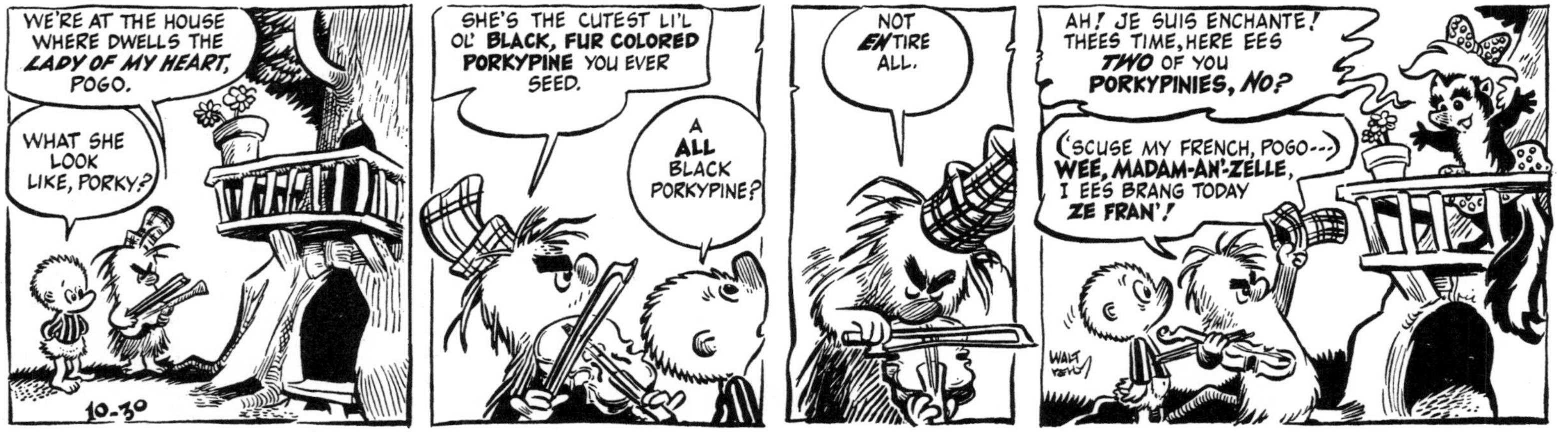
WE'RE AT THE HOUSE WHERE DWELLS THE *LADY OF MY HEART,* POGO.
WHAT SHE LOOK LIKE, PORKY?
10-30
SHE'S THE CUTEST LI'L OL' **BLACK, FUR COLORED PORKYPINE** YOU EVER SEED.
A **ALL** BLACK PORKYPINE?
NOT *EN*TIRE ALL.
AH! JE SUIS ENCHANTE! THEES TIME, HERE EES *TWO* OF YOU **PORKYPINIES, *NO?***
('SCUSE MY FRENCH, POGO--) **WEE, MADAM-AN'-ZELLE,** I EES BRANG TODAY **ZE FRAN'!**

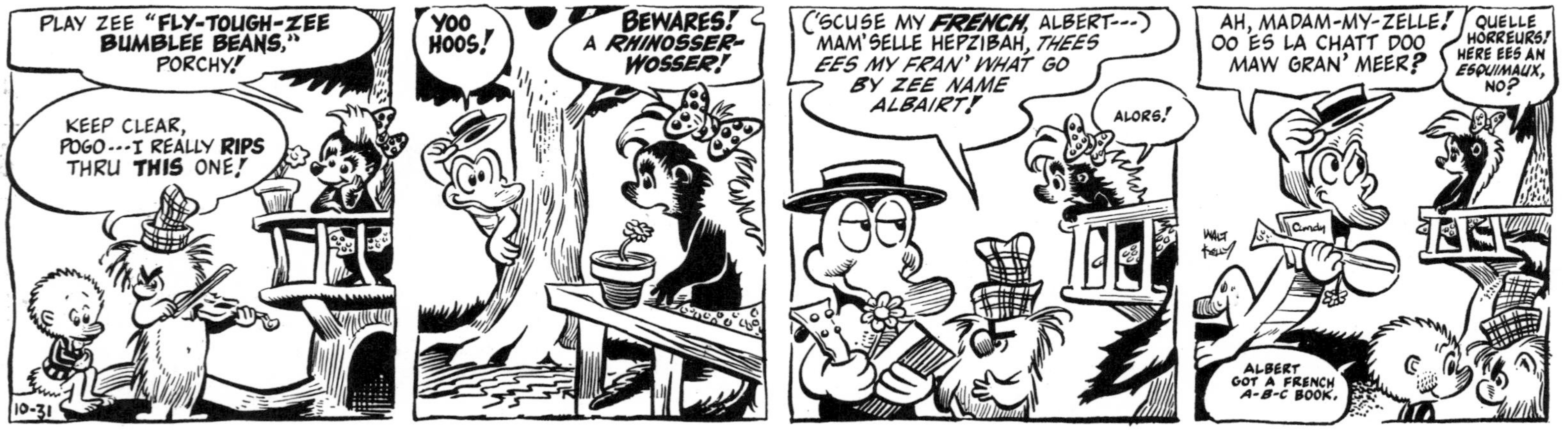
PLAY ZEE "**FLY-TOUGH-ZEE BUMBLEE BEANS,**" PORCHY!
KEEP CLEAR, POGO---I REALLY **RIPS** THRU **THIS** ONE!
10-31
YOO HOOS!
BEWARES! A ***RHINOSSER-WOSSER!***
('SCUSE MY ***FRENCH,*** ALBERT---) MAM'SELLE HEPZIBAH, *THEES EES MY FRAN' WHAT GO BY ZEE NAME ALBAIRT!*
ALORS!
AH, MADAM-MY-ZELLE! OO ES LA CHATT DOO MAW GRAN' MEER?
QUELLE HORREURS! HERE EES AN ESQUIMAUX, NO?
Candy
ALBERT GOT A FRENCH A-B-C BOOK.

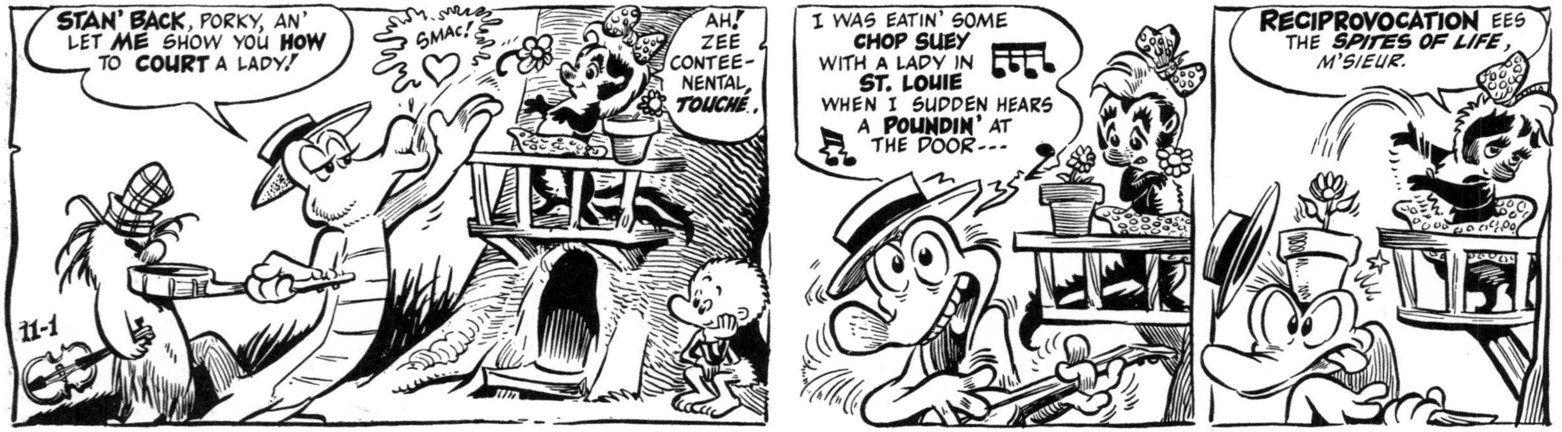
STAN' BACK, PORKY, AN' LET **ME** SHOW YOU **HOW** TO **COURT** A LADY!
SMAC!
AH! ZEE CONTEE-NENTAL, ***TOUCHÉ.***
11-1
I WAS EATIN' SOME **CHOP SUEY** WITH A LADY IN **ST. LOUIE** WHEN I SUDDEN HEARS A **POUNDIN'** AT THE DOOR---
RECIPROVOCATION EES THE ***SPITES OF LIFE,*** *M'SIEUR.*

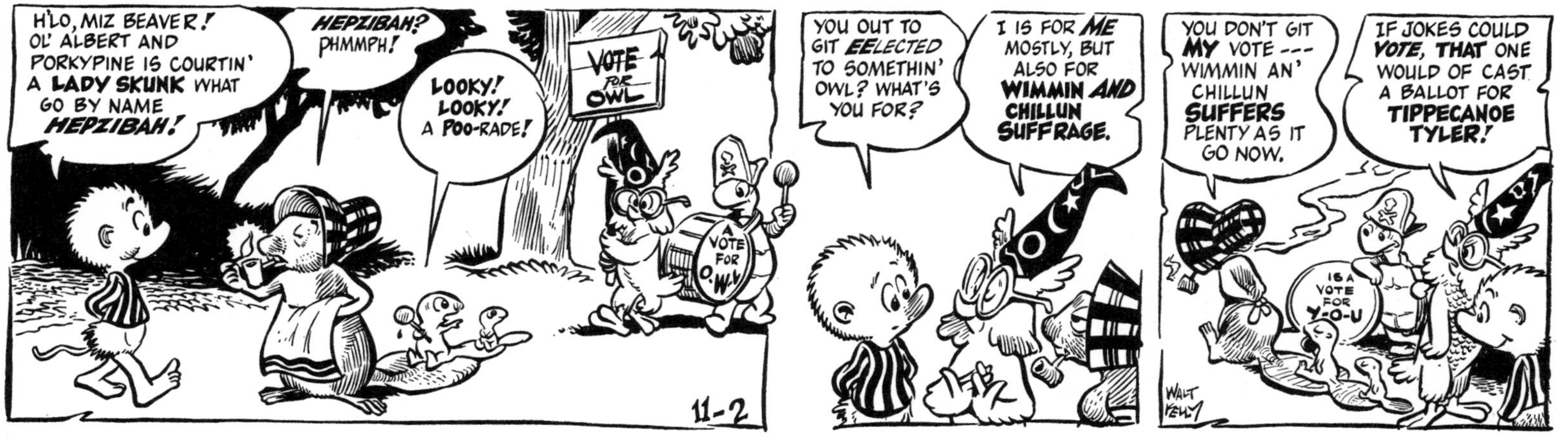
H'LO, MIZ BEAVER! OL' ALBERT AND PORKYPINE IS COURTIN' A LADY SKUNK WHAT GO BY NAME HEPZIBAH!
HEPZIBAH? PHMMPH!
LOOKY! LOOKY! A POO-RADE!
VOTE FOR OWL
A VOTE FOR OWL
11-2
YOU OUT TO GIT EELECTED TO SOMETHIN' OWL? WHAT'S YOU FOR?
I IS FOR ME MOSTLY, BUT ALSO FOR WIMMIN AND CHILLUN SUFFRAGE.
YOU DON'T GIT MY VOTE --- WIMMIN AN' CHILLUN SUFFERS PLENTY AS IT GO NOW.
IF JOKES COULD VOTE, THAT ONE WOULD OF CAST A BALLOT FOR TIPPECANOE TYLER!
IS A VOTE FOR Y-O-U
WALT KELLY

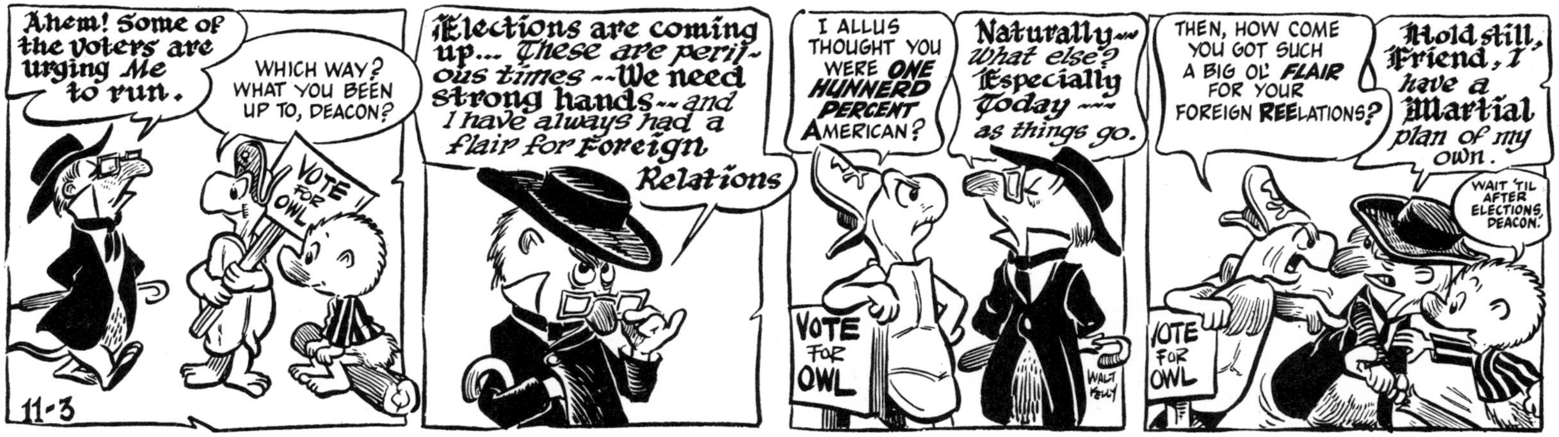
Ahem! Some of the voters are urging Me to run.
WHICH WAY? WHAT YOU BEEN UP TO, DEACON?
VOTE FOR OWL
11-3
Elections are coming up... These are perilous times --We need strong hands-- and I have always had a flair for Foreign Relations
I ALLUS THOUGHT YOU WERE ONE HUNNERD PERCENT AMERICAN?
Naturally-- What else? Especially Today --- as things go.
VOTE FOR OWL
WALT KELLY
THEN, HOW COME YOU GOT SUCH A BIG OL' FLAIR FOR YOUR FOREIGN REELATIONS?
Hold still, Friend, I have a Martial plan of my own.
WAIT 'TIL AFTER ELECTIONS, DEACON.
VOTE FOR OWL

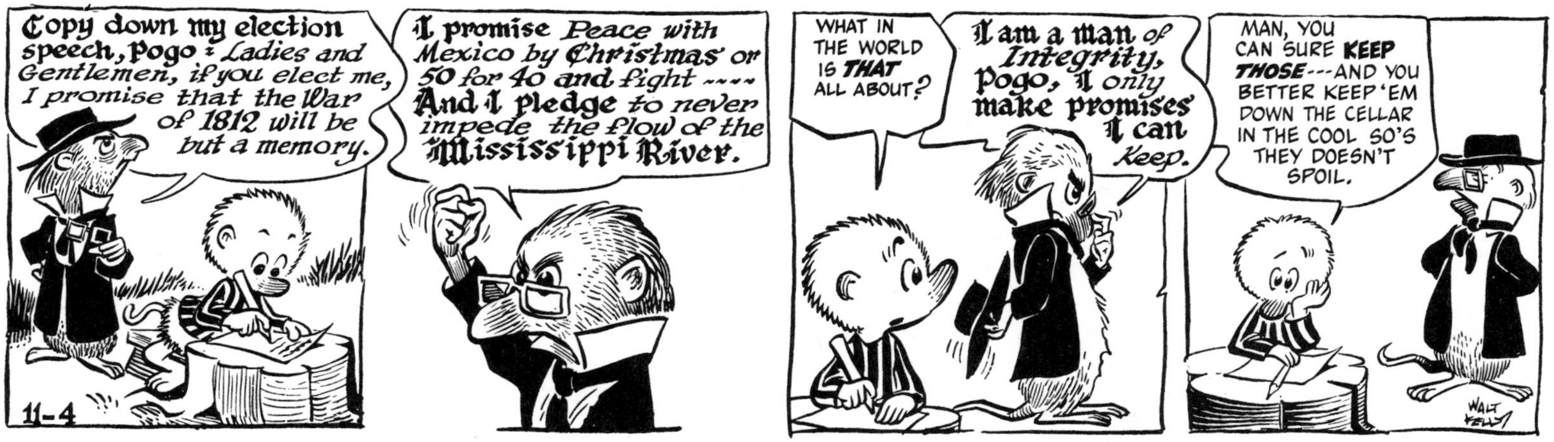
Copy down my election speech, Pogo: Ladies and Gentlemen, if you elect me, I promise that the War of 1812 will be but a memory.
I promise Peace with Mexico by Christmas or 50 for 40 and fight ---- And I pledge to never impede the flow of the Mississippi River.
11-4
WHAT IN THE WORLD IS THAT ALL ABOUT?
I am a man of Integrity, Pogo, I only make promises I can Keep.
MAN, YOU CAN SURE KEEP THOSE---AND YOU BETTER KEEP 'EM DOWN THE CELLAR IN THE COOL SO'S THEY DOESN'T SPOIL.
WALT KELLY

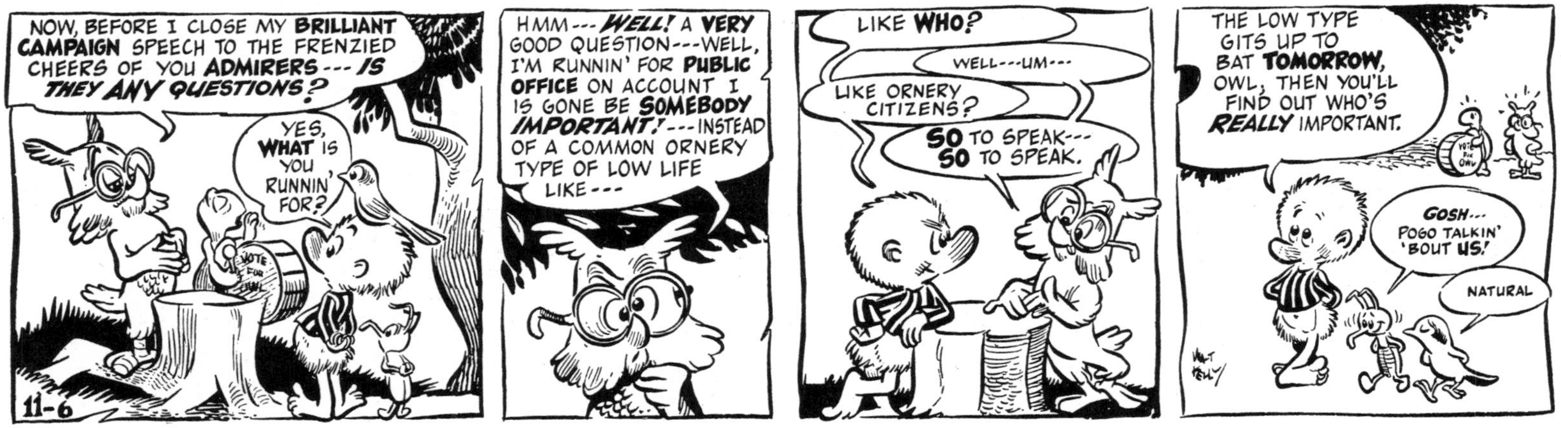
NOW, BEFORE I CLOSE MY **BRILLIANT CAMPAIGN** SPEECH TO THE FRENZIED CHEERS OF YOU **ADMIRERS**--- ***IS THEY ANY QUESTIONS?***
YES, **WHAT** IS YOU RUNNIN' FOR?
VOTE FOR
11-6
HMM--- ***WELL!*** A **VERY** GOOD QUESTION---WELL, I'M RUNNIN' FOR **PUBLIC OFFICE** ON ACCOUNT I IS GONE BE **SOMEBODY *IMPORTANT!*** ---INSTEAD OF A COMMON ORNERY TYPE OF LOW LIFE LIKE---
LIKE **WHO?**
WELL---UM---
LIKE ORNERY CITIZENS?
SO TO SPEAK--- **SO** TO SPEAK.
THE LOW TYPE GITS UP TO BAT **TOMORROW,** OWL, THEN YOU'LL FIND OUT WHO'S ***REALLY*** IMPORTANT.
GOSH--- POGO TALKIN' 'BOUT **US!**
NATURAL
WALT KELLY

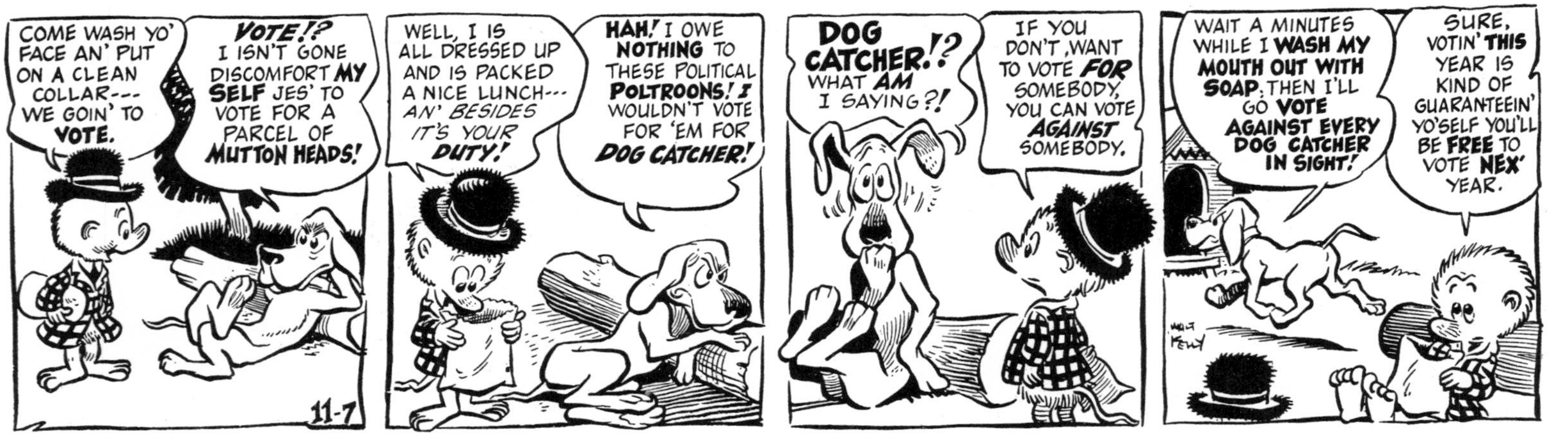
COME WASH YO' FACE AN' PUT ON A CLEAN COLLAR--- WE GOIN' TO **VOTE.**
VOTE!? I ISN'T GONE DISCOMFORT **MY SELF** JES' TO VOTE FOR A PARCEL OF **MUTTON HEADS!**
11-7
WELL, I IS ALL DRESSED UP AND IS PACKED A NICE LUNCH--- *AN' BESIDES IT'S YOUR* ***DUTY!***
HAH! I OWE **NOTHING** TO THESE POLITICAL **POLTROONS! *I*** WOULDN'T VOTE FOR 'EM FOR ***DOG CATCHER!***
DOG CATCHER!? WHAT ***AM*** I SAYING?!
IF YOU DON'T WANT TO VOTE ***FOR*** SOMEBODY, YOU CAN VOTE ***AGAINST*** SOMEBODY.
WAIT A MINUTES WHILE I **WASH MY MOUTH OUT WITH SOAP,** THEN I'LL GO **VOTE AGAINST EVERY DOG CATCHER IN SIGHT!**
SURE, VOTIN' **THIS** YEAR IS KIND OF GUARANTEEIN' YO'SELF YOU'LL BE **FREE** TO VOTE **NEX'** YEAR.
WALT KELLY

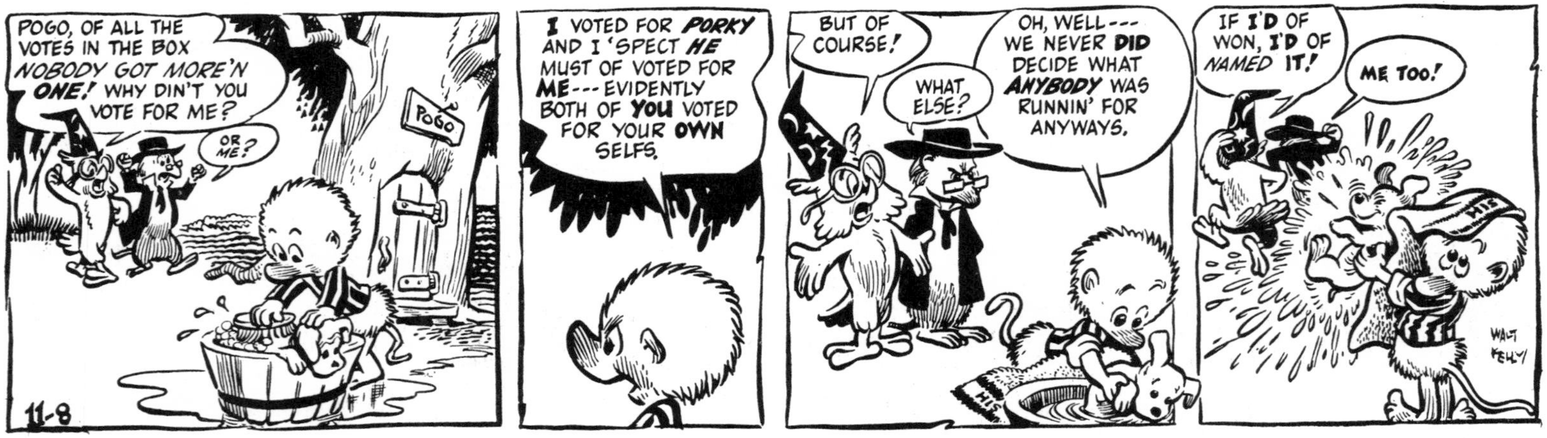
POGO, OF ALL THE VOTES IN THE BOX *NOBODY GOT MORE'N* ***ONE!*** WHY DIN'T YOU VOTE FOR ME?
OR ME?
POGO
11-8
I VOTED FOR ***PORKY*** AND I 'SPECT ***HE*** MUST OF VOTED FOR **ME**---EVIDENTLY BOTH OF **YOU** VOTED FOR YOUR **OWN** SELFS.
BUT OF COURSE!
WHAT ELSE?
OH, WELL--- WE NEVER **DID** DECIDE WHAT ***ANYBODY*** WAS RUNNIN' FOR ANYWAYS.
IF **I'D** OF WON, **I'D** OF *NAMED* **IT!**
ME TOO!
WALT KELLY

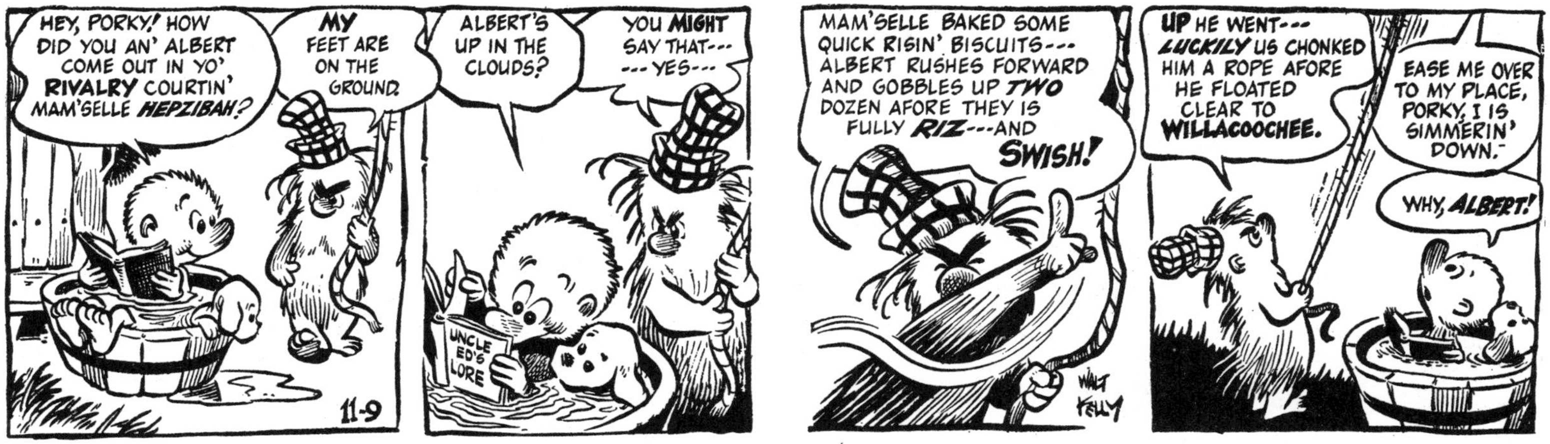
HEY, PORKY! HOW DID YOU AN' ALBERT COME OUT IN YO' RIVALRY COURTIN' MAM'SELLE HEPZIBAH?
MY FEET ARE ON THE GROUND.
11-9
ALBERT'S UP IN THE CLOUDS?
YOU MIGHT SAY THAT--- ---YES---
UNCLE ED'S LORE
MAM'SELLE BAKED SOME QUICK RISIN' BISCUITS--- ALBERT RUSHES FORWARD AND GOBBLES UP TWO DOZEN AFORE THEY IS FULLY RIZ---AND
SWISH!
WALT KELLY
UP HE WENT--- LUCKILY US CHONKED HIM A ROPE AFORE HE FLOATED CLEAR TO WILLACOOCHEE.
EASE ME OVER TO MY PLACE, PORKY, I IS SIMMERIN' DOWN.
WHY, ALBERT!

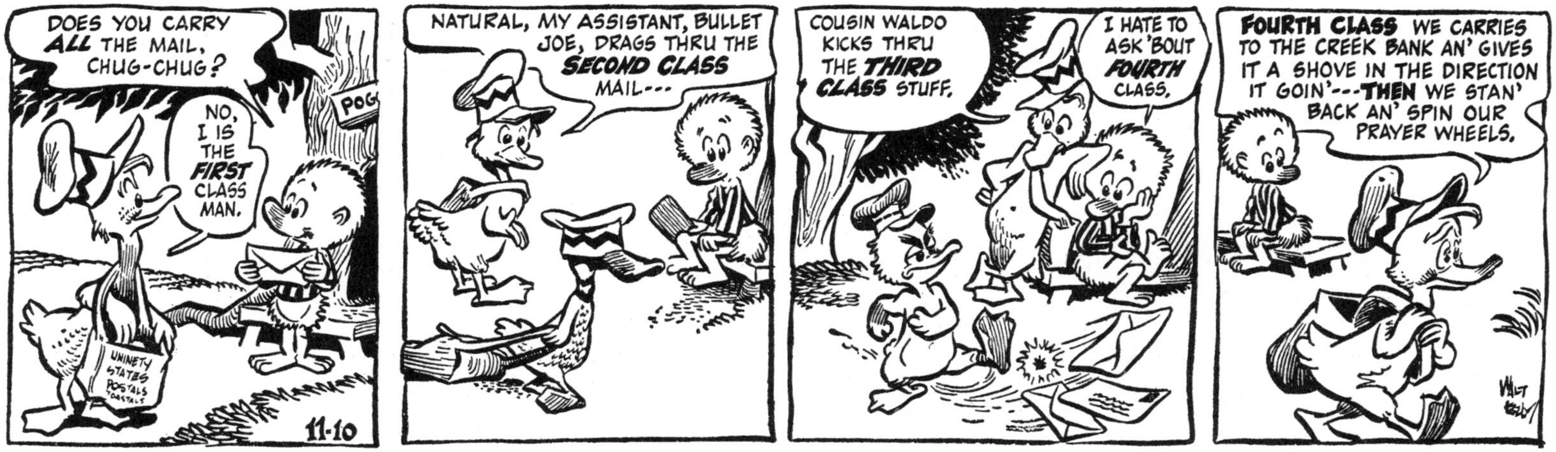
DOES YOU CARRY ALL THE MAIL, CHUG-CHUG?
NO, I IS THE FIRST CLASS MAN.
POG
UNINETY STATES POSTALS
11-10
NATURAL, MY ASSISTANT, BULLET JOE, DRAGS THRU THE SECOND CLASS MAIL---
COUSIN WALDO KICKS THRU THE THIRD CLASS STUFF.
I HATE TO ASK 'BOUT FOURTH CLASS.
FOURTH CLASS WE CARRIES TO THE CREEK BANK AN' GIVES IT A SHOVE IN THE DIRECTION IT GOIN'---THEN WE STAN' BACK AN' SPIN OUR PRAYER WHEELS.
WALT KELLY

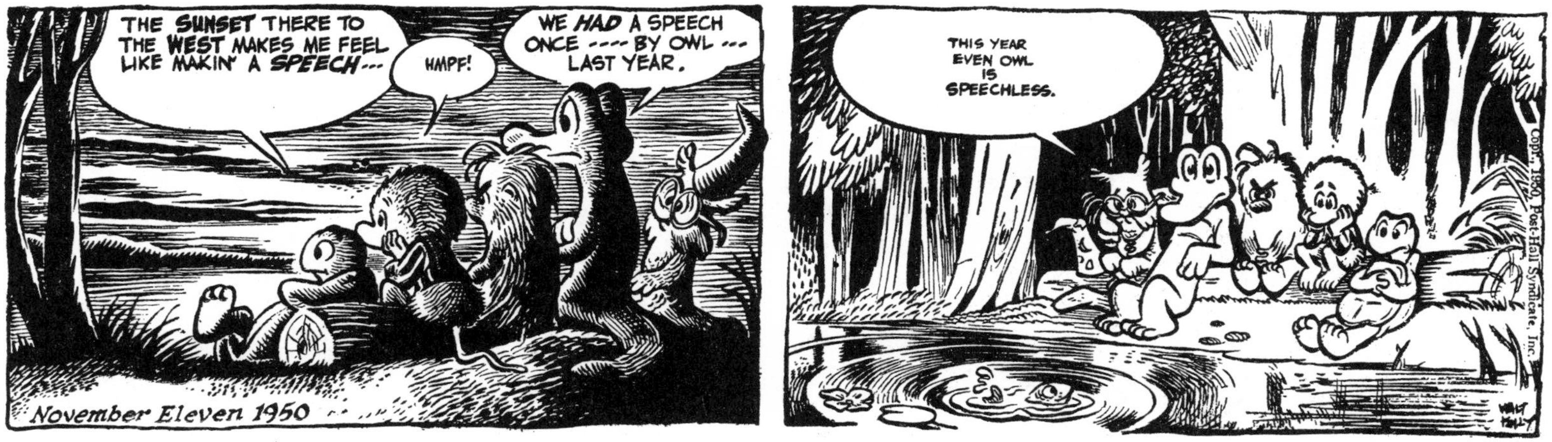
THE SUNSET THERE TO THE WEST MAKES ME FEEL LIKE MAKIN' A SPEECH---
HMPF!
WE HAD A SPEECH ONCE ---- BY OWL --- LAST YEAR.
November Eleven 1950
THIS YEAR EVEN OWL IS SPEECHLESS.
Copr. 1950 Post-Hall Syndicate, Inc.
WALT KELLY

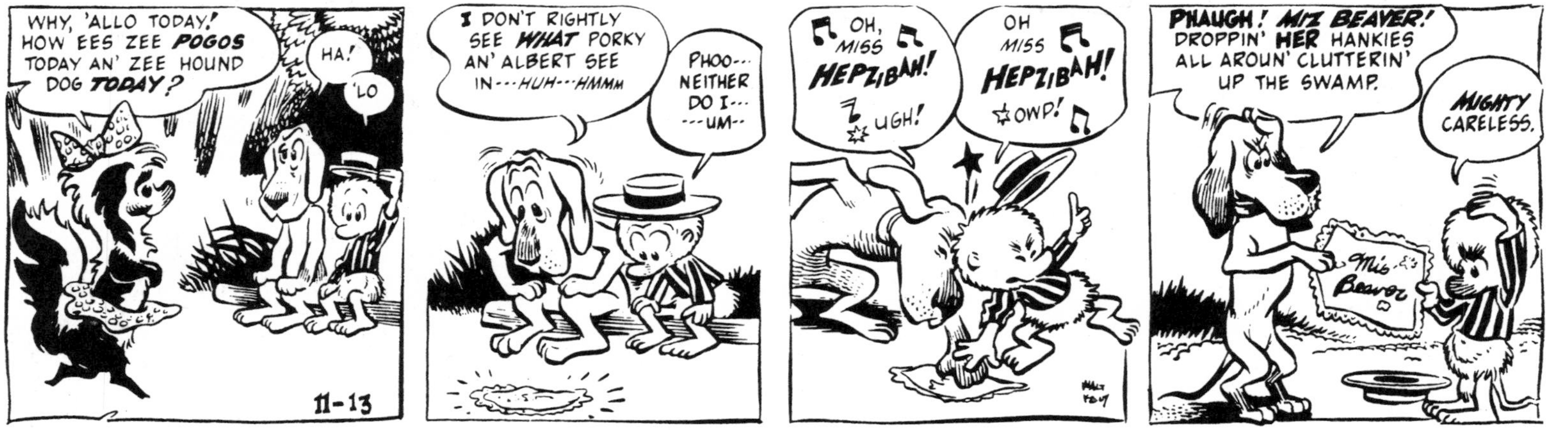
WHY, 'ALLO TODAY! HOW EES ZEE POGOS TODAY AN' ZEE HOUND DOG TODAY?
HA!
'LO
I DON'T RIGHTLY SEE WHAT PORKY AN' ALBERT SEE IN---HUH---HMMM
PHOO--- NEITHER DO I--- ---UM--
OH, MISS HEPZIBAH!
UGH!
OH MISS HEPZIBAH!
OWP!
PHAUGH! MIZ BEAVER! DROPPIN' HER HANKIES ALL AROUN' CLUTTERIN' UP THE SWAMP.
MIGHTY CARELESS.
Mis Beaver
11-13

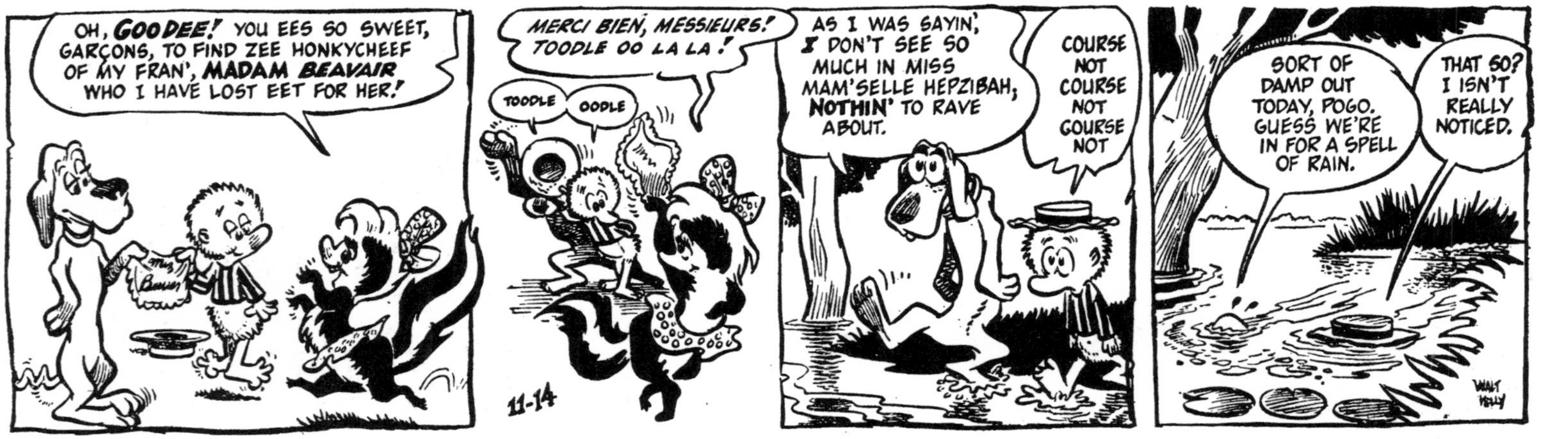
OH, GOODEE! YOU EES SO SWEET, GARÇONS, TO FIND ZEE HONKYCHEEF OF MY FRAN', MADAM BEAVAIR WHO I HAVE LOST EET FOR HER!
MERCI BIEN, MESSIEURS! TOODLE OO LA LA!
TOODLE
OODLE
AS I WAS SAYIN', I DON'T SEE SO MUCH IN MISS MAM'SELLE HEPZIBAH, NOTHIN' TO RAVE ABOUT.
COURSE NOT COURSE NOT COURSE NOT
SORT OF DAMP OUT TODAY, POGO. GUESS WE'RE IN FOR A SPELL OF RAIN.
THAT SO? I ISN'T REALLY NOTICED.
11-14

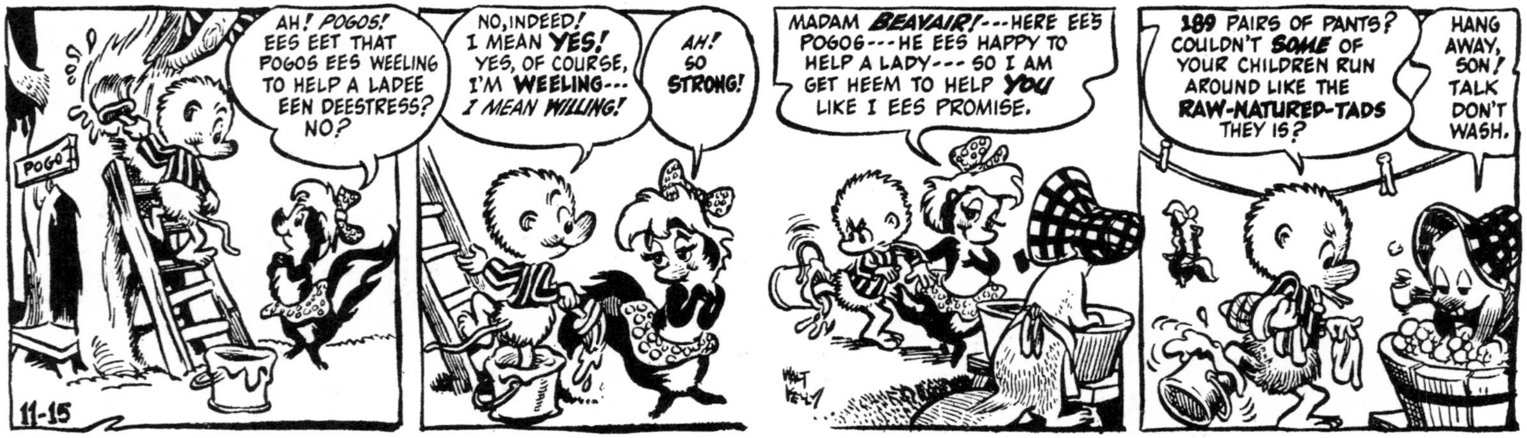
AH! POGOS! EES EET THAT POGOS EES WEELING TO HELP A LADEE EEN DEESTRESS? NO?
POGO
NO, INDEED! I MEAN YES! YES, OF COURSE, I'M WEELING--- I MEAN WILLING!
AH! SO STRONG!
MADAM BEAVAIR!---HERE EES POGOS---HE EES HAPPY TO HELP A LADY--- SO I AM GET HEEM TO HELP YOU LIKE I EES PROMISE.
189 PAIRS OF PANTS? COULDN'T SOME OF YOUR CHILDREN RUN AROUND LIKE THE RAW-NATURED-TADS THEY IS?
HANG AWAY, SON! TALK DON'T WASH.
11-15

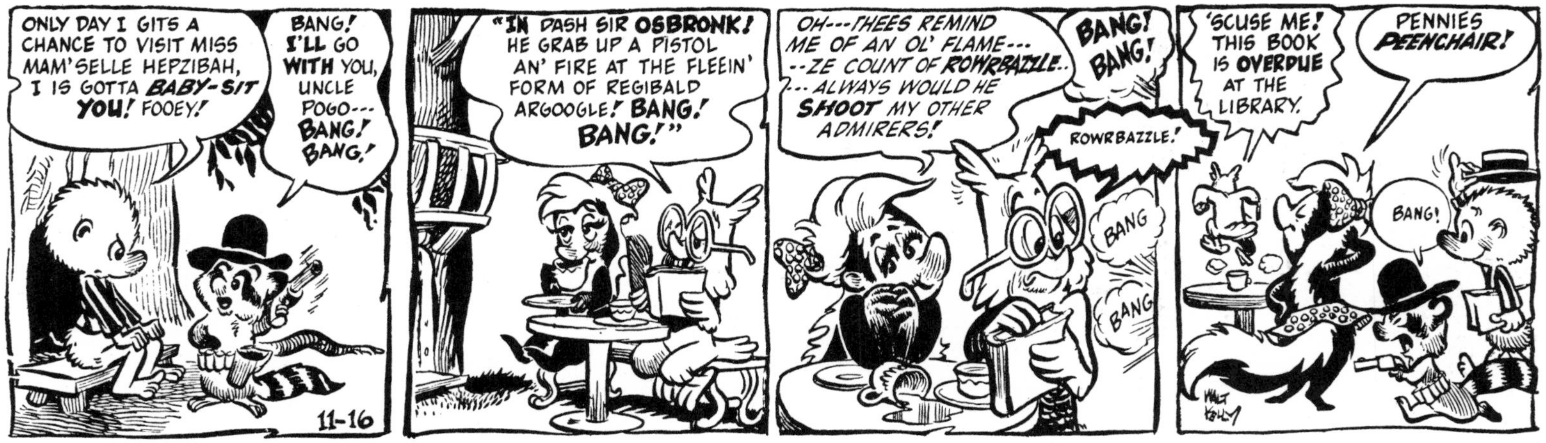
ONLY DAY I GITS A CHANCE TO VISIT MISS MAM'SELLE HEPZIBAH, I IS GOTTA BABY-SIT YOU! FOOEY!
BANG! I'LL GO WITH YOU, UNCLE POGO--- BANG! BANG!
11-16
"IN DASH SIR OSBRONK! HE GRAB UP A PISTOL AN' FIRE AT THE FLEEIN' FORM OF REGIBALD ARGOOGLE! BANG! BANG!"
OH---THEES REMIND ME OF AN OL' FLAME--- --ZE COUNT OF ROWRBAZZLE... ... ALWAYS WOULD HE SHOOT MY OTHER ADMIRERS!
BANG! BANG!
ROWRBAZZLE!
BANG
BANG
'SCUSE ME! THIS BOOK IS OVERDUE AT THE LIBRARY.
PENNIES PEENCHAIR!
BANG!
WALT KELLY

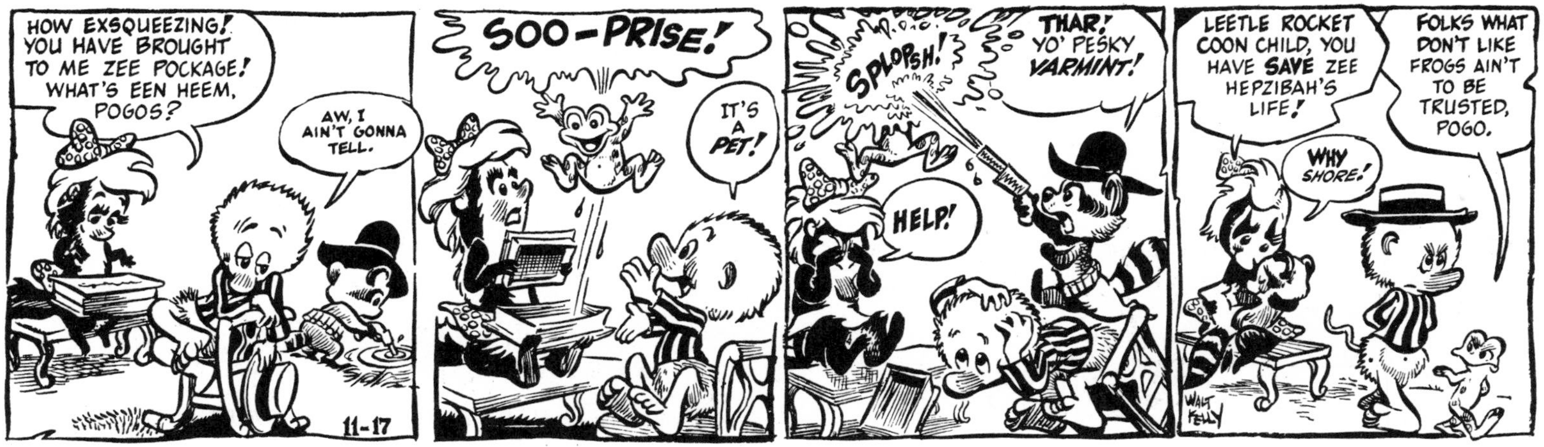
HOW EXSQUEEZING! YOU HAVE BROUGHT TO ME ZEE POCKAGE! WHAT'S EEN HEEM, POGOS?
AW, I AIN'T GONNA TELL.
11-17
SOO-PRISE!
IT'S A PET!
SPLOPSH!
THAR! YO' PESKY VARMINT!
HELP!
LEETLE ROCKET COON CHILD, YOU HAVE SAVE ZEE HEPZIBAH'S LIFE!
FOLKS WHAT DON'T LIKE FROGS AIN'T TO BE TRUSTED, POGO.
WHY SHORE!
WALT KELLY

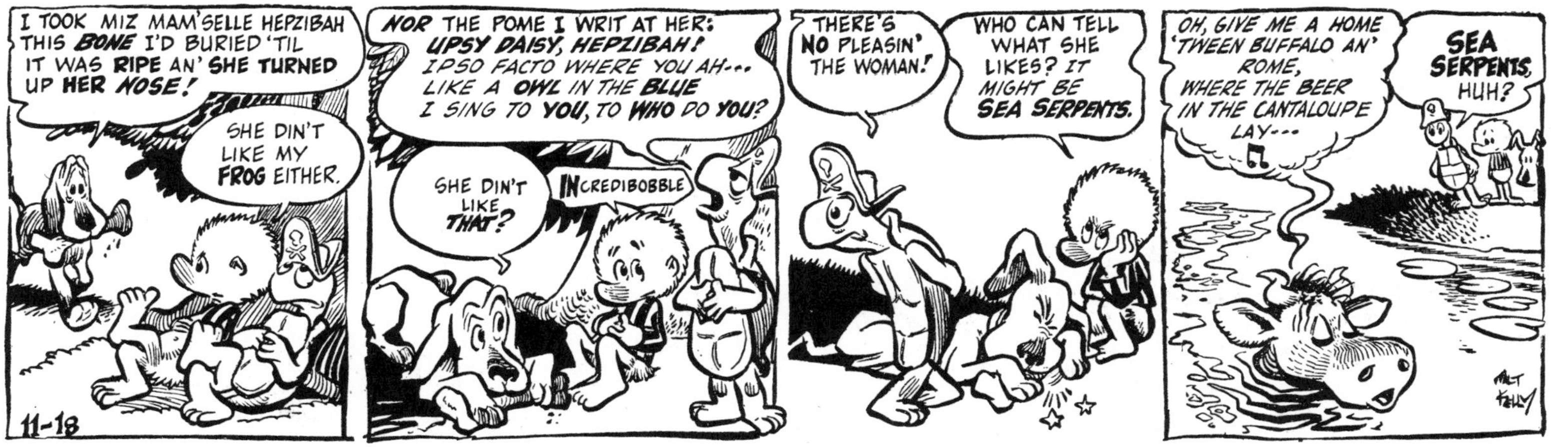
I TOOK MIZ MAM'SELLE HEPZIBAH THIS BONE I'D BURIED 'TIL IT WAS RIPE AN' SHE TURNED UP HER NOSE!
SHE DIN'T LIKE MY FROG EITHER.
11-18
NOR THE POME I WRIT AT HER: UPSY DAISY, HEPZIBAH! IPSO FACTO WHERE YOU AH--- LIKE A OWL IN THE BLUE I SING TO YOU, TO WHO DO YOU?
SHE DIN'T LIKE THAT?
INCREDIBOBBLE
THERE'S NO PLEASIN' THE WOMAN!
WHO CAN TELL WHAT SHE LIKES? IT MIGHT BE SEA SERPENTS.
OH, GIVE ME A HOME 'TWEEN BUFFALO AN' ROME, WHERE THE BEER IN THE CANTALOUPE LAY---
SEA SERPENTS, HUH?
WALT KELLY

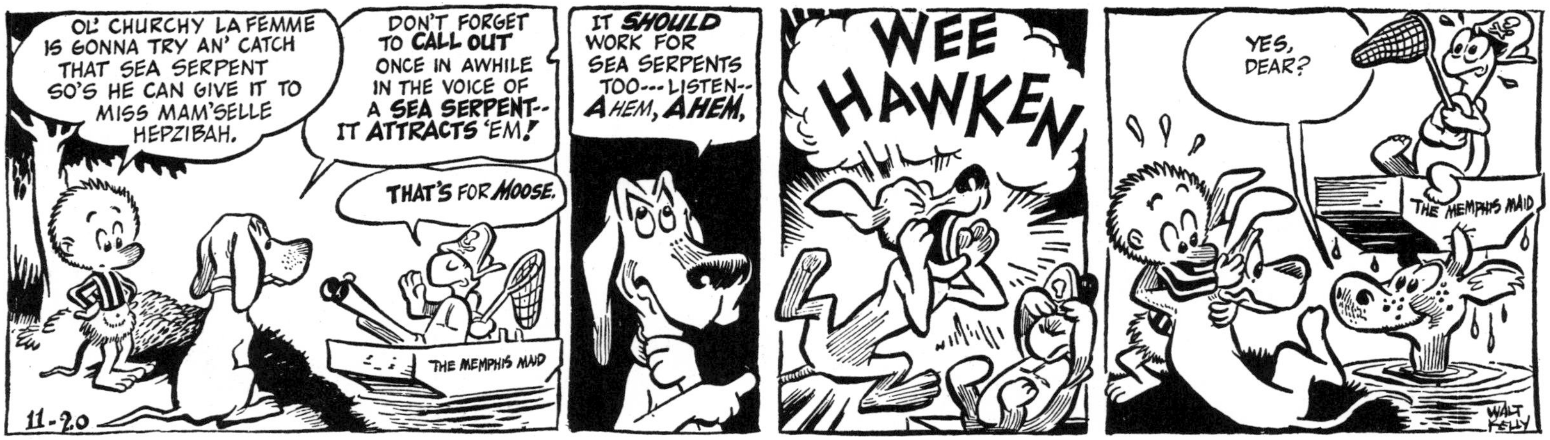
OL' CHURCHY LA FEMME IS GONNA TRY AN' CATCH THAT SEA SERPENT SO'S HE CAN GIVE IT TO MISS MAM'SELLE HEPZIBAH.
DON'T FORGET TO CALL OUT ONCE IN AWHILE IN THE VOICE OF A SEA SERPENT-- IT ATTRACTS 'EM!
THAT'S FOR MOOSE.
THE MEMPHIS MAID
IT SHOULD WORK FOR SEA SERPENTS TOO--- LISTEN-- AHEM, AHEM,
WEE HAWKEN
YES, DEAR?
THE MEMPHIS MAID
WALT KELLY
11-20

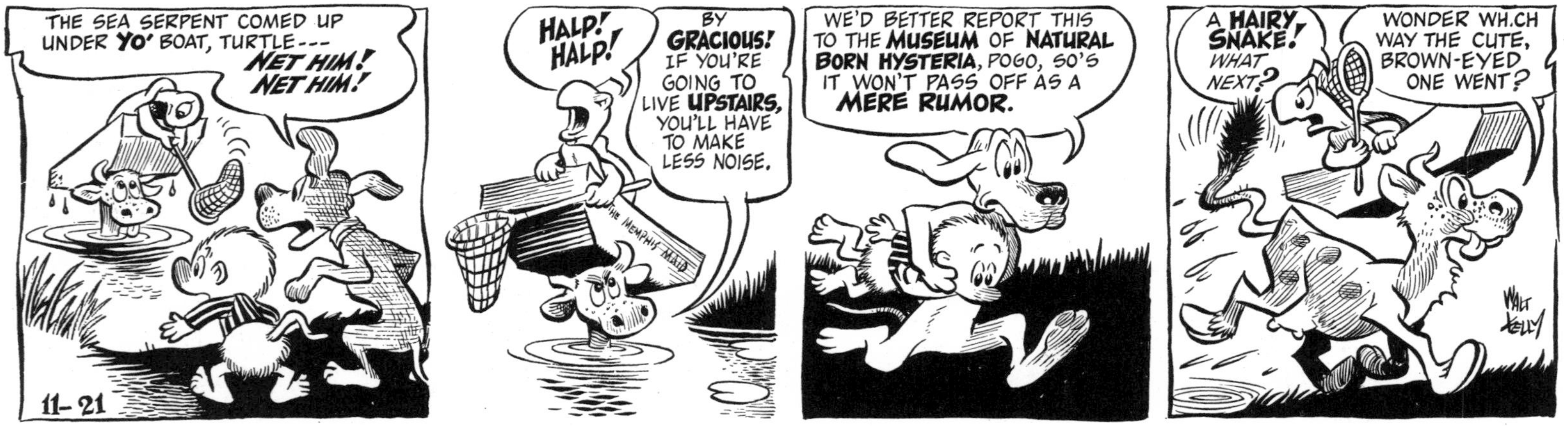
THE SEA SERPENT COMED UP UNDER YO' BOAT, TURTLE--- NET HIM! NET HIM!
HALP! HALP!
BY GRACIOUS! IF YOU'RE GOING TO LIVE UPSTAIRS, YOU'LL HAVE TO MAKE LESS NOISE.
THE MEMPHIS MAID
WE'D BETTER REPORT THIS TO THE MUSEUM OF NATURAL BORN HYSTERIA, POGO, SO'S IT WON'T PASS OFF AS A MERE RUMOR.
A HAIRY SNAKE! WHAT NEXT?
WONDER WH.CH WAY THE CUTE, BROWN-EYED ONE WENT?
WALT KELLY
11-21

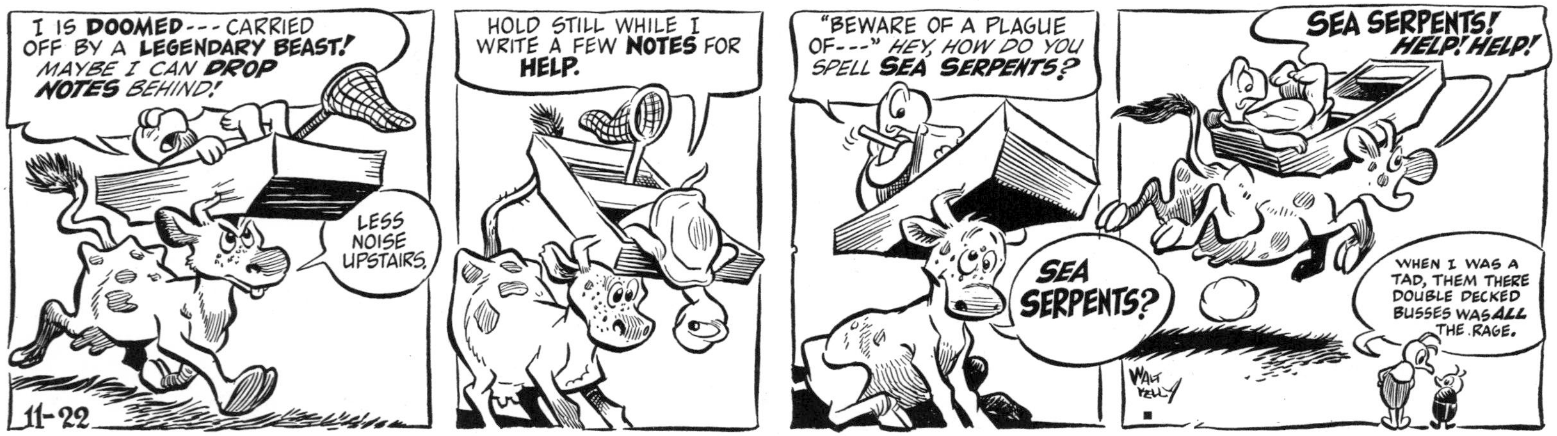
I IS DOOMED--- CARRIED OFF BY A LEGENDARY BEAST! MAYBE I CAN DROP NOTES BEHIND!
LESS NOISE UPSTAIRS.
HOLD STILL WHILE I WRITE A FEW NOTES FOR HELP.
"BEWARE OF A PLAGUE OF---" HEY, HOW DO YOU SPELL SEA SERPENTS?
SEA SERPENTS?
WALT KELLY
SEA SERPENTS! HELP! HELP!
WHEN I WAS A TAD, THEM THERE DOUBLE DECKED BUSSES WAS ALL THE RAGE.
11-22

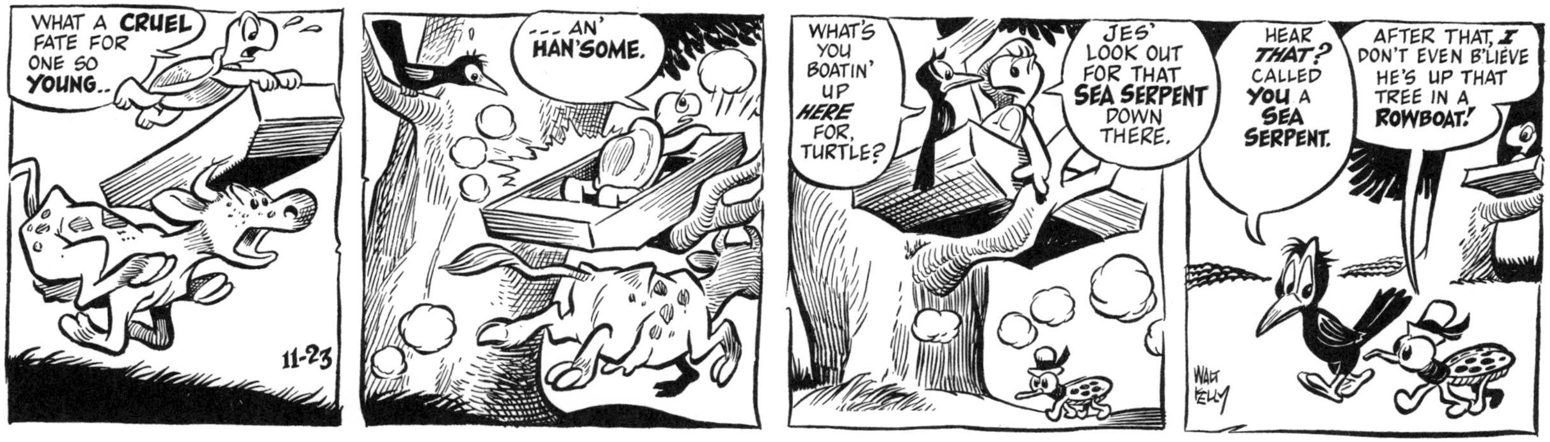
WHAT A CRUEL FATE FOR ONE SO YOUNG..
11-23
--- AN' HAN'SOME.
WHAT'S YOU BOATIN' UP HERE FOR, TURTLE?
JES' LOOK OUT FOR THAT SEA SERPENT DOWN THERE.
HEAR THAT? CALLED YOU A SEA SERPENT.
AFTER THAT, I DON'T EVEN B'LIEVE HE'S UP THAT TREE IN A ROWBOAT!
WALT KELLY

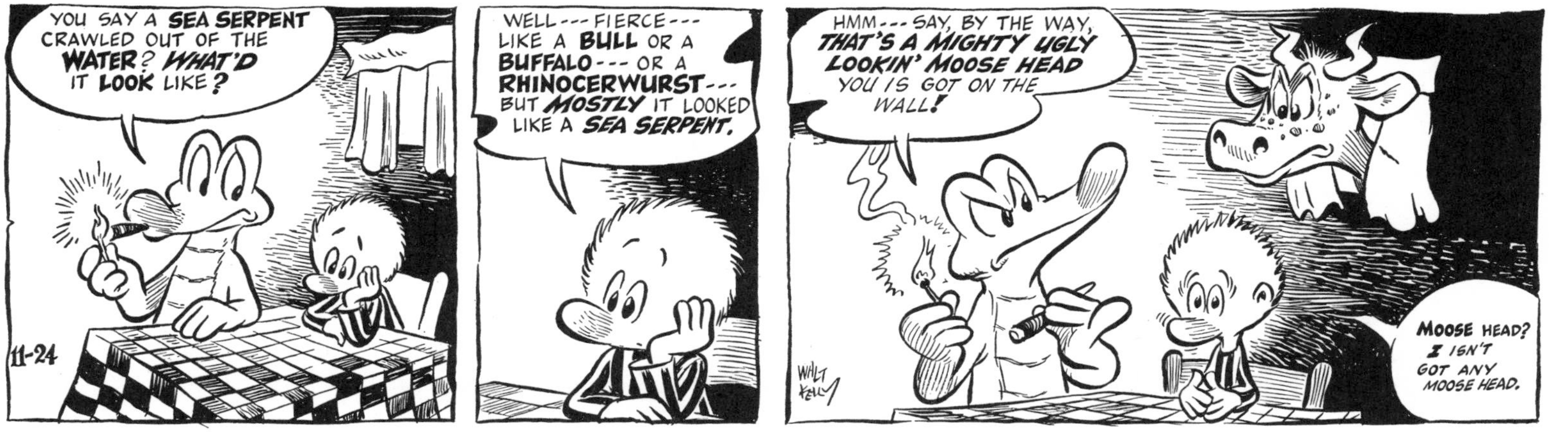
YOU SAY A SEA SERPENT CRAWLED OUT OF THE WATER? WHAT'D IT LOOK LIKE?
11-24
WELL---FIERCE--- LIKE A BULL OR A BUFFALO---OR A RHINOCERWURST--- BUT MOSTLY IT LOOKED LIKE A SEA SERPENT.
HMM---SAY, BY THE WAY, THAT'S A MIGHTY UGLY LOOKIN' MOOSE HEAD YOU IS GOT ON THE WALL!
MOOSE HEAD? I ISN'T GOT ANY MOOSE HEAD.
WALT KELLY

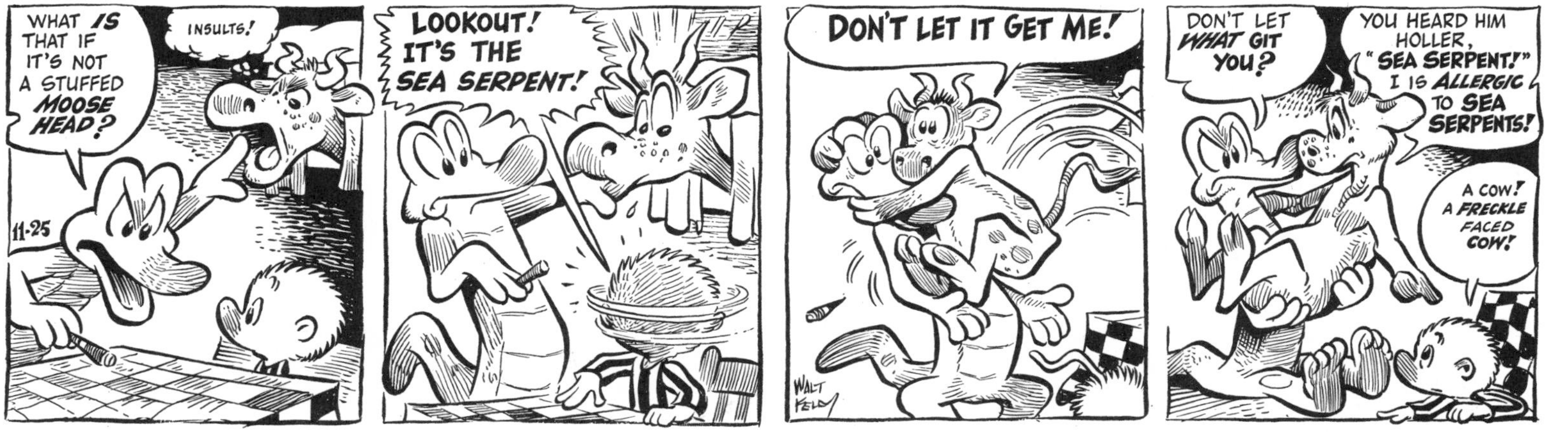
WHAT IS THAT IF IT'S NOT A STUFFED MOOSE HEAD?
INSULTS!
11-25
LOOKOUT! IT'S THE SEA SERPENT!
DON'T LET IT GET ME!
WALT KELLY
DON'T LET WHAT GIT YOU?
YOU HEARD HIM HOLLER, "SEA SERPENT!" I IS ALLERGIC TO SEA SERPENTS!
A COW! A FRECKLE FACED COW!

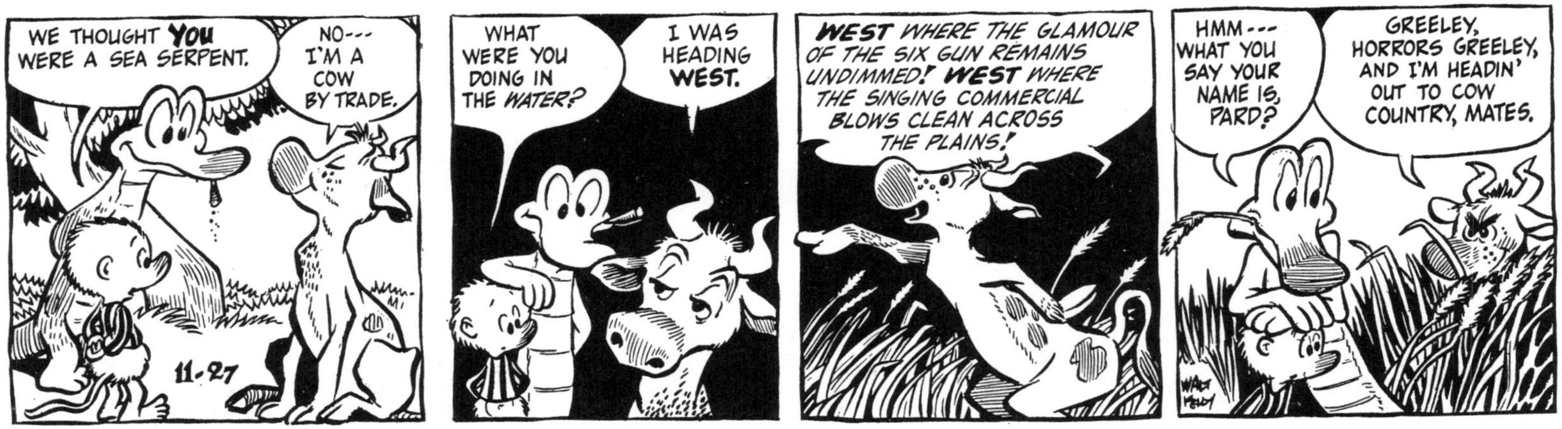
WE THOUGHT YOU WERE A SEA SERPENT.
NO--- I'M A COW BY TRADE.
11-27
WHAT WERE YOU DOING IN THE WATER?
I WAS HEADING WEST.
WEST WHERE THE GLAMOUR OF THE SIX GUN REMAINS UNDIMMED! WEST WHERE THE SINGING COMMERCIAL BLOWS CLEAN ACROSS THE PLAINS!
HMM--- WHAT YOU SAY YOUR NAME IS, PARD?
GREELEY, HORRORS GREELEY, AND I'M HEADIN' OUT TO COW COUNTRY, MATES.
WALT KELLY

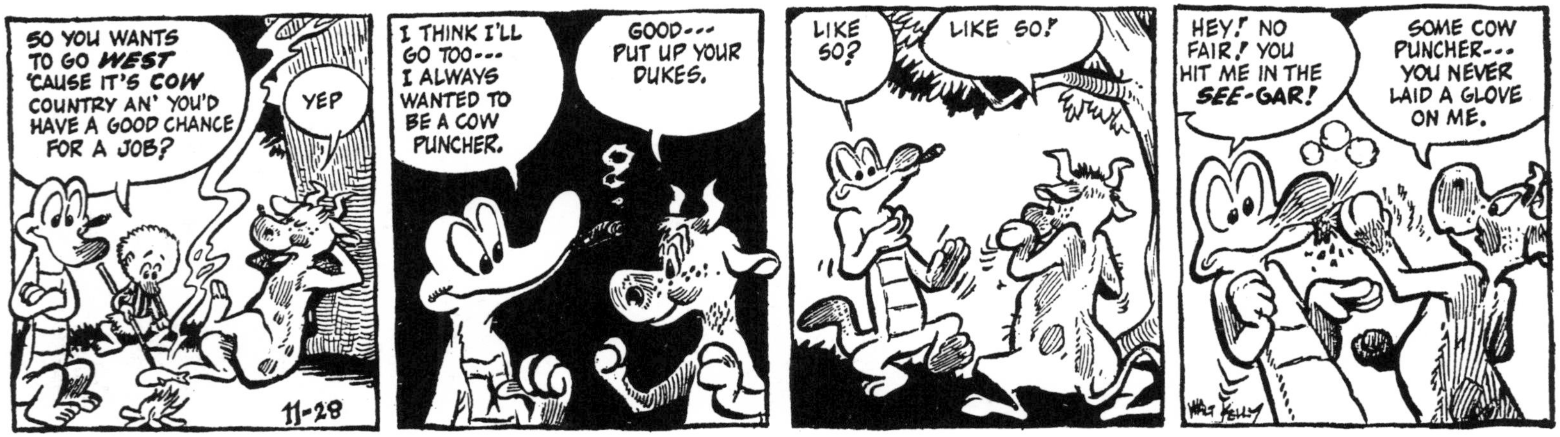
SO YOU WANTS TO GO WEST 'CAUSE IT'S COW COUNTRY AN' YOU'D HAVE A GOOD CHANCE FOR A JOB?
YEP
11-28
I THINK I'LL GO TOO--- I ALWAYS WANTED TO BE A COW PUNCHER.
GOOD--- PUT UP YOUR DUKES.
LIKE SO?
LIKE SO!
HEY! NO FAIR! YOU HIT ME IN THE SEE-GAR!
SOME COW PUNCHER--- YOU NEVER LAID A GLOVE ON ME.
WALT KELLY

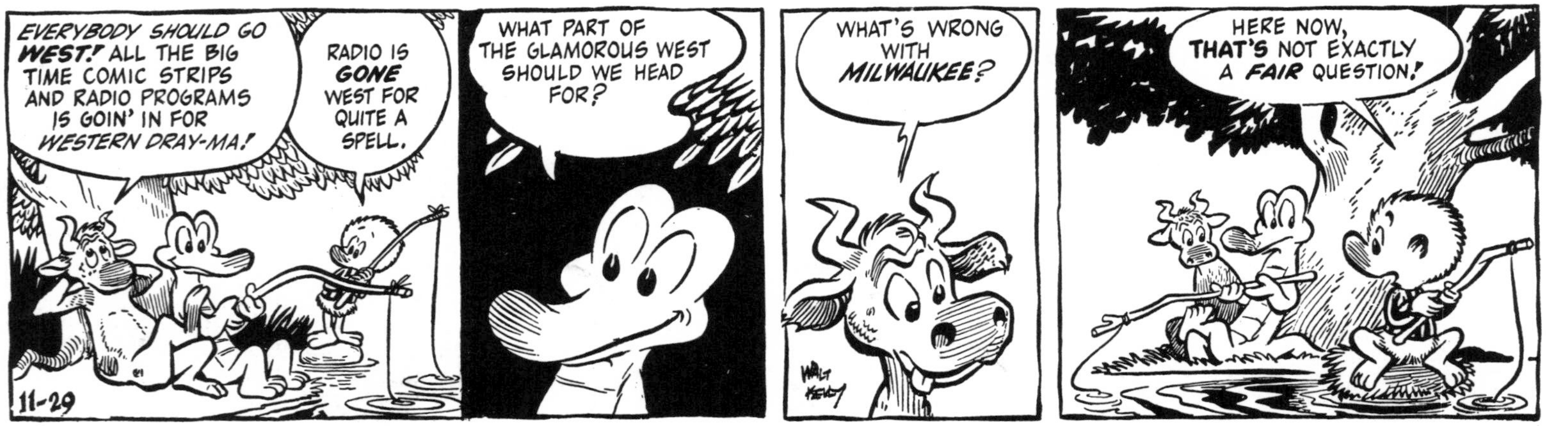
EVERYBODY SHOULD GO WEST! ALL THE BIG TIME COMIC STRIPS AND RADIO PROGRAMS IS GOIN' IN FOR WESTERN DRAY-MA!
RADIO IS GONE WEST FOR QUITE A SPELL.
11-29
WHAT PART OF THE GLAMOROUS WEST SHOULD WE HEAD FOR?
WHAT'S WRONG WITH MILWAUKEE?
WALT KELLY
HERE NOW, THAT'S NOT EXACTLY A FAIR QUESTION!

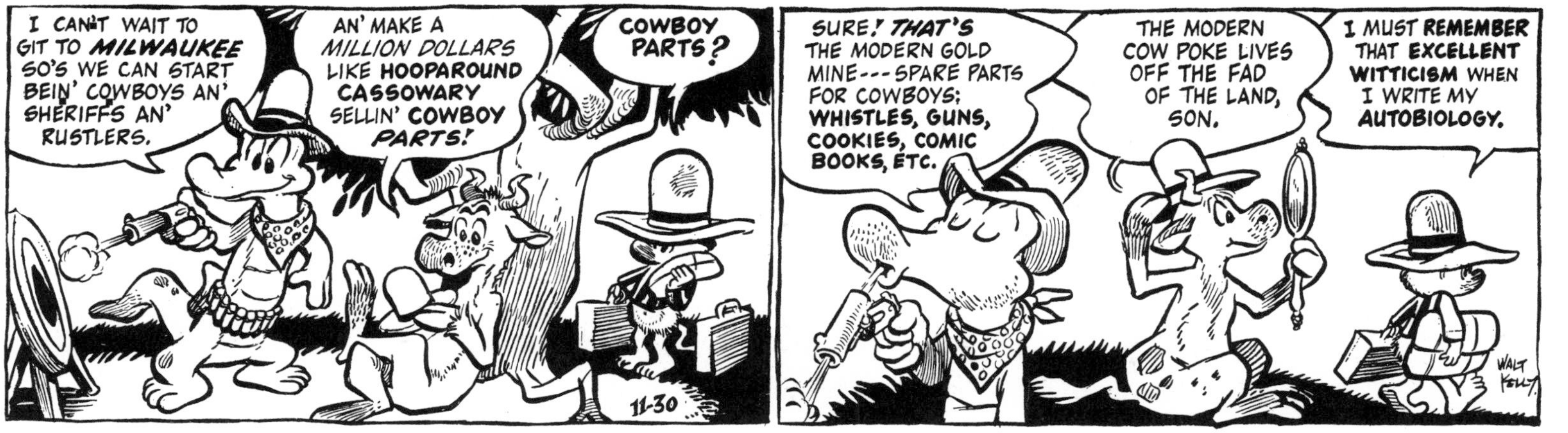
I CAN'T WAIT TO GIT TO MILWAUKEE SO'S WE CAN START BEIN' COWBOYS AN' SHERIFFS AN' RUSTLERS.
AN' MAKE A MILLION DOLLARS LIKE HOOPAROUND CASSOWARY SELLIN' COWBOY PARTS!
COWBOY PARTS?
11-30
SURE! THAT'S THE MODERN GOLD MINE--- SPARE PARTS FOR COWBOYS: WHISTLES, GUNS, COOKIES, COMIC BOOKS, ETC.
THE MODERN COW POKE LIVES OFF THE FAD OF THE LAND, SON.
I MUST REMEMBER THAT EXCELLENT WITTICISM WHEN I WRITE MY AUTOBIOLOGY.
WALT KELLY

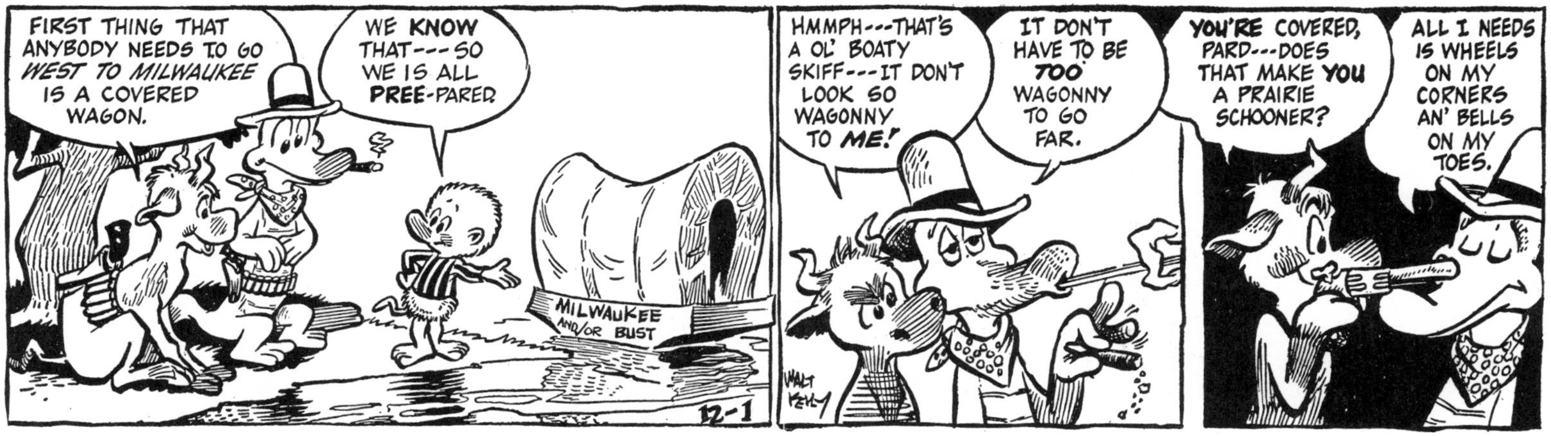
FIRST THING THAT ANYBODY NEEDS TO GO WEST TO MILWAUKEE IS A COVERED WAGON.
WE KNOW THAT--- SO WE IS ALL PREE-PARED
MILWAUKEE AND/OR BUST
12-1
HMMPH---THAT'S A OL' BOATY SKIFF---IT DON'T LOOK SO WAGONNY TO ME!
IT DON'T HAVE TO BE TOO WAGONNY TO GO FAR.
YOU'RE COVERED, PARD---DOES THAT MAKE YOU A PRAIRIE SCHOONER?
ALL I NEEDS IS WHEELS ON MY CORNERS AN' BELLS ON MY TOES.
WALT KELLY

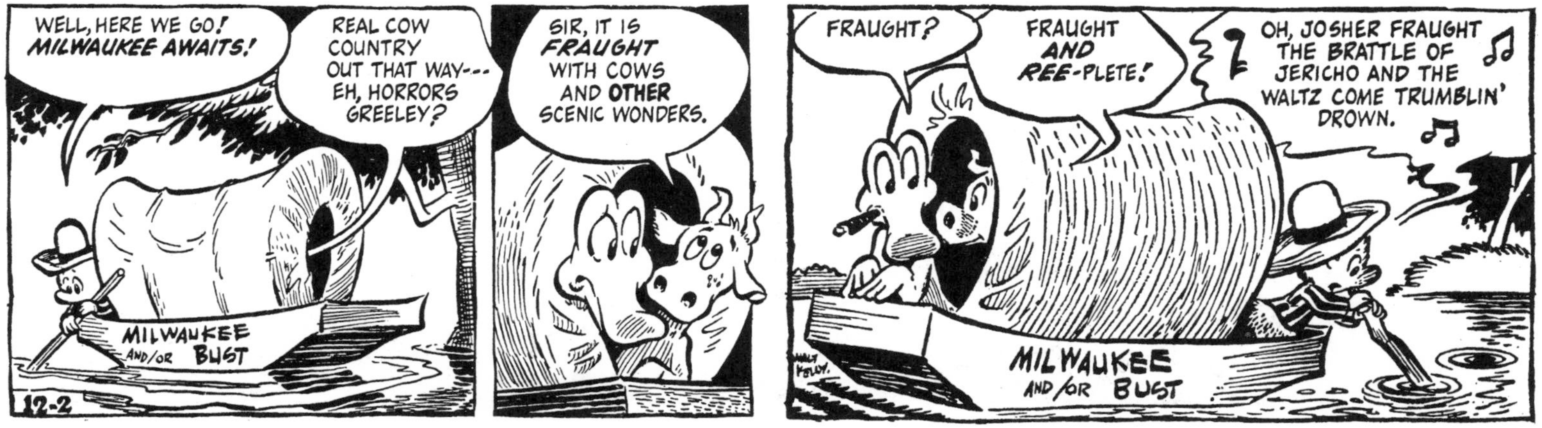
WELL, HERE WE GO! MILWAUKEE AWAITS!
REAL COW COUNTRY OUT THAT WAY--- EH, HORRORS GREELEY?
MILWAUKEE AND/OR BUST
12-2
SIR, IT IS FRAUGHT WITH COWS AND OTHER SCENIC WONDERS.
FRAUGHT?
FRAUGHT AND REE-PLETE!
OH, JOSHER FRAUGHT THE BRATTLE OF JERICHO AND THE WALTZ COME TRUMBLIN' DROWN.
MILWAUKEE AND/OR BUST
WALT KELLY

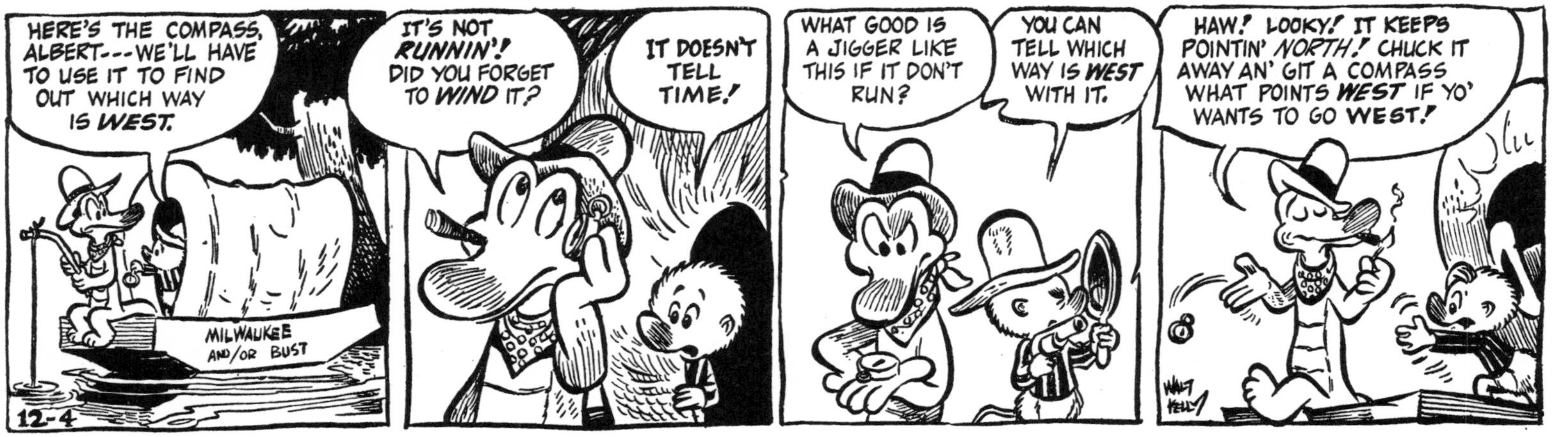
HERE'S THE COMPASS, ALBERT---WE'LL HAVE TO USE IT TO FIND OUT WHICH WAY IS **WEST.**
MILWAUKEE AND/OR BUST
12-4
IT'S NOT **RUNNIN'!** DID YOU FORGET TO **WIND** IT?
IT DOESN'T TELL TIME!
WHAT GOOD IS A JIGGER LIKE THIS IF IT DON'T RUN?
YOU CAN TELL WHICH WAY IS **WEST** WITH IT.
HAW! LOOKY! IT KEEPS POINTIN' **NORTH!** CHUCK IT AWAY AN' GIT A COMPASS WHAT POINTS **WEST** IF YO' WANTS TO GO **WEST!**
WALT KELLY

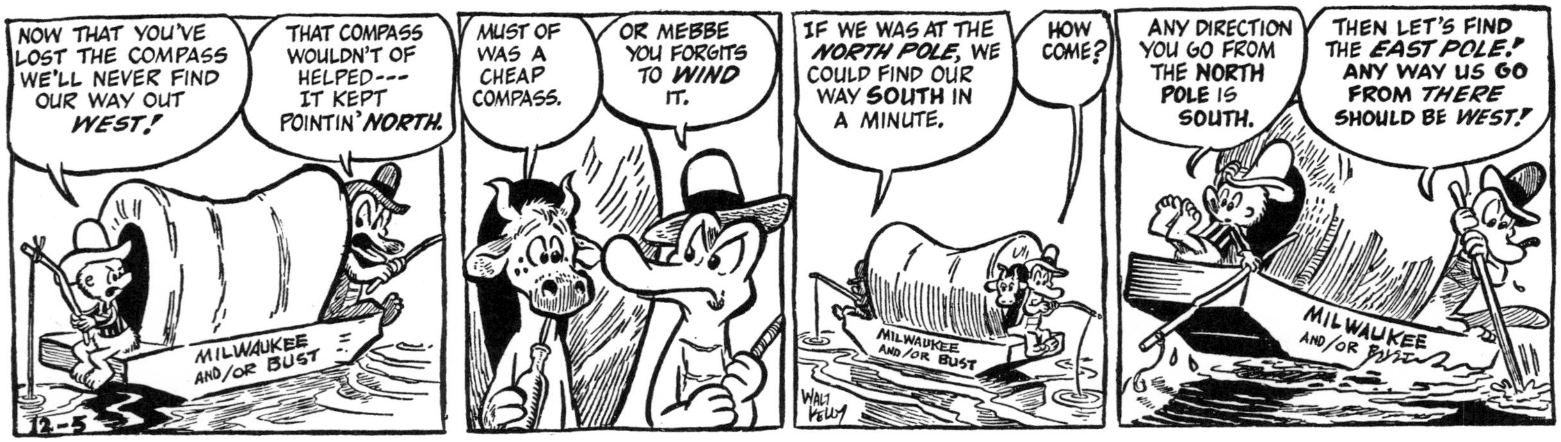
NOW THAT YOU'VE LOST THE COMPASS WE'LL NEVER FIND OUR WAY OUT **WEST!**
THAT COMPASS WOULDN'T OF HELPED--- IT KEPT POINTIN' **NORTH.**
MILWAUKEE AND/OR BUST
12-5
MUST OF WAS A CHEAP COMPASS.
OR MEBBE YOU FORGITS TO **WIND** IT.
IF WE WAS AT THE **NORTH POLE,** WE COULD FIND OUR WAY **SOUTH** IN A MINUTE.
HOW COME?
MILWAUKEE AND/OR BUST
WALT KELLY
ANY DIRECTION YOU GO FROM THE **NORTH POLE** IS **SOUTH.**
THEN LET'S FIND THE **EAST POLE!** ANY WAY US GO FROM **THERE** SHOULD BE **WEST!**
MILWAUKEE AND/OR BUST

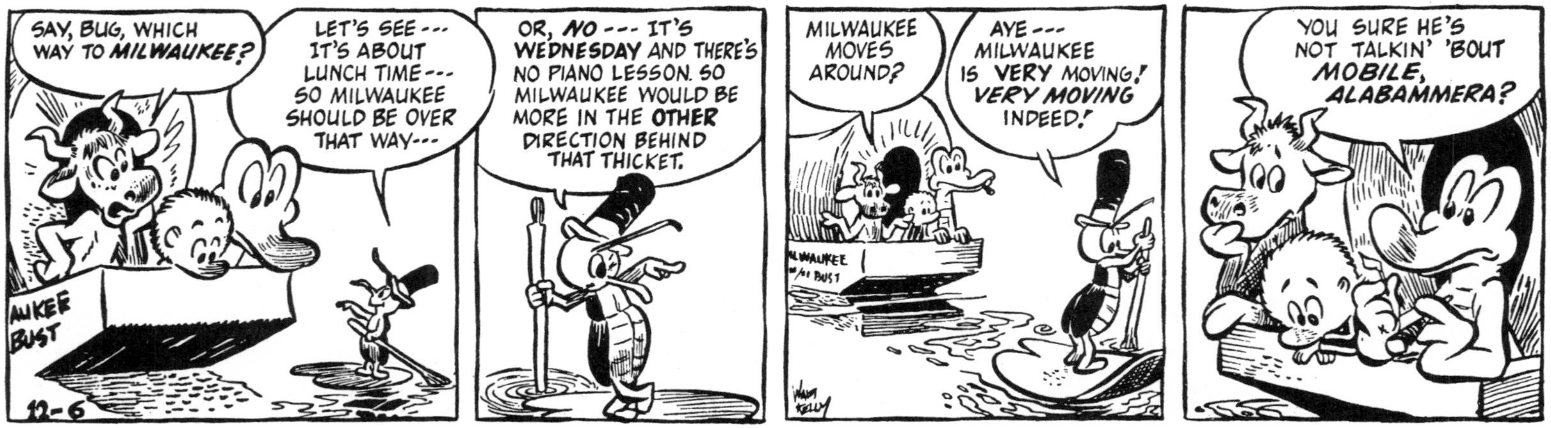
SAY, BUG, WHICH WAY TO **MILWAUKEE?**
LET'S SEE--- IT'S ABOUT LUNCH TIME--- SO MILWAUKEE SHOULD BE OVER THAT WAY---
AUKEE BUST
12-6
OR, **NO**--- IT'S **WEDNESDAY** AND THERE'S NO PIANO LESSON. SO MILWAUKEE WOULD BE MORE IN THE **OTHER** DIRECTION BEHIND THAT THICKET.
MILWAUKEE MOVES AROUND?
AYE--- MILWAUKEE IS **VERY** MOVING! **VERY MOVING** INDEED!
WALT KELLY
YOU SURE HE'S NOT TALKIN' 'BOUT **MOBILE, ALABAMMERA?**

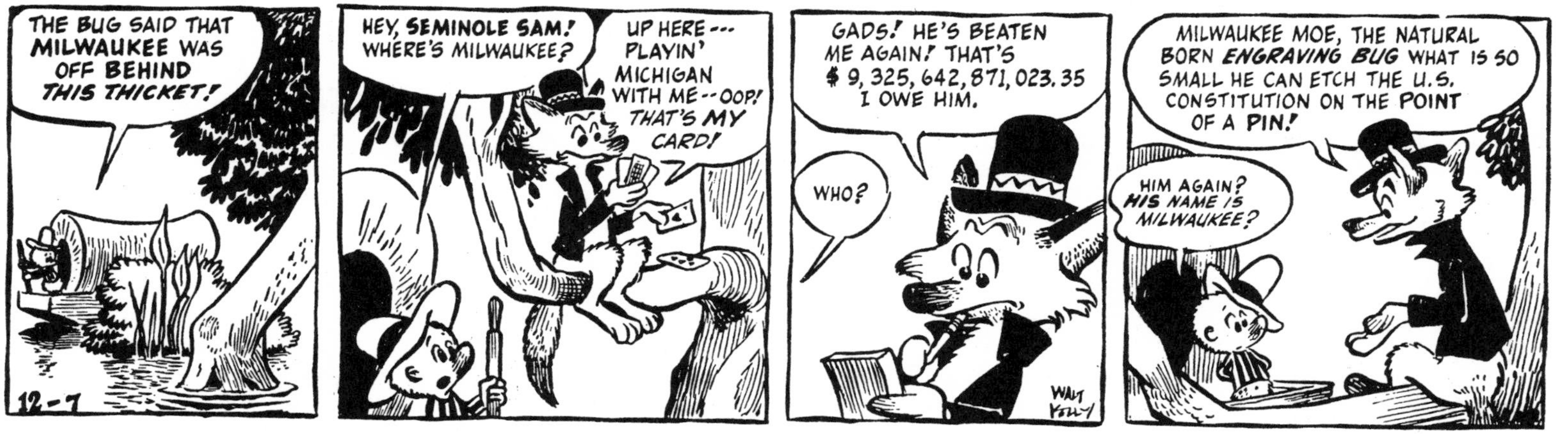
THE BUG SAID THAT MILWAUKEE WAS OFF BEHIND THIS THICKET!
HEY, SEMINOLE SAM! WHERE'S MILWAUKEE?
UP HERE--- PLAYIN' MICHIGAN WITH ME--OOP! THAT'S MY CARD!
GADS! HE'S BEATEN ME AGAIN! THAT'S $ 9,325,642,871,023.35 I OWE HIM.
WHO?
MILWAUKEE MOE, THE NATURAL BORN ENGRAVING BUG WHAT IS SO SMALL HE CAN ETCH THE U.S. CONSTITUTION ON THE POINT OF A PIN!
HIM AGAIN? HIS NAME IS MILWAUKEE?
12-7

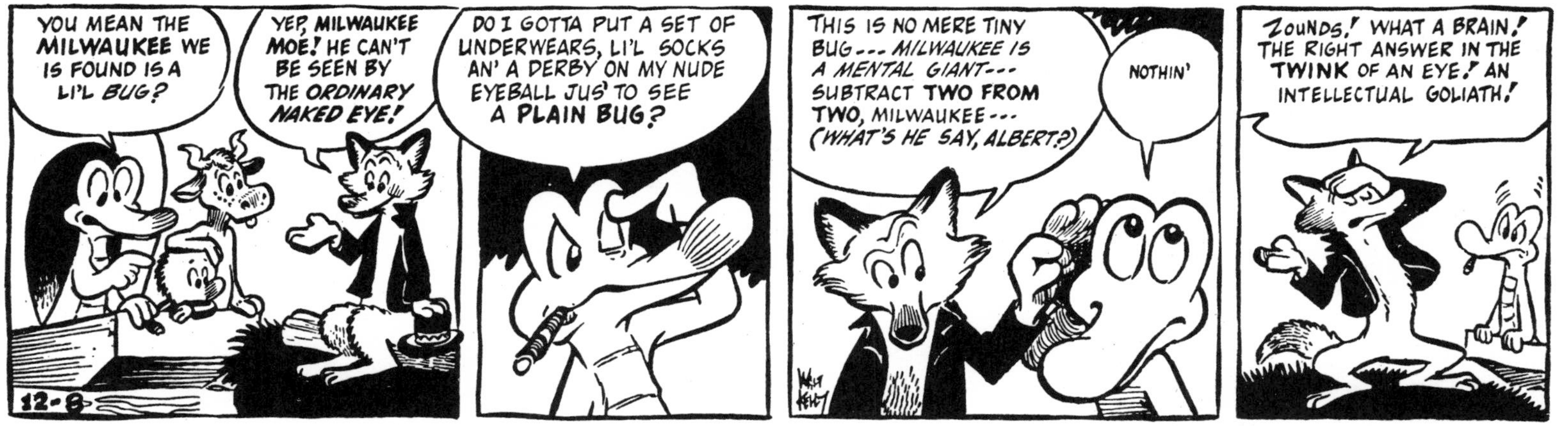
YOU MEAN THE MILWAUKEE WE IS FOUND IS A LI'L BUG?
YEP, MILWAUKEE MOE! HE CAN'T BE SEEN BY THE ORDINARY NAKED EYE!
DO I GOTTA PUT A SET OF UNDERWEARS, LI'L SOCKS AN' A DERBY ON MY NUDE EYEBALL JUS' TO SEE A PLAIN BUG?
THIS IS NO MERE TINY BUG--- MILWAUKEE IS A MENTAL GIANT--- SUBTRACT TWO FROM TWO, MILWAUKEE--- (WHAT'S HE SAY, ALBERT?)
NOTHIN'
ZOUNDS! WHAT A BRAIN! THE RIGHT ANSWER IN THE TWINK OF AN EYE! AN INTELLECTUAL GOLIATH!
12-8

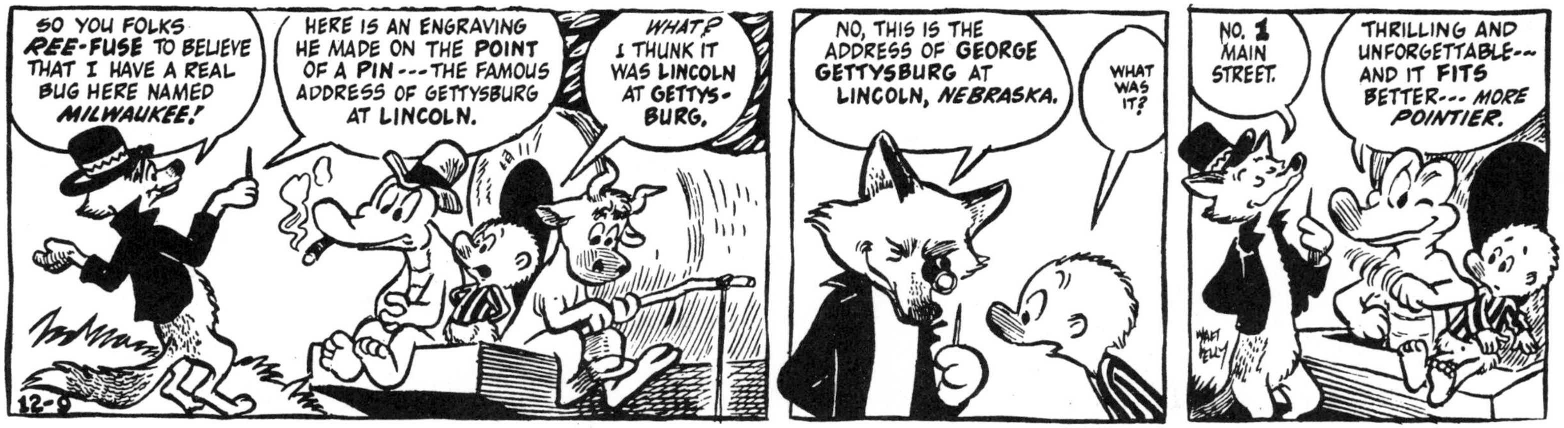
SO YOU FOLKS REE-FUSE TO BELIEVE THAT I HAVE A REAL BUG HERE NAMED MILWAUKEE!
HERE IS AN ENGRAVING HE MADE ON THE POINT OF A PIN---THE FAMOUS ADDRESS OF GETTYSBURG AT LINCOLN.
WHAT? I THUNK IT WAS LINCOLN AT GETTYS-BURG.
NO, THIS IS THE ADDRESS OF GEORGE GETTYSBURG AT LINCOLN, NEBRASKA.
WHAT WAS IT?
NO. 1 MAIN STREET.
THRILLING AND UNFORGETTABLE-- AND IT FITS BETTER--- MORE POINTIER.
12-9

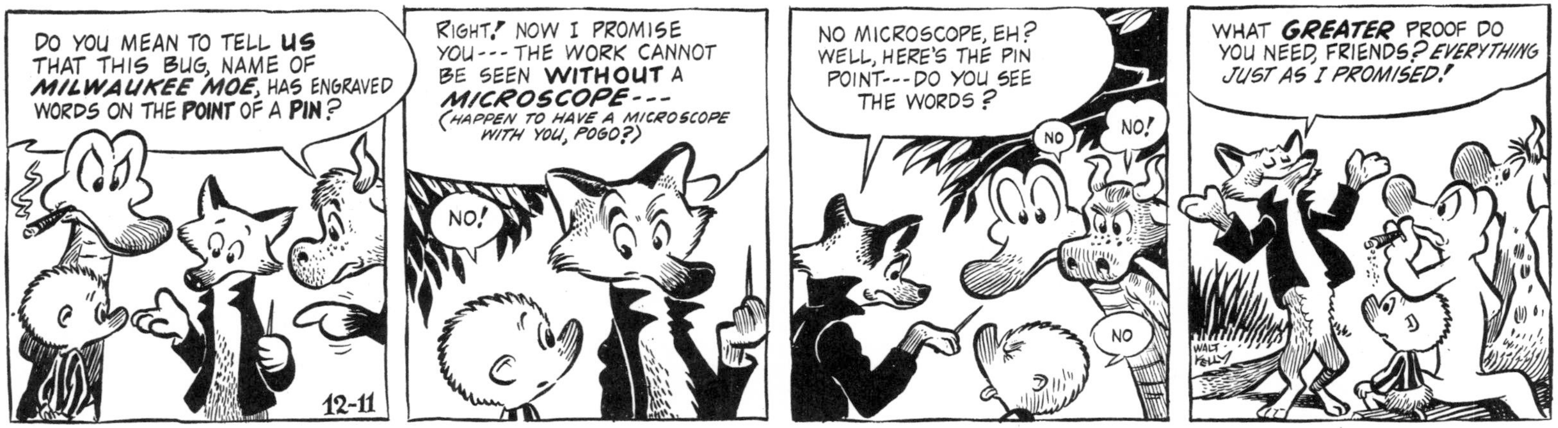
DO YOU MEAN TO TELL US THAT THIS BUG, NAME OF MILWAUKEE MOE, HAS ENGRAVED WORDS ON THE POINT OF A PIN?
12-11
RIGHT! NOW I PROMISE YOU--- THE WORK CANNOT BE SEEN WITHOUT A MICROSCOPE--- (HAPPEN TO HAVE A MICROSCOPE WITH YOU, POGO?)
NO!
NO MICROSCOPE, EH? WELL, HERE'S THE PIN POINT---DO YOU SEE THE WORDS?
NO
NO!
NO
WHAT GREATER PROOF DO YOU NEED, FRIENDS? EVERYTHING JUST AS I PROMISED!
WALT KELLY

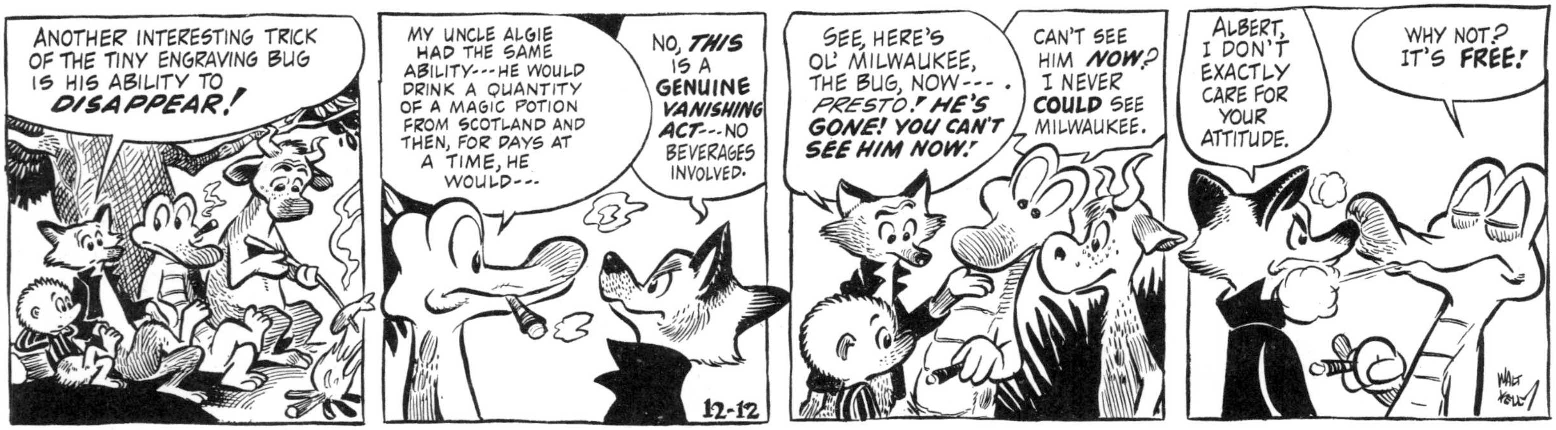
ANOTHER INTERESTING TRICK OF THE TINY ENGRAVING BUG IS HIS ABILITY TO DISAPPEAR!
MY UNCLE ALGIE HAD THE SAME ABILITY---HE WOULD DRINK A QUANTITY OF A MAGIC POTION FROM SCOTLAND AND THEN, FOR DAYS AT A TIME, HE WOULD---
NO, THIS IS A GENUINE VANISHING ACT---NO BEVERAGES INVOLVED.
12-12
SEE, HERE'S OL' MILWAUKEE, THE BUG, NOW---. PRESTO! HE'S GONE! YOU CAN'T SEE HIM NOW!
CAN'T SEE HIM NOW? I NEVER COULD SEE MILWAUKEE.
ALBERT, I DON'T EXACTLY CARE FOR YOUR ATTITUDE.
WHY NOT? IT'S FREE!
WALT KELLY

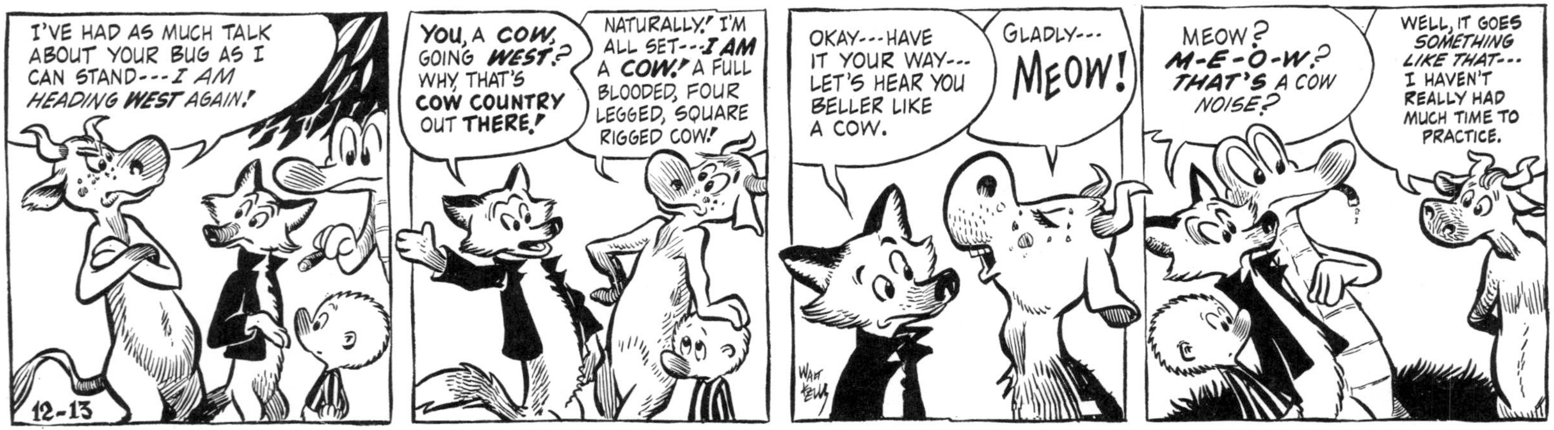
I'VE HAD AS MUCH TALK ABOUT YOUR BUG AS I CAN STAND---I AM HEADING WEST AGAIN!
12-13
YOU, A COW, GOING WEST? WHY, THAT'S COW COUNTRY OUT THERE!
NATURALLY! I'M ALL SET---I AM A COW! A FULL BLOODED, FOUR LEGGED, SQUARE RIGGED COW!
OKAY---HAVE IT YOUR WAY--- LET'S HEAR YOU BELLER LIKE A COW.
GLADLY---
MEOW!
WALT KELLY
MEOW? M-E-O-W? THAT'S A COW NOISE?
WELL, IT GOES SOMETHING LIKE THAT--- I HAVEN'T REALLY HAD MUCH TIME TO PRACTICE.

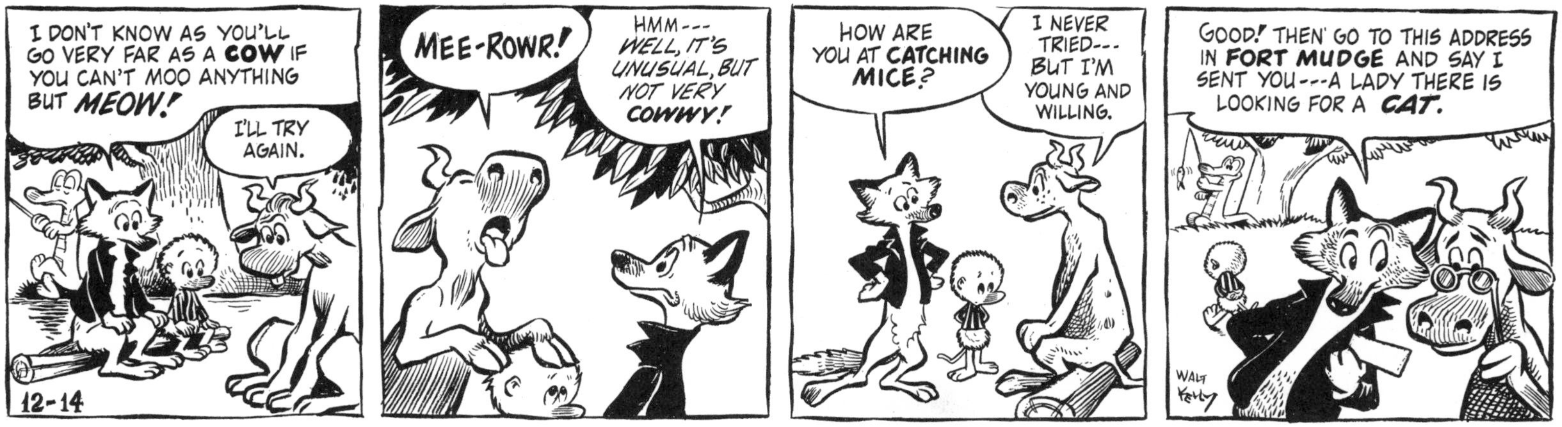
I DON'T KNOW AS YOU'LL GO VERY FAR AS A **COW** IF YOU CAN'T MOO ANYTHING BUT ***MEOW!***
I'LL TRY AGAIN.
12-14
MEE-ROWR!
HMM--- *WELL, IT'S UNUSUAL, BUT NOT VERY* ***COWWY!***
HOW ARE YOU AT **CATCHING MICE**?
I NEVER TRIED--- BUT I'M YOUNG AND WILLING.
GOOD! THEN GO TO THIS ADDRESS IN **FORT MUDGE** AND SAY I SENT YOU---A LADY THERE IS LOOKING FOR A ***CAT***.

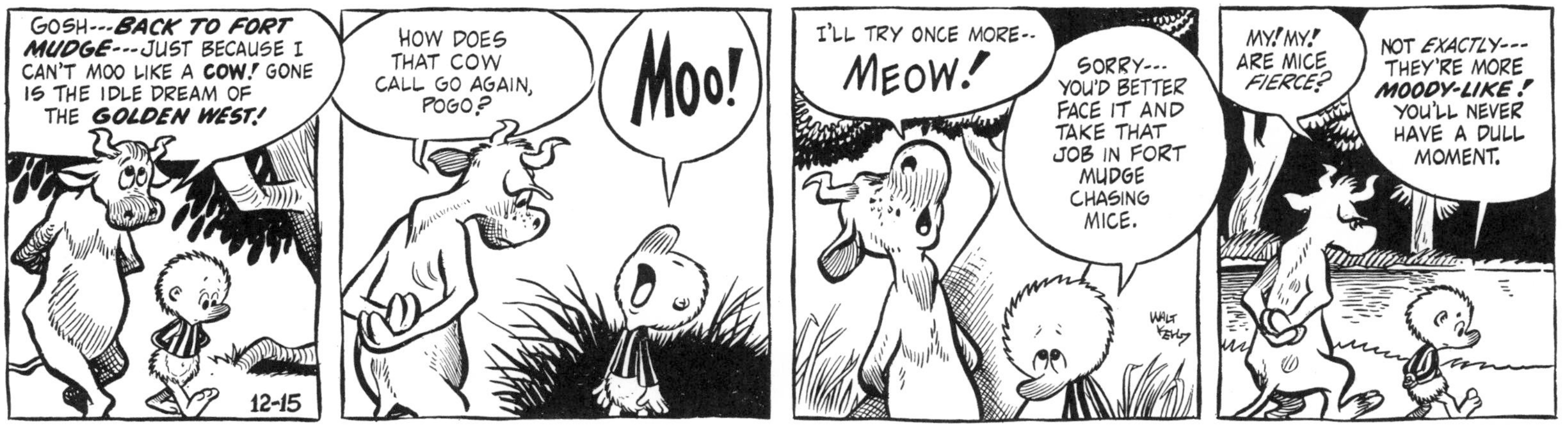
GOSH---***BACK TO FORT MUDGE***---JUST BECAUSE I CAN'T MOO LIKE A **COW!** GONE IS THE IDLE DREAM OF THE ***GOLDEN WEST!***
12-15
HOW DOES THAT COW CALL GO AGAIN, POGO?
MOO!
I'LL TRY ONCE MORE--
MEOW!
SORRY--- YOU'D BETTER FACE IT AND TAKE THAT JOB IN FORT MUDGE CHASING MICE.
MY! MY! ARE MICE *FIERCE*?
NOT *EXACTLY*--- THEY'RE MORE ***MOODY-LIKE!*** YOU'LL NEVER HAVE A DULL MOMENT.

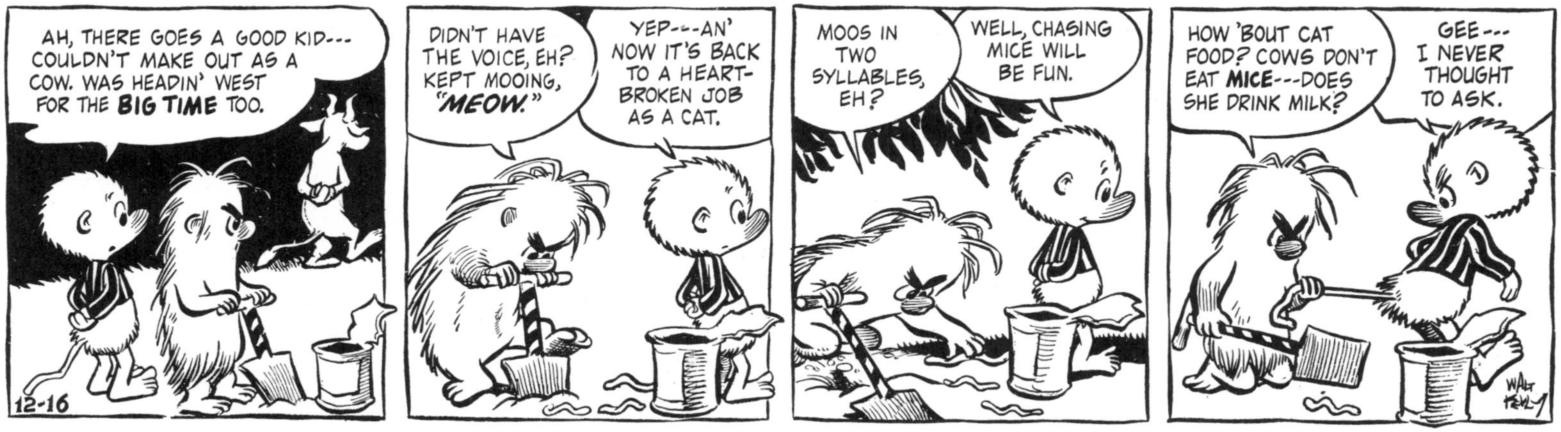
AH, THERE GOES A GOOD KID--- COULDN'T MAKE OUT AS A COW. WAS HEADIN' WEST FOR THE **BIG TIME** TOO.
12-16
DIDN'T HAVE THE VOICE, EH? KEPT MOOING, ***"MEOW."***
YEP---AN' NOW IT'S BACK TO A HEART-BROKEN JOB AS A CAT.
MOOS IN TWO SYLLABLES, EH?
WELL, CHASING MICE WILL BE FUN.
HOW 'BOUT CAT FOOD? COWS DON'T EAT **MICE**---DOES SHE DRINK MILK?
GEE--- I NEVER THOUGHT TO ASK.

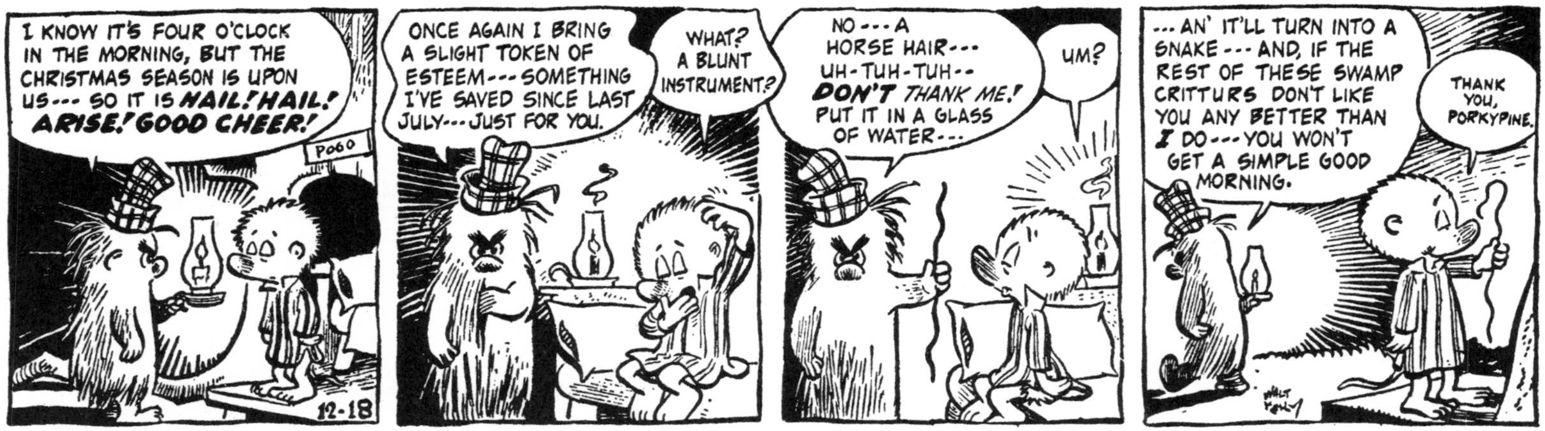
I KNOW IT'S FOUR O'CLOCK IN THE MORNING, BUT THE CHRISTMAS SEASON IS UPON US--- SO IT IS **HAIL! HAIL! ARISE! GOOD CHEER!**
POGO
12-18
ONCE AGAIN I BRING A SLIGHT TOKEN OF ESTEEM--- SOMETHING I'VE SAVED SINCE LAST JULY--- JUST FOR YOU.
WHAT? A BLUNT INSTRUMENT?
NO--- A HORSE HAIR--- UH-TUH-TUH-- **DON'T** *THANK ME!* PUT IT IN A GLASS OF WATER---
UM?
--- AN' IT'LL TURN INTO A SNAKE--- AND, IF THE REST OF THESE SWAMP CRITTURS DON'T LIKE YOU ANY BETTER THAN **I** DO--- YOU WON'T GET A SIMPLE GOOD MORNING.
THANK YOU, PORKYPINE.

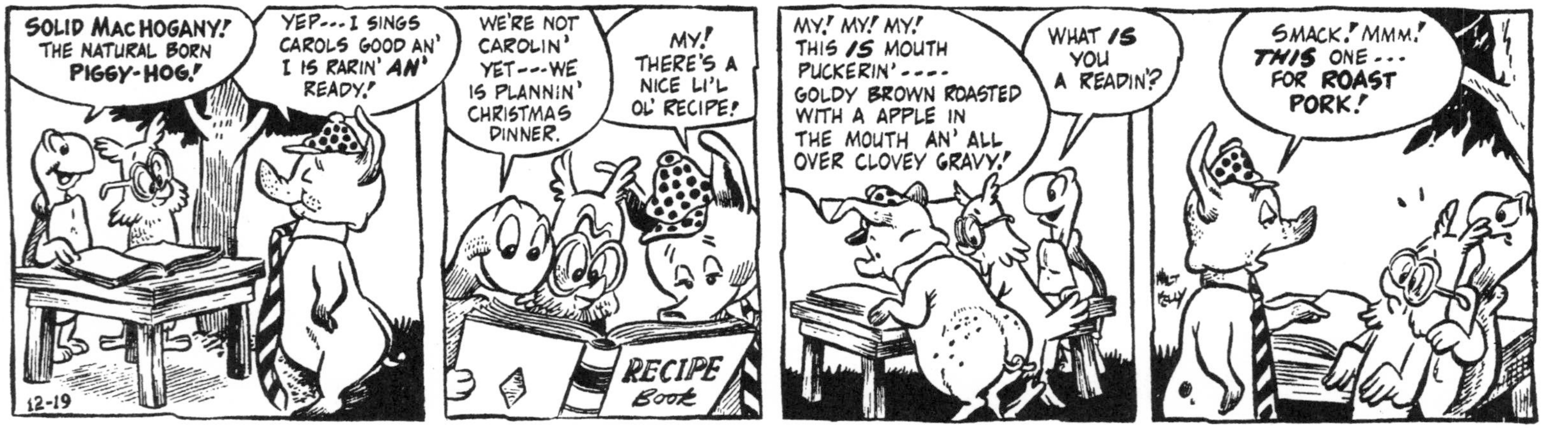
SOLID MACHOGANY! THE NATURAL BORN PIGGY-HOG!
YEP--- I SINGS CAROLS GOOD AN' I IS RARIN' **AN'** READY!
12-19
WE'RE NOT CAROLIN' YET--- WE IS PLANNIN' CHRISTMAS DINNER.
MY! THERE'S A NICE LI'L OL' RECIPE!
RECIPE Book
MY! MY! MY! THIS **IS** MOUTH PUCKERIN'---- GOLDY BROWN ROASTED WITH A APPLE IN THE MOUTH AN' ALL OVER CLOVEY GRAVY!
WHAT **IS** YOU A READIN'?
SMACK! MMM! **THIS** ONE--- FOR **ROAST PORK!**

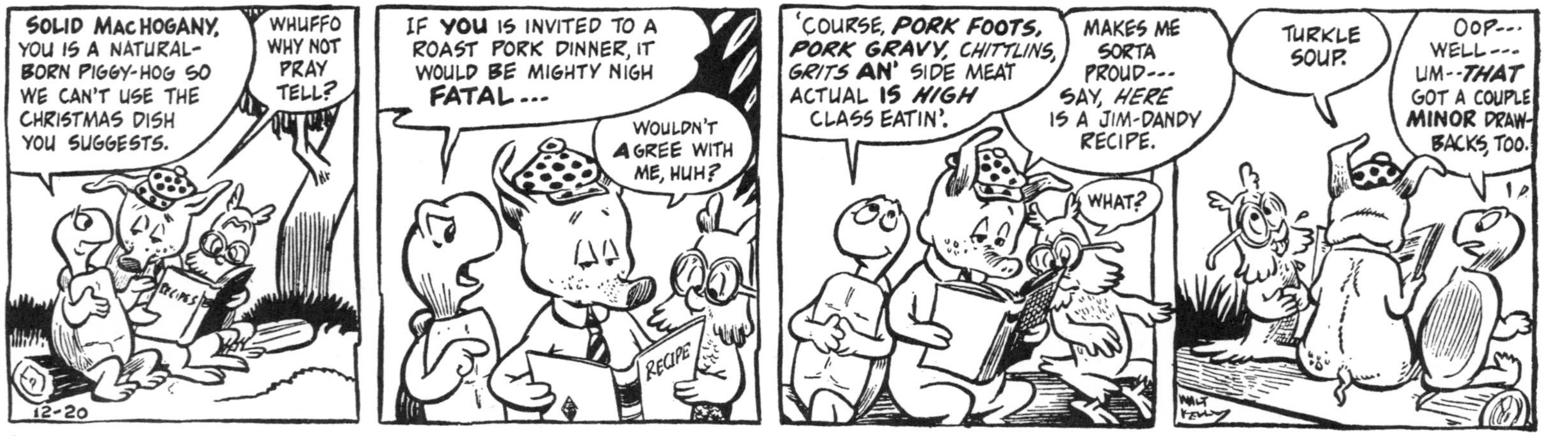
SOLID MACHOGANY, YOU IS A NATURAL-BORN PIGGY-HOG SO WE CAN'T USE THE CHRISTMAS DISH YOU SUGGESTS.
WHUFFO WHY NOT PRAY TELL?
RECIPES
12-20
IF **YOU** IS INVITED TO A ROAST PORK DINNER, IT WOULD **BE** MIGHTY NIGH **FATAL**---
WOULDN'T **A**GREE WITH ME, HUH?
RECIPE
'COURSE, ***PORK FOOTS, PORK GRAVY,*** *CHITTLINS, GRITS* **AN'** SIDE MEAT ACTUAL **IS *HIGH*** CLASS EATIN'.
MAKES ME SORTA PROUD--- SAY, *HERE* IS A JIM-DANDY RECIPE.
WHAT?
TURKLE SOUP.
OOP--- WELL--- UM--***THAT*** GOT A COUPLE **MINOR** DRAW-BACKS, TOO.

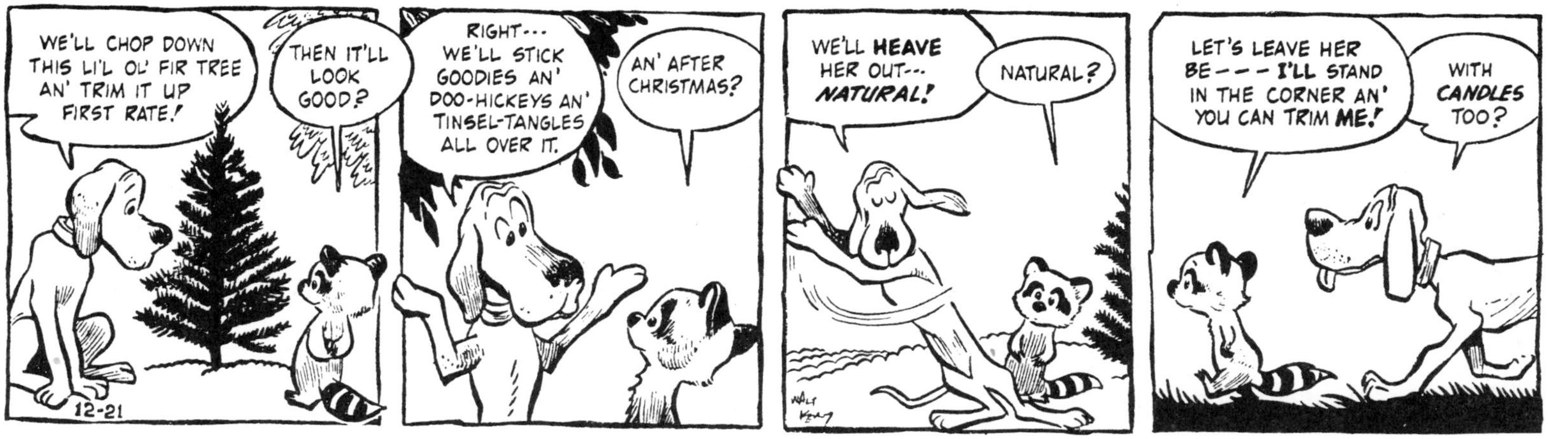
WE'LL CHOP DOWN THIS LI'L OL' FIR TREE AN' TRIM IT UP FIRST RATE!
THEN IT'LL LOOK GOOD?
RIGHT--- WE'LL STICK GOODIES AN' DOO-HICKEYS AN' TINSEL-TANGLES ALL OVER IT.
AN' AFTER CHRISTMAS?
WE'LL **HEAVE** HER OUT--- ***NATURAL!***
NATURAL?
LET'S LEAVE HER BE--- **I'LL** STAND IN THE CORNER AN' YOU CAN TRIM **ME!**
WITH ***CANDLES*** TOO?
12-21
WALT KELLY

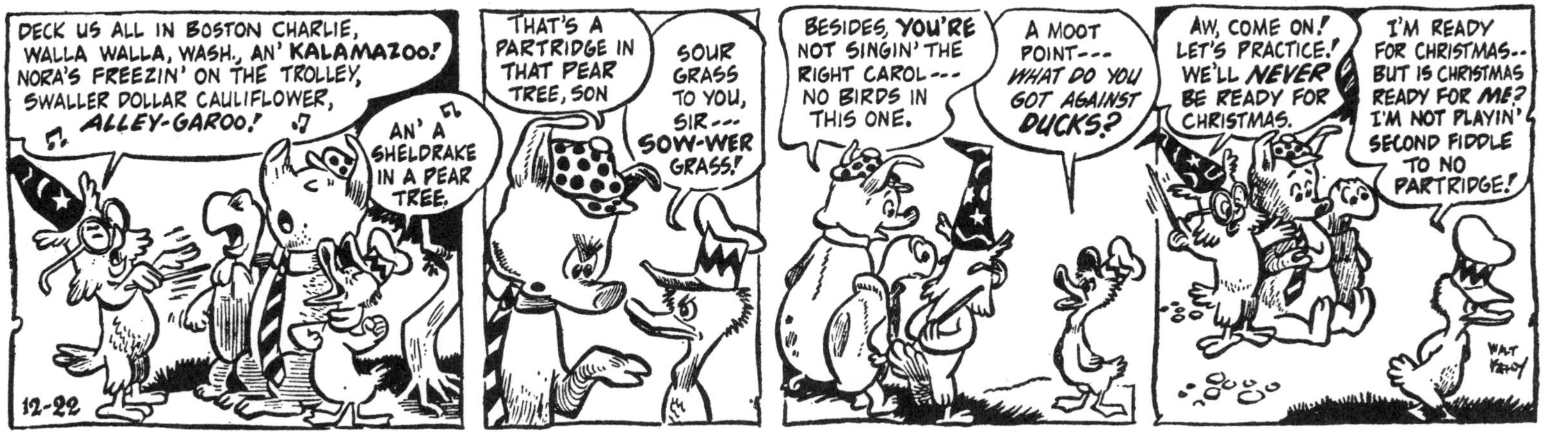
DECK US ALL IN BOSTON CHARLIE, WALLA WALLA, WASH., AN' **KALAMAZOO!** NORA'S FREEZIN' ON THE TROLLEY, SWALLER DOLLAR CAULIFLOWER, ***ALLEY-GAROO!***
AN' A SHELDRAKE IN A PEAR TREE.
THAT'S A PARTRIDGE IN THAT PEAR TREE, SON
SOUR GRASS TO YOU, SIR--- **SOW-WER** GRASS!
BESIDES, **YOU'RE** NOT SINGIN' THE RIGHT CAROL--- NO BIRDS IN THIS ONE.
A MOOT POINT--- *WHAT DO YOU GOT AGAINST* ***DUCKS?***
AW, COME ON! LET'S PRACTICE! WE'LL ***NEVER*** BE READY FOR CHRISTMAS.
I'M READY FOR CHRISTMAS.. BUT IS CHRISTMAS READY FOR **ME?** I'M NOT PLAYIN' SECOND FIDDLE TO NO PARTRIDGE!
12-22
WALT KELLY

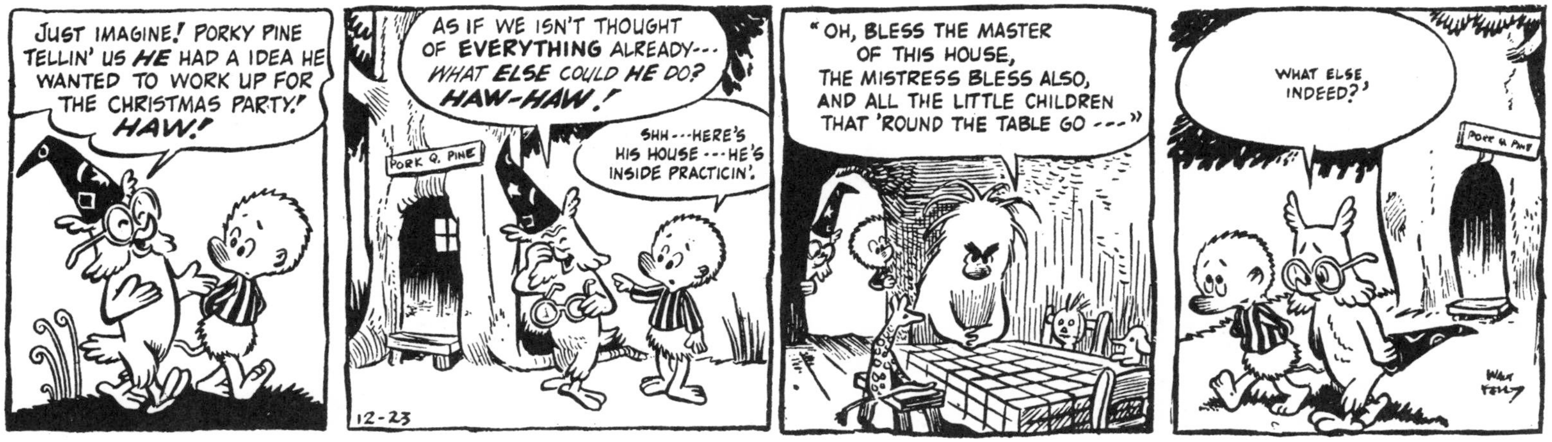
JUST IMAGINE! PORKY PINE TELLIN' US ***HE*** HAD A IDEA HE WANTED TO WORK UP FOR THE CHRISTMAS PARTY! ***HAW!***
AS IF WE ISN'T THOUGHT OF **EVERYTHING** ALREADY--- *WHAT* ***ELSE*** *COULD* ***HE*** *DO?* ***HAW-HAW!***
PORK Q. PINE
SHH---HERE'S HIS HOUSE---HE'S INSIDE PRACTICIN'.
"OH, BLESS THE MASTER OF THIS HOUSE, THE MISTRESS BLESS ALSO, AND ALL THE LITTLE CHILDREN THAT 'ROUND THE TABLE GO---"
WHAT ELSE INDEED?
PORK Q. PINE
12-23
WALT KELLY

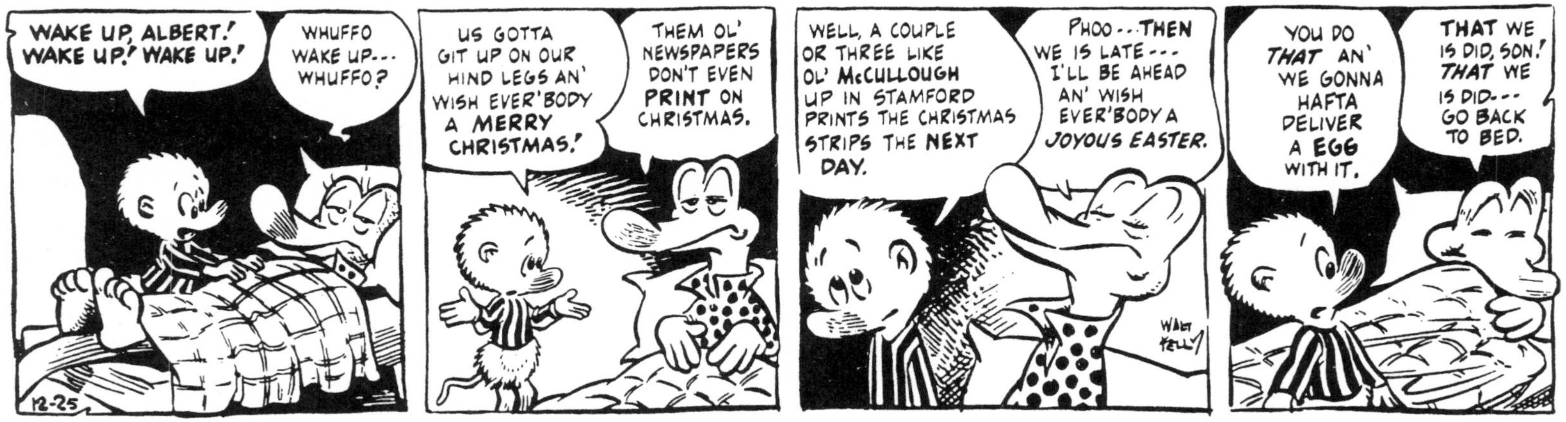
WAKE UP, ALBERT! WAKE UP! WAKE UP!
WHUFFO WAKE UP--- WHUFFO?
US GOTTA GIT UP ON OUR HIND LEGS AN' WISH EVER'BODY A MERRY CHRISTMAS!
THEM OL' NEWSPAPERS DON'T EVEN PRINT ON CHRISTMAS.
WELL, A COUPLE OR THREE LIKE OL' McCULLOUGH UP IN STAMFORD PRINTS THE CHRISTMAS STRIPS THE NEXT DAY.
PHOO--THEN WE IS LATE--- I'LL BE AHEAD AN' WISH EVER'BODY A JOYOUS EASTER.
WALT KELLY
YOU DO THAT AN' WE GONNA HAFTA DELIVER A EGG WITH IT.
THAT WE IS DID, SON! THAT WE IS DID--- GO BACK TO BED.
12-25

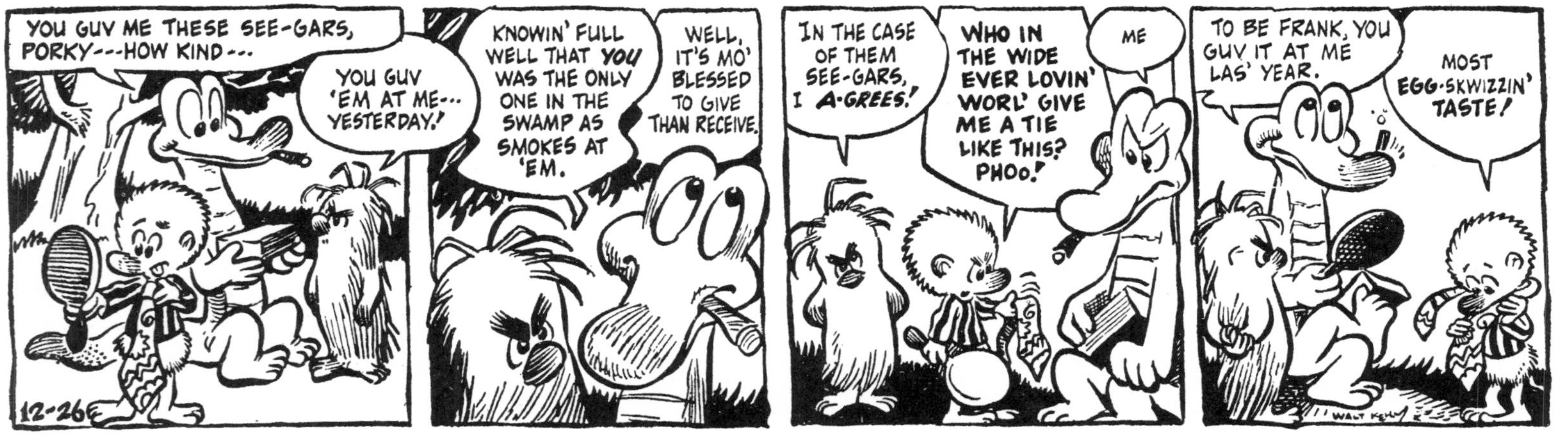
YOU GUV ME THESE SEE-GARS, PORKY---HOW KIND---
YOU GUV 'EM AT ME--- YESTERDAY!
KNOWIN' FULL WELL THAT YOU WAS THE ONLY ONE IN THE SWAMP AS SMOKES AT 'EM.
WELL, IT'S MO' BLESSED TO GIVE THAN RECEIVE.
IN THE CASE OF THEM SEE-GARS, I A-GREES!
WHO IN THE WIDE EVER LOVIN' WORL' GIVE ME A TIE LIKE THIS? PHOO!
ME
TO BE FRANK, YOU GUV IT AT ME LAS' YEAR.
MOST EGG-SKWIZZIN' TASTE!
WALT KELLY
12-26

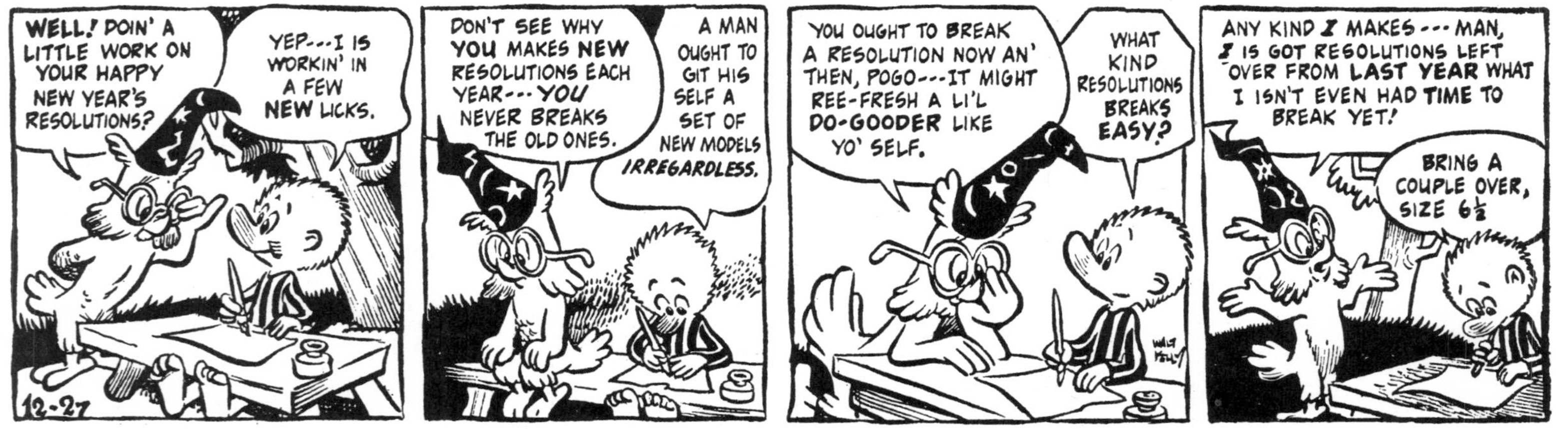
WELL! DOIN' A LITTLE WORK ON YOUR HAPPY NEW YEAR'S RESOLUTIONS?
YEP---I IS WORKIN' IN A FEW NEW LICKS.
DON'T SEE WHY YOU MAKES NEW RESOLUTIONS EACH YEAR--- YOU NEVER BREAKS THE OLD ONES.
A MAN OUGHT TO GIT HIS SELF A SET OF NEW MODELS IRREGARDLESS.
YOU OUGHT TO BREAK A RESOLUTION NOW AN' THEN, POGO---IT MIGHT REE-FRESH A LI'L DO-GOODER LIKE YO' SELF.
WHAT KIND RESOLUTIONS BREAKS EASY?
WALT KELLY
ANY KIND I MAKES --- MAN, I IS GOT RESOLUTIONS LEFT OVER FROM LAST YEAR WHAT I ISN'T EVEN HAD TIME TO BREAK YET!
BRING A COUPLE OVER, SIZE 6½
12-27

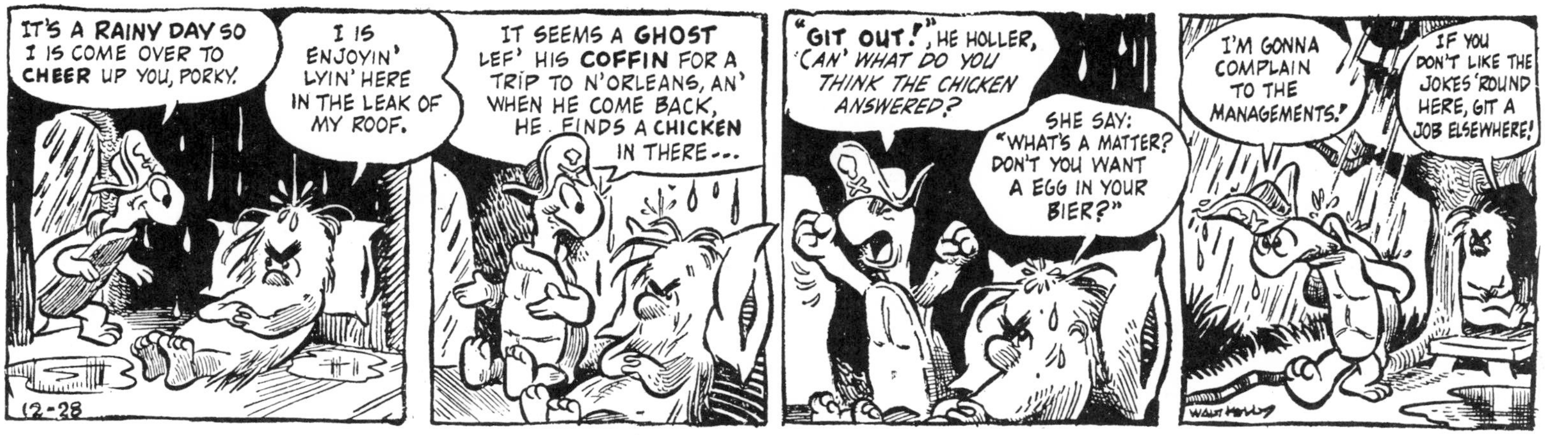
IT'S A RAINY DAY SO I IS COME OVER TO CHEER UP YOU, PORKY.
I IS ENJOYIN' LYIN' HERE IN THE LEAK OF MY ROOF.
12-28
IT SEEMS A GHOST LEF' HIS COFFIN FOR A TRIP TO N'ORLEANS, AN' WHEN HE COME BACK, HE FINDS A CHICKEN IN THERE---.
"GIT OUT!", HE HOLLER, 'CAN' WHAT DO YOU THINK THE CHICKEN ANSWERED?
SHE SAY: "WHAT'S A MATTER? DON'T YOU WANT A EGG IN YOUR BIER?"
I'M GONNA COMPLAIN TO THE MANAGEMENTS.
IF YOU DON'T LIKE THE JOKES 'ROUND HERE, GIT A JOB ELSEWHERE!
WALT KELLY

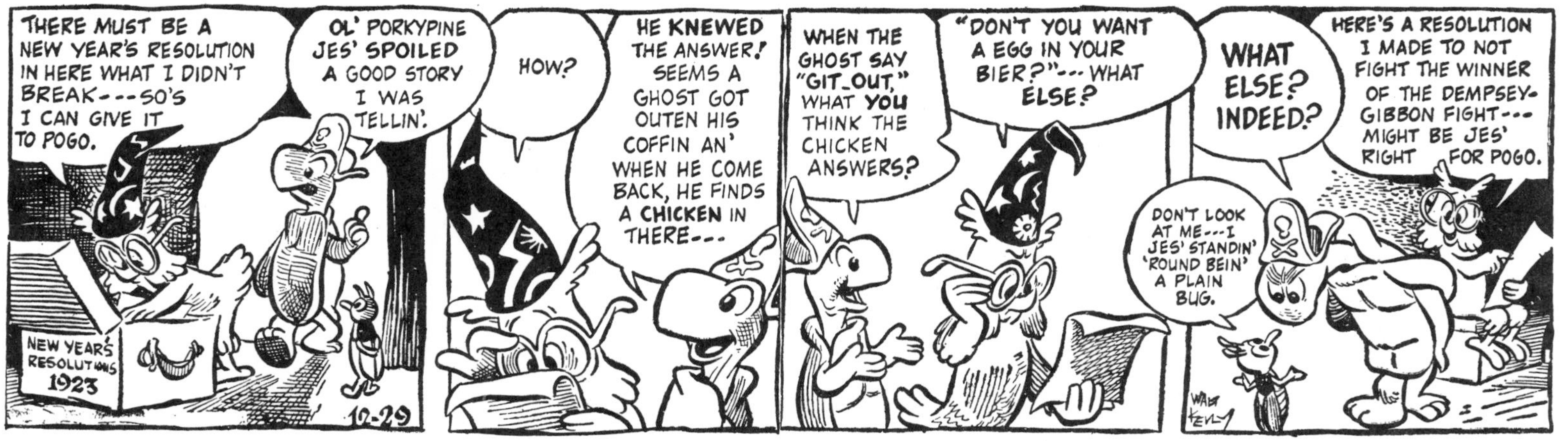
THERE MUST BE A NEW YEAR'S RESOLUTION IN HERE WHAT I DIDN'T BREAK---SO'S I CAN GIVE IT TO POGO.
OL' PORKYPINE JES' SPOILED A GOOD STORY I WAS TELLIN'.
NEW YEAR'S RESOLUTIONS 1923
12-29
HOW?
HE KNEWED THE ANSWER! SEEMS A GHOST GOT OUTEN HIS COFFIN AN' WHEN HE COME BACK, HE FINDS A CHICKEN IN THERE---
WHEN THE GHOST SAY "GIT OUT," WHAT YOU THINK THE CHICKEN ANSWERS?
"DON'T YOU WANT A EGG IN YOUR BIER?"--- WHAT ELSE?
WHAT ELSE? INDEED?
HERE'S A RESOLUTION I MADE TO NOT FIGHT THE WINNER OF THE DEMPSEY-GIBBON FIGHT--- MIGHT BE JES' RIGHT FOR POGO.
DON'T LOOK AT ME---I JES' STANDIN' 'ROUND BEIN' A PLAIN BUG.
WALT KELLY

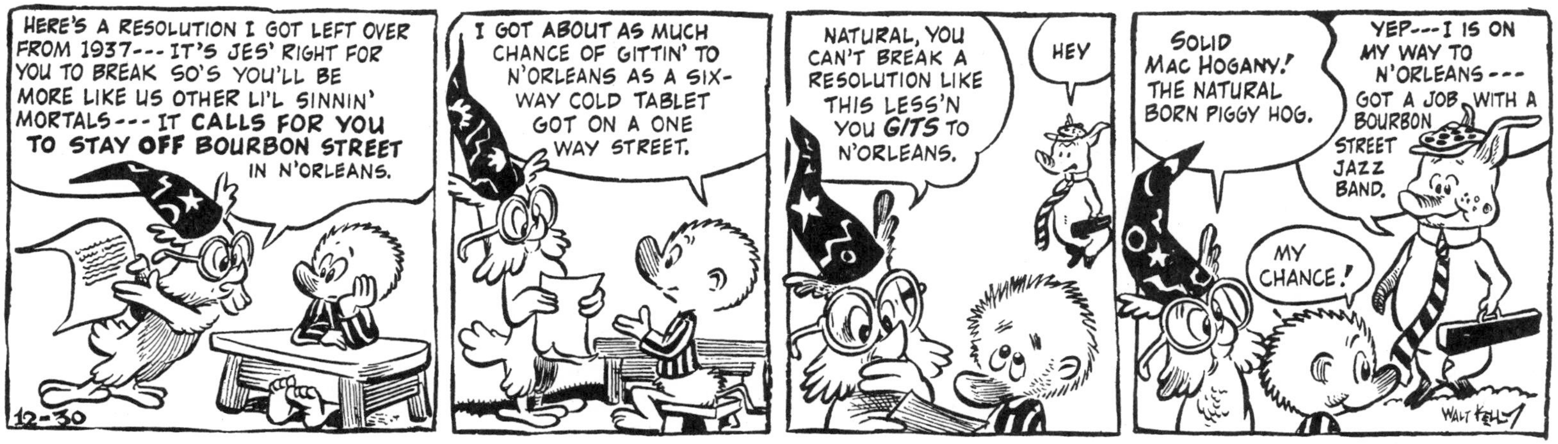
HERE'S A RESOLUTION I GOT LEFT OVER FROM 1937--- IT'S JES' RIGHT FOR YOU TO BREAK SO'S YOU'LL BE MORE LIKE US OTHER LI'L SINNIN' MORTALS--- IT CALLS FOR YOU TO STAY OFF BOURBON STREET IN N'ORLEANS.
12-30
I GOT ABOUT AS MUCH CHANCE OF GITTIN' TO N'ORLEANS AS A SIX-WAY COLD TABLET GOT ON A ONE WAY STREET.
NATURAL, YOU CAN'T BREAK A RESOLUTION LIKE THIS LESS'N YOU GITS TO N'ORLEANS.
HEY
SOLID MAC HOGANY! THE NATURAL BORN PIGGY HOG.
YEP---I IS ON MY WAY TO N'ORLEANS--- GOT A JOB WITH A BOURBON STREET JAZZ BAND.
MY CHANCE!
WALT KELLY

ABOUT THE SUNDAYS

By Mark Evanier

The Hall Syndicate began syndicating the daily *Pogo* strip in May of 1949. Response among client newspapers must have been positive right out of the starting gate because pretty soon, Kelly was also drawing a Sunday page which began appearing the following January. It bolstered his income but probably doubled his weekly workload.

A Sunday installment is a lot more labor for a cartoonist than merely drawing that many more panels per week. For one thing, the panels are at least published if not drawn larger and so seem to cry out for more elaborate, pleasing illustration. Even on the dailies, Kelly worked larger than many of his contemporaries.

For another, the Sunday page represented (and does today on some strips) a series of scheduling challenges and mechanical requirements. Syndicates like their cartoonists to be 4-6 weeks ahead of publication for daily strips – more if they can manage it. Kelly would usually and deliberately deliver close to publication, especially later as the strip grew more political and what was occurring in the news often impacted what was occurring in his swamp. Sunday pages were generally not the place for timely satire. They had to be turned in a minimum of ten weeks ahead of release date and there was less wiggle room if one fell tardy. He also wanted that day's *Pogo* to be more for children.

The *Pogo* Sundays did not often reflect the continuity, when there was any, in the concurrently-appearing daily strips. Which was fortunate for Kelly since at the time he composed a Sunday page, he rarely had written (or probably even decided on) what would be appearing in the dailies that ran the day before and after. The separation was for marketing reasons. It enabled the syndicate salesmen to sell only the dailies or only the Sunday page to a newspaper that could not accommodate both.

Most of the Sunday pages are standalone gags, but from time to time he would briefly get a separate storyline going from Sunday to Sunday. At other times, the Sunday pages might share a thematic bond with what was simultaneously occurring in the dailies. And every now and then, Kelly would find himself in a daily storyline that seemed to demand the color and larger canvas of a Sunday page. What that happened, he'd go to the trouble of planning ahead so a storyline could run straight through the weekend. Even then, they were engineered to make sense if one's local paper didn't subscribe to both offerings.

The Sunday page was more complicated to write than the dailies. It had to be structured so it could be sliced and diced to fit the needs of various newspapers' Sunday formats. The Sunday pages reproduced in this collection show each strip in its entirety but not every client newspaper ran them in full.

The full strip – all three tiers – could be run as a half-page in a paper. But as with most strips, it was written so the top tier was expendable. A newspaper, wanting to save space, might then wedge three strips onto one page by lopping off their top tiers. In every Sunday page that follows, you could start reading at the beginning of the second tier without feeling you were missing anything. But of course, you'd be missing a lot. Some of Kelly's cleverest lines, as well as his best swamp panoramas, were in the top third which went unseen in many cities.

It was also necessary to write and design the strip to allow for a "dropout" panel – a panel of a specified size which could be omitted so the strip could be jig-sawed and rearranged into a tabloid format. In *Pogo*, it was usually a panel of fixed size at the center on the second tier. In the first Sunday page (1/29/50), it's the one where Pogo says, "Go ahead, tree, say 'Ah!'"

The space before and after it on that tier could be carved into one, two or three panels but that one center panel had to be a standard size. More importantly, it had to be written so it could be omitted and tabloid readers would not notice its absence. Dialogue had to segue seamlessly from the panel before to the panel after. In that first page, Kelly merely has Pogo repeat what he said in the previous panel. Later, he would become cleverer in how he utilized that space.

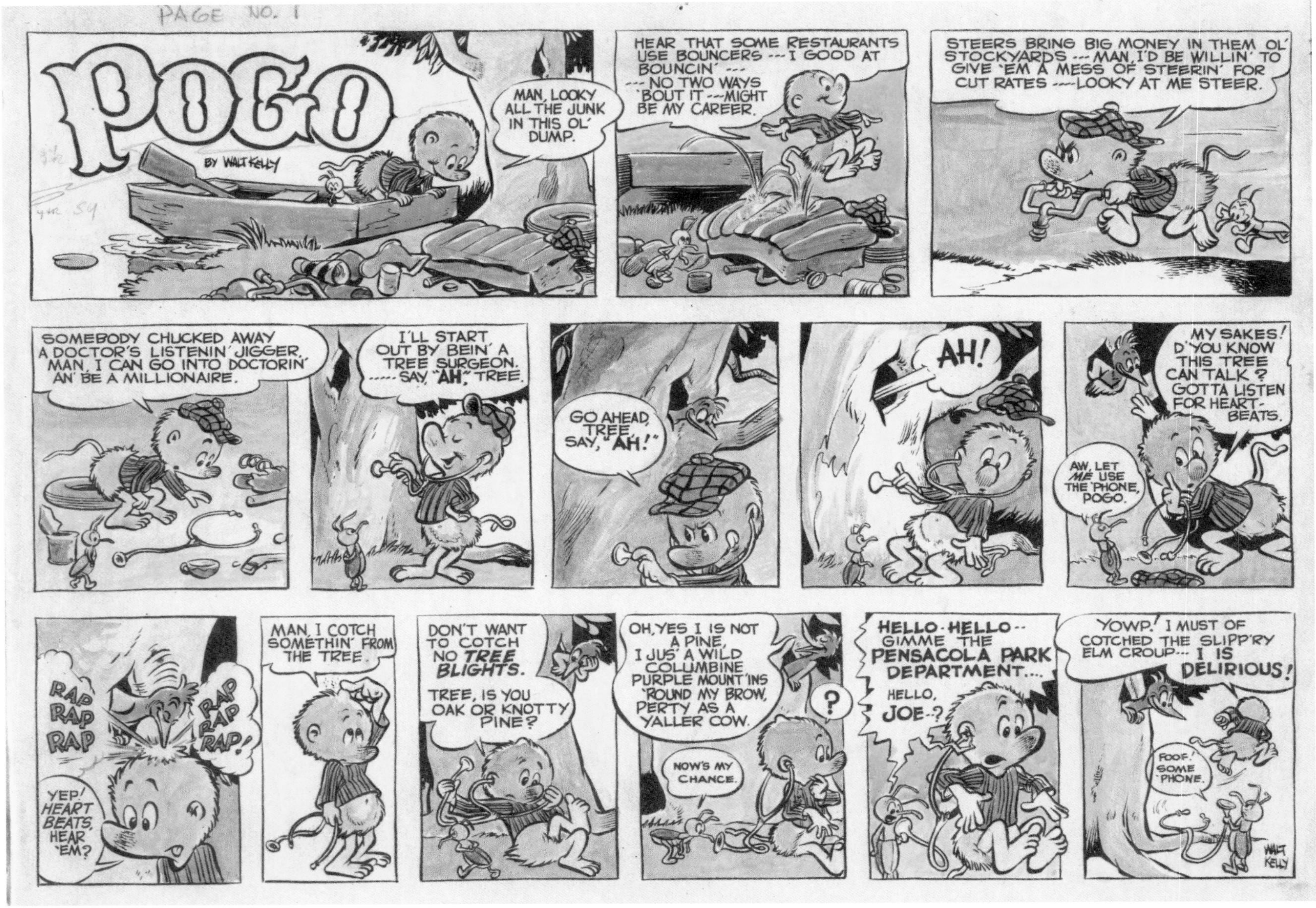
PAGE NO. 1
POGO
BY WALT KELLY
MAN, LOOKY ALL THE JUNK IN THIS OL' DUMP.
HEAR THAT SOME RESTAURANTS USE BOUNCERS --- I GOOD AT BOUNCIN' --- --- NO TWO WAYS 'BOUT IT --- MIGHT BE MY CAREER.
STEERS BRING BIG MONEY IN THEM OL' STOCKYARDS --- MAN, I'D BE WILLIN' TO GIVE 'EM A MESS OF STEERIN' FOR CUT RATES ---- LOOKY AT ME STEER.
SOMEBODY CHUCKED AWAY A DOCTOR'S LISTENIN' JIGGER. MAN, I CAN GO INTO DOCTORIN' AN' BE A MILLIONAIRE.
I'LL START OUT BY BEIN' A TREE SURGEON. ..... SAY, "AH," TREE.
GO AHEAD, TREE, SAY, "AH!"
AH!
MY SAKES! D'YOU KNOW THIS TREE CAN TALK? GOTTA LISTEN FOR HEART-BEATS.
AW, LET ME USE THE 'PHONE, POGO.
RAP RAP RAP
RAP RAP RAP!
YEP! HEART BEATS, HEAR 'EM?
MAN, I COTCH SOMETHIN' FROM THE TREE.
DON'T WANT TO COTCH NO TREE BLIGHTS.
TREE, IS YOU OAK OR KNOTTY PINE?
OH, YES I IS NOT A PINE, I JUS' A WILD COLUMBINE PURPLE MOUNT'INS 'ROUND MY BROW, PERTY AS A YALLER COW.
?
NOW'S MY CHANCE.
HELLO-HELLO -- GIMME THE PENSACOLA PARK DEPARTMENT....
HELLO, JOE --?
YOWP! I MUST OF COTCHED THE SLIPP'RY ELM CROUP--- I IS DELIRIOUS!
FOOF! SOME 'PHONE.
WALT KELLY

Kelly's color guide for his first Sunday page (1/29/50) shows a rather conservative approach...and a final (for now) decision on exactly what color our favorite possum would be. Earlier appearances in Dell comic books varied, partly because Kelly had little control and partly because printing techniques of the day were so inconsistent. Pogo was supposed to be light gray but usually came out some pale shade of purple...a sad compromise he shared with Batman. The published version of this strip is on page 192.

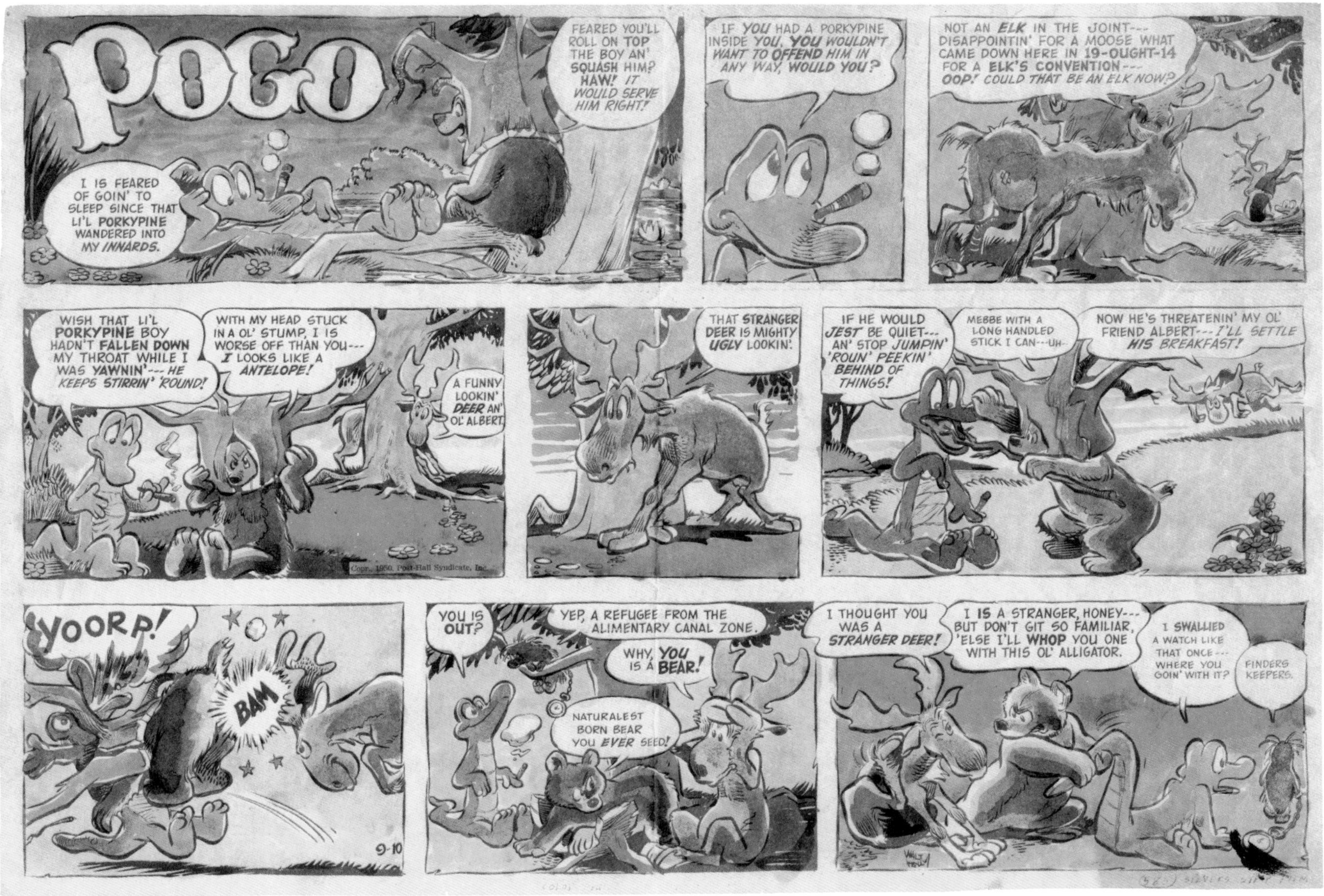
POGO
I IS FEARED OF GOIN' TO SLEEP SINCE THAT LI'L PORKYPINE WANDERED INTO MY INNARDS.
FEARED YOU'LL ROLL ON TOP THE BOY AN' SQUASH HIM? HAW! IT WOULD SERVE HIM RIGHT!
IF YOU HAD A PORKYPINE INSIDE YOU, YOU WOULDN'T WANT TO OFFEND HIM IN ANY WAY, WOULD YOU?
NOT AN ELK IN THE JOINT--- DISAPPOINTIN' FOR A MOOSE WHAT CAME DOWN HERE IN 19-OUGHT-14 FOR A ELK'S CONVENTION--- OOP! COULD THAT BE AN ELK NOW?
WISH THAT LI'L PORKYPINE BOY HADN'T FALLEN DOWN MY THROAT WHILE I WAS YAWNIN'--- HE KEEPS STIRRIN' 'ROUND!
WITH MY HEAD STUCK IN A OL' STUMP, I IS WORSE OFF THAN YOU--- I LOOKS LIKE A ANTELOPE!
A FUNNY LOOKIN' DEER AN' OL' ALBERT.
THAT STRANGER DEER IS MIGHTY UGLY LOOKIN'.
IF HE WOULD JEST BE QUIET--- AN' STOP JUMPIN' 'ROUN' PEEKIN' BEHIND OF THINGS!
MEBBE WITH A LONG HANDLED STICK I CAN---UH---
NOW HE'S THREATENIN' MY OL' FRIEND ALBERT--- I'LL SETTLE HIS BREAKFAST!
YOORP!
BAM
YOU IS OUT?
YEP, A REFUGEE FROM THE ALIMENTARY CANAL ZONE.
WHY, YOU IS A BEAR!
NATURALEST BORN BEAR YOU EVER SEED!
I THOUGHT YOU WAS A STRANGER DEER!
I IS A STRANGER, HONEY--- BUT DON'T GIT SO FAMILIAR, 'ELSE I'LL WHOP YOU ONE WITH THIS OL' ALLIGATOR.
I SWALLIED A WATCH LIKE THAT ONCE--- WHERE YOU GOIN' WITH IT?
FINDERS KEEPERS.
9-10

Eight months later, as seen in this color guide for 9/10/50, Kelly's palette has deeper, richer colors...and less literal ones, as witness the deep violet trees. He also was willing to take the risk that the person hand-cutting the color separations could approximate his hand-painted pattern behind the moose in the center (and made-for-dropping-out) panel. The published version appears over on page 224.

Sunday strips were also more work than dailies because, of course, they had to be composed with consideration of color and then they had to be colored. Whereas many in Kelly's job description feel they have enough to do and so fob off the task of painting color guides to an assistant or some stranger at their syndicate, he did his own. Two examples appear on the preceding pages. An engraver followed Kelly's color choices and indications on these hand-tinted stats when the printing plates were fashioned.

His approach to color was bold and in the years following, it would grow even bolder. The low-budget process did not serve the material (or any newspaper comic strip) well. Color separations were done by hand by (often) low-paid non-artists. They'd try to follow Kelly's directions and sometimes they got close. But even then, the printing was usually done onto the cheapest available newsprint paper on presses that never seemed quite able to get all four colors in register. A lesser cartoonist – and even some good ones – might have opted for similar, predictable color schemes, figuring those had the best chance for survival.

Kelly didn't take the safe, easy route there or anywhere. His color guides challenged the engravers to freehand in highlights and gradations; to place one bright color chockablock with an opposite but equal hue. It wasn't just the characters in the Okefenokee Swamp who were so colorful. It was the swamp, itself. The first color guide on the preceding spread shows a fairly conventional application of color. By the second, just a few months later, he'd stopped coloring *Pogo* like most other strips and was growing ever more unconventional in his approach. No one but the artist

himself would have so gambled with his own readability...and despite the cheapjack reproduction, he succeeded far more often than not.

Still, he worked in a medium with a "throwaway" mentality... one where even the finest practitioners – the journalists with whom Kelly consorted and bonded – joked about their output being used to wrap fish and accepted such a fate. The work was easily discarded when it seemed to have no further marketplace. Originals were trashed or given away. Printing plates were smelted down. Assembling "keeper" volumes now – especially on good paper and with good printing – is a frustrating effort but one that has to be done.

The search for the best possible source material delayed the launch of this series for years. Scattered original artwork and proof sheets exist but after a thorough dragnet and much discussion, the only complete source material was determined to be the newspaper pages themselves. They were printed in the first place as cheaply as possible, true, but that turns out to be the only complete record of Walt Kelly's *Pogo*.

So pages have been lovingly and painstakingly restored by hand and computer, always with an eye on the original intention of the artist. Like a vintage movie that has been restored not to the standards of current technology but to the way it was originally projected, this is how *Pogo* appeared to its intended audience. That the work can suffer such handicaps and still delight has a lot to do with how witty and talented Walt Kelly was. In fact, it has everything to do with it.

SUNDAY FUNNIES

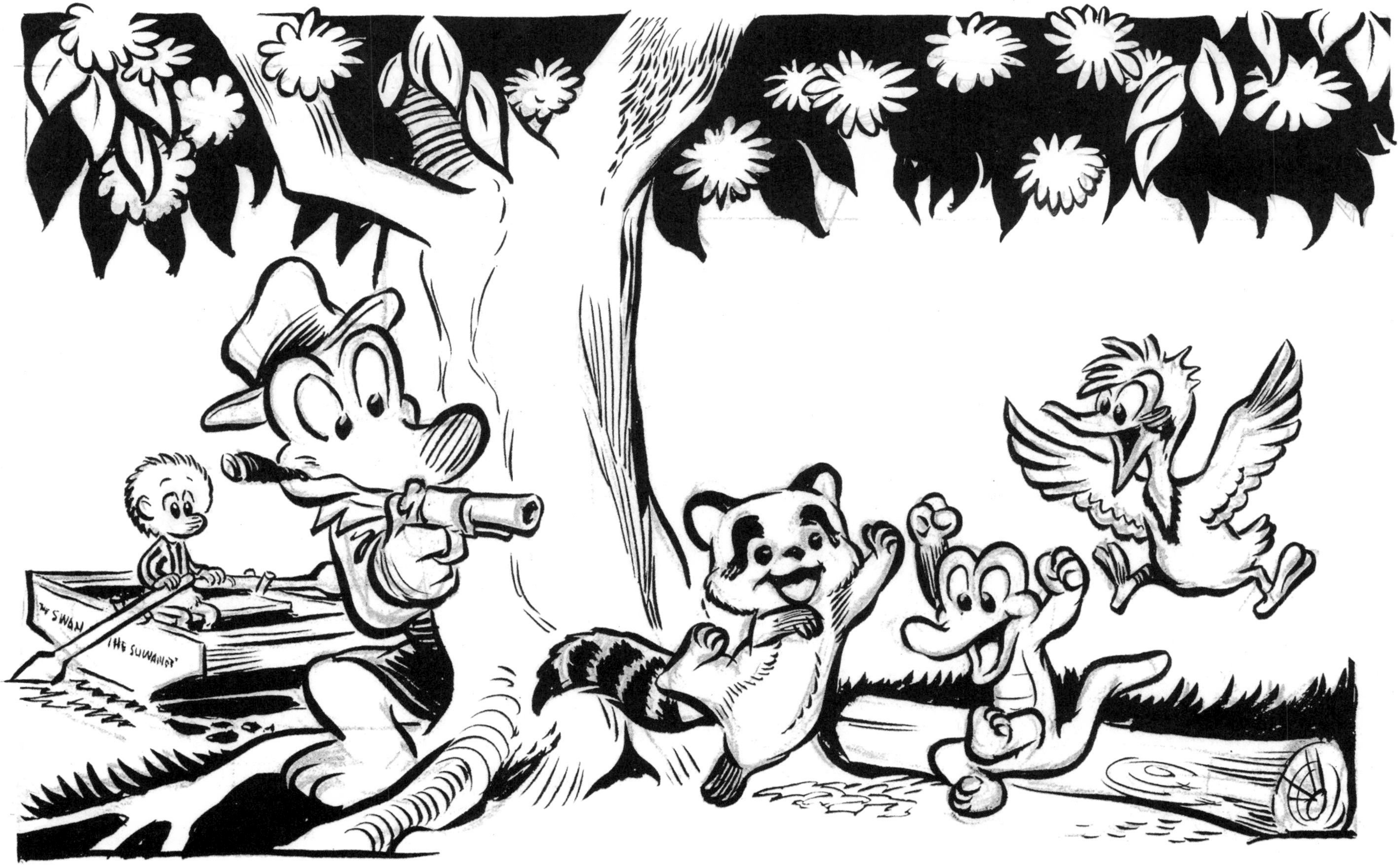
SWAN

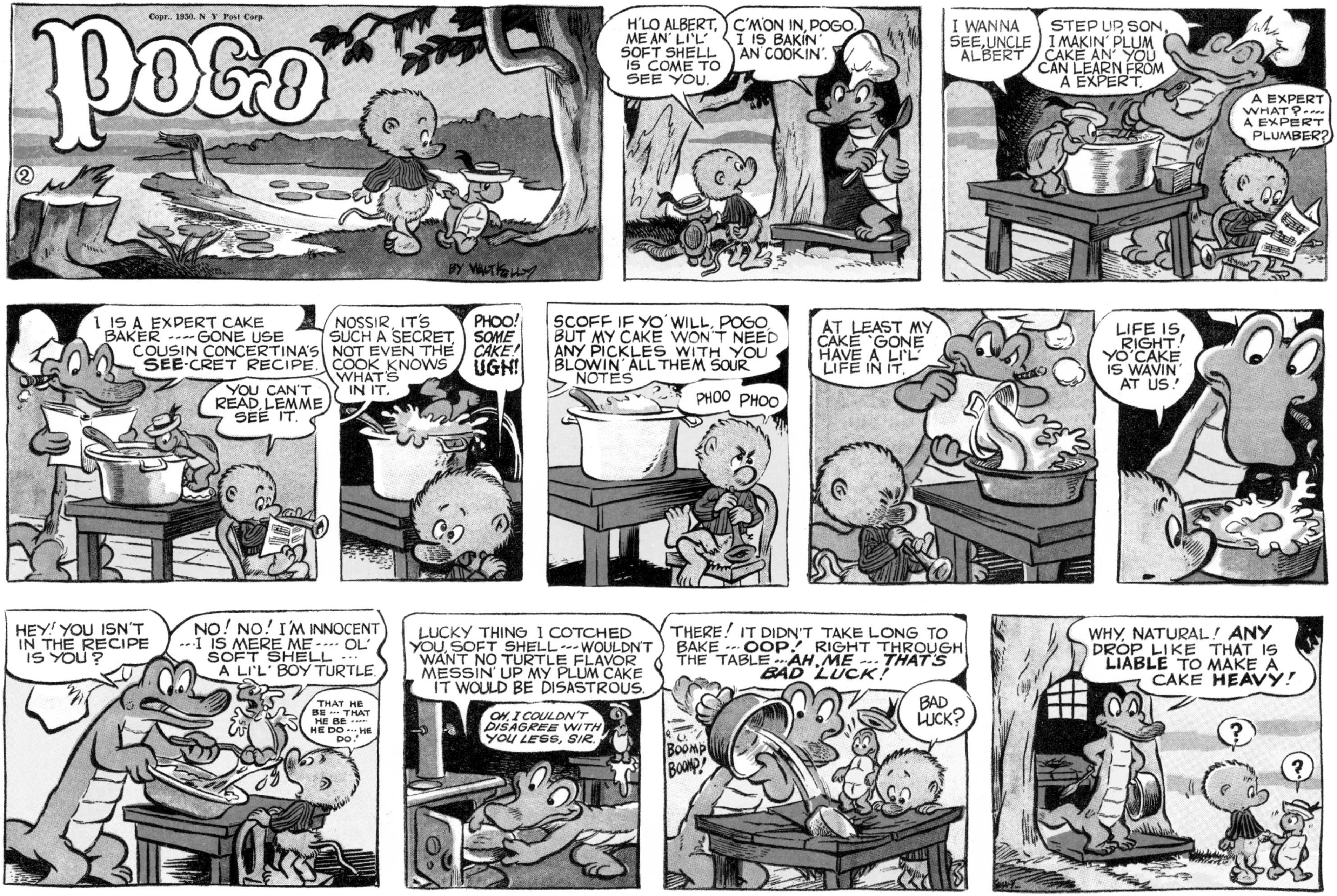
Copr., 1950, N Y Post Corp.
POGO
②
BY WALT KELLY
H'LO ALBERT, ME AN' LI'L' SOFT SHELL IS COME TO SEE YOU.
C'MON IN, POGO. I IS BAKIN' AN' COOKIN'.
I WANNA SEE, UNCLE ALBERT
STEP UP, SON, I MAKIN' PLUM CAKE AN' YOU CAN LEARN FROM A EXPERT.
A EXPERT WHAT?---- A EXPERT PLUMBER?
I IS A EXPERT CAKE BAKER ---- GONE USE COUSIN CONCERTINA'S **SEE**-CRET RECIPE.
YOU CAN'T READ, LEMME SEE IT.
NOSSIR, IT'S SUCH A SECRET, NOT EVEN THE COOK KNOWS WHAT'S IN IT.
PHOO! SOME CAKE! UGH!
SCOFF IF YO' WILL, POGO, BUT MY CAKE WON'T NEED ANY PICKLES WITH YOU BLOWIN' ALL THEM SOUR NOTES
PHOO PHOO
AT LEAST MY CAKE 'GONE HAVE A LI'L' LIFE IN IT.
LIFE IS RIGHT! YO' CAKE IS WAVIN' AT US!
HEY! YOU ISN'T IN THE RECIPE IS YOU?
NO! NO! I'M INNOCENT --I IS MERE ME ---- OL' SOFT SHELL --- A LI'L' BOY TURTLE.
THAT HE BE --- THAT HE BE ---- HE DO --- HE DO.'
LUCKY THING I COTCHED YOU, SOFT SHELL --- WOULDN'T WANT NO TURTLE FLAVOR MESSIN' UP MY PLUM CAKE IT WOULD BE DISASTROUS.
OH, I COULDN'T DISAGREE WITH YOU LESS, SIR.
THERE! IT DIDN'T TAKE LONG TO BAKE -- **OOP!** RIGHT THROUGH THE TABLE -- **AH, ME --- THAT'S BAD LUCK!**
BOOMP BOOMP!
BAD LUCK?
WHY, NATURAL! **ANY** DROP LIKE THAT IS **LIABLE** TO MAKE A CAKE **HEAVY**!
?
?

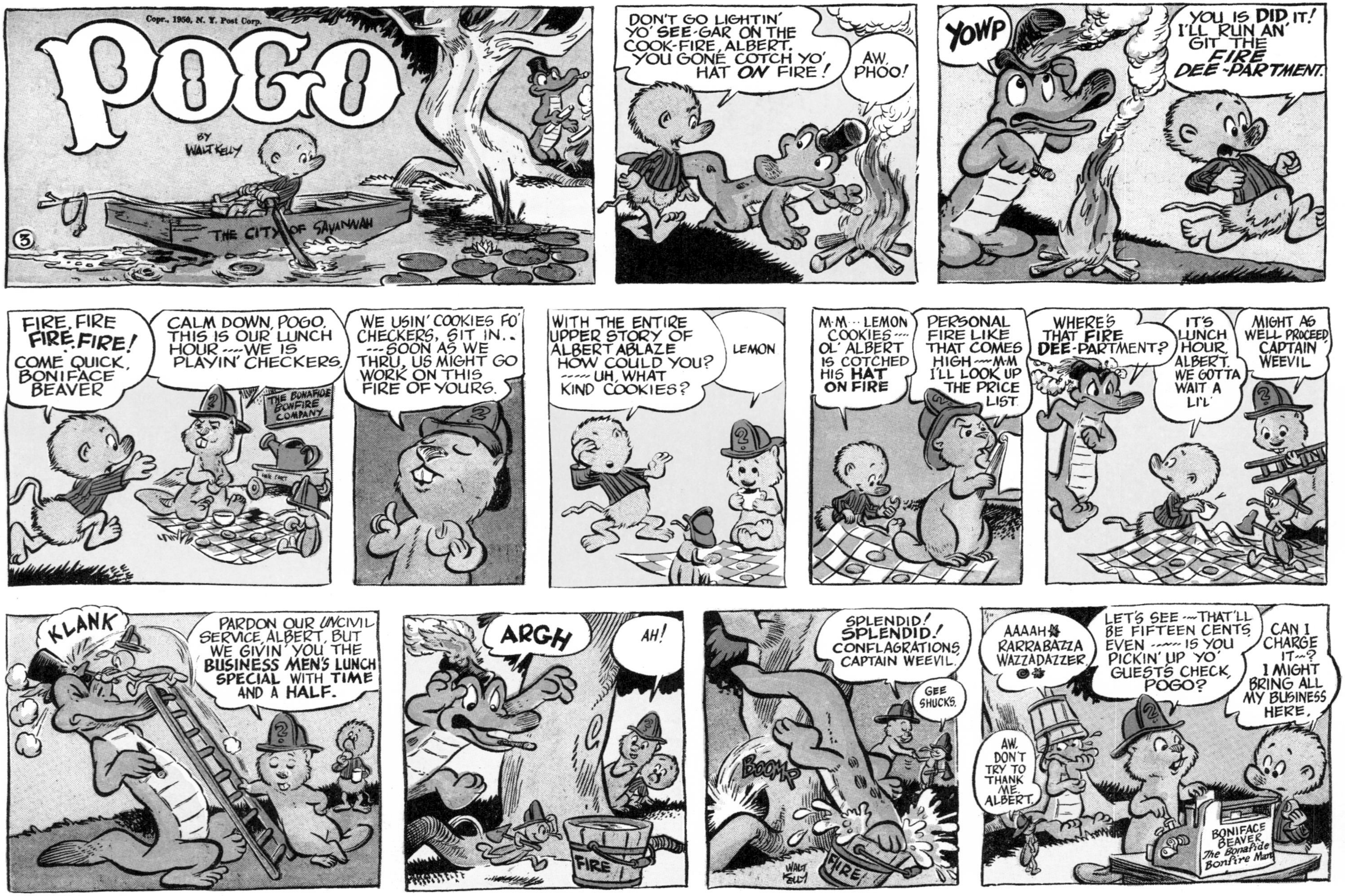
Copr., 1950, N. Y. Post Corp.
POGO
BY WALT KELLY
THE CITY OF SAVANNAH
3
DON'T GO LIGHTIN' YO' SEE-GAR ON THE COOK-FIRE, ALBERT. YOU GONE COTCH YO' HAT ON FIRE!
AW. PHOO!
YOWP
YOU IS DID IT! I'LL RUN AN' GIT THE FIRE DEE-PARTMENT.
FIRE, FIRE FIRE. FIRE! COME QUICK, BONIFACE BEAVER
CALM DOWN, POGO. THIS IS OUR LUNCH HOUR ---- WE IS PLAYIN' CHECKERS.
THE BONAFIDE BONFIRE COMPANY
WE USIN' COOKIES FO' CHECKERS, SIT IN.. ---SOON AS WE THRU, US MIGHT GO WORK ON THIS FIRE OF YOURS.
WITH THE ENTIRE UPPER STORY OF ALBERT ABLAZE HOW COULD YOU? ----- UH, WHAT KIND COOKIES?
LEMON
M-M ... LEMON COOKIES ---- OL' ALBERT IS COTCHED HIS HAT ON FIRE
PERSONAL FIRE LIKE THAT COMES HIGH ---- M-M I'LL LOOK UP THE PRICE LIST
WHERE'S THAT FIRE DEE-PARTMENT?
IT'S LUNCH HOUR, ALBERT. WE GOTTA WAIT A LI'L
MIGHT AS WELL PROCEED, CAPTAIN WEEVIL
KLANK
PARDON OUR UNCIVIL SERVICE, ALBERT, BUT WE GIVIN' YOU THE BUSINESS MEN'S LUNCH SPECIAL WITH TIME AND A HALF.
ARGH
AH!
FIRE
SPLENDID! SPLENDID! CONFLAGRATIONS, CAPTAIN WEEVIL.
GEE SHUCKS.
BOOMP
FIRE
WALT KELLY
AAAAH RARRABAZZA WAZZADAZZER
LET'S SEE --- THAT'LL BE FIFTEEN CENTS EVEN ----- IS YOU PICKIN' UP YO' GUESTS CHECK, POGO?
CAN I CHARGE IT --? I MIGHT BRING ALL MY BUSINESS HERE.
AW. DON'T TRY TO THANK ME, ALBERT.
BONIFACE BEAVER The Bonafide Bonfire Man

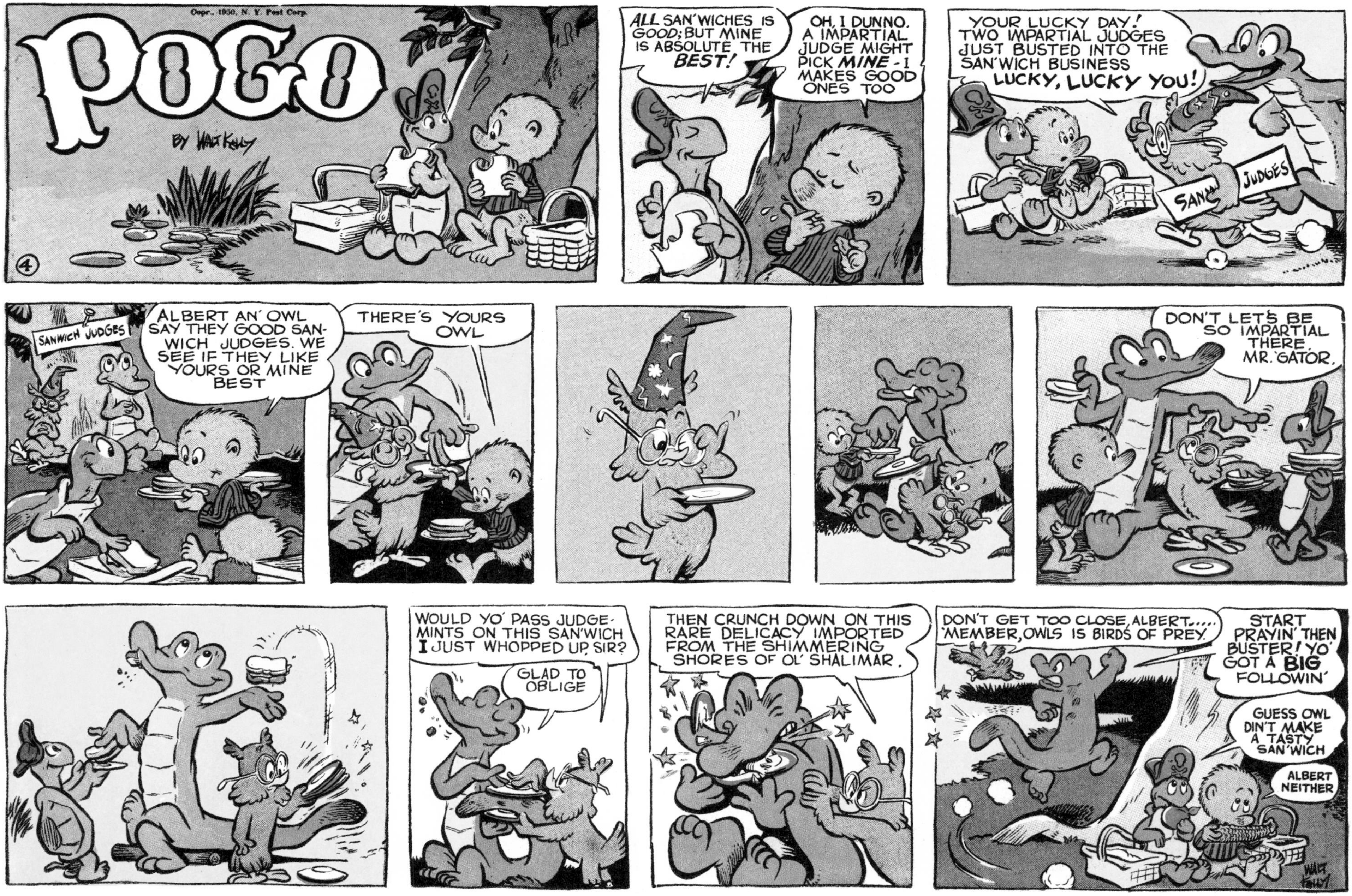
Copr., 1950, N. Y. Post Corp.
POGO
BY WALT KELLY
4
ALL SAN'WICHES IS GOOD; BUT MINE IS ABSOLUTE THE BEST!
OH, I DUNNO. A IMPARTIAL JUDGE MIGHT PICK MINE - I MAKES GOOD ONES TOO
YOUR LUCKY DAY! TWO IMPARTIAL JUDGES JUST BUSTED INTO THE SAN'WICH BUSINESS LUCKY, LUCKY YOU!
JUDGES
SANWICH JUDGES
ALBERT AN' OWL SAY THEY GOOD SAN-WICH JUDGES. WE SEE IF THEY LIKE YOURS OR MINE BEST
THERE'S YOURS OWL
DON'T LET'S BE SO IMPARTIAL THERE, MR. GATOR.
WOULD YO' PASS JUDGE-MINTS ON THIS SAN'WICH I JUST WHOPPED UP, SIR?
GLAD TO OBLIGE
THEN CRUNCH DOWN ON THIS RARE DELICACY IMPORTED FROM THE SHIMMERING SHORES OF OL' SHALIMAR.
DON'T GET TOO CLOSE, ALBERT..... 'MEMBER, OWLS IS BIRDS OF PREY.
START PRAYIN' THEN BUSTER! YO' GOT A BIG FOLLOWIN'
GUESS OWL DIN'T MAKE A TASTY SAN'WICH
ALBERT NEITHER
WALT KELLY

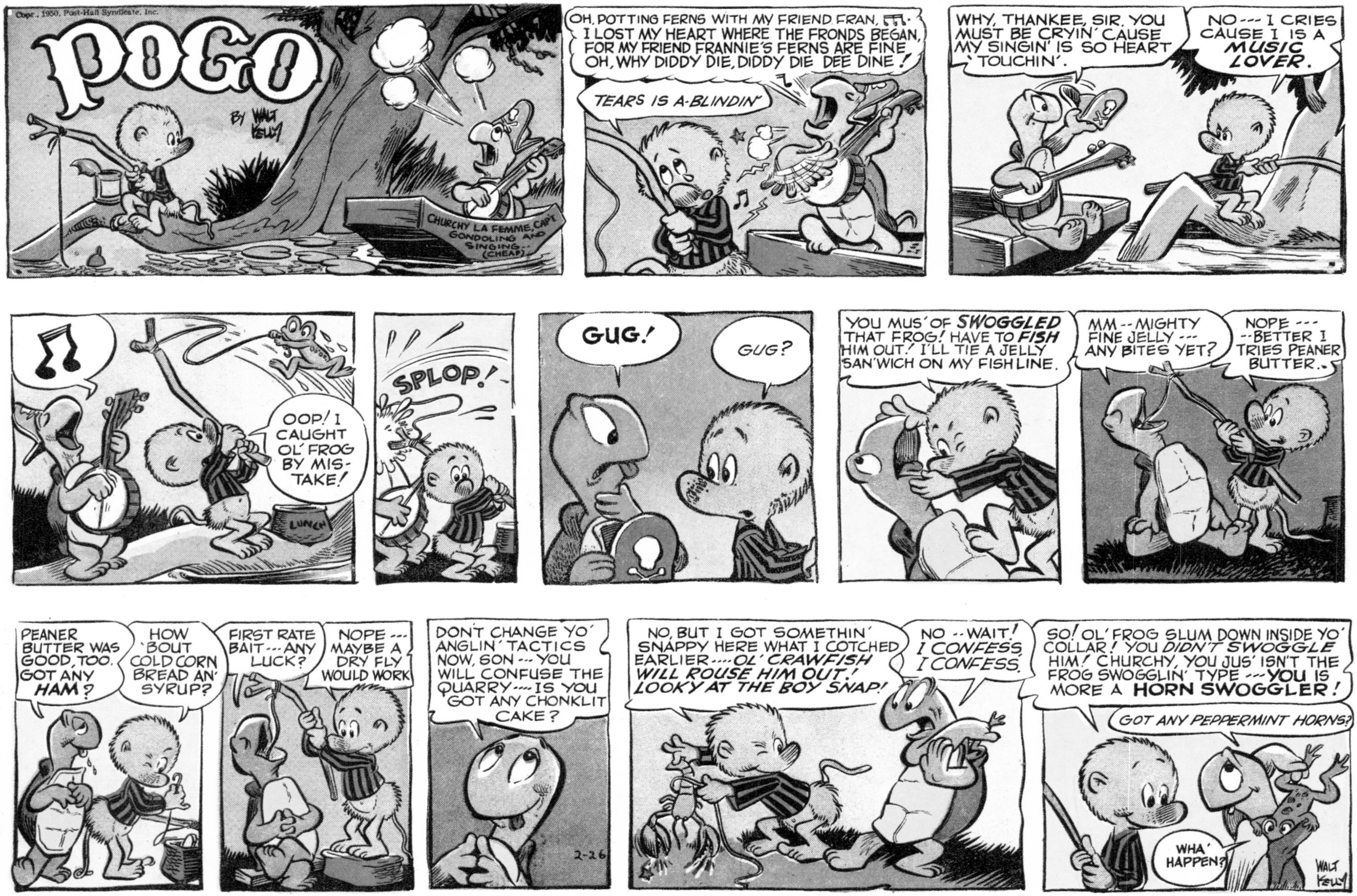
Copr., 1950, Post-Hall Syndicate, Inc.
POGO
BY WALT KELLY
CHURCHY LA FEMME, CAPT. GONDOLING AND SINGING.. (CHEAP)
OH, POTTING FERNS WITH MY FRIEND FRAN, I LOST MY HEART WHERE THE FRONDS BEGAN, FOR MY FRIEND FRANNIE'S FERNS ARE FINE OH, WHY DIDDY DIE, DIDDY DIE DEE DINE!
TEARS IS A-BLINDIN'
WHY, THANKEE, SIR. YOU MUST BE CRYIN' CAUSE MY SINGIN' IS SO HEART 'TOUCHIN'.
NO --- I CRIES CAUSE I IS A MUSIC LOVER.
OOP! I CAUGHT OL' FROG BY MIS-TAKE!
LUNCH
SPLOP!
GUG!
GUG?
YOU MUS' OF SWOGGLED THAT FROG! HAVE TO FISH HIM OUT! I'LL TIE A JELLY SAN'WICH ON MY FISHLINE.
MM -- MIGHTY FINE JELLY --- ANY BITES YET?
NOPE --- --BETTER I TRIES PEANER BUTTER.
PEANER BUTTER WAS GOOD, TOO. GOT ANY HAM?
HOW 'BOUT COLD CORN BREAD AN' SYRUP?
FIRST RATE BAIT --- ANY LUCK?
NOPE --- MAYBE A DRY FLY WOULD WORK
DON'T CHANGE YO' ANGLIN' TACTICS NOW, SON --- YOU WILL CONFUSE THE QUARRY --- IS YOU GOT ANY CHONKLIT CAKE?
2-26
NO, BUT I GOT SOMETHIN' SNAPPY HERE WHAT I COTCHED EARLIER ---- OL' CRAWFISH WILL ROUSE HIM OUT! LOOKY AT THE BOY SNAP!
NO -- WAIT! I CONFESS I CONFESS.
SO! OL' FROG SLUM DOWN INSIDE YO' COLLAR! YOU DIDN'T SWOGGLE HIM! CHURCHY, YOU JUS' ISN'T THE FROG SWOGGLIN' TYPE --- YOU IS MORE A HORN SWOGGLER!
GOT ANY PEPPERMINT HORNS?
WHA' HAPPEN?
WALT KELLY

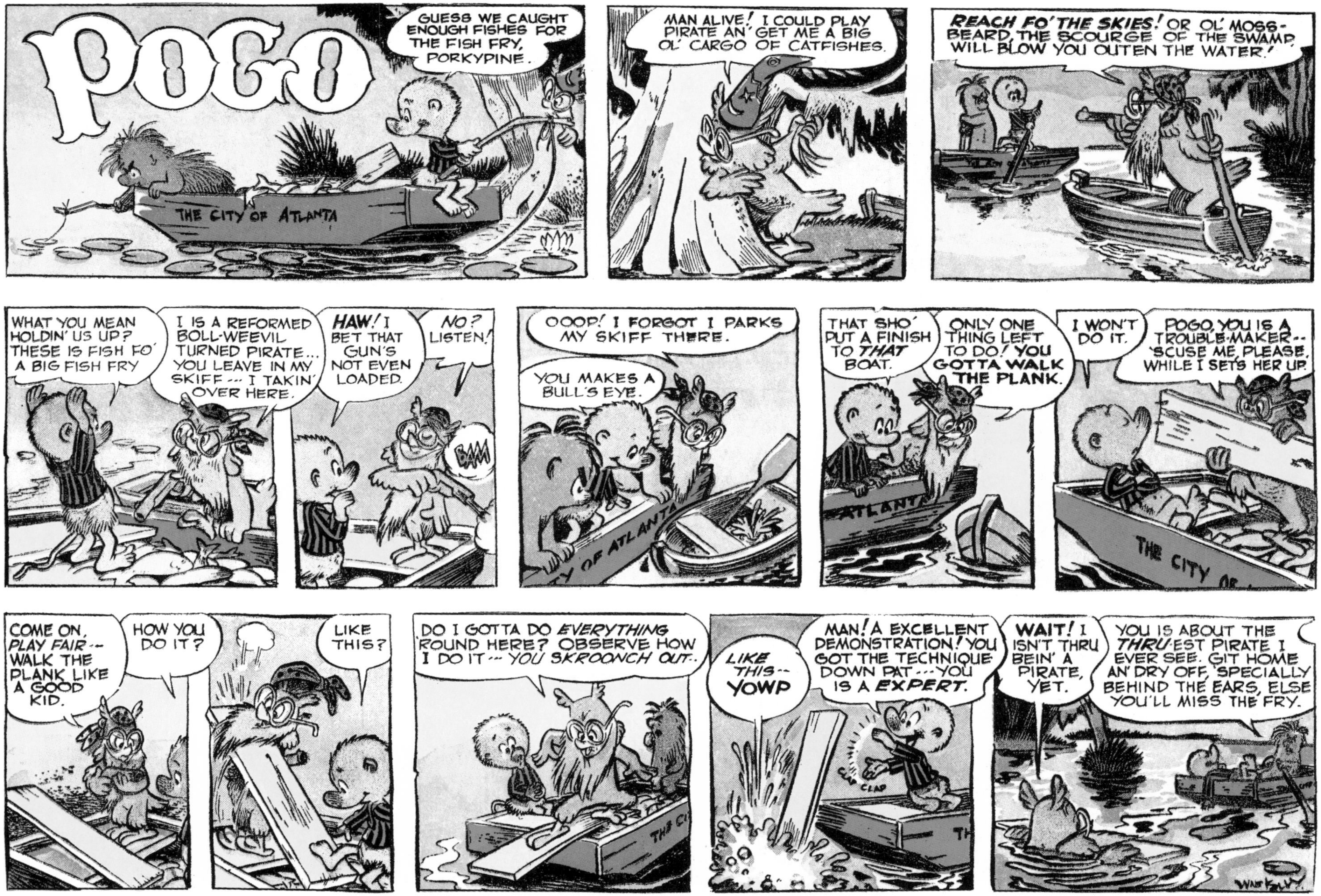
POGO
GUESS WE CAUGHT ENOUGH FISHES FOR THE FISH FRY, PORKYPINE.
THE CITY OF ATLANTA
MAN ALIVE! I COULD PLAY PIRATE AN' GET ME A BIG OL' CARGO OF CATFISHES.
REACH FO' THE SKIES! OR OL' MOSS-BEARD, THE SCOURGE OF THE SWAMP WILL BLOW YOU OUTEN THE WATER!
WHAT YOU MEAN HOLDIN' US UP? THESE IS FISH FO' A BIG FISH FRY
I IS A REFORMED BOLL-WEEVIL TURNED PIRATE... YOU LEAVE IN MY SKIFF --- I TAKIN' OVER HERE.
HAW! I BET THAT GUN'S NOT EVEN LOADED.
NO? LISTEN!
BAM
OOOP! I FORGOT I PARKS MY SKIFF THERE.
YOU MAKES A BULL'S EYE.
OF ATLANTA
THAT SHO' PUT A FINISH TO THAT BOAT.
ONLY ONE THING LEFT TO DO! YOU GOTTA WALK THE PLANK.
ATLANT
I WON'T DO IT.
POGO, YOU IS A TROUBLE-MAKER-- 'SCUSE ME, PLEASE, WHILE I SETS HER UP.
THE CITY OF
COME ON, PLAY FAIR-- WALK THE PLANK LIKE A GOOD KID.
HOW YOU DO IT?
LIKE THIS?
DO I GOTTA DO EVERYTHING 'ROUND HERE? OBSERVE HOW I DO IT --- YOU SKROONCH OUT..
LIKE THIS-- YOWP
MAN! A EXCELLENT DEMONSTRATION! YOU GOT THE TECHNIQUE DOWN PAT --- YOU IS A EXPERT.
CLAP CLAP
WAIT! I ISN'T THRU BEIN' A PIRATE, YET.
YOU IS ABOUT THE THRU-EST PIRATE I EVER SEE. GIT HOME AN' DRY OFF, SPECIALLY BEHIND THE EARS, ELSE YOU'LL MISS THE FRY.

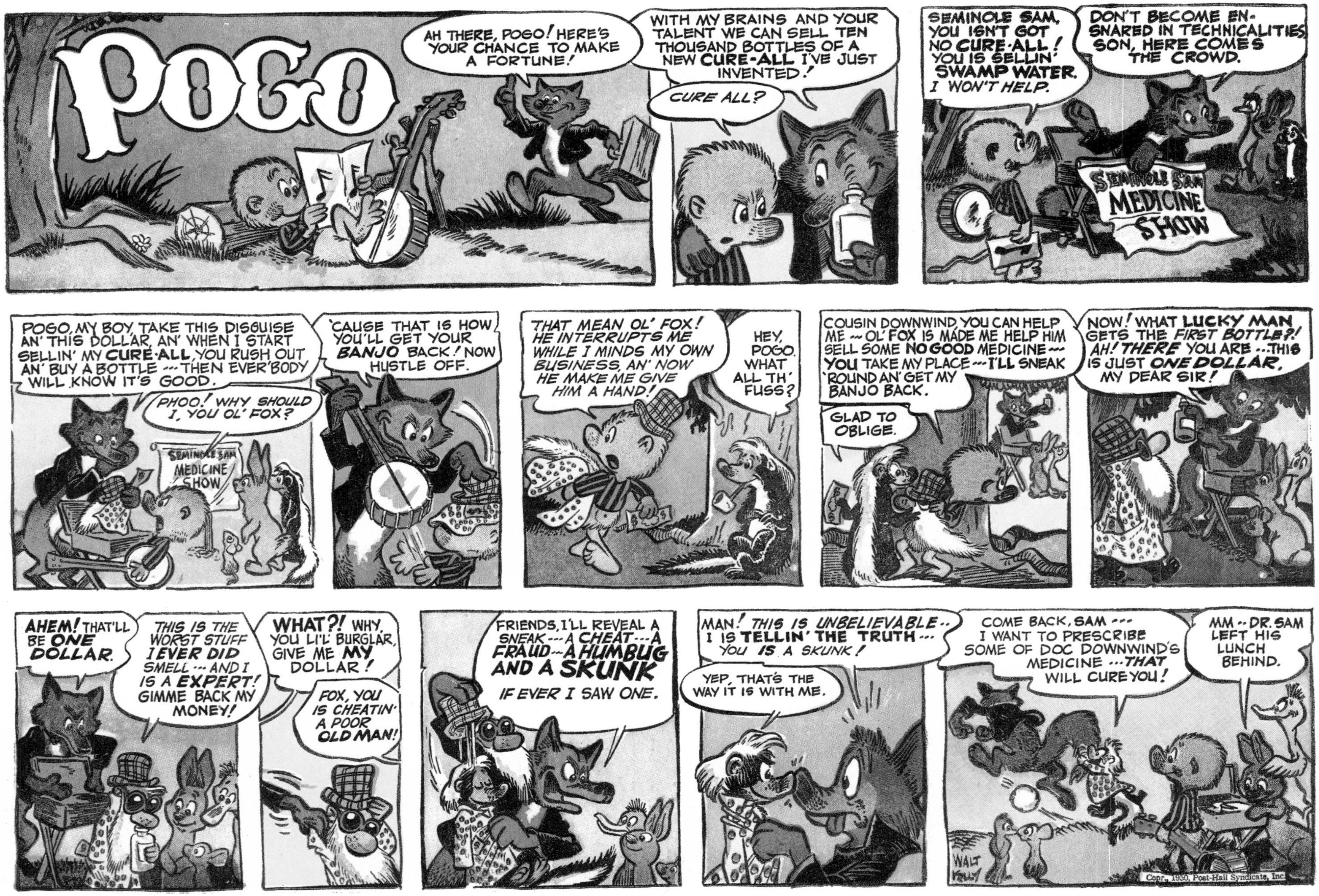
POGO
AH THERE, POGO! HERE'S YOUR CHANCE TO MAKE A FORTUNE!
WITH MY BRAINS AND YOUR TALENT WE CAN SELL TEN THOUSAND BOTTLES OF A NEW CURE-ALL I'VE JUST INVENTED.!
CURE ALL?
SEMINOLE SAM, YOU ISN'T GOT NO CURE-ALL! YOU IS SELLIN' SWAMP WATER. I WON'T HELP.
DON'T BECOME EN-SNARED IN TECHNICALITIES SON, HERE COMES THE CROWD.
SEMINOLE SAM MEDICINE SHOW
POGO, MY BOY, TAKE THIS DISGUISE AN' THIS DOLLAR, AN' WHEN I START SELLIN' MY CURE-ALL, YOU RUSH OUT AN' BUY A BOTTLE --- THEN EVER'BODY WILL KNOW IT'S GOOD.
PHOO! WHY SHOULD I, YOU OL' FOX?
SEMINOLE SAM MEDICINE SHOW
'CAUSE THAT IS HOW YOU'LL GET YOUR BANJO BACK! NOW HUSTLE OFF.
THAT MEAN OL' FOX! HE INTERRUPTS ME WHILE I MINDS MY OWN BUSINESS, AN' NOW HE MAKE ME GIVE HIM A HAND!
HEY, POGO. WHAT ALL TH' FUSS?
COUSIN DOWNWIND, YOU CAN HELP ME -- OL' FOX IS MADE ME HELP HIM SELL SOME NO GOOD MEDICINE --- YOU TAKE MY PLACE --- I'LL SNEAK 'ROUND AN' GET MY BANJO BACK.
GLAD TO OBLIGE.
NOW! WHAT LUCKY MAN GETS THE FIRST BOTTLE?! AH! THERE YOU ARE --- THIS IS JUST ONE DOLLAR, MY DEAR SIR!
AHEM! THAT'LL BE ONE DOLLAR.
THIS IS THE WORST STUFF I EVER DID SMELL --- AND I IS A EXPERT! GIMME BACK MY MONEY!
WHAT?! WHY, YOU LI'L BURGLAR, GIVE ME MY DOLLAR!
FOX, YOU IS CHEATIN' A POOR OLD MAN!
FRIENDS, I'LL REVEAL A SNEAK --- A CHEAT --- A FRAUD --- A HUMBUG AND A SKUNK IF EVER I SAW ONE.
MAN! THIS IS UNBELIEVABLE -- I IS TELLIN' THE TRUTH --- YOU IS A SKUNK!
YEP, THAT'S THE WAY IT IS WITH ME.
COME BACK, SAM --- I WANT TO PRESCRIBE SOME OF DOC DOWNWIND'S MEDICINE --- THAT WILL CURE YOU!
MM -- DR. SAM LEFT HIS LUNCH BEHIND.
WALT KELLY
Copr., 1950, Post-Hall Syndicate, Inc.

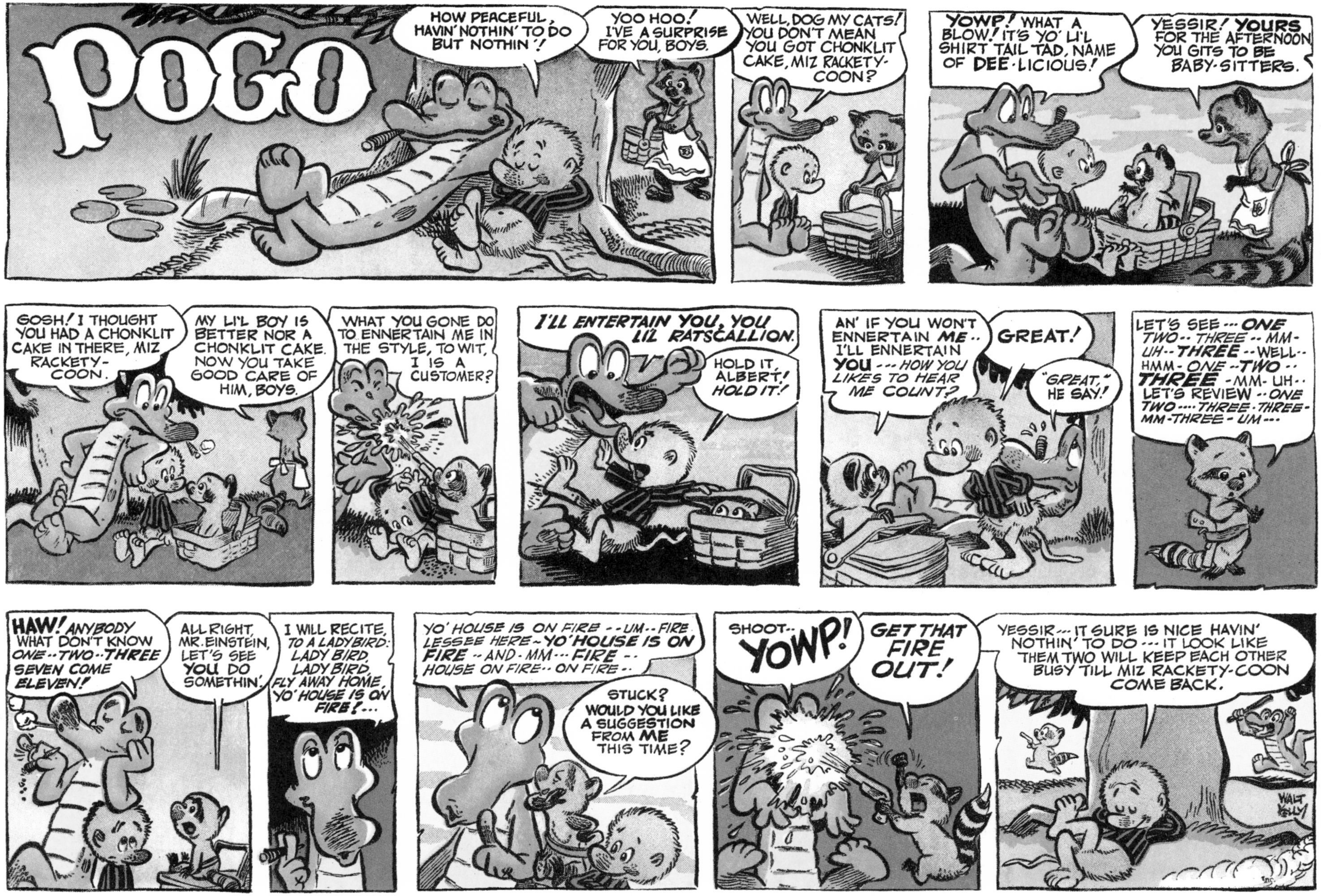
POGO
HOW PEACEFUL, HAVIN' NOTHIN' TO DO BUT NOTHIN'!
YOO HOO! I'VE A SURPRISE FOR YOU, BOYS.
WELL, DOG MY CATS! YOU DON'T MEAN YOU GOT CHONKLIT CAKE, MIZ RACKETY-COON?
YOWP! WHAT A BLOW! IT'S YO' LI'L SHIRT TAIL TAD, NAME OF DEE-LICIOUS!
YESSIR! YOURS FOR THE AFTERNOON YOU GITS TO BE BABY-SITTERS.
GOSH! I THOUGHT YOU HAD A CHONKLIT CAKE IN THERE, MIZ RACKETY-COON.
MY LI'L BOY IS BETTER NOR A CHONKLIT CAKE. NOW YOU TAKE GOOD CARE OF HIM, BOYS.
WHAT YOU GONE DO TO ENNERTAIN ME IN THE STYLE, TO WIT, I IS A CUSTOMER?
I'LL ENTERTAIN YOU, YOU LI'L RATSCALLION.
HOLD IT, ALBERT! HOLD IT!
AN' IF YOU WON'T ENNERTAIN ME.. I'LL ENNERTAIN YOU --- HOW YOU LIKES TO HEAR ME COUNT?
GREAT!
"GREAT," HE SAY!
LET'S SEE --- ONE TWO -- THREE -- MM-UH -- THREE -- WELL -- HMM - ONE -- TWO -- THREE - MM - UH -- LET'S REVIEW -- ONE TWO .... THREE - THREE - MM - THREE - UM ---
HAW! ANYBODY WHAT DON'T KNOW ONE -- TWO -- THREE SEVEN COME ELEVEN!
ALL RIGHT, MR. EINSTEIN, LET'S SEE YOU DO SOMETHIN'.
I WILL RECITE, TO A LADYBIRD: LADY BIRD, LADY BIRD, FLY AWAY HOME, YO' HOUSE IS ON FIRE! ...
YO' HOUSE IS ON FIRE -- UM -- FIRE LESSEE HERE -- YO' HOUSE IS ON FIRE -- AND - MM --- FIRE -- HOUSE ON FIRE -- ON FIRE --.
STUCK? WOULD YOU LIKE A SUGGESTION FROM ME THIS TIME?
SHOOT..
YOWP!
GET THAT FIRE OUT!
YESSIR --- IT SURE IS NICE HAVIN' NOTHIN' TO DO --- IT LOOK LIKE THEM TWO WILL KEEP EACH OTHER BUSY TILL MIZ RACKETY-COON COME BACK.
WALT KELLY

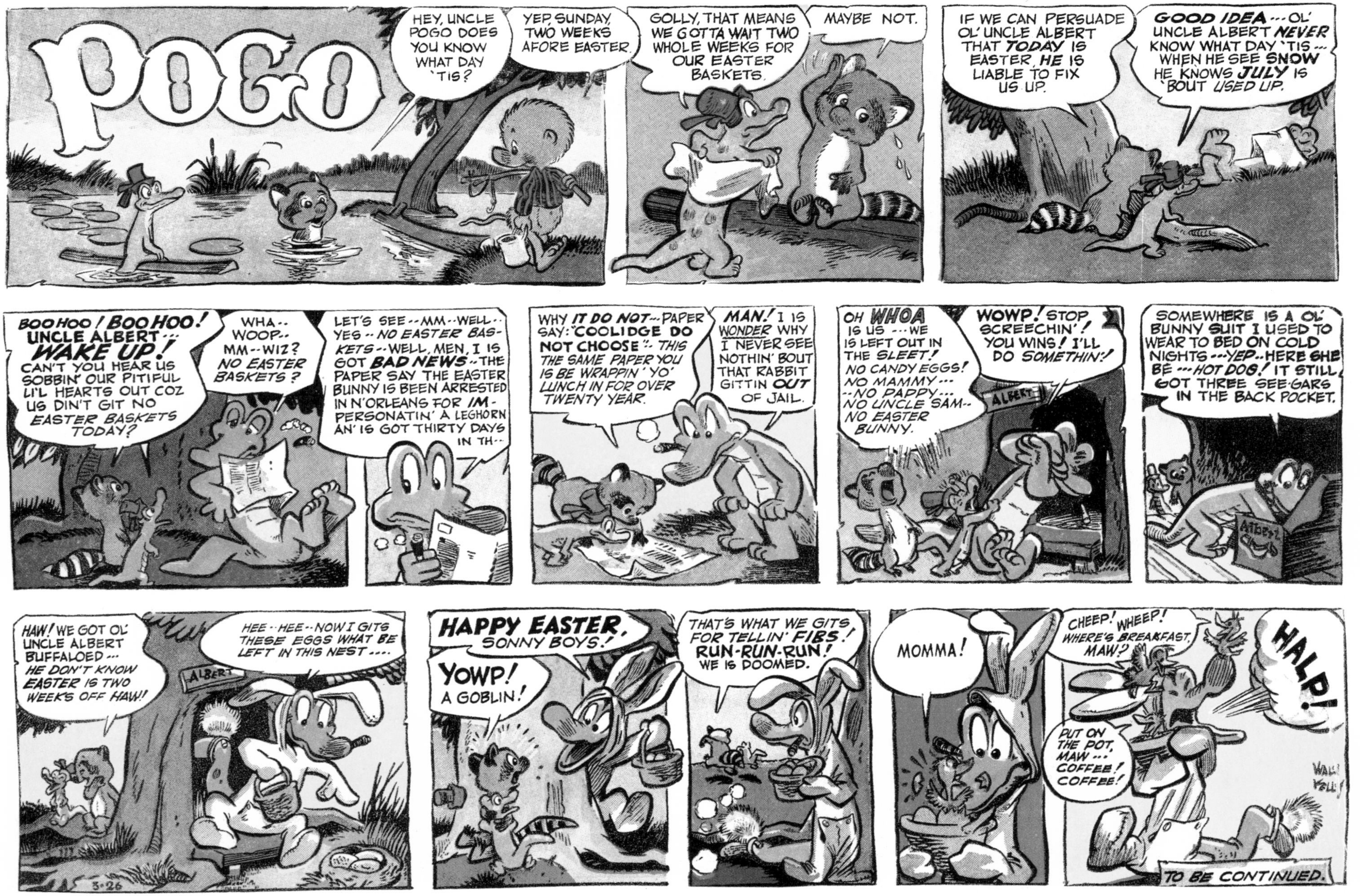
POGO
HEY, UNCLE POGO DOES YOU KNOW WHAT DAY 'TIS?
YEP, SUNDAY, TWO WEEKS AFORE EASTER.
GOLLY, THAT MEANS WE GOTTA WAIT TWO WHOLE WEEKS FOR OUR EASTER BASKETS.
MAYBE NOT.
IF WE CAN PERSUADE OL' UNCLE ALBERT THAT TODAY IS EASTER, HE IS LIABLE TO FIX US UP.
GOOD IDEA --- OL' UNCLE ALBERT NEVER KNOW WHAT DAY 'TIS --- WHEN HE SEE SNOW HE KNOWS JULY IS 'BOUT USED UP.
BOO HOO! BOO HOO! UNCLE ALBERT ... WAKE UP! CAN'T YOU HEAR US SOBBIN' OUR PITIFUL LI'L HEARTS OUT COZ US DIN'T GIT NO EASTER BASKETS TODAY?
WHA -- WOOP -- MM -- WIZ? NO EASTER BASKETS?
LET'S SEE -- MM -- WELL -- YES -- NO EASTER BASKETS -- WELL, MEN, I IS GOT BAD NEWS -- THE PAPER SAY THE EASTER BUNNY IS BEEN ARRESTED IN N'ORLEANS FOR IMPERSONATIN' A LEGHORN AN' IS GOT THIRTY DAYS IN TH --
WHY IT DO NOT -- PAPER SAY: "COOLIDGE DO NOT CHOOSE" -- THIS THE SAME PAPER YOU IS BE WRAPPIN' YO' LUNCH IN FOR OVER TWENTY YEAR.
MAN! I IS WONDER WHY I NEVER SEE NOTHIN' 'BOUT THAT RABBIT GITTIN OUT OF JAIL.
OH WHOA IS US --- WE IS LEFT OUT IN THE SLEET! NO CANDY EGGS! NO MAMMY --- -- NO PAPPY --- NO UNCLE SAM -- NO EASTER BUNNY.
WOWP! STOP SCREECHIN'! YOU WINS! I'LL DO SOMETHIN'!
ALBERT
SOMEWHERE IS A OL' BUNNY SUIT I USED TO WEAR TO BED ON COLD NIGHTS --- YEP -- HERE SHE BE --- HOT DOG! IT STILL GOT THREE SEE-GARS IN THE BACK POCKET.
HAW! WE GOT OL' UNCLE ALBERT BUFFALOED --- HE DON'T KNOW EASTER IS TWO WEEKS OFF HAW!
HEE -- HEE -- NOW I GITS THESE EGGS WHAT BE LEFT IN THIS NEST ....
ALBERT
3-26
HAPPY EASTER, SONNY BOYS!
YOWP! A GOBLIN!
THAT'S WHAT WE GITS FOR TELLIN' FIBS! RUN-RUN-RUN! WE IS DOOMED.
MOMMA!
CHEEP! WHEEP! WHERE'S BREAKFAST, MAW?
PUT ON THE POT, MAW --- COFFEE! COFFEE!
HALP!
WALT KELLY
TO BE CONTINUED.

POGO
WOWIE! ALBERT, YOU SURE GIVED ME A SCARE!
GIMME THE BORRY OF YO' BAIT, POGO, WHILST I FEEDS THESE BIRD CHILLUN AN' I TELLS YOU HOW COME I DRESS UP LIKE A JACK RABBIT.
PARDON MY BEG TO DIFFERMINT, BUT YOU LOOK MORE LIKE A JACKASS.
THANK YOU, MOMMA.... THANK YOU, MOMMA.
CALM DOWN, YOU LI'L SPRAT, AFORE MAMMY FORGIT SHE A GENTLEMINT--. TWO TADS TOLE ME LAST WEEK THAT IT WAS EASTER, SO I DRESS UP LIKE A OL' BUNNY AN' GITS 'EM SOME EGGS -- THE TADS RUN OFF --- THE EGGS HATCH AN' NOW I IS A MAMMY BOAT TAILED GRACKLE.
KOOTCHIE KOOTCHIE.
ALBERT, AS LONG AS YOU PUT ON YOUR BUNNY SUIT TOO SOON, LEAVE IT ON WHILE YOU LOOKS FOR MIZ CHLOE, THE MAMMY OF THEM LI'L BOAT-TAILED GRACKLES.
I'LL DO IT.
MUST OF PUT MY SUIT ON BACKSIDE FRONT--- I'LL JUS' STUFF THE BIRD CHILLUN INTO THE POCKET.
ALBERT'S A GOOD KID --- ONLY REASON HE'S STUCK WITH THEM BABY BOAT-TAILED GRACKLES IS 'CAUSE HE TRIED TO DO A GOOD TURN FOR SOMEBODY.
MAN'S BEST FRIEND, TO WIT, THE DOG, AWAITS WITH CALM DIGNITY TO HUNT THE EASTER RABBIT--- TIME IS OF THE ESSENCE BUT THE NOBLE DOG URGES NOT --- NEITHER DOES HE PROD --- HIS PATIENT LIPS ARE SEALED---
SHH-- WE IS COUNTIN' OUR LUNCH
THE FAITHFUL BEAST IS LONG SUFFERING -- AH, HE CAN WAIT, THO' HIS LIFE'S SPAN IS LESS THAN A SCORE "TAKE YOUR TIME," HIS SOFT BROWN EYES SEEM TO SAY......
THE CHASE GROWS STALE -- THE TRAIL LIES FALLOW--- BUT WHY HURRY? THE DOG CHAMPS AT THE BIT, BUT IF YOU MUST COMPARE SANDWICHES, PRAY BE THOROUGH ----.
BEE HOLD! A KING-SIZED JACK RABBIT! THERE'S A RARE BIT TO CHAMP ON. CHAMP -- SIC 'IM!
CHLO-EE!
AIN'T NO CHAINS GONE BIND ME -- THAT IS A BONAFINE KANG-GAY-ROO!
IS YOU KIDS SEED MIZ CHLOE, THE BOAT-TAIL GRACKLE? HMMF--- THEY LEFT THEY LUNCH!
THE TALENTS OF A TRUE RETRIEVER DO NOT INCLUDE THE HARRYING OR BEAGLING OF STRANGE AUSTRALIANS.
CHOMP-- CHOMP-- CHLOE -- YOO-HOO!
PHOO! YOU IS A-SCAIRT OF A BIG BUNNY.
YEAH-- JUS 'CAUSE IT'S A KANGAROO
WALT KELLY

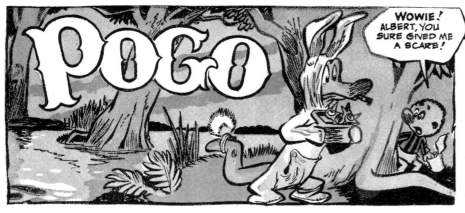

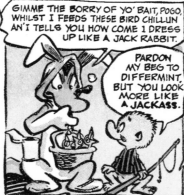

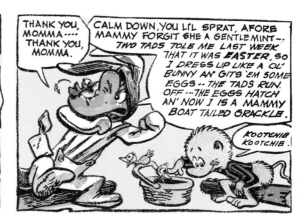

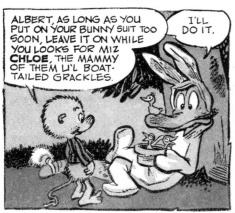

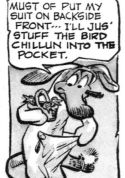

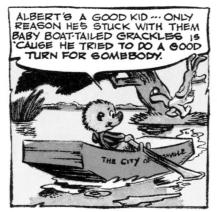

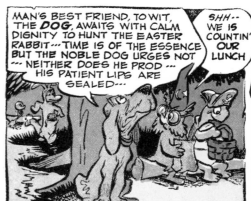

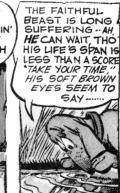

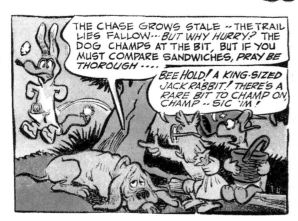

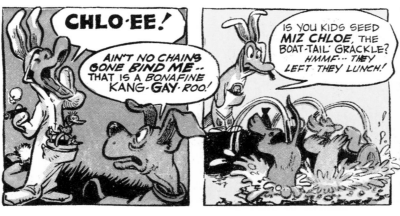

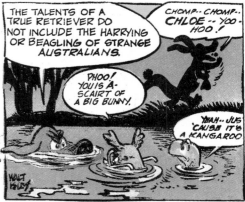

SUNDAY, APRIL 9, 1950

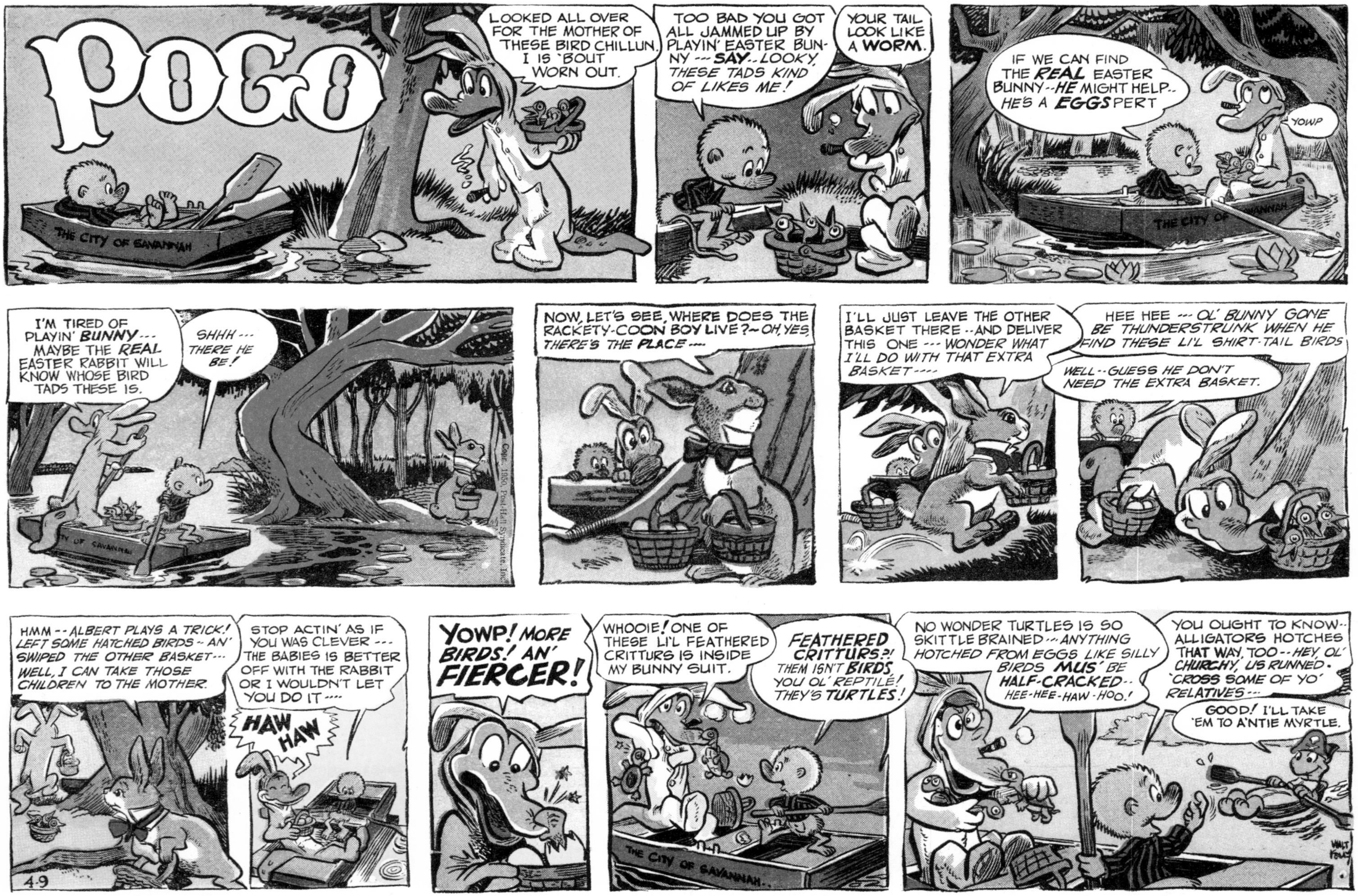
POGO
THE CITY OF SAVANNAH
LOOKED ALL OVER FOR THE MOTHER OF THESE BIRD CHILLUN. I IS 'BOUT WORN OUT.
TOO BAD YOU GOT ALL JAMMED UP BY PLAYIN' EASTER BUNNY --- SAY.. LOOKY, THESE TADS KIND OF LIKES ME!
YOUR TAIL LOOK LIKE A WORM.
IF WE CAN FIND THE REAL EASTER BUNNY--HE MIGHT HELP.. HE'S A EGGSPERT
YOWP
I'M TIRED OF PLAYIN' BUNNY--- MAYBE THE REAL EASTER RABBIT WILL KNOW WHOSE BIRD TADS THESE IS.
SHHH--- THERE HE BE!
Copr. 1950, Post-Hall Syndicate, Inc.
NOW, LET'S SEE, WHERE DOES THE RACKETY-COON BOY LIVE?~ OH, YES, THERE'S THE PLACE----
I'LL JUST LEAVE THE OTHER BASKET THERE--AND DELIVER THIS ONE --- WONDER WHAT I'LL DO WITH THAT EXTRA BASKET----
HEE HEE --- OL' BUNNY GONE BE THUNDERSTRUNK WHEN HE FIND THESE LI'L SHIRT-TAIL BIRDS
WELL--GUESS HE DON'T NEED THE EXTRA BASKET.
HMM--ALBERT PLAYS A TRICK! LEFT SOME HATCHED BIRDS--AN' SWIPED THE OTHER BASKET--- WELL, I CAN TAKE THOSE CHILDREN TO THE MOTHER.
STOP ACTIN' AS IF YOU WAS CLEVER --- THE BABIES IS BETTER OFF WITH THE RABBIT OR I WOULDN'T LET YOU DO IT----
HAW HAW
4-9
YOWP! MORE BIRDS! AN' FIERCER!
WHOOIE! ONE OF THESE LI'L FEATHERED CRITTURS IS INSIDE MY BUNNY SUIT.
FEATHERED CRITTURS?! THEM ISN'T BIRDS, YOU OL' REPTILE! THEY'S TURTLES!
NO WONDER TURTLES IS SO SKITTLE BRAINED--ANYTHING HOTCHED FROM EGGS LIKE SILLY BIRDS MUS' BE HALF-CRACKED.. HEE-HEE-HAW-HOO.!
YOU OUGHT TO KNOW.. ALLIGATORS HOTCHES THAT WAY, TOO--HEY, OL' CHURCHY, US RUNNED. 'CROSS SOME OF YO' RELATIVES---
GOOD! I'LL TAKE 'EM TO A'NTIE MYRTLE.
WALT KELLY

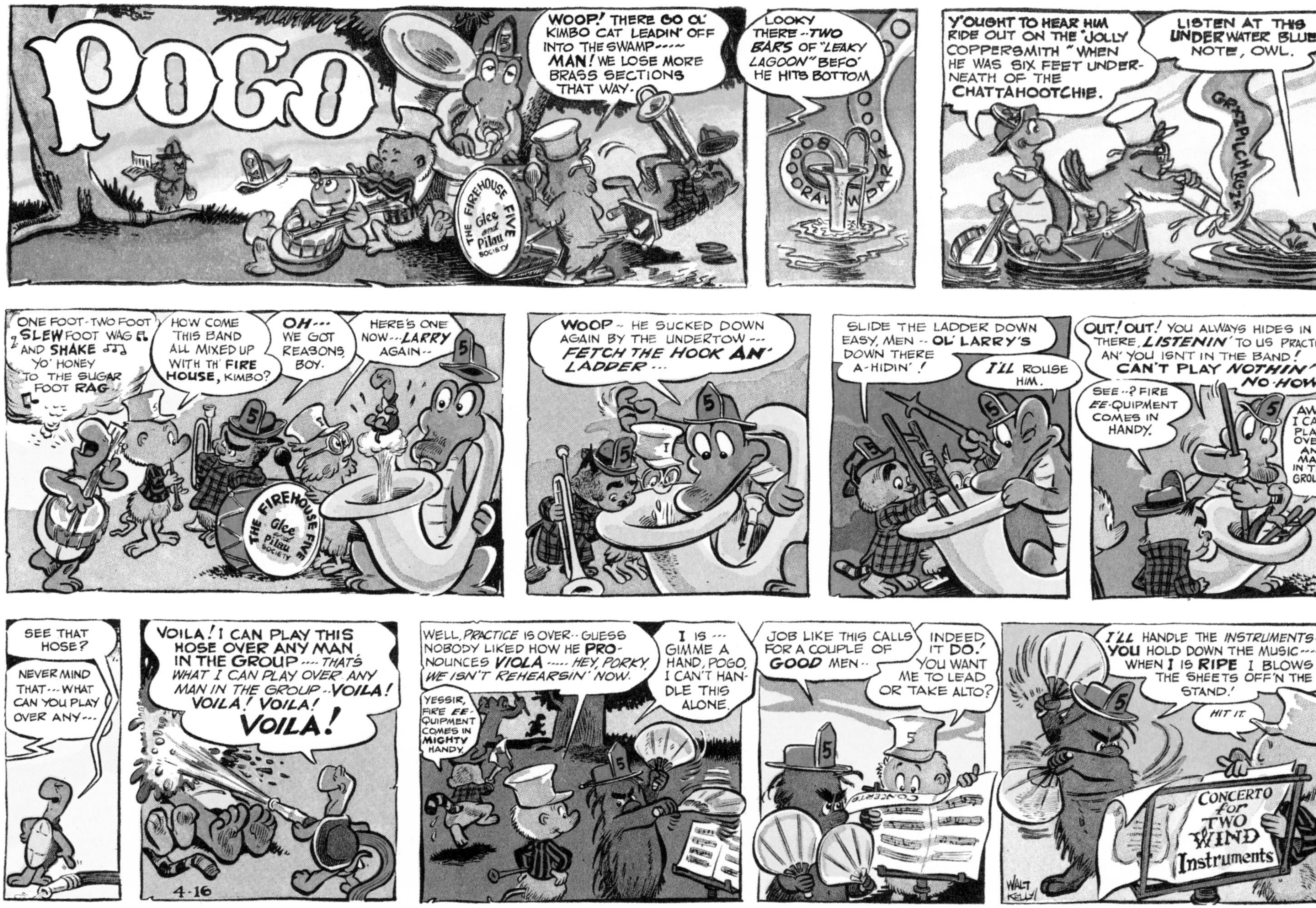
POGO
WOOP! THERE GO OL' KIMBO CAT LEADIN' OFF INTO THE SWAMP---- MAN! WE LOSE MORE BRASS SECTIONS THAT WAY.
THE FIREHOUSE FIVE Glee and Pilau SOCIETY
LOOKY THERE--TWO BARS OF "LEAKY LAGOON" BEFO' HE HITS BOTTOM
Y'OUGHT TO HEAR HIM RIDE OUT ON THE "JOLLY COPPERSMITH" WHEN HE WAS SIX FEET UNDERNEATH OF THE CHATTAHOOTCHIE.
LISTEN AT THIS UNDERWATER BLUE NOTE, OWL.
ONE FOOT-TWO FOOT SLEW FOOT WAG AND SHAKE YO' HONEY TO THE SUGAR FOOT RAG
HOW COME THIS BAND ALL MIXED UP WITH TH' FIRE HOUSE, KIMBO?
OH--- WE GOT REASONS, BOY.
HERE'S ONE NOW---LARRY AGAIN--
THE FIREHOUSE FIVE Glee and Pilau SOCIETY
WOOP-- HE SUCKED DOWN AGAIN BY THE UNDERTOW--- FETCH THE HOOK AN' LADDER---
SLIDE THE LADDER DOWN EASY, MEN -- OL' LARRY'S DOWN THERE A-HIDIN'!
I'LL ROUSE HIM.
OUT! OUT! YOU ALWAYS HIDES IN THERE, LISTENIN' TO US PRACTICE AN' YOU ISN'T IN THE BAND! CAN'T PLAY NOTHIN' NO-HOW.
SEE--? FIRE EE-QUIPMENT COMES IN HANDY.
AW, I CAN PLAY OVER ANY MAN IN THE GROUP!
SEE THAT HOSE?
NEVER MIND THAT---WHAT CAN YOU PLAY OVER ANY---
VOILA! I CAN PLAY THIS HOSE OVER ANY MAN IN THE GROUP---- THAT'S WHAT I CAN PLAY OVER ANY MAN IN THE GROUP--VOILA! VOILA! VOILA! VOILA!
4-16
WELL, PRACTICE IS OVER--GUESS NOBODY LIKED HOW HE PRONOUNCES VIOLA----- HEY, PORKY, WE ISN'T REHEARSIN' NOW.
I IS--- GIMME A HAND, POGO, I CAN'T HANDLE THIS ALONE.
YESSIR, FIRE EE-QUIPMENT COMES IN MIGHTY HANDY.
JOB LIKE THIS CALLS FOR A COUPLE OF GOOD MEN--
INDEED IT DO.! YOU WANT ME TO LEAD OR TAKE ALTO?
I'LL HANDLE THE INSTRUMENTS-- YOU HOLD DOWN THE MUSIC---- WHEN I IS RIPE I BLOWS THE SHEETS OFF'N THE STAND.!
HIT IT.
CONCERTO for TWO WIND Instruments
WALT KELLY

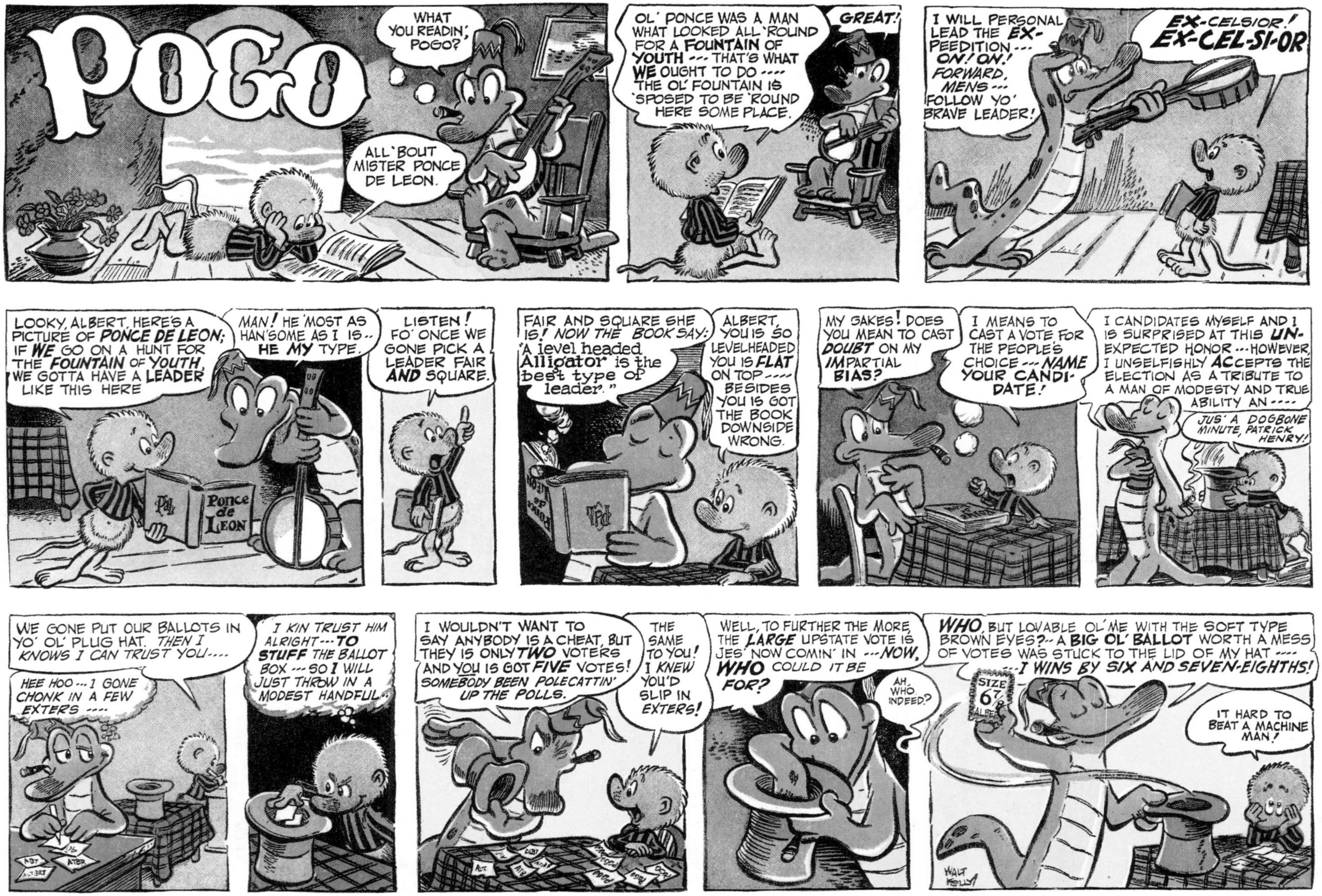
POGO
WHAT YOU READIN', POGO?
ALL 'BOUT MISTER PONCE DE LEON.
OL' PONCE WAS A MAN WHAT LOOKED ALL 'ROUND FOR A FOUNTAIN OF YOUTH --- THAT'S WHAT WE OUGHT TO DO ---- THE OL' FOUNTAIN IS 'SPOSED TO BE 'ROUND HERE SOME PLACE.
GREAT!
I WILL PERSONAL LEAD THE EX-PEEDITION --- ON! ON! FORWARD, MENS --- FOLLOW YO' BRAVE LEADER!
EX-CELSIOR! EX-CEL-SI-OR
LOOKY, ALBERT, HERE'S A PICTURE OF PONCE DE LEON; IF WE GO ON A HUNT FOR THE FOUNTAIN OF YOUTH, WE GOTTA HAVE A LEADER LIKE THIS HERE
MAN! HE 'MOST AS HAN'SOME AS I IS.. HE MY TYPE.
Ponce de Leon
LISTEN! FO' ONCE WE GONE PICK A LEADER FAIR AND SQUARE.
FAIR AND SQUARE SHE IS! NOW THE BOOK SAY: "A level headed Alligator is the best type of leader."
ALBERT, YOU IS SO LEVELHEADED YOU IS FLAT ON TOP ---- BESIDES YOU IS GOT THE BOOK DOWNSIDE WRONG.
MY SAKES! DOES YOU MEAN TO CAST DOUBT ON MY IMPARTIAL BIAS?
I MEANS TO CAST A VOTE FOR THE PEOPLE'S CHOICE --- NAME YOUR CANDI-DATE!
I CANDIDATES MYSELF AND I IS SURPRISED AT THIS UN-EXPECTED HONOR --- HOWEVER, I UNSELFISHLY ACCEPTS THE ELECTION AS A TRIBUTE TO A MAN OF MODESTY AND TRUE ABILITY AN ----
JUS' A DOGBONE MINUTE, PATRICK HENRY!
WE GONE PUT OUR BALLOTS IN YO' OL' PLUG HAT. THEN I KNOWS I CAN TRUST YOU ----
HEE HOO --- I GONE CHONK IN A FEW EXTERS ----
I KIN TRUST HIM ALRIGHT --- TO STUFF THE BALLOT BOX --- SO I WILL JUST THROW IN A MODEST HANDFUL.
I WOULDN'T WANT TO SAY ANYBODY IS A CHEAT, BUT THEY IS ONLY TWO VOTERS AND YOU IS GOT FIVE VOTES! SOMEBODY BEEN POLECATTIN' UP THE POLLS.
THE SAME TO YOU! I KNEW YOU'D SLIP IN EXTERS!
WELL, TO FURTHER THE MORE, THE LARGE UPSTATE VOTE IS JES' NOW COMIN' IN --- NOW, WHO COULD IT BE FOR?
AH, WHO INDEED?
WHO, BUT LOVABLE OL' ME WITH THE SOFT TYPE BROWN EYES?-- A BIG OL' BALLOT WORTH A MESS OF VOTES WAS STUCK TO THE LID OF MY HAT ---- --- I WINS BY SIX AND SEVEN-EIGHTHS!
SIZE 6⅞
IT HARD TO BEAT A MACHINE MAN!
WALT KELLY

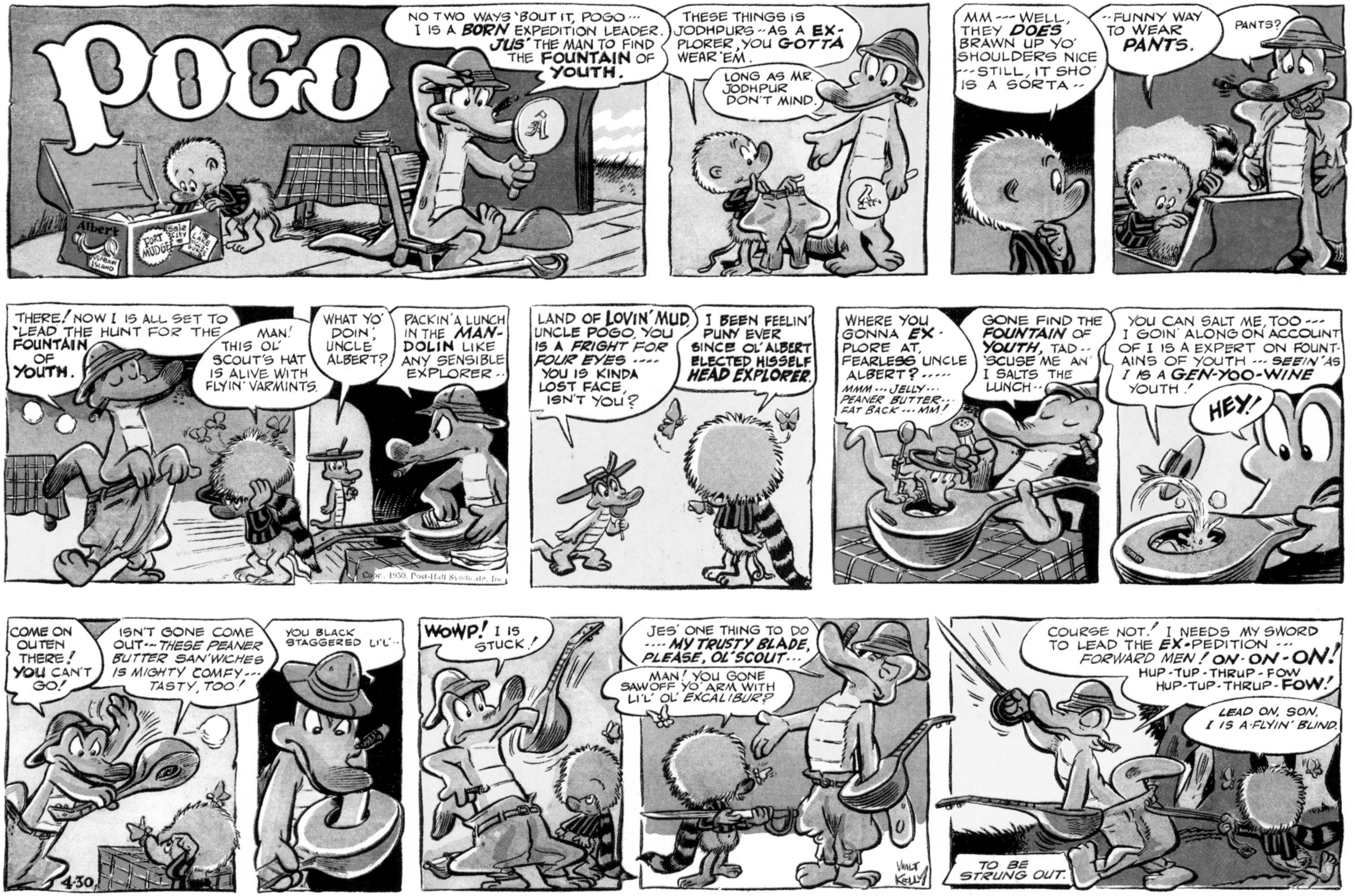
POGO
NO TWO WAYS 'BOUT IT, POGO --- I IS A BORN EXPEDITION LEADER. JUS' THE MAN TO FIND THE FOUNTAIN OF YOUTH.
Albert
PORT MUDGE
THESE THINGS IS JODHPURS -- AS A EX-PLORER, YOU GOTTA WEAR 'EM.
LONG AS MR. JODHPUR DON'T MIND.
MM --- WELL, THEY DOES BRAWN UP YO' SHOULDERS NICE --- STILL, IT SHO' IS A SORTA --
-- FUNNY WAY TO WEAR PANTS.
PANTS?
THERE! NOW I IS ALL SET TO 'LEAD' THE HUNT FOR THE FOUNTAIN OF YOUTH.
MAN! THIS OL' SCOUT'S HAT IS ALIVE WITH FLYIN' VARMINTS.
WHAT YO' DOIN', UNCLE ALBERT?
PACKIN' A LUNCH IN THE MAN-DOLIN LIKE ANY SENSIBLE EXPLORER --
Copr. 1950, Post-Hall Syndicate, Inc.
LAND OF LOVIN' MUD, UNCLE POGO, YOU IS A FRIGHT FOR FOUR EYES ---- YOU IS KINDA LOST FACE, ISN'T YOU?
I BEEN FEELIN' PUNY EVER SINCE OL' ALBERT ELECTED HISSELF HEAD EXPLORER.
WHERE YOU GONNA EX-PLORE AT, FEARLESS UNCLE ALBERT? -----
MMM --- JELLY --- PEANER BUTTER --- FAT BACK --- MM!
GONE FIND THE FOUNTAIN OF YOUTH, TAD -- 'SCUSE ME AN' I SALTS THE LUNCH --
YOU CAN SALT ME, TOO --- I GOIN' ALONG ON ACCOUNT OF I IS A EXPERT ON FOUNT-AINS OF YOUTH --- SEEIN' AS I IS A GEN-YOO-WINE YOUTH.
HEY!
COME ON OUTEN THERE! YOU CAN'T GO!
ISN'T GONE COME OUT -- THESE PEANER BUTTER SAN'WICHES IS MIGHTY COMFY --- TASTY, TOO!
4-30
YOU BLACK STAGGERED LI'L' --
WOWP! I IS STUCK!
JES' ONE THING TO DO ---- MY TRUSTY BLADE, PLEASE, OL' SCOUT ---
MAN! YOU GONE SAWOFF YO' ARM WITH LI'L' OL' EXCALIBUR?
WALT KELLY
COURSE NOT! I NEEDS MY SWORD TO LEAD THE EX-PEDITION --- FORWARD MEN! ON-ON-ON! HUP-TUP-THRUP-FOW HUP-TUP-THRUP-FOW!
LEAD ON, SON. I IS A FLYIN' BLIND.
TO BE STRUNG OUT.

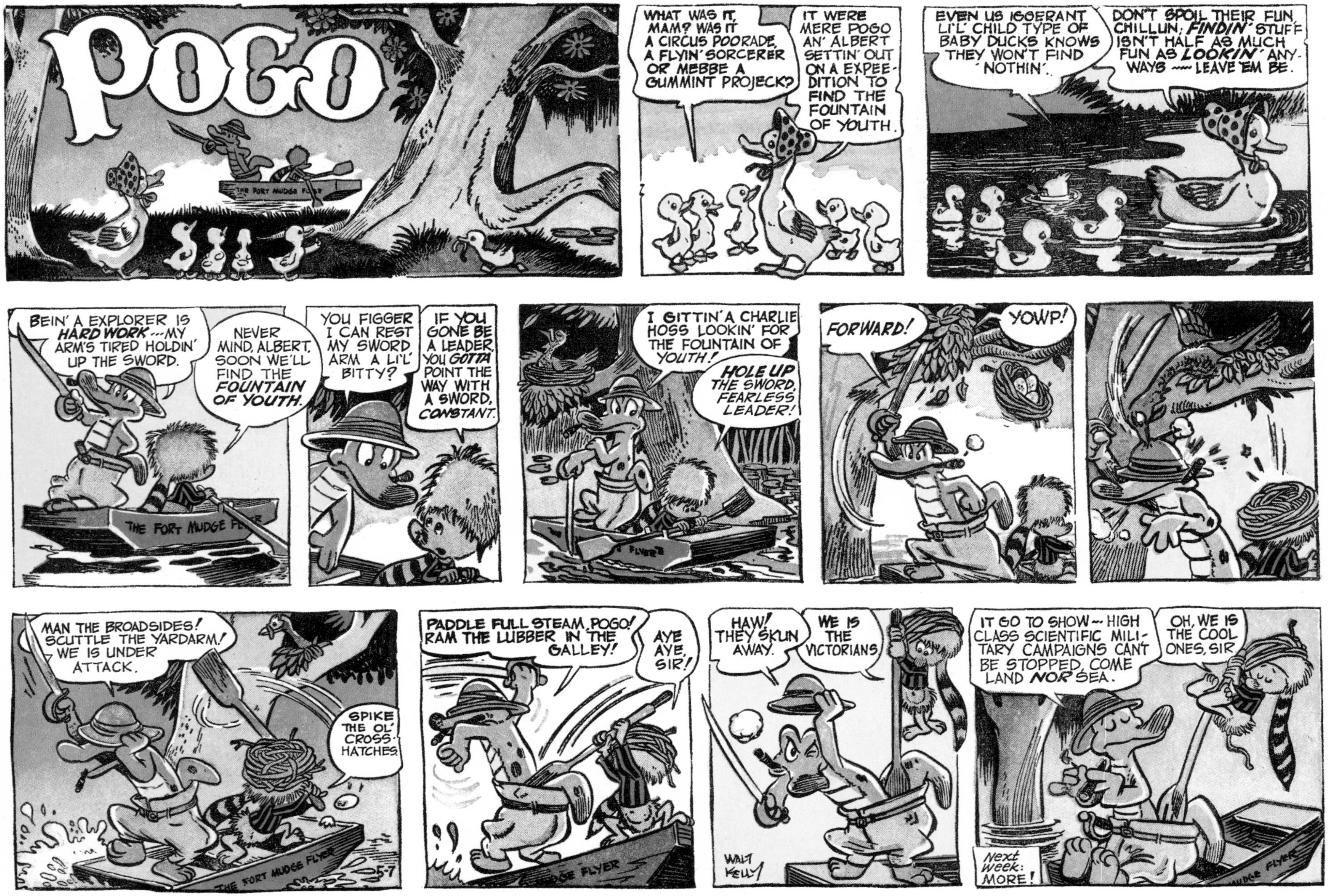
POGO
THE FORT MUDGE FLYER
WHAT WAS IT, MAM? WAS IT A CIRCUS POORADE, A FLYIN' SORCERER OR MEBBE A GUMMINT PROJECK?
IT WERE MERE POGO AN' ALBERT SETTIN' OUT ON A EXPEEDITION TO FIND THE FOUNTAIN OF YOUTH.
EVEN US IGGERANT LI'L' CHILD TYPE OF BABY DUCKS KNOWS THEY WON'T FIND 'NOTHIN'.
DON'T SPOIL THEIR FUN, CHILLUN; FINDIN' STUFF ISN'T HALF AS MUCH FUN AS LOOKIN' ANYWAYS — LEAVE 'EM BE.
BEIN' A EXPLORER IS HARD WORK... MY ARM'S TIRED HOLDIN' UP THE SWORD.
NEVER MIND, ALBERT. SOON WE'LL FIND THE FOUNTAIN OF YOUTH.
THE FORT MUDGE FLYER
YOU FIGGER I CAN REST MY SWORD ARM A LI'L' BITTY?
IF YOU GONE BE A LEADER, YOU GOTTA POINT THE WAY WITH A SWORD, CONSTANT.
I GITTIN' A CHARLIE HOSS LOOKIN' FOR THE FOUNTAIN OF YOUTH!
HOLE UP THE SWORD, FEARLESS LEADER!
FORWARD!
YOWP!
MAN THE BROADSIDES! SCUTTLE THE YARDARM! WE IS UNDER ATTACK.
SPIKE THE OL' CROSS-HATCHES.
THE FORT MUDGE FLYER
5-7
PADDLE FULL STEAM, POGO! RAM THE LUBBER IN THE GALLEY!
AYE AYE, SIR!
HAW! THEY SKUN AWAY.
WE IS THE VICTORIANS
WALT KELLY
IT GO TO SHOW — HIGH CLASS SCIENTIFIC MILITARY CAMPAIGNS CAN'T BE STOPPED, COME LAND NOR SEA.
OH, WE IS THE COOL ONES, SIR.
Next week: MORE!

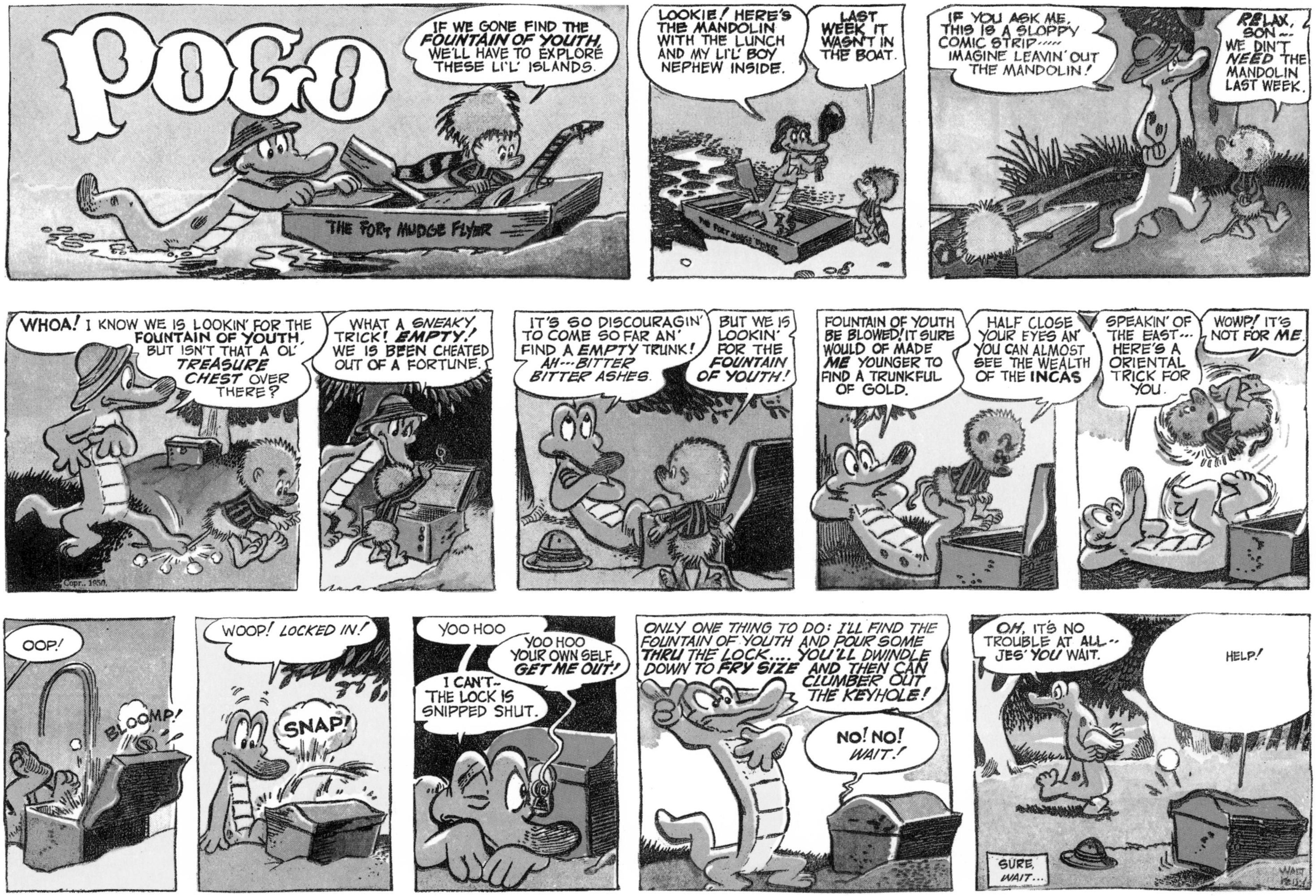
POGO
IF WE GONE FIND THE FOUNTAIN OF YOUTH, WE'LL HAVE TO EXPLORE THESE LI'L' ISLANDS.
THE FORT MUDGE FLYER
LOOKIE! HERE'S THE MANDOLIN WITH THE LUNCH AND MY LI'L' BOY NEPHEW INSIDE.
LAST WEEK IT WASN'T IN THE BOAT.
IF YOU ASK ME, THIS IS A SLOPPY COMIC STRIP..... IMAGINE LEAVIN' OUT THE MANDOLIN!
RELAX, SON -- WE DIN'T NEED THE MANDOLIN LAST WEEK.
WHOA! I KNOW WE IS LOOKIN' FOR THE FOUNTAIN OF YOUTH, BUT ISN'T THAT A OL' TREASURE CHEST OVER THERE?
Copr., 1950.
WHAT A SNEAKY TRICK! EMPTY! WE IS BEEN CHEATED OUT OF A FORTUNE.
IT'S SO DISCOURAGIN' TO COME SO FAR AN' FIND A EMPTY TRUNK! AH--- BITTER BITTER ASHES.
BUT WE IS LOOKIN' FOR THE FOUNTAIN OF YOUTH!
FOUNTAIN OF YOUTH BE BLOWED! IT SURE WOULD OF MADE ME YOUNGER TO FIND A TRUNKFUL OF GOLD.
HALF CLOSE YOUR EYES AN' YOU CAN ALMOST SEE THE WEALTH OF THE INCAS
SPEAKIN' OF THE EAST--- HERE'S A ORIENTAL TRICK FOR YOU.
WOWP! IT'S NOT FOR ME.
OOP!
BLOOMP!
WOOP! LOCKED IN!
SNAP!
YOO HOO
YOO HOO YOUR OWN SELF, GET ME OUT!
I CAN'T-- THE LOCK IS SNIPPED SHUT.
ONLY ONE THING TO DO: I'LL FIND THE FOUNTAIN OF YOUTH AND POUR SOME THRU THE LOCK.... YOU'LL DWINDLE DOWN TO FRY SIZE AND THEN CAN CLUMBER OUT THE KEYHOLE!
NO! NO! WAIT!
OH, IT'S NO TROUBLE AT ALL -- JES' YOU WAIT.
HELP!
SURE, WAIT...
WALT KELLY

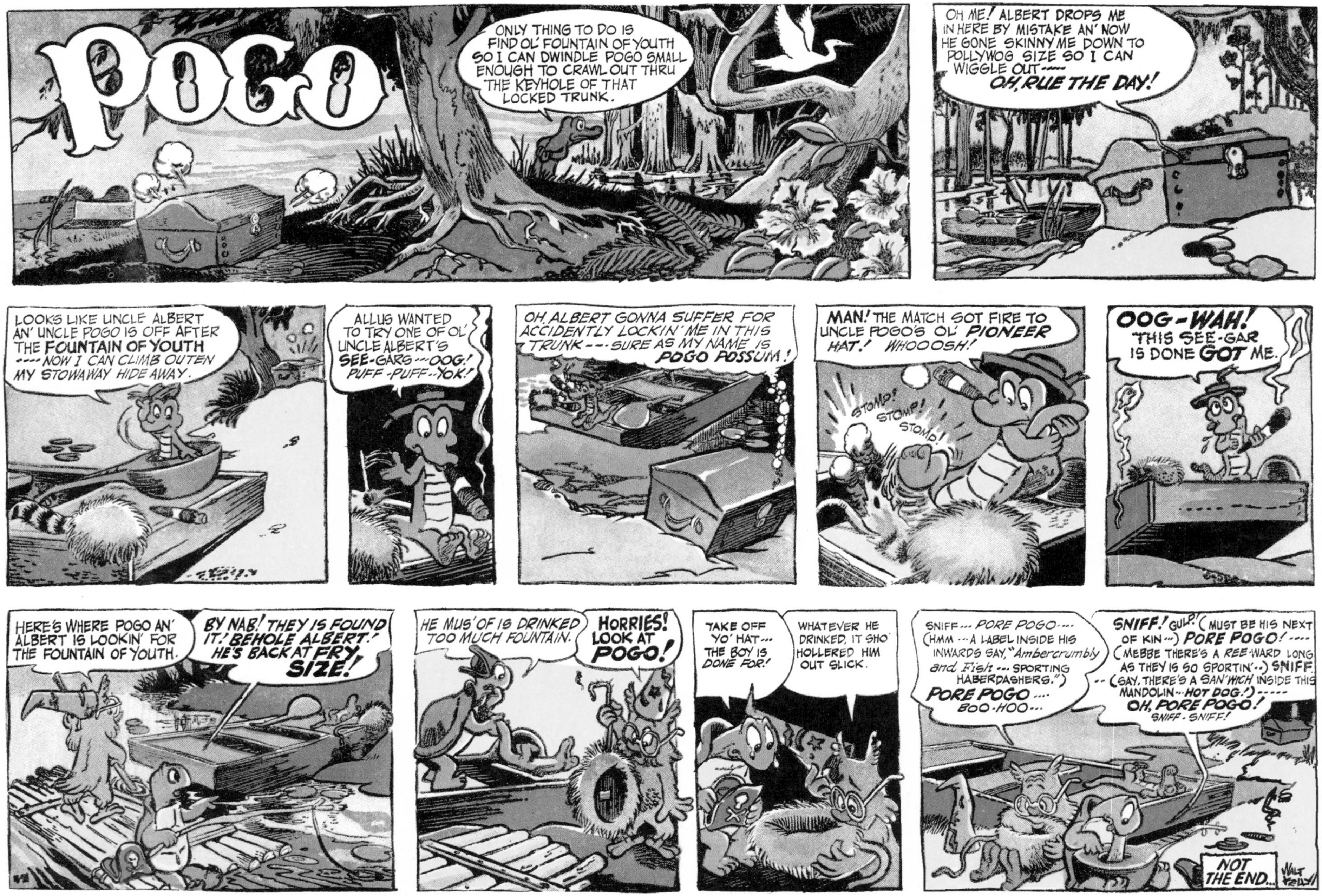
POGO
ONLY THING TO DO IS FIND OL' FOUNTAIN OF YOUTH SO I CAN DWINDLE POGO SMALL ENOUGH TO CRAWL OUT THRU THE KEYHOLE OF THAT LOCKED TRUNK.
OH ME! ALBERT DROPS ME IN HERE BY MISTAKE AN' NOW HE GONE SKINNY ME DOWN TO POLLYWOG SIZE SO I CAN WIGGLE OUT---- OH, RUE THE DAY!
LOOKS LIKE UNCLE ALBERT AN' UNCLE POGO IS OFF AFTER THE FOUNTAIN OF YOUTH ---- NOW I CAN CLIMB OUTEN MY STOWAWAY HIDE AWAY.
ALLUS WANTED TO TRY ONE OF OL' UNCLE ALBERT'S SEE-GARS---OOG! PUFF-PUFF--YOK!
OH, ALBERT GONNA SUFFER FOR ACCIDENTLY LOCKIN' ME IN THIS TRUNK----SURE AS MY NAME IS POGO POSSUM!
MAN! THE MATCH GOT FIRE TO UNCLE POGO'S OL' PIONEER HAT! WHOOOSH!
STOMP! STOMP! STOMP!
OOG-WAH! THIS SEE-GAR IS DONE GOT ME.
HERE'S WHERE POGO AN' ALBERT IS LOOKIN' FOR THE FOUNTAIN OF YOUTH.
BY NAB! THEY IS FOUND IT! BEHOLE ALBERT! HE'S BACK AT FRY SIZE!
HE MUS' OF IS DRINKED TOO MUCH FOUNTAIN.
HORRIES! LOOK AT POGO!
TAKE OFF YO' HAT--- THE BOY IS DONE FOR!
WHATEVER HE DRINKED, IT SHO' HOLLERED HIM OUT SLICK.
SNIFF--- PORE POGO---- (HMM---A LABEL INSIDE HIS INWARDS SAY, "Ambercrumbly and Fish--- SPORTING HABERDASHERS.") PORE POGO.... BOO-HOO---
SNIFF! GULP! (MUST BE HIS NEXT OF KIN---) PORE POGO!---- (MEBBE THERE'S A REE-WARD LONG AS THEY IS SO SPORTIN'--) SNIFF. --(SAY, THERE'S A SAN'WICH INSIDE THIS MANDOLIN---HOT DOG!)----- OH, PORE POGO! SNIFF-SNIFF!
NOT THE END...
WALT KELLY

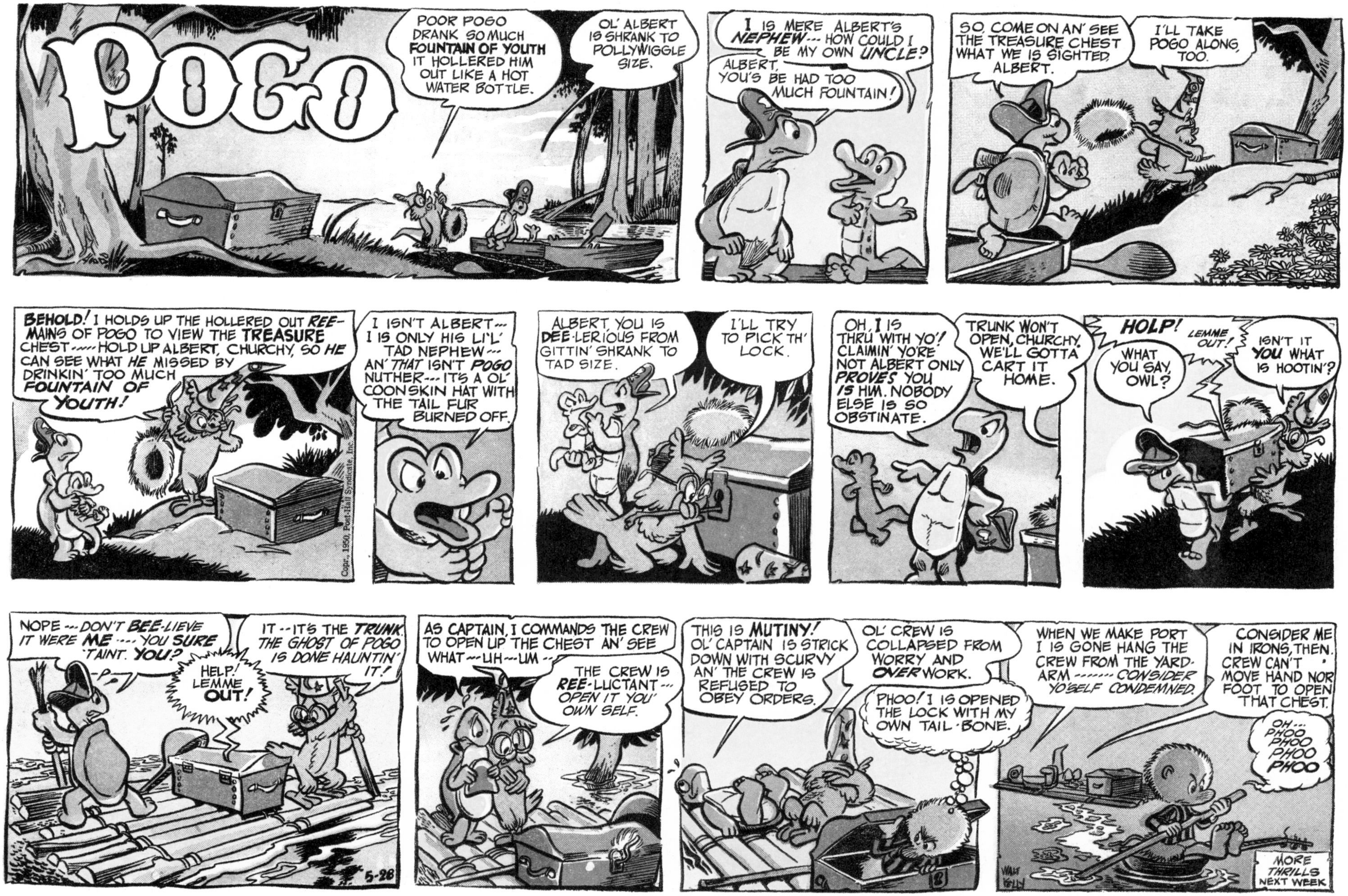
POGO
POOR POGO DRANK SO MUCH FOUNTAIN OF YOUTH IT HOLLERED HIM OUT LIKE A HOT WATER BOTTLE.
OL' ALBERT IS SHRANK TO POLLYWIGGLE SIZE.
I IS MERE ALBERT'S NEPHEW--- HOW COULD I BE MY OWN UNCLE?
ALBERT, YOU'S BE HAD TOO MUCH FOUNTAIN!
SO, COME ON AN' SEE THE TREASURE CHEST WHAT WE IS SIGHTED, ALBERT.
I'LL TAKE POGO ALONG, TOO.
BEHOLD! I HOLDS UP THE HOLLERED OUT REE-MAINS OF POGO TO VIEW THE TREASURE CHEST---- HOLD UP ALBERT, CHURCHY, SO HE CAN SEE WHAT HE MISSED BY DRINKIN' TOO MUCH FOUNTAIN OF YOUTH!
Copr. 1950, Post-Hall Syndicate, Inc.
I ISN'T ALBERT--- I IS ONLY HIS LI'L' TAD NEPHEW--- AN' THAT ISN'T POGO NUTHER--- IT'S A OL' COONSKIN HAT WITH THE TAIL FUR BURNED OFF.
ALBERT, YOU IS DEE-LERIOUS FROM GITTIN' SHRANK TO TAD SIZE.
I'LL TRY TO PICK TH' LOCK.
OH, I IS THRU WITH YO'! CLAIMIN' YO'RE NOT ALBERT ONLY PROVES YOU IS HIM. NOBODY ELSE IS SO OBSTINATE.
TRUNK WON'T OPEN, CHURCHY. WE'LL GOTTA CART IT HOME.
HOLP!
LEMME OUT!
WHAT YOU SAY, OWL?
ISN'T IT YOU WHAT IS HOOTIN'?
NOPE --- DON'T BEE-LIEVE IT WERE ME ---- YOU SURE 'TAINT. YOU?
HELP! LEMME OUT!
IT -- IT'S THE TRUNK. THE GHOST OF POGO IS DONE HAUNTIN' IT!
AS CAPTAIN, I COMMANDS THE CREW TO OPEN UP THE CHEST AN' SEE WHAT --- UH --- UM --
THE CREW IS REE-LUCTANT --- OPEN IT YOU' OWN SELF.
THIS IS MUTINY! OL' CAPTAIN IS STRICK DOWN WITH SCURVY AN' THE CREW IS REFUSED TO OBEY ORDERS.
OL' CREW IS COLLAPSED FROM WORRY AND OVERWORK.
PHOO! I IS OPENED THE LOCK WITH MY OWN TAIL-BONE.
WHEN WE MAKE PORT I IS GONE HANG THE CREW FROM THE YARD-ARM ------- CONSIDER YO'SELF CONDEMNED.
CONSIDER ME IN IRONS, THEN. CREW CAN'T MOVE HAND NOR FOOT TO OPEN THAT CHEST.
OH... PHOO PHOO PHOO PHOO
5-28
WALT KELLY
MORE THRILLS NEXT WEEK

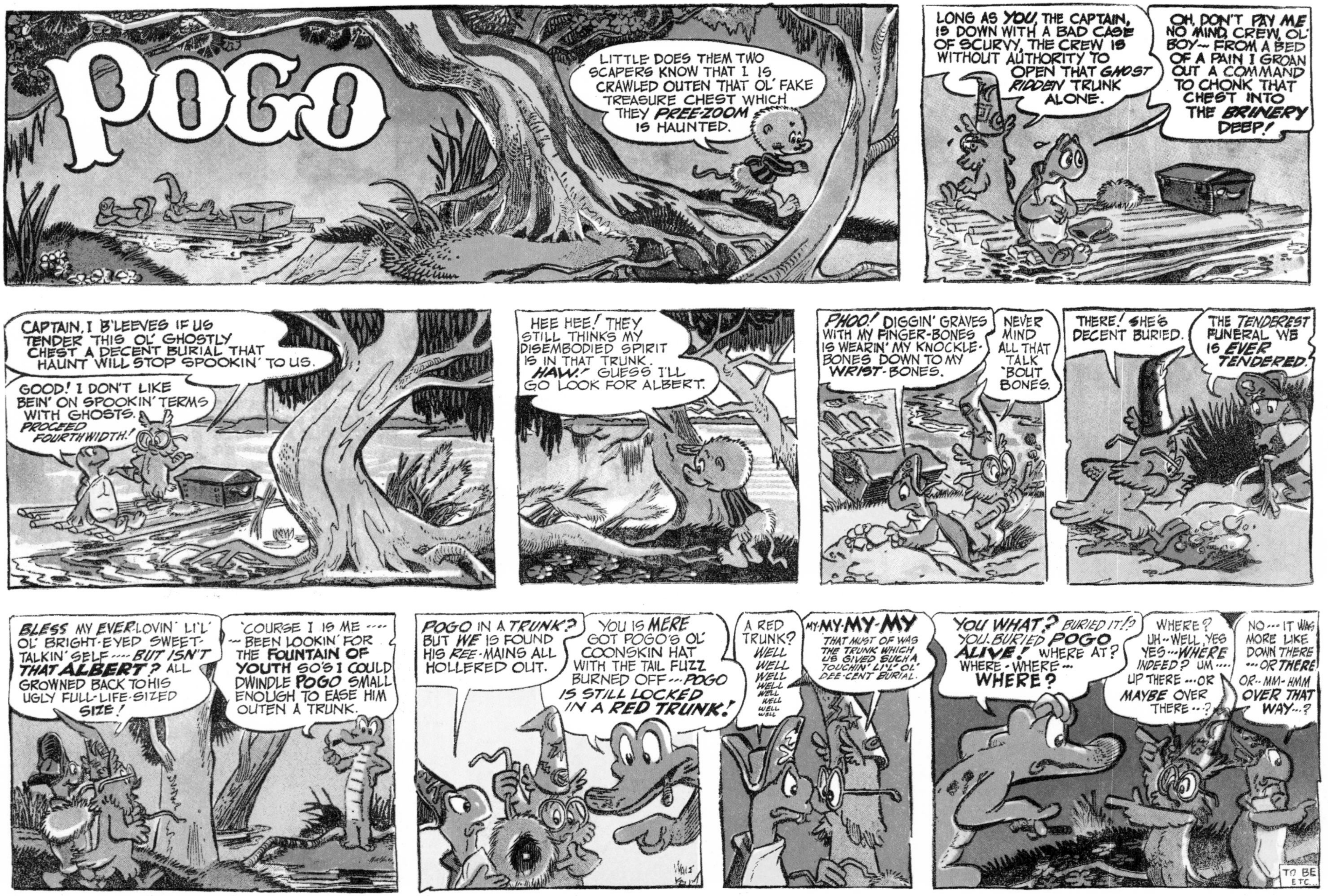
POGO
LITTLE DOES THEM TWO SCAPERS KNOW THAT I IS CRAWLED OUTEN THAT OL' FAKE TREASURE CHEST WHICH THEY PREE-ZOOM IS HAUNTED.
LONG AS YOU, THE CAPTAIN, IS DOWN WITH A BAD CASE OF SCURVY, THE CREW IS WITHOUT AUTHORITY TO OPEN THAT GHOST RIDDEN TRUNK ALONE.
OH, DON'T PAY ME NO MIND, CREW, OL' BOY— FROM A BED OF A PAIN I GROAN OUT A COMMAND TO CHONK THAT CHEST INTO THE BRINERY DEEP!
CAPTAIN, I B'LEEVES IF US TENDER THIS OL' GHOSTLY CHEST A DECENT BURIAL THAT HAUNT WILL STOP SPOOKIN' TO US.
GOOD! I DON'T LIKE BEIN' ON SPOOKIN' TERMS WITH GHOSTS. PROCEED FOURTHWIDTH!
HEE HEE! THEY STILL THINKS MY DISEMBODIED SPIRIT IS IN THAT TRUNK. HAW! GUESS I'LL GO LOOK FOR ALBERT.
PHOO! DIGGIN' GRAVES WITH MY FINGER-BONES IS WEARIN' MY KNOCKLE-BONES DOWN TO MY WRIST-BONES.
NEVER MIND ALL THAT TALK 'BOUT BONES.
THERE! SHE'S DECENT BURIED.
THE TENDEREST FUNERAL WE IS EVER TENDERED.
BLESS MY EVER-LOVIN' LI'L' OL' BRIGHT-EYED SWEET-TALKIN' SELF···· BUT ISN'T THAT ALBERT? ALL GROWNED BACK TO HIS UGLY FULL-LIFE-SIZED SIZE!
'COURSE I IS ME ···· ··BEEN LOOKIN' FOR THE FOUNTAIN OF YOUTH SO'S I COULD DWINDLE POGO SMALL ENOUGH TO EASE HIM OUTEN A TRUNK.
POGO IN A TRUNK? BUT WE IS FOUND HIS REE-MAINS ALL HOLLERED OUT.
YOU IS MERE GOT POGO'S OL' COONSKIN HAT WITH THE TAIL FUZZ BURNED OFF ··· POGO IS STILL LOCKED IN A RED TRUNK!
A RED TRUNK? WELL WELL WELL WELL WELL WELL WELL WELL
MY-MY-MY-MY THAT MUST OF WAS THE TRUNK WHICH US GIVED SUCH A TOUCHIN' LI'L' OL' DEE-CENT BURIAL.
YOU WHAT? BURIED IT!? YOU BURIED POGO ALIVE! WHERE AT? WHERE-WHERE··· WHERE?
WHERE? UH··WELL, YES YES···WHERE INDEED? UM···· UP THERE ···OR MAYBE OVER THERE··?
NO··· IT WAS MORE LIKE DOWN THERE ···OR THERE OR··MM-HMM OVER THAT WAY··?
TO BE ETC.

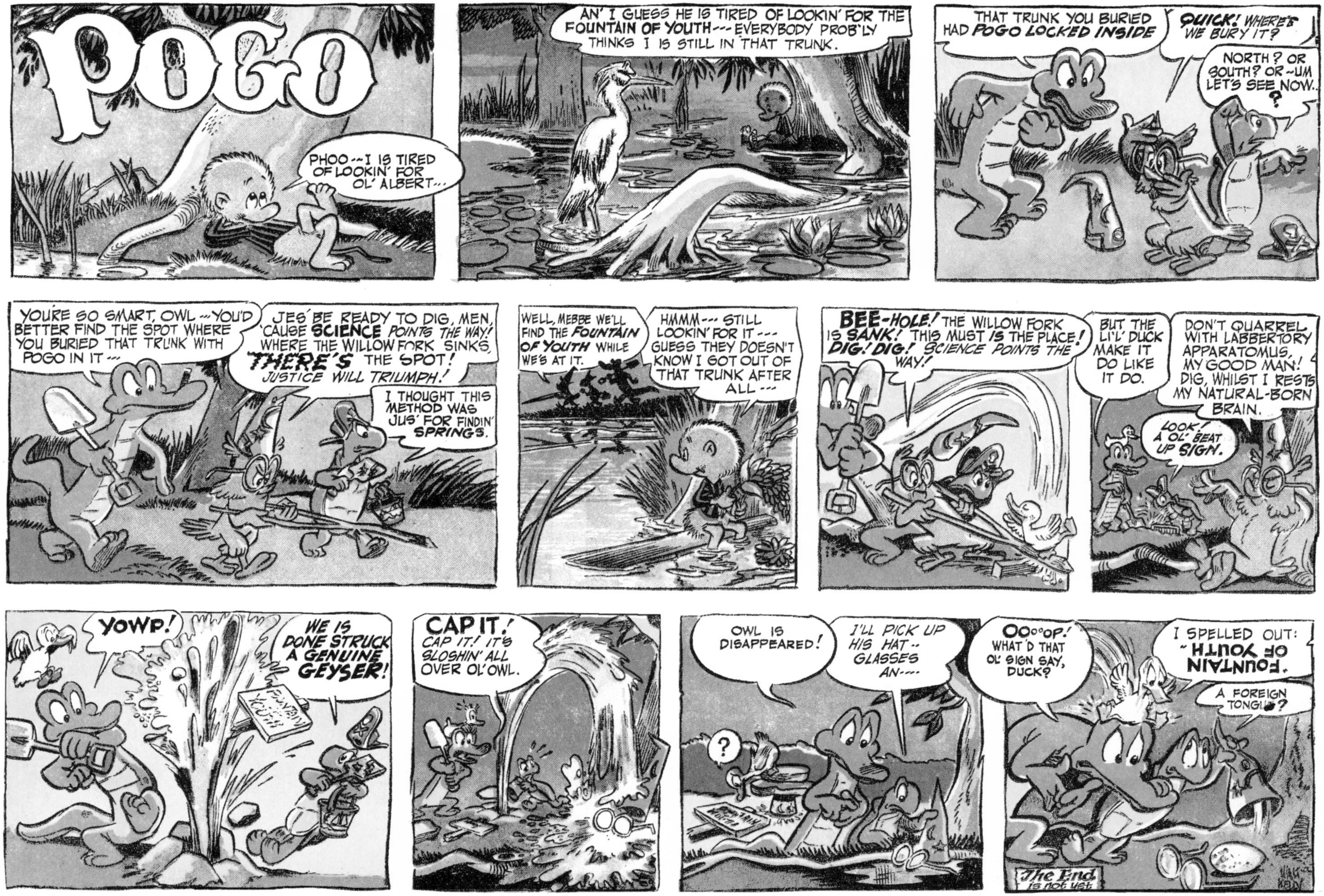
POGO
PHOO--I IS TIRED OF LOOKIN' FOR OL' ALBERT...
AN' I GUESS HE IS TIRED OF LOOKIN' FOR THE FOUNTAIN OF YOUTH--- EVERYBODY PROB'LY THINKS I IS STILL IN THAT TRUNK.
THAT TRUNK YOU BURIED HAD POGO LOCKED INSIDE
QUICK! WHERE'S WE BURY IT?
NORTH? OR SOUTH? OR--UM LET'S SEE NOW..
?
YOU'RE SO SMART, OWL --YOU'D BETTER FIND THE SPOT WHERE YOU BURIED THAT TRUNK WITH POGO IN IT---
JES' BE READY TO DIG, MEN, 'CAUSE SCIENCE POINTS THE WAY! WHERE THE WILLOW FORK SINKS, THERE'S THE SPOT! JUSTICE WILL TRIUMPH!
I THOUGHT THIS METHOD WAS JUS' FOR FINDIN' SPRINGS.
WELL, MEBBE WE'LL FIND THE FOUNTAIN OF YOUTH WHILE WE'S AT IT.
HMMM--- STILL LOOKIN' FOR IT--- GUESS THEY DOESN'T KNOW I GOT OUT OF THAT TRUNK AFTER ALL---
BEE-HOLE! THE WILLOW FORK IS SANK! THIS MUST IS THE PLACE! DIG! DIG! SCIENCE POINTS THE WAY!
BUT THE LI'L' DUCK MAKE IT DO LIKE IT DO.
DON'T QUARREL WITH LABBERTORY APPARATOMUS, MY GOOD MAN! DIG, WHILST I RESTS MY NATURAL-BORN BRAIN.
LOOK! A OL' BEAT UP SIGN.
YOWP!
WE IS DONE STRUCK A GENUINE GEYSER!
CAP IT! CAP IT! IT'S SLOSHIN' ALL OVER OL' OWL.
OWL IS DISAPPEARED!
?
I'LL PICK UP HIS HAT-- GLASSES AN---
OO°°OP! WHAT'D THAT OL' SIGN SAY, DUCK?
I SPELLED OUT: FOUNTAIN OF YOUTH.
A FOREIGN TONGUE?
The End is not yet.

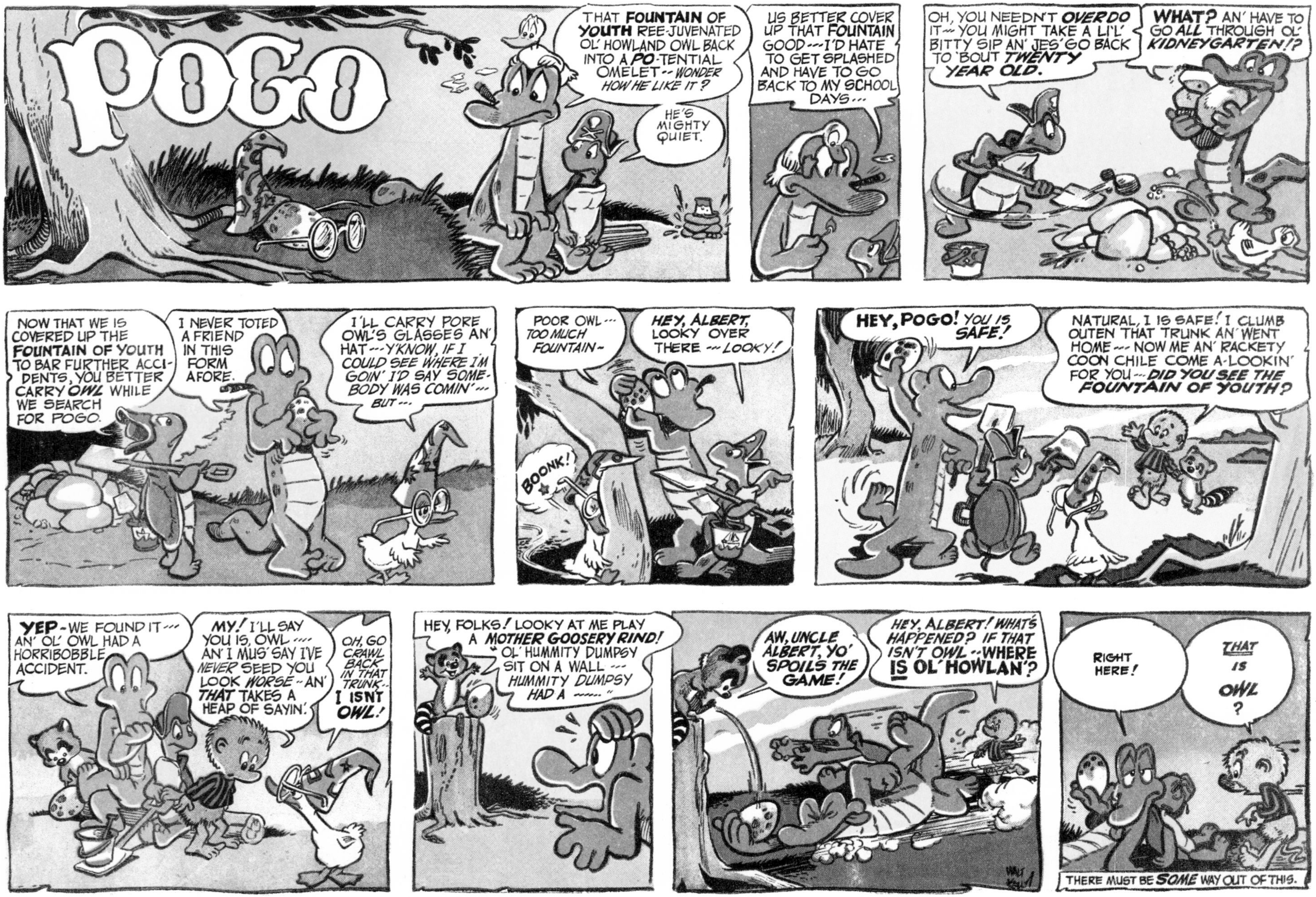
POGO
THAT FOUNTAIN OF YOUTH REE-JUVENATED OL' HOWLAND OWL BACK INTO A PO-TENTIAL OMELET -- WONDER HOW HE LIKE IT?
HE'S MIGHTY QUIET.
US BETTER COVER UP THAT FOUNTAIN GOOD --- I'D HATE TO GET SPLASHED AND HAVE TO GO BACK TO MY SCHOOL DAYS...
OH, YOU NEEDN'T OVERDO IT -- YOU MIGHT TAKE A LI'L' BITTY SIP AN' JES' GO BACK TO 'BOUT TWENTY YEAR OLD.
WHAT? AN' HAVE TO GO ALL THROUGH OL' KIDNEYGARTEN!?
NOW THAT WE IS COVERED UP THE FOUNTAIN OF YOUTH TO BAR FURTHER ACCI-DENTS, YOU BETTER CARRY OWL WHILE WE SEARCH FOR POGO.
I NEVER TOTED A FRIEND IN THIS FORM AFORE.
I'LL CARRY PORE OWL'S GLASSES AN' HAT --- Y'KNOW, IF I COULD SEE WHERE I'M GOIN' I'D SAY SOME-BODY WAS COMIN' --- BUT ---
POOR OWL --- TOO MUCH FOUNTAIN --
HEY, ALBERT, LOOKY OVER THERE -- LOOKY!
BOONK!
HEY, POGO! YOU IS SAFE!
NATURAL, I IS SAFE! I CLUMB OUTEN THAT TRUNK AN' WENT HOME --- NOW ME AN' RACKETY COON CHILE COME A-LOOKIN' FOR YOU -- DID YOU SEE THE FOUNTAIN OF YOUTH?
YEP - WE FOUND IT --- AN' OL' OWL HAD A HORRIBOBBLE ACCIDENT.
MY! I'LL SAY YOU IS, OWL ---- AN' I MUS' SAY I'VE NEVER SEED YOU LOOK WORSE -- AN' THAT TAKES A HEAP OF SAYIN'.
OH, GO CRAWL BACK IN THAT TRUNK -- I ISN'T OWL!
HEY, FOLKS! LOOKY AT ME PLAY A MOTHER GOOSERY RIND!
"OL' HUMMITY DUMPSY SIT ON A WALL --- HUMMITY DUMPSY HAD A ----- "
AW, UNCLE ALBERT, YO' SPOILS THE GAME!
HEY, ALBERT! WHAT'S HAPPENED? IF THAT ISN'T OWL -- WHERE IS OL' HOWLAN'?
RIGHT HERE!
THAT IS OWL?
WALT KELLY
THERE MUST BE SOME WAY OUT OF THIS.

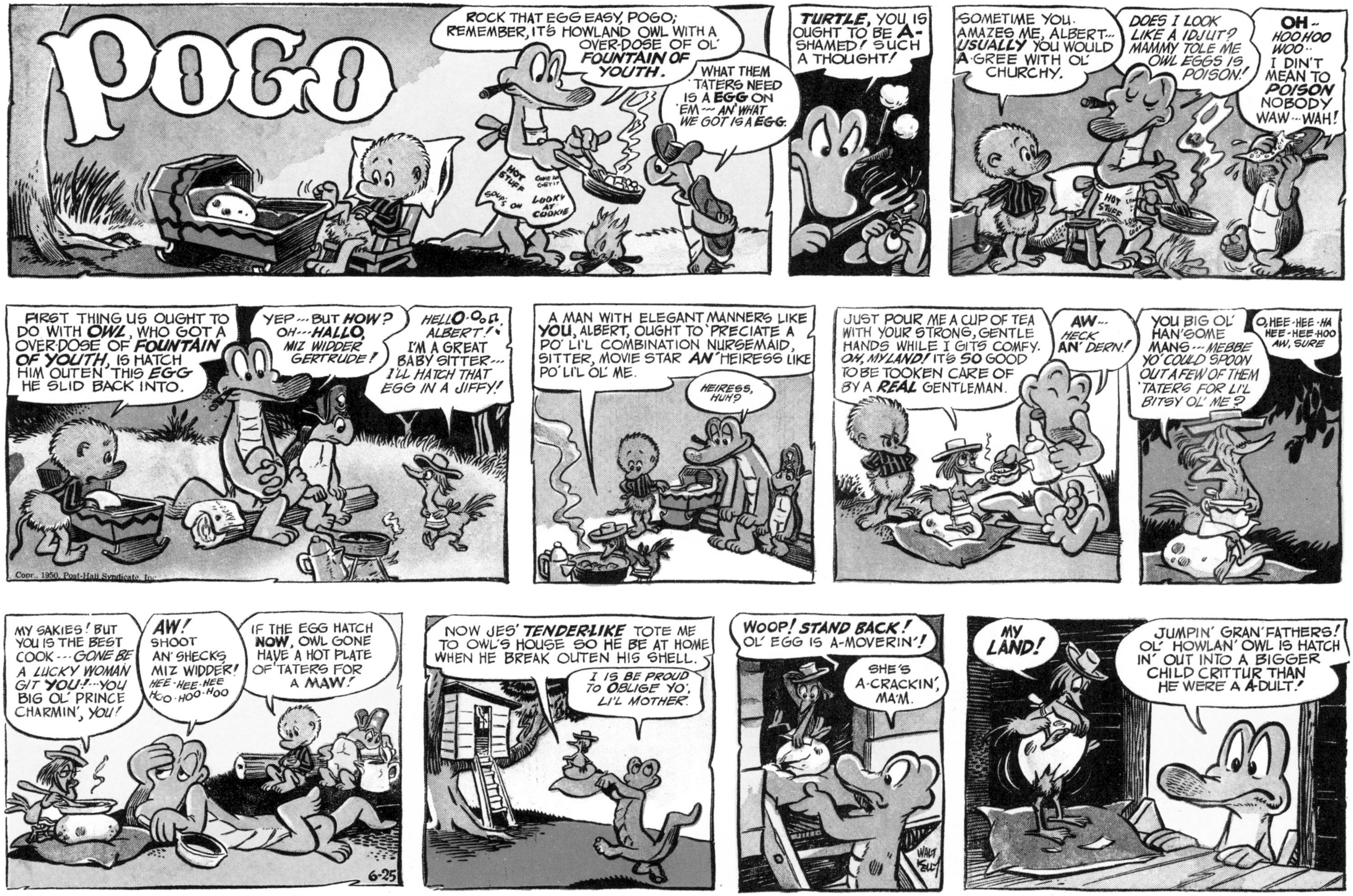
POGO
ROCK THAT EGG EASY, POGO; REMEMBER, IT'S HOWLAND OWL WITH A OVER-DOSE OF OL' **FOUNTAIN OF YOUTH.**
WHAT THEM 'TATERS NEED IS A **EGG** ON 'EM — AN' WHAT WE GOT IS A **EGG.**
HOT STUFF
SOUP'S ON
LOOKY AT COOKIE
TURTLE, YOU IS OUGHT TO BE **A-**SHAMED! SUCH A THOUGHT!
SOMETIME YOU AMAZES ME, ALBERT... **USUALLY** YOU WOULD A-GREE WITH OL' CHURCHY.
DOES I LOOK LIKE A IDJUT? MAMMY TOLE ME OWL EGGS IS POISON!
OH-- HOO HOO WOO-- I DIN'T MEAN TO **POISON** NOBODY WAW---WAH!
FIRST THING US OUGHT TO DO WITH **OWL,** WHO GOT A OVER-DOSE OF **FOUNTAIN OF YOUTH,** IS HATCH HIM OUTEN THIS **EGG** HE SLID BACK INTO.
YEP---BUT **HOW?** OH---**HALLO,** MIZ WIDDER GERTRUDE!
HELLO-O-O! ALBERT! I'M A GREAT BABY SITTER--- I'LL HATCH THAT EGG IN A JIFFY!
A MAN WITH ELEGANT MANNERS LIKE **YOU,** ALBERT, OUGHT TO 'PRECIATE A PO' LI'L COMBINATION NURSEMAID, SITTER, MOVIE STAR **AN'** HEIRESS LIKE PO' LI'L OL' ME.
HEIRESS, HUH?
JUST POUR ME A CUP OF TEA WITH YOUR STRONG, GENTLE HANDS WHILE I GITS COMFY. *OH, MY LAND!* IT'S **SO** GOOD TO BE TOOKEN CARE OF BY A **REAL** GENTLEMAN.
AW--- HECK **AN'** DERN!
YOU BIG OL' HAN'SOME MANS--- MEBBE YO' COULD SPOON OUT A FEW OF THEM 'TATERS FOR LI'L BITSY OL' ME?
O, HEE-HEE-HA HEE-HEE-HOO AW, SURE
Copr., 1950, Post-Hall Syndicate, Inc.
MY SAKIES! BUT YOU IS THE BEST COOK--- GONE BE A LUCKY WOMAN GIT **YOU!**---YOU BIG OL' PRINCE CHARMIN', YOU!
AW! SHOOT AN' SHECKS MIZ WIDDER! HEE-HEE-HEE HOO-HOO-HOO
IF THE EGG HATCH **NOW,** OWL GONE HAVE A HOT PLATE OF 'TATERS FOR A **MAW!**
6-25
NOW JES' **TENDER-LIKE** TOTE ME TO OWL'S HOUSE SO HE BE AT HOME WHEN HE BREAK OUTEN HIS SHELL.
I IS BE PROUD TO OBLIGE YO', LI'L MOTHER.
WOOP! **STAND BACK!** OL' EGG IS A-MOVERIN'!
SHE'S A-CRACKIN', MA'M.
WALT KELLY
MY LAND!
JUMPIN' GRAN'FATHERS! OL' HOWLAN' OWL IS HATCH IN' OUT INTO A BIGGER CHILD CRITTUR THAN HE WERE A **A-**DULT!

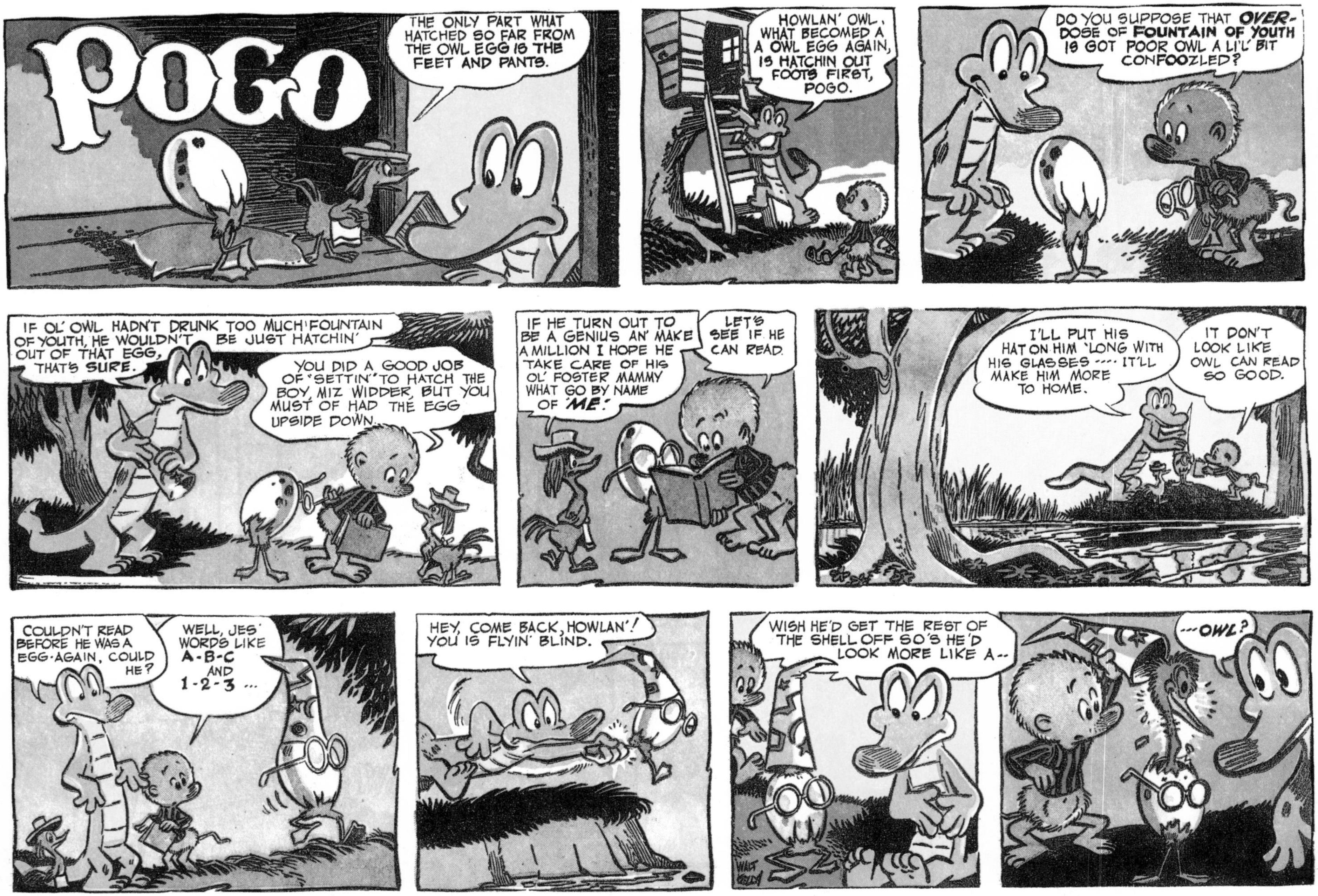
POGO
THE ONLY PART WHAT HATCHED SO FAR FROM THE OWL EGG IS THE FEET AND PANTS.
HOWLAN' OWL, WHAT BECOMED A A OWL EGG AGAIN, IS HATCHIN OUT FOOTS FIRST, POGO.
DO YOU SUPPOSE THAT OVER-DOSE OF FOUNTAIN OF YOUTH IS GOT POOR OWL A LI'L' BIT CONFOOZLED?
IF OL' OWL HADN'T DRUNK TOO MUCH FOUNTAIN OF YOUTH, HE WOULDN'T BE JUST HATCHIN' OUT OF THAT EGG, THAT'S SURE.
YOU DID A GOOD JOB OF "SETTIN'" TO HATCH THE BOY, MIZ WIDDER, BUT YOU MUST OF HAD THE EGG UPSIDE DOWN.
IF HE TURN OUT TO BE A GENIUS AN' MAKE A MILLION I HOPE HE TAKE CARE OF HIS OL' FOSTER MAMMY WHAT GO BY NAME OF 'ME.'
LET'S SEE IF HE CAN READ.
I'LL PUT HIS HAT ON HIM 'LONG WITH HIS GLASSES ---- IT'LL MAKE HIM MORE TO HOME.
IT DON'T LOOK LIKE OWL CAN READ SO GOOD.
COULDN'T READ BEFORE HE WAS A EGG AGAIN, COULD HE?
WELL, JES' WORDS LIKE A-B-C AND 1-2-3 ...
HEY, COME BACK, HOWLAN'! YOU IS FLYIN' BLIND.
WISH HE'D GET THE REST OF THE SHELL OFF SO'S HE'D LOOK MORE LIKE A--
---OWL?
WALT KELLY

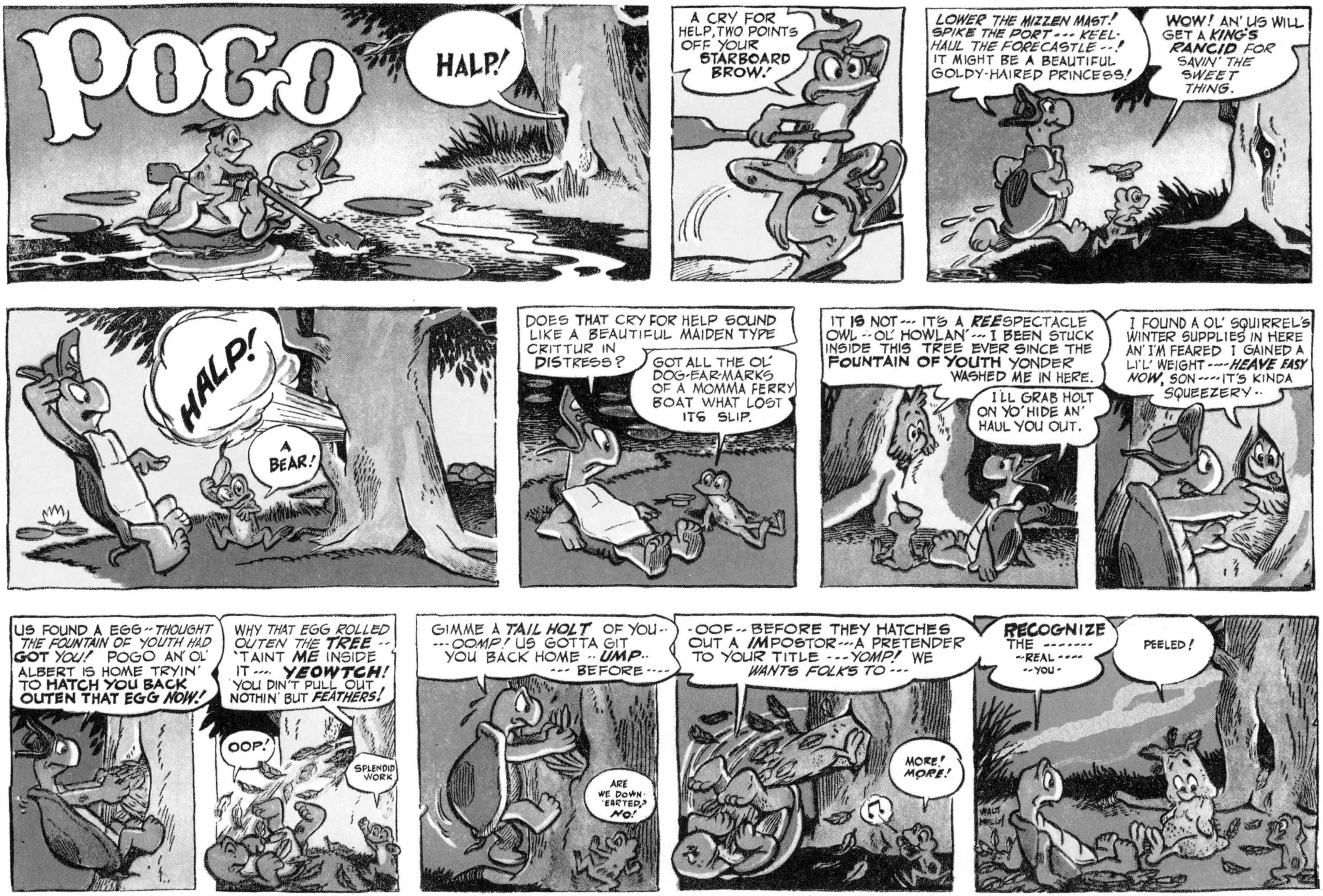
POGO
HALP!
A CRY FOR HELP, TWO POINTS OFF YOUR STARBOARD BROW!
LOWER THE MIZZEN MAST! SPIKE THE PORT --- KEEL-HAUL THE FORECASTLE --! IT MIGHT BE A BEAUTIFUL GOLDY-HAIRED PRINCESS!
WOW! AN' US WILL GET A KING'S RANCID FOR SAVIN' THE SWEET THING.
HALP!
A BEAR!
DOES THAT CRY FOR HELP SOUND LIKE A BEAUTIFUL MAIDEN TYPE CRITTUR IN DISTRESS?
GOT ALL THE OL' DOG-EAR-MARKS OF A MOMMA FERRY BOAT WHAT LOST ITS SLIP.
IT IS NOT --- IT'S A REESPECTACLE OWL -- OL' HOWLAN' --- I BEEN STUCK INSIDE THIS TREE EVER SINCE THE FOUNTAIN OF YOUTH YONDER WASHED ME IN HERE.
I'LL GRAB HOLT ON YO' HIDE AN' HAUL YOU OUT.
I FOUND A OL' SQUIRREL'S WINTER SUPPLIES IN HERE AN' I'M FEARED I GAINED A LI'L' WEIGHT ---- HEAVE EASY NOW, SON ---- IT'S KINDA SQUEEZERY ..
US FOUND A EGG -- THOUGHT THE FOUNTAIN OF YOUTH HAD GOT YOU! POGO AN' OL' ALBERT IS HOME TRYIN' TO HATCH YOU BACK OUTEN THAT EGG NOW!
WHY THAT EGG ROLLED OUTEN THE TREE -- 'TAINT ME INSIDE IT ---. YEOWTCH! YOU DIN'T PULL OUT NOTHIN' BUT FEATHERS!
OOP!
SPLENDID WORK
GIMME A TAIL HOLT OF YOU -- --- OOMP! US GOTTA GIT YOU BACK HOME -- UMP -- --- BEFORE ---
ARE WE DOWN-'EARTED? NO!
-OOF -- BEFORE THEY HATCHES OUT A IMPOSTOR --- A PRETENDER TO YOUR TITLE --- YOMP! WE WANTS FOLKS TO ---
MORE! MORE!
RECOGNIZE THE ------- --REAL ---- --YOU-
PEELED!
WALT KELLY

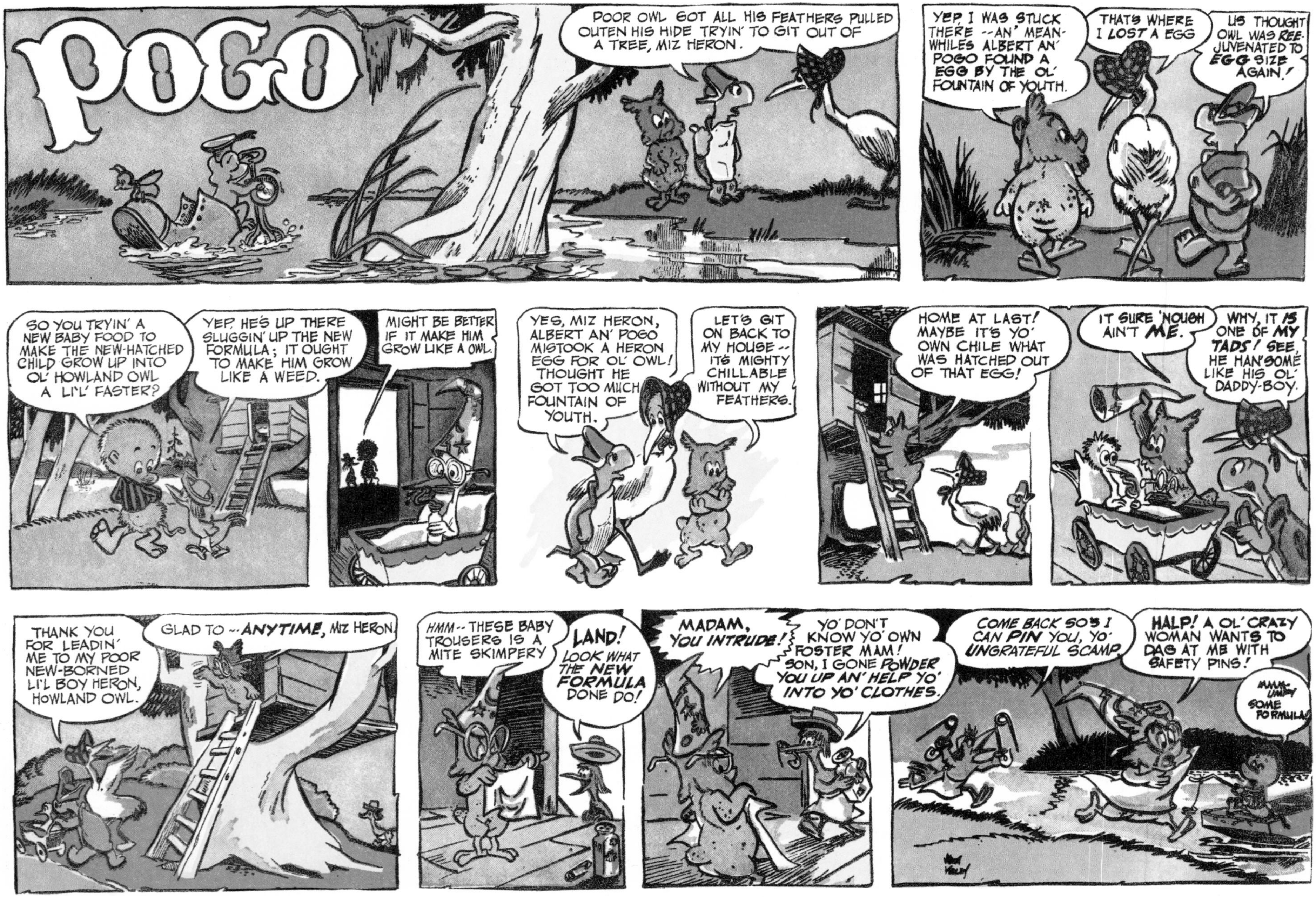
POGO
POOR OWL GOT ALL HIS FEATHERS PULLED OUTEN HIS HIDE TRYIN' TO GIT OUT OF A TREE, MIZ HERON.
YEP, I WAS STUCK THERE --AN' MEANWHILES ALBERT AN' POGO FOUND A EGG BY THE OL' FOUNTAIN OF YOUTH.
THAT'S WHERE I LOST A EGG
US THOUGHT OWL WAS REE-JUVENATED TO EGG SIZE AGAIN!
SO YOU TRYIN' A NEW BABY FOOD TO MAKE THE NEW-HATCHED CHILD GROW UP INTO OL' HOWLAND OWL A LI'L' FASTER?
YEP. HE'S UP THERE SLUGGIN' UP THE NEW FORMULA; IT OUGHT TO MAKE HIM GROW LIKE A WEED.
MIGHT BE BETTER IF IT MAKE HIM GROW LIKE A OWL.
YES, MIZ HERON, ALBERT AN' POGO MISTOOK A HERON EGG FOR OL' OWL! THOUGHT HE GOT TOO MUCH FOUNTAIN OF YOUTH.
LET'S GIT ON BACK TO MY HOUSE -- IT'S MIGHTY CHILLABLE WITHOUT MY FEATHERS.
HOME AT LAST! MAYBE IT'S YO' OWN CHILE WHAT WAS HATCHED OUT OF THAT EGG!
IT SURE 'NOUGH AIN'T ME.
WHY, IT IS ONE OF MY TADS! SEE, HE HAN'SOME LIKE HIS OL' DADDY-BOY.
THANK YOU FOR LEADIN' ME TO MY POOR NEW-BORNED LI'L BOY HERON, HOWLAND OWL.
GLAD TO -- ANYTIME, MIZ HERON.
HMM -- THESE BABY TROUSERS IS A MITE SKIMPERY
LAND! LOOK WHAT THE NEW FORMULA DONE DO!
MADAM, YOU INTRUDE!
YO' DON'T KNOW YO' OWN FOSTER MAM! SON, I GONE POWDER YOU UP AN' HELP YO' INTO YO' CLOTHES.
COME BACK SO'S I CAN PIN YOU, YO' UNGRATEFUL SCAMP.
HALP! A OL' CRAZY WOMAN WANTS TO DAG AT ME WITH SAFETY PINS!
SOME FORMULA!

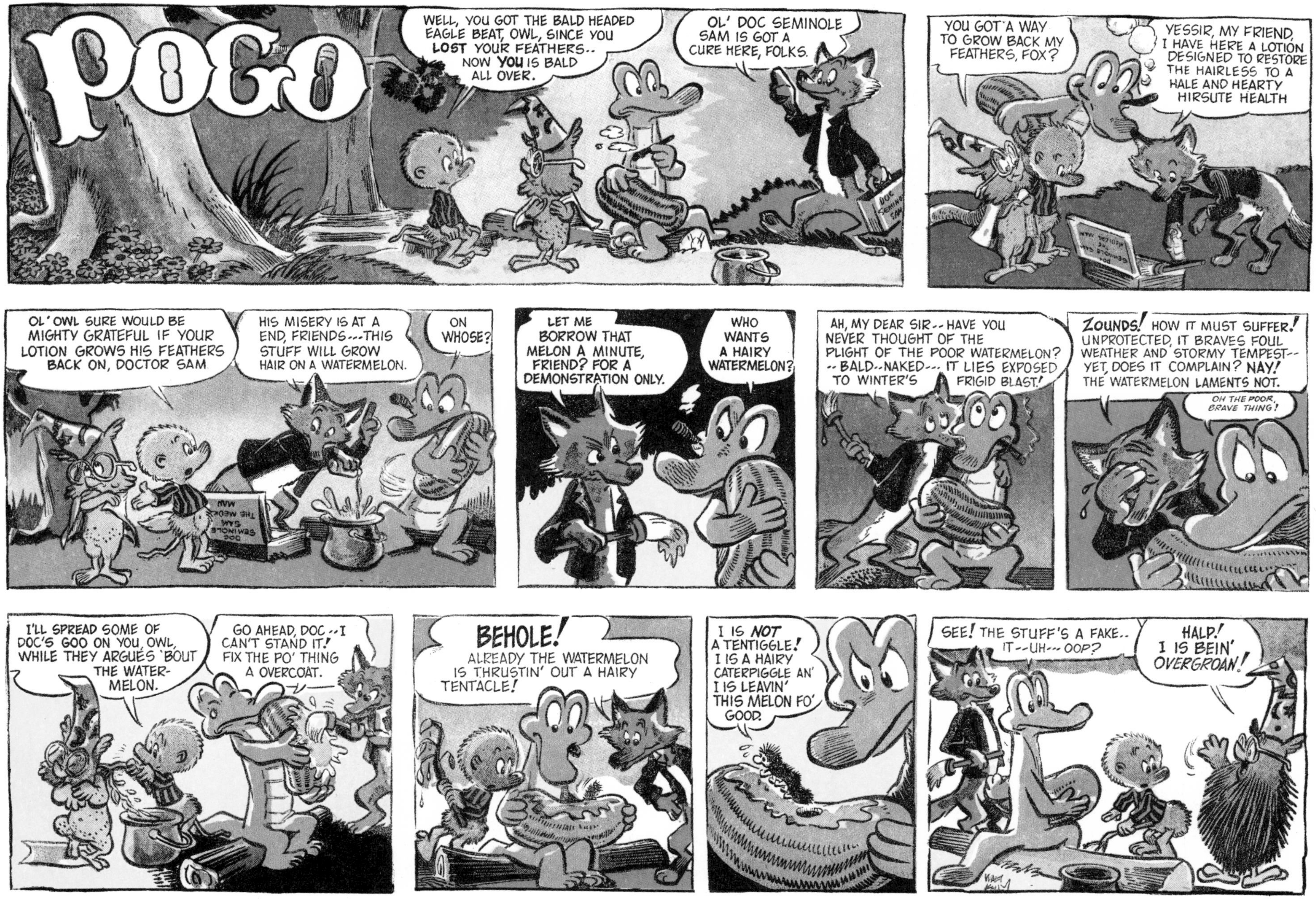
POGO
WELL, YOU GOT THE BALD HEADED EAGLE BEAT, OWL, SINCE YOU LOST YOUR FEATHERS.. NOW YOU IS BALD ALL OVER.
OL' DOC SEMINOLE SAM IS GOT A CURE HERE, FOLKS.
DOC SEMINOLE SAM
YOU GOT A WAY TO GROW BACK MY FEATHERS, FOX?
YESSIR, MY FRIEND, I HAVE HERE A LOTION DESIGNED TO RESTORE THE HAIRLESS TO A HALE AND HEARTY HIRSUTE HEALTH
OL' OWL SURE WOULD BE MIGHTY GRATEFUL IF YOUR LOTION GROWS HIS FEATHERS BACK ON, DOCTOR SAM
HIS MISERY IS AT A END, FRIENDS---THIS STUFF WILL GROW HAIR ON A WATERMELON.
ON WHOSE?
LET ME BORROW THAT MELON A MINUTE, FRIEND? FOR A DEMONSTRATION ONLY.
WHO WANTS A HAIRY WATERMELON?
AH, MY DEAR SIR--HAVE YOU NEVER THOUGHT OF THE PLIGHT OF THE POOR WATERMELON? --BALD--NAKED---IT LIES EXPOSED TO WINTER'S FRIGID BLAST!
ZOUNDS! HOW IT MUST SUFFER! UNPROTECTED, IT BRAVES FOUL WEATHER AND STORMY TEMPEST--YET, DOES IT COMPLAIN? NAY! THE WATERMELON LAMENTS NOT.
OH THE POOR, BRAVE THING!
I'LL SPREAD SOME OF DOC'S GOO ON YOU, OWL, WHILE THEY ARGUES 'BOUT THE WATER-MELON.
GO AHEAD, DOC--I CAN'T STAND IT! FIX THE PO' THING A OVERCOAT.
BEHOLE! ALREADY THE WATERMELON IS THRUSTIN' OUT A HAIRY TENTACLE!
I IS NOT A TENTIGGLE! I IS A HAIRY CATERPIGGLE AN' I IS LEAVIN' THIS MELON FO' GOOD.
SEE! THE STUFF'S A FAKE.. IT--UH---OOP?
HALP! I IS BEIN' OVERGROAN!

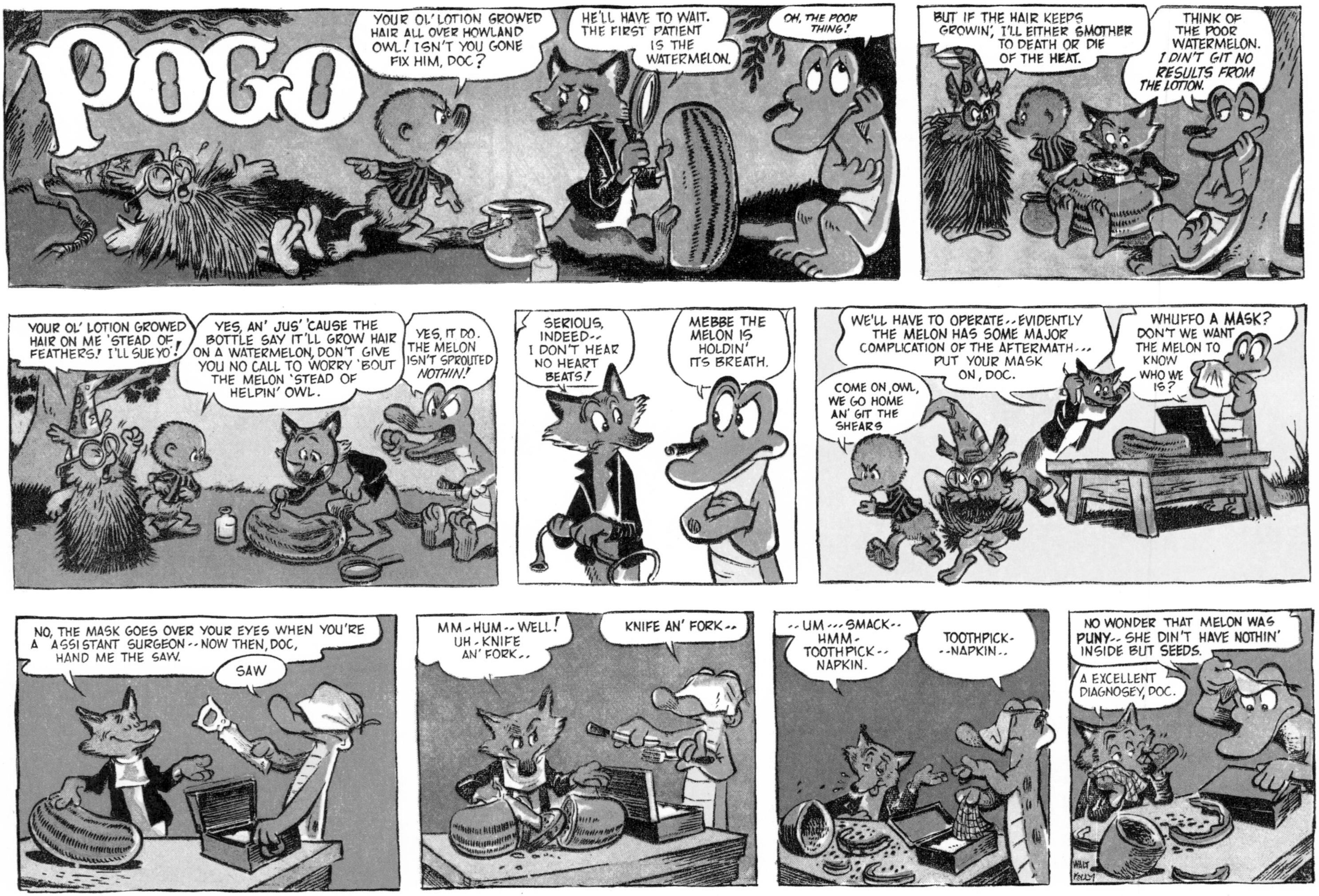
POGO
YOUR OL' LOTION GROWED HAIR ALL OVER HOWLAND OWL! ISN'T YOU GONE FIX HIM, DOC?
HE'LL HAVE TO WAIT. THE FIRST PATIENT IS THE WATERMELON.
OH, THE POOR THING!
BUT IF THE HAIR KEEPS GROWIN', I'LL EITHER SMOTHER TO DEATH OR DIE OF THE HEAT.
THINK OF THE POOR WATERMELON. I DIN'T GIT NO RESULTS FROM THE LOTION.
YOUR OL' LOTION GROWED HAIR ON ME 'STEAD OF FEATHERS! I'LL SUE YO'!
YES, AN' JUS' CAUSE THE BOTTLE SAY IT'LL GROW HAIR ON A WATERMELON, DON'T GIVE YOU NO CALL TO WORRY 'BOUT THE MELON 'STEAD OF HELPIN' OWL.
YES, IT DO. THE MELON ISN'T SPROUTED NOTHIN!
SERIOUS, INDEED-- I DON'T HEAR NO HEART BEATS!
MEBBE THE MELON IS HOLDIN' ITS BREATH.
WE'LL HAVE TO OPERATE--EVIDENTLY THE MELON HAS SOME MAJOR COMPLICATION OF THE AFTERMATH--- PUT YOUR MASK ON, DOC.
WHUFFO A MASK? DON'T WE WANT THE MELON TO KNOW WHO WE IS?
COME ON, OWL, WE GO HOME AN' GIT THE SHEARS
NO, THE MASK GOES OVER YOUR EYES WHEN YOU'RE A ASSISTANT SURGEON--NOW THEN, DOC, HAND ME THE SAW.
SAW
MM-HUM--WELL! UH-KNIFE AN' FORK--
KNIFE AN' FORK--
--UM---SMACK-- HMM-TOOTHPICK-- NAPKIN.
TOOTHPICK- --NAPKIN--
NO WONDER THAT MELON WAS PUNY--SHE DIN'T HAVE NOTHIN' INSIDE BUT SEEDS.
A EXCELLENT DIAGNOSEY, DOC.
WALT KELLY

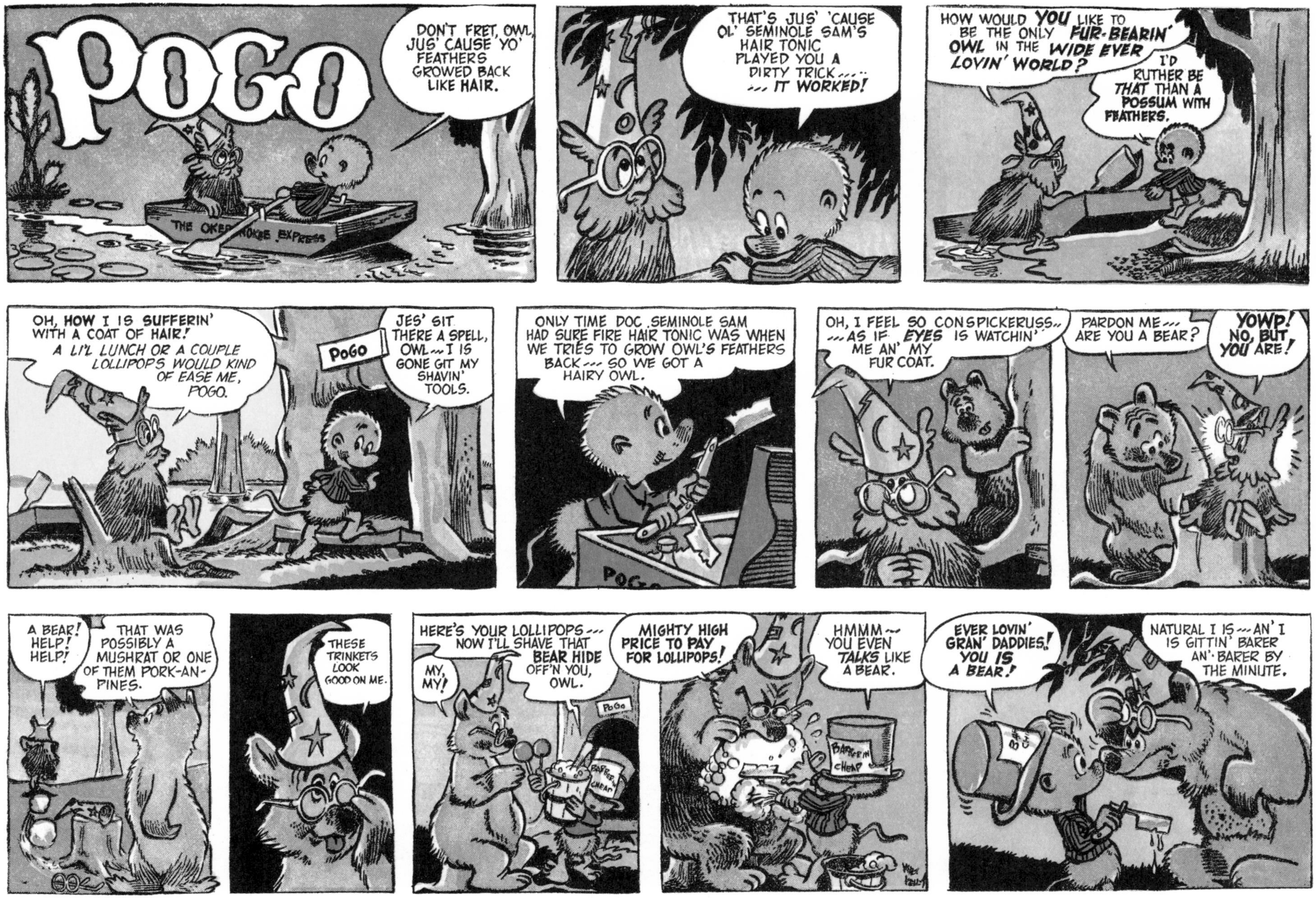
POGO
DON'T FRET, OWL, JUS' CAUSE YO' FEATHERS GROWED BACK LIKE HAIR.
THE OKEFENOKEE EXPRESS
THAT'S JUS' 'CAUSE OL' SEMINOLE SAM'S HAIR TONIC PLAYED YOU A DIRTY TRICK..... ...IT WORKED!
HOW WOULD YOU LIKE TO BE THE ONLY FUR-BEARIN' OWL IN THE WIDE EVER LOVIN' WORLD?
I'D RUTHER BE THAT THAN A POSSUM WITH FEATHERS.
OH, HOW I IS SUFFERIN' WITH A COAT OF HAIR! A LI'L LUNCH OR A COUPLE LOLLIPOPS WOULD KIND OF EASE ME, POGO.
POGO
JES' SIT THERE A SPELL, OWL...I IS GONE GIT MY SHAVIN' TOOLS.
ONLY TIME DOC SEMINOLE SAM HAD SURE FIRE HAIR TONIC WAS WHEN WE TRIES TO GROW OWL'S FEATHERS BACK... SO WE GOT A HAIRY OWL.
OH, I FEEL SO CONSPICKERUSS.. ...AS IF EYES IS WATCHIN' ME AN' MY FUR COAT.
PARDON ME... ARE YOU A BEAR?
YOWP! NO, BUT YOU ARE!
A BEAR! HELP! HELP!
THAT WAS POSSIBLY A MUSHRAT OR ONE OF THEM PORK-AN-PINES.
THESE TRINKETS LOOK GOOD ON ME.
HERE'S YOUR LOLLIPOPS... NOW I'LL SHAVE THAT BEAR HIDE OFF'N YOU, OWL.
MY, MY!
POGO
MIGHTY HIGH PRICE TO PAY FOR LOLLIPOPS!
HMMM... YOU EVEN TALKS LIKE A BEAR.
BARGEIN CHEAP
EVER LOVIN' GRAN' DADDIES! YOU IS A BEAR!
NATURAL I IS...AN' I IS GITTIN' BARER AN' BARER BY THE MINUTE.

SUNDAY, AUGUST 13, 1950

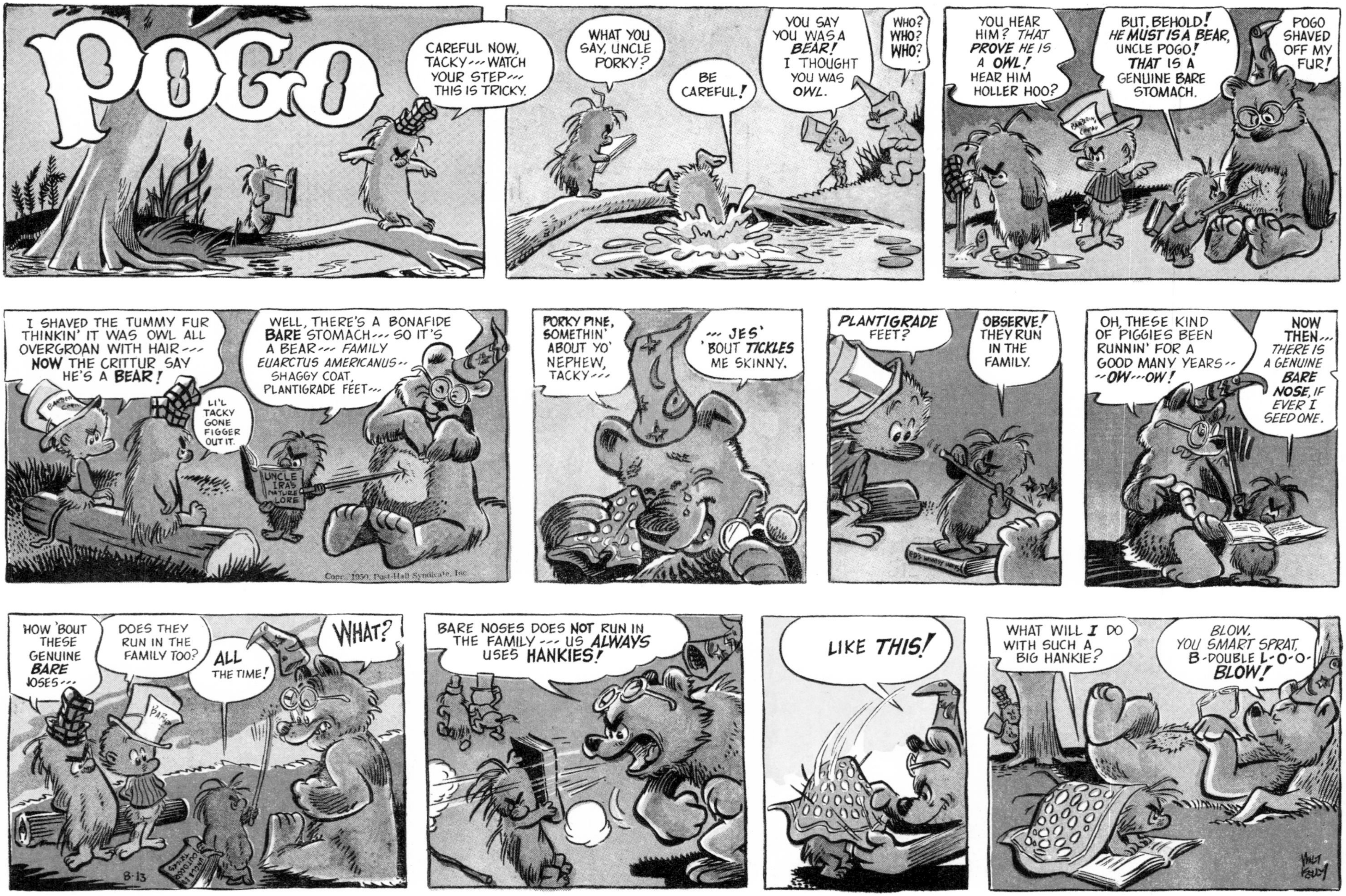
POGO
CAREFUL NOW, TACKY --- WATCH YOUR STEP --- THIS IS TRICKY.
WHAT YOU SAY, UNCLE PORKY?
BE CAREFUL!
YOU SAY YOU WAS A BEAR! I THOUGHT YOU WAS OWL.
WHO? WHO? WHO?
YOU HEAR HIM? THAT PROVE HE IS A OWL! HEAR HIM HOLLER HOO?
BUT, BEHOLD! HE MUST IS A BEAR, UNCLE POGO! THAT IS A GENUINE BARE STOMACH.
POGO SHAVED OFF MY FUR!
I SHAVED THE TUMMY FUR THINKIN' IT WAS OWL ALL OVERGROAN WITH HAIR --- NOW THE CRITTUR SAY HE'S A BEAR!
WELL, THERE'S A BONAFIDE BARE STOMACH --- SO IT'S A BEAR --- FAMILY EUARCTUS AMERICANUS -- SHAGGY COAT, PLANTIGRADE FEET ---
LI'L TACKY GONE FIGGER OUT IT.
UNCLE IRA'S NATURE LORE
Copr. 1950, Post-Hall Syndicate, Inc.
PORKY PINE, SOMETHIN' ABOUT YO' NEPHEW, TACKY ---
--- JES' 'BOUT TICKLES ME SKINNY.
PLANTIGRADE FEET?
OBSERVE! THEY RUN IN THE FAMILY.
OH, THESE KIND OF PIGGIES BEEN RUNNIN' FOR A GOOD MANY YEARS -- -- OW --- OW!
NOW THEN --- THERE IS A GENUINE BARE NOSE, IF EVER I SEED ONE.
HOW 'BOUT THESE GENUINE BARE JOSES ---
DOES THEY RUN IN THE FAMILY TOO?
ALL THE TIME!
WHAT?
8-13
BARE NOSES DOES NOT RUN IN THE FAMILY --- US ALWAYS USES HANKIES!
LIKE THIS!
WHAT WILL I DO WITH SUCH A BIG HANKIE?
BLOW, YOU SMART SPRAT, B-DOUBLE L-O-O-BLOW!
WALT KELLY

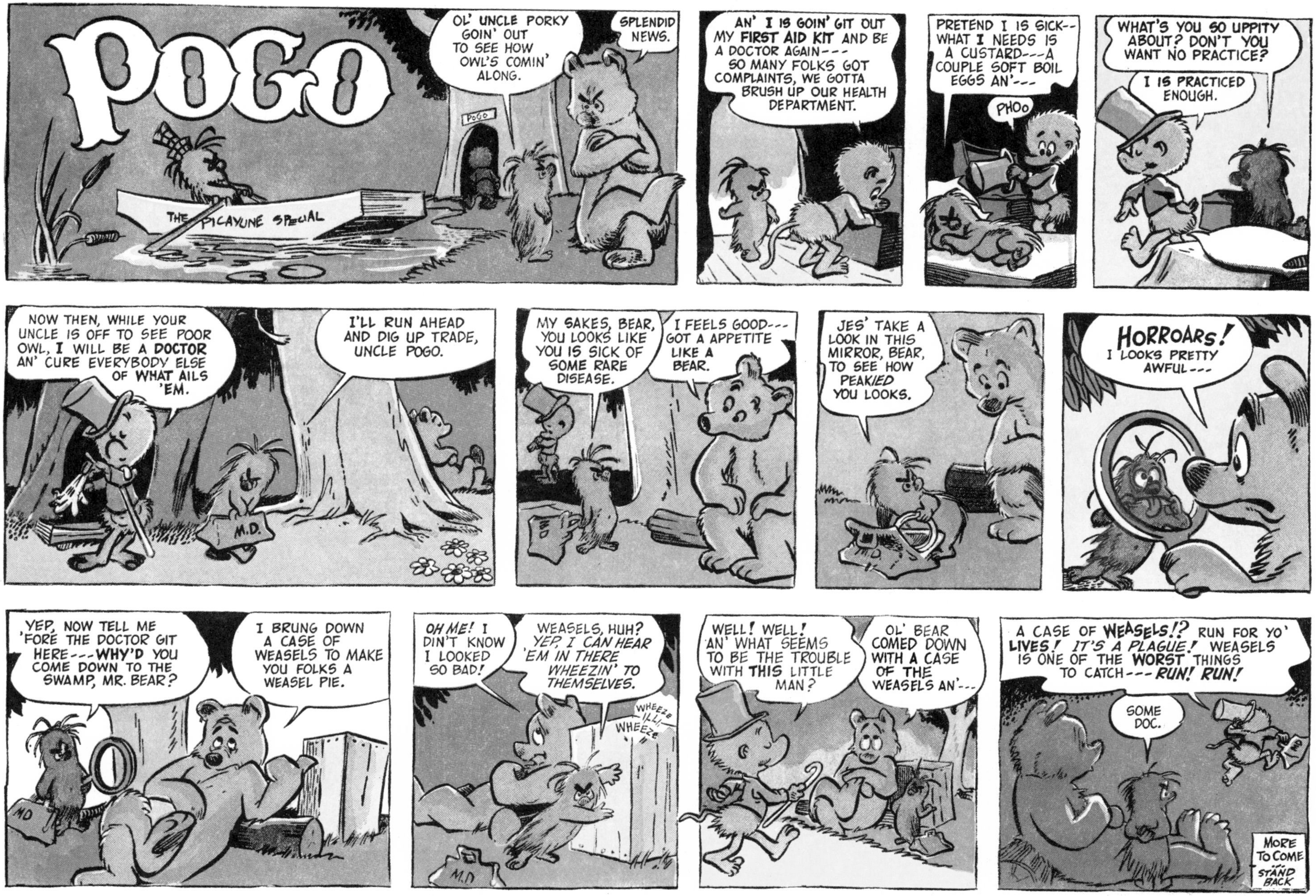
POGO
THE PICAYUNE SPECIAL
POGO
OL' UNCLE PORKY GOIN' OUT TO SEE HOW OWL'S COMIN' ALONG.
SPLENDID NEWS.
AN' I IS GOIN' GIT OUT MY FIRST AID KIT AND BE A DOCTOR AGAIN--- SO MANY FOLKS GOT COMPLAINTS, WE GOTTA BRUSH UP OUR HEALTH DEPARTMENT.
PRETEND I IS SICK-- WHAT I NEEDS IS A CUSTARD---A COUPLE SOFT BOIL EGGS AN'---
PHOo
WHAT'S YOU SO UPPITY ABOUT? DON'T YOU WANT NO PRACTICE?
I IS PRACTICED ENOUGH.
NOW THEN, WHILE YOUR UNCLE IS OFF TO SEE POOR OWL, I WILL BE A DOCTOR AN' CURE EVERYBODY ELSE OF WHAT AILS 'EM.
I'LL RUN AHEAD AND DIG UP TRADE, UNCLE POGO.
M.D.
MY SAKES, BEAR, YOU LOOKS LIKE YOU IS SICK OF SOME RARE DISEASE.
I FEELS GOOD--- GOT A APPETITE LIKE A BEAR.
JES' TAKE A LOOK IN THIS MIRROR, BEAR, TO SEE HOW PEAKIED YOU LOOKS.
HORROARS! I LOOKS PRETTY AWFUL---
YEP, NOW TELL ME 'FORE THE DOCTOR GIT HERE---WHY'D YOU COME DOWN TO THE SWAMP, MR. BEAR?
I BRUNG DOWN A CASE OF WEASELS TO MAKE YOU FOLKS A WEASEL PIE.
MD
OH ME! I DIN'T KNOW I LOOKED SO BAD!
WEASELS, HUH? YEP, I CAN HEAR 'EM IN THERE WHEEZIN' TO THEMSELVES.
WHEEZE
WHEEZE
M.D
WELL! WELL! AN' WHAT SEEMS TO BE THE TROUBLE WITH THIS LITTLE MAN?
OL' BEAR COMED DOWN WITH A CASE OF THE WEASELS AN'---
A CASE OF WEASELS!? RUN FOR YO' LIVES! IT'S A PLAGUE! WEASELS IS ONE OF THE WORST THINGS TO CATCH---RUN! RUN!
SOME DOC.
MORE TO COME ... STAND BACK

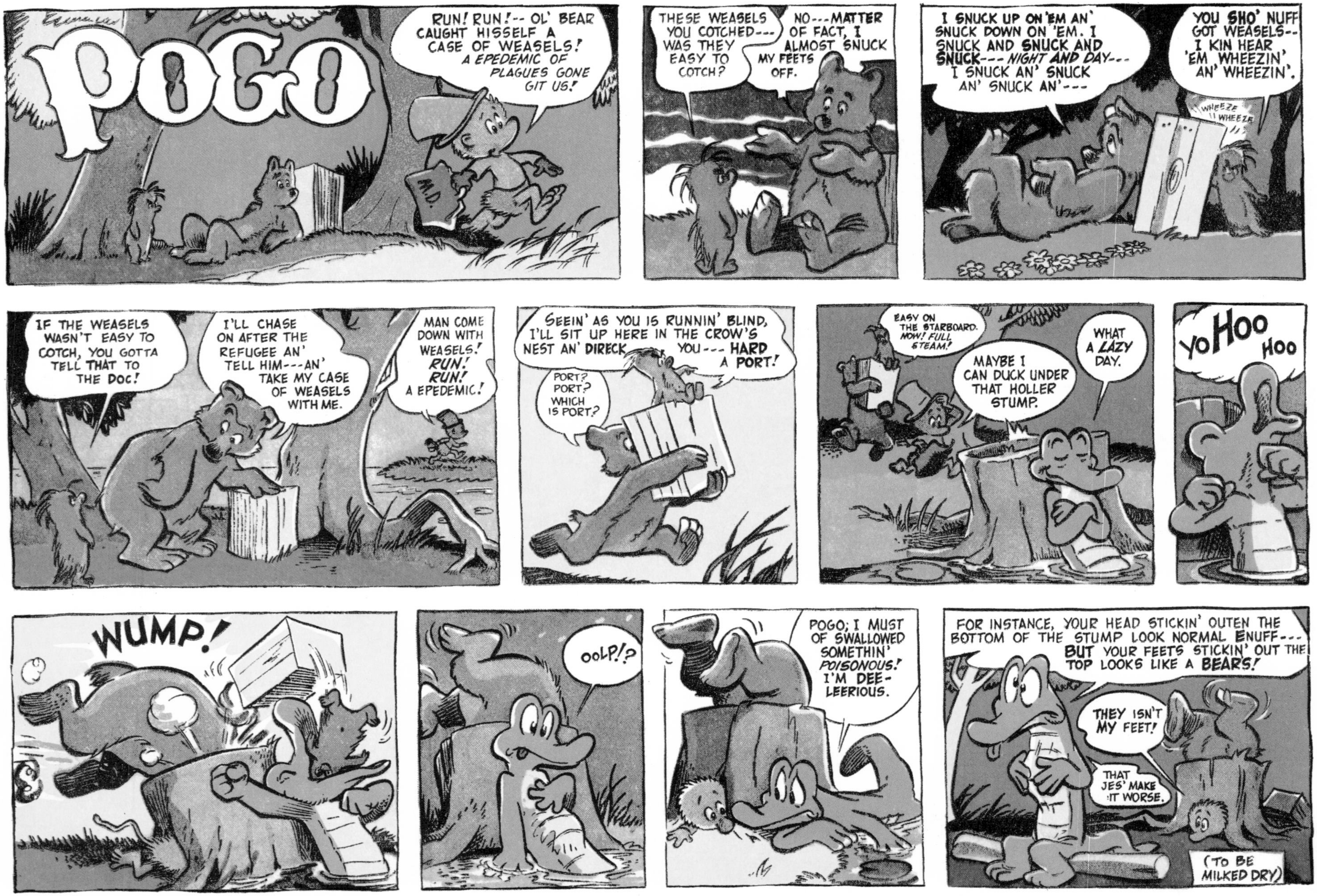
POGO
RUN! RUN!-- OL' BEAR CAUGHT HISSELF A CASE OF WEASELS! A EPEDEMIC OF PLAGUES GONE GIT US!
M.D.
THESE WEASELS YOU COTCHED--- WAS THEY EASY TO COTCH?
NO---MATTER OF FACT, I ALMOST SNUCK MY FEETS OFF.
I SNUCK UP ON 'EM AN' SNUCK DOWN ON 'EM. I SNUCK AND SNUCK AND SNUCK--- NIGHT AND DAY--- I SNUCK AN' SNUCK AN' SNUCK AN'---
YOU SHO' NUFF GOT WEASELS-- I KIN HEAR 'EM WHEEZIN' AN' WHEEZIN'.
WHEEZE WHEEZE
IF THE WEASELS WASN'T EASY TO COTCH, YOU GOTTA TELL THAT TO THE DOC!
I'LL CHASE ON AFTER THE REFUGEE AN' TELL HIM---AN' TAKE MY CASE OF WEASELS WITH ME.
MAN COME DOWN WITH WEASELS! RUN! RUN! A EPEDEMIC!
SEEIN' AS YOU IS RUNNIN' BLIND, I'LL SIT UP HERE IN THE CROW'S NEST AN' DIRECK YOU--- HARD A PORT!
PORT? PORT? WHICH IS PORT?
EASY ON THE STARBOARD. NOW! FULL STEAM!
MAYBE I CAN DUCK UNDER THAT HOLLER STUMP.
WHAT A LAZY DAY.
YO HOO HOO
WUMP!
OOLP!?
POGO; I MUST OF SWALLOWED SOMETHIN' POISONOUS! I'M DEE-LEERIOUS.
FOR INSTANCE, YOUR HEAD STICKIN' OUTEN THE BOTTOM OF THE STUMP LOOK NORMAL ENUFF--- BUT YOUR FEETS STICKIN' OUT THE TOP LOOKS LIKE A BEARS!
THEY ISN'T MY FEET!
THAT JES' MAKE IT WORSE.
(TO BE MILKED DRY)

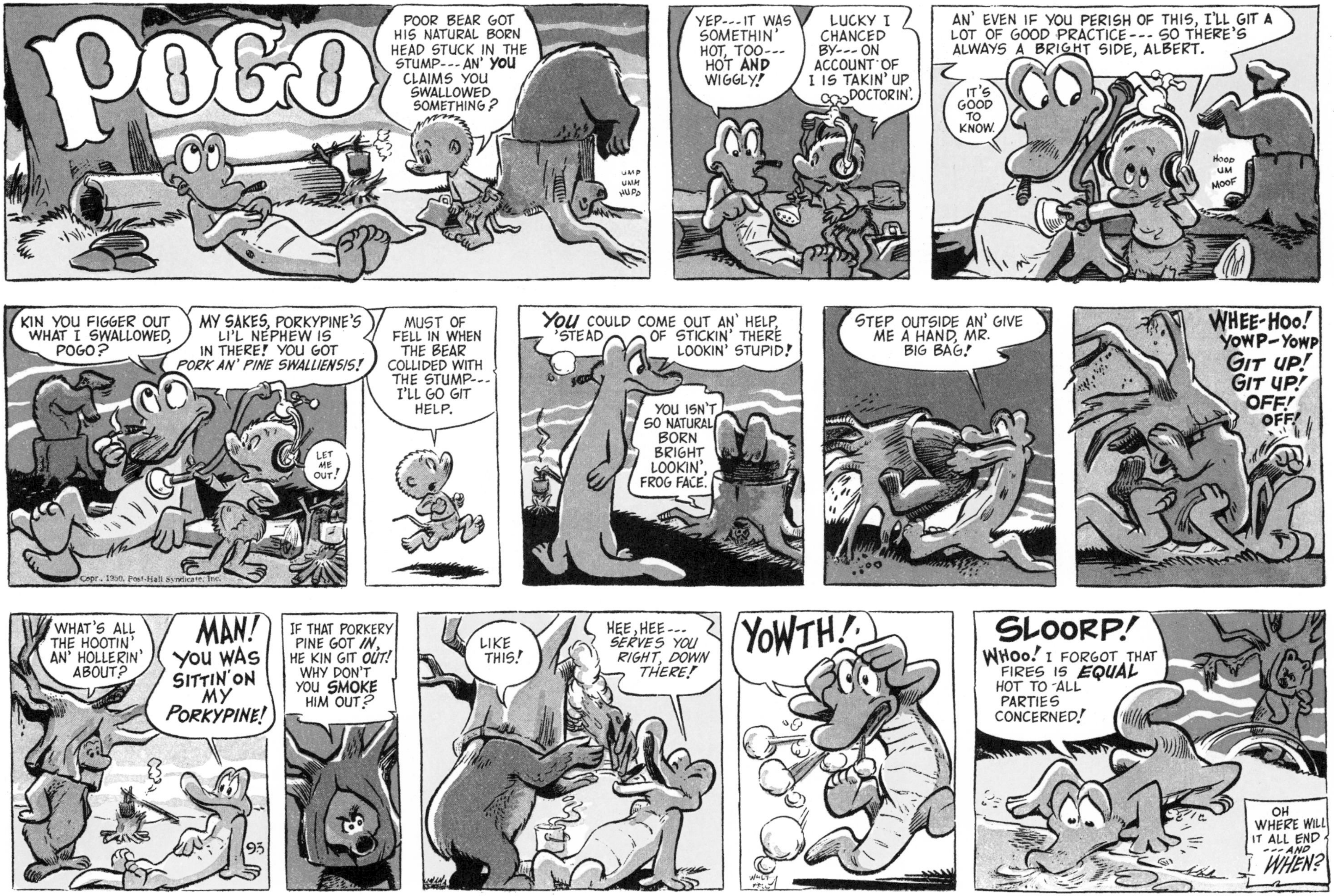
POGO
POOR BEAR GOT HIS NATURAL BORN HEAD STUCK IN THE STUMP--- AN' **YOU** CLAIMS YOU SWALLOWED SOMETHING?
UMP UMM HUPP
YEP---IT WAS SOMETHIN' HOT, TOO--- HOT **AND** WIGGLY!
LUCKY I CHANCED BY--- ON ACCOUNT OF I IS TAKIN' UP DOCTORIN'.
AN' EVEN IF YOU PERISH OF THIS, I'LL GIT A LOT OF GOOD PRACTICE--- SO THERE'S ALWAYS A BRIGHT SIDE, ALBERT.
IT'S GOOD TO KNOW.
HOOD UM MOOF
KIN YOU FIGGER OUT WHAT I SWALLOWED, POGO?
MY SAKES, PORKYPINE'S LI'L NEPHEW IS IN THERE! YOU GOT *PORK AN' PINE SWALLIENSIS!*
LET ME OUT!
Copr., 1950, Post-Hall Syndicate, Inc.
MUST OF FELL IN WHEN THE BEAR COLLIDED WITH THE STUMP--- I'LL GO GIT HELP.
YOU COULD COME OUT AN' HELP, 'STEAD OF STICKIN' THERE LOOKIN' STUPID!
YOU ISN'T SO NATURAL BORN BRIGHT LOOKIN', FROG FACE.
STEP OUTSIDE AN' GIVE ME A HAND, MR. BIG BAG!
WHEE-HOO! YOWP-YOWP GIT UP! GIT UP! OFF! OFF!
WHAT'S ALL THE HOOTIN' AN' HOLLERIN' ABOUT?
MAN! YOU WAS SITTIN' ON MY PORKYPINE!
9-3
IF THAT PORKERY PINE GOT *IN*, HE KIN GIT *OUT!* WHY DON'T YOU **SMOKE** HIM OUT?
LIKE THIS!
HEE, HEE--- *SERVES YOU RIGHT, DOWN THERE!*
YOWTH!
SLOORP! WHOO! I FORGOT THAT FIRES IS ***EQUAL*** HOT TO ALL PARTIES CONCERNED!
OH WHERE WILL IT ALL END ---AND *WHEN?*

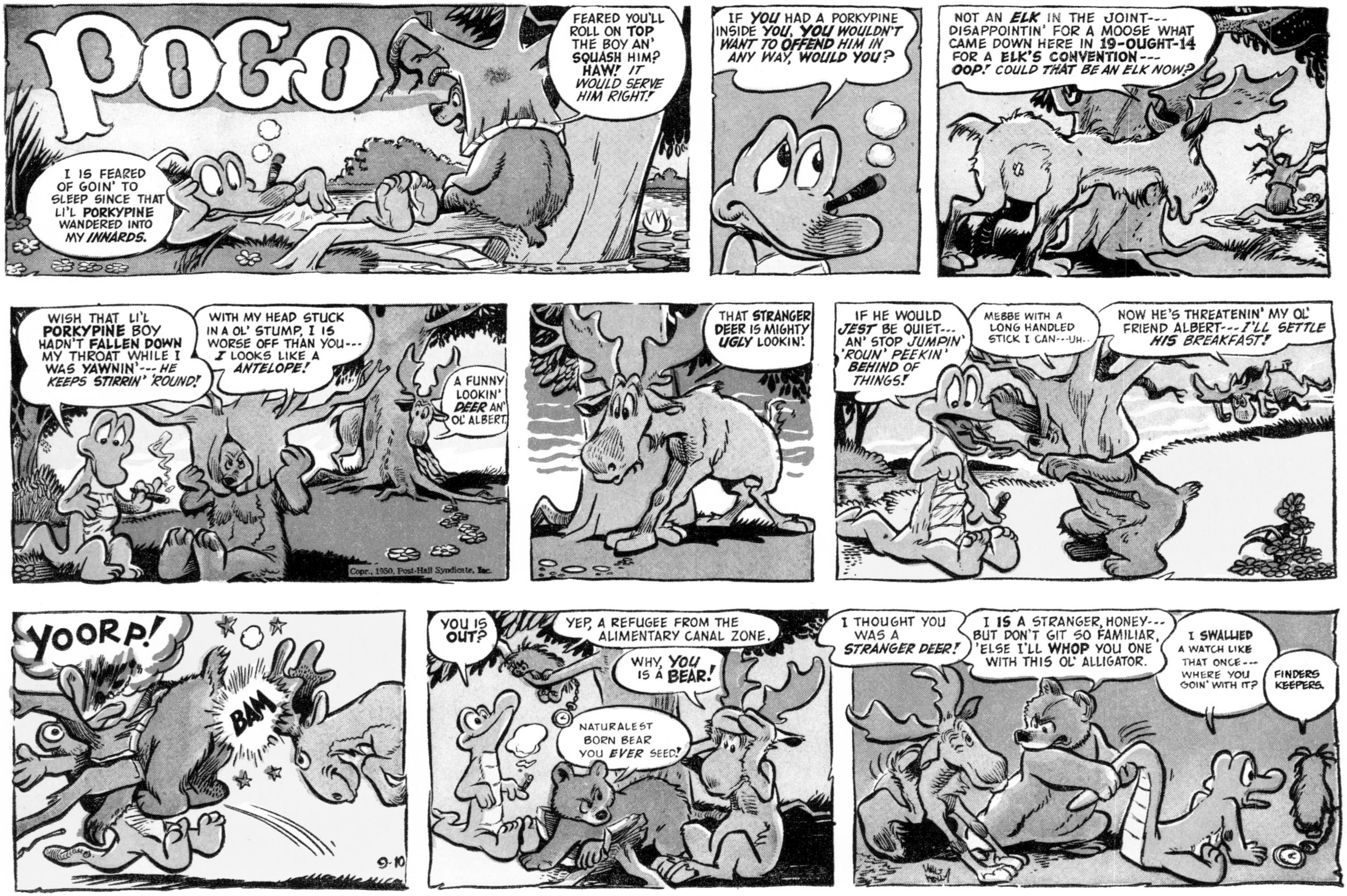
POGO
I IS FEARED OF GOIN' TO SLEEP SINCE THAT LI'L PORKYPINE WANDERED INTO MY INNARDS.
FEARED YOU'LL ROLL ON TOP THE BOY AN' SQUASH HIM? HAW! IT WOULD SERVE HIM RIGHT!
IF YOU HAD A PORKYPINE INSIDE YOU, YOU WOULDN'T WANT TO OFFEND HIM IN ANY WAY, WOULD YOU?
NOT AN ELK IN THE JOINT--- DISAPPOINTIN' FOR A MOOSE WHAT CAME DOWN HERE IN 19-OUGHT-14 FOR A ELK'S CONVENTION--- OOP! COULD THAT BE AN ELK NOW?
WISH THAT LI'L PORKYPINE BOY HADN'T FALLEN DOWN MY THROAT WHILE I WAS YAWNIN'--- HE KEEPS STIRRIN' 'ROUND!
WITH MY HEAD STUCK IN A OL' STUMP, I IS WORSE OFF THAN YOU--- I LOOKS LIKE A ANTELOPE!
A FUNNY LOOKIN' DEER AN' OL' ALBERT.
Copr., 1950, Post-Hall Syndicate, Inc.
THAT STRANGER DEER IS MIGHTY UGLY LOOKIN'.
IF HE WOULD JEST BE QUIET--- AN' STOP JUMPIN' 'ROUN' PEEKIN' BEHIND OF THINGS!
MEBBE WITH A LONG HANDLED STICK I CAN---UH..
NOW HE'S THREATENIN' MY OL' FRIEND ALBERT--- I'LL SETTLE HIS BREAKFAST!
YOORP!
BAM
9-10
YOU IS OUT?
YEP, A REFUGEE FROM THE ALIMENTARY CANAL ZONE.
WHY, YOU IS A BEAR!
NATURALEST BORN BEAR YOU EVER SEED!
I THOUGHT YOU WAS A STRANGER DEER!
I IS A STRANGER, HONEY--- BUT DON'T GIT SO FAMILIAR, 'ELSE I'LL WHOP YOU ONE WITH THIS OL' ALLIGATOR.
I SWALLIED A WATCH LIKE THAT ONCE--- WHERE YOU GOIN' WITH IT?
FINDERS KEEPERS.
WALT KELLY

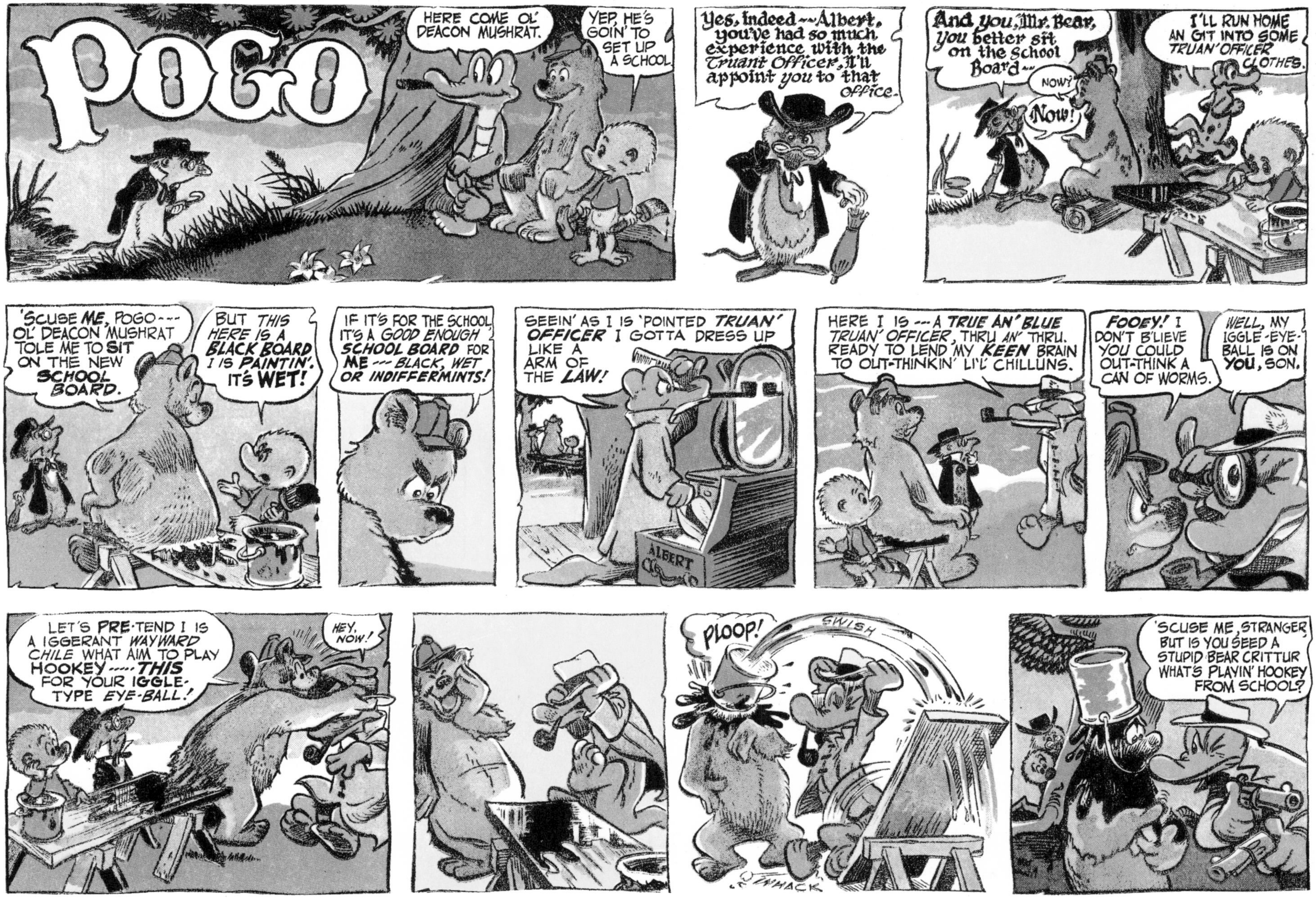
POGO
HERE COME OL' DEACON MUSHRAT.
YEP, HE'S GOIN' TO SET UP A SCHOOL.
Yes, indeed -- Albert, you've had so much experience with the Truant Officer, I'll appoint you to that office --
And you, Mr. Bear, you better sit on the School Board --
NOW?
Now!
I'LL RUN HOME AN GIT INTO SOME TRUAN' OFFICER CLOTHES.
'SCUSE ME, POGO --- OL' DEACON MUSHRAT TOLE ME TO SIT ON THE NEW SCHOOL BOARD.
BUT THIS HERE IS A BLACK BOARD I IS PAINTIN'. IT'S WET!
IF IT'S FOR THE SCHOOL, IT'S A GOOD ENOUGH SCHOOL BOARD FOR ME --- BLACK, WET OR INDIFFERMINTS!
SEEIN' AS I IS 'POINTED TRUAN' OFFICER I GOTTA DRESS UP LIKE A ARM OF THE LAW!
ALBERT
HERE I IS --- A TRUE AN' BLUE TRUAN' OFFICER, THRU AN' THRU. READY TO LEND MY KEEN BRAIN TO OUT-THINKIN' LI'L CHILLUNS.
FOOEY! I DON'T B'LIEVE YOU COULD OUT-THINK A CAN OF WORMS.
WELL, MY IGGLE-EYE-BALL IS ON YOU, SON.
LET'S PRE-TEND I IS A IGGERANT WAYWARD CHILE WHAT AIM TO PLAY HOOKEY..... THIS FOR YOUR IGGLE-TYPE EYE-BALL!
HEY, NOW!
PLOOP!
SWISH
WHACK
'SCUSE ME, STRANGER, BUT IS YOU SEED A STUPID BEAR CRITTUR WHAT'S PLAYIN' HOOKEY FROM SCHOOL?

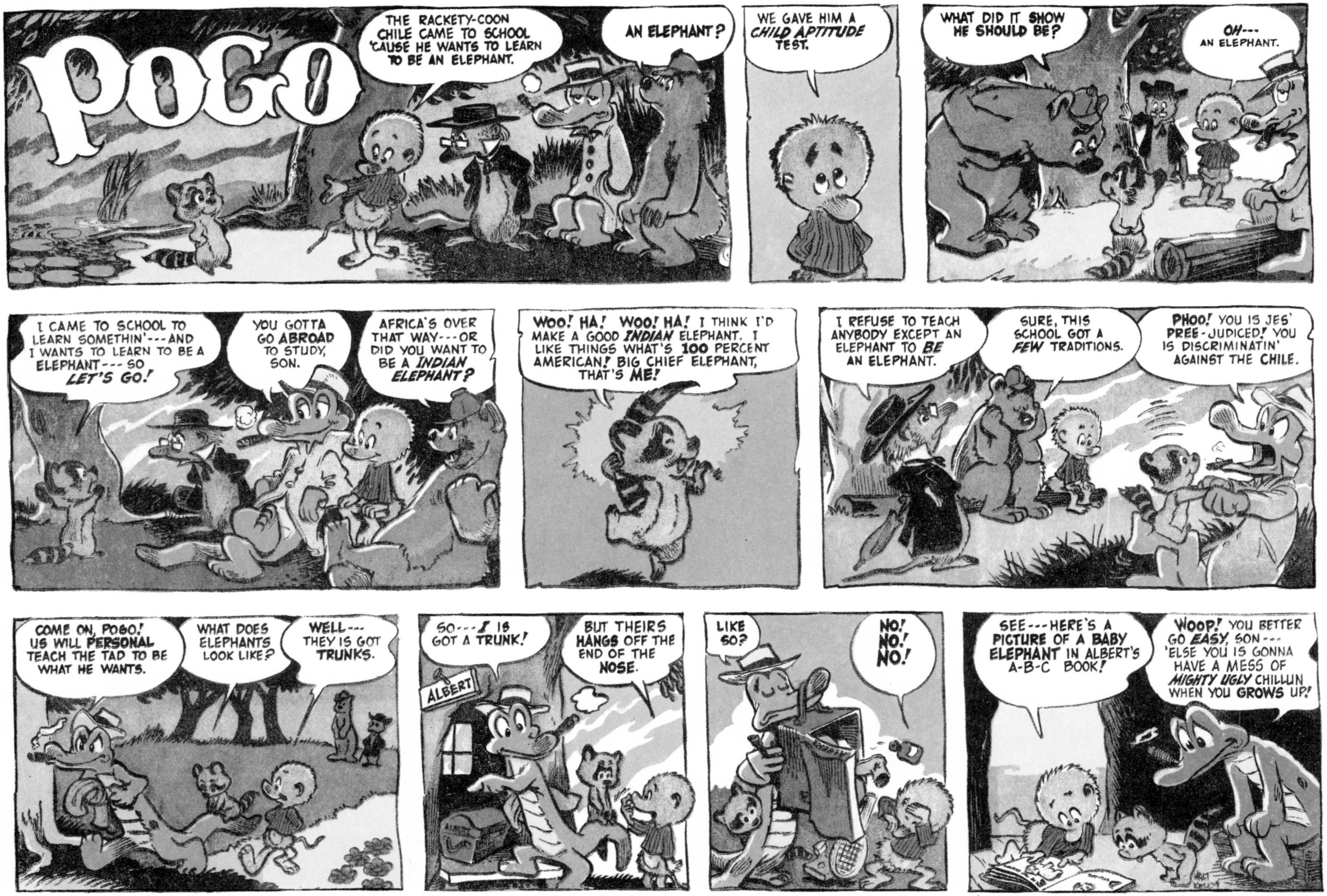
POGO
THE RACKETY-COON CHILE CAME TO SCHOOL 'CAUSE HE WANTS TO LEARN TO BE AN ELEPHANT.
AN ELEPHANT?
WE GAVE HIM A CHILD APTITUDE TEST.
WHAT DID IT SHOW HE SHOULD BE?
OH--- AN ELEPHANT.
I CAME TO SCHOOL TO LEARN SOMETHIN'---AND I WANTS TO LEARN TO BE A ELEPHANT--- SO LET'S GO!
YOU GOTTA GO ABROAD TO STUDY, SON.
AFRICA'S OVER THAT WAY---OR DID YOU WANT TO BE A INDIAN ELEPHANT?
WOO! HA! WOO! HA! I THINK I'D MAKE A GOOD INDIAN ELEPHANT. I LIKE THINGS WHAT'S 100 PERCENT AMERICAN! BIG CHIEF ELEPHANT, THAT'S ME!
I REFUSE TO TEACH ANYBODY EXCEPT AN ELEPHANT TO BE AN ELEPHANT.
SURE, THIS SCHOOL GOT A FEW TRADITIONS.
PHOO! YOU IS JES' PREE-JUDICED! YOU IS DISCRIMINATIN' AGAINST THE CHILE.
COME ON, POGO! US WILL PERSONAL TEACH THE TAD TO BE WHAT HE WANTS.
WHAT DOES ELEPHANTS LOOK LIKE?
WELL--- THEY IS GOT TRUNKS.
SO---I IS GOT A TRUNK!
ALBERT
BUT THEIRS HANGS OFF THE END OF THE NOSE.
LIKE SO?
NO! NO! NO!
SEE---HERE'S A PICTURE OF A BABY ELEPHANT IN ALBERT'S A-B-C BOOK!
WOOP! YOU BETTER GO EASY, SON--- 'ELSE YOU IS GONNA HAVE A MESS OF MIGHTY UGLY CHILLUN WHEN YOU GROWS UP!

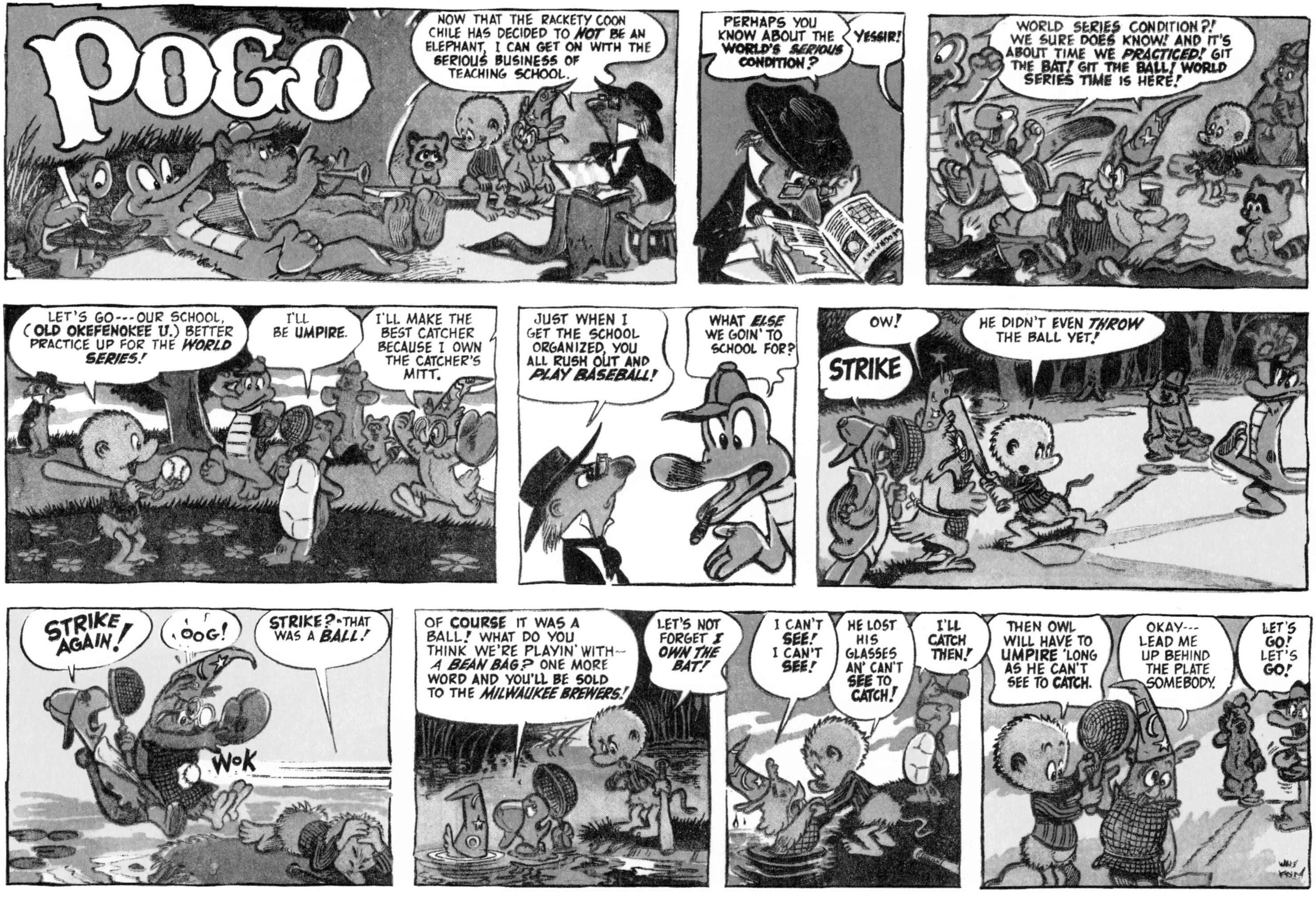
POGO
NOW THAT THE RACKETY COON CHILE HAS DECIDED TO NOT BE AN ELEPHANT, I CAN GET ON WITH THE SERIOUS BUSINESS OF TEACHING SCHOOL.
PERHAPS YOU KNOW ABOUT THE WORLD'S SERIOUS CONDITION?
YESSIR!
WORLD SERIES CONDITION?! WE SURE DOES KNOW! AND IT'S ABOUT TIME WE PRACTICED! GIT THE BAT! GIT THE BALL! WORLD SERIES TIME IS HERE!
LET'S GO---OUR SCHOOL, (OLD OKEFENOKEE U.) BETTER PRACTICE UP FOR THE WORLD SERIES!
I'LL BE UMPIRE.
I'LL MAKE THE BEST CATCHER BECAUSE I OWN THE CATCHER'S MITT.
JUST WHEN I GET THE SCHOOL ORGANIZED, YOU ALL RUSH OUT AND PLAY BASEBALL!
WHAT ELSE WE GOIN' TO SCHOOL FOR?
OW!
HE DIDN'T EVEN THROW THE BALL YET!
STRIKE
STRIKE AGAIN!
OOG!
STRIKE? THAT WAS A BALL!
WOK
OF COURSE IT WAS A BALL! WHAT DO YOU THINK WE'RE PLAYIN' WITH-- A BEAN BAG? ONE MORE WORD AND YOU'LL BE SOLD TO THE MILWAUKEE BREWERS!
LET'S NOT FORGET I OWN THE BAT!
I CAN'T SEE! I CAN'T SEE!
HE LOST HIS GLASSES AN' CAN'T SEE TO CATCH!
I'LL CATCH THEN!
THEN OWL WILL HAVE TO UMPIRE 'LONG AS HE CAN'T SEE TO CATCH.
OKAY--- LEAD ME UP BEHIND THE PLATE SOMEBODY.
LET'S GO! LET'S GO!

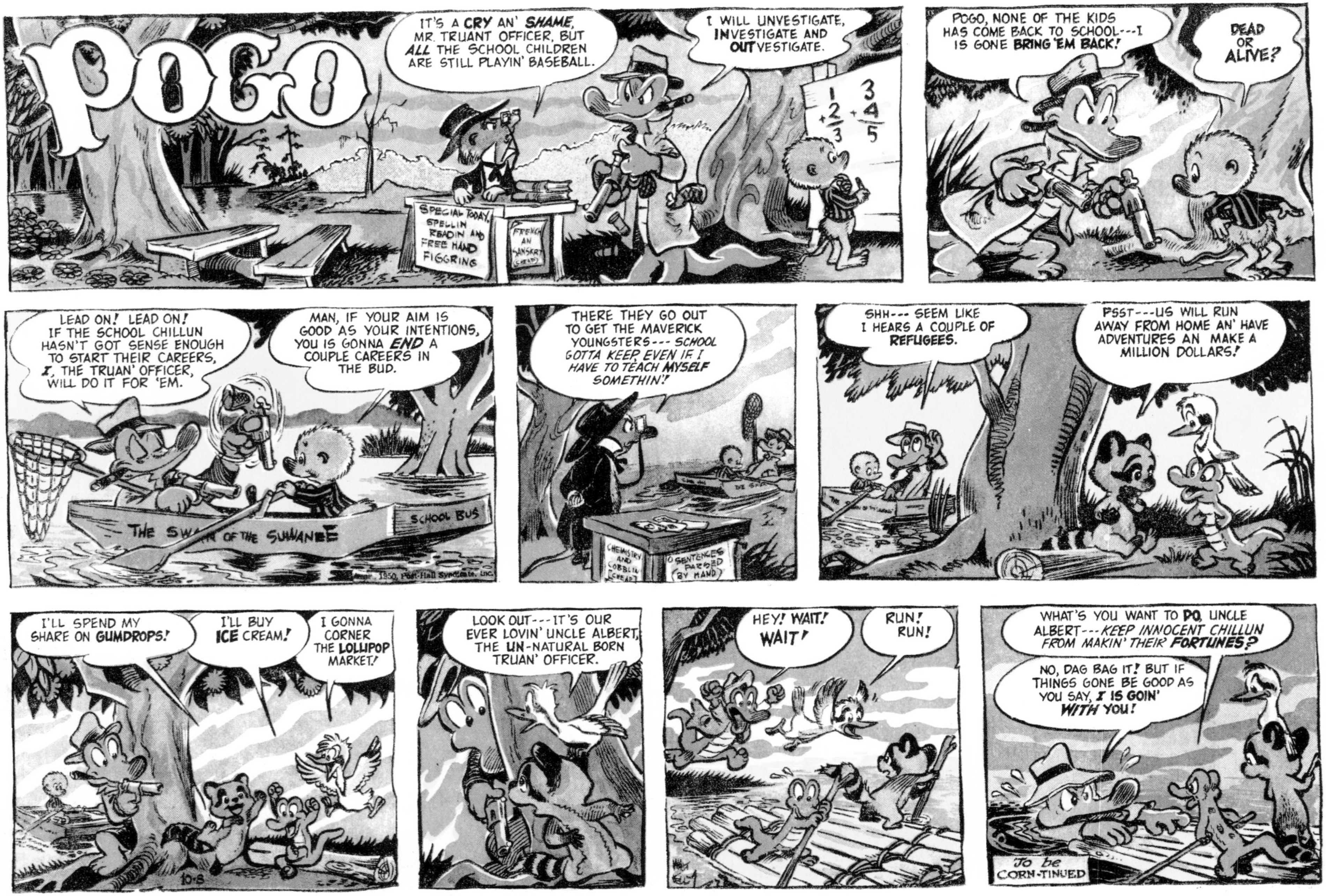
POGO
IT'S A CRY AN' SHAME, MR. TRUANT OFFICER, BUT ALL THE SCHOOL CHILDREN ARE STILL PLAYIN' BASEBALL.
I WILL UNVESTIGATE, INVESTIGATE AND OUTVESTIGATE.
SPECIAL TODAY, SPELLIN READIN AND FREE HAND FIGGRING
FRENCH AN SANSKRIT (CHEAP)
POGO, NONE OF THE KIDS HAS COME BACK TO SCHOOL---I IS GONE BRING 'EM BACK!
DEAD OR ALIVE?
LEAD ON! LEAD ON! IF THE SCHOOL CHILLUN HASN'T GOT SENSE ENOUGH TO START THEIR CAREERS, I, THE TRUAN' OFFICER, WILL DO IT FOR 'EM.
MAN, IF YOUR AIM IS GOOD AS YOUR INTENTIONS, YOU IS GONNA END A COUPLE CAREERS IN THE BUD.
SCHOOL BUS
THERE THEY GO OUT TO GET THE MAVERICK YOUNGSTERS--- SCHOOL GOTTA KEEP EVEN IF I HAVE TO TEACH MYSELF SOMETHIN'!
CHEMISTRY AND COBBLIN (CHEAP)
SENTENCES PARSED BY HAND
SHH--- SEEM LIKE I HEARS A COUPLE OF REFUGEES.
PSST---US WILL RUN AWAY FROM HOME AN' HAVE ADVENTURES AN MAKE A MILLION DOLLARS!
I'LL SPEND MY SHARE ON GUMDROPS!
I'LL BUY ICE CREAM!
I GONNA CORNER THE LOLLIPOP MARKET!
LOOK OUT---IT'S OUR EVER LOVIN' UNCLE ALBERT, THE UN-NATURAL BORN TRUAN' OFFICER.
HEY! WAIT! WAIT!
RUN! RUN!
WHAT'S YOU WANT TO DO, UNCLE ALBERT---KEEP INNOCENT CHILLUN FROM MAKIN' THEIR FORTUNES?
NO, DAG BAG IT! BUT IF THINGS GONE BE GOOD AS YOU SAY, I IS GOIN' WITH YOU!
To be CORN-TINUED

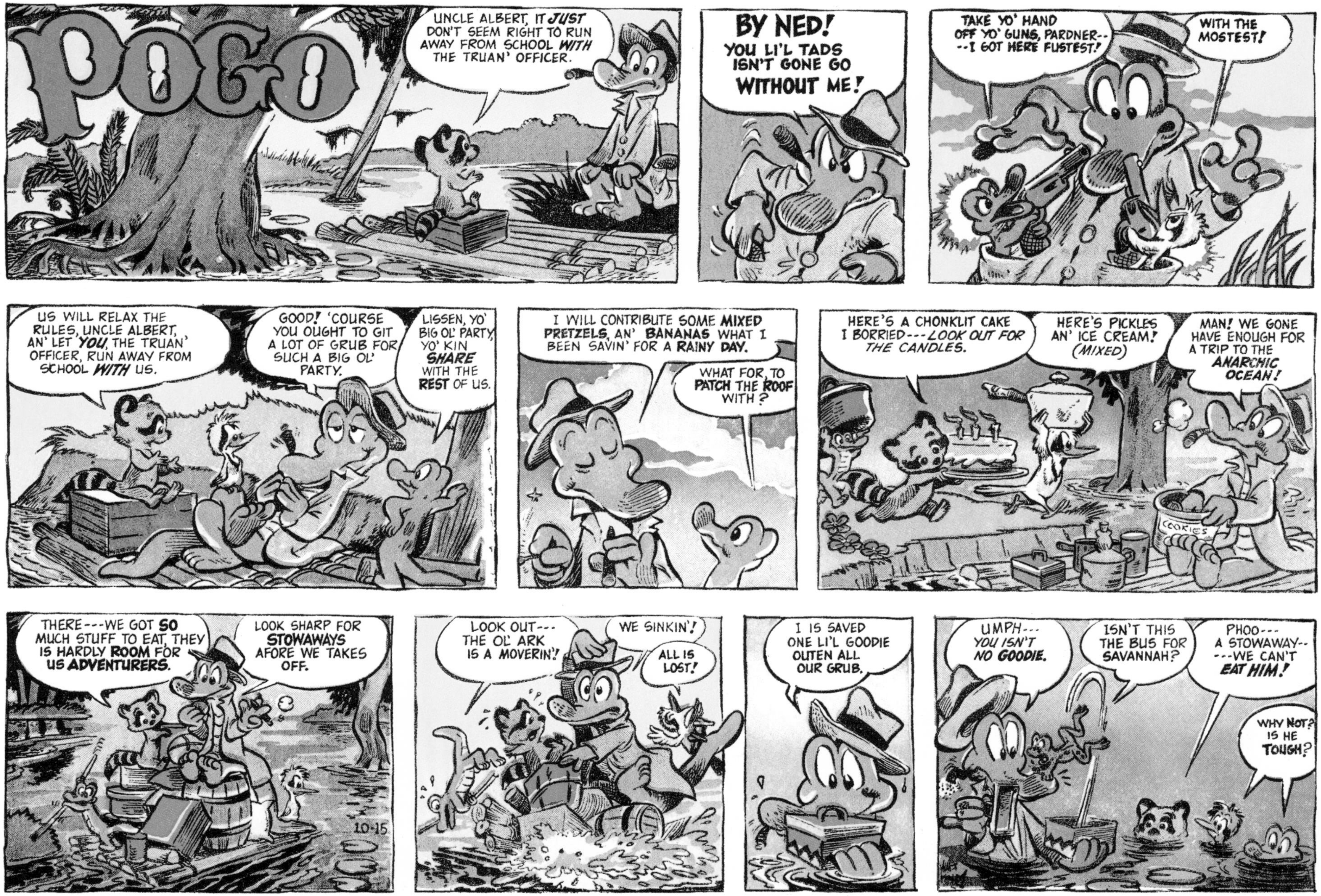
POGO
UNCLE ALBERT, IT JUST DON'T SEEM RIGHT TO RUN AWAY FROM SCHOOL WITH THE TRUAN' OFFICER.
BY NED! YOU LI'L TADS ISN'T GONE GO WITHOUT ME!
TAKE YO' HAND OFF YO' GUNS, PARDNER-- --I GOT HERE FUSTEST!
WITH THE MOSTEST!
US WILL RELAX THE RULES, UNCLE ALBERT, AN' LET YOU, THE TRUAN' OFFICER, RUN AWAY FROM SCHOOL WITH US.
GOOD! 'COURSE YOU OUGHT TO GIT A LOT OF GRUB FOR SUCH A BIG OL' PARTY.
LISSEN, YO' BIG OL' PARTY, YO' KIN SHARE WITH THE REST OF US.
I WILL CONTRIBUTE SOME MIXED PRETZELS, AN' BANANAS WHAT I BEEN SAVIN' FOR A RAINY DAY.
WHAT FOR, TO PATCH THE ROOF WITH?
HERE'S A CHONKLIT CAKE I BORRIED---LOOK OUT FOR THE CANDLES.
HERE'S PICKLES AN' ICE CREAM! (MIXED)
MAN! WE GONE HAVE ENOUGH FOR A TRIP TO THE ANARCHIC OCEAN!
COOKIES
THERE---WE GOT SO MUCH STUFF TO EAT, THEY IS HARDLY ROOM FOR US ADVENTURERS.
LOOK SHARP FOR STOWAWAYS AFORE WE TAKES OFF.
10-15
LOOK OUT--- THE OL' ARK IS A MOVERIN'!
WE SINKIN'!
ALL IS LOST!
I IS SAVED ONE LI'L GOODIE OUTEN ALL OUR GRUB.
UMPH--- YOU ISN'T NO GOODIE.
ISN'T THIS THE BUS FOR SAVANNAH?
PHOO--- A STOWAWAY-- ---WE CAN'T EAT HIM!
WHY NOT? IS HE TOUGH?

SUNDAY, OCTOBER 22, 1950

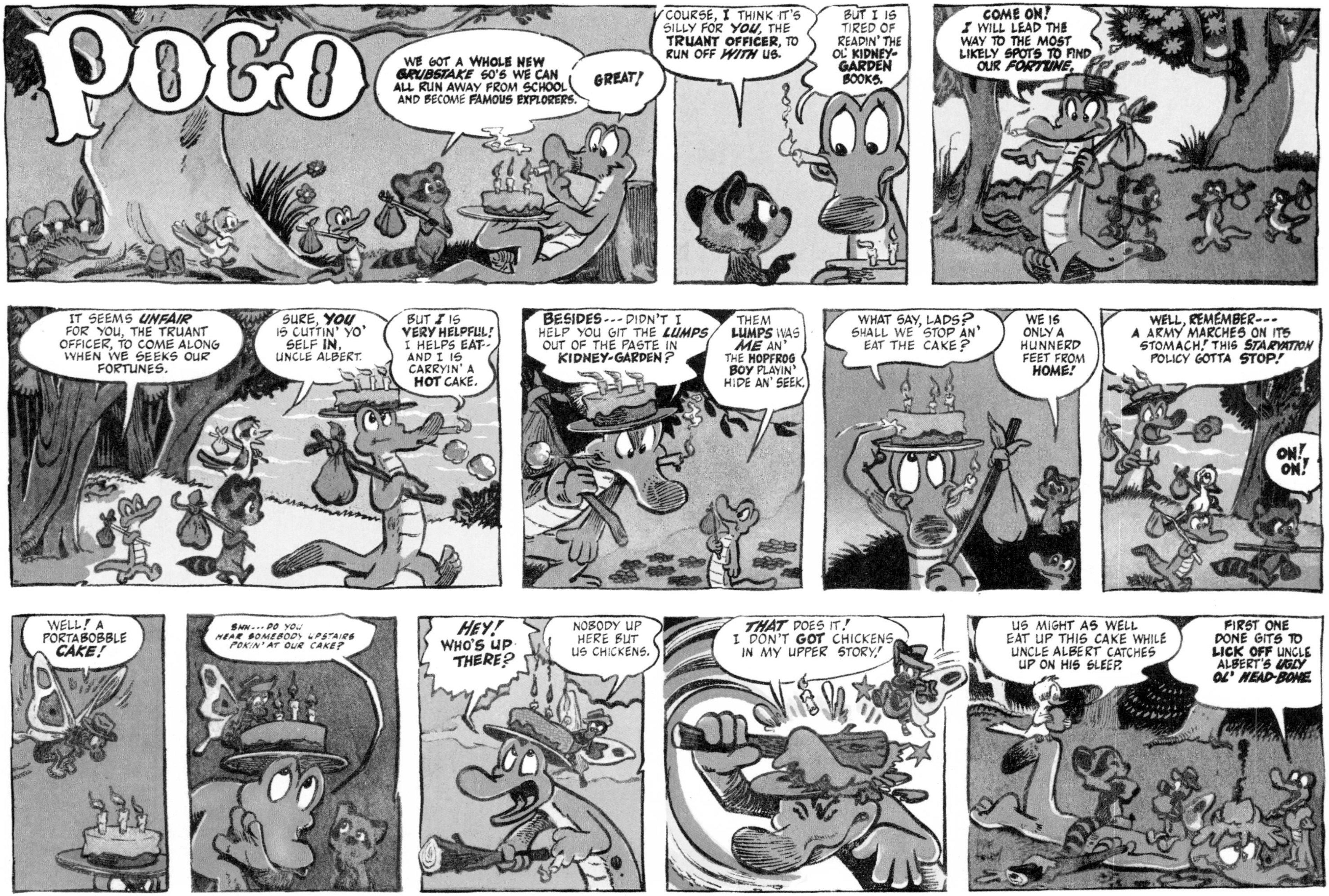

POGO
WE GOT A WHOLE NEW GRUBSTAKE SO'S WE CAN ALL RUN AWAY FROM SCHOOL AND BECOME FAMOUS EXPLORERS.
GREAT!
COURSE, I THINK IT'S SILLY FOR YOU, THE TRUANT OFFICER, TO RUN OFF WITH US.
BUT I IS TIRED OF READIN' THE OL' KIDNEY-GARDEN BOOKS.
COME ON! I WILL LEAD THE WAY TO THE MOST LIKELY SPOTS TO FIND OUR FORTUNE.
IT SEEMS UNFAIR FOR YOU, THE TRUANT OFFICER, TO COME ALONG WHEN WE SEEKS OUR FORTUNES.
SURE, YOU IS CUTTIN' YO' SELF IN, UNCLE ALBERT.
BUT I IS VERY HELPFUL! I HELPS EAT-- AND I IS CARRYIN' A HOT CAKE.
BESIDES--- DIDN'T I HELP YOU GIT THE LUMPS OUT OF THE PASTE IN KIDNEY-GARDEN?
THEM LUMPS WAS ME AN' THE HOPFROG BOY PLAYIN' HIDE AN' SEEK.
WHAT SAY, LADS? SHALL WE STOP AN' EAT THE CAKE?
WE IS ONLY A HUNNERD FEET FROM HOME!
WELL, REMEMBER--- A ARMY MARCHES ON ITS STOMACH! THIS STARVATION POLICY GOTTA STOP!
ON! ON!
WELL! A PORTABOBBLE CAKE!
SHH--- DO YOU HEAR SOMEBODY UPSTAIRS POKIN' AT OUR CAKE?
HEY! WHO'S UP THERE?
NOBODY UP HERE BUT US CHICKENS.
THAT DOES IT! I DON'T GOT CHICKENS IN MY UPPER STORY!
US MIGHT AS WELL EAT UP THIS CAKE WHILE UNCLE ALBERT CATCHES UP ON HIS SLEEP.
FIRST ONE DONE GITS TO LICK OFF UNCLE ALBERT'S UGLY OL' HEAD-BONE.

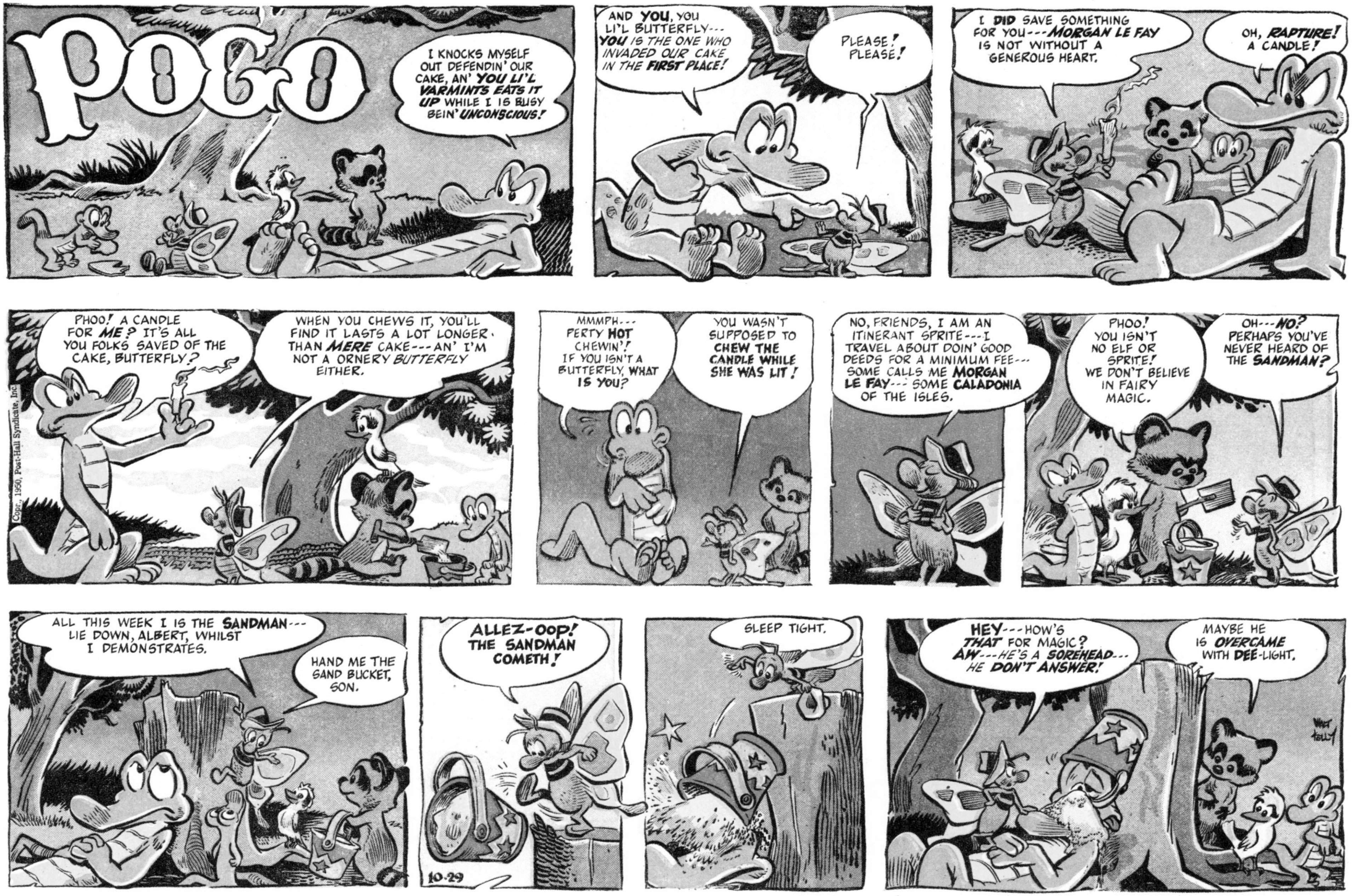
POGO
I KNOCKS MYSELF OUT DEFENDIN' OUR CAKE, AN' YOU LI'L VARMINTS EATS IT UP WHILE I IS BUSY BEIN' UNCONSCIOUS!
AND YOU, YOU LI'L BUTTERFLY--- YOU IS THE ONE WHO INVADED OUR CAKE IN THE FIRST PLACE!
PLEASE! PLEASE!
I DID SAVE SOMETHING FOR YOU---MORGAN LE FAY IS NOT WITHOUT A GENEROUS HEART.
OH, RAPTURE! A CANDLE!
PHOO! A CANDLE FOR ME? IT'S ALL YOU FOLKS SAVED OF THE CAKE, BUTTERFLY?
WHEN YOU CHEWS IT, YOU'LL FIND IT LASTS A LOT LONGER THAN MERE CAKE---AN' I'M NOT A ORNERY BUTTERFLY EITHER.
Copr. 1950, Post-Hall Syndicate, Inc.
MMMPH--- PERTY HOT CHEWIN'! IF YOU ISN'T A BUTTERFLY, WHAT IS YOU?
YOU WASN'T SUPPOSED TO CHEW THE CANDLE WHILE SHE WAS LIT!
NO, FRIENDS, I AM AN ITINERANT SPRITE---I TRAVEL ABOUT DOIN' GOOD DEEDS FOR A MINIMUM FEE--- SOME CALLS ME MORGAN LE FAY--- SOME CALADONIA OF THE ISLES.
PHOO! YOU ISN'T NO ELF OR SPRITE! WE DON'T BELIEVE IN FAIRY MAGIC.
OH---NO? PERHAPS YOU'VE NEVER HEARD OF THE SANDMAN?
ALL THIS WEEK I IS THE SANDMAN--- LIE DOWN, ALBERT, WHILST I DEMONSTRATES.
HAND ME THE SAND BUCKET, SON.
ALLEZ-OOP! THE SANDMAN COMETH!
10-29
SLEEP TIGHT.
HEY---HOW'S THAT FOR MAGIC? AW---HE'S A SOREHEAD--- HE DON'T ANSWER!
MAYBE HE IS OVERCAME WITH DEE-LIGHT.
WALT KELLY

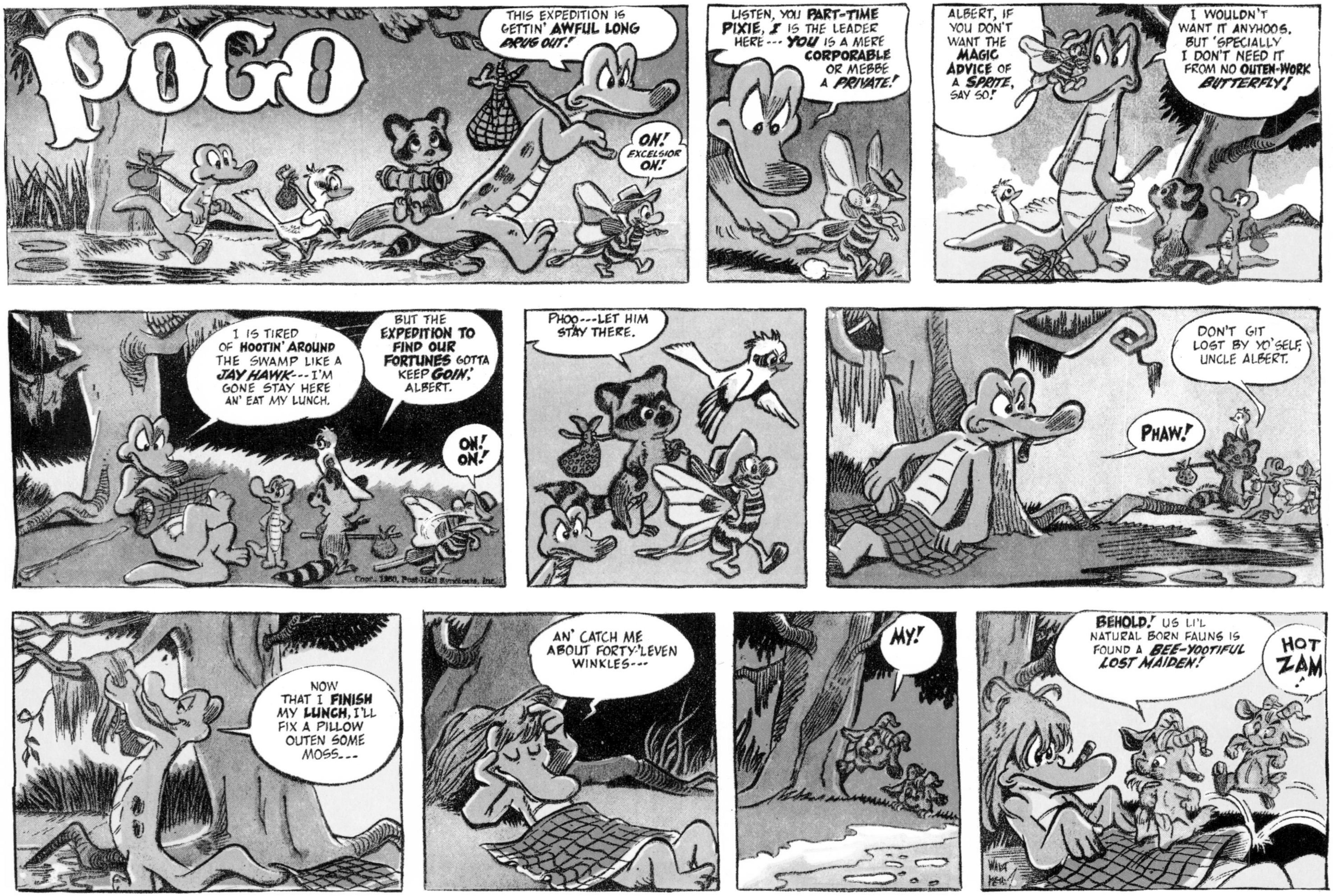
POGO
THIS EXPEDITION IS GETTIN' AWFUL LONG DRUG OUT!
ON! EXCELSIOR ON!
LISTEN, YOU PART-TIME PIXIE, I IS THE LEADER HERE--- YOU IS A MERE CORPORABLE OR MEBBE A PRIVATE!
ALBERT, IF YOU DON'T WANT THE MAGIC ADVICE OF A SPRITE, SAY SO!
I WOULDN'T WANT IT ANYHOOS. BUT 'SPECIALLY I DON'T NEED IT FROM NO OUTEN-WORK BUTTERFLY!
I IS TIRED OF HOOTIN' AROUND THE SWAMP LIKE A JAY HAWK--- I'M GONE STAY HERE AN' EAT MY LUNCH.
BUT THE EXPEDITION TO FIND OUR FORTUNES GOTTA KEEP GOIN', ALBERT.
ON! ON!
Copr. 1950, Post-Hall Syndicate, Inc.
PHOO---LET HIM STAY THERE.
DON'T GIT LOST BY YO'SELF, UNCLE ALBERT.
PHAW!
NOW THAT I FINISH MY LUNCH, I'LL FIX A PILLOW OUTEN SOME MOSS---
AN' CATCH ME ABOUT FORTY-'LEVEN WINKLES---
MY!
BEHOLD! US LI'L NATURAL BORN FAUNS IS FOUND A BEE-YOOTIFUL LOST MAIDEN!
HOT ZAM!

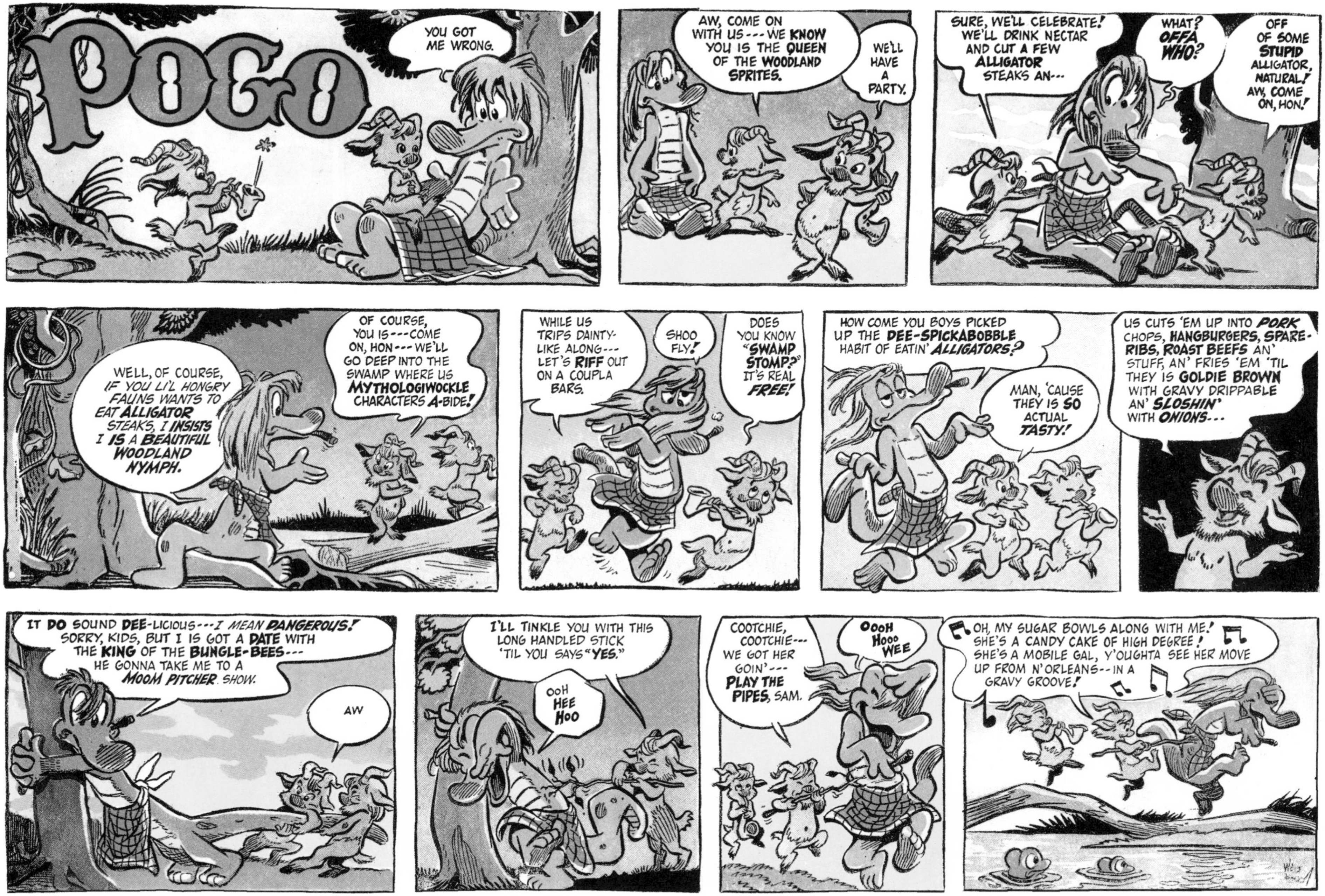
POGO
YOU GOT ME WRONG.
AW, COME ON WITH US--- WE KNOW YOU IS THE QUEEN OF THE WOODLAND SPRITES.
WE'LL HAVE A PARTY.
SURE, WE'LL CELEBRATE! WE'LL DRINK NECTAR AND CUT A FEW ALLIGATOR STEAKS AN---
WHAT? OFFA WHO?
OFF OF SOME STUPID ALLIGATOR, NATURAL! AW, COME ON, HON!
WELL, OF COURSE, IF YOU LI'L HONGRY FAUNS WANTS TO EAT ALLIGATOR STEAKS, I INSISTS I IS A BEAUTIFUL WOODLAND NYMPH.
OF COURSE, YOU IS---COME ON, HON--- WE'LL GO DEEP INTO THE SWAMP WHERE US MYTHOLOGIWOCKLE CHARACTERS A-BIDE!
WHILE US TRIPS DAINTY-LIKE ALONG--- LET'S RIFF OUT ON A COUPLA BARS.
SHOO FLY!
DOES YOU KNOW "SWAMP STOMP?" IT'S REAL FREE!
HOW COME YOU BOYS PICKED UP THE DEE-SPICKABOBBLE HABIT OF EATIN' ALLIGATORS?
MAN, 'CAUSE THEY IS SO ACTUAL TASTY!
US CUTS 'EM UP INTO PORK CHOPS, HANGBURGERS, SPARE-RIBS, ROAST BEEFS AN' STUFF, AN' FRIES 'EM 'TIL THEY IS GOLDIE BROWN WITH GRAVY DRIPPABLE AN' SLOSHIN' WITH ONIONS---
IT DO SOUND DEE-LICIOUS---I MEAN DANGEROUS! SORRY, KIDS, BUT I IS GOT A DATE WITH THE KING OF THE BUNGLE-BEES--- HE GONNA TAKE ME TO A MOOM PITCHER SHOW.
AW
I'LL TINKLE YOU WITH THIS LONG HANDLED STICK 'TIL YOU SAYS "YES."
OOH HEE HOO
COOTCHIE, COOTCHIE--- WE GOT HER GOIN'--- PLAY THE PIPES, SAM.
OOOH HOOO WEE
OH, MY SUGAR BOWLS ALONG WITH ME! SHE'S A CANDY CAKE OF HIGH DEGREE! SHE'S A MOBILE GAL, Y'OUGHTA SEE HER MOVE UP FROM N'ORLEANS--IN A GRAVY GROOVE!

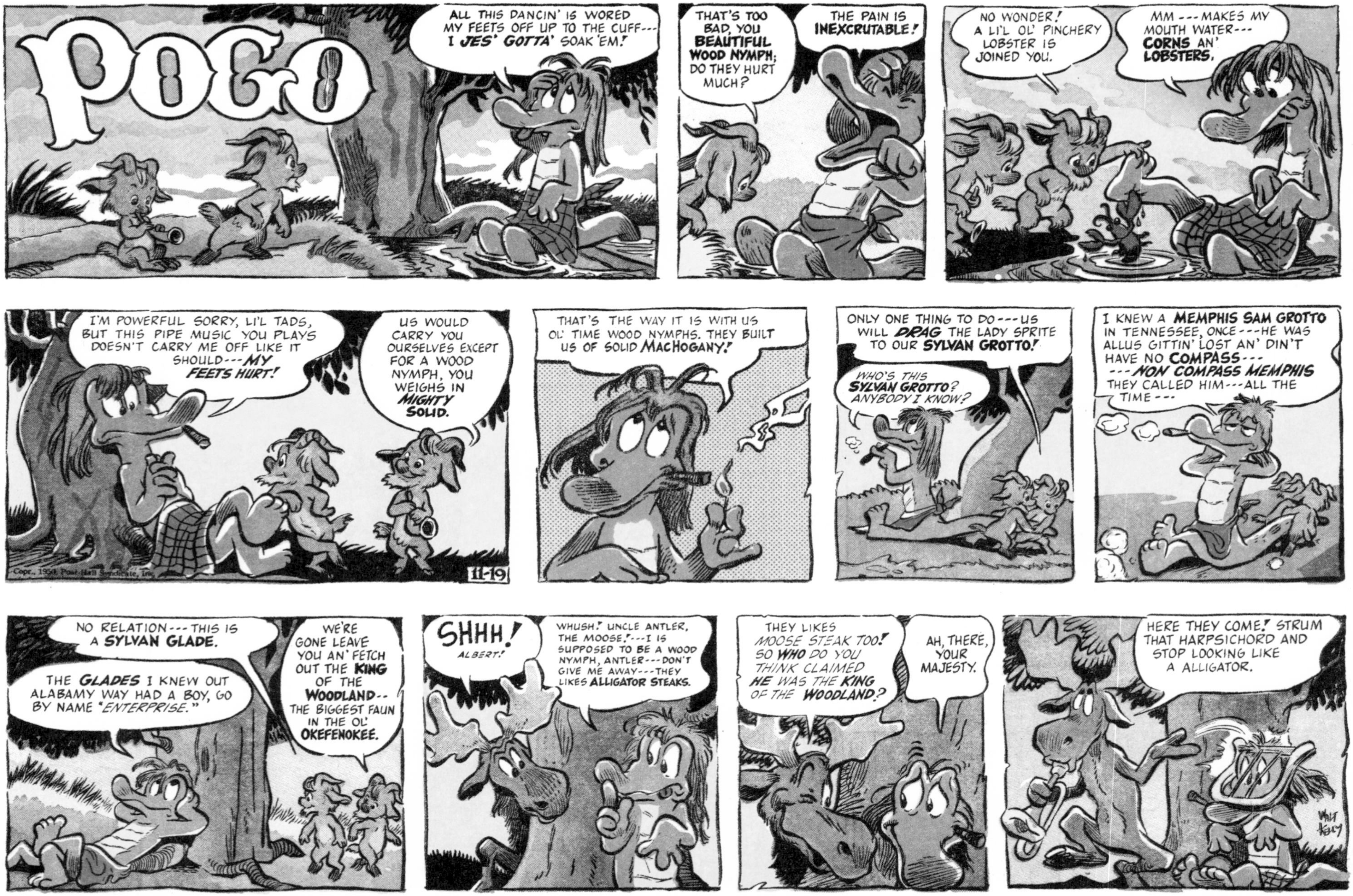
POGO
ALL THIS DANCIN' IS WORED MY FEETS OFF UP TO THE CUFF--- I JES' GOTTA' SOAK 'EM!
THAT'S TOO BAD, YOU BEAUTIFUL WOOD NYMPH; DO THEY HURT MUCH?
THE PAIN IS INEXCRUTABLE!
NO WONDER! A LI'L OL' PINCHERY LOBSTER IS JOINED YOU.
MM---MAKES MY MOUTH WATER--- CORNS AN' LOBSTERS.
I'M POWERFUL SORRY, LI'L TADS, BUT THIS PIPE MUSIC YOU PLAYS DOESN'T CARRY ME OFF LIKE IT SHOULD---MY FEETS HURT!
US WOULD CARRY YOU OURSELVES EXCEPT FOR A WOOD NYMPH, YOU WEIGHS IN MIGHTY SOLID.
11-19
THAT'S THE WAY IT IS WITH US OL' TIME WOOD NYMPHS. THEY BUILT US OF SOLID MACHOGANY!
ONLY ONE THING TO DO---US WILL DRAG THE LADY SPRITE TO OUR SYLVAN GROTTO!
WHO'S THIS SYLVAN GROTTO? ANYBODY I KNOW?
I KNEW A MEMPHIS SAM GROTTO IN TENNESSEE, ONCE---HE WAS ALLUS GITTIN' LOST AN' DIN'T HAVE NO COMPASS--- ---NON COMPASS MEMPHIS THEY CALLED HIM---ALL THE TIME---
NO RELATION---THIS IS A SYLVAN GLADE.
THE GLADES I KNEW OUT ALABAMY WAY HAD A BOY, GO BY NAME "ENTERPRISE."
WE'RE GONE LEAVE YOU AN' FETCH OUT THE KING OF THE WOODLAND-- THE BIGGEST FAUN IN THE OL' OKEFENOKEE.
SHHH! ALBERT!
WHUSH! UNCLE ANTLER, THE MOOSE!---I IS SUPPOSED TO BE A WOOD NYMPH, ANTLER---DON'T GIVE ME AWAY---THEY LIKES ALLIGATOR STEAKS.
THEY LIKES MOOSE STEAK TOO! SO WHO DO YOU THINK CLAIMED HE WAS THE KING OF THE WOODLAND?
AH, THERE, YOUR MAJESTY.
HERE THEY COME! STRUM THAT HARPSICHORD AND STOP LOOKING LIKE A ALLIGATOR.
WALT KELLY

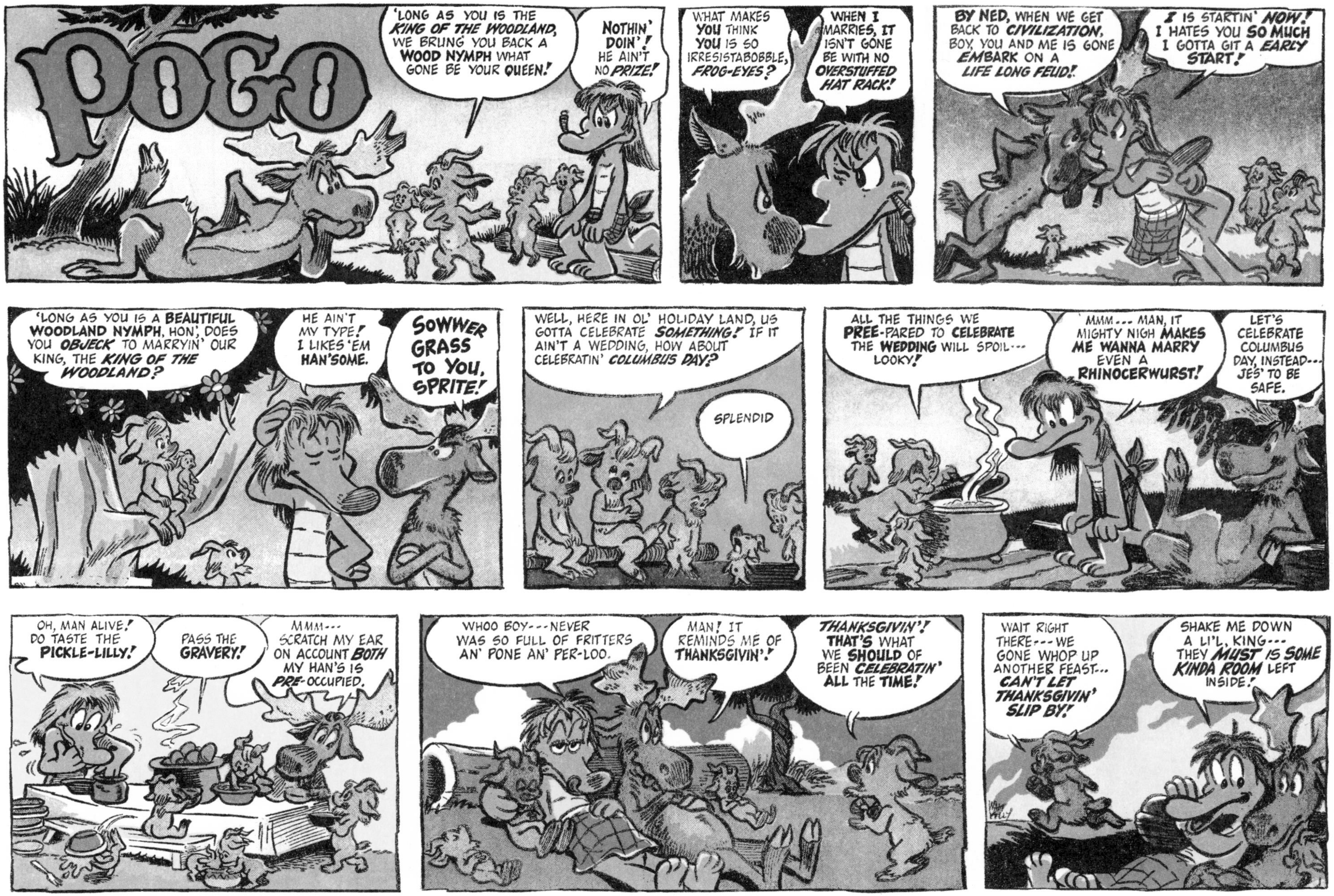
POGO
'LONG AS YOU IS THE KING OF THE WOODLAND, WE BRUNG YOU BACK A WOOD NYMPH WHAT GONE BE YOUR QUEEN!
NOTHIN' DOIN'! HE AIN'T NO PRIZE!
WHAT MAKES YOU THINK YOU IS SO IRRESISTABOBBLE, FROG-EYES?
WHEN I MARRIES, IT ISN'T GONE BE WITH NO OVERSTUFFED HAT RACK!
BY NED, WHEN WE GET BACK TO CIVILIZATION, BOY, YOU AND ME IS GONE EMBARK ON A LIFE LONG FEUD!
I IS STARTIN' NOW! I HATES YOU SO MUCH I GOTTA GIT A EARLY START!
'LONG AS YOU IS A BEAUTIFUL WOODLAND NYMPH, HON', DOES YOU OBJECK TO MARRYIN' OUR KING, THE KING OF THE WOODLAND?
HE AIN'T MY TYPE! I LIKES 'EM HAN'SOME.
SOWWER GRASS TO YOU, SPRITE!
WELL, HERE IN OL' HOLIDAY LAND, US GOTTA CELEBRATE SOMETHING! IF IT AIN'T A WEDDING, HOW ABOUT CELEBRATIN' COLUMBUS DAY?
SPLENDID
ALL THE THINGS WE PREE-PARED TO CELEBRATE THE WEDDING WILL SPOIL--- LOOKY!
MMM--- MAN, IT MIGHTY NIGH MAKES ME WANNA MARRY EVEN A RHINOCERWURST!
LET'S CELEBRATE COLUMBUS DAY, INSTEAD--- JES' TO BE SAFE.
OH, MAN ALIVE! DO TASTE THE PICKLE-LILLY!
PASS THE GRAVERY!
MMM--- SCRATCH MY EAR ON ACCOUNT BOTH MY HAN'S IS PRE-OCCUPIED.
WHOO BOY---NEVER WAS SO FULL OF FRITTERS AN' PONE AN' PER-LOO.
MAN! IT REMINDS ME OF THANKSGIVIN'!
THANKSGIVIN'! THAT'S WHAT WE SHOULD OF BEEN CELEBRATIN' ALL THE TIME!
WAIT RIGHT THERE--- WE GONE WHOP UP ANOTHER FEAST... CAN'T LET THANKSGIVIN' SLIP BY!
SHAKE ME DOWN A LI'L, KING--- THEY MUST IS SOME KINDA ROOM LEFT INSIDE!

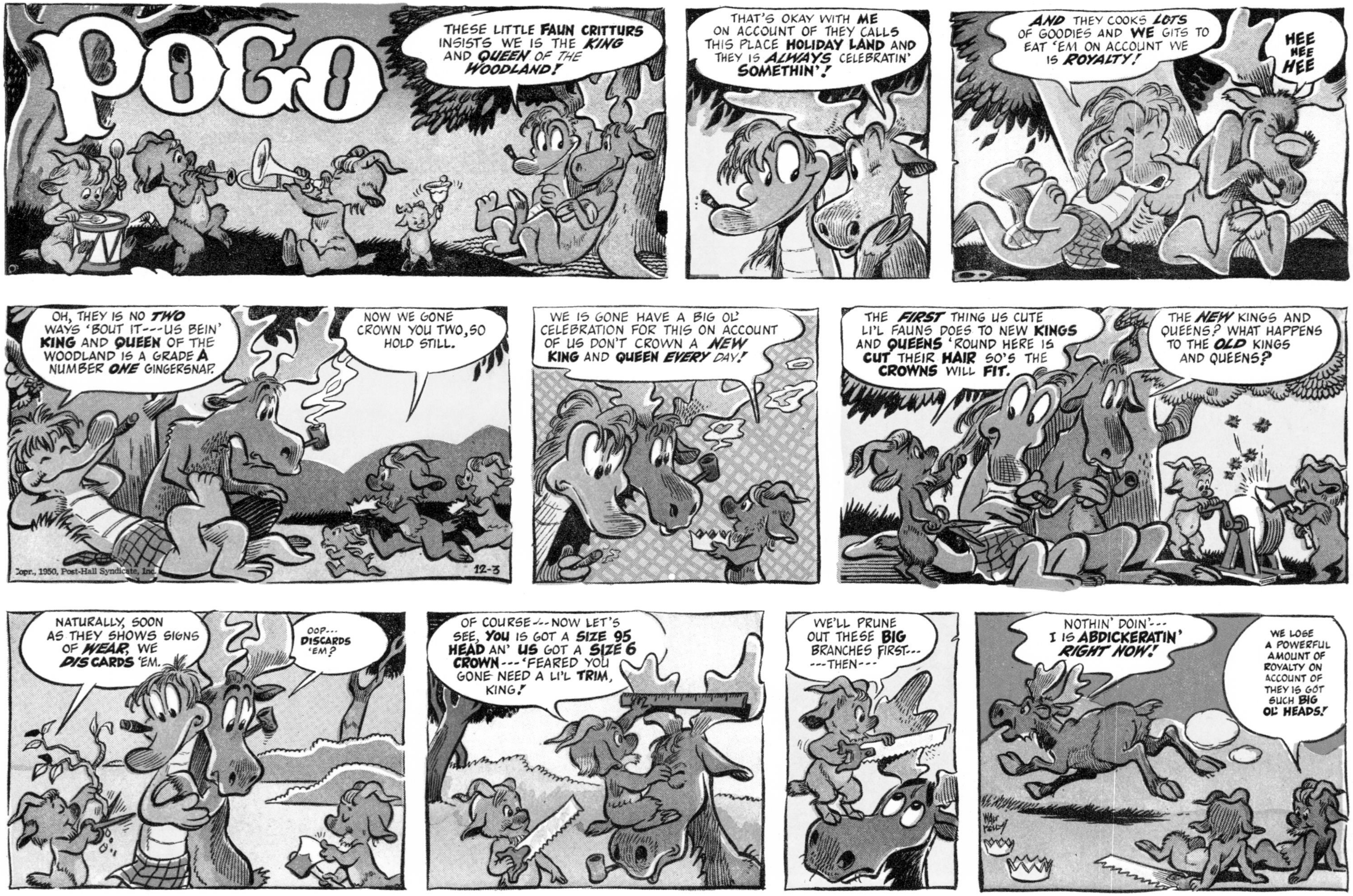
POGO
THESE LITTLE FAUN CRITTURS INSISTS WE IS THE KING AND QUEEN OF THE WOODLAND!
THAT'S OKAY WITH ME ON ACCOUNT OF THEY CALLS THIS PLACE HOLIDAY LAND AND THEY IS ALWAYS CELEBRATIN' SOMETHIN'!
AND THEY COOKS LOTS OF GOODIES AND WE GITS TO EAT 'EM ON ACCOUNT WE IS ROYALTY!
HEE HEE HEE
OH, THEY IS NO TWO WAYS 'BOUT IT---US BEIN' KING AND QUEEN OF THE WOODLAND IS A GRADE A NUMBER ONE GINGERSNAP.
NOW WE GONE CROWN YOU TWO, SO HOLD STILL.
Copr., 1950, Post-Hall Syndicate, Inc.
12-3
WE IS GONE HAVE A BIG OL' CELEBRATION FOR THIS ON ACCOUNT OF US DON'T CROWN A NEW KING AND QUEEN EVERY DAY!
THE FIRST THING US CUTE LI'L FAUNS DOES TO NEW KINGS AND QUEENS 'ROUND HERE IS CUT THEIR HAIR SO'S THE CROWNS WILL FIT.
THE NEW KINGS AND QUEENS? WHAT HAPPENS TO THE OLD KINGS AND QUEENS?
NATURALLY, SOON AS THEY SHOWS SIGNS OF WEAR, WE DISCARDS 'EM.
OOP... DISCARDS 'EM?
OF COURSE---NOW LET'S SEE, YOU IS GOT A SIZE 95 HEAD AN' US GOT A SIZE 6 CROWN---'FEARED YOU GONE NEED A LI'L TRIM, KING!
WE'LL PRUNE OUT THESE BIG BRANCHES FIRST--- ---THEN---
WALT KELLY
NOTHIN' DOIN'--- I IS ABDICKERATIN' RIGHT NOW!
WE LOSE A POWERFUL AMOUNT OF ROYALTY ON ACCOUNT OF THEY IS GOT SUCH BIG OL' HEADS!

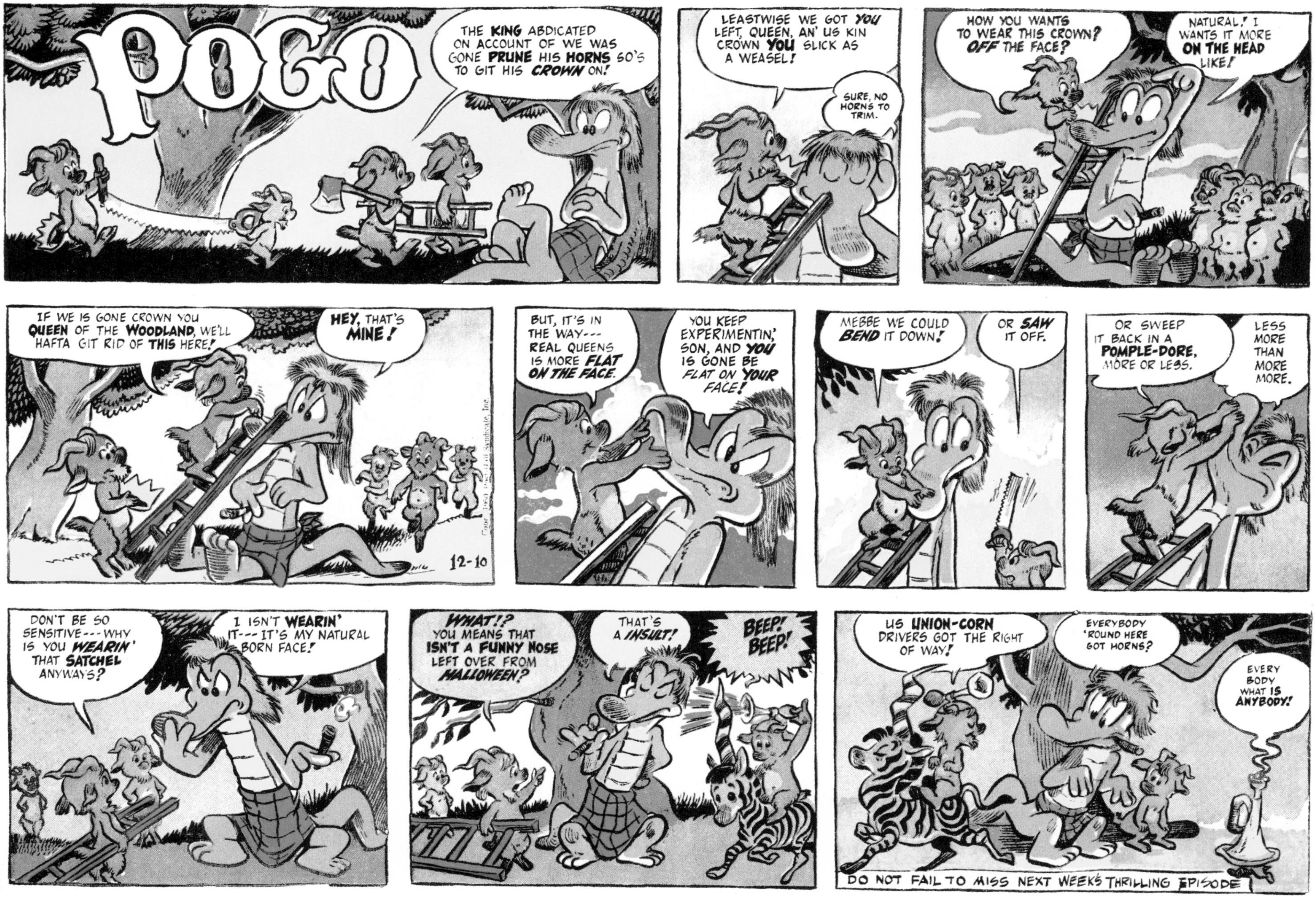
POGO
THE KING ABDICATED ON ACCOUNT OF WE WAS GONE PRUNE HIS HORNS SO'S TO GIT HIS CROWN ON!
LEASTWISE WE GOT YOU LEFT, QUEEN, AN' US KIN CROWN YOU SLICK AS A WEASEL!
SURE, NO HORNS TO TRIM.
HOW YOU WANTS TO WEAR THIS CROWN? OFF THE FACE?
NATURAL! I WANTS IT MORE ON THE HEAD LIKE!
IF WE IS GONE CROWN YOU QUEEN OF THE WOODLAND, WE'LL HAFTA GIT RID OF THIS HERE!
HEY, THAT'S MINE!
12-10
BUT, IT'S IN THE WAY--- REAL QUEENS IS MORE FLAT ON THE FACE.
YOU KEEP EXPERIMENTIN', SON, AND YOU IS GONE BE FLAT ON YOUR FACE!
MEBBE WE COULD BEND IT DOWN!
OR SAW IT OFF.
OR SWEEP IT BACK IN A POMPLE-DORE, MORE OR LESS.
LESS MORE THAN MORE MORE.
DON'T BE SO SENSITIVE---WHY IS YOU WEARIN' THAT SATCHEL ANYWAYS?
I ISN'T WEARIN' IT--- IT'S MY NATURAL BORN FACE!
WHAT!? YOU MEANS THAT ISN'T A FUNNY NOSE LEFT OVER FROM HALLOWEEN?
THAT'S A INSULT!
BEEP! BEEP!
US UNION-CORN DRIVERS GOT THE RIGHT OF WAY!
EVERYBODY 'ROUND HERE GOT HORNS?
EVERY BODY WHAT IS ANYBODY!
DO NOT FAIL TO MISS NEXT WEEK'S THRILLING EPISODE

SUNDAY, DECEMBER 17, 1950

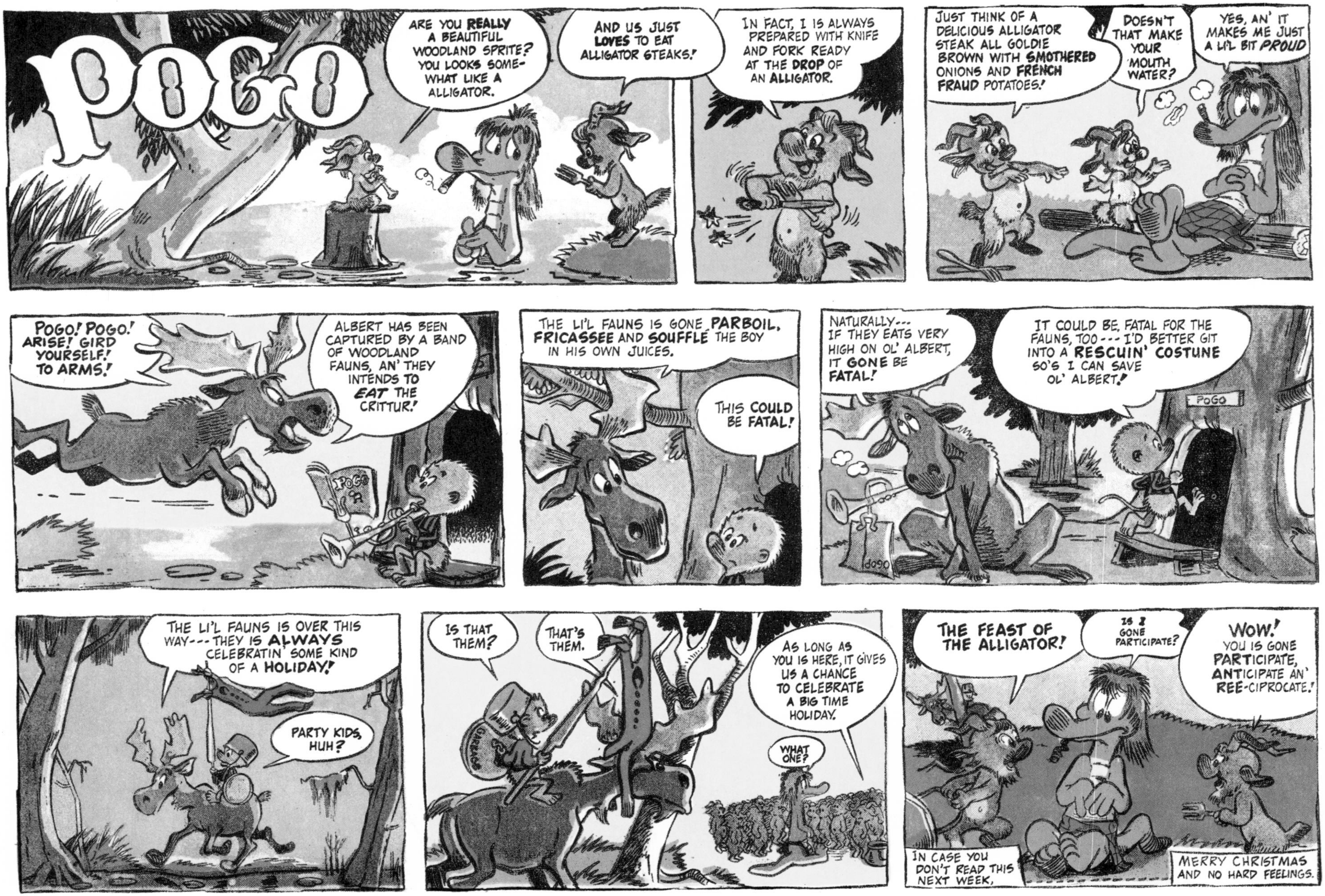

POGO
ARE YOU REALLY A BEAUTIFUL WOODLAND SPRITE? YOU LOOKS SOME-WHAT LIKE A ALLIGATOR.
AND US JUST LOVES TO EAT ALLIGATOR STEAKS!
IN FACT, I IS ALWAYS PREPARED WITH KNIFE AND FORK READY AT THE DROP OF AN ALLIGATOR.
JUST THINK OF A DELICIOUS ALLIGATOR STEAK ALL GOLDIE BROWN WITH SMOTHERED ONIONS AND FRENCH FRAUD POTATOES!
DOESN'T THAT MAKE YOUR MOUTH WATER?
YES, AN' IT MAKES ME JUST A LI'L BIT PROUD
POGO! POGO! ARISE! GIRD YOURSELF! TO ARMS!
ALBERT HAS BEEN CAPTURED BY A BAND OF WOODLAND FAUNS, AN' THEY INTENDS TO EAT THE CRITTUR!
POGO
THE LI'L FAUNS IS GONE PARBOIL, FRICASSEE AND SOUFFLÉ THE BOY IN HIS OWN JUICES.
THIS COULD BE FATAL!
NATURALLY--- IF THEY EATS VERY HIGH ON OL' ALBERT, IT GONE BE FATAL!
IT COULD BE FATAL FOR THE FAUNS, TOO --- I'D BETTER GIT INTO A RESCUIN' COSTUNE SO'S I CAN SAVE OL' ALBERT!
POGO
POGO
THE LI'L FAUNS IS OVER THIS WAY--- THEY IS ALWAYS CELEBRATIN' SOME KIND OF A HOLIDAY!
PARTY KIDS, HUH?
IS THAT THEM?
THAT'S THEM.
AS LONG AS YOU IS HERE, IT GIVES US A CHANCE TO CELEBRATE A BIG TIME HOLIDAY.
WHAT ONE?
THE FEAST OF THE ALLIGATOR!
IS I GONE PARTICIPATE?
WOW! YOU IS GONE PARTICIPATE, ANTICIPATE AN' REE-CIPROCATE!
IN CASE YOU DON'T READ THIS NEXT WEEK,
MERRY CHRISTMAS AND NO HARD FEELINGS.

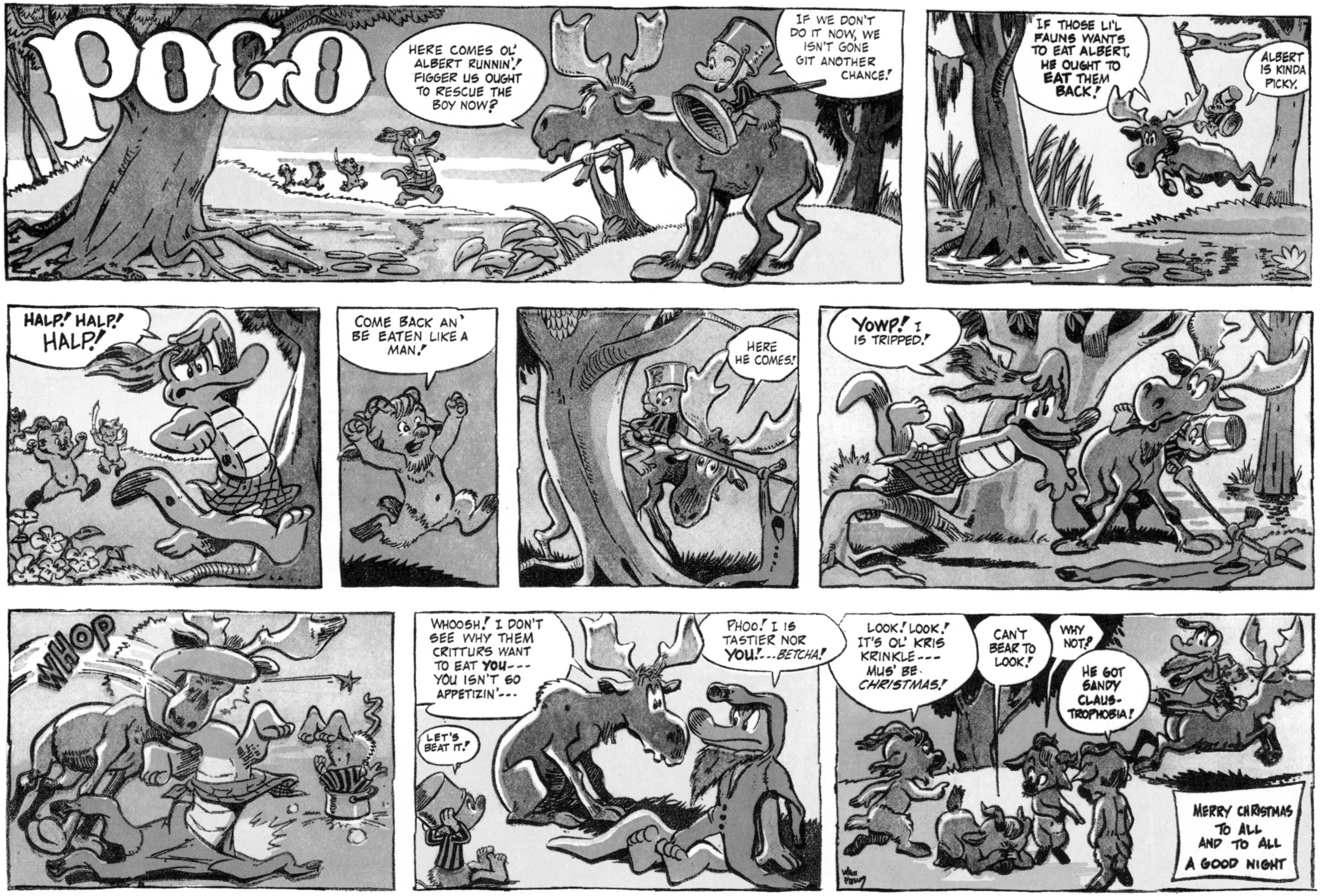
POGO
HERE COMES OL' ALBERT RUNNIN'! FIGGER US OUGHT TO RESCUE THE BOY NOW?
IF WE DON'T DO IT NOW, WE ISN'T GONE GIT ANOTHER CHANCE!
IF THOSE LI'L FAUNS WANTS TO EAT ALBERT, HE OUGHT TO EAT THEM BACK!
ALBERT IS KINDA PICKY.
HALP! HALP! HALP!
COME BACK AN' BE EATEN LIKE A MAN!
HERE HE COMES!
YOWP! I IS TRIPPED!
WHOP
WHOOSH! I DON'T SEE WHY THEM CRITTURS WANT TO EAT YOU--- YOU ISN'T SO APPETIZIN'---
PHOO! I IS TASTIER NOR YOU!...BETCHA!
LET'S BEAT IT!
LOOK! LOOK! IT'S OL' KRIS KRINKLE--- MUS' BE CHRISTMAS!
CAN'T BEAR TO LOOK!
WHY NOT?
HE GOT SANDY CLAUS-TROPHOBIA!
MERRY CHRISTMAS TO ALL AND TO ALL A GOOD NIGHT

SUNDAY, DECEMBER 31, 1950

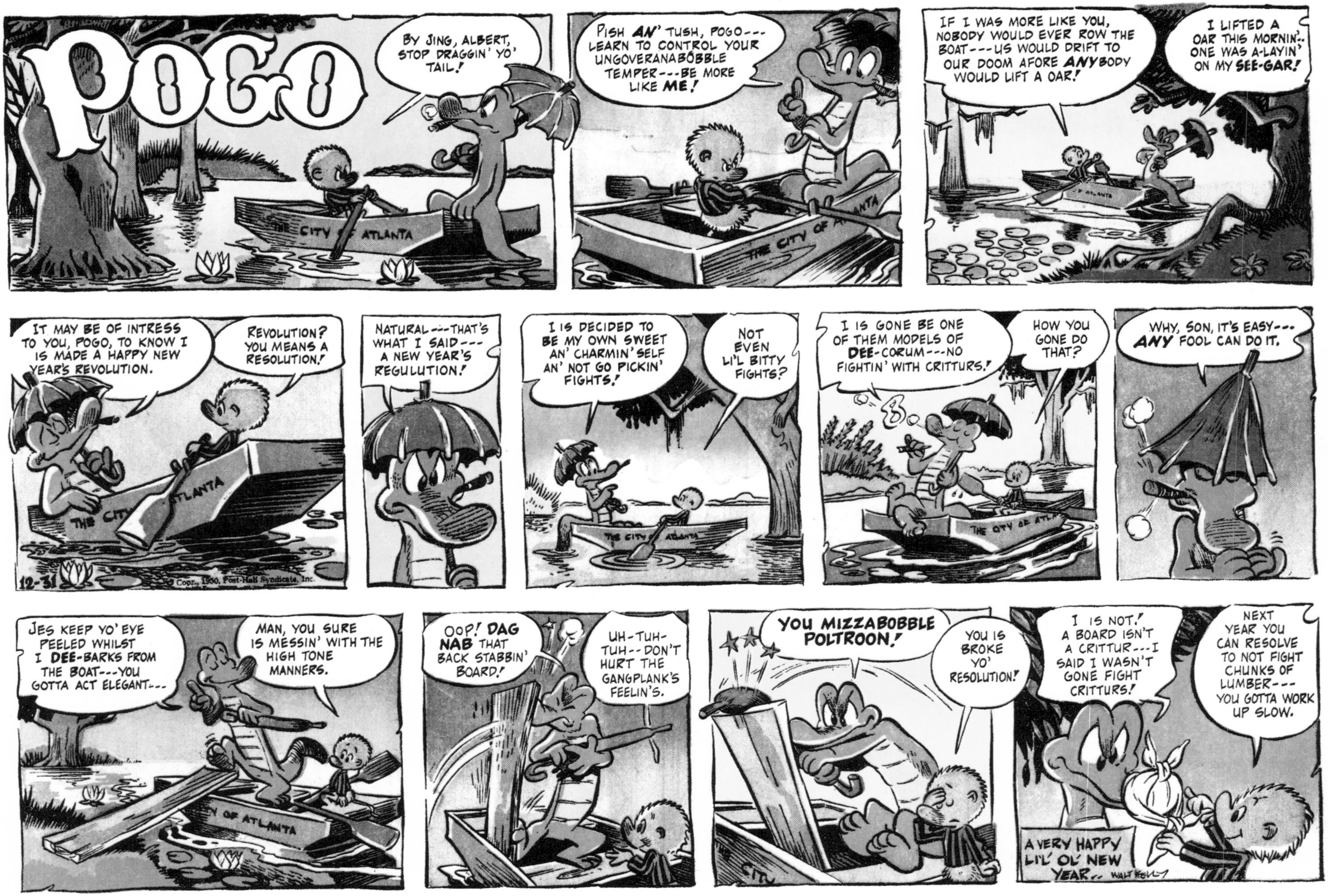

POGO
BY JING, ALBERT, STOP DRAGGIN' YO' TAIL!
THE CITY OF ATLANTA
PISH AN' TUSH, POGO--- LEARN TO CONTROL YOUR UNGOVERANABOBBLE TEMPER---BE MORE LIKE ME!
THE CITY OF ATLANTA
IF I WAS MORE LIKE YOU, NOBODY WOULD EVER ROW THE BOAT---US WOULD DRIFT TO OUR DOOM AFORE ANYBODY WOULD LIFT A OAR!
I LIFTED A OAR THIS MORNIN'. ONE WAS A-LAYIN' ON MY SEE-GAR!
IT MAY BE OF INTRESS TO YOU, POGO, TO KNOW I IS MADE A HAPPY NEW YEAR'S REVOLUTION.
REVOLUTION? YOU MEANS A RESOLUTION!
THE CITY OF ATLANTA
12-31
Copr., 1950, Post-Hall Syndicate, Inc.
NATURAL---THAT'S WHAT I SAID--- A NEW YEAR'S REGULUTION!
I IS DECIDED TO BE MY OWN SWEET AN' CHARMIN' SELF AN' NOT GO PICKIN' FIGHTS!
NOT EVEN LI'L BITTY FIGHTS?
THE CITY OF ATLANTA
I IS GONE BE ONE OF THEM MODELS OF DEE-CORUM---NO FIGHTIN' WITH CRITTURS!
HOW YOU GONE DO THAT?
THE CITY OF ATL
WHY, SON, IT'S EASY--- ANY FOOL CAN DO IT.
JES KEEP YO' EYE PEELED WHILST I DEE-BARKS FROM THE BOAT---YOU GOTTA ACT ELEGANT---
MAN, YOU SURE IS MESSIN' WITH THE HIGH TONE MANNERS.
Y OF ATLANTA
OOP! DAG NAB THAT BACK STABBIN' BOARD!
UH-TUH-TUH--DON'T HURT THE GANGPLANK'S FEELIN'S.
YOU MIZZABOBBLE POLTROON!
YOU IS BROKE YO' RESOLUTION!
I IS NOT! A BOARD ISN'T A CRITTUR---I SAID I WASN'T GONE FIGHT CRITTURS!
NEXT YEAR YOU CAN RESOLVE TO NOT FIGHT CHUNKS OF LUMBER--- YOU GOTTA WORK UP SLOW.
A VERY HAPPY LI'L' OL' NEW YEAR..
WALT KELLY

Cloudy, Rain

NEW YORK STAR

CITY EDITION

VOL. I. No. 112   (Copyright, 1948, New York *Star*, Inc.)   **TUESDAY, NOVEMBER 2, 1948**   **FIVE CENTS**

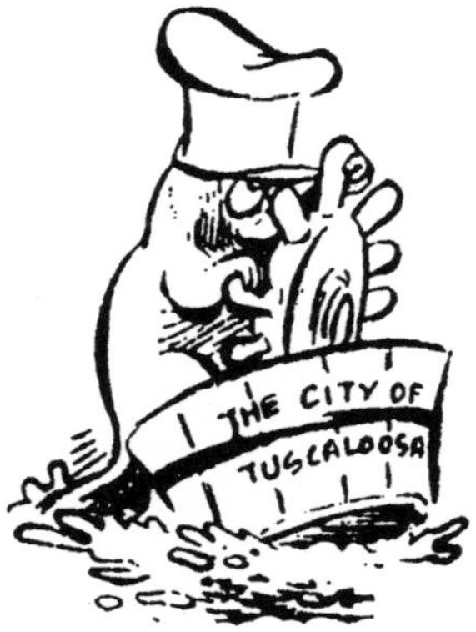
THE CITY OF
TUSCALOOSA

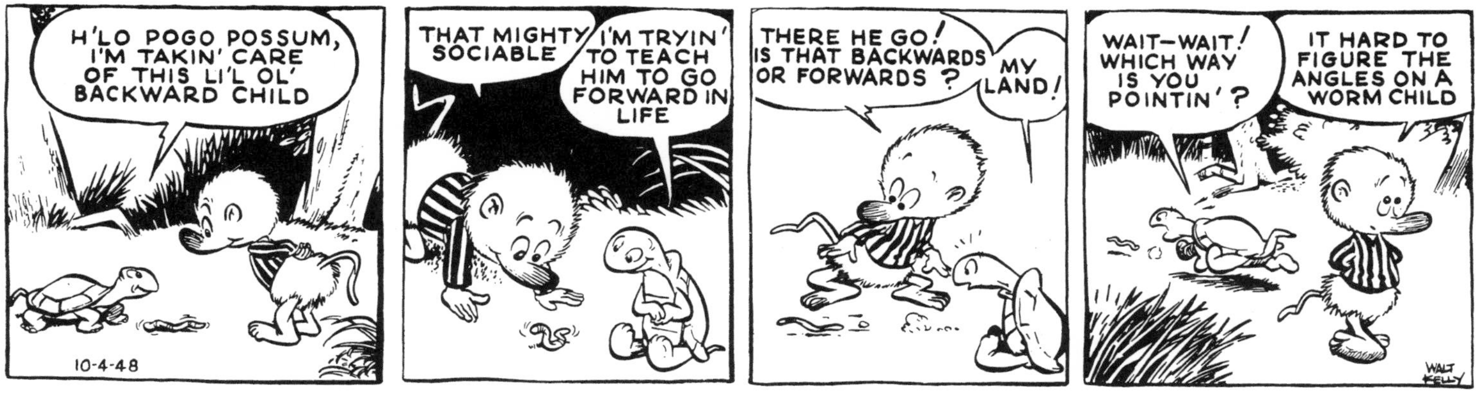
H'LO POGO POSSUM, I'M TAKIN' CARE OF THIS LI'L OL' BACKWARD CHILD
10-4-48
THAT MIGHTY SOCIABLE
I'M TRYIN' TO TEACH HIM TO GO FORWARD IN LIFE
THERE HE GO! IS THAT BACKWARDS OR FORWARDS ?
MY LAND!
WAIT—WAIT! WHICH WAY IS YOU POINTIN' ?
IT HARD TO FIGURE THE ANGLES ON A WORM CHILD
WALT KELLY

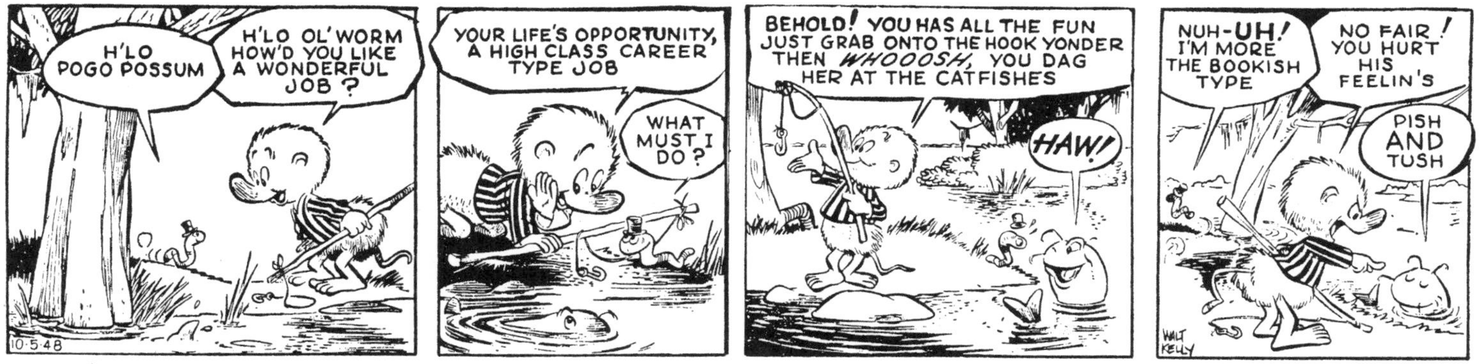
H'LO POGO POSSUM
H'LO OL' WORM HOW'D YOU LIKE A WONDERFUL JOB ?
10-5-48
YOUR LIFE'S OPPORTUNITY, A HIGH CLASS CAREER TYPE JOB
WHAT MUST I DO ?
BEHOLD! YOU HAS ALL THE FUN JUST GRAB ONTO THE HOOK YONDER THEN WHOOOSH, YOU DAG HER AT THE CATFISHES
HAW!
NUH-UH! I'M MORE THE BOOKISH TYPE
NO FAIR! YOU HURT HIS FEELIN'S
PISH AND TUSH
WALT KELLY

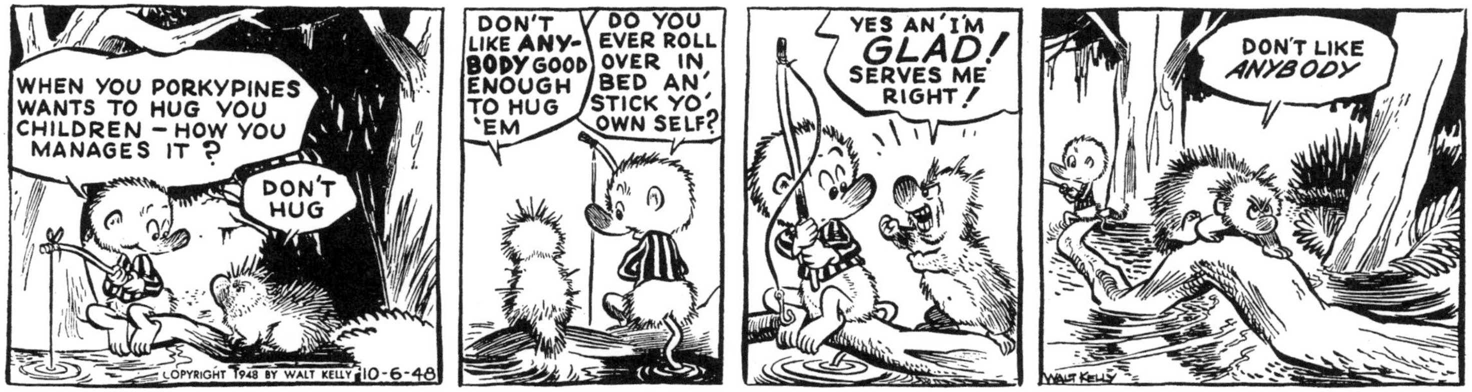
WHEN YOU PORKYPINES WANTS TO HUG YOU CHILDREN – HOW YOU MANAGES IT ?
DON'T HUG
COPYRIGHT 1948 BY WALT KELLY
10-6-48
DON'T LIKE ANYBODY GOOD ENOUGH TO HUG 'EM
DO YOU EVER ROLL OVER IN BED AN' STICK YO' OWN SELF?
YES AN' I'M GLAD! SERVES ME RIGHT!
DON'T LIKE ANYBODY
WALT KELLY

WHY SO GLUM POGO POSSUM?
H'LO CAP'N CHURCHY LAFEMME I CAN'T FIND NO CATFISH BAIT
COME ON IN YOUR HOUSE. GOT ANY BREAD?
POGO
MADE HER THIS MORNING
SQUEEZEY ROLL OUT SOME MORE BREAD BALL BAIT— THEN YOU AN' ME IS EQUAL PARTNERS IN YOUR FISHIN' BUSINESS
BUT THIS IS MY BREAD
JUST FOR THAT YOU KEEPS A COOL FIVE PER CENT OF THE FISH. THAT BAIT IS MADE OF YOUR BREAD AND MY BRAINS
YASSIR! IT ALL SOLID DOUGH
CITY OF NASHVILLE
WALT KELLY
10-7-48

THAT'S THIRTY-NINE FISHES YOU IS CAUGHT — SO HOW YOU LIKES TO HEAR A POEM, POGO?
CRUNCH HER OUT, CHURCHY
CITY OF NASHVILLE
"OH BY THE BAYOU BY YOU SIDE I WILL BUY YOU A BY-YOO-TIFFLE BOUQUET, MAME."
MAME? WHAT SHE DOIN' IN THERE?
CITY OF NASHVILLE
LET'S US LEAVE MAME'S NAME OUT OF THIS HERE!
I WILL LEAVE BOTH OF YOU OUT---YOU IS SCARE THE CAT-FISHES
I'M NOT GONE LET OL' MAME BE INSULT FORE AN' AFT---- --GOOD DAY!
36-37-38-39 RIGHT
PERCHANCE I WAS HASTY
WALT KELLY
10-8-48

DON'T SEEM LIKE OL' TURTLE LEFT ME MY FAIR SHARE
H'LO POGO POSSUM
HOWLAND OWL. YOU'RE A SCIENTIST IS THIS HERE FISH FIVE PER CENT OF THIRTY-NINE?
MM-I LEFT MY SLIDE RULE IN MY SUNDAY PANTS- ---LESSEE---HEY, IS YOU FIVE PER CENT?
HE DON'T SAY— BUT MY PROFESSIONAL SUSPICION IS HE'S A LI'L SKIMPY
A SKIMPY? ALL THE TIME I FIGURES HE'S A CATFISH!
WALT KELLY
10-10-48

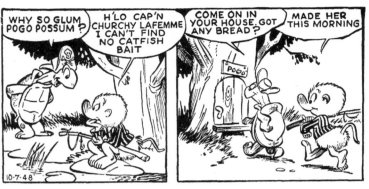

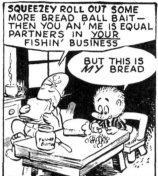

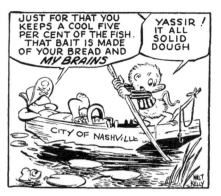

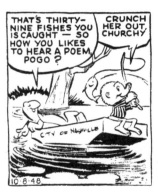

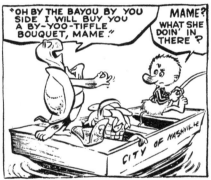

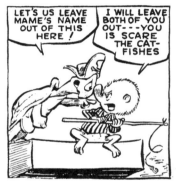

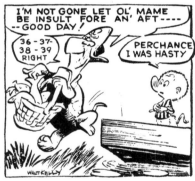

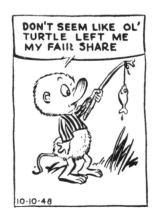

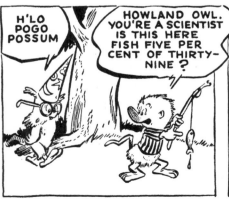

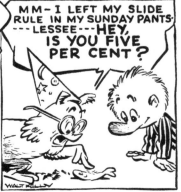

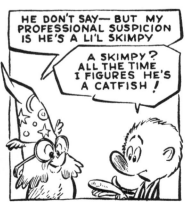

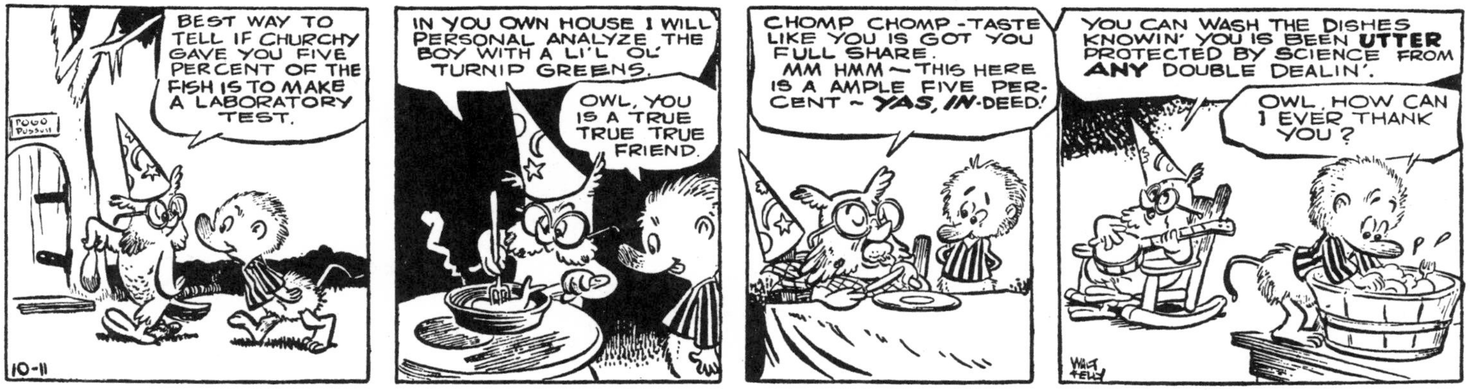
BEST WAY TO TELL IF CHURCHY GAVE YOU FIVE PERCENT OF THE FISH IS TO MAKE A LABORATORY TEST.
POGO POSSUM
10-11
IN YOU OWN HOUSE I WILL PERSONAL ANALYZE THE BOY WITH A LI'L OL' TURNIP GREENS.
OWL, YOU IS A TRUE TRUE TRUE FRIEND.
CHOMP CHOMP - TASTE LIKE YOU IS GOT YOU FULL SHARE.
MM HMM ~ THIS HERE IS A AMPLE FIVE PER-CENT ~ YAS, IN-DEED!
YOU CAN WASH THE DISHES KNOWIN' YOU IS BEEN UTTER PROTECTED BY SCIENCE FROM ANY DOUBLE DEALIN'.
OWL, HOW CAN I EVER THANK YOU?
WALT KELLY

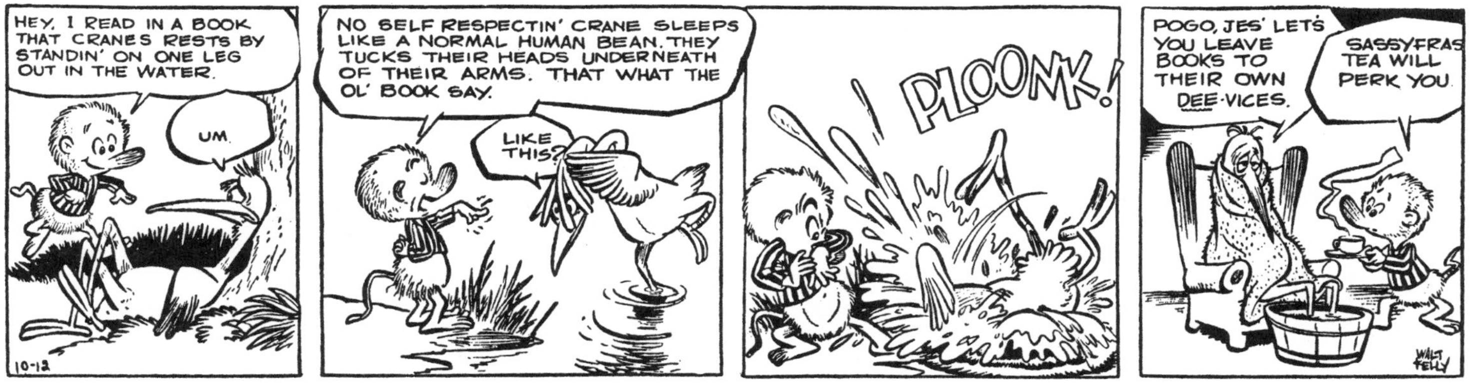
HEY, I READ IN A BOOK THAT CRANES RESTS BY STANDIN' ON ONE LEG OUT IN THE WATER.
UM.
10-12
NO SELF RESPECTIN' CRANE SLEEPS LIKE A NORMAL HUMAN BEAN. THEY TUCKS THEIR HEADS UNDERNEATH OF THEIR ARMS. THAT WHAT THE OL' BOOK SAY.
LIKE THIS?
PLOONK!
POGO, JES' LETS YOU LEAVE BOOKS TO THEIR OWN DEE-VICES.
SASSYFRAS TEA WILL PERK YOU.
WALT KELLY

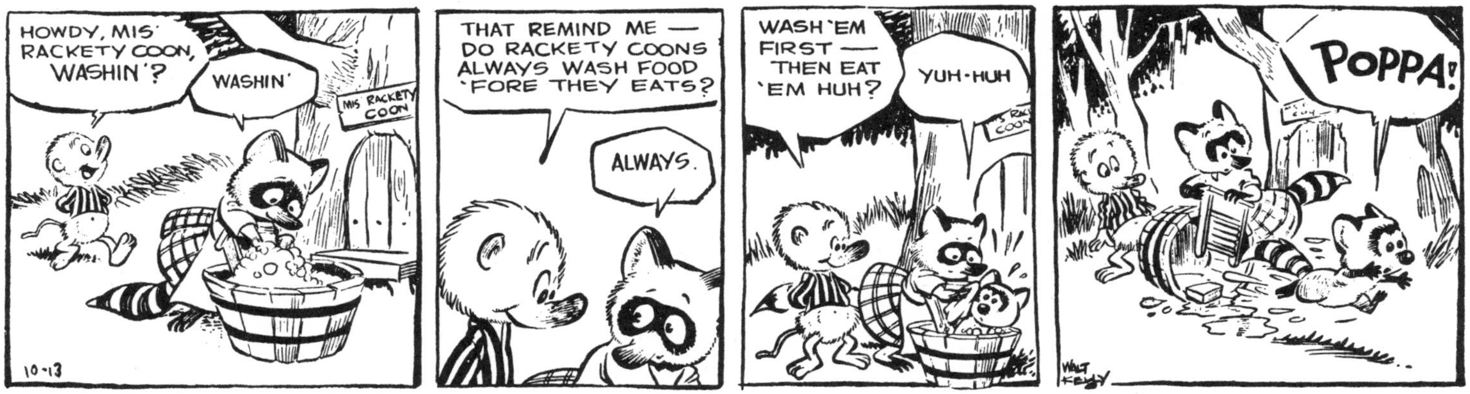
HOWDY, MIS' RACKETY COON, WASHIN'?
WASHIN'
MIS RACKETY COON
10-13
THAT REMIND ME — DO RACKETY COONS ALWAYS WASH FOOD 'FORE THEY EATS?
ALWAYS.
WASH 'EM FIRST — THEN EAT 'EM HUH?
YUH-HUH
POPPA!
WALT KELLY

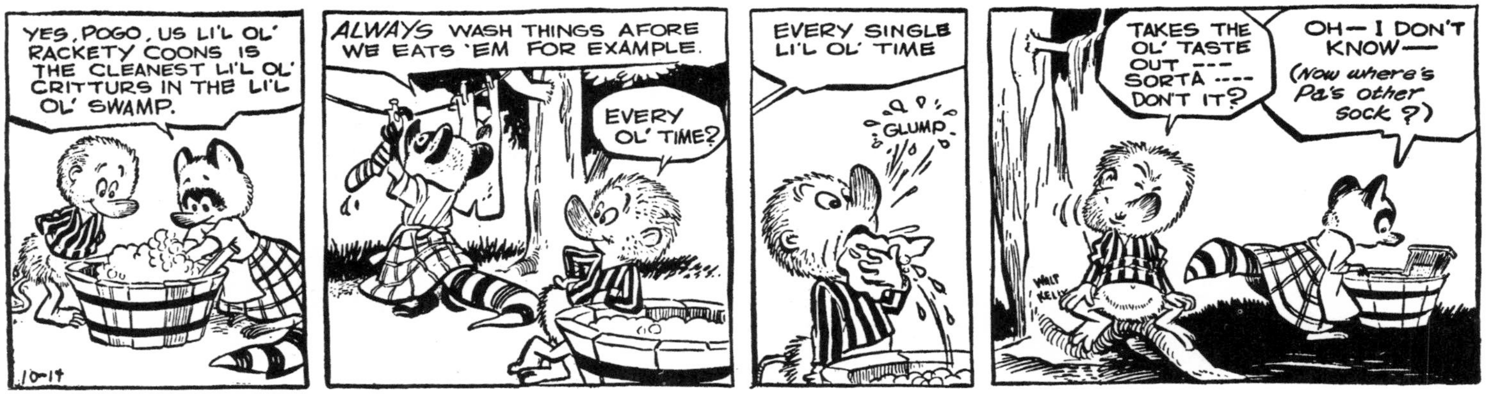
YES, POGO, US LI'L OL' RACKETY COONS IS THE CLEANEST LI'L OL' CRITTURS IN THE LI'L OL' SWAMP.
10-14
ALWAYS WASH THINGS AFORE WE EATS 'EM FOR EXAMPLE.
EVERY OL' TIME?
EVERY SINGLE LI'L OL' TIME
GLUMP
TAKES THE OL' TASTE OUT --- SORTA ---- DON'T IT?
OH — I DON'T KNOW —
(Now where's Pa's other sock?)
WALT KELLY

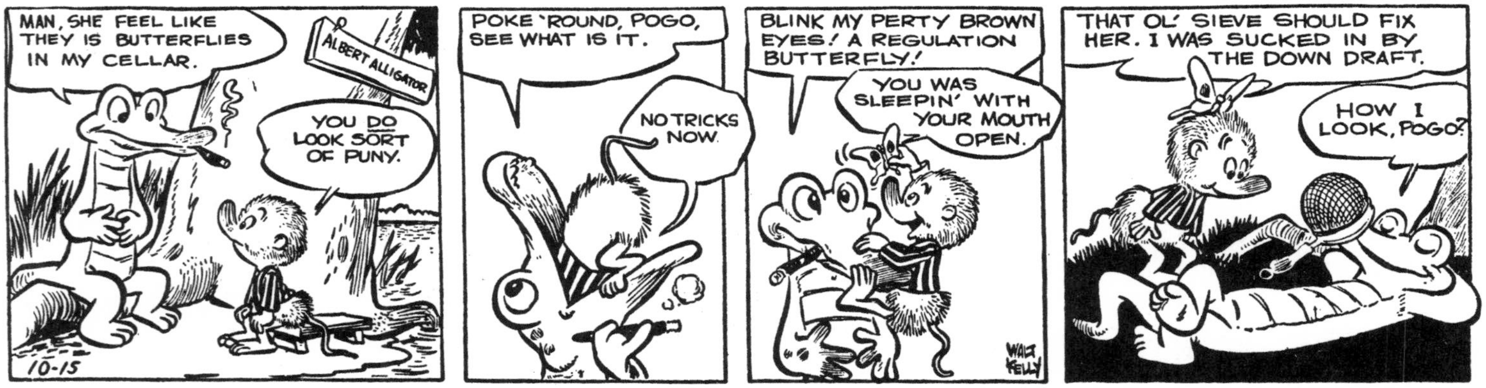
MAN, SHE FEEL LIKE THEY IS BUTTERFLIES IN MY CELLAR.
ALBERT ALLIGATOR
YOU DO LOOK SORT OF PUNY.
10-15
POKE 'ROUND, POGO, SEE WHAT IS IT.
NO TRICKS NOW.
BLINK MY PERTY BROWN EYES! A REGULATION BUTTERFLY!
YOU WAS SLEEPIN' WITH YOUR MOUTH OPEN.
WALT KELLY
THAT OL' SIEVE SHOULD FIX HER. I WAS SUCKED IN BY THE DOWN DRAFT.
HOW I LOOK, POGO?

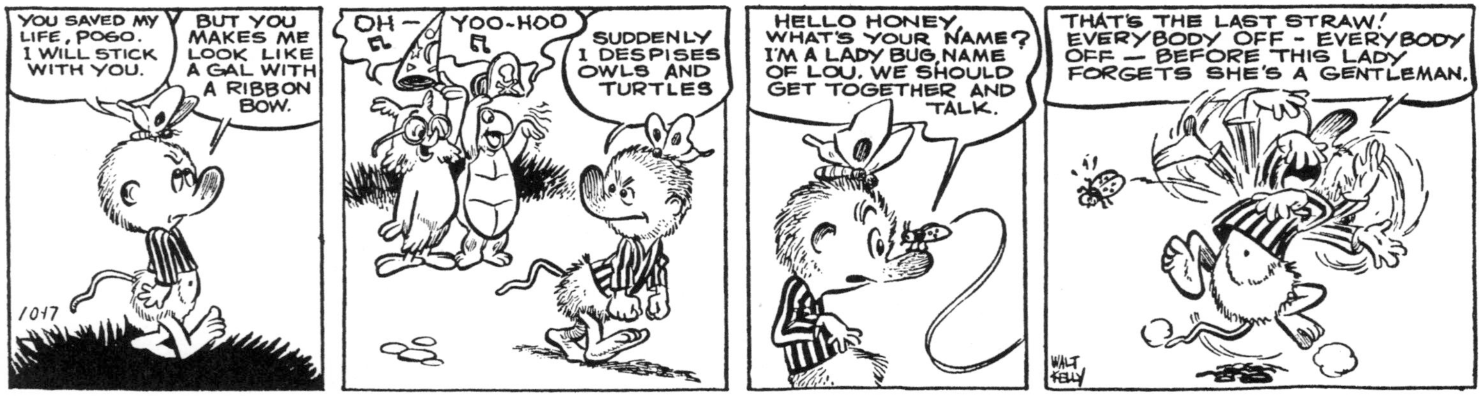
YOU SAVED MY LIFE, POGO. I WILL STICK WITH YOU.
BUT YOU MAKES ME LOOK LIKE A GAL WITH A RIBBON BOW.
1017
OH —
YOO-HOO
SUDDENLY I DESPISES OWLS AND TURTLES
HELLO HONEY, WHAT'S YOUR NAME? I'M A LADY BUG NAME OF LOU. WE SHOULD GET TOGETHER AND TALK.
THAT'S THE LAST STRAW! EVERYBODY OFF - EVERYBODY OFF — BEFORE THIS LADY FORGETS SHE'S A GENTLEMAN.
WALT KELLY

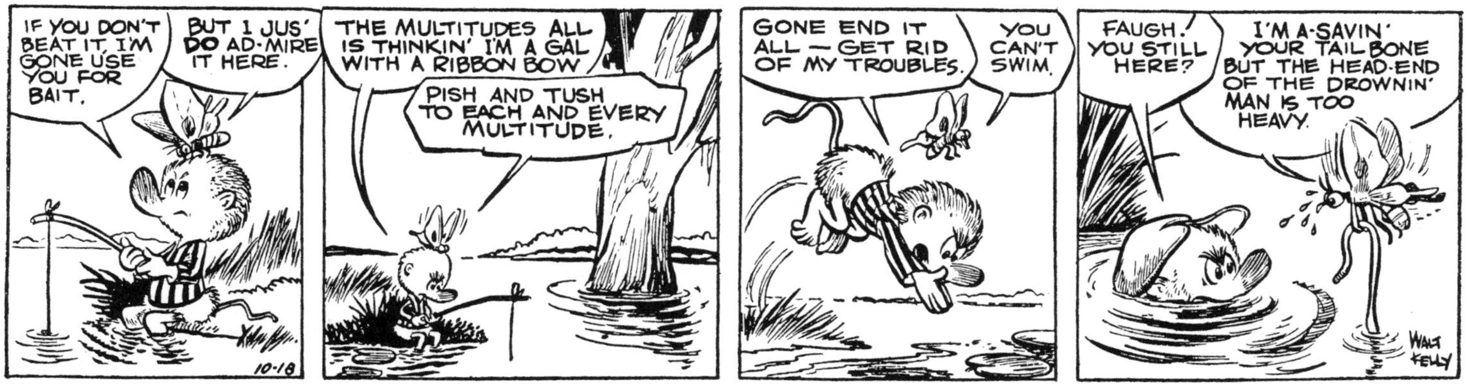
IF YOU DON'T BEAT IT, I'M GONE USE YOU FOR BAIT.
BUT I JUS' **DO** AD-MIRE IT HERE.
10-18
THE MULTITUDES ALL IS THINKIN' I'M A GAL WITH A RIBBON BOW
PISH AND TUSH TO EACH AND EVERY MULTITUDE.
GONE END IT ALL — GET RID OF MY TROUBLES.
YOU CAN'T SWIM.
FAUGH! YOU STILL HERE?
I'M A-SAVIN' YOUR TAIL BONE BUT THE HEAD-END OF THE DROWNIN' MAN IS TOO HEAVY.
WALT KELLY

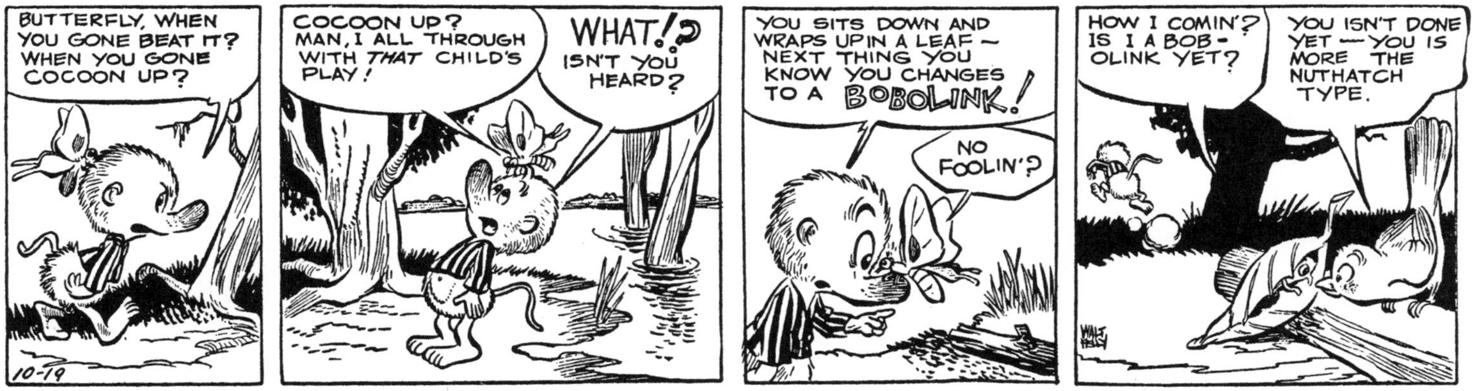
BUTTERFLY, WHEN YOU GONE BEAT IT? WHEN YOU GONE COCOON UP?
10-19
COCOON UP? MAN, I ALL THROUGH WITH *THAT* CHILD'S PLAY!
WHAT!? ISN'T YOU HEARD?
YOU SITS DOWN AND WRAPS UP IN A LEAF — NEXT THING YOU KNOW YOU CHANGES TO A BOBOLINK!
NO FOOLIN'?
WALT KELLY
HOW I COMIN'? IS I A BOB-OLINK YET?
YOU ISN'T DONE YET — YOU IS MORE THE NUTHATCH TYPE.

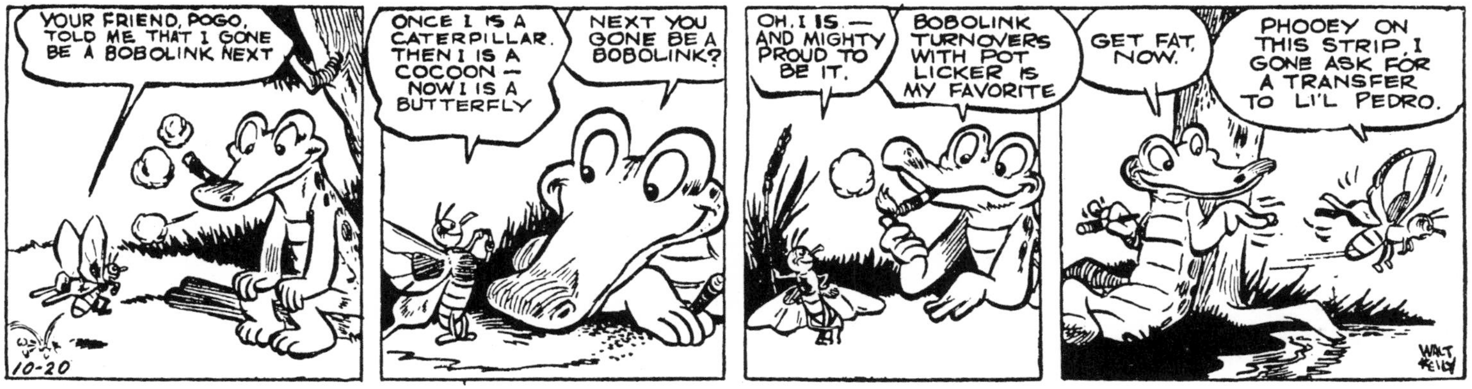
YOUR FRIEND, POGO, TOLD ME THAT I GONE BE A BOBOLINK NEXT
10-20
ONCE I IS A CATERPILLAR. THEN I IS A COCOON — NOW I IS A BUTTERFLY
NEXT YOU GONE BE A BOBOLINK?
OH, I **IS**. — AND MIGHTY PROUD TO BE IT.
BOBOLINK TURNOVERS WITH POT LICKER IS MY FAVORITE
GET FAT, NOW.
PHOOEY ON THIS STRIP. I GONE ASK FOR A TRANSFER TO LI'L PEDRO.
WALT KELLY

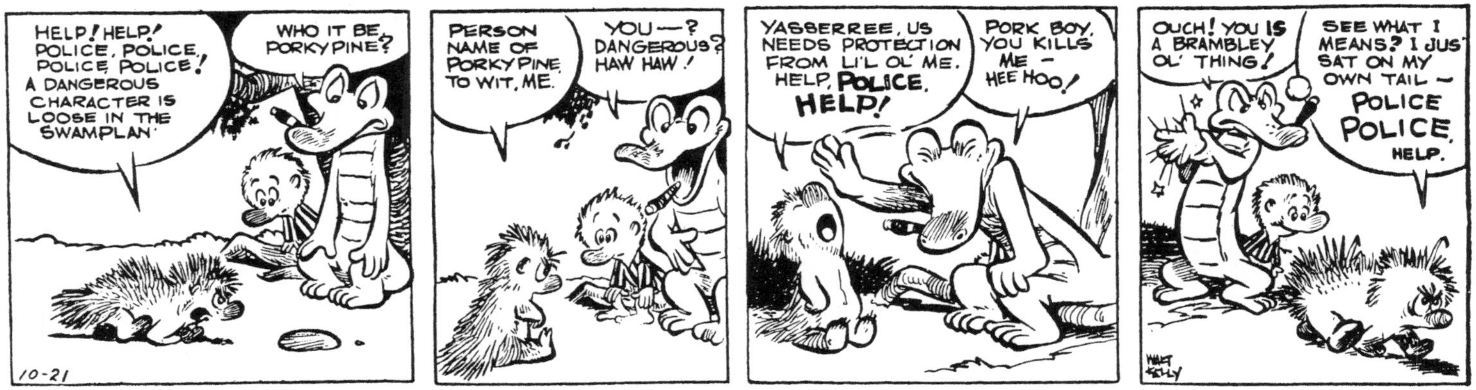
HELP! HELP! POLICE, POLICE, POLICE, POLICE! A DANGEROUS CHARACTER IS LOOSE IN THE SWAMPLAN'
WHO IT BE, PORKYPINE?
PERSON NAME OF PORKYPINE, TO WIT, ME.
YOU—? DANGEROUS? HAW HAW!
YASSERREE, US NEEDS PROTECTION FROM LI'L OL' ME. HELP, POLICE, HELP!
PORK BOY, YOU KILLS ME — HEE HOO!
OUCH! YOU IS A BRAMBLEY OL' THING!
SEE WHAT I MEANS? I JUS' SAT ON MY OWN TAIL — POLICE POLICE, HELP.
10-21
WALT KELLY

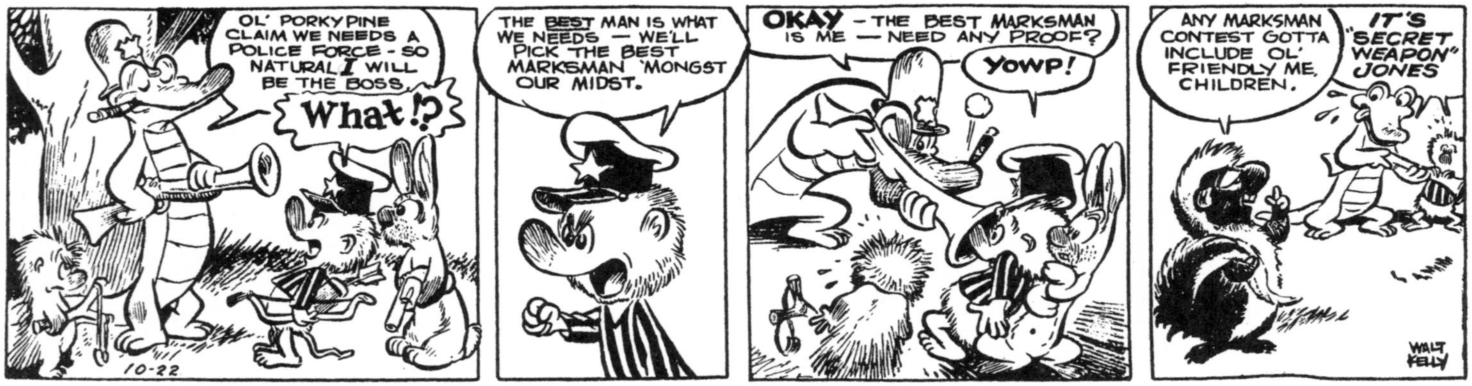
OL' PORKYPINE CLAIM WE NEEDS A POLICE FORCE - SO NATURAL I WILL BE THE BOSS.
What!?
THE BEST MAN IS WHAT WE NEEDS — WE'LL PICK THE BEST MARKSMAN 'MONGST OUR MIDST.
OKAY — THE BEST MARKSMAN IS ME — NEED ANY PROOF?
YOWP!
ANY MARKSMAN CONTEST GOTTA INCLUDE OL' FRIENDLY ME, CHILDREN.
IT'S "SECRET WEAPON" JONES
10-22
WALT KELLY

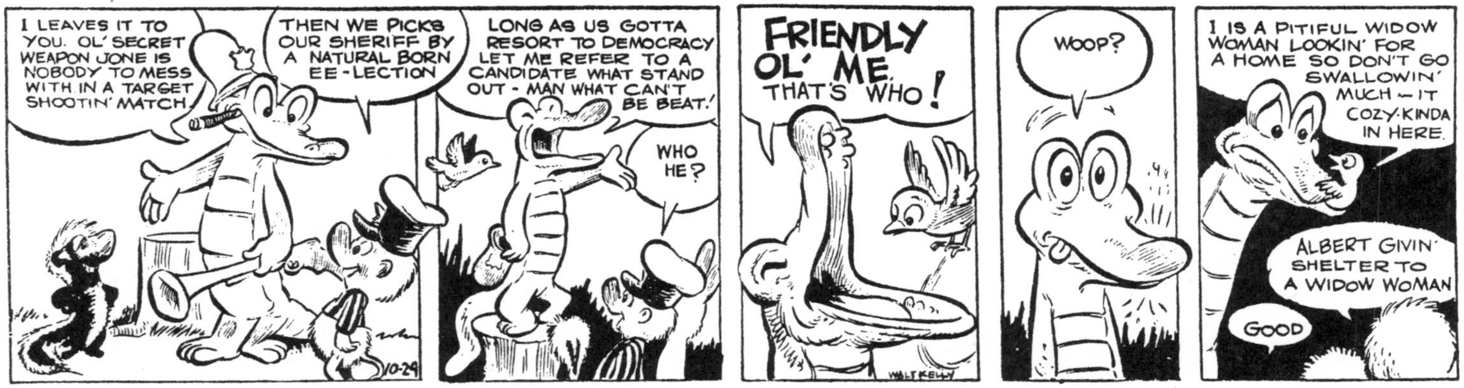
I LEAVES IT TO YOU. OL' SECRET WEAPON JONE IS NOBODY TO MESS WITH IN A TARGET SHOOTIN' MATCH.
THEN WE PICKS OUR SHERIFF BY A NATURAL BORN EE-LECTION
LONG AS US GOTTA RESORT TO DEMOCRACY LET ME REFER TO A CANDIDATE WHAT STAND OUT - MAN WHAT CAN'T BE BEAT.
WHO HE?
FRIENDLY OL' ME, THAT'S WHO!
WOOP?
I IS A PITIFUL WIDOW WOMAN LOOKIN' FOR A HOME SO DON'T GO SWALLOWIN' MUCH — IT COZY-KINDA IN HERE.
ALBERT GIVIN' SHELTER TO A WIDOW WOMAN
GOOD
10-24
WALT KELLY

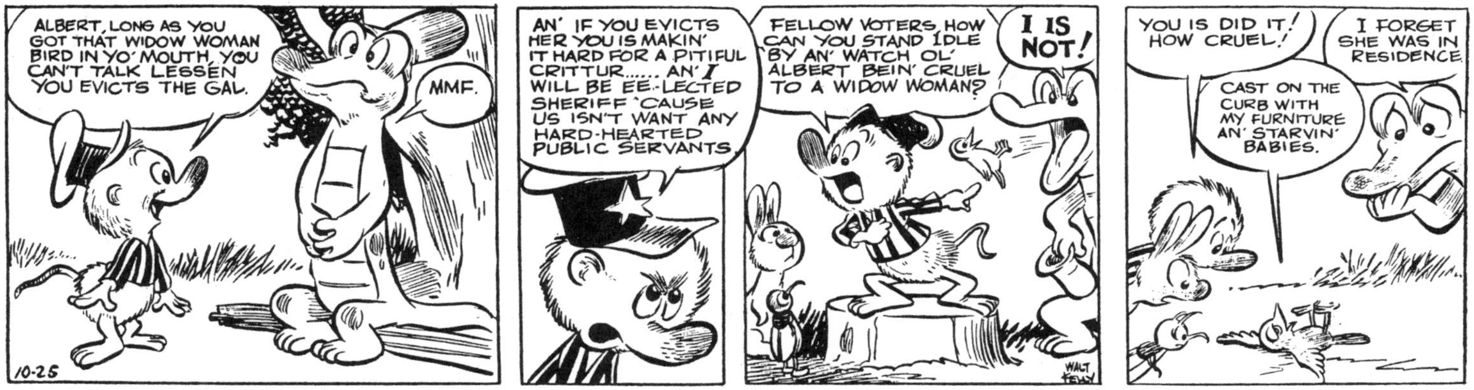
ALBERT, LONG AS YOU GOT THAT WIDOW WOMAN BIRD IN YO' MOUTH, YOU CAN'T TALK LESSEN YOU EVICTS THE GAL.
MMF.
10-25
AN' IF YOU EVICTS HER YOU IS MAKIN' IT HARD FOR A PITIFUL CRITTUR...... AN' I WILL BE EE-LECTED SHERIFF 'CAUSE US ISN'T WANT ANY HARD-HEARTED PUBLIC SERVANTS.
FELLOW VOTERS, HOW CAN YOU STAND IDLE BY AN' WATCH OL' ALBERT BEIN' CRUEL TO A WIDOW WOMAN?
I IS NOT!
WALT KELLY
YOU IS DID IT! HOW CRUEL!
CAST ON THE CURB WITH MY FURNITURE AN' STARVIN' BABIES.
I FORGET SHE WAS IN RESIDENCE.

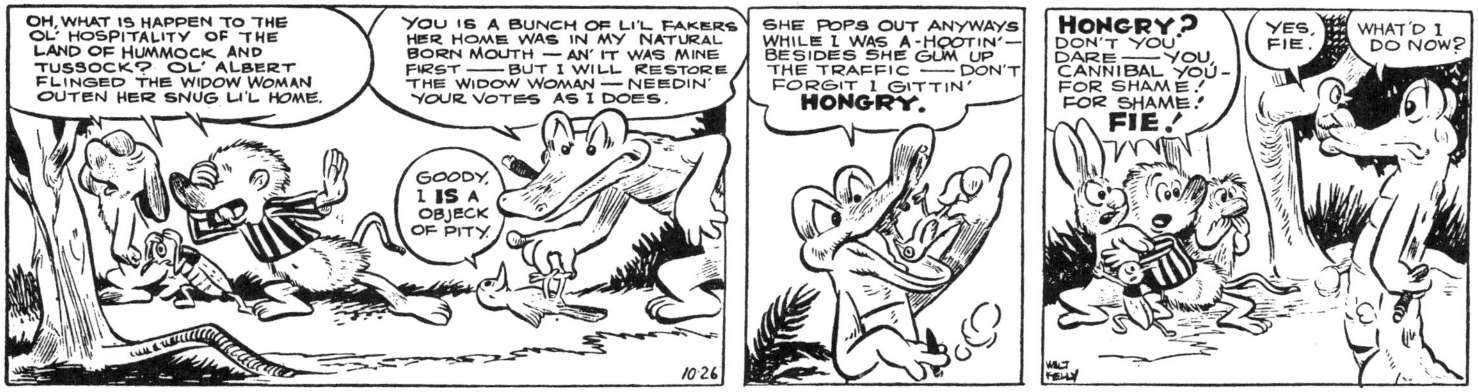
OH, WHAT IS HAPPEN TO THE OL' HOSPITALITY OF THE LAND OF HUMMOCK AND TUSSOCK? OL' ALBERT FLINGED THE WIDOW WOMAN OUTEN HER SNUG LI'L HOME.
YOU IS A BUNCH OF LI'L FAKERS HER HOME WAS IN MY NATURAL BORN MOUTH — AN' IT WAS MINE FIRST — BUT I WILL RESTORE THE WIDOW WOMAN — NEEDIN' YOUR VOTES AS I DOES.
GOODY, I IS A OBJECK OF PITY.
10-26
SHE POPS OUT ANYWAYS WHILE I WAS A-HOOTIN' — BESIDES SHE GUM UP THE TRAFFIC — DON'T FORGIT I GITTIN' HONGRY.
HONGRY? DON'T YOU DARE — YOU CANNIBAL YOU — FOR SHAME! FOR SHAME! FIE!
YES, FIE.
WHAT'D I DO NOW?
WALT KELLY

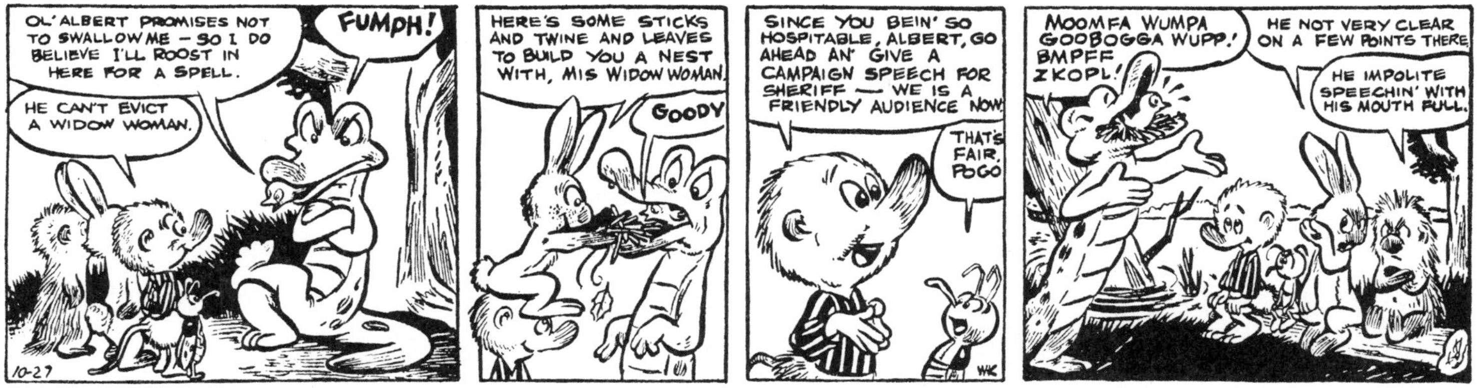
OL' ALBERT PROMISES NOT TO SWALLOW ME — SO I DO BELIEVE I'LL ROOST IN HERE FOR A SPELL.
FUMPH!
HE CAN'T EVICT A WIDOW WOMAN.
10-27
HERE'S SOME STICKS AND TWINE AND LEAVES TO BUILD YOU A NEST WITH, MIS WIDOW WOMAN.
GOODY
SINCE YOU BEIN' SO HOSPITABLE, ALBERT, GO AHEAD AN' GIVE A CAMPAIGN SPEECH FOR SHERIFF — WE IS A FRIENDLY AUDIENCE NOW.
THAT'S FAIR, POGO
WK
MOOMFA WUMPA GOOBOGGA WUPP! BMPFF ZKOPL!
HE NOT VERY CLEAR ON A FEW POINTS THERE.
HE IMPOLITE SPEECHIN' WITH HIS MOUTH FULL.

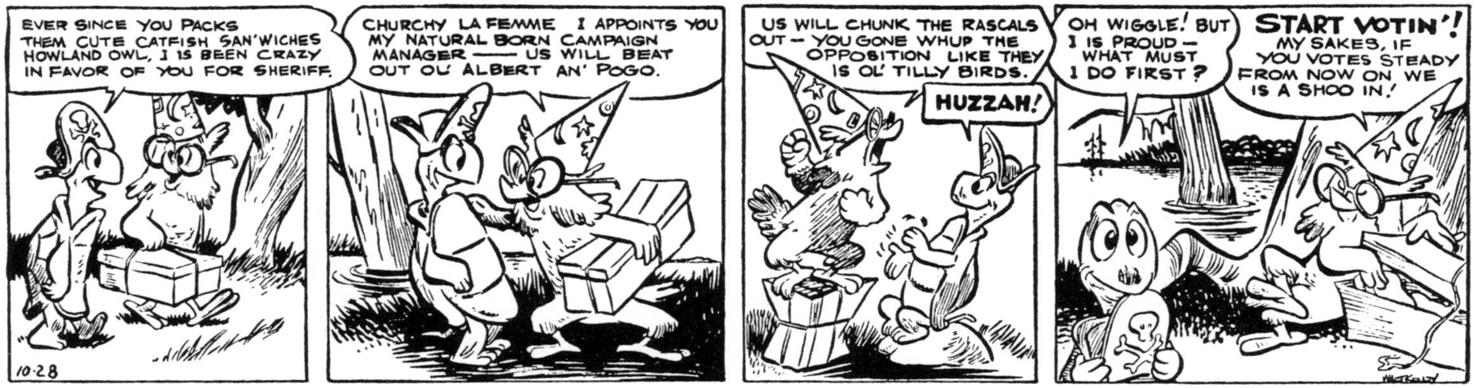
EVER SINCE YOU PACKS THEM CUTE CATFISH SAN'WICHES HOWLAND OWL, I IS BEEN CRAZY IN FAVOR OF YOU FOR SHERIFF.
10-28
CHURCHY LA FEMME I APPOINTS YOU MY NATURAL BORN CAMPAIGN MANAGER —— US WILL BEAT OUT OL' ALBERT AN' POGO.
US WILL CHUNK THE RASCALS OUT — YOU GONE WHUP THE OPPOSITION LIKE THEY IS OL' TILLY BIRDS.
HUZZAH!
OH WIGGLE! BUT I IS PROUD — WHAT MUST I DO FIRST?
START VOTIN'! MY SAKES, IF YOU VOTES STEADY FROM NOW ON WE IS A SHOO IN!

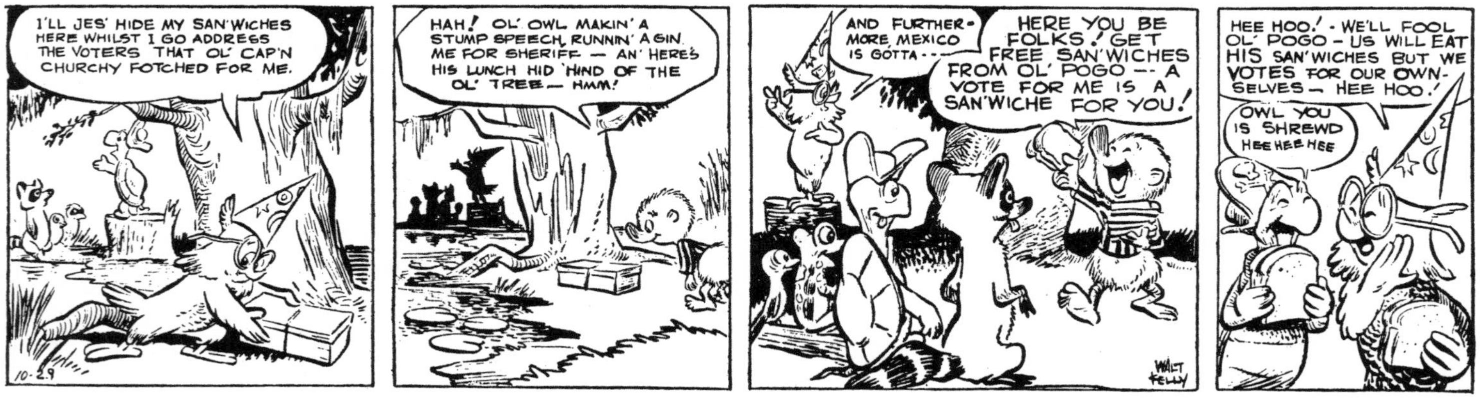
I'LL JES' HIDE MY SAN'WICHES HERE WHILST I GO ADDRESS THE VOTERS THAT OL' CAP'N CHURCHY FOTCHED FOR ME.
10-29
HAH! OL' OWL MAKIN' A STUMP SPEECH, RUNNIN' A GIN. ME FOR SHERIFF — AN' HERE'S HIS LUNCH HID 'HIND OF THE OL' TREE — HMM!
AND FURTHERMORE, MEXICO IS GOTTA---
HERE YOU BE FOLKS! GET FREE SAN'WICHES FROM OL' POGO -- A VOTE FOR ME IS A SAN'WICHE FOR YOU!
WALT KELLY
HEE HOO! - WE'LL FOOL OL' POGO - US WILL EAT HIS SAN'WICHES BUT WE VOTES FOR OUR OWN-SELVES — HEE HOO!
OWL YOU IS SHREWD HEE HEE HEE

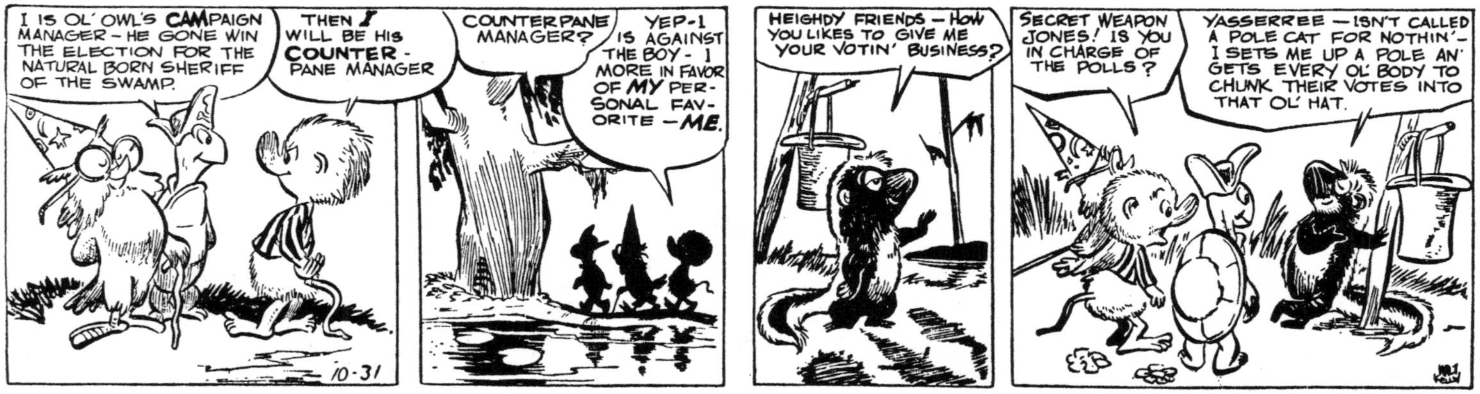
I IS OL' OWL'S CAMPAIGN MANAGER - HE GONE WIN THE ELECTION FOR THE NATURAL BORN SHERIFF OF THE SWAMP.
THEN I WILL BE HIS COUNTER-PANE MANAGER
10-31
COUNTERPANE MANAGER?
YEP-I IS AGAINST THE BOY - I MORE IN FAVOR OF MY PERSONAL FAVORITE — ME.
HEIGHDY FRIENDS — HOW YOU LIKES TO GIVE ME YOUR VOTIN' BUSINESS?
SECRET WEAPON JONES! IS YOU IN CHARGE OF THE POLLS?
YASSERREE — ISN'T CALLED A POLE CAT FOR NOTHIN' - I SETS ME UP A POLE AN' GETS EVERY OL' BODY TO CHUNK THEIR VOTES INTO THAT OL' HAT.

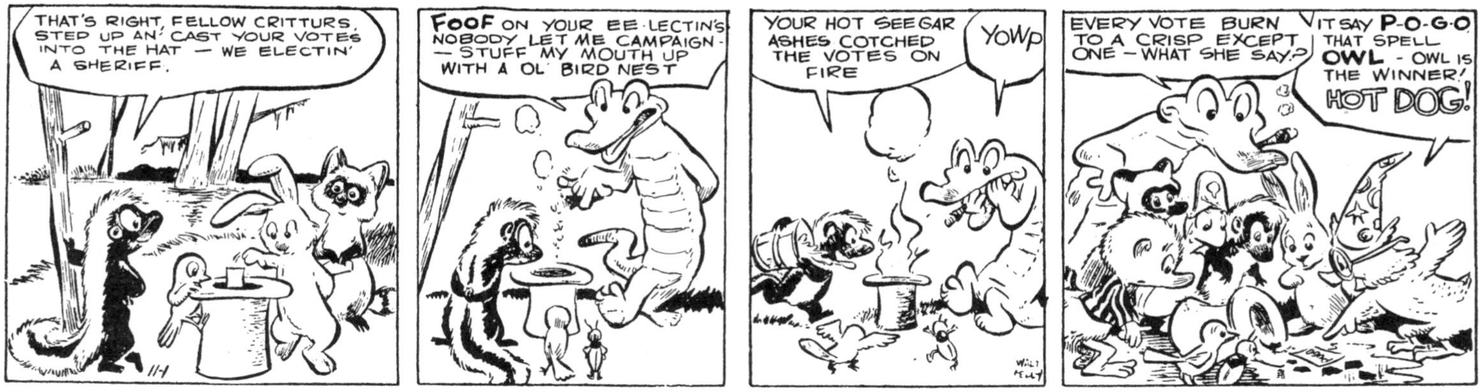
THAT'S RIGHT, FELLOW CRITTURS. STEP UP AN' CAST YOUR VOTES INTO THE HAT — WE ELECTIN' A SHERIFF.
11-1
FOOF ON YOUR EE-LECTIN'S NOBODY LET ME CAMPAIGN — STUFF MY MOUTH UP WITH A OL' BIRD NEST
YOUR HOT SEEGAR ASHES COTCHED THE VOTES ON FIRE
YOWP
WALT KELLY
EVERY VOTE BURN TO A CRISP EXCEPT ONE — WHAT SHE SAY?
IT SAY P-O-G-O THAT SPELL OWL - OWL IS THE WINNER! HOT DOG!

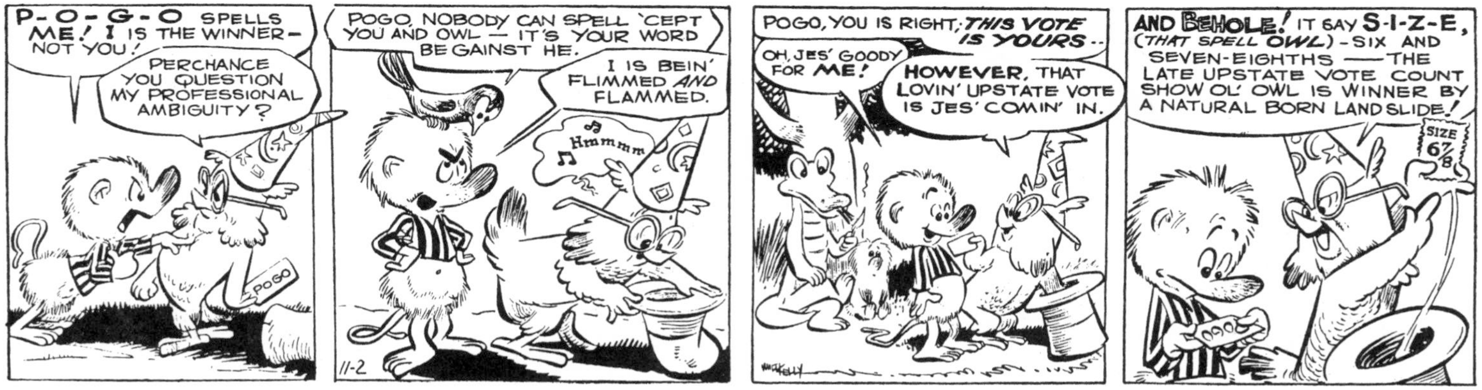
P-O-G-O SPELLS ME! I IS THE WINNER — NOT YOU!
PERCHANCE YOU QUESTION MY PROFESSIONAL AMBIGUITY?
POGO
POGO, NOBODY CAN SPELL 'CEPT YOU AND OWL — IT'S YOUR WORD BE GAINST HE.
I IS BEIN' FLIMMED AND FLAMMED.
Hmmmm
11-2
POGO, YOU IS RIGHT, THIS VOTE IS YOURS..
OH, JES' GOODY FOR ME!
HOWEVER, THAT LOVIN' UPSTATE VOTE IS JES' COMIN' IN.
WALT KELLY
AND BEHOLE! IT SAY S-I-Z-E, (THAT SPELL OWL) - SIX AND SEVEN-EIGHTHS — THE LATE UPSTATE VOTE COUNT SHOW OL' OWL IS WINNER BY A NATURAL BORN LANDSLIDE!
SIZE 6 7/8

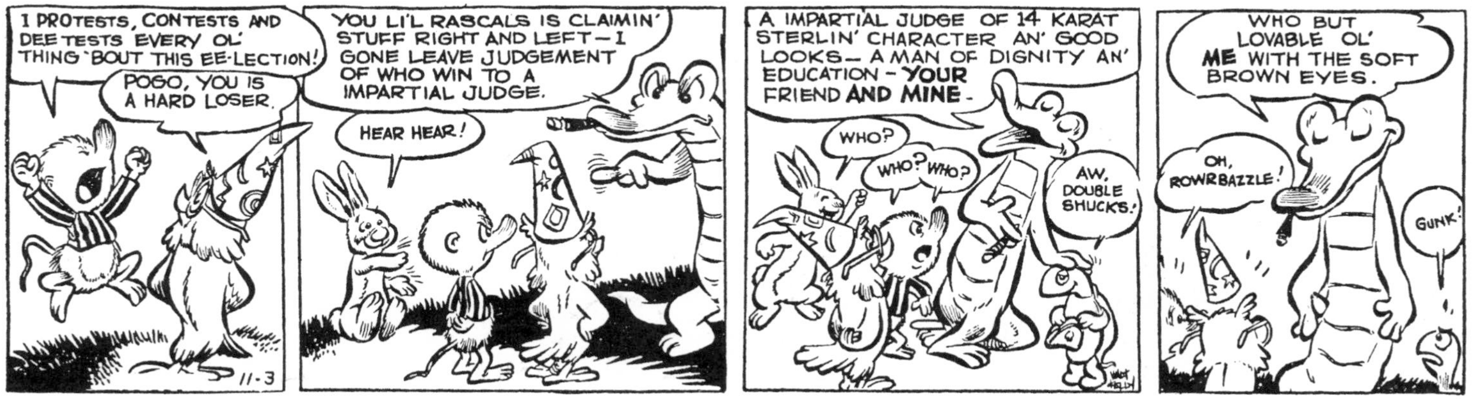
I PROTESTS, CONTESTS AND DEE-TESTS EVERY OL' THING 'BOUT THIS EE-LECTION!
POGO, YOU IS A HARD LOSER.
11-3
YOU LI'L RASCALS IS CLAIMIN' STUFF RIGHT AND LEFT — I GONE LEAVE JUDGEMENT OF WHO WIN TO A IMPARTIAL JUDGE.
HEAR HEAR!
A IMPARTIAL JUDGE OF 14 KARAT STERLIN' CHARACTER AN' GOOD LOOKS — A MAN OF DIGNITY AN' EDUCATION — YOUR FRIEND AND MINE —
WHO?
WHO? WHO?
AW, DOUBLE SHUCKS!
WALT KELLY
WHO BUT LOVABLE OL' ME WITH THE SOFT BROWN EYES.
OH, ROWRBAZZLE!
GUNK!

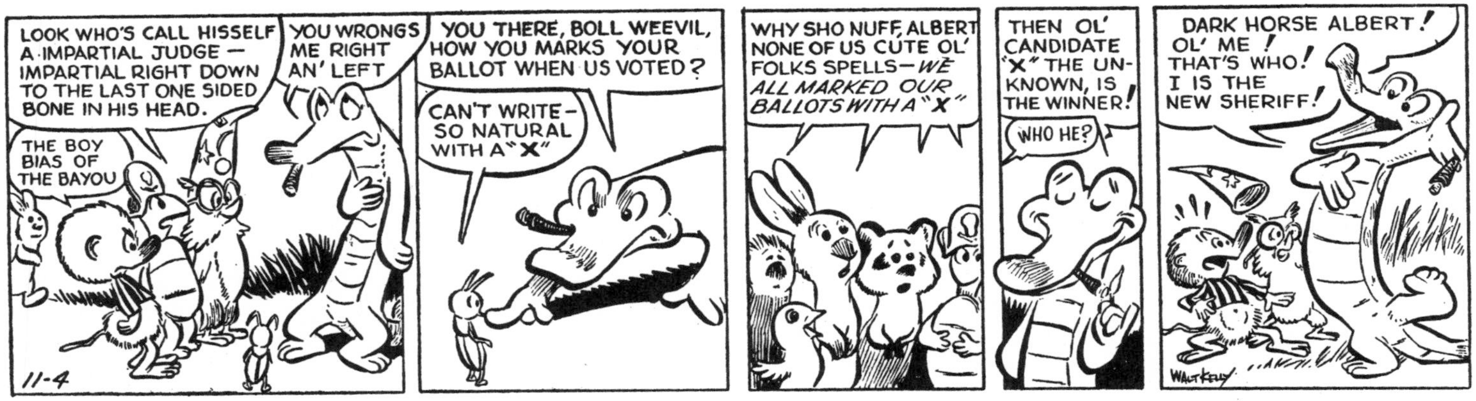
LOOK WHO'S CALL HISSELF A·IMPARTIAL JUDGE — IMPARTIAL RIGHT DOWN TO THE LAST ONE SIDED BONE IN HIS HEAD.
YOU WRONGS ME RIGHT AN' LEFT
THE BOY BIAS OF THE BAYOU
11-4
YOU THERE, BOLL WEEVIL, HOW YOU MARKS YOUR BALLOT WHEN US VOTED?
CAN'T WRITE-SO NATURAL WITH A "X"
WHY SHO NUFF, ALBERT NONE OF US CUTE OL' FOLKS SPELLS—*WE ALL MARKED OUR BALLOTS WITH A "X"*
THEN OL' CANDIDATE "X" THE UN-KNOWN, IS THE WINNER!
WHO HE?
DARK HORSE ALBERT! OL' ME! THAT'S WHO! I IS THE NEW SHERIFF!
WALT KELLY

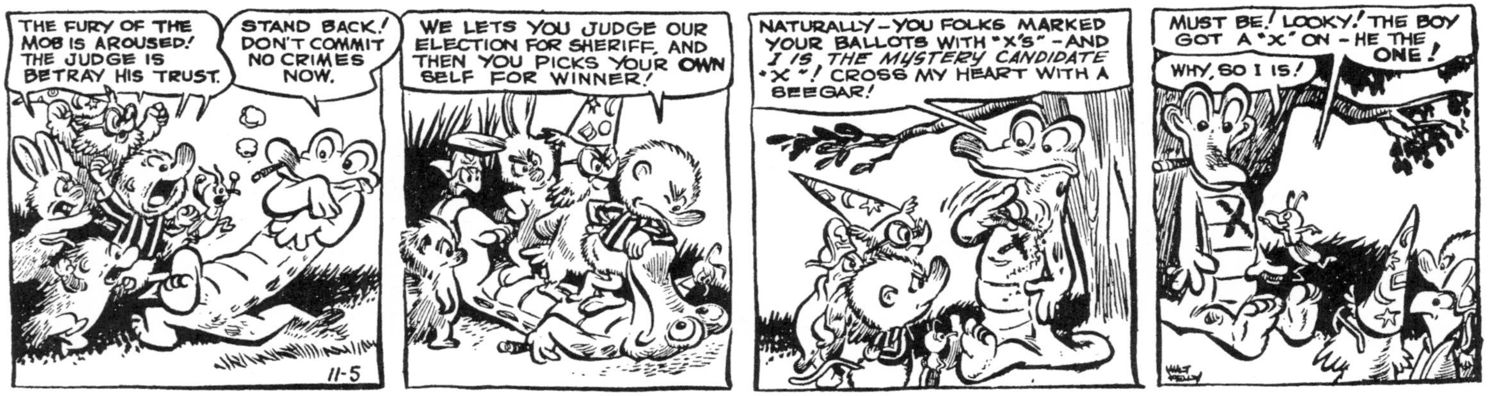
THE FURY OF THE MOB IS AROUSED! THE JUDGE IS BETRAY HIS TRUST.
STAND BACK! DON'T COMMIT NO CRIMES NOW.
11-5
WE LETS YOU JUDGE OUR ELECTION FOR SHERIFF, AND THEN YOU PICKS YOUR **OWN** SELF FOR WINNER!
NATURALLY—YOU FOLKS MARKED YOUR BALLOTS WITH "X'S"—AND *I IS, THE MYSTERY CANDIDATE "X"*! CROSS MY HEART WITH A SEEGAR!
MUST BE! LOOKY! THE BOY GOT A "X" ON—HE THE **ONE**!
WHY, SO I IS!
WALT KELLY

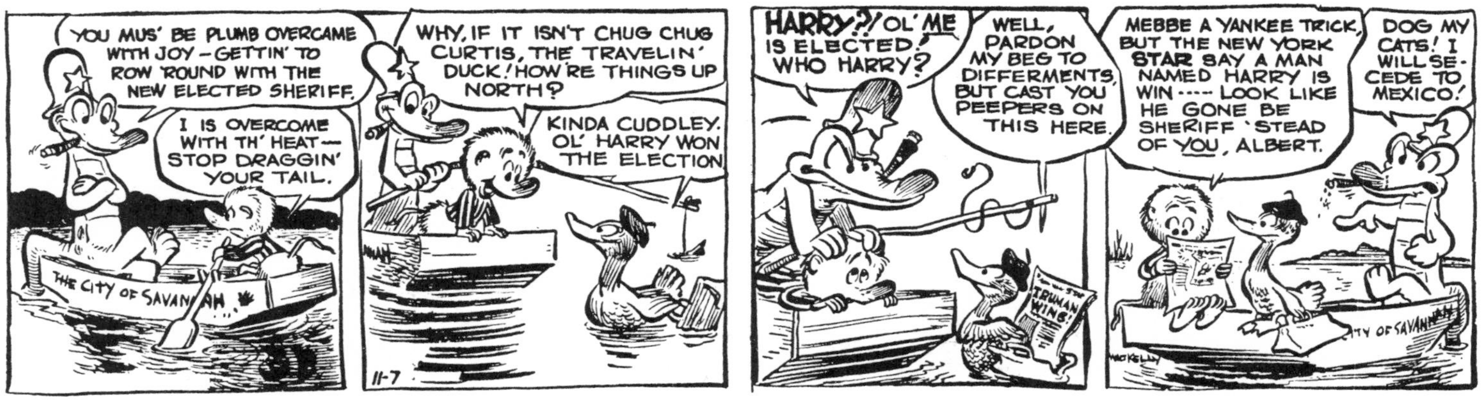
YOU MUS' BE PLUMB OVERCAME WITH JOY—GETTIN' TO ROW 'ROUND WITH THE NEW ELECTED SHERIFF.
I IS OVERCOME WITH TH' HEAT— STOP DRAGGIN' YOUR TAIL.
THE CITY OF SAVANNAH
WHY, IF IT ISN'T CHUG CHUG CURTIS, THE TRAVELIN' DUCK! HOW'RE THINGS UP NORTH?
KINDA CUDDLEY. OL' HARRY WON THE ELECTION
11-7
HARRY?!! OL' ME IS ELECTED! WHO HARRY?
WELL, PARDON MY BEG TO DIFFERMENTS, BUT CAST YOU PEEPERS ON THIS HERE.
TRUMAN WINS!
MEBBE A YANKEE TRICK, BUT THE NEW YORK **STAR** SAY A MAN NAMED HARRY IS WIN---- LOOK LIKE HE GONE BE SHERIFF 'STEAD OF YOU, ALBERT.
DOG MY CATS! I WILL SE-CEDE TO MEXICO!
CITY OF SAVANNAH

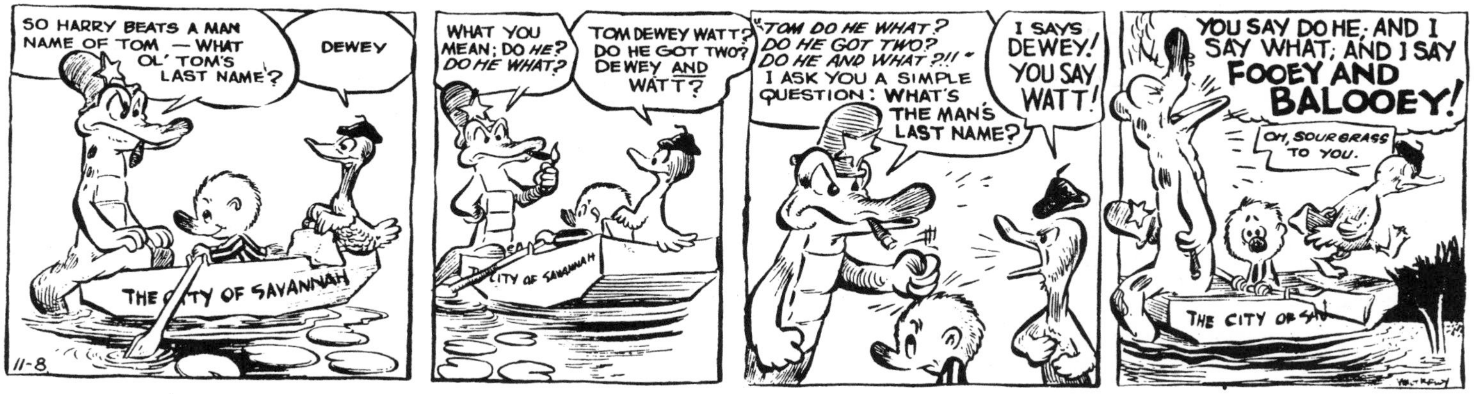
SO HARRY BEATS A MAN NAME OF TOM — WHAT OL' TOM'S LAST NAME?
DEWEY
THE CITY OF SAVANNAH
11-8
WHAT YOU MEAN; DO HE? DO HE WHAT?
TOM DEWEY WATT? DO HE GOT TWO? DEWEY AND WATT?
CITY OF SAVANNAH
"TOM DO HE WHAT? DO HE GOT TWO? DO HE AND WHAT?!!" I ASK YOU A SIMPLE QUESTION: WHAT'S THE MAN'S LAST NAME?
I SAYS DEWEY! YOU SAY WATT!
YOU SAY DO HE; AND I SAY WHAT; AND I SAY FOOEY AND BALOOEY!
OH, SOURGRASS TO YOU.
THE CITY OF SA

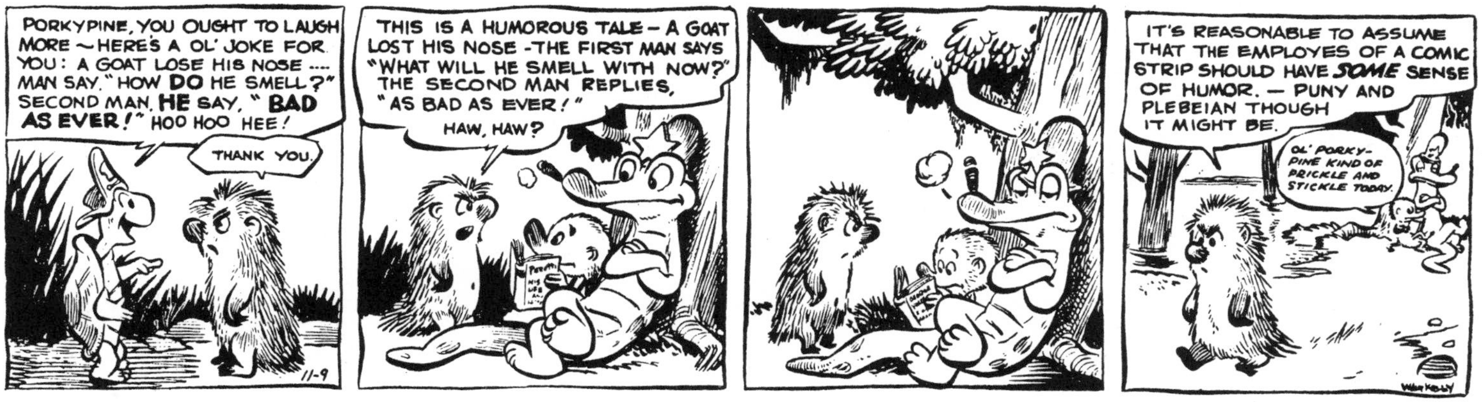
PORKYPINE, YOU OUGHT TO LAUGH MORE ~ HERE'S A OL' JOKE FOR YOU: A GOAT LOSE HIS NOSE .... MAN SAY, "HOW DO HE SMELL?" SECOND MAN, HE SAY, "BAD AS EVER!" HOO HOO HEE!
THANK YOU.
11-9
THIS IS A HUMOROUS TALE - A GOAT LOST HIS NOSE - THE FIRST MAN SAYS "WHAT WILL HE SMELL WITH NOW?" THE SECOND MAN REPLIES, "AS BAD AS EVER!"
HAW, HAW?
IT'S REASONABLE TO ASSUME THAT THE EMPLOYES OF A COMIC STRIP SHOULD HAVE SOME SENSE OF HUMOR. — PUNY AND PLEBEIAN THOUGH IT MIGHT BE.
OL' PORKY-PINE KIND OF PRICKLE AND STICKLE TODAY.

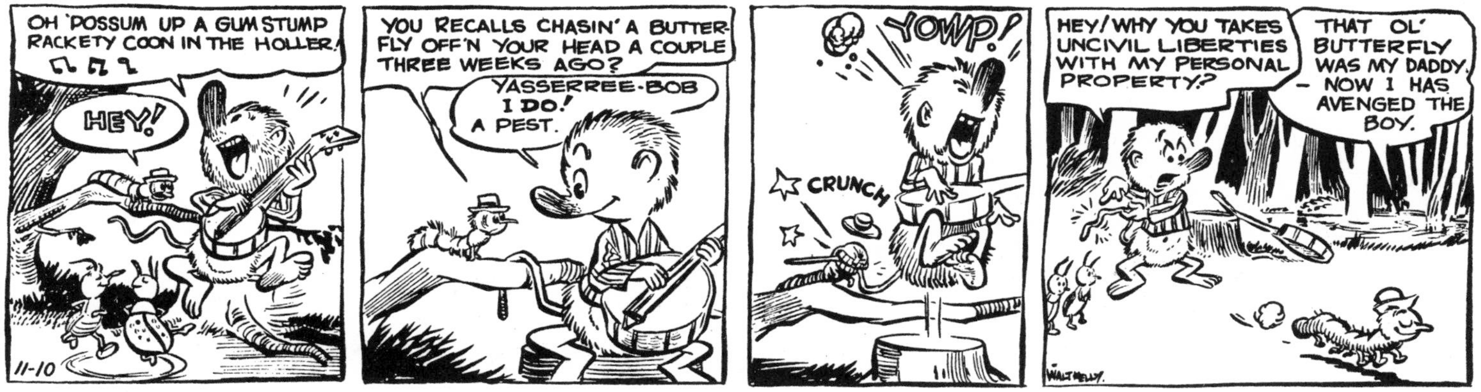
OH 'POSSUM UP A GUM STUMP RACKETY COON IN THE HOLLER!
HEY!
11-10
YOU RECALLS CHASIN' A BUTTER-FLY OFF'N YOUR HEAD A COUPLE THREE WEEKS AGO?
YASSERREE-BOB I DO! A PEST.
YOWP!
CRUNCH
HEY! WHY YOU TAKES UNCIVIL LIBERTIES WITH MY PERSONAL PROPERTY?
THAT OL' BUTTERFLY WAS MY DADDY. - NOW I HAS AVENGED THE BOY.

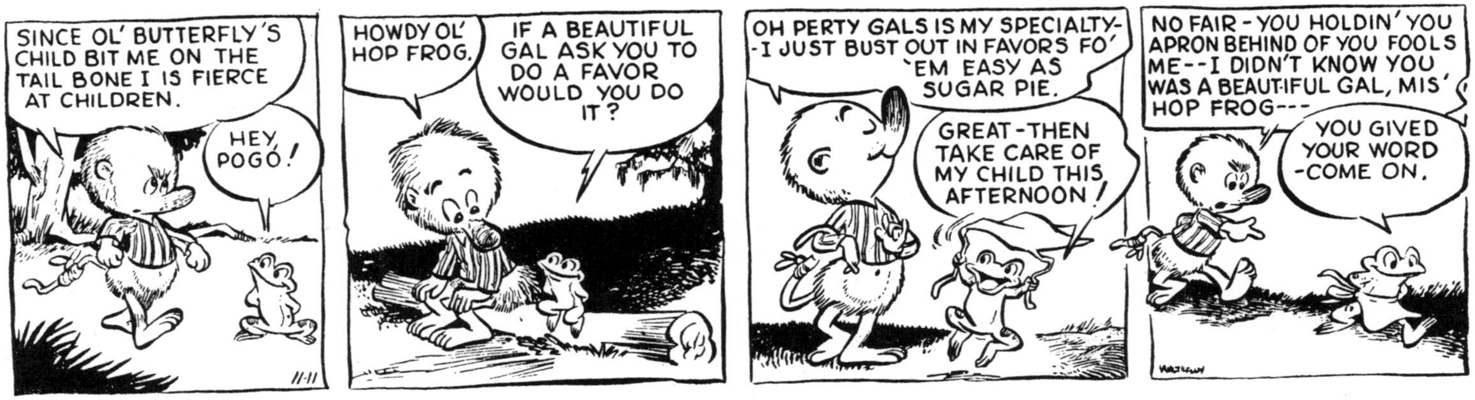
SINCE OL' BUTTERFLY'S CHILD BIT ME ON THE TAIL BONE I IS FIERCE AT CHILDREN.
HEY, POGO!
11-11
HOWDY OL' HOP FROG.
IF A BEAUTIFUL GAL ASK YOU TO DO A FAVOR WOULD YOU DO IT?
OH PERTY GALS IS MY SPECIALTY- -I JUST BUST OUT IN FAVORS FO' 'EM EASY AS SUGAR PIE.
GREAT-THEN TAKE CARE OF MY CHILD THIS AFTERNOON!
NO FAIR - YOU HOLDIN' YOU APRON BEHIND OF YOU FOOLS ME--I DIDN'T KNOW YOU WAS A BEAUTIFUL GAL, MIS' HOP FROG---
YOU GIVED YOUR WORD -COME ON.

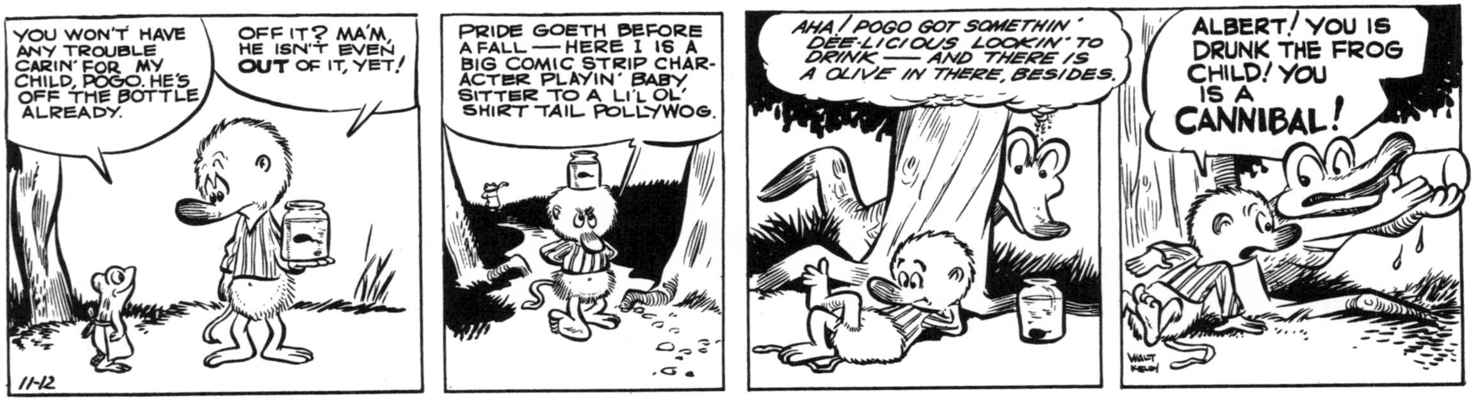
YOU WON'T HAVE ANY TROUBLE CARIN' FOR MY CHILD, POGO. HE'S OFF THE BOTTLE ALREADY.
OFF IT? MA'M, HE ISN'T EVEN OUT OF IT, YET!
11-12
PRIDE GOETH BEFORE A FALL — HERE I IS A BIG COMIC STRIP CHARACTER PLAYIN' BABY SITTER TO A LI'L OL' SHIRT TAIL POLLYWOG.
AHA! POGO GOT SOMETHIN' DEE-LICIOUS LOOKIN' TO DRINK — AND THERE IS A OLIVE IN THERE, BESIDES.
ALBERT! YOU IS DRUNK THE FROG CHILD! YOU IS A CANNIBAL!
WALT KELLY

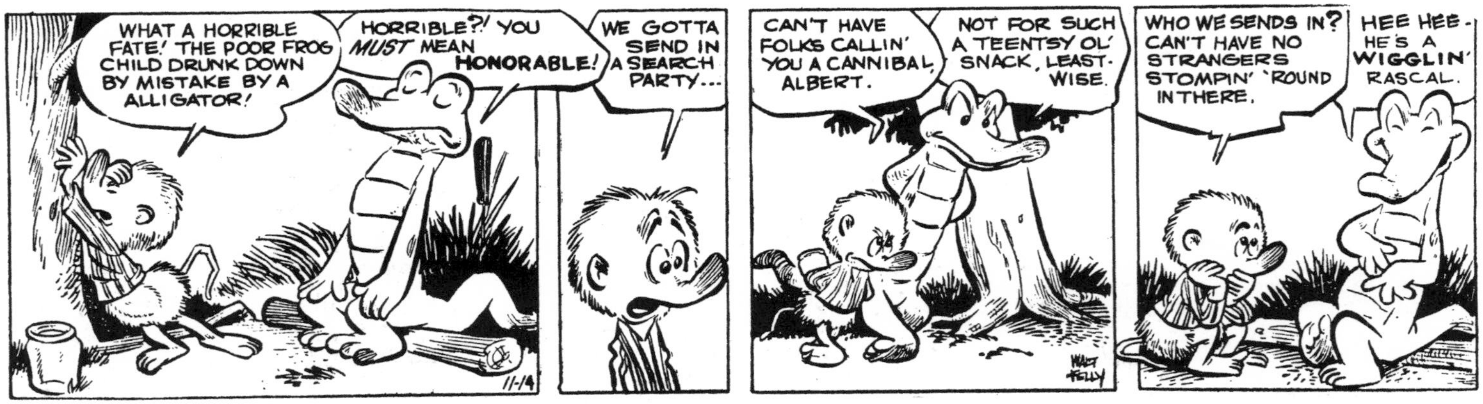
WHAT A HORRIBLE FATE! THE POOR FROG CHILD DRUNK DOWN BY MISTAKE BY A ALLIGATOR!
HORRIBLE?! YOU MUST MEAN HONORABLE!
11-14
WE GOTTA SEND IN A SEARCH PARTY...
CAN'T HAVE FOLKS CALLIN' YOU A CANNIBAL, ALBERT.
NOT FOR SUCH A TEENTSY OL' SNACK, LEAST-WISE.
WALT KELLY
WHO WE SENDS IN? CAN'T HAVE NO STRANGERS STOMPIN' 'ROUND IN THERE.
HEE HEE - HE'S A WIGGLIN' RASCAL.

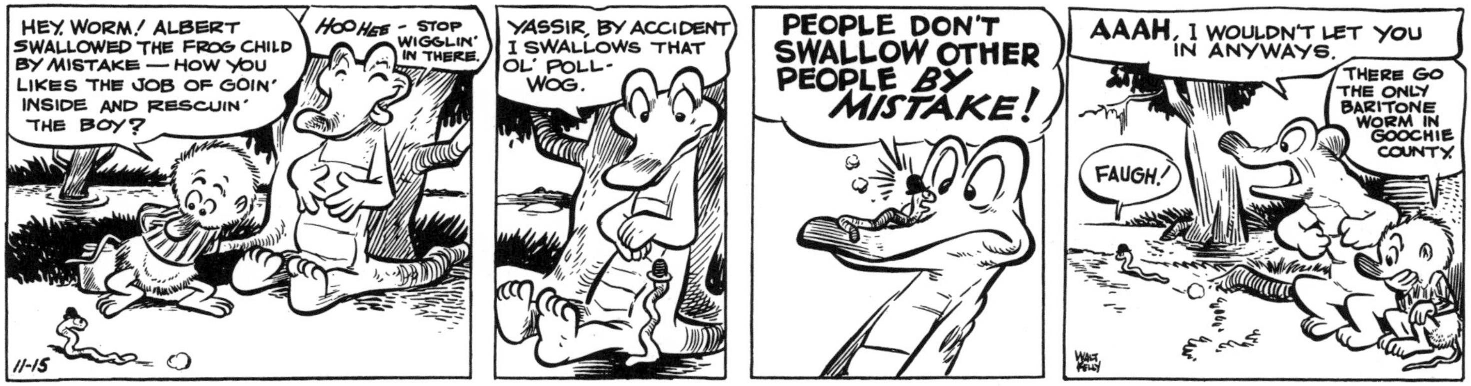
HEY, WORM! ALBERT SWALLOWED THE FROG CHILD BY MISTAKE — HOW YOU LIKES THE JOB OF GOIN' INSIDE AND RESCUIN' THE BOY?
HOO HEE - STOP WIGGLIN' IN THERE.
11-15
YASSIR, BY ACCIDENT I SWALLOWS THAT OL' POLL-WOG.
PEOPLE DON'T SWALLOW OTHER PEOPLE BY MISTAKE!
AAAH, I WOULDN'T LET YOU IN ANYWAYS.
THERE GO THE ONLY BARITONE WORM IN GOOCHIE COUNTY.
FAUGH!
WALT KELLY

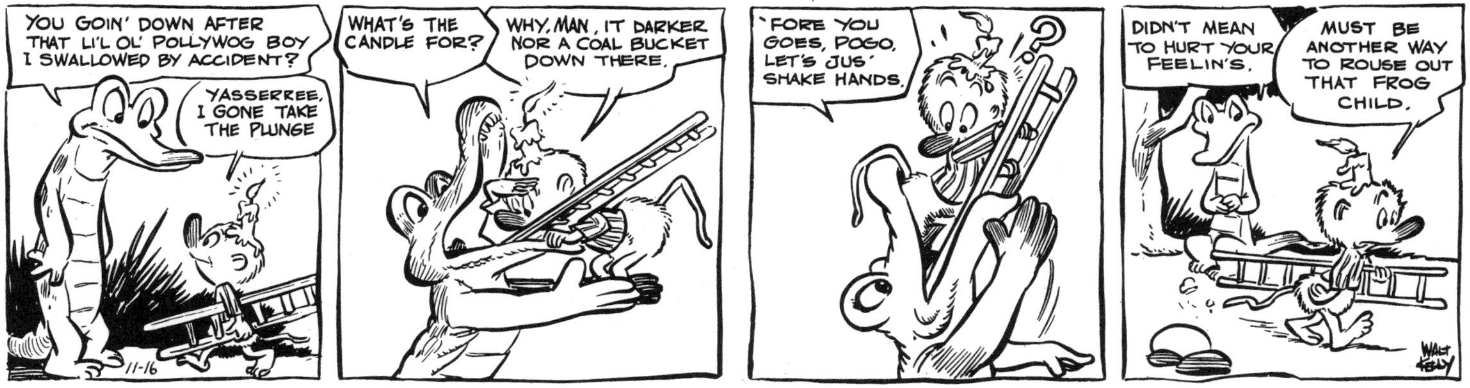
YOU GOIN' DOWN AFTER THAT LI'L OL' POLLYWOG BOY I SWALLOWED BY ACCIDENT?
YASSERREE, I GONE TAKE THE PLUNGE
11-16
WHAT'S THE CANDLE FOR?
WHY, MAN, IT DARKER NOR A COAL BUCKET DOWN THERE.
'FORE YOU GOES, POGO, LET'S JUS' SHAKE HANDS.
DIDN'T MEAN TO HURT YOUR FEELIN'S.
MUST BE ANOTHER WAY TO ROUSE OUT THAT FROG CHILD.
WALT KELLY

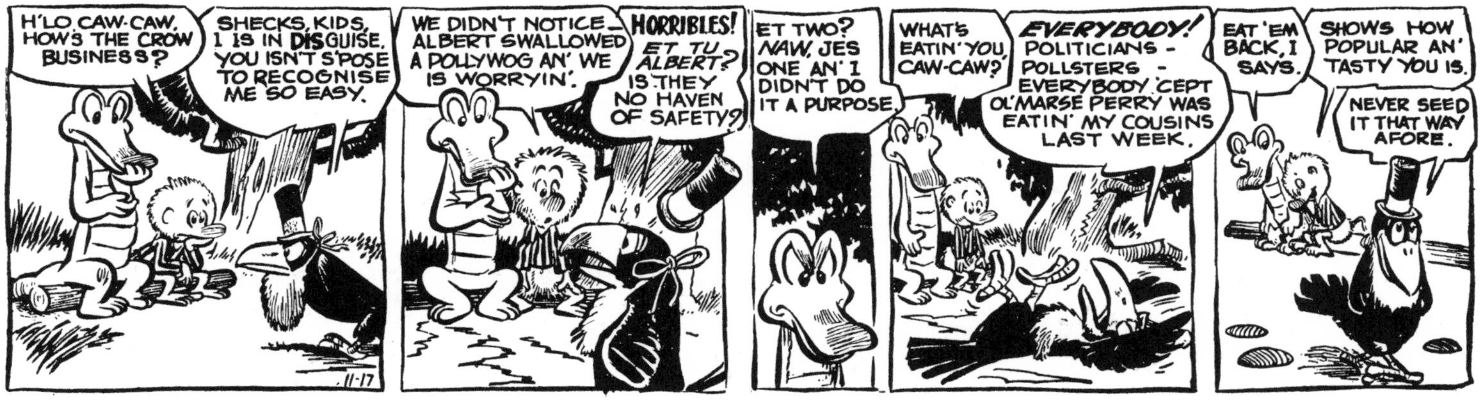
H'LO CAW-CAW, HOW'S THE CROW BUSINESS?
SHECKS, KIDS, I IS IN DISGUISE. YOU ISN'T S'POSE TO RECOGNISE ME SO EASY.
WE DIDN'T NOTICE — ALBERT SWALLOWED A POLLYWOG AN' WE IS WORRYIN'.
HORRIBLES! ET TU ALBERT? IS THEY NO HAVEN OF SAFETY?
11-17
ET TWO? NAW, JES ONE AN' I DIDN'T DO IT A PURPOSE.
WHAT'S EATIN' YOU, CAW-CAW?
EVERYBODY! POLITICIANS - POLLSTERS - EVERYBODY 'CEPT OL' MARSE PERRY WAS EATIN' MY COUSINS LAST WEEK.
EAT 'EM BACK, I SAYS.
SHOWS HOW POPULAR AN' TASTY YOU IS.
NEVER SEED IT THAT WAY AFORE.

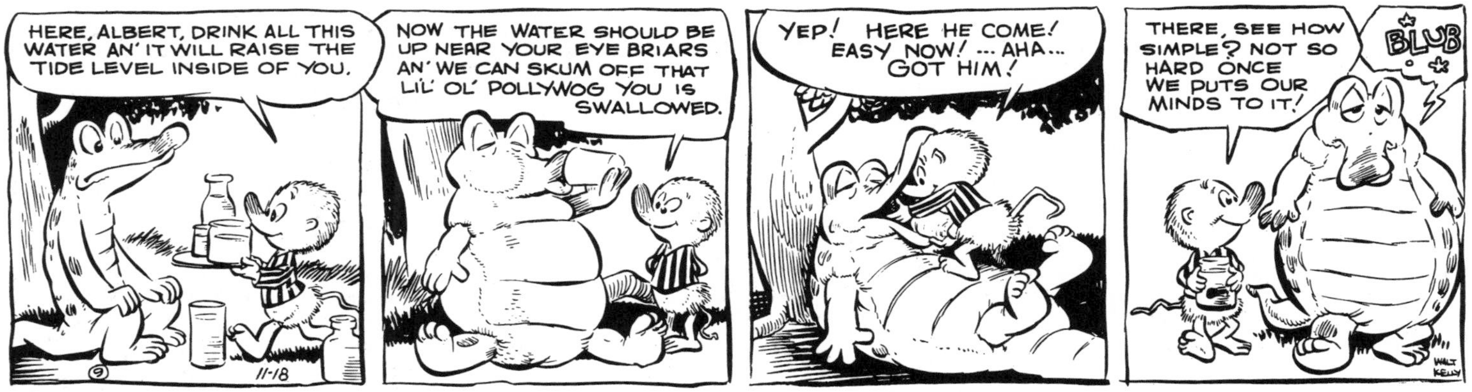
HERE, ALBERT, DRINK ALL THIS WATER AN' IT WILL RAISE THE TIDE LEVEL INSIDE OF YOU.
11-18
NOW THE WATER SHOULD BE UP NEAR YOUR EYE BRIARS AN' WE CAN SKUM OFF THAT LIL' OL' POLLYWOG YOU IS SWALLOWED.
YEP! HERE HE COME! EASY NOW! --- AHA... GOT HIM!
THERE, SEE HOW SIMPLE? NOT SO HARD ONCE WE PUTS OUR MINDS TO IT!
BLUB
WALT KELLY

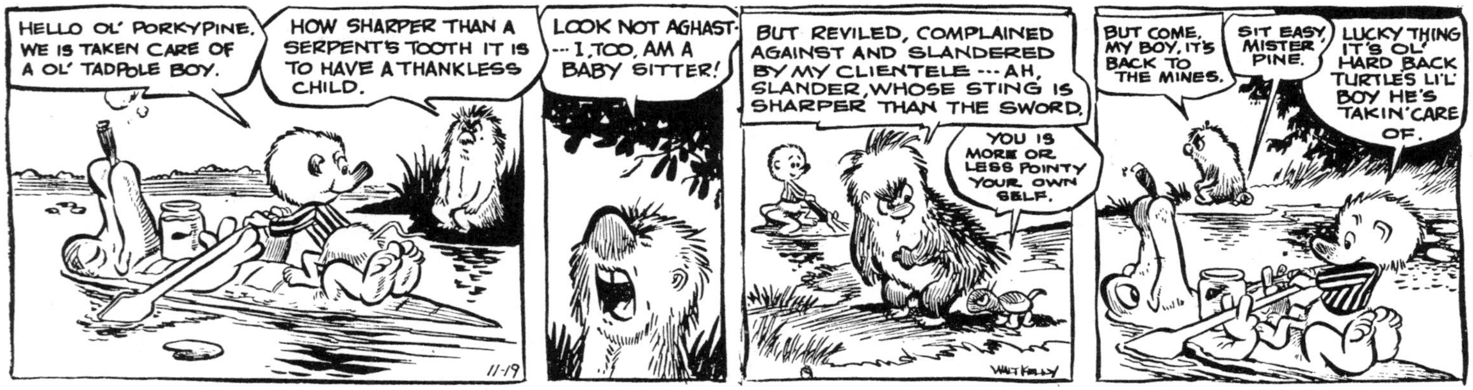
HELLO OL' PORKYPINE. WE IS TAKEN CARE OF A OL' TADPOLE BOY.
HOW SHARPER THAN A SERPENT'S TOOTH IT IS TO HAVE A THANKLESS CHILD.
11-19
LOOK NOT AGHAST --- I, TOO, AM A BABY SITTER!
BUT REVILED, COMPLAINED AGAINST AND SLANDERED BY MY CLIENTELE --- AH, SLANDER, WHOSE STING IS SHARPER THAN THE SWORD.
YOU IS MORE OR LESS POINTY YOUR OWN SELF.
WALT KELLY
BUT COME, MY BOY, IT'S BACK TO THE MINES.
SIT EASY, MISTER PINE.
LUCKY THING IT'S OL' HARD BACK TURTLE'S LI'L BOY HE'S TAKIN' CARE OF.

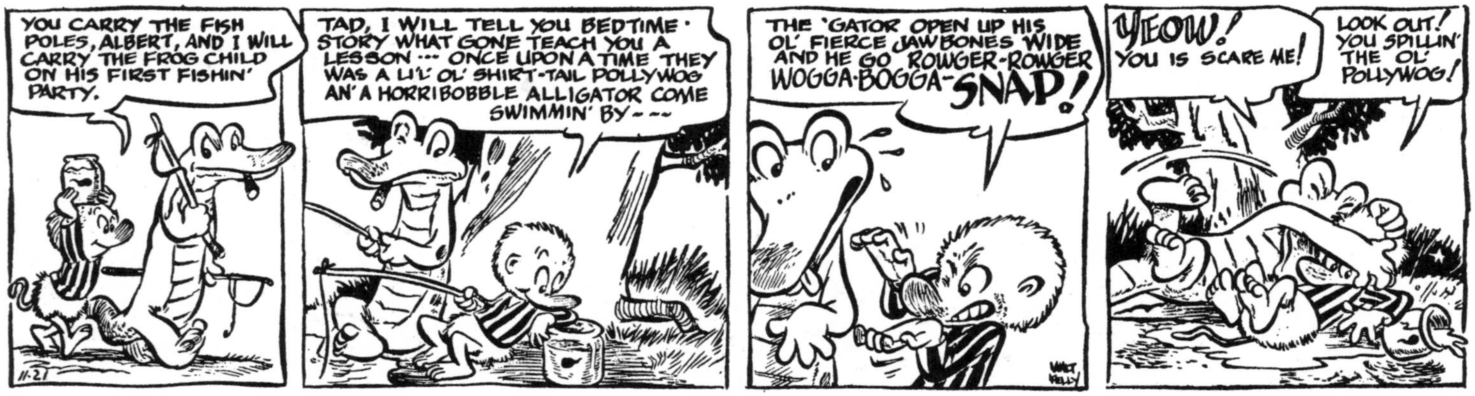
YOU CARRY THE FISH POLES, ALBERT, AND I WILL CARRY THE FROG CHILD ON HIS FIRST FISHIN' PARTY.
11-21
TAD, I WILL TELL YOU BEDTIME STORY WHAT GONE TEACH YOU A LESSON --- ONCE UPON A TIME THEY WAS A LI'L' OL' SHIRT-TAIL POLLYWOG AN' A HORRIBOBBLE ALLIGATOR COME SWIMMIN' BY---
THE 'GATOR OPEN UP HIS OL' FIERCE JAWBONES WIDE AND HE GO ROWGER-ROWGER WOGGA-BOGGA-SNAP!
WALT KELLY
YEOW! YOU IS SCARE ME!
LOOK OUT! YOU SPILLIN' THE OL' POLLYWOG!

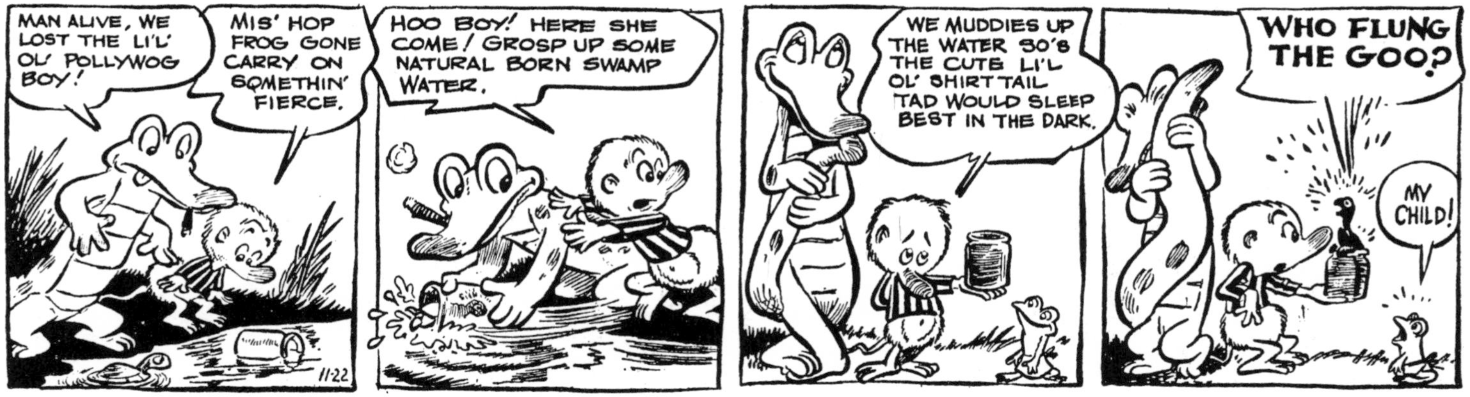
MAN ALIVE, WE LOST THE LI'L' OL' POLLYWOG BOY!
MIS' HOP FROG GONE CARRY ON SOMETHIN' FIERCE.
HOO BOY! HERE SHE COME! GROSP UP SOME NATURAL BORN SWAMP WATER.
11-22
WE MUDDIES UP THE WATER SO'S THE CUTE LI'L OL' SHIRT TAIL TAD WOULD SLEEP BEST IN THE DARK.
WHO FLUNG THE GOO?
MY CHILD!

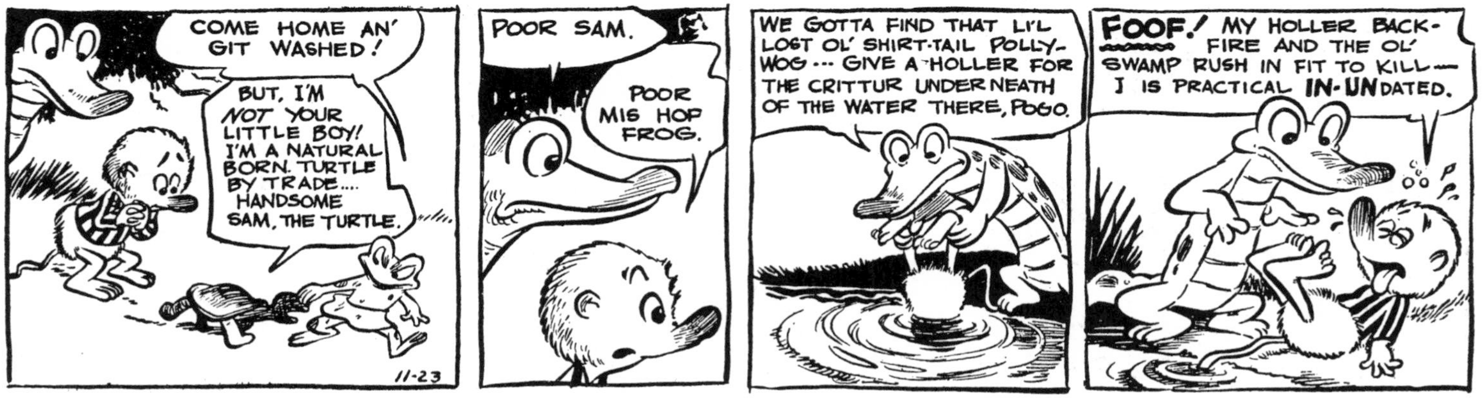
COME HOME AN' GIT WASHED!
BUT, I'M NOT YOUR LITTLE BOY! I'M A NATURAL BORN TURTLE BY TRADE.... HANDSOME SAM, THE TURTLE.
11-23
POOR SAM.
POOR MIS HOP FROG.
WE GOTTA FIND THAT LI'L LOST OL' SHIRT-TAIL POLLY-WOG --- GIVE A HOLLER FOR THE CRITTUR UNDERNEATH OF THE WATER THERE, POGO.
FOOF! MY HOLLER BACK-FIRE AND THE OL' SWAMP RUSH IN FIT TO KILL— I IS PRACTICAL IN-UNDATED.

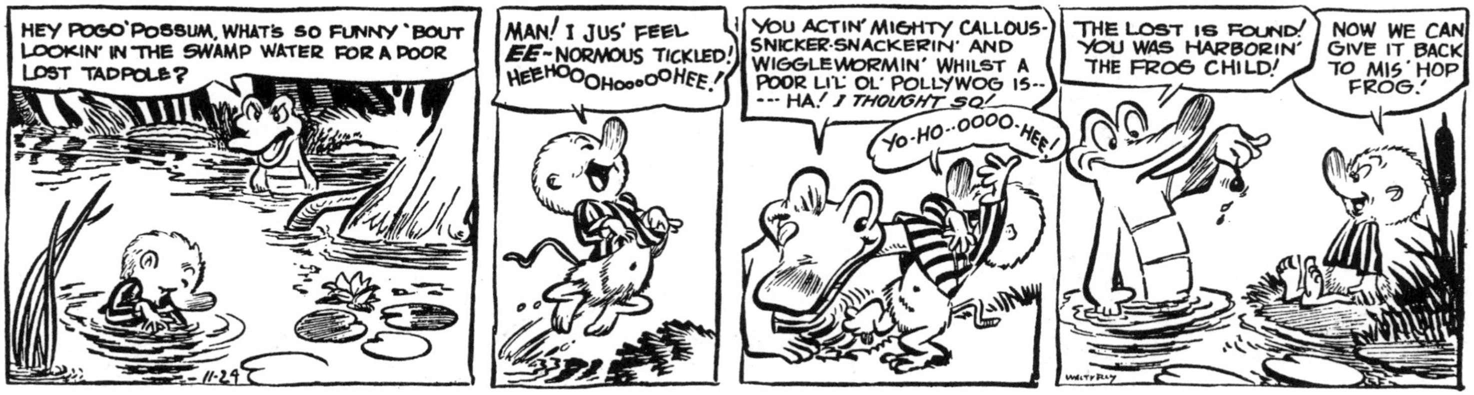
HEY POGO'POSSUM, WHAT'S SO FUNNY 'BOUT LOOKIN' IN THE SWAMP WATER FOR A POOR LOST TADPOLE?
11-24
MAN! I JUS' FEEL EE-NORMOUS TICKLED! HEEHOOOOHoooOOHEE!
YOU ACTIN' MIGHTY CALLOUS-SNICKER-SNACKERIN' AND WIGGLEWORMIN' WHILST A POOR LI'L OL' POLLYWOG IS-- --- HA! I THOUGHT SO!
YO-HO--OOOO-HEE!
THE LOST IS FOUND! YOU WAS HARBORIN' THE FROG CHILD!
NOW WE CAN GIVE IT BACK TO MIS' HOP FROG!

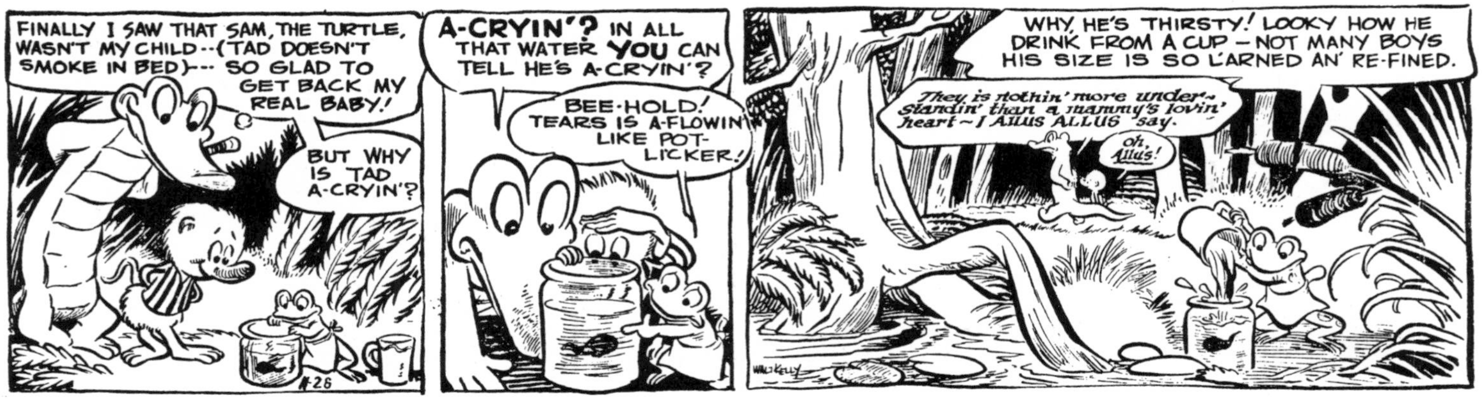
FINALLY I SAW THAT SAM, THE TURTLE, WASN'T MY CHILD--(TAD DOESN'T SMOKE IN BED)--- SO GLAD TO GET BACK MY REAL BABY!
BUT WHY IS TAD A-CRYIN'?
11-26
A-CRYIN'? IN ALL THAT WATER YOU CAN TELL HE'S A-CRYIN'?
BEE-HOLD! TEARS IS A-FLOWIN' LIKE POT-LICKER!
WHY, HE'S THIRSTY! LOOKY HOW HE DRINK FROM A CUP – NOT MANY BOYS HIS SIZE IS SO L'ARNED AN' RE-FINED.
They is nothin' more under-standin' than a mammy's lovin' heart ~ I Allus ALLUS say.
Oh, Allus!
WALT KELLY

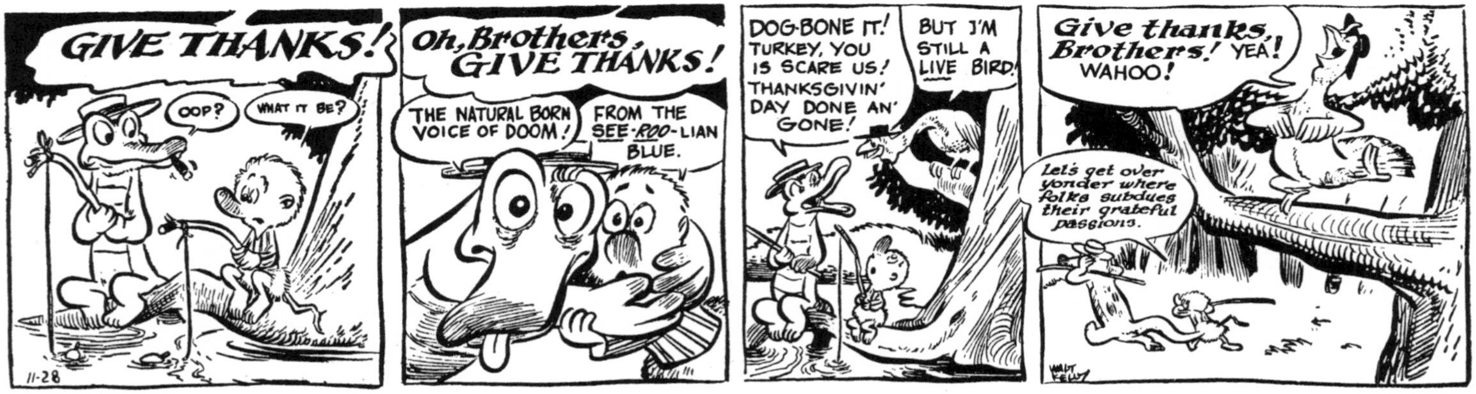
GIVE THANKS!
OOP?
WHAT IT BE?
11-28
Oh, Brothers, GIVE THANKS!
THE NATURAL BORN VOICE OF DOOM!
FROM THE SEE-ROO-LIAN BLUE.
DOG-BONE IT! TURKEY, YOU IS SCARE US! THANKSGIVIN' DAY DONE AN' GONE!
BUT I'M STILL A LIVE BIRD!
Give thanks, Brothers! YEA! WAHOO!
Let's get over yonder where folks subdues their grateful passions.
WALT KELLY

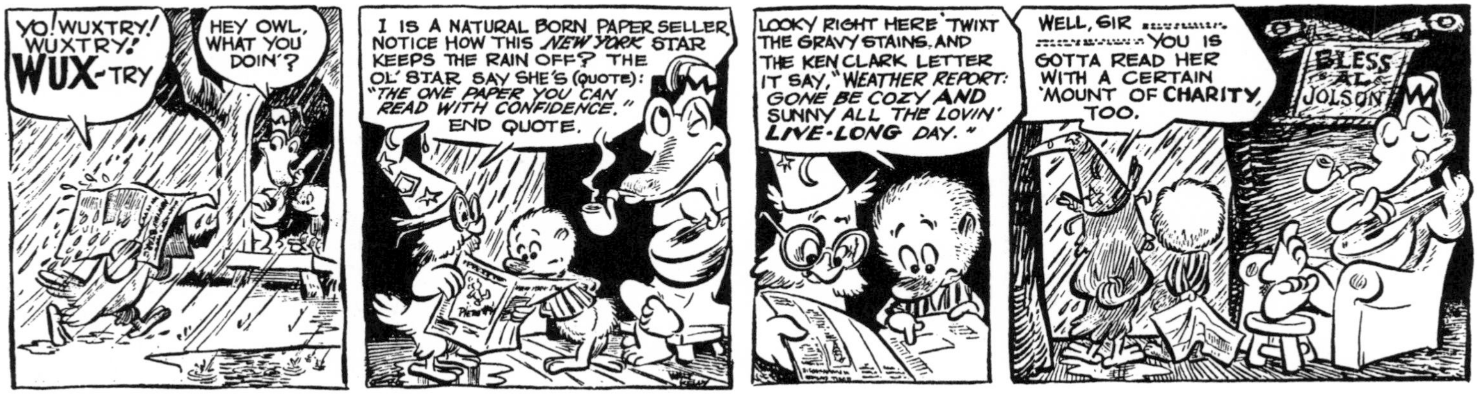
YO! WUXTRY! WUXTRY! WUX-TRY
HEY OWL, WHAT YOU DOIN'?
I IS A NATURAL BORN PAPER SELLER NOTICE HOW THIS NEW YORK STAR KEEPS THE RAIN OFF? THE OL' STAR SAY SHE'S (QUOTE): "THE ONE PAPER YOU CAN READ WITH CONFIDENCE." END QUOTE.
LOOKY RIGHT HERE 'TWIXT THE GRAVY STAINS AND THE KEN CLARK LETTER IT SAY, "WEATHER REPORT: GONE BE COZY AND SUNNY ALL THE LOVIN' LIVE-LONG DAY."
WELL, SIR .... YOU IS GOTTA READ HER WITH A CERTAIN 'MOUNT OF CHARITY, TOO.
BLESS AL JOLSON

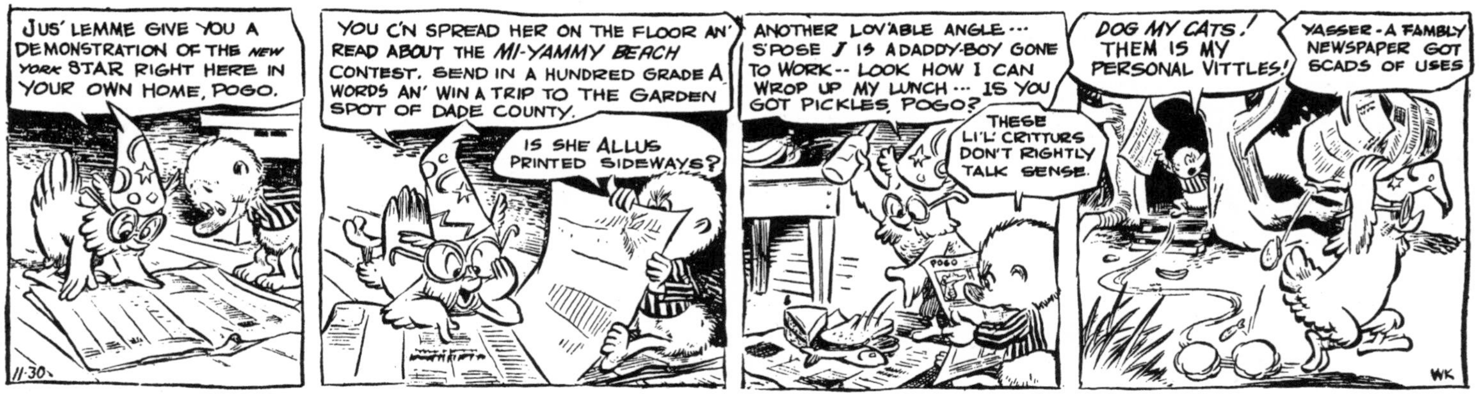
JUS' LEMME GIVE YOU A DEMONSTRATION OF THE NEW YORK STAR RIGHT HERE IN YOUR OWN HOME, POGO.
YOU C'N SPREAD HER ON THE FLOOR AN' READ ABOUT THE MI-YAMMY BEACH CONTEST. SEND IN A HUNDRED GRADE A WORDS AN' WIN A TRIP TO THE GARDEN SPOT OF DADE COUNTY.
IS SHE ALLUS PRINTED SIDEWAYS?
ANOTHER LOV'ABLE ANGLE... S'POSE I IS A DADDY-BOY GONE TO WORK-- LOOK HOW I CAN WROP UP MY LUNCH... IS YOU GOT PICKLES, POGO?
THESE LI'L' CRITTURS DON'T RIGHTLY TALK SENSE.
DOG MY CATS! THEM IS MY PERSONAL VITTLES!
YASSER - A FAMBLY NEWSPAPER GOT SCADS OF USES
11-30

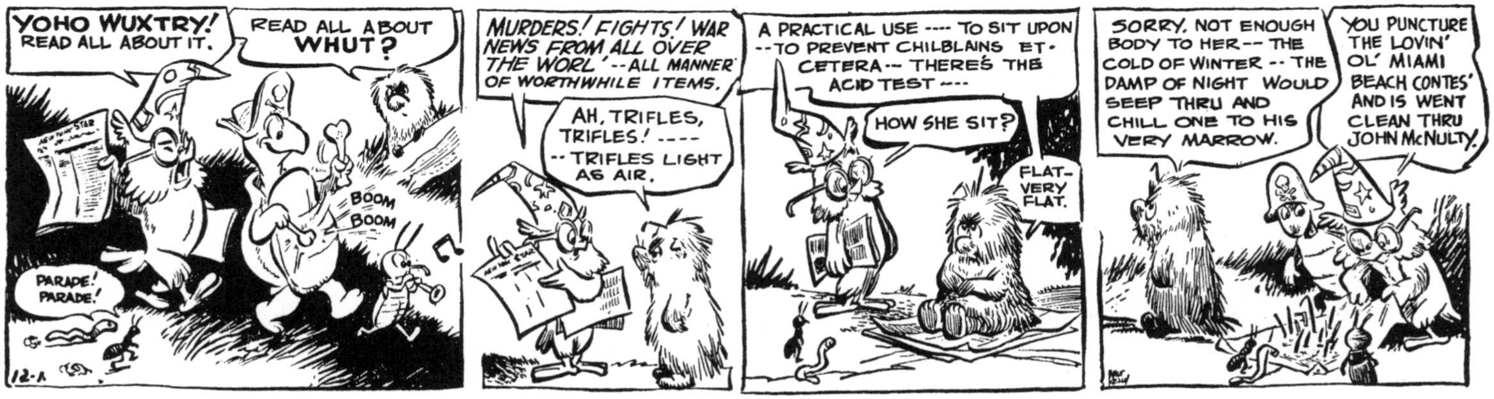
YOHO WUXTRY! READ ALL ABOUT IT.
READ ALL ABOUT WHUT?
PARADE! PARADE!
BOOM BOOM
MURDERS! FIGHTS! WAR NEWS FROM ALL OVER THE WORL' -- ALL MANNER OF WORTHWHILE ITEMS.
AH, TRIFLES, TRIFLES! ---- -- TRIFLES LIGHT AS AIR.
A PRACTICAL USE ---- TO SIT UPON -- TO PREVENT CHILBLAINS ET-CETERA -- THERE'S THE ACID TEST ---
HOW SHE SIT?
FLAT-VERY FLAT.
SORRY, NOT ENOUGH BODY TO HER -- THE COLD OF WINTER -- THE DAMP OF NIGHT WOULD SEEP THRU AND CHILL ONE TO HIS VERY MARROW.
YOU PUNCTURE THE LOVIN' OL' MIAMI BEACH CONTES' AND IS WENT CLEAN THRU JOHN McNULTY.
12-1

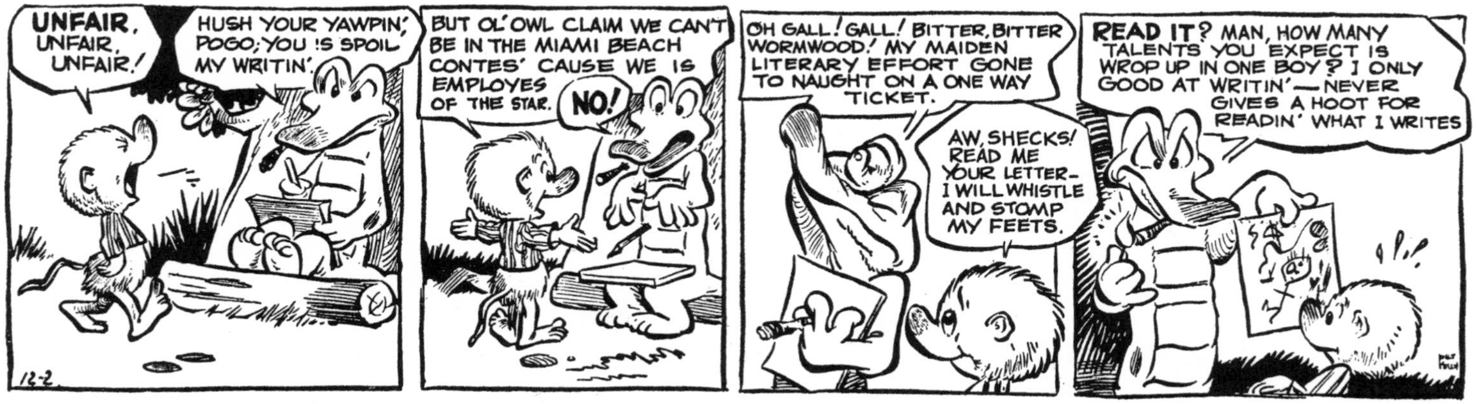
UNFAIR, UNFAIR, UNFAIR!
HUSH YOUR YAWPIN', POGO; YOU IS SPOIL' MY WRITIN'.
BUT OL' OWL CLAIM WE CAN'T BE IN THE MIAMI BEACH CONTES' CAUSE WE IS EMPLOYES OF THE STAR.
NO!
OH GALL! GALL! BITTER, BITTER WORMWOOD! MY MAIDEN LITERARY EFFORT GONE TO NAUGHT ON A ONE WAY TICKET.
AW, SHECKS! READ ME YOUR LETTER-I WILL WHISTLE AND STOMP MY FEETS.
READ IT? MAN, HOW MANY TALENTS YOU EXPECT IS WROP UP IN ONE BOY? I ONLY GOOD AT WRITIN'— NEVER GIVES A HOOT FOR READIN' WHAT I WRITES
12-2

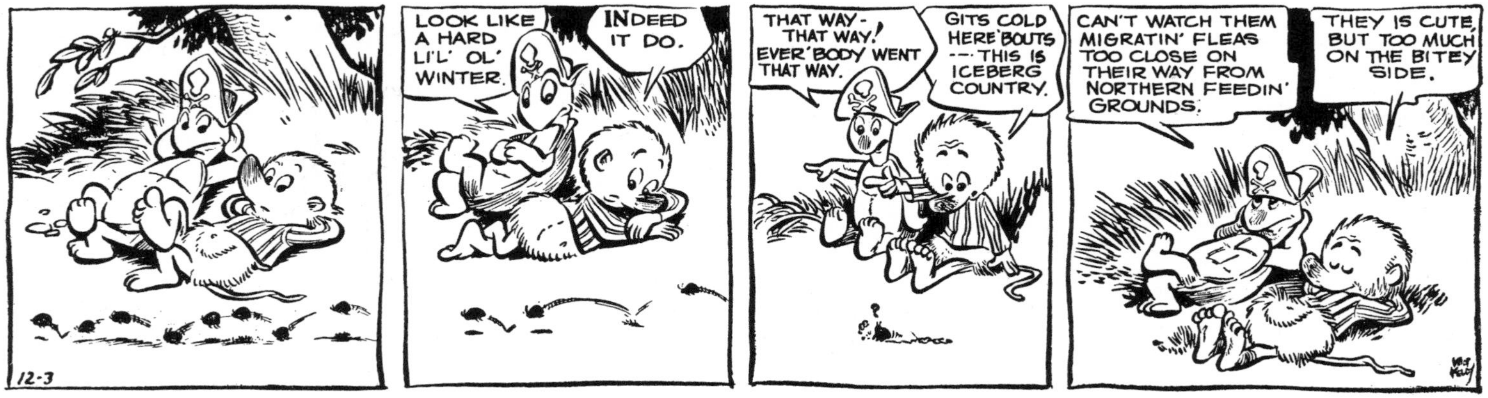
12-3
LOOK LIKE A HARD LI'L' OL' WINTER.
INDEED IT DO.
THAT WAY - THAT WAY! EVER'BODY WENT THAT WAY.
GITS COLD HERE'BOUTS -- THIS IS ICEBERG COUNTRY.
CAN'T WATCH THEM MIGRATIN' FLEAS TOO CLOSE ON THEIR WAY FROM NORTHERN FEEDIN' GROUNDS.
THEY IS CUTE, BUT TOO MUCH ON THE BITEY SIDE.

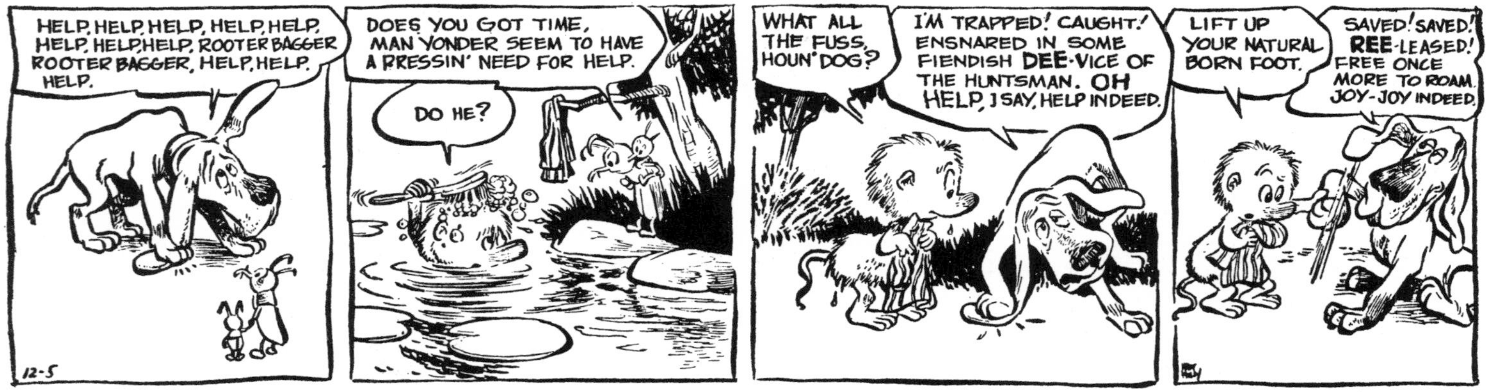
12-5
HELP, HELP, HELP, HELP, HELP, HELP, HELP, HELP, ROOTER BAGGER ROOTER BAGGER, HELP, HELP, HELP.
DOES YOU GOT TIME, MAN YONDER SEEM TO HAVE A PRESSIN' NEED FOR HELP.
DO HE?
WHAT ALL THE FUSS, HOUN' DOG?
I'M TRAPPED! CAUGHT! ENSNARED IN SOME FIENDISH DEE-VICE OF THE HUNTSMAN. OH HELP, I SAY, HELP INDEED.
LIFT UP YOUR NATURAL BORN FOOT.
SAVED! SAVED! REE-LEASED! FREE ONCE MORE TO ROAM. JOY-JOY INDEED.

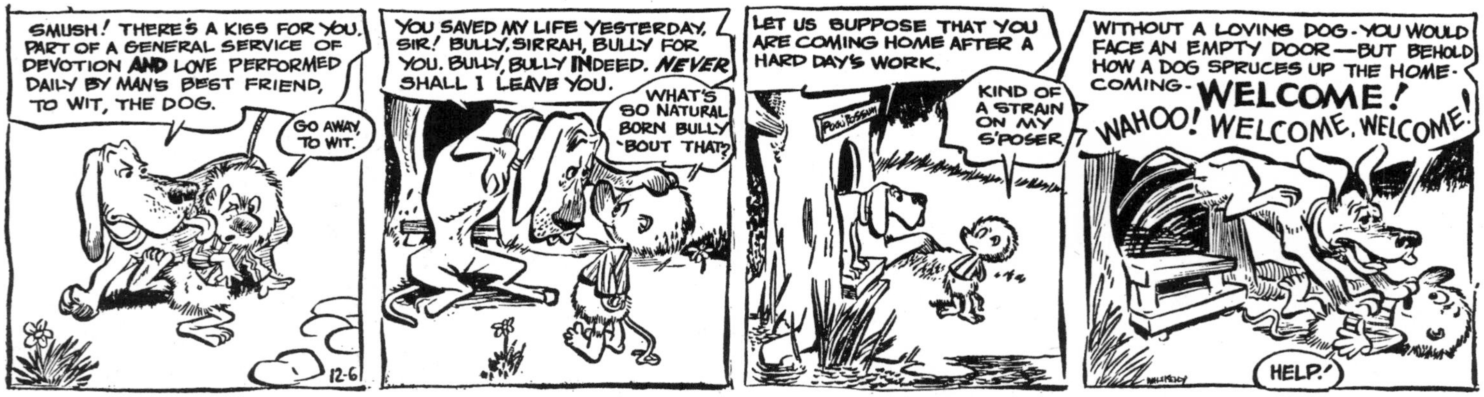
SMUSH! THERE'S A KISS FOR YOU. PART OF A GENERAL SERVICE OF DEVOTION AND LOVE PERFORMED DAILY BY MAN'S BEST FRIEND, TO WIT, THE DOG.
GO AWAY, TO WIT.
12-6
YOU SAVED MY LIFE YESTERDAY, SIR! BULLY, SIRRAH, BULLY FOR YOU. BULLY, BULLY INDEED. NEVER SHALL I LEAVE YOU.
WHAT'S SO NATURAL BORN BULLY 'BOUT THAT?
LET US SUPPOSE THAT YOU ARE COMING HOME AFTER A HARD DAY'S WORK.
KIND OF A STRAIN ON MY S'POSER
WITHOUT A LOVING DOG - YOU WOULD FACE AN EMPTY DOOR — BUT BEHOLD HOW A DOG SPRUCES UP THE HOME-COMING - WELCOME!
WAHOO! WELCOME, WELCOME!
HELP!

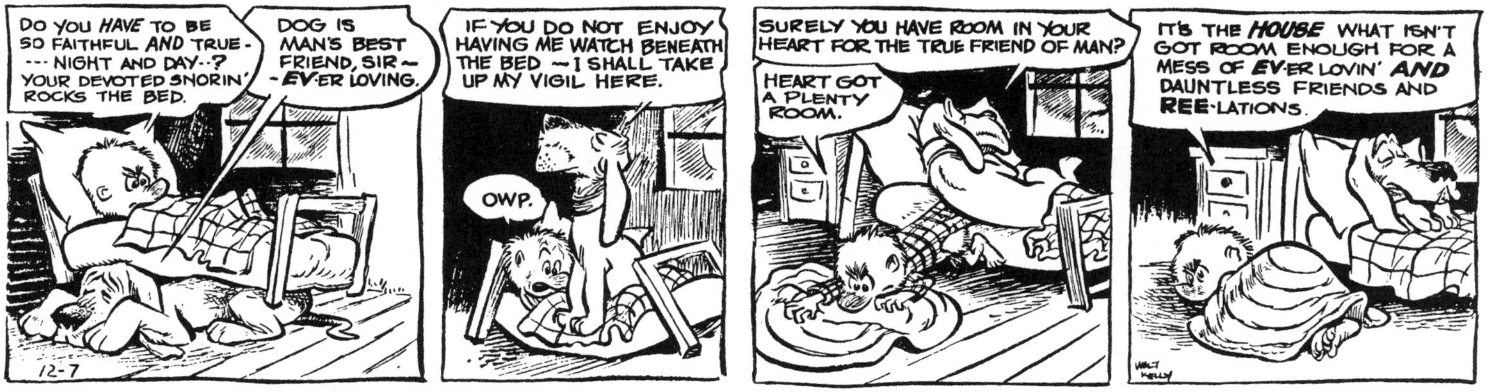
DO YOU *HAVE* TO BE SO FAITHFUL *AND* TRUE - --- NIGHT AND DAY--? YOUR DEVOTED SNORIN' ROCKS THE BED.
DOG IS MAN'S BEST FRIEND, SIR ~ -*EV*-ER LOVING.
12-7
IF YOU DO NOT ENJOY HAVING ME WATCH BENEATH THE BED ~ I SHALL TAKE UP MY VIGIL HERE.
OWP.
SURELY YOU HAVE ROOM IN YOUR HEART FOR THE TRUE FRIEND OF MAN?
HEART GOT A PLENTY ROOM.
IT'S THE *HOUSE* WHAT ISN'T GOT ROOM ENOUGH FOR A MESS OF *EV*-ER LOVIN' *AND* DAUNTLESS FRIENDS AND **REE**-LATIONS.
WALT KELLY

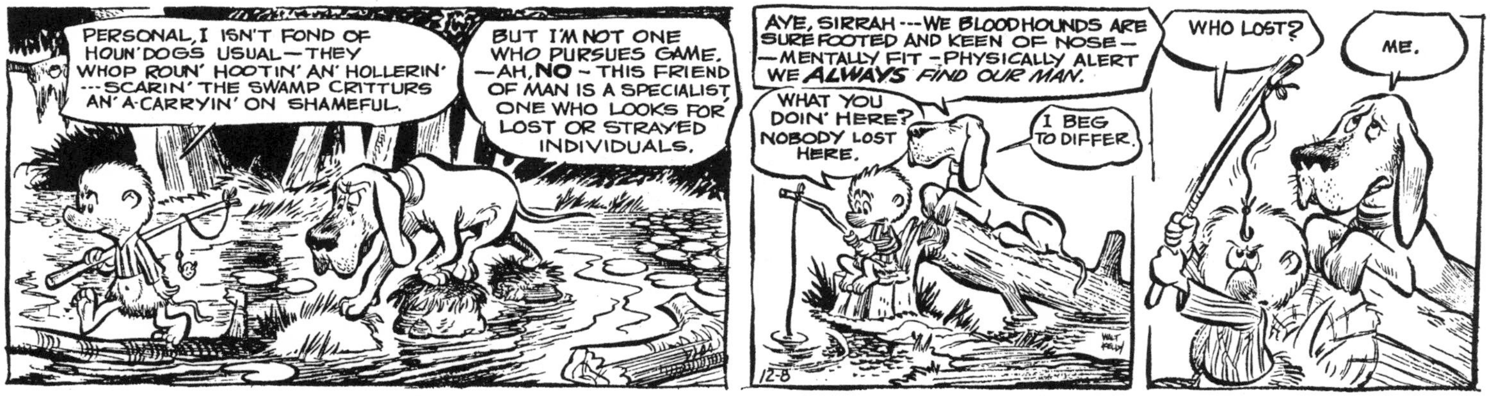
PERSONAL, I ISN'T FOND OF HOUN'DOGS USUAL — THEY WHOP ROUN' HOOTIN' AN' HOLLERIN' ---SCARIN' THE SWAMP CRITTURS AN' A-CARRYIN' ON SHAMEFUL.
BUT I'M NOT ONE WHO PURSUES GAME. —AH, **NO** ~ THIS FRIEND OF MAN IS A SPECIALIST, ONE WHO LOOKS FOR LOST OR STRAYED INDIVIDUALS.
AYE, SIRRAH ---WE BLOODHOUNDS ARE SURE FOOTED AND KEEN OF NOSE— —MENTALLY FIT —PHYSICALLY ALERT WE *ALWAYS FIND OUR MAN.*
WHAT YOU DOIN' HERE? NOBODY LOST HERE.
I BEG TO DIFFER.
12-8
WALT KELLY
WHO LOST?
ME.

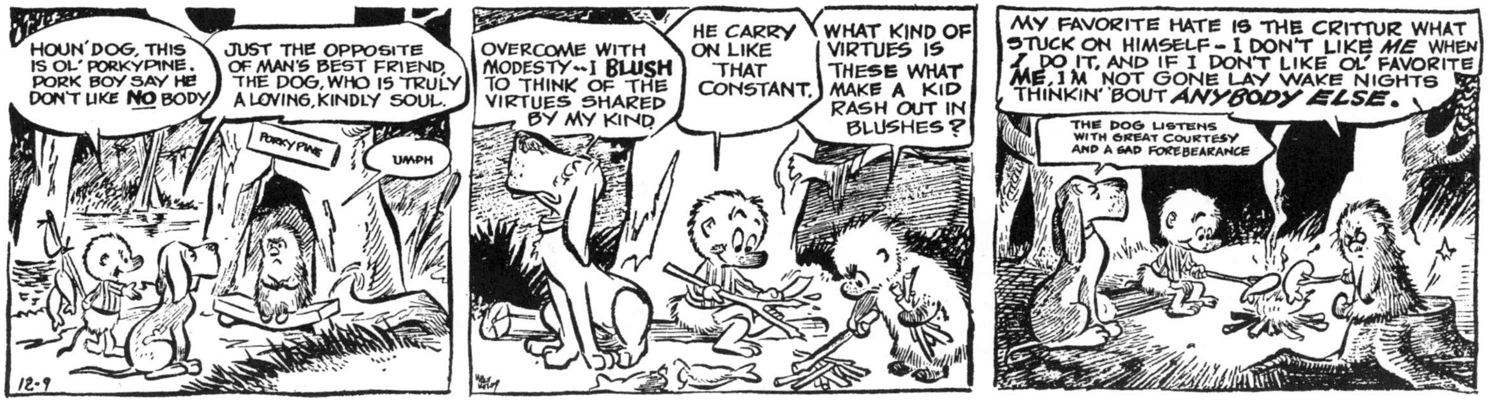
HOUN'DOG, THIS IS OL' PORKYPINE. PORK BOY SAY HE DON'T LIKE NO BODY.
JUST THE OPPOSITE OF MAN'S BEST FRIEND, THE DOG, WHO IS TRULY A LOVING, KINDLY SOUL.
PORKY PINE
UMPH
12-9
OVERCOME WITH MODESTY--I **BLUSH** TO THINK OF THE VIRTUES SHARED BY MY KIND.
HE CARRY ON LIKE THAT CONSTANT.
WHAT KIND OF VIRTUES IS THESE WHAT MAKE A KID RASH OUT IN BLUSHES?
WALT KELLY
MY FAVORITE HATE IS THE CRITTUR WHAT STUCK ON HIMSELF - I DON'T LIKE *ME* WHEN *I* DO IT, AND IF I DON'T LIKE OL' FAVORITE *ME*, I'M NOT GONE LAY WAKE NIGHTS THINKIN' 'BOUT *ANYBODY ELSE*.
THE DOG LISTENS WITH GREAT COURTESY AND A SAD FOREBEARANCE

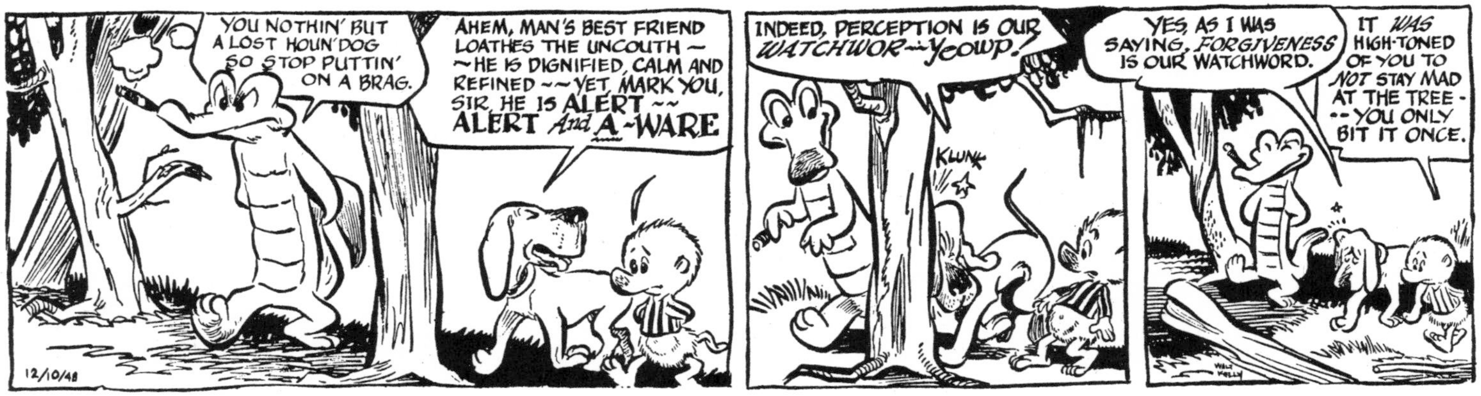
YOU NOTHIN' BUT A LOST HOUN'DOG SO STOP PUTTIN' ON A BRAG.
AHEM, MAN'S BEST FRIEND LOATHES THE UNCOUTH ~ ~HE IS DIGNIFIED, CALM AND REFINED ~~ YET, MARK YOU, SIR, HE IS ALERT ~~ ALERT And A-WARE
INDEED, PERCEPTION IS OUR WATCHWOR-- YEOWP!
KLUNK
YES, AS I WAS SAYING, FORGIVENESS IS OUR WATCHWORD.
IT WAS HIGH-TONED OF YOU TO NOT STAY MAD AT THE TREE - -YOU ONLY BIT IT ONCE.
12/10/48

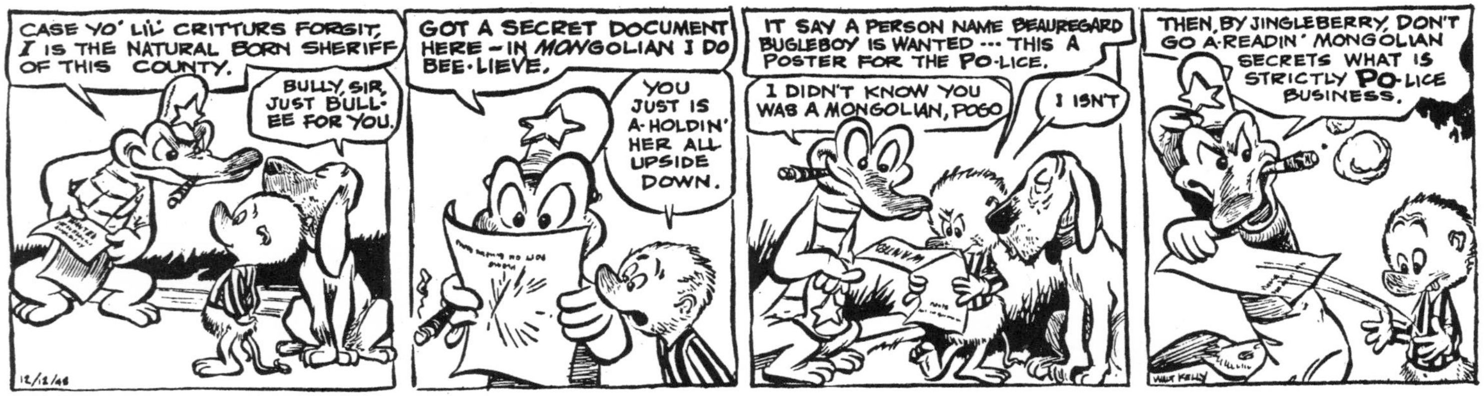
CASE YO' LIL' CRITTURS FORGIT, I IS THE NATURAL BORN SHERIFF OF THIS COUNTY.
BULLY, SIR, JUST BULL-EE FOR YOU.
GOT A SECRET DOCUMENT HERE - IN MONGOLIAN I DO BEE-LIEVE.
YOU JUST IS A-HOLDIN' HER ALL UPSIDE DOWN.
IT SAY A PERSON NAME BEAUREGARD BUGLEBOY IS WANTED --- THIS A POSTER FOR THE PO-LICE.
I DIDN'T KNOW YOU WAS A MONGOLIAN, POGO
I ISN'T
THEN, BY JINGLEBERRY, DON'T GO A-READIN' MONGOLIAN SECRETS WHAT IS STRICTLY PO-LICE BUSINESS.
12/11/48
WALT KELLY

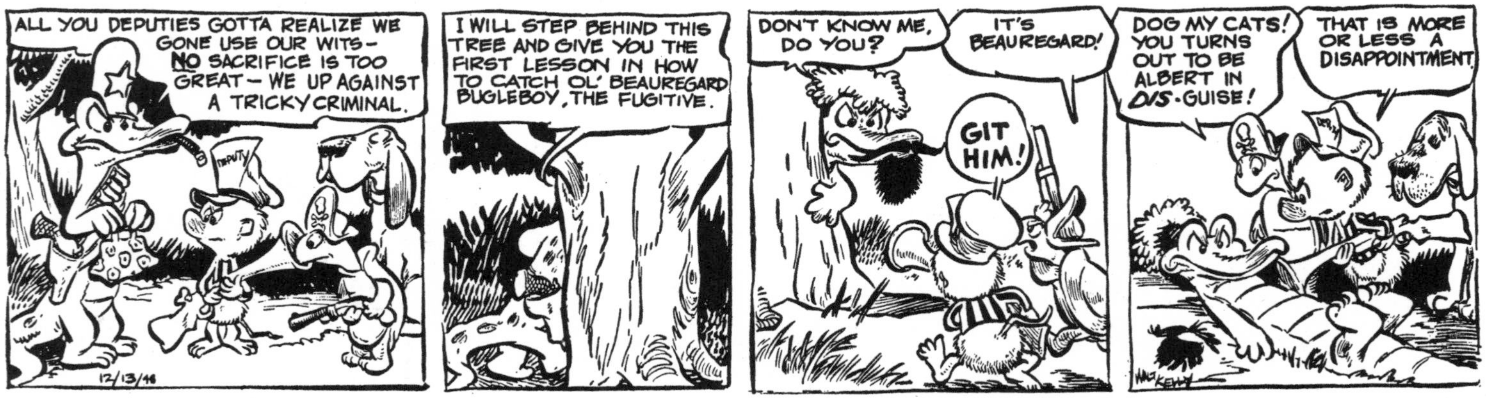
ALL YOU DEPUTIES GOTTA REALIZE WE GONE USE OUR WITS- NO SACRIFICE IS TOO GREAT - WE UP AGAINST A TRICKY CRIMINAL.
DEPUTY
I WILL STEP BEHIND THIS TREE AND GIVE YOU THE FIRST LESSON IN HOW TO CATCH OL' BEAUREGARD BUGLEBOY, THE FUGITIVE.
DON'T KNOW ME, DO YOU?
IT'S BEAUREGARD!
GIT HIM!
DOG MY CATS! YOU TURNS OUT TO BE ALBERT IN DIS-GUISE!
THAT IS MORE OR LESS A DISAPPOINTMENT.
12/13/48
WALT KELLY

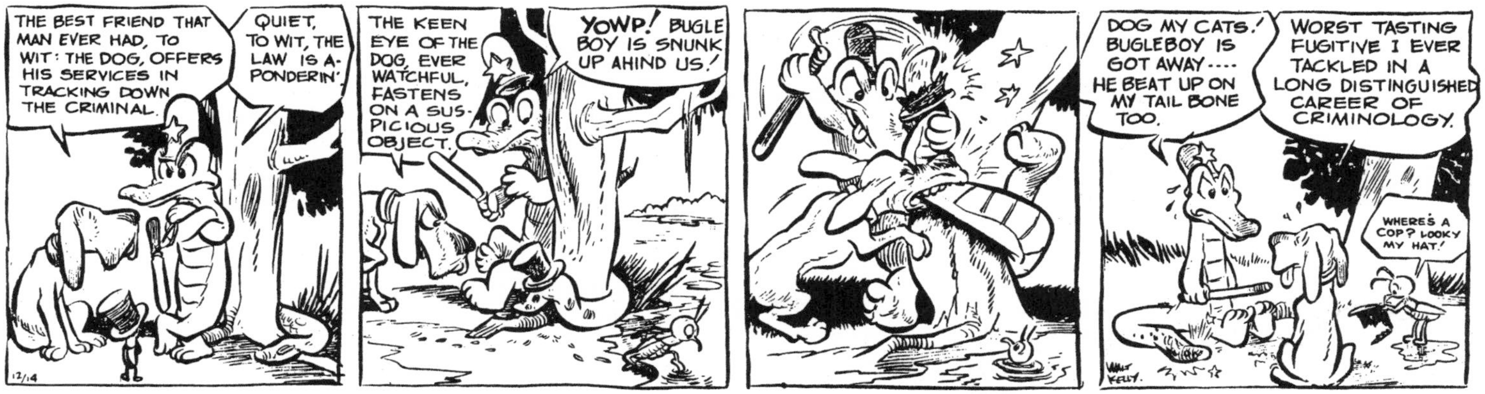
THE BEST FRIEND THAT MAN EVER HAD, TO WIT: THE DOG, OFFERS HIS SERVICES IN TRACKING DOWN THE CRIMINAL.
QUIET, TO WIT, THE LAW IS A-PONDERIN'.
12/14
THE KEEN EYE OF THE DOG, EVER WATCHFUL, FASTENS ON A SUSPICIOUS OBJECT.
YOWP! BUGLE BOY IS SNUNK UP AHIND US!
DOG MY CATS! BUGLEBOY IS GOT AWAY---- HE BEAT UP ON MY TAIL BONE TOO.
WORST TASTING FUGITIVE I EVER TACKLED IN A LONG DISTINGUISHED CAREER OF CRIMINOLOGY.
WHERE'S A COP? LOOKY MY HAT!
WALT KELLY

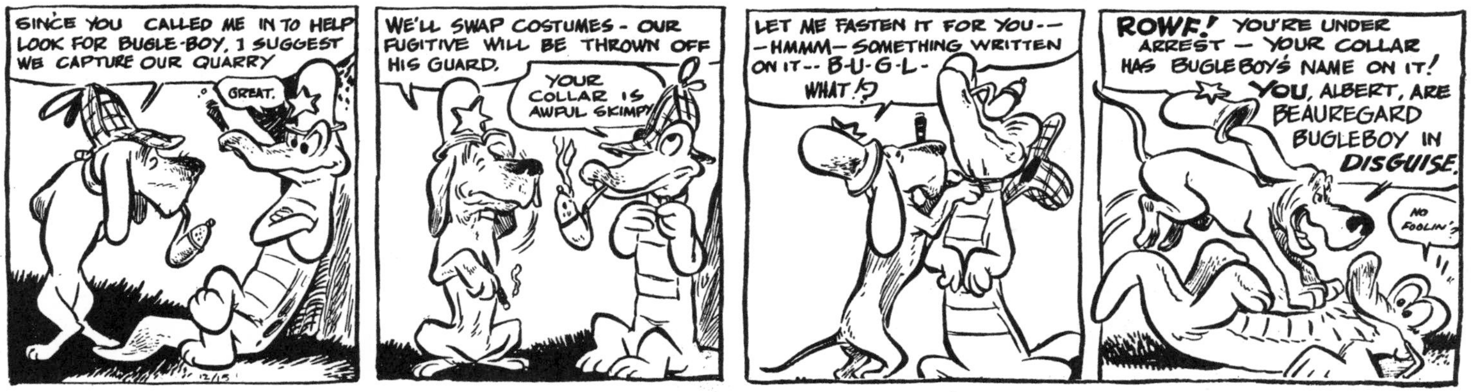
SINCE YOU CALLED ME IN TO HELP LOOK FOR BUGLE-BOY, I SUGGEST WE CAPTURE OUR QUARRY
GREAT.
12/15
WE'LL SWAP COSTUMES - OUR FUGITIVE WILL BE THROWN OFF HIS GUARD.
YOUR COLLAR IS AWFUL SKIMPY
LET ME FASTEN IT FOR YOU-- -HMMM- SOMETHING WRITTEN ON IT-- B-U-G-L-
WHAT!?
ROWF! YOU'RE UNDER ARREST - YOUR COLLAR HAS BUGLEBOY'S NAME ON IT! YOU, ALBERT, ARE BEAUREGARD BUGLEBOY IN DISGUISE.
NO FOOLIN'

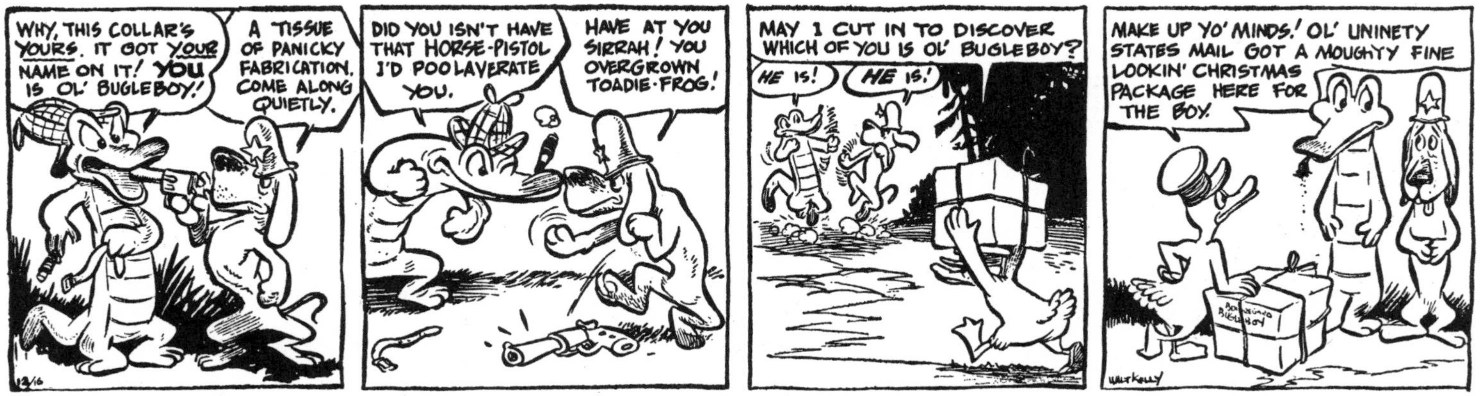
WHY, THIS COLLAR'S YOURS. IT GOT YOUR NAME ON IT! YOU IS OL' BUGLEBOY!
A TISSUE OF PANICKY FABRICATION. COME ALONG QUIETLY.
12/16
DID YOU ISN'T HAVE THAT HORSE-PISTOL I'D POOLAVERATE YOU.
HAVE AT YOU SIRRAH! YOU OVERGROWN TOADIE-FROG!
MAY I CUT IN TO DISCOVER WHICH OF YOU IS OL' BUGLEBOY?
HE IS!
HE IS!
MAKE UP YO' MINDS! OL' UNINETY STATES MAIL GOT A MOUGHTY FINE LOOKIN' CHRISTMAS PACKAGE HERE FOR THE BOY.
WALT KELLY

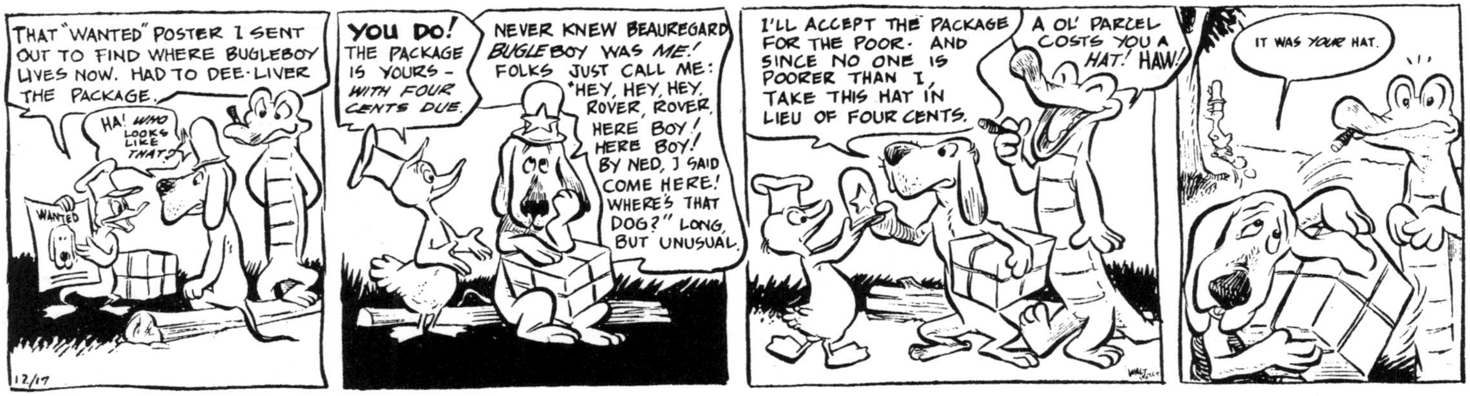
THAT "WANTED" POSTER I SENT OUT TO FIND WHERE BUGLEBOY LIVES NOW. HAD TO DEE-LIVER THE PACKAGE.
HA! WHO LOOKS LIKE THAT?
WANTED
12/17
YOU DO! THE PACKAGE IS YOURS - WITH FOUR CENTS DUE.
NEVER KNEW BEAUREGARD BUGLEBOY WAS ME! FOLKS JUST CALL ME: "HEY, HEY, HEY, ROVER, ROVER, HERE BOY! HERE BOY! BY NED, I SAID COME HERE! WHERE'S THAT DOG?" LONG, BUT UNUSUAL.
I'LL ACCEPT THE PACKAGE FOR THE POOR- AND SINCE NO ONE IS POORER THAN I, TAKE THIS HAT IN LIEU OF FOUR CENTS.
A OL' PARCEL COSTS YOU A HAT! HAW!
IT WAS YOUR HAT.

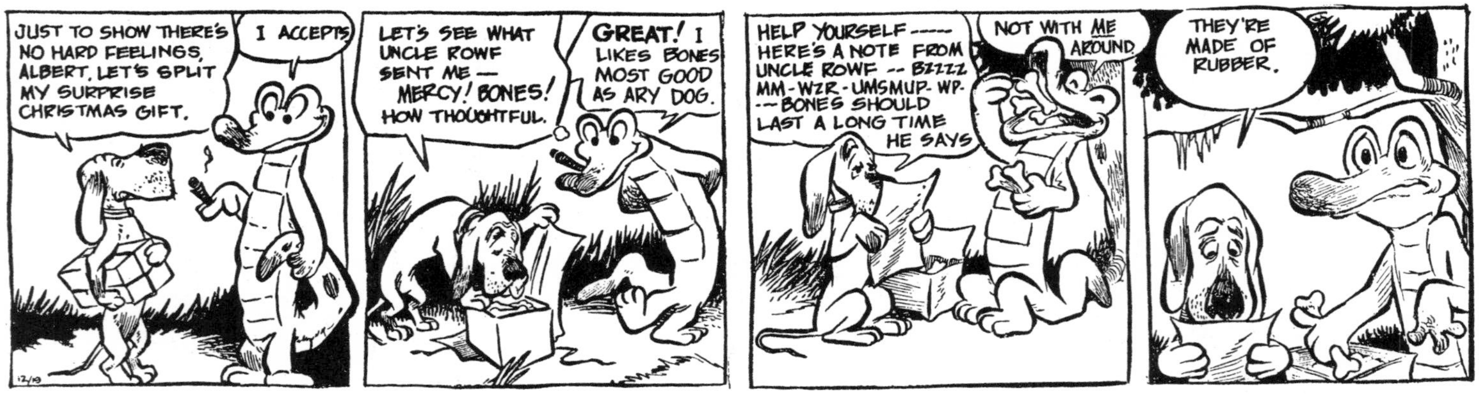
JUST TO SHOW THERE'S NO HARD FEELINGS, ALBERT, LET'S SPLIT MY SURPRISE CHRISTMAS GIFT.
I ACCEPTS
12/19
LET'S SEE WHAT UNCLE ROWF SENT ME — MERCY! BONES! HOW THOUGHTFUL.
GREAT! I LIKES BONES MOST GOOD AS ARY DOG.
HELP YOURSELF ----- HERE'S A NOTE FROM UNCLE ROWF -- BZZZZ MM-WZR-UMSMUP-WP- --BONES SHOULD LAST A LONG TIME HE SAYS
NOT WITH ME AROUND.
THEY'RE MADE OF RUBBER.

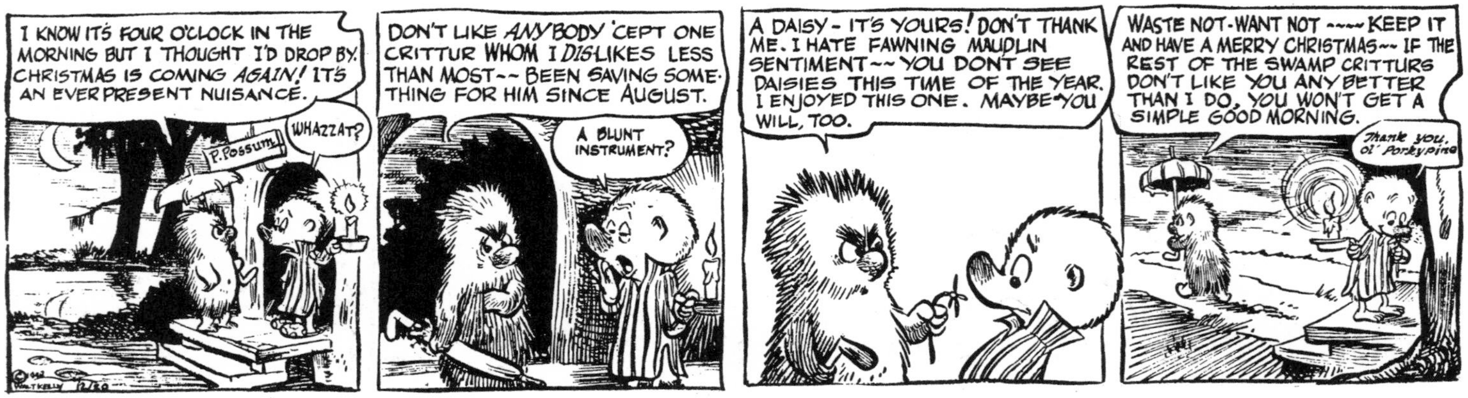
I KNOW IT'S FOUR O'CLOCK IN THE MORNING BUT I THOUGHT I'D DROP BY. CHRISTMAS IS COMING AGAIN! IT'S AN EVERPRESENT NUISANCE.
P. Possum
WHAZZAT?
DON'T LIKE ANYBODY 'CEPT ONE CRITTUR WHOM I DISLIKES LESS THAN MOST-- BEEN SAVING SOME-THING FOR HIM SINCE AUGUST.
A BLUNT INSTRUMENT?
A DAISY - IT'S YOURS! DON'T THANK ME. I HATE FAWNING MAUDLIN SENTIMENT-- YOU DONT SEE DAISIES THIS TIME OF THE YEAR. I ENJOYED THIS ONE. MAYBE YOU WILL, TOO.
WASTE NOT-WANT NOT ---- KEEP IT AND HAVE A MERRY CHRISTMAS-- IF THE REST OF THE SWAMP CRITTURS DON'T LIKE YOU ANY BETTER THAN I DO, YOU WON'T GET A SIMPLE GOOD MORNING.
Thank you, ol' Porkypine

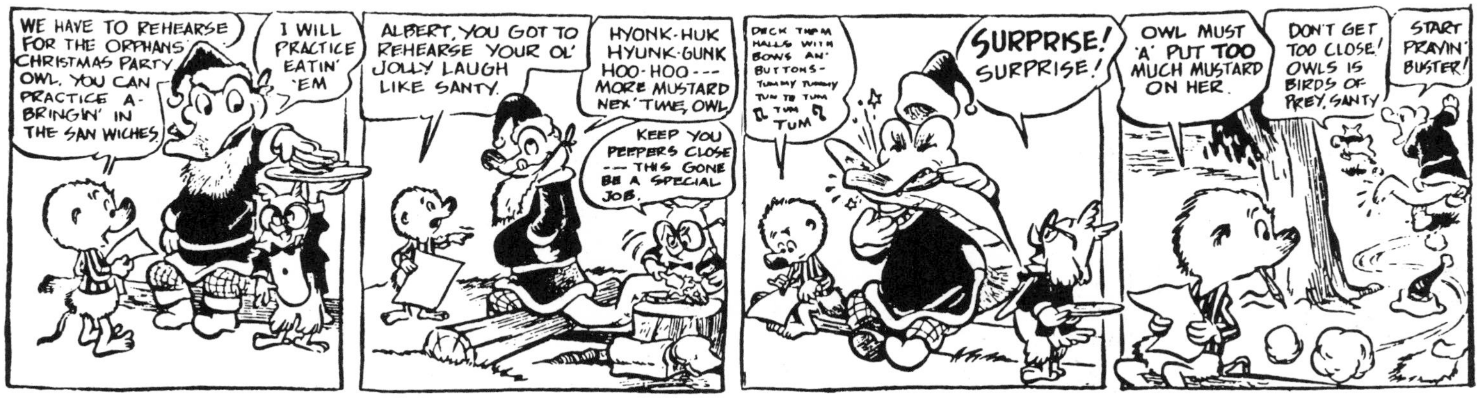
WE HAVE TO REHEARSE FOR THE ORPHANS CHRISTMAS PARTY OWL. YOU CAN PRACTICE A-BRINGIN' IN THE SAN WICHES.
I WILL PRACTICE EATIN' 'EM
ALBERT, YOU GOT TO REHEARSE YOUR OL' JOLLY LAUGH LIKE SANTY.
HYONK-HUK HYUNK-GUNK HOO-HOO--- MORE MUSTARD NEX' TIME, OWL
KEEP YOU PEEPERS CLOSE --- THIS GONE BE A SPECIAL JOB.
DECK THEM HALLS WITH BOWS AN' BUTTONS- TUMMY TUMMY TUM TE TUM TUM TUM
SURPRISE! SURPRISE!
OWL MUST 'A' PUT TOO MUCH MUSTARD ON HER.
DON'T GET TOO CLOSE! OWLS IS BIRDS OF PREY, SANTY
START PRAYIN' BUSTER!

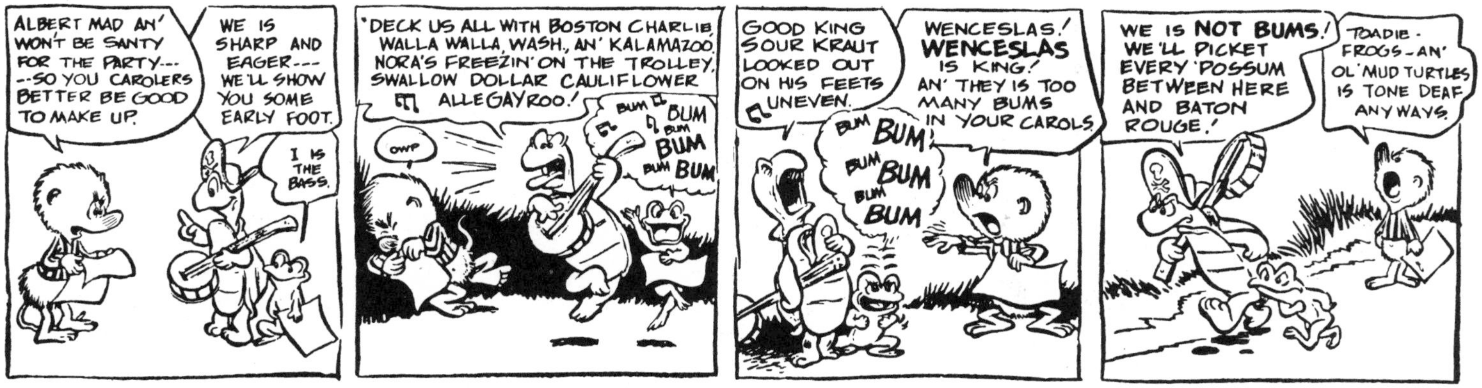
ALBERT MAD AN' WON'T BE SANTY FOR THE PARTY--- --SO YOU CAROLERS BETTER BE GOOD TO MAKE UP.
WE IS SHARP AND EAGER--- WE'LL SHOW YOU SOME EARLY FOOT.
I IS THE BASS.
"DECK US ALL WITH BOSTON CHARLIE WALLA WALLA, WASH., AN' KALAMAZOO. NORA'S FREEZIN' ON THE TROLLEY, SWALLOW DOLLAR CAULIFLOWER ALLEGAYROO.'
OWP
BUM BUM BUM BUM BUM BUM BUM
GOOD KING SOUR KRAUT LOOKED OUT ON HIS FEETS UNEVEN.
BUM BUM BUM BUM BUM BUM
WENCESLAS! WENCESLAS IS KING! AN' THEY IS TOO MANY BUMS IN YOUR CAROLS.
WE IS NOT BUMS! WE'LL PICKET EVERY 'POSSUM BETWEEN HERE AND BATON ROUGE.'
TOADIE-FROGS-AN' OL' MUD TURTLES IS TONE DEAF ANYWAYS.

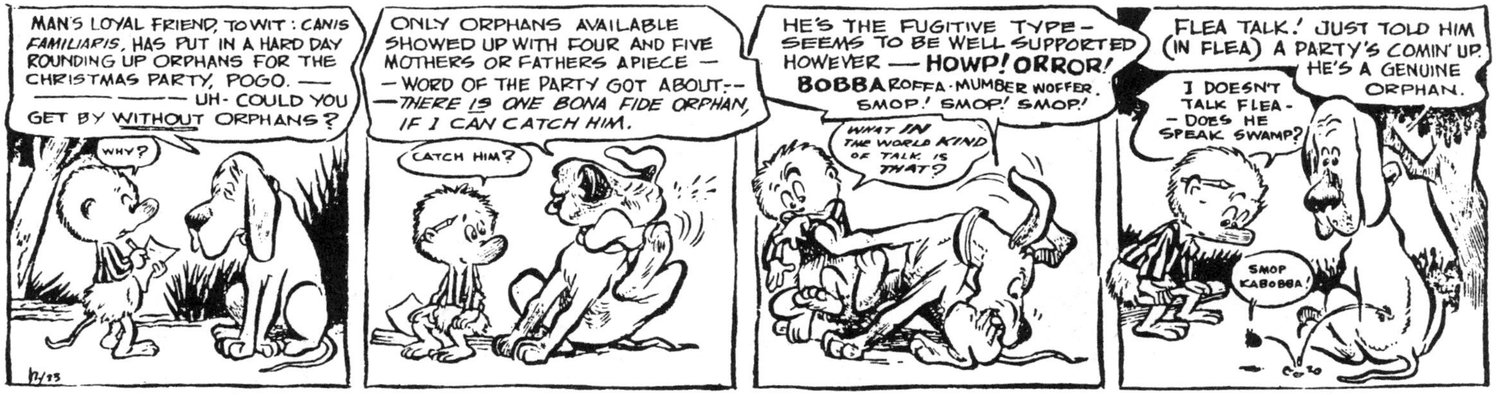
MAN'S LOYAL FRIEND, TO WIT: CANIS FAMILIARIS, HAS PUT IN A HARD DAY ROUNDING UP ORPHANS FOR THE CHRISTMAS PARTY, POGO. ——— ——— UH- COULD YOU GET BY WITHOUT ORPHANS?
WHY?
ONLY ORPHANS AVAILABLE SHOWED UP WITH FOUR AND FIVE MOTHERS OR FATHERS APIECE — — WORD OF THE PARTY GOT ABOUT.-- — THERE IS ONE BONA FIDE ORPHAN, IF I CAN CATCH HIM.
CATCH HIM?
HE'S THE FUGITIVE TYPE- SEEMS TO BE WELL SUPPORTED HOWEVER — HOWP! ORROR! BOBBA ROFFA-MUMBER WOFFER. SMOP! SMOP! SMOP!
WHAT IN THE WORLD KIND OF TALK IS THAT?
FLEA TALK! JUST TOLD HIM (IN FLEA) A PARTY'S COMIN' UP. HE'S A GENUINE ORPHAN.
I DOESN'T TALK FLEA- - DOES HE SPEAK SWAMP?
SMOP KABOBBA!

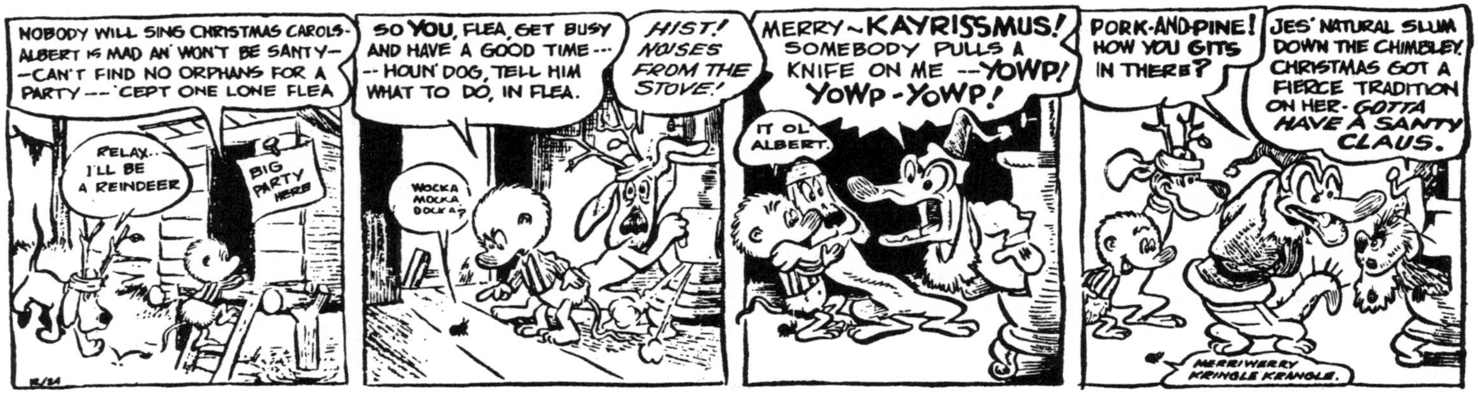
NOBODY WILL SING CHRISTMAS CAROLS-ALBERT IS MAD AN' WON'T BE SANTY--CAN'T FIND NO ORPHANS FOR A PARTY--'CEPT ONE LONE FLEA
RELAX.. I'LL BE A REINDEER
BIG PARTY HERE
12/24
SO YOU, FLEA, GET BUSY AND HAVE A GOOD TIME---HOUN' DOG, TELL HIM WHAT TO DO, IN FLEA.
WOCKA MOCKA DOCKA?
HIST! NOISES FROM THE STOVE!
MERRY~KAYRISSMUS! SOMEBODY PULLS A KNIFE ON ME --YOWP! YOWP-YOWP!
IT OL' ALBERT.
PORK-AND-PINE! HOW YOU GITS IN THERE?
JES' NATURAL SLUM DOWN THE CHIMBLEY. CHRISTMAS GOT A FIERCE TRADITION ON HER- GOTTA HAVE A SANTY CLAUS.
MERRIWERRY KRINGLE KRANGLE.

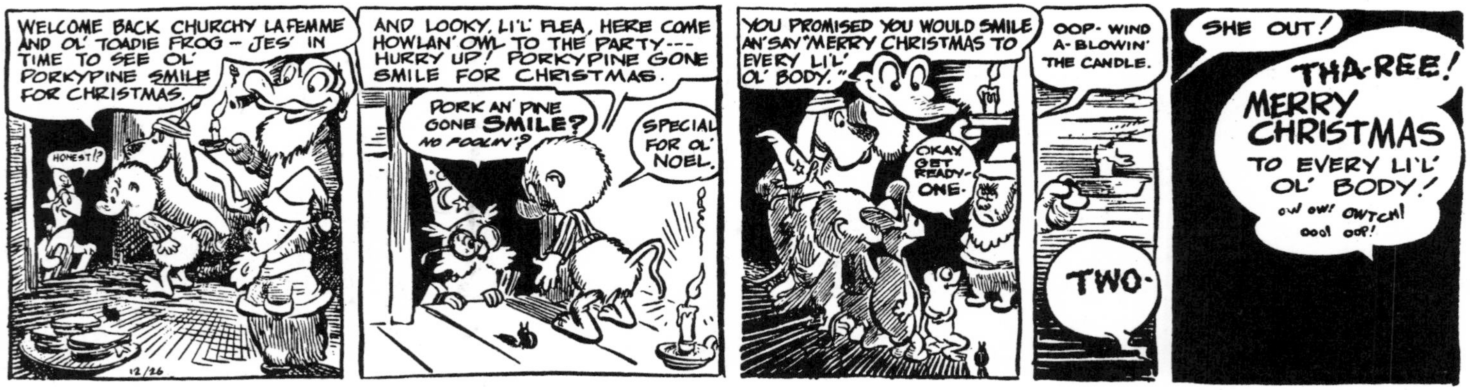
WELCOME BACK CHURCHY LA FEMME AND OL' TOADIE FROG- JES' IN TIME TO SEE OL' PORKYPINE SMILE FOR CHRISTMAS.
HONEST!?
12/26
AND LOOKY, LI'L' FLEA, HERE COME HOWLAN' OWL TO THE PARTY---HURRY UP! PORKYPINE GONE SMILE FOR CHRISTMAS.
PORK AN' PINE GONE SMILE? NO FOOLIN'?
SPECIAL FOR OL' NOEL.
YOU PROMISED YOU WOULD SMILE AN' SAY "MERRY CHRISTMAS TO EVERY LI'L' OL' BODY."
OKAY GET READY- ONE.
OOP- WIND A-BLOWIN' THE CANDLE.
TWO-
SHE OUT!
THA-REE! MERRY CHRISTMAS TO EVERY LI'L' OL' BODY!
OW OW! OWTCH! OOO! OOP!

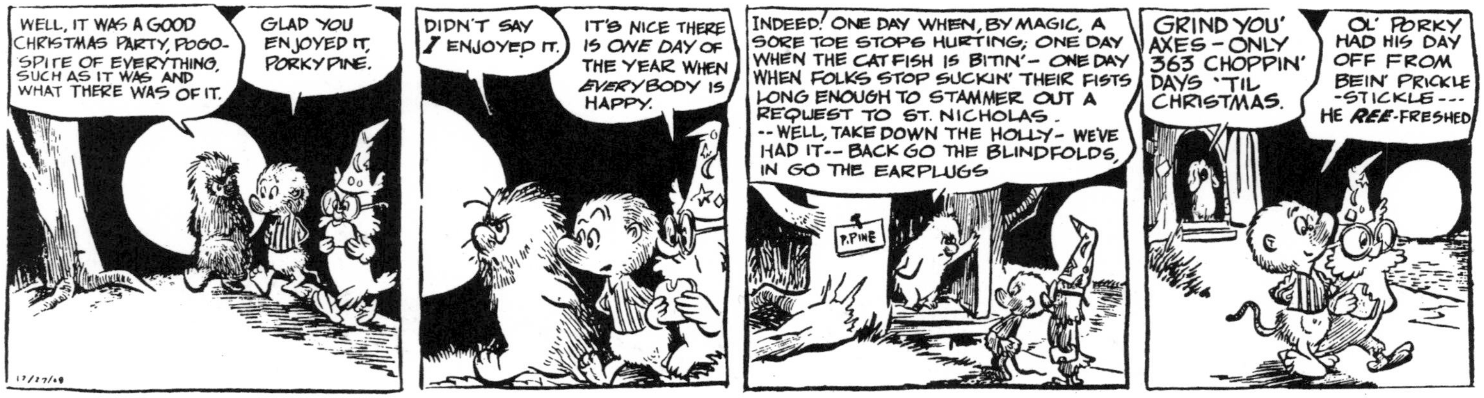
WELL, IT WAS A GOOD CHRISTMAS PARTY, POGO-SPITE OF EVERYTHING, SUCH AS IT WAS AND WHAT THERE WAS OF IT.
GLAD YOU ENJOYED IT, PORKYPINE.
12/27/48
DIDN'T SAY I ENJOYED IT.
IT'S NICE THERE IS ONE DAY OF THE YEAR WHEN EVERYBODY IS HAPPY.
INDEED! ONE DAY WHEN, BY MAGIC, A SORE TOE STOPS HURTING; ONE DAY WHEN THE CATFISH IS BITIN'- ONE DAY WHEN FOLKS STOP SUCKIN' THEIR FISTS LONG ENOUGH TO STAMMER OUT A REQUEST TO ST. NICHOLAS. --WELL, TAKE DOWN THE HOLLY- WE'VE HAD IT-- BACK GO THE BLINDFOLDS, IN GO THE EARPLUGS
P. PINE
GRIND YOU' AXES - ONLY 363 CHOPPIN' DAYS 'TIL CHRISTMAS.
OL' PORKY HAD HIS DAY OFF FROM BEIN' PRICKLE-STICKLE--- HE REE-FRESHED

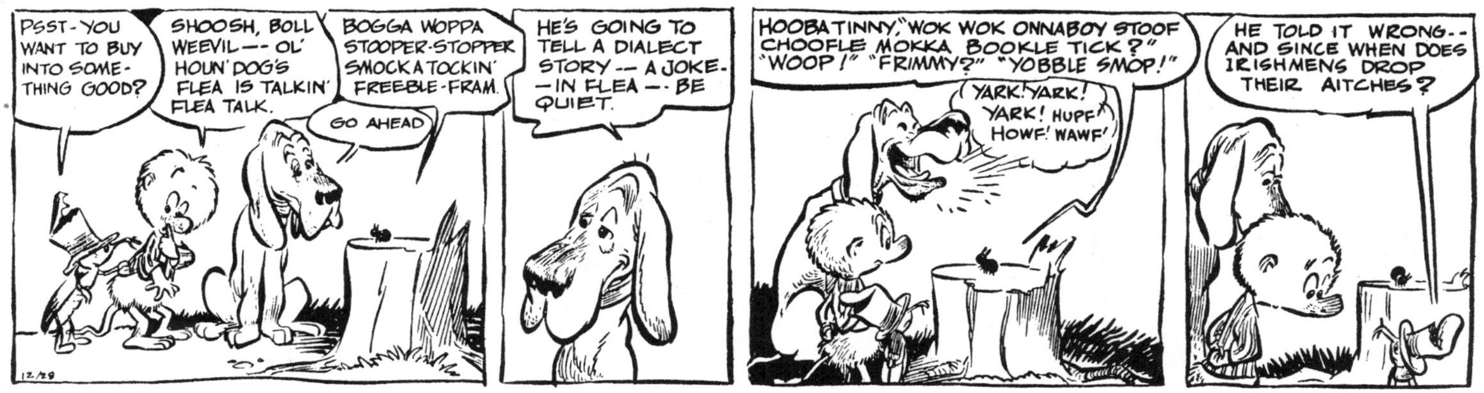
PSST-YOU WANT TO BUY INTO SOME-THING GOOD?
SHOOSH, BOLL WEEVIL—OL' HOUN' DOG'S FLEA IS TALKIN' FLEA TALK.
BOGGA WOPPA STOOPER-STOPPER SMOCKATOCKIN' FREEBLE-FRAM.
GO AHEAD
HE'S GOING TO TELL A DIALECT STORY—A JOKE—IN FLEA—BE QUIET.
HOOBATINNY,"WOK WOK ONNABOY STOOF CHOOFLE MOKKA BOOKLE TICK?" "WOOP!" "FRIMMY?" "YOBBLE SMOP!"
YARK! YARK! YARK! HUPF' HOWF' WAWF'
HE TOLD IT WRONG--AND SINCE WHEN DOES IRISHMENS DROP THEIR AITCHES?
12/28

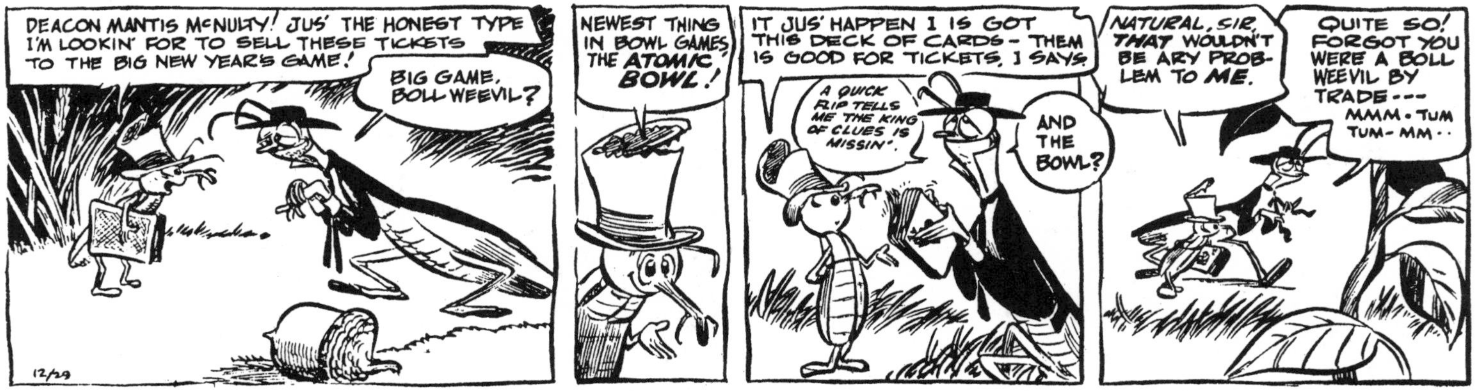
DEACON MANTIS McNULTY! JUS' THE HONEST TYPE I'M LOOKIN' FOR TO SELL THESE TICKETS TO THE BIG NEW YEAR'S GAME!
BIG GAME, BOLL WEEVIL?
NEWEST THING IN BOWL GAMES THE ATOMIC BOWL!
IT JUS' HAPPEN I IS GOT THIS DECK OF CARDS - THEM IS GOOD FOR TICKETS, I SAYS.
A QUICK RIP TELLS ME THE KING OF CLUES IS MISSIN'.
AND THE BOWL?
NATURAL, SIR, THAT WOULDN'T BE ARY PROB-LEM TO ME.
QUITE SO! FORGOT YOU WERE A BOLL WEEVIL BY TRADE--- MMM-TUM TUM-MM--
12/29

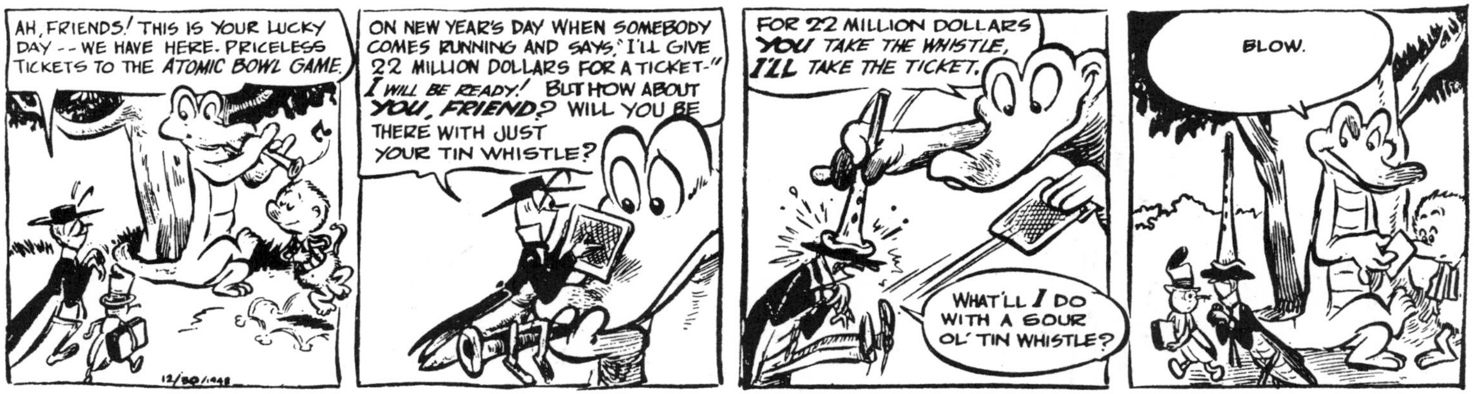
AH, FRIENDS! THIS IS YOUR LUCKY DAY--WE HAVE HERE. PRICELESS TICKETS TO THE ATOMIC BOWL GAME.
ON NEW YEAR'S DAY WHEN SOMEBODY COMES RUNNING AND SAYS,"I'LL GIVE 22 MILLION DOLLARS FOR A TICKET-" I WILL BE READY! BUT HOW ABOUT YOU, FRIEND? WILL YOU BE THERE WITH JUST YOUR TIN WHISTLE?
FOR 22 MILLION DOLLARS YOU TAKE THE WHISTLE, I'LL TAKE THE TICKET.
WHAT'LL I DO WITH A SOUR OL' TIN WHISTLE?
BLOW.
12/30/1948

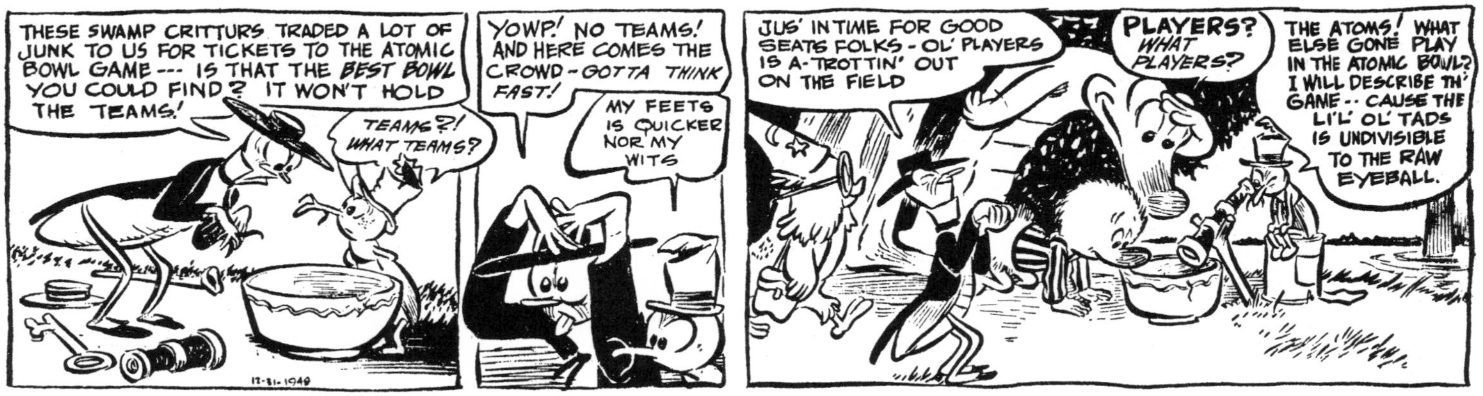
THESE SWAMP CRITTURS TRADED A LOT OF JUNK TO US FOR TICKETS TO THE ATOMIC BOWL GAME --- IS THAT THE BEST BOWL YOU COULD FIND? IT WON'T HOLD THE TEAMS!
TEAMS?! WHAT TEAMS?
YOWP! NO TEAMS! AND HERE COMES THE CROWD - GOTTA THINK FAST!
MY FEETS IS QUICKER NOR MY WITS
JUS' IN TIME FOR GOOD SEATS FOLKS - OL' PLAYERS IS A-TROTTIN' OUT ON THE FIELD
PLAYERS? WHAT PLAYERS?
THE ATOMS! WHAT ELSE GONE PLAY IN THE ATOMIC BOWL? I WILL DESCRIBE TH' GAME -- CAUSE THE LI'L' OL' TADS IS UNDIVISIBLE TO THE RAW EYEBALL.
12-31-1948

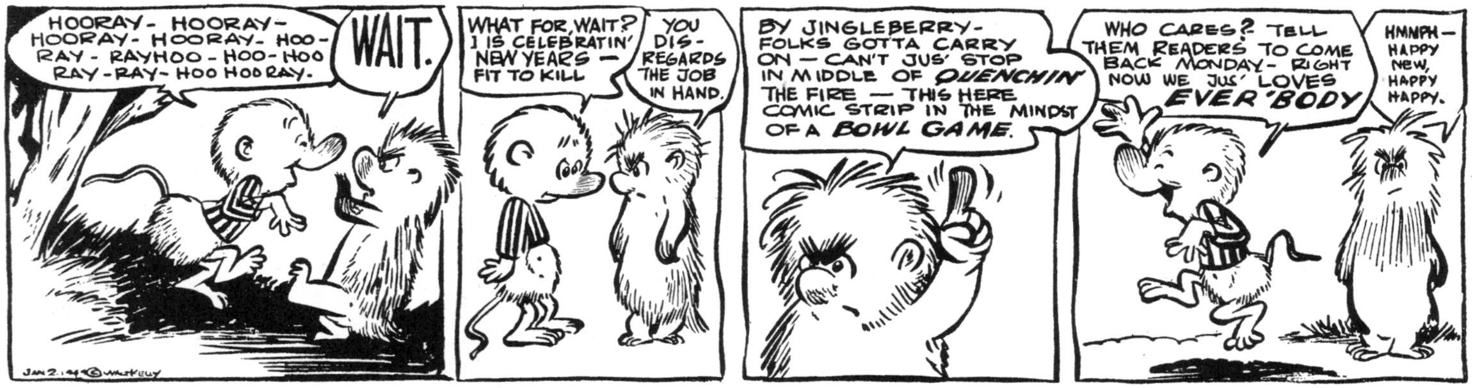
HOORAY- HOORAY- HOORAY- HOORAY- HOO-RAY - RAYHOO - HOO-HOO RAY-RAY- HOO HOORAY.
WAIT.
WHAT FOR, WAIT? I IS CELEBRATIN' NEW YEARS — FIT TO KILL
YOU DIS-REGARDS THE JOB IN HAND.
BY JINGLEBERRY- FOLKS GOTTA CARRY ON — CAN'T JUS' STOP IN MIDDLE OF QUENCHIN' THE FIRE — THIS HERE COMIC STRIP IN THE MINDST OF A BOWL GAME.
WHO CARES? TELL THEM READERS TO COME BACK MONDAY- RIGHT NOW WE JUS' LOVES EVER'BODY
HMMPH — HAPPY NEW, HAPPY HAPPY.

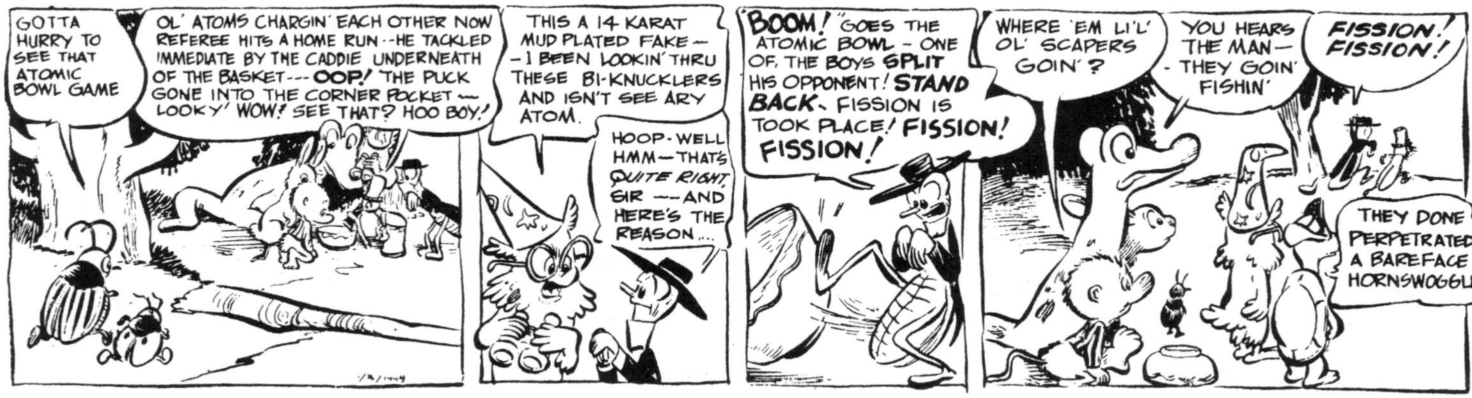
GOTTA HURRY TO SEE THAT ATOMIC BOWL GAME
OL' ATOMS CHARGIN' EACH OTHER NOW REFEREE HITS A HOME RUN --HE TACKLED IMMEDIATE BY THE CADDIE UNDERNEATH OF THE BASKET --- OOP! THE PUCK GONE INTO THE CORNER POCKET — LOOKY! WOW! SEE THAT? HOO BOY!
THIS A 14 KARAT MUD PLATED FAKE — — I BEEN LOOKIN' THRU THESE BI-KNUCKLERS AND ISN'T SEE ARY ATOM.
HOOP- WELL HMM — THAT'S QUITE RIGHT, SIR --- AND HERE'S THE REASON ....
BOOM! GOES THE ATOMIC BOWL - ONE OF THE BOYS SPLIT HIS OPPONENT! STAND BACK. FISSION IS TOOK PLACE! FISSION! FISSION!
WHERE 'EM LI'L' OL' SCAPERS GOIN'?
YOU HEARS THE MAN — - THEY GOIN' FISHIN'
FISSION! FISSION!
THEY DONE PERPETRATED A BAREFACE HORNSWOGGLE.

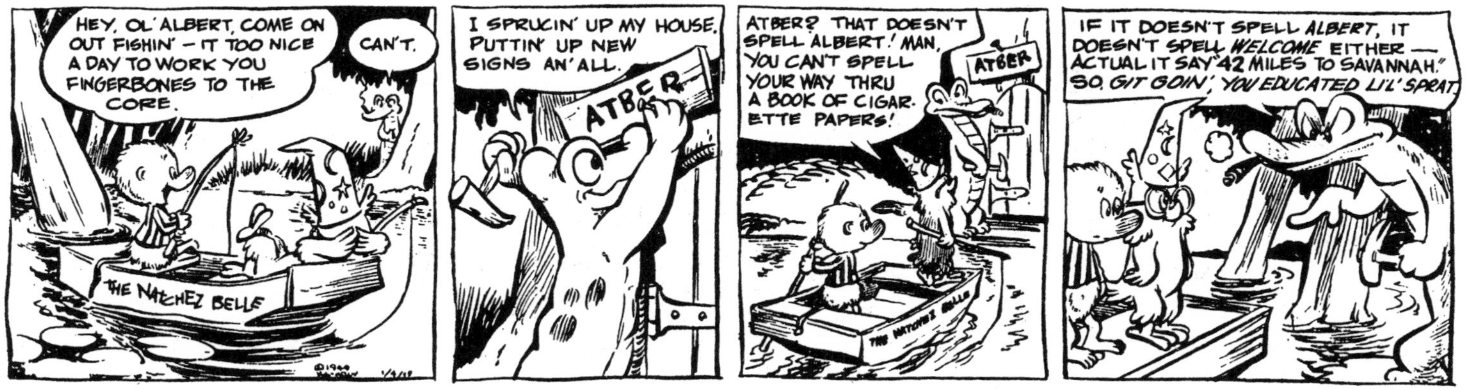
HEY, OL' ALBERT, COME ON OUT FISHIN' — IT TOO NICE A DAY TO WORK YOU FINGERBONES TO THE CORE.
CAN'T.
THE NATCHEZ BELLE
I SPRUCIN' UP MY HOUSE, PUTTIN' UP NEW SIGNS AN' ALL.
ATBER
ATBER? THAT DOESN'T SPELL ALBERT! MAN, YOU CAN'T SPELL YOUR WAY THRU A BOOK OF CIGAR-ETTE PAPERS!
ATBER
IF IT DOESN'T SPELL ALBERT, IT DOESN'T SPELL WELCOME EITHER — ACTUAL IT SAY "42 MILES TO SAVANNAH." SO, GIT GOIN', YOU EDUCATED LI'L' SPRAT.

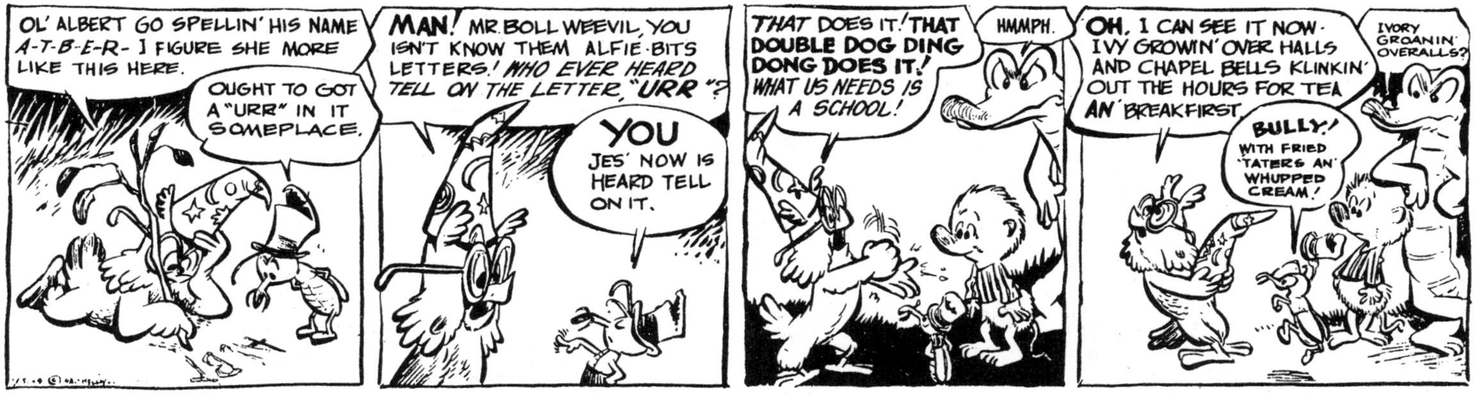
OL' ALBERT GO SPELLIN' HIS NAME A-T-B-E-R- I FIGURE SHE MORE LIKE THIS HERE.
OUGHT TO GOT A "URR" IN IT SOMEPLACE.
MAN! MR. BOLL WEEVIL, YOU ISN'T KNOW THEM ALFIE-BITS LETTERS! WHO EVER HEARD TELL ON THE LETTER "URR"?
YOU JES' NOW IS HEARD TELL ON IT.
THAT DOES IT! THAT DOUBLE DOG DING DONG DOES IT! WHAT US NEEDS IS A SCHOOL!
HMMPH.
OH, I CAN SEE IT NOW - IVY GROWIN' OVER HALLS AND CHAPEL BELLS KLINKIN' OUT THE HOURS FOR TEA AN' BREAKFIRST.
IVORY GROANIN' OVERALLS?
BULLY! WITH FRIED 'TATERS AN' WHUPPED CREAM!

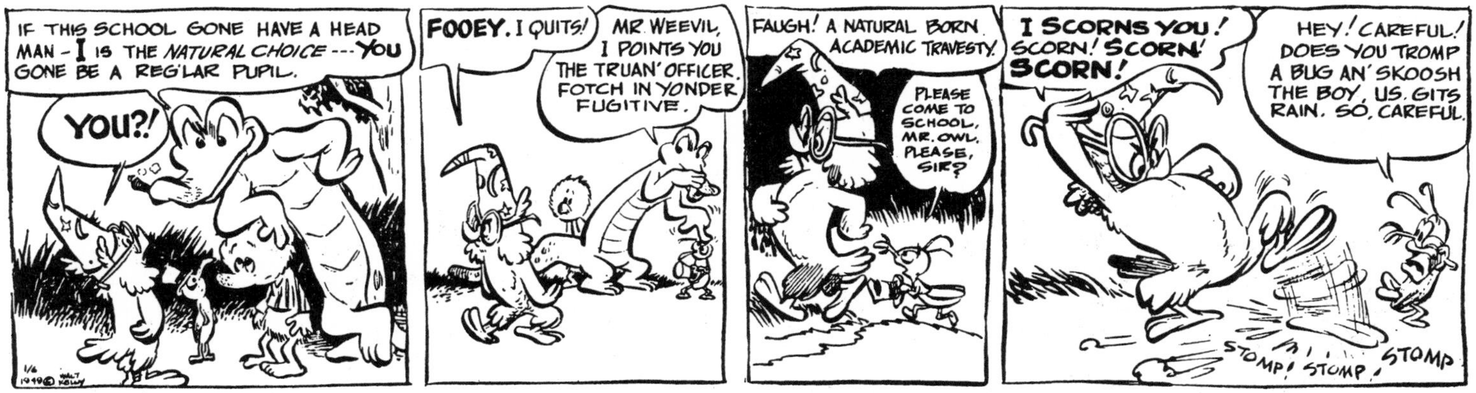
IF THIS SCHOOL GONE HAVE A HEAD MAN - I IS THE NATURAL CHOICE --- YOU GONE BE A REG'LAR PUPIL.
YOU?!
FOOEY. I QUITS!
MR. WEEVIL, I POINTS YOU THE TRUAN' OFFICER. FOTCH IN YONDER FUGITIVE.
FAUGH! A NATURAL BORN ACADEMIC TRAVESTY.
PLEASE COME TO SCHOOL, MR. OWL. PLEASE, SIR?
I SCORNS YOU! SCORN! SCORN! SCORN!
HEY! CAREFUL! DOES YOU TROMP A BUG AN' SKOOSH THE BOY, US. GITS RAIN. SO, CAREFUL.
STOMP! STOMP! STOMP

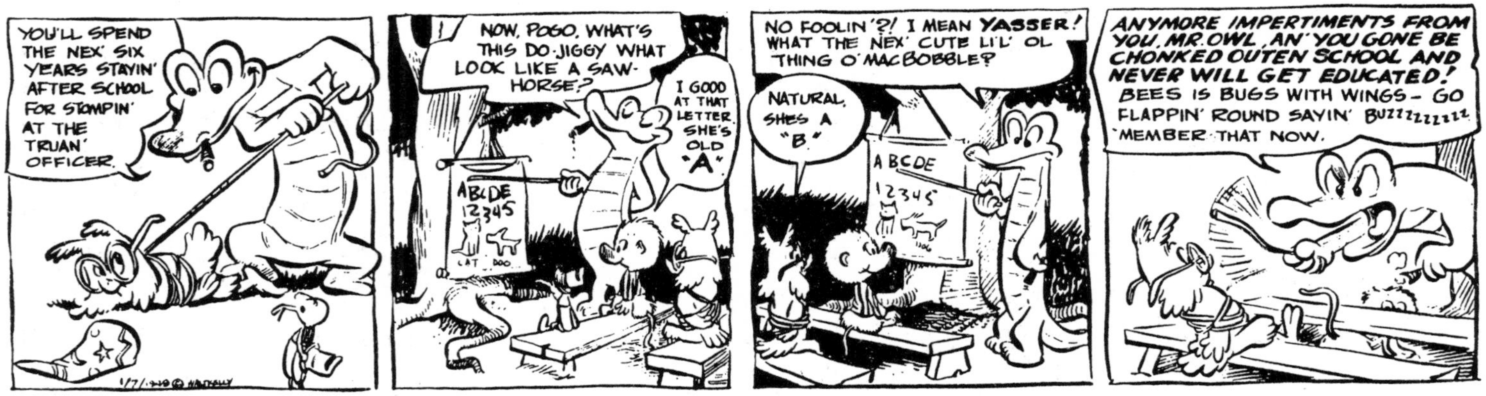
YOU'LL SPEND THE NEX' SIX YEARS STAYIN' AFTER SCHOOL FOR STOMPIN' AT THE TRUAN' OFFICER.
NOW, POGO, WHAT'S THIS DO-JIGGY WHAT LOOK LIKE A SAW-HORSE?
I GOOD AT THAT LETTER. SHE'S OLD "A"
NO FOOLIN'?! I MEAN YASSER! WHAT THE NEX' CUTE LI'L' OL THING O' MACBOBBLE?
NATURAL, SHES A "B"
ANYMORE IMPERTIMENTS FROM YOU, MR. OWL, AN' YOU GONE BE CHONKED OUTEN SCHOOL AND NEVER WILL GET EDUCATED! BEES IS BUGS WITH WINGS - GO FLAPPIN' ROUND SAYIN' BUZZZZZZZZ 'MEMBER THAT NOW.

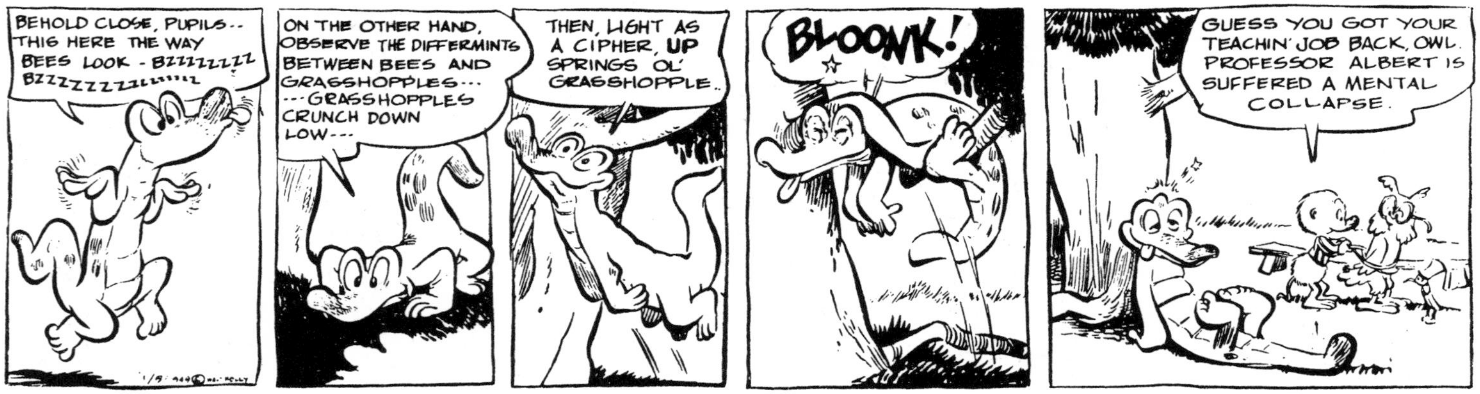
BEHOLD CLOSE, PUPILS-- THIS HERE THE WAY BEES LOOK - BZZZZZZZZ BZZZZZZZZZZZZ
ON THE OTHER HAND, OBSERVE THE DIFFERMINTS BETWEEN BEES AND GRASSHOPPLES--- ---GRASSHOPPLES CRUNCH DOWN LOW---
THEN, LIGHT AS A CIPHER, UP SPRINGS OL' GRASSHOPPLE.
BLOONK!
GUESS YOU GOT YOUR TEACHIN' JOB BACK, OWL. PROFESSOR ALBERT IS SUFFERED A MENTAL COLLAPSE.

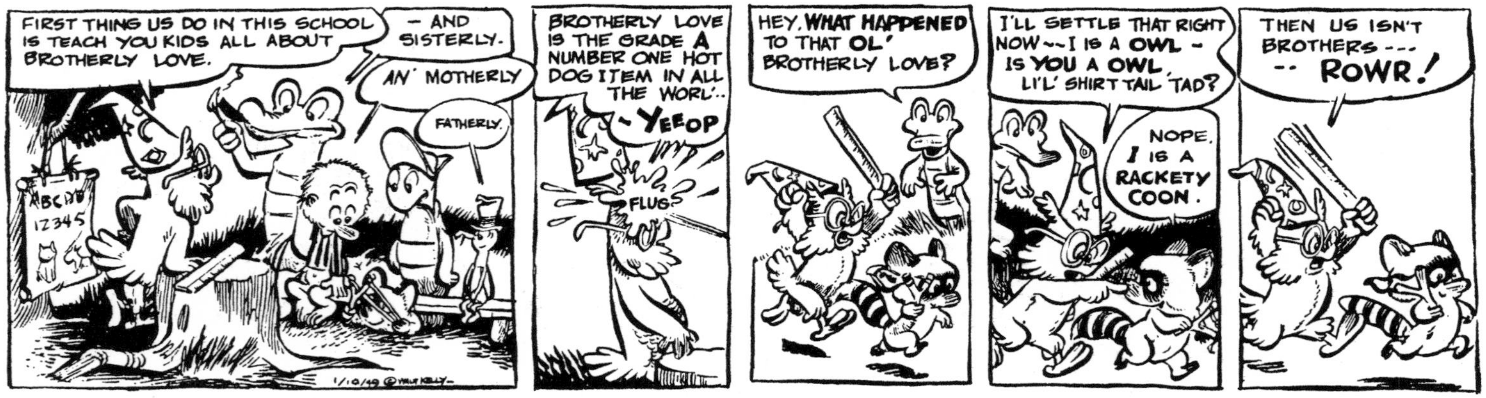
FIRST THING US DO IN THIS SCHOOL IS TEACH YOU KIDS ALL ABOUT BROTHERLY LOVE.
- AND SISTERLY.
AN' MOTHERLY
FATHERLY.
BROTHERLY LOVE IS THE GRADE A NUMBER ONE HOT DOG ITEM IN ALL THE WORL'..
-YEEOP
FLUG!
HEY, WHAT HAPPENED TO THAT OL' BROTHERLY LOVE?
I'LL SETTLE THAT RIGHT NOW--I IS A OWL - IS YOU A OWL, LI'L' SHIRT TAIL TAD?
NOPE. I IS A RACKETY COON.
THEN US ISN'T BROTHERS--- -- ROWR!

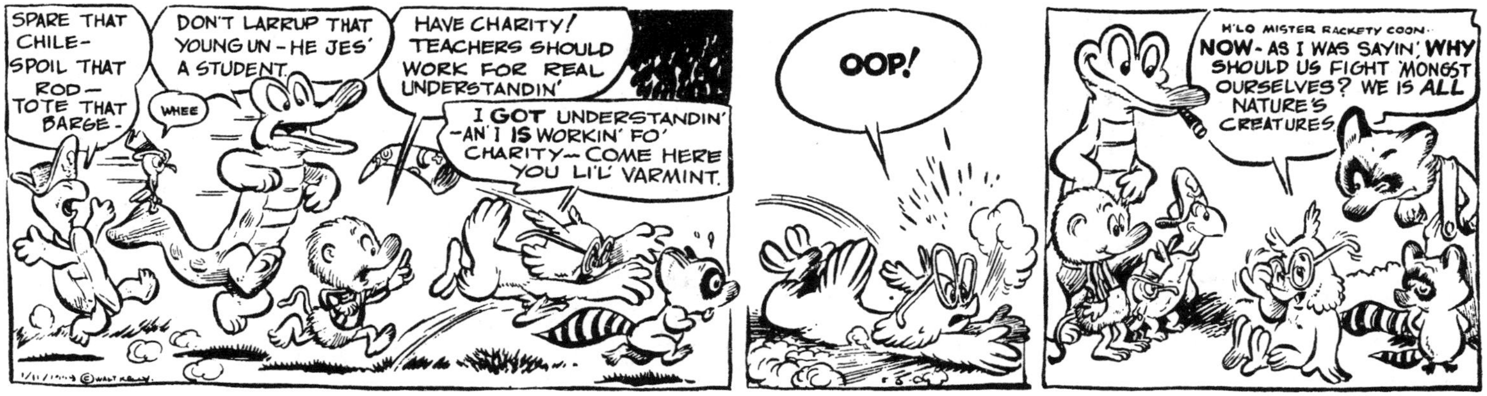
SPARE THAT CHILE- SPOIL THAT ROD— TOTE THAT BARGE-
WHEE
DON'T LARRUP THAT YOUNG UN - HE JES' A STUDENT.
HAVE CHARITY! TEACHERS SHOULD WORK FOR REAL UNDERSTANDIN'
I GOT UNDERSTANDIN' -AN' I IS WORKIN' FO' CHARITY— COME HERE YOU LI'L' VARMINT.
OOP!
H'LO MISTER RACKETY COON..
NOW- AS I WAS SAYIN', WHY SHOULD US FIGHT 'MONGST OURSELVES? WE IS ALL NATURE'S CREATURES.

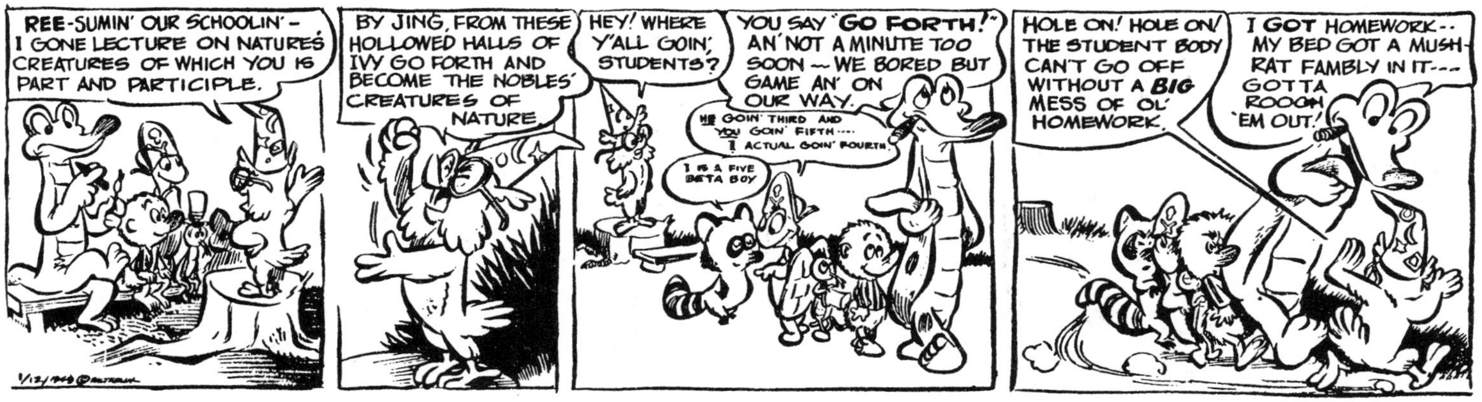
REE-SUMIN' OUR SCHOOLIN'- I GONE LECTURE ON NATURE'S CREATURES OF WHICH YOU IS PART AND PARTICIPLE.
BY JING, FROM THESE HOLLOWED HALLS OF IVY GO FORTH AND BECOME THE NOBLES' CREATURES OF NATURE.
HEY! WHERE Y'ALL GOIN', STUDENTS?
YOU SAY "GO FORTH!" AN' NOT A MINUTE TOO SOON — WE BORED BUT GAME AN' ON OUR WAY.
HE GOIN' THIRD AND YOU GOIN' FIFTH---- I ACTUAL GOIN' FOURTH.
I IS A FIVE BETA BOY
HOLE ON! HOLE ON! THE STUDENT BODY CAN'T GO OFF WITHOUT A BIG MESS OF OL' HOMEWORK.
I GOT HOMEWORK-- MY BED GOT A MUSH-RAT FAMBLY IN IT--- GOTTA ROOON 'EM OUT!

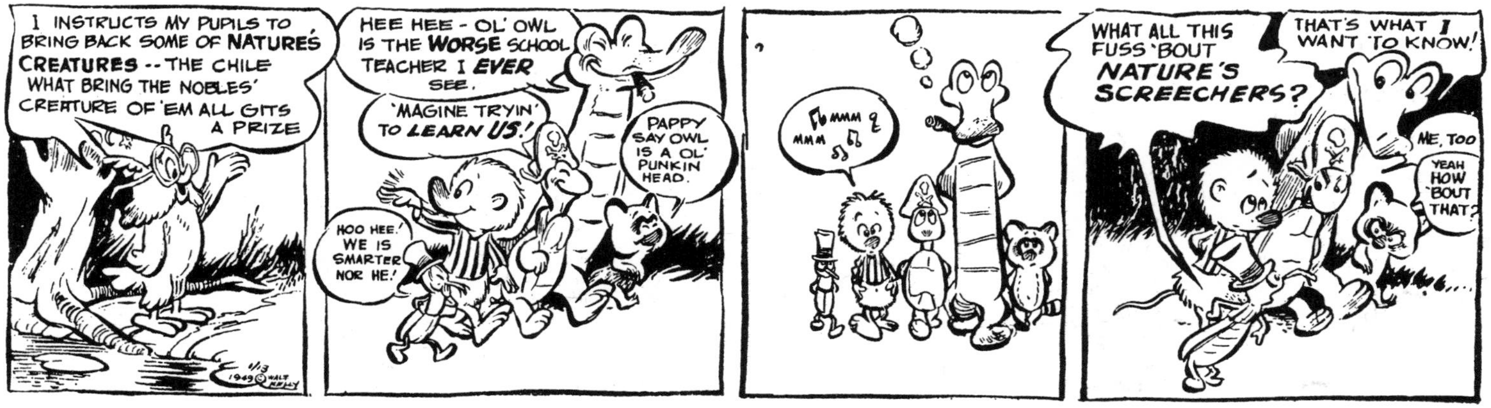
I INSTRUCTS MY PUPILS TO BRING BACK SOME OF NATURE'S CREATURES -- THE CHILE WHAT BRING THE NOBLES' CREATURE OF 'EM ALL GITS A PRIZE
HEE HEE - OL' OWL IS THE WORSE SCHOOL TEACHER I EVER SEE.
'MAGINE TRYIN' TO LEARN US!
PAPPY SAY OWL IS A OL' PUNKIN HEAD.
HOO HEE! WE IS SMARTER NOR HE!
MMM MMM
WHAT ALL THIS FUSS 'BOUT NATURE'S SCREECHERS?
THAT'S WHAT I WANT TO KNOW!
ME, TOO
YEAH HOW 'BOUT THAT?

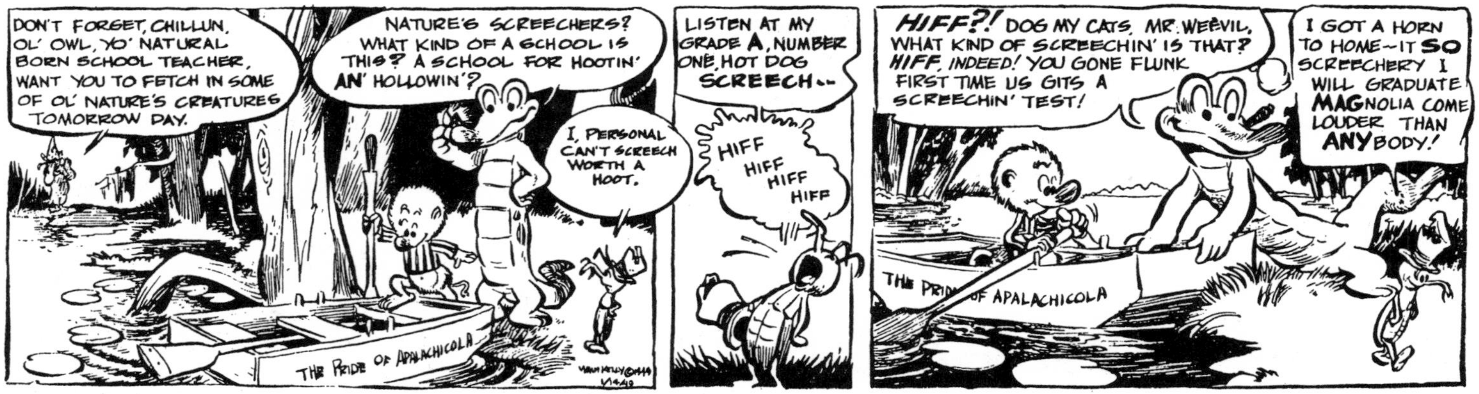
DON'T FORGET, CHILLUN, OL' OWL, YO' NATURAL BORN SCHOOL TEACHER, WANT YOU TO FETCH IN SOME OF OL' NATURE'S CREATURES TOMORROW DAY.
NATURE'S SCREECHERS? WHAT KIND OF A SCHOOL IS THIS? A SCHOOL FOR HOOTIN' AN' HOLLOWIN'?
I, PERSONAL CAN'T SCREECH WORTH A HOOT.
THE PRIDE OF APALACHICOLA
LISTEN AT MY GRADE A, NUMBER ONE, HOT DOG SCREECH..
HIFF HIFF HIFF HIFF
HIFF?! DOG MY CATS, MR. WEEVIL, WHAT KIND OF SCREECHIN' IS THAT? HIFF, INDEED! YOU GONE FLUNK FIRST TIME US GITS A SCREECHIN' TEST!
I GOT A HORN TO HOME--IT SO SCREECHERY I WILL GRADUATE MAGNOLIA COME LOUDER THAN ANYBODY!
THE PRIDE OF APALACHICOLA

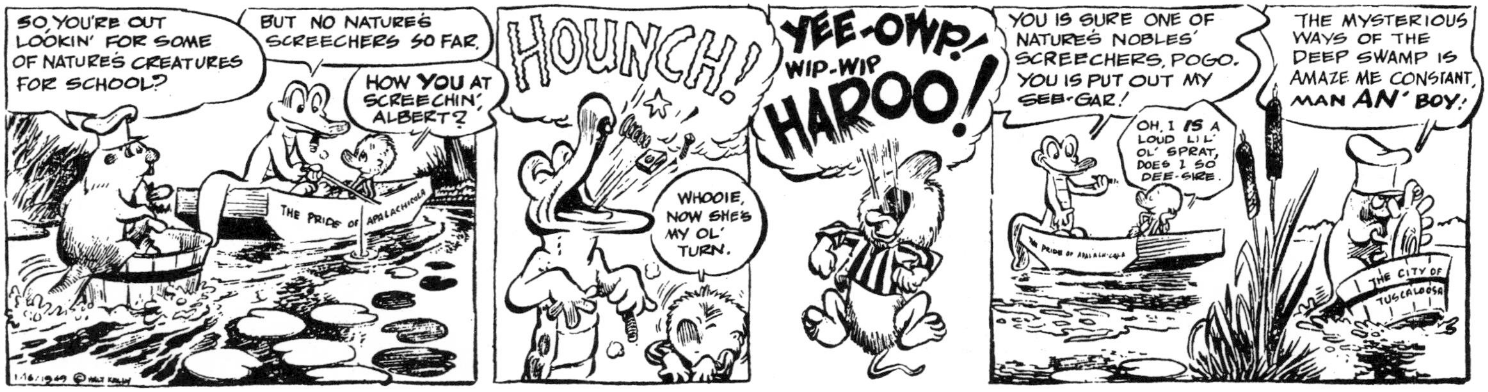
SO, YOU'RE OUT LOOKIN' FOR SOME OF NATURE'S CREATURES FOR SCHOOL?
BUT NO NATURE'S SCREECHERS SO FAR.
HOW YOU AT SCREECHIN', ALBERT?
THE PRIDE OF APALACHICOLA
HOUNCH!
WHOOIE, NOW SHE'S MY OL' TURN.
YEE-OWP! WIP-WIP HAROO!
YOU IS SURE ONE OF NATURE'S NOBLES' SCREECHERS, POGO. YOU IS PUT OUT MY SEE-GAR!
OH, I IS A LOUD LIL' OL' SPRAT, DOES I SO DEE-SIRE.
THE MYSTERIOUS WAYS OF THE DEEP SWAMP IS AMAZE ME CONSTANT, MAN AN' BOY!
THE CITY OF TUSCALOOSA

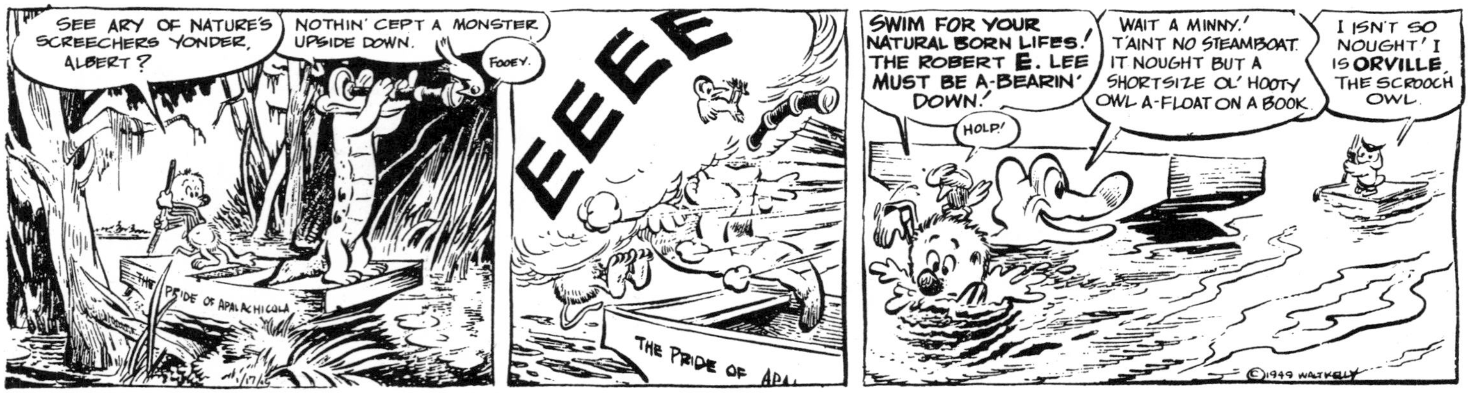
SEE ARY OF NATURE'S SCREECHERS YONDER, ALBERT?
NOTHIN' CEPT A MONSTER UPSIDE DOWN.
FOOEY.
THE PRIDE OF APALACHICOLA
EEEE
THE PRIDE OF APA
SWIM FOR YOUR NATURAL BORN LIFES! THE ROBERT E. LEE MUST BE A-BEARIN' DOWN!
HOLP!
WAIT A MINNY! T'AINT NO STEAMBOAT. IT NOUGHT BUT A SHORTSIZE OL' HOOTY OWL A-FLOAT ON A BOOK.
I ISN'T SO NOUGHT! I IS ORVILLE THE SCROOCH OWL.
©1949 WALT KELLY

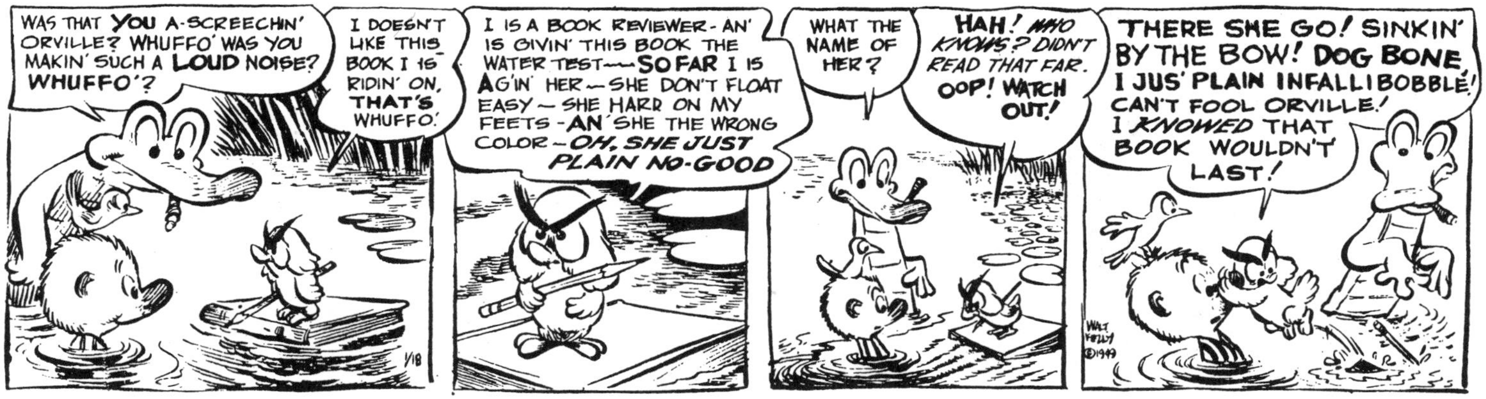
WAS THAT YOU A-SCREECHIN' ORVILLE? WHUFFO' WAS YOU MAKIN' SUCH A LOUD NOISE? WHUFFO'?
I DOESN'T LIKE THIS BOOK I IS RIDIN' ON, THAT'S WHUFFO.'
I IS A BOOK REVIEWER - AN' IS GIVIN' THIS BOOK THE WATER TEST---SO FAR I IS AG'IN' HER -- SHE DON'T FLOAT EASY -- SHE HARD ON MY FEETS - AN' SHE THE WRONG COLOR -- OH, SHE JUST PLAIN NO-GOOD
WHAT THE NAME OF HER?
HAH! WHO KNOWS? DIDN'T READ THAT FAR. OOP! WATCH OUT!
THERE SHE GO! SINKIN' BY THE BOW! DOG BONE, I JUS' PLAIN INFALLIBOBBLE! CAN'T FOOL ORVILLE! I KNOWED THAT BOOK WOULDN'T LAST!

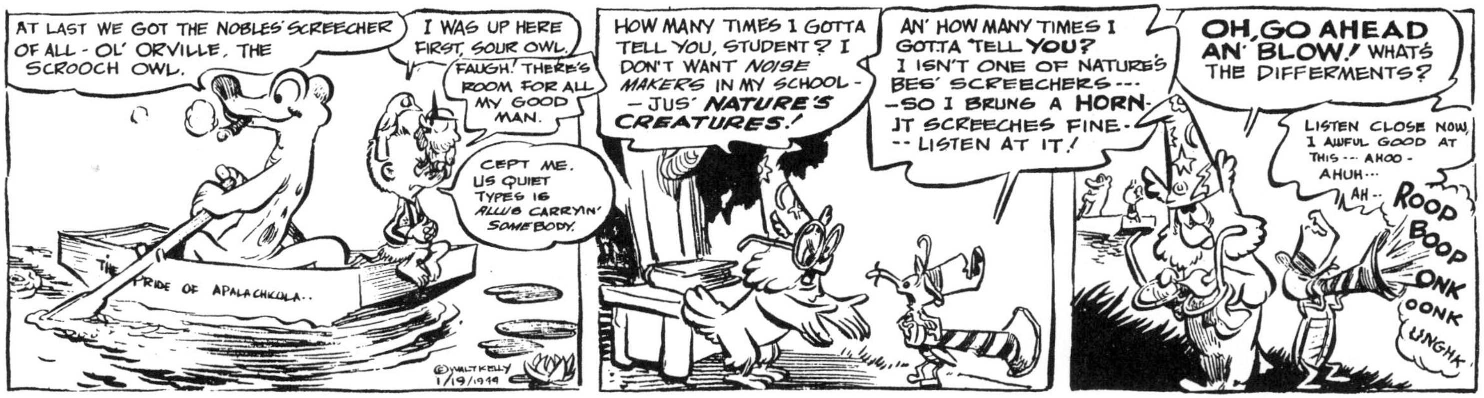
AT LAST WE GOT THE NOBLES' SCREECHER OF ALL - OL' ORVILLE, THE SCROOCH OWL.
I WAS UP HERE FIRST, SOUR OWL.
FAUGH! THERE'S ROOM FOR ALL MY GOOD MAN.
CEPT ME. US QUIET TYPES IS ALLUS CARRYIN' SOMEBODY.
THE PRIDE OF APALACHICOLA
HOW MANY TIMES I GOTTA TELL YOU, STUDENT? I DON'T WANT NOISE MAKERS IN MY SCHOOL - - JUS' NATURE'S CREATURES!
AN' HOW MANY TIMES I GOTTA TELL YOU? I ISN'T ONE OF NATURE'S BES' SCREECHERS--- -SO I BRUNG A HORN. IT SCREECHES FINE- -- LISTEN AT IT!
OH, GO AHEAD AN' BLOW! WHAT'S THE DIFFERMENTS?
LISTEN CLOSE NOW, I AWFUL GOOD AT THIS--- AHOO - AHUH--- AH--
ROOP BOOP ONK OONK UNGHK

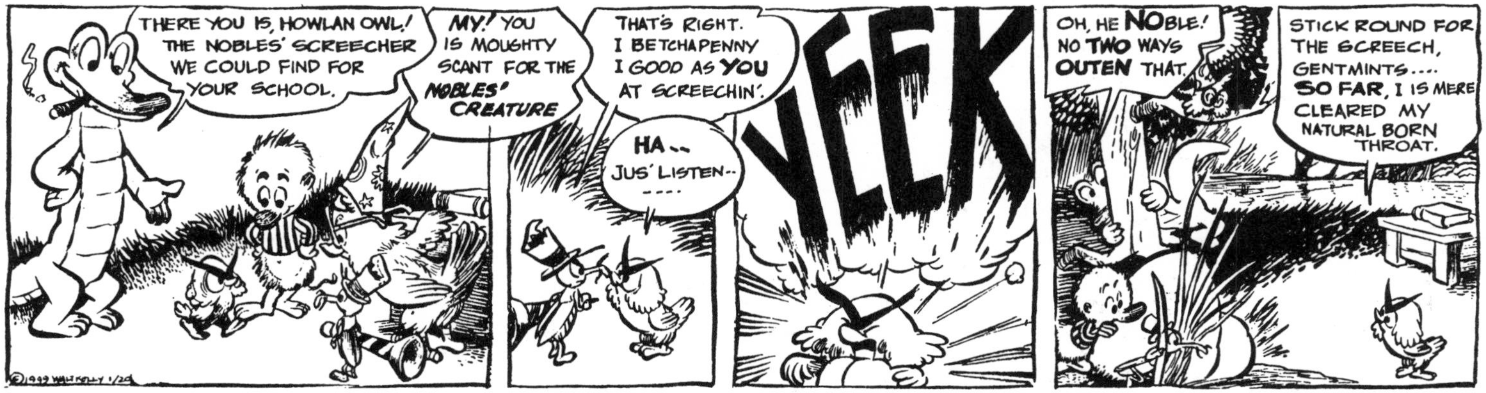
THERE YOU IS, HOWLAN OWL! THE NOBLES' SCREECHER WE COULD FIND FOR YOUR SCHOOL.
MY! YOU IS MOUGHTY SCANT FOR THE NOBLES' CREATURE
THAT'S RIGHT. I BETCHAPENNY I GOOD AS YOU AT SCREECHIN'.
HA -- JUS' LISTEN-- ----
YEEK
OH, HE NOBLE! NO TWO WAYS OUTEN THAT.
STICK ROUND FOR THE SCREECH, GENTMINTS.... SO FAR, I IS MERE CLEARED MY NATURAL BORN THROAT.

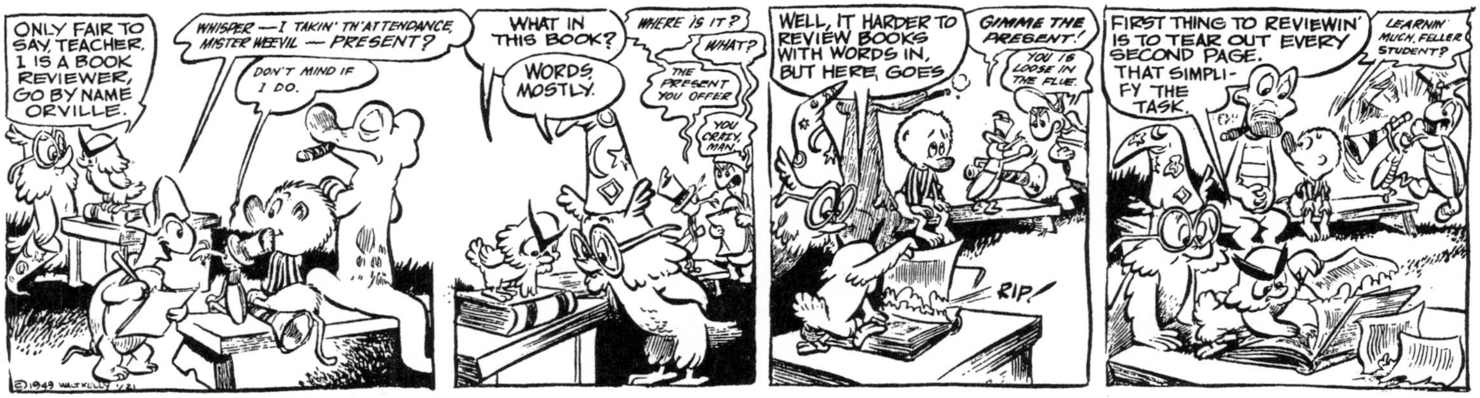
ONLY FAIR TO SAY, TEACHER, I IS A BOOK REVIEWER, GO BY NAME ORVILLE.
WHISPER — I TAKIN' TH' ATTENDANCE, MISTER WEEVIL — PRESENT?
DON'T MIND IF I DO.
WHAT IN THIS BOOK?
WORDS MOSTLY.
WHERE IS IT?
WHAT?
THE PRESENT YOU OFFER
YOU CRAZY, MAN.
WELL, IT HARDER TO REVIEW BOOKS WITH WORDS IN, BUT HERE, GOES
GIMME THE PRESENT!
YOU IS LOOSE IN THE FLUE.
RIP!
FIRST THING TO REVIEWIN' IS TO TEAR OUT EVERY SECOND PAGE. THAT SIMPLIFY THE TASK.
LEARNIN' MUCH, FELLER STUDENT?
©1949 WALT KELLY 1/21

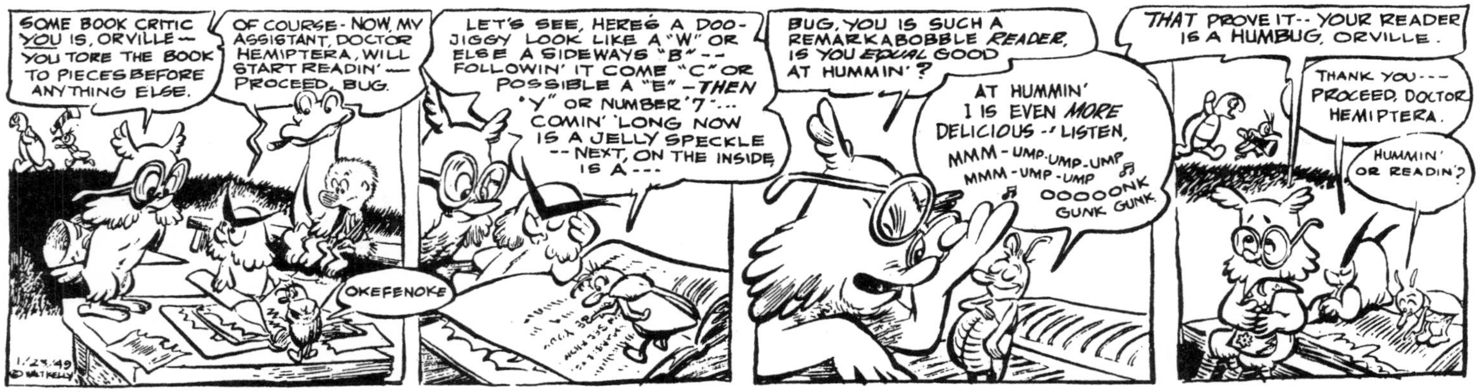
SOME BOOK CRITIC YOU IS, ORVILLE — YOU TORE THE BOOK TO PIECES BEFORE ANYTHING ELSE.
OF COURSE - NOW, MY ASSISTANT, DOCTOR HEMIPTERA, WILL START READIN' — PROCEED, BUG.
OKEFENOKE
1/23/49 © WALT KELLY
LET'S SEE, HERE'S A DOO-JIGGY LOOK LIKE A "W" OR ELSE A SIDEWAYS "B" — FOLLOWIN' IT COME "C" OR POSSIBLE A "E" — THEN "Y" OR NUMBER '7'... COMIN' 'LONG NOW IS A JELLY SPECKLE — NEXT, ON THE INSIDE IS A —
BUG, YOU IS SUCH A REMARKABOBBLE READER, IS YOU EQUAL GOOD AT HUMMIN'?
AT HUMMIN' I IS EVEN MORE DELICIOUS -' LISTEN, MMM-UMP-UMP-UMP MMM-UMP-UMP OOOOOONK GUNK GUNK
THAT PROVE IT -- YOUR READER IS A HUMBUG, ORVILLE.
THANK YOU — PROCEED, DOCTOR HEMIPTERA.
HUMMIN' OR READIN'?

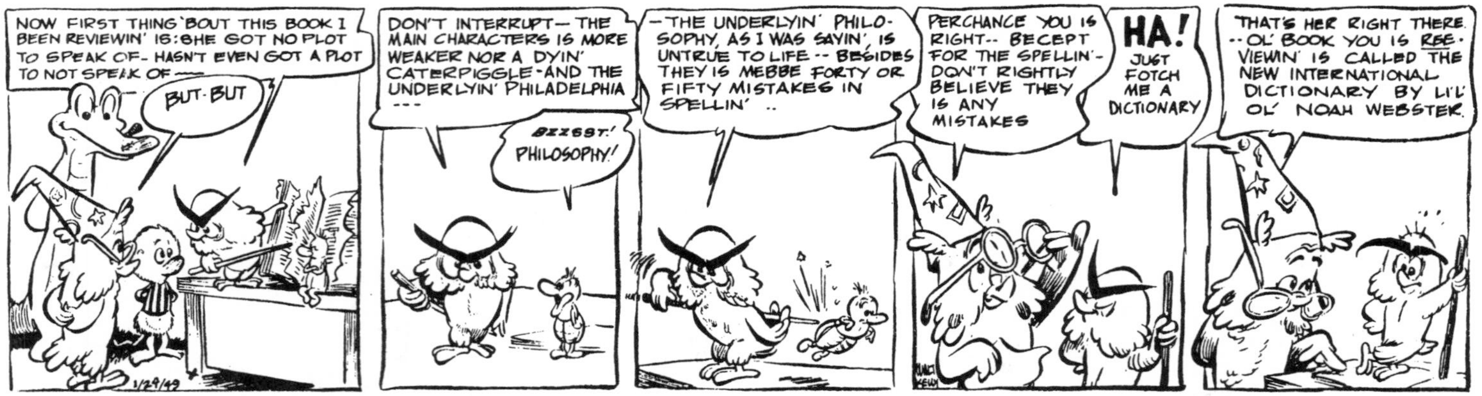
NOW FIRST THING 'BOUT THIS BOOK I BEEN REVIEWIN' IS: SHE GOT NO PLOT TO SPEAK OF - HASN'T EVEN GOT A PLOT TO NOT SPEAK OF —
BUT-BUT
1/24/49
DON'T INTERRUPT — THE MAIN CHARACTERS IS MORE WEAKER NOR A DYIN' CATERPIGGLE - AND THE UNDERLYIN' PHILADELPHIA —
BZZSST! PHILOSOPHY!
— THE UNDERLYIN' PHILOSOPHY, AS I WAS SAYIN', IS UNTRUE TO LIFE -- BESIDES THEY IS MEBBE FORTY OR FIFTY MISTAKES IN SPELLIN' ..
WALT KELLY
PERCHANCE YOU IS RIGHT -- BECEPT FOR THE SPELLIN' - DON'T RIGHTLY BELIEVE THEY IS ANY MISTAKES
HA! JUST FOTCH ME A DICTIONARY
THAT'S HER RIGHT THERE -- OL' BOOK YOU IS REE-VIEWIN' IS CALLED THE NEW INTERNATIONAL DICTIONARY BY LI'L OL' NOAH WEBSTER.

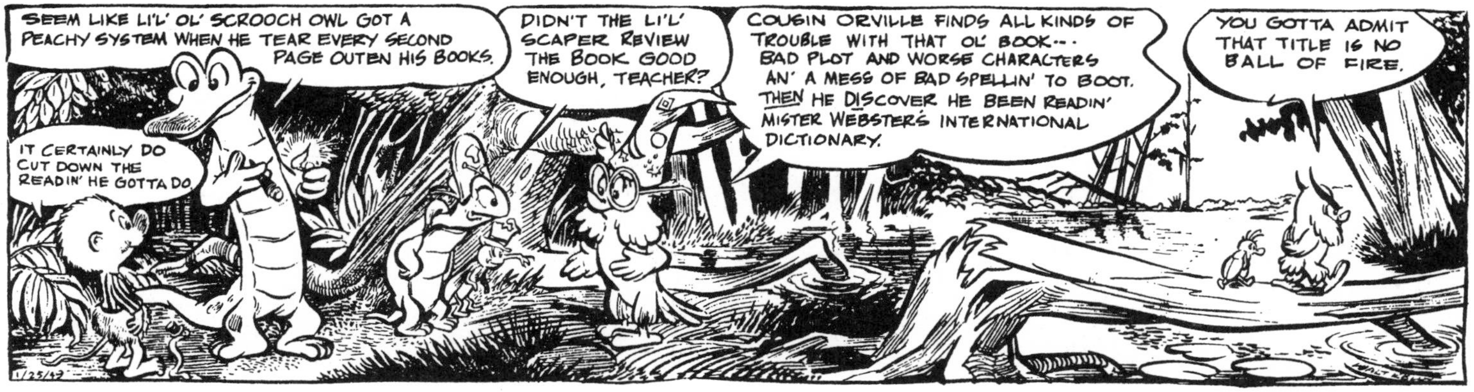
SEEM LIKE LI'L' OL' SCROOCH OWL GOT A PEACHY SYSTEM WHEN HE TEAR EVERY SECOND PAGE OUTEN HIS BOOKS.
IT CERTAINLY DO CUT DOWN THE READIN' HE GOTTA DO.
DIDN'T THE LI'L' SCAPER REVIEW THE BOOK GOOD ENOUGH, TEACHER?
COUSIN ORVILLE FINDS ALL KINDS OF TROUBLE WITH THAT OL' BOOK--- BAD PLOT AND WORSE CHARACTERS AN' A MESS OF BAD SPELLIN' TO BOOT. THEN HE DISCOVER HE BEEN READIN' MISTER WEBSTER'S INTERNATIONAL DICTIONARY.
YOU GOTTA ADMIT THAT TITLE IS NO BALL OF FIRE.

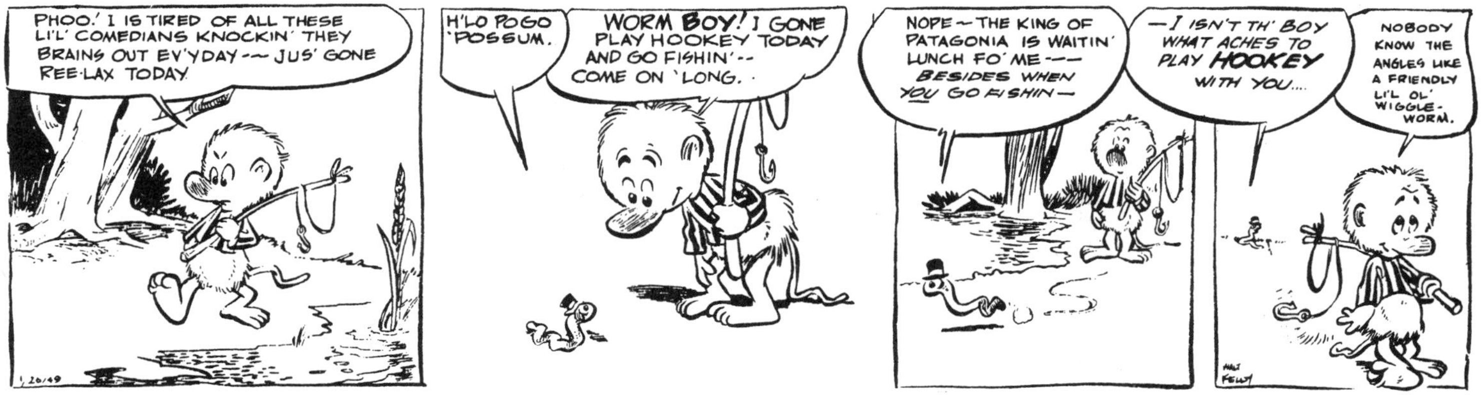
PHOO! I IS TIRED OF ALL THESE LI'L' COMEDIANS KNOCKIN' THEY BRAINS OUT EV'YDAY -- JUS' GONE REE·LAX TODAY.
H'LO POGO 'POSSUM.
WORM BOY! I GONE PLAY HOOKEY TODAY AND GO FISHIN'-- COME ON 'LONG.
NOPE -- THE KING OF PATAGONIA IS WAITIN' LUNCH FO' ME --- BESIDES WHEN YOU GO FISHIN --
-- I ISN'T TH' BOY WHAT ACHES TO PLAY HOOKEY WITH YOU....
NOBODY KNOW THE ANGLES LIKE A FRIENDLY LI'L OL' WIGGLE-WORM.

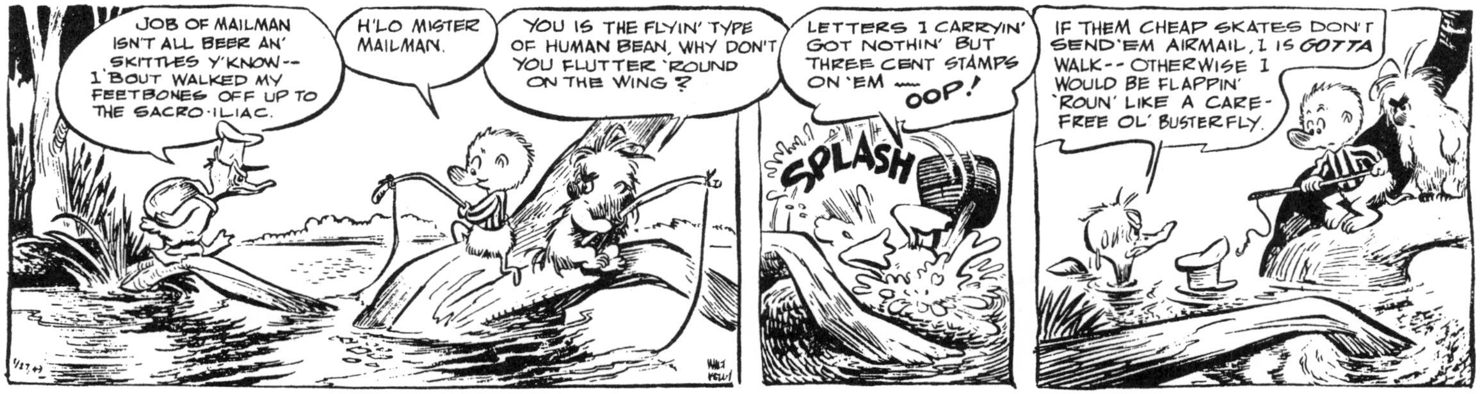
JOB OF MAILMAN ISN'T ALL BEER AN' SKITTLES Y'KNOW-- I 'BOUT WALKED MY FEETBONES OFF UP TO THE SACRO·ILIAC.
H'LO MISTER MAILMAN.
YOU IS THE FLYIN' TYPE OF HUMAN BEAN, WHY DON'T YOU FLUTTER 'ROUND ON THE WING?
LETTERS I CARRYIN' GOT NOTHIN' BUT THREE CENT STAMPS ON 'EM — OOP!
SPLASH
IF THEM CHEAP SKATES DON'T SEND 'EM AIRMAIL, I IS GOTTA WALK -- OTHERWISE I WOULD BE FLAPPIN' 'ROUN' LIKE A CARE-FREE OL' BUSTERFLY.

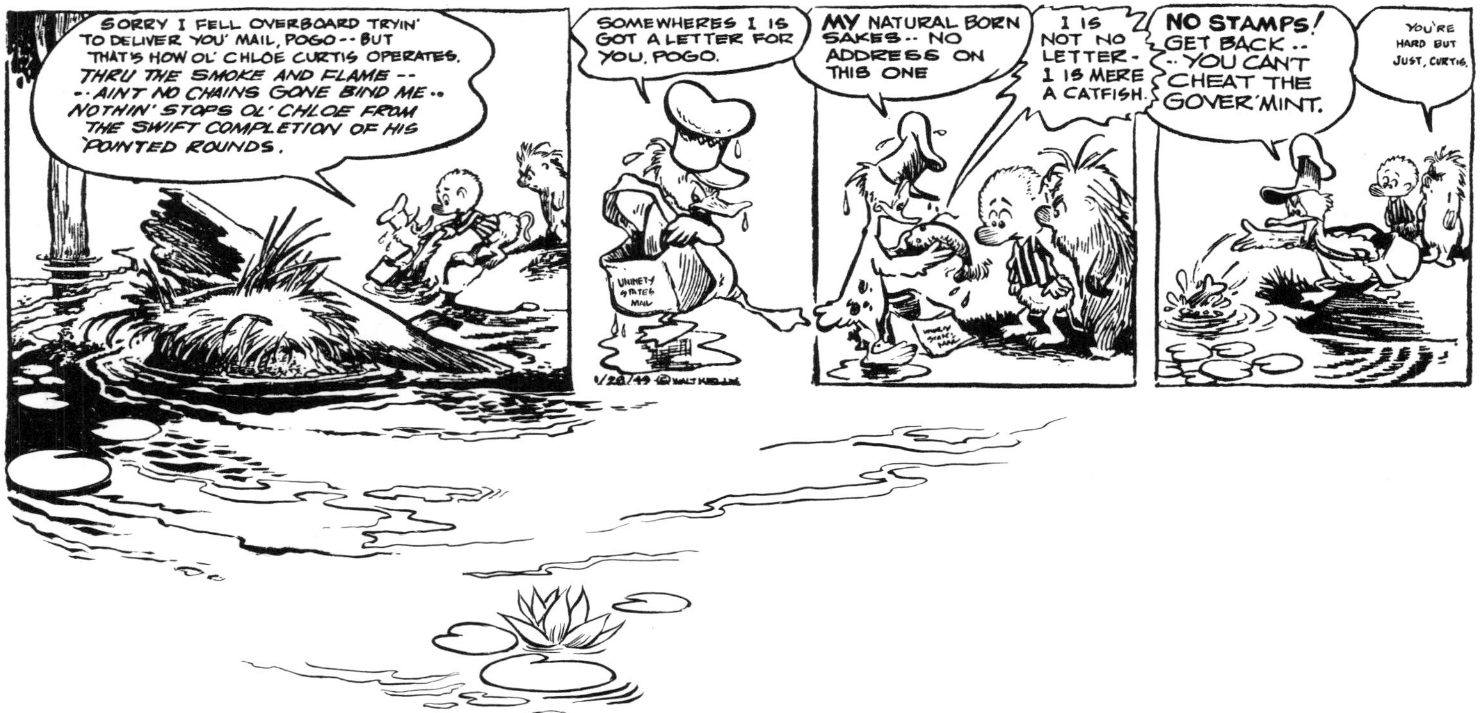
SORRY I FELL OVERBOARD TRYIN' TO DELIVER YOU' MAIL, POGO -- BUT THAT'S HOW OL' CHLOE CURTIS OPERATES. THRU THE SMOKE AND FLAME -- -- AINT NO CHAINS GONE BIND ME -- NOTHIN' STOPS OL' CHLOE FROM THE SWIFT COMPLETION OF HIS 'POINTED ROUNDS.
SOMEWHERES I IS GOT A LETTER FOR YOU, POGO.
UNINETY STATES MAIL
MY NATURAL BORN SAKES -- NO ADDRESS ON THIS ONE
I IS NOT NO LETTER - I IS MERE A CATFISH.
NO STAMPS! GET BACK -- -- YOU CAN'T CHEAT THE GOVER'MINT.
YOU'RE HARD BUT JUST, CURTIS.

SWAMP TALK

Annotations and Historical Data
By R.C. Harvey

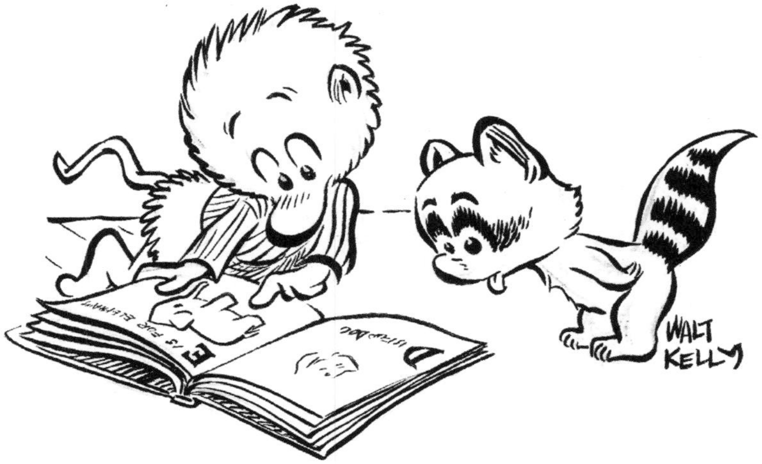
WALT KELLY

Walt Kelly is admired – and revered in some quarters (this one, for instance) – for his deft blending of the verbal and visual resources of the comic strip medium for the purposes of vaudevillian slapstick and other irreverences, chiefly political satire. And for much of the quarter-century run of *Pogo* under Kelly's hand, the strip commented pointedly on the antics in Washington, ridiculing the pomposities of American political life by dragging off into its panels portraits of the miscreants themselves, albeit disguised, slightly, as warm and cuddly swamp critters. But initially, and for the first couple years of its run, Pogo wasn't ridiculing specific public figures, and the kind of political satire that distinguished Kelly's later work was, with a couple notable exceptions, nearly absent. For the sake of those exceptions, we offer the following annotations. Some of them explain topical references to events, some of them political, that we may have long forgotten or which newer readers never knew. Others pick up threads of cultural history or illuminate obscure corners of lexicography. Altogether, these notes are intended to enrich the reading of the strip, reminding all of the time and world in which it was created. Kelly's work is a classic that speaks for itself but perhaps a little historical context can add to the experience.

1948

10/4 – *Pogo* started on this date in the *New York Star*, a daily newspaper described by *The New Yorker* as "the semi-official outlet of advanced liberal thought" put out by "a staff of indefatigable crusaders." The *Star* was a rejuvenated version of the determinedly independent *PM*, a leftist newspaper published in New York from 1940 through 1948. After *PM* folded, the *Star* began in the summer of '48, and Kelly joined the staff as art director, which meant he drew everything that needed drawing, including editorial cartoons. Devotees of Pogo know that this most pleasant of possums was born in October. He debuted in the first issue of *Animal Comics* (dated December 1942 – January 1943) in a story entitled "Albert Takes the Cake" wherein Albert the Alligator steals Pogo's birthday cake. The very first picture of Pogo shows him tearing a page off a wall calendar for October to reveal the next page that proclaims it's Pogo's birthday. The exact day isn't cited but now we know – it's October 4.

10/7 – Churchy LaFemme first appeared, in a somewhat more cantankerous aspect, in *Animal Comics* No. 13. His name is a Southern fried version of "cherchez la femme," or, less

Frenchified, "look for the woman," an expression used in France, where people are much more liberal about such matters, as the reason for a man's otherwise inexplicable behavior: it can be explained by assuming he is trying to cover up an illicit affair or to impress a woman.

10/20 – *Little Pedro* was a comic strip by William de la Torre, one of the short roster of comic strips running in the *New York Star*. Crockett Johnson's *Barnaby* (drawn at the time by Jack Morley) was another, as was Jack Sparling's *Claire Voyant*.

10/22 – References to an election echo the national presidential campaign going on simultaneously in which incumbent Democrat Harry S Truman was being challenged by Republican Thomas E. Dewey, a former prosecuting attorney and governor of New York. No one expected Truman, the "Missouri jackass," to win the presidency, but the liberal *Star* was an avid Truman supporter. Kelly drew editorial cartoons supporting Truman and ridiculing Dewey, whose stiff demeanor Kelly captured with a recurring caricature of him as a robotic adding machine. Dewey was everyone's favorite to win: Republican party regulars, pollsters, pundits – everyone, including lots of Democrats – expected Dewey to win. And Dewey shared that view.

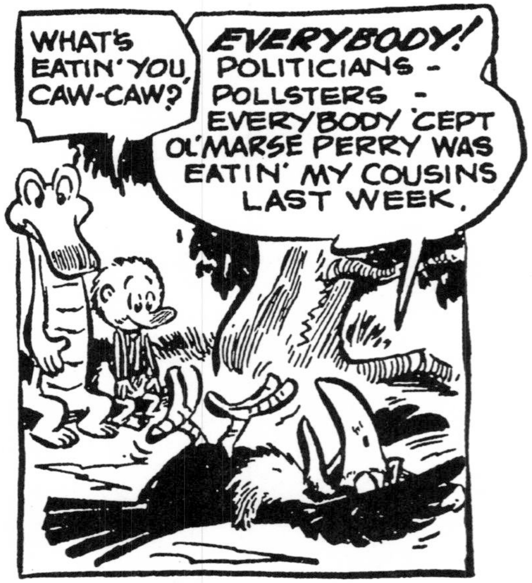
WHAT'S EATIN' YOU, CAW-CAW?
EVERYBODY! POLITICIANS - POLLSTERS - EVERYBODY 'CEPT OL' MARSE PERRY WAS EATIN' MY COUSINS LAST WEEK.

11/7 – To the surprise of many (Tom Dewey included) Harry Truman beat Thomas Dewey in the election held November 2, the Tuesday preceding this strip. This one was published on Sunday as the *Star* published only six days a week, Sunday through Friday with no Saturday edition.

The news-bearing duck, Chug Chug Curtis, gets his last name from the father of Maggie Thompson *nee* Curtis (presently senior editor of the *Comics Buyer's Guide)*: Ed Curtis and his spouse were fans of Kelly's work in *Mother Goose* and fairy tale comic books in the mid-1940s, and friends of the Kelly family.

11/17 – In the wake of the Truman victory, the pundit brothers Alsop wrote: "There is only one question on which professional politicians, polltakers, political reporters and other wiseacres and prognosticators can any longer speak with much authority. That is how they want their crow cooked." Only "ol' Marse Perry" wasn't eating crow. That was Jennings Perry, a political columnist for the *Star*, who, nearly alone among legions of his brethren, did not predict a Dewey win, holding out instead for a Truman triumph.

11/28 – This strip was published on the Sunday after Thanksgiving, which was celebrated on Thursday, November 25. The *Star* didn't publish on the holiday.

12/1- John McNulty was a fellow New York journalist and friend of Kelly's.

12/5 – Another of the strip's mainstays, Houn'dog, shows up for the first time. We learn on 12/12 that his actual name is Beauregard Bugleboy – a great name for a bloodhound – but he is almost always to be referred to as Houn'dog.

12/20 – The first Porky Pine and Pogo Christmas strip. These will become an "anyule" event.

12/22 – Every Yuletide beginning with this one, Kelly deployed his strip to commemorate the occasion and succeeded in infecting the entire nation with the joyous spirit of the season by encoring his cast's rendition of "Deck the Halls with Boughs of Holly," which invariably came out "Deck Us All with Boston Charlie," here performed for the first time.

12/29 – Bowl celebrations of the arts and crafts of football were not as numerous in those days as they are in these, but they were nonetheless fervently attended to, and here and for the next few days, Kelly likens the gridiron competition to that which will undoubtedly occur between the U.S. and the Soviet Union should the latter ever develop the atom bomb (which it did, as we shall see, before the new year was out.)

1949

1/2 – The *New York Star* didn't publish on Saturday, so Pogo observes New Year's Day on Sunday.

1/28 – The *New York Star* ceased publication on this date, and *Pogo*, for the nonce, ceased, too.

5/16 – *Pogo* became a syndicated comic strip on this date, having been picked up by the Post-Hall Syndicate. It's interesting to compare the syndicated *Pogo* with the *New York Star* version collected at the back of this book. Although at first glance, the syndicated *Pogo* does not appear much different than the earlier effort – the inaugural strip here is pretty much *deja vu* all over again, or so it seems – a slightly more prolonged scrutiny reveals that Kelly's graphic style had matured somewhat between October 1948 and May 1949.

5/25 – Carries forward the story introduced in the last *Star* strips, 1/28-29.

8/18 – Albert first uttered the extravagance of the second panel in *Animal Comics* No. 12 and will repeat the comment again and again. The expression on his face in the second panel is priceless.

9/5-6 – Without electricity in the swamp, Kelly couldn't do gags about radio or, later, television when the next wave of electronic entertainment swept across the nation. This would prove to be a considerable inhibition once so much of American civilization emerged from the tube. This episode may be the only time Kelly tried to establish a mechanism in the strip that would permit him to tap into the electronic media. He quickly abandoned it on September 7. It was apparently too mechanical, too artificial and strained, to suit him.

10/1 – The World Series usually comes to the swamp in the fall; this is its first appearance in the strip.

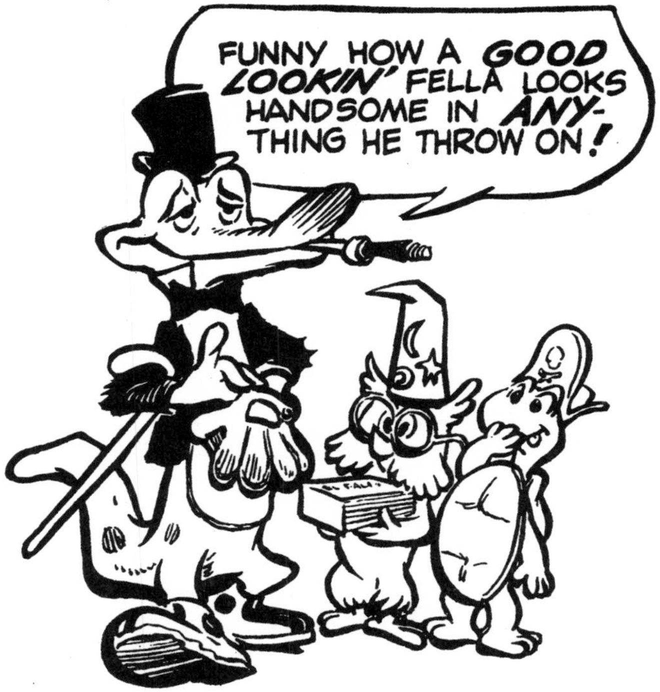
FUNNY HOW A GOOD LOOKIN' FELLA LOOKS HANDSOME IN ANY-THING HE THROW ON!

11/11 – November 11 is the U.S. holiday Veterans Day, also known as Armistice Day (or Remembrance Day) and it commemorates the end of World War I. A minute of silence is a traditional act to honor the war dead.

12/16 – Perloo is a traditional rice dish – a distant cousin of jambalaya – that traces its origins to the family of Middle Eastern dishes known as pilaws or pilafs. In the American South, there were many spellings of the word but they all seemed to be pronounced "Perloo" with the accent on the first syllable, so Perloo it was in *Pogo*.

12/26 – Walt's friend John McNulty was one of Porky's early devoted fans. Once he told Kelly: "Don't ever let the little bum smile." And Kelly never did...except in this strip and in occasional repeats of the same scenario.

12/30 – Perhaps the worst pun in the world: "If I were," "Fire." Terrible, just terrible. But treasured as a pearl beyond compare.

1950

1/16 – The Salk vaccine, discovered in 1952 and announced in 1955, soon eradicated infantile paralysis, polio, as the scourge of American childhood. Annual fund drives were conducted to raise money to fight the disease, and comic strip cartoonists often touted for the fabled March of Dimes, which had been founded as the National Foundation for Infantile Paralysis in 1938 by President Franklin D. Roosevelt, himself crippled by the disease. The fund drives were dubbed the March of Dimes by singer/comedian Eddie Cantor as a play on the name of a widely circulated weekly newsreel feature called The March of Time.

1/31 – Houn'dog is quoting Edward FitzGerald's *Rubaiyat of Omar Khayam;* ditto the woodchuck (aka, ground hog).

2/5 – Almost from the first of the Sunday strips, Kelly began lavishing artwork on the opening splash panel, drawing elaborately gnarled and festooned swamp trees and wild grasses and lily pads galore.

2/14 – It is rumoured he thought of himself as a newspaperman first and as a cartoonist somewhat after that. Kelly easily slipped into short continuities about newspapering.

2/22 – On this date, we celebrate the birthday of the Father of Our Country, George Washington.

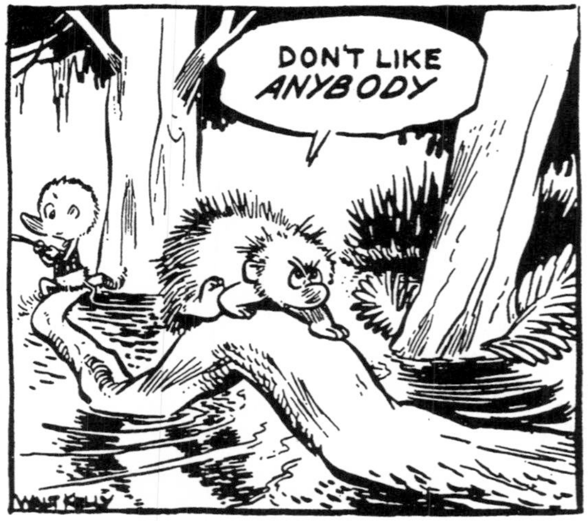
DON'T LIKE ANYBODY

2/23 – Man...lookit all that scrumptious art in the last panel!

3/3 – Kelly is taking a friendly poke at another of the comic strip genre, serious adventure strips, or, perhaps more accurately, at comic books, particularly crime comics, which were coming under increasingly hostile fire at the time. Kelly had once written an autobiography, "The Land of Elephant Squash," in which he writes about himself in the third person, describing his reaction to comic books at the time he began drawing them. The comics he describes sound like the one Owl is imagining:

"He [Kelly] read with growing horror the kinds of comic books being left about where children could reach them and decided that real juvenile work was his forte rather than the adventure type of business. 'It was impossible for me to draw a naked woman,' he explains. 'It was blinding work. I would no sooner have her clothes off than I would remove my hat, out of respect. With my eyes unshaded, I couldn't see what I was doing. Besides, the editor said that as an adventure man, I had better stick to drawing mice. So I concentrated on puppies, kittens, mice and elves – every once in a while glancing back at the men who were grimly penciling out the Pueriles of Pauline, taking clothes off and dagging people with butcher knives.'"

3/11 – Etaoin Shurdlu is a nonsense name or phrase that originated with linotype operators back in the days of "hot type" printing. The letters ETAOIN SHURDLU were those in the first two vertical columns on the left-hand side of the keyboard.

3/13 – Kelly makes a foray into somewhat pointed political satire for the first time in the syndicated strip. By the dawn of 1950, America's two worst Cold War fears about Russia had materialized. The Soviets developed an atomic bomb, which the U.S. had thought was its exclusive possession; and China fell into the hands of Mao Tse-tung and his Red Army, strenuously implying that the global ambitions of Communism might not be so far-fetched after all. Pogo had not yet celebrated its first anniversary as a nationally syndicated feature, and Kelly, like all syndicated cartoonists of the day, avoided making political commentary in his strip because newspaper editors who might have different views could drop the strip. And as he lost papers, the cartoonist's income would drop accordingly. Kelly would eventually throw such caution to the winds. At present, however, he followed the customs of his craft. Still, he devoted most of March's strips to Owl's researches into the secrets of the atom. Owl's moronic grasp of nuclear physics is highly comical. His fear of "foreign powers," however, is so extreme as to ridicule those who promoted fright at the prospect of the Communist atomic threat.

3/23 – Albert alludes to a famous animal movie star, a German Shepherd named Rin Tin Tin, whose career began in 1922 in silent films and was stretched through the thirties and into the forties by a succession of German Shepherds named Rin Tin Tin.

3/26 – For the first time, Kelly devises a Sunday storyline that won't end in one swoop and must, therefore, be continued to next Sunday. It won't be the only such incident.

3/30 – Owl falls into the satirical trap Kelly has been building for several days: he sees a Communist anywhere he sees a hammer and sickle, even if he provided the hammer himself and the sickle is but a sample of the skill of the neighborhood scissors grinder. (Albert in false whiskers is obviously the fearsome bearded Bolshevik; but the beard, remember, is false. So, perhaps, are some of the alarums raised by rabid Republicans who blamed the Democrats for the loss of the U.S. nuclear monopoly.) Kelly's first foray into political commentary in the spring of 1950 was more good-natured kidding than cutting satire.

4/16 – The heavily-browed "Kimbo cat" is a caricature of Disney animator Ward Kimball. Kelly was Kimball's assistant in the studio from 1939 until Walt's departure in '41 and his good friend for the rest of his life. Both loved Dixieland jazz and Kimball satisfied his musical urges by collecting a number of like-minded would-be musicians from the Disney staff to form a band. At first, it was called the Hugga-Jeedy Eight ("because that was the sound my old Model T Ford made while idling," Kimball explained), then the San Gabriel Valley Blue Blowers, and finally, towards the end of the forties, the Firehouse Five Plus Two, the ensemble we see reincarnated here. The group made several record albums to which Kelly sometimes contributed liner notes and/or cover art.

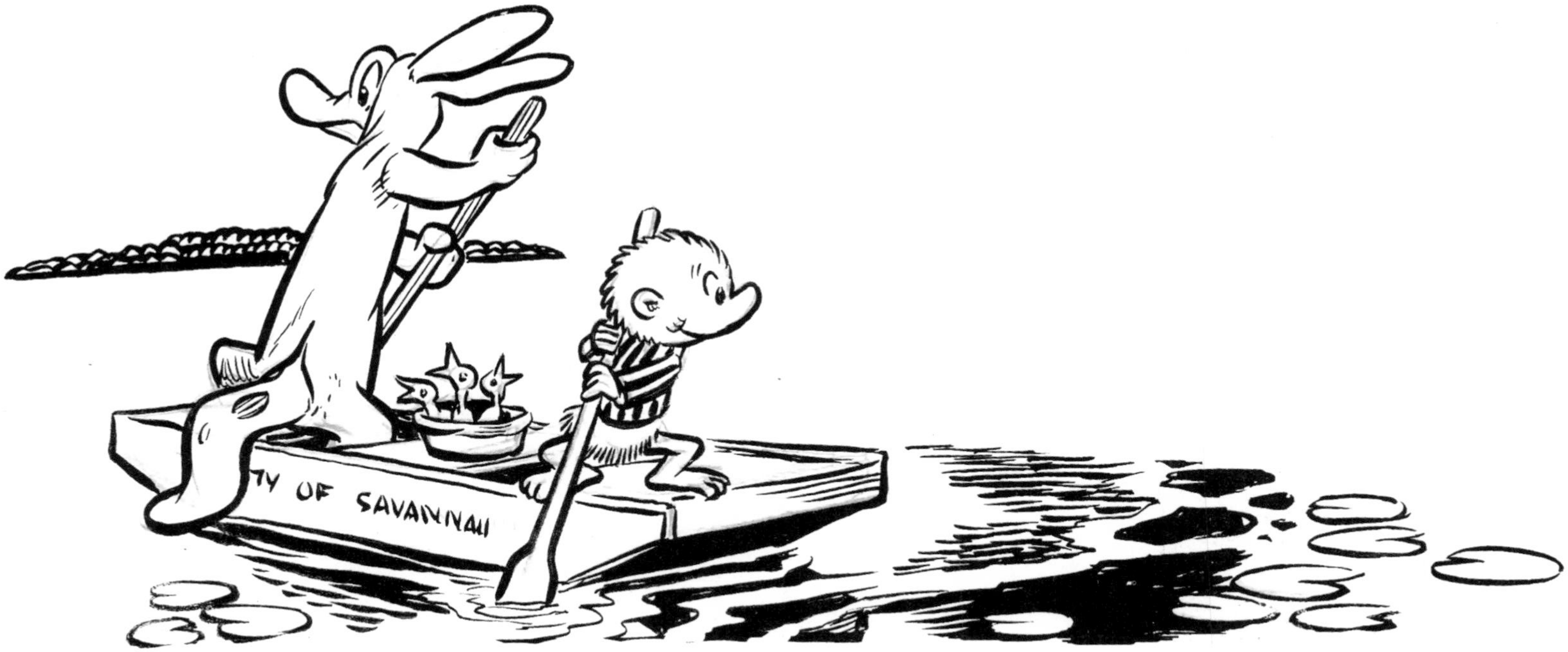
TY OF SAVANNAH

4/17 – John Stanley, whose name becomes the name of a bird in this strip, achieved cartooning immortality by writing and sometimes drawing Little Lulu stories for the Dell/Western series. In the early-to-mid-1940s, Stanley, like Kelly, worked for Oskar Lebeck, Western's east coast editor, producing numerous comic book titles aimed at young readers.

5/9 – The cuckoo is quoting a traditional English round, estimated to date from 1260 and so possibly the oldest instance of counterpoint in existence, saith Wikipedia. The title, translated, means "summer has come in" or "summer has arrived."

5/20 – May 20, 1950 was the first Armed Forces Day, which unified previously separate Army, Navy and Air Force Days and signaled the 1947 unification of America's armed forces into one department, the Department of Defense, replacing the Department of War and the Department of the Navy (founded as the British-sounding Board of Admiralty in 1780); the Air Force was created as a new military service at the same time as the DOD, removing it from the Army, where it had been called the Army Air Force.

5/29 – Deacon Mushrat is the first Pogo companion whose tone of voice and locution and, hence, personality are implied by the style of lettering in his speech balloons – in this case, a Gothic font suggesting stodginess accompanied by an overweening sense of propriety.

6/7 – Hawgshaw and Cully are, respectively, caricatures of William Randolph Hearst and Robert McCormick, two of the nation's most prominent and outspoken newspaper publishers.

6/11 – A novel variation on the situation in 5/21.

6/16ff. – The hue and cry about the "loss" of China and about the Russians having obtained atomic secrets by underhanded espionage rather than by honest toil in their own fiendish laboratories inflamed American imaginations. Spies, great quantities of the citizenry believed, were everywhere, lurking with sinister designs. In the House of Representatives, the Un-American Activities Committee, HUAC, investigated labor unions, liberal organizations, peace groups, and New Deal agencies, holding highly visible public hearings and proving the subversive intent of hapless citizens by reason of their associations – the organizations to which they belonged or the friends whose company they kept. When the panic was at its height, livelihoods and lives were blasted on the basis of the most nebulous "evidence": mere rumor was sufficient to destroy a person's reputation. The fevers of this sort of groundless accusatory hysteria were eventually christened "McCarthyism" in honor of Joseph R. McCarthy, the junior senator from Wisconsin who perfected the smear techniques for which he became notorious in his witch-hunt for communists in government.

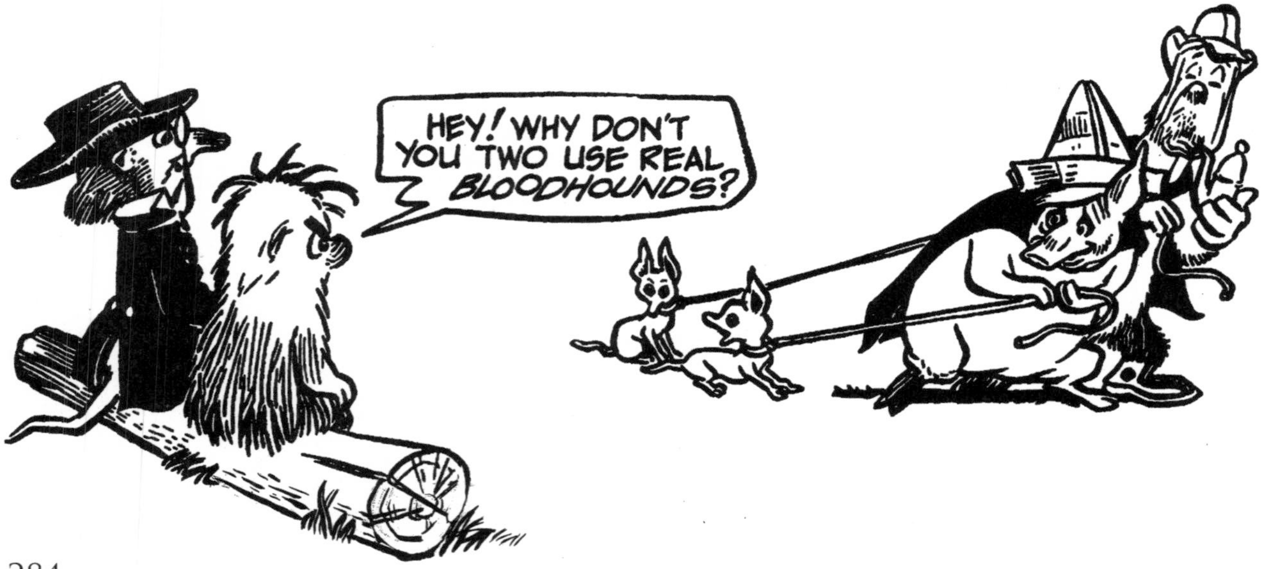
HEY! WHY DON'T YOU TWO USE REAL BLOODHOUNDS?

Kelly had pitched into the HUAC and its vigilante tactics when doing editorial cartoons for the *New York Star* in 1948-49. McCarthy, he perceived, was just one more self-promoting drum major in the parade of sensation-mongers that had used fear of Communism to advance their political fortunes. And so he turned the lost Pup Dog episode into a mini-mockery of the witch-hunters.

The allegation of Ol' Albert's cannibalism rests entirely upon the sort of flimsy unprovoked evidence that Commie-hunters delighted in, and Albert's accusers are every bit as fanatic as the anti-Communist crusaders, jumping to conclusions so rapidly that they arrive at a guilty verdict before the trial rather than during it (6/16). And as McCarthy was already doing, they fabricate the evidence in support of their accusations (6/29-30).

After ridiculing the folly in such proceedings, Kelly brings his moral lesson to a close by establishing Albert's absolute innocence and then putting the vigilantes to rout in rousing Hollywood style, the good guy in the white hat galloping in at the last minute to drive the evil rumor mongers out (7/11-12). In a final dig at the fanaticism of the witch-hunters, he depicts the most extreme of them clinging to their case even after the live-liness of the *corpus delicti* proves that no crime has been committed: desperate, the fanatics now move to make a case against Albert on the grounds that he *could* have eaten Pup Dog (7/10).

This sequence is the most sustained effort at political satire in the strip since its inception. The episode also includes the first use of a satirical device for which Kelly later became widely celebrated. In Cully and Hawgshaw, as I mentioned earlier, Kelly deploys caricatures of actual personages to underscore his satire.

Cully, the tall creature, is the spitting image of the aristocratic proprietor of the *Chicago Tribune*, Colonel Robert McCormick (called, by his relatives and detractors, "Bertie.") And Cully's behavior mocks the eccentricities and sometimes arrogant ignorance of the publisher. McCormick had been appointed a colonel during World War I, and he was therefore convinced that he was a military expert *non pareil* (and he employed his military title ever after as a way of reminding everyone of his qualifications), but his pronouncements often revealed his utter naivete in military matters. When Cully explains (6/13) that he doesn't use bloodhounds to track his quarry because they're too bossy and go where they want to go, he is giving voice to a typical McCormick attitude.

And in the Colonel's voice, Kelly provides one more clue as to Cully's identity in real life: the Colonel, schooled briefly in Britain, affected a British accent all his life, and in Cully's speech, reverberating with the ostentatious extra syllables of British upper crust – "notcherwelly" and "utterwelly" – Kelly is clearly mocking McCormick. Even the name "Cully" is an English word denoting someone easily tricked or duped.

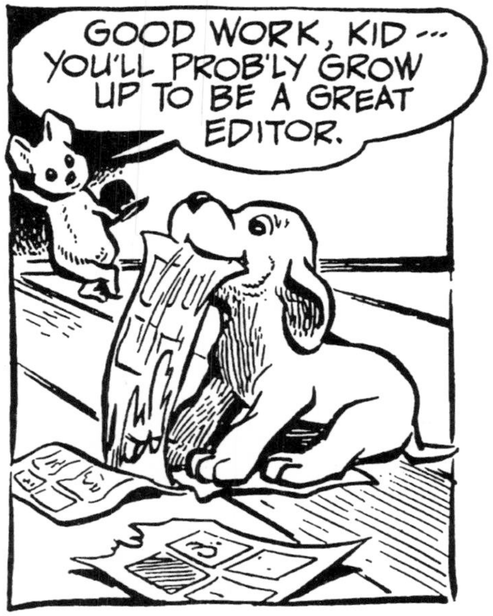
GOOD WORK, KID--- YOU'LL PROB'LY GROW UP TO BE A GREAT EDITOR.

Cully's companion, Hawgshaw the pig, is undoubtedly William Randolph Hearst; the length of his snout distorts the likeness somewhat, but the eyes are clearly Hearst's; and the lock of hair on the brow likewise. The admiral's hat made from a folded-up newspaper evokes Hearst's role in the Spanish American War at the turn of the 20th century, when, as the chief war monger, Hearst seemed virtually in command of U.S. military forces from the editorship of the *New York Journal*. By 1950, Hearst was sick and dying, but his world had grown smaller, and he might be seen as tending pretty carefully to his own knitting.

In singling out these two press lords for ridicule, Kelly enriches his satire without much risk. By 1950, McCormick and Hearst were well-worn shibboleths for the power of the press gone mad. Still, neither McCormick nor Hearst were toothless foes; both could still muster blistering attacks on their enemies if they so desired. But Kelly used the two fading fanatics as targets not so much for their personal or political proclivities but as representatives of their newspapers, which were enthusiastic supporters of anti-Communist enterprises. Journalists working in these papers comprised a noisy cheering section on the sidelines of the witch-hunts, and their early support of McCarthy secured him a foothold that enabled him to rise to power. And McCarthy, despite his boorishness and his political gaffes, was on the rise.

7/3 – Comic books were coming under increasing fire as the cause of juvenile delinquency because of their often gruesome crime stories. Publishers, however, maintained that such stories always ended with the capture or death of crooks, proving that crime does not pay. What could be more moral?

7/11 – *Suspensus per collum* means "hung by the neck"; *ne quid nimis*, "not anything in excess"; *silent leges inter arma*, "laws are silent amidst arms"; to all of which, Albert quips sarcastically, *non omnis moriar* – "I shall not completely die" (Horace). Or perhaps "I'm not dead yet." Thanks in part to Houn'dog's casual explication (7/6-7, coupled to the scalawags' performance on 6/8), we know, now, that Cully and Hawgshaw kidnapped Pup Dog to hold him for ransom, then, inexplicably, tried to drown him but wanted him back when they heard a reward was offered.

7/14 – Albert's ordeal concludes satisfactorily with feast and fellowship, Kelly's warmly felt recipe for the ills of any society, a prescription he invokes throughout the strip's run with ritual regularity.

8/4 – *Hoc opus hic labor est* is loosely translated to mean "this is the problem, this is the hard task," quoted from Virgil's *Aenead.*

8/7 – Albert says, "Hic – Hic – Jacet – Hic – Et – Ubique – Hic." *Hic Jacet* is Latin for "here lies" and is often used on tombstones. *Hic Et Ubique* is Latin for "here and everywhere."

8/9 – *De profundis* ("out of the depths") is the name of an essay on spirituality and faith arising from despair and degradation that was written in prison by Oscar Wilde. It also refers to Psalm 129, written perhaps during the suffering of the Babylonian Exile.

8/13 – "Plantigrade" refers to creatures that walk with the entire lower surface of the foot on the ground, as humans and bears do.

8/15 – Skittles is a game similar to nine pins, so beer and skittles usually implies a pleasant time, intoxication and playfulness; the typical usage, however, is, as the butterfly has it, "not all beer and skittles" – *i.e.*, not as pleasant as you might suppose.

8/23 – An object lesson in how many successive actions a cartoonist can depict in a single panel.

8/30 – Pup Dog's mastery of the poltergeist nonsense expression has no particular significance that I can discover. If googled, the results are all *Pogo,* so it apparently originated with Kelly, and it means exactly what it appears to mean.

9/13 – The name on the stern of the boat doubtless invokes a weepy Victorian novel, *East Lynn,* by Mrs. Henry Wood. The book was ferociously popular, being translated into thousands of foreign languages and the stage, but it was so awful that *East Lynn* became in later, more sophisticated times an international literary exemplar of terribly bad prose fiction.

9/17 – A rare instance of the Sunday *Pogo* meshing with the action of the dailies; Kelly probably planned this two-week sequence far in advance because Sunday strips are usually due at the syndicate 4-5 weeks earlier than dailies.

9/28 – Waycross, Georgia, should anyone ask, is the town situated at the northern entrance to Okefenokee Swamp, ostensibly the swamp in which Pogo and his cohorts live (although

at one time for the benefit of *Life* magazine, Kelly said the name of the strip's swamp was Pogofenokee).

10/2 – More evidence that Kelly had worked out a rare seven-day continuity: Owl lost his glasses just the day before, a Sunday.

10/29 – "Le Fay" is an ancient word for "fairy," and Morgan Le Fay, we learn by Googling, is "popularly known as an Arthurian sorceress and enchantress.

10/30 – Hepzibah is a Biblical personage, wife of King Hezekiah of Judah. The name means "my delight is in her," which may account for Kelly's choice of the name for the siren skunk who will be the only romantic interest in the whole of *Pogo.*

11/3 – Deacon Mushrat says, "... as things go": in the paranoia of the times, no one would admit to being anything but one hundred percent American because everything "foreign" was suspicious: it could be Communist. Deacon Mushrat's closing reference to a "martial plan" twists the meaning of the Marshall Plan, a post-World War II American program (1948-51) to aid the recovery of war-torn Europe and named after Truman's Secretary of State, George Marshall, who was awarded the Nobel Peace Prize for the Marshall Plan.

11/4 – Voting in the off-year election for members of the House of Representatives and a third of the U.S. Senate took place on November 7, 1950.

11/5 – Kansas is the home of the Jayhawks, the mascot of the University of Kansas, but the origin of the term lies in struggles during the 1850s over whether the Kansas Territory would a slave state or a free state. Ruffians on both sides of the issue, called jayhawks, rampaged across the countryside, attacking settlements and looting and killing to make their point. The name refers to two birds – the noisy, quarrelsome blue jay with a reputation of robbing other birds' nests, and the sparrow hawk, a stealthy hunter. Albert's casual reference evokes the notion of dashing around, to and fro, perhaps to no lasting effect.

Fauns in Roman mythology are place spirits of untamed woodland. Romans associated them with the Greek satyrs, which resemble goats in the lower half of their bodies but are also drunken orgiastic followers of Bacchus. Kelly had the gentler version in mind, and while these wood sprites seem entirely at home in the woody swamp, they never appeared in the strip after this sequence.

11/7 – *Poltroon* is defined as "a spiritless coward."

11/11 – Pogo and his pals are unusually morose on this year's Veterans Day because American soldiers were once again dying on the field of battle. North Korea invaded South Korea on June 25, the United Nations had asked for help, and by the end of the month, President Truman sent ground troops and bombers into war where they remained on this Veterans Day.

11/26 – Thanksgiving was the previous Thursday.

12/17 – "In case you don't read this next week..." Next Sunday is December 24, Christmas Eve, and some newspapers did not publish on that day.

12/25 – A few newspapers published on holidays, and some, like the Stamford paper referred to here, published holiday strips the next day thereby offering readers a double dose of their favorite funnies. Here, Kelly provides friendly acknowledgment to publisher McCullough.

12/30 – A story fragment that will be consummated in the ensuing volume of this series.

ACKNOWLEDGEMENTS

A book such as this doesn't happen without a great many
people offering their help.

For generously supplying the comic strip images
in this collection, thanks to Rick Norwood, to
Steve Thompson, president of the POGO Fan Club, and
to Lucy Caswell, curator of the Ohio State University
Billy Ireland Cartoon Library and Museum.

For supplying the 1950 Sunday original art used in
full-size scans throughout the book, we are grateful to
Kathleen, Carolyn and Pete Kelly.

And we'd like to thank Jeff Smith for his support
and advice, Steve Rude for his artistic wisdom,
Rick Rogers for his preliminary assistance
and many others who, like Gordon Kent
and Mike Rees, contributed aid
and encouragement.